PHOENIX

A COMPLETE HISTORY OF THE LUFTWAFFE
1918-1945

Volume 1 - The Phoenix is Reborn 1918-1934

DEDICATION

This book, and indeed the whole Phoenix Project, is dedicated to

Rosemarie Anne Meredith

without whom this would not have been possible

PHOENIX

A COMPLETE HISTORY OF THE LUFTWAFFE 1918-1945

Volume 1 - The Phoenix is Reborn 1918-1934

Richard Meredith

Helion & Company

Helion & Company Limited
26 Willow Road
Solihull
West Midlands
B91 1UE
England
Tel. 0121 705 3393
Fax 0121 711 4075
Email: info@helion.co.uk
Website: www.helion.co.uk
Twitter: @helionbooks
Visit our blog http://blog.helion.co.uk/

Published by Helion & Company 2016
Designed and typeset by Battlefield Design, Gloucester (www.battlefield-design.co.uk)
Cover designed by Paul Hewitt, Battlefield Design (www.battlefield-design.co.uk)
Printed by Gutenberg Press Limited, Tarxien, Malta

Front cover: Fokker D-XIII *Jagdflugzeug Nr.11* of the *Fliegerschule Stahr* at the *Reichswehr's* secret
Lipetsk air base, 1926-28. Bundesarchiv RH2 Bild-02292-073 Photo: o.Ang.
Rear cover: Flight students tug a glider into the air on the heights near Berlin-Gatow.
Bundesarchiv Bild 102-14452 Photo: Georg Pahl.

ISBN 978-1-910294-50-5

British Library Cataloguing-in-Publication Data.
A catalogue record for this book is available from the British Library.

For details of other military history titles published by Helion & Company
Limited contact the above address, or visit our website: http://www.helion.co.uk.

We always welcome receiving book proposals from prospective authors.

Contents

List of Photographs

Plate Section 2

List of Figures

List of Maps

List of Charts

List of Tables

Glossary

A-Boot	Small Torpedo Boat (Minesweeper)
A-Stand	Defensive position in the nose of an aircraft
Abschuss(e)	Shoot down(s) or Air Combat Claim(s)
Abteilung(en)	Battalion(s), Staff(s) & Ministerial Branch(es)
Abteilungschef	Branch Chief (Ministry)
Abwehrwaffen	Defensive armament
Abwurfmunition	Drop ordnance
Abwurfwaffen	Drop ordnance
Abzeichen	Badge
Amphibienflugzeug	Amphibious aircraft
Altmarker	Wartime Pilots
Alte Adler	Old Eagles – *Luftstreitkräfte* officers
Amt(er)	Ministerial Office(s)
Arbeitsplan	Plan of Works
Arbeitsprogramm	Programme of Works
Arbitur	University Matriculation Certificate
Armee	Army
Armee-Abteilung	Army detachment
Armeekorps	Army Corps
Artikel	Article (Treaty of Versailles)
Artillerie	Artillery
Artillerieflugboot	Naval gunnery spotter
Artillerie-Schiessplatzes	Artillery Range
Artillerieschule	School of Artillery
Aufklärungsflugzeuge	Reconnaissance aircraft
Aufklärungsschiffe	Reconnaissance Ships
Aufklärungsstaffel(n)	Reconnaissance Squadron(s)
Aufklärungsstreitkräfte	Naval Reconnaissance Forces
Aufschlagzünder	Impact fuse for drop ordnance
Aufstellungsplan	Unit Activation Plan
Ausbildung	Training
Ausbildungsleiter	Head of Training
Ausbildungsstabes	Training Staff
Ausrüstung	Military equipment
Ausrüstungsperiod	Rearmament Period
B-Stand	Defensive position in the upper fuselage of an aircraft
Balkankreuz	Balkan Cross
Ballistische	Ballistics
Ballon-Abwehr-Kanon (BAK)	Anti-Balloon Gun
Bataillon(e)	Battalion(s)

Batterie	Artillery Battery
Bauaufsicht	Construction supervision, control
Baureihe	Construction series, batch
Bauschreibung	Construction specification
Bay.Militär-Max-Josef-Orden	Bavarian Military Order of *Max Josef*
Bedienungsvorschrift So.	Special armament directive
Begleit	Escort
Behelfs	Auxiliary
Behelfskampfgeschwader	Auxiliary Bomber Wing
Beobachter	Observer (inc.aircrew)
Beobachterschule	Aerial Observer School
Beobachtungskursus	Observer training course (Artillery Officers)
Bericht	Report
Beschaffung	Procurement
Besoldungs	Payrolls
Betriebsstoffbehalteranlage	Fuel system
Bildgeräte	Photographic equipment
Bildoffizier	Photographic Officer
Bildschule	Photographic School
Bildstelle	Photographic Station, Department
blau	blue
Blaukreuzkampstoffen	Blue Cross Gases (Chemical Agents)
Bombe(n)	Bomb(s)
Bombenmagazin	Internal vertical bomb rack
Bombengeschwader des OHL	Bomber Wing/Army High Command (Imperial period)
Bordausrüstung	Aircraft equipment
Bordflugzeug(e)	Shipboard aircraft
Bordfunker	Wireless Operator (Aircrew)
Bordfunkermachiniste(n)	Wireless Operator/Mechanic(s)
Bordmechaniker	Flight Engineer (Aircrew)
Bordschutz	Air Gunner (Aircrew)
Botschaft	Embassy
Brandbombe(n)	Incendiary bomb(s)
Brückengerät	Bridging equipment
Brückenkopf	Bridgehead
Bundesarchiv	German National Archives
Büro	Secretariat
C-Stand	Defensive position in the lower fuselage of an aircraft
Chefkonstrukteur	Chief Designer
Chefpilot	Chief Pilot
Dampfschiff, Dampfer	Steam ship
Denkschrift	Memorandum
deutschen (Dt./Dtsch.)	German
Diktat	Direction
Division(en)	Division(s)
Doppeltrommel	Saddle magazine for machine gun
Drehkranz	Rotatable gun mount

Dreizweckeflugzeug	Three-seat multi-role aircraft
Duralumin	Light metal aluminium alloy
Einbau-und Prufvorschrift d.So	Installation and test schedule for special equipment
Einheitslafette	Single pedestal gun mount
Einsatz Ausbildung	Operational training
Einsatzkommando	Operational Detachment
Einsatzposition	Operational location
Eisenbahn	Railway
Eisenbahn Panzerzug	Armoured Train
Eisernen Kreuz	Iron Cross - two classes: EK 2 & EK 1 (EK II & I)
Elektrischer Zunder	Electrical fuse for drop ordnance
Elektron	Magnesium alloy
Elektronbrandbombe	Magnesium based incendiary bomb
Emfanger	Light indicator (Artillery fire control)
Empfanger	Wireless Receiver
Entfernungsmesser	Range finder
Entwicklung	Development
Entwicklungsprogramm	Development Programme
Ersatz	Replacement/Substitute
Eskadron	Cavalry Squadron
Expert(en)	Fighter Ace (5 or more air victories)
F-Boot	Motorboat minesweeper
Fahrgestell	Vehicle mounting
Fahrtruppe(n)	Supply troop(s) – mounted
Fahrnen	Horsemen
Fallschirm und Sicherheitswarte	Parachute Packer and Safety Equipment
Feindflug(e)	Operational sortie(s)
Feld	Field
Feldflugplatz(e)	Forward Airfield(s)
Feldhaubitze	Field Howitzer
Feldheer	Field Army
Feldkanone	Field Gun
Feldluftschiffer Abteilung	Field Airship Detachment (Imperial period)
Feldwebel-Lehrgange	Senior NCO Instructional Course
Fernaufklärer	Long range reconnaissance crew (aircraft)
Fernaufklärungsstaffel	Long range reconnaissance squadron
Flakabteilung(en)	Anti-Aircraft Artillery Battalion(s)
Flakartillerie-Schule	Ant-Aircraft Artillery School
Flakgeschütz(en)	Anti-Aircraft Gun(s)
Flakscheinwerfer	Anti-Aircraft Searchlight
Flakverbände	Anti-Aircraft Artillery Units
Flakwaffe	Anti-Aircraft Artillery Arm
Flieger	Aviator or Flier
Flieger Abteilung	Flight Detachment (Imperial period)
Fliegerabzeichen	Pilot's badge
Fliegerbodenpersonal	Air Technical personnel
Fliegerdivision(en)	Air Division(s)

Fliegerführer(n)	Air Commander(s)
Fliegergeschwader (See)	Naval Air Wing
Fliegergruppe(n)	Air Group(s)
Fliegerhorst(en)	Airfield(s)
Fliegerkurierstaffeln(n)	Air communications squadron(s)
Fliegeroffizier(e)	Flying officer(s)
Fliegerschule(n)	Flight training School(s)
Fliegerschützenlehrgang	Aerial Gunnery Instructional Course
Fliegerstammabteilung	Airmen's Cadre Battalion
Fliegerstation	Air Station (Imperial period)
Fliegertruppe	Aviation Personnel
Fliegerverbände	Aviation units
Fliegerwaffe	Air Arm
Fliegerwaffenschulen	Operational Training Units
Flottille	Flotilla
Flottenerkunder	Fleet scout
Flugabwehrkanon(en)	Anti-Aircraft Gun(s)
Flugabwehrmesswesen	Air Defence Survey Service
Flugbetriebsboot	Flight Servicing Craft, Boat
Flugboot	Flying boat
Flugerprobung	Flight testing
Flughafen	Airport
Flugkäpitan	Air Captain (DLH)
Fluglagegerät	Flight Attitude Indicator, Artificial Horizon
Flugleiter	Chief of Flying
Flugleitung	Air Traffic Control
Flugmeldedienst	Aircraft monitoring/reporting service
Flugmotorenschlosser	Engine Mechanic
Flugpionier	Pioneer of Flight
Flugplatz(e)	Aerodrome(s)
Flugplatz-Kommandantur	Airfield Commandant
Flugschiff	Very large flying boat
Flugschuler	Flight student
Flugsicherungsschiff	Aircraft Recovery Vessel
Flugtechnisches Personal	Aircraft technical personnel
Flugüberwachung	Police Flight Monitoring
Flugwesens	Flying
Flugwettbewerb	Air Meeting
Flugzeug(e)	Aircraft
Flugzeugbergungsschiffe	Aircraft Recovery Vessel
Flugzeugfeinmech'ker u.Elektriker	Aircraft Instrument Mechanic & Electrician
Flugzeugführer	Pilot (Aircrew)
Flugzeugführerschein	Pilot's Licence
Flugzeug-Geräteverwalter	Aircraft Equipment Administrator
Flugzeughandbuch	Aircraft Handbook
Flugzeughandwerker	Aircraft Craftsman
Flugzeugkanone	Aircraft cannon
Flugzeugklempner	Aircraft sheet metal worker
Flugzeugkonstrukteur	Aircraft designer

Flugzeugmaler	Aircraft painter
Flugzeugmechaniker	Aircraft Mechanic
Flugzeugmuster	Aircraft type, model
Flugzeugmutterschiff	Seaplane Tender (Imperial period)
Flugzeugsattler	Aircraft leather worker
Flugzeugtischler	Aircraft carpenter
Flugzeugwarte(n)	Aircraft mechanic(s)
Flugzeugzerstörer	Long range heavy fighter
Frachtflugzeug	Freight aircraft
Freiwilligen	Volunteers
Freikorps	Volunteer Corps (Weimar period)
Fremde Heer	Enemy armies
Fremde Luftmachte	Enemy air forces
Friedensstandort(e)	Peacetime garrison or bases
FT Navigation	Wireless navigation
Führergehilfen	Command Assistants (General Staff)
Führung	Leadership
Führungsabteilung	Command - Leadership Branch
Funk	Wireless
Funkfeuer	Non-directional wireless (radio) beacons
Funkpersonal	Wireless personnel
Fursorge-Offizier	Welfare Officer
für beweglichen Einbau	for flexible installation (machine guns)
für starren Einbau	for fixed installation (machine guns)
Gasbombe(n)	Gas filled bomb(s)
Gaskampfschule	Chemical Warfare School
Gasschutzdienst	Gas Defence Service
Gefechtsübungen	Battle Training
geheime	secret
geheime Fliegerliste	secret pilot roster (*Weimar* period)
geheime Kommandosache	Top secret command matter
gehobene Luftamter	Higher Air Offices
gelb	yellow
gemischte (gem.)	mixed
Generalstabs	General Staff
geräte	equipment
Gerätemapp	Equipment Catalogue
Geschaftsführer	Executive Director
Geschwader	Wing
Grenadier	Grenadier
Grenzschutz	Border troops
Größe	Large
Größe Generalstab	Imperial General Staff
Großlinienschiffe	Dreadnought Battleship (Imperial period)
Größflugtag	Major Air Day
Größflugzeug(e)	Large aircraft
Größraumflugel	Flying Wing
grun	green

Grundschuler	Ground student – technical trades
Gruppe	Group, Staff or Ministerial Department
Gruppenkommando	Army Group Command (*Weimar* period)
Halbflottille	Half Flotilla
Hakenkreuz	Swastika
Handelsmarine	Merchant Navy
Handkamera	Hand-held Camera for aerial use
Hauptbildstelle	Main Photographic Centre
Hauptkampflinie (HKL)	Main Battle Line
Haushalt	Budget
Heer(es)	Army - Branch of *Wehrmacht*
Heeresabteilung	Army Group (small size)
Heeresaufklärungsstaffel(n)	Army reconnaissance squadron(s)
Heeresgruppe(n)	Army Group(s)
Heimat	Homeland, Metropolitan Germany
Heimatschützjäger	Home Defence Fighter
Hellblau	Light Blue
Hilfslehrer	Assistant Instructor
Hilfschiff(e)	Naval Auxiliary Vessel
Hochrot	Bright red
Hochseeflotte	High Seas Fleet (Imperial period)
Hochseefahiger-F-Aufkl-Flugb't	Oceanic Reconnaissance Flying Boat
Hochseestreitkräfte	High Seas Forces (Imperial period)
Hohenzollern	Imperial Royal House
Hohere Flg.Technische Schule	Higher Air Technical School
Hoherer (Höheren)	Higher
Horch und Scheinwerfereinsatz	Sound Locator and Searchlight Operations
Infanterie	Infantry
Infanterieschule	School of Infantry
Ingenieur(e)	Engineer(s)
Ingenierbüro	Engineering team
Inspekteur	Inspector
Inspektion	Inspectorate
Jagdflieger	Fighter pilot(s)
Jagdflieger-Lehrgang	Instructional course for fighter pilots
Jagdregiment	Fighter Regiment
Jagdstaffel	Fighter squadron
Jagdflugzeuge	Fighter aircraft
Jagdgruppe	Fighter Group
Jagdverbände	Fighter units
Jagdwaffe	Fighter Arm
Jagdeinsitzer	Single-seat fighter aircraft
Jagdzweisitzer	Two-seat fighter aircraft
Jäger	Air - Fighter pilots
Jungmarker	Young officer candidate pilots

Kaiserliche Marine	Imperial Navy
Kampfeinsitzer	Single-seat combat aircraft
Kampfflieger	Bomber crews
Kampfflugzeuge	Bomber aircraft
Kampfgruppe	Battlegroup, Bomber Group
Kampfgeschwader	Bomber Wing
Kampfgeschwader des OHL	Bomber Wing/Army High Command (Imperial period)
Kampffliegerstaffel	Bomber squadron (Imperial period)
Kampfgruppe(n)	Bomber Group(s)
Kampfregiment	Bomber Regiment
Kampfschulgeschwader	Bomber Training Wing
Kampfstoffbomb(en)	Gas Bomb(s)
Kampfstofftank(en)	Gas Tank(s)
Kampf-Verkehrsflugzeug	Bomber/Transport aircraft
Kampfwagenschule	Armoured Vehicle School
Kanal	Canal
Kanon(en)	Cannons(s) Gun(s)
Kanonenmotor	Engine mounted cannon
Kanoniere	Gunners
Kasino	Officers' Mess
Katapult	Catapult
Kavallerie	Cavalry
Kavallerieschule	School of Cavalry
Kennblatt	General arrangement drawing
Kette	Formation of three aircraft
Kettenhund	Wingman to *Kette* leader
Klass(e)	Class(es) (warships)
kleine	small
Kleinflugboot	small Flying Boat
Kleinflugzeuge	Small aircraft
Kolonne	Column
Kommandeur der Flieger	Air Commander attached to a higher army command
Kommandierenden Admiral	Admiral Officer Commanding
Kommandierenden General	General Officer Commanding
Kommandogerate	Fire Control Equipment
Kommando-Hilfs-Gerat	Auxiliary Fire Director
Konstruktionsbüros	Construction Team
Korps	Corps
Korpstruppen	Corps Troops
Kraftfahr	Motor
Kraftfahr-Lehrgang	Motor Vehicle Instructional Course
Kraftfahrlehrer	Motor vehicle instructor
Kraftfahrtruppe	Motor Vehicle Troops
Kraftfahrzeug(e) (Kfz)	Motor Vehicle
Kraftwagenflak	Lorry mounted anti-aircraft gun
Kraftwagengeschütz	Lorry mounted gun
Kraftwagenversuchs	Motor vehicle test
Kreisflugpark	Regional Air Depot
Kreuzer (Kreuziere)	Cruiser(s)

Kreuz-lafette	Cruciform gun platform
Krieg	War
Kriegsakademie	War Academy (general staff officer training)
Kriegsmarine	Navy - Branch of *Wehrmacht*
Kriegschule	War School (officer training)
Kriegspiel(en)	War Game(s)
Kriegswehrmacht	Armed forces on a wartime footing
Kunstflugmeister	Aerobatic Champion
Kurier (-maschine)	Courier (aircraft)
Küsten (-flieger)	Coastal (aviators)
Küstenartillerieschule	Naval Coastal Gunnery School
Küstenwehr-Abteilung	Naval Coast Defence Battalion
Landespolizei	Territorial Police
Langstrecken	Long distance
Langstrecken-Größbomber	Long Range Heavy Bomber (Ural Bomber)
Langenstreckenschule	Long distance route school (German Railways)
Lazarett	Hospital
Lehrer	Instructor
Lehrgangsleiter	Course leader
leichte (lei.)	light
Leichtsportflugzeuge	Light sports aircraft
Leuchtbombe(n)	Illumination flare(s)
Leuchtfeuer	Aerial light beacon (later)
Linealvisier	Gun sight (Iron Sight)
Linienschiff(e)	Ship(s) of the Line – Battleship(s) (Imperial period)
Luftamt(er)	Air Office(s)
Luftfahrt	Aviation
Luftfahrtfeuer	Aviation light beacon (early)
Luftfahrtindustrie	German Aviation Industry
Luftfahrzeugrolle	List of German Aircraft Registrations
Luftkreis	Air Region
Luftpark	Air Depot
Luftpolizei	Air Police
Luftschiff(e)	Airship(s)
Luftschiffertruppe	Imperial Navy's Airship Division
Luftschütz	Air defence
Luftsieg(e)	Aerial victory(ies)
Luftsperr	Barrage Balloon, Balloon barrage
Luftstreitkräfte	Military Air Service (Imperial period)
Lufttaktik	Air tactics
Luftwaffe	Air Force - Branch of *Wehrmacht*
Lotfernrohr	Telescopic bomb sight
Luftaufsichtwachen	Air traffic observation stations
Luftbildschule	Aerial photography school
M-Boot	Minesweeper (Navy)
M-Boot	Motor Boat (Engineers)
Marine	Naval

Marineakademie	Naval Academy
Marinearchiv	Naval Archives
Marineartillerie	Naval artillery
Marineflieger	Naval aviators
Marinefliegerverbände	Naval air units
Marine-Luftschiff-Abteilung	Naval Airship Battalion (Imperial period)
Marineluftstreitkräfte	Naval Air Arm (Imperial period)
Marineschule	Naval School (officer training)
Marinestation der Nordsee	North Sea Naval Station (*Wilhelmshaven*)
Marinestation der Ostsee	Baltic Sea Naval Station (*Kiel*)
Maschinen-Gewehr	Machine Gun
Masterprüfung	Type Test - engines
Matrosen-Artillerie	Naval artillery
Meerbusen	Bay
Mehrzweckstaffel	Naval multi-role squadron
Messtruppen	Survey Troops (Artillery)
Militär(ische)	military
Militärische Erpobung	Military aircraft testing
Militärflieger	Military aviator (Imperial period)
Minensuchboote	Minesweeping vessels
Minensucher	Minesweeper
Modell	Model
moteur canon	Engine mounted cannon (French)
Motoren	Engines
motorisiert (mot.)	motorised
Motorsegler	Motor glider
Munitionsanstalt	Munitions Depot
Munitionstrommel	Ammunition Drum
Nachrichten	Signals
Nachtbomber-Land	Land-based night bomber (*Weimar* period)
Nachtflugbetriebes	Night Flying Organisation
Nachtjagdflugzeug	Night fighter aircraft
Nachschub	Supply
Nachschubeinheiten	Supply units
Nachstrecke	Nocturnal commercial air route
Nahaufklärungsflieger	Short range reconnaissance crews
Nahaufklärungsflugzeug	Tactical reconnaissance aircraft
nord	north
Notlandeplätze	Emergency Landing Grounds
Notrüstung	Emergency armament
Nummer(n)	Number(s)
I.Offizier(e)	Executive Officer(s)
Offizierkorps	Officer corps
Operativer Luftkrieg	operational air war doctrine
Ordnung	Order (placement)
Ortsfesten-Flakbatterie	Fortress emplaced anti-aircraft battery
ost	east

Ozeanflieger	Trans-oceanic flier
Panzerschiff(e)	lit. Armoured Ship, Heavy Cruiser
Panzerschule	Armour (Tank) School
Parabellum	7.92 mm Modell 13 machine gun used in aircraft
Peilempfanger	Direction finding equipment
Pionier	Engineers
Pionierschule	School of Engineering
Polizei	Police
Polizeifliegerstaffel	Police Air Squadron (*Weimar* period)
Ponton	Pontoon (bridge)
Postflugzeug	Postal aircraft
Pour le Mérite	Blue Max – for meritorious service
preus.Militär-FF Abzeichen	Prussian Military Pilot's Badge
Provisorische	Provisional
Rauchzylinder (RZ)	Rotating cylindrical projectile
Referate	Ministerial Staffs or Desk(s)
Referent	Staff Advisor
Reflexnivier (Revi)	Reflector gun sight
Regierungsstaffel	Government transport squadron
Regiment(er)	Regiment(s)
Reichsbahn	German Railways
Reichsbahnstrecke	German Railways Air Route (numbered)
Reichsbahn-Streckenschule	Route flying school (German Railways)
Reichsbahn-Streckenstaffel	Route flying squadron (German Railways)
Reichsheer	German Army (*Weimar* period)
Reichsluftwaffe	German Air Force (*Weimar* period)
Reichsmarine	German Navy (*Weimar* period)
Reichsmark	German Mark (currency)
Reichstag	German Parliament
Reichswehr	German Armed Forces (*Weimar* period)
Reihe	Model (of aircraft)
Reihenmotor	In-line engine
Reinhardt-Lehrgang	General staff officer training course – introduced in 1931
Reiseflugzeug(e)	Touring aircraft
Reitend	mounted
Reiter	Cavalry (alternative name)
Reklamestaffeln	Advertising Squadron
Rentenmark	German Mark introduced in 1923
Reparaturanleitung	Workshop Manual
Rhonvater	*Rhon* Father
Richtfernrohr	Periscopic Bomb Sight
Richtlinien	Directives
Richtungshorer	Sound locator
Risiko Flotte	Risk Fleet – *Adm. Tirpitz*, later *Staatssekretär Milch*
RK d.kon.H'ord.v.Hohenzollern	Knights Cross of the Royal House of *Hohenzollern*
rot	red
Rote	Formation of two aircraft

Rotenflieger	Wingman to Rote Leader
Ruckstossverstarker	Recoil booster for a machine gun
Sachbearbeiter	Official in Charge
Sammelmagazinen	Internal racks for small drop ordnance
Schein	Licence (A, B, A/B & C)
scheinwerfer	searchlight
Schiessausbildung	Gunnery training
Schiessübungen	Gunnery practice
Schiff(e)	ship(s)
Schiffsartillerieschule	Naval Gunnery Shool
Schiffstammdivision	Shore-based training and replacement Division
Schlachtflieger(ie)	Assault crews
Schlachtflugzeug	Assault aircraft
Schlachtgruppe(n)	Assault Group(s)
Schlachtschiff(e)	Battleship(s)
Schleppsegel	Trailing sail or mat to recover a seaplane
Schnellboot (S-Boot)	Motor Torpedo Boat
Schule(n)	School(s)
Schulflugzeug	Training aircraft
Schulmaschine	Training machine
Schulschiff(e)	Training vessel(s)
Schuttkasten	Canister for drop ordnance
Schützpolizei	Armed police
Schwarm	Formation of four aircraft – two Roten
schwarz	black
Schwere (schw.)	heavy
See	Sea - large inland lake
Seeaufklärer	Reconnaissance seaplane
Seeaufklärungsstaffel	Naval reconnaissance squadron
Seeflieger	Naval aviator
Seeflugstation	Naval air station (Imperial period)
Seeflugzeuge	Naval Aircraft
Seeflugzeughalle	Seaplane hangar
Seejagdeinsitzer	Single-seat fighter seaplane
Seejagdstaffel	Naval fighter squadron
Seejagdzweisitzer	Two-seat fighter seaplane
Seekadett(e)	Naval cadet(s)
Seekampfflieger	Naval combat pilot (Imperial period)
See-Kampfzweisitzer	Two-seat combat seaplane
Sender	Wireless Transmitter
Serie	Series
Seeübungsstaffel	Naval Proficiency Squadron
Segelflugschule(n)	Glider School(s)
Segel-Lehrgang	Instructional glider course
Segelschulschiff	Sail training ship
Serie	Series (of aircraft)
Sicherung der Nordsee	North Sea Coastal Forces
Skagerrakschlacht	Battle of Jutland – May 1916

Soldatenrats	Soldiers' Councils
Sonderanhanger	Special trailer/limber
Sonderausbildung	Special training – flight personnel
Sonderausrüstungen	Special equipment
Sondergruppe	Special Department, Special Group
Sondermunition	Special ordnance
Sperrballonen	Barrage Balloons
Splitterbomb(en)	Fragmentation Bomb(s)
Sportsflieger	Sport Fliers
Sportsflugzeuge	Sports Aircraft
Sprengbomb(en)	High explosive bomb(s)
Stab(es)	Headquarters
Stabsbildabteilung	Headquarters Photographic Branch
Stabskompanie	Headquarters company
Stabstaffel	Headquarters Squadron
Staffel	Squadron or formation of 12 aircraft – four *Ketten*
Stationsleiter	Commander of an Air Station
Steilbeobachterlehrgange	Mountain Observer training course
Stielhandgranate	Hand Grenade (Stick Grenade)
Stellung	Position or Line
Sternmotor	Radial engine
Stielhandgranate	Stick Hand Grenades
Stosstrupp	Assault unit
Streuflugzeug	Agricultural aircraft (crop sprayer)
Sturzkampfflugzeug	Dive bomber aircraft
Sturzkampfgruppe	Dive Bomber Group
Sturzkampfregiment	Dive Bomber Regiment
süd	south
T-Boot	Torpedo Boat
Taktik Ausbildung	Tactical Training
Tarnlehrgang	Camouflage demonstration course
Technik	Technology
Technische Hochschule(n)	Technical University(ies)
Technischen Büros	Technical Bureau
Technischer Mitarbeiter	Technical Director
Technische Schule d.Lw.	Air Force Technical School
Telefongesprach	Telephone conversation
Tiefangriff	Low level attack
Torpedoboot(e)	Torpedo Boat
Torpedoflugzege	Torpedo Bomber Aircraft
Torpedo-Seeflugzeuge	Torpedo Bomber Seaplane
Torpedostaffel(n)	Torpedo Bomber Squadron(s)
Truppenübungsplatz	Military Exercise Area
Turbinen-Schnelldampfer	High speed turbine-powered merchantman
Typ	Type
Typennummern	Type numbers
Übungsflugzeug	Proficiency Trainer

Unternehmen	Operation (military)
Unteroffizier-Lehrgang	Junior NCO Training Course
Unterseeboot(e) U-Boot	Submarine(s)
Untersetzungsgetriebe	Geared engine – reduction gear
Verkehrsabteilung	Transport Branch
Verkehrsflugboot	Transport Flying Boat
Verkehrsflugzeug(e)	Commercial transport aircraft
Verkehrslandeplatz(e)	Commercial landing grounds
verlegefahigen	transportable
Vermessungsschiff	Survey Vessel
Verordnungsblatt	Gazette
Versuchsbatterie	Experimental Artillery Battery
Versuchsgruppe	Test Department, Test Group
Versuchspark	Test Depot
Versuchsstelle	Test Centre
Verwaltung	Administration
Verwundeten-Abzeichen	Wound badge (in Black, Silver & Gold)
Vorkommando	Advanced, Preliminary Command
Vorpostenboot(en)	Escort/Patrol vessel(s)
Vorschriften	Directives
Waffen	Weapons, Ordnance, Arm of Service
Waffenfarbe	Arm of Service colour
Wasserflugzeug	Seaplane
Wehrkreis	Military Region
Wehrwirtschaft	Defence economics
Weltmeister	World Champion
Werkenummer	Works Number, Construction Number
west	west
Wetterdienst	Meteorological services
Wetterflug	Meteorological observation flight
Wetterflugstelle(n)	Weather Station(s)
Wetterzug	Meteorological Platoon (Artillery)
Wirtschaftliche	Economics
Zeitungsflugzeug(e)	Newspaper transport aircraft
Zentralflughafen	Central airport (*Berlin-Tempelhof*)
Zeppelinhalle	Airship hangar
Zerstörer(n)	Destroyer(s)
Zug(e)	Platoon(s)
Zugkraftwagen	Half-Track Vehicle
Zunder	Fuse for drop ordnance
Zweigstelle	Organisational Branch
Zwillingsmagazinen	Twin magazine

Abbreviations

Abt(n)	*Abteilung(en)*	Battalion
AFF	*Ansteuerungsfunkfeuer*	Instrument landing system beacon
AG	*Aktiengesellschaft*	Joint stock company
AK	*Armee Korps*	Army Corps
AOK	*Armee Oberkommando*	Army
AON	*Aviatsiya Osobovo Naznacheniya*	Soviet long range bomber aviation
APK	*Artillerieprüfungskommission*	Artillery Testing Commission
Art.	*Artillerie*	Artillery
Art.Offz.	*Artillerie-Offizier*	Gunnery Officer (Naval)
B	*Militärische Klasseneinteilung B*	Unarmed biplanes - Imperial
BAK	*Ballon-Abwehr-Kanon*	Anti-Balloon Gun
BK	*Bordkanone*	Fixed mounted aircraft cannon
BM	*Bordmechaniker*	Flight Engineer
BoGOHL	*Bombengeschwader d.Oberste-Heeresl.*	Bomber Wing, Army High Comd.
BO	*Beobachter*	Observer
BS	*Bordschutz*	Air Gunner
Btl.	*Bataillon*	Battalion
C	*Militärische Klasseneinteilung C*	Armed biplanes - Imperial
CdS	*Chef des Stabes*	Chief of Staff
CL	*Militärische Klasseneinteilung CL*	Assault biplanes - Imperial
D	*Militärische Klasseneinteilung D*	Fighter biplanes - Imperial
Dr.	*Militärische Klasseneinteilung Dr*	Fighter Triplanes - Imperial
Div.	*Division*	Division
Dtsch.	*Deutschen*	German
E	*Militärische Klasseneinteilung E*	Armed monoplanes - Imperial
(E)	*Eisenbahn*	Railway mounted
E-Stelle	*Erprobungsstelle*	Experimental Test Centre
Erg.	*Ergänzungs*	Replacement
Erkudista	*Erkundsflugzeuge f.d.Div.Nahaufkl.Staf.*	Army Co-operation aircraft
Erkunigros	*Erkundungsf'zg f.mit.Hoh.u.gros.Entfern'n*	Long range Recce-Bomber
ESAC	*Elect.Senkrecht Aufhangung f.Cyl.bom.*	Elect.Vertical Magazine for C-Bombs
ETC	*Elektrische Tragervorrichtung f.C-Bomb*	Elect.operated racks for C-Bombs
(F)	*Fernaufklärungsstaffel*	Long range Reconnaissance Sqdrn.
FA	*Flieger Abteilung*	Flight Detachment (Imperial period)
FA	*Flakabteilung*	Anti-Aircraft Artillery Battalion
FdL	*Führer der Marineluftstreitkräfte*	Naval Air Commander
FEA	*Flieger-Ersatz-Abteilung*	Aircrew Replacement Battalion
FF	*Flugzeugführer*	Pilot
Fhr.	*Führer*	Leader
Flak	*Flakartillerie*	Anti-Aircraft Artillery

FlaK	*Flakabwehrkanone*	Anti-Aircraft Gun
Fl.-Div.	*Flieger-Division*	Air Division
FR	*Flakregiment*	Anti-Aircraft Artillery Regiment
FuG	*Funk-Great(e)*	Wireless equipment
G	*Militärische Klasseneinteilung G*	Multi-engine bombers - Imperial
GAZ	*Gosudarstvenny aviatsionny zavod*	Soviet State Aircraft Factory
Gefu	*Ges.f.Ford.Gewerblicher Unter'gen Ausland*	Foreign Industrial Activities Ltd.
gem.	*gemischte*	mixed
gef.	*gefallen*	Killed in action (KIA)
gefang.	*Gefangen*	Prisoner of War (PoW)
gem.	*gemisst*	Missing in action (MIA)
gew.	*verwundet*	Wounded in action (WIA)
GmbH	*Gesellschaft mit beschrankter Haftung*	Limited Company (Ltd.)
Gr.Kdo.	*Gruppenkommando*	Army Group Command
Gronabo	*Größnachtbomber*	Heavy Night Bomber
GUAP	*Glavnoe upravlenie aviatsionnoi promyshlennosti*	CD of the Aircraft Industry
GU-RKKVVF	*Glavnoe upravlenie-RKKVVF*	Chief Directorate of the Air Force
(H)	*Heeresaufklärungstaffel*	Army Reconnaissance Squadron
HDv.	*Heeresdienstvorschrift*	Army Regulation (numbered)
Heitag	*Heimatjagdeinsitzer*	Home defence day fighter
Henaja	*Hellnachtjagd*	Illuminated Night Fighting
HEZ	*Haupt-Einflugzeichensenders*	Inner marker transmitter (ILS)
HK	*Handkamera*	Hand-held aerial camera
HKL	*Hauptkampflinie*	Main Battle Line
Hr.Gr.	*Heeresgruppe*	Army Group
i.G.	*im Generalstab*	in the General Staff
ILS	Instrument Landing System	Beam Approach System
ILUK	*Inter.Luftfahrt-Uberwachungs Kom.*	Inter-allied Aviation Control Com'n
IMKK	*Interallierte Militär-Kontroll Kommission*	Inter-allied Military Control Com'n
Inf.	*Infanterie*	Infantry
Jasta	*Jagdstaffel*	Fighter squadron
J	*Militärische Klasseneinteilung J*	Armoured aircraft - Imperial
JG	*Jagdgeschwader*	Fighter Wing
JGr.	*Jagdgruppe*	Fighter Group
K	*Kanonier*	Gunner
KaGOHL	*Kampfgeschwader d.Oberste-Heersl.*	Bomber wing, Army High Comd.
Kar.	*Karabiner*	Carbine - Rifle
Kap.	*Käpitan*	Squadron Commander
Kasta	*Kampffliegerstaffel*	Bomber squadron
Kav.	*Kavallerie*	Cavalry
KdE	*Kommando der Fliegererprobungsstelle*	Flight Testing Stations Command
Kdo.	*Kommando*	Small unit command
Kdr.	*Kommandeur*	Gruppe Commander
Kdre.	*Kommodore*	Wing Commodore

KFS	*Kampffliegerschule*	Bomber Aircrew School
Kfw.	*Kraftwagen*	Motor vehicle
Kfz.	*Kraftfahrzeug*	Motor vehicle
KoFl.	*Kommandeur der Flieger*	Army Air Commander
KoFlak	*Kommandeur der Flakartillerie*	Anti-aircraft Artillery Commander
KoFlug	*Kommandant der Flughafen*	Airfield Commandant
KoGenLuft	*Kom.Gen.d.Luftstreitkräfte*	General Commanding Air Service
Kp.	*Kompanie*	Company
(L)	*Luftstreitkräfte, Luftwaffen*	Air Service, Air Force
Lu.	*Luft*	Air
Ia	*Operations Offizier*	First Staff Officer - Operations
lei.	*leichte*	light
LGK	*Luftfahrt Garantie Komitee*	Aerial Guarantee Commission
LS-Amt	*Luftschützamt*	Air Defence Office
Lw.	*Luftwaffe*	Luftwaffe
Maga	*Magazin*	Internal Bomb Carrier
MG	*Maschinengewehr*	Machine Gun
Minabo	*Mittlere Nachtbomber*	Medium night bomber
(mot.)	*motorisiert*	motorised
MS	*Minensuch(er)*	Minesweeper
MS	*Motorschiff*	Motor Ship (Diesel powered)
m.V.	*mit Verzogerung*	with delay (Bomb Fuse)
NACA	National Advisory Committee for Aeronautics (USA)	
Nachr.	*Nachrichten*	Signals
NAGr.	*Nahaufklärungsgruppe*	Short range Reconnaissance Group
Nav.Offz.	*Navigations Offizier*	Navigating officer (Naval)
NII	*Nauchno-ispytatel'ny institute*	Soviet Test Institute
Najaku	*Nachtjagd und Erkundungsflugzeug*	Night fighter Recce aircraft
OHL	*Oberste Heeresleitung*	Imperial High Command
OQu	*Oberquartiermeister*	Senior General Staff Officer - Army
PeilG	*Peilempfanger-Geräte*	Direction finding equipment
Pio.	*Pionier*	Engineers
Plm	*Pour le Mérite*	For meritorious service (Blue Max)
PuW	*Prüfanstalt und Werft der Fliegertruppe*	Air Evaluation Institute and Works
PVC	*Pulver-Elektrische Aufhangevorrichtung*	Chemical-Electrical activated ord'ce rack
Pz.	*Panzer*	Tank - Armour
Qu	*Quartiermeister*	Quartermaster
R	*Militärische Klasseneinteilung R*	Long range multi-engine bomber – I.
RdL	*Reichsminister der Luftfahrt*	German Air Minister
RdLI (RDL)	*Reichsverband d.dtsch.Luftfahrtindustrie*	Association of Ger.Aviation Industry
Revi	*Reflexnivier*	Reflector gun sight
Rgt.	*Regiment*	Regiment

RKKVF	*Raboche-Krest'yanski Krasny vozdushny flot.*	Red Air Fleet
RLM	*Reichsluftfahrtministerium*	German Air Ministry
RMS	*Reichsmarine Schiff*	German Navy's Ship
RVM	*Reichsverkehrsministerium*	German Transport Ministry
RWM	*Reichswehrministerium*	German Armed Forces Ministry
Ru.	*Rüstungs*	Armaments
RZ	*Rauchzylinder*	Rotating cylindrical projectile
Samag	*Sammelmagazinen*	Internal racks for small bombs
San.	*Sanitäts*	Medical
Schlasta	*Schlachtstaffel*	Assault squadron
Schusta	*Schützstaffel*	Escort Squadron (Imperial period)
schw.	*schwere*	heavy
SC	*Sprengbomben cylindrische*	High explosive bombs (cylindrical)
SD	*Splitterbomben*	Fragmentation Bombs
SES	*Seeflugzeug-Erprobungsstelle*	Seaplane Testing Centre
SG	*Schlachtgeschwader*	Assault Wing
SGr.	*Schlachtgruppe*	Assault Group (Imperial period)
Sich.	*Sicherungs*	Security
SMH	*Seiner Majestat Hilfschiff*	His Majesty's Auxiliary (HMA)
SMS	*Seiner Majestat Schiff*	His Majesty's Ship (HMS)
So	*Sonderausrüstung*	Special armament
Stabia	*Stabsbildabteilung*	Headquarters Photographic Branch
SVK	*Seeflugzeug-Versuchskommando*	Seaplane Testing Command
T 2 III (L)	*Truppenamt-Organisation (Luft)*	Organisation Br.,Troop Off.Air Staff
T 2 V (L)	*Truppenamt-Organisation (Luft)*	Organisation Br.,Troop Off.Air Staff
TA (L) T-Luft	*Truppenamt (Luft)*	Troop Office Air Staff
TO	*Technisches Offizier*	Technical Officer
TS	*Turbinen-Schiff*	Turbine Ship
TsAGI	*Tsentral'ny aerogidroinamicheski institute*	Central Aero & Hydrodynamics Inst.
TuF	*Tank und Flieger*	Heavy machine gun for ground spt.
TVA	*Torpedo-Versuchsanstalt*	Torpedo Test Institute
(v.)	*verlegefahigen*	transportable
VEZ	*Vor-Einflugzeichensenders*	Outer marker transmitter (ILS)
VZ	*Verzugszundung*	safety time delay (Bomb Fuse)
WaA	*Heeres-Waffenamt*	Army Ordnance Office
Wa.L	*Waffenamt-Org.Pruf.u.Beschaffung Luft*	Ord.Office-Org,Test & Procurement
Wa Wi L	*Waffenamt-Wirtschaftliche Luft*	Ord.Office-Foreign air economies
Wekusta	*Wettererkungdungstaffel*	Meteorological Squadron
WeWi	*Wehrwirtschaft*	Military Economics
zbV	*zur besonderen Verwendung*	for special Purposes
Z.Mo.	*Zentrale Moskau*	Moscow Centre
Zwimag	*Zwillingsmagazinen*	Twin internal bomb carrier

AVIATION AND MILITARY ORGANISATIONS & EVENTS

Abteilung I, Luftverkehr/RVM	Branch I, Air Transport, Transport Ministry
Abteilung Beschaffung (LC III)/RLM	(Technical) Procurement Branch
Abteilung Bodenorg.u.Flugsicherung (LB V)/RLM	Ground organisation & Flight Safety Branch
Abteilung Elektrotechnik u.Funkwesen/DLV	Electronic & Wireless Branch/Aviation Inst.
Abteilung Entwicklung (LC II)/RLM	(Technical) Development Branch
Abteilung Forschung (LC I)/RLM	(Technical) Research Branch, Air Ministry
Abteilung Fremde Luftstreitkräfte/TA	Enemy Air Forces Branch, Troop Office
Abteilung für Luft-und Kraftfahrwesen/RVM	Air and Motor Vehicle Branch, Transport Min.
Abteilung für zivilen Luftschütz (ZL)/RLM	Civil Air Defence Branch, Air Ministry
Abteilung Haushalt (LC IV)/RLM	(Technical) Budget Branch, Air Ministry
Abteilung Küstenflug/DLH	Coastal Flying Branch/National Airline
Abteilung Luftbildwesen (LB IV)/RLM	Aerial Photography Branch, Air Ministry
Abteilung Luftfahrwesen/Admiralitat	Aviation Branch/Imperial Admiralty
Abteilung Luftoheit (LB II)/RLM	Air Sovereignty Branch, Air Ministry
Abteilung Luftverkehr (LB I)/RLM	Commercial Aviation Branch, Air Ministry
Abteilung Wetterdienst (LB III)/RLM	Meteorological Service Branch, Air Min.
Abt.Nachrichtenverbindungswesens (LA/NVW)	Signals Branch, Air Command Office
Abteilung Zivilen Luftschütz (LA/ZL)	Civil Air Defence Branch, Air Comd.Office
Abwehrgruppe/ZA	Passive Air Defence Dept., Central Branch
Aerodynamische Abteilung/DVL	Aerodynamics Branch/Exp.Inst.for Aviation
Aerodynamische Versuchsanstalt (AVA)	Aerodynamic Research Institute
Aerosport GmbH	Aerosport Ltd.
Akamedischen Fliegergruppen (Akaflieg)	Academic Flying Groups - Universities
Allgemeines Heeresamt (AHA)/Heeresleitung	General Office, Army High Command
Allgemeines Luftamt (LB)/RLM	General Air Office, Air Ministry
Amtes Ausland/Abwehr/RWM	Foreign Office, Security, Armed Forces Min.
Armee-Oberkommando (AOK)	Army Command
Artillerie-Prüfungs-Kommission (APK)	Artillery Testing Commission
Attachegruppe/ZA	Air Attache Department, Central Branch
Ausbildungsabteilung (LA II)/RLM	Training Branch, Air Command Office
Bayerische Luft Lloyd	Bavarian Air Lloyd
Beamten-und Besoldungsabteilung (LD II)/RLM	State Servants and Payroll Branch, Air Min.
Beauftrager für Industriepersonal	Commissioner for Industrial Personnel
Begriffsbestimmungen f.d.dtsch.Luftfahrzeugbau	Definitions on German Aircraft Construction
Beschwerdeordnung	Military complaint procedures
Bio.Reichsanstalt für Land-und Forstwirtschaft	Biological Institute for Agriculture & Forestry
Buerodirektor des RLM	Air Ministry Secretariat
Bund der Frontsoldaten "Stahlhelm"	Steel Helmet – German Veterans Asson.
Büros für Industriearbeiter/RLM	Industrial Personnel Bureau, Air Ministry
BZ-Preis der Lufte	Berliner Zeitung Air Prize 1925
Chef(s) der Heeresleitung/RWM	Army High Command, Armed Forces Min'try
Chef(s) der Marineleitung/RWM	Naval High Command, Armed Forces Min'try
Chemisch-Technische Reichsanstalt	German Chemical-Technical Research Inst.
Coup Mondiale d'Acrobatie Aerienne	World Aerobatic Competition
Deutsch-Russische Luftverkehr GmbH (Deruluft)	German-Russian Air Transport Ltd.
Deutscher Aero Lloyd AG (DAL)	German Air Lloyd Airline Co.Ltd.
Deutsch Forschungsanstalt für Segelflug (DFS)	German Research Institute for Gliding

Deutschesluftamt	German Aviation Office (1919)
Deutsche Luftfahrt GmbH	German Aviation Ltd.
Deutsche Luftfahrtsammlung	German Aviation Collection (Museum)
Deutsche Luftfahrtverband eV (DLV)	German Aviation Association
Deutsche Luft Hansa AG (DLH)	German State Airline Co.Ltd.
Deutsche Luft-Reederei GmbH (DLR)	German Airways Ltd.
Deutsche Luftsportverband eV (DLV)	German Air Sport Association
Deutsche Verkehrsfliegerschule GmbH (DVS)	German Commercial Flight School Ltd.
Deutsche Versuchsanstalt für Luftfahrt	German Research Institute for Aviation
Deutsche Zeppelinreederei	German Zeppelin Airways
Deutschen Aero Clubs	German National Aero Club
Deutschen Modell-und Segelflug Verbände	German Model and Gliding Association
Deutscher Rundflug	German air touring competition
Deutschlandflug	Biennual German air touring competition
Die Pflichten des Soldaten	The Obligations of the Soldier
Eprobungsstellen der Luftfahrt	Aviation Testing Stations
Europa-Rundflug	Biennual European air touring competition
Federation Aeronautique Internationale (FAI)	International Federation for Aeronautics
Fertigungs GmbH	Construction Ltd.
Fliegergerate-Inspizient/LS Amt	Air Equipment Inspectorate/Air Defence Off.
Fliegerjugend/DLV	Youth Wing, Air Sport Association
Fliegerlandesgruppe/DLV	Regional Flight Group, Air Sports Assocn.
Fliegers von Tsingtau	Shanghai Airmen (Film)
Flieger-Versuchs und Lehranstalt (FVL)	Flight Research and Development Institute
Flotten-Abteilung/Marineleitung	Fleet Branch, Naval High Command
Flugbereitschaft des RLM	RLM Flight Readiness Section
Flugkommando Berlin	Berlin Air Command
Flugzentrum Lipetsk	Lipetsk Flight Centre
Flugzeug Beschaffungs Programm 1934	1934 Aircraft Procurement Programme
Flugzeugführer-Ausbildungsstelle/DLV	Pilot training centre, Air Sport Assocn.
Flugzeugführer-Übungsstelle/DLV	Pilot Proficiency Centre, Air Sports Assocn.
Flugzeugführer-Vorbereitungs-Lehrgang	Pilot's Preliminary Training Course
Flugzeugmeisterei	Aircraft Engineering Centre
Forschungsamtes	Communications Intercept Office
Freiwilligen Korps	Volunteer Corps
Führer der Marineluftstreitkräfte	Commander of the Naval Air Service
Führungsabteilung (LA I)/RLM	Command Branch/Air Command Office
Führungs Abteilung (I)/Höheren Luftamter	Command Branch/Higher Air Office
Funkversuchskommando (FVK)	Naval wireless experimental Command
Generalkommando (GK)	Corps Command
Gerichts Abteilung (III)/Höheren Luftamtes	Legal Branch/Higher Air Office
Ges.z.Forderung gewerblicher Unternehmen Ausland	Foreign Industrial Activities Ltd.
Geschütz Prufungs Kommission (GPK)	Gun Testing Commission
Gruppe Abwehr/ZA	Passive Air Defence Dept., Central Branch
Gruppe BSx	Dept.X, Sea Transport Branch, B-Office
Gruppe Politische Angelegenheiten/ZA	Political Affairs Department, Central Branch
Gruppe Rechtwesen/ZA	Legal Department, Central Branch
Gruppe Sanitätswesen/ZA	Medical Department, Central Branch
Hamburgische Luftverkehrs GmbH	Hamburg Air Transport Ltd.

Hansa-Luft (Flug) dienst GmbH	Hansa Air Services Ltd.
Hauptbildstelle, Bildabteilung/LS Amt	Main Photographic Branch /Air Defence Off.
Haushalts-und Wirtschaftsabteilung (LD I)/RLM	Budget and Economics Branch, Air Ministry
Heeres-Friedenskommission	Military Peace (Armistice) Commission
Heeres-Personalamtes (HPA)/Heeresleitung	Personnel Office/Army High Command
Heeressanitäts-Inspektion/RWM	Army Medical Inspectorate, War Ministry
Heeres-Verwaltungsamtes (HVA)/Heeresleitung	Administrative Office/Army High Command
Heeres-Waffenamt (WaA)/Heeresleitung	Ordnance Office, Army High Command
Inspekteur des Bildungswesens der Marine	Naval Training Inspectorate
Inspekteur der Heimat Luftschütz	Metropolitan Air Defence Inspectorate
Inspekteur der Luftschütztruppen/LS Amt	Air Defence Troops Inspectorate/Air Defence
Inspektion der Fliegertruppe	Air Troops Inspectorate
Inspektion des Lichtbildwesens	Aerial Photography Inspectorate
Inspektion des Militärischen Verkehrswesens	Military Transport Inspectorate
Inspektion für Waffen und Geräte/RWM	Weapons and Equipment Inspectorate
Inspektion Torpedo-und Minenwesens	Torpedo and Minewarfare Inspectorate
Interalliierte Luftfahrt-Überwachungs-Kommission	Inter-allied Aviation Supervisory Com'n
Interallierte Militär-Kontroll Kommission (IMKK)	Inter-allied Military Control Commission
Internationale Luftfahrtausstellung (ILA) Berlin	International Aviation Exhibition, Berlin
Intern'le Studienkommission f.motorlosen Flug	Intern'l Commission for Motorless Flight
Junkers Luftverkehr AG	Junkers Air Transport Co.Ltd.
Kaiserlicher Deutscher Aero-Club	Imperial German Aero Club
Kampfmittel-Versuchsplatz	Chemical (Gas) Warfare Establishment
Kommandant des RLM	RLM Headquarters Command
Kommandeur der Flieger der Flotte	Air Commander, Imperial High Seas Fleet
Kommando der Fliegererprobungsstelle (KdE)	Flight Testing Stations Command
Kommando der Heeresflieger	Army Aviation Command
Kommando der (Flieger) Schulen (KdS)/RLM	Schools Command, Air Ministry
Koniglich-bayerischen Luftstreitkräfte	Royal Bavarian Air Service
Koniglich-Preußische Fliegertruppe	Royal Prussian Air Arm
Kriegsamt	Imperial War Office
Landesgruppen/DLV	Regional Group/Air Sports Assocn.
Lehr-und Versuchsanstalt für Militärflugwesen	Military Training and Test Institute
Liegenschafts-u.Unterkunftswesen (LD III)/RLM	Real Estate and Housing Branch, Air Min.
Liste der Einheiten (LA)	List of Units, Air Command Office
Luftamt(es)	Regional Air Office
Luftdienst eV	Air Services Association
Luftfahrtabteilung/RVM	Aviation Branch, Transport Ministry
Luftfahrt Abteilung (V)/Höheren Luftamter	Aviation Branch, Higher Air Office
Luftfahrt-Garantie Kommission (LGK)	Allied Aviation Guarantee Commission
Luftfahrtindustrie	German Aviation Industry
Luftfahrt Nachrichten	Aviation News (Periodical)
Luftfahrzeugrolle (LFR)	German Civil Aircraft Registry
Luftkommando Amt (LA)/RLM	Air Command Office, Air Ministry
Luft-Magazins	Air Magazine (Periodical)
Luftpersonalamt (LP)/RLM	Air Personnel Office, Air Ministry
Luftschützamt/RWM	Air Defence Office, Armed Forces Ministry
Luftschützgruppe/Heeresleitung	Air Defence Dept., Army High Command
Luftschützgruppe/Marineleitung	Air Defence Dept, Naval High Command

Luftverkehrs AG Westfalen	Air Transport Co.Ltd. Westfalen
Luftverkehrsgesellschaft mbH	Air Transport Ltd.
Luftverkehrsgesellschaft Ruhrgebiet AG	Ruhr Region Air Transport Ltd.
Marineluft Fabrikationsprogramm	Naval Air Construction Programme
militärarztlichen Akademie des Heeres	Army Medical Academy
Militärstrafgesetzbuch	Code of Military Justice (
Militärwochenblatt	Military Monthly (Periodical)
Motoren-Abteilung/DVL	Propulsion Branch/Exp.Inst.for Aviation
Motoren-Kommission/RVM	Aero-engine commission, Transport Min.
Nachrichten für Luftfahrer	Notices to Airmen or NOTAM
Nachschubabteilung (LA V)/RLM	Supply Branch, Air Command Office
Nationalsozialist Flugschau	National Socialist Air Show
Nordbayerischen Verkehrsflug GmbH	North Bavarian Air Transport Ltd.
Oberschlesischen Flughäfen GmbH	Upper Silesian Airports Ltd.
Oberschlesischen Luftverkehrs AG	Upper Silesian Air Transport Co.Ltd.
Organisationsabteilung (LA II)/RLM	Organisation Branch, Air Command Office
österreichische Armee	Austro-Hungarian Army
österreichischen Fliegertruppe	Austro-Hungarian Air Arm
ostmanischen Armee	Turkish Army
Pariser Luftfahrtabkommens	Paris Air Agreements – 21 May 1926
Personal Abteilung (II)/Höheren Luftamter	Personnel Branch/Higher Air Office
Personal Amt (LP)/RLM	Personnel Office, Air Ministry
Pressegruppe/ZA	Press Department, Central Branch
Pruf-Abteilung/DVL	Test Branch/Experimental Inst.for Aviation
Prufstelle für Luftfahrzeuge/DVL	Aircraft Testing Centre/Exp.Inst.for Aviation
Reichsamt für Luft-und Kraftfahrwesen (RVM)	Air and Motor Vehicle Branch, Transport Min.
Reichskommissars für die Luftfahrt	German Commissioner for Aviation
Reichsleistungsgesetz	German Military Service Law
Reichsluftamt	German Aviation Office
Reichsluftfahrtministerium (RLM)	German Air Ministry
Reichsluftsportführer	German Air Sport Leader
Reichsmarineamt	Imperial Naval Office
Reichsminister der Luftfahrt	German Minister of Aviation
Reichsverband d.deutschen Luftfahrtindustrie	Association of the German Aviation Industry
Reichsverkehrsministerium (RVM)	German Transport Ministry
Reklameabteilung/DLV	Advertising Branch, Air Sport Assocn.
Reklamestaffeln(n)/DLV	Advertising squadron(s), Air Sport Assocn.
Rheinland Programm	Rhineland Programme – January 1934
Rhön-Rossitten Gesellschaft (RRG)	Rhön-Rossitten Ltd.
Ring Deutscher Flieger	German Fliers Network
SA-Fliegersturme	SA Flying Unit
Schlesische Luftverkehrs AG	Silesian Air Transport Ltd.
Schwarz Reichswehr	Black (Covert) Armed Forces
Seeflug-Wettbewerb Warnemünde	Seaplane Competition, Warnemünde 1926
Seetransportabteilung/B-Amt	Naval Transport Branch/Gen.Naval Office
Seeversuchsabteilung GmbH (Severa)	Naval Experimental Branch Ltd.
See-Versuchskommando (SVK)	Seaplane Experimental Command
Segelflugabteilung(en)/DLV	Gliding School(s), Air Sports Assocn.
Sondergruppe R (Russland)	Special Department Russia

Sperrversuchskommando (SVK)	Mine Warfare Experimental Command
Sportflug GmbH	Sport Fliers Ltd.
SS-Fliegersturme	SS Flying Unit
Starke-u.Ausrüstungsnachweisung (LA IV)/RLM	Strength and Equipment Branch, Air Comd.
Statische Abteilung/DVL	Statistical Branch/Exp.Inst.for Aviation
Strafregisterverordnung vom 17.2.1934	Criminal Records Regulations of 17.2.1934
Strafvollstreckungsvorschrift für die Reichswehr	Execution of imprisonment of 27.11.1933
Sturmvogel	Stormbird Association
Südwestdeutschen Luftverkehrs AG	South-West German Airlines
Technische Abteilung/RRG	Technical Branch/Rhön-Rossitten Ltd.
Technisches Amt (LC)/RLM	Technical Office, Air Ministry
Torpedo-Versuchs-Anstalt (TVA) (Eckernförde)	Naval Torpedo Research Institute
Torpedo Versuchsverband	Torpedo Research Unit
Trans-Europa Union	Trans-Europe Union Airline
Truppenamt (TA)/Heerseleitung	Troop Office, Army High Command
Reichswehr Vereinfachungskommissar	Comm'r for Retrenchment & Simplification
Verwaltungs Abteilung (IV)/Höheren Luftamter	Administrative Branch/Higher Air Office
Verein Alte Adler	Old Eagles Association
Verkehrinspektion der DLH	Transport Inspectorate, German Airlines
Verpflegung und Bekleidung (LD IV)/RLM	Food and Clothing Branch, Air Ministry
Verwaltungsamt (LD)/RLM	Administrative Office, Air Ministry
Volksflugtag	People's Air Day
Vorläufige Reichsheer	Provisional German Army (1919-20)
Vorläufige Reichsmarine	Provisional German Navy (1919-20)
Waffen Amt	Army Ordnance Office
Waffen Prüfwesens Abteilung (WaPrw)/WaA	Weapons Experimental Branch, Ord.Off.
Waffen Beschaffung Abteilung (WuB)/WaA	Weapons Procurement Branch, Ord.Off.
Wehrmachtamtes/RWM	Armed Forces Office/War Ministry
Wissenschaftliche Vers.-u.Prüfs't f.Luftfahrzeuge	Aircraft Scientific Test & Evaluation Institute
Zentralabteilung/RMA	Central Branch, General Naval Office
Zentral-Abteilung (ZA)/RLM	Central Branch, Air Ministry
Zentrale Moskau (Z.Mo.)	Moscow Centre
Zentral für Wetterflug (ZfW)	Meteorological Flight Centre

GOVERNMENT POSITIONS, POLITICAL ORGANISATIONS & EVENTS

Bayerische Volkspartei (BVP)	Bavarian People's Party
Burgermeister	Town Mayor
Der Sieg des Glaubens	Victory of Faith (Film)
Deutsches Reichsbahn	German State Railways
Die Nacht der langen Messer	Night of the Long Knives – 30 June 1934
Eiserner Front	Left wing political group
geheime Staats Poliziei (Gestapo)	State Secret Police
Harzburger Front	Right wing political group
Kabinett	Cabinet
Kaiserliches Patentamt	Imperial Patent Office
Kapp Putsch	Kapp Putsch (13-15 March 1920)
Kommunistische Partei Deutschlands	German Communist Party
Kraftfahr-und Landstrassenwesen/RVM	Motor vehicle and Highways Branch
Ministerpräsident	Presidential Minister

Mitglied des Vorstandes	Managing Director
München Putsch	Munich Putsch (9 November 1923)
Nationalsozialist(ische) (NS)	National Socialist
NS Deutsche Arbeiterpartei	German National Socialist Workers Party
Oberburgermeister	Mayor
Präsidenten des Deutschen Reichstags	President of the German Parliament
Preußischen Innernminister	Prussian Interior Minister
Preußischen Landesversammlung	Prussian State Assembly
Preußischen Staatsrates	Prussian State Minister
Rasse-und Siedlungshaupt Leiter	Leader of Race and Settlement
Rat der Volksbeauftragten	People' Council
Reichsarbeitsminister	German Employment Minister
Reichsbanner	German Socialist Group
Reichsbauernführer	German Agricultural Leader
Reichsforstmeister	Master of the German Forests
Reichsführer SS	German Leader of the Security Troops
Reichsjustizminister (ium)	German Minister of Justice (Ministry)
Reichskanzler	German Chancellor
Reichskriegsminister (ium)	German War Minister (Ministry)
Reichskommissar für die Luftfahrt	German Commissioner for Aviation
Reichsluftfahrtminister (ium)	German Air Minister (Ministry)
Reichsminister des Auswärtigen (Ausland)	German Minister for Foreign Affairs
Reichsminister des Innern	German Interior Minister (Home Office)
Reichsminister ohne Geschaftsbereich	German Minister without Portfolio
Reichsparteitage des Sieges	NSDAP Party Days of the Victors (Sep 1933)
Reichspostminister (ium)	German Postal Minister (Ministry)
Reichspräsident	German President
Reichspropagandaminister (ium)	German Propaganda Minister (Ministry)
Reichstagsabgerordneter	Member of Parliament
Reichstagpräsident	President of the Reichstag
Reichsstatthalters in Preussen	Reichs Governor in Prussia
Reichswirtschaftsminister	German Economics Minister
Reichverteidigungsrat	Reichs Defence Council
Reichswehrminister (ium)	German Armed forces Minister (Ministry)
Rotfrontorganisation	Communist Red Front Organisation
Ruhrfond	Ruhr Funds – donations 1923
Ruhrkrise	Ruhr Crisis 1923
Schütz Staffel (SS)	NSDAP Security troops
Sicherheitsdienst (SD)	NSDAP Political Security Service
Spartakists	Spartacist League
staatlichen Naturschutzgebeit	State Nature Reserve
Staatsminister	Minister of State
Staatssekretär für die Luftfahrt	State Secretary for Aviation
Stabschef	Chief of Staff
Sturmabteilung (SA)	NSDAP Stormtroopers
Verfassungsfeier	Anniversary of the founding of the Republic
Vizekanzler	German Vice Chancellor
Winterhilfswerkes	Winter Relief Charity
Zentrum Partei	Centre Party

GERMAN AVIATION INDUSTRY

AGO-Flugzeugwerke GmbH	AGO Aircraft Works Ltd.
Albatros Flugzeugwerke GmbH	Albatros Aircraft Works Ltd.
Allgemeine Fluggesellschaft Memel mbH	General Aircraft Memel Ltd.
Arado-Flugzeugwerke GmbH	Arado Aircraft Works Ltd.
Arado Handelsgesellschaft mbH	Arado Merchant Ltd.
Argus Motoren Gesellschaft mbH	Argus Motor Ltd.
ATG-Maschinen GmbH	ATG Machinery Ltd.
Walter Bachmann Flugzeugbau	Walter Bachmann Aircraft Construction
Bäumer-Aero GmbH	Bäumer Aero Ltd.
Bayerische Flugzeugwerke AG (BFW)	Bavarian Aircraft Works Co.
BMW Flugmotorenbau GmbH	Bavarian Motor Construction Ltd.
Bucker Flugzeugbau GmbH	Bucker Aircraft Construction Ltd.
Caspar-Werke AG	Caspar Works Co.
Daimler-Benz AG	Daimler-Benz Co.
Dietrich-Gobiet Flugzeugbau AG	Dietrich Gobiet Aircraft Construction Co.
Dornier-Metallbauten GmbH	Dornier Metal Boats Ltd.
Dornier-Werke GmbH	Dornier Works Ltd.
Flettner-Flugzeugbau	Flettner Aircraft Construction
Focke-Wulf Flugzeugbau AG	Focke Wulf Aircraft Construction Co.
Flugzeugbau Friedrichshafen GmbH	Friedrichshafen Aircraft Construction Ltd.
Gotha Waggonfabrik AG	Gotha Waggon Works Co.
Halberstadter Flugzeugwerke GmbH	Halberstadt Aircraft Works Ltd.
Flugzeugbau Halle GmbH	Halle Aircraft Construction Ltd.
Hamburger Flugzeugbau	Hamburg Aircraft Construction
Hannoverische Waggonfabrik AG	Hannover Waggon Works Co.
Hanns Klemm Flugzeugbau GmbH	Hanns Klemm Aircraft Construction Ltd.
Hansa und Brandenburgische Flugzeugwerke GmbH	Hansa-Brandenburg Aircraft Works Ltd.
Ernst Heinkel Flugzeugwerke AG	Ernst Heinkel Aircraft Works Co.
Ernst Heinkel Flugzeugwerke GmbH	Ernst Heinkel Aircraft Works Ltd.
Henschel Flugmotorenwerke GmbH	Henschel Aircraft Engine Works Ltd.
Henschel Flugzeug-Werke AG	Henschel Aircraft Works Co.
Hirth-Motoren GmbH	Hirth Motors Ltd.
Junkers-Fokker AG (JFA)	Junkers-Fokker Co.
Junkers Flugzeugwerke GmbH	Junkers Aircraft Works Ltd.
Junkers Flugzeug-und Motorenwerke AG	Junkers Aircraft and Motor Works Co.
Junkers Motorenbau GmbH	Junkers Motor Construction Ltd.
Flugzeugbau Kiel GmbH	Kiel Aircraft Construction Ltd.
Luft-Fahrzeug-Gesellschaft (LFG)	Air Vehicles Ltd.
Luftschiffbau Zeppelin GmbH	Zeppelin Airship Construction Ltd.
Luftverkehrsgesellschaft (LVG)	Air Transport Ltd.
Maybach Motorenbau GmbH	Maybach Motor Construction Ltd.
Messerschmitt Flugzeugbau GmbH	Messerschmitt Aircraft Construction Ltd.
Mitteldeutsche Motorenwerke	Central Germany Motor Works
Muhlenbau und Industrie AG	Muhlen Construction and Manufacturing Co.
Niedersachsische Werke	Lower Saxony Works
Ostdeutsche Albatros Werke GmbH	Eastern Germany Albatros Works Ltd.
Pommerische Motorenwerke	Pommeranian Motor Works

Raab-Katzenstein Flugzeugwerke GmbH		Raah-Katzentsein Aircraft Works Ltd.
Rohrbach Metall-Flugzeugbau GmbH		Rohrbach Metal Aircraft Construction Ltd.
Segel-Flugzeugbau Kassel		Kassel Sailplane Construction
Siemens und Halske AG		Siemens and Halske Co.
Udet Flugzeugbau GmbH		Udet Aircraft Construction Ltd.
Weser Flugzeugbau GmbH		Weser Aircraft Construction Ltd.

MILITARY POSITIONS & TITLES

aD	*ausser Dienst*	Retired
Adj.	*Adjutant(ur)*	Adjutant
aK	*auf Kriegsdauer*	War commission
aktiv.	*Aktive (liste)*	Active (list)
Arzt	*Arzt*	Medical officer
Beamte(n)	*Beamte(n)*	Uniformed officials
Bfr.	*Befehlshaber*	Commander
char.	*Charakterisierung*	Honorary Rank
Chef	*Chef*	Chief or Commander
CdGS	*Chef des Generalstabes*	Chief of the General Staff
CdS	*Chef des Stabes*	Chief of Staff
Dipl.	*Diplomierter*	Certificated - Diploma
Dr.	*Doktor*	Doctor
Edler	*Edler*	Noble
Erg.	*Ergänzungs (liste)*	Replacement (list)
Erg.Offz.	*Ergänzungsoffizier(e)*	Replacement Officer(s)
Fl.Fhr	*Fliegerführer*	Air Commander
Frhr.	*Freiherr*	Baron
Fhr.	*Führer*	Tactical Commander
Fhr.Res.	*Führerreserve*	Command reserve - officers
Furst	*Furst*	First in line
gef.	*Gefallene*	Killed in action
Graf	*Graf*	Count
Herr	*Herr*	Mr.
Hoh.	*Hoherer*	Higher or Senior
Ing.	*Ingenieur*	Engineer
Insp. Inspiz.	*Inspekteur – Inspizient*	Inspector
Kap.	*Käpitan*	Squadron Commander
Kdr.	*Kommandeur*	Commander
Kdre.	*Kommodore*	Commodore
Kdt.	*Kommandant(ur)*	Commandant
Kom.Gen.	*Kommandierender General*	Commanding General (Corps)
Ltr.	*Leiter*	Leader, Head of
Mann.	*Mannschaften*	Enlisted personnel
med.	*medizine*	Medical
OB	*Oberbefehlshaber*	Commander-in-Chief
Offz	*Offizier*	Officer
OffziG	*Generalstabsoffizier*	General Staff Officer
Offz.Stv.	*Offizier Stellvertreter*	Officer Aspirant (NCO)
OQu.	*Oberquartiermeister*	Quartermaster General

phil.	*philosophie*	Philosophy
Prinz	*Prinz*	Prince
Qu.	*Quartiermeister*	Quartermaster
Res. (R.)	*Reserve (liste)*	Reserve (list)
RDA	*Rangsdienstalter (liste)*	Seniority (list)
Stv.	*Stellvertrener*	Deputy
Uffz.	*Unteroffizier*	Non-Commissioned Officer
verl.	*verluste*	lost in action
verm.	*vermisste*	missing in action
verw.	*verwundete*	wounded in action
vet.	*Veterinarie*	Veterinary
von	*von*	Esquire
zV	*zu Verfugung*	available over age officers

GEOGRAPHICAL AREAS

Bayern (bayerische)	Bavaria (Bavarian)
Braunschweig	Brunswick
Deutschland	Germany
Franken (Mittel-)(Ober-)	Franconia
München	Munich
Ostpreussen	East Prussia
Pfalz (Ober-)	Palatinate
Pommern	Pommerania
Preussen (preußischen)	Prussia (Prussian)
Rheinland	Rhineland
Sachsen (sächische)	Saxony (Saxon)
Schlesien (schlesische)	Silesia (Silesian)
Württemberg (isches)	Württemberg (Württembergian)

ITEMS OF UNIFORM

Dienstanzug	Service Dress
Fliegerdolch	Dress Dagger
Fliegermesser	Dress Knife
Größer Gesellschaftsanzug	Formal Full-Dress
Kleiner Gesellschaftsanzug	Informal Full-Dress
Kragenspiegel	Coloured collar patches
Stahlhelm	Steel Helmet
Strassenanzug	Walking-Out Dress

Chronology 1918-1935

11 Nov 18	*Waffenstillstand* – Armistice
Jan 19	*Spartakist* Uprising
11 Feb 19	Ebert becomes *Reichspräsident;* Noske appointed *Reichswehminister*
31 Mar 19	*Adm.*Trotha appointed *Chef d.Marineleitung*
21 Jun 19	Former *Hochseeflotte* scuttled at Scapa Flow
28 Jun 19	Treaty of Versailles signed
11 Aug 19	Weimar Constitution signed
Oct 19	*Hptm.*Wilberg appointed *Luftschütz-Referat* (in the *Truppenamt*)
10 Jan 20	Terms of Versailles in force – Military Aviation forbidden
30 Jan 20	*TA* proposes the organisation of *Fliegerhorsten* within all *Wehrkreisen* and the formation of three *Fliegerstaffeln* and *Flakbatterien*
22 Feb 20	Beginning of activity by the *IMKK* in Germany
Feb 20	Organisation of a *Fliegerreferats* in the *Marineleitung* (*KptLt.*Faber)
1 Mar 20	Organisation of a *Fliegerreferats* in the *Truppenamt* of the *Heeresleitung* (*Hptm.* Wilberg), of the *Referats Flugtechnik* in the *Inspektion für Waffen und Gerat* and the *Referats "Fremdes Flugwesen"* in *T3*
Mar 20	*Gen.d.Inf.*von Seeckt appointed *Chef d.Heeresleitung*
Mar 20	*Kapp Putsch*
27 Mar 20	Noske replaced by *Dr.*Gessler as *Reichswehrminister*
6 May 20	Seeckt's edict dissolving the *Fliegertruppe*
Aug 20	First glider course on the Rhön with the participation of former *Fliegeroffiziere*
30 Aug 20	*Adm.*Behncke appointed *Chef d.Marineleitung*
1 Oct 20	*Luftschiffertruppe* disbanded
31 Oct 20	Report by *Hptm.*Wilberg for *Gen.*von Seeckt regarding the development of glider aviation
21 Jul 21	*Linienschiff Ostfriesland* sunk by USAAS bombers
Sep 21	German-Soviet discussions over the establishment of a German armaments factory in the USSR (*Obst.*Hasse, *Maj.*von Schleicher)
8 Dec 21	First Conference between Seeckt and Soviet negotiators
13 Dec 21	Washington Naval Treaty signed by former Allied powers
1 Feb 22	Start of the three month ban on the import and construction of aircraft
16 Apr 22	Rapello Treaty signed – Establishment of *Luftfahrtgarantiekommitees (LGK)*
22	First theoretical *Fliegerlehrgang* for *Fahnriche zur See* at Stralsund
Dec 22	*Maj.a.D.*Brandenburg appointed as *Ministerialrat* in the *RVM*
1 Jan 23	Germany regains air sovereignty over the Reichs territory
11 Jan 23	France occupies the Ruhr; purchase of 100 Fokker D.XIII fighters arranged by the *RWM* using the *Ruhrfonds*
Feb 23	*RWM* Commision under *GenMaj.*Hasse in the Soviet Union
Feb 23	Establishment of *Zentrale Moskau (ZMo). Leiter Obst.a.D.*von der Lieth-Thomsen until 1929
Feb 23	Second naval *Fliegerlehrgang*

26 Mar 23	*KptLt.*Ritter takes over the leadership of the *Fliegerreferats* in the *Marineleitung*
23	Seeckt Memorandum regarding the creation of a *Luftamtes* within the *RWM* and the formation of an independent *Reichsluftwaffe*
22 Jun 23	Hyper-inflation destroys German economy
26 Sep 23	Passive resistance in the Ruhr ends
8-9 Nov 23	*München Putsch*; Hitler arrested, Göring flees to Sweden
Dec 23	*ILUK* reports a total of 128 aircraft are employed in civil air traffic with 64 aircraft under construction
Jan 24	Discussions between *the Infanterie-Divisonen Referenten zbV* and the *TA's Fliegerreferenten* re: flying training with powered aircraft in the *Reichswehr*
Oct 24	*Adm.*Zenker appointed *Chef d.Marineleitung*
Oct 24	*Hptm.*Felmy was *Sachbearbeiter* (Official in Charge) of air questions in *T 1*
24	Responsibility for the *Reichsamtes für Luftfahrt* rests with the *RVM*
1 Apr 24	*Maj.a.D.*Brandenburg appointed *Leiter of the Abteilung Luftfahrt/RVM*
24	Establishment of the *Flugzentrum* in Lipetsk
Jun 24	Formation of *Sportflug GmbH* with ten *Fliegerschulen* in the seven *Wehrkreisen*
24	Creation of the *Severa GmbH* for the benefit of the *Reichsmarine*. Beginning of *Seebeobachterlehrgange* with *Severa*. First training of naval pilots by *Aerosport GmbH* at Warnemünde
24	*Hptm.*Student, *Referent Leiter Fliegertechnik (Entwicklung)* in the *WaA* discusses with the *Bayerischen Motorenwerk* the development of a German aero-engine
24	c.*RM* 200,000 allocated from the *Reichsmarine* budget for the *Seefliegerei*
22 Jan 25	Formation of the *Gruppe T 2 III (L)* as the central office for aviation matters within the *Reichsheeres*
28 Feb 25	Death of *Reichspräsident* Ebert
1 Apr 25	Creation of the *Deutsche Verkehrsfliegerschule (DVS) Berlin-Staaken* under *Maj.a.D.*Keller – for marine aircrew at Warnemünde under *Oblt.z.S.a.D.*von Gronau; the Warnemünde centre has a satellite at Stettin-Altdamm under *KorvKpt.a.D.*Goltz. Establishment of the *Seeflugstation List* under *KptLt.a.D.*Scheurlen
26 Apr 25	*GFM.a.D.*Hindenburg becomes *Reichspräsident*
Jun 25	*Fliegerschule* established at Lipetsk: *Leiter Maj.a.D.*Stahr until 1930, beginning of training, including all fighter pilot training, at Lipetsk
4 Jun 25	*Gruppe T 2 III (L)* forbidden by Allied monitors
14 Jul 25	French evacuate Ruhr
Jul 25	*Kpt.z.S.*Lahs *appointed Leiter* of the *Gruppe BSx* in the *Reichsmarine's Seetransportabteilung*
31 Aug 25	Beginning of negotiations with the *IMKK* for permission to create a *Luftschützreferates*
25	*Erprobungsstelle Rechlin des Reischverbändes der deutschen Luftfahrt* established; testing begins in Summer 1926
25	Annual budget of the *Heeresfliegergruppe* established at c.*RM* 10 million
6 Jan 26	Amalgamation of *Junkers Luftverkehr* and *Deutscher Aero Lloyd* to create *Deutsche Luft Hansa*
21 May 26	Signing of the Paris Air Agreement. Dissolution of *Sportflug GmbH*
May 26	Publication of the *Richtlinien für die operativen Luftkriegs* by *T 1*
1 Sep 26	Completion of the work of the *Luftfahrtgarantiekommitees*
Sum 26	*2.Deutscher Seeflugzeugwettbewerb*
8 Sep 26	Germany becomes a member of the League of Nations
Sep 26	Discussions between the *RWM* and the *RVM* over plans to provide flying training for *Offiziersanwarten (Jungmarker)*

8 Oct 26	Seeckt dismissed; *Gen.d.Inf.*Heye becomes *Chef d.Heeresleitung*
29 Nov 26	Selection and training of the *Jungmarker* ordered
30 Dec 26	Publication of the *Liste der Offiziere des Reichsheeres* who were assigned to *Sportflug*
26	Formation of *Fertigungs GmbH* by the *RWM*
26	*Kpt.z.S.*Lohmann, *Leiter Seetransportabteilung der Reichsmarine* purchases a controlling share of the *Caspar-Werke AG* for the *Reichsmarine*
30 Jan 27	Initial draft aircraft acquisition plan for the *Reichswehr* in the event of mobilisation (*A-Plan*)
Jan 27	Agreement by the *IMKK* to the creation of a *Luftschütz-Referats*
31 Jan 27	Completion of the work of the *IMKK* in Germany
1 Apr 27	Formation of the *Gruppe T 2 V (L)* as the central agency for aviation matters within the *Reichsheeres*
1 Apr 27	The first *Jungmarker* begin flight training with the *DVS*
1 Apr 27	Formation of the *Deutsche Luftfahrt GmbH*
30 Jun 27	First schedule for the *A-Planes* – including the *Luftstreitkräfte* and the *ReichsLuftschütz Luft-Heimatverbände*
15 Aug 27	*Maj.*Sperrle replaces *Maj.*Wilberg as *Leiter des Fliegerstabes* in the *TA*
27	*Hptm.*Student, *Referent Leiter Fliegertechnik (Entwicklung)* orders the initiation of the development of military aircraft types (*Heitag, Erkudista, Najaku* & *Erkunigros*) by the Aircraft Industry
27	Development of the *Größflugbootes* Do X by the *Reichsmarine*
27	The training of *Heeresfliegerei* by the *DVS* moves from Berlin-Staaken to Schleißheim and Braunschweig
20 Jan 28	*Dr.*Gessler forced to resign and replaced by *GenLt.a.D.*Groener as *Reichswehrminister*
1 Feb 28	Amalgamation of all *Fliegertechnischen* elements of the WaA into the *Gruppe Wa (L)*
1 Apr 28	Purchase of the *Caspar-Werke AG* by the *Reichsmarine*; formation of the *Seeflugzeug-Eprobungsstelle (SES) Travemünde*
10 Jul 28	First *Heeresleitung* Order regarding the formation of *Fliegerkurierstaffeln*
Sum 28	Beginning of *Beobachter* training and technical testing at Lipetsk
Sum 28	The first *Jungmarker* begin their fighter pilot training at Lipetsk
1 Oct 28	*Adm.*Zenker obliged to retire – in part of Lohmann Affair; *Adm.*Raeder appointed *Chef d.Marineleitung*
1 Oct 28	Beginning of *Seebeaobachterausbildung* at the DVS Warnemünde
1 Nov 28	*Maj.*Volkmann replaces *Hptm.*Student as *Chef Gruppe Wa.L*
Aut 28	Memorandum by *Maj.*Sperrle on the merits of a central *Fliegerinspektion*
14 Dec 28	Rejection by *Maj.*Keitel of the *Keßelring* recommendations within the *Truppenamt*
28	Beginning of *Beobachterausbildung* at Voronezh (Woronesh)
1 Jan 29	Official formation of the *Erprobungsstelle Travemünde der deutschen Luftfahrtindustrie*
1 Feb 29	*Obstlt.*Felmy appointed *Chef Gruppe T 2 V (L)*
1 Apr 29	Beginning of the *1st Ausrüstungsperiod*
20 Sep 29	*Kap.z.S.*Zander becomes the *Leiter d.Luftschützgruppe* in the *Marineleitung*
1 Oct 29	Transformation of the *Gruppe T 2 V (L)* as the *Inspektion der Luftwaffe* in the *Inspektion der Waffenschulen*; transformation of the *Gruppe Wa.L* into the *Wa.Prw.8F*; appointment of *Obstlt.*Wimmer in succession to *Maj.*Volkmann
24 Oct 29	Wall Street Crash; beginning of the World economic crisis
Dec 29	Announcement of aircraft development within the *2nd Ausrüstungsperiode*
29	*Maj.a.D.Dr.*Niedermeyer becomes *Leiter d.ZMo* until 1932
29 Jan 30	Assignment of the *Fahrabteilung 2* as the troop cadre for the *Luftwaffe*
Mar 30	*WaA* plan for the establishment of an *A-Luftwaffe*

30 Mar 30	Fall of the Müller Government; *Reichspräsident* Hindenburg appoints Bruning as *Reichskanzler* under an evolving form of presidential government
1 Apr 30	*Aufstellungsplan der Wehrmacht* in the case of mobilisation agreed
30 Jun 30	Allies complete evacuation of the Rheinland
1 Oct 30	Beginning of the formation of the *Reklamestaffeln*; return of the necessary personnel from Lipetsk to Germany
1 Nov 30	*Gen.d.Inf.*von Hammerstein-Equord appointed *Chef d.Heeresleitung*; *Geheime Fliegerliste des Reichsheeres* shows 168 names (See App.1J)
Dec 30	Draft *Richtlinien für die Ausbildung in der Reichswehr auf dem Gebiet der Luftwaffe*
Jan 31	*Reichsheer* possesses c.300 trained *Fliegeroffiziere* and *Offiziersanwarter*; the *Reichsmarine* has 40 to 50 *Fliegeroffiziere*
20 Jan 31	The *Reklamestaffeln* were earmarked as *Fliegerkurierstaffeln* in the event of mobilisation (First military air units of the *Reichsheeres*)
1 Feb 31	*Richtlinien für die Ausbildung in der Reichswehr auf dem Gebiet der Luftwaffe* promulgated
Sum 31	High point of secret flight testing at Lipetsk with staffing of over 300 men
27 Oct 31	New Standing Deployment Plan within *Inspektion 1*
19 Dec 31	Principles for Operations by the *Luftstreitkräfte* established
Dec 31	Transfer of *Beobachterausbildung* from Lipetsk to Braunschweig
31	*Maj.*Müller was *Leiter Lipetsk* until 1933
1 Feb 32	*Inspektion 1 Planstudie* for the *A-Luftwaffe 1938* (1,056 aircraft)
2 Feb 32	Geneva Disarmament Conference begins
24 Feb 32	Final instruction for the establishment of the notional *Luftwaffe* by the *Chef d.Heeresleitung*
4 Apr 32	*Inspektion 1* report on the current situation of the German aviation industry
1 Jun 32	*Reichspräsident* Hindenburg replaces Bruning with von Papen as *Reichskanzler* and Groener with *GenLt.a.D.*von Schleicher as *Reichswehrminister*
1 Jul 32	*Planstudie "Wehrmachtluftabteilung"*
9 Jul 32	Lausanne Conference ends, ending of German war reparations
26 Jul 32	Loss of the *Segelschulschiff Niobe* with most of the *Reichsmarine's* 1932 Class of *Fahnriche zur See*
28 Jul 32	Formation instruction for the *Luftstreitkräfte* within the new *Friedensheer* (peacetime Army)(See App.2J)
31 Jul 32	*NSDAP* becomes largest party in the Reichstag elections
10 Aug 32	The organisational basis for the formation of the *Luftstreitkräften* agreed
Aug 32	Memorandum on the necessary requirements to bring together all aspects of German Aviation under the *Reichswehrminister*
1 Oct 32	*FregKpt.*Wenninger appointed *Leiter d.Luftschützgruppe* in the *Marineleitung*
11 Oct 32	Beginning of negotiations over independence for the planned *Luftwaffe*
11 Nov 32	Report by *Inspektion 1* in respect of the current situation of the personnel and equipment of the *Luftwaffe*
3 Dec 32	*Reichspräsident* Hindenburg replaces von Papen as *Reichskanzler* with von Schleicher
32	*Obst.*Hartmann became *Leiter d.ZMo*
30 Jan 33	*Reichspräsident* Hindenburg appoints *Reichskanzler* with von Papen as *Vizekanzler* and replaces von Schleicher with *Gen.d.Inf.*von Blomberg as *Reichswehrminister*
1 Feb 33	Separation of the *Inspektion der Luftwaffe* from the *Inspektion der Waffenschulen*
2 Feb 33	Decree establishing the position of the *Reichskommissars für di Luftfahrt*
8 Feb 33	Order by the *Reichswehrministers* bringing together the *Flieger* and *Luftschütz* of both the *Heeres* and the *Marine*

9 Feb 33	Cabinet discussion over the acceleration of the formation period for the *Luftwaffe*
Mar 33	Speech by Göring at Rechlin to the leading officers of the *Heeres-*and *Marineleitung* over aviation questions
31 Mar 33	Eight *Aufklärungstaffeln,* four *Jagdstaffeln* and *Behelfsbomberstaffeln* in formation
1 Apr 33	Creation of the *Luftschützamtes* in the *RWM* under *Obst.*Bohnstedt from the *Inspektion 1 (L)* and the *Luftschützgruppe/Marineleitung;*
10 Apr 33	Directive for the formation of a peacetime air arm (*Friedensfliegerwaffe*)
27 Apr 33	Establishment of the *Luftfahrtministeriums* under the *Reichsverteidigungsminister* and *Befehlshaber der gesamten Wehrmacht*
9 May 33	Conclusion of discussion over the independence of the *Luftwaffe*
15 May 33	Transfer of the *Luftschützamtes/RWM* to the *Luftfahrtministerium* (See App.2K). *RM* 7.3 million for the *Seefliegerei;* the *Reichsheer* has trained over 500 *Fliegeroffizierie* and *Offziersanwarter*
19 Jun 33	Calls by *Staatssekretär* Milch/*RLM* for an Air Fleet (*Riskio-Flotte*) of 600 aircraft
29 Jun 33	Order for a new *Aufstellungsprogramm* for the *Luftwaffe*
12 Jul 33	Activation order for the *Friedensluftwaffe* (See App.2L)
14 Aug 33	Order for the formation of the *Fliegerschulen*
28 Aug 33	Order for the 2nd *Ausrüstungsperiod* for the *Luftwaffe*
1 Sep 33	Transformation of the *Luftschützamtes* into the *Luft-Kommandoamt (LA)* in the *RLM; Obst.*Bohnstedt replaced by *Obst.*Wever
Aut 33	Disbandment of the *Flugzentrums Lipetsk.* Handing over of the infrastructure and serviceable Fokker D.XIII to the Soviet Air Force
1 Jan 34	*Reichspräsident* Hindenburg selects *Gen.d.Art.*von Fritsch as *Chef d.Heeresleitung*
May 34	*E-Stellen Rechlin* and *Travemünde* become military installations
2 Aug 34	Death of *Reichspräsident* Hindenburg; *Reichskanzler* Hitler becomes *Oberbefehlshaber der Reichswehr*
26 Feb 35	Directive by the *Führer and Reichskanzlers* over the formation of a *Reichs-Luftwaffe*
16 Mar 35	National Conscription re-introduced

Introduction

A great deal has been written about the *Luftwaffe*. In the first instance these publications were holistic histories - attempts to understand the *Luftwaffe* and in particular its spectacular rise, operational employment during the *Blitzkrieg* years and its subsequent fall in the face of overwhelming Allied air superiority. By the sixties literary interest had shifted to the *Luftwaffe's* aircraft, its technical expertise and its seemingly lost opportunities at a time of massive scientific and technical development. This interest was manifest in a wide range of volumes looking at the whole spectrum of German aviation development. This interest has continued undiminished by the passage of time although in many cases more recent works have concentrated on a single aircraft type. At the same time there was a significant change in emphasis in other *Luftwaffe* topics with a growing interest in the men and units in which they served. To a point campaign histories also emerged with a particular emphasis on those linked to American and British operations. Most recently a range of more focused books have emerged that examine in more detail quite specialised areas of *Luftwaffe* endeavour, a focus that includes pre-war developments, *Luftwaffe* ground forces, aerial tactics and aircraft camouflage schemes. As it has become more acceptable to publish these works in Germany the growth of German literature in particular has become very noticeable and welcome.

The Phoenix Project seeks to go beyond a simple re-working of earlier publications. It certainly intends to be a synthesis. This is a very necessary step given the increasingly focused nature of most recent books. It also seeks to provide balance. Many aspects of *Luftwaffe* activity have been neglected. This is particularly true of non-aviation activities and this work seeks to give proper emphasis to the *Luftnachrichtentruppe* (*Luftwaffe* Signals Service), the *Santitatswesens der Luftwaffe* (*Luftwaffe* Medical Services), the *Flakartillerie* (Anti-Aircraft Artillery) and the *Luftwaffenfeldverbände* (*Luftwaffe* Ground Forces). It also seeks to restore the balance between aircrews and their aircraft and the vital work of the Luftwaffe's huge technical organisation – the *Fliegerbodenpersonal*. Quite simply to date nearly all modern literature has focused on a very small element of the *Luftwaffe's* overall organisation and in the Phoenix Project I hope to put the record straight. Balance is also required in the geographical coverage of *Luftwaffe* activity. Nearly all that has been written covers the *Luftwaffe's* role and activity within the context of the western Allies. Yet for three years the *Luftwaffe's* war had been mainly focused in the east and it was always the war against the Soviet Union that was always more urgent and more vital to the *Wehrmacht*.

To understand the *Luftwaffe*, its training and tactics, organisation, equipment and employment one must also see the big picture. The *Luftwaffe* did not act in isolation. It was an integral part of the wider *Wehrmacht* and given the essentially continental aspect of German military operations this primarily meant the ground war. In all cases I have sought to place *Luftwaffe* activity back within its proper context and to this end a good part of this history will reflect military and naval operations to which there was an aerial dimension.

However this work does not seek to make judgements. The rights and the wrongs, the lost opportunities, the "might have beens" have been debated endlessly elsewhere. Put simply this book seeks to return the *Luftwaffe* to its proper historical context, to draw together its many disparate components and to provide a better balance of its diverse activities. The reader is left to form what ever opinion (s)he may wish - there is an abundance of raw material in the pages that follow.

Project Structure

A Project of this complexity requires a structure that will guide the reader through its myriad pages. Chronologically the work has been divided into a number of periods.

Within Volume 1 *The Phoenix is Reborn* there are two chronological sections:

The Years of Secrecy 1918-32
The Rise of Hitler 1933-1935

Within the context of this volume each period has then been divided into five parallel themes:

Strategy and Command
Ministerial Activity
Technical Developments and Production
Infrastructure and Training
Operational Activity

Each period can represent a separate volume within the overall history, whilst within the history as a whole the five separate themes can be followed separately from each other. As the Project is inter-connected both by chronological period and by theme the work has been extensively cross-referenced throughout. The reader can follow these connections or ignore them according to individual interest and purpose. It is only by adopting such a structure that proper weight can be given to each aspect of *Luftwaffe* activity and that each component part can be seen within its proper historical context.

In addition to the primary narrative there is also a further story. To their credit the publishers have supported the inclusion of a great number of photographs, diagrams and maps. The photographic material provides a parallel and important story that is a visual narrative in its own right and one that allows the reader to either dip into the history and structure of the period or to supplement the key messages within the written narrative. Detailed captions have been provided in every case thus avoiding the disjointed approach to the inclusion of visual material that is evident elsewhere. In essence the photographs have been re-connected to the actual events of the period.

The primary narrative is further supplemented by notes which seek to elaborate on the event or issue. Related decisions, alternative perspectives and technical developments, particularly those made outside of Germany, have been included at this point rather than interrupt the main story. Where an individual appears for the first time and/or drops out of the central story further biographical detail may be given in the notes. Due to the work's overall structure some material has been covered more than once but usually with a different emphasis and on occasion this will mean that material may appear in the main narrative in one section and as a source or note in another. The author accepts that there has been some repetition but its inclusion has been justified as it enables the overall work to be used in different ways by different readers.

Much detail has been provided in a series of appendices. These summarise information from the main narrative and are also intended as reference sources which can be used to discover more about particular individuals, organisations and units. To this end all officers with the rank of full *General* or above together with all highly decorated personnel have been given their own biography within the appendices of later volumes. All flying units of *Gruppe* size or larger and all *Regimenter* in the case of other *Luftwaffe* branches have been given their own historical summaries.

Style and Sources
This work seeks to recreate past realities so that the reader can better understand the decisions that were made at that time. Where possible an attempt has also been made to better understand the human aspects of this period. After all the *Luftwaffe* was primarily a large group of individuals who collectively represented the social, economic and political circumstances within Germany during this tumultuous period of history. This has been achieved through the extensive use of first hand accounts and diary entries together with a liberal sprinkling of contemporary documents and publications. The style seeks to emulate that used during the period. All ranks, positions and organisational terms have been left in their German form and *italicised*. At first this may seem confusing to the English reader but immersion in the work makes their use logical and self-explanatory. A comprehensive Glossary is also included at the front of each volume.

Inevitably massive use has been made of secondary sources. Post-war analysis by former *Luftwaffe* officers on behalf of the British and particularly the American intelligence programmes has proved to be especially valuable in this respect. More recent publications have been cross-checked to establish the most accurate account. Where sources clash the author has of necessity made a judgement and alternative views have then been included in the accompanying notes. Recently a great deal of material has been made available on the Internet and this has been used to update earlier thinking where this is appropriate.

With the exception of the photo captions, all statements that are seated in fact have been sourced so that the reader can check the veracity of the work and follow up specific areas of personal interest. Given the author's wish to achieve balance a considerable amount of detail - particularly in technical issues - has been omitted as this information can be obtained from the quoted source. A detailed Bibliography is included at the end of each volume.

Referencing
Where ever possible sources have been identified by page number(s). As this volume was originally written some ten years ago without page numbers, this has proved to be a mammoth task. As a result there are a small number of instances where page numbers have not been included: where a general source has been used and to include all the page numbers would be meaningless and confusing; where the book is no longer available to me to reference – originally accessed via a library, museum or loaned. I ask for the reader's forbearance in this respect.

Acknowledgements

It has always been my intention to include a wide range of quotes in the Project. As we become more divorced from the events of this period it is essential that we re-connect with those who were present through their diaries, memoirs and personal accounts. Unfortunately this has proved very difficult to achieve as many witnesses are now dead, many publishing houses have ceased to trade and rights have been difficult to trace. My thanks go those authors and publishers who have freely given their permission for me to quote from their works: Chevron Publishing for Erik Mombeeck, Erik Mombeeck for ASBL Linkebeek, Ian Allan Publishing for Hanfried Schliephake, the Imperial War Museum for Basil Collier, Lionel Leventhal/Greenhill Books for David Isby and Rudolph Stark, Pavilion Books Co.Ltd. (Batsford) for Kenneth Macksey and Peter Kilduff via Grubb Street for Carl Degelow. My thanks also go the University Press of Kansas for permission to quote from James Corum's *The Luftwaffe: Creating the Operational Air War 1918-1940* (copyright 1997 by the University of Kansas) and Edward Westermann's *Flak: German Anti-aircraft Defenses 1914-1945* (copyright 2001 by the University Press of Kansas) as well as to Judy and Jerry Crandall (Eagle Publications) to quote extensively from Wolfgang Falck's *Wolfgang Falck: The Happy Falcon – An Autobiography of the Father of Night Fighters* (copyright 2002 Eagle Editions Ltd.). Full credit lines have been given in the footnotes and a further reference to the publishers in the bibliography.

Unfortunately extensive and sincere attempts over the last year to contact a number of other authors have been less successful. It has been agreed with the Orion Publishing Group that I may quote from David Irving *The Rise and Fall of the Luftwaffe: The Life of Luftwaffe Marshal Erhard Milch* (Copyright 1973 Futura Publications Limited - Weidenfeld & Nicolson), Herbert Molloy Mason *The Rise of the Luftwaffe 1918-1940* (Coyright 1973 Cassell & Collier Macmillan Publishers Ltd.), Leonard Mosley *The Reich Marshal: A Biography of Hermann Göring* (Copyright 1974 Weidenfeld and Nicolson) and Peter Townsend *Duel of Eagles* (Copyright 1970 Weidenfeld & Nicolson). For the purposes of historical completeness it is possible that I may have unintentionally included other material which is under the copyright of a copyright holder who is presently unknown to me. In case of justified claims for copyright, please contact the author/publisher.

All photographs used in this volume have been sourced from the Bundesrepublik Deutschland's on-line Bundesarchiv and printed with permission from that source. Specific credits are provided for each photograph within the captions. Given sufficient interest in the Project it may be possible to publish a separate addendum with additional captioned photographs from this period from a range of other sources.

Since the Phoenix Project began in 1976 a wide reaching programme of research has been completed and it would not be possible to list all those who have contributed. However my special thanks go to the Department of Printed Books at the Imperial War Museum which provided a valuable impetus during the early stages of my research. Access to their copy of the *BA/MA RL 2 III Gen.Qu.(6.Abt.)'s Meldungen über Flugzeugunfalle und Verluste bei den fliegenden Verbände (taglich)* accessible on micro fiche was also invaluable. Thereafter my personal collection of *Luftwaffe* related books grew steadily and in this respect both Simon and Roly of the Aviation Bookshop deserve a special mention. More recently the wealth of material on the Internet has become significant.

In this respect Michael Holm's magnificent *Luftwaffe 1939-45* has been of tremendous assistance in respect of the *Luftnachrichtentruppe, Sanitätswesens der Luftwaffe* and the *Flakartillerie*, whilst his links to more specialised areas include Tony Wood's synthesis of the *Abschussmeldungen, Chef f.Ausz.u.Dizsiplin/LP (A) V* and to Henry de Zeng IV and Douglas Stankey's more recent analysis of the *Abteilung Propaganda/OKW Personalveranderungen für Apr 39-Oct 43 NARA RG242/T-77 Films 937-963* in respect of Luftwaffe officer career summaries. On a more personal level I must recognise the contributions that were made by the late Mary Ta'Bois, a former Y Station Operative, who assisted with some of the early translation and to my late wife Rosemarie to whom the whole Phoenix Project is dedicated.

The Author
February 2015

Part 1

The Years of Secrecy 1918-1932

1A1

Germany in Chaos 1918-1920

At eleven o'clock on the morning of the 11 November 1918 the guns finally fell silent along the entire length of the Western Front.[1] More than four years of bloody conflict on an unprecedented scale had cost the nations of Europe some ten million lives and more than twice that number wounded and disabled. The cost to Germany had been particularly severe with 1,950,000 dead from a total mobilised force of 13,250,000 men.[2] Moreover the nation had been forced to capitulate, an action which many of its fighting men had considered to be premature; in their minds Germany had not been defeated on the battlefield, it had been sold out by the politicians.[3]

Within hours of the cease fire the evacuation of the occupied territories had begun. In a masterful example of thorough staff work the three million men who made up the *Feldheer* (Field Army) in the west were brought home to their garrison towns in the Fatherland, all of this being accomplished within the thirty one days allowed by the Allied powers.[4] In nearly every case strict military discipline, the hallmark of the German soldier, was maintained and the remnants of regiments and divisions passed over the Rhein bridges in perfect order and often to the sound of glockenspiels and snare drums.[5] To the Allied observers it too hardly seemed to be the withdrawal of a defeated foe.

1   Shirer W.L. 1969 *The Collapse of the Third Republic: An Inquiry into the Fall of France in 1940* (hereafter cited as Shirer 1969) p.131. The Armistice was signed at 5 am in a railway car within a small clearing in the Forest of Compiegne at Rethondes - see also *App.I The Armistice Convention with Germany of 11th November 1918, and Annexes* in Edmonds J.E. 1944 *History of the Great War: The Occupation of the Rhineland 1918-1929* (hereafter cited as Edmonds 1944) pp.327-332.

2   Barraclough G. (Ed.) 1978 *The Times Atlas of World History* (hereafter cited as Barraclough (Ed.) 1978) pp.252-253. This represented a loss rate of 14.7%. During 1914-18 the *Luftstreitkräfte* had trained 17,000 men as pilots and aircrew. Of these: 4,600 had been killed in action, 2,000 had been killed in accidents or though other causes, 3,100 were missing or prisoners of war and 4,300 had been wounded (82% of those trained) - see Hermann 1943 *The Rise and Fall of the Luftwaffe* (hereafter cited as Hermann 1943) p.14. *Hptm.*Hermann was in reality *Hptm.*Hermann Steiner. As an anti-Nazi there was a very real threat to this author and his family at the time this book was first published in 1943.

3   Mason H.M. 1973 *The Rise of the Luftwaffe 1918-1940* (hereafter cited as Mason 1973) p.16, 20 & 22.

4   *Annexe No.1 I. The Evacuation of the Invaded Territories of Belgium, France and Luxembourg, as well as of Alsace Lorraine and II "The Evacuation of the Rhine Lands in App. I The Armistice Convention with Germany of 11th November 1918, and Annexes* in Edmonds 1944 pp.332-334. Groener's swift and orderly withdrawal of the three million strong *Feldheer* across the Rhine has been described as the last great achievement of the old imperial army. see Seaton A. 1982 *The German Army 1933-1945* (hereafter cited as Seaton 1982) p.1. Wilhelm Groener had been the last *OQu.i.OHL* - see Groener-Geyer D. 1955 *General Groener* & Snyder L.L. 1976 *Encyclopaedia of the Third Reich* (hereafter cited as Snyder 1976) p.128.

5   Churchill W.S. 1948 *The Second World War Vol.I The Gathering Storm* (hereafter cited as Churchill 1948) p.5 & Seaton 1982 p.1. However on reaching their home garrisons the bulk the rank and file deserted to their homes, often taking their personal weapons with them. Demobilised men received new boots, a new greatcoat and a small sum of money - see Mason 1973 p.22. Many rear echelon troops had in fact already fallen under the influence of the communists and had elected *Soldatenrats* (Soldier's Councils) - see Hoeppner von, E. W. Gen.d.Kav.a.D. 1921 *Germany's War in the Air: The Development and Operations of German Military Aviation in the World War* pp.172-173 (hereafter cited as Hoeppner 1921) p.169-172, *Hptm.*Erhard Milch (*Fhr.JGr.6*) in Irving D. 1973 *The Rise and Fall of the Luftwaffe: The Life of Luftwaffe Marshal Erhard Milch* (hereafter cited as Irving 1973) p.10 & *Lt.*Hanns-Gerd Rabe (*Fl.Abt.(A) 253*) in Kilduff P. 1991 *Germany's First Air Force 1914-1918* (hereafter cited as Kilduff 1991) p.151, whilst some highly decorated officers felt: *"If the call ever goes out again to fight for the Fatherland, I will gladly leave it to others"* (*Lt.d.Res.*Carl Degelow). Degelow was the last member of the *Luftstreitkräfte* to be awarded the

However the disciplined order of the *Feldheer* was not to be found in the *Heimat* (Homeland) of 1918; indeed the returning soldiers came home to find a nation impoverished by hunger and racked by political unrest.[6] The Allied blockade had particularly hit the civilian population and it was estimated that as many as half a million people had died of the cumulative effects of malnutrition during the last eighteen months of the war. The increasing uncertainty over the supply of food had led to an uncharacteristic outbreak of rioting and this escalating level of civil unrest had encouraged the *Spartakists*, the members of the German Communist Party, to emerge into open rebellion on the streets of Berlin.[7] Meanwhile their covert activities within the frustrated and discontented lower deck of the moribund *Kaiserliche Marine* (Imperial Navy) had led to the mutiny at Kiel.[8]

The new German Republic, led by the socialist Friedrich Ebert, was powerless to restore order without the support of the *Heer*; a truly ironical position as the senior army officers were almost unanimously opposed to the Republican politicians whom they believed had stabbed them in the back in reaching an armistice with the allied powers *(Photo 1A-1)*.[9] In any case the rapid, and at times almost uncontrolled, demobilisation soon made it apparent that there were simply not enough troops loyal to the state to influence the course of events. An attempt to employ the Imperial Horse Guards for the suppression of mutinous sailors in the capital in late December 1918 ended in debacle.[10]

This was the situation that faced the returning pilots of the *Luftstreitkräfte* (Army Air Service). Whereas only months some pilots had been national heroes they were now the subject of abuse and maltreatment from the communist mobs who actively sought out the most highly decorated officers:

> The impressions I gained in Trier were the worst possible; the town was a hot bed of mutiny and disorder. We were not prepared for anything of that sort, because we were accustomed to the good spirit shown by our men and could not believe that all discipline would crumble away so quickly.
>
> All the streets were full of riot and uproar, red flag processions and revolutionary oratory. The greater part of the demonstrations was composed of women and young lads.

coveted *Pour le Mérite* for 30 aerial victories (8 Nov 18) - see Degelow C. 1979 *Germany's Last Knight of the Air: The Memoirs of Major Carl Degelow* (hereafter cited as Degelow 1979) p.187 & Angolia J.R. and Hackney C.R. 1984 *The Pour le Mérite and Germany's First Aces* (hereafter cited as Angolia and Hackney 1984) pp.272-273.

6   Shirer W.L. 1963 *The Rise and Fall of the Third Reich: A History of Nazi Germany* (hereafter cited as Shirer 1963) p.52 & Mason 1973 p.21. To avoid anarchy the ruling Social Democrats would have needed to act decisively against the monarchists, feudal landowners, industrial magnates, the officials of the imperial civil service, the military caste as well as the political revolutionaries of both the right and the left.

7   Mason 1973 pp.24-25 & Henig R. 1998 *The Weimar Republic 1919-1933* (hereafter cited as Henig 1998) pp.9-10. The revolution followed the pattern of the Bolshevik uprising in the former Russia. The communists, independents, radicals as well as some moderates amongst the majority Social-Democrats did their utmost to destroy Ebert's provisional government. Their mistake was in trying to undermine the vestigial authority of the *OHL* and the status of army officer - see Seaton 1982 pp.1-2. The *Spartakists* were the forerunners of the *Kommunistische Partei Deutschlands (KPD)* - see Snyder 1976 p.199.

8   Padfield P. 1984 *Donitz: The Last Führer* (hereafter cited as Padfield 1984) pp.114-115. The enforced inactivity of the *Kaiserliche Marine's Hochseeflotte* following the *Skagerrakschlacht* (Battle of Jutland) of May 16 had fostered increasing resentment amongst the ratings on the lower decks. This provided a fertile breeding ground for political radicalism and in particular communist ideas. The matter came to a head in Nov 18 when *Adm.*von Scheer and other leading senior officers proposed a "death ride" for the *Hochseeflotte* in one final sortie against the British Grand Fleet in a symbolic action that would restore the Navy's "honour" in the eyes of the German people. The rebellion that followed was inevitable.

9   Snyder 1976 p.77 & Seaton 1982 p.2. Ebert was the leader of the majority Socialist Democratic Party from 1913. He was named provisional *Präsident* by the Weimar National Assembly on the 11 Feb 19. Whilst in office he attempted to steer a middle course between the radical left (communists) and right (nationalists) - see also Kotowski G. 1963 *Friedrich Ebert: eine politische Biographie*.

10   Mason 1973 pp.23-24 & Henig 1998 p.10.

I saw a mob assault an officer at a street corner. I went for them at once, but my help came too late. I found the old officer lying on the ground, with his head bleeding from several wounds. His uniform was in tatters; the epaulettes that had been torn off lay in the mud. I was in time to rescue him and carry him off to safety in a neighbouring hotel.

I could not understand the hatred shown by those people. What harm had the old officer done them? Was it their hatred of the system under which the individual had to suffer?[11]

Leutnant der Reserve Rudolph Stark
Käpitan Jasta 35b

Ordered to report to stipulated collecting points, usually the *Flieger-Ersatz-Abteilungen* (Replacement Air Depots) such as Alsfeld, Darmstadt and Halle, so that their aircraft could be handed over intact to the forces of occupation many pilots chose to deliberately wreck their aircraft in ham-fisted landings:

After the destruction of our planes we were told to report to Aschaffenburg, which was close to Frankfurt am Rhein, where the remnants of the *Oberste Heeresleitung* were assembled. Hermann (Göring) and Ernst Udet stayed in the house of an industrialist on the outskirts of the town, and we set up our headquarters in a paper making factory. I had a large courtyard suitable for mustering the officers and men, and there was plenty of storage space for luggage. While we were waiting the disbandment of the *Geschwader* and our own discharge, I and my clerks had plenty to do, bringing the records up to date. But for the pilots there was nothing to do but wait, and they did most of their waiting in the local restaurant, and they were often very drunk and always very bitter. It was understandable. The Germany we had known and loved and fought for was going to pieces before our eyes, and we helpless to do anything about it. Officers were being insulted in the streets by their men, the medals they had risked their lives to earn torn from their breasts.[12]

Oberleutnant Karl Bodenschatz
Adjutant Jagdgeschwader Nr. 1

In other cases aircraft left unattended in the open were cannibalised by the populace whilst fuel and spare parts were often sold-off locally:

The next few weeks - my next weeks - were full of burning planes, of planes reduced to scrap... During my retreat I saw planes abandoned in France and Belgium because they were no longer fit to be flown or had been damaged deliberately by the hostile population or by the revolutionary ground personnel or just because there was no fuel. Also abandoned were

11   Quoted from Stark R. 1988 *Wings of War – A German Airman's Diary of the Last Year of the Great War* pp.222-223 with the kind permission of Greenhill Books, Lionel Leventhal Ltd. *Lt.*Stark served with *Fl.Abt.296, Jasta 34b, Jasta 77b* & *Jasta 35b*. He had *11 Luftsiege* - see also Franks N., Bailey F. and Duiven R. 1996 *The Jasta Pilots: Detailed listings and histories August 1916 - November 1918* (hereafter cited as Franks et al 1996) p.271.

12   Quoted from Mosley L. 1974 *The Reich Marshal: A Biography of Hermann Göring* (hereafter cited as Mosley 1974) p.44 with the knowledge of the Orion Publishing Group. *Oblt.*Bodenschatz served with *Fl.Abt.3b* & *Jasta 2* before being appointed *Rittm.*Manfred Frhr.von Richthofen's *Adjutant* in JG 1 in Jul 17 - see also Bodenschatz K. Oblt. 1935 *Jagd in Flanderns Himmel – Aus den sechsen Kampfmonaten des Jagdgeschwaders Freiherr von Richthofen* & service record for Karl Bodenschatz in Hildebrand K.F.1990 *Die Generale der deutschen Luftwaffe 1935-1945 Band 1 A-G* (hereafter cited as Hildebrand 1990) pp.89-90 & Franks et al 1996 p.106. See also Hoeppner 1921 p.170, Ries K. 1970 *Luftwaffe Bd.1 Die Maulwurfe 1919-1935* (hereafter cited as Ries 1970) pp.11-12 & Mason p.16.

immense amounts of spare engines, spare parts, tools, ammunition, instruments - every kind of equipment farther behind in the reserve depots and in the repair centres, nearly all of which were located in the occupied countries. Nobody thought of salvaging this material; nobody seemed interested.

A great many planes and engines were lost in the Rheinland and indeed everywhere in Germany, training planes and also fighters and bombers which were about to be sent to the front. They were abandoned and pillaged and looted by souvenir hunters and by scrap thieves. Many of the planes which had already been put on freight trains were simply broken to bits - for scrap, for firewood, by the starving population. You couldn't blame these people. They needed the wood. They needed the few Pfennig they got for the scrap. And anyhow, planes to them were the very symbol of war - which they hated above all.[13]

Hauptmann ausser Dienst Hermann Steiner
Bombengeschwader der Obersten Heeresleitung

Indeed in the east one unit sold its entire inventory of fuel, aircraft and maintenance equipment to a group of Polish "customers", whilst in 1919 Anthony Fokker even managed to transfer most of the contents of his factory at Schwerin back to the Netherlands.[14] Not surprisingly the Allied demands for the transfer of 2,600 aircraft and engines quickly became quite impossible and even the revised figure of 1,700 machines and 2,000 aero-engines by the 1 December 1918 proved difficult to satisfy.[15] In fact by the 13 December only 730 aircraft had been handed over, mostly by rail, and nearly all were unserviceable.[16]

On the 21 January 1919 *GenLt.*Ernst-Wilhelm von Hoeppner, the *Kommandierenden General der Luftstreitkräfte*, formally disbanded the office of *KoGenLuft* in accordance with the armistice agreement:

13   Quoted from Hermann 1943 *The Rise and Fall of the Luftwaffe* pp.15-16 John Long Ltd. See also Ries 1970 p.11.
14   Ries 1970 p.11, Mason 1973 p.74-76 & Postma T. 1979 *Fokker: Aircraft Builders to the World* p.44. Following the Armistice Fokker had acted quickly to conceal 220 airframes and 400 engines in cellars and farm buildings. These were subsequently evacuated to the Netherlands by rail by Heinrich Mahn, his head of transportation. Meanwhile in the new nation state of Poland a considerable amount of aviation material was seized from the German and Austo-Hungarian authorities from base facilities at Lwow, Przemysl, Lublin, Warsaw & Poznan. During its battles with Ukrainian and later Soviet forces during 1919-21 the newly formed Army Air Force was equipped almost exclusively with former German and Austrian military aircraft - see Belcarz B. and Peczkowski R. 2001 *White Eagles: The Aircraft, Men and Operations of the Polish Air Force 1918-1939* p.36-45. Seizures are estimated at 250 machines, purchases at 20 machines – see Hooton E.R. 1994 *Phoenix Triumphant: The Rise and Rise of the Luftwaffe* (hereafter cited as Hooton 1994) p.21.
15   Edmonds 1944 p.44. The Allied knew that most operational aircraft had been transferred by the Germans to the eastern territories. The German response to Allied pressure varied: *"The first excuse was bad flying weather; then that the machines flown home had been dismantled; next that the revolutionaries had destroyed large numbers - actually in the Cologne area a number were destroyed by German air troops, as they had not the pilots available to fly them home."* However it has been claimed that the *Luftstreitkräfte's* front line strength was far stronger that credited by the Allies and that only by delivering brand new aircraft from the depots and factories could the overall target figure be reached - see Hoeppner 1921 p.169.
16   Ries 1970 p.11. *Artikel 4* of the Armistice Convention stipulated the surrender in good condition by the German armies of 1,700 fighting and bombing aeroplanes - in the first place, all Fokker D-VIIs and all night bombing aeroplanes - see *App.I The Armistice Convention with Germany of 11th November 1918, and Annexes in Edmonds 1944* p.327. On the 12 Dec 18 the German authorities claimed that they had handed over all their serviceable aircraft. The Allies later discovered that this amounted to just 516 land and 58 seaplanes of a force in excess of 9,000 machines - this being the figure secretly admitted to the Ebert Government on the 2 Mar 19 - see Morrow J.H. 1982 *German Air Power in World War I* p.146.

To the *Luftstreitkräfte*!

By a decree of the *Reichswehrministerium* dated 16 January 1919, the office of the *Kommandierenden General* has been discontinued.

And so I take leave of the leaders and troops of the *Luftstreitkräfte* which I had the high honour and pleasure of commanding during two years of the war.

Comrades! I thank you for what you did during the war!

The *Flieger, Flakartillerie* and *Feldluftschiffertruppen*, aided by the sure-working meteorological service, did excellent work at the front, and in a measure that was constantly increasing. The home defence work, monotonous in its constant watch, protected the sections of our country that were threatened by air attacks and prevented great loss of life and much material destruction.

All this was made possible by your incomparable valour, your vigilance, and your devotion to duty. Frequently you had to make a difficult flight against enemies far superior in numbers, but in spite of this you were able to win. Our *Luftstreitkräfte* entered the armistice undefeated and it merits the thanks of the *Heer* and the Fatherland.

With pensive sorrow and true respect I turn to our fallen heroes - their glorious picture will always be revered.

We are now facing serious and difficult days. I am confident that all of you, using the happy valour and industry which you displayed in gaining your successes during the war, will now make a whole-hearted effort to reconstruct Germany and to assure her a glorious future.[17]

The Kommandierenden General
von Hoeppner
Generalleutnant

However a good many units were still active in support of the increasing number of *Freiwilligen Korps* (Volunteer Corps); ad hoc military formations led by professional army officers and consisting mainly of tough veterans of the Great War for whom the national descent into anarchy could no longer be tolerated.[18] The first clash came in January 1919 when a *Freikorps Bataillon* of some 1,200 volunteers took on the *Spartakists* in the capital. Rapidly joined by at least 3,000 more ex-soldiers fierce fighting raged for more than three days and by the 15 January Berlin was once again in Government hands and Karl Liebknecht, the *Spartakist* leader, was amongst those summarily

---

17   Quoted from Hoeppner 1921 *Germany's War in the Air: The Development and Operations of German Military Aviation in the World War* pp.172-173 with the knowledge of the Battery Press. Although lacking aeronautical experience it was Hoeppner's organisational talents that led to his appointment as *KG.d.Luftstreitkräfte (KoGenLuft)* in Nov 16. In this duty he was outstandingly effective and by the end of the war the *Luftstreitkräfte* had evolved into a formidable fighting force totalling 2,709 aeroplanes in 284 *Abteilungen u.Staffeln* - see service record for Ernst von Hoeppner in Hildebrand 1990 p.xix-xxi & Angolia and Hackney 1984 pp.128-129. See also Imrie A. 1971 *Pictorial History of the German Army Air Service* (hereafter cited as Imrie 1971) pp.39-40 & Corum J.S. 1997 *The Luftwaffe: Creating the Operational Air War 1918-1940* (hereafter cited as Corum 1997) p.26.

18   Snyder 1976 p.98 & Henig 1998 p.11. Taking its inspiration from the first use of the term in 1813 during the Napoleonic Wars *"a new Freikorps, composed of former officers, demobilised soldiers, military adventurers, fanatical nationalists and unemployed youths, was organised by Hptm.Kurt von Schleicher. Rightist in political philosophy, blaming Social Democrats and Jews for Germany's plight, the Freikorps called for the elimination of traitors to the Fatherland."* Many members of the *Freikorps* were serving soldiers and sailors. It has been estimated that between 2-300 of these detachments were formed during the period 1918-23. Certainly they varied greatly in size and efficiency and were not all active simultaneously - see Pipes J. *Reichswehr - The Armed Forces 1918-35* in www.feldgrau.com. (hereafter cited as Pipes in www.feldgrau.com) The *Reichswehrministerium* maintained personnel records, arranged pay and provided supplies and equipment - see Hooton 1994 p.20.

executed.[19] During these actions air support was provided by *Feld-Flieger-Abteilungen 420* (*Hptm.* Ulrich Grauert) and *423* (*Hptm.* Victor Krocker).[20]

The fighting then moved north-west to the Nordsee ports of Wilhelmshaven, Cuxhaven, Bremen and Hamburg but no sooner had these towns and cities been secured than the communists took over in other parts of the country and fighting followed in Düsseldorf, Erfurt, Gotha and Halle *(Photo 1A-2)*:

> As the attempted revolution wore on, however, one had to put one's personal feelings aside and the show the world one was made of sterner stuff. Glutted with success in Russia, the communists tried to export their brand of liberation to Germany. It soon got so far out of hand that the civilian police were virtually powerless to stop marauding gangs of Reds who roamed the streets looking to overcome by force what they could not win politically. During one such encounter, the great German fighter *experte* Rudolf Berthold (44 *abschusse*) was seized by some communists, one of whom grabbed the silver threaded ribbon of his *Pour le Mérite* and strangled him to death with it.
>
> Fight fire with fire became the watchword. As I was living in Hamburg after I was discharged from the *Luftstreitkräfte*, I joined with several other former soldiers who wanted to form a private, semi-military organisation to effectively deal with the Reds. Together we formed the *Hamburger Zeitfreiwillger-Korps* and chased the rascals out of the city.[21]

Leutnant der Reserve Carl Degelow
Member of *Hamburger Zeitfreiwillger-Korps*

In March the *Spartakists* made a further bid for control of the capital and the equivalent of two full-strength infantry divisions had to be sent into the city by local *Freikorps* commanders. On this occasion the volunteers had the benefit of both armoured cars and air support but the fighting still raged for ten days before the professionalism of the *Freikorps* again prevailed and the rising was effectively crushed *(Photo 1A-3)*.[22] In March the conflict spread south to Bayern where the communists had seized München and had declared the establishment of an autonomous Soviet Republic. On this occasion the air units were able to play a more decisive role when they reported

---

19   Shirer 1963 pp.54-55 & Henig 1998 p.11. The *Freikorps* rarely took prisoners. Most captured *Spartakists* were lined up against a wall and shot - see Mason 1973 p.25. However Germany was not alone in experiencing violence on the streets following the ending of hostilities. Even in Britain there were riots and strikes, demonstrations in London and tanks on the streets of Glasgow. Some less responsible elements of the press whipped up concerns over the rise of Bolshevism and anarchy - see Marwick A. 1965 *The Deluge*.

20   Hooton 1994 pp.21-22. *Hptm.* Grauert had enjoyed a very varied flying career as a *Beobachter* with the *Aufklärungsverbände, Kampfflieger* & *Balloneinheiten*. He ended the war on the staff of *Kofl 18.Armee* - see service record for Ulrich Grauert in Hildebrand 1990 pp.385-386; *Hptm.* Krocker had learned to fly before the war and had subsequently served with the *Aufklärungsflieger* finishing the war as *Kdr.Armee Fl.Abt.18* - see service record for Victor Krocker in Hildebrand K.F.1991 *Die Generale der deutschen Luftwaffe 1935-1945 Band 2 H-N* (hereafter cited as Hildebrand 1991) pp.248-249.

21   Quoted from Degelow 1979 *Germany's Last Knight of the Air: The Memoirs of Major Carl Degelow* p.187 with kind permission of Grubb Street Publishing (re-published as *Black Fokker Leader – The First World War's last airfighter knight* (Peter Kilduff, 9781906502287, Grub Street Publishing 2009). Berthold had previously fought in the Ostsee region as part of the *Freikorps "Eisern Schar"*. His gravestone bore the inscription *"Honoured by his enemies - slain by his German brethren"* - see Angolia and Hackney 1984 pp.110-111. The *Freikorps* on the Nordsee coast were supported by *FFA 419* (*Hptm.* Creydt), *420* (Grauert) & *422* (Loewe) - see Hooton 1994 p.22, Mason 1973 p.44 & Henig 1998 p.12.

22   Mason 1973 pp.25-26. The communists attempted to secure power via a general strike which deprived the populace of utilities and transportation. However more radical elements seized the capital's 32 police stations as well Berlin's Police headquarters. This led to a massive response from the *Freikorps*. More than 2,000 revolutionaries were killed in the fighting.

on the movements of the *Spartakists* and attacked their units in open country. No less than 30,000 *Freikorps* troops were involved in these battles which lasted for more than a week before victory for the Government forces was once again secured.[23]

However internal turmoil was not the only threat to the new Republic for in the east Soviet forces sought to exploit the civil war which raged in Germany's towns and cities by driving back the German *8. Armee* from the towns of Riga and Mitau in Kurland (Baltic States) *(Map 1)*.[24] Several air units were mobilised to assist the regular army and *Freikorps* detachments in the east, including *Freiwilligen Flieger Abteilungen 424, 425* and *426* together with *Feld Flieger Abteilung 433*.[25] Equipped with the most modern products of the German aircraft industry such as the Junkers D.I and CL.I monoplanes, the Fokker D.VII and Siemens Schuckert D-IV biplane fighters and the L.V.G. C-VI and Halberstadt CL-V two-seaters, the units were manned by some of the former *Luftstreitkräfte's* most experienced pilots including *Hptm.*Bruno Loerzer and *Oblt.*Oskar Freiherr von Boenigk (See also 1C1).[26] Another important unit was the *Kampfgeschwader Sachsenberg* which formed at Jüterbog under the command of *Oblt.z.See* Gotthard Sachsenberg, the former *Kdr.Marine Jagdgeschwader Flandern*. This *Geschwader* consisted of a *Jagdstaffel (FFA 416), Schlachtstaffel (FFA 417)* and an *Aufklärungsstaffel (FFA 413)* together with ground troops, a balanced force which gave notable service in Kurland in support of the *Eisernen-Division* (Iron Division) during the spring and early summer of 1919.[27]

Although the success of the German ground and air forces gave cause for satisfaction their sacrifice would be totally nullified in June 1919 with the signing of the Treaty of Versailles.[28] Many Germans

23   Mason 1973 p.26. Red units in the open were bombed and strafed without mercy. Air support was provided by *FFA 409, 421* & *422* under *Hptm.*Steffen as KoFl. A number of *Bayerische Fliegerabteilungen* were also in action: *FFA Furth, Schmalschlager, Kriegelsteiner* & *Dessloch* plus *FA Krauser* & *Hafner* together with *Schlasta Anschutz* - see Pletschlacher P. 1978 *Die Koniglich Bayerischen Fliegertruppen* p.152 & Hooton 1994 p.22.

24   Reynolds C.G. 1974 *Command of the Sea: The History and Strategy of Maritime Empires* pp.476-477.

25   Imrie 1971 p.61 & Suchenwirth R. 1968 *The Development of the German Air Force 1919-1939* USAF Historical Studies No.160 (hereafter cited as Suchenwirth 1968) p.3. These units were formed specifically for this purpose in Dec 18 & Jan 19. At least 12 units operated against the Poles: *Feld-Fl.Abtn.400, 402-418, 411, 412, 431* & *432*. Air operations in Ostpreussen were co-ordinated by *Fliegergeschwader von Bredow*; in Schlesien by *Hptm.*Hugo Sperrle, the former *Kofl.AOK 7*. In total some 35 *Staffeln* with 250-300 aircraft were formed to support the *Freikorps* although not all in existence at the same time- see Hooton 1994 pp.23-24. During this period the Allies were happy for German forces to take the field against Bolshevik Russia. British forces had been deployed via Murmansk, whilst other allied units were active in southern Russia until Sum 20 when the White Forces finally succumbed to the Red revolutionaries - see Taylor J.W.R. and Moyes P.J.R. 1968 *Pictorial History of the R.A.F. Vol.One 1918-1939* pp.21-22.

26   Ries 1970 p.13, Imrie 1971 p.61 & Hooton 1994 p.23. *Fl.Abt.425* was attached to *AOK 10* and flew in support of the *Freiwilligen Reserve Korps Kowno*; *Fl.Abt.433* was attached to the *Ostpreussische Freiwillgen Korps* in Kurland. See also Grey C.G. 1943 *The Luftwaffe* p.85, and for details of the aircraft employed see Lamberton W.M. 1960 *Fighter Aircraft of the 1914-1918 War* & Lamberton W.M. 1962 *Reconnaissance and Bomber Aircraft of the 1914-1918 War*. *Hptm.*Loerzer was the former *Kdr.JG 3*. He served with the *Baltikum-Freikorps* until Apr 20 - see service record for Bruno Loerzer in Hildebrand 1991 pp.309-310. *Oblt.*Boenigk was the former *Kdr.JG 2*. He was *Fhr.Freiwilligen-Fl.-Abt.418* in the *Grenzschutz Ost* between Dec 18 - Sep 19 - see service record for Oskar Boenigk in Hildebrand 1990 pp.95-96. Both men were not formally discharged from the *Heer* until the 31 Mar 20. Other experienced officers included *Hptm.*Joachim von Schroder (*Bogohl 7*), *Oblt.*Otto Dessloch (*Jasta 17*), *Lt.*Werner Junck (*Jasta 8*), *Lt.*Carl-August von Schoenebeck (*Jasta 33*) - see Franks et al 1996 & Hooton 1994 p.23.

27   Ries 1970 p.13-14 & Hooton 1994 p.23. The *KG Sachsenberg* was formed from former military aviators who had answered the Government's call of Dec 18 for volunteers to protect the eastern borders (*Grenzschutz Ost*) and the German population of the Ostsee states. See also Imrie A. 1989 *German Naval Air Service* pp.87-88. *Oblt.z.S.*Sachsenberg was the *Marineluftstreitkräfte's* leading *Experte* with 31 *abschusse*. He was awarded the *Plm* on the 5 Aug 18 - see Angolia and Hackney 1984 p.228-230.

28   Edmonds 1944 p.183 & Henig 1998 pp.17-19. Prior to this the Armistice had been prolonged on three separate occasions since Nov 18. The last time was on the 16 Feb 19 in response to continued German military operations in Poland – Edmonds 1943 pp.42-43. In the meantime the heads of the victorious allied powers gathered in Paris in Jan 19 to agree the peace settlement that would be imposed on Germany. The French in particular would press for economic reparations, military occupation of the Rheinland and a massive reduction in Germany's military capability. Parisians had heard the thunder of *Preussen* artillery on 5 occasions in the previous century and had

had hoped for a tolerable settlement, particularly in the light of President Woodrow Wilson's famous "Fourteen Points" which had been first pronounced in January 1918; however these optimists had not counted on the depth of public feeling in France and Britain.[29] Both countries had suffered dearly in the four years of trench warfare which had devastated a sizeable part of the French countryside, whilst the flower of their youth had also died in that epic struggle.[30] The civilian population not been spared either and in a new dimension to warfare the *Marine Luftschiff Abteilung* (Naval Airship Battalion) and the *Luftstreitkräfte* had both bombed London and Paris from as early as 1915.[31] The politicians of both nations were therefore determined that the Germans would never again be able to inflict such suffering on the nations of Europe and the terms of the Treaty were written with this aim very much in mind. As issued to the German delegation in the Trianon at Versailles on the 7 May 1919 the Treaty consisted of no less than 440 separate articles totalling 75,000 words, a coherent package of directives which would relegate the German nation to the status of a minor European power:

THE TREATY OF VERSAILLES - A SUMMARY OF THE MAIN POINTS

- Germany was to admit sole responsibility for starting the Great War. She was also to produce for trial before an Allied tribunal some 900 officers and other ranks who had been accused of war crimes. Leading this list was the former *Kaiser*, Wilhelm II, for *"a supreme offence against international morality and the sanctity of treaties"* (Article 227);
- All planning then in progress for a new **Reichswehr** was to stop. The *Oberste Heeresleitung* was to be dissolved (Article 160) and all military academies were to be closed. The new *Reichsheer* would have a maximum strength of 100,000 men of which only 4,000 could be officers. Seven infantry and three cavalry divisions would be permitted but artillery support would be restricted to just 300 pieces of small calibre. Possession of armoured vehicles was prohibited and the manufacture of poison gas declared illegal;
- To prevent the build-up of trained reserves, service in the **Reichsheer** was to be restricted to volunteers who signed on for twelve years, or in the case of officers for a minimum of twenty-five years. Once discharged neither group could join a reserve force, whilst even membership of veterans' organisations was prohibited. Conscription was declared illegal;
- The **Reichsmarine** was to be reduced to a few pre-Dreadnought battleships, light cruisers and a handful of destroyers and torpedo boats, all other warships being handed over to the Allied powers (Article 185). Submarines were forbidden and new construction was limited to specific tonnages and was only possible when existing warships had reached an age of between fifteen and twenty years. Some existing coastal fortifications were per-

---

suffered occupation on three of those occasions: 1814, 1815, 1870, 1914 & 1918 - see Shirer 1969 p.142.

29   Mason 1973 pp.30-31. President Wilson had declared: *"We have no quarrel with the German people. We have no feeling toward them except sympathy and friendship"*. If his 14 points had been adopted Germany would have quickly returned to economic and political normality within a new more open international framework. However the US Senate refused to ratify the French proposal for a permanent military occupation of the Rheinland. This was regarded as a betrayal by the French Government.

30   Barraclough (Ed.) 1978 pp.252-253. French losses totalled 1.5 million from a mobilised force of 8.2 million (18.2%), whilst British losses totalled 1 million from 9.5 million (10.5%). However these figures do not take account of the detail: France had suffered 1,357,800 KIA, 537,000 POW/MIA & no less than 4,266,000 WIA - 73 % of the 8,410,000 mobilised. Of those wounded 1.5 million were permanently maimed. There was a very real concern about the birth rate. It was estimated that there had been 1.4 million fewer births because of the war. In 1919 France had a total population of just 39 million compared to Germany's 63 million. State sponsored immigration was necessary to help rebuild the French economy - see Shirer 1969 pp.139-140 & Hooton 1994 p.26.

31   Hoeppner 1921 pp.54-57, Imrie 1971,p p.29-30, Cole C. and Cheesman E.F. 1984 *The Air Defence of Great Britain 1914-1918*, Kilduff 1991 pp.70-73 & Corum 1997 p.24 & pp.34-36.

mitted but their modernisation was not allowed. A total of 15,000 officers and men were authorised with the same conditions of service as that of the *Reichsheer*;

- No **air arm** of any kind was permitted (Article 198) and all stocks of air material not already handed over to the Allied authorities were to be destroyed (Article 202). Even civil aviation was to be restricted *"during the six months following the date on which the present Treaty comes into force, the manufacture and importation of aircraft, parts of aircraft, engines for aircraft and parts of engines for aircraft shall be forbidden in all German territory"* (Article 201);

- The Germans were to pay war reparations totalling $130 billion with $5 billion to be paid in gold within two years of the signing of the Treaty. Large amounts of coal and iron ore were to be turned over to the French who would also occupy the Rheinland and the Saar industrial region for a period of fifteen years. Total blast furnace capacity was to be reduced by one third. All merchant ships above 1,600 tons were to be surrendered to the Allied powers;

- The political map of Europe was re-drawn and Germany was to be physically reduced in size losing territories to Poland, France and Belgium, whilst in 1920 Schleswig-Holstein was divided with Denmark. The former German territory of Memel was placed under Allied occupation until 1923 when it was annexed by Lithuania *(Map 1-1)*. All overseas colonies were to be surrendered.[32]

So shocked were the German politicians and such was the outrage felt by much of the German populace that serious thought was given to military defiance as an alternative to compliance with the Treaty's regulations. *GFM*.Paul von Hindenburg, the *Chef d.OHL* at Kolberg, advised his political masters that:

We can re-conquer the province of Posen and defend our frontiers in the East...in the West we can scarcely count upon being able to withstand a serious offensive on the part of the enemy in view of the numerical superiority of the *Entente* and their ability to outflank us on both wings. The success of the operation as a whole is therefore very doubtful, but as a soldier I cannot help feeling that it were better to perish honourably rather than accept a disgraceful peace.[33]

Generalfeldmarschall Paul von Hindenburg
Chef der Obersten Heeresleitung 17 June 1919

However the *Feldmarschall* was astute enough to realise that such an honourable course would have no more support than did *Admiral* von Scheer's planned "death ride" of 1918 and on the 24 June he went into voluntary retirement thus distancing himself from the Weimar politicians and the *Versailles Diktat*.[34] Given the presence of a large Allied army of occupation already across the

---

32   Shirer 1963 p.142, Shirer 1969 pp.57-59 & Mason 1973 pp.34-38. See also *Auswartigen Amt 1919 Der Friedensvertrag zwischen Deutschland und den Allierten und Assozierten Maechten nebst dem Schlussprotokoll und der Vereinbarung betreffend die militärische Besetzung der Rheinlande & App.XXI Peace Treaty of Versailles; Military Clauses* in Edmonds 1944 pp.396-401. However it was Article 231 the so-called "war guilt" clause that caused the new Weimar Government and the German people as a whole the greatest distress. Germany was not allowed to join the League of Nations and she was to pay substantial yet unspecified reparations to the Allied powers for the damage caused by the aggression of Germany and her allies. The subsequent loss of territory represented 13.5% of the pre-war area of Germany with 13% of her economic productivity and c.10% of its population. Heavy industry was particularly affected with the loss of 74% of domestic iron ore and 25% of her coal – see Henig 1998 pp.18-20.

33   Sourced from Shirer 1963 *The Rise and Fall of the Third Reich: A History of Nazi Germany* p.58 Martin Secker & Warburg Ltd. President Wilson remarked to one of his advisers: *"If I were a German, I think I should not sign it"* - see Mason 1973 p.39.

34   Seaton 1982 p.2. By distancing himself from the Weimar Government Hindenburg effectively assumed the moral

Rhein, *Reichspräsident* Ebert had little option but to agree to all the Allies' terms and four days later at Versailles the German delegation formally signed the Treaty *(Photo 1A-4)*.[35]

The terms of the Treaty formally came into force on the 1 January 1920 and within three months the mounting frustration within the right-wing elements of the *Reichswehr* had boiled over into open rebellion. On the night of the 12 March three *Freikorps* regiments together with some units of the regular army moved into Berlin where they pronounced the end of the Weimar Government. Led by *General* Walther von Lüttwitz, the *Kommandierenden General III (Berlin) Korps*, the militarists sought to reject the Versailles Treaty and to install a nationalist government under Wolfgang Kapp within an overall framework that would enhance the power of the *Reichswehr* and might even lead to a reinstatement of the Hohenzollern dynasty *(Photo 1A-5)*.[36] However the putsch proved as short-lived as its communist predecessors and within five days a general strike together with a lack of support from abroad had caused the revolt to collapse.[37] The pendulum than swung back briefly and violently to the left and there was another upsurge of communist activity. Within a week this too been extinguished in a series of bloody engagements between the rebels and the *Reichsheer* who had been given carte blanche by the Weimar Government to quash the revolution.[38]

The same events that had brought about the military up-rising in Berlin were to also result in the final disbandment of the *Reichswehr's* remaining flying units, a painful duty which was completed by the 9 April 1920 *(Photo 1A-6)*.[39] A last-minute request by the German authorities to the Ambassadors Conference, then in session in Paris, for the retention of a single *Staffel* together with eight airfields was predictably refused and the Allied powers also insisted on the disbandment of the *Polizei-Fliegerstaffeln* which had been formed during the previous year at Königsberg-Seerappen, Breslau-Gandau, Berlin-Karlshorst, Gotha-Erfurt, Paderborn, Allenstein-Deuthen, Kitzingen, Schleißheim, Größenhain, Boblingen, Schwerin and Hamburg.[40] The formal disbandment of the *Luftstreitkräfte* quickly followed, an event which was marked by the new *Chef des Heeresleitung* in an order of the day, dated 6 May 1920:

high ground over the *Versailles Diktat*. This added fuel to the *"Stab in the back"* accusations that many officers directed toward Ebert's Government.

35   Mason 1973 p.40. The "war guilt" and "extradition" clauses virtually split the new German assembly and *Präsident* Ebert nearly resigned. On the 22 June 1919 the National Assembly returned a vote of 237 to 138 in favour of accepting the Treaty terms with the exception of the two above clauses – see Henig 1998 p.20. As a result the *Versailles Diktat* was for ever associated with Friedrich Ebert and the socialist politicians of the Weimar Republic.

36   Suchenwirth 1968 p.4 & Mason 1973 pp.41-42. A naval *Freikorps* under *Kpt.z.S.*Hermann Ehrhardt played a pivotal role in the *Putsch* - see also Padfield 1984 pp.119-121. Ebert's Government fled the city and called on the populace to strike: *"Strike, stop working, prevent the return of bloody reaction. Not a hand must move, not a single worker must help the military dictatorship. General strike all along the line! Workers, unite"*. Kapp fled to Sweden - see Snyder 1976 p.191.

37   Mason 1973 p.42-43 & Henig 1998 pp.25-26. The *Reichswehr* had refused to act against the *Freikorps* and the Berlin Garrison. *GenLt.*Hans von Seeckt informed Ebert: *"Truppe schiesst nicht auf Truppe"* (Troops do not fire on Troops). The *Reichswehr* had been established on the 6 Mar 19 - see Suchenwirth 1968 p.3.

38   Mason 1973 pp.43-45.

39   Ries 1970 p.12.

40   *Dokumente 6 Polizeifliegerstaffeln Stand: 31 Mar 20* in Volker K.H. 1968 *Dokumente und Documentarfotos zue Geschichte der deutschen Luftwaffe* (hereafter cited as Volker 1968), Ries 1970 p.15, Schliephake H. 1971 *The Birth of the Luftwaffe* (hereafter cited as Schliephake 1971) p.12 & Schilling F. and Rettinghaus H. 1994 *Die Geschichte der Luftpolizei* pp.13-18 & 21-28. On the 21 Jan 20 the 14 *Polizeifliegerstaffeln* then in existence had a total of 280 aircraft on charge though not all had engines (10 B-Type, 198 C-Type, 58 D-Type & 14 G-Type) – Schilling and Rettinghaus 1994 p.20. It is therefore not surprising that the Allied authorities viewed the *Polizeifliegerstaffeln* as an "air force in waiting". *Hptm.* Milch was *Fhr.d.Polizeifliegerstaffel* Königsberg from 5 Sep 19 to 4 Dec 19. Milch was a career officer who had entered military service in Feb 10, received flight training as a *Beobachter* at Jüterbog in Jul-Aug 15 and had thereafter served in a number of *Fliegerabteilungen* and staff positions - see Irving 1973 p.11-12 and service record for Erhard Milch in Hildebrand 1991 pp.394-395. The German Government tried hard to retain the *Polizeifliegerstaffeln*. They were finally downgraded to non-flying units (*Luftüberwachungs-Abteilungen*) on the 30 Jun 21 - see Hooton 1994 p.31.

As from May 8 1920, a young branch of the armed forces, which has served with bravery in action and earned fame in the course of its relatively short history, will lay down its arms in silence and with pride. On this day, the *Luftstreitkräfte* fulfils the demand laid down in the Peace Treaty for the complete disbanding of all its formations and establishments.[41]

Then following a review of the *Luftstreitkräfte's* accomplishments during the Great War and in recognition of the General's own ambitions for the future of German military aviation, the order ended on a more defiant note:

We shall not abandon the hope of one day seeing the *Luftstreitkräfte* come to life again. The fame of the *Luftstreitkräfte* engraved in the history of the German armed forces will never fade. It is not dead, its spirit lives on!
Charged with the carrying out of this order.

Generalleutnant Hans von Seeckt
Chef der Heeresleitung

However given the realities of 1920 any such developments would have to be shrouded in secrecy and within both the *Heeres* and *Marineleitung* plans were soon laid to provide a basis for future air arms (See 1A2 & 1E3).[42] In the meantime, following the violent excesses of 1919-20, a degree of political stability had at last been achieved within the new German Republic. The *Reichsheer* had, by its actions in the suppression of the communists, revealed itself to be a significant political force, a strength which would allow a degree of independence in the years ahead that far exceeded the bounds which the Allies had originally intended under the Treaty regulations (See 1E1).[43] This reality, together with a fundamental hostility by large segments of the population for both the Treaty of Versailles and for the Republican politicians who had agreed to its terms, was appreciated by some but ignored by many. The British Prime Minister of the time was amongst the more perceptive:

You may strip Germany of her colonies, reduce her armaments to a mere police force and her navy to that of a fifth rate power; all the same in the end if she feels that she has been unjustly treated in the peace of 1919 she will find means of exacting retribution on her conquerors.[44]

David Lloyd George

41   Quoted from Schliephake 1971 *The Birth of the Luftwaffe* p.12 with kind permission of Ian Allan Publishing. Seeckt had been a military adviser to the German authorities at Versailles. He was a keen advocate of an independent air arm - see Corum 1997 p.52-55.
42   Hooton 1994 p.28-29 & Corum 1997 p.55-58. In May 19 *Hptm.* Helmuth Wilberg had already drawn up plans for a peacetime air force of c.1,800 aircraft and 10,000 officers and men - see Cooper M. 1981 *The German Air Force 1933-1945: An Anatomy of Failure* p.379.
43   Seaton 1982 pp.3-4.
44   Quoted from Mason 1973 *The Rise of the Luftwaffe 1918-1940* p.47 with the knowledge of the Orion Publishing Group. Winston Churchill would later write *"The economic clauses of the Treaty were malignant and silly to an extent that made them obviously futile... the victors imposed upon the Germans all the long-sought ideals of the liberal nations of the West... emperors having been driven out, nonentities were elected... wise policy would have crowned and fortified the Weimar Republic with a constitutional sovereign in the person of the infant grandson of the Kaiser, under a Council of Regency. Instead a gaping void was opened in the national life of the German people. All the strong elements, military and feudal, which might have rallied to a constitutional monarchy and for its sake respected and sustained the new democratic and Parliamentary processes, were for the time being unhinged "* - quoted from Churchill 1948 *The Second World War Vol.I The Gathering Storm* p.7 Cassell & Co.Ltd.

In the meantime within Germany there were many who were more than ready to speak openly of their feelings toward the new Government. On the occasion of a large meeting of officers called by *GenMaj.*Hans-Georg Reinhardt in support of the new regime in December 1918 the former *Kommandeur der Jagdgeschwader "Freiherr von Richthofen" Nr.1* took the opportunity to express the views of many of his comrades *(Photo 1A-7)*:

We officers did our duty for four long years. We risked our bodies for the Fatherland. Now we come home - and how do they treat us? They spit on us and deprive us of what we gloried in wearing. I therefore implore you to cherish hatred, a profound, abiding hatred of those animals who have outraged the German people. But the day will come when we drive them out of Germany. Prepare for that day. Arm yourselves for that day. Work for that day.[45]

Oberleutnant Hermann Göring
December 1918

Unfortunately for the World, Göring's impassioned comments would prove to be an accurate forecast for Germany's future.

---

45   Quoted from Mosley 1974 *The Reich Marshal: A Biography of Hermann Göring* p.46 with the knowledge of the Orion Publishing Group. Reinhardt had called the meeting in the Berlin Philharmonic Hall to encourage members of the *Offizierkorps* to back Ebert's provisional government. He had removed his rank insigne and medals in accordance with the latest edict. Predictably Göring's address was well received by most of those present. However Göring did not remain in Germany for the internal battles that followed. In 1919 he left for Denmark and Sweden as a display pilot. Reinhardt was Ebert's nominee as *Chef d.Heeresleitung* for the new *Vorläufige Reichsheer* which was formed on the 6 Mar 19 - see Pipes in www.feldgrau.com. & Seaton 1982 p.3.

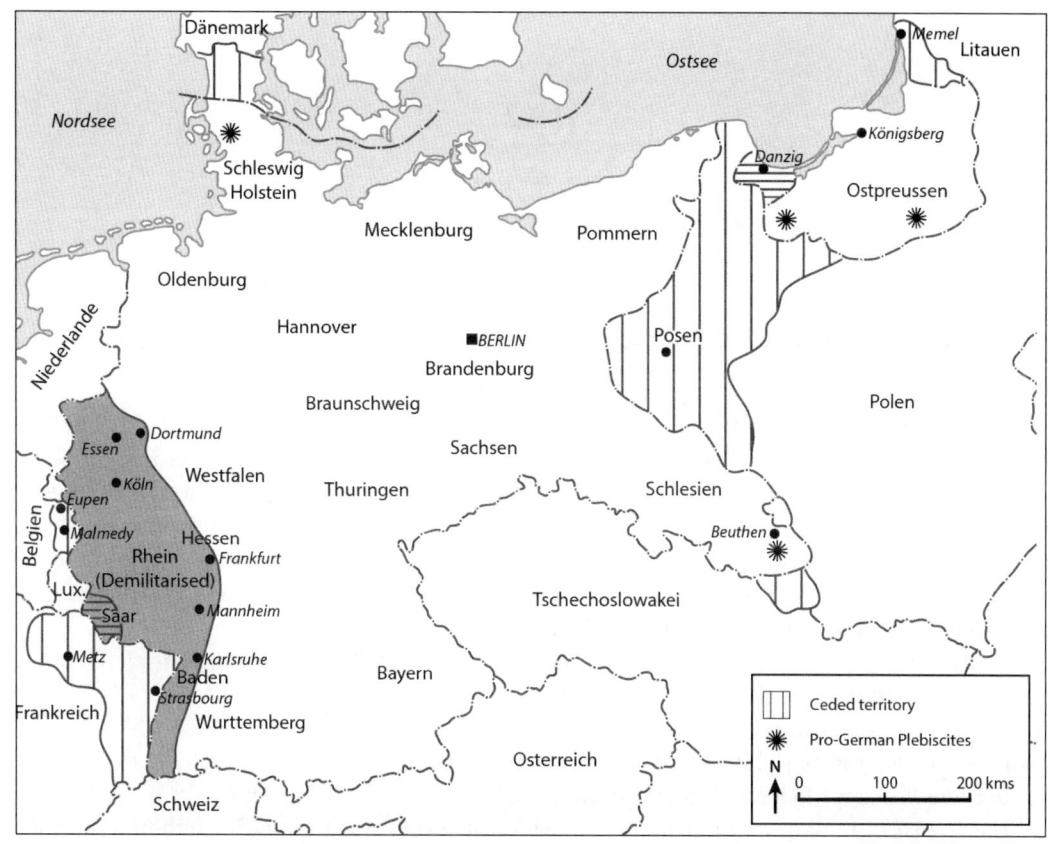

I-1   Changes to the territorial boundaries of the German Reich following the peace treaties of 1919.

1A2

The Need for Secrecy

The key roles of Seeckt and Wilberg, 1920-1926

The *Reichswehrministerium (RWM)* was a product of Versailles being created on the 1 October 1919 through the amalgamation of the four previously separate war ministries of the German Empire.[1] The *RWM* in turn controlled the *Reichswehr's* two principal arms: the newly created *Reichsheer* and the *Reichsmarine*. The *Reichswehrminister* was a political appointment: *Präsident* Friedrich Ebert nominated his former deputy Gustav Noske to this crucial post, whilst *GenLt.*Hans-Georg Reinhardt was appointed as *Chef der Heeresleitung*.[2] The *Chef der Admiralitat* was *VizAdm.*Adolph von Trotha.[3] The new *RWM* was located in Berlin's Bendlerstrasse.

Neither Noske, Reinhardt nor Trotha would survive the turmoil of early post-war German politics and attempted revolution (See 1A1). In the wake of the *Kapp Putsch* in March 1920 Ebert replaced Noske as *Reichswehrminister* with the more right-wing Otto Karl Gessler, whilst *GenLt.* Hans von Seeckt was moved into the key role of *Chef der Heeresleitung*.[4] Trotha was briefly replaced by *KonAdm.*William Michaelis and ultimately by *Adm.*Paul Behncke (See 1E3).

The *Heeresleitung* (Army Command) was established as one of two executive authorities for the *Vorläufige Reichsheer* (Provisional Army) on the 6 March 1919.[5] To perpetuate the role of the banned *Oberste Heeresleitung* (Greater General Staff) the *Truppenamt* (Troop Office) was established under

---

1   Seaton A. 1982 *The German Army 1933-1945* (hereafter cited as Seaton 1982) p.3. These were the war ministries of Preussen, Bayern, Wurttemburg & Sachsen. Also amalgamated into the *RWM* was the previously distinct naval ministry.

2   Seaton 1982 p3. See also Pipes J. *Reichswehr - The German Armed Forces 1919-1935* in www.feldgrau.com. (hereafter cited as Pipes Reichswehr).

3   Sieche W. *Germany* p.218 in Gardiner R. and Chesneau R. (Ed.) 1980 *Conway's All the World's Fighting Ships 1922-1946*. See also Pipes J. *The Reichsmarine 1919-1935* in www.feldgrau.com & *Reichsmarine* in www.wikipedia.org.de (hereafter cited as Wikipedia Reichsmarine).

4   Mason H.M. 1973 *The Rise of the Luftwaffe 1918-1940* (hereafter cited as Mason 1973) p.88, Seaton 1982 p.3, Pipes Reichswehr & Pipes J. *Reichsheer* in www.feldgrau.com. On the 16 May 20 *GenLt.*Reinhardt was appointed *Bfr.Wehrkreis V* Stuttgart. Seeckt had previously been *C.d.GS.i.OHL* - see Corum J.S. 1997 *The Luftwaffe: Creating the Operational Air War 1918-1940* (hereafter cited as Corum 1997) pp.50-51. Gessler, a former lawyer from Nürnberg, was described by members of the *Truppenamt* as *"a man of straw"* and *"a purely ornamental being"*; Gen. Nollet of the *IKK* commented: *"He confined himself to signing the decisions of General von Seeckt... It was under the cover of his name and of his political authority that von Seeckt carried out his work of reorganisation"* - quoted from Mason 1973 *The Rise of the Luftwaffe 1918-1940* p.95 with the knowledge of the Orion Publishing Group. From the point of view of the *Reichswehr* it was a truly admirable arrangement. Unfortunately Seeckt treated Gessler quite badly and this would eventually result in Seeckt's enforced retirement from the post of *Chef d.Heeresleitung* - see Seaton 1982 p.16. Trotha's support for the *Marinefreikorps* and the *Lüttwitz-Kapp Putsch* would lead to his dismissal in Mar 20. He was eventually succeeded as *Chef d.Marineleitung* by *Adm.*Paul Behncke in Sep 20 - see Wikipedia Reichsmarine.

5   Suchenwirth R. Prof. 1968 *The Development of the German Air Force 1919-1939* USAF Historical Studies No.160 (hereafter cited as Suchenwirth 1968) p.3. The Decree of the 6 Mar 19 established the *Vorläufige Reichswehr* (Provisional Defence Forces) of which the *Vorläufige Reichsheer* was a part - see Pipes Reichswehr.

Seeckt on the 11 October 1919 with an initial establishment of some 60 officers.[6] The *Truppenamt* was divided into seven numbered *Abteilungen: T1* (*Heeres* – Command & Policy), *T2* (*Organisation*), *T3* (*Fremde Heere* – Enemy Armies), *T4* (*Lehr* – Tactical Training), *T5* (*Wehr* – Recruitment & Personnel), *T6* (*Erziehungs-u.Bildungswesen* – Education and Training) & *T7* (*Transport*) (*Chart I-1*).[7] Although Article 198 had specifically banned all aspects of military aviation in Germany, Seeckt moved quickly to establish the following covert aviation agencies within the *Heeresleitung*:[8]

COVERT AVIATION AGENCIES WITHIN THE HEERESLEITUNG -1 MARCH 1920

- The ***Luftschütz-Referat*** (Air Organisation and Training Desk)(TA L). This was the central office for all matters relating to the development of military aviation. Given their wartime association *Hptm.*Helmuth Wilberg's appointment as *Referent* (Staff Advisor) met with Seeckt's full approval. Wilberg had served as Seeckt's *Kommandeur der Flieger* (*KoFl.*) in Macedonia during 1915 before seeing service on the Western Front during 1917-18 as *KoFl.AOK 4*; he had also been Seeckt's choice as his aviation adviser during the military discussions in Paris during 1919.[9]

- The ***Fremde Luftstreitkräfte-Referat*** (Foreign Air Desk) within *T 3* (*Fremde Heere*). Staffed by *Hptm.*Wolfgang Weese, its task was to maintain files on foreign air forces.[10]

- The ***Flugtechnik-Referat*** (Air Technical Desk) within the *Inspektion für Waffen und Gerat* (Weapons and Equipment Inspectorate) of the *Heereswaffenamt* (*HWA*) (Army Ordnance Office). *Hptm.*Kurt Student was tasked with monitoring technical developments abroad (See also 1C1).[11]

6   Goerlitz W. 1953 *History of the German General Staff 1657-1945* pp.218-219, 225-228 & 241-243 & Seaton 1982 p.6. The *OHL* was banned under Article 160 of the Versailles Treaty - see *App.XXI Peace Treaty of Versailles: Military Clauses* in Edmonds J.E. 1944 *History of the Great War: The Occupation of the Rhineland 1918-1929* (hereafter cited as Edmonds 1944) p.397. It was replaced in Oct 19 by the *Truppenamt*, initially under *GenMaj.*Hans von Seeckt until his promotion in Mar 20 - see Corum 1997 p.50 & www.wikipedia.org. *Truppenamt* (hereafter cited as wikipedia Truppenamt). Indeed the activities of the *Generalstabsoffioziere* assigned to the *Divisionstabes* (Divisional Staffes) were concealed under the new title *Führergehilfen* (Command Assistants) - see Seaton 1982 p.6 & Corum 1997 pp.66-67. The *Truppenamt* was mainly staffed by former *Offiziere.i.G.*(General Staff Officers) - see Nielsen A. 1959 *The German Air Force General Staff* USAF Historical Studies No.173 p.18-19. It has been suggested that *GenMaj.*Otto Hasse was the first *Chef d.Truppenamt*. However see Seaton 1982 p.15.

7   Seaton 1982 p.15. Seeckt was replaced as *Chef.d.Truppenamt* by *GenLt.*Wilhelm Heye on the 26 Mar 20 - see wikipedia Truppenamt.

8   *Army Aviation Organisation 1 March 1920 to 31 March 1927* in Beauvais H., Kossler K., Mayer M. and Regel C. 2002 *German Secret Flight Test Centres to 1945: Johannisthal, Lipetsk, Rechlin, Travemünde, Tarnewitz, Peenemunde-West* (hereafter cited as Beauvais et al 2002) p.50. See also Hertel W. Dipl.Ing.GenIng.a.D.1955 *Procurement in the German Air Force* USAF Historical Studies No.170 (hereafter cited as Hertel 1955) p.5 & Maass B. GenLt.a.D. *Organisation der Fliegerstellen im RWM 1920-1933* in A/I/2, Karlsruhe Document Collection in Suchenwirth 1968 p.6. *Gen.*Ritter von Haack, a former *Insp.d.Koniglich bayerische Luftstreitkräfte* (Inspector of the Royal Bavarian Air Service), and Seeckt's personal *Chef des Stabes* (Chief of Staff), was an influential officer in these covert developments - see Cooper M. 1981 *The German Air Force 1933-1945: An Anatomy of Failure* (hereafter cited as Cooper 1981) p.380.

9   Suchenwirth 1968 p.6 & Volker K-H. 1962 *Die Entwicklung der militärischen Luftfahrt in Deutschland Germany 1920-1933* (hereafter cited as Volker 1962) p.p.136-137. *Hptm.*Wilberg was one of the founders of the *Luftstreitkräfte*. He took the field in Aug 14 as *Fhr.Feldflieger-Abt.11* and from Jul 15 was a *Kofl.AOK* initially with Seeckt in the Balkans - see service record for Helmuth Wilberg in Hildebrand K.F.1992 *Die Generale der deutschen Luftwaffe 1935-1945 Band 3 O-Z* (hereafter cited as Hildebrand 1992) pp.513-514 & Corum 1997 p.21, pp.30-32 34, p.52 & pp.57-58.

10   Suchenwirth 1968 p.6. *Hptm.*Weese was a *Referent* in *T 3* from 1 Mar 20 to his discharge on the 9 Oct 20. He had been a bomber pilot with *Bogohl 3* until the 6 Jun 18 when he was captured by the French - see service record for Wolfgang Weese in Hildebrand 1992 pp.482-483.

11   Hertel 1955 pp.5-6 & Suchenwirth 1968 p.6. *Hptm.*Student obtained his *Flugzeugführerschein* on the 8 Aug 13 and had served in reconnaissance, bomber and fighter units throughout the war. He ended the war as *Ltr.d.Abt.f.Versuche*

- The ***Fliegerrüstungwirtschaftliches Referat*** (Foreign Air Armament Economies Desk) Also located with the *HWA* where it was referred to as the *Wa Wi L. Hptm.* Leopold Vogt's task was to compile and evaluate information on the aviation sector of foreign armament economies.[12]

A procurement office was planned but due to the imposition of international restrictions on the manufacture and operation of military aircraft in Germany this office was effectively still born.[13]

Seeckt was an admirable choice as *Chef der Heeresleitung*:

Hans von Seeckt was one of the most influential military thinkers of the twentieth century. He rebuilt and reorganised the German Army in the chaotic situation of post-war Germany, and imbued that force with his own vision of warfare. It is testimony to the German general staff tradition that, at a time when the German nation had been brought low, it put forward a man of genuine vision, with a first rate strategic mind, and great tactical and operational competence, to command the army. Von Seeckt was considered by the officer corps to be a logical choice to be post-war chief of the general staff. During World War I, von Seeckt had earned a reputation as a superior tactician.[14]

James Corum
The Luftwaffe: Creating the Operational Air War, 1918-1940

Drawing on his wartime experiences in the Balkans, Russia and the Near East, Seeckt was convinced that the future form of warfare would be dominated by mobility and manoeuvre. This was in direct contrast to the thinking of those officers who had served exclusively in the trenches of the Western Front.[15] Likewise his consistently successful employment of small forces of better-led, better trained and better equipped troops against much larger but less flexible opponents only served to underline the many advantages of a small professional force as proposed by the Allied Powers. Indeed it could be argued that the enforced re-structuring of the *Reichsheer* around a 100,000 man force structure was to be in Germany's long term interests.[16] In this respect Seeckt recognised that

u. Wissenschaft Adlershorst (Leader of the Adlershorst Research Branch) - see service record for Kurt Student in Hildebrand 1992 pp.363-365.

12   Wimmer W. Gen.d.Flg.a.D. *Stellungnahme zu Luftfahrt-Ausbildung in der Reichswehr von Hellmuth Felmy, Teil I* in B/III/1a, Karlsruhe Document Collection in Suchenwirth 1968 p.7.

13   Suchenwirth 1968 p.7. Article 201 prohibited the production and import of aircraft for a period of 6 months following the signing of the Versailles Treaty; Article 198 prohibited the maintenance of a military air arm - see Ries K. 1970 *Luftwaffe Bd.1 Die Maulwurfe 1919-1935* (hereafter cited as Ries 1970) p.12.

14   Quoted from Corum 1997 *The Luftwaffe: Creating the Operational Air War 1918-1940* p.50 with the kind permission of the University Press of Kansas. Commissioned in 1887 Seeckt's early promise led to him being accepted by the *Kriegsakademie* (War Academy) for training as an *Offizier i.G.* in 1897. Cultured and sophisticated he travelled widely prior the Great War. He spoke English and French fluently. He was comfortable in a range of political, academic and intellectual circles. His wartime service was remarkable in that he was almost exclusively associated with mobile warfare in the Balkans, Russia and the Near East. As such he escaped the restrictions imposed on those who served against the western Allies - see Seeckt von H. GenOb.a.D. 1938 *Aus Meinem Leben 1866-1917* & Meier-Welcker H. 1967 *Seeckt* in Corum p.50-51.

15   Corum 1997 p.50. In contrast the post-war thinking and writings of many Allied commanders (Petain, Haig & Pershing) would emphasise the power of the defence against which success could only be achieved via overwhelming force and fire power. A war of annihilation as opposed to a war of manoeuvre – Corum 1997 p.51.

16   Corum 1997 p.51-52. Seeckt correctly realised that trench warfare was not inevitable in any future conflict. It had come into being in 1914 due to the peculiar circumstances of that period - the effectiveness of machine guns and barbed wire had temporarily overcome the traditional mobility of the cavalry. Even before the Versailles Treaty

military aircraft would have an important role to play in any future conflict *(Photo 1A-8)*.[17]

Seeckt also recognised the importance of air power, not just as an adjunct to terrestrial military operations but as an independent force in its own right. During the military discussions prior to the Versailles judgement he had supported this cause with the Allied powers in Paris.[18] In a further discussion document of 1923 Seeckt had again proposed, albeit hypothetically given the political realities of the period, that the air arm should be independent from both the *Reichsheer* and *Reichsmarine*.[19] Nonetheless his thinking diverged from that emerging in Britain and the USA where a strategic role for air power was proposed by such officers as Air Marshal Sir Hugh Trenchard and Col. William Mitchell.[20] Seeckt saw the future of air power in *"operational"* terms. Air power would be used to break the military power of an enemy rather than the economic basis of its military power and more controversially, as suggested by *General* Giulio Douhet in his 1921 treatise *"La conquista del dominio dell'aria"*, the moral strength of its civilian population. In 1929 Seeckt went so far as to suggest:

> The war will begin with a simultaneous attack of the air fleets - the weapon which is most prepared and fastest means of attacking the enemy. Their enemy is, however, not the major cities or industrial power, but the enemy air force. Only after its suppression can the offensive arm be directed against other targets. If both sides have roughly equal force, decision will not be reached quickly. Even if one side is pushed onto the defence, it will employ every means to destroy the attacker. The degree of material and moral success of the superior attacker against the enemy sources of power depends upon the passive and moral powers of resistance of the defenders. Thereby, it is stressed that all the major troop assembly points are worthwhile and easy targets. The disruption of the personnel and material mobilisation is a primary mission of the aerial offensive.
>
> Alongside the air force led attack will be the prepared field force, essentially the regular army, which will attack with all possible speed. The higher the quality of the army, the

Seeckt had advocated a smaller professional army of 21 divisions totalling 200-300,000 men.

17   Messenger C. 1991 *The Art of Blitzkrieg* (hereafter cited as Messenger 1991) p.58. *"The whole future of warfare appears to me to be in the employment of mobile armies, relatively small but of high quality, and rendered distinctly more effective by the addition of aircraft."* – quoted from Seeckt von H. GenOb.a.D. 1930 *Thoughts of a Soldier* p.62 Verlag für kulturpolitik.

18   Cooper 1981 p.379. In May 19 *Hptm.* Wilberg had presented Seeckt with a memorandum for an independent force of some 1,800 aircraft staffed by 8,000 military and 1,200 naval personnel.

19   *Seeckt Denkschrift, 1923* in Volker 1962. To what extent Seeckt was influenced by the emergence of the *RAF* as an independent air arm in Apr 18 is unclear. In this respect Trenchard's White Paper Comd.467 *Permanent Organisation of the Royal Air Force - Note by the Secretary of State for Air on a Scheme outlined by the Chief of the Air Staff 11 Dec 19*, HMSO would have been of interest to German planners. However this precedent was not followed by other nations during this formative period. See Grey C.G. 1940 *A History of the Air Ministry* pp.75-80 & Taylor J.W.R. and Moyes P.J.R. 1968 *Pictorial History of the R.A.F. Vol. One 1918-1939* (hereafter cited as Taylor and Moyes 1968) p.18.

20   Roberston B. 1978 *The RAF: A Pictorial History* p.64-65 & Messenger 1991 pp.33-37. As the former commander of the Independent Air Force during 1918 Trenchard was convinced of the importance of bombing as the prime function of air power - see *App.26 The 41st Wing R.F.C./R.A.F. and the Independent Air Force R.A.F.* in Moyes P.J.R. 1964 *Bomber Squadrons of the R.A.F. and their aircraft* pp.314-317 & Sinnott C. 2001 *The RAF and Aircraft Design 1923-1939: Air Staff Operational Requirements* (hereafter cited as Sinnott 2001) pp.48-49. However the financial realities of the twenties actually produced a more balanced force structure - see *Table 9B United Kingdom: Regular Squadrons by type and year* in James J. 1990 *The Paladins: A Social History of the RAF up to the outbreak of World War II* p.249. In the USA Mitchell and others had fought for an independent air arm following their return from France. Mitchell had argued that an independent air arm was more effective and economic solution to the problem of national defence than spending huge sums on a new generation of battleships. To prove his point he carried out a series of trials against captured German warships (1921) and obsolete American battleships (1921-23) - see Craven W.F. and Cate J.L. (Ed.) 1948 *The Army Air Forces in World War II Vol.1 Plans and early operations January 1939 to August 1942* pp.24-29.

greater its mobility, the more competent its leadership, the greater its chances of driving the opposing forces quickly from the field, the more rapidly it can disrupt the development and deployment of further forces, and the faster the enemy can be pushed to sue for peace.[21]

Generaloberst ausser Dienst Hans von Seeckt
"Gedanken eines Soldaten"
1929

In keeping with German General Staff tradition Seeckt ordered a thorough post-mortem of the performance of the *Feldheer* in the recently concluded war. Numerous committees were established to undertake this important work:

It is absolutely necessary to put the experience of the war in a broad light, and to collect this experience while the impressions won on the battlefield are still fresh, and the major proportion of the experienced officers are still in leading positions.[22]

However rather than an academic exercise, this endeavour was a formative process aimed at improving tactics. To this end the authors of these reports were instructed to consider:

What new situations arose in the war that had not been considered before the war?
How effective were our pre-war views in dealing with the above situations?
What new guidelines have been developed from the use of new weaponry in war?
Which new problems, put forward by the war, have not yet found a solution?[23]

Wilberg had already initiated a similar exercise within the *Luftstreitkräfte*.[24] Prior to Seeckt's directive this had involved 83 officers in 21 committees and sub-committees that collectively would report on the effectiveness of air unit organisation, combat tactics and technical developments.[25] Following Seeckt's directive additional committees were formed and ultimately 130 officers were engaged in this exhaustive examination of the effectiveness of German air power during the Great War. Officers engaged in this important process included *Maj.*Streccius (*KoFl.AOK 18*), *Hptlte.* Ernst Brandenburg (*Kdr.Kagohl 3*), Hermann Hoth (*Stab KoGenLuft*), Erhard Milch (*Fhr.JGr.6*), Hugo Sperrle (*Kofl.AOK 7*), Kurt Student (*Ltr.Abt.f. Versuche u. Wissenschaft Adlershorst*), *Rittm.*Karl Bolle (*Kap.Jasta Boelcke*), *Oblt.*Ernst Udet (*Kap.Jasta 4*)and *Lte.*Carl Degelow (*Kap.Jasta 35b*) & Josef Jacobs (*Kap.Jasta 7*)(*Photo 1A-9*).[26] Wilberg, who contributed to a report on the effectiveness

21   Quoted from Seeckt von H. 1929 *Gedanken eines Soldaten* in Corum 1997 *The Luftwaffe: Creating the Operational Air War 1918-1940* p.54 with the kind permission of the University Press of Kansas. Douhet's book was first published in 1921 and revised in 1927. It was published in German in 1929 and therefore its content would have been known to the concealed air staff in the *Truppenamt* - see Douhet G. 1972 *Command of the Air* (reprint of 1927 edition) & Grabmann W. GenMaj.a.D. 1956 *German Air Force Air Defence Operations" Vol.I 1933-41* USAF Historical Studies No.164 pp.19-21. See also Messenger 1991 pp.32-33.

22   *Seeckt, letter to Truppenamt et al, 1 Dec 1919* in BA/MA 2/2275 in Corum 1997 p.59. In all there were 57 committees and sub-committees with over 400 officers by the middle of 1920.

23   Quoted from *Seeckt, letter to Truppenamt et al, 1 Dec 1919* in BA/MA 2/2275 in Corum 1997 *The Luftwaffe: Creating the Operational Air War 1918-1940* p.59 with the kind permission of the University Press of Kansas.

24   *Flugmusterei, Letter 13 Nov 19* in BA/MA RH 2/2275 in Corum 1997 *The Luftwaffe: Creating the Operational Air War 1918-1940* p.59 with the kind permission of the University Press of Kansas.

25   *Flugmusterei, Letter 4 Dec 19* in BA/MA RH 2/2275 in Corum 1997 *The Luftwaffe: Creating the Operational Air War 1918-1940* p.60 with the kind permission of the University Press of Kansas.

26   Corum 1997 p.60. See also Angolia J.R. and Hackney C.R. 1984 *The Pour le Mérite and Germany's First Aces*, Hildebrand K.F.1990-92 *Die Generale der deutschen Luftwaffe 1935-1945 Band 1-3* & Franks N., Bailey F. and

of fighter group tactics, was also the author of a report on the effectiveness of the air supply service during 1918.[27]

The result of all this endeavour was the incorporation into *Heeresdienstvorschrift Nr.487: Führung und Gefecht der Verbundenen Waffen, 1921* (Leadership and Combat with Combined Arms), of a considerable body of operational air doctrine. For the most part this doctrine followed accepted principles, particularly in the concentration of all available air assets at the point of decision - the *Schwehrpunkt*:

> During operations the leadership has the responsibility for determining the most important objective for reconnaissance, as well as the decision to assemble and deploy superior aerial forces, in co-ordination with the ground forces, over the most important sector of the ground battle. All possible forces must be employed at this decisive point. Troop units who are not directly involved in combat at this decisive point cannot generally count upon receiving air support.[28]

Heeresdienstvorschrift Nr.487, para.71

This reflected operational practice within the *Luftstreitkräfte* during the last year of the war when fighter units were increasingly assembled into *Jagdgeschwadern* (Fighter Wings) and *Jagdgruppen* (Fighter Groups) and deployed flexibly at key points along the Western Front with the aim of securing local air superiority.[29] Similar arrangements had been in use in respect of twin-engine bombing aircraft since October 1917 when most of the existing *Kampfstaffeln* (Bomber Squadrons) were reorganised into *Bombengeschwadern der Obersten Heeresleitung (Bogohl)* (High Command Bomber Wings) under the direct command of Army General Staff, whilst the newly formed *Schlachtstaffeln* had also been grouped together in *Schlachtgruppen* and *Geschwadern* to support the German counter-offensive in March 1918 *(Photo 1A-10)*.[30]

However Seeckt's pre-occupation with mobile operations required a new emphasis on the part of the air arm. Operations on the Western Front had been primarily defensive, for example fighters had rarely crossed the lines in search of the enemy air force.[31] In *H.Dv.487* the battle for air superiority was made the primary objective:

> The battle for air superiority is an offensive one. The enemy aviation is to be sought out and attacked forward of the zone of troops. The opponent is to be pushed onto the defensive, and his power and aggressiveness broken by the destruction of numerous aircraft.

Duiven R. 1996 *The Jasta Pilots: Detailed listings and histories August 1916 - November 1918*.

27   Corum 1997 p.62.

28   Quoted from *H.Dv.487 Führung und Gefecht der Verbundenen Waffen, 1921, Part I, para 71* in Corum 1997 *The Luftwaffe: Creating the Operational Air War 1918-1940* p.64 with the kind permission of the University Press of Kansas.

29   It seems likely that *Hptm.*Walter Stahr, *Flieger-Referent* within *T 4* during 1920, would have played a part in the formulation of *H.Dv.487* - see service record for Walter Stahr in Hildebrand 1992 pp.341-342.

30   Hoeppner von, E. W. *1921 Germany's War in the Air: The Development and Operations of German Military Aviation in the World War* p.109 & Imrie A. 1971 *Pictorial History of the German Army Air Service* (hereafter cited as Imrie 1971) pp.44 & 51. *JG 1 (Rittm.*Manfred Frhr.von Richthofen) was formed on the 24 Jun 17, whilst *JG 2 (Hptm.* Adolf Ritter von Tutschek) & *JG 3 (Oblt.*Bruno Loerzer) were formed on the 2 Feb 18. *JG 4* and various ad hoc *Jagdgruppen* would follow during 1918 - see Johnson J.E. AVM.(Rtd.) 1964 *Full Circle: The Story of Air Fighting* (hereafter cited as Johnson 1964) pp.79-80, Nowarra H.J. in Robertson B. (Ed.) 1959 *Air Aces of the 1914-1918 War* pp.165-166 & Baker D. 1990 *Manfred von Richthofen: The man and the aircraft he flew* p.84.

31   Hoeppner 1921 p.104 & Imrie 1971 p.46. This reorganisation had the particular support of *Gen.d.Inf.*Erich von Ludendorff, the new *OQu.I*. By Nov 17 144 *G-Typ* bombers had been concentrated into seven *Bogohl*. All *Geschwader* bar *Bogohl 3* had 18 aircraft, whilst the *England-Geschwader* had 36 machines - see also Kilduff P. 1991 *Germany's First Air Force 1914-1918* (hereafter cited as Kilduff 1991) p.69.

Defensive screens or sector barriers are made essentially impossible by the nature of the air battle. Strong numerical superiority cannot permanently eliminate aerial activity - only hinder it, and restrict its periods of action. It is therefore recommended that measures to restrict enemy aerial observation be carried out on the ground.[32]

Heeresdienstvorschrift Nr.487, para.77

To this end a considerable part of the 1921 regulations was devoted to the employment of anti-aircraft artillery (See 1E2).[33] This is not surprising as the *Flakartillerie* (Anti-Aircraft Artillery) had proved to be highly effective, particularly during the closing stages of the conflict when large numbers of Allied aircraft had been in action over the German front line and rear areas.[34] *H.Dv.487* required *"each army unit (to) be responsible for its own air defence, and set up an aircraft spotter system"*.[35] There was also an understanding that the heavy anti-aircraft gun was a valuable anti-tank weapon in its own right, the high muzzle velocity of such weapons making engagements with ground targets possible over considerable distances.[36]

For the first two years of its existence the *Reichswehr* had to operate alongside the activities of the *Interallierten Militär-Kontroll-Kommission (IMKK)* (Allied Military Control Commission) whose task was to ensure that the disarmament clauses of the Versailles Treaty were carried out to the satisfaction of the Allied powers.[37] There was an understandable lack of co-operation on the part of the German authorities whose liaison committee, the *Heeres-Friedenskommission* (Military Peace Commission), under *Gen.*von Cramon was obstructive from its very first meeting with the *IMKK's* officials on the 29 January 1920.[38] Nonetheless the work of destruction went ahead, this being particularly true in the case of military aviation (Article 202), although this task was to take far longer than had originally been anticipated.[39]

---

32   Imrie 1971 pp.48 & 58. See also Orange V. Prof. 2001 *Park – Then Biography of Air Chief Marshal Sir Keith Park* p.36.

33   Quoted from *H.Dv.487 Führung und Gefecht der Verbundenen Waffen, 1921, Part I, para 77* in Corum 1997 *The Luftwaffe: Creating the Operational Air War 1918-1940* p.64 with the kind permission of the University Press of Kansas. The "offensive" employment of air power had been the basis for British aerial doctrine during the Great War - see Johnson 1964 pp.67 & 77.

34   Corum 1997 p.64. By the end of the Great War the German ground based air defence forces totalled 2,770 guns and 718 searchlights manned by 2,800 officers and 55,000 other ranks - see Eberhard von W. (Ed.) 1930 *Unsere Luftstreitkräfte 1914-1918: Ein Denkmal deutschen Heldentums.*

35   Lange von C. (Ed.) 1941 *Flakartillerie greift an: Tatsachenbereite in Wort und Bild* p.127. During the Great War German Flak accounted for 1,588 enemy aircraft, a figure which exceeded the combined total for the French, Italian and British forces. In fact during the first 10 months of 1918 German Flak was responsible for 47% of all allied air losses - see Hoeppner 1921 p.160 & Westermann E.B. 2001 *Flak: German Anti-aircraft Defenses 1914-1945* (hereafter cited as Westermann 2001) pp.26-27.

36   Quoted from *Heeresdienstvorschrift Nr.487, 1921* in Westermann 2001 *Flak: German Anti-aircraft Defenses 1914-1945* p.32 with the kind permission of the University of Kansas.

37   Hoeppner 1921 p.123. German anti-aircraft artillery was used to good effect against British tanks on the Somme (1916) and at Cambrai (1917). Hoeppner claims that 8 British tanks were knocked out by the *7 Flak Batterie* on the 23 Nov 17. See also Seydel Hptm.a.D. 1921 *Flak in Militärwochenblatt Nr.33* in Corum p.63.

38   Mason 1973 pp.76-87. During the winter of 1919-20 the Allied powers sent a total of 383 officers and 737 other ranks to Germany to supervise the dismantling of the armament industry and the effective disarming of the *Reichswehr*. See also *App.XXI "Peace Treaty of Versailles; Military Clauses* in Edmonds 1944 p398-399.

39   Mason 1973 pp.78-79 & 85. The *Reichswehr* had expected a dictatorial approach and officials were amazed when the *IKK* insisted that a German liaison committee be formed to "assist" their work. Like most officers Cramon was rabidly opposed to Versailles and in particular the military clauses. At the first meeting the two sides did not even get to sit down as both Cramon and Gen.Nollet (*IKK*) claimed jurisdiction over the proceedings. Allied officers were often subjected to obstructive behaviour and at times intimidation during their visits to military establishments. The German Government was fined for these excesses. Nonetheless in 1921 the *IKK* was reduced in size to 174 officers and 400 other ranks.

ARTICLE 202

On the coming into force of the present treaty, all military and naval aeronautical material, except the machines mentioned in the second and third paragraphs of Art.198, must be delivered to the Governments of the Principal Allied and Associated Powers. Delivery must be effected to such places as the Allied Governments may select, and must be completed within three months.

In particular, this material will include all items under the following heads which are or have been or were designed for warlike purposes:

- Complete aeroplanes and seaplanes, as well as those being manufactured, repaired or assembled
- Dirigibles able to take to the air, being manufactured, repaired or assembled
- Plant for the manufacture of hydrogen
- Dirigible sheds and shelters for every kind of aircraft
- Pending their delivery, dirigibles will, at the expense of Germany, be maintained inflated with hydrogen; the plant for the manufacture of hydrogen, as well as the sheds for the dirigibles, may at the discretion of the Allied Powers, be left to Germany until the time when the dirigibles are handed over
- Engines for aircraft
- Nacelles and fuselages
- Armament (guns, machine guns, light machine guns, bomb-dropping apparatus, torpedo-dropping apparatus, synchronisation apparatus, aiming apparatus)
- Munitions (cartridges, shells, bombs loaded or unloaded, stocks of explosives or material for their manufacture)
- Instruments for use on aircraft
- Wireless apparatus and photographic or cinematograph apparatus for use on aircraft
- Component parts of any of the items under the preceding heads
- The material referred to above shall not be removed without special permission from the Allied Governments.

Once again the Allies, on this occasion in the form of the *Interalliierte Luftfahrt-Überwachungs-Kommission (ILUK)* (Allied Aerial Control Commission), met with German subversion and it has been estimated that around 1,000 aircraft and 2,500 engines were sold to foreign customers instead of being surrendered as part of Germany's war reparations.[40] When it became obvious that air material was being deliberately hidden from the control teams the Allied powers applied further pressure on the *RWM* by extending the provisions of Article 201, the ban on civil aviation, a measure which hit the remaining aircraft manufacturers who were waiting with mounting impatience to restart operations (See 1B1).[41] As this was very much against the *Reichswehr's* long-term interests, Gessler had little option but to instruct the *Reichsheer* to report and hand-over such hidden equipment as a matter of urgency.[42] The *ILUK's* disarmament work was officially completed on the 24 September 1921, more than a year after the dissolution of the

---

40   *Article 202, Treaty of Versailles Part V. Section III Air Clauses* in Hermann 1943 *The Rise and Fall of the Luftwaffe* (hereafter cited as Hermann 1943) p.39.

41   Ries 1970 p.11 & Mason 1973 p.84. Large amounts of material was hidden in barns, cellars etc. It is known that former German military aviation equipment was sold to Norway, Sweden, Denmark, Finland, Turkey and the Netherlands. Some even found its way to South America.

42   Hermann 1943 p.40. This is one of the reasons why the firms of AEG (Berlin), DFW (Leipzig), Gotha, Friedrichshafen, Pfalz (Speyer) & Siemens-Schuckert (Berlin) were closed. See also Hertel 1955 p.1.

Luftstreitkräfte and the Commission never did discover the fate of some equipment including 136 aircraft and 337 aero-engines. On the 5 May 1922 the *ILUK* was dissolved, its work then being assumed by the *Luftfahrt Garantie Komitee (LGK)* (Aerial Guarantee Commission) whose task was to supervise the civilian clauses of the peace treaty.[43]

FIGURE 1A-1 REPORT BY THE ALLIED CONTROL COMMISSION TO THE AIR MINISTRY, LONDON 24 SEPTEMBER 1921		
Items	**Surrendered**	**Destroyed**
Landplanes	516	14,617
Seaplanes	58	
Balloons	24	65
Airships	8	9
Engines	4,091	25,037
Machine Guns	6,923	7,626
Bombs	17,044	214,042
Hangars/Sheds	116	196

In the meantime the *Truppenamt (T 4)* subjected the *Reichsheer* to a rigorous training programme in which all personnel, whatever their trade, were expected to have a combat role.[44] There was still a very real danger from Poland and the *Heeresleitung* decided to concentrate the *Reichsheer's* limited resources in the east under *Gruppenkommando 1 (Gen.d.Inf.* Walter von Bergmann).[45] The loss of Posen and a substantial area of Preussen to this new state had, understandably, inflamed German feelings towards an emergent Poland:

> Poland's existence is intolerable and incompatible with the survival of Germany. Poland must disappear, and will disappear through her own inner weakness and through Russia - with our help. With Poland collapses one of the strongest pillars of the Peace of Versailles, France's advance outpost of power... The attainment of this objective must be one of the firmest guiding principles of German policy; it is capable of achievement - but only through Russia or with her help.[46]

General der Infanterie Hans von Seeckt
Chef der Heeresleitung

---

43   Hermann 1943 p.40. At a conference at Boulogne on the 22 Jun 20 the Allied Powers decided that Germany would not be allowed to begin the construction of any aeronautical material until 3 months after the final surrender of all military aviation equipment.

44   Ries 1970 p.15.

45   Seaton 1982 p.7. To maximise the *Reichsheer's* operational effectiveness Seeckt ordered that all non-combative tasks such as military history be re-assigned to other governmental or civilian agencies.

46   Pipes Reichswehr. In the expectation of being permitted a peacetime army of some 300,000 men the Reich had been divided into four operational commands in 1919. However in accordance with the Versailles Treaty two of these were subsequently disbanded on the 30 Apr 20 leaving Gr.Kdo.1 Berlin & Gr.Kdo.2 Kassel - see App. XXI *Peace Treaty of Versailles: Military Clauses* in Edmonds 1944 p.396-397 & www.axishistory.com (hereafter cited as Axis History). Bergmann could also count on members of the *Stahlhelm* - a veteran's association - who had volunteered for service with the *Grenzschutz Ost*. Officers, known as *Kreiskommissare*, were provided by the *Reichsheer*. Equipment and weapons came from hidden stocks held in defiance of the *IKK* - see Seaton 1982 p.8.

Seeckt therefore allocated Bergmann six of the ten available *Divisionen: 1.Division* (Königsberg/Ostpr.), *2.Division* (Stettin), *3.Division* (Berlin), *4.Division* (Dresden), *1.Kavallerie-Division* (Frankfurt a.d.Oder) and *2.Kavallerie-Division* (Breslau).[47] Despite obvious ideological differences he also moved swiftly to forge closer links with Germany's former eastern adversary. During the early spring of 1921 he was instrumental in securing Government approval for further talks with Lenin's Government which had sought German military support in the planned overhaul of the Red Army (*RKKA*).[48] These covert staff discussions took place under the cover provided by the signing of the Germano-Soviet Commercial Agreement in May of that year and to co-ordinate these developments Seeckt established the highly secret *Sondergruppe R (Russland)* (Special Group Russia) within the *Truppenamt*, this being led by *Obst.*Walther Nicolai, the former *Chef d.Ob. Qu.IIIb (Fremde Heere)*.[49] Other senior officers involved in these negotiations included *GenLt.*Otto Hasse and *Obstlt.*Kurt von Schleicher.[50]

Given the restrictions imposed by the *IMKK* it was considered desirable that in return for German technical and training assistance that facilities should be made available in the USSR for clandestine use by the *Reichswehr*.[51] Responsibility for these secret negotiations was to rest with the *Zentrale Moskau* (Moscow Centre), a covert military mission which was led by former *Chef des Generalstabes der Kommandierenden General der Luftstreitkräfte (Chief of the General Staff of the Commanding General of the Air Service), Obst.i.G.a.D.*Hermann von der Lieth-Thomsen (See also 1D1).[52] On the 16 April 1922 German and Soviet diplomats formally signed the Treaty of Rapello which provided for the mutual renunciation of reparations, expansion of trade relations

47   Quoted from Mason 1973 *The Rise of the Luftwaffe 1918-1940* p.97 with the knowledge of the Orion Publishing Group. This proved to be a remarkably prophetic statement given the events of Sep 39. There was a very real concern that Germany's geo-political position had been greatly disadvantaged by the creation of Poland in the east and Czechoslovakia in the south - see Schwabedissen W. GenLt.a.D. *Problems of Fighting a Three-Front War* USAF Historical Studies No.178 p.2-3.

48   Seaton 1982 pp.7-8 & Pipes Reichswehr. Although these were structured as *Infanterie-Divisionen* (Infantry Divisions), in contemporary documents there were simply referred to as *Divisionen* - see Hildebrand 1990-92.

49   Mason 1973 pp.98-99 & Seaton 1982 pp.8-9. These diplomatic ambitions were facilitated by the Allies' earlier intervention (in 1919) in support of the Russian White Army, actions that had effectively driven a wedge between France and her traditional ally in eastern Europe - see Shirer W.L. 1969 *The Collapse of the Third Republic: An Inquiry into the Fall of France in 1940* (hereafter cited as Shirer 1969). Bolshevik plans to subjugate Poland had come to a premature and unexpected end with the defeat of the Red Army at the gates of Warszawa in Aug 20. This setback led to an appreciation on the part of the Russian Commander, Mikahil Tuchachevski, that the emergent Red Army had to be trained and re-organised along professional lines. However there were those in Bolshevik Russia, notably Trotsky, that saw a place for a larger militia based army (*RKKA*) which was ideologically more in keeping with the spirit of the 1917 Revolution - see Messenger 1991 p.61. During the course of 1920 the Soviets had placed Victor Kopp, a capable diplomat of Estonian heritage, in Berlin to begin secret negotiations with the German authorities. A number of joint Soviet-German ventures would result from his work - see Vercamer A. and Pipes J. *German Military in the Soviet Union 1918-1933* in www.feldgrau.com (hereafter cited as Vercamer and Pipes). Soviet pragmatism is evidenced by Leonid Lenin: *"I am not fond of the Germans by any means, but at the present time it is more advantageous to use them than to challenge them. An independent Poland is very dangerous to Soviet Russia; it is an evil, however (it) also has its redeeming features; for while it exists we may safely count on Germany, because the Germans hate Poland and will at any time make common cause with us in order to strangle Poland"* – quoted from Mason 1973 *The Rise of the Luftwaffe 1918-1940* p.99 with the knowledge of the Orion Publishing Group.

50   Suchenwirth 1968 pp.11-12. The Germano-Soviet Trade Agreement was signed on the 6 May 21. Leonid Krassin, the chief Soviet negotiator, had approached the *RWM* with a view to securing German industrial backing for a revitalisation of the Soviet armament industry.

51   Suchenwirth 1968 p.12 & Mason 1973 p.103. Seeckt was personally engaged in discussions with Karl Radek but it was *GenLt.*Otto Hasse who was mainly responsible for these negotiations - see Rabenau von F. Gen.a.D. 1940 *Seeckt: Aus seinem Leben* p.308. In Feb 23 Hasse had replaced Heye as the *Chef d.Truppenamt* - see Seaton 1982 p.15 & wikipedia Truppenamt.

52   Suchenwirth 1968 p.13. Seeckt was particularly keen to see these facilities developed to circumvent the restrictions imposed on German military aviation by the *Versailles Diktat* - see also Vercamer and Pipes.

and the immediate resumption of diplomatic relations.[53] The secret military clauses, agreed later in 1922, included the progressive establishment of clandestine facilities for German use at Lipetsk, Orenberg and Kazan together with a manufacturing facility for the *Junkers Flugzeugwerke AG* at Fili deep inside the USSR (See also 1C1).[54] The first official *Reichswehr* mission to Moskva followed in February 1923 under the direction of Hasse, the *Chef der Truppenamt*. It is notable that this mission included *Hptm.*Kurt Student, the *HWAs' Flugtechnickreferent.*[55]

Germany's principal aims in entering into this secret agreement with the emergent Soviet Union were *(Photo 1A-11)*:

REICHSWEHR OBJECTIVES UNDER THE RAPELLO AGREEMENT

- Development of advanced military technologies, theoretical studies and training programmes free for foreign scrutiny
- Development of proscribed weapons and their tactical applications - principally aircraft, tanks and chemical warfare
- Development of an experienced cadre of military specialist in a range of fields who would later lead technological developments in Germany[56]

The banned air arm was the major beneficiary of these agreements. As preparations went ahead to establish a secret training and technical base in the Soviet Union, *Maj.*Wilberg reorganised the *TA (L)* to handle the increased work load. Four distinct *Referate* (Desks) were created: I - *Einsatz Ausbildung* (Operational Training), II - *Personal* (Personnel), III - *Technik* (Technical) and IV - *Verwaltung* (Administration). In 1925 two additional *Referate* were added: V - *Organisation* and VI - *Luftschütz* (Air Defence).[57] To meet the needs of this new organisation the *Heeres-Personalamt (HPA)* (Army Personnel Office) posted a number of former *Fliegeroffiziere* to the *TA (L)*; *Hptm.* Hugo Sperrle together with *Rittm.*Bruno Maaß and Heinz-Hellmuth von Wuhlisch were all assigned during 1925 when the *TA (L)* was itself transferred to the *Truppenamt's* Organisation Branch as *T 2 III (L) (Chart I-1).*[58]

In the meantime economic problems within Germany had left the Weimar Government with no alternative but to inform the Allied Reparations Commission that it would be impossible to meet the instalment due at the end of 1922; indeed it was the German wish that the whole reparations

53   Suchenwirth 1968 p.13 & Mason 1973 p.103. *Maj.*Lieth-Thomsen had been the prime mover behind the emergence of the *Luftstreitkräfte* as an independent arm of the *Heer* in 1915. From Nov 16 he was *C.d.GS.d.KoGenLuft* and as such was Hoeppner's right hand man in the development of the military air arm. Decorated with the *Plm* on the 8 Apr 17 he was retired on the 11 Aug 19 - see Angolia and Hackney 1984 pp.126-127 and service record for Hermann von der Lieth-Thomsen in Hildebrand K.F.1991 *Die Generale der deutschen Luftwaffe 1935-1945 Band 2 H-N* (hereafter cited as Hildebrand 1991) pp.296-297.

54   Suchenwirth 1968 p.12. The Allied Powers, notably France, had been pressing the Soviets to demand war reparations from Germany. This treaty was therefore incredibly significant for diplomatic, economic and military reasons - see also Shirer 1969 p.144. The military clauses were agreed on the 11 Aug 22 - see Vercamer and Pipes.

55   *Memorandum from GenOb.Hans von Seeckt to Reichskanzler, Dr.Wilhelm Cuno, dated 23 Nov 22* & Thomsen GenIng.a.D. *Junkers Flugzeugwerke Fili in der Naehe von Moskau 1924-127* in C/III/1, Karlsruhe Document Collection in Suchenwirth 1968 p.12.

56   Suchenwirth 1968 p.13 & Hooton E.R. 1994 *Phoenix Triumphant: The Rise and Rise of the Luftwaffe* (hereafter cited as Hooton 1994) p.37.

57   Vercamer and Pipes.

58   Beauvais et al 2002 p.50. *Herr* von Meyern-Hohenberg was Wilberg's *Adjutant*. He also handled all personnel matters; *Herr* Wille was the *Referent Haushalt* (Budget); *Herr* Seldner handled covert equipment procurement - see *App.2 Air Force Agencies in 1921-28* (Integration with the *Reichswehr*) in Hertel 1955 p.269.

question should be re-examined with a view to its reduction.[59] The proposal drew little reaction from Britain, whilst the Americans responded by withdrawing their remaining personnel.[60] The French and the Belgians on the other hand were incensed and immediately occupied the Ruhr with a view to securing their reparations quota *(Photo 1A-12)*.[61] This was met in turn by a state sponsored total strike in the collieries, steel works and on the railways and as passions increased, by several acts of sabotage.[62] These the French attempted to quash by summary executions, imprisonment and the import of labour from France and Belgium to reactivate the Ruhr industries.[63]

Not surprisingly there was considerable pressure on the Government, and therefore on Seeckt, to adopt a course of military action against the French in the Ruhr.[64] German forces in the west comprised just four divisions under *Gen.d.Inf.*Arnold Ritter von Mohl's *Gruppenkommando 2* (Kassel): *5.Division* (Stuttgart), *6.Division* (Münster), *7.Division* (München) and *3.Kavallerie-Division* (Weimar).[65] To his credit, Seeckt was able to resist these pressures in the knowledge that the *Reichsheer* could not have beaten the French in an open battle.[66] He therefore supported the policy of passive resistance.[67] Nevertheless behind the scenes measures were taken to improve the *Reichsheer's* fighting capability and amongst these was the secret acquisition by Wilberg of 100 modern fighters from Fokker's *Nederlandsche Vliegtuigenfabriek* in Amsterdam. The deal was brokered by the industrialist Hugo Stinnes from his offices in Hamburg but the money was diverted from the "*Ruhrfond*", a Government fund that had been set up to subsidise the strikers' families in the occupied industrial area.[68] Readily available was the Fokker D.XI, a derivative of the famous

---

59   Service records in Hildebrand 1990-92.

60   Mason 1973 pp.119-120. It was proposed *"that reparation should be reduced to tolerable dimensions, that Germany should be released from all payments, both in cash and in goods such as coal and lumber, for a period of several years, given a bank credit, and restored to trade equality".*

61   Mason 1973 p.120. The Americans had already concluded their peace settlement with Germany on the 11 Nov 21. The USA would henceforth return to its earlier isolationist stance and progressively distance itself from European affairs.

62   Shirer 1969 p.147 & Mason 1973 p.120. The French despatched a force of five combat divisions supported by light and heavy tanks, artillery and aircraft under Gen.Degoutte into the Ruhr on the 9 Jan 23. The Belgians contributed a further division. In Jul 24 the *Aviation Militaire* element comprised the *5eme.Brigade Aerienne* in Rheinland-Pfalz with 214 aircraft: *33 Regt.d'aviation mixtes d'observation* (Mainz) & *12 Regt.d'aviation de bombardement de jour* (Neustadt) - see Christienne C. and Lissarague P.1980 *A History of French Military Aviation* (hereafter cited as Christienne and Lissarague 1980) p.212.

63   Mason 1973 pp.122-123: *"Organised bands of saboteurs roamed throughout the countryside, blowing up bridges, cutting lines, and derailing troop trains."* One such saboteur was Leo Schlageter, a former officer, who was eventually caught in the act of blowing up a railway bridge. He was shot by the French Army - see also Caldwell D. 1996 *The JG 26 War Diary Vol.1 1939-1942* pp.3-4.

64   Shirer 1969 p.147 & Mason 1973 pp.122-123. More than 15,000 French, Belgian and Italian civilian engineers, signalmen and railway personnel were drafted into the Ruhr to secure some $106 million worth of goods, the balance of which was taken by France after deducting expenses.

65   Mason 1973 pp.120-125. Within the *Reichsheer* there was considerable pressure to act. *Obstlt.*Edwin von Stulpnagel wrote to Seeckt to remind him that *"from the national and soldierly point of view, it is the duty of the soldier to act."* A bewildering number of patriotic groups supported armed intervention. The *Ring Deutscher Flieger* gave useful moral support to this cause. Certainly the nation was, momentarily at least, united behind the Weimar Government in its outrage toward the French. Both Britain and the USA were opposed to the French decision to take control of the Ruhr industries.

66   Pipes Reichswehr. Mohl assumed command of *Gr.Kdo.2* on the 1 Jan 23 - the moment of crisis. See also Axis History.

67   Mason 1973 p.121. On the 1 Jan 23, prior to the deployment of Degoutte's forces, the French had a total of 87,991 troops in the Rhineland. These forces were supplemented by 30,704 Belgians and 8,730 British troops. By this time the British occupied a compact zone around Köln, whilst the Belgians occupied the west bank of the Rhein up to their own border and that of neighbouring Holland - see *Sketch 5 Rhineland Occupation Areas January 1924* in Edmonds 1944 p.247. One interesting aside to the French occupation was a declaration by Cramon to *Gen.*Nollet of the *IKK* that he could no longer guarantee the safety of allied inspectors. The supervisory activities of the *IKK* therefore effectively stopped on the 9 Jan 23.

68   Mason 1973 p.123. There is evidence to suggest that the *Reichsheer* also covertly supported the saboteurs. Certainly small groups of volunteers received short-term military training with a view to them forming a mobilisable reserve - see Seaton 1982 p.8.

D.VII, but a more advanced design was also projected - the Fokker D.XIII, a fighter with a greatly improved performance.[69] The Germans ordered fifty of each but as events were to unfold neither type would be available before 1924 and the D.XIs were subsequently diverted to Romania. The Fokker D.XIII on the other hand was test flown by *Ing.*Hans Leutert and *Hptm.*Kurt Student and the entire order was subsequently shipped to Leningrad en route to the secret base at Lipetsk deep within the Soviet Union (See 1C3 & 1D1).[70]

Unfortunately Ebert's policy of passive resistance in the Ruhr was economically unsustainable and as the value of the *Reichsmark* plummeted during 1923 it became obvious that the strike would have to end.[71] In August Wilhelm Cuno was replaced as *Reichskanzler* by Gustav Stresemann and on the 26 September passive resistance in the Ruhr was terminated as nationalist fervour again took hold in the city streets.[72] Once again the *Reichsheer* was given sweeping powers to quash the rebellions and attempts to form separate republics in both the Rheinland and Bayern were both swiftly neutralised.[73] The final flicker of resistance occurred in München on the 9 November when armed police shot dead sixteen members of the *Nationalsozialistische Deutsche Arbeiter-Partei (NSDAP)*; members of a mob who were attempting to take-over the city.[74] Amongst the wounded was *Hptm.a.D.*Hermann Göring, the former *Kommandeur JG 1*.[75]

The period following the French occupation of the Ruhr had seen a temporary suspension of the *LGK's* work and when inspections were resumed in 1924 the Allied teams found that German attitudes had become far more obstructive.[76] In fact it would not be until September 1924 that a general inspection was initiated. A 500 page report followed in January 1925 which revealed a

69   Mason 1973 pp.123-125. Ebert and Cuno were behind Seeckt's decision to purchase fighter aircraft. *GenLt.*Hasse was responsible for financing these arrangements. It was estimated that Hugo Stinnes controlled as much as 20% of Germany's post-war resources; he was already involved in the financing of the *Reichswehr's* involvement in the Soviet Union. Fokker was advised that the fighters were destined for the Argentine and as such all the technical manuals were written in Spanish - see Constable T.J. and Toliver R.F. 1968 *Horrido! Fighter Aces of the Luftwaffe* p.133.

70   Morse S. (Ed.) 1982 *The Illustrated Encylopedia of Aircraft* p.1875. The Fokker D.XI (300 hp Hispano Suiza) was a derivative of the famous D.VII of 1918. It was exhibited at the International Air Exhibition in Sweden in 1923 and 125 were built for the Soviet Union, whilst others were exported to Argentina, Romania, Spain, Switzerland and the USA. The Fokker D.XIII was fitted with the far more powerful Napier Lion of 450 hp and was capable of 260 kph - making it the fastest fighter in the world at that time.

71   Mason 1973 p.126 & Postma T. 1979 *Fokker: Aircraft Builders to the World* pp.59 & 61.

72   Shirer W.L. 1963 *The Rise and Fall of the Third Reich: A History of Nazi Germany* (hereafter cited as Shirer 1963) p.51. The stability of the *Reichsmark,* already precarious in 1922, quickly collapsed during 1923. In 1921 the $ had been worth 75 Marks, in 1922 this dropped to 400 Marks, whilst the events of 1923 precipitated an ever increasing decline from 7,000 Marks in Jan 23 to 160,000 Marks by Jul 23. German currency had become worthless, wiping out at a stroke the life savings of the working and middle classes. The faith of the German people in the economic system as well as the Weimar Republic as an institution was also destroyed.

73   Mason 1973 p.127. The Government could no longer fund payments to workers who did not work and did not pay taxes.

74   Mason 1973 p.127. Additionally in Berlin some 600 former officers and men of the so-called *Schwarz Reichswehr* briefly occupied three old forts. After 48 hours they surrendered to the regular army without a fight.

75   Shirer 1963 pp.68-75. Led by Adolf Hitler some 600 members of the *Sturmabteilung (SA)* attempted an ill-planned and ill-considered local coup when they surrounded the *Burgerbrau Keller* in München during the evening of the 8 Nov 23 where Gustav Ritter von Kahr, *Staatskommissar f.Bayern,* was speaking to a crowd of some 3,000. Also present was *GenLt.*Otto von Lossow, *Bfr.Wehkreis VII* (Officer Commanding Military District VII) & *PolObst.* Hans von Seisser, the *Chef d.bayersiche Staatspolizei* (Chief of the Bavarian State Police). Hitler had hoped to enlist the support of both the Police and the Army but in this in he was unsuccessful. At 11 am on the 9 Nov 23 the assembled *Putschists,* led by Hitler, Göring and *Gen.*Erich Ludendorff, marched toward the Marienplatz in central München where they were stopped by armed police who opened fire on Hitler's party. Following his capture Hitler was incarcerated in Landsberg Prison - see also Snyder L.L. 1976 *Encyclopaedia of the Third Reich* (hereafter cited as Snyder 1976) p.20-21. Following this round of rebellions an even greater apolitical stance was adopted by the *Reichswehr* - see Cooper M. 1978 *The German Army 1933-1945: It's Political and Military Failure* p.6.

76   Mosley L. 1974 *The Reich Marshal: A Biography of Hermann Göring* pp.85-86 & Irving D. 1989 *Göring: A Biography* pp.62-64.

catalogue of concerns that ranged from secret stockpiles of weapons to the existence of a General Staff in being. There was also a very strong suspicion that the *Reichswehr* was in the process of establishing a covert air arm.[77]

Although Allied concerns led to the brief suppression of Wilberg's *T 2 III (L)* in the autumn of that year such was the political and social climate that it was possible for these issues to be dismissed by *Reichskanzler* Stresemann as "petty details".[78] Indeed such was the willingness of the Allied powers to seek a new relationship with Weimar Germany that negotiations were initiated between the various European powers during the course of the year. These discussions culminated in the signing of the Locarno Pact on the 1 December 1925 when the governments of France, Britain, Italy, Belgium and Germany all agreed to a thirty year period of non-aggression.[79] Furthermore both France and Britain agreed to guarantee Germany's post-Versailles frontiers, whilst the French Government accepted the need to open negotiations with the Germans on issues of mutual concern. As part of this general process of rehabilitation, Germany was accepted as a member of the League of Nations in 1926.[80]

Throughout this turbulent period Wilberg had played a key role in keeping the spirit of German military aviation alive, an objective which was initially accomplished by encouraging serving officers to participate in the various gliding organisations of the time (See 1D2). He also maintained close links with the *Ring Deutschen Flieger*, a veteran's organisation which enjoyed the patronage of *Gen.d.Kav.a.D.*Ernst von Hoeppner, the former *Kom.Gen.d.Luftstreitkräfte (Commanding General of the Air Service)*, until his death in September 1922.[81] Thereafter it was administered by *Obst.a.D.*Wilhelm Siegert, the former *Inspekteur der Flieger* (Inspector of Flight Troops), who maintained comprehensive files on around 2,500 former aircrew of the wartime *Luftstreitkräfte*.[82] In the event of war these men would provide a valuable reservoir of trained and experienced manpower and there is evidence to suggest that during the Ruhr Crisis a number of these former officers were given refresher flying training at the few private flying schools that then existed in Germany.[83]

To reinforce this capability Wilberg, acting on a proposal by Friedrich-Wilhelm (Fritz) Siebel that a domestic flying training organisation was required prior to the opening of the Lipetsk facility, secretly used *Reichswehr* funding to establish *Sportflug GmbH* in 1924.[84] Outwardly a sports flying operation, *Sportflug's* training curriculum was actually geared to meeting the needs of military pilots and the first of the new *Fliegerschulen* were located within each of the *Reichsheer's* seven territorial *Wehrkreise* (See 1D2 & 1E1).[85] This was an increasingly important objective as the number of serving officers actually

---

77   Mason 1973 pp.136-137. On the 12 Mar 24 the front pages of *Der Tag* carried the story: *"The National Union of German Officers, the German Officers' league and the Naval Officers' Union take the strongest exception to the latest Note of the Ambassadors' Conference in Paris. Our associations demand of the Government of the German Reich that the Note be decisively rejected. The unanimous shout of the German people must ring in the ears of the foreigner: Out with all these Control Commissions! Clear them out of Germany!"*

78   Mason 1973 pp.137-138. Published in 1925 the Commissioner's Report revealed that a store of 113,000 rifles had been discovered, that the banned General Staff had been re-created within the *Truppenamt*, that new artillery pieces had been installed on the Polish frontier, that non-authorised firms were engaged in the manufacture of munitions, the replacement budget for infantry weapons was ten times that required by the authorised force, and that the establishment of the armed police was 30,000 in excess of that permitted.

79   Hooton 1994 p.49 & Beauvais et al 2002 p.50. See also Mason 1973 p.138.

80   Shirer 1963 pp.112 & 136 & Snyder 1976 p.214.

81   Shirer 1963 pp.112 & 136.

82   Hooton 1994 p.29. See also the service record for Ernst Hoeppner in Hildebrand K.F.1990 *Die Generale der deutschen Luftwaffe 1935-1945 Band 1 A-G* pp.xix-xxi.

83   Mason 1973 pp.124-125, Hooton 1994 p.29 & Corum 1997 pp.77-78. Siegert was a highly respected and effective staff officer - see Kilduff 1991 pp.18-23. Although offered a key post in post war civil aviation Siegert felt unable to work with the new Social Democrat Government. He would lead the *Ring Deutschen Flieger* until his own death in 1929.

84   Hooton 1994 p.39. Training was provided on the ageing Albatros B-II, and possibly the new Dietrich DP II *Bussard* - see also Lange B. 1970 *Das Buch der deutschen Luftfahrtechnik* p.191.

85   Suchenwirth 1968 p.15 & Mason 1973 p.135. Siebel had been to the Soviet Union following the signing of the

available for flying duties steadily decreased. By 1926 only 100 of the original 180 *Fliegeroffiziere* were still eligible for this work; a situation brought about by retirement, illness and accident (See also 1E1).[86] For example both *Oblte.*Werner Junck and Carl-August Schoenebeck left the *Reichsheer* during this period to pursue other opportunities in aviation.[87] The 1926 Paris Aviation Convention permitted primary flying training for up to six serving officers per annum, provided that they paid for the training themselves (See 1B1 & 1D2).[88] To circumvent these restrictions Wilberg arranged for around 40 *Fahnenjunker* (Officer Candidates) per year to receive *ab initio* flying instruction prior to their official entry into the *Reichswehr*.[89] It was a neat trick and not essentially illegal.

Wilberg also played a pivotal role in the evolution of a new doctrine for air power, concepts that reached maturity in May 1926 with the publication of the *Richtlinien für die Führung des operativen Luftkrieges* (Directives for the leadership of the operational air war).[90] The need to reach a favourable decision in the face of overwhelming French air power had already led to the adoption of a new approach to the employment of air power by the *TA (L)* in such a conflict. In the mid-to late twenties the French *Aviation Militaire* was without doubt the most powerful air arm in the world:[91]

FIGURE 1A-2 AVIATION MILITAIRE (METROPOLITAN FRANCE) - ORDER OF BATTLE
SUMMER 1925

1ere. Division Aerienne (Metz)

2eme.Brigade Aerienne (Thionville)	11eme. Brigade Aerienne (Metz)
38 Regiment d'aviation mixtes d'observation	11 Regiment d'aviation de bombardement de jour
2 Regiment d'aviation de chasse	21 Regiment d'aviation de bombardement de nuit

2eme.Division Aerienne (Paris)

1ere.Brigade Aerienne (Le Bourget)	6eme.Brigade Aerienne (Tours)
24 Regiment d'aviation mixtes d'observation	31 Regiment d'aviation d'observation
22 Regiment d'aviation de bombardement de nuit	2 Regiment d'aviation de chasse

Treaty of Rapello to help with the planning of the Lipetsk facility. Siebel had proposed to the *RWM* that civilian flying schools be established in Germany at which serving and former officers could undertake flying training - see Hooton 1994 p.57.

86   Kreipe W. Gen.d.Flg.a.D. and Koester R. Obst.a.D. 1955 *Technical Training within the German Luftwaffe* USAF Historical Studies No.169 pp.7-8, Ries 1970 p.41 & Mason 1973 p.135.

87   Hooton 1994 p.57.

88   Service records for Werner Junck in Hildebrand 1991 pp.142-143 and Carl-August von Schoenebeck in Hildebrand 1992 pp.213-214. Junck was discharged on the 31 May 23 and left for Colombia and Venezuela to work as an airline pilot. He had pleaded with Wilberg to be allowed to go - see Townsend P. 1970 *Duel of Eagles* pp.79-80. Schoenebeck was discharged on the 30 Jun 24 and gained employment in the *Firma Motorwagen AG* in Kassel.

89   Schliephake H. 1971 *The Birth of the Luftwaffe* (hereafter cited as Schliephake 1971) p.16.

90   Schliephake 1971 p.16.

91   *Truppenamt T-Luft "Richtlinien für die Führung des operativen Luftkrieges"* in Corum 1997 (hereafter cited as T-Luft 1926) p.81. It has been suggested that *Hptm.*Hellmuth Felmy played a pivotal role in the writing of these directives - see Hooton 1994 p.62. Certainly he was a *Referent* within *T 1 (Führung)* from 1 Oct 24 until 5 Nov 26 - see service record for Hellmuth Felmy in Hildebrand 1990 pp.273-275. Within the *TA (L) Hptm.*Walter Lackner was engaged in the writing of *Flieger-Vorschriften* (Air Directives) during Jun 22 - Oct 25 - see service record for Walter Lackner in Hildebrand 1991 pp.278-279.

Regiments d'aviation autonme
5eme.Brigade Aerienne (Mayence)
33 Regiment d'aviation mixtes d'observation
12 Regiment d'aviation de bombardement de jour

3eme.Brigade Aerienne (Dijon)	4eme.Brigade Aerienne (Lyons)
32 Regiment d'aviation mixtes d'observation	35 Regiment d'aviation mixtes d'observation

Clearly a conventional clash with the *Aviation Militaire* was unthinkable, even in the medium term. Wilberg's staff therefore advocated an interdiction campaign that would seek to destroy the sources of its military power - its key aircraft and armament factories. To this end a well- researched target list was drawn up and the theory tested during *Luftschützübungsreise* (Aerial War Games) within the *Truppenamt* in 1924.[92]

Such thinking became the basis for the 1926 Directives, a thirty-nine page document that laid out the proposed organisation, targeting strategy and operational parameters for a bombing campaign, a concept that was referred to as *operativer Luftkrieg* (operational air war):

The air force allows the supreme commander to carry out the war simultaneously to the innermost political, moral, economic and military sources of the power of the state. The attack of the air force is directed against the population, industry, and transportation net as well as against the enemy armed forces and the facilities that sustain them. By attacks against the enemy's major cities and industrial centres, it will be attempted to crush the enemy's moral resistance and will to fight by targeting his armaments industry and food distribution.[93]

Richtlinien für die Führung des operativen Luftkrieges
Truppenamt-Luft May 1926

The indivisibility of the civilian and industrial components of the modern nation state were acknowledged and it was accepted that civilian casualties were both inevitable and advantageous in the prosecution of total war:

The requirements for civilian life are closely tied to the necessary requirements of the military. Civilian machinery that is brought to a standstill by attacks of the operational air force will also have a decisive effect upon the war industries and the total support of the armed forces.[94]

Richtlinien für die Führung des operativen Luftkrieges
Truppenamt-Luft May 1926

92   Green W. and Fricker J. 1958 *The Air Forces of the World: Their History, Development and Present Strength* p.98 & Christienne and Lissarague 1980 pp.219-222. Material such as this was contained in the *TA-L, Referat* VI publication *"Militärische Faktoren für die Bewertung der modernen Luftmachte" dated 9 Apr 1926*, in BA/MA RH 2279. On the 1 Jul 24 the *Aviation Militaire* in Metropolitan France had a strength of 100 Escadrilles with an establishment of 900 combat aircraft: 270 fighters, 30 night fighters, 200 day bombers, 96 night bombers, 80 reconnaissance and 224 observation aircraft. In the event of an armed conflict with Germany, the 5eme.*Brigade Aerienne* would support the ground forces already deployed within the Reich, whilst the 1ere.*Division Aerienne*, which was held at a high degree of readiness in eastern France, would be available for a range of operations including air superiority, support of the ground forces and night bombardment.
93   *Luftschützübungsreise 1924* in BA/MA RH 2/2244 in Corum 1997 pp.74-75. It was estimated that just 8 factories supported the French *Aviation Militaire*.
94   Quoted from *para 4, T-Luft 1926* in Corum 1997 *The Luftwaffe: Creating the Operational Air War 1918-1940* p.82 with the kind permission of the University of Kansas.

There was considerable discussion over targeting rationale and in this respect the *Richtlinien* provide evidence of the *T-Luft's* on-going analysis of the complex economic-military infrastructure of a modern industrial nation such as France. The armament factories, transportation networks and sea ports were seen as primary targets.[95] However their dependence on the electricity grid and in particular the generating stations was seen of especial importance to a force that would lack numerical strength, although in possession of superior equipment and tactics.[96]

It was proposed that the *Reichswehr's* future air arm should be divided into two parts: a force of reconnaissance and close support aircraft, control of which would be delegated to the local *Reichsheer* or *Reichsmarine* commander; and an independent force of bombing aircraft that would be under the direct control of the supreme commander.[97] Heavy bomber and reconnaissance *Staffeln* (Squadrons) would each have six aircraft, whilst fighter *Staffeln* would have an establishment of fifteen machines. Three or more *Staffeln* would constitute a *Geschwader* (Wing) and it was expected that all flying units would be highly mobile, their ground echelons being fully motorised.[98] This was very much in accordance with *Luftstreitkräfte* practice in the final year of the Great War.[99] The strategic force would be organised into *Brigaden* (Brigades), several of which would constitute a *Flieger-Division* (Air Division). These units would be equipped with long range bombers which themselves would be protected by long range, heavily armed two-seat escort fighters.[100] In certain circumstances the independent force could be directed to support ground or naval forces by attacking key installations and lines of communication. However the authors of the *Richtlinien* were at pains to note that such missions should only be attempted at *"the critical moment of decision"*. As the *Reichswehr's* decisive force it was vital that the bomber force be conserved and not frittered away in an expensive and potentially protracted campaign of attrition.[101] Interestingly, unlike some foreign theorists, Wilberg's staff chose also to emphasise the importance of a strong and unified air defence system to protect the homeland from similar actions by the enemy.[102]

The 1926 *Richtlinien* were an important step in the resurgence of military air power in Germany. Although the *Reichswehr* lacked the physical resources to form an actual air arm, the

---

95   *Para 68 & 70, T-Luft 1926* in Corum 1997 p.82. In this respect Wilberg's thinking was not vastly different from that of the British Air Staff: *"the main objective for an air force lies in the aircraft factories and productive centres of the enemy's country, his seat of government and his supply and transport system"* - see *Air Staff Memorandum August 1923 (Supplement in March 1924) "Air Strategy in Home Defence: The Correct Objective"*. Interestingly the RAF's "enemy" at that time was also France! - see Sinnott 2001 pp.58 & 134.

96   *Para 69, T-Luft 1926* in Corum p.82. The electrification of the railways was becoming a feature in various parts of Europe at this time. In Germany the Berlin-Lichterfelde Ost line was electrified in 1903 and this was followed by part of the Hamburg suburban network during 1908-11. By the end of the thirties 4% of the *Reichsbahn* would be electrified compared to 32% in Italy & 77% in Switzerland where cheap HEP was utilised. France had electrified 7.8% of its network by that time - see Naval Intelligence Division 1945 *Germany Vol.IV Ports and Communications* pp.236-241.

97   *Para 5, T-Luft 1926* in Corum 1997 p.82. Such diversions did not concern the British Air Staff. Geographically isolated from invasion air operations in the context of home defence were seen primarily as an offensive strategy. Air defence was not considered to be sufficiently effective as to prevent enemy air attacks on targets in the southern half of Great Britain. The only effective defence was offence - see Taylor and Moyes 1968 pp.52-53 & Sinnott 2001 pp.3 & 6.

98   *Truppenamt "Zusammenstellung der Gesamtstarken und Ausrüstung der Kommandobehorden und Truppeneinheiten des Feldheers"* National Archives, von Seeckt Papers File M-132, Roll 340 in Corum 1997 p.121.

99   Imrie 1971 pp.57-59 & Kilduff 1991 p.76.

100   *Para 11, T-Luft 1926* in Corum 1997 pp.82-83. British planners did not see a role for escort aircraft, be they heavily armed bombers or long range fighters. British air strategy rested on the assumptions: 1. That accurate bombing was possible, 2. That it would be effective, 3.That it would be carried out by self-defending formations of bombers, and 4. That continuous, day and night, bombing was essential and possible" - see Sinnott 2001 p.11.

101   *Paras 91, 92 & 95, T-Luft 1926* in Corum 1997 p.83.

102   *Paras 106-127, T-Luft 1926* in Corum 1997 p.83. British planners called for only a small fighter force, just 17 of the planned 52 squadrons - see Collier B. 1957 *The Defence of the United Kingdom* p.15 & Sinnott 2001 p.10.

Richtlinien provided the framework within which the planning for such a force could be developed. Specifications for new combat aircraft could be issued to the aircraft manufacturers (See 1C2 & 1C3), an appropriate training curriculum could be established for the secret flying schools (See 1D1 & 1D2), and tactics and weapons could be evaluated under simulated operational conditions at the secret air base in the Soviet Union (See 1D1). The *Richtlinien* also formed the basis for further discussion and debate within the *Reichswehr* and even at this early stage German air strategy showed signs of independent thought. The publications and opinions of Mitchell, Trenchard and Douhet as well as such emerging military theorists as Fuller and Liddell Hart had been read and reported to an official audience via such journals as the *Militärwochenblatt* and *Luftfahrt Nachrichten.*[103] However the resulting doctrine was almost uniquely German, a military concept that sought to blend tactical and strategic operations under the single umbrella of *operativer Luftkrieg.*

The *Richtlinien* marked a watershed in the development of the new air arm. It was the end of the beginning, a stage that had of necessity to be cloaked in secrecy. By 1926 Germany had finally been accepted into the international community of nations. The economic disasters of 1923-24 were becoming something of a memory and the next four years would be a period of steadily increasing prosperity. Within this optimistic framework there would be further funding for secret developments in the Soviet Union.[104] However the future development of military aviation would lie in the hands of others. In October 1926 Seeckt was forced to resign as *Chef der Heeresleitung* following his ill-advised decision to permit the Kaiser's grandson, Prinz Wilhelm von Preussen, to attend the *Reichsheer's* annual manoeuvres in the uniform of the old Imperial First Foot Guards without informing or obtaining permission from Gessler as *Reichswehrminister (Photo 1A-13).*[105] He was replaced by *Gen.d.Inf.*Wilhelm Heye.[106] Then in December 1926 disaffected elements within the *Junkers Flugzeugwerke* leaked information to the liberal Social Democrat deputy Philip Scheidemann on the activities of *Sondergruppe "R"* and in particular *GenLt.*Otto Hasse:

---

103   Corum 1997 pp.89-91 & 98-101. The *TA (L)* subscribed to all the major German and foreign aviation journals - for example the Italian *Rivista Aeronautica* and the French *Revue du Aeronautique Militaire*. The *Militärwochenblatt* was the primary journal of the *Reichswehr*; it served as the means of transmitting the latest thinking on a range of military subjects to all interested parties within the *Reichsheer* and *Reichsmarine*. It contained a section entitled *Luftfahrwesen* which reported specifically on foreign military aviation. The *Luftfahrt Nachrichten* was issued by the *TA (L)* and dealt with developments in aviation technology and intelligence on foreign air forces. Hans Ritter's *Der Zukunftskrieg und seine Waffen* of 1924 provided a useful synthesis on the theoretical application of air power. Col.J.F.C.Fuller was the British Army's main exponent of mechanised warfare; Capt.B.Liddell Hart was a leading thinker in infantry tactics. Significant publications included Fuller's *Tanks in the Great War* & *The Reformation of War* and Liddell Hart's *Paris, or the Future of War* & *The Remaking of Modern Armies* - see Messenger 1991 p.32-66 & Delaney J. 2000 *The Blitzkreig Campaigns: Germany's Lightning War Strategy in Action* p.18-25.

104   Mason 1973 p.145. Through Seeckt's apolitical stance the *Reichswehr* had retained the confidence of the highest echelons within the Weimar Government, a view which now led President Ebert to support the allocation of additional funding for the development of new weapons.

105   Mason 1973 p.154 & Seaton 1982 p.16. By this time Seeckt's independent and at time high-handed attitude toward the Republican Government in general and to Gessler in particular had become intolerable. Even the new *Präsident*, Paul von Hindenburg, had little time for the *Chef der Heeresleitung*, commenting: *"von Seeckt's insufferable conceit was ruining the army."* Seeckt was sent to China as head of a German Military Mission before returning to Germany to write extensively on his thinking on the future form of military operations - see Seeckt H. 1928 *Gedanken eines Soldaten*, Seeckt H. 1933 *Die Reichswehr* & Seeckt H. 1938 *Aus Meinem Leben, 1866-1917.* He died in Feb 37. *GFM.a.D.*Paul von Hindenburg succeeded as *Präsident* of the Republic following the death of Ebert in 1925. The re-appearance of Hindenburg changed the relationship between the *Reichswehr* and the Weimar Government as the *Generalfeldmarschall's* role as *Oberbefehlshaber* was more real than titular. This had caused friction with Seeckt who saw the *Reichsheer* to be very much "his creation" and this was undoubtedly a contributory factor to his replacement by the amiable *GenOb.*Wilhelm Heye. However it would be incorrect to conclude that Hindenburg played an active role in the affairs of the *Reichsheer* for he did not, however it did prevent Seeckt's successors, namely Heye and from 1930 *Gen.d.Inf.*Kurt Freiherr von Hammerstein-Equord, from ever having quite the power that Seeckt had enjoyed.

106   www.wilkipedia.org Heye had previously been *Bfr. WK I* Ostpreussen - see Pipes Reichswehr.

I would like to prove through several pertinent facts that the *Reichswehr* has become more and more a state within the State, obeying its own laws and following its own politics. Based on a memorandum from the house of Junkers which has come to our attention, it seems there exists within the *Reichswehrministerium* a special section known as *Sondergruppe R* whose members are, for the most part, serving army officers. They have spent since 1923 sums mounting in the neighbourhood of eighty million gold marks. And there exists in a large Berlin bank an account upon which one of the *Reichswehr* functionaries, *Herr* Spangenburg, executes the necessary payments... This Spangenburg is in close contact with the so-called...., or *Gefu*, among whose directors one finds a certain Otto zur Leien, who resides always abroad, notably in Russia. Through Spangenburg, several millions of marks have been paid through the treasury of *Gefu*, clearly demonstrating the collusion between the *Reichswehr* and this society.

The task of *Gefu* is the building of an armaments industry abroad, chiefly in Russia. Contracts have been signed with false names. The go-between for the Junkers contracts, signed on the 14 March 1922, was none other than General Hasse. We know for certainty that Russian made munitions have arrived by boat from Leningrad at the end of September and in October of this year... The communist cell at the port (of Stettin) is perfectly aware of these things.

It is neither clean nor honest to see Soviet Russia preaching world disarmament on one hand, while the same time she is actively rearming the *Reichswehr*. We must put an end to this scandal! We can no longer tolerate a state of things contrary to the creation of a truly republican and democratic army. The *Reichswehr* needs to be completely shaken up and reformed.[107]

Philipp Scheidemann
Social Democrat Deputy to the *Reichstag*
16 December 1926

However this dramatic public disclosure achieved very little except the closure of the *Gefu* organisation which had arranged for the supply of Soviet-made munitions to the *Reichsheer*. Hasse, by this time a *General der Infanterie*, had already been transferred to become *Befehlshaber der Wehrkreis III* (Berlin).[108] He was replaced as *Chef.d. Truppenamt* by *GenMaj.*Georg Wetzell.[109]

---

107   Quoted from Mason 1973 *The Rise of the Luftwaffe 1918-1940* pp.155-156 with the knowledge of the Orion Publishing Group. This followed on the decision to close down Junker's Fili factory following a lack of orders from the *VVS-RKKA*. See also Schmitt G. 1988 *Hugo Junkers and his Aircraft* p.135 & Hooton 1994 p.48. Of course the Ebert Government and its successors were fully aware of the *Reichswehr's* activities in the Soviet Union - see Seaton 1982 p.8. A contemporary source suggests that the money that had been promised to Junkers by the *Reichswehr* had been lost in speculative ventures by Niedermayer and Hasse - see Herrmann 1943 p.52. This source also suggests that Hasse shot himself but this is not substantiated elsewhere - Hasse was assigned to Berlin as *Bfr.Gr.Kdo.1* during Apr 29 - Sep 32 - see www.axishistory.com. *Gefu - Gesellschaft zur Forderung gewerblicher Unternehmen Ausland* - a front company for the *RWM* to channel funds to firms operating in the USSR - see Schmidt 1988 p.132.

108   Pipes Reichswehr. This appointment had taken effect on the 1 Feb 26.

109   Seaton 1982 p.15. Georg not Wilhelm Wetzell – see service record for Georg Wetzell in www.Lexicon-der-Wehrmacht.de.

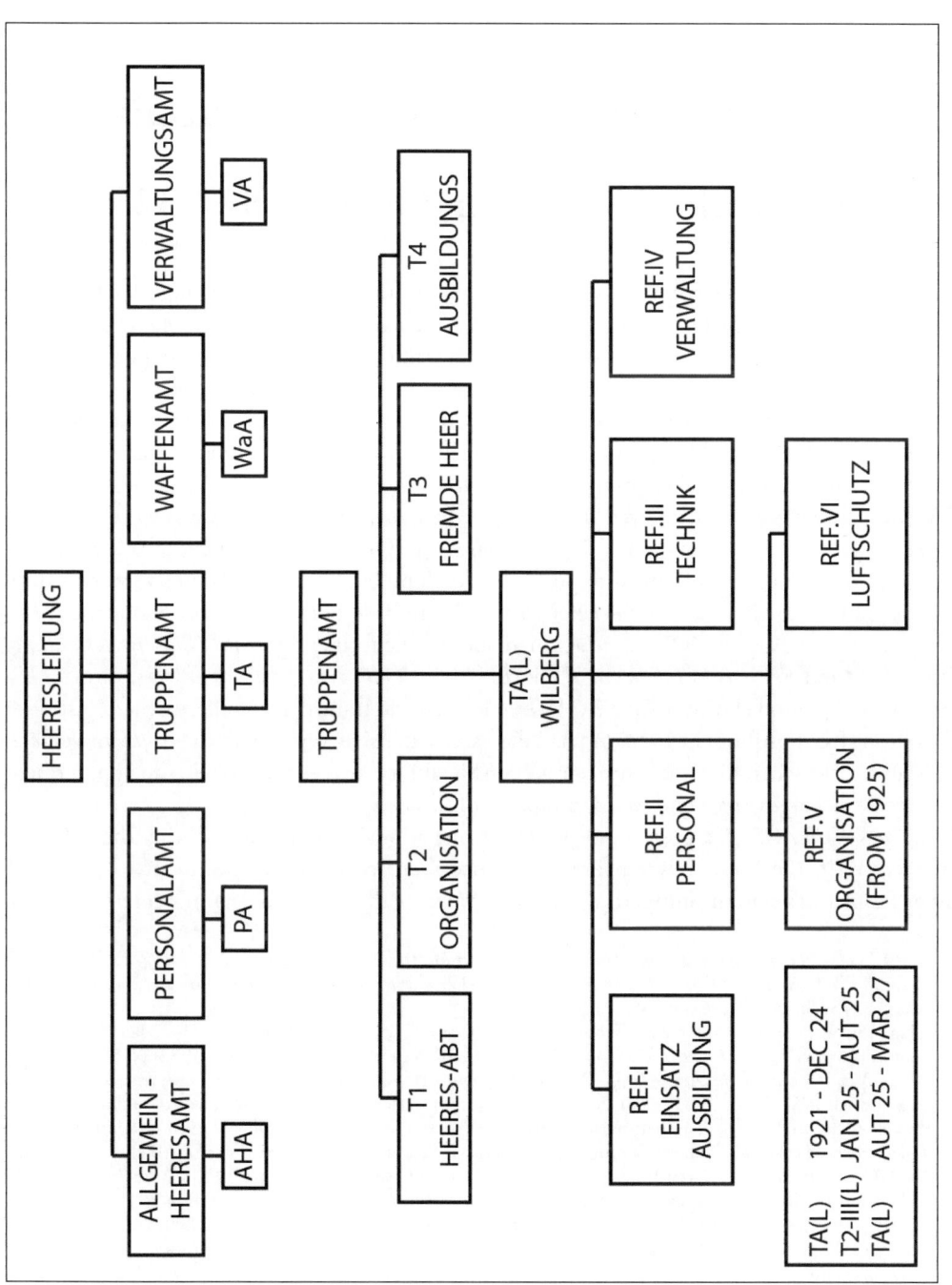

I-1 Covert military aviation agencies within the *Truppenamt* 1920-27

1A3

Developing a Military Aviation Capability

The work of Sperrle and Felmy 1927-33

In the autumn of 1925 *Abteilung T 2 III (L)* had been outwardly dissolved following Allied concerns about the secret development of military aviation in Germany.[1] In reality it simply reverted to its former status of an independent and totally covert department - the *TA (L)* - that reported directly to the new *Chef des Truppenamt* (Chief of the Troop Office), *GenMaj.*Georg Wetzell (See 1A2).[2] Continuity in air staff matters was assured through *Maj.*Helmuth Wilberg's continued leadership of the *TA (L)* and it is notable that there were few changes in his clandestine air staff during this transitional period. The formal dissolution of the *Interalliierte Luftfahrt-Überwachungs-Kommission (ILUK)* in January 1927 then allowed the *TA (L)* to be returned to *T 2 (Organisation)* in April of that year under the new designation *T 2 V (L)(Chart I-2).*[3] Promoted to the rank of *Oberstleutnant* on the same date, Wilberg continued to guide the development of German military aviation until his re-assignment to the *Stab Infanterie-Regiment 18* at Paderborn on the 30 September.[4] His successor on the 15 August 1927 was *Maj.*Hugo Sperrle, the former *Referent I (Einsatz Ausbildung)* within *TA (L)* and *Referent I (Taktik)* in *T 2 V (L).*[5]

Sperrle was a sound choice as *Chef T 2 V (L).* He had been trained as a military aviator just prior to the outbreak of hostilities in 1914 and had then seen extensive service with the *Aufklärungsflieger* until March 1917 when his experience and leadership ability was recognised with an appointment to a staff post as *Fliegergruppenführer 13* in support of *Armeeoberkommando (AOK) 7.* From January 1918 he was *KoFl.AOK 7*, a position of particular operational responsibility during the *Feldheer's* final offensive in the West. His wartime experience then led to his appointment to *Gen.d.Inf.* Walther Reinhardt's staff at Stuttgart as *Flieger-Referent* (Staff Advisor – Air) in September 1920.

---

1   *Chart 1 Offices within the Army Troop Office dealing with Air Matters, 1 March 1920 - 31 March 1927* in Suchenwirth R. 1968 *The Development of the German Air Force 1919-1939* USAF Historical Studies No.160 (hereafter cited as Chart 1 in Suchenwirth 1968) p.246.

2   Chart 1 in Suchenwirth 1968 p.246. Georg Wetzell was *Chef d. Truppenamt* between Oct 25 - 27 Jan 27 - see www. wikipedia.org. & Seaton A. 1982 *The German Army 1933-1945* (hereafter cited as Seaton 1982) p.15.

3   *Chart 2 Offices within the Army Troop Office dealing with Air Matters, 1 April 1927 - 30 September 1929* in Suchenwirth 1968 p.247. The work of the *ILUK* ended on the 31Jan 27. *T 2 V (L)* was formed on the 1 Apr 27 as the central department for all military aviation matters - see also *App.I Air Force Agencies in 1928 (Integration with the Reichswehr)* in Hertel W. Dipl.Ing.GenIng.a.D.1955 *Procurement in the German Air Force* USAF Historical Studies No.170 (hereafter cited as Hertel 1955) p.268 & *Army Aviation Organisation 1st April 1927 to 30th September 1929* in Beauvais H., Kossler K., Mayer M. and Regel C. 2002 *German Secret Flight Test Centres to 1945: Johannisthal, Lipetsk, Rechlin, Travemünde, Tarnewitz, Peenemunde-West* (hereafter cited as Beauvais et al 2002) p.50.

4   Service record for Helmuth Wilberg in Hildebrand K.F.1992 *Die Generale der deutschen Luftwaffe 1935-1945 Band 3 O-Z* (hereafter cited as Hildebrand 1992 pp.513-514. Following familiarisation with his new role Obstlt.Wilberg was appointed *Bataillons-Kdr.i.IR 18* on the 1 Feb 28, a position which he was to hold until the 30 Sep 29 when he was appointed *Kdt.Festung Breslau.*

5   Service record for Hugo Sperrle in Hildebrand 1992 pp.325-326 & Hooton E.R. 1994 *Phoenix Triumphant: The Rise and Rise of the Luftwaffe* (hereafter cited as Hooton 1994) p.51. Sperrle took up post as *Chef T 2 V (L)* on the 15 Aug 27.

Following a brief period of *Truppendienst* with *Artillerie-Regiment 4* he had then joined Wilberg's air staff in March 1925.[6]

As *Referent I (Einsatz Ausbildung)* Sperrle had played an important part in the formulation of the influential *1926 Richtlinien für die Führung des operativen Luftkrieges*.[7] During the following years such concepts were evaluated in the *Reichswehr's* annual *Kriegspiele* (War Games) which were held in Berlin between January and March, often in the presence of invited foreign military observers.[8] *T 2 V (L)* was responsible specifically for the first *Operativer Kriegspiel* (Operational War Game) which was held over several days in January 1927. The second series, held in February to March, were all-embracing and engaged the whole of Wetzell's *Truppenamt*.[9] The *1927 Kriegspiel* used the scenario of a Polish attack on eastern Germany, which required the Blue Forces under *Obstlt.* Werner von Fritsch *(Chef T 1)*, to conduct defensive operations prior to mounting a counter-offensive into Poland. Officers from *T 2 V (L)* deployed hypothetical German air forces in defence of German cities and also operationally in support of the *Reichsheer* in the field.[10]

During the late twenties and early thirties the *Truppenamt* maintained close links with a number of foreign armies. Chief amongst these was the Red Army where relations had been especially close following the signing of the Treaty of Rapello in 1922 and where *Reichsheer* officers had been sent for training from 1924 (See 1A2 & 1D1).[11] It is noteworthy that *GenMaj.* Werner von Blomberg, Wetzell's successor as *Chef des Truppenamt*, visited the Soviet Union in the late twenties where he was impressed by both the Red Army and the totalitarian form of government in which the military enjoyed the power and respect denied to officers in Weimar Germany.[12] At the same time a large number of *Reichsheer* officers could speak English and this favoured visits to and discussion with officers in the U.S. Army.[13] In 1928 following just such a visit *Maj.* Oskar von dem Hagen, the *Reichsheer's* senior air officer within *T 3 Fremde Heere*, wrote an extensive report on the US Army Air Corps *(USAAC)*.[14] In the following year *Hptm.* Wilhelm Speidel, who had recently returned from secret flying training at Lipetsk, was attached to the *USAAC* where was attached to the Air Corps Tactical School, Air Corps Engineering School and the Air Corps Technical School, in each case for a period of around six weeks.[15] Over the course of a year he was able to visit primary and advanced

6   Service record for Hugo Sperrle in Hildebrand 1992 pp.325-326. See also Hooton 1994 p.51 & Corum J.S. 1997
     The Luftwaffe: Creating the Operational Air War 1918-1940 (hereafter cited as Corum 1997) p.86. Sperrle was
     assigned to *AR 4* at Dresden on the 1 Mar 24 and remained there until posted to the *TA (L)* on the 1 Mar 25.
7   Corum 1997 pp.81-83 & 86.
8   *T 1, letter of November 1926*, in BA/MA RH 12-1/15 in Corum 1997 p.109.
9   *T 1, letter of November 1926*, in BA/MA RH 12-1/15 in Corum 1997 p.109.
10   Citino R. 1987 *The Evolution of Blitzkrieg Tactics: Germany defends itself against Poland, 1918-1933* pp.147-150. &
     Corum 1997 p.109.
11   Messenger C. 1991 *The Art of Blitzkrieg* p.63. Numerous high-ranking German officers were able to freely visit the
     USSR in the twenties to observe Red Army manoeuvres and to discuss military affairs. For example *Hptm.* Walter
     Model studied the technical aspects of rearmament in the USSR - see Mellenthin von F.W. 1977 *German Generals
     of World War Two* p.148. See also Teske H. (Ed.) 1966 *General Ernst Kostring: Der militärische Mittler zwischen dem
     deutschen Reich und der Sowjetunion* & Corum 1997 p.101.
12   Wheeler-Bennett J.W. 1964 *The Nemesis of Power: The German Army in Politics, 1918-1945* p.296 & Mitcham
     S.W.1988 *Hitler's Field Marshals and their Battles* (hereafter cited as Mitcham 1988) pp.21-22. Blomberg was
     recorded as saying *"I was not far short of becoming a complete Bolshevik myself!"* – quoted from Snyder L.L. 1976
     Encyclopaedia of the Third Reich (hereafter cited as Snyder 1976) pp.29-30 Bookmart Limited.
13   Corum 1997 p.99. English was the primary foreign language in German schools during the Weimar Republic. US
     officers seemed to have few qualms about speaking to serving German officers. Following the Treaty of Versailles the
     USA had quickly withdrawn from European politics, hoping that the League of Nations would be strong enough to
     resolve any further international disagreements in Europe - see Barraclough G. (Ed.) 1978 *The Times Atlas of World
     History* pp.264-265.
14   Hagen von dem Maj., November 1928 *Reisebericht* in BA/MA RH 2/1822 in Corum 1997 p.100.
15   Mondey D.1971 *Pictorial History of the USAF* (hereafter cited as Mondey 1971) pp.29-31. The *USAAC* was formed
     out of the *USAAS* on the 2 Jul 26. Although an expansion plan was authorised on the 1 Jul 27 this was restricted

flying training schools before being attached to attack, observation, bomber and fighter squadrons where he was given the chance to fly some of the latest combat types. One useful outcome of this visit was the large stock of current official books and manuals which Speidel sent back to Germany for detailed analysis by air officers within *T 2 V (L)* and *T 3*.[16] Upon his return to Germany in May 1930, Speidel was attached to *T 3* for a month to write a detailed report on the *USAAC*.[17]

Although denied close links with both France and Britain, the *Reichsheer* was able to develop a relationship with Benito Mussolini's Italy. For a period of six months from April 1929 *Hptm. Dr.Ing.*Wolfram Freiherr von Richthofen was attached to the *Regia Aeronautica* where his brief was to examine the doctrine, tactics, equipment and training of this emerging air arm.[18] His success in this mission led to his assignment to the *Deutschen Botschaft* in Rome as a military attache.[19] A particular interest at this time were the air power theories of Giulio Douhet whose views were well known to the secret air staff via a range of different professional journals and in particular the *Militärwochenblatt* (See also 1A2).[20]

From his appointment as a civilian in March 1926, *Maj.a.D.*Hilmer Freiherr von Bülow was responsible for the co-ordination of the air intelligence effort within *T 2 V (L)*. Bülow was yet another experienced *Luftstreitkräfte* officer who had joined *Feldflieger-Abteilung 1* in August 1914 and had thereafter served as the acting *KoFl AOK 9* in 1917 and as *Fliegergruppenführer 24* in 1918.[21] Reports from officers such as Speidel and Richthofen were collated with secondary material from an increasingly wide range of specialist military and technical periodicals to produce a current picture of foreign developments in the emerging field of military aviation. Bülow quickly expanded *Referat VI Fremde Luftstreitkräfte* (Enemy Air Services) to maintain accurate orders of battle (Tables of Strength and Organisation) for such air arms as the French *Aviation Militaire*, the Polish *Lotnictwo Armijne* and the Czech *Cs.letecky sbor*:

from 1929 by the Wall Street Crash and it's economic after effects. Throughout the 20s the offensive strength of the USAAC failed to exceed 1 Pursuit, 1 Attack & 1 Bombardment Group. Like so many European air arms the emphasis at this time was on observation aircraft for the direct support of the ground forces - see also Anderton D.A. 1981 *The History of the US Air Force* (hereafter cited as Anderton 1981) p.40.

16   Corum 1997 p.100. *Hptm.*Speidel had not been a member of the *Luftstreitkräfte*; his wartime service had been with the *Grenadiere* & *Sturm-Bataillonen*. He had undergone secret staff officer training with both the *5.Division* (1924/25) & *T 2* (1926/27) before going to Lipetsk in 1928. The fact that he was not overtly an air officer may have served to make his attachment to the *USAAC* more politically acceptable - see service record for Wilhelm Speidel in Hildebrand 1992 pp.320-322.

17   Speidel *Hptm, Berichte* in MA/DBR, R 06 10/4 in Corum p.100.

18   Neulen H.W. 2000 *In the Skies of Europe: Air Forces allied to the Luftwaffe 1939-1945* (hereafter cited as Neulen 2000) pp.17-22. The *Regia Aeronautica*, formed on the 28 Mar 23, was a child of Mussolini's new Fascist Italy. Initially Mussolini had acted as air minister but by the time of Richthofen's visit the *RA* and the Air Ministry were in the hands of *Gen.d.Armata* Italo Balbo and under his leadership civil aviation in Italy had flourished. By 1930 Italy was third in importance within Europe in terms of air transport (following Germany & France). The Italian aircraft industry also blossomed with a succession of record breaking flights together with Italian involvement in such international competitions as the Schneider Trophy - see Barker R. 1981 *The Schneider Trophy Races*. Following long range formation flights with seaplanes in the Mediterranean during 1928 (W.Med.) & 1929 (E.Med & Black Sea), Balbo personally led another flight to South America in 1930 (10,400 kms by 14 Savoia S.55A seaplanes) - see also Corum 1997 p.101.

19   Corum J.S. 2008 *Wolfram von Richthofen – Master of the German Air War* pp.94-97. During this period Richthofen got to know the senior and mid-ranking officers of the *Regia Aeronautica*. He visited their bases, flew their aircraft and toured Italy's aircraft factories. *Lt.*Wolfram Frhr.von Richthofen had served in *Jasta 11* within *JG 1* where he scored 8 *Abschusse* during 1918 - see Franks N., Bailey F. and Duiven R. 1996 *The Jasta Pilots: Detailed listings and histories August 1916 - November 1918* p.241 and service record for Wolfram Frhr.von Richthofen in Hildebrand 1992 pp.107-108.

20   Corum 1997 pp.89-91.

21   Service record for Hilmer Frhr.von Bülow in Hildebrand K.F.1990 *Die Generale der deutschen Luftwaffe 1935-1945 Band 1 A-G* (hereafter cited as Hildebrand 1990) pp.127-128.

In 1927 *Major* Wilberg, who was then *Chef T V (L)* in the *Reichswehrministerium*, instructed me to form an intelligence agency *(Referat VI)* to determine and research the organisational structure, strength, distribution, and material of foreign air forces. To assist me, he assigned two additional officers to the agency: *Obstlt.a.D.*Prager and *Maj.a.*D.Morell. Also assigned to *Referat VI* was *Hptm.a.D.*Kirschner, publisher of the magazine *Der Luftwacht* that was financed by the *Reichsverkehrsministerium*. This magazine printed information on strength figures and organisation as well as on technological progress made in the field of aviation in foreign countries. This information provided the *Reichswehr* with valuable data, and later also the *Wehrmacht* establishment.

No preparatory work or precedence for accomplishing this mission was available. The only sources were the foreign press, specialised periodicals and other publications. No service directive was issued for the activation of this intelligence agency nor was any issued subsequently. Obtaining classified information through counter-intelligence channels was initially interdicted. Under these difficult circumstances, it was impossible to attain the objective of obtaining precise information on all foreign military and civilian aviation in order to establish their potential at that time. Initially, the intelligence agency remained therefore a collecting agency for publicised foreign information instead of being an organisation that evaluated and interpreted essential material. On operating procedures, organisational structures, and operational potentials of foreign air forces. The officers assigned to the intelligence agency had all been regular *Luftstreitkräfte* officers in the Great War, after which they had been retired and later re-activated. Their excellent linguistic ability could not compensate for their lack of recent practical experience in combat and their inability to give a factual interpretation of technological progress in foreign aircraft production. Repeated references to these shortcomings were not acknowledged by higher echelons, because the small number of regular air officers then available did not permit the transfer of individual officers to *Referat VI*.

Referat VI concentrated its efforts on the countries adjacent to Germany, especially France, Great Britain and Russia; also of interest was the U.S.A. and all other countries that were then major air powers such as Italy and Japan. Gradually, the network of air force collection efforts spread over the entire globe. Thus, by 1930 the *Referat* employed about ten officers and several clerical personnel, so that the *Referat* was re-designated the *Abteilung Fremde Luftstreitkräfte*.

Aside from checking on foreign aviation developments, contacts with the German press were intensified upon instruction from the *Chef TA (L)*. Numerous lectures were held for meetings of officers, military associations etc., and also on the wireless. The subject was foreign aviation, with particular emphasis being placed on vividly describing the unfavourable air-geographic position of Germany in the centre of Europe. In this manner, the audience was made aware of the untenable situation and the need for air power was propagated. Moreover, personnel of the *Abteilung* wrote articles on foreign aviation, describing the steady progress in the production of airframes and engines as well as in air force organisational matters, that is to say in spheres that were either interdicted to Germany by the peace treaty or severely restricted.[22]

22   Quoted from Bülow Frhr.von H. GenLt.a.D. Undated *Die Abteilung Fremde Luftmachte im Reichswehr-und Reichsluftfahrtministerium 1927-1937* Karlsruhe Document Collection. For information on other European air arms - see Christienne C. and Lissarague P.1980 *A History of French Military Aviation* (hereafter cited as Christienne and Lissarague 1980) pp.236-238, Belcarz B. and Peczkowski R. 2001 *White Eagles: The Aircraft, Men and Operations of the Polish Air Force 1918-1939* pp.88-98 & Titz Z. 1971 *Czechoslovakian Air Force 1918-1970* Arco Aircam Aviation No.30 pp.4-5. See also Green W. and Fricker J. 1958 *The Air Forces of the World: Their History, Development and Present Strength* pp.78, 98 & 224-225.

By 1931 bombing target files had been created as part of the *Reichswehr's* contingency planning for a future war in Europe.[23]

Although the *Reichswehr* lacked military aircraft at this time, steps had been taken by the *Heereswaffenamt* in 1926 to develop an initial generation of such machines (See 1C2 & 1C3). In response to the Air Staff's *Richtlinien für die Führung des operativen Luftkrieges Hptm.*Kurt Student's *Wa.Prw.6F* had called for a single seat fighter aircraft for home defence duties *(Heitag)*, a two-seat tactical reconnaissance aircraft *(Erkudista)*, a two-seat night fighter and reconnaissance aircraft *(Najuku)* and a long-range, medium altitude reconnaissance aircraft that could also double as a bomber *(Erkunigros)*.[24] From 1927 these types were secretly tested at the *Erprobungsstelle Albatros* at Rechlin and the *Wissenschaftliche Versuchs-und Prüfanstalt für Luftfahrzeuge (Wivupal)* at Lipetsk (See also 1D1).[25]

The emergence of the new states of Lithuania, Poland and Czechoslovakia, as well as the presence of an openly hostile Franco-Belgian army in the Rheinland combined to produce a feeling of insecurity within the Reich. The 1923 crisis had revealed the need for contingency plans to deal with a variety of possible scenarios and this work was an annual pre-occupation for the various departments of the *Truppenamt*. After much deliberation *T 2* drew up an emergency mobilisation plan, the *Aufstellungsplan einer Kriegswehrmacht* or *A-Plan* on the 30 June 1927.[26] This envisaged an enlarged field force *(Feldheer)* which was to be supported by an air arm of eight reconnaissance *Staffeln*, three fighter *Staffeln* and a provisional bomber unit made up of three bomber *Staffeln*, whilst the seven existing divisional *Referenten z.b.V.* would be transformed into *Kommandeure der Flieger (KoFl)*.[27] Plans also existed for the creation of a motorised force of *Flakartillerie*. This would consist of a total of sixty-four 8.8 cm *FlaK* weapons supplemented by thirty sound locators, sixty searchlights and ninety anti-aircraft machine guns (See 1E2).[28] In addition it was agreed on the 10 July 1928 that the *DLH* would activate a total of nine *Fliegerkurierstaffeln* to provide a communications and liaison service within and between the various *Wehrkreise* (See 1D2).[29]

To equip the projected air units *Hptm.*Hellmuth Volkmann's *Wa.B.6F,* a secret air procurement office within the *Heereswaffenamt*, produced a plan to acquire a force of 247 combat aircraft in the event of mobilisation (See also 1C2).[30] The proposed *Jagdstaffeln* would be armed with the remaining Fokker D.XIII fighters, whilst the remaining units would have to have been equipped with converted civilian types.[31] In an emergency these aircraft and their crews would have been requisitioned from the *DLH* and the *DVS* using the powers available to the *Reichswehrminister* under the *Reichsleistungsgesetz* (Reich Service Law).[32] In the meantime to prove the practicality

23   Kahn D. 1978 *Hitler's Spies: German Military Intelligence in the World War II* p.381-382. One of Bülow's early desk officers was *Hptm.a.D.*Morell who specialised in military aviation within the western states.

24   Hertel 1955 p.13 & Hooton 1994 pp.64-65.

25   Beauvais et al 2002 pp.43-46. Front line testing at Lipetsk began in the summer of 1928.

26   Suchenwirth 1968 p.37, Hooton 1994 p.63 & Corum 1997 p.121. Initial plans for an emergency mobilisation *(Mobilmachungsfall)* had been drafted on the 30 Jan 27. Each *Division* would be based on one of the 21 existing *Infanterie-Regimenter* - see Seaton 1982 pp.27-28. Earlier contingency planning by Seeckt had envisaged a much larger force of 64 *Divisionen*.

27   Suchenwirth 1968 p.37 & Hooton 1994 p.63. The mobilised air arm would be known under its earlier wartime name of *Luftstreitkräfte*.

28   Hooton 1994 p.63.

29   Suchenwirth 1968 p.38 & Andersson L. 1989 'Secret Luftwaffe: German Military Aviation Build-up between the Wars' in *Air Enthusiast* No.41 1989 (hereafter cited as Andersson 1989) p.41. It was anticipated that the *Fliegerkurierstaffeln* would be formed by 1929 as civilian organisations each with 6 aircraft and 30 employees - see Hooton 1994 p.63.

30   Andersson 1989 p.41. See also Koos V. 2006 *Typenbucher Deutsche Luftfahrt: Ernst Heinkel Flugzeugwerke 1922-1932* p.83.

31   Suchenwirth 1968 p.38. Favoured types included the Albatros L 75 as *Aufklärungsflugzeuge* together with the Rohrbach Ro VIII and Junkers G 24 as *Behelfsnachtbomber-Flugzeuge* - see also Beauvais et al 2002 pp.43-46.

32   Suchenwirth 1968 p.38.

of the *Behelfsnachtbomber* (Auxiliary Night Bomber) concept *Hptm.*Wilhelm Wimmer's *Referat III Technik* arranged for single examples of both the Rohrbach Ro VIII Roland and Junkers G 24 airliners to be converted into auxiliary bombers and tested at Lipetsk during the summer months of 1928 (See 1C2 & 1D1).[33]

Surprisingly given the small scale and relatively intimate nature of the *Reichsheer's* aviation programme, co-operation between *T 2 V (L)* and the *Heereswaffenamt's Wa (L)* had not always been harmonious. In 1928 in an effort to solve this problem *Maj.*Albert Keßelring, the *Vereinfachungskommissar (Reichswehr* Commissioner for Retrenchment and Simplification), recommended that the existing organisations be replaced by a single *Flieger-Inspektion* (Air Inspectorate) to co-ordinate all planning, development and procurement work in the field of military aviation.[34] *Maj.*Wilhelm Keitel, then *Chef T 2,* agreed that the idea had much to commend it but the idea of consolidating the work of *T 2 V (L)* and *Wa.Prw.8* was shelved for fear of an adverse foreign reaction should the existence of such a major department for military aviation become publicly known.[35]

At this point there was a further routine change of leadership within the *Truppenamt* when *Maj.* Hellmuth Felmy replaced Sperrle as *Chef T 2 V (L)* on the 1 February 1929. Felmy had already been involved with the *Reichsheer's* secret aviation programme as a *Referent* alongside Sperrle within the *5.Division* at Stuttgart during 1921-24 and then as a *Referent* within *T 1 (Führungs)* during 1924-26. His credentials were good; he had trained as a military aviator in 1912 and had seen continuous war service as a member of the *Luftstreitkräfte* in both Europe and the Middle East.[36] Together with Sperrle he was acknowledged by his peers and superiors as a knowledgeable, capable and competent officer. Furthermore Felmy was considered by many to possess one of the finest brains in the *Reichsheer.*[37] His appointment was therefore even more appropriate when sixth months later the whole of his department was transferred to the newly established *Inspektion der Waffenschulen, Insp.1 (W),* under *Obst.*Hilmar Ritter von Mittelberger as *Inspektion 1 (L).*[38]

This reorganisation was doubly significant. Firstly it provided Felmy with a greater level of control over the development of military aviation than had been enjoyed by either Sperrle or Wilberg, and secondly it placed the development of military aviation directly under the *Heeresleitung.* Through Mittelberger, his immediate superior, Felmy had direct access to *GenOb.*Wilhelm Heye, the *Chef des Heeresleitung* who remained in this position until 31 October 1930 when he was replaced by *Gen.d.Inf.*Kurt Freiherr von Hammerstein-Equord.[39]

---

33 Beauvais et al 2002 pp.43-46.

34 Suchenwirth 1968 p.18 & Hertel 1955 p.12. Concern over bureaucracy, duplication and the diversion of serving officers from *Truppendienst* had contributed to *Maj.*Keßelring's assignment to the *Wehramt/RWM* in Oct 26 - see service record for Albert Keßelring in Hildebrand K.F.1991 *Die Generale der deutschen Luftwaffe 1935-1945 Band 2 H-N* (hereafter cited as Hildebrand 1991) pp.165-167. His tasks were to (1) release soldiers from office work and thereby increase the active strength and (2) to reduce internal and external correspondence through a wider delegation of authority - see Keßelring A. GFM.a.D. 1974 *The Memoirs of Field-Marshal Keßelring* pp.23-24.

35 Goerlitz W. (Ed.) 2000 *The Memoirs of Field Marshal Keitel, Chief of the German High Command 1938-1945* pp.15-17. Keitel was also very aware of financial restrictions within the *Reichsheer* and he was a known conservative - see also Suchenwirth 1968 pp.18-19 & Mitcham 1988 pp.162-163.

36 Service record for Hellmuth Felmy in Hildebrand 1990 pp.273-275. He had successively been *Fhr.d.Feld-Fl.Abt.51, Fl.Abt.300, Fl.Abt. A 256* and on the staff of the *Reichskolonialamt/Schütztruppe.*

37 Mitcham S.W. 1989 *Eagles of the Third Reich - Hitler's Luftwaffe* p.30 & Corum 1997 p.86.

38 Homze E.L. 1976 *Arming the Luftwaffe: The Reich Air Ministry and the German Aircraft Industry 1919-1939* (hereafter cited as Homze 1976) p.24 , Hooton 1994 p.51 & Corum 1997 p.87. Mittelberger's position has often been confused with that of Felmy. As *In.1 Waffenschulen* Mittelberger had responsibility for the *Infanterie-Schule Dresden, Kavallerie-Schule Hannover, Artillerie-Schule Jüterbog* & the *Pioniere Schule München.* Born in 1878, Mittelberger was a leader of considerable ability. He would be promoted to *GenMaj.* in 1930 and to *GenLt.* on the 1 Jan 32 - see Suchenwirth 1968 p.229.

39 Suchenwirth 1968 p.19 & Hooton 1994 p.51. Wilhelm Heye had been *Chef d.Heeresleitung* since 1926, he

Felmy's *Inspektion 1 (L)* was a larger department than any of its predecessors. The new organisation had a total of nine *Referate* (Desks), whilst for the first time it was also responsible for the *Flieger-Referate* and *Referate z.b.V.* who were attached to each of the seven *Infanterie-Divisionen* and the three *Kavallerie-Divisionen* (See also 1E1)*(Chart 1-3).*[40] *Referate I (Taktik Ausbildung), V (Organisation)* and *VII (Luftschütz)* were all nominally to be staffed by air officers with general staff training *(Führergehilfen-Ausbildung).* For the first time some of these officers were not wartime pilots or observers but had been trained secretly by the *Reichsheer* as aircrew at Lipetsk or in other countries including the USA *(Jungmarker)*(See 1D1). To retain continuity their assistant advisors *(Hilfs-Referent)* were all former members of the *Luftstreitkräfte (Altmarker).*[41] At much the same time a special *Ausbildungsstab* was formed within *Inspektion 4 Artillerie* to look after the emerging needs of the *Flakartillerie*; *Obstlt.*Günther Rüdel was assigned as *Kommandeur Ausbildungsstabes III* (Commander of Training Staff III) on the 1 February 1930 (See also 1E2).[42]

FIGURE 1A-3 STAFF POSITIONS WITHIN THE INSPEKTION 1 (L) 1930		
Chef d.Inspektion 1 (L) - Maj.Hellmuth Felmy		
Referat I (Taktik Ausbildung)	-	Hptm.Walter Schwabedissen
Referat II (Personal u.Tradition)	-	Maj.Ulrich Grauert
Referat III (Technik)	-	Hptm.Karl Drum
Referat IV (Verwaltung)	-	Minamt.Wichterich
Referat V (Organisation u.Haushalt)	-	Hptm.Wilhelm Speidel
Referat VI (Nachr.u.Auswertung)	-	Maj.a.D.Hilmer Frhr.von Bülow
Referat VII (Luftschütz)	-	Maj.Rudolf Bogatsch
Referat VIII (Bürodienst)	-	Hptm.a.D.von Karmainsky
Referat IX (Ausbildung)	-	Hptm.Ludwig Keiper

Later in 1930 it was also decided to secretly acquire and operate military aircraft within the Reich territory despite the specific restrictions of the Versailles settlement. This decision was reached at a significant meeting on the 29 November between *Reichswehrminister GenLt.a.D.*Wilhelm Groener, Mittelberger and *Maj.a.D.*Ernst Brandenburg of the *RVM* and soon afterwards a *Reklamefliegerabteilung* (Air Publicity Department) was formed within the auspices of *Inspektion 1 (L)* under the direction of *Maj.(char)* Gustav Kastner-Kirdorf.[43] *Reklamestaffeln* were created at

was promoted to *GenOb.* on the 1 Jan 30 & retired on the 31 Oct 30. *GenLt.*Frhr.von Hammerstein had been *C.d.S.3.Division* (1924-29), *C.d.S.Hr.Gr.Kdo.I* (1929) & *C.d.Truppenamt* from Oct 29 - see Seaton 1982 p.296 & service record for Hammerstein-Equord in AxisBiographicalResearch. In most respects the *Inp.1 (L)* continued to report to the *Truppemant* - at that time led by *GenLt.*Werner von Blomberg, an officer who was sympathetic to the needs of aviation - see Seaton 1982 p.30.

40   Nowarra H.J. 1980 *Die Verbotenen Flugzeuge 1921-1935 – Die getarnte Luftwaffe* (hereafter cited as Nowarra 1980) p.40. See also Suchenwirth 1968 pp.20-21.

41   *Chart 3 Offices within the Army Troop Office dealing with Air Matters, 1 October 1929 - 31 March 1933* in Suchenwirth 1968 (hereafter cited as Chart 3 in Suchenwirth 1968) p,248.

42   Westermann E.B. 2001 *Flak: German Anti-aircraft Defenses 1914-1945* (hereafter cited as Westermann 2001) p.44. *Obstlt.*Rüdel had been associated with the wartime *Flakverbände* as *Kdr.d.Kraftwagen-Geschützkommandos Ostende*, (Commander of Motorised-Artillery Ostende) later the *Ballon-Abwehrkanonen-Schule Ostende* (Anti-Balloon Artillery School) from Oct 15. Retained by the *Reichsheer* his last position prior to joining *In.4* was as a *Referent* in *T 1* dealing with supply issues - see service record for Günther Rüdel in Hildebrand 1992 pp.146-147.

43   Ries 1970 p.113 & Hooton 1994 p.69. The *Reklamestaffeln* were formed in response to Groener's own observations

Königsberg-Neuhausen, Berlin-Staaken and Nürnberg-Fürth*(Photo 1A-14)*. Ostensibly these three units belonged to the *Luftfahrt GmbH* but in reality they were staffed by experienced instructor pilots from Lipetsk and were officially subordinate to *Wehrkreis I* (Königsberg), *III* (Berlin) and *VII* (München) respectively. Each *Staffel* consisted of four aircraft, initially trainers and sports machines, and these were employed to provide a degree of realism during military manoeuvres whilst at other times they maintained an overt cover by towing banners which advertised a variety of different consumer products (See also 1E1).[44]

Although the *Reklamestaffeln* were an important initial step in the resurgence of German military aviation they were but a token force and in the short term the key objectives for Felmy's *Inspektion 1 (L)* were the resolution of four key questions: (1) which agency was to command and control German military aviation; (2) what was to be the future size and force structure of the *Fliegertruppe*; (3) what was to be its doctrine and tactics, and (4) how were answers to these questions determine the nature of its equipment - in particular the type of bomber that was required. Underpinning all of these questions was the central issue of doctrine.

In common with contemporary air power enthusiasts and theorists many of Felmy's staff favoured the bomber as the primary instrument of air warfare and possibly of warfare itself.[45] The *Richtlinien für die Ausbildung in der Reichswehr auf dem Gebiet der Luftstreitkräfte* (Principles for the Employment of Air Forces within the German Armed Forces) published by *Inspektion 1 (L)* on the 20 December 1930 argued that the role of the bomber force was to *"battle for the air against the military and economic sources of power of the enemy"*.[46] To achieve this goal it was considered essential that *"the mass of the bombers be united under a commander of the Bomber Force and should be employed in the conduct of the operational air war under the direction of the High Command"*.[47] The importance of the Fighter Force was recognised but primarily in terms of the way in which it could support the offensive power of the bombers. With this in mind the principal role of the fighters was to achieve aerial superiority, whilst a secondary role was the protection of the *Heimat* (Homeland) from air attack in conjunction with strong anti-aircraft artillery forces.[48] Only after these duties had been completed would fighters be released to conduct low-level attacks in the direct support of the *Feldheer*; tactics that had recently been proven to be effective during the course of tactical trials at Lipetsk (See 1D1).[49]

during the 1929 autumn manoeuvres when enemy aircraft had been simulated by freely drifting balloons – see Suchenwirth 1968 p.32 & Mason 1973 p.163. *Gen.*Wilhem Groener had been the last *ObQu.* within the *OHL* in 1918 and as such had planned the successful withdrawal of the *Feldheer* from the occupied territories. A loyal supporter of the Weimar Government he served successively as *Reichsverkehrsminister* (20-23), *Reichswehrminister* (28-32) and concurrently *Reichsminister des Innern* (31-32). Suffering from diabetes he resigned from Government on the 13 May 32 following a violent clash in the *Reichstag* with Göring and other *NSDAP* deputies - see Groener-Geyer D. 1955 *General Groener Soldat und Staatsmann* (hereafter cited as Groener-Geyer 1955) pp.301-325, Shirer W.L. 1963 *The Rise and Fall of the Third Reich: A History of Nazi Germany* (hereafter cited as Shirer 1963) p.162 & Snyder 1976 p.128. The *Insp.1 (L)* was responsible for the *Reklamestaffeln* from 1931 - see Chart 3 in Suchenwirth 1968 p.248. See also service record for Gustav Kastner-Kirdorf in Hildebrand 1991 pp.153-154. The *Käpitane* were: *Königsberg* – Friedrich-Karl Knust later Lothar von Janson; *Berlin-Staaken* later Döberitz – Edgar Petersen; *Fürth*– Gerhard Ulbricht – see Zeng IV H. de and Stankey D. 2013 *Luftwaffe Officer Career Summaries* in www.ww2.dk.

44   Ries 1970 p.113 & Hooton 1994 p.69.

45   Corum 1997 p.105.. In 1925 Basil Liddell Hart theorised that air power had become the dominant form of military power and that it would eventually prove to be the decisive weapon in a future conflict - see Liddell Hart B.H. 1925 *Paris, The Future of War.*

46   Quoted from *Grundsatze für den Einsatz der Luftstreitkräfte 1930* in BA/MA RL 2/II 364 Entwurf in Corum 1997 *The Luftwaffe: Creating the Operational Air War 1918-1940* p.120 with the kind permission of the University Press of Kansas.

47   Quoted from *Grundsatze für den Einsatz der Luftstreitkräfte 1930* in BA/MA RL 2/II 364 Entwurf in Corum 1997 *The Luftwaffe: Creating the Operational Air War 1918-1940* p.120 with the kind permission of the University Press of Kansas

48   *Grundsatze für den Einsatz der Luftstreitkräfte 1930* in BA/MA RL 2/II 364 Entwurf in Corum 1997 p.120.

49   Corum 1997 p.120 & Beauvais et al 2002 p.48.

The *1930 Richtlinien* were significant in that they demonstrated the thinking of the air staff and their uniquely German view of the employment of airpower (*operativer Luftkrieg*). They confirmed *Maj.*Helmuth Wilberg's earlier thinking as expressed in the *1926 Richtlinien für die Führung des operativen Luftkrieges* (See 1A2). The *Richtlinien* were undoubtedly influenced by the earlier work of the Soviet theoreticians *Gen.*Mikhail Frunze and *Marshall* Mikhail Tukhacheveskii, thoughts and ideas that were well known to the *Reichsheer* through its continuing close relationship with the Red Army.[50] Both of these officers were imbued with the power of the offence; both saw air power as a vital part of that strategy. Although Tukhachevskii argued for the use of air power in support of the ground forces he saw the main employment of air forces to be in depth rather than simply on the battlefield. Like contemporary German theoreticians Tukhachevskii appreciated the unique capacity of air power to successfully interdict lines of communication and destroy enemy headquarters, troop concentrations and supply depots well behind the front line.[51]

There was also evidence of other influences from France, Britain and Italy (See 1A2).[52] Indeed as part of Richthofen's assignment to the *Deutsch Botschaft* in Rome, Felmy had specifically instructed him to report on the *Regia Aeronautica's* response to Douhet's theories.[53] Similarly the *Inspektion 1 (L)* was certainly aware of contemporary American thinking on strategic bombing from Hagen and Speidel's reports. Many *USAAC* officers viewed Douhet's enthusiasm for an attack on enemy cities with distaste, considering it to be fundamentally immoral.[54] By contrast American thinking had crystallised around the most efficient way of dislocating or disrupting the industrial potential of an enemy nation through pinpoint air attack. Examination of the industrial infrastructure of the U.S.A. had revealed its essential vulnerability to attacks on the electricity generation and distribution system.[55] Such views helped to reinforce the *Inspektion's* view that the emerging *Fliegertruppe* should be directed toward a purely military role in the prosecution of any future war. The prevailing Douhetian strategy of terror bombing, including the use of chemical warfare against civilian targets, was totally rejected: *"the bombardment of undefended cities, as well as the use of poison*

---

50   Corum 1997 p.95. *Hptm.a.D.*Martin Fiebig was engaged in the instruction of Soviet air force officers during the early twenties and he was well aware of their enthusiasm for strategic bombing. Soviet military leaders displayed a tremendous interest in the potential of airpower. Douhet's books had been translated into Russian and had been widely read by the late 20s. No less than 39 *Reichswehr* officers visited the USSR during 1926-27 - see Messenger 1991 p.63.

51   Simpkin R. 1987 *Deep Battle: The Brainchild of Marshall Tukhacheveskii* p.43.

52   Corum 1997 pp.91-95. Italy was considered to be at the cutting edge as an air power in the late 20s & early 30s. Between 1927-33 the air power theories and doctrines of all the leading military powers were discussed in some detail in the *Reichswehr's* monthly periodical - the *Militärwochenblatt*.

53   Corum 1997 p.101. The *Regia Aeronautica* had commissioned the six-engine Caproni Ca 90 heavy bomber. Completed in 1929 this was briefly the largest aircraft in the world and it remained the largest landplane until the advent of the Tupolev ANT-20 Maxim Gorky in 1934. Interestingly Italian military doctrine was as much moulded by *Maj.*Amadeo Mecozzi's ideas about tactical air power as it was by Douhet. Mecozzi envisaged a future air force as having (1) a strategic bomber force to directly oppose the enemy nation, (2) a naval air force to attack the enemy nation & (3) a tactical air force to support the army of the battlefield. He argued that it was the third element that should be the primary branch of the *Regia Aeronautica* - see Mecozzi A.Maj. 'Les Grandi Unita Aviatori' in *Rivista Aeronautica* Mar 29 & Hallion R.P. 1989 *Strike from the Sky: The History of Battlefield Air Attack 1911-1945* p.82 & Corum 1997 pp.94-95.

54   Corum 1997 pp.97-98. Within Italy the influential *Gen.di Armata Aerea* Italo Balbo thought well of Douhet but tended to support Mecozzi's concepts for assault aviation. In 1929 he was instrumental in establishing tactical assault units which were then evaluated in a series of exercises and manoeuvres - see also Segre C. *Balbo and Douhet: Master and Disciple* in Pozzuoli C. 1988 *La Figura e l'Opera di Giulio Douhet* p.58. Mecozzi on the other hand opposed Douhet's view on both moral and practical grounds. Given Italy's geo-political realities within the Mediterranean this conviction was not only understandable but realistic - see Neulen 2000 p.24.

55   Futrell R.F. 1989 *Ideas, Concepts, Doctrine; Basic Thinking in the United States Air Force, 1907-1960 Vol.I.*p.39. Interestingly the *USAAC* was also interested in the development of attack aviation and to this end had established the 3rd Attack Group in 1921 - see Maurer M. 1969 *Combat Squadrons of the Air Force World War II* pp.29-31. In many respects the development of military aviation in USA and Italy was conditioned by similar geo-political realities. Both nations were primarily maritime powers and there were few potential opponents whose industrial centres were close enough to home bases for strategic attack to be a practical proposition at that time.

gas, are forbidden by international treaty".[56]

The future role of the bomber was central to this pivotal discussion and in this respect Germany's lack of military hardware actually worked to the air staff's advantage as it encouraged continued analysis and reflection. The earlier decision by *T 2 V (L)* to order the development of a four-engine *Größnachtbomber (Gronabo)* in 1927 must be seen in this light.[57] The aim was to produce an experimental aircraft that would then form the basis for further development. Student's *Wa.Prw.6F* awarded the contract to the *AG für Dornier-Flugzeuge* at Altenrhein in Switzerland, an acknowledged leader in the design and manufacture of large all-metal aircraft.[58] The Do P was of mixed construction and unusual for its time in being a cantilever monoplane. In this respect it is pertinent to note that contemporary British, French and American heavy night bombers were all biplanes.[59] The first example of the Do P was completed in 1930 but it was not tested at Lipetsk until 1932 by which time it had been overtaken by more recent thinking on the advantages of a smaller twin-engine night bomber (See 1C2 & 1C3).[60]

The concept of a twin-engine *mittlere Nachtbomber (Minabo)* appears to have evolved at a time when both the British and the French seemed to be moving away from the heavy night bomber per se, a trend that had to be set against a general international desire for disarmament.[61] Certainly the peace movement was a powerful force for change within the European democracies; there was even talk in Britain of totally disbanding the *RAF*.[62] It is pertinent to note that Germany was a signatory of the Kellogg-Briand Pact of August 1928 in which all parties had formally rejected

---

56   Quoted from *Grundsatze für den Einstatz der Luftstreitkräfte 1930* in BA/MA RL 2/II 364 Entwurf in Corum 1997 *The Luftwaffe: Creating the Operational Air War 1918-1940* p.120 with the kind permission of the University Press of Kansas. Whilst supporting the development of chemical warfare at Saratov in the USSR, Felmy's staff rejected the widespread employment of poison gas as proposed by some theorists - see Liddell Hart B.H. 1927 *The Remaking of Modern Armies* pp.83-87 & Fleischer W. 2003 *German Air-Dropped Weapons to 1945* (hereafter cited as Fleischer 2003) pp.23-25 & 27.

57   Hooton 1994 pp.64-65.

58   Lange B. 1970 Das *Buch der deutschen Luftfahrtechnik* (hereafter cited as Lange 1970) p.199. Dornier had previously designed the Do N heavy bomber on behalf of the Imperial Japanese Army - see also Sekigawa E. 1974 *Pictorial History of Japanese Military Aviation* p.22. The Do P was essentially a landplane version of the proven Do R Superwal – see Nowarra 1980 p.192.

59   Lange 1970 p.199. In truth the Vickers Virginia was evolved from an earlier 1920 requirement for a heavy night bomber. However it was progressively modified and improved throughout this period and it remained in first line service until 1937 - see Andrews C.F. 1969 *Vickers Aircraft since 1908* pp.130-150 & Thetford O. 1976 *Aircraft of the Royal Air Force since 1918* (hereafter cited as Thetford 1976) pp.508-512. The Liore et Olivier LeO 20 BN 3 on the other hand was the winning design for the *Aviation Militaire's 1926 Concours d'Avions de Bombardement* requirement. Initial aircraft were twin-engined, whilst later aircraft powered by four Gnome-Rhône Titan engines. In all 311 aircraft were built during 1926-32 - see Cross R. 1964 *The Bomber Aircraft Pocketbook* (hereafter cited as Cross 1964) pp.68-69 & Morse S. (Ed.) 1982 *The Illustrated Encyclopedia of Aircraft* (hereafter cited as Morse (Ed.) 1982) pp.2320 & 2332.

60   Beauvais et al 2002 p.48.

61   Beauvais et al 2002. p.47. British service bombers were divided into two groups: day and night. The day bomber category was further sub-divided into single and twin engine. From the beginning the *RAF* had sought a dual role day and night bomber however the technology of the time had resulted in large long range heavy bombers which were inevitably too slow for successful operation by day, hence the continued need for fast light bombers for day operations - see Sinnott C. *2001 The RAF and Aircraft Design 1923-1939: Air Staff Operational Requirements* (hereafter cited as Sinnot 2001) p.51 & pp.57-60. In 1930 the RAF's bomber squadrons were equipped with the Hawker Hart (single-engine day), Boulton & Paul Sidestrand (twin-engine day) and the Vickers Virginia, Handley Page Hyderabad and Hinaidi (twin-engine night) - see Moyes P.J.R. 1964 *Bomber Squadrons of the R.A.F. and their aircraft* & Thetford 1976. French thinking favoured the multi-role *BCR (Bombardement, Combat et Reconnaissance)* type as advocated by Douhet. This thinking would result in the selection of the Potez 54 series as the standard type for the *Plan des 1,010 avions* in 1932 - see Cross 1964 pp.84-85, Christienne and Lissarague 1980 pp.259-262, Morse (Ed.) 1982 p.2774 & Coum 1997 p.93.

62   Terraine J. 1985 *The Right of the Line: The Royal Air Force in the European War 1939-1945* (hereafter cited as Terraine 1985) pp.7-8 & 12-13.

aggressive war as an instrument of foreign policy.[63] In February 1932 the first of several World Disarmament Conferences opened in Geneva; German interests were represented by *Gen.d.Inf.* Werner von Blomberg, the former *Chef des Truppenamt.*[64] There was also a degree of pragmatism in the move away from night bombing. It was recognised that the accuracy of aerial navigation by night was questionable, whilst the few bombing trials that had been carried out by other air arms during this period had revealed a lamentable lack of bombing accuracy even by aircraft operating by day.[65] It is notable that despite their doctrinal beliefs neither the *RAF* nor the *Aviation Militaire* carried out much night flying training at this time.[66]

The Do F of 1932 was therefore something of a compromise between what the air staff thought they wanted and what was politically and economically viable at that point in time. It certainly was not a true heavy bomber as exemplified by the contemporary French Liore et Olivier LeO 206 BN4 and the Soviet Tupolev TB-3 (ANT 6) four-engine behemoths.[67] Nor was it a light day bomber, a type that still dominated the force structure of many of Europe's air arms. It's closest relatives was the Martin Model 123 (XB-907), a twin-engine all-metal monoplane bomber, which had been delivered to the *USAAC* in March 1932 and the French Bloch MB 200 BN 4 which would enter service in the same year.[68] These aircraft in their refined production form would form the basis of their respective air arm's increased emphasis on bombardment aviation during the decade to come.[69]

The ability to strike political and economic targets as well as those of a strictly military nature located well behind the front line gave weight to the developing argument that air power could and would be deployed independently of either the *Reichsheer* or the *Reichsmarine*. Given this new reality many air officers wanted nothing less than an independent military air arm. On the 17 May 1930, as *Chef des Truppenamt*, Hammerstein-Equord began a debate that would rage for nearly two years when he requested views on the future status of the planned *Fliegertruppe (Photo 1A-15).*[70] It was a debate that was given added impetus in November with Groener's decision to begin the production and stock-piling of the aviation equipment (See also 1B1 & 1C2).[71]

63   Terraine 1985 p.7. Also known as the Pact of Paris and signed by Germany, Britain, France, Italy, Japan, the USA and nine other states on the 27 Aug 28. Eventually this accord was signed by a further 45 nations world wide. See also Grey C.G. 1940 *A History of the Air Ministry* pp.222-224 & Hooton 1994 p.72.

64   Hooton 1994 p.72. Blomberg, who was then *Bfr.i.Wehrkreis I*, was accompanied by *Maj.a.D.*Ernst Brandenburg of the *RVM*. Blomberg had been *Chef d.Truppenamt* from 1 Apr 27 - 30 Sep 29 - see service record for Werner von Blomberg in AxisBiographicalResearch. The abolition of all kinds of aerial bombing was a particular focus for these disarmament conferences. As such it led to a delay in the development of new bombers for the *RAF* as there was an understandable concern that such expense might be wasted by a world wide ban on bombing operations - see Sinnot 2001 p.8, 134 & pp.138-139.

65   Spies R. 1927 *Report on Bombing Accuracy and Patterns* in BA/MA RH 2/2187 in Corum 1997 p.105. See also Fleischer 2003 p.27. *Lt.d.Res.a.D.*Dip.Ing.Rudolf Spies was employed in a civilian capacity by *T 2 V (L)* as a *Hilfsreferent* from Feb 25 - Mar 27 when he transferred to the *LS/Marineleitung* - see service record for Rudolf Spies in Hildebrand 1992 pp.327-328.

66   Hooton 1994 p.90. As late as 1938 the *Armée de l'Air* flew just 75 hrs at night compared to 17,600 hrs by day - see SHAA File 2B133. The situation in the RAF was little better.

67   Morse (Ed.) 1982 p.2332. In fact only 40 LeO 206 bombers were built for the *Aviation Militaire* from 1932. By contrast 818 TB-3 aircraft were built for the *VVS* during 1932-39 - see Gordon Y. and Khazanov D. 1999 *Soviet Combat Aircraft of the Second World War Vol.2 Twin-Engined Fighters, Attack Aircraft and Bombers* pp.140-144.

68   Swanborough G. and Bowers P.M. *1989 United States Military Aircraft since 1909* pp.433-436. The Martin 123 had been designed and built as a private venture in order to get Martin back into the bomber business following the *USAAC's* procurement in quantity of the Keystone LB series. It incorporated all the latest thinking in advanced combat aircraft design - see also Hooton E. *Military Aviation - the Slow Developer* in Jarrett P. (Ed.) 1997 *Biplane to Monoplane: Aircraft development 1919-39* pp.62-63.

69   Mondey 1971 p.35 & Anderton 1981 pp.40-41. The Bloch MB 200 BN4 was another BCR type. In all 200 would be delivered to the *Armée de l'Air* between1932-35 - see Cross 1964 pp.78-79.

70   Hooton 1994 pp.71-72. At that time *GenLt.*Hammerstein-Equord was still *Chef d.Truppenamt.*

71   Hooton 1994 p.61 & 71. This was the outcome of a necessarily secret meeting in Berlin between *Reichswehrminister* Groener, *Auslandminister* Curtius and *Reichsverkehrsminister* von Guerard on the 29 Nov 30. *GenMaj.*Mittelberger

Several influential officers feared that an independent air arm along the lines suggested by contemporary theorists would lead to the neglect of the needs of the ground forces. Such views were particularly promoted by *Obst.*Hermann Geyer *(Chef T 1)* and *Obstlt.*Keitel *(Chef T 2)*. Such officers, and it is appropriate to note that these included *GenMaj.*Wilhelm Adam *(Chef des Truppenamt)* and Hammerstein-Equord himself, did not favour an independent force under the auspices of the *RWM*. However they did concede that the position of *Kommandierenden General der Luftstreitkräfte (KoGenLuft)* would be required within the *Reichsheer*.[72] There was a real concern that there were simply not enough trained staff officers to sustain an independent air arm whilst providing for the planned three-fold growth of the *Feldheer*. Even at the operational level the needs of the planned force would necessitate the transfer of 320 trained pilots and observers together with a further 2,000 technical personnel, an unwelcome and dangerous dilution of the restricted pool of trained officers and men available to the *Reichsheer* in the early thirties.[73]

Despite these obstacles the strength of Felmy's arguments coupled to Mittelberger's diplomacy allowed progress to be made.[74] On the 21 April 1931 Adam recognised the indivisibility of military aviation and the anti-aircraft artillery and that their continued development should be focused within a single organisation. Then on the 19 December the *Heeresleitung* issued a set of ground rules for the wartime employment of air forces. The *Grundsatze für den Einsatz der Luftstreitkräfte* covered the role of Reconnaissance Aviation, Fighter Aviation, Bomber Aviation, Communications, Ground Organisation and Meteorological Services.[75] Hammerstein-Equord's plan envisaged the division of military aviation into three groups, the largest part coming under the direct control of the *Heeresleitung* for operations in support of the *Feldheer*. A second smaller group would come under the *KoGenLuft* for the air defence of the Reich and as such would report to the Reichswehrminister. The third group would be assigned to the support of the *Reichsmarine*.[76] Finally on the 24 February 1932 the *Chef des Heeresleitung* accepted that the proposed air arm should be a separate service, equal in status with the *Reichsheer* and *Reichsmarine* within the overall framework provided by the *RWM*.[77] Unfortunately further rearguard action by both Keitel and Geyer ensured that Felmy was still denied control over all equipment development, this being left within *Wa.Prw.8* and the various *Waffen-Inspektion: In.2 Infanterie, In.4 Artillerie* and *In.7 Nachrichten* (See1C2).[78]

Insofar as the actual force structure was concerned early plans fluctuated between the original 14 *Staffeln-Plan* authorised in 1927 and the 22 *Staffel-Plan* as authorised by Hammerstein-Equord in a 1929 revision to the overall *Aufstellungs-Plan*.[79] In this larger force the number of night bomber units was unchanged but the fighter force was doubled to six *Staffeln* whilst the number of reconnaissance units was increased to 13 *Staffeln*. Each *Staffel* was to be equipped with six aircraft, making a force of 132 aircraft together with 50% reserves to produce a *Fliegertruppe* of some 200 combat aircraft.

and *Maj.a.D.*Ernst Brandenburg were in attendance.

72   Hooton 1994 pp.71-72. Hammerstein-Equord had earlier insisted that all aviation training must continue to stress the importance or army support - see Corum 1997 p.87. Adam had been *C.d.S.Hr.Gr.Kdo.I* in 1929-30. He was *C.d.Truppenamt* from 1 Oct 30 & was promoted to *GenLt.* on the 1 Dec 31 - see service record for Wilhelm Adam in AxisBiographicalResearch. An earlier study by *T 1* on strategic air operations had concluded that air forces would be of little practical effect in a future conflict. Given the technology of the period this was not an unreasonable conclusion.

73   Hooton 1994 p.73. Both *T 1* & *T 2* were particularly concerned about the manpower issue.

74   Hooton 1994 pp.72-73. Recognising the strength of conservative opposition to an independent air arm Mittelberger had wisely assured his colleagues on the 1 Apr 31 that even an autonomous air arm would always act in co-operation with the *Feldheer*.

75   Hooton 1994 p.72.

76   *Chef d.Heeresleitung in a letter to the Waffenamt, Juli 1931* in BA/MA RH 8/v.993 in Corum 1997 pp.87-88.

77   Hooton 1994 p.72.

78   Hooton 1994 p.72. *Obst.*Keitel was usually most reluctant to change; he was also very unwell during this period suffering from pneumonia and a heart condition - see Mitcham 1988 p.163.

79   Hooton 1994 p.63, 71 & 73. Hammerstein-Equord was *C.d.Truppenamt* at this time.

To support the front line it was proposed that a *Flieger-Ersatzabteilung* (Training and Replacement Unit) be formed in each of the seven *Wehrkreise*.[80] A few months later pressure from Geyer's *T 1* led to the adoption of a smaller but more balanced force of just 18 *Staffeln* with six *Staffeln* each of bombers, fighter and reconnaissance machines.[81] It took Felmy over two years to get the plans changed back to include an air arm of 22 *Staffeln*. His arguments together with those of Adam as *Chef der Truppenamt* were finally accepted by the *Heeresleitung* on the 14 July 1932. Formal approval followed and *GenLt.a.D.*Kurt von Schleicher, the new *Reichswehrminister*, set a new completion date of 1936.[82] It was agreed that the *Flieger-Ersatzabteilungen* would be established in the year beginning 1 April 1933, these being followed by two fighter and four reconnaissance *Staffeln* in 1934, whilst the remaining sixteen *Staffeln* would be phased-in during 1935 and 1936. By the end of this programme the new *Reichsluftwaffe* would have achieved a strength of 630 officers and 4,000 other ranks.[83] Schleicher also agreed to the re-creation of an anti-aircraft artillery arm from 1933, the funds for which were also to be diverted from the secret allocation for the *A-Heer*.[84]

However by this point *Obstlt.*Felmy was thinking in terms of a far larger air force.[85] On the 1 February 1932, as part of a detailed forward planning exercise, he submitted proposals for an eighty *Staffel* air arm to be achieved by 1938, thus quadrupling his own earlier study.[86] By this time it was anticipated that the *Reichsheer* would itself have expanded to a total force of 21 *Divisionen* and the *Inspektion 1 (L)'s* plan called for a front-line of 720 machines with a further 240 aircraft in reserve plus 96 trainers. Furthermore in keeping with *Inspektion 1 (L)'s* published doctrine, Felmy proposed that half of this force (42 *Staffeln*) should comprise bomber aircraft whose first aim in the event of hostilities was the destruction of the enemy air force prior to further strategic bombing operations against the enemy homeland.[87] Although not ratified by the *Chef des Heeresleitung*, Felmy's new proposals were of significance in demonstrating the strength and coherence of the links between doctrine, force size and force structure that had been achieved by *Inspektion 1 (L)* by 1933.

Nonetheless there still were very real political and economic constraints to such an ambitious programme, not the least of which was the manufacturing capacity of the German aircraft industry.

---

80   Hooton 1994 p.72. On the 19 May 30 Felmy issued an order that detailed the deployment of the planned *Fliegertruppe*. It also mentioned the formation of the *Reklamestaffeln* for the first time - see Schliephake H. 1971 *The Birth of the Luftwaffe* (hereafter cited as Schliephake 1971) p.27.

81   Hooton 1994 p.72. This plan dated from the 15 Apr 30.

82   Hooton 1994 p.73. Felmy first wrote to Heye in support of the original 22 *Staffeln* Plan on the 19 May 30. This would have provided for a force of 150 first-line aircraft with 50 reserves, whilst the *Fliegerschulen* would have 62 trainers with 18 reserves giving a total force of 280 machines and 4,600 officers and men. Kurt Schleicher replaced Groener as *Reichswehrminister* in Jun 32 after a period of political in-fighting within the Government. *GenLt.a.D.* Schleicher had been an increasingly powerful player in the early years of the Weimar Republic playing an important role in the formation of the *Freikorps* (19-20), working alongside Seeckt as a political *referent* (23-24) before becoming Groener's *Chef d.Ministeramt/RWM* (26-32). A powerful figure within the *Reichswehr* he ensured that the position of *Chef d.Heeresleitung* went to his own protégé Hammerstein-Equord, whilst Blomberg, the natural successor, was side tracked to Ostpressuen as *Bfr.WK I*. In company with his patron *Reichswehrminister* Groener he was successful in influencing Hindenburg's decision to appoint Heinrich Bruning as *Reichskanzler* on the 28 Mar 30 and then in his replacement by Franz von Papen on the 30 May 32. In terms of his own advancement he ruthlessly replaced Groener as *Reichswehrminister* in May 32 and then Papen as *Reichskanzler* on the 3 Dec 32 - see Groener-Geyer 1955 p.301, Shirer 1963 pp.150-152 & 160-164, Synder 1976 p.310-311 & Seaton 1982 pp.23-26.

83   Hooton 1994 p.73.

84   Hooton 1994 p.73 & Westermann 2001 pp.45-46.

85   Service record for Hellmuth Felmy in Hildebrand 1990 pp.273-275. Felmy had been promoted to *Obstlt.* on the 1 Feb 31.

86   Homze 1976 pp.34-35 & Corum 1997 p.122. This force would have included 6 *Fernaufklärungsstaffeln* (Long Range Recce Squadrons), 14 *Nahaufklärungsstaffeln* (Short Range Recce Squadrons), 18 *Jagdstaffeln* (Fighter Squadrons) and 42 *Kampfstaffeln* (Bomber Squadrons).

87   Homze 1976 pp.34-35 & Corum 1997 p.122. By 1938 the 42 bomber squadrons would have a combined strength of 370 aircraft plus 126 reserves.

Experts within the *Inspektion 1 (L)* had assessed this as only 100 single-engine machines per month nine months after mobilisation.[88] The depressed state of the world economy had caused a drop in the sales of commercial aircraft throughout Europe and in the absence of substantial military contracts several firms had been forced to suspend operations whilst others were in dire financial difficulties (See 1C2).

It was against this difficult economic context that Mittelberger proposed on the 15 July 1932 the formation of a unified Air Ministry to co-ordinate the development of both military and civil aviation.[89] Within days Schleicher had added weight to this argument by stating in a wireless broadcast that in view of the financial situation it was essential that the nation should get value for money on its defence spending.[90] The *Inspektion 1 (L)'s* formal view was expressed in August when *Hptm.*Hans Jeschonnek, *Referent I (Taktisch Ausbildung)*, submitted a memorandum which proposed that either the existing *Abteilung Luftfahrt* (Aviation Department) under Brandenburg be brought under the direct control of the *RWM* or that the existing *Reichswehr* aviation departments be transferred to join Brandenburg in the *RVM* whilst remaining under the overall direction of the *Reichswehrministerium* (See also 1B1).[91] Jeschonnek argued that substantial savings could be achieved by such an amalgamation as it would allow military programmes to be advanced using funds already voted by the Government to the development of civil aviation.[92]

That the *Marineleitung* agreed, albeit reluctantly, to these proposals was a sign of the *Reichswehr's* growing concern over the increasing political instability within Germany (See 1E3). It was widely recognised that the established order was beginning to break down as the World Economic Depression produced a downturn in economic activity throughout the nation.[93] Unemployment rose and in the absence of state benefits social conditions within the industrial cities quickly became a fertile breeding ground for extremist political factions from both the left and the right.[94] In the September 1930 elections to the *Reichstag* Adolf Hitler's *NSDAP* increased its holding from 12 to

---

88   Suchenwirth 1968 p.23 & pp.35-37 & Hooton 1994 p.76.

89   Hooton 1994 p.75. Mittelberger felt that Germany should follow the example set by Britain and France who had both established independent air ministries. In France this had been established on the 14 Sep 28 – see Christienne and Lissarague 1980 p.240.

90   Hooton 1994 p.75.

91   Hooton 1994 p.75. *Oblt.*Hans Jeschonnek, the brother of *Hptm.*Paul Jeschonnek, had been assigned as *Referat I (Taktik und Ausbildung)* (Tactics and Training) in Oct 31. His service in the *Reichsheer* had been almost associated almost entirely with the development of military aviation. Assigned to the *Insp. Waffen u.Gerat* in Dec 23 he joined Student's clandestine *Wa.Prw.6F.* Following the completion of his general staff officer training in 1928 - where he graduated as top of his class - he was transferred to Felmy's *T 2 V (L)*, later *Insp.1 (L)*. He was promoted to *Hptm.* on the 1 Jun 32 - see Suchenwirth R. 1969 *Command and Leadership in the German Air Force* USAF Historical Studies No.174 pp.213-214 & service record for Hans Jeschonnek in Hildebrand 1991 pp.138-139.

92   Hooton 1994 p.75 & Corum 1997 p.88. This was in fact nothing new as Brandenburg had been more than generous in the support of military aviation through the judicious, and at times illegal, use of *RVM* funding.

93   Shirer 1963 pp.135-136. The Wall Street Crash (New York Stock Exchange) occurred on the 24 Oct 29. The ripples spread quickly outward being most felt in those countries that were dependant on international trade. Germany was a leading mercantile nation and its industries relied to a greater or lesser extent on imported raw materials and overseas exports. In 1928 Germany ranked third in the world in terms of its share of foreign trade: USA 15.6%, Great Britain 12.5% & Germany 8.8%. The German Mercantile Marine ranked sixth overall with some 3.5 m BRT of largely modern shipping - See Blanchard W.O. and Visher S.S. 1931 *Economic Geography of Europe* pp.125-126, p.129, 131 & 79. Industrial production in Germany fell by nearly 50% between 1929-32 throwing millions out of work and many more on to reduced working. Many small businesses went under.

94   Seaton 1982 pp.21-22. By the early 30s political activists had polarised around the rightist *Harzburger Front* (the *NSDAP Sturmabteilung* & the Nationalist *Stahlhelm* organisations) and the leftist *Eiserner Front* (the Socialist *Reichsbanner* and Communist *Rotfrontorganisation*). Clashes between these extremist factions were increasingly frequent and bloody. On the eve of the Jul 32 elections a wave of political violence and murder swept Germany. In Preussen alone there were 461 pitched battles which resulted in the deaths of 82 and severe injuries to 400 more activists between the 1-20 Jun 32 - see Shirer 1963 p.165. By this time the SA had a strength of 445,000 men, more than four times the size of the *Reichsheer* - see Irving D. 1989 *Göring: A Biography* (hereafter cited as Irving 1989) p.104.

107 seats.[95] In July 1932 this holding was increased again to 230 seats, a number that made *NSDAP* support vital to any Parliamentary vote in a House of 608 seats.[96] In August *Hptm.a.D.*Hermann Göring was elected *Präsidenten des Deutschen Reichstags*, a position which gave him and the National Socialists considerable control over Parliamentary business.[97] However few in either the political or military establishment wished to see Hitler made *Reichskanzler* and it was into this political maelstrom that Schleicher made his successful, although short-lived, bid for power when he outflanked the incumbent, Franz von Papen, to secure this key post at the beginning of December 1932 *(Photo 1A-16)*.[98]

It was hoped that Schleicher would now use the very powers that he had denied Papen to deal with the political extremists. He enjoyed the full support of his protege Hammerstein-Equord and it was appreciated that as *Reichskanzler* and *Reichswehrminister* Schleicher had the power to bring the *Reichswehr* on to the streets against the National Socialist *Sturmabteilung (SA)* and the Communist *Rotfrontorganisation* whose violence and intimidation were clearly beyond the capacity of the Police to control.[99] However with such powers there was the real concern that Schleicher might attempt to take over the Presidency in addition to his other positions.[100] *Präsident GFM.a.D.*Paul Hindenburg decided to act *(Photo 1A-17)*. On the 1 January 1933 Blomberg was brought back to Berlin from Königsberg/Ostpressuen as Schleicher's replacement as *Reichswehrminister*,[101] whilst on the 30 January Hindenburg replaced the generally despised Schleicher with Hitler as *Reichskanzler (Photo 1A-18)*.[102]

Hitler and Göring had made no secret of their desire to control the military.[103] To safeguard

95   Shirer 1963 p.138. In the 1930 elections the *NSDAP* polled 6,409,600 votes (107 seats), whilst the *KPD* polled 4,592,000 votes (77 seats). It was significant that the *NSDAP* had made ground at the expense of the more moderate centre-line parties.

96   Shirer 1963 p.138 & Irving 1989 p.105. In the 1932 elections the *NSDAP* polled 13,732,779 votes (230 seats). The *KPD* also increased its vote to earn 89 seats - mainly from the working classes.

97   Shirer 1963 p.170 & Absolon R. (Ed.) 1984 *Rangliste der Generale der deutschen Luftwaffe nach dem stand vom 20.April 1945* (hereafter cited as Absolon (Ed.) 1984) p.105. Although in his acceptance address to the *Reichstag* Göring had stated that he would perform his duties *"justly and impartially according to Reichstag rules"* he was soon bending those same rules to the overall benefit of the *NSDAP* - quoted from Lee A. 1972 *Goering; Air Leader* p.37 Gerald Duckworth & Company Limited. In Aug 32 he successfully prevented Papen's attempt to dissolve the *Reichstag* by taking an unexpected vote. This action also served to hasten Papen's fall from office - see Irving 1989 pp.105-106.

98   Shirer 1963 pp.173-175 & Seaton 1982 p.26. Throughout 1931-32 Schleicher had manoeuvred between the different political factions in an attempt to achieve his own ends. He thought he could control the *NSDAP* and he had enlisted the support of prominent Nazis in his machinations. However Hitler and Göring proved to be more than a match for him in the end - see Irving 1989 p.108.

99   Groener-Geyer 1955 p.296. In a letter on the 22 May 32, shortly after his resignation from the Government, Groener noted: *"Schleicher is not interested in getting the Nazis into power - he wants it for himself through Hindenburg and his close friend Oskar (Hindenburg's son) who has the greatest influence there...Schleicher has for some time been harbouring the notion to govern without the Reichstag but with the support of the Reichswehr...Hammerstein follows his friend Schleicher around like a well-trained lapdog."* – quoted from Groener-Geyer 1955 p.325 Societats Verlag.

100   Seaton 1982 pp.26-27. There is the suggestion that Göring primed Oskar von Hindenburg with this idea as a way of bringing Schleicher down. See also Shirer 1963 p.181 & Irving 1989 p.108.

101   Seaton 1982 p. 27. In a final attempt to hold on to some aspect of power Schleicher had tried to obtain Hitler's support for him to remain on as *RWM* in the new Cabinet. In this he was unsuccessful as Blomberg enjoyed the support of the *Präsident* and Papen, the former *Reichskanzler* - see Mitcham 1988 p.24.

102   Shirer 1963 p182 & Irving 1989 p.108. In this Hitler enjoyed the support of Papen who had helped topple Schleicher. In recognition of this support Papen was made *Vizekanzler* in Hitler's new Cabinet - see Snyder 1976 pp.266-267.

103   Shirer 1963 pp.139-140. *NSDAP* attempts to infiltrate the *Reichswehr* had resulted in the 1930 show trial of three young *Reichsheer* officers from *AR 5 (Obst.*Ludwig Beck) at Ulm. In 1927 Groener had forbidden the recruitment of *NSDAP* members into the *Reichsheer* and even banned their employment in civilian capacities. Göring was active in German aviation matters from his election to the *Reichstag* in 1927. In an undated speech he demonstrated his support for a centralised air ministry: *"Everything will be in the hands of one responsible individual, and this will greatly help to promote all technical developments. The whole industry will become the instrument of a leader who knows from his own practical experiences what we need most. Technical centralisation of air development will help the army and the*

the *Reichswehr's* aviation interests Blomberg moved the *Inspektion 1 (L)* from the *Inspektion der Waffenschulen* to the direct control of the *RWM* on the 24 January 1933 (See 2A1).[104] Just over a week later the growing strength of the emergent National Socialists was confirmed when Göring was appointed *Reichskommisar für die Luftfahrt* (Reichs Commissioner for Aviation) on the 2 February 1933.[105] He quickly sought to extend his control to cover all aviation matters including military developments. An early example of this policy was Göring's success in having *Obstlt. Wilhelm Wimmer's Wa.Prw.8* transferred from the *Heereswaffenamt* to his new office.[106] However the new *Reichskommissar* was forced to concede that, for the time being at least, the *Flakartillerie* would remain under the control of the *Reichsheer*.[107]

It was at this time that the air staff were advised that the *Inspektion 1 (L)* would be shortly reorganised along the lines previously outlined by Jeschonnek in his memorandum of August 1932. The new office, to be known as the *Luftschützamt* (Air Defence Office), would be jointly staffed by officers from the *Reichsheer* and the *Reichsmarine*:[108]

FIGURE 1A-4 ORGANISATION OF THE LUFTSCHÜTZAMT	
1 APRIL 1933	
Amt Chef - Obst.i.G.Eberhard Bohnstedt	
Chef des Stabes - FregKpt.Rudolf Wenninger	
Verbindungsoffizier by R.d.L. - Hptm.Hans Jeschonnek	
Abteilung 1L (Heer) - Obstlt.Hellmuth Volkmann	
Gruppe I (Taktik)	- Hptm.Josef Kammhuber
Gruppe II (Organisation)	- Hptm.Wilhelm Speidel
Gruppe III (Ausbildungs)	- Hptm.Gerd von Massow
Abteilung 1L (Marine) - FregKpt.Rudolf Wenninger	
Gruppe I (Taktik)	- KorvKpt.Ulrich Kessler (?)
Gruppe II (Organisation)	- FregKpt.Wolfgang Weigand
Gruppe III (Ausbildungs)	- FregKpt.Hans Geisler (?)

Felmy had not been surprised to be told that he would be re-assigned as *Kommandeur Infanterie-Regiment Nr.17* at Braunschweig, after all he had seen continuous service with the air staff in its

---

navy. Even at first there might be some interdepartmental difficulties" - quoted from Hermann 1943 *The Rise and Fall of the Luftwaffe* p.65 John Long Ltd. The leader in question would of course by Göring.

104   Maass B. GenLt.a.D. 1955 *The Organisation of the German Air Force High Command and Higher Echelon Headquarters within the German Air Force* USAF Historical Studies No.190 (hereafter cited as Maass 1955) p.15.

105   Absolon (Ed.) 1984 p.105 & Irving 1989 p.113.

106   Maass 1955 p.14.

107   Westermann 2001 p.56. Nonetheless an element of operational control over the *Flakartillerie* was achieved on the 16 Sep 33 when Blomberg agreed to GenMaj.Rüdel becoming responsible to Göring on matters concerning the organisation, training, augmentation and equipping of air defence forces. Rüdel's primary duty was *"the standardised co-ordination of all military and civil preparedness measures for air defence in the field and in the homeland as well as the systematic continued development of air defence tactics and technical matters"* - see *Unterstellung der Luftschütztruppen (September 16, 1933)* in T-405/Reel 1/Frames 4828144-46, NARA in Westermann 2001 p.56.

108   Maass 1955 p.15 & Volker K-H. 1967 *Die deutsche Luftwaffe 1933-1939: Aufbau, Führung und Rüstung der Luftwaffe sowie die Entwicklung der deutschen Luftkriegstheorie* pp.11-12. The *LS Amt* was established on the 1 Apr 33 in accordance with *Direktive Nr.401/33 Geheim, 21 Mar 33* as issued by the *Inspektion 1 (L) i.RWM* and later confirmed by *Reichsverteidigungsminister und Befehlshaber der gesamten Wehrmacht Nr.1007/33 vom 15.5.1933.* For staff positions - see Hildebrand 1990-92.

various forms since February 1929.[109] The majority of his *Referate* were also re-assigned. However he must have been astonished and dismayed to learn that the chief of the new office would be *Obst.*Eberhard Bohnstedt, a staff officer without any previous aviation experience.[110] In the final reckoning it seemed that the conservatives had won the day and that in April 1933 an independent future for military aviation within Germany seemed as far away as ever. [111]

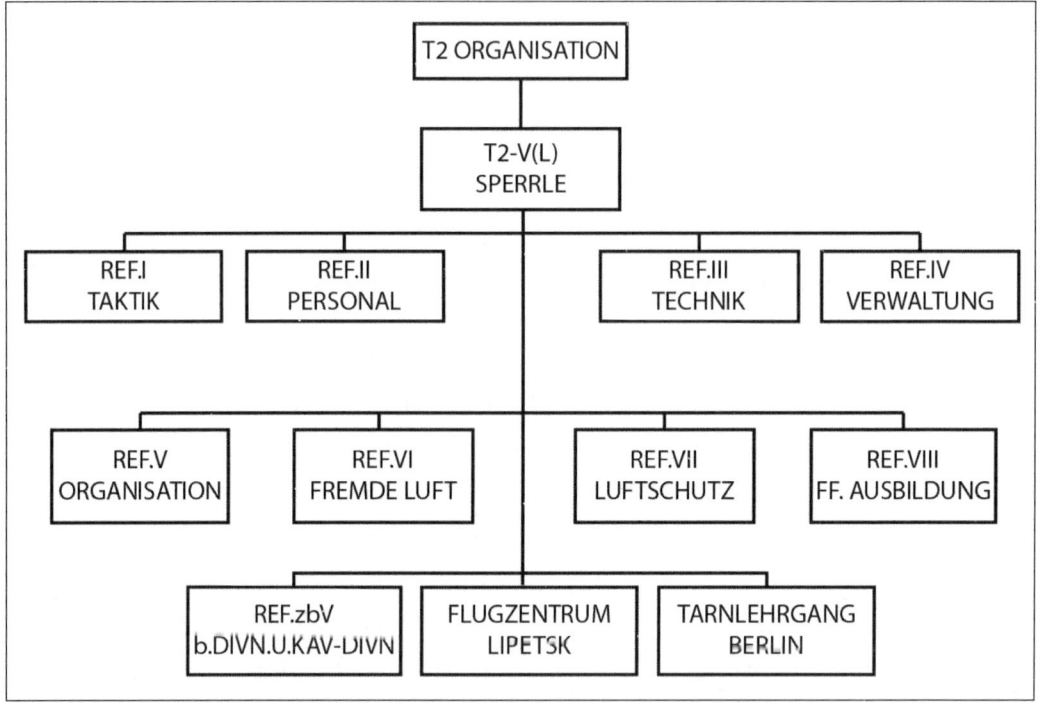

I-2   Organisation of *T 2 V (L)*, 1 April 1927 until the 30 September 1929

109   Service record for Hellmuth Felmy in Hildebrand 1990 pp.273-275. To familiarise himself with his new assignment *Obstlt.*Felmy was attached to the *Stab IR 15* at Kassel for four months from the 1 Apr 33. He assumed command of *IR 17* on the 1 Aug 33.

110   Service record for Eberhard Bohnstedt in www.reocities.com/~orion47/WEHRMACHT/HEER. Bohnstedt's war service had been exclusively as a junior staff officer. In the *Reichsheer* he had served on the staff of the *3.Division* (Berlin) and the *2.Kav.Div.*(Breslau) as well as with *T 4 (Ausbildungs)*. Prior to his new appointment he had been *Kdr.II./IR 6* at Lübeck.

111   Irving D. 1973 *The Rise and Fall of the Luftwaffe: The Life of Luftwaffe MarshallErhard Milch* pp.31-32. Bohnstedt replaced Felmy. Unfortunately he had none of the foresight or drive of his predecessor. He had been appointed by Hammerstein-Equord as a means of preventing the *Luftwaffe* from emerging as a distinct service within the *Reichswehr*. *GenMaj.*Walther von Reichenau, Blomberg's *C.d.GS.*, later advised Milch that Hammerstein-Equord viewed Bohnstedt as *"the stupidest clot I could find in my general staff"*. The most logical appointment would have been *GenMaj.*Helmuth Wilberg but he had retired just 4 months earlier - see service record for Helmuth Wilberg in Hildebrand 1992 pp.513-514.

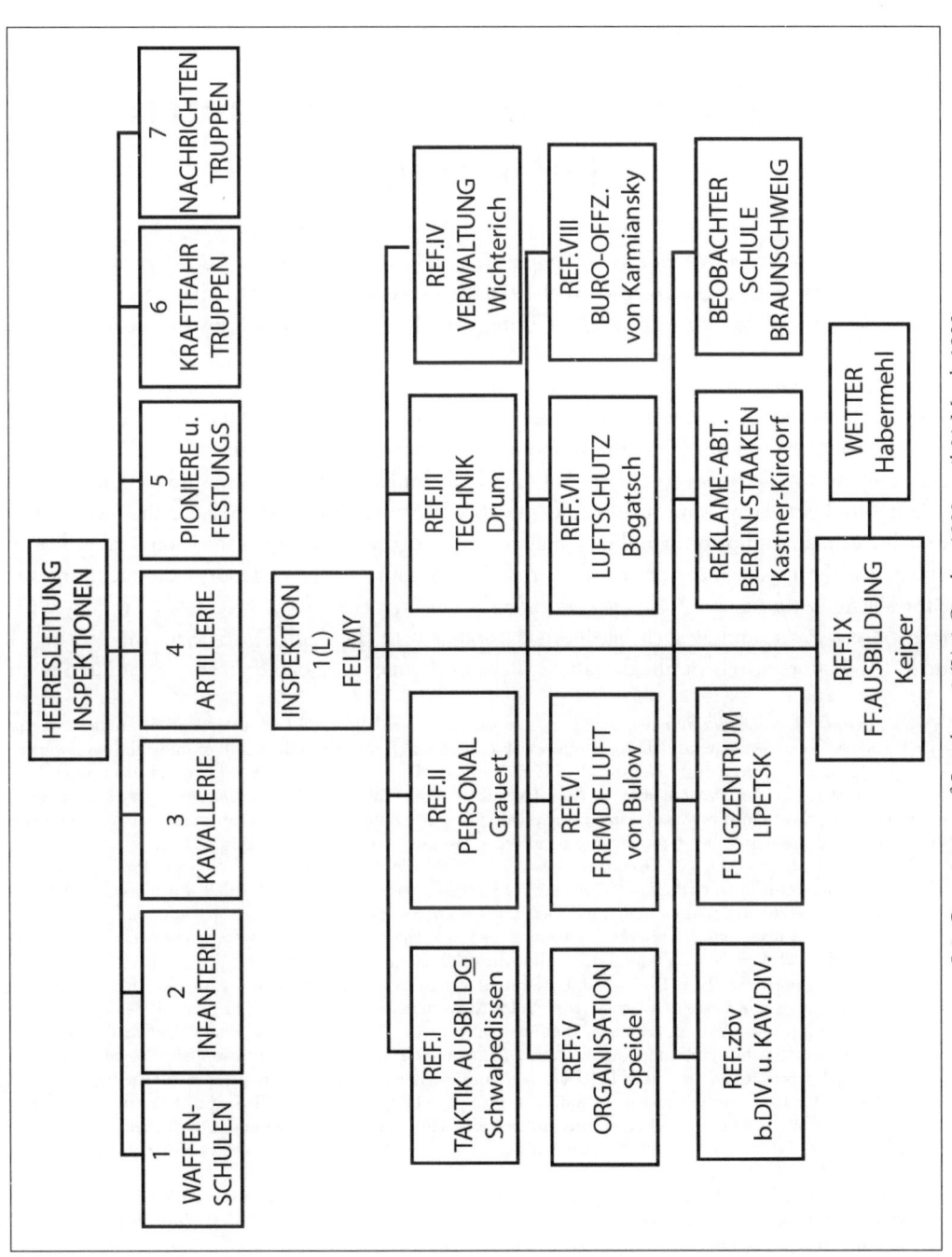

I-3 Organisation of *Inspektion 1 (L)*, 1 October 1929 until 31 March 1933

Brandenburg and the Luftfahrtabteilung 1919-1933

Although the *Rat der Volksbeauftragten* (People's Council) had organised a *Reichsluftamt* (German Aviation Office) as early as the 26 November 1918 this office appears to have to have been subsumed into the *Reichsverkehrsministerium* (Reichs Transport Ministry) *(RVM)* almost immediately with August Euler at its head.[1] Euler enjoyed the support of Heinrich Albert, the *Reichsminister des Innern* (Reichs Interior Minister), as well as several prominent aircraft manufacturers. He also had the distinction of holding the *FAI Deutschland Nr.1*, dated 1 February 1910 (German Pilots Licence Nr.1).[2] However he did not enjoy the support or confidence of the militarists. To officers such as *Obst.*Hermann von der Lieth-Thomsen and *Maj.*Wilhelm Haehnelt, Euler was nothing more than an "irritating lightweight" and in December both officers made it clear to Euler they would not accept his civilian authority in military matters.[3] Part of the solution to this potentially thorny problem was the appointment of *Maj.a.D.*Ernst Brandenburg as Euler's deputy.[4] Brandenburg was the former *Kommandeur der 3.Kampfgeschwader der Obersten Heeresleitung (Kagohl 3)*, the so-called *England-Geschwader*, and as such had been decorated with the *Pour le Mérite* on the on the 14 June 1917.[5] Unfortunately on the day after his award Brandenburg had been severely injured in an

1   Suchenwirth R. 1968 *The Development of the German Air Force 1919-1939* USAF Historical Studies No.160 (hereafter cited as Suchenwirth 1968) p.9. The earliest attempt to form an air ministry to promote the development of civil aviation had been on 11 Nov 18 when Paul Gohre, the Under-Secretary of State for War, had authorised the creation of a *Deutschesluftamt*. Gohre had hoped to interest *Obst.*Wilhelm Siegert, the *Inspekteur der Fliegertruppen*, into leading this Branch but Siegert had no sympathy for the Socialist Government nor the Republic. Siegert was in fact totally exhausted by an unrelenting period of active duty. He was discharged from the *Heer* on the 4 Mar 19 - see also Morrow J.H. 1982 *German Air Power in World War I* (hereafter cited as Morrow 1982) p.150. The *Reichsluftamt* formed part of the *Reichsministerium des Innern* between 4 Dec 18 – 8 Jan 20 when it was transferred to the *Reichsverkehrsministerium*. From the 1 Oct 19 it was known as the *Reichsamt für Luft-und Kraftfahrwesen* – see Vogt E. Dr. *Zulassung und Kennzeichnung der deutschen Zivilflugzeuge 1914-1945 4.Die deutsche Luftfahrzeugrolle 1920-1934 (LFR B)* in www.adl-luftfahrthistori.de (hereafter cited as Vogt Undated).
2   Morrow 1982 pp.56-59, 99-101, 146-148. For a listing of pre-war German aviators - see Angolia J.R. and Hackney C.R. 1984 *The Pour le Mérite and Germany's First Aces* (hereafter cited as Angolia and Hackney 1984) pp.14-23.
3   Morrow 1982 p.144. *Obst.*von der Lieth-Thomsen had been *GenLt.*Ernst von Hoeppner's *Chef des Generalstabes*. On the 12 Jan 19 he would be appointed *Chef der Luftfahrt-Abteilung (Abt.A7L) im preußische Kriegsministerium* - an almost rival organisation to Euler's Reichsluftamt. *Maj.*Haehnelt replaced Siegert as *Inspekteur der Fliegertruppen* on the 15 Dec 18, a position that he would hold until the 31 Dec 19. He was discharged from the *Reichsheer* a year later on the 31 Dec 20 - see service records for Hermann von der Lieth-Thomsen & Wilhelm Haehnelt in Hildebrand K.F.1991 *Die Generale der deutschen Luftwaffe 1935-1945 Band 2 H-N* (hereafter cited as Hildebrand 1991) pp.296-297 & 7-8.
4   Morrow 1982 pp.146-148. Brandenburg had briefly headed-up the *Deutschesluftamt* before joining the *Reichsluftamt*. See also conversation between *MinRat.*Willy Fisch and *Prof.*Richard Suchenwirth, 20 Dec 57 in Suchenwirth 1968 (hereafter cited as Fisch in Suchenwirth 1968) p.10.
5   Kilduff P. 1991 *Germany's First Air Force 1914-1918* pp.69-73. *Kagohl 3* was formed as a result of a secret *Kriegsministerium Direktive* of the 25 Apr 17. Unlike the other *Kagohl* it consisted of six *Kampfstaffeln* and as such was the most powerful German bomber unit of the war. For the attacks on Britain - see Cole C. and Cheesman E.F. 1984 *The Air Defence of Great Britain 1914-1918*. Despite his injuries Brandenburg returned to command *Bogohl 3* in Dec 17. He was discharged in 1919 with the rank of *Major a.D.* - see service record Ernst Brandenburg in www.frontflieger.de.

air accident and was still on crutches at the end of the war. He joined Euler in the newly formed *Reichsluftamt* in December 1918.[6]

The emerging status of civil aviation did not initially justify separate ministerial status and therefore Euler's re-named *Reichsamt für Luft-und Kraftfahrwesen* remained within the newly created *RVM*.[7] The *Reichsminister* was *GenLt.a.D.* Wilhelm Groener, the former *ObQu.d.OHL* and the master mind behind Germany's efficient transportation system during the Great War.[8] His responsibilities covered the well-developed network of inland waterways and railways and to a lesser extent the emerging national road network.[9] The nationalisation of the railway network in 1924 as the *Deutsche Reichsbahn GmbH* formed a major part of *RVM* activity during the immediate post-war years but equally important was the development and regulation of commercial aviation (See also 1D2).[10] Notwithstanding the impending peace settlement the *Reichsluftamt* provided support for *Deutsche Luft-Reederei (DLR)*, the first of Germany's airlines which was granted its operating licence on the 8 January 1919.[11] Formed in 1917, the company operated its first scheduled services in 1919 from Berlin to Weimar and by the end of the year other routes had been established to Hannover and the Rheinland, Hamburg and Westerland auf Sylt, and to Warnemünde and Swinemünde in northern Germany.[12] To further boost the development of civil aviation Euler arranged for Government subsidies to be made available and this financial support led to the emergence of a number of new airlines, notably *Lloyd Luftverkehr Sablatnig, Lloyd Ostflug* and the *Deutsche Luft-Lloyd*.[13]

The *DLR* was a founding member of the International Air Traffic Association (IATA), an organisation established on the 28 August 1919 to help promote international air travel. With support from the *Reichsluftamt* a number of international arrangements were successfully concluded, the first with the Dutch *KLM* and Danish *DDL* to open the Malmo-Kopenhagen-Hamburg-Amsterdam route in 1920.[14] In the meantime the terms of the Treaty of Versailles, signed in June 1919, specifically accorded commercial airlines of the victorious Allied Powers the same right to operate in German sovereign airspace as those of indigenous origin.[15] This was an important

---

6   Vogt Undated, Suchenwirth 1968 p.10 & Angolia and Hackney 1984 pp.140-141. Brandenburg was the oldest military aviator to be awarded the *Plm*. He had joined the *Fliegertruppe* as a pilot in Nov 15 and his performance was such that he was chosen to form *Kagohl 3* on the 5 Mar 17 - see service record for Ernst Brandenburg in www.frontflieger.de.

7   Grey C.G. 1943 *The Luftwaffe* (hereafter cited as Grey 1943) p.107. The *RVM* was created under Article 7, para 19 of the Constitution of the new Republic of Germany.

8   Snyder L.L. 1976 *Encyclopaedia of the Third Reich* (hereafter cited as Snyder 1976) p.128. Groener had replaced Ludendorff in this key position on the 26 Oct 18 and it was under his direction that the *Feldheer* was withdrawn in good order to Germany following the Armistice (See 1A1). Unlike many career officers Groener was a loyal supporter of the democratic republican government. See also Seaton A. 1982 *The German Army 1933-1945* pp.1-3 & Hooton E.R. 1994 *Phoenix Triumphant: The Rise and Rise of the Luftwaffe* (hereafter cited as Hooton 1994) p.27.

9   Naval Intelligence Division 1945 *Germany Vol.IV Ports and Communications* (hereafter cited as NID 1945) pp. 192-194, p.435 & 449. The *Deutsche Reichsbahn* had a route mileage greater than any other European nation with the exception of the USSR.

10   *Chapter III Railways* in NID 1945 pp.215-216. The nationalisation of the railways formed part of the reparations agreements - the operating profit being siphoned off to help "pay for the war".

11   Hooks M. 1999 *Images of Aviation: Luft Hansa* (hereafter cited as Hooks 1999) p.7.

12   *App.I Civil Aviation* in NID 1945 pp.621-622. See also Jackson R. 1983 *The Sky their Frontier: The Story of the World's Pioneer Airlines and Routes 1920-40* (hereafter cited as Jackson 1983) p.101, Hooton 1994 pp.31-32 & Hooks 1999 p.7.

13   *App.I Civil Aviation* in NID 1945 p.622. However Euler did face unexpected opposition from the *Reichswehr*. In Feb 19 he learned that Thomsen and Haehnelt had started a military courier service based at Döberitz and Weimar with connections to Dresden, Stuttgart and later München. In an attempt to undermine Euler the military offered the use of this service to civilian concerns. This only stopped following the disbandment of *A7L* later in 1919 - see Hooton 1994 p.31.

14   Hooks 1999 p.7.

15   Hermann 1943 *The Rise and Fall of the Luftwaffe* (hereafter cited as Hermann 1943) pp.38-39. The aerial navigation clauses of the Treaty were included in Articles 313-320.

concession for the French who sought to extend their influence into central and south-eastern Europe. On the 23 April 1920 the *Cie Franco-Roumaine de Navigation Aerienne* was established with Romanian finance and French technical expertise.[16] Meanwhile in France the *Societe Generale de Transports Aeriens*, more popularly known as *Les Lignes Farman*, extended its route network eastward from Paris to Brussels in 1920, to Amsterdam in 1921 and to Berlin shortly afterwards.[17]

In February 1920 the *Interalliierte Luftfahrt-Überwachungs-Kommission (ILUK)* began to supervise the aerial disarmament of Germany in accordance with Article 202 of the Versailles Treaty and the *RVM* became embroiled in the tug of war between the *Reichswehr* and the Allied powers (See also 1A2).[18] Aerial disarmament was due to be completed by the 10 June 1920 by which date all aircraft manufacture had to cease within German territory:

> During the six months following the coming into force of the present treaty, the manufacture and importation of aircraft, parts of aircraft, engines for aircraft, and parts of engines for aircraft, shall be forbidden in all German territory.[19]

Article 201
Versailles Treaty

However the Allied inspection teams were met by obstruction and subterfuge and five months later it was clear that both the *Reichswehr* and many aircraft manufacturers had hidden away large quantities of aviation material.[20] The Allied response was to extend the ban on civil aircraft construction for a further six months, a measure that was very damaging to the remaining aircraft constructors as well as to the emergent airlines.[21] The German Government protested about the Allied decision to use Article 201 as a means of forcing the Germans to surrender their remaining stocks of military aircraft and engines. Nonetheless a decree made non-compliance with Article 202 a punishable offence and the surrender of military equipment was speeded up. A tug of war then ensued with German protests and evasion being punished with further extensions of the construction ban. In the end *ILUK's* disarmament work was not officially completed until the 24 September 1921 and on the 5 May 1922 the team was dissolved to be replaced by the *Luftfahrt Garantie Komitee (LGK)* whose task was to supervise the civilian clauses of the peace treaty.[22]

16   Jackson 1983 p.117. In 1925 this company was re-titled *Compagne Internationale de Navigation Aerienne (CINA)*.
17   Stroud J.1966 *European Transport Aircraft since 1910* (hereafter cited as Stroud 1966) p.106. Aerial navigation rights over Germany were of less consequence to the British with their pre-occupation with their Empire routes. As late as 1927 Imperial Airways (established in 1924) had only 5 European routes of which only one was to a German destination: Köln - see Jackson 1983 p.109.
18   Schmitt G. 1988 *Hugo Junkers and his Aircraft* (hereafter cited as Schmitt 1988) pp.49-50. The *ILUK* was known in Britain as the Inter-Allied Aeronautical Control Commission (*IAACC*) - see Hooton 1994 p.32.
19   Quoted from *Article 201, Treaty of Versailles Part V. Section III Air Clauses* in Hermann 1943 *The Rise of the Luftwaffe* p.39 John Long Ltd.
20   Ries K. 1970 *Luftwaffe Bd.1 Die Maulwurfe 1919-1935* (hereafter cited as Ries 1970) p.11 & Mason H.M. 1973 *The Rise of the Luftwaffe 1918-1940* (hereafter cited as Mason 1973) pp.78-80 & 84-85. According to *Col.*Rorand of the French delegation only 6,730 landplanes, 262 seaplanes and 8,039 engines had been destroyed by the 1 Apr 20 - see *SHAT File 4N96-I* in Hooton 1994 pp.32-33. In fact significant quantities of air material were being sold to foreign customers instead of being surrendered as part of Germany's war reparations. In Jan 21 the *RWM* issued an order to all units that the location of all hidden aircraft was to reported prior to these machines being handed over.
21   Hermann 1943 p.40. This is one of the reasons why the firms of *AEG* (Berlin), *DFW* (Leipzig), *Gotha, Friedrichshafen, Pfalz* (Speyer) & *Siemens-Schuckert* (Berlin) ceased trading. The one off *RVM* payment of *RM* 150 million in compensation for lost profits and wages came too late - see Hooton 1994. For conditions in Germany at this time - see Heinkel E. 1956 *He 1000* (hereafter cited as Heinkel 1956).
22   Ries 1970 p.12, Schmitt 1988 p.50 & Hooton 1994 p.33.

Unfortunately the twenty-four months that it had taken to complete the aerial disarmament of Germany had led to a hardening of attitudes on the part of the Allied powers. The Boulogne Conference of 22 June 1920 had been followed by a further conference in November of that year and the issue of the London Ultimatum on the 5 May 1921.[23] A further conference on the 14 April 1922 was used to draw up the new *Begriffsbestimmungen für den deutschen Luftfahrzeugbau* (Definitions of Categories of German Aircraft Construction) that were subsequently handed over to the *RVM*. In an accompanying note the Ambassadors stated:

To ensure the application of Article 198 of the Treaty, which forbids it to possess any aerial forces, whether controlled by the army or by the navy; Germany must recognise the definitions of categories as established by the allied governments differentiating civil aviation from military aviation, the latter being forbidden by Article 198. The allied governments will ascertain that Germany fulfils its obligations through continuous supervision.[24]

The *RVM* had no choice but to accept these definitions which were formalised in an order concerning aircraft construction on the 5 May 1922:

TERMS FOR GERMAN AIRCRAFT CONSTRUCTION
MAY 1922

HEAVIER THAN AIR MACHINES

Rule 1: Every single seater with a performance of more than 60 hp will be regarded as military and as an instrument of war.

Rule 2: Every unmanned aircraft will be regarded as military and therefore as an instrument of war.

Rule 3: Every aircraft with armour or any other form of protection or any equipment which allows it to be armed: guns, bomb release mechanism or sighting device, will be regarded as military and as an instrument of war.

The following specifications are maximum figures for all heavier than air machines and all those which exceed these limits will be regarded as military and therefore as instruments of war.

Rule 4: Maximum climbing power fully loaded 4,000 m. (An engine fitted with a device providing super-compression puts the aircraft furnished with it into the military category).

Rule 5: Speed with maximum load and at an altitude of 2,000 m: 170 kph. (The engines at full power and which accordingly develop their maximum performance).

Rule 6: The maximum amount of oil and fuel (highest grade aviation gasoline), carried must not exceed 800 x 170 grams per unit horsepower when divided by the maximum velocity of the aircraft with maximum load and at maximum performance at an altitude of 2,000 m.

---

23   Schmitt 1988 p.50. The manufacture of civilian aircraft was finally permitted from the 5 May 22 - see Hooton 1994 p.34.

24   Quoted from Trautvetter 'Über die Begriffsbestimmungen für den deutschen Luftfahrzeugbau' in *Der Luftweg H.8/1922* p.78.

Rule 7: Every aircraft capable of carrying a payload of more than 600 kg, including pilot, flight mechanic and instruments inasmuch as the maximum conditions of rules 4, 5 and 6 are reached is regarded as military and is therefore an instrument of war. [25]

MANOEUVRABLE AIRSHIPS

Those manoeuvrable airships the volume of inflatable gas of which exceeds the following specifications are regarded as military in character and are therefore instruments of war:

I	rigid airships:	cubic metres 30,000
II	semi-rigid airships	cubic metres 25,000
III	non-rigid airships	cubic metres 20,000

Rule 8: Factories which produce equipment must be registered. All planes, pilots and trainee pilots must be registered under the conditions laid down in the Convention of 13th October 1919. These lists are to be at the disposal of the Guarantee Committee.

Rule 9: Stockpiles of aircraft engines, spare parts and engine accessories are not allowed in excess of what is thought necessary to cover the needs of civil air travel. The level of amounts is established by the Guarantee Committee.

These continued restrictions only served to increase the pressure on Euler and his successor Traugott Bredow, even though it was the *Reichswehr* that was very much to blame for the obstructive behaviour encountered by the *ILUK*. Nonetheless *Gen.d.Inf.*Hans von Seeckt, the *Chef der Heeresleitung*, was instrumental in the final replacement of Bredow by Brandenburg. Brandenburg had initially acted as a Ministerial Advisor for aviation within Groener's *RVM*. On the 1 April 1924 he was appointed *Leiter der Abteilung für Luft-und Kraftfahrwesen* (Leader of the Aviation and Motor Vehicle Branch) within the *RVM* under *Reichsminister* Rudolf Oeser, later Rudolf Krohne *(Photo 1B-1)*.[26]

German air sovereignty was nominally restored on the 1 January 1923 but France in particular continued to flout German airspace, no doubt emboldened by the military occupation of the Rheinland by Franco-Belgian forces in the same month.[27] Brandenburg retaliated by seizing any foreign airliner that was obliged to land on German Territory in accordance with Articles 313-315. These clearly stated that *"Allied aircraft shall enjoy the same privileges as German aircraft.., that any regulations made by Germany shall be applicable equally to the aircraft of Germany and to those of the Allied and Associated countries.., and that aircraft of the Allied and Associated Powers... shall be treated on a footing of equality with German aircraft"*.[28] Put simply if German aircraft were restricted in terms of size, speed and carrying capacity so must any foreign aircraft that occupied German airspace. Thus all foreign aircraft that were forced to land in Germany due to technical difficulties were immediately impounded as they were in contravention of Articles 313-315. In this way no less than

---

25   Quoted from Poturzyn von J.M.1924 *Jahrbuch für den Luftverkehr 1924* Münchenp.133.

26   Hooton 1994 p.35.See also Rabenau von F. Gen.d.Art. 1940 *Seeckt: Aus seinem Leben.* Euler resigned in Dec 20 and retired to a life of obscurity. He is commemorated today by the *Flughäfen August Euler*, formerly Darmstadt-Griesheim - the site where he learned to fly and became Germany's pioneer aviator. See also *Reichsverkehrsministerium* in www.wikipedia.org . He was replaced on the 1 Mar 21 by Traugott Bredow – see Vogt Undated.

27   Shirer W.L. 1969 *The Collapse of the Third Republic: An Inquiry into the Fall of France in 1940* p.147 & Mason 1973 pp.120-123.

28   Quoted from *Articles 313-315, Treaty of Versailles Part V. Section III Air Clauses* in Hermann 1943 *The Rise of the Luftwaffe* pp.50-51 John Long Ltd.

thirteen *Franco-Roumaine* airliners were confiscated and the *Cie Franco-Roumaine de Navigation Aerienne* was one of those airlines that was soon putting pressure on the Allied authorities to have all the technological restrictions on German aircraft removed.[29]

Interestingly the forced landings of so many airliners, often in southern Germany close to the Czechoslovak border, gave substance to the ideas that German scientists had perfected some form of "Death Ray" which could cause an aircraft's engines to fail thus forcing the airliner to land in German territory. The truth was more mundane. Engine failure was quite common in the twenties and in this case it seems that the magnetos fitted to a particular type of engine had a tendency to fail after so many hours in the air, hence the similar area of Germany where transiting airliners had come to grief. However acting under the instructions of the *Abteilung für Luft-und Kraftfahrwesen* the apologetic officials of the *Luftüberwachungsdienst* had no option but to oblige the *Cie Franco-Roumaine de Navigation Aerienne* to arrange for its aircraft to be dismantled and returned to France by rail.[30]

The early to mid-twenties were a time of particular hardship for the German aircraft industry and for the struggling German airlines. The Allied restrictions on domestic aircraft manufacture coupled to hyper inflation which resulted from the German Government's attempt to oppose the Franco-Belgian occupation of the Rheinland through strikes and passive resistance, quickly resulted in the devaluation of the *Reichsmark*. Indeed by the summer of 1923 German currency was effectively worthless, wiping out at a stroke the life savings of the working and middle classes and making it virtually impossible for any form of commercial activity to continue.[31] A number of aircraft manufacturers simply moved aircraft manufacture and assembly abroad; Junkers and Heinkel established Swedish subsidiaries, Rohrbach opened a facility in Denmark, whilst Dornier moved across Lake Constance to Altenrhein in Switzerland and also established subsidiaries in Italy, Spain, the Netherlands and Japan (See 1C1).[32]

The domestic airlines were also in trouble. The number of airliners in service had increased from 50 machines in 1921 to 70 aircraft in 1922, however thereafter the route distance flown by these airliners plummeted from 1,197,000 kms in 1922 to just 714,000 kms in 1923, a drop of 40%. The number of passengers flown actually increased from 7,700 to 8,500 but this was not the most important element of the airline's traffic (See 1D2).[33] Many small airlines simply folded whilst *Aero-Union AG* and *Lloyd Luftdienst GmbH* joined forces in 1923 to create *Deutscher Aero Lloyd AG (DAL)*, whilst the only other major airline in Germany to survive was *Junkers Luftverkehr AG*.[34] The continued survival of both these airlines was highly dependent on Government subsidies and postal contracts.[35] It was a powerful lever that Brandenburg would soon be asked to use for the benefit of the *Reichswehr*.

29   Hermann 1943 p.51, Suchenwirth 1968 p.8, Mason 1973 p.141 & Hooton 1994 pp.53-54.

30   Grey 1943 pp.91-92 & Mason 1973 p.141. Issues of aerial sovereignty were the concern of the *Luftpolizei* which was a specialist arm of the Reich's conventional police forces and as such the responsibility of the *Reichsministerium des Innern* - see also Schilling F. and Rettinghaus H. 1994 *Die Geschichte der Luftpolizei* pp.29-34.

31   Shirer W.L. 1963 *The Rise and Fall of the Third Reich: A History of Nazi Germany* pp.61-62. In 1921 the US $ had been worth 75 Marks, in 1922 this dropped to 400 Marks, whilst the events of 1923 precipitated an ever increasing decline from 7,000 Marks in Jan 23 to 160,000 Marks by Jul 23. See also Hooton 1994 p.34.

32   Heinkel E. 1956 *He 1000* (hereafter cited as Heinkel 1956) pp.72-74, Ries 1970 pp.24-25 & Lange B. 1970 *Das Buch der deutschen Luftfahrtechnik* p.192, 242, 271 & pp.350-351.

33   *Statistisches Jahrbuch für das Deutsche Reich Band 1922 & Band 1923* in App.I Civil Aviation in NID 1945 p.623.

34   *App.I Civil Aviation* in NID 1945 p.622, Jackson 1983 p.101 & Schmitt 1988 p.82. *DLR* had formed the basis for *Aero-Union* which had absorbed a number of smaller airlines in 1921. As many as 38 small airlines had been in existence within Germany in 1919-20 - see Irving D. 1973 *The Rise and Fall of the Luftwaffe: The Life of Luftwaffe Marshal Erhard Milch* (hereafter cited as Irving 1973) p.16.

35   Irving 1973 p.16. By 1925 the survival of both *DAL* & *Junkers Luftverkehr* was dependent on Government subsidies.

In the knowledge that the airlines were being forced to operate increasingly obsolete and inefficient ex-military aircraft types, Brandenburg and his team had worked tirelessly to get the Allied restrictions on domestic aircraft construction reduced. On the 24 June 1923 the maximum authorised speed (Rule 5) was increased to 180 kph and the permitted payload (Rule 7) to 900 kgs.[36] The continued dispute over foreign airlines' operating rights over Germany also laid the foundations for German participation in the Ambassador's Conference in Paris in 1926.[37] German interests were represented by the *RVM's Dr.jur.*Alfred Wegerdt and *MinRat.*Willy Fisch.[38] Six weeks of hard bargaining culminated in the Paris Air Agreement of the 21 May 1926 which finally lifted all technological restrictions on the construction of German aircraft including lighter than air machines. German air sovereignty was also internationally recognised.[39] On the other hand the German Government had to agree to the continued prohibition in the construction and acquisition of military aircraft, to continued restrictions on the training of military pilots, and to certain special regulations in respect of air transport over the Rheinland (See also 1E1). The *LGK* was withdrawn and the *Zeppelin Luftschiffbau* works at Friedrichshafen was restored to German control. An international agreement on air transport between Germany and France quickly followed.[40]

Although Fisch expressed disappointment in the final form of the Paris Air Agreement, the outcome was nothing less than a triumph for the Germans.[41] It was now possible for German aircraft manufacturers to openly build aircraft of any size in Germany and the need for foreign subsidiaries disappeared overnight (See 1C2). This led to the assembly of the capable Junkers G 23 airliner at Dessau instead of at Limhamn, whilst Heinkel could build the HE 5 floatplanes ordered for the *Deutsche Verkehrsfliegerschule (DVS)* (German Commercial Flying School) at Warnemünde instead of Lidingo (See also 1C4 & 1D2)*(Photo 1B-2).*[42] It was also possible to build a number of military prototypes, although of necessity the true nature of these machines still had to be concealed. Such machines included the Heinkel HE 7 *Torpedoflugzeug und Seeaufklärer* of 1927 which was later tested at the *SFS Travemünde* as a photographic aircraft, the HD 15 *Bordaufklärer* of 1926/27 whose naval credentials were barely concealed under the official designation *Versuchsflugboot* (Experimental Flying Boat) and the earlier HD 33 *Fernaufklärungs-und Tagbombenflugzeug* (Long Range Reconnaissance Aircraft and Day Bomber) of 1925/26 which masqueraded as a *Postflugzeug* (Postal Aircraft)(See 1C3 & 1C4). The HD 33 had originally been assembled in Sweden but immediately following the signing of the Paris Air Agreement this aircraft was returned to Germany where it was considered by *Maj.*Helmuth Wilberg's *TA (L)* to be the production prototype for a planned batch of 24 aircraft.[43]

36   Schmitt 1988 p.52

37   Suchenwirth 1968 p.15 & Hooton p.54. The Locarno Pact was instrumental in helping to relieve the political tensions that had been building-up in Europe following the Franco-Belgian occupation of the Ruhr.

38   Suchenwirth 1968 p.15. *Maj.a.D.*Fisch had been the *1.Adj.d.Insp.d.Fliegertruppen* (Oct 16-Sep 17) before joining the *Kriegsministerium* as a *Referent* (Sep 17-Jan 19). As a *MinRat.* within the *Abt.Luftfahrt* he represented German aviation interests on the *LGK* and at the Paris Conference - Service record for Willy Fisch in Hildebrand K.F.1990 *Die Generale der deutschen Luftwaffe 1935-1945"Band 1 A-G* pp.286-287. Alfred Wegerdt had seen war service as a *Lt.d.Res.* in *Jag.Btl.13.* He was employed by the *RVM* in a legal capacity from Apr 21 - see service record for Alfred Wegerdt in Hildebrand K.F.1992 *Die Generale der deutschen Luftwaffe 1935-1945 Band 3 O-Z* (hereafter cited as Hildebrand 1992) pp.484-485.

39   Suchenwirth 1968 p.15 & Hooton 1994 p.54.

40   *App. I Civil Aviation* in NID 1945 p.622. This gave the *Les Lignes Farman* the same operating rights as the newly formed *DLH* over the Paris-Köln-Berlin route.

41   Fisch to Suchenwirth, 7 Sep 54 in Suchenwirth 1968 p.15. Fisch was to write: *"and we struggled six hard weeks to reach this trivial result."*

42   Schmitt 1988 pp.96-98 & 146-150 and Koos V. 2006 *Typenbucher Deutsche Luftfahrt: Ernst Heinkel Flugzeugwerke 1922-1932* (hereafter cited as Koos 2006) pp.23-25. *AB Flygindustrie* was established in 1924 to assemble the Junkers G 23 from parts supplied by the parent firm at Dessau. Following the Paris Air Agreement this work ceased in May 26.

43   Koos 2006 pp.28-29, 42-43 & 82-83. Due to political and military circumstances the HD 33 was destined not to be manufactured in series.

Brandenburg was certainly sympathetic to the needs of the *Reichswehr*, an attitude that can be explained by his earlier status as a career officer and the patronage he had since enjoyed from Seeckt. One of his first acts in support of the *Reichswehr* was to suggest to Hugo Junkers that the Professor become involved in the development of a military aircraft manufacturing facility inside the USSR (See 1A2 & 1C1).[44] When this enterprise collapsed in 1925 he was once again a key player.[45] Junkers faced financial ruin over the Fili Affair and had threatened legal proceedings against *Maj.*Oskar Ritter von Niedermayer and *GenLt.*Otto Hasse of the *Truppenamt* in an attempt to recoup his investment. The scandal would certainly expose the murky activities of the mysterious *Sondergruppe R* and by implication the *Reichswehrministerium* (Reichs Defence Ministry). However in the knowledge that Junkers was deeply in debt, Brandenburg proposed a merger between *Junkers Luftverkehr* and *Aero Lloyd* to produce a single new national airline - *Deutsche Luft Hansa (DLH)*. In return for giving up his airline Junkers would be given a cash settlement that would ensure the survival of the *Junkers Flugzeug-und Motorenwerke* at Dessau. He would also be able to sell his assets at Fili to the Soviet authorities, whilst his control over his foreign airline interests, which were extensive, would remain unaltered.[46] The alternative was bankruptcy and the loss of his life's work. Junkers agreed, the immediate crisis for the *Reichswehr* was avoided and *DLH* was born.[47] Brandenburg was later to admit that the whole affair was *"one of the most hateful and grievous experiences in my life"*.[48]

DLH was established on the 6 January 1926 with a share capital of *RM* 25 million. The share allocation was: the *Reichs Government* (26%), the individual German states (19%), regional air transport companies (27.5%) and private investors (27.5%).[49] Brandenburg as *Ltr.d.Luftfahrtabteilung* was given a seat on the Board of Directors together with the chief *Burgermeisteirei* of Köln, Essen, Munich and other cities, sundry bankers and the heads of the major aircraft manufacturing firms; in all sixty-six board members.[50] The *Präsident* of the Board was *Dr.*Emil-Georg von Stauss of the *Deutsche Bank*, whilst the *Vizepräsident* was *Herr* Heck, formerly *Präsident* of *Junkers Luftverkehr AG*. The executive directors were *Dr.*Otto Merkel and *Maj.a.D.*Martin Wronsky of *DAL* together with *Hptm.a.D.*Erhard Milch of the *Junkers Luftverkehr* (See also 1D2).[51] As a state sponsored monopoly *DLH* enjoyed a handsome annual subsidy, a sum that averaged *RM* 18 million during the late twenties. This represented 38% of all *RVM* aviation subsidies during 1926-29.[52]

The formation of *DLH* helped to re-vitalise the aircraft manufacturing industry. Junkers received orders for eighteen G 24 airliners, a further example being acquired in 1927, whilst seven

---

44   Hermann 1943 p.52.
45   Schmitt 1988 pp.133-135. The Soviet authorities ordered very few aircraft from Junkers, whilst the promised
        Reichswehr orders never materialised - see also Hermann 1943 p.52.
46   Hermann 1943 p.53, Mason 1973 pp.144-145 & Irving 1973 p.14. The Fili Plant was taken over the Soviet
        authorities on the 1 Mar 27 and placed under the direction of the designer Andrei Tupolev - see Hooton 1994 p.48.
47   Hermann 1943 p.53 & Hooks 1999 p.7. However many Junkers employees were embittered by this affair and
        in Dec 26 information on the *Sondergruppe R's* activities was leaked to the liberal Social Democrat deputy Philip
        Scheidemann who sought to expose the *RWM's* illegal activities - see Mason 1973 pp.155-156. In Britain a similar
        process of consolidation had led to the formation of Imperial Airways in Mar 24 - see Nayler J.L. and Ower E. 1930
        Aviation of To-Day: Its History and Development pp.426-427 & Jackson 1983 p.108.
48   *Affidavit Dr.Ernst Brandenburg, 29 Oct 49* in Irving 1973 p.17.
49   *App.I Civil Aviation* in NID 1945 p.622.
50   Irving 1973 p.17. On the 1 Jan 26 the *Abt.f.Luft-u.Kraftfahrwesen* was reorganised as the *Luftfahrtabteilung* – see
        Vogt Undated.
51   Grey 1943 pp.110-111. Supporters of *Prof.*Junkers, notably Gotthard Sachsenberg and Hermann Steiner, later
        claimed that Milch was the only one of their number to agree to a position in *DLH* - see Hermann 1943 p.53.
        However Heck's position as *Vizepräsident* belies this view. Milch later stated that he only accepted this executive
        position with Junkers' blessing - see *Milch Diary 14 Nov 25* in Irving 1973 p.17. Milch had been asked to fill this
        position by Koch & Fisch who were acting on Brandenburg's behalf at the *RVM*.
52   Homze E.L.1976 *Arming the Luftwaffe: The Reich Air Ministry and the German Aircraft Industry 1919-1939* pp.29-31.

more G 24s were supplied by the *RVM* in the same year.[53] The *Rohrbach Metall-Flugzeugbau GmbH* as awarded an order for six Ro VIII *Roland* airliners, with three Ro VIIIa following in 1928 and a further nine Roland IIs in 1929 *(Photo 1B-3).*[54] However of equal importance were the *RVM's* orders for training aircraft, placed on behalf of the *DVS* (See 1D2):[55]

<table>
<tr><td colspan="5">FIGURE 1B-1 DVS TRAINING AIRCRAFT - ACQUISITIONS BY THE RVM
1925-1932</td></tr>
<tr><td>Type</td><td>A.U.W.</td><td>Engine(s)</td><td>Power</td><td>Qty.</td></tr>
<tr><td>Udet U 12</td><td>810 kgs</td><td>One Siemens</td><td>85 hp</td><td>60</td></tr>
<tr><td>Arado SC I</td><td>1,500 kgs</td><td>One BMW</td><td>230 hp</td><td>10</td></tr>
<tr><td>Junkers A 20/35</td><td>1,500 kgs</td><td>One BMW</td><td>230 hp</td><td>20</td></tr>
<tr><td>Albatros L 75</td><td>1,785 Kgs</td><td>One BMW</td><td>320 hp</td><td>30</td></tr>
<tr><td>Junkers F 13</td><td>1,850 kgs</td><td>One Junkers</td><td>230 hp</td><td>15</td></tr>
<tr><td>Arado SC II</td><td>1,985 Kgs</td><td>One BMW</td><td>360 hp</td><td>10</td></tr>
<tr><td>Junkers W 33/34</td><td>2,500 kgs</td><td>One Junkers</td><td>310 hp</td><td>11</td></tr>
<tr><td>Junkers G 24</td><td>6,155 kgs</td><td>Three Junkers</td><td>310 hp</td><td>5</td></tr>
</table>

Brandenburg recognised that well-trained pilots, engineers and wireless operators were a key element to the establishment of an efficient national air transport system. To meet this objective he had supported the formation of the *DVS* on the 1 April 1925.[56] Following the signing of the Paris Air Agreement, *Sportflug GmbH* was dissolved and its assets re-allocated to the *DVS* and to the newly formed *Akademischen Fliegergruppen* (University Flying Groups).[57] Under the early leadership of *Maj.a.D.*Alfred Keller, Berlin-Staaken was developed as the main operating base of the *DVS*, whilst a *Zweigstelle-See* was later opened at Warnemünde on the Ostsee for the training of seaplane pilots.[58] The *DVS* specialised in commercial pilot training *(Flugzeugführerschein Land and See-C).* To meet the wider needs of German civil aviation including that of sport aviation Brandenburg encouraged the development of privately operated flying schools throughout the country and the number of student pilots rose steadily from 183 in December 1924 to 341 in March 1926 (See 1D2). On that date the *LGK* noted that there were 968 fully qualified pilots in Germany whilst a further 172 qualified pilots were enrolled on refresher courses. Of the 1,481 pilots and student pilots in March 1926, 94 were serving officers of the *Reichswehr* (6%) whilst a further 48 were members of the *Luftpolizei* (Air Police)(3%).[59]

53   Stroud 1966 pp.303-306 & Schmitt 1988 pp.103-104. Nine of these aircraft were subsequently converted to single-engine configuration as the F 24 freight aircraft – see Stroud 1966 pp.306-307 & Schmidt 1988 pp.105-106.
54   Stroud 1966 pp.357-360.
55   Lange 1970 & Ries 1970 pp.41-44.
56   Suchenwirth 1968 p.15, Ries 1970 p.41 & Ries K. 1988 *Deutsche Flugzeugführerschulen und ihre Maschinen 1919-1945* (hereafter cited as Ries 1988) pp.10-11
57   Suchenwirth 1968 pp.15-16. The *Akademischen Fliegergruppen* were attached to the *Technischen Hochschulen* (Technical High Schools - Universities) at Aachen, Berlin-Charlottenburg, Braunschweig, Breslau, Darmstadt, Dresden, Königsberg/Ostpr. and München and were instrumental in the training of a new generation of German design engineers for the aircraft industry. Many of these *Fliegergruppen* actually designed and built their own aircraft, those of the *Akaflieg Darmstadt* being amongst the most successful - see Lange 1970 pp.155-158.
58   Ries 1988 pp.10-11. In Jan 27 Keller was replaced by Dr.Günther Ziegler - see service records for Alfred Keller in Hildebrand 1991 pp.163-164 & Günther Ziegler in Hildebrand 1992 pp.567-568. Additional *Zweigstellen* would be established at Schleißheim and List auf Sylt, whilst in 1929 the original *Zweigstelle* Staaken would move to Braunschweig.
59   *SHAT File 4N97, Dossier 2* in Hooton 1994 p.52. Newly qualified pilots and their skill levels were listed in the

The creation of the *DVS* and *DLH* were both important in military terms. Germany was still denied any form of military aviation and its serving officers continued to be severely restricted in terms of the flying training that they could receive. The dissolution of *Sportflug GmbH* outwardly confirmed this view but in reality the professional training of covert military aviators had actually improved with students being secretly enrolled on the *DVS's Flieger-Lehrgange* at Staaken and Warnemünde (See 1E1 & 1E3). The creation of a single national airline also made it easier for this organisation to be integrated into the *Truppenamt's* contingency planning in the event of war (See 1A3). From 1928 operational testing of both the Junkers G 24 and the Rohrbach Ro VIII as *Behelfsnachtbomber* (Auxiliary Night Bombers) was secretly carried out at Lipetsk, deep within the USSR (See 1C2 & 1D1). The *Aufstellungsplan einer Kriegswehrmacht* or *A-Plan* (Wartime Mobilisation Plan) of the 30 June 1927 envisaged the mobilisation of sizeable elements of both the *DLH* and *DVS* to provide a limited bombing and reconnaissance capability in the event of war. To this force would be added the Fokker D.XIII fighters then based in the Soviet Union. Graduates of the *Fliegerschule Lipetsk* would form the basis for this force but experienced instructors and airline personnel would also have to play their part. To achieve this aim Brandenburg's *Luftfahrtabteilung* worked closely with the *Truppenamt's T 2 V (L)* under *Maj.*Hugo Sperrle (See 1A3).

DLH's early G 24 and Ro VIII airliners had been entered on to the *Luftfahrtabteilung's Luftfahrzeugrolle* (Aircraft Registration Roll) with numbers in the 900-*Serie*, for example both the G 24 D-901 and 903 were used by the airline for a proving flight to Peking in the summer of 1926, whilst the prototype Ro VIII D-991 was delivered to the airline later in the same year (See 1D2).[60] By international agreement all civil aircraft had to be registered, German registered aircraft being accorded the prefix D for *Deutschland*. For the most part such arrangements formed part of the legislation associated with the Paris Convention of 1919 which had created the International Commission for Air Navigation (ICAN) with a membership of thirty-three nations.[61] However as a defeated nation Germany had been excluded and was subject to international supervision by the *ILUK*. To assist the *Kommission* with its work it was decreed that all German registered aircraft would be numbered in a strict sequence thus enabling a close watch to be maintained of the actual number of aircraft in commission at any given time. In 1922 there were just 111 registered aircraft, whilst in March 1926 there were 511 registered machines.[62] Appropriately the first aircraft to be registered as D-1 was Junkers F 13 WNr.531 although it has to be acknowledged that this aircraft also carried the provisional registration D-183 prior to the 18 July 1919 *(Photo 1B-4)*.[63]

The impact of Allied restrictions on aircraft production and ownership can be seen through

weekly bulletins issued by the RVM - see *Reichsverkehrsministerium* 1929 *Nachrichten für Luftfahrer* (hereafter cited as RVM 1929). The *Luftfahrtabteilung* was responsible for all licensing and approvals both of aircraft and aircrew. For the different types of Flight Licence - see Hooton 1994 p.58 & Ketley B. and Rolfe M. 1996 *Luftwaffe Fledglings 1935-1945: Luftwaffe Training Units and their Aircraft* pp.4-7

60   Stroud 1966 p.360, Ries 1970 p.46, Schmitt 1988 pp.101-104 & Hooks 1999 p.9.

61   Desouetter D.M. Undated *All About Aircraft* (hereafter cited as Desouetter Undated) p.321-322 . As the *ICAN* was seen as a European organisation it is not surprising that the USA, USSR & China were not members.

62   Ries K. 1977 *Recherchen zur Deutschen Luftfahrzeugrolle Teil 1: 1919-1934* (hereafter cited as Ries 1977). This author has done a great deal of valuable work in re-constructing the pre-war German aircraft roll. It should be noted that not all allocated numbers were actually taken up, whilst some aircraft were re-registered more than once. Nonetheless the *LGK* was able to ascertain that there were 111 German registered aircraft in 1922, 192 in 1923, and 511 in Mar 26 - see *SHAT File 4N97, Dossier 2* in Hooton 1994 p.40 & 52. See also more recent research by Dr.Ernst Vogt in Vogt Undated.The *LFR-B* was initiated in May 20 and ran until Mar 34. The last aircraft to be registered in this sequence was D-3463.

63   Schmitt 1988 p.46. Junkers F 13 WNr.531 was the prototype of this enormously successful light transport. WNr.531 was initially registered to the *Junkers Flugzeugwerke* but on the 13 Apr 22 it passed to the *Bayerischen Luft Lloyd*. In 1926 it was transferred to *DLH* to whom it was re-registered as D-OJOP in 1934. Eventually no less than 110 F 13 aircraft would be entered on the *Deutsche Luftfahrzeugrolle*.

examination of the *Luftfahrzeugrolle*. By the winter of 1925/26 registrations had only reached the 600-*Serie* and for the most part these were light sports aircraft and trainers such as the Albatros L 67, Bahnbedarf D II and the Udet U 7. One exception was the Focke Wulf A 16, a small three passenger light transport, five of which received registrations in the 600-*Serie*: D-646 & 647, 658 & 659 and 671.[64] Just over a year later entries on the *Luftfahrzeugrolle* had exceeded 1000, whilst by late 1928 the 1500-*Serie* was in use.[65] D-1000 was appropriately Junkers G 24a WNr.931, the final production aircraft from Limhamn and as such originally registered as S-AABA in 1926. It had then been re-registered in Germany.[66] Weekly changes to the *deutschen Luftfahrzeugrolle* were published by the *RVM* in the *Nachrichten für Luftfahrer* (Notices to Airmen or NOTAM). For example the entry for the week beginning the 19 January 1929 *(Nachrichten für Luftfahrer 29/Nr.3)* showed, amongst the twenty entries, that Dietrich DP IX WNr.153 D-802 had been re-registered to the *DVS* where it was joined by the newly registered Arado SC II WNr.45 D-1542 and Arado W II WNr.48 D-1544, whilst Junkers W 33 D-1383 had been one of five aircraft destroyed and the Heinkel HD 21 WNr.7 D-677 had been re-engined with the Daimler D IIa.[67]

Paradoxically overall aircraft production in Germany had actually declined in the years following the Paris Air Agreements although the light aircraft market, dominated by such firms as the *Hanns Klemm Flugzeugbau* and the *Udet Flugzeugbau*, remained buoyant.[68] However the increasing complexity of the larger airliners made construction progressively more time-consuming and expensive, whilst the adherence by such firms as the *Junkers Flugzeugwerke, Dornier-Werke* and *Rohrbach Metall-Flugzeugbau* to modern all-metal construction techniques resulted in high unit costs which could not be reduced through worth-while production runs (See also 1C1 & 1C2).[69]

Type certification of new designs was the responsibility of the *Deutsche Versuchsanstalt für Luftfahrt (DVL)* at Berlin-Adlershof and it was this organisation that formed the basis for the *Eprobungsstelle Rechlin* which was established in 1925-26 to form the basis for a secret military test centre (See also 1C1).[70] In fact the testing of military prototypes and equipment had already begun

64   Ries 1977. In all 23 A 16 transports were built for airline use between 1924-26. Focke Wulf A 16b D-658 & 659 were registered to *Junkers Luftverkehr AG*, A 16a D-647 to *Bremer Luftverkehr AG* whilst A 16a D-671 was owned by *Luftverkehr AG Niedersachsen* - see Stroud 1966 pp.263-264 & Smith J.R. 1973 *Focke Wulf: An Aircraft Album* (hereafter cited as Smith 1973) pp.12-13.

65   *Flugzeuge, Verzeichnis der in die deutsche Luftfahrzeugrolle eingetragenen Flugzeuge* in RVM 1929.

66   *Construction and employment of G 23/G 24 aircraft from Dessau and Limhamm 2nd Construction Series* in Schmitt 1988 p.153. Construction of the G 24 in Sweden ceased in May 26. This source suggests that WNr.931 was re-registered in Germany as D-1000 in the same year. However a number of later aircraft types were entered in the 900-Serie - see also Ries 1977.

67   *Flugzeuge, Verzeichnis der in die deutsche Luftfahrzeugrolle eingetragenen Flugzeuge* in RVM 1929. Of interest was the continued existence of the wartime machines such as the LVG B III WNr.375 which was re-engined with the Daimler D II as D-1148. This aircraft was registered to the *Unterfrankische Sportflug GmbH* at Würzburg. New registrations were reported in the *Nachrichten für Luftfahrer* from the 1 Feb 28 – see Vogt Undated.

68   Vajda F.A. & Dancey P.1998 *German Aircraft Industry and Production 1933-1945* (hereafter cited as Vajda & Dancey 1998) p.9. Klemm would build 450 *Sportflugzeuge* during 1927-33, whilst *Udet* built 219 between 1921-26 - see also Herlin H. 1958 *Udet - eines Mannes Leben* p.123, Lange 1970 pp.307-314 & 357-359 and Ishoven van A. 1977 *The Fall of an Eagle: The Life of Fighter Ace Ernst Udet* pp.88-97.

69   *Table 3: German Aircraft Production, 1924-1929* in Hooton 1994 p.54, Vajda and Dancey 1998 p.9 & Stinton D. *The Structural Revolution* in Jarrett P. (Ed.) 1997 *Biplane to Monoplane: Aircraft development 1919-39* p.132-136. In the USA it was estimated that the introduction of all-metal aircraft increased total manufacturing costs by as much as 48% - see Holley I.B. 1964 *Buying Aircraft: Material Procurement for the Army Air Forces* US Army in World War II Special Studies p.20.

70   Beauvais H., Kossler K., Mayer M. and Regel C. 2002 *German Secret Flight Test Centres to 1945: Johannisthal, Lipetsk, Rechlin, Travemünde, Tarnewitz, Peenemunde-West* (hereafter cited as Beauvais et al 2002) pp.37-38 & 53-57. The *DVL's Abteilung M (Militärische)* consisted of *Dipl.Ing.*Wilhelm Degen, *Dr.*Karl Genthe, *Ing.*Bruno Gollhammer & *Dipl.Ing.*Schaper. The *DVL* carried out a great deal of applied research work on behalf of the German aircraft industry. It was led by *Dr.Ing.*Wilhelm Hoff from 1919 and *Dr.Ing.*Georg Madelung from 1926. It was divided into 5 major Branchs: *Aerodynamische* (Aerodynamics), *Statische* (Statistics), *Motoren* (Power plants), *Elektrotechnik und*

in 1925 at both Adlershof and the *Erprobungsstelle Staaken* although this work had of necessity to be shrouded in secrecy to escape the scrutiny of the *LGK*. The test programme from February to June 1925 included weapons testing of the Lubbe and GAST machine guns, variable pitch propellers, an experimental exhaust gas turbine and the evaluation Albatros L 70 *Aufklärer* (See also 1C5).[71] During the latter part of the decade type testing was carried out at both Staaken and Rechlin for landplanes and at Travemünde for seaplanes (See also 1C3). The three *Eprobungsstellen* were registered to the *Reichsverband der Deutschen Luftfahrtindustrie (RDL)*.[72]

FIGURE 1B-2 GERMAN AIRCRAFT PRODUCTION 1924 - 1932			
Year	Hooton	Vajda	Event
1924	248		German financial stability secured
1925	585	406	
1926	168		Paris Air Agreement May 1926
1927	301		
1928	355	409	Decline of German economy
1929	330	379	
1930		332	World Economic Recession
1931		310	World Economic Recession
1932		231	World Disarmament Conference

During 1926-32 Brandenburg promoted the growth of the indigenous aircraft industry through the provision of subsidies worth *RM* 321.22 million, this money being used to develop new aircraft and engines and also to procure new equipment. In some cases the *RVM* even bought shares in aircraft companies to provide them with investment capital.[73] Elements of this funding were also re-directed to support specific military programmes and in the 1928-29 fiscal year this funding totalled *RM* 3.38 million. In contrast the *Reichsheer* could devote very little of its budget to covert aircraft development and procurement. In fact during the period 1925-29 this averaged just *RM* 5.62 million annually (See also 1A3).[74] The contribution made by the *RVM* to the development of the aircraft industry was therefore of massive significance.

Brandenburg was particularly concerned about Germany's relatively weak aero-engine sector where the *BMW Flugmotorenbau GmbH (BMW)* at München-Allach and the *Junkers Motorenwerke AG* at Dessau were the only firms capable of making the powerful engines that were required for both *DLH's* advanced airliners and the *Reichswehr's* planned combat aircraft (See 1C3). As a short

Funkwesen (Electrical and Wireless) & *Pruf* (Testing). In 1928 some of the *DVL's* work was shown publicly at the *Berlin ILA (Internationale Luftfahrt Ausstellung)* - see Grey 1943 pp.122-123 & Lange 1970 pp.188-191.

71   *Test Programme 1.2.25-30.6.25 Bb.Nr.25/2.25.F BA/MA Freiburg, Document RM8v/3604* in Beauvais et al 2002 p.55 & 111. The planned test programme also included the Junkers J 28 *Jagdzweisitzer* but this did aircraft not get past the design stage; the Albatros L 70 was completed in 1924/25 and was powered by a Napier Lion. Only prototypes were completed - see Lange 1970 p.159.

72   Beauvais et al 2002 p.54-55.

73   Smith J.R. 1971 *Messerschmitt: An Aircraft Album* p.8. The *RVM* had shares in the *Bayerische Flugzeugbau* at Augsburg. Brandenburg's policies appear to have had cross party support from successive *Reichsministers (RVM)*: Wilhelm Koch *(DNVP)*, Theodor von Guerard *(Zentrum)*, Georg Schatzel *(BVP)*, Adam Stegerwald *(Zentrum)* & Theodor von Guerard *(Zentrum)* during 1927-31 – see *Reichsverkehrsministerium* in www.wikipedia.org.

74   Hooton 1994 pp.74-75.

term solution Brandenburg advocated the import and licence production of proven aero-engines from abroad and in 1927/28 *BMW* secured the rights to manufacture both the Pratt and Whitney Wasp and Hornet radials.[75] At the same time the Berlin based firm of *Siemens und Halske AG* opted to build the equally successful Gnome-Rhône (Bristol) Jupiter.[76] Together with the indigenous BMW VI, these foreign engines would be widely employed by *Deutsche Luft Hansa* and by the *Reichswehr* in the early thirties (See 1C2). To ensure a more advantageous longer term position Brandenburg then placed a development contract with *BMW* for a new 30 litre engine in the 1,000 hp class, this being followed by a contract for *Junkers* to develop an intermediate 20 litre engine.[77] Similarly support was given to Junkers for the development of a heavy oil engine in response to a *DLH* requirement (See 1C2 & 1C4). The first type to use this type of engine commercially was the Junkers F 24, a single-engine conversion of the successful G 24 airliner. These were used primarily by *DLH* for freight transport (See 1D2).[78]

Throughout the twenties the officials and employees of the *Luftfahrtabteilung* had worked to facilitate the growth of commercial air transport through the development of an increasingly comprehensive ground infrastructure. Nowhere was this more obvious than in the case of the new international airport at Berlin-Tempelhof which was officially opened in October 1923 as a replacement for Berlin-Staaken as the national hub (See also 1D2).[79] Over the next five years the airfield was extensively re-developed with financial assistance being provided by the *RVM*. A large new terminal building was erected on the northern perimeter of the circular flying field, this being flanked on either side by two massive hangars.[80] In 1928 the newly completed terminal handled 31,451 passengers, 250,591 kgs of post and parcels, and 894,783 kgs of freight and packages in the course of 9,916 aircraft movements, the vast majority of these being carried by the three main German airlines: principally *DLH* together with *Nordbayerische Verkehrsflug* and the *Deutsch-Russische Luftverkehrs-gesellschaft*.[81] The *Luftfahrtabteilung* classified Germany's civil aviation facilities into three categories: *Flughäfen* (Airports) of which there were very few,

75   Gunston B. 1995 *World Encyclopaedia of Aero Engines* (hereafter cited as Gunston 1995) p.26 & pp.118-120. By 1929 both the Wasp and Hornet radials were important engines with a string of world records. They were in series production for both the *USAAC* & *USN* and powered 90% of American commercial transports. In the end the smaller 13.4 Litre Wasp was not manufactured in Germany. See also Gersdorff von K. and Grasmann K. 1985 *Die Deutsche Luftfahrt 2: Flugmotoren und Strahltriebwerke* (hereafter cited as Gersdorff and Grasmann 1985) pp.53-56.

76   Lange 1970 pp.423-425, Gunston 1995 p.32 & pp.30-31 and Lumsden A.S.C. 1994 *British Piston Aero-Engines and their Aircraft* pp.93-94. The Bristol Jupiter was eventually licence built by 17 different firms powering a staggering 262 different aircraft types. See also Gersdorff and Grasmann 1985 pp.47-49.

77   Suchenwirth 1968 pp.22-23. The *RVM* later awarded *Daimler-Benz* a contract for a 30-litre engine. With the exception of its very large LOF 6 diesel engines for use aboard the *LZ 129 & 130, Daimler-Benz* was mainly engaged in automotive design and manufacture at this time - see also Gunston 1995 p.49 & Vajda and Dancey 1998 p.235.

78   Stroud 1966 pp.306-307, Gersdorff and Grasmann 1985 pp.88-91 & Schmitt 1988 pp.206-208.

79   Hooks 1999 pp.57-60. Staaken was situated 16-18 kms to the west of Berlin's city centre, whereas Tempelhof was just 6 kms to the south. Tempelhof opened on the 8 Oct 23. Following the formation of *DLH*, Staaken became that airline's main maintenance facility - see Zapf J. 2001 *Flugplatze der Luftwaffe 1934-1945 und was davon ubrig blieb Bd.1 Berlin & Brandenburg* (hereafter cited as Zapf 2001) p.56.

80   Zapf 2001 pp.54-56. A contemporary author described the development of Tempelhof in most favourable terms: *"With the coming of the Reichsverkehrsministerium it was made the great central air-station of Germany and one might say the great aerial air-junction of Europe. During 1915-26 buildings of impressive size and of pleasing aspect were built, and they were formally opened on the April 9th, 1927. At that time it was quite the most complete airport in the world. One excellent feature about it was the enormous open-air restaurant arranged on a sloping terrace right alongside the gates through which passengers passed to or from the machines. And the machines were always drawn up opposite the terrace. One could go and sit there in the sun and have a good meal, or sit over glasses of beer or coffee for hours on end, for a few pence. It was a very sound way of encouraging air-mindedness among the people. And it did so. Compared with it, or out-of-the-way, dirty, uncomfortable, inhospitable Terminal Aerodrome at Croydon was a tragedy of incompetence."* - quoted from Grey 1943 *The Luftwaffe* pp.117-118 Faber and Faber Ltd.

81   *Anhang "Statistik des planmassigen deutschen Luftverkehrs im Kalenderjahr 1928" in RVM 1929.*

Verkehrslandeplätze (Commercial Landing Grounds) of which there were nearly fifty in operation by 1927 and *Notlandeplätze* (Emergency Landing Grounds) of which there were 139 in operation in May 1929.[82]

FIGURE 1B-3 PRINCIPAL FLUGHÄFEN AND VERKEHRSLANDEPLÄTZE 1928					
Airport	Province	Passengers		Movements	
		German	Foreign	German	Foreign
Berlin-Tempelhof	Brandenburg	8,744	1,172	27,573	3,878
Bremen-Neulanderfeld	Nord Sachsen	2,116	360	4,261	1,035
Breslau-Gandau	Schlesien	2,727		5,428	
Chemnitz	Sachsen	2,457		3,525	
Dortmund	Nordrhein-Westfalen		4,868		5,191
Dresden-Heller	Sachsen	2,714	678	4,687	1,312
Düsseldorf-Lohausen	Nordrhein-Westfalen	2,450			2,576
Erfurt	Thüringen	4,184		5,597	
Essen-Mülheim	Nordrhein-Westfalen	7,087	408	7,685	76
Frankfurt am Main	Hessen	6,392	146	14,904	304
Halle-Nietleben	Sachsen	7,457		13,477	
Hamburg-Fühlsbuttel	Nord Sachsen	3,257	1,869	9,275	3,430
Hannover	Nord Sachsen	6,712	328	10,064	125
Kassel-Waldau	Hessen	2,616	270	2,815	138
Köln-Butzweilerhof	Nordrhein-Westfalen	5,909	1,842	11,934	4,406
Lübeck-Travemünde	Schleswig-Holstein	2,104	4	3,269	8
Mannheim-Stadt	Bad Württemberg	3,057		2,425	
München-Oberweisenfeld	Bayern	3,900	593	12,743	2,023
Nürnberg	Bayern	4,116	1,226	6,171	232
Plauen	Vogtland	2,130		2,303	
Stuttgart-Böblingen	Bad Württemberg	3,744	291	9,343	477
Statistics show movements by German & Foreign registered aircraft and the passengers carried by each category.					

82   *Verzeichnis der deutschen Notlandeplatze nach dem Stande vom 1.Mai 1929* in RVM 1929. This source provided detailed co-ordinates for each landing ground, together with geographical details, airfield dimensions and its suitability for aircraft of different types.

The high point insofar as commercial aviation was concerned was 1928. Thereafter passenger numbers fell sharply from 120,700 to 96,800 persons in 1929, whilst freight traffic fell slightly from 2,164 tons to 2,070 tons. Postal services increased a little before falling more significantly in 1930.[83] As the *RVM's* budgetary situation worsened in response to the developing economic crisis there had to be a commensurate reduction in *DLH's* subsidies which were halved in 1929, whilst there was also a reduction in the overall number of commercial airfields within Germany from sixty-six to just fifty-two by the end of the year (See 1D2).[84]

The *RVM's* support for a nation wide wireless telegraphy and direction finding network seems to have been less effected by these developments. By the late-twenties a network of light and wireless beacons had already been established. These had been influenced by earlier developments in the USA where a federal airways system had been constructed with a system of ground based lights to facilitate nocturnal navigation.[85] *Luftfahrtfeuer*, later *Leuchtfeuer* (light beacons), worked in the same way as nautical lighthouses with an illuminated signal being shown that allowed the flight crew to fix their position. In Germany one of the first illuminated routes was the 148 km *Nachtflugstrecke* (Night Air Route) between Berlin-Tempelhof and Leipzig-Schkeuditz in Sachsen.[86] *Funkfeuer* (radio beacons) on the other hand were non-directional radio beacons (NDBs) which transmitted a morse identifier on a specific wavelength that was followed by a longer aural transmission for D/F purposes. This facilitated radio navigation above cloud and in bad weather when light beacons were not visible.[87] The *Funkfeuer* was a relatively short range navigational aid (32 kms) and initially their use was confined to the major terminal airfields *(Map I-2)*.[88]

To detect the signal from such beacons the aircraft had to be equipped with a direction finding loop which was rotated by the *Bordfunker* (wireless operator) to achieve the strongest signal. A bearing could then be taken and the aircraft flown along that heading to over fly the *Funkfeuer*. Alternatively if two or more beacons could be identified the aircraft's position could be fixed by triangulation.[89] The development of airborne wireless and direction finding equipment was energetically pursued by both *Lorenz* and *Telefunken* from 1925, the installation of a 70 W-Größ-station Spez.205 F on Dornier *Merkur* aircraft employed on the Berlin-Königsberg night service

83   *ICAO and Statistisches Jahrbuche für das Deutsches Reich Band 1928-33* in *App.I Civil Aviation* in NID 1945 p.623.

84   *App.I Civil Aviation* in NID 1945 pp.622-623 & Hooton 1994 p.53. In 1928 the *RVM's* budget was *RM* 55.5 m; in 1929 it was only *RM* 42.8 m. Faced with financial ruin *DLH* managers had appealed to the *RVM* to resist the halving of subsidies in 1929. Brandenburg responded by suggesting that they "buy" their own deputies in the *Reichstag* to offset the political pressure of the socialist anti-aviation lobby - see Irving 1973 pp.20-25.

85   Hirst M. *Sophisticated Systems* in Jarrett P. (Ed.) 1997 (hereafter cited as Hirst in Jarrett (Ed.) 1997) pp.160-161. On the 29 Jan 29 the first airway to be lit stretched between New York & Los Angeles. Thereafter development had been rapid. Light beacons were located at intervals of 24-48 kms and by 1933 there were 1,550 light beacons along 28,800 kms of airway - see Naylor and Ower 1930 p.246.

86   *Luftfahrfeuer der Nachtflugstrecke Berlin-Schkeuditz in 29/38, dated 21 Sep 29* in RVM 1929. Each of the five lights along this 148 km route used the same signal: Blink (0.2 sec), Pause (2.8 sec).

87   Hirst in Jarrett (Ed.) 1997 pp.161-163 & Wakefield K.1999 *Pfadfinger: Luftwaffe Pathfinder Operations over Britain 1940-44* (hereafter cited as Wakefield 1999) p.5. The first practical use of radio beacons also occurred in the USA where the "Radio Range" system was introduced to back up the light beacons on certain airways. Each radio beacon emitted two focused slightly overlapping energy lobes, frequency modulated to produce either the Morse letter A (dot-dash) for left of track or N (dash-dot) for right of track. Where the two lobes overlapped the AN modulation produced a continuous tone in the pilot's earphones thus indicating he was on track - see also Naylor and Ower 1930 p.246.

88   *Funkverkehrsbezirke der deutschen Flughafenfunkstellen, 6 Apr 29* in RVM 29/15.

89   Desouetter Undated pp.157-159. *NDBs* continued as a widely employed radio navigation aid into the 21st. Century. They are low powered 10/200W transmitters in the 200-1750 kc/s frequency band. NDBs for over-water tracking are more powerful and may give a useful range of up to 740 kms. However they are affected by precipitation, diurnal changes - dawn and dusk being particular problem times when the signal can fade, atmospheric disturbances - particularly thunderstorms, and the local effect of a coastline or mountain range - see Trenkle F. 1986 *Bordfunkgerate - Vom Funksender zum Bordradar" Die deutsche Luftfahrt 7* (hereafter cited as Trenkle 1986) p. & Wakefield 1999 pp.83-84.

in 1926 being an early example of its operational use.[90] By the 26 October 1929 there were 142 wireless equipped aircraft in Germany: *DLH* (85), *DVS* (26), *Luftdienst GmbH* (25) and the remainder to the *RDL*.[91] Germany was a signatory of the *Betriebsordnung für den internationalen Flugfunkdienst*, an international agreement that sought to standardise European wireless services for aviation and during the autumn and winter of 1929 the *Nachrichten für Luftfahrer* contained a great deal of information on ground based radio aids, the wireless routes and the new Q-Codes for the expeditious transmission of weather and flight safety information.[92]

FIGURE 1B-4 WIRELESS DIRECTION FINDING STATIONS (FUNKPEILANLANGEN) APRIL 1929			
Established	**Code**	**Planned**	**Code**
Hamburg	ddm	Breslau	ddu
Hannover	ddv	Stettin	ddn
Dortmund	dde	Stolp	ddj
Frankfurt	ddf	Königsberg	ddw
Erfurt	dda	Halle-Leipzig	ddl
Stuttgart	ddt	Hof	ddo
Nürnberg	ddg	Köln	ddk
München	ddp		
Dresden	ddr		
Berlin	ddx		

The provision of accurate meteorological forecasts had always been an important service for aviators. The use of aircraft to take temperature and humidity readings in the lower atmosphere was resumed in 1921 when the *ILUK* permitted the employment of a few de-militarised Fokker D.VII fighters and Rumpler high altitude photo-reconnaissance aircraft for this purpose by the *Deutsche Seewarte* at Hamburg-Fühlsbuttel and by the *Aeronautisches Observatorium Lindenburg (AOL)* at Berlin-Adlershof, later Berlin-Staaken.[93] From 1926 additional TEMP (Temperature & Pressure) ascents were made by the *Rhön-Rossitten-Gesellschaft* at Darmstadt, whilst in the latter part of the

90   Trenkle 1986 p.24.
91   *Betriebsordnung für den internationalen Flugfunkdienst nebst Ausführungbestimmungen für den deutschen Flugfernmeldediesnst Anhang IV* in 29/43 RVM 1929. In the absence of a letter based registration system each aircraft was given a five character wireless identification code eg. the veteran Friedrichshafen FF.49 D-49 was given the code *danap*, whilst Junkers W 33d D-1741, the most recent aircraft to be registered at the time of this survey, was given the code *dangd*.
92   *Betriebsordnung für den internationalen Flugfunkdienst 29/40* in RVM 1929. The other six signatories to this agreement were: Belgium, France, Great Britain, the Netherlands, Switzerland and Czechoslovakia. The adoption of common wireless procedures was a massive step forward in the development of international air transport. For example an airliner flying from Berlin to Croydon would route via the following *Funkfeuer*: Berlin (ddx), Hannover (ddv), Dortmund (ddc), Rotterdam (phr), & Croydon (ged) - see *Betriebsordnung für den internationalen Flugfunkdienst 29/50* in RVM 1929. The Q-Codes were a form of wireless shorthand that also overcame aspects of foreign languages at a time when Morse was used for all transmissions eg *QRA What is the name of your wireless station?, QRF Where have you come from?* - see also *Anhang XI Zusammenstellung der im Funkverkehr anzuwendenden Abkurzungen* in 29/44 RVM 1929 & *Betriebsordnung für den internationalen Flugfunkdienst* in 29/52 RVM 1929.
93   Kington J.A. and Selinger F. 2006 *Wekusta: Luftwaffe Meteorological Reconnaissance Units and Operations 1938-1945* (hereafter cited as Kington and Selinger 2006) p.11.

twenties *Wetterflugstellen* were also established by the *RVM* at München (Bayern) and Königsberg (Ostpreussen).[94] To co-ordinate the work of these weather stations the *Luftfahrtabteilung* financed the establishment of the *Zentral für Wetterflug (ZfW)* in Berlin on the 1 April 1929. A variety of aircraft types were inevitably used for this important work including obsolete military aircraft and newer types such as the Junkers A 20 and A 35 but in December 1930 the *RVM* supported a request by *Dr.*Kurt Wegener of the *ZfW* for a specialist meteorological aircraft. This would result in the design and construction of the unique Focke Wulf A 47, which first flew in June 1932.[95]

The key role of the *RVM* in the development of the German aircraft industry can perhaps be best seen in its financial support for the initial operation of the remarkable Junkers G.38. This large capacity transport had its origins in the even more ambitious J 1000 project of 1923-24 which was built around *Prof.*Junkers' patented flying wing design.[96] Work on the G.38 began with private finance in 1927, the prototype beginning flight trials on the 10 November 1929 when Junkers held the first of many press days to publicise what was then the world's largest landplane *(Photo 1B-5)*. Of all-metal construction the G.38 was of conventional configuration with a shoulder-mounted wing, fuselage and tailplane. However the wing was immense in span, chord and thickness. The four engines and four of the aircraft's nineteen passengers were totally enclosed by this single structure which also provided work stations for the *Bordmechaniker* (flight mechanics) who were able to service both the inboard Junkers L 55 and outboard Junkers L 8 engines in flight. Appropriately registered D-2000 the G.38a began its acceptance trials in March 1930 and quickly established a number of speed records with a measured payload of 5,000 kgs. Prestigious publicity flights within Germany and throughout Europe followed with most of these costs being borne by the *RVM* on account of Junkers' increasingly parlous financial position.[97]

As with so many innovatory designs the G.38 was never destined to be a commercial success (See also 1D2). Instead it would be the Ju 52/3m that would eventually see the *Junkers Flugzeug-und Motorenwerke AG* emerge as the most successful European aircraft manufacturing firm of its era.[98] This variant of the basic Junkers design owed much to the influence of Erhard Milch and his engineering staff at *DLH*.[99] Milch was also the favoured candidate for the position of *Staatssekretär für die Luftfahrt* (State Secretary for Aviation) when this position was created in February 1933 despite the more obvious candidacy of Brandenburg (See 2A2 & 2B1). The reasons for this are not entirely clear. *MinRat.*Willy Fisch later commented: *"Both as a person (an excellent comrade!) and as an organiser, Brandenburg was outstanding. Between 1925 and 1933 he covered himself with glory... he was reliable, cautious, and skilful worker as well as an outstanding promoter of civilian aviation and sport flying".*[100] Moreover Milch did not really want a Government post being very happy with his position as Managing Director of *Luft Hansa*.[101] He proposed that both Brandenburg and

94   Kington and Seeliger 2006 pp.11-12.

95   Wagner W. 1980 *Kurt Tank - Konstrukteur und Testpilot bei Focke Wulf" Die deutsche Luftfahrt 1* p.43-44. The Focke Wulf A 47 had begun life on the drawing boards of the Albatros concern. *Prof.*Heinrich Focke's contribution to the design was the incorporation of the *"Zanonia"* wing which made the aircraft virtually unspinnable - see also Smith 1973 p.32-33.

96   Stroud J. 1984 'Die Junkers Größflugzeuge' in *Air Enthusiast* No.24 (hereafter cited as Stroud 1984) pp.32-34 & Schmitt 1988 pp.88-90.

97   Stroud 1984 pp.34-39 & 78 & Schmitt 1988 pp.125-129. By 1931 Junkers was on the verge of bankruptcy such was the cumulative effects of the economic downturn. However a second aircraft, the G.38b, was commissioned by *DLH* as the type had proved an interesting novelty with the fare paying public. The G.38b had seats for 34 passengers and was registered as D-2500. It was used on a number of different European routes from Jul 32.

98   Nowarra H.J. 1987 *Aircraft & Legend: Junkers Ju 52* pp.17-21, 26-42 & 51-64.

99   Irving 1973 p.25 & Schmitt 1988 p.172.

100   Interview of MinDirektor a.D.Wilhelm Fisch by Prof.Richard Suchenwirth, 20 Dec 1957 in Suchenwirth 1968 p.10.

101   Suchenwirth R. 1969 *Command and Leadership in the German Air Force* USAF Historical Studies No.174 p.18-21.

*KonAdm.a.D.*Rudolf Lahs, the *Präsident des RDL*, were more appropriate candidates. However Lahs had been unenthusiastic.[102] Adolf Hitler, the new *Reichskanzler*, clearly favoured Milch, probably on account of his support for the *NSDAP* during the 1932 election campaign when *DLH* airliners flew Party candidates and officials some 35,000 kms free of charge, and it seems likely that this was the deciding factor in the decision not to place Brandenburg as head of the emerging *RLM* (See 2A2).[103] Instead Brandenburg was offered and accepted the post of *Leiter der Abteilung Kraftfahr- und Landstrassenwesen* (Leader of the Motor Vehicle and Highways Branch) within the *RVM*. For his services to aviation he would later be given the honorary rank of *Luftwaffe Oberst* but in many respects this was scant recognition for the massive contribution that he had made to the development of German aviation during the Weimar period.[104]

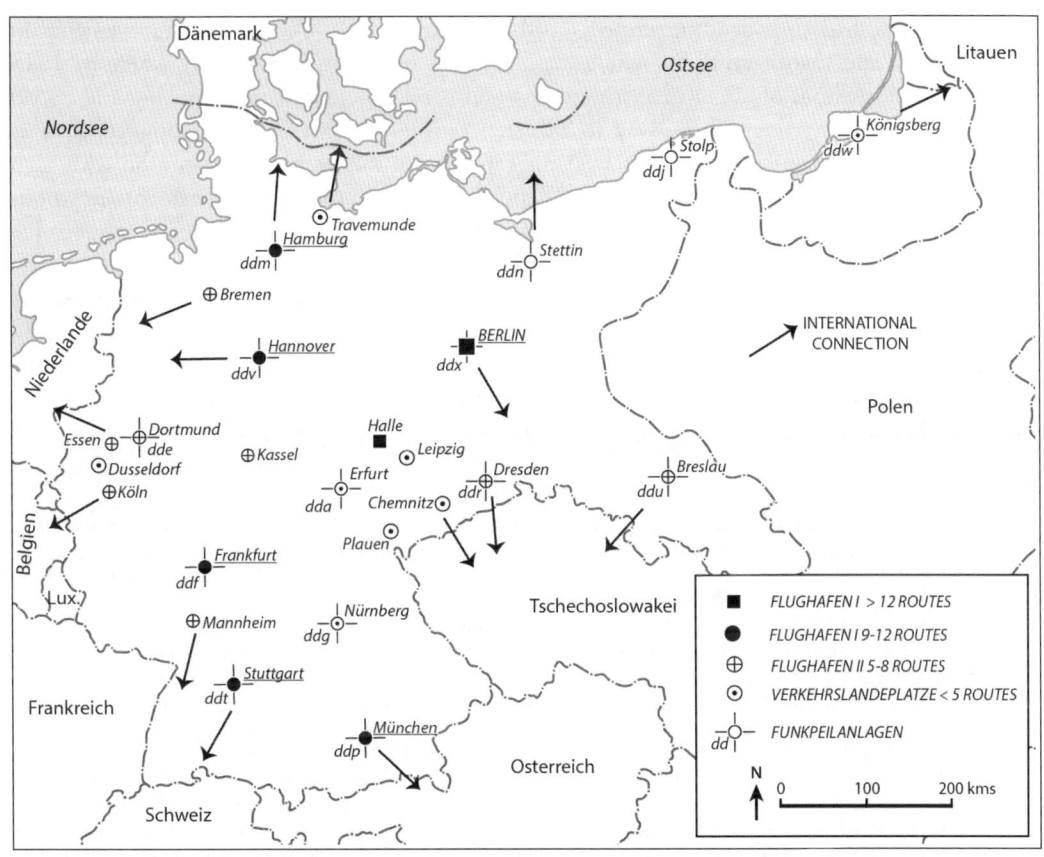

I-2   *Funkpeilanlagen* and main commercial *Flughäfen* of the German Reich Apr 1929

    Milch was in fact concerned amongst other things of Göring's earlier morphine addiction - see Irving 1973 p.29.

102 Heinkel 1956 p.154.This source states that Lahs had been Göring's preferred candidate but the Admiral had been unenthusiastic.

103 Hermann 1943 pp.54-55, Irving 1973 p.29 & Sweeting C.G. 2001 *Hitler's Squadron: The Führer's Personal Aircraft and Transport Unit 1933-45* pp.10-14.

104 Service record for Ernst Brandenburg in www.frontflieger.de. And Wikipedia.de He was given the rank *Min. Direktor (Char)* and decorated with the *RK.KVK.m.Schwerten* - see www.feldgrau.com. He was replaced by *MinDir.* Willy Fisch as *Ltr.d.Abteilung I Luftverkehr* which was formed on the 30 Jan 33 from the *Luftfahrtabteilung* – see Vogt Undated.

1C1

Clandestine Military Developments 1919-1926

The Great War had provided the impetus and the pressure for spectacular improvements in aircraft design and manufacture. Nowhere was this more true than in Germany where by 1918 the traditional methods of aircraft construction: wood, steel-tube, struts, wire bracing and doped fabric, had already starting to give way to all-metal cantilever construction.[1] Designers such as Hugo Junkers and Claudius Dornier were at the forefront of this technical innovation with such designs as the Junkers D.I and CL.I and the Zeppelin D.I.[2] Meanwhile improvements in wood-working technology by designers at LFG-Roland and Pfalz had resulted in advanced monocoque fuselage structures using plywood skins over wooden frames.[3]

Initially some factories continued to fulfil existing orders for military aircraft. For example the *Siemens-Schuckert* completed the manufacture of the last of 119 D-IV fighters, whilst both *BFW* and the *Hannoverische Waggonfabrik* completed batches of 200 aircraft.[4] In other cases attempts were made to modify existing military types into commercial transports. Good examples were the AEG J-II, Friedrichshafen G.IIIa, Junkers J 10, LVG C-*Serie*, Rumpler C-*Serie* and Sablatnig P-I

---

1   Munson K. *The Biplane's Fall from Favour* in Jarrett P. (Ed.) 1997 *Biplane to Monoplane: Aircraft development 1919-39* pp.15-16. To illustrate the proclivity of German designers no less than 167 different types of fighter aircraft had been built during 1914-18: 106 biplanes, 15 triplanes (or more wings) & 46 monoplanes - see Kosin R. 1983 *Die Entwicklung der deutschen Jagdflugzeuge* (hereafter cited as Kosin 1983) p.43.

2   Kosin 1983 p.42, Nowarra H.J. 1980 *Die Verbotenen Flugzeuge 1921-1935 – Die getarnte Luftwaffe* (hereafter cited as Nowarra 1980) pp.68-70 & 76-78, Dornier 1983 *Dornier: Die Chronik des ältesten deutschen Flugzeugwerks* (hereafter cited as Dornier 1983) p.78 & Schmitt G. 1988 *Hugo Junkers and his Aircraft* (hereafter cited as Schmitt 1988) pp.23-38. *Prof.*Junkers' enthusiasm for all metal aircraft had begun with the construction of the J 1 in 1915. In 1916 iron gave way to the new material duralumin which was used on the uncompleted J 3 and the successful J 4. The J 4 first flew at Döberitz on the 28 Jan 17 and formed the basis of the J-I of which 210 were manufactured as infantry support aircraft - see Lamberton W.M. 1962 *Reconnaissance and Bomber Aircraft of the 1914-1918 War* (hereafter cited as Lamberton 1962) pp.150-151. The J 7 was a single seat fighter which first flew in Oct 17. It was further developed into the J 9 which entered production as the D.I after Mar 18. However only 41 examples reached the front where they were used operationally - see Lamberton W.M. 1960 *Fighter Aircraft of the 1914-1918 War* (hereafter cited as Lamberton 1960) pp.146-147. The CL.I also grew out of the J 7. The J 8 formed the basis for the improved J 10 which first flew on the 4 May 18. However only 47 of these advanced close support aircraft were completed in 1918 - see Lamberton 1960 pp.144-145 & Schmitt 1988 pp.37-38. The Zeppelin D.I was an equally radical departure from accepted design philosophy. Unfortunately a structural weakness in the wing attachments led to the death of *Hptm.*Wilhelm Reinhard, the *Kdr.JG 1*, during the Adlershof trials on the 3 Jul 18 and the type was rejected - see Lamberton 1960 pp.118-119. Duralumin was an aluminium based alloy with copper (3.7-4.7%), magnesium (0.6-1%), manganese (0.2-0.4%) and silicon (0.3-0.7%) together with traces of iron, titanium and zinc - see Schneider H. 1940 *Flugzeug-Typenbuch: Handbuch der Deutschen Luftfahrt und Zubehor-Industrie Hauptausgabe A 1939/40* p.556.

3   Lamberton 1960 pp.148-159 & Kosin 1983 pp.47-48. Both *Roland and Pfalz* used plywood skins on a succession of single and two seat fighters and reconnaissance aircraft during 1916-18.

4   Hooton E.R. 1994 *Phoenix Triumphant: The Rise and Rise of the Luftwaffe* (hereafter cited as Hooton 1994) p.19. *Junkers* completed 37 CL.I close support aircraft; however it has not been possible to substantiate a claim that *Zeppelin* built the six-engined R-VIII - see Lamberton 1962 p.154.

(See 1D2).[5] Purely commercial projects followed. Examples include the Albatros L 57 (160 hp Daimler D IIIa), Dornier L 1 *Delphin* (185 hp BMW IIIa), the LFG V 13 *Strela-See* (185 hp BMW IIIa or 200 hp Benz Bz IV) and Sablatnig P-III (200 hp Benz Bz IV or 260 hp Maybach Mb IVa).[6] At Dessau *Professor* Junkers had called for two new types to be developed specifically to meet the projected civil markets for air transport. From these projects would emerge the superb F 13 (230 hp Junkers L 2, later 320 hp BMW IV & 310 hp Junkers L 5) all-metal four seat transport aircraft which first flew on the 25 June 1919 and which was produced in quantity.[7] Less fortunate was the remarkable Zeppelin E.4/20, a four engine (245 hp Maybach) high wing monoplane which had been designed by *Dr.Ing.*Adolf Rohrbach for use on the projected Berlin-Friedrichshafen route. The arrival of the *Interalliierte Luftfahrt-Überwachungs-Kommission (ILUK)* in 1920 led to an immediate suspension of all test flying by this large aircraft (See 1A2). Later in November 1922, at the Commission's orders, the prototype was destroyed.[8]

The restrictive practices of the *ILUK* effectively shut down much of the German aircraft industry. Only 95 aircraft were produced during 1920, 74 of these being manufactured by Junkers at Dessau.[9] By the beginning of 1921 many of the famous names in German aviation had closed their doors or had made the transfer to other types of manufacturing; *AEG, Aviatik, Halberstadt, Hannover, LVG, Rumpler* and *Siemens-Schuckert* had all ceased aircraft manufacture.[10] Other German designers and technicians had been driven abroad, either to work for foreign firms or to establish foreign subsidiaries where German designs could be manufactured and sold.[11] Following his decision to destroy his innovative Gs I twin-engine (260 hp Maybach Mb IVa) flying boat at Kiel in 1920 Claudius Dornier established an Italian subsidiary, the *Construzioni Meccaniche Aeronautiche SA (CMASA)* at the Marina di Pisa in 1922, specifically to manufacture his larger G I flying boat.[12] The first Dornier Do J *Wal* (360 hp Rolls Royce Eagle or 300 hp Hispano Suiza) was completed by *CMASA* in 1923 and over the next decade 150 aircraft of this type were built in Italy for world-wide employment *(Photo 1C-1)*.[13] Another German designer who established a foreign subsidiary at this

5   Stroud J.1966 *European Transport Aircraft since 1910* (hereafter cited as Stroud 1966) pp.218-219, 277-278, 293-294, 347-349 & 363-366 & Jackson R. 1983 *The Sky their Frontier: The Story of the World's Pioneer Airlines and Routes 1920-40* p.102. This was common practice in France and Britain. A number of Handley Page 0/400 and Airco DH 4 bombers were modified for the air mail and passenger transport role for use by the *RAF* during the Versailles Treaty negotiations and for communications duties with the British Army of Occupation in the Rheinland - see Roberston B. 1978 *The RAF: A Pictorial History* pp.34-35.

6   Stroud 1966 p.221, pp.234-237, 343-345 & 366-368. See also Nowarra 1980 pp.88-89 & Dornier 1983 p.81.

7   Stroud 1966 pp.294-300, Nowarra 1980 pp.92-94 & Schmitt 1988 pp.42-47 & p.66. *Junkers* called a meeting of his senior staff on the 11 Nov 18 to cancel all further work on military projects and concentrate the Company's efforts entirely on the design and manufacture of civil air transports. Some 12 F 13 aircraft were completed in 1919, these being followed by a further 80 in 1920-21. Thereafter production fluctuated with good years in 1923-24. In all around 370 examples of the F 13 were completed between 1919 and 1932, a third (110) of these being registered to German operators.

8   Stroud 1966 pp.357-358 & Imrie A. 1973 'The Staaken E./420' in *Aircraft Illustrated* Vol.6 No.4 pp.140-143. Work on the projected Junkers JG 1 also ceased - see Schmitt 1988 p.88.

9   Vajda F.A. & Dancey P.1998 *German Aircraft Industry and Production 1933-1945* (hereafter cited as Vajda & Dancey 1998) p.9. See also Hertel W. Dipl.Ing.GenIng.a.D.1955 *Procurement in the German Air Force* USAF Historical Studies No.170 (hereafter cited as Hertel 1955) pp.1-2.

10   Hooton 1994 p.35.

11   Grey C.G. 1943 *The Luftwaffe* (hereafter cited as Grey 1943) p.86 & 95. Many German technicians moved to the USA where they became some of the brightest stars in the California Technical University (Caltech). See also Hermann 1943 *The Rise and Fall of the Luftwaffe* (hereafter cited as Hermann 1943) pp.37-41 & Ries K. 1970 *Luftwaffe Bd.1 Die Maulwurfe 1919-1935* (hereafter cited as Ries 1970) pp.24-25.

12   Stroud 1966 pp.233-234. The Dornier Gs I first flew on the 31 Jul 19. Intended for commercial operation by the Swiss *Ad Astra Aero* firm the design had also attracted interest from both the Netherlands and Sweden. However under pressure from the *ILUK* for the aircraft to be surrendered to them, *Dornier* elected to its destruction at Kiel on the 25 Apr 20 - see Dornier 1983 p.80.

13   Stroud 1966 pp.239-243 & Nowarra 1980 pp.90-91. The Do J was built by *CMASA* & *Piaggio* (Italy), *Kawasaki*

time was *Dr.Ing.*Rohrbach. In 1922 he set up the *Rohrbach Metall-Flugzeugbau GmbH* in Berlin, but all production of his large metal aircraft was assigned to a Danish subsidiary: the *Rohrbach Metall Aeroplan Co. A/S* in Copenhagen.[14]

Paradoxically the *ILUK's* laudable efforts to neutralise Germany's capacity to develop military aircraft were to an extent negated by the covert activities of some erstwhile allies.[15] As latecomers to military aeronautics both Japan and the USA were keen to obtain technical information and know how from the Germans.[16] Denied access to a German military airship the US Military Commission put pressure on their British and French contemporaries to allow the *Luftschiffbau Zeppelin* to design and manufacture a new large capacity commercial vessel for employment by the US Navy (*USN*).[17] After much argument and deliberation this proposal was finally agreed in December 1921. The result was the LZ126 (Five 400 hp Maybach VL 1) which was completed in August 1924 and delivered to the *USN* at Lakehurst Naval Air Station on the 15 October 1924.[18] The *USN* was also very interested in another area of German expertise: the design of small submarine-borne reconnaissance aircraft. In 1917 Ernst Heinkel, a young designer with the *Hansa und Brandenburgische Flugzeugwerke*, had designed the W.20 for use aboard the *U-139* and *U-155 Klassen*. The W 20/2 had been moderately successful although never used operationally.[19] Following the armistice *Oblt.d.Res.a.D.*Friedrich Christiansen had brought the idea to the attention of the US Naval authorities in Berlin and the result was a secret contract for two new submarine-borne scouts. These were built covertly at the *Caspar-Werke AG* at Travemünde and delivered as the U-1 (62 hp Siemens Sh 4) despite the activities of the Allied Inspection teams. It would seem that Christiansen was also responsible for selling a further two examples to the Imperial Japanese Navy as the U-2 (*IJN*).[20]

(Japan), the *Construcciones Aeronauticas SA* (Spain) & *Aviolanda* (Netherlands) before production returned to Friedrichshafen in 1932 - see also Dornier 1983 p.87 & pp.96-97.

14   Stroud 1966 p.357.

15   Grey 1943 pp.89-90, Mason H M, 1973 *The Rise of the Luftwaffe 1918-1940* (hereafter cited as Mason 1973) pp.114-116 & Hooton 1994 p.33.

16   Swanborough G. and Bowers P.M. 1989 *United States Military Aircraft since 1909* p.694. In 1919 the US Military shipped no less than 347 surrendered German aircraft to the USA. Some were used for experimental work at McCook Field but many of the 142 Fokker D.VII fighters were used by the USAAS & USMC as second line fighters and fighter trainers. In Britain a number of German types had been evaluated at the Aeroplane Experimental Establishment (Home) Martlesham Heath and at other establishments such as Farnborough (Royal Aeronautical Establishment) & Pulham (Airship Experimental Establishment) - see Mason T. 1993 *British Flight Testing: Martlesham Heath 1920-1939* (hereafter cited as Mason 1993) p.199. Types evaluated at Martlesham in 1920-22 included the Fokker D.VIII, Roland D-Vlb & Junkers J 10. The airships L-64 & L-71 were surrendered to Britain - see Chamberlain G. 1984 *Airships - Cardington: A history of Cardington airship station and its role in world airship development* (hereafter cited as Chamberlain 1984) p.85.

17   Grey 1943 pp.88-90 & Chamberlain 1984 pp.98-106 & p.110. All the surviving airships had been destroyed in the naval mutinies of 1918 or by the *ILUK*. The French authorities were particularly keen to see the destruction of *Zeppelin's* Friedrichshafen works. Britain was not supportive of the American proposal as it had already agreed to supply a new airship (the Royal Airship Works R 38) to the *USN*. However in Aug 21 the R 38 was lost over Hull and in Dec 21 the American request for a new German commercial airship was agreed by the Allies as part of Germany's war reparations - see also Althoff W.F. 1990 *Sky Ships: A History of the Airship in the United States Navy* (hereafter cited as Althoff 1990) p.3, pp.16-18 & p.51.

18   Althoff 1990 pp.51-82. The LZ126 represented the pinnacle of airship technology when completed in 1924. Named ZR-3 *Los Angeles* she gave good service until 1932 by which time she had logged 4,181 hrs. The ZR-3 did more than any other airship to advance *USN* airship operations. See also Chamberlain 1984 p.110.

19   Treadwell T.C. 1985 *Submarines with wings: The past, present and future of aircraft carrying submarines* (hereafter cited as Treadwell 1985) pp.8-10. A second design, the LFG V 19 was produced in 1918 although it did not fly until after the armistice. Despite its simplicity it was not a success as it took far too long to re-assemble and it required 5 waterproof steel containers – see also Nowarra 1980 pp.96-97.

20   Heinkel E. 1956 He 1000 (hereafter cited as Heinkel 1956) pp.71-72, Lange B. 1970 *Das Buch der deutschen Luftfahrtechnik* (hereafter cited as Lange 1970) pp.181-182, Nowarra 1980 pp.86-87 & Treadwell 1985 pp.11-12. Heinkel had first met Christiansen in 1917 when he was *Stationsleiter Zeebrugge*. Christiansen flew Heinkel's W.12 two seat floatplane fighter with great effect during the last two years of the war and was decorated for these exploits

The US Navy was responsible for another clandestine development, the Dornier Do H *Falke* (320 hp BMW IV), a single seat fighter that was designed and built at the *Flugzeugbau Friedrichshafen's* Manzell factory alongside less belligerent types as the *Delphin* (185 hp BMW IIIa), *Komet* (185 hp BMW IIIa later 320 hp BMW IV) and Do A *Libelle* (55 hp Siemens Sh 4).[21] The *Falke* owed much to Dornier's earlier D.I in its all-metal construction and multi-sparred wing. To escape detection the *Falke* was assembled across the border in Switzerland and made its first flight on the 1 November 1922 at Dubendorf. It was then disassembled and shipped to the USA where it was fitted with a Wright built Hispano Suiza H3 engine of 300 hp and entered into the *USN* Fighter Competition at McCook Field in April 1923 as the Wright Pursuit 1.[22] Although it demonstrated a remarkable performance its monoplane layout and metal construction were considered too advanced for service employment and no further production was undertaken.[23]

In May 1922 Heinkel broke away from Caspar to form his own company, the *Ernst Heinkel Konstruktionsbüro*, which in turn metamorphosed in to the *Ernst Heinkel Flugzeugwerke* at Warnemünde in December of that year.[24] Initially Heinkel concentrated on improving his earlier wartime seaplane designs. As these aircraft could not be built in Germany he acted on a suggestion by KptLt.a.D.Carl Clemens Bucker that they be manufactured at the *Svenska Aero AB* at Stockholm-Lidingo.[25] The HE 1 and later HE 2 (360 hp Rolls Royce Eagle) were built in some numbers for the Swedish Navy as the S 1 and S 2 respectively, whilst the HE 1 was also built in small number for the *Reichsmarine* following the Ruhr Crisis of 1923 (See 1E3).[26] On the basis of this work and his earlier collaboration over the U-2, Heinkel was then approached by a Japanese naval delegation in 1925 with a commission to design a number of superior land and seaplane types for use by the *IJN*.[27] A

with the *Plm* on the 11 Dec 17 - see Angolia J.R. and Hackney C.R. 1984 *The Pour le Mérite and Germany's First Aces* pp.174-176. After the war he did some flying in Norway before joining the *Caspar-Flugzeugwerke* as test pilot on the 1 Apr 19. It was in this capacity that he solicited work from the Americans and recruited Heinkel to design the U-1 - see service record for Friedrich Christiansen in Hildebrand K.F.1990 *Die Generale der deutschen Luftwaffe 1935-1945 Band 1 A-G* pp.157-158.

21   Green W. 1970 *The War Planes of the Third Reich* (hereafter cited as Green 1970) p.109. See also Stroud 1966 pp.234-239, Nowarra 1980 pp.86-87 & 90-91 and Dornier 1983 p.83.

22   Dornier 1983 p.88 & Kosin 1983 pp.55-57. Dornier was assisted by Richard Vogt and Alexander Lippisch. In 1925 a *Falke* was shipped to Argentina where it was demonstrated to the Argentinian Army. It was then flown by *Oblt.a.D.*Carl-August von Schoenebeck across the Andes to Chile where it competed with a Curtiss P-1C Hawk for a Chilean military contract. Despite its superiority no further orders were forthcoming and Chile bought 8 P-1A in 1926 and 8 P-1B in 1927, almost certainly on grounds of cost and availability - see Bowers P.M. 1979 *Curtiss Aircraft 1907-1947* p.278. Meanwhile a float equipped version, the *Falke-See* was produced at the new Italian plant at Marine di Pisa, the development of which was passed to *Kawasaki* in Aug 24 - see Nowarra 1980 pp.92-93 & Dornier 1983 p.89.

23   Swanborough G. and Bowers P.M. 1976 *United States Navy Aircraft since 1911* p.496. In its American form the Dornier *Falke* was referred to as the Wright WP-1. For further details of its construction - see Kosin 1983 pp.56-57 & Dornier 1983 p.88.

24   Green 1970 p.258.

25   Green 1970 p.258. Bucker was a wartime *Marineluftstreitkräfte* pilot. See also Heinkel 1956 p.72 & pp.74-75.

26   Lange 1970 p.243, Nowarra 1980 pp.88-89 & 98-99 and Koos V. 2006 *Typenbucher Deutsche Luftfahrt: Ernst Heinkel Flugzeugwerke 1922-1932* (hereafter cited as Koos 2006) pp.13-17.These were improvements of the wartime W 29 & W 33 designs. The S 1 was built by *Flygkompaniets verkstader*, whilst the S 2 was manufactured by *Svenska Aero* - see also Nowarra H.J. 1966 *Marine Aircraft of the 1914-1918 War* p.75. The Swedes were very pleased with their new aircraft, commenting in 1924: *"The S 1 seaplanes have shown the greatest efficiency and manoeuvrability, although they have operated away from the Station for along time. The best proof of the airworthiness of the planes is that after a period of four months with a total flying time of 705 hours, during which they took part in all the manoeuvres of the Coastal Fleet, they were still in perfectly good flying order"* - quoted from Heinkel 1956 *He 1000* p.74 Hutchinson & Co. (Publishers) Ltd. The German HE 1 floatplanes (WNr.202-211) were placed in store in a warehouse in Stockholm harbour until they could be utilised in Germany - see Mason 1973 p.125 & 145 and Beauvais et al 2002 p.42. Initial Heinkel designs were either prefixed by the abbreviation HE (*Heinkel Eindecker*) or HD (*Heinkel-Doppledecker*) - see Lange 1970 pp.243-247 & Koos 2006.

27   Heinkel 1956 pp.91-92 & Koos 2006 pp.66-67. The Japanese delegation was led by *Capt.*Kaga and included

torpedo bomber was required, together with two types of shipboard seaplane for use aboard the Imperial Navy's capital ships. The result was the unsuccessful HD 14 (600 hp Fiat) torpedo plane and the HD 25 (450 hp Napier Lion) and HD 26 (300 hp Hispano Suiza) shipboard floatplanes.[28] Heinkel later recalled that an anonymous telephone call would immediately precede the arrival of an *ILUK* inspection team at Warnemünde. In this way the parts of the secret Japanese aircraft could be spirited away into the local area until the coast was clear for work to resume.[29]

However Japanese interest was not confined to Heinkel's activities at Travemünde and Warnemünde. During 1923 Adolf Rohrbach's all-metal Ro II (360 hp Rolls Royce Eagle) flying boat was evaluated by the Japanese as an armed bomber, whilst several examples of the improved Ro III (360 hp Rolls Royce Eagle IX) were later assembled at Rohrbach's Danish subsidiary for use by the *IJN*.[30] The British Air Ministry was also complicit in breaking the terms of the 1922 restrictions on German aircraft construction. In 1923 Specification 445337/23 was issued to William Beardmore & Co.Ltd. covering the construction of a large all-metal landplane in accordance with Rohrbach structural methodology.[31] In the following year two Ro IV (450 hp Napier Lion) flying boats were also ordered, the first of these actually being fabricated in Berlin before assembly at Copenhagen-Kastrup. It was delivered for testing at the MAEE at Felixstowe on the 18 September 1925.[32]

Into this already murky world of deceit and subterfuge came the *Reichsheer* in the form of *Hptm.* Kurt Student.[33] In 1920 Student had been given control of the *Flugtechnikreferat* (Flight Technical Desk) within the *Heereswaffenamt's Inspektion für Waffen und Gerat* (Weapons and Equipment

Engineer Yonezawa of the *Aichi Tokei Denki*. Kaga would later command the *Nagato*, one of two new battleships for the *IJN* - see Friedman N. & Sturton I. *Japan* in Sturton I. (Ed.) *Conway's Battleships – The Definitive Visual Reference to the World's All-Big-Gun Ships* pp.164-165.

28   Koos 2006 pp.40-41 & 66-69, Lange 1970 pp.244-245, Sekigawa E.1974 *Pictorial History of Japanese Military Aviation* (hereafter cited as Sekigawa 1974) p.25 & Nowarra 1980 pp.114-117. Sixteen examples of the HD 25 were built in Japan as the Aichi Type 2 Reconnaissance Seaplane. In addition to the *Nagato*, two cruisers: the heavy cruiser *Furutaka* & the light cruiser *Nagara* were also equipped with launching rails. The launching rail and later catapults were designed by Karl Schwarzler of the *Ernst Heinkel Flugzeugwerke* - see Heinkel 1956 pp.89-90.

29   Heinkel 1956 p.80. However on one visit the 720 hp Fiat A-14 engine, intended for the HD 14, was discovered during an *ILUK* inspection. Heinkel passed it off as an old engine which was being used for training purposes by the factory apprentices.

30   Lange 1970 p.351 & Nowarra 1980 pp.96-98 & 120-121. The young Kurt Tank was employed by *Rohrbach* to re-design the hull of the Ro IIA. The new hull design was incorporated into the improved Ro IIIA, later to be named the *Rodra* (Ro drei-A) - see Conradis H. 1960 *Design for Flight: The Kurt Tank Story* p.15 & Wagner W. 1980 *Kurt Tank - Konstrukteur und Testpilot bei Focke Wulf Die deutsche Luftfahrt 1* pp.13-15.

31   Jarrett P. 1990 'Beardmore's Heavy Metal Monsters Pt.2' in *Aircraft Monthly* Vol.18 No.3 pp136-142. This interest seems to have followed a lecture by *Dr.Ing.*Rohrbach to the Royal Aeronautical Society. Beardmore entered into a licence agreement with the *Rohrbach Metall-Flugzeugbau GmbH* in 1924. Rohrbach appears to have been directly involved in the design of the Inflexible although it was not allocated the designation Ro VII as suggested by this source - see Lange 1970 p.351. It was built by Beardmore at Dalmuir before being assembled and test flown at the *AAEE* Martlesham Heath on the 5 Mar 28. Tests showed the aircraft's flying characteristics to be *"quite good in calm weather"* although it was slow to respond to control inputs, particularly at slow speed. Unfortunately the unavailability of sufficiently powerful engines prevented the type from carrying a useful role and the prototype (J7557) was scrapped in 1930. See also Mason 1993 pp.201-202 & Spec.18/23 in Meekcoms K.J. and Morgan E.B. 1994 *The British Aircraft Specifications File: British Military and Commercial Aircraft Specifications 1920-1949* (hereafter cited as Meekcoms and Morgan 1994) p.66.

32   Jarrett P. 1990 'Beardmore's Heavy Metal Monsters Pt.1' in *Aircraft Monthly* Vol.18 No.2 pp.74-79 & Nowarra 1980 pp.122-123. The Inverness was not a success. It was under-powered, sluggish in response at slow speeds, subject to corrosion and was difficult to maintain. The improved Beardmore built N184 was not completed until 1928, It was also judged by the *MAEE* as unsuitable for either service or commercial use and was subsequently scrapped - see also Kinsey G. 1978 *Seaplanes - Felixstowe: The Story of the Air Station 1913-1963* p.93 & 101 & Spec.20/24 in Meekcoms and Morgan 1994 pp.83-84.

33   Heinkel 1956 pp.78-79. A pre-war military aviator, *Hptm.*Student had seen considerable wartime service as a reconnaissance, bomber and fighter pilot. During Oct 15-May 17 he was *Fhr.Jasta 9*; between Jul 17-Feb 18 he was *Kdr.JGr.b.AOK 3* - see service record for Kurt Student in Hildebrand K.F.1992 *Die Generale der deutschen Luftwaffe 1935-1945 Band 3 O-Z* pp.363-365.

Inspectorate within the Army Ordnance Office).[34] *Hptm.*Student's last position within the wartime *Luftstreitkräfte* (German Air Service) had been as *Leiter der Abteilung für Versuche und Wissenschaft Adlershof* (Leader of the Adlershof Test Department) within *Maj.*Felix Wagenführ's *Kommando der Flugzeugmusterei* (Aircraft Engineering Centre). This command had been responsible for the flight testing and writing of associated technical reports on new military aircraft; Student's department had concentrated on experimental work.[35] A key part of *Gen.d.Kav.*Hans von Seeckt's *Heeresleitung* (Army Command), the *HWA* (known internally as the *WaA*) was responsible for supervising the design, development, testing and acceptance of all new ordnance equipment for the *Reichsheer*. It was divided into two parts: (1) development and testing (*Wa.Prüfwesens*), and (2) industrial development and procurement (*Wa.Beschaffungs*). The *Flugtechnikreferat (In.WG 6F)* was a covert department within the *Wa.A.*[36] Given Allied restrictions its work was initially restricted to the compilation of information and the preparation of summaries of significant foreign aviation publications on behalf of the *Truppenamt* (Troop Office) (See also 1A2).[37] In these duties Student was assisted by a number of serving and non-serving officers. These included *Hptm.*Heinrich Lorenz, *Rittm.*Adolf Baeumker, *Oblt.*Paul Jeschonnek and from December 1923 his younger brother *Lt.*Hans Jeschonnek.[38] Baeumker, a former *Feldluftschiffertruppe* (Field Airship Troops) observer, served within the *Flugtechnikreferat* as an air armament specialist, whilst *Oblt.a.D.Dipl.Ing.*Ernst Marquard joined the team in October 1924 as an adviser in drop ordnance and chemical warfare (See 1D1).[39]

Student was an important player in the emergent German glider movement. In August 1920, accompanied by his wife, he visited the young gliding enthusiasts on the Wasserkuppe and thereafter channelled secret *Reichswehr* funds to the more promising *Verein* (Associations) and groups (See 1D2).[40] The Ruhr Crisis of 1923 then witnessed a more overt role during the secret acquisition of Fokker D.XI and D.XIII (450 hp Napier Lion) fighters from the Netherlands. Student was personally involved in the flight testing of the new fighters prior to their transfer to the newly established

34   Suchenwirth R. 1968 *The Development of the German Air Force 1919-1939* USAF Historical Studies No.160 (hereafter cited as Suchenwirth 1968) p.6.

35   Beauvais H., Kossler K., Mayer M. and Regel C. 2002 *German Secret Flight Test Centres to 1945: Johannisthal, Lipetsk, Rechlin, Travemünde, Tarnewitz, Peenemunde-West* (hereafter cited as Beauvais et al 2002) p.37. See also the service record for Kurt Student in Hildebrand 1992 p.364.

36   Seaton A. 1982 *The German Army 1933-1945* p.29. Internally the *Flugtechnikreferat* was known as *IWG 6F - Inspektion für Waffen und Gerat 6F* - see Beauvais et al 2002 p.37.

37   Hertel 1955 p.5 & Suchenwirth 1968 p.6. Specifically foreign air armament activities, the performance of foreign aircraft and the compilation of material on foreign operational air doctrine. The material so gathered was often published for wider consumption in the *Militärwochenblatt* (Ed.Gen.Konstantin von Altrock) which was printed fortnightly - see Corum J.S. 1997 *The Luftwaffe: Creating the Operational Air War 1918-1940* (hereafter cited as Corum 1997) p.69.

38   Hildebrand K.F.1990-92 *Die Generale der deutschen Luftwaffe 1935-1945 Band 1-3*. Heinrich Lorenz was a former fighter pilot *(Fhr.Jasta 33, 10 & 7)* and *Ltr.d.Fliegerschule b.Armeeflugpark 4*; unfortunately nothing is known of Paul Jeschonnek's service history; Hans Jeschonnek had served with *Jasta 40* in 1918. Within *In.W.G.6F* Hans Jeschonnek would focus on aircraft development in neighbouring countries. During the course of the decade he would attend many air shows and exhibitions whilst through the generosity of officials in the Netherlands, Sweden and Switzerland he was able to actually evaluate a number of foreign aircraft types - see Interview of *GenOb.a.D.*Kurt Student with Prof.Richard Suchenwirth, 12 Mar 55 in D/II/1 Karlsruhe Document Collection in Suchenwirth R. Prof. 1969 *Command and Leadership in the German Air Force* USAF Historical Studies No.174 p.214.

39   Service record for Adolf Baeumker in *www.dir.de.* & for Ernst Marquard in Hildebrand K.F.1991 *Die Generale der deutschen Luftwaffe 1935-1945 Band 2 H-N* pp.356-357. Marquard had been too late to see active service as a fighter pilot in the wartime *Luftstreitkräfte*. He had been discharged in Jan 19 and enrolled in the *Maschinenbau-Studium an der Technischen Hochschule Stuttgart* where he was awarded his *Dipl.Ing.* on the 6 Jul 22. In May 22 he gained employment at the *Allgemeinen Vergaser-Gesellschaft* in Berlin before being recruited for secret work in the *RWM* in Oct 24. Civilians included Boehme (Airframes), Bullinger (Engines), Grosch (Equipment), Schwarz (Construction) & Wegner (Military Economics) - see *App.2 Air Force Agencies in 1921-28 (Integration with the Reichswehr)* in Hertel 1955 p.269.

40   Hermann 1943 pp.17-19.

secret base at Lipetsk in the USSR (See 1A2).[41] Meanwhile in Germany, working under an assumed identity and always in civilian clothes, Student progressively established a network of contacts with key individuals in the surviving aircraft manufacturing firms whose output had continued to decline, reaching just 47 machines during the course of 1922.[42] These contacts in turn led to an order for the first new combat aircraft for the *Reichsheer* when Student asked Ernst Heinkel to provide a two-seat short-range reconnaissance aircraft (*Nahaufklärungsflugzeug*) (See 1C3).[43] Despite a lack of *Reichswehr* funding - Heinkel recalled that he was expected to finance this work himself - the HD 17 (450 hp Napier Lion) appeared in 1924. In addition to the two prototypes (WNr.216 & 217), parts for seven production aircraft (WNr.239-245) were produced under conditions of the greatest secrecy. Final assembly was carried out in Sweden prior to the machines being shipped to Lipetsk in 1926 (See 1D1).[44] Meanwhile in Germany a similar secret agreement appears was concluded with the *Albatros Flugzeugwerke GmbH* at Berlin-Johannisthal as this firm produced two experimental reconnaissance aircraft in the following year.[45] To avoid allied restrictions the Albatros L 65 (450 hp Napier Lion) was assembled and test flown by the *Allgemeine Fluggesellschaft Memel mbH*. The other reconnaissance aircraft was the Albatros L 70 (450 hp Napier Lion).[46]

Of equal significance were Student's orders for training aircraft and aero-engines.[47] It seems likely that some assistance was provided to the *Dietrich-Gobiet Flugzeugbau AG* which had been obliged to relocate from Mannheim to Kassel as a result of the French occupation of the Rheinland in 1923.[48] Certainly his DP IIa *Bussard* (85-125 hp Siemens Sh 5, 11, 12 & 14) was suitable for clandestine fighter training.[49] In 1924 Heinkel produced two training aircraft to meet *Reichswehr* contracts.[50] These were the HE 18 (85 hp Siemens Sh 5), a two-seat development of the HE 3L *Sportflugzeug* (Sportsplane) that had gained first prize in the international *Flugwettbewerb* (Air Meeting) at Goteborg in Sweden in 1923, and the HD 21 two seat biplane (105-160 hp Daimler D.I, D-II & D-III).[51] Relatively few HE 18 aircraft were built but the HD 21 proved a commercial success and the type was built under licence by the newly established *Werft Warnemünde der Arado Handelsgesellschaft* which was located at Warnemünde in Mecklenburg.[52] The creation of *Sportflug*

41   Mason 1973 pp.125-126, Postma T. 1979 *Fokker: Aircraft Builders to the World* p.59 & 61 & Nowarra 1980 pp.100-101. The Fokker D.XI fighters were subsequently sold to Romania.

42   Heinkel 1956 pp.80-81, Mason 1973 pp.118-119. Interestingly seven of these were covert military aircraft, the first to be completed in Germany - see Vajda and Dancey 1998 p.9.

43   Heinkel 1956 p.79. Student wanted a land biplane with a maximum speed of 224 kph and a service ceiling of at least 6,000 m. The first development orders were issued in 1923 - see Nowarra H.J. 1981 *Nahaufklärer 1910-1945: Die Augen des Heeres* pp.33-34 & 134.

44   Lange 1970 pp.244-245, Koos 2006 pp.46-48 & Nowarra 1980 pp.106-108. There is some dispute as to whether these machines were actually assembled at Warnemünde or Lidingo. The answer may be both locations - see also Ries 1970 p.86.

45   Beauvais et al 2002 pp.48-49. Heinkel produced the HD 32 & HD 35 trainers - improvements of the basic HD 21, the HD 17 reconnaissance aircraft; Albatros the L 65 reconnaissance aircraft and BMW the BMW VI high powered aero-engine - see also Lange 1970 pp.158-159, 244-246 & 396-397, Koos 2006 pp.46-48, 80-81 & 86-87 and Nowarra 1980 pp.110-111 & 134-135.

46   Lange 1970 pp.158-159 & Nowarra1980 pp.110-112.

47   Andersson L. 1989 'Secret Luftwaffe: German Military Aviation Build-up between the Wars' in *Air Enthusiast* No.41 1989 p.39. According to one source the first clandestine military order was for 5 single-seat monoplane trainers (50 hp) placed with *Albatros*. Although Andersson suggests that these were L 60 trainers, it is more likely that they were L 66 or L 67 aircraft - see Lange 1970 p.159.

48   Hooton 1994 p.39.

49   Lange 1970 p.191 & Nowarra 1980 pp.98-99.

50   Heinkel 1956 p.81.

51   Lange 1970 p.245, Nowarra 1980 pp.108-109 & Koos 2006 pp.49-50 & 55-56. The HE 3 had been designed to be quickly interchangeable between land and sea landing gear. The HE 18 was a productionised version with a conventional steel tube fuselage with fabric covering which was built in small numbers.

52   Lange 1970 p.245, Green 1970 p.25 & Kosin 1983 p.65. In 1921 the wealthy industrialist and entrepreneur Hugo

GmbH in April 1924 resulted in a general expansion of flying training and a number of low-powered two-seat trainers were legitimately produced in Germany to meet this need over the following two years (See 1A2 & 1D2). These included the Albatros L 68 (96-125 hp Siemens Sh 11 & 12), Arado S 1 (100 hp Bristol Lucifer & 125 hp Siemens Sh 12), Caspar C 26 (100 hp Bristol Lucifer), LFG V 39 (105-120 hp Daimler D.I & D-II) and the Udet U 12a *Flamingo* (75-85 hp Siemens Sh 5, later Sh 10).[53] During the course of 1925 no less than 406 aircraft were produced in Germany by 17 manufacturers.[54] Nearly all of these were light *Sportflugzeuge*. The general growth in aircraft manufacturing during 1924-26 acted as a stimulus to the creation of new companies. On the 1 January 1924 Heinrich Focke, Georg Wulf and *Dr.*Werner Naumann established the *Focke Wulf Flugzeugbau GmbH* at Bremen.[55] One of their earliest designs was the S 1 (55 hp Siemens Sh 5) of 1925. This two seat elementary trainer featured side-by-side seating for the student and instructor. However it was not a commercial success.[56]

Student's substantial order for the BMW IIIa and its more powerful development the BMW IV did a great deal to restore the fortunes of the German aero-engine industry.[57] By 1921 the former thirty aero-engine works had been reduced in number to just five factories.[58] The big two during the Great War had been the *Daimler AG* and *Benz & Cie*.[59] These firms had focused on the production of high-powered engines in the 180-240 hp class. Allied restrictions hit this product area particularly severely and in 1919 both firms ceased aero-engine production and turned their attention to the growing automobile market where they traded jointly as *Mercedes Benz*.[60] The much smaller *BMW Flugmotorenbau GmbH (BMW)* also struggled to stay afloat in the face of the restrictive activities of the *ILUK*.[61] During 1918 its 185 hp six-cylinder in-line BMW IIIa engine had been particularly

Stinnes had acquired the former *Werft Warnemünde des Flugzeugbaus Friedrichshafen* with the aim of re-starting aircraft production following the relaxation of the allied restrictions. In 1924 he acquired the services of *Ing.*Walter Rethel who had previously been employed by Fokker in the Netherlands and in 1925 the *Arado Handelsgesellschaft* was formed at Warnemünde. *Arado* completed 15 examples of the HD 21 and 4 examples of the HD 32. The Managing Director was known other than *Obstlt.a.D.*Felix Wagenführ, the former *Flugzeugmusterei* and Student's former superior in the *Luftstreitkräfte* - see Kranzhoff J A 1997 *Arado: Geschichte eines Flugzeugwerks* (hereafter cited as Kranzhoff 1997) pp.8-10.

53   Ries 1970 p.41, Lange 1970 p.159, 161, 182 & pp.358-359, Nowarra 1980 pp.112-113, 124-125 & 140-142 and Kranzhoff 1997 pp.17-18. The *Udet Flugzeugbau GmbH* was established at Milbertshofen, nr.Muchen-Oberweisenfeld, by Ernst Udet (*Plm* with 62 *abschusse*) in the summer of 1921. In 1922 he joined forces with his friend Erich Scheuermann and moved his operation to München-Ramersdorf. However in 1925 Udet returned to his first love "flying" and left the day to day operation of the *Udet Flugzeugbau* in the hands of Heinz Pohl - see Ishoven van A. 1977 *The Fall of an Eagle: The Life of Fighter Ace Ernst Udet* (hereafter cited as Ishoven 1977 Udet) pp.86-99.

54   Vajda and Dancey 1998 p.9. However the larger figure of 585 machines for 1925 is cited in another source - see *Table 3: German Aircraft Production, 1924-1929* in Hooton 1994 p.54.

55   Smith J.R. 1973 *Focke Wulf: An Aircraft Album* (hereafter cited as Smith 1973) p.7 & Vajda and Dancey 1998 p.197. The new firm's first product was in fact the A 16 light transport. First flown on the 23 Jun 24 the A 16 WNr.2 D-437 was powered by a 75 hp Sh 11 radial. A total of 24 A 16 transports were built at Bremen during 1924-26.

56   Lange 1970 pp.221-222 & Smith 1973 p.14.

57   Hooton 1994 p.48. In reality these engines were ordered on behalf of the Soviet authorities - see also Boyd A. 1977 *The Soviet Air Force since 1918* (hereafter cited as Boyd 1977) p.10.

58   Gersdorff von K. and Grasmann K. 1985 *Die Deutsche Luftfahrt 2: Flugmotoren und Strahltriebwerke* (hereafter cited as Gersdorff and Grasmann 1985) p.42.

59   Vajda and Dancey 1998 p.235. During the Great War *Daimler* produced 19,876 engines (45%), whilst *Benz* produced 11,360 engines (26%). See also Gersdorff and Grasmann 1985 pp.28-29. Karl Benz had produced the world's first motor car in Jul 86 and both companies had been in the forefront of automotive developments during the period leading up to the Great War. The *Maybach Motorenbau GmbH* was another firm that stopped aero-engine production at the end of the war and turned its attention to automobile manufacture - see Lange 1970 pp.421-422.

60   Hertel 1955 pp.78-79, Hooton 1994 p.56 & Vajda and Dancey 1998 p.235.

61   Vajda and Dancey 1998 p.234. Until 1921 *BMW* had to find additional work by making brakes for railway wagons. Later on it produced motorcycles for *Victoria Werke*. With support from the Austrian financier Castiglioni *BMW* amalgamated with *Victoria* to form the *BMW AG* on the 22 May 22.

successful, being the preferred engine for the superlative Fokker D.VII fighter (See 1A1).[62] The *Pour le Mérite* expert Ernst Udet noted that his Fokker D.VII 4253/18 could attain 2,000 m in 6 minutes, 4,000 m in 12 minutes and 6,000 m in 21 minutes. After 82 flying hours this particular engine was overhauled with very little wear and tear being found; remedial work was confined to re-seating the valves and renewing the piston rings.[63] Post war *BMW* managed to preserve its winning design team under the leadership of *Ing.*Helmut Sachse. By increasing the overall engine capacity from 19 to 22.9 litres the BMW III was developed into the more powerful BMW IVa of 250 hp. However production of this engine was delayed until 1924 by the Allies' prohibition of more powerful aero-engines.[64] In response to a secret *Reichswehr* requirement the team followed this engine with its first vee-twelve power-plant in 1925.[65] The liquid-cooled BMW VI was in essence two BMW IVa engines with a total capacity of 46.9 litres aligned at 60 degrees on a common crankcase. Initially rated at 600 hp at 1,500 rpm the BMW VI weighed 510 kgs and as such offered a greater power output per kilogram (0.74 kg/hp) than its predecessor (0.95 kg/hp).[66] Previously dependent on such imported engines as the British Napier Lion and Rolls Royce Eagle, the new BMW VI at last gave German airframe designers an indigenous high-powered aero-engine.[67]

However during the extended period of allied restrictions it was the low powered engines that were of more practical employment. These ranged from the 34 hp two cylinder Haacke-Boxermotor HFM 2a that was used to power the Udet U 1 of 1922 and the similar 24 hp Daimler F 7502b two-cylinder boxer of 1925 which was fitted to the Klemm L 20A1 & B1 to the larger radial engine designs of the *Siemens und Halske Flugmotorenwerk AG*.[68] *Siemens und Halske* at Berlin-Spandau had been a minor engine producer during the Great War, but their low-powered radials found a small but steady market in post-war Germany when aircraft were limited in size and performance.[69] Using aluminium cylinders with screwed-on heads, steel liners and in-line valves the company produced the five-cylinder Sh 4 (62 hp) in 1921, the seven-cylinder Sh 5 (85 hp) in 1923, together with the seven-cylinder Sh 11 (96 hp) and nine-cylinder Sh 12 (125 hp) in 1925.[70] It can be argued that it was these low-powered radials rather than the larger in-line engines that provided the basis for a German resurgence in the air. The Siemens radial engine family powered, amongst others, the Albatros L 59 and L 60 *Sportflugzeuge*, the Dornier A *Libelle Sportflugboot* (Sport Flying Boat), the Heinkel HE 3 and HE 18 *Sportflugzeuge*, Junkers K 16 *Reiseflugzeug* (Touring Aircraft), LFG V 23, V 28 and V 40 *Sportflugzeuge* and the Udet U 3, U 4, U 6 & U 10 *Sportflugzeuge* and the U 5 & U 8 *Reiseflugzeuge*.[71]

The only new aero-engine manufacturer was the *Junkers Motorenbau GmbH* of Dessau which

---

62   Gersdorff and Grasmann 1985 pp.36-37 & Gunston B. 1995 *World Encyclopaedia of Aero Engines* (hereafter cited as Gunston 1995) p.26.

63   Ishoven 1977 pp.65-66. Udet considered the BMW IIIa to be the pinnacle of engine performance in the last stages of the war.

64   Gersdorff and Grasmann 1985 pp.57-59 & Gunston 1995 p.26. The BMW IV had been test flown in 1919 in a DFW F 37. It was developed to meet a requirement by *Aero Lloyd* - see Hertel 1955 p.24-25 & Lange 1970 p.396.

65   Beauvais et al 2002 p.42. This requirement, placed by Student, dated from 1924 - see Hertel 1955 pp.24-25.

66   Gersdorff and Grasmann 1985 pp.58-59 & Gunston 1995 p.26. The 6-cylinder in-line BMW V was also under development at this time. It featured light metal cylinder heads and water jacket in an attempt to reduce overall engine weight when compared to the earlier BMW IVa.

67   Gunston 1995 p.26. See also *Langs-und Querschnitt des Wassergekuhlten 12-Zylinder-V-Motors BMW VI mit dem Schmierstoffkreislauf* in Gersdorff and Grasmann 1985 p.64-I.

68   Gersdorff and Grasmann 1985 pp.44-48 & 130-133. *Siemens und Halske*, together with the *Siemens Schuckert Werke*, formed part of the giant *Siemens* electrical conglomerate - see Vajda and Dancey 1998 p.234.

69   Vajda and Dancey 1998 p.234. Wartime production had totalled just 569 aero-engines.

70   Lange 1970 p.424, Gersdorff and Grasmann 1985 pp.44-48, Gunston 1995 p.30 & Vajda and Dancey 1998 p.234. Production of the Sh 4 was 70 units, whilst production of the larger Sh 5 totalled 110 units.

71   Lange 1970 pp.158-159, p.194, pp.243-245, p.315 & 358. The *Reiseflugzeug* was a touring aircraft as opposed to a sports plane.

began to design and produce its own series of water-cooled six-cylinder in-line petrol aero-engines in November 1923 *(Photo 1C-2)*.[72] The L 1 was rated at 77 hp at 1,800 rpm, whilst the L 2 began life at 195 hp.[73] However the most important of the early engines was the much larger L 5 of 1925 which employed six 160 x 190 mm cylinders to give a total swept capacity of 22.92 litres. Initially the L 5 only developed 280 hp at 1,450 rpm, but later versions were rated at 310 and even 340 hp.[74] With a ready market supplied by the parent company's aircraft designs the L 5 would become an important production engine during the mid-to late-twenties. It was used by the Junkers F 13, G 24, G 31 and A 20.[75]

Meanwhile the German-Russian rapprochement had encouraged *Reichswehr* planners to explore the idea of opening an aircraft manufacturing facility, far from prying eyes, in the USSR (See 1A2). To this end *Maj.a.D.*Oskar Ritter von Niedermayer had visited Professor Junkers at Dessau in July 1921.[76] However the Professor, by then aged 62, had been non-committal, an attitude which stemmed in part from his pacifist beliefs and partly from his deep distrust of both politicians and the military. However the continuing Allied ban on civil aviation had forced him to scrapping his advanced G 1 monoplane airliner and reduce his former workforce of 710 to a core of less than 200, the wages of which he had to personally finance (See also 1B).[77] Clearly such economic realities could not be ignored and when *Obst.*Otto Hasse, the *Chef der Truppenamt*, visited Junkers in the autumn of that year he found the eccentric aircraft manufacturer in a more receptive mood *(Photo 1C-3)*. Detailed discussions lasted through the winter and on the 15 March 1922 these culminated in an agreement with the *Sondergruppe "R" (Russland)* (Special Group Russia) for Junkers to establish an aircraft manufacturing facility at Fili on the western outskirts of Moskva.[78] In return Junkers was promised the equivalent of $10 million from secret *Reichswehr* funds plus a further $25 million for capital developments, the allocation of these funds to be spread over several years. To conceal *Reichswehr* involvment these funds were made available to Junkers via a "front" company, the *Gesellschaft zur Forderung gewerblicher Unternehmen Ausland (Gefu)*.[79] Junkers undertook to provide the design team together with the required industrial expertise, whilst the Soviet authorities were responsible for the workforce. It was also agreed that Soviet aircraft engineers would be allowed in the plant as observers; the young Andrei Tupolev being one of those seconded to Fili from the *Tsentral'ny Aerogidrodinamicheski Institut (Ts.AGI.)* (Central Aero and Hydrodynamics Institute) for this purpose.[80]

---

72 Lange 1970 p.415, Gersdorff and Grasmann 1985 pp.71-75 & Vajda and Dancey 1998 pp.236-237. The dates given in another source are inaccurate in this respect - see Gunston 1995 p.89. The *Junkers Motorenbau* was established on the 27 Nov 23 - see Schmitt 1988 p.201.

73 Gersdorff and Grasmann 1985 pp.71-75 & Gunston 1995 p.89.

74 Gersdorff and Grasmann 1985 pp.72-75 & Schmitt 1988 pp.203-204.

75 Lange 1970 pp.274-277 & Schmitt 1988 p.94, pp.103-104 & 109-112.

76 Mason 1973 pp.111-112. See also Hermann 1943 p.25 & 52. *Hptm.a.D.*Hermann Steiner was a Junkers employee and as such his observations are highly biased in favour of *Prof.*Junkers who he greatly admired.

77 Mason 1973 p.111 & Hooton 1994 p.37.

78 Schmitt 1988 pp.132-135. *Junkers* was assigned the former Russo-Baltic Automobile Works (founded in 1917) at Fili on the outskirts of Moskva. It appears that a similar arrangement was concluded with the *Albatros Flugzeugwerke* although details remain obscure - see Hooton 1994 p.37.

79 Mason 1973 p.111. *Gefu* was controlled by *Gen.d.Inf.a.D.*Karl von Borries and *Maj.*Fritz Tschunke. It had a working capital of *RM* 75 m - see Hooton 1994 pp.37-38. *Gen.d.Flg.a.D.*Hellmuth Felmy has since stated that the *Reichswehr* contributed RM 100 million to the Fili venture - see Suchenwirth 1968 p.13. Junkers had protested to Hasse that he did not want anything to do with military aviation. He was eventually won round by the promise that insofar as the military aspects of the deal went these would only be to the benefit of the Soviets. In addition he was excited by the prospect of a concession to organise civilian airlines throughout the USSR. - see Hermann 1943 pp.51-53. Further discussions with the *Sovnarkom*, the Council of People's Commissars, led to the ratification of the arrangement on the 23 January 1923 - see Boyd 1977 p.9.

80 Boyd 1977 pp.9-10. The Soviet workforce reached 1,350 men at peak production. The Soviet engineers and

It was expected that as many as 300 aircraft per year would be built at Fili once full production was reached, sixty of these being specifically for the *RKKVF*, whilst a proportion of the remainder would be for German use at Lipetsk.[81] One of the first types to be manufactured at Fili was the F 13, production of which had been only recently reinstated at Dessau following the lifting of some of the Allied restrictions.[82] A few A 20 *Postflugzeuge* were also assembled from parts made at Dessau, these being armed for use by the *RKKVF* as reconnaissance aircraft.[83] However the Soviet authorities were more interested in the H 21 two-seat reconnaissance fighter and its single-seat derivative, the H 22. These two machines were purpose-built for Soviet service and although the H 22 was not produced in quantity, the *GU-RKKVVF* having decided to purchase 100 Martinsyde F.4 Buzzard fighters from Britain as an interim type, the Fili plant did go on to build 122 examples of the H 21.[84] These aircraft saw considerable use during the twenties and were employed for counter-insurgency operations over Soviet Central Asia.

The Junkers aircraft built at Fili were all powered by 6-cylinder in-line BMW engines, these being imported from Germany. However the Soviet authorities had hoped that Junkers would also establish an aero-engine factory in Moskva (*GAZ-4*) where a small Soviet engineer team had been created with this development in mind.[85] Junkers, on the other hand, was becoming increasingly disillusioned with the situation at Fili. He had invested heavily at both this plant and at Dessau having been assured by the German authorities that large contracts would be forthcoming. However with the exception of the H 21 the Soviets were to place few orders for his designs and in Germany the economic situation had deteriorated.[86] He therefore resisted further pressure from the *Sondergruppe "R"* and not only refused to co-operate in the matter of an aero-engine plant, but in 1926 he even threatened to pull-out of Fili altogether (See 1A2 & 1D2).[87] Anxious not to lose German expertise the Soviets moved quickly to stabilise the situation through the injection of funds from the Chief Directorate of the Aircraft Industry (*GUAP*) but in reality the arrangement was doomed as it promised little in the way of future mutual advantage.[88] The concession was finally cancelled on the 1 March 1927 after the

technicians proved exacting task masters despite the technical expertise of the *Junkers* men - see Schmitt 1988 p.135.

81   Hooton 1994 p.38. The first Soviet order was placed on the 4 Dec 22 - 20 J 20 floatplanes, 50 J 21 reconnaissance aircraft & 30 J 22 fighters.

82   Stroud 1966 p.297 & Schmitt 1988 pp.139-142. The diminutive Ju 13 (F 13) made a considerable contribution to the development of civil aviation in the *USSR* despite the fact that only twenty were built for use by the airline *Dobrolyot*, these aircraft being employed on the Moskva-Gorkii-Kazan route, in the Crimea and around Tashkent in Soviet Central Asia - see also Stroud 1966 p.

83   Nowarra 1980 pp.94-95 & Schmitt 1988 pp.135-136. These aircraft were produced in 1924. The A 20 had been designed and built at Dessau as a mail and freight transport for use by *Junkers Luftverkehr*. It was also built by Junkers Swedish subsidiary *AB Flygindustri* - see Stroud 1966 pp.301-302.

84   Boyd 1977 p.8. The Soviets purchased large numbers of *Fokker* aircraft including the D.XI & C-IV. A number of BMW IIIa engines were assembled at Fili - see Schmitt 1988 p.135.

85   Boyd 1977 p.10. The Soviet team at *GAZ-4* included future engine designers Arkadi Shvetsov & Aleksandr Mikulin. The *RKKVF* ordered 380 BMW engines in late 1923 - see Hooton 1994 p.48. Approximately 170 all-metal aircraft were built or assembled at Fili. *Junkers* invested heavily in Fili: *RM* 500-600 m. working capital, 150 m special machinery, 150 m support materials, 100 m production expertise, 100 m administration and day to day running costs - in all *RM* 1,100 m - see Schmitt 1988 p.132. However see Felmy in Suchenwirth 1968 p.13 & Lichte A. 1976 'Der Reichseingriff in die Junkers-Werke' in *Junkers Nachrichten* H5/6 1976. Later Soviet contracts included another 20 J 20 floatplanes, 72 J 21 reconnaissance aircraft & 23 K 30 bombers – see Nowarra 1980 pp.94-96 & Hooton 1994 p.48. However not all of these were delivered and parts for the J 20 were built at Dessau, whilst the K 30 was built in Sweden – see Schmitt 1988 pp.143-145.

86   Mason 1973 pp.144-145. It was at this point that disaffected Junkers employees leaked information of the Fili agreement to opposition politicians. However little long term harm was caused to the *Reichswehr*. Junkers on the other hand had lost heavily and this enabled *Maj.a.D.*Brandenburg of the *RVM* to successfully apply pressure on the Professor for him to relinquish control of *Junkers Luftverkehr* and thus create a national airline - *Deutsche Lufthansa*.

87   Boyd 1977 p.18.

88   Boyd 1977 p.25.

final delivery of a small batch of K 30 bombers.[89] These were again regarded as interim machines but they did see some service as the JuG-1 with the *VVS-RKKA's Tyazhelyi Bombardirovshchik Brigada* (Heavy Bomber Brigade) pending deliveries of the indigenous Tupolev TB-1 (ANT-4). Following the withdrawal of the *Junkers Flugzeugwerke* from Fili the plant reverted to Soviet control as the *GAZ-22* being subsequently employed for the construction of the TB-1. However the Soviet Union still had to rely on imported aero-engines, the TB-1 itself being powered by the BMW VI which was produced under licence in the USSR as the M-17 from 1928.[90]

Prior to the general relaxation of allied restrictions in 1926 the only way by which the struggling German aircraft industry could engage in the design, development and construction of large commercial transports, flying boats or new military prototypes was to carry out such work abroad. To this end all of the major aircraft firms had established foreign subsidiary companies by the mid-twenties as shown below:[91]

FIGURE 1C-1 GERMAN OWNED FOREIGN AIRCRAFT MANUFACTURING SUBSIDIARIES 1925		
Albatros GmbH	Berlin-Johannisthal	Allgemeine Fluggesellschaft Memel mbH
Caspar-Werke AG	Lübeck-Travemünde	Dansk Aero, Copenhagen
Dornier-Werke GmbH	Friedrichshafen	AG für Dornier-Flugzeuge, Altenrhein
Ernst Heinkel Flugzeugwerke GmbH	Rostock-Warnemünde	Svenska Aero AB, Lidingo
Junkers Flugzeug-u.Motorenwerke AG	Dessau	A.B.Flygindustri, Limhamn
Rohrbach Metall-Flugzeugbau GmbH	Berlin	Rohrbach Metal-Aeroplan Co.A/S.

The importance of these arrangements can be best seen in the work of Claudius Dornier who was engaged in the development of a number of military prototypes in the mid-twenties. These included the Do D *Torpedoseeflugzeug* (Torpedo Bomber Seaplane), completed in 1924 which was evaluated by the *Reichsmarine* and the Do N *Kampfflugzeug* (Bomber) which had been designed on behalf of the Kawasaki to meet a Imperial Japanese Army requirement (See 1E3).[92] The unusual all-metal Do N owed a great deal to contemporary Do J Wal design philosophy with a parasol wing, boat-like fuselage and two engines in tandem on the wing centre-section. Completed in 1926 it was subsequently built under licence by Kawasaki as the Type 87 Heavy Bomber, with a total of 28 examples being completed. It would see operational use over Manchuria from 1931.[93]

89   Schmitt 1988 pp.143-145. The parts for these aircraft were actually manufactured at Dessau, assembled in Sweden as the R 42 and delivered to Fili as the JuG 1 for final fitting out as bombers. In all 15 aircraft were delivered in 1926. In the early 30s they were modified for civil use.
90   Boyd 1977 pp.26-27.
91   Lange 1970 p.158, 181, 192, 242, 271 & 350.
92   Lange 1970 pp.194-195 & Nowarra 1980 pp.146-147. The Do D was based on the earlier Do *Komet III* was produced on behalf of Kawasaki to meet an *IJN* requirement. It was subsequently developed into the Do D Bas and 24 were built for the Yugoslav Navy, whilst the *RVM* purchased 3 aircraft on behalf of the *RWM* - see also Dornier 1983 p.92 & Thiele H. 2004 *Luftwaffe Aerial Torpedo Aircraft and Operations in World War Two* pp.9-10.
93   Lange 1970 p.199, Nowarra 1980 pp.126-128 & Dornier 1983 p.103. The Do N was the *IJA's* first all-metal bomber and it was used to establish the Army's first dedicated bomber unit. As part of the development work a small German team was despatched to Kobe, including for a time *Prof.Dr.*Dornier himself. *Kawasaki* had also engaged the services of German designer *Dr.Ing.*Richard Vogt. In 1928 his KDA-2, powered by a licence built BMW VI, would be selected as the *IJA's* Type 88 Reconnaissance Bomber with production totalling 710 machines – see Sekigawa 1974 pp.21-23.

1C2

Laying the Foundations for Military Aviation 1926-1932

The Paris Agreement of May 1926 promised the ending of all restrictions on the design, testing and manufacture of civil aircraft within Germany (See 1B1). Of equal significance was the dissolution of the *Interalliierte Luftfahrt-Überwachungs-Kommission (ILUK)* (Allied Aviation Supervisory Commission) in January 1927 and the withdrawal of all Allied inspection teams from the Reich territory.[1] One of the many responses to these developments was the reorganisation and expansion of the existing covert *Flugtechnikreferat* (Flight Technical Desk) inside the *Inspektion für Waffen und Geräte* (Weapons and Equipment Inspectorate) within the *Heereswaffenamt* (Army Ordnance Office) *(WaA)* (See 1C1). From October 1925 responsibility for the development of military aircraft had been divided between *Hptm.*Kurt Student's *Waffen Prüfwesens 6 Flugzeuge* (Weapons Development Department 6 – Aircraft) (formerly *In.W.G. 6F*) and *Hptm.*Hellmuth Volkmann's *Waffen Beschaffungs 6 Flugzeuge* (Weapons Procurement Department 6 - Aircraft). *Referate* (Desks) in both departments which dealt with *Flugzeuge* (Airframes), *Motoren* (Engines), *Ausrüstung* (Equipment), *Bauaufsicht* (Construction Control) and *Wehrwirtsch* (Economics)*(Chart 1-4).*[2] To preserve secrecy the individual *Entwicklungsreferate* (Advisory Development Boards) were camouflaged as civilian firms, for example the *Flugzeugreferat* was outwardly known as the *Ingenierbüro Nicolaus.*[3] *Wa.B.6F* on the other hand was responsible for economic planning and procurement. Volkmann was a former fighter pilot who had been assigned to *Infanterie-Regiment 14* at Konstanz from January 1921 prior to being appointed to the *Stab 5.Division* at Stuttgart in March 1924. He took up his new position in October 1925.[4]

1   Hertel W. Dipl.Ing.GenIng.a.D.1955 *Procurement in the German Air Force* USAF Historical Studies No.170 (hereafter cited as Hertel 1955) p.2, Nowarra H.J. 1980 *Die Verbotenen Flugzeuge 1921-1935 – Die getarnte Luftwaffe*, (hereafter cited as Nowarra 1980) p.33 & Beauvais H., Kossler K., Mayer M. and Regel C. 2002 *German Secret Flight Test Centres to 1945: Johannisthal, Lipetsk, Rechlin, Travemünde, Tarnewitz, Peenemunde-West* (hereafter cited as Beauvais et al 2002) p.37 & 57.

2   Hertel 1955 pp.6-9, Andersson L. 1989 'Secret Luftwaffe: German Military Aviation Build-up between the Wars' in *Air Enthusiast* No.41 1989 (hereafter cited as Andersson 1989) p.38 & Hooton E.R. 1994 *Phoenix Triumphant: The Rise and Rise of the Luftwaffe* (hereafter cited as Hooton 1994) p.50. *Hptm.*Student had been the *Flugtechnikreferat* within the *Insp.d.Waffen u.Gerat* since Apr 20 - see service record for Kurt Student in Hildebrand K.F.1992 *Die Generale der deutschen Luftwaffe 1935-1945 Band 3 O-Z* (hereafter cited as Hildebrand 1992) pp.363-365. *Hptm.* Volkmann took over his new duties on the 1 Oct 25 - see Hildebrand 1992 pp.450-451. Within the *WaA* covert military aviation development was concealed with *Wa.Prw.6 Kraftfahrzeuge* (Motor Vehicles) - see *App.A Structure of Organisation for Co-operation between the Reichswehr and Red Army* in Schliephake H. 1971 *The Birth of the Luftwaffe* (hereafter cited as Schliephake 1971 p.61 & Fleischer W. 2003 *German Air-Dropped Weapons to 1945* (hereafter cited as Fleischer 2003) p.6.

3   Beauvais et al 2002 p.37. The *Referate* were headed by: Boehme *(Flugzeuge)*, Bullinger *(Motoren)*, Grosch *(Ausrüstung)*, Schwarz *(Bauaufsicht)* & Wegner *(Wehrwirtsch)*; the *Büros* were headed by: Nicolaus *(Flugzeuge)*, Lorenz *(Motoren)*, Genthe *(Bord-Ausrüstung)*, Schulz *(Waffen)*, Gela *(Bomber)*, Schwartz *(FT)*, Spieweck *(Bildgeräte)*, Grosch *(Ausrüstung)* - see *App.2 Air Force Agencies in 1921-28* (Integration with the *Reichswehr*) in Hertel 1955 p.269 & *Organisationsplan der für die getarnte Luftrüstung verantwortlichen Stellen im Reichswehrministerium* in Nowarra 1980 p.33.

4   Beauvais et al 2002 p.37 & Service record for Hellmuth Volkmann in Hildebrand 1992 pp.450-451. *Hptm.*

Student's staff were primarily concerned with the transformation of *Maj.*Helmuth Wilberg's *Richtlinien für die Führung des operativen Luftkrieges* (Directives for the leadership of the operational air war), published in May 1926, into operational requirements for new aircraft and their associated equipment and weapons (See 1A2).[5] The *TA (L)'s* priorities were (1) covert operational training, (2) the design and testing of emergency equipment, to be followed when appropriate by (3) the acquisition of operational combat aircraft.[6] Within the context of the *Notrüstung-Programm* (Emergency Equipment Programme) *Wa.Prw.6F* issued four operational requirements for new military aircraft later in the same year.[7] These were for a single-seat day fighter for Homeland Defence *(Heitag)*, a two-seat tactical reconnaissance aircraft *(Erkudista)*, a two-seat night fighter and reconnaissance aircraft *(Najuku)* and a long-range, medium altitude reconnaissance aircraft that could also double as a bomber *(Erkunigros)*:[8]

FIGURE 1C-2 WA.PRW.6F OPERATIONAL REQUIREMENTS 1926	
Codename	**Operational Requirement**
Heitag	Heimatjagdeinsitzer
Erkudista	Erkundsflugzeuge für die Divisionsnahaufklärungsstaffeln
Najuku	Nachtjagd und Erkundungsflugzeug
Erkunigros	Erkundungsflugzeug für mittlere Hohen und größte Entfernungen

In the following year a further requirement was issued by *Wa.Prw.6F* for a four-engine *Größnachtbomber (Gronabo)*. Five firms were invited to tender for these five aircraft types: the *Albatros Flugzeugwerke* at Berlin-Johannisthal, the *Arado Handelsgesellschaft* at Warnemünde, the newly established *Bayerische Flugzeugwerke* at Augsburg, the *AG für Dornier-Werke* at Altenrhein

---

Volkmann, was pre-war military pilot who saw war service with *Feldflieger-Abtn.25 & 71*, before joining *Jasta 6* in Aug 16. He was briefly *Fhr.Jasta 10* in late 16 before being re-assigned as *Fhr.d.Kampfeinsitzer-Schulen Köln, Paderborn, Warschau & II*. He ended the war as *Fhr.Fl.Abt. A 211*.

5   Andersson 1989 p.41. *Maj.*Wilberg was *Ltr.T 2 III (L)* and as such was responsible for the development of a military air doctrine. See also *Truppenamt T-Luft "Richtlinien für die Führung des operativen Luftkrieges"* in Corum J.S. 1997 *The Luftwaffe: Creating the Operational Air War 1918-1940* (hereafter cited as Corum 1997) pp.81-83. The role of *T 2 V (L)* can be seen as "tactical requirements" whilst that of *Wa.Prw.6F* was "technical solutions" - see Suchenwirth R. 1968 *The Development of the German Air Force 1919-1939* USAF Historical Studies No.160 (hereafter cited as Suchenwirth 1968) p.18.

6   Hertel 1955 p.11.

7   Kosin R. 1983 *Die Entwicklung der deutschen Jagdflugzeuge* (hereafter cited as Kosin 1983) p.65. One source gives 1927 as the date for these operational requirements - see Caspari H.A. Dr. (Ed.) Undated *E-Stellen Travemünde und Tarnewitz 3.Band – Die Geschichte der Seeflugzeug-Erprobungsstelle Travemünde und daraus hervorgegangenen E-Stelle für Flugzeugbewaffnung Tarnewitz Anhang C: Zeittafel* (hereafter cited as Caspari (Ed.) Undated) p.294, whilst another source suggests that these requirements were not issued until 1928, however this was the year that the actual trials and evaluation programme began - see Hooton 1994 p.65. The term *"Notrusting-Programm"* may be inaccurate, although this period was known as the *Notrüstung-Periode* and these aircraft were referred to as *Notrüstung* types - see Suchenwirth 1968 pp.24-25. & Beauvais et al 2002 p.42. Fearing a repetition of the 1926 Fili scandal the *RWM* forbade any open reference to the term "bomber" in testing circles until 1929 - see Hooton 1994 p.64.

8   Hertel 1955 p.13, Nowarra 1980 p.27 & Hooton 1994 p.64. Surprisingly the *Wa.Prw.6F* and its successors the *Wa (L)* and *Wa.Prw.8*, do not appear to have used a numerical system for its Operational Requirements nor for the more detailed Specifications that were issued to individual manufacturers. For details of the British system - see Sinnott C. 2001 *The RAF and Aircraft Design 1923-1939: Air Staff Operational Requirements* (hereafter cited as Sinnott 2001) pp.25-27 & Meekcoms K.J. and Morgan E.B. 1994 *The British Aircraft Specifications File: British Military and Commercial Aircraft Specifications 1920-1949* pp.21-23. Apart from in the use of specific engines the designers were given free reign in producing their responses to the military requirements - see Hertel 1955 pp.13-14.

and the *Heinkel Flugzeugwerke* at Warnemünde.[9] The absence of the *Junkers Flugzeugwerk* at Dessau in this line-up may be explained by *Professor* Junkers' known antithesis towards the development of military aircraft, to the fall-out from the contemporary Fili Affair or more probably to the perceived expense and complexity of his all-metal designs (See 1C1 & 1D2).[10] The use of the new 600 hp BMW VI vee-twelve or the Siemens und Halske licence built 530 hp Bristol Jupiter nine-cylinder radial was specified in each case. Six different designs were produced, these being: the Arado SD I single-seat fighter (BMW VI), the Albatros L 76, later L 77v, two-seat fighter (BMW VI), the Albatros L 78 two-seat tactical reconnaissance aircraft (BMW VI), the BFW M.22 (Jupiter) and Heinkel HD 34 (BMW VI) bombers, the Dornier Do P (Jupiter) heavy night bomber and the Heinkel HD 41 (BMW VI, later Jupiter) two-seat reconnaissance bomber.[11] The first of these prototypes were ready for testing in 1927 (See 1C3).[12]

Since the war the testing of new commercial aircraft had been carried out quite openly at the *Reichsverband der deutschen Luftfahrtindustrie (RdL)'s* (Reich Association of the German Aircraft Industry) *Eprobungsstelle* (Testing Station) at Berlin-Staaken and by the *Deutsche Versuchsanstalt für Luftfahrt (DVL)* (German Experimental Institute for Aviation) at Berlin-Adlershof.[13] However the testing of military aircraft within Germany was expressly prohibited by the Versailles Treaty (See also 1B1). To help overcome these restrictions Student encouraged the formation of a special *Abteilung M Militärische Eprobung* (Department M Military Testing) within the *DVL* to oversee the development and activities of a new test facility at Rechlin on the Muritzsee *(Photo 1C-4)*.[14] In 1925, with government support, the resident *Luftfahrtverein Waren eV* purchased further land together with the former facilities of the wartime *Flieger-Versuchs und Lehranstalt (FVL)* (Flight Research and Development Institute) at this remote Mecklenburg site as the basis for a new *Eprobungsstelle* (See also 1B1).[15] Limited building work followed with the erection of single hangar (42m x 21m) which incorporated a workshop and living quarters.[16] Almost immediately a secret

9   Hooton 1994 pp.64-65. The requirement was for a four engine heavy night bomber, for long range operations, a speed of 212 kph and an operational ceiling of 4,500 m - see Schliephake 1971 p.28.

10   Hermann 1943 *The Rise and Fall of the Luftwaffe* (hereafter cited as Hermann 1943) p.51 & Schmitt G. 1988 *Hugo Junkers and his Aircraft* pp.135-135. Given the military design activity at Dessau at this time it is difficult to ascribe a pacifist attitude on the part of Junkers as a reason for his company not being invited to tender for these requirements. In 1925 the A 20 had been re-designed as the R 02 reconnaissance bomber for the Turkish military - a total of 64 military versions of the A 20 (R 02), A 25 (R 41) & A 35 (R 42) were delivered during 1925/26. In 1926 Dessau completed two examples of the A 32 a three seat multi-purpose monoplane; in the following year this aircraft was converted to the bomber-reconnaissance role as the K 39 at Limhamn in Sweden - see Schmitt 1988 pp.153-156. The fact that Junkers' all-metal constructional techniques were not favoured by Wa.Prw.6F or its successors was almost certainly significant - see Kosin 1983 pp.70-71 – whilst it has also been suggested that the *RWM* considered Junkers' military products to have a poor reputation – see Hooton 1994 p.62.

11   Lange B. 1970 *Das Buch der deutschen Luftfahrttechnik* (hereafter cited as Lange 1970) p.160, pp.161-162, p.191, pp.246-247 & p.320, Nowarra 1980 pp.144-145, 160-162, 172-174, 182-183, 186-187 & 192-193, Dornier GmbH 1983 *Dornier: Die Chronik des altesten deutschen Flugwerks* p.112, Hooton 1994 p.65, Kranzhoff J A 1997 *Arado: Geschichte eines Flugzeugwerks* pp.25-26 & Koos V. 2006 *Typenbucher Deutsche Luftfahrt: Ernst Heinkel Flugzeugwerke 1922-1932* (hereafter cited as Koos 2006) pp.84-85 & 99-100. It was not intended that these types be produced in series. Instead the aim was to construct a few test models to clarify the technical possibilities that existed within Germany at that time and to ascertain the performance achieved - see Hertel 1955 pp.12-14.

12   Nowarra 1980 p.144. This was the Albatros L 76.

13   Andersson 1989 p.41 & Beauvais et al 2002 p.53.

14   Beauvais et al 2002 p.41. Berlin-Adlershof was more commonly known as Berlin-Johannisthal - see Zapf J. 2001 *Flugplatze der Luftwaffe 1934-1945 und was davon ubrig blieb Bd.1 Berlin & Brandenburg* (hereafter cited as Zapf 2001) p.39. The *DVL* was an important centre for theoretical scientific research and experiment in aeronautical subjects - see Hertel 1955 p.2 & Lange 1970 pp.188-191.

15   Zapf J. 2006 *Flugplatze der Luftwaffe 1934-1945 und was davon ubrig blieb Bd.5 Mecklenburg-Vorpommern* pp.315-341 & Beauvais et al 2002 p.53. Prior to this military prototypes had been tested abroad. In 1925 the Albatros L 65 I & II were tested in Memelland, whilst the Do C & Do H Falke were test flown at Dubendorf in Switzerland.

16   Beauvais et al 2002 pp.52-53. This facility had originally been opened in Aug 18 as a complex of 3 airfields: Larz

test programme was agreed and implemented. This work included tests with fire proof fuel tanks, variable pitch propellers, test firing with the GAST and Lubbe machine guns, air tests of the BMW IV and endurance tests for the new BMW VI as well as trials with exhaust gas turbines (See 1C3 & 1C5).[17] In the following year there was a greater emphasis on engine development, in particular the BMW VI (See 1C1) as well as the evolution of a more powerful petrol engine in the 800 - 1,200 hp class and a diesel engine for aircraft use (See 1C3).[18] At the end of 1927 the *Albatros Flugzeugwerke* assumed control of the airfield with operations being controlled by the *Erprobungs-Abteilung der Albatros Flugzeugwerke GmbH, Johannisthal* and under this new authority further improvements were then made to the site during the following two years.[19] In the meantime more extensive testing together with tactical trials were carried out at the Soviet Union at the even more highly classified *Wissenschaftliche Versuchs-und Prüfanstalt für Luftfahrzeuge (Wivupal)* (Aircraft Scientific Research and Test Institute) at Lipetsk (See 1D1).[20]

In the meantime the necessarily secret work of *Wa.Prw.6F* and *Wa.B.6F* was concealed from the inquisitive eyes of the international community within the *Firma Fertigungs GmbH* (Manufacturing Ltd.). *Fertigungs GmbH* was a "front" company which was established by the *RWM* in 1926 through which orders could be placed with the various aircraft and aero-engine firms for a new generation of military aircraft.[21] Managing Director of the *Firma Fertigungs GmbH* was *Ing.* Heinrich Bauer, a former Managing Director of the *Albatros Flugzeugwerke* at Berlin-Johannisthal.[22] A *Technischen Büros* (Technical Bureau) was established under *Dipl-Ing.*Otto Maashoff, this office being responsible for the detailed assessment and examination of the design data submitted by the aircraft manufacturers prior to the finalisation of a prototype order.[23] Initially a specific firm was invited to submit plans to meet each specification but by the end of the decade a process of open tendering had been adopted and several firms would offer competing designs.[24]

To equip *T 2 V (L)'s* projected air units Volkmann's *Wa.B.6F* produced a plan in 1927 to acquire, in the event of an emergency, a total force of 247 aircraft (See 1A3).[25] With the exception

(Wireless Telegraphy), Rechlin (Aviation) & Roggentin (Engines). *Hptm.*August Joly was placed in command. Its isolation was made all the more secure as it could not be accessed overland by any main traffic artery - see Suchenwirth 1968 p.29.

17   BA/MA Freiburg, Dokument RM8v/3604: *Preliminary Draft, Test Programme 1.2.1925 to 30.6.1925* in Beauvais et al 2002 p.55 & 111.

18   BA/MA Freiburg, Dokument RM8v/3604: *Preliminary Draft, Test Programme 1925/26* in Beauvais et al 2002 p.56 & 111.

19   Beauvais et al 2002 pp.53-55.

20   Schliephake 1971 pp.16-17 & Beauvais et al 2002 p.43. The official affiliation to the *DVL* via *Abt.M* was dropped although the majority of the *E-Stelle's* technical personnel continued to be provided by this organisation.

21   Suchenwirth 1968 p.25 & Nowarra 1980 p.27. *"The purpose of the newly established section (Fertigung) was to create the necessary conditions for serial production under licence through the establishment of uniform standards and specifications in the preparation and execution of construction data"* - quoted from Hertel 1955 *Procurement in the German Air Force* p.67 USAF Historical Studies No.170. Front line testing at Lipetsk began in the summer of 1928 with the arrival at that site of a 16 man team headed by Ernst Marquard and Emil Thuy – see Beauvais et al 2002 pp.42-44.

22   Service record for Heinrich Bauer in Hildebrand K.F.1990 *Die Generale der deutschen Luftwaffe 1935-1945 Band 1 A-G* pp.53-54. *Ing.*Bauer, the former Managing Director of *Albatros-Flugzeugwerke* entered *Reichsdienst* on the 16 Jul 26 as *Beratender Ingenieur* (Consultant Engineer) *d.Firma Fertigungs GmbH*. In Sep 26 he was appointed *Direktor d.Fertigungs GmbH*, a position he held until Sep 33.

23   Service record for Otto Maashoff in Hildebrand K.F.1991 *Die Generale der deutschen Luftwaffe 1935-1945 Band 2 H-N* (hereafter cited as Hildebrand 1991) pp.331-332. *Lt.d.Res.a.D.Dipl-Ing.*Maashoff had entered *Reichsdienst* on the 1 Apr 26 and was assigned to *Wa L* within the *HWA*. In Aug 26 he was appointed *Ltr.d.Technischen Büros d.Firma Fertigung GmbH*, a position he held until Jul 32.

24   Hertel 1955 pp.11-12. This requirement had been generated in response to *Rittm.*Adolf Baeumker's theoretical memorandum which had been prepared to meet a possible Polish attack on Ostpreussen. *Hptm.*Volkmann felt that such a requirement was out of all proportion to the capacity of the German aero-industry to produce these machines in 1927 and he had protested as such in the strongest terms to the *T 2 V (L)*.

25   Andersson 1989 p.41.

of the fighter units that would make use of the remaining Lipetsk based Fokker D.XIII fighters, the other units would have to have been equipped with converted types then in use by the *DVS* for training or by the *DLH* for transport duties (See also 1D2):[26]

FIGURE 1C-3 PROJECTED AIRCRAFT PROCUREMENT UNDER THE HEERESWAFFENAMT'S NOTPROGRAMM 1927-28		
Albatros L 65	Reconnaissance	47
Albatros L 70	Reconnaissance	72
Heinkel HD 33	Reconnaissance	24
Fokker D.XIII	Fighter	47
Dornier Merkur	Auxiliary Bomber	37
Junkers G 24	Auxiliary Bomber	20

In the event such a substantial procurement did not occur; primarily because of continued allied surveillance, but also due to a lack of funds. Funding for the development of military aircraft and associated equipment only averaged *RM* 3 million annually during the mid-to late-twenties. However this figure was supplemented by average annual *RVM* subsidies to the Industry of *RM* 45.88 million (See also 1B1).[27] On a more pragmatic level it was in any case doubtful whether the aircraft industry actually possessed the capacity to produce these additional aircraft whilst fulfilling existing commercial contracts.

On the 1 February 1928 both *Wa.B.6F* and *Wa.Prw.6F* were removed from the immediate jurisdiction of the *Inspektion für Waffen und Geräte* and amalgamated to produce a single department, the *Gruppe Wa (L)* (Ordnance Group – Military Aviation) within the *Heereswaffenamt*.[28] This was partly in response to the need to more effectively co-ordinate the development of military aircraft and partly in response to the recommendations of the *Reichswehr Vereinfachungskommissar* (German Armed Forces Commissioner for Retrenchment and Simplification)(See 1A3).[29] After eight years in the vanguard of covert military aviation technology, Student was re-assigned to *Infanterie-Regiment 2* at Allenstein/ Ostpreussen for a period of *Truppendienst* (Troop Service). In recognition of his major contribution to the development of military aviation his seniority *(RDA)* as a Hauptmann was back dated from 20 June 1918 to the 5 October 1916.[30] Volkmann took over as *Chef Wa (L)*. His enlarged department consisted of three *Gruppen* (Departments) which dealt with

26 Suchenwirth 1968 p.38 & Andersson 1989 p.41. Favoured types included the Albatros L 75 as *Aufklärungsflugzeuge* together with the Rohrbach Ro VIII and Junkers G 24 as *Behelfsnachtbomber-Flugzeuge* - see also Beauvais et al 2002 pp.43-44.

27 Hooton 1994 pp.61-62..

28 *HWA Nr.2840/28, geh.Kdo. "Z" Wa B 6* in Suchenwirth 1968 p.18. The date of 1 Feb 26 is thought to be a typo and should be 1 Feb 28 which would be supported by *Anhang C: Zeittafel* in Caspari (Ed.) Undated p.294. However another source suggests 29 Nov 28 – see Zeitler M. *The Reichswehr und Rote Armee, 1920-33* in Beauvais et al 2002 p.37 – whilst *Hptm.*Student was posted on the 1 Nov 28 – see service record for Kurt Student in Hildebrand 1992 p.364.

29 Keßelring A. GFM.a.D. 1974 *The Memoirs of Field-Marshal Keßelring* pp.23-24. This had been one of *Maj.*Albert Keßelring's proposals as *Reichswehr* Commissioner for Retrenchment and Simplification *(Vereinfachungskommissar)* - see Suchenwirth 1968 p.18. Previously Development (Prüfwesen) and Procurement *(Beschaffungs)* had been separate departments within the *Waffenamt* and this had led to inefficiency, duplication and to a degree of discord. *Maj.*Keßelring had been assigned to the *Wehramt/RWM* in Oct 26 - see service record for Albert Keßelring in Hildebrand 1991 pp.165-167.

30 Service record for Kurt Student in Hildebrand 1992 pp.363-365. Following a period of refresher training with the *Ausbildungs-Bataillon* & *10./IR 2* he became a *Kompaniechef* within *IR 2*. Promoted to *Maj.* on the 1 Jan 30 he was later appointed *Kdr.I./IR 3* at Marienburg on the 1 Feb 31.

Entwicklung (Development), *Beschaffung* (Procurement) and *Wehrwirtschaft Rüstung* (Armament Economics). The three *Gruppen* were headed respectively by *Hptm.Dr.*Paul Jeschonnek, *Hptm.* Eduard Seldner and *Herr* Wegner.[31] There were also several *Referate* with specific responsibilities for *Flugzeuge* (Aircraft), *Motoren* (Engines), *Bord Ausrüstung* (Aircraft Equipment), *FT Gerat* (Wireless Equipment), *Bildgerät* (Photographic Equipment), *Waffen* (Armament), *Bomben* (Drop Ordnance) and *Bauaufsicht* (Construction Supervision) *(Chart I-5).*[32] As before the task of *Wa.(L)* was to translate the operational requirements of the *Truppenamt's* (Troop Office) secret air staff then under *Maj.*Hellmuth Felmy, the new *Chef T2 V (L)*, into effective combat aircraft (See 1A3). It was therefore responsible for all military aviation development and procurement and its officers worked closely with the *Erprobungsstellen Rechlin* and *Lipetsk* as well as with the larger aircraft manufacturers. *Hptm.Dr.*Paul Jeschonnek was appointed *Leiter Erprobung* (Head of Testing) *(Wa (L)Prw.)* within the new organisation.[33] Other suitably qualified officers were seconded to the major aviation firms, for example *Oblt.Dipl-Ing.*Gerhard Bassenge, a former *Jagdflieger* with 7 *Abschusse*, was seconded to the *AG für Dornier-Flugzeuge* as a military advisor whilst the company was engaged in the construction of a new heavy bomber for the *Reichsheer*, the Do P (See 1C3).[34] In all *Wa.(L)* employed 48 officers, officials and civilians at this time.[35]

In the meantime evaluation of the *Notrüstung* prototypes at Rechlin and Lipetsk had proved disappointing. None of the new types were to exhibit particularly pleasant handling characteristics and in some cases the aircraft were simply dangerous (See 1C3).[36] The Arado SD I was lost during a test flight from Rechlin on the 11 October 1927. Its pilot, Dr-*Ing.*Theodor Bienen, was killed.[37] The Albatros L 76 proved to be prone to spin accidents; an L 76a was lost with its crew of two due to this cause during a wireless test at Berlin-Rudow on the 22 July 1927, whilst *Hptm.Dr.*Paul Jeschonnek was killed when it became impossible to escape from an inverted spin in another L 76 on the 13 June 1929.[38] The BFW M 22, designed by Willy Messerschmitt, was not completed until March 1930 but it too had a short life. It crashed at Augsburg on the 14 October 1930 during a test flight by *Oblt.a.D.*Eberhard Mohnicke. Mohnicke, the *Käpitan Fliegerstaffel Rechlin* was killed.[39] The HD

---

31   *App.3 Air Force Agencies in 1928-29 (Integration with the Reichswehr)* in Hertel 1955 p.270 & *Organisatorischer Aufbau der für die geplante Luftrüstung verantwortlichen Stellen im Reichswehrminsiterium 1928/29* in Nowarra 1980 p.41. *Hptm.*Seldner was an experienced pilot who had flown bombers, close support aircraft and fighters in the *Luftstreitkräfte* during 1916-18. His final position had been as *Fhr.Jasta 31* with the rank of *Hptm*. Post war he had served with *IR 14* at Konstanz prior to appointment to the *WaA* as a *Referent* in Oct 26 - see service record for Eduard Seldner in Hildebrand 1992 pp.293-294.

32   *App.3 Air Force Agencies in 1928-29 (Integration with the Reichswehr)* in Hertel 1955 p.270 & Beauvais et al 2002 pp.37-38.

33   Beauvais et al 2002 p.37 & 127. *Hptm.*Student had been *Ltr.Erprobung* prior to his re-assignment. Prior to his appointment *Hptm.*Paul Jeschonnek had obtained extensive experience of military aircraft development within *Wa.Prw.6F.*

34   Service record for Gerhard Bassenge in Hildebrand K.F.1990 *Die Generale der deutschen Luftwaffe 1935-1945 Band 1 A-G* (hereafter cited as Hildebrand 1990) pp.51-52. Bassenge had been a member of the prestigious *Jasta Boelcke* and had been wounded in action in Nov 17. Post war he had been a *Kp.Offz.* within *IR 3* at Deutsch-Eylau in Ostpr. before training as an *Ingenieur* at the *Technischen Hochschule Hannover* between 1922-27. A period at the *RWM* followed, almost certainly with either *Wa.Prw.6F* or *Wa.B.6F.* In Oct 28 he was posted to the *Stab IR 6* at Lübeck.

35   *Waffenamt, Organisation and Personnel Roster 1928/29* in BA/MA RH 8/v.3667. Detailed examination of the roster revealed 3 *Offiziere*, 11 *Offiziere a.D.* & 15 *Ingenieure*.

36   Nowarra 1980 pp.162-163, Kosin 1983 pp.65-66, Hooton 1994 p.65 & Kranzhoff 1997 pp.25-28. The unregistered Arado SD I was WNr.31 at the Warnemünde works. It was powered by a 425 hp Bristol radial and had made 20 flights by the time of the fatal crash.

37   Beauvais et al 2002 p.57. It had completed 20 flights. This was also the first recorded aircraft crash at Rechlin. However it would not be the last!

38   Nowarra 1980 p.144-145, Kosin 1983 pp.68-69 & Beauvais et al 2002 pp.46-49 & p.57.

39   Smith J.R. 1971 *Messerschmitt: An Aircraft Album* (hereafter cited as Smith 1971) p.22, Nowarra 1980 pp.182-183 & Beauvais et al 2002 pp.56-57. Mohnicke had previously served with *Kagohl 2* and *Jasta 11* where he had scored *9 Abschusse* - see Franks N., Bailey F. and Duiven R. 1996 *The Jasta Pilots: Detailed listings and histories August 1916 -*

41 was one of the few to have exhibited acceptable handling characteristics but only four examples were completed, these being used for engine and equipment trials.[40] In the meantime Albatros had attempted to resolve the longitudinal instability of the L 76a by deepening the rear fuselage and increasing the area of the fin and rudder. The modified aircraft was designated the L 77v and six of the type were ordered for weapons trials at Lipetsk in the *Jagdzweisitzer* (two seat fighter role).[41] Fortunately for Albatros its less innovatory L 78 *Erkudista*, based on the earlier L 75 *B 2 Schulflugzeug* (Basic Trainer), was more successful and a small quantity were ordered for training purposes.[42]

In October 1929 Volkmann was promoted to Major and simultaneously transferred to the *Stab Artillerie-Führers II* (Headquarters Artillery Commander II) in Stettin.[43] His replacement as *Chef Wa (L)*, or *Wa.Prw.8* as it was soon to be known, was *Maj.*Wilhelm Wimmer, an experienced air officer who had seen extensive war service with the *bayerischen Luftstreitkräfte* (Bavarian Air Service) and who had previously been employed as *Referat III Technik* (Head of Desk 3 Technical) within the *T 2 V (L)* (See 1A3).[44]

In the summer of 1929 a major re-structuring of the *Heereswaffenamt* led to the re-organisation of the *Wa (L)* into five *Gruppen* under *Hptm.Dipl.Ing.*Eduard Riesch, *Hptm.Dipl.Ing.*August Ploch, *Dipl.Ing.*Dietrich Frhr.von Massenbach, *Hptm.*Seldner and *Herr* Wegner *(Chart 1-6)*.[45] The increased importance of aircraft development was recognised by the grouping of the previously separate *Referate* for *Flugzeuge, Motoren* and *Bord-Ausrüstung* into *Gruppe 1 Entwicklung Flugzeuge*, whilst the remaining *Waffen, Bildgeräte* and *FT Navigation Referate* were joined by *Referate* for *Bomber* (Bomber Aircraft), *Chemische Kampfstoffe* (Chemical Weapons) and *Sondermunition* (Special munitions) to form *Gruppe 2 Ausrüstung*. Both of these Gruppen were now led by recently qualified *Diplom-Ingenieure*.[46] The importance of testing was also recognised by the creation of *Gruppe 3 Eprobung* which supervised the myriad activities of the *Erprobungsstellen Rechlin, Albatros, Staaken* and *Lipetsk*. Procurement was handled by *Gruppe 4 Beschaffung* with separate *Referate* for *Flugzeuge, Motoren* and *Ausrüstung. Fertigungs GmbH* was also absorbed into this Gruppe. Economic planning and industrial matters were handled by *Gruppe 5 Wehrwirtschaft Rüstung*.[47]

November 1918 p.216. Prior to his appointment as *Kap.Fliegerstaffel Rechlin*, he had been *Ref.VII Taktische Auftrage Ausbildungs* (Tactical Tasks Training) within *Wa.Prw.6F* - see *Organisation of the E-Stelle Rechlin 1928 to 1945* in Beauvais et al 2002 p.127.

40   Lange 1970 p.247, Nowarra 1980 pp.186-187, Beauvais et al 2002 pp.48-49 & p.57 & Koos 2006 pp.99-100.

41   Lange 1970 p.160, Nowarra 1980 pp.160-161, Kosin 1983 pp.68-69 & Beauvais et al 2002 p.49 & pp.56-57.

42   Lange 1970 p.160 & Nowarra 1980 p.160-162.

43   Service records for Hellmuth Volkmann in Hildebrand 1992 pp.450-451.

44   Service record for Wilhelm Wimmer in Hildebrand 1992 pp,526-527. Wimmer had learned to fly in 1914 and his war service had included *Truppendienst* with *bay.Fl.Abt.4, preus.FeldFl.Abt.51* & *bay.Fl.Abt.294*, as well as *Stabsdienst* with the *StoFl.AOK Strantz* and the *bayerischen Inspektion d.Luftstreitkräfte*. He was discharged on the 30 Sep 20 but re-engaged on the 1 Jan 21 seeing service with *IR 20, Kraftfahr-Abt.7* & *IR 19*. From Oct 26 he had been a *Referent* in the *RWM*. This source suggests that he was not assigned to the *HWA* until May 30.

45   *Army Ordnance Office Aviation Organisation 1st October 1929 to 31st March 1933* in Beauvais et al 2002 p.51. It seems likely that this internal re-organisation was first affected as the *Wa (L) I* (Aircraft Development), *Wa (L) II* (Weapons, Photographic and F.T. Development) and *Wa (L) III* (Testing). The *HWA* had itself been reorganised in 1927 and its internal structure simplified to incorporate just four major *Abteilungen* (Departments). It was at this point that the various *Inspektionen*, including the *In.WG*, were removed from the direct jurisdiction of the *Heeresleitung* and incorporated into the *HWA* - see Corum 1997 pp.86-87.

46   *App.4 Air Force Agencies in 1929-33 (Integrated with Reichswehr)* in Hertel 1955 p.272. *Hptm.*Ploch was a former reconnaissance pilot with *Fl.Abt.202* who had studied as a *Dipl.Ing* at the *Technischen Hochschule Charlottenburg* during 1922-27 whilst assigned to *Art.Rgt.1*. He had then served in the *Stab Art.Rgt.3* in Berlin prior to assuming leadership of *Gr.2 Entwicklung-Ausrüstung*. *Hptm.*Riesch was also a reconnaissance pilot who had served with bay. *Fl.Abt.294* prior to becoming *Fhr.Fliegerschule b.Armeeflugpark 6* in Aug 18. He had studied at the *Technischen Hochschule München* during 1923-28 and was assigned to the *WaA* in Apr 28 as a *Rittm.*in *RR 17* - see service records for August Ploch & Eduard Riesch in Hildebrand 1992 pp.44-45 & 114-115.

47   *App.4 Air Force Agencies in 1929-33 (Integrated with Reichswehr)* in Hertel 1955 p.272 & *Lezte Organisationsformen*

FIGURE 1C-4 ORGANISATION OF WAFFEN PRÜFWESENS ABTEILUNG 8F
1929-1933

Abteilungs-Leiter - Maj.Wilhelm Wimmer

Haushalt (Budget) - Herr Wille

Ingenieur bei Stabe - Nicolaus

Gruppe 1 Entwicklung-Flugzeuge	Gruppe 2 Entwicklung-Ausrusting	Gruppe 4 Beschaffung
Hptm.Eduard Riesch	Hptm.August Ploch	Hptm.Eduard Seldner
1a Flugzeuge (Lucht)	2a Waffen (Thuy)	4a Flugzeuge (Boehme)
1b Motoren (Sachse)	2b Bomber (Marquard)	4b Motoren (Bullinger)
1c Bordausrüstung (Genthe)	2c Chem.Kraftstoffe (Voelker)	4c Ausrüstung (Grosch)
	2d Bildgeräte (Spieweck)	4d Bauaufsicht (Schwarz)
	2e FT u.Navigation (Schwartz)	4e Best.Verwalt. (Grosch)
	2f Sonder Munition u.Schütz (Viereck)	

Gruppe 3 Erprobungs	Gruppe 5 Wehrwirtschaft Rüstung
Dipl-Ing.Dietrich von Massenbach	Herr Wegner

Following the tragic death of *Hptm.*Jeschonnek in June 1929, *Dipl-Ing.*Dietrich Frhr.von Massenbach was promoted to *Leiter Erprobung* at both Staaken and Rechlin. He had previously been *Referat VIa Flugzeuge* at Rechlin.[48] In December the *RdL* agreed to formally take over responsibility for the *Eprobungsstelle Rechlin*, although its aircraft were still registered to the *RdL E-Stelle Staaken*.[49] The internal organisation of the *Eprobungstelle Rechlin* continued to mirror that of *Wa.Prw.8*.[50]

After the summer of 1928 aerial weapons testing does not appear to have taken place at Rechlin, this being the dedicated function of the *Wivupal*.[51] Aircraft destined for military trials were delivered to Berlin-Staaken where they were covertly fitted with their military equipment, for example bomb carriers, bomb sights, bomb release gear and defensive gun positions. Following functional tests this special equipment *(Sonderausrüstung)* was removed, packed in crates and despatched for the three week journey by sea and rail to Lipetsk.[52] Meanwhile aircraft with sufficient endurance were secretly to Lipetsk flown along *Deruluft's* airline route to Moskva and from Velikye Luki south

---

der für die technische Entwicklung der Luftrüstung der Reichswehr zustandigen Gruppe im Reichswehrministerium 1932 in Nowarra 1980 p.48.

48 *Losses of the E-Stelle Rechlin and its Predecessors 1926 to 1945 in Organisation of the E-Stelle Rechlin 1928 to 1945"* in Beauvais et al 2002 p120. *Hptm.*Jeschonnek was test flying Albatros L 76 WNr.10111 D-1210 when it failed to recover from an inverted spin to the north of Kotzow. Paul Jeschonnek had been highly regarded by his contemporaries - see *Felmy H. Gen.d.Flg.a.D. interview with Suchenwirth R. Prof., 16 Feb 54* in Suchenwirth 1968 p.26 & 201. A number of sources suggests that he had been selected as Volkmann's successor as *Chef TA.L./ Wa.Prw.8* - see Suchenwirth 1968 pp.25-26 & Hooton 1994 p.52.

49 *Aircraft at the DVL, Abteilung M, Eprobungsstelle Albatros, E-Stelle RDL Staaken & Rechlin, 1926 to 1934* in Beauvais et al 2002 pp.113-115.

50 *Organisation of the E-Stelle Rechlin 1928 to 1945* in Beauvais et al 2002 p.127.

51 Suchenwirth 1968 p.29. However see Beauvais et al 2002 pp.43-48.

52 Beauvais et al 2002 p.43.

FIGURE 1C-5 ORGANISATION OF THE RDL E-STELLEN STAAKEN AND RECHLIN		
1930		
Ltr.Gruppe III (Erprobungs) Wa.Prw.8 - Dipl-Ing.Dietrich von Massenbach		
Referat Flugzeuge	Aircraft	Chef Pilot Hoppe
Referat Motor	Powerplants	Not appointed (was Ing.Sachse)
Referat Ausrüstung	Aircraft Equipment	Dipl-Ing.Dietrich Schwenke
Referat F.T.	Wireless Telegraphy	Dr.von Seelen
Referat L.B.	Photography	Rittm.a.D.Poetsch
Ltr.d.Betriebsgruppe (Operating) - Dipl-Ing.von Gerlach		
Betriebs Rechlin	E-Stelle Rechlin	Dip-Ing.Karl Bader
Betriebs Staaken	E-Stelle Staaken	Ing.Karl Leutert
Ltr.Verwaltungsreferat (Administration) - Hptm.a.D.Arthur Brandt		

into the Ukraine.[53] Prior to the manufacture of dedicated military aircraft there was considerable official interest by *T 2 V (L)* in the practicality of quickly converting *Deutsche Luft Hansa's* existing airliners into *Behelfsnachtbomber* (Auxiliary Night Bombers)(See also 1D2).[54] This concept was evaluated by a special sixteen man test unit under the joint leadership of *Oblt.(char.) Dipl-Ing.* Ernst Marquard and *Oblt.a.D.*Emil Thuy at Lipetsk in the summer of 1928.[55] Two modified airliners were employed: the Rohrbach Ro VIIIMb *Roland* WNr.18 D-991 and the Junkers G 24ge WNr.844 D-878.[56] Each aircraft flew ten sorties during which forty releases of practice ordnance was made, whilst eight releases of live *PuW* bombs were also conducted.[57] Further tests were carried out at Lipetsk the following summer by a reinforced twenty man team. During July and August

53   Beauvais et al 2002 p.43. Short range aircraft were usually crated and sent by sea and then overland by rail to avoid the necessity for intermediate refuelling stops inside the Soviet Union.

54   Suchenwirth 1968 p.38 & Hooton 1994 p.63. In the event of mobilisation the whole of *DLH* and the *DVS* (aircraft, crews, airfields, spare parts, workshops and facilities) were to be requisitioned by the *RWM* using the powers available to the Minister under the *Reichsleistungsgesetz* (Reichs Service Law).

55   Beauvais et al 2002 pp.43-46 & Fleischer 2003 pp.25-27. Ernst Marquard trained as a pilot at Boblingen and Diest in 1917-18. He was too late for war service and was discharged on the 20 Jan 19. Service in the *Freikorps* was followed by his *Dipl-Ing.* course at the *Technischen Hochschule Stuttgart.* He secured employment with the *Allgemeinen Vergaser-Gesellschaft* in Berlin in Jun 22. He entered *Reichsdienst* in Oct 24 where his speciality was chemical weapons and drop ordnance and from Jun 26 he was assigned to *Wa.Prw.6F as Referat IIc* - see service record Ernst Marquard in Hildebrand 1991 pp.356-357. Emil Thuy had trained as a military pilot at Johannisthal and Boblingen. He served with *Fl.Abt.53,* before joining *Jasta 21.* He was *Kap.Jasta 28* and was decorated with the *Plm* on the 30 Jun 18. His final score was *32 abschusse.* Post war he worked for *Siemens Schukert* in Finland before joining the *RWM.* Tragically he was killed on the 11 Jun 30 when his L 76a WNr.10 101 D-1127 crashed on take off from an emergency landing field near Smolensk - see service record for Emil Thuy in Angolia J.R. and Hackney C.R. 1984 *The Pour le Mérite and Germany's First Aces* pp.218-219 & *Losses of the E-Stelle Rechlin and its Predecessors 1926 to 1945* in Beauvais et al 2002 p.120.

56   Beauvais et al 2002 p.49. The aircraft arrived at Lipetsk in Jun 28 and were then fitted with their military equipment - *Sonderausrüstung.* Roland Ro VIII WNr.18 was the prototype which had been flight tested at Staaken in 1926 prior to service with *DLH* as D-991*Zugspitze* until 1928 when it was withdrawn for modification as a *Behelfsnachtbomber* - see Stroud J.1966 *European Transport Aircraft since 1910* (hereafter cited as Stroud 1966) pp.358-360 & Nowarra 1980 pp.176-178. Junkers G 24 WNr.844 had been originally completed at Dessau in 1925 as a G 23. To avoid *ILUK* restrictions it was then delivered to Limhamn where it was brought up to G 24 standard with three Junkers L5 engines as a G 24ge prior to registration as S-AAAM. In 1926 it returned to Germany via Holland as H-NADA. It joined *DLH* in 1926 as D-878 *Haarlem.* Following military trials in 1928-29 it was scrapped in 1931 - see *Construction and employment of G 23/G 24 aircraft from Dessau and Limhamm 1st Construction Series* in Schmitt 1988 p.151.

57   Beauvais et al 2002 p.44. Unfortunately the elderly *PuW* ordnance proved totally unsatisfactory above 3,000 m as the bombs broke up - see also Fleischer 2003 p.25.

1929 over 1,200 practice bombs were dropped, whilst tests were also carried out on a wide range of *Sonderausrüstungen*: bomb-release mechanisms, new bomb sights and the practicality of the improvised defensive machine gun positions (See also 1C5 & 1D1). In its final report the team concluded that in an emergency both aircraft could be employed successfully in the bombing role, although the G 24 was judged the better of the two types for this unexpected role.[58]

The reorganisation of the *Wa (L)* and the appearance of *Wa.Prw.8* was timely. The first *Rüstungsperiode* (Rearmament Period) had started on the 1 April 1929, whilst in October a parallel reorganisation of the *Truppenamt's* air staff had led to the creation of the *Inspektion 1 (L)* (Air Inspectorate) under *GenMaj.*Hilmar Ritter von Mittelberger with Felmy as his *Chef des Stabes* (See 1A3).[59] The enhanced importance of military aviation was recognised with demands from the *Heeresleitung* (Army High Command) in 1930 for a *Fliegertruppe* (Flight Troops) of 22-*Staffeln* (Squadrons): 13 *Aufklärer-* (Reconnaissance), 6 *Jäger-* (Fighter) and 3 *Bomber-Staffeln*.[60] In the same year the *RWM* released *RM* 110 million for the further development and purchase of aircraft and aviation equipment as part of its earlier plans for secret rearmament (*Aufstellungsplan einer Kriegswehrmacht*).[61] Additional funding was made available for active and passive air defence measures (See 1E2).

Given this financial backing a new generation of more capable military aircraft could be developed and Wimmer therefore issued a set of new requirements to the aircraft industry, these being in part based on the *Reichsheer's* earlier experiences with the *Notrüstung Program*.[62] The *Heitag* requirement was eventually met by the Arado Ar 64 (Jupiter VI), a design which could trace its design lineage via the interim SD III and SD II to the original SD I of 1927, whilst also at Warnemünde *Heinkel* further developed the earlier HD 41 to produce the thoroughly acceptable HD 45 (BMW VIu). This type was judged more capable than the rival Focke Wulf S 39 (Jupiter VI) to meet the *Erkunigros* requirement.[63] *Focke Wulf* had hoped to win the updated *Erkudista* requirement with its advanced A 40 (Jupiter), but once again *Heinkel* won the day with its parasol wing HE 46 (Jupiter VI), a new type which had been developed via an initial biplane configuration (See 1C3).[64]

---

58   Beauvais et al 2002 p.48. This is not surprising. The G 24 had formed the basis for the K 30 bomber which had been built in series at Limhamn as the R 42 - see Nowarra 1980 pp.118-120 & Schmitt 1988 pp.154-155.

59   *Anhang C: Zeittafel* in Caspari (Ed.) Undated p.295. The first *Rüstungsperiode* was to last until 1933.

60   Nowarra 1980 p.37 & Hooton 1994 pp.71-72. On the 15 Apr 30 this plan was reduced to 18 *Staffeln* which included 6 *Gronabo Staffeln*. The proposed air am was variously known as the *Luftstreitkräfte, Flugwaffe* & *Fliegertruppe* in the early 30s - see also Vajda F.A. & Dancey P.1998 *German Aircraft Industry and Production 1933-1945* (hereafter cited as Vajda & Dancey 1998) p.9. The decision to actually procure military aircraft was made possible by the *Reichs* Government's decision on the 29 Nov 30 to lift the confining ban on aircraft stockpiling - see *Aktennotiz des Reichswehrministers Groener vom 3.12.1930* in Suchenwirth 1968 p.37.

61   Müller-Hildebrand B. 1954 *Das Heer bis zum Kriegsbeginn*. This was 22.7% of the total rearmament budget and clearly showed the importance attached to military aviation. During 1928-29 *RM* 3.38 million had been diverted from *RVM* funds to directly support the development of military aircraft and aero-engines - see Hooton 1994 p.62. There was of course a great deal of cross-over between civil and military development of new equipment and technology.

62   Kosin 1983 p.73 & Beauvais et al 2002 p.48. Some sources suggest that there were two *Rüstungsperiode*: the first being from 1925-29 and the second from 1930-34. An authoritative source has stated the first *Rüstungsperiode* did not begin until the 1 Apr 29 - see *Anhang C: Zeittafel* in Caspari (Ed.) Undated p.295. Shortly before he was re-assigned in 1929 Volkmann issued a new set of performance requirements to the Industry - 350 kph for fighters, 250 kph for reconnaissance aircraft & 220 kph for bombers - see Hertel 1955 p.14, Nowarra 1980 p.27 & Hooton 1994 p.65. The new requirements appear to have been issued in 1929 - see also Vajda and Dancey 1998 p.9.

63   Hertel 1955 pp.15-16, Lange 1970 p.162, 224 & 247, Smith J.R. 1973 *Focke Wulf: An Aircraft Album* (hereafter cited as Smith 1973) p.27, Wagner W. 1980 *Kurt Tank - Konstrukteur und Testpilot bei Focke Wulf Die deutsche Luftfahrt 1* pp.36-37, Nowarra 1980 pp.178-180, 186-187, 190-192, 204-206 & 216-217, Hooton 1994 p.78 & Koos 2006 pp.99-100 & 107-108.

64   Hertel 1955 pp.15-16, Lange 1970 p.224 & 247, Hooton 1994 p.65 & Koos 2006 pp.109-110. The A 40 proved very unstable and despite intensive remedial work the type remained unsatisfactory. Only one example was completed - see Conradis H. 1960 *Design for Flight: The Kurt Tank Story* (hereafter cited as Conradis 1960) p.48, Smith 1973 pp.27-28, Nowarra 1980 pp.206-209 & 212-213 and Wagner 1980 p.37.

To meet the *Najuku* requirement *Albatros* returned to the fray with its L 84 (BMW VIu) *Jagdzweisitzer* (Two-seat Fighter). However the first example crashed in 1932 and only one other aircraft was built.[65] Competing designs emerged from both *Dornier* and *Junkers*. The Do C4 (BMW VI) appears to have been a new design built specifically for the *RWM*, whilst the Junkers K 47 (Hornet) was a military version of the existing A 48 *Schul-und Versuchsflugzeug* (Training and Development Aircraft).[66] Three K 47 *Jagdzweisitzer* were purchased by the *Reichsheer* for testing at Travemünde and Lipetsk where they quickly proved very popular amongst the pilots. However despite their many virtues neither the Do C4 nor the K 47 found official favour, almost certainly on account of their expensive all-metal structures.[67] Thus as a result of the failure of the L 84 *Wa.Prw.8* decided against placing any orders to meet the *Najuku* requirement.

In the bomber field *Dornier* reigned supreme. The first prototype of the four-engine Do P was completed in 1930 but it was not tested at Lipetsk until 1932.[68] By this time it had been superseded by the Do F, a two-engine design that had been produced to meet a new *Wa.Prw.8* requirement for a *Mittlere Nachtbomber (Minabo)*.[69] The declining economic position of the early thirties was certainly a factor in turning Mittelberger's air staff away from the *Gronabo* concept, but there were also real concerns by influential members of the German Government about the international repercussions that might accrue from the acquisition of such an offensive weapon.[70] Nonetheless both Felmy and Wimmer supported the development of the bomber as part of the planned force structure and it was to meet this requirement that the development contract for a *Minabo* was issued.[71] In contrast to the conservatism evident in the earlier requirements, the *Dornier* engineers were allowed free reign with their response. The resulting Do F, which flew the first time on the 7 May 1932 at Altenrhein, was therefore in advance of all contemporary bomber design in both the USA and Europe.[72] The tried and trusted biplane layout, never favoured by *Dornier*, was abandoned in favour of an advanced semi-cantilever wing structure with the two Jupiter VI radial engines being mounted in faired nacelles on the leading edge. It also featured the novel feature of a retractable main undercarriage, the first of its kind to be fitted to a European bomber aircraft (See also 1C3).[73]

65   Lange 1970 p.161, Nowarra 1980 p.198 & Hooton 1994 p.78.

66   Lange 1970 p.201, Nowarra 1980 pp.200-201, Dornier 1983 p.117 & Kosin 1983. In some publications the Do C4 appears to have been listed as the Do 10. This aircraft actually preceded the Do-C3 float-sesquiplane that had been produced to meet a Colombian Navy requirement - see Lange 1970 p.201, Dornier 1983 p.115 & Hooton 1994 p.78. The Do 10 first flew 25 Jul 31 and 2 examples were built for the *RWM* WNr.226 D-1592 & WNr.227 D-1898.

67   Lange 1970 p.283, Nowarra 1980 pp.174-176, Kosin 1983 pp.69-72 & Hooton 1994 p.78. In 1927 *Junkers* designer Karl Plauth, a former *Jagdflieger*, had begun design work on a military version of the all-metal A 48 training and research monoplane. Following his death in a flying accident on the 3 November this work was continued by his colleague Herrmann Pohlmann. Components for the K 47 two-seat fighter were built at Dessau prior to assembly at Junker's Swedish subsidiary *AB Flygindustri* at Malmo – see Schmitt 1988 p.159. Several examples were sold to China. Three examples were purchased and registered to the *RdL* as the A 48 - see Andersson 1989 p.43.

68   Dornier 1983 p.112, Hooton 1994 p.78 & Beauvais et al 2002 p.48. By this time outmoded in the bomber role the Do P was used by the *RVM* as a transport aircraft from Mar 31.

69   Nowarra 1980 pp.212-214, Hooton 1994 p.78, Corum 1997 p.122 & Beauvais et al 2002 p.48.

70   Hooton 1994 p.73.

71   Hooton 1994 pp.72-73. The evolution of the German bomber force must be set against a rising tide of international opinion against war and against the bomber in particular following the Kellogg-Briand Pact of 1928 to which the German Government was a signatory. The first World Disarmament Conference was held in Geneva in Feb 32. For Wimmer's strongly argued views on the importance of the bomber in a future war - see *Waffenamt Correspondence: Conference Memo, 18 Februar 1932 in BA/MA RH 8/v 9916* in Corum 1997 pp.119-120.

72   Green W. 1970 *The War Planes of the Third Reich* (hereafter cited as Green 1970) p.110, Nowarra 1980 pp.212-214 & Dornier 1983 p.124.

73   Munson K. *The Biplane's Fall from Favour* in Jarrett P. (Ed.) 1997 *Biplane to Monoplane: Aircraft development 1919-39* (hereafter cited as Jarrett (Ed.) 1997) pp.18-20. In creating the Do F *Dornier* was a trend setter rather than a follower. The oft-remarked Boeing Model 200 Monomail that influenced the later development of the Boeing B-9 & the Boeing Model 247 airliner did not fly until the 6 May 30 by which time the design of the Do F was already

With the exception of the Do F it was *Wa.Prw.8* policy to develop aircraft types that utilised conventional airframe and engine technology, indeed this had been a specific requirement in the case of both the *Erkudista* and the *Erkunigros* requirements.[74] This reflected the prevailing industrial practice and manufacturing skills of most German firms with the notable exception of *Dornier, Junkers* and *Rohrbach*.[75] In 1930 there were still only eight airframe and four aero-engine manufacturers capable of undertaking the manufacture of military aircraft and even this number would be reduced during the following two years with the collapse of the *Albatros, BFW* and *Rohrbach* concerns in the face of an escalating World Economic Depression:[76]

FIGURE 1C-6 GERMAN AIRFRAME AND AERO-ENGINE MANUFACTURERS 1930	
Albatros-Flugzeugwerke GmbH	Berlin-Johannisthal
Arado Handelsgesellschaft	Rostock-Warnemünde
Bayerischen Flugzeugwerke AG	Augsburg
Dornier-Werke GmbH	Friedrichshafen
Focke Wulf Flugzeugbau GmbH	Bremen
Ernst Heinkel Flugzeugwerke GmbH	Rostock-Warnemünde
Junkers Flugzeug-und Motorenwerke AG	Dessau
Rohrbach Metall-Flugzeugbau GmbH	Berlin
Argus Motoren Gesellschaft	Berlin-Reinickendorf
BMW Flugmotorenwerke GmbH	München-Allach
Junkers Motorenwerke AG	Dessau
Siemens und Halske Flugmotorenwerk AG	Berlin-Spandau

under way - see Bowers P.M. 1966 *Boeing Aircraft since 1916* p.176-178. The first British monoplane night bomber was the Fairey Hendon, a marginally earlier design, but this did not fly until the 25 Nov 30 - see Taylor H.A. 1974 *Fairey Aircraft since 1915* pp.208-216. The first French monoplane night bomber was the Bloch MB.200, however it did not fly until Jul 33 and was actually a contemporary of later British bombers - the Bristol Bombay & Handley Page Harrow - see Morse S. (Ed.) 1982 *The Illustrated Encyclopedia of Aircraft* p.734. None of these European types had retractable landing gear although this had been a feature of the experimental American Douglas XB-7 and Fokker XB-9 of 1931 and would be a feature of the B-9 and the later Martin B-10 - see Swanborough G. and Bowers P.M. 1989 *United States Military Aircraft since 1909* pp.101-102, 433-436, p.635 & 646. The Do F was actually evolved in parallel with the 3 engined Do Y. The Do Y flew first on the 17 Jan 31 but was rejected by *Wa.Prw.8* - see Nowarra 1980 pp.202-203, Dornier 1983 p.121, Dressel J. and Griehl M.1997 *The Luftwaffe Album: Bomber and Fighter Aircraft of the German Air Force 1933-1945* pp.12-13. See also Stroud J. *The Evolution of the Transport Aircraft* pp.41-43 & Hooton E.R. *Military Aviation - the slow developer* in Jarrett (Ed.) 1997 pp.62-63.

74   Green 1970 p.110 & Hooton 1994 p.78. The *Wa.Prw.8's* lack of interest in the K 47 needs to be seen in this light.
75   Suchenwirth 1968 pp.21-22 & 35 and Hooton 1994 pp.76-77.
76   Hertel 1955 p.76, Suchenwirth 1968 p.23 & Vajda and Dancey 1998 pp.9-10. Interestingly this listing did not include Germany's most prolific aircraft manufacturer - the *Hanns Klemm Flugzeugbau* (later the *Leichtflugzeugbau Klemm*) at Boblingen which produced some 450 light aircraft for private owners, club use and training between 1926-32. Its most notable product was the L 25 of 1928 - see Vajda and Dancey 1998 p.221. Hanns Klemm was an avowed pacifist - see Hermann 1943 pp.30-31. The assets of the *Albatros Flugzeugwerke* were amalgamated with those of *Focke Wulf* at Bremen - see Conradis 1960 p.38, Lange 1970 p.158 & Smith 1973 p.9; *BFW* filed for bankruptcy in Jun 31 although Willy Messerschmitt managed to salvage some assets from this collapse to re-establish the *Messerschmitt Flugzeugbau GmbH* - see Smith 1971 p.10 & Ishoven van A. 1975 *Messerschmitt – Aircraft Designer* pp.65-68.; Adolf Rohrbach had been in financial trouble from 1929. Nonetheless he declined the offer of work in the USSR - see Hermann 1943 pp.33-34 & Boyd A. 1977 *The Soviet Air Force since 1918* p.29; *Junkers* was almost taken over by *Henschel* - see Smith 1973 p.9. In return for covert *Reichswehr* contracts Arado was obliged to accept military nominees on to its board of directors, notably *Dipl.Ing.*Walter Blume who was appointed Technical Director in Jan 32 in place of Walter Rethel. Seven of Blume's former colleagues were also moved into positions of responsibility - see Kranzhoff 1997 pp.49-51.

Manufacturing capacity with its emphasis on the production of light aircraft for private ownership and club use was totally inadequate to support even a modest military programme. Indeed the production figures for the years following the relaxation of Allied restrictions in 1926 were less than that achieved in 1925.[77] The best year was 1928 when 409 aircraft had been produced.[78] Thereafter the worsening economic position had taken its toll and by the 4 April 1932, when Mittelberger published an industrial survey of the aircraft industry for the benefit of the *Truppenamt*, he warned that with just 3,800 employees in seven airframe and four aero-engine plants the Industry was quite incapable of even meeting the *Reichswehr's* minimum mobilisation plans.[79] At that time only *Junkers* and *Heinkel* could undertake limited series production and even then on a strictly limited basis not exceeding some six aircraft per month. Despite the best efforts of *Fertigungs GmbH* to standardise manufacturing methods and equipment installation it was a fact that the majority of airframe firms still hand-built their aircraft on a custom basis.[80]

The aero-engine situation was especially worrying. Despite the financial support provided by the *RVM* overall investment in this sector had been far too low for far too long. The domestic market was simply not large enough to support the development and manufacture of the high-powered aero-engines that were needed to support the planned military programme.[81] For example only 100 examples of the *Reichswehr* sponsored 600 hp BMW VI vee-twelve had been built in the four years prior to March 1930.[82] At the same time the *Argus Motoren Gesellschaft's* attempts to produce two new high-powered engines had been unsuccessful. Neither the truly massive 94 litre 1,500 hp As 5, a water-cooled engine with six rows of four cylinders in double W form of 1926, nor the much smaller but potentially more efficient 16 litre As 6 vee-twelve of 650 hp of 1927/28 found production orders and in both cases only prototypes were completed.[83] Even the established *Junkers Motorenwerke* enjoyed only slightly more success. In 1928 the company emulated *BMW's* earlier practice with the BMW VI to produce the 650 hp L 55 by joining two L 5 engine banks together to form a vee-twelve.[84] Then by increasing the running speed of its tried and tested six-cylinder L 5 engine from 1,500 rpm to 2,100 rpm it produced the L 8 which offered 420 hp for take off in contrast to the 310 hp of the L 5. Finally in 1930 it combined two L 8s to produce the L 88 which

77   *Table 3: German Aircraft Production, 1924-1929* in Hooton 1994 p.54. However this source is consistently at variance with Vajda and Dancey 1998 p.9.

78   Vajda and Dancey 1998 p.9. Alternative figures are: 1926 (168), 1927 (301), 1928 (355) & 1929 (330) - see *Table 3: German Aircraft Production, 1924-1929* in Hooton 1994 p.54.

79   Hooton 1994 p.76.

80   Hooton 1994 pp.76-77. One of the main missions of *Fertigungs GmbH* had been to standardise aviation parts so as to facilitate licence production of chosen types - *"The advantage of standardised construction data was that all engineering personnel, once they had become familiar with that data, would find the same terminology and so forth in all agencies concerned with air armament. Each individual one of the thousands of parts making up an aircraft, its engine, and its equipment was systematically catalogued by a numbering system and through this system could be traced to its origin.* – quoted from Hertel 1955 *Procurement in the German Air Force* p.69 USAF Historical Studies No.170.

81   Hooton 1994 p.77. Indeed many German firms had preferred to invest in motor vehicle and engine production. This enjoyed bigger sales to the *Reichswehr* and was in any case linked to a much larger civilian market.

82   Vajda and Dancey 1998 p.233.The As 5 had been developed to meet a *Wa.Prüf.6F* requirement for an engine in the 1,500-1,800 hp class. *"from the tactical and technical viewpoint this was a long range project far ahead of the standards then reached in the technological field. It was found, however, that industrial techniques were not yet far enough advanced to handle problems of this type, so that the development project had to be cancelled...it was too heavy and large for installation in any of the fuselages then in existence"* - quoted from Hertel 1955 *Procurement in the German Air Force* pp.25-26 USAF Historical Studies No.170.

83   Lange 1970 p.393 & Gersdorff von K. and Grasmann K. 1985 *Die Deutsche Luftfahrt 2: Flugmotoren und Strahltriebwerke* (hereafter cited as Gersdorf and Grasmann 1985) p.119. The As 5 was produced to meet a *RVM* requirement. Another authoritative source suggests that the As 5 was a 43.5 litre vee-twelve - see Gunston B. 1995 *World Encyclopaedia of Aero Engines* (hereafter cited as Gunston 1995) p.15.

84   Gersdorff and Grasmann 1985 pp.74-75 & Schmitt 1988 pp.204-206. The L 55 was used on the K 39 *Aufklarer* which was built in Sweden in 1926/27 - see Lange 1970 p.282, Nowarra 1980 pp.134-135 & Schmitt p.156.

was rated at 800 hp. However none of these engines were built in quantity.[85]

In the meantime a second *Junkers* engine design team under *Dr.-Ing.*Gasterstatt had struggled to solve the many practical problems associated with *Junkers'* original 1907 patent for a *"Junkers Doppelkolben-Schwerolmotor"* (Twin-cylinder Heavy Oil Motor).[86] The "heavy oil" engine had many advantages over the conventional petrol engine, specifically better fuel economy over long distances, lower fire risk in the event of an accident due to the use of a less volatile fuel and lower overall installation and running costs (See also 1B1 & 1C3).[87] The first manifestation of this new technology was the massive FO 3 five-cylinder in-line heavy oil engine of 1926. Using a two stroke cycle with opposed pistons, the FO 3 could produce 830 hp at just 1,200 rpm.[88] However the great weight of the engine precluded it commercial employment and during 1927 trials began on a smaller six-cylinder engine, the FO 4. This engine was first flown aboard the Junkers F 24 (W 41) and after further development it went into commercial service with *Deutsche Luft Hansa* in December 1931 as the 720 hp Jumo 4 to support cargo operations between Berlin and Amsterdam.[89] At the same time as production of the Jumo 4 began at Dessau, Gasterstatt's oil-team began work on the even smaller Jumo 5 in a further attempt to improve the power to weight ratio of the heavy oil engine. By using smaller cylinders the weight could be reduced, whilst by raising the engine's operating speed from 1,700 to 2,200 rpm rated output could be increased. Thus for an engine weight of just 500 kgs, 550 hp could be achieved. Bench testing began in 1932 and the engine was installed in a Focke Wulf A 17c *Möwe* in the following year.[90]

Lacking the financial means to develop new engines both *BMW* and *Siemens und Halske* elected to enter into negotiations with successful foreign companies to build their proven engines under licence. During 1927/28 *BMW* secured the rights to manufacture both the Pratt and Whitney Wasp and Hornet radials.[91] Licence production of the Hornet began in 1930.[92] In the meantime *Siemens und Halske* opted to build the equally successful 28.6 litre Bristol Jupiter radial from 1928.[93] The

---

85   Gersdorff and Grasmann 1985 pp.74-75 & Schmitt 1988 pp.204-206. The L 8 & L 88 were both used to power the giant G.38 airliner, whilst the L 88 was used on the prototype Ju 52 WNr.4001. *Mitsubishi* took out a manufacturing licence for the L 88 to power its Ki 20 heavy bomber - itself a variant of the G.38.

86   Gersdorff and Grasmann 1985 pp.88-89 & Schmitt 1988 pp.206-207.

87   Nayler J.L. and Ower E. 1930 *Aviation of To-Day: Its History and Development* pp.393-395. However it must be stated that it was *DLH* rather than *Wa.Prw.8* that was interested in this line of engine development - see Schliephake 1971 p.29.

88   Gersdorff and Grasmann 1985 p.89. The Fo 3 was first demonstrated in public at the *1928 Internationalen Luftfahrtausstellung* in Berlin. See also Schmitt 1988 p.207 & Gunston 1995 p.89.

89   Gersdorff and Grasmann 1985 pp.89-90, Schmitt 1988 pp.207-208 & Gunston 1995 p.89. The F 24 was a single engine variant of the multi-engine G 24. Fitted with either the BMW VI or VII this conversion had resulted from a dispute between *Junkers* and the *DLH* over the continued safety of the Junkers L 5 powered G 24 airliner at is designed all up weight. Milch's solution was to remove all three L 5 engines and replace them with a single BMW engine of more power. The converted aircraft were then employed on cargo operations - see Irving D. 1973 *The Rise and Fall of the Luftwaffe: The Life of Luftwaffe Marshal Erhard Milch* pp.20-21. The heavy oil conversion was known at Dessau as the W 41 - see Schmitt 1988 pp.105-106. The aircraft was former G 24 WNr.832 D-1051 - see Stroud 1966 pp.306-307 & *Construction and employment of G 23/G 24 aircraft from Dessau and Limhamm 1st Construction Series* in Schmitt 1988 p.151.

90   Gersdorff and Grasmann 1985 p.90 & Schmitt 1988 pp.208-210. The Focke Wulf A 17c *Möwe* WNr.50 D-1444 *Münster* was used as a test bed for the Jumo 5 heavy oil engine - see Stroud 1966 p.266.

91   Gunston 1995 pp.26-27. It has been suggested that licences for foreign radials were sought in response to a suggestion by the *Wa.Prüf 6F*. However it was *DLH* that sought the licences in anticipation of a further growth of commercial air transport - see Hertel 1955 p.27. By 1929 the P&W Wasp and Hornet radials had set a string of world records, were in series production for both the *US Army* & *USN* and powered 90% of American commercial transports. The 13.4 Litre Wasp was not manufactured in Germany but the larger 18.6 Litre Hornet was considered an ideal type in the 500-600 hp class and was the preferred type for *DLH* operations.

92   Lange 1970 p.395 & 396 and Gersdorff and Grasmann 1985 pp.53-56. The 27.7 litre BMW Hornet produced 525 hp at 1,900 rpm for take off. It became *DLH's* preferred engine for the Ju 52/3m - see Nowarra H.J. 1987 *Aircraft & Legend: Junkers Ju 52* p.35 & Schmitt 1988 pp.172-174.

93   Lange 1970 p.425. The Bristol Jupiter was eventually licence built by 17 different firms powering a staggering 262

British Jupiter VI of 1925, employed on several German prototypes, had introduced a drop-forged duralumin crankcase and a Bristol Triplex carburettor.[94] However the Siemens Jupiter was based on the Gnome et Rhône version with its superior Farman gearing that allowed a higher engine speed with less vibration. In this form the *Siemens* manufactured Jupiter engines would produce 530 hp and were widely employed by both *Deutsche Luft Hansa* and by the *Reichswehr*.[95]

The availability of such engines as the Jupiter, Hornet and BMW VI coupled to the increasingly optimistic reports from the various *Erprobungsstellen* finally enabled Wimmer's *Wa.Prw.8* to issue limited military contracts to a number of firms during the latter part of 1932. Including those destined for export fifty six military aircraft had been manufactured in 1931, a further fifty five in 1932.[96] In 1933 a total of forty two were required, a figure that included military trainers and the additional aircraft shown below:[97]

FIGURE 1C-7 COVERT MILITARY AIRCRAFT CONTRACTS 1932-33	
Arado Handelsgesellschaft	SD IV (6), SD V (2)
Dornier-Werke GmbH	Do P (1), Do C4 (1), Do F (1)
Focke Wulf Flugzeugbau GmbH	SD IV & HD 45 (12)
Ernst Heinkel Flugzeugwerke GmbH	HD 38 (5), HD 45 (7), HD 59 (2), HE 70 (3)

The covert construction of military aircraft during the early thirties was a significant step for both the *Reichswehr* and the fledgling German aircraft industry and although these modest plans would quickly be superseded it remained a fact that the aircraft types and equipment that would equip a resurgent *Luftwaffe* now existed.

---

different aircraft types.

94   Gunston 1995 p.32. In Britain Farman gearing was introduced on the Bristol Jupiter VIII of 1928. The ultimate geared and supercharged Jupiter X would produce 525 hp at 4,870 m. *Gnome et Rhône* held the European licence for the Jupiter. A particular advantage of this version was its metric engineering - see Hertel 1955 p.27.

95   Gersdorff and Grasmann 1985 pp.47-49. *DLH* purchased c.90 examples, the *Reichswehr* a further 30 for use by *Heinkel*. In all 131 engines were built under licence and it formed the basis for the later Sh 22 radial.

96   Vajda and Dancey 1998 p.9.

97   Vajda and Dancey 1998 pp.9-10. *Heinkel* were also contracted to deliver 2 training aircraft - presumably either HD 24 or HD 72. See also Kosin 1983 pp.79-80.

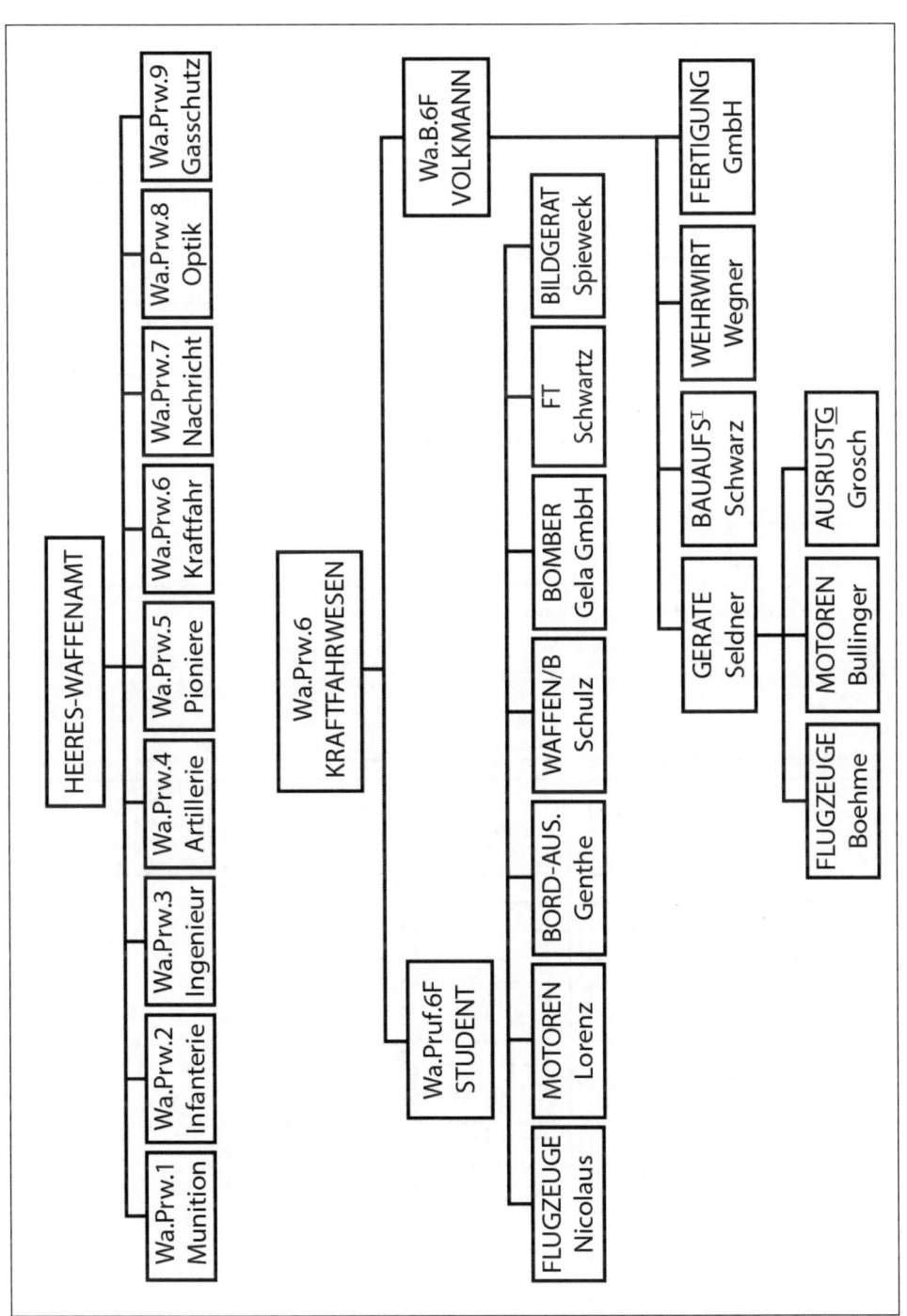

I-4 *Heereswaffenamt* Aviation Organisation – *Wa.Pru.6*, October 1925 - February 1928

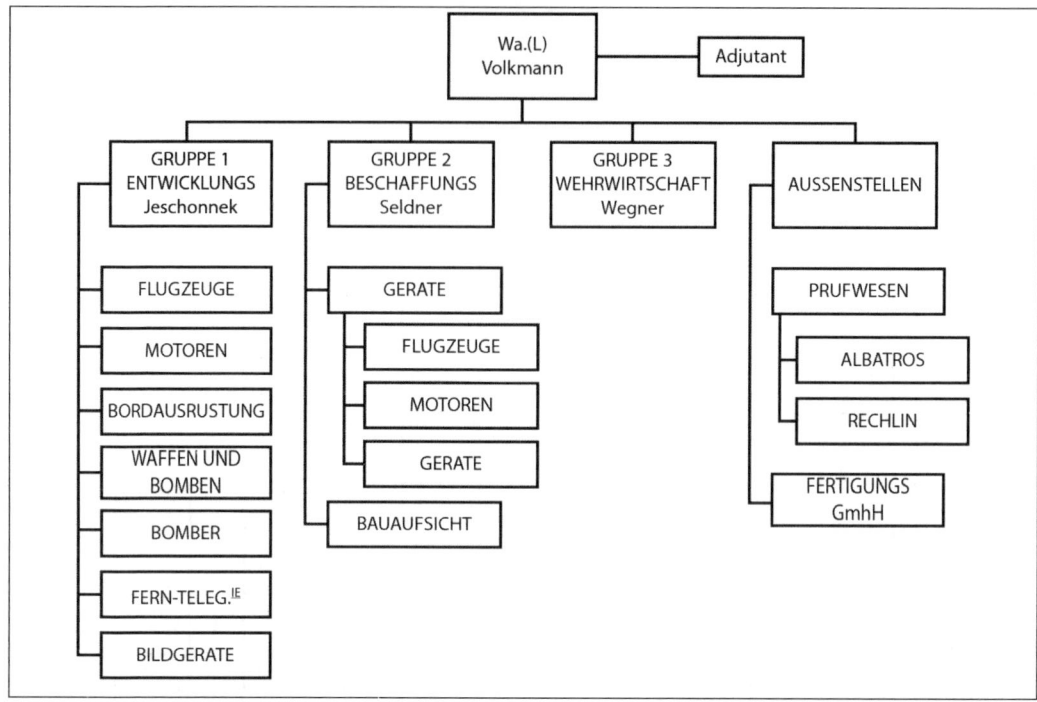

I-5   *Heereswaffenamt* Aviation Organisation – *Wa.(L) 1*, March 1928 – September 1929

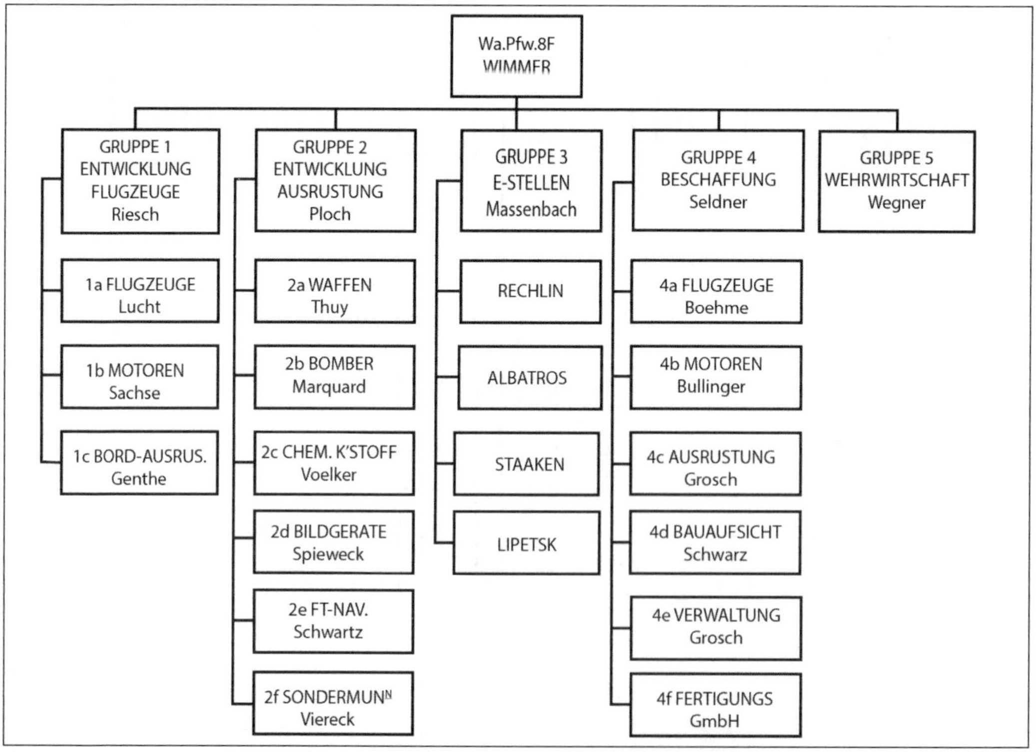

I-6 *Heereswaffenamt* Aviation Organisation – *Wa.Prw.8*, October 1929 - March 1933

1C3

Military Development and Production Programmes 1923-1932

During the period 1920-32 the German aircraft industry produced a total of 3,284 aircraft, an average of 253 per year.[1] Despite Allied restrictions 365 of these were military (including naval) types: 207 reconnaissance aircraft *(Aufklärungsflugzeuge)*, 93 bombers and torpedo aircraft *(Bomben, Torpedo-und Kampfflugzeuge)* and 65 fighters *(Jagdflugzeuge)*.[2] For the most part these were prototypes *(Versuchsmuster)* and given this context it can be seen just how prolific the German aircraft industry had been in terms of military developments during this period.

German military aircraft fell into two broad categories: designs produced in response to foreign military requirements and those produced to meet covert *Reichswehr* requirements. Up to the beginning of 1927 all military aircraft were assembled outside of Germany to evade the restrictive activities of the *Interalliierte Luftfahrt-Überwachungs-Kommission (ILUK)* although much design work and some fabrication certainly took place within Germany.[3] Thereafter the manufacture and assembly of military types took place increasingly within Germany although under subterfuge due to the international restrictions that were still in force.[4] Thus military designs were openly referred to as experimental or developmental types or even as postal or transport aircraft.[5] As it was impossible for the *Reichswehr* to actually operate military aircraft within Germany there was understandably very little series production although the clandestine air staff continually updated contingency plans as to which types would be manufactured in an emergency (See 1A3 & 1C2).[6] As late as 1932 there were only contracts for 40 military and naval aircraft from a total of four manufacturers (See 1C2).[7] With so little internal demand German manufacturers eagerly sought foreign contracts as means of ensuring their financial survival. The major markets for military

---

1   Vajda F.A. & Dancey P.1998 *German Aircraft Industry and Production 1933-1945* (hereafter cited as Vajda & Dancey 1998) p.9.

2   Vajda and Dancey 1998 p.9.

3   Hertel W. Dipl.Ing.GenIng.a.D.1955 *Procurement in the German Air Force* USAF Historical Studies No.170 (hereafter cited as Hertel 1955) p.2. The Allied inspection teams were withdrawn in Jan 27.

4   Auswartigen Amt 1919 *Der Friedensvertrag zwischen Deutschland und den Allierten und Assoziierten Maechten nebst dem Schlussprotokoll und der Vereinbarung betreffend die militärische Besetzung der Rheinlande" & App.XXI "Peace Treaty of Versailles; Military Clauses* in Edmonds J.E. 1944 *History of the Great War: The Occupation of the Rhineland 1918-1929* pp.396-401.

5   Ries K. 1970 *Luftwaffe Bd.1 Die Maulwurfe 1919-1935* (hereafter cited as Ries 1970) p.25, Mason H.M. 1973 *The Rise of the Luftwaffe 1918-1940* (hereafter cited as Mason 1973) pp.117-118, Nowarra H.J. 1980 *Die Verbotenen Flugzeuge 1921-1935 – Die getarnte Luftwaffe* (hereafter cited as Nowarra 1980) pp.104-105 & Koos V. 2006 *Typenbucher Deutsche Luftfahrt: Ernst Heinkel Flugzeugwerke 1922-1932* (hereafter cited as Koos 2006) pp.13-15, 16-17, 38-39, 46-48, 63-65 & 70-71.

6   Thomas G. 1966 *Geschichte der deutsche Wehr und Rüstungswirtschaft, 1918 to 1945* pp.53-57, Suchenwirth R. 1968 *The Development of the German Air Force 1919-1939* USAF Historical Studies No.160 (hereafter cited as Suchenwirth 1968) pp.24-25, App. *German Military Aviation, 1919-1933* in Cooper M. 1981 *The German Air Force 1933-1945: An Anatomy of Failure* p.385 & Corum J.S. 1997 *The Luftwaffe: Creating the Operational Air War 1918-1940* (hereafter cited as Corum 1997) p.78 & pp.121-122.

7   Vajda and Dancey 1998 p10. These were Arado (8), Dornier (3), Focke Wulf (12) and Heinkel (17).

aircraft were Sweden where both the *Ernst Heinkel Flugzeugwerke* and the *Junkers Flugzeug-und Motorenwerke* had subsidiaries, the Soviet Union with which there was a close military relationship and Imperial Japan which had ambitions to dominate the Pacific Ocean in the post-war period (See also 1C1).[8] Of all the German manufacturers it was *Heinkel* that enjoyed the greatest commercial success in these markets and it was through that company's continuous development of a range of military and naval aircraft that Germany was able to re-appear so suddenly on the world stage of military aviation following the advent of the National Socialists under Adolf Hitler in 1933 (See also 1A3 & 2C2 & 2C3)*(Photo 1C-5)*.[9]

A. RECONNAISSANCE AIRCRAFT
(AUFKLÄRUNGSFLUGZEUGE)

The secret military agreements with the Soviet Union in 1922 together with the *Ruhr Krise* of 1923 provided the impetus for the first covert military contracts for military aircraft (See 1A2 & 1C1).[10] In 1923 *Hptm.*Kurt Student, *Flugtechnikreferat 6F* within the *Heereswaffenamt's Inspektion für Waffen und Geräte (WaA In.WuG)*, approached both the *Albatros* and *Heinkel* concerns with a proposal that they each design a two-seat *Aufklärungsflugzeug* for possible employment at the *Reichswehr's* planned military facility at Lipetsk in the Ukraine (See 1D1).[11] In the absence of a suitably powerful German power plant Student specified the use of the 450 hp Napier Lion broad-arrow engine.[12] However Student was also aware that the planned Fokker D.XIII fighters would also be powered by the Lion and this would enable a degree of standardisation to be achieved at Lipetsk (See below).The *Albatros-Flugzeugwerke GmbH* at Berlin-Johannisthal responded with the L 65-I which was assembled at the company's foreign subsidiary the *Allgemeine Fluggesellschaft Memel mbH*.[13] The **L 65-I Memel I** was a biplane of conventional design and wooden construction. The wing span was 10.3 m and "I" interplane struts were employed. The prototype was completed

---

8   Heinkel E. 1956 *He 1000* (hereafter cited as Heinkel 1956) pp.68-82, Lange B. 1970 *Das Buch der deutschen Luftfahrtechnik* (hereafter cited as Lange 1970) p.242 & 271, Mason 1973 pp.114-119 & Schmitt G. 1988 *Hugo Junkers and his Aircraft* (hereafter cited as Schmitt 1988) pp.130-161. Claudius Dornier followed a more cosmopolitan route with the Do J *Wal* in particular being widely used by air arms from around the world – see Dornier GmbH 1983 *Dornier: Die Chronik des altesten deutschen Flugwerks* (hereafter cited as Dornier 1983) pp.16-19. See also Green W. and Fricker J. 1958 *The Air Forces of the World: Their History, Development and Present Strength* p.179, 267 & 246, Boyd A. 1977 *The Soviet Air Force since 1918* pp.8-10 & Sekigawa E.1974 *Pictorial History of Japanese Military Aviation* (hereafter cited as Sekigawa 1974) pp.21-25.

9   Hertel 1955 pp.86-88, Heinkel 1956 pp .89-118, Corum 1997 pp.122-123, Vajda and Dancey 1998 p.10 & Koos 2006 pp.107-114 & 124-127. See also Seaton A. 1982 *The German Army 1933-1945* pp.29-31.

10   Suchenwirth 1968 p.7, Mason 1973 p.145, Hooton E.R. 1994 *Phoenix Triumphant: The Rise and Rise of the Luftwaffe* (hereafter cited as Hooton 1994) p.39 & Corum 1997 p.76.

11   Heinkel 1956 p.79, Nowarra H.J. 1981 *Nahaufklärer 1910-1945: Die Augen des Heeres* (hereafter cited as Nowarra 1981) p.33 & Schliephake H. *Secret Flight Testing in Lipetsk, Russia* in Beauvais H., Kossler K., Mayer M. and Regel C. 2002 *German Secret Flight Test Centres to 1945: Johannisthal, Lipetsk, Rechlin, Travemünde, Tarnewitz, Peenemunde-West* (hereafter cited as Schliephake in Beauvais et al 2002) p.42. The *Caspar-Werke AG* at Lübeck-Travemünde may also have been approached at this time as the company produced a Napier Lion engined *Aufklärer* - the CS 14 - in its Danish subsidiary at around this time - see Lange 1970 p.182 & Nowarra 1980 p.18 & pp.102-104.

12   Lumsden A.S.C. 1994 *British Piston Aero-Engines and their Aircraft* (hereafter cited as Lumsden 1994) pp.165-166. The Napier Lion was designed by A.J.Rowledge in 1916-17. It was compact 12 cylinder engine in which the cylinders were arranged in 3 rows of 4 cylinders each. These rows were themselves arranged at 60 degrees to each other in a W or broad arrow configuration. The Lion was rated at 450 hp and the type used by the Germans in the Fokker D.XIII, Albatros L 65 & Heinkel HD 17 was the Mk.II. The Lion was very widely used and was a hard-working and reliable engine. See also Gunston B. 1995 *World Encyclopaedia of Aero Engines* (hereafter cited as Gunston 1995) p.112.

13   Lange 1970 pp.158. The Memelland had been separated from Germany as part of the complex pattern of treaties that had brought the Great War to a close. It lay immediately adjacent to the Reich province of Ostpreussen.

in 1925.[14] Further development resulted in the **L 65-II and III**. These machines were powered by a 565 hp Lion. The L 65-III was scaled up with an increased wing span of 12.4 m and a fuselage length of 7.58 m. With a loaded weight of 1,340 kgs the L 65-III had a maximum speed of 240 kph. The L 65 appears to have found some favour with the *WaA* as it was included in *Wa.B.6F's 1927 Notrüstung Programm* (Emergency Equipment Programme) with a projected order for 47 machines. The contemporary L 70 *Aufklärer* was also favoured with a projected order for 72 aircraft.[15] The **L 70** was also a biplane but with a reduced gap between the wings when compared to the L 65. It was also powered by the Napier Lion II and a prototype was completed in 1924/25.[16]

Heinkel's response was the HD 17, two examples of which were supplied to the American Cox-Klemin company for submission as the CO-2 in the *USAAS'* competition for a Corps Observation aircraft in 1924.[17] Production of the HD 17 for the *Reichswehr* did not occur until 1926 when seven aircraft were completed, these being WNr.239 to 245.[18] The **Heinkel HD 17** was a robust and reliable aircraft of thoroughly conventional design and appearance. The *Reichswehr* aircraft differed from those exported in having "N" rather than "I" interplane struts and a revised vertical stabiliser and rudder, the latter having a different type of horn balance. In its production form the HD 17 had a loaded weight of 2,148 kgs, a top speed of 225 kph at 1,220 m and a service ceiling 6,360 m. It could climb to 3,000 m in 11 minutes.[19]

However its flying characteristics appear to have been less than desired with one pilot commenting that the HD 17 was *"rather large and clumsy"* and it must be said that *Maj.*Helmuth Wilberg's *Luftschützreferat* regarded the type as a training aircraft not suitable for operational employment.[20] A new requirement was therefore issued by *Wa.Prw.6F* (formerly In.WuG.6F) in 1926 for a two-seat ***Erkundsflugzeuge für die Divisions-nahaufklärungsstaffeln*** or **Erkudista** (Tactical Reconnaissance Aircraft) to be powered by either the new 600 hp BMW VI water-cooled vee-twelve or the 530 hp Gnome et Rhône (Jupiter) 9A nine-cylinder radial.[21] Once again the *Albatros-Flugzeugwerke* was the favoured contractor and their earlier work on the L 65-III was used as the basis for a new type - the L 76 *Aufklarer*. Completed during the winter of 1927/28 the **Albatros L 76 Aeolus** was an interesting unequal span biplane, the lower wing being of smaller span and chord than the upper to improve downward visibility for the crew - an essential requirement for a *Heeresaufklärer*. The upper wing had a span of 12.76 m. The aircraft was of mixed construction with a steel tube fuselage and a plywood covered wing. The weight fully loaded was 2,440 kgs.

14   Lange 1970 pp.158-159 & Nowarra 1980 pp.110-111.
15   Lange 1970 p.159. It is not clear what Lion variant was used in the L 65-II & III as none are listed with a rating of 450 hp – see Lumsden 1994 pp.165-169. The *Notrustings Programm* was a basis for aircraft procurement in the event of an attack by one of Germany's neighbours - see Andersson L. 1989 'Secret Luftwaffe: German Military Aviation Build-up between the Wars' in *Air Enthusiast* No.41 1989 (hereafter cited as Andersson 1989) p.41.
16   Lange 1970 p.159 & Nowarra 1980 p.112.
17   Heinkel 1956 p.79, Nowarra 1980 pp.106-108 & Koos 2006 pp.46-48. This competition, divided into two parts, was won by the Douglas XO-2 (Liberty engine) & the Curtiss XO-1 (Packard engine) - see Swanborough G. and Bowers P.M. 1989 *United States Military Aircraft since 1909* pp.249-254 & 219-223.
18   Koos 2006 p.47.
19   Nowarra 1981 p.134 & Koos 2006 p.48. The 7 production aircraft served well. Only one was lost - WNr.245 in a crash landing on the 7 Oct 27.
20   Kosin R. 1983 *Die Entwicklung der deutschen Jagdflugzeuge* (hereafter cited as Kosin 1983) p.61. The HD 17 was not included in the *1927 Notrustüngs Programm* - see Andersson 1989 p.41. The *Luftschützreferat* was responsible for the overall development of military aviation and as such was located in the *Truppenamt* - see Suchenwirth 1968 p.6 & Corum 1997 p.57.
21   Kosin 1983 p.65 & Beauvais et al 2002 p.42 & 56. This was one of four operational requirements within the *Notrüstung-Programm* (Emergency Equipment Programme) of 1926-28. The requirements stemmed from *T 2 III (L)'s "Richtlinien für die Führung des operativen Luftkrieges"* (Directives for the Conduct of the Operational Air War) which were published in May 26 - see Corum 1997 pp.81-83.

The L 76 was powered by the BMW VI which gave the aircraft a top speed of 235 kph.[22] A small batch of L 76 aircraft was built, these machines being deployed to Lipetsk for operational testing from 1928.[23] Unfortunately the new aircraft displayed some adverse flying characteristics especially when spinning and in all there were seven fatalities (See also 1C2).[24] In an attempt to resolve these difficulties *Dipl.Ing.*Walter Blume's team introduced revised tail surfaces. In this form the aircraft was known as the **L 76a** but even so a number of these modified aircraft were also lost.[25]

As the difficulties with the L 76 became apparent Blume's design team produced an upgraded version of the contemporary L 75 *Ass B 2 Schulflugzeug* (Basic Trainer).[26] The result was the **Albatros L 78** six examples of which were sent to Lipetsk to supplement the earlier L 76 aircraft.[27] The L 78 was of more conventional appearance than the L 76 but it retained the distinctive tail surfaces and it was powered by the same 600 hp BMW VI water-cooled engine. It was also noteworthy in being the first military aircraft to be built to incorporate a range of standardised components, a measure introduced by *Fertigungs GmbH*, the civilian cover for *Wa.Prw.8F*, in an attempt to ease production through more effective sub-contracting within the industry (See also 1C2).[28] The performance of the L 78 was satisfactory although not spectacular and a small production batch was later built for the clandestine *Fliegertruppe*.[29]

In the meantime the *Heinkel Flugzeugwerke* had been engaged in a different line of development in response to *Wa.Prw.6F's* 1926 requirement for a long-range, medium altitude reconnaissance aircraft that could also double as a bomber without any modification other than the installation of special equipment. This was known within the *WaA* as the **Erkunigros** or **Erkundungsflugzeug für mittlere Hohen und größte Entfernungen**.[30] *Heinkel's* proposal for this machine was the HD 41, two examples of which were completed to evaluate the respective merits of the specified power plants. The **Heinkel HD 41a** WNr.321 D-1694 was fitted with the BMW VI, whilst the **HD 41b** WNr.342 D-1795 employed the *Siemens* built Gnome et Rhône (Jupiter) 9A.[31] Ostensibly both aircraft were engine test beds *(Triebwerkseprobungsflugzeug)* and as such they could be tested extensively within Germany at the *RdL's Erprobungsstellen* at Rechlin and Staaken.[32] However it

---

22   Lange 1970 p.160 & Nowaara 1980 pp.144-145.

23   Schliephake in Beauvais et al 2002 p.46 & 49. The first aircraft to be deployed to Lipetsk was L 76a WNr.10 101 D-1127. The six production L 76 aircraft were WNr.10 102 (D-1113), 103 (D-1209), 122 (D-1210), 123 (D-1283), 124 (D-1288) & 125 (D-1289) – see Nowarra 1980 p.144.

24   Lange 1970 p.160. The following pilots are known to have been killed in accidents associated with the L 76: Paul Jeschonnek, Fritz Mulhahn & Emil Thuy - see also Regel C. *The Eprobungsstelle Rechlin* in Beauvais et al 2002 (hereafter cited as Regel in Beauvais et al 2002) p.57 & 93 and *Losses of the E-Stelle Rechln and its Predecessors 1926 to 1945* in Beauvais et al 2002 p.120. The sprung rear legs of the undercarriage gave rise to some interesting behaviour on landing if one wheel touched first - see Kosin 1983 p.68.

25   Lange 1970 p.158. *Dipl.Ing.*Blume joined the *Konstruktionsbüro* at *Albatros* in Oct 26. The following L 76a aircraft are known to have been registered: WNr.10 101 (D-1127), WNr.10 104 (D-1128) & WNr.10 107 (D-1130) - see Nowarra 1980 p.144 & *Aircraft at the DVL, Abteilung M, Eprobungsabteilung Albatros, E-Stelle RDL Staaken & Rechlin, 1926 to 1934* in Beauvais et al 2002 p.113.

26   Lange 1970 p.160 & Nowarra 1980 pp.158-160. The prototype of the L 75 was D-1348 which first flew in 1928. It was powered by a 320 hp BMW IV engine although production aircraft were generally fitted with the 360 hp BMW Va. Most aircraft were used by the DVS - see Ries 1970 pp.43-44 & Ries K. 1988 *Deutsche Flugzeugführerschulen und ihre Maschinen 1919-1945* (hereafter cited as Ries 1988) p.10.

27   Schliephake in Beauvais et al 2002 pp.48-49. The six L 78 aircraft sent to Lipetsk were: WNr.10 151-156.

28   Regel in Beauvais et al 2002 p.58. See also Hertel 1955 p.69 & Hooton 1994 p.47 & 65.

29   Lange 1970 p.160. These aircraft saw service with the DVS as trainers. The 12 production aircraft were registered as D-1791, 1988, 2093, 2094, 2098, 2099, 2131, 2132, 2173, 2174, 2467 & 2487 – see Nowarra 1980 p.162. Those at the *DVS Zweigstelle Cottbus* subsequently formed the equipment of the *Fliegerstaffel Cottbus* in 1934 - see Ries K. 1986 *Luftwaffe Photo-Report 1919-1945* p.24.

30   Hertel 1955 p.13, Kosin 1983 p.65 & Regel in Beauvais et al 2002 pp.56-57.

31   Nowarra 1980 pp.186-187 & Koos 2006 pp.99-100.

32   Regel in Beauvais et al 2002 p.57 & Koos 2006 p.99.

was as a two-seat reconnaissance bomber that the HD 41 found particular favour. In the summer of 1930 the first prototype underwent operational test flying at Lipetsk where it was fitted with an internal Bombenmagazin Mag 6W 12/IIIa, whilst the effectiveness of both the Goerz-Richtfernrohr Fl.218 and 220 mechanical bomb sights were evaluated with this aircraft (See also 1C5). The 600 hp BMW VI conferred the HD 41a with a top speed of 240 kph and a maximum cruising speed of 220 kph at ground level, whilst the aircraft could be climbed to 3,000 m in 14.8 minutes. The service ceiling was 5,000 m. As a long range type it had a fuel capacity of 550 litres which gave the aircraft an optimal range of 1,070 kms.[33] Provisional planning in January 1930 called for the manufacture of 261 of these aircraft in the event of a national emergency.[34]

In the meantime two more prototypes were completed. These were initially known as the HD 41c WNr.363 and 364 but were re-designated HD 45a prior to their completion in 1931. The **Heinkel HD 45a** featured a 660 hp BMW VI 5,5 ZU engine and as the pace of rearmament increased the second prototype WNr.364 D-2064 was quickly dispatched to Lipetsk for four months of weapons trials beginning in June of that year.[35] For bomb dropping the HD 45a could either be fitted with a Bomben-Magazinen Maga 3 C 50/II for three SC 50 Sprengbomben (High Explosive Bombs) or a Sammelmagazinen Samag 16 C 10/V for 16 SC 10 Splitterbomben (Fragmentation Bombs)(See 1C5).[36] The initial production aircraft was the **HD 45b**, ten of which were ordered by the *WaA* in 1932. This variant was fitted with 660 hp BMW VI 7,3 high compression engine which improved performance still further. The maximum speed was 274 kph at sea level and 248 kph at 4,000 m where a maximum cruising speed of the 210 kph could be sustained. Fuel capacity for 520 litres gave the aircraft a range of 960 kms at 4,000 m. For defensive purposes the HD 45b was armed with a fixed lu.MG 08/15 machine gun with 500 rounds and a flexibly mounted MG 15 machine gun in the *B-Stand* (Dorsal Gun Position) with 750 rounds in 10 Doppeltrommel 15 magazines (See 3C4). A *FuG* II wireless transceiver was also fitted in the rear cockpit the associated wires being carried above the wing on three antenna (See 4D4). For the reconnaissance role cameras could be installed, whilst for offensive operations up to 160 kgs of bombs could be carried internally. Fully loaded the HD 45b weighed 2,985 kgs.[37]

However the HD 45 was not the only type developed to meet the *Erkunigros* requirement. In 1929 Heinrich Focke began the design of a parasol wing variant of the parallel A 36 *Postflugzeug* (Mail Carrier) to meet the *WaA* specification.[38] The **Focke Wulf S 39** featured a substantial fabric covered steel tube fuselage with ample room for the crew of two in tandem open cockpits. The parasol wing was supported by broad bracing struts, whilst a strut braced wide track undercarriage was provided below the fuselage. The only concession to modernity was the clean NACA cowling for the 510 hp Siemens (Gnome et Rhône) Jupiter VI radial.[39] This gave the S 39 a maximum

---

33   Koos 2006 pp.99-100.
34   Koos 2006 p.99.
35   Green W. 1970 *The War Planes of the Third Reich* (hereafter cited as Green 1970) p.259, Nowarra 1980 pp.216-217 & Koos 2006 pp.107-108.
36   Fleischer W. 2003 *German Air-Dropped Weapons to 1945* (hereafter cited as Fleischer 2003) pp.29-33 & Koos 2006 p.107.
37   Nowarra 1981 pp.139-141 & Koos 2006 p.108.
38   Hooton 1994 p.78. It is not entirely clear whether the S 39 was designed to meet *the Erkudista* or *Erkunigros* requirement.
39   Lange 1970 p.224. In an attempt to reduce the form drag caused by the exposed cylinders and valve gear of radial engines the American National Advisory Committee for Aeronautics (NACA) used their large wind tunnel at Langley, Va. to experiment with a range of different circular cowlings for these engines. It was found that NACA Cowling No.10 not only reduced drag by 66% but actually improved engine cooling. Flight trials in the late 20s largely confirmed these findings and the closely fitting NACA cowling became a feature of many new designs in the years that followed - see Pearcy A. 1993 *Flying the Frontiers: NACA and NASA Experimental Aircraft* p.18 & Hassell P. *Advances in Aerodynamics* in Jarrett P. (Ed.) 1997 *Biplane to Monoplane: Aircraft development 1919-39* (hereafter

speed of 265 kph, a commendable performance in view of the relatively low power provided by the Jupiter radial.[40] The single prototype WNr.98 D-1708 was tested at Lipetsk in 1931 but was not judged good enough to be included in the *WaA's* procurement plans. Instead the *Focke Wulf Flugzeugbau* was given a small contract for the licence production of the HD 45b.[41]

Despite the merits of the Albatros L 78 *Wa.Prw.8F* was still anxious to achieve a more satisfactory solution to its basic **Erkudista** requirement and new development contracts were placed in 1930 with both *Focke Wulf* and *Heinkel*.[42] The **Focke Wulf A 40** was broadly similar to the parallel S 39 in that it was a parasol wing monoplane powered by a Siemens (Gnome et Rhône) Jupiter VI radial. Once again the fuselage was constructed of welded steel tube with a fabric covering, whilst the wing was constructed of spruce with a plywood covering. The earlier broad chord wing struts were replaced by more slender bracing units. The undercarriage geometry was also changed to make the type more suitable for short field operations with oil damped oleos. The main wheels were faired but the engine was uncowled.[43] Unfortunately the A 40 quickly exhibited some unpleasant flight characteristics which were never fully eradicated. Only the prototype WNr.99 D-1908 was built.[44] The type was therefore passed over in favour of the rival HE 46.

In its initial form the **Heinkel HD 46** was a biplane.[45] Two prototypes were ordered in 1930, the HD 46a WNr.376 D-1702 and the HD 46b WNr.377 D-1082. The second aircraft differed only in having a horn balanced rudder. Both were powered by an uncowled Siemens (Gnome et Rhône) Jupiter VI radial and were of mixed wood, metal and fabric construction as preferred by the *Wa.Prw.8F*. The HD 46a first flew on the 23 April 1931 and early in the summer it was sent to Lipetsk for operational trials with the new SC 10 Splitterbomben, these being carried internally in a Zwillingsmagazinen Zwimag 6 C 10 (See 1C5). In its initial form the HD 46 had a top speed of 198 kph at sea level and an optimal range of 890 kms on 390 litres of fuel. The landing speed was 102 kph.[46] Despite the HD 46's overall merits it was decided that the parasol wing layout would provide a far better view downwards for both crew members and *Heinkel* was therefore instructed to modify the aircraft accordingly. The result was the HE 46c which began test flying in the spring of 1932. Wing span was increased from 11.5 m to 14 m and the Siemens (Gnome et Rhône) Jupiter VI was replaced by the more powerful 650 hp Siemens und Halske Sh 22B radial which drove a larger 3.65 m fixed-pitch wooden airscrew. In addition to its internal *Zwimag 6 C 10* magazine, the HE 46c was equipped with a *Handkamera* (Hand-held Camera), *FuG I* wireless, a fixed lu.MG 08/15 machine gun firing forwards and a MG 15 machine gun on a *Drehkranzes D.30* ring mount in the B-Stand. Fully loaded the HE 46c weighed 2,300 kgs in comparison to the earlier HD 46a's 2,170 kgs.[47]

cited as Hassell in Jarrett (Ed.) 1997) pp.145-146.

40   Smith J.R. 1973 *Focke Wulf: An Aircraft Album* (hereafter cited as Smith 1973) p.27, Nowarra 1980 pp.204-205 & Wagner W. 1980 *Kurt Tank - Konstrukteur und Testpilot bei Focke Wulf Die deutsche Luftfahrt 1* (hereafter cited as Wagner 1980) pp.36-37. The A 36 & S 39 had the same fuselage and tail surfaces. The prototype S 39 was later re-registered D-IQIM and evaluated at Rechlin as the Fw 39B.

41   Smith 1973 p.27 & Vajda and Dancey 1998 p.10.

42   Smith 1973 pp.27-28.

43   Smith 1973 p.27-28, Nowarra 1980 pp.212-213 & Wagner 1980 p.37. This source suggests that the A 40 was fitted with a Siemens Sh 22B of 660 hp. However this seems unlikely, at least in 1931 and the installation of a Siemens Jupiter VI is more likely - see Lange 1970 p.224.

44   Conradis H. 1960 *Design for Flight: The Kurt Tank Story* p.48. Kurt Tank, recently employed at *Focke Wulf*, recalled that the A 40 was an advanced design but it had some tricky problems that could not be fully resolved. The prototype was later re-registered as D-IJEF and evaluated as the Fw 40 at Berlin-Staaken - see Wagner 1980 p.37.

45   Koos 2006 pp.109-110. This had been specifically requested by the *Wa.Prw.8F*. At that time *Heinkel* had no experience in parasol wing monoplanes.

46   Nowarra 1980 pp.206-209 & Koos 2006 pp.109-110.

47   Green 1970 p.261 & Nowarra 1980 pp.208-209

B. FIGHTER AIRCRAFT

The *Ruhr Krise* of 1923 lent urgency to the *Reichswehr's* plans to acquire a military air capability (See 1A2). Funding was agreed to purchase 100 Fokker fighters from the Netherlands, the negotiations being placed in the hands of the *Flugtechnikreferat* and during the course of 1923 Student placed orders for 50 Fokker D.XI and 50 Fokker D.XIII fighters to be manufactured at the *Nederlandsche Vliegtuigenfabriek's* Amsterdam works.[48] The Fokker D.XI first flew on the 5 May 1923 and 125 were ordered by the Soviet authorities for the *VVS-RKKA*, a decision that would have influenced Student's recommendation that a further 50 be ordered for the *Reichswehr* for initial employment inside the Soviet Union.[49] The **Fokker D.XI** was sesquiplane, a biplane with a large top wing and a much smaller bottom wing. It was of mixed construction and powered by a 300 hp Hispano Suiza 8Fb vee-eight water cooled engine.[50] However Student was also interested in a more powerful variant of this basic design and the D.XIII was developed by Fokker to incorporate a 450 hp Napier Lion II twelve-cylinder engine to meet this specific *Reichswehr* requirement. The **Fokker D.XIII** did not fly until the 12 September 1924 but it displayed a remarkable turn of speed with 270 kph being recorded. The initial climb rate was 1.7 mins to 1,000 m and the aircraft had a range of 600 kms; loaded weight was 1,650 kgs (See also 1D1).[51] An order for 50 D.XIII fighters was placed with the *Nederlandsche Vliegtuigenfabriek* for delivery in 1925.[52]

In the year following the delivery of the Fokker D.XIII fighters to Lipetsk the *Wa.Prw.6F* issued a request for proposals for a home defence fighter or **Heimatjagdeinsitzer (Heitag)**. Somewhat surprisingly this contract went to the newly established *Arado Handelsgesellschaft* at Warnemünde.[53] A few months earlier a small design team had been created under the leadership of *Ing.*Walter Rethel, a former colleague of Anthony Fokker at Schwerin, and it was either his experience of wartime fighter aircraft design or the influence of *Obstlt.a.D.*Felix Wagenführ that influenced Student's staff officers (See 1C1).[54] Advanced monoplane fighters such as the Rohrbach Ro IX *Rofix* were not favoured by *Wa.Prw.6F* possibly on account of their expense but equally because of their difficulty of manufacture.[55] It is notable that *Wa.Prw.6F* and its successor *Wa.Prw.8F* consistently favoured conventional designs during this period, designs that used welded metal tube fuselage structures with wooden wings with plywood or fabric or covering, and in the case of fighter aircraft a braced biplane layout.[56]

48   Mason 1973 pp.125-126 & Postma T. 1979 F*okker: Aircraft Builders to the World* (hereafter cited at Postma 1979) p.59.

49   Postma 1979 p.59 & Green W. and Swanborough G. 1980 'Fighter A to Z' in *Air International* Vol.18 No.2 (hereafter cited as Green and Swanborough 1980) p.93.

50   Green and Swan/borough 1980 p.93 & Morse S. (Ed.) 1982 *The Illustrated Encylopedia of Aircraft* (hereafter cited as Morse (Ed.) 1982) pp.1874-1875.

51   Postma 1979 p.59 & 61. It has been suggested that the D.XIII was powered by a 575 hp Lion XI - see Green W. and Swanborough G. 1980 'Fighter A to Z' in *Air International* Vol.18 No.3 p.149, Morse (Ed.) 1982 p.1875 & Kosin 1983 p.58. However this variant of the prolific Lion Srs was not developed until 1930 – see Lumsden 1994 p.169.

52   Mason 1973 p.126 & Postma 1979 p.59.

53   Kosin 1983 p.65. *Arado* had been established in Apr 25 as part of the Hugo Stinnes empire - see also Kranzhoff J A 1997 *Arado: Geschichte eines Flugzeugwerks* (hereafter cited as Kranzhoff 1997) pp.8-10 & Vajda and Dancey 1998 p.158.

54   Kosin 1983 pp.65-66. Wagenführ had previously been *Chef d.Flugmusterei* (Aircraft Engineering Centre) within the *Luftstreitkräfte* – see Koos V. *Flight Testing to the End of World War* One in Beauvais et al 2002 p.29 & 32 & Regel in Beauvais et al 2002 p.52. *Dornier, Junkers* and *Rohrbach* had never been favoured as they were proponents of all-metal aircraft design. In 1922 *Junkers* had produced the H 22 fighter for the *VVS-RKKA* – see Nowarra 1980 pp.96-97 & Schmitt 1988 p.137, whilst *Dornier* had sought sales for his advanced Do-H *Falke* in the USA and South America – see Nowarra 1980 pp.90-93 & Dornier 1983 pp.88-89. In 1926 *Rohrbach* had the Ro IX *Rofix* under test but this aircraft was subsequently lost in a spinning accident - see Nowarra 1980 pp.140-141 & Wagner 1980 pp.17-19.

55   Nowarra 1980 pp.140-141 & Wagner 1980 pp.17-19 & Kosin 1983 pp.63-65.

56   Kosin 1983 p.71. The Germans were not alone in this respect. During the twenties aircraft of biplane configuration

Rethel designed his proposal around an imported 425 hp Gnome et Rhône (Jupiter) 9A radial. The **Arado SD I** WNr.31 was a cantilever sesquiplane of conventional construction.[57] It first flew in 1927 but failed to meet the *WaA* requirements and the prototype was lost in a crash at the *E-Stelle Rechlin* on the 11 October 1927 which claimed the life of its test pilot *Dr.Ing.*Theodor Bienen.[58] With an all up weight of 1,230 kgs the SD I had a top speed of 275 kph at 5,000 and 242 kph at sea level, hardly an improvement over the D.XIII already in service.[59] Concerns about the inadequate structural strength of the SD I led to an entirely new design in 1929. The **Arado SD II** was a slightly larger aircraft with a wing span of 9.9 m and a length of 7.4 m. Loaded weight rose to 1,770 kgs. The fuselage was deeper, particularly at mid-length, and the pilot sat high up with a good view over the top wing and downwards in front of the lower wing. A more powerful engine was also installed in the form of the 530 hp Gnome et Rhône (Jupiter) 9A geared radial but this did not help overall performance which was in fact worse than the SD I.[60] A second prototype of the SD II featured the direct drive 490 hp Siemens Jupiter VI. In this form it was known as the **Arado SD III** WNr.53 D-1973 and because the slow running engine required the use of a larger three blade airscrew the length of the main undercarriage legs had to be increased to provide sufficient ground clearance for the propeller.[61] Notwithstanding its difficult ground handling the performance of the SD III was even more disappointing than that of the SD II and following operational testing at Lipetsk during the summer of 1930 it was decided that still further development work was required.[62]

*Ing.*Rethel and his team seem to have been undeterred by these setbacks and in 1930 the broadly similar **Arado Ar 64a** appeared powered by a 530 hp Siemens (Gnome et Rhône) Jupiter VI radial. Apart from a massive four blade wooden fixed pitch airscrew there was very few differences between this aircraft and its ancestor the SD III.[63] Two modified examples, the Ar 64b WNr.65 D-2470 and

with mixed construction techniques reigned supreme. In the case of fighters low wing loadings and a high degree of manoeuvrability were considered to be primary objectives and this was particularly achievable by using a biplane layout - see Jarrett P. (Ed.) 1997 *Biplane to Monoplane: Aircraft development 1919-39* pp.55-56. Where innovation occurred it could take different forms. For example in the RAF interest in the heavily armed bomber destroyer resulted in aircraft designed to carry the 37 mm Coventry Ordnance Works recoilless cannon and in the re-examination of the "pusher" layout to overcome the problems of flying biplane fighters safely and efficiently at night within F.29/27 – see Sinnott C. 2001 *The RAF and Aircraft Design 1923-1939: Air Staff Operational Requirements* pp.52-56 & Meekcoms K.J. and Morgan E.B. 1994 *The British Aircraft Specifications File: British Military and Commercial Aircraft Specifications 1920-1949* (hereafter cited as Meekcoms and Morgan 1994) p.127. However it is pertinent to note that Britain, France and the USA were all actively pursuing monoplane fighters in the early thirties – see Sinnott 2001 pp.77-78 & Meekcoms and Morgan 1994 p.147, Morse (Ed.) 1982 p.1439 & Swanborough G. and Bowers P.M. 1989 *United States Military Aircraft since 1909* (hereafter cited as Swanborough and Bowers 1989) pp.99-100.

57   Kosin 1983 pp.65-66. The SD I utilised cantilever wings of wooden construction, plywood covering over wooden ribs. A single "V" strut separated the two wings. The fuselage was of welded steel tube, skinned in sheet aluminium over the forward fuselage and by doped fabric to the rear. The suspension was based on V-shaped rubber chords which provided some progressive springing effect as the angle of the V altered under compression. See also Kranzhoff 1997 pp.25-26.

58   Regel in Beauvais et al 2002 p.57. Bienen was a member of the *Abteilung M* of the *DVL*. The SD I was lost at Rechlin where it had been under-going evaluation as a *Heitag*. Its loss was kept secret for more than a year when it was eventually reported in the *Berliner Illustrierte Flugwoche* as an *"Arado Sportsflugzeug"* - see Kranzhoff 1997 pp.26-28.

59   Lange 1970 p.162, Green W. and Swanborough G. 1971 'Fighter A to Z' in *Air Enthusiast* Vol.1 No.7 (hereafter cited as Green and Swanborough 1971) p.390, Nowarra 1980 pp178-180. & Kosin 1983.

60   Lange 1970 p.162, Green and Swanborough 1971 p.390, Nowarra 1980 pp.179-180, Kosin 1983 p.66 & Kranzhoff 1997 p.28.

61   Kosin 1983 p.66 & Kranzhoff 1997 pp.28-29. Due to the massive torque of the propeller the SD III tended to ground loop on take off and landing unless the pilot exercised considerable care.

62   Lange 1970 p.162, Green and Swanborough 1971 p.391, Kosin 1983 p.66 & Schliephake in Beauvais et al 2002 pp.48-49

63   Kens K. and Nowarra H.J. 1961 *Die deutschen Flugzeuge 1933-1945: Deutschlands Luftfahrt-Entwicklungen bis ende des Zweiten Weltkrieges* (hereafter cited as Kens and Nowarra 1961) pp.41-42 & p.650, Lange 1970 p.162, Green

WNr.66 D-2338, both powered by the 640 hp BMW VI 6,3 vee twelve were tested at Lipetsk in 1931 where a top speed of 250 kph was recorded. However it is unlikely that the planned armament of two lu.MG 08/15 machine guns was fitted to either aircraft due to problems with weapon-engine synchronisation associated with a four blade airscrew.[64] Minor structural changes followed and the next prototype (Ar 64c) reverted to the Jupiter radial and there is evidence to suggest that three aircraft were eventually completed to this standard.[65] However the first real attempt to resolve the type's continued handling difficulties, particularly during take-off and landing, came with the next Jupiter prototype (Ar 64d). This aircraft featured a revised undercarriage together with a re-designed fin and rudder to improve longitudinal stability and rudder response.[66] Finally in the last prototype, the Ar 64e, a two-blade fixed-pitch airscrew was fitted to overcome the armament installation problems previously encountered and it was one of these aircraft that was tested at Rechlin in the latter part of 1932.[67]

To help in the decision making process *Maj.*Wilhelm Wimmer's *Wa.Prw.8F* held a fly-off fighter competition at the *E-Stelle Rechlin* in November 1932. The Ar 64, Ar 65, HD 38 and HD 49 were all represented together with a Fokker D.XIII for comparative purposes (See also 1C4). Initially the new aircraft were pitted against the D.XIII but in the later stages they were flown against each other as well as in range of other operational situations including low level flight and formation flying.[68] As a result of these trials the Ar 65 was chosen as the best interim type and small production orders were placed for both Arado fighters.[69]

The **Arado Ar 65a** WNr.71(?) D-2218 first flew in 1931. It differed in many ways from the earlier Ar 64 series: larger wings of 11.2 m span, ailerons on all four wings, a deeper rear fuselage and a strut braced horizontal stabiliser. The liquid-cooled 750 hp BMW VI 7,3 was fitted as standard and this gave the new fighter a maximum speed of 300 kph and an initial climb rate of 10.6m/sec. Loaded weight was 1,930 kgs. The standard fighter armament of twin lu.MG 08/15 machine guns was fitted together with an internal Zwimag 6 C 10 bomb magazine for six SC 10 Splitterbomben (See 1C5). The initial three prototypes (Ar 65a-c) embodied equipment changes and minor structural improvements.[70] Ar 65a D-2218 took part in the 1932 fighter competition at Rechlin where it was judged to be superior to both the competing HD 38 and HD 49.[71] The initial production aircraft was the Ar 65d which appeared in 1933. This was fitted with two of the new MG 17 machine guns with 500 rpg (Rounds per Gun)(See 3C4).[72]

and Swanborough 1971 p.391, Nowarra 1980 pp.190-192 & Kosin 1983 pp.73-75. In the literature this aircraft is consistently referred to as the Ar 64 even though this designation was not adopted until 1933 - see Hooton 1994 p.78.

64   Schliephake in Beauvais et al 2002 pp.48-49. These aircraft were given the Lipetsk *Nummern* 103 & 104. See also Lange 1970 p.162.

65   *Aircraft at the DVL, Abteilung M, Eprobungsabteilung Albatros, E-Stelle RDL Staaken & Rechlin, 1926 to 1934* in Beauvais et al 2002 pp.113-115. The Ar 64c were registered D-2766, 2767 & 2768 - possibly with the WNr.86-88. These aircraft were used at Rechlin for 100 hrs each of test flying with the new Siemens Sh 22 radial.

66   Green and Swanborough 1971 p.391.

67   Green and Swanborough 1971 p.391 & Ries 1988 p.65.

68   Regel in Beauvais et al 2002 p.60. The comparative "air battles" were held on the 9th, 10th & 12th Nov 28 with additional flights both before and after these dates to cover performance, low level and formation flying.

69   Regel in Beauvais et al 2002 p.60. In 1932 *Arado* received an order for 6 SD IV & 2 SD V fighters – see Vajda and Dancey 1998 p.10.

70   Kens and Nowarra 1961 p.42, Lange 1970 p.162, Green and Swanborough 1971 p.391, Nowarra 1980 pp.198-200, Kosin 1983 pp.74-75 & Kranzhoff 1997 p.48. The Ar 65b was registered D-1898.

71   Regel in Beauvais et al 2002 p.60. Heinkel had produced a separate lineage of single seat fighters beginning with the HD 37 and HD 43 for the *VVS-RKKA*. From this the HD 38 was developed to meet a *Reichsmarine* requirement for a float fighter (See 1C4) and from that the improved HD 49 had emerged (See 2C3) – see Kosin 1983 p.66, 68 & pp.73-76 and Koos 2006 pp.90-94, 103-104 & 111-112.

72   Green and Swanborough 1971 p.391. Due to shortage of manufacturing capacity 12 of the early production Ar 65

In addition to calling for the development of single-seat home defence day fighter, *Wa.Prüf.6F* also sought a two seat combat aircraft capable of night fighting and armed reconnaissance - the **Nachtjagd und Erkundungsflugzeug (Najuku)** requirement.[73] The basis for this specification is obscure as such an aircraft had not been specifically operated by the wartime *Luftstreitkräfte* although there were of course many instances of the crews of *C-* and *CL-Flugzeuge* successfully defending their machines against enemy fighters.[74] Within post-war Germany the cause of the armed two-seat combat aircraft was taken up by *Dipl.Ing.*Walter Blume who had joined the reorganised *Albatros Flugzeugwerke* as designer in October 1926.[75]

The first *Najuku* type to be officially recognised as such was the **Albatros L 77v.** This was nothing more than a re-designated L 76a (See above) and as such was powered by a 600 hp BMW VI. For its *Jagdzweisitzer* role the L 77v was armed with two lu.MG 08/15 machine guns synchronised to fire through the propeller arc together with a single flexible lu.MG 08/15 on a Scarff Drehkranz D.29 mount in the rear cockpit (See also 1C5).[76] Six L 77v aircraft were built, four from the parent firm: WNr.10 136-139, and two from the *Ernst Heinkel Flugzeugwerke*: WNr.303 & 304.[77] This order reflected *Fertigungs GmbH's* plans to carry out licence production of key types in the event of an emergency and to standardise where ever possible manufacturing techniques (See 1C2).[78] A number of L 77v aircraft were sent to Lipetsk for trials purposes and in 1931 one aircraft was modified to carry a flexibly mounted 2 cm Oerlikon cannon in the rear cockpit (See 1C5).[79]

Despite the known shortcomings of the basic L 76 design Blume persisted with the *Jagdzweisitzer* concept with the **Albatros L 84.** Powered by the more powerful 660 hp BMW VIu this aircraft introduced "V" form interplane struts but was otherwise similar to the L 77v.[80] The first prototype WNr.10 187 D-1899 appeared in 1931 and was sent to Lipetsk for trials during the same year.[81]

	were completed by *Erla* - see Kranzhoff 1997 p.48.
73	Kosin 1983 p.65, Hooton 1994 p.64 & Regel in Beauvais et al 2002 p.56.
74	Imrie A. 1971 *Pictorial History of the German Army Air Service* p. 40-41, 45, 47-48, 51-53, 56-57 & 59. The vulnerability of the *Luftstreitkräfte's C-Typen* to fighter attack led to the development of the *Schusta* in in 1916 as escorts for the *Korps* aircraft – the Roland C-II proving to be one of the more effective *C-Typen* in the fighter role. A year later the role changed to that of close support and the *Schusta* were removed from the regular *Fliegerabteilungen* and redesignated as *Schlasta*. They were then progressively re-equipped with a new range of small and manoeuvrable two-seat *CL-Typen* the most notable of which were the Halberstadt and Hannover CL-*Serie*, Although not primarily employed as fighters they were to prove formidable opponents. The final aircraft to emerge in this new class was the highly advanced Junkers CL.I in the closing months of the war – see Lamberton W.M. 1960 *Fighter Aircraft of the 1914-1918 War* pp.132-133, 136-137, 144-145 & 148-149. Without doubt the most successful two-seat fighter of the Great War was the Bristol F2B Fighter which saw extensive service with the RFC & RAF from 1917. This had been developed as the R2A reconnaissance machine and its employment in the fighter role was almost accidental - see Lamberton 1960 pp.32-33 & Barnes C.H. 1970 *Bristol Aircraft since 1910* pp.104-108.
75	Lange 1970 p.158 & Kosin 1983 p.68. Blume had transferred to the *Fliegertruppe* from the *Infanterie* in 1915. Initially an NCO he was commissioned into the *Reserve* in Jan 17 and later in that year he was selected by *Oblt.* Bruno Loerzer to join *Jasta 26*. Wounded in action on the 29 Nov 17 he returned to service as *Kap.Jasta 9* in 1918. A successful *Jagdflieger* he was awarded the *Plm* on the 30 Sep 18 and ended the war with *28 abschusse* - see Angolia J.R. and Hackney C.R. 1984 *The Pour le Mérite and Germany's First Aces* pp.244-245.
76	Lange 1970 p.160, Nowarra 1980 pp.160-161 & Kosin 1983 p.68.
77	Lange 1970 p.160. The L 77v aircraft were registered: 10 136 D-1546, 10 137 D-1547, 10 138 D-1548, 10 139 D-1549, 303 D-1573 & 304 D-1574 - see also R.V.M. 1929 *Nachrichten für Luftfahrer 1929* & *Aircraft at the DVL, Abteilung M, Eprobungsabteilung Albatros, E-Stelle RDL Staaken & Rechlin, 1926 to 1934* in Beauvais et al 2002 p.114.
78	Hertel 1955 p.67 & Suchenwirth 1968 p.25.
79	Schliephake in Beauvais et al 2002 pp.48-49. This may have been one of the two *Heinkel* built aircraft which were delivered with rotatable gun mountings.
80	Lange 1970 p.161 & Nowarra 1980 p.198.
81	Schliephake in Beauvais et al 2002 p.48 & 49. L 84 D-1899 was assigned to the *RdL* in 1931 and was still on charge of the *E-Stelle Rechlin* in 1935 - *Aircraft at DVL, Abteilung M, Erprobungsstelle Albatros, E-Stelle RDL Staaken & Rechlin, 1926 to 1934* in Beauvais et al 2002 p.114.

Subsequently the *Focke Wulf Flugzeugbau*, into which *Albatros* had been absorbed, completed a second aircraft, WNr.10 190 D-2086, in February 1933 but no further development of this type was undertaken.[82]

Other types that appeared at Lipetsk in the summer of 1931 were the innovative Junkers K 47 and the Dornier Do C 1 *Kampfzweisitzer*. The **Junkers K 47** had been developed from *Dipl. Ing.*Karl Plauth's experimental A 48 *Schul-und Versuchsflugzeug* (Training and Research Aircraft) which first appeared in 1928 *(Photo 1C-6)*.[83] Unlike contemporary Junkers' aircraft the A 48 was an all-metal aircraft with a smooth fuselage skin and as such it was considered too advanced for the fledgling air arm. Corrugated metal skins continued to be used for the wings and the empennage. Powered by a 520 hp Bristol Jupiter VI the A 48 demonstrated a top speed of 275 kph and given the military potential for such an aircraft the parent company at Dessau completed as many as seven aircraft which were despatched to *AB Flygindustri* at Limhamn in Sweden where they were developed into the Pratt and Whitney Hornet engined K 47 *Kampfzweisitzer*.[84] In view of the advanced nature of this design three aircraft were ordered for operational testing at Lipetsk where WNr.3361-3363 arrived in 1930.[85] The flying characteristics of the K 47 were judged to be good and the type was favoured by the test crews. Less appears to be known about the **Dornier Do C 1** which was completed in 1931. Powered by a 710 hp BMW VI, the Do C 1 was a fabric covered parasol wing monoplane of otherwise metal construction. First flown on the 25 July 1931, only two examples were completed, the *Wa.Prw.8F* considering the metal structure of both the K 47 and the Do C 1 to be too complex and expensive for series production.[86]

C. BOMBER AIRCRAFT

Of the three main types of combat aircraft under development for the *Reichsheer* the bomber category was the least important as it was very difficult to disguise their true purpose at a time when Germany was not allowed to operate military aircraft of any type. Therefore in the first instance the bomber requirement was subsumed within the ***Erkunigros (Erkundungsflugzeug für mittlere Hohen und größte Entfernungen)*** specification which it was hoped would produce a medium altitude reconnaissance aircraft that could also double as a bomber.[87] Proposals were received from both the *Bayerische Flugzeugwerke (BFW)* and the *Ernst Heinkel Flugzeugwerke* and work began on these twin-engine aircraft in 1927.

In the meantime the 1926 Paris Air Agreement had finally permitted the operation of larger more powerful aircraft within Germany and a number of erstwhile combat types were imported albeit under the guise of some civilian application (See also 1B1). One such aircraft was the **Heinkel HD 33** which had been secretly developed in Sweden at the behest of *Wa.Prw.6F* with work beginning in 1925. Initially powered by a 240 hp Armstrong Siddeley Puma this large single-

82   Lange 1970 p.158. The *Albatros Flugzeugwerke* was a casualty of the economic recession. The development and production of a number of its aircraft was continued by *Focke Wulf* – see Wagner 1980 p.36.

83   Lange 1970 p.283, Nowarra 1980 pp.174-176 & Schmitt 1988 p.165, 145 & 159.

84   Schmitt 1988 p.159. An order for 12 K 47 aircraft was received from China. This source suggests that the Jupiter VI was rated at 600 hp. However this seems unlikely as even the Bristol Jupiter IXF of 1930 was only rated at 550 hp - see Lumsden 1994.

85   Kosin 1983 pp.69-72 & Schliephake in Beauvais et al 2002 pp.48-49.

86   Nowarra 1980 pp.200-201 & Dornier 1983 p.117. The Do C 2a was a floatplane version which found some favour in South America – see Nowarra 1980 pp.200-203 & Dornier 1983 p.123. Do C 1 WNr.226 D-1592 was assigned to the *RdL* in 1931 – see *Aircraft at DVL, Abteilung M, Erprobungsstelle Albatros, E-Stelle RDL Staaken & Rechlin, 1926 to 1934* in Beauvais et al 2002 p.114. The structural complexity and cost of the K 47 and Do C 1 were reasons why these models were passed over – see Kosin 1983 pp.70-71.

87   Hooton 1994 p.64 & Regel in Beauvais et al 2002 p.57.

engine biplane first flew in September of that year. It was then re-engined with the 300 hp BMW IV six-cylinder in-line engine and re-appeared in February 1926 as a long range reconnaissance and day bombing aircraft - *Fernaufklärungs-und Tagbombenflugzeug*. In May 1926 the HD 33 arrived at Warnemünde as a prospective postal aircraft and was quickly fitted with one of the first 660 hp BMW VI vee-twelve engines together with a revised engine cooling system. In this form the HD 33 had a loaded weight of 2,730 kgs, a top speed of 246 kph, and a service ceiling of 6,200 m. A tactical radius of 200 kms was possible on the 900 litres of fuel carried.[88] HD 33 WNr.237 was registered to the *DVL* as the D-1205 which continued to covertly evaluate the aircraft on behalf of the TA (L). Although only one aircraft was actually built the *WaA's 1927 Notrustüngs-Programm* included a planned order of 24 aircraft of this type for emergency use by the *Reichswehr*.[89]

In August 1927 Student approved Heinkel's plans for a new twin-engine bomber and reconnaissance aircraft.[90] Substantially larger than the HD 33 the **Heinkel HD 34** was a large biplane of conventional construction powered by two BMW VI 7,3 high compression liquid-cooled engines. A crew of three or four men could be carried and plans existed for the type to be armed with two fixed lu.MG 08/15 machine guns in the nose and two similar weapons on a flexible mounting in the rear fuselage (B-Stand). HD 34 WNr.287 was ready for testing by the following summer but it crashed at Warnemünde on the 25 June 1928 and no further development was undertaken.[91]

The more limited resources of *BFW* delayed completion of the **BFW M 22** WNr.444 until the following year. Once again this was a large biplane of conventional construction. The upper wing was supported by a central fairing above the fuselage and by large "I" interplane struts between the wings. Willy Messerschmitt opted for two 530 hp Siemens (Gnome et Rhône) Jupiter VI radials which were mounted between the wings driving two-blade fixed-pitch propellers. The wheels of the substantial main undercarriage were neatly spatted. Defensive gun positions were provided in the nose and in the rear fuselage and the pilot sat forward of the wing with a good view to the front of the aircraft. Test flying occupied the summer months of 1930. A top speed of 220 kph was recorded, the normal range being just 500 kms. The all up weight was 3,800 kgs.[92] Unfortunately the M 22 was destroyed in a crash near Augsburg on the 14 October 1930, *Oblt.a.D.*Eberhard Mohnicke a test pilot from the *RdL* being killed (See also 1C2 & 1D1). No further development was undertaken.[93]

In the meantime work had begun at the *Dornier-Werke* at Friedrichshafen and Altenrhein on a far larger four-engine long range night bomber. In 1927 *Wa.Prw.6F* had placed a requirement for such an aircraft or *Größnachtbomber (Gronabo)* capable of long range operations, a speed of 212 kph and an operational ceiling of not less than 4,500 m.[94] The selection of *Dornier* for such a project was logical in the light of its previous experience with the Do N twin-engine bomber which had been designed to meet an Imperial Japanese Army requirement.[95] The **Dornier Do P**

---

88   Lange 1970 p.246, Nowarra 1980 pp.118-119 & Koos 2006 pp.82-83.
89   Andersson 1989 p.41.
90   Koos 2006 p.84. The type was also known as the *Land-Mehrzweckflugzeug* or land based multi-role aircraft.
91   Nowarra 1980 pp.172-173 & Koos 2006 pp.84-85. It was hoped that the HD 34 would have a top speed of 266 kph and a service ceiling of 7,600 m.
92   Lange 1970 p.320, Smith J.R. 1971 *Messerschmitt: An Aircraft Album* p.22 & Nowarra 1980 pp.182-183.
93   *Losses of the E-Stelle Rechlin and its predecessors 1926 to 1945* in Beauvais et al 2002 p.120.
94   Schliephake H. 1971 *The Birth of the Luftwaffe* (hereafter cited as Schliephake 1971) p.28. In this requirement *Wa.Prw.6F* was undoubtedly influenced by contemporary developments in France - Liore et Olivier LeO 20, and in Britain - Vickers Virginia. The twin engine Vickers Virginia had entered service with the RAF in late 24 and it would remain in first line service until 1937 - see Andrews C.F. 1969 *Vickers Aircraft since 1908* pp.130-150 & Thetford O. 1976 *Aircraft of the Royal Air Force since 1918* pp.508-512. The Liore et Olivier LeO 20 BN 3 on the other hand was the successful entrant in the *Aviation Militaire's 1926 Concours d'Avions de Bombardement*. Initial aircraft were twin-engine, whilst later aircraft were powered by four Gnome-Rhône Titan engines – see Morse (Ed.) 1982 p.2320 & 2332.
95   Lange 1970 p.199, Nowarra 1980 pp.126-127 & Dressel J. and Griehl M.1997 *The Luftwaffe Album: Bomber and*

Gronabo followed a similar design concept, the four 510 hp Jupiter radial engines being mounted in tandem pairs on the high wing; the wing itself being faired into the upper part of the fuselage. Two prototypes were built and the first of these WNr.180, later registered D-1982, was evaluated at Lipetsk during 1931 and 1932. Unfortunately by this time the type was outmoded and *Wa.Prw.8F* interest had switched to the development of a more flexible and cheaper twin-engine design (See 1A3). The Do P had open gun positions in the nose and rear fuselage and these were used for armament trials with the new MG 15 machine gun whilst in the Ukraine (See 1D1). A further problem with the aircraft was its inability to carry the new *SC Sprengbomben* without extensive modification - it had been designed around the earlier and now obsolescent *PuW* ordnance (See 1C5). No further development was therefore undertaken.[96]

In 1929 *Wa.Prw.8F* issued a new requirement for a **mittlere Nachtbomber (Minabo)** to which *Dornier's* design team made two proposals *(Photo 1C-7)*.[97] The first of these was the three-engine **Dornier Do Y**. Powered by three Bristol Jupiter VI engines, later replaced by more powerful Gnome et Rhône (Jupiter) 9A engines, the Do Y had a very respectable maximum speed of 300 kph, a maximum bomb load of 1,200 kgs and a still air range of 1,500 kms. Test flying began on the 17 October 1931.[98] The structurally similar **Dornier Do F** was powered by two 530 hp Siemens (Gnome et Rhône) Jupiter VI radials semi-enclosed by Townend style cowlings. To maximise the thrust from these engines large fixed-pitch four blade wooden propellers were installed. The Do F was also the first European bomber to feature a retractable main undercarriage, an innovation that was also a feature of the contemporary Boeing Y1B-9A, and one that again helped to boost performance, a top speed of 250 kph being reported.[99] Defensive positions with the new MG 15 machine gun were provided in the nose *(A-Stand)*, the upper rear fuselage *(B-Stand)* and under the rear fuselage *(C-Stand)*.[100] From the outset the Do F was designed around the new SC 50 and SC 250 ordnance which was stored internally in six vertical bomb magazines. The planned bomb load was either 6 SC 250 Sprengbomben, 30 SC 50 Sprengbomben or 120 SC 10 Splitterbomben for a total of 1,500 kgs (See also 1C5).[101] Following a detailed technical evaluation at the *Erprobungsstelle Rechlin* the prototype Do F (Do 11a) WNr.230 D-2270 arrived a Lipetsk in 1932 and operational trials continued into the following year.[102] A small production order, ostensibly for use by *Deutsche Luft Hansa* as a *Frachtflugzeug* (Freighter) was placed by the *RVM* in 1932. However in reality it was expected that most of the production aircraft would be for the *Reichswehr*. Production aircraft (Do 11C) would be powered by the newly developed 650 hp Siemens und Halske Sh 22B radial.[103]

Fighter Aircraft of the German Air Force 1933-1945 (hereafter cited as Dressel and Griehl 1997) pp.12-13. The prototype of the Do N first flew at Altenrhein in 1926. The success of the design led to its licensed manufacture in Japan as the Kawasaki Type 87 Bomber. In all 28 were built - see Sekigawa 1974 p.22 & Dornier 1983 p.103.

96   Lange 1970 p.199, Nowarra 1980 pp.192-193 & Dornier 1983 p.112. It is reported that the Do P at Lipetsk was handed over the *VVS* in 1933 as a gift - see Schliephake in Beauvais el 2002 p.48. The remaining example was acquired by the *RVM* in Mar 31 - see Dornier 1983 p.112.

97   Dressel and Griehl 1997 p.13. Junkers offered the existing but ageing K 30 *Kampflugzeug* to meet the requirements of this specification. The K 30 was a bomber version of the G 24 airliner which had been produced in small numbers as the JuG 1 in Sweden during the late 20s for the *VVS-RKKA* - see Nowarra 1980 pp.118-120 & Schmitt 1988 pp.154-156 & 143-145.

98   Lange 1970 p.201, Nowarra 1980 pp.202-203 & Dressel and Griehl 1997 pp.13-14. Three defensive positions were planned, the upper *A & B-Standen* having twin machine guns, whilst a pivot-mounted machine gun was to be installed in the ventral C-Stand. The 3 Do Y bombers built were delivered to the Yugoslav Air Force - see Dornier 1983 p.121.

99   Dornier 1983 p.124. Retractable landing gear was a feature of the experimental American Douglas XB-7 and Fokker XB-8 of 1931 and it would be a feature of the Boeing B-9 and the later Martin B-10. See also Green 1970 p.110 & Swanborough and Bowers 1989 p.635 & 646 and pp.101-102 & 433-436.

100   Lange 1970 p.201 & Dressel and Griehl 1997 pp.14-15.

101   Dressel and Griehl 1997p.14 & Schliephake in Beauvais et al 2002 p.48.

102   Schliephake in Beauvais et al 2002 pp.48-49.

103   Stroud J.1966 *European Transport Aircraft since 1910* (hereafter cited as Stroud 1966), Green 1970 p.110 & Dressel

D. HIGH POWERED AERO-ENGINES

During the Great War the *Luftstreitkräfte* had relied on a range of four and six cylinder water-cooled in-line engines, supplemented to a small extent by nine cylinder air-cooled rotary engines. The major manufacturers had been the *Daimler-Werke* and *Benz & Cie* with, to a far lesser extent, the *BMW Flugmotorenwerke (BMW)*. The rotary engines were built by the *Oberursel-Motorenwerke*.[104] The design and construction of the in-line engines followed the automotive tradition and the majority of the wartime engines could trace their lineage back to *Dr.Ing.*Ferdinand Porsche's pre-war work.[105] The six-cylinder Austro-Daimler employed a shallow aluminium crankcase with dry sump lubrication, a scavenger pump being used to return the surplus oil to an external tank from which a pressure pump delivered it to the bearings. The cylinders with their integral heads were formed from cast or welded steel and these were bolted as separate units to the crankcase. The water-jackets were fabricated from sheet steel stampings and were welded to each cylinder. The pistons drove a heavy and relatively rigid crankshaft which was supported by seven main bearings. The associated camshaft used eight main bearings and was connected to the overhead valves by long push rods, the valves being inclined outward at 30 degrees to the vertical. The cylinders were 130 x 175 mm with an overall capacity of 13.9 litres. The pre-war engine was rated at 120 hp at 1,200 rpm. The engine had a weight of 262 kgs.[106]

The slow revving Austro-Daimler proved to be reliable and efficient with excellent fuel economy, smoothness of operation and effective cooling. The separate bolted cylinders simplified maintenance. Wartime design improvements would result in a 225 hp six cylinder in-line engine.[107] Elsewhere German designers would achieve similar outputs using this basic layout by the end of hostilities.[108] In contrast to developments in France and Britain there was far less interest within the *Luftstreitkräfte* in the rotary engine. This engine was far lighter than the large in-line designs. Effective cooling was ensured through the actual rotation of the engine itself around a fixed crankshaft. The rotation of the engine also negated the need for a carburettor as the turbulence and heat to which the fuel and air was submitted as they entered the engine was quite sufficient to provide the right mixture. This arrangement also did away with the throttle as the engine was run at full power throughout the flight, landing being facilitated by either a blip switch which cut off the ignition or by a selective device that ran the engine on 7, 5 or 3 cylinders.[109] The Oberursel UR IIIa of 1917 produced 160 hp at 1,300 rpm for a weight of just 170 kgs. This engine was used with the Fokker Dr.I fighter.[110]

Post-war the lack of aviation work within Germany quickly resulted in the loss of established manufacturers such as *Benz* and *Daimler*.[111] This difficult situation was then aggravated by the enforcement of the new *Begriffsbestimmungen für den deutschen Luftfahrzeugbau* (Definitions of Categories of German Aircraft Construction) in May 1922 that effectively removed the indigenous

---

and Griehl 1997 pp.14-15. See also Vajda and Dancey 1998 p.10.

104   *Flugmotoren des Ersten Weltkrieges* in Gersdorff von K. and Grasmann K. 1985 *Die Deutsche Luftfahrt 2: Flugmotoren und Strahltriebwerke* (hereafter cited as Gersdorff and Grasmann 1985) pp.28-29. Other manufacturers included the *Siemens und Halske AG, Basse und Selve*, the *Maybach Motorenbau GmbH* and the *Maschinenfabrik Augsburg-Nürnberg (MAN)*. See also Lange 1970 p.381, 395 & 402 and Vajda and Dancey 1998 p.233 & 235.

105   Smith H. 1981 *Aircraft Piston Engines: From the Manly Balzer to the Continental Tiara* (hereafter cited as Smith 1981) pp.29-30. & Gunston 1995 pp.20-21. *Siemens* did produce a rotary engine that was fitted to the Siemens Schukert D-IV fighter. The engine tended to over-heat and was not particularly successful in service.

106   Smith 1981 p.30 & Gunston 1995 p.21.

107   Gunston 1995 p.21.

108   *Der BMW IIIa setzt sich durch* in Gersdorff and Grasmann 1985 pp.36-37. The 1916 Benz Bz III was rated at 195 hp, whilst the 1916 Daimler D IIIa produced 180 hp and the 1917 BMW IIIa was rated at 226 hp.

109   Smith 1981 pp.57-65. The French Clerget and British Bentley rotaries used a selector switch to reduce the number of cylinders that would develop power during an approach to land.

110   Gersdorff and Grasmann 1985 pp.27-31. See also Lumsden 1994 pp.21-22 & 87-88.

111   Vajda and Dancey 1985 p.235.

civil market for high-powered aero-engines (See 1B1). For their developments abroad the German aircraft designers therefore turned to the use of foreign engines, notably the Napier Lion, Bristol Jupiter and Rolls Royce Eagle.[112] Of these the 450 hp Lion Mk.II was the *WaA's* favoured type in the early to mid-twenties and this engine was used for a variety of military prototypes as well as production types such as the Fokker D.XIII and Heinkel HD 17 (See above).

The **Napier Lion II** was a twelve cylinder "broad arrow" or "W" engine that had been developed from July 1916. The initial prototypes appeared in the following year but only 35 engines had been delivered by the end of hostilities and existing contracts were cancelled.[113] Post war the Lion Mk.II was widely used from 1919 with a slightly more powerful variant the Mk.IIB being introduced in 1925. In the broad arrow layout the cylinders were arranged in three banks of four, a configuration that reduced the engine's overall length and resulted in a compact layout. The Lion was a water-cooled 23.9 litre poppet valve engine. The cylinders had a bore of 137.5 mm with a stroke of 128 mm (137 x 128). The dry weight was 470 kgs. The Lion proved to be a very reliable engine in service. Using 74 octane fuel it could produce 450 hp at 2,000 rpm at an altitude of up to 1,530 m.[114]

Marine aircraft such as the Dornier Do J *Wal* and the Heinkel HE 1 were powered by the **Rolls Royce Eagle**. First developed meet a British Admiralty requirement the Eagle entered service in 1916. It was twelve cylinder upright vee engine with the two banks of six cylinders aligned at 60 degrees to each other. It was a water-cooled poppet valve engine with a capacity of 20.32 litres. Individual cylinders were 114.3 x 165.1 mm in size. The 360 hp Eagle IX was a modified "civil" engine with a slightly reduced compression ratio, a strengthened crankshaft, improved camshaft-drive and improved altitude mixture control. Ignition was via four magnetos and fuel induction via two carburettors (40-50 octane fuel). The Eagle was a geared engine and this allowed both left and right hand propeller drive for use in the tandem Do J *Wal* layout. Overall dry weight was 437 kgs.[115]

Not withstanding the use of these imported engines the *In.W.G.6F* was understandably keen to promote the development of an indigenous high-powered aero engine. As early as 1924 Helmut Sachse's successful *BMW* design team at München-Allach had been approached by Student with a development contract for an aero engine in the 600 hp class.[116] The basis for this new development was the new 300 hp **BMW IVa** six cylinder in-line water-cooled engine that would enter production once the Allied restrictions had been lifted and for which an order had already been placed by the *In.W.G.6F* on behalf of the Soviet authorities (See 1C1).[117] The secret to the BMW IVa's success was the decision to employ a new larger 160 x 190 mm cylinder of 3.82 litre capacity in place of the wartime BMW IIIa's 150 x 180 mm cylinder of 3.17 litre capacity whilst simultaneously increasing the engine's running speed from 1,440 rpm to 1,650 rpm.[118] The BMW IVa quickly became a commercial success and aircraft powered by this engine would secure 5 world records in 1926 and a further 17 world records in 1927.[119]

112   Hertel 1955 p.24.
113   Lumsden 1994 pp.164-165. The initial contract for the Napier Lion had been 100 units. Some of the production engines were used on prototype aircraft; an unofficial British altitude record of 9,300 m was achieved in a Lion powered DH 9 on the 2 Jan 19.
114   Lumsden 1994 pp.165-166. See also Gunston 1995 p.112.
115   Lumsden 1994 pp.183-187. See also Gunston 1995 p.140. For use on the Do J – see Lange 1970 pp.195-197.
116   Hertel 1955 p.24-25.
117   Gersdorff and Grasmann 1985. For a short period following the end of the Great War *BMW* had turned its attention away from aviation to marine engines and motor cycles. Work resumed on aero-engine development in 1922. The *VVS-RKKA* had placed an order for 380 BMW II/III/IV engines which were to be manufactured at *Junkers'* Fili plant in the USSR - see Boyd A. 1977 *The Soviet Air Force since 1918* p. & Hooton 1994 p.48.
118   Gersdorff and Grasmann 1985 pp.57-59. The BMW IVa was used by all the major German aircraft manufacturers including *Junkers* which had its own aero-engine department.
119   Gersdorff and Grasmann 1985 p.58.

The new 600 hp **BMW VI** appeared in prototype form in 1925. It was a twelve cylinder vee water-cooled engine, in effect a combination of two BMW IV cylinder banks mounted at 60 degrees to each other on a common crankcase.[120] Overall capacity was a formidable 46.95 litres with an initial compression ratio of 5.5:1. Whilst the cylinders were fabricated from steel with welded water jackets, the crankcase was formed from cast aluminium or from *Elektron* - a new light weight magnesium alloy.[121] Partly through the use of this material the overall weight of the new twelve cylinder engine at 510 kgs was considerably less than that of two BMW IVs (570 kgs). However light metal alloys were not used for the cylinder heads or the water jackets even though these were a feature of the parallel six-cylinder BMW V.[122] The new BMW VI passed its *Masterprüfung* (Type Test) successfully in February 1926 just in time for commercial production to begin following the lifting of restrictions in May.[123]

Relatively few BMW VI engines were built during the latter part of the twenties; demand from both the airlines and the military for this type of engine being limited during this period.[124] Nonetheless *Wa.Prw.6F* had specified the use of this power plant as one of two standard types of aero-engine for future military aircraft and as such it was subject to further development at München-Allach (See 1C2). As the **BMW VI 6,3** the compression ratio was increased via an engine driven mechanical compressor and the use of higher 87 octane fuel. This together with a slight increase in engine speed resulted in 640 hp being available for take-off, whilst a maximum continuous cruise rpm of 1,530 rpm output produced 580 hp.[125] In a parallel development BMW-Farman reduction gearing was introduced to produce the **BMW VI U** *(Untersetzungsgetriebe)*. The introduction of such gearing allowed larger diameter propellers to be fitted than would have otherwise been the case with a high powered engine. In the case of the BMW VI U the gearing reduced propeller speed to approximately two thirds of the engine speed (0.6:1).[126] Engine speed for take-off was increased from 1,500 rpm to 1,700 rpm which in turn resulted in a higher short term power rating of 750 hp. Maximum continuous power was 585 hp at 1,530 rpm. Overall weight increased to 546 kgs for those engines fitted with an *Elektron* crankcase.[127]

The need for a higher power rating, particularly at greater altitudes, for use with fighter aircraft then led to the **BMW VI 7,3.** In this engine the compression ratio was raised still further to 7.3:1 which was sufficient to produce 700 hp at 1,550 rpm for take off. The maximum continuous rating was preserved at 500 hp at 1,390 rpm. In the early thirties further detailed improvements were made to both the production BMW VI 6,0 and BMW VI 7,3 engines. From *Baureihe* (Production

120   Lange 1970 pp.396-397, Gersdorff and Grasmann 1985 pp.58-59 & Gunston 1995 p.26.
121   Schneider H. 1940 *Flugzeug-Typenbuch: Handbuch der Deutschen Luftfahrt und Zubehor-Industrie Hauptausgabe A 1939/40* p.566. *Elektron A 9 V* was manufactured by *Rudolf Rautenbach Leichtmetall-Giessereien* of Solingen. It was a magnesium based alloy with 8-9% Aluminium, 0.3% Silicon, 0.1-0.5% Manganese & 0.1-0.8% Zinc. It proved ideal for the complex castings associated with high powered aero-engines.
122   Lange 1970 p.396. The BMW V was a 6-cylinder in-line water-cooled engine rated at 410 hp at 1650 rpm which was completed in 1926/27. In a modified form with a weight of 285 kgs, the BMW Va, it entered commercial use in 1927. By comparison the overall dry weight of the BMW VI with an aluminium crank case was 546 kgs.
123   Lange 1970 p.397 & Gersdorff and Grasmann 1985 p.58.
124   Lange 1970 p.397 & Gersdorff and Grasmann 1985 p.58. The BMW VI was put on show at both the Berlin *ILA* and Paris Salon in 1928. Licence production of the engine would later be arranged in Japan, Czechoslovakia and the USSR.
125   Lange 1970 p.397 & Gersdorff and Grasmann 1985 p.58. The major problem with higher compression ratios was the tendency of the fuel to pre-detonate. This was prevented through the use of additives such as lead-tetraethyl and iron-carbonyl. At the time these blends were referred to as "dopes". A disadvantage of such fuels was the fouling that they caused inside the cylinders - see Stern W.J. *Aircraft Engines* in Nayler J.L. and Ower E. 1930 *Aviation of To-Day: Its History and Development* (hereafter cited as Stern in Nayler and Ower 1930) p.392 & Lumsden 1994 p.33.
126   Lange 1970 p.397 & Lumsden 1994 pp.39-40.
127   Lange 1970 p.397 & Gersdorff and Grasmann 1985 pp.58-59.

Series) 6 the BMW carburettor was replaced by the superior Zenith type on VI 7,3 an improvement that led to the use of the designation **BMW VI 6,0 Z** or **7,3 Z** (Zenith), whilst liquid cooling using Ethyl-Glycol was introduced in place of the earlier water cooling in *Baureihe 7*.[128] Production at München-Allach steadily increased during this period; the BMW VI U was employed as a power plant on the Heinkel HD 45A/B *Aufklarer*, the BMW VI 6,0 Z on the Heinkel HD 59A/B and HD 60A/B *Marineflugzeuge*, whilst the BMW VI 7,3 Z was used by the Arado Ar 65 and Heinkel HD 38 *Jagdflugzeuge*.[129]

The *WaA's* other "standard" engine was the Bristol Jupiter VI radial, albeit in its licence built **Gnome et Rhône (Jupiter) 9A** form.[130] The Jupiter was another British engine of wartime origin although series production had not really got underway in Great Britain until the Jupiter III of 1923.[131] Unlike the earlier rotaries the radial was a fixed engine with the crankshaft driving the propeller either directly or through some form of reduction gearing. Radial engines were certainly attractive in the twenties as they offered superior power to weight ratios to the far heavier and larger water-cooled in-line, broad arrow and vee configurations.[132] They were also more compact, less complex, easier to service and less prone to breakdown or damage in operation. The vibration associated with many in-line engines of this era was largely absent in the radial. Vibration in water cooled engines could be particularly disruptive to coolant lines and connections and this was one of the reasons that the US Navy for example specified radial engines for its shipboard aircraft.[133]

The basic Jupiter was a nine-cylinder radial of 28.73 litres capacity; cylinder dimensions were 146 x 190 mm. Overall weight was in excess of 350 kgs. The cylinders were fabricated from steel, the outer surfaces being deeply finned to cool the engine. The cylinder heads were machined flat to accept a cast aluminium "poultice" type head complete with valve guides and the two vertical inlet and two exhaust seats and passages; the BMW VI by comparison had only single inlet and exhaust valves of much greater size. The aluminium head was also finned to assist cooling. Initially rated at 400 hp with a compression ratio of 5:1 the performance of the Jupiter was then steadily improved to reach 520 hp in the Jupiter VI of 1927. Military engines had a compression ratio of 6.3:1. This gave optimum power at 1,220 later 1,520 m but required the use of a gated throttle below these altitudes to prevent engine damage through detonation associated with the use of 74-octane petrol.[134] The metric engineered Gnome et Rhône 9A introduced the superior Farman bevel epicyclic reduction gear, this being later introduced as standard by the parent company with the Bristol Jupiter VIII of 1929.[135]

In Germany the Gnome et Rhône 9A was built by the *Siemens und Halske Flugmotorenwerk AG* at Berlin-Spandau as the **Siemens Jupiter VI**.[136] To enable the engine to be used in both tractor and pusher installations, for example aboard the giant Dornier Do X *Flugschiff*, the Siemens design team

128   Lange 1970 p.397 & Gersdorff and Grasmann 1985 pp.58-59.
129   Lange 1970 p.162 & pp.246-249.
130   Hertel 19955 p.27. The *Societe des Moteurs Gnome et Rhône* took out a licence production agreement for the Bristol Jupiter radial in Oct 21. Interestingly the company's chief engineer and chief designer were both Bristol employees - see also Lumsden 1994 p.92 & Gunston 1995 p.77.
131   Nayler and Ower 1930 pp.381-382 & 383-386 & Hertel 1955 p.27. The failure of the ABC Dragonfly of 1918 resulted in a loss of confidence in Britain in the radial engine and for a period in the early twenties water-cooled engines such as the Rolls Royce Eagle and the Napier Lion were preferred for service use - see also Stern in Nayler and Ower pp,381-382 & Lumsden 1994 pp.52-53 & 93-94. The Bristol Jupiter was formally chosen as the first new post-war engine for the *RAF* in Oct 23 when an order for 81 engines was signed – see Gunston 1995 p.32.
132   Stern in Nayler and Ower 1930 pp.384-387 & Smith 1981 pp.97-103 & 108-109.
133   Smith 1981 p.106.
134   Nayler and Owen 1930 pp.383-386 & Lumsden 1994 pp.93-101.
135   Hertel 1955 p.27 & Gunston 1995 pp.30-31.
136   Gunston 1995 p.77. This licence was obtained from *Gnome et Rhône* rather than Bristol in a rather interesting commercial arrangement. *Gnome et Rhône* were not always paying the expected royalties to Bristol by this time !

introduced a truly circular cylinder design in which the depth of the external finning was constant; the Bristol built cylinders had deeper finning at the rear than at the front of the engine so as to even out the cooling. The 28.6 litre *Siemens* engine developed 530 hp at 2,100 rpm with a compression ratio of 6.3:1 and most engines were delivered with a 0.5:1 Farman reduction gearing as the **Jupiter VI U**. In all 131 Siemens Jupiter VI engines were built, these being used mainly by *Deutsche Luft Hansa* but also for a number of military prototypes including the Arado Ar 64, Dornier Do F and Focke Wulf S 39.[137]

In the meantime *Hptm.*Student had asked *RegBauMtr.a.D.*Becker's design team at Berlin-Spandau to improve on the licence built Jupiter with Germany's first indigenous high powered radial, the **Siemens und Halske Sh 20**. Work began in 1928 and the resulting Sh 20 was a supercharged nine-cylinder radial of 31.5 litres capacity with new cylinders of 154 mm bore and 188 mm stroke fitted with sintered aluminium oxide spark plugs. The dry weight was 415 kgs.[138] The Sh 20B completed its *Masterprüfung* on the 8 February 1930 and was thereafter test flown for 175 hours using the HD 41b WNr.342 D-1795 during which 450 hp and 500 hp were obtained.[139] Thereafter further test flying was carried out with two Junkers W 34 machines but output was disappointing, only 540 hp being obtained at 1,850 rpm. Only thirty three Sh 20B and 20/U engines were produced during the period 1930-32.[140]

To increase engine speed and boost performance Becker's team then reduced the stroke of the Sh 20B to 160 mm, the new engine being referred to as the **Siemens und Halske Sh 22**.[141] The super-charged Sh 22 had a smaller capacity but a greater output than the Sh 20B, being initially rated at 600 hp at 2,000 rpm. Unlike the Jupiter, from which it was essentially derived, the Sh 22 had a Duralumin cylinder head with a single inlet and two exhaust valves. To keep weight to a minimum the crank case was also formed from Duralumin although this was quickly replaced by *Elektron*. The dry weight was 450 kgs. With Farman reduction gearing (0.62:1) fitted as standard the Sh 22 became the preferred engine for both the Dornier Do F *Nachtbomber* and the Heinkel He 46 *Nahaufklärer* from 1933.[142]

Wimmer's engine specialists, Helmut Sachse and Franz Mahnke, both appreciated that despite the availability of the BMW VI and Siemens Sh 22 there was a pressing need to develop a range of more powerful engines to support of the second phase of aerial rearmament.[143] To co-ordinate the diverse and at times conflicting requirements of the *Reichsheer, Reichsmarine*, the *DVS* and *DLH* it was decided to form a *Motoren-Kommission* under the chairmanship of *RegRat* Adolf Baeumker of the *RVM* to co-ordinate future plans and focus development funding (See also 1B1).[144] Two

137   Gersdorff and Grasmann 1985 pp.47-49. *DLH* used the Siemens Jupiter for the Focke Wulf *Möwe*, the Do *Wal* & *Superwal* and the Do X. About 30 engines were allocated for military purposes - see also Lange 1970 p.425.

138   Hertel 1955 p.26 & 28, Lange 1970 p.425, Gersdorff and Grasmann 1985 p.47 & Gunston 1995 pp.30-31. The Sh 20 was fitted with a single-stage supercharger. The compression ratio was 5.6:1.

139   Lange 1970 p.425 & Gersdorff and Grasmann 1985 p.47. The HD 41b had been previously employed by Siemens und Halske for test flying the licence built Jupiter - see also Koos 2006 pp.99-100.

140   Gersdorff and Grasmann 1985 pp.47-49. The Sh 20/U was fitted with reduction gearing for the propeller, this variant weighing an additional 60 kgs. The Sh 20 was tested in Junkers W 34fao, whilst the Sh 20U was tested aboard the W 34fei - see Schmitt 1988 p.124.

141   Gersdorff and Grasmann 1985 p.47 & Gunston 1995 p.31.

142   Lange 1970 p.425, Gersdorff and Grasmann 1985 pp.47-49 & Gunston 1995 p.31. The Sh 22 was also test flown using the HD 41b D-1795 - see Koos 2006.

143   Hertel 1955 p.29. *Ref.1b (Motoren)* was headed, first by Sachse and later by Mahnke. Mahnke had studied at the *Technischen Hochschule Berlin* between 1920-26 and had then been employed as a *Konstrukteur u.Versuchs-Ingenieur* by the *Firma Werkzeugmaschinenbau Drescher* at Wittstock prior to joining the WaA as a civilian in Sep 27 - see service record for Franz Mahnke in Hildebrand K.F.1992 *Die Generale der deutschen Luftwaffe 1935-1945 Band 3 O-Z* pp.344-345.

144   Hertel 1955 p.30. Funding was a particular concern at a time of a world economic downturn. *RVM* resources were

different engines were proposed: (1) a 30 litre liquid cooled engine with inverted cylinders to improve forward visibility when fitted to a fighter aircraft. This 12-cylinder engine was to have a small stroke and high engine speed to give a thrust of 800 hp; and (2) a high-powered twin-row radial for use in bomber aircraft and large transports. The firms of *Daimler-Benz* and *Junkers* were contracted to develop the liquid cooled engine, whilst those of *BMW* and *Siemens* concentrated on the radial development (See 3C2).[145]

Interestingly the *Reichsmarines* engine specialists considered the leap to a 30 litre engine to be too ambitious and in response to these concerns a further requirement was subsequently issued to both *Junkers* and *BMW* for a smaller 20 litre engine of similar configuration (See 3C2).[146]

co-ordinated by *MinRat.*Albert Muhlig-Hoffmann & *RegRat.*Baeumker. Representatives of all these agencies were included on the *Motoren Kommission. Dipl.Ing.*Oskar Kurtz's *Motorenabteilung* of the *DVL* was also represented, its research work being of especial value in future planning - see Lange 1970 pp.189-190.

145   Hertel 1955 pp.31-32.
146   Hertel 1955 p.32. There does seem to be some confusion as to the origin of the 20 Litre requirement as Hertel states: *"At the request of the Reichsmarine, the firms of Junkers and BMW nevertheless were given specifications and directives for development of a 20-litre engine"*, whilst Wimmer has stated that: *"the Navy raised no objections against the 20-litre engine, which was intended for twin-engine aircraft, but considered the jump to 30-litre engines too great"* – quoted from Hertel 1955 *Procurement in the German Air Force* p.31 USAF Historical Studies No.170. The *Luftschützgruppe's Referat Technik* appear to have been influenced by the new Rolls Royce Kestrel, a 21.25 litre vee twelve in the 500 hp class, that had entered production in 1927 as the Rolls Royce F - see Lumsden 1994 pp.190-192.

1C4

Naval Development and Production Programmes 1926-1932

During the *Reichswehr* period the *Gruppe BSx (B-Amt Seetransportabteilung Gruppe x)* (Gruppe x, Sea Transport Branch, B-Office) under *Kpt.z.See* Rudolf Lahs and its successor the *Luftschützgruppe* (Air Defence Group) under *Kpt.z.See* Konrad Zander pursued an entirely separate and distinctive aircraft development programme to that of the *Reichsheer* (See also 1E3).[1] Technical matters were initially the preserve of *KptLt.*Joachim Coeler assisted, amongst others, by former *Marineflieger Lt.z.See a.D.Dipl. Ing.*Wolfram Eisenlohr who specialised in airframes and power plants, and *Lt.d.Res a.D.Dipl.Ing.* Rudolf Spies who was an expert in marine airframe design.[2] Not surprisingly naval interest centred on the development of water borne aircraft or seaplanes *(Seeflugzeuge)* and recurrent themes during the late twenties and early thirties were reconnaissance floatplanes for both coastal and shipboard employment *(See-Aufklärungsflugzeuge)*, reconnaissance flying boats of greater endurance for work with the Fleet during operations in the *Nordsee (Aufklärungs-Flugbooten)* and Torpedo Bomber *(Torpedo-und Bomben Flugzeuge)* for anti-shipping missions in both the Nordsee and Ostsee (See also 1E3).

The *Marineleitung* (Naval High Command) had responded quickly to the relaxation of the Allied restrictions on technical developments in German aviation. Immediately prior to the creation of the *Gruppe BSx, KptLt.*Hans Ritter, the *Referent für Flugwesen und Luftschütz (Referent A II 1)* (Staff Advisor for Aviation and Air Defence), had secured sufficient funding to sponsor a major seaplane competition at Warnemünde for a modern *"Postflugzeug"* (Mail Carrying Aircraft).[3] No less than

---

1   Caspari H.A. *Vorgeschichte der deutschen Seefliegerei* in Caspari H.A. Dr. (Ed.) Undated *E-Stellen Travemünde und Tarnewitz 2.Band – Die Geschichte der Seeflugzeug-Eprobungsstelle Travemünde und daraus hervorgegangenen E-Stelle für Flugzeugbewaffnung Tarnewitz* (hereafter cited as Caspari in Caspari (Ed.) Bd.2) p.23 & 31 and Andersson L. 1989 'Secret Luftwaffe: German Military Aviation Build-up between the Wars' in *Air Enthusiast* No.41 1989 (hereafter cited as Andersson 1989) p.43 & Hooton E.R. 1994 *Phoenix Triumphant: The Rise and Rise of the Luftwaffe* (hereafter cited as Hooton 1994) p.29, 33 & 59. In 1926 *Adm.*Paul Zenker authorised the upgrading of the *Referent für Flugwesen und Luftschütz* to the status of a distinct yet covert *Gruppe* within *Kpt.z.See* Günther Lohmann's *Seetransport-Abteilung*. The *Gruppe-LS* was formed from the *Gruppe BSx* in 1929.

2   Caspari in Caspari (Ed.) Bd.2 p.23 & 25. Coeler's team consisted of: *Dipl.Ing.*Spies *(Flugzeugwelle)*, *Dipl. Ing.*Dr.Harmsen *(Flugzeugschwimmer u.Boote)*, *Dipl.Ing.*Eisenlohr *(Flugmotoren)*, *Dr.*Mader *(Flugzeuggerate u.Instrumente)* & *Ing.*Bock *(Funkentelegraphie)*. See also service records for Joachim Coeler & Wolfram Eisenlohr in Hildebrand K.F.1990 *Die Generale der deutschen Luftwaffe 1935-1945 Band 1 A-G* pp.163-164 & 242-243 and Rudolf Spies in Hildebrand K.F.1992 *Die Generale der deutschen Luftwaffe 1935-1945 Band 3 O-Z* pp.327-328. Joachim Coeler had served as a pilot with the *I.Seeflieger-Abt.* before being retained by the *Reichsmarine* in a training capacity with the *Schiffstammdivision der Nordsee*. He subsequently saw service afloat aboard the *Linienschiff Braunschweig* and in coastal defence with *Küstenwehr-Abt.II*. He was *Ref.Technik* in the *Gruppe BSx* from Jun 26-Mar 28 and within the *Luftschützgruppe/Marineleitung* from Apr 28-Mar 30. *Lt.d.Res.a.D.*Rudolf Spies had been employed as a pilot and service engineer by *Svenska Aero AB* in Sweden from Jan 23 until Sep 24 when he joined the *Heinkel Flugzeugwerke* at Warnemünde. In Feb 25 he was employed by the *Reichsheer* in a civilian role as a *Hilfsreferent* and pilot within *Maj.*Wilberg's *T2 V (L)* - see also Schliephake H. 1971 *The Birth of the Luftwaffe* (hereafter cited as Schliephake 1971) p.24.

3   Caspari in Caspari (Ed.) Bd.2 p.19 & 22 and Kossler K. *The E-Stelle (See) Travemünde* in Beauvais H., Kossler K., Mayer M. and Regel C. 2002 *German Secret Flight Test Centres to 1945: Johannisthal, Lipetsk, Rechlin, Travemünde, Tarnewitz, Peenemunde-West* (hereafter cited as Kossler in Beauvais et al 2002) p.131. The *Referat A II 1* was led by

360,000 *Marks* was offered in prize money for the design which proved most suitable as a replacement for the earlier HE 1 *See-Aufklärungsflugzeug*.[4] The possibility of future orders provided the stimulus that the German aircraft industry so desperately needed and it was no surprise that eight manufacturers offered a total of fourteen different designs for the *Seeflug-Wettbewerb* (Seaplane Competition) which was held at Warnemünde between the 11th and 31st July 1926. The winning aircraft was the HE 5a WNr.247 D-937 flown by *Oblt.z.See a.D.*Wolfgang Gronau, whilst second place went to the Junkers W 33/See D-921 which was also rated as the best aircraft fitted with a German engine.[5] Heinkel's HD 24 biplane was also successful and Spies gained third place in the overall event:[6]

FIGURE 1C-8 ENTRIES FOR THE SEEFLUG-WETTBEWERB WARNEMÜNDE 1926			
LFG	V 59	1	D-918
LFG	V 60	2	D-923
LFG	V 61	3	D-925
Caspar	C 29		D-...
Rohrbach	Ro VII	5	D-926
Rohrbach	Ro VII	6	D-927
Junkers	W 33	7	D-921
Junkers	W 34	8	D-922
Heinkel	HE 5a	9	D-937
Heinkel	HE 5b	10	D-938
Heinkel	HD 24	11	D-934
Heinkel	HD 24	12	D-935
Gerbrecht	W 3	13	D-941
Dornier	Do E		D-932
Dornier	Do E		D-...
Junkers	A 20	16	D-826
Heinkel	HE 1	17	D-939
Udet	U 13	18	D-945

*KapLt.*Walther Faber until the 23 Mar 23 when *KapLt.*Hans Ritter was appointed to this post. Ritter had trained as a naval aviator in 1916 and saw extensive war service thereafter with the *Marineluftsreitkrafte-* see service record for Hans Ritter in Hildebrand 1992 pp.116-117. Walther Faber was posted to the *kleine Kreuzer Medusa* as *Nav.Offz.* before being re-assigned as a *Referent* in the *Insp.Torpedo-u.Minenwesens.* After a period as *1.Offz.* aboard the *kleine Kreuzer Emden*, he was promoted to *Kpt.z.S.* in Oct 32 as *C.d.S.d.Insp.Torp.u-Minenwesens.* He then undertook a series of shore positions with the *Marinestation d.Ostsee.* From the 28 Aug 38 he was a *Gr.Ltr.i.Kriegswissenschahtliche-Abt.d.OKM* (Naval War History Branch) with the honorary rank of *Kon.Adm.* from 31 Mar 40 – see service record for Walther Faber in Axis Biographical Research in www.reocities.com.

4   Lange B. 1970 *Das Buch der deutschen Luftfahrtechnik* (hereafter cited as Lange 1970) pp.140-141. See also Heinkel E. 1956 *He 1000* (hereafter cited as Heinkel 1956) pp.102-103, Schliephake 1971 p.24, Jung D., Wenzel B. and Abendroth A. 1977 *Die Schiffe und Boote der deutschen Seeflieger 1912-1976* (hereafter cited as Jung et al 1977) pp.44-45 & Kossler in Beauvais et al 2002 p.132.

5   Lange 1970 p.140, Nowarra H.J. 1980 *Die Verbotenen Flugzeuge 1921-1935 – Die getarnte Luftwaffe* (hereafter cited as Nowarra 1980) pp.114-115 & 134-136, Schmitt G. 1988 *Hugo Junkers and his Aircraft* (hereafter cited as Schmitt 1988) p.113 & Koos V. 2006 *Typenbucher Deutsche Luftfahrt: Ernst Heinkel Flugzeugwerke 1922-1932* (hereafter cited as Koos 2006) pp.23-25. From Oct 25 *Oblt.z.S.*Wolfgang von Gronau had been attached to the *Marineleitung* as an advisor on flying training - see service record for Wolfgang Gronau in Hildebrand 1990 pp.395-396.

6   Nowarra 1980 pp.130-133 & Koos 2006 pp.63-65. See also Lange 1970 pp.140-141.

Through the auspices of the *RVM* small production orders were later placed for both the HE 5 and the HD 24 with nine and eighteen respectively of these aircraft being built for use by the *Deutsche Verkehrsfliegerschule (DVS)* (German Commercial Flying School) (See also 1D2).[7] The competition also provided the basis for the later commercial success of the Junkers W 33 and W 34, whilst a dozen of these utility transports were delivered to the *Luftdienst GmbH* between 1927 and 1933 (See 1E3).[8] In the meantime *Heinkel* continued to refine the basic HE 5 design and the HE 8 saw widespread service with the Yugoslav, Norwegian, Swedish and Danish navies whilst the HE 9 was placed in production for the *DVS*.[9] Naval interest in the flying boat also continued to increase with support for the Rohrbach Ro V and VII, but it was the outstanding performance of the Dornier Do J *Wal* that was to dominate developments in this particular field.[10] This outstanding design had first appeared in 1922 and due to the Allied restrictions the first production aircraft were manufactured by the *CMASA* in Italy in 1923. Ultimately some 300 *Wals* were built, but it would not be until 1932 that the first aircraft were produced in Germany for naval employment. In the meantime production lines had been established in Switzerland, Japan, Spain and the Netherlands in addition to those in Italy where more than half of the total number of *Wals* were eventually made.[11]

In 1927 German naval interest in the large flying boat culminated with a remarkable secret contract for a *Flugschiff* capable of trans-oceanic operations, long-range maritime reconnaissance, mine-laying and torpedo-bombing.[12] The result was the incredible Do X D-1929 which was built at *Dornier's* Altenrhein plant in Switzerland and which first flew on 12 July 1929 *(Photo 1C-8)*.[13] Although capable of carrying 150 passengers and 10 crew the Do X was ultimately found to be lacking as a long-range maritime reconnaissance aircraft as its service ceiling was restricted to just 500 metres and its range was only 1,700 kms.[14] During 1930-31 the Do X crossed the South Atlantic and visited Argentina and Brazil before flying north to New York, the *Käpitan* for this flight being *Oblt.d.Res.a.D.*Friedrich Christiansen, a very successful former *Marinejagdflieger* (Naval Fighter Pilot).[15]

7   Ries K. 1988 *Deutsche Flugzeugführerschulen und ihre Maschinen 1919-1945* (hereafter cited as Ries 1988) p.10 & Koos 2006 p.64.
8   Nowarra 1980 pp.134-138 & Schmitt 1988 pp.113-124.
9   Nowarra 1980 pp.166-168, Ries 1988 p.10 & Koos 2006 pp.33-35.
10 Ries K. 1970 *Luftwaffe Bd.1 Die Maulwurfe 1919-1935* (hereafter cited as Ries 1970) p.24 & 38, Lange 1970 pp.195-198 & Nowarra 1980 pp.90-91.
11 Dornier 1983 *Dornier: Die Chronik des altesten deutschen Flugzeugwerks* (hereafter cited as Dornier 1983) p.87 & 96-97. See also Stroud J.1966 *European Transport Aircraft since 1910* (hereafter cited as Stroud 1966) pp.239-243, Ries 1970 p.24 & Lange 1970 p.197.
12 Lange 1970 pp.199-200, Schliephake 1971 pp.24-25, Jung et al 1977 p.45, Nowarra 1980 pp.184-186, Hooton 1994 p.65 & Kossler in Beauvais et al 2002 p.132. However another authoritative source suggests that the *Reichsmarine* was never very interested in this project - see Weal J. 1980 'Dr Dornier's Great White Wal' in *Air Enthusiast* No.13 (hereafter cited as Weal 1980) pp.1-4.
13 Stroud 1966 pp.249-252, Weal 1980 p.6 & Dornier 1983 p.111. Claudius Dornier shared a passion for giant aircraft with his contemporary Hugo Junkers. However Dornier was primarily interested in seaplanes and he had already gained a great deal of expertise and financial success with the *Wal* family. Prior to the easing of restrictions Dornier had just completed the construction of a major manufacturing facility at Altenrhein on the southern (Swiss) shore of the Muggelsee.
14 Ries 1970 p.114, Weal 1980 p.6 & Dornier 1983 pp.22-25. On the 25 July 1929 the Dornier Do X *Flugschiff* D-1929 had left the water for the first time. This behemoth of the air was powered by no less than twelve Siemens Jupiter VI radials each delivering 530 hp. In October in a short record breaking flight was made during which a staggering 169 persons were carried. At the time it was claimed that 170 passengers had been carried - including 9 stowaways!
15 Lange 1970 p.200 & Weal 1980 pp.7-11 & Dornier 1983 p.114. Following re-engining with twelve 650 hp Curtiss Conqueror vee-twelves the Do X then began on the 5 November 1930 a protracted cruise to New York via the South Atlantic to Brazil and Argentina before heading north to the USA and ultimately back to Europe across the North Atlantic reaching the Muggelsee near Berlin on the 24 May 1931. This flight had originally been advertised as a *Europarundflug*. There was in fact no fixed agenda or objectives. However the media expected more and this was to

Both *Dipl.-Ing.*Claudius Dornier and *Dr.Ing.*Adolf Rohrbach were both keen proponents of all-metal aircraft design (See 1C1). However the *Reichsmarine*, like the *Reichsheer*, preferred more traditional methods of construction and it was to Ernst Heinkel and Karl Caspar that the *Gruppe BSx's Referent Technik* (Air Technical Advisor) turned for its secret naval aircraft developments in the mid to late twenties (See 1C3). The *Ernst Heinkel Flugzeugwerke* was particularly prolific with a range of shipboard biplanes and shore-based torpedo-bombers in addition to its reconnaissance floatplanes.[16] Much of this can be attributed to the energy and foresight of Heinkel himself. When a rival questioned *KorvKpt.*Hans Siburg, the new *Referent Technik*, over the perceived unfairness of the *Reichsmarine's* procurement policy he replied:

> The little fellow over there has shorter legs than you, but he runs faster. You're scared of any slippery ground, while he goes on skates. While you are still debating whether you can carry out a contract, he has already built the 'planes, so naturally I have to give him the majority of the contracts.[17]

Heinkel's former employer, the *Caspar-Werke GmbH* at Travemünde, was soon in trouble. Very few of its designs were destined to be produced in series and this was especially true of its naval prototypes, the CJ 14 *Jagdflugzeug* and the CS 14 *Marine-Aufklärungsflugzeug*.[18] Not surprisingly the company's financial fortunes quickly declined and on the 8 April 1927 the *Caspar-Werke* was transformed into an *Allgemeine Gesselschaft (AG)* or public limited company with covert funding being provided by the *Reichsmarine*. With nearly all of its work coming from Coeler's *Referent Technik* the final take-over at the end of that year was a foregone conclusion and in January 1928 the *Caspar-Werke* was officially re-christened the *Seeflug-Erprobungsstelle Travemünde (SES)* (Marine Aircraft Experimental Establishment Travemünde) with 60 employees *(Photo 1C-9)*.[19] Although

result in much criticism when protracted work had to be made at Lisbon (due to a fire), in the Canaries (following an abortive take off), in Brazil (overhaul, refit and engine repairs) and finally in the USA (complete overhaul). For this epic journey of 45,000 kms the Do X was at times commanded by *Oblt.d.Res.a.D.*Friedrich Christiansen and Fritz Hammer *(Syndicato Condor)*, whilst *Dipl.Ing.*Horst Merz, Cramer von Clausbruch, Clarence Schildhauer (General Motors) and Walter Diele all acted as pilots on various legs of the journey. In 1931 two further examples were built for use by the Italian carrier *SANA* although they saw only restricted employment before being scrapped – see Weal 1980 p.12. As *Ltr.Seeflugstation Zeebrugge Oblt.d.Res.*Christiansen had been decorated with the *Plm* on the 11 Dec 17 - see Angolia J.R. and Hackney C.R. 1984 *The Pour le Mérite and Germany's First Aces* pp.174-177 & Kilduff P. 1991 *Germany's First Air Force 1914-1918* (hereafter cited as Kilduff 1991) pp.91-94.

16   Heinkel 1956 pp.89-118.

17   Quoted from Heinkel 1956 *He 1000* p.101 Hutchinson & Co. (Publishers) Ltd. Ernst Heinkel had been a successful wartime designer with the *Hansa Brandenburgische Flugzeugwerke GmbH* and he had later worked for *Caspar* before setting up his own company in 1922 - see Heinkel 1956 pp.48-88. Hans Siburg was a former pilot with the *I.Seeflieger-Abt.*, his last wartime position being *Flugstationsleiter* for the seaplane tender *Oswald*. He was retained by the post-war *Reichsmarine* and saw considerable sea service aboard the Survey Vessels *Panther* & *Meteor*, the *Kreuzer Berlin* and the *Linienschiff Hessen*. Between Apr 26-Sep 28 he was *Luftschütz Rererent in Stab d.Marinestation Ostsee* - see service record for Hans Siburg in Hildebrand 1992 pp.302-304. See also Haagen R. & Caspari H.A. *Rohrbach-Flugboote* in Caspari H.A. Dr. (Ed.) Undated *E-Stellen Travemünde und Tarnewitz 3.Band – Die Geschichte der Seeflugzeug-Eprobungsstelle Travemünde und daraus hervorgegangenen E-Stelle für Flugzeugbewaffnung Tarnewitz* (hereafter cited as Caspari (Ed.) Bd.3) pp.67-82.

18   Lange 1970 p.182.

19   Caspari in Caspari (Ed.) Bd.2 p.26, Lange 1970 p.181, Schliephake 1971 p.24, Nowarra 1980 pp.102-104 & Kossler in Beauvais et al 2002 p.132. The *Caspar Werke* had produced a great many prototypes and a few aircraft that were built in small numbers. However financial success had eluded the company and by 1927 it was short of both work and finance. The firm had been unlucky in the 1926 *Seeflug-Bewerbe* as its planned entrant, the C 29 *Seeaufklärer*, had crashed prior to the event – see Nowarra 1980 pp.126-127. In the meantime the collapse of the *Phoebus AG*, one of Germany's largest companies, in 1927 had led to a media expose of Lohmann's involvement in illegal naval developments. The affair acutely embarrassed the *Reichswehr* and led to the resignation of the *Reichswehrminister, Dr.*Gessler, and somewhat later in September 1928 to *Adm.*Zenker who accepted a degree of

the *SES* was a civilian concern under *KorvKpt.a.D.*Hermann Moll it was in reality a fully functional naval flight test centre.[20] In the years that followed a variety of prototypes were evaluated by the *SES* including the Dornier Do J *Wal* and its derivatives, the Rohrbach Ro X *Romar* long-range flying boat, the Heinkel HE 7 torpedo bomber, the Focke Wulf W 4 reconnaissance floatplane, and the new Arado SSD I fighter floatplane *(Photo 1C-10)*.[21] To meet the projected needs of the giant Do X a large new hangar had been constructed on the northern edge of the Priwall. At the same time - 1927 - a contract had been placed with the *Flenderwerft-Lübeck* for a 100-tonne floating dock (Bau-Nr.173) for use at the *Travemünde Eprobungsstelle*. Large enough to accommodate the Do X, the dock was also fitted with catapult equipment for training and trials purposes, this being supplied by the *Deutsche Werke Kiel*.[22] On the 1 January 1929 the *SES* was officially re-titled *RDL, Gruppe Flugzeugbau, Travemünde Eprobungsstelle* (The Reichs Aircraft Industry Aircraft Construction Group, Travemünde Testing Station) and at the same time *Dipl.-Ing.*Kurt Fritsche was appointed *Technische Leiter* (Technical Director) *(Photo 1C-11)*.[23]

The development of advanced aeronautical technology gathered pace under *Kpt.z.See* Zander, Lahs's successor as *Chef Gruppe BSx*. In addition to a number of new aircraft development contracts, for example in 1930 design proposals were sought for a *See-Mehrzweckflugzeug* (Naval Multi-role Aircraft) and a new *See-Aufklärer* (Naval Reconnaissance Aircraft), Siburg's *Referent Technik* also pushed forward the development of wireless telegraphy, compression-ignition engines and a number of aircraft weapons (See 1C5). *Ing.*Bock placed orders with *Telefunken* and *Lorenz* for sophisticated wireless equipment which was tested at the *Funks-Versuchs-Kommando Warnemünde (FVK)* (Wireless Research Command Warnemünde) and in a series of trial oceanic flights over the Atlantic using the Junkers G 24he WNr.923 D-1230, the Heinkel HE 6 WNr.286 D-1220 and the HE 10 WNr.317 D-1731. HE 6 D-1220 reached the Azores from Lisbon in October 1927 before being damaged in an accident on take-off during an attempted east-west crossing of the Atlantic Ocean.[24] The importance of this work to the *Reichsmarine* can be seen by the successive

responsibility for Lohmann's activites. Zenker was succeeded as *Chef der Marineleitung* by *VizeAdm.*Erich Raeder. Inevitably Lohmann was another casualty of the *Phoebus Affair*. He retired from naval service and died soon after in 1928 - see Siche E. *Germany* in Gardiner R. and Chesneau R. (Ed.) 1980 *Conway's All the World's Fighting Ships 1922-1946* p.219.

20   Wolle H. *Entstehung der Seeflugzeug-Erprobungsstelle Travemünde des RDL* in Caspari (Ed.) Bd.2 (hereafter cited as Wolle in Caspari (Ed.) Bd.2) pp.35-50. Service record for Hermann Moll in Hildebrand K.F.1991 *Die Generale der deutschen Luftwaffe 1935-1945 Band 2 H-N* (hereafter cited as Hildebrand 1991) pp.400-401 . Moll had entered the *Kaiserliche Marine* in Apr 08 and had been trained as a *Beobachter* in 1914. He had ended the war on the staff of the *Abt.Luftfahrwesen/Admiralitat* and had been discharged in Jan 20. Moll had been *Caspar's* Commercial Director from April 1925 after earlier employment with the Warnemünde based *Dinos-Werft* and the *Friedrichshafen Flugzeugbau.*

21   *Seetuchtigkeitserprobung des Rohrbach Romar in Travemünde* in Caspari (Ed.) Bd.2 pp.253-258 & Kossler in Beauvais et al 2002 p.132. The *SES* acted in the same way as the wartime *Seeflugzeug-Versuchskommando (SVK)* at Warnemünde. In 1928 the *Arbeitsprogramm BSx* listed a total of 11 separate development programmes which ranged from the Do X to the HD 15 – see *Arbeitsprogramm BS x b 1928* in Seifert K-D. 1999 *Die deutsche Luftfahrt 28: Der deutsche Luftverkehr 1926-1945 – auf dem Weg zum Weltverkehr* p.141. See also Smith J.R. 1973 *Focke Wulf: An Aircraft Album* (hereafter cited as Smith 1973) pp.20-21, Nowarra 1980 pp.150-151 & 180-181, Wagner W. 1980 *Kurt Tank - Konstrukteur und Testpilot bei Focke Wulf Die deutsche Luftfahrt 1* (hereafter cited as Wagner 1980) pp.29-33 & Koos 2006 pp.28-29.

22   Wolle in Caspari Bd.2 pp.37-45 & Kossler in Beauvais et al 2002 p.132.

23   Kossler in Beauvais et al 2002 p.134.

24   Schliephake 1971 p.25, Trenkle F. 1986 *Bordfunkgerate - Vom Funksender zum Bordradar Die deutsche Luftfahrt 7* pp.23-26, Andersson 1989 p.43 & Hooton 1994 p.66. The HE 6 was used for an attempt on the east-west crossing of the Atlantic Ocean in Oct-Nov 27. A private venture design which cost Ernst Heinkel 180,000 Marks the aircraft left Lisbon for Horta on the Azores on the 4 Nov 27- a distance of 1,680 kms which was completed in 9 hrs 35 mins. Unfortunately the much longer crossing to Newfoundland was thwarted by large waves on take off and the HE 6 was destroyed -see Heinkel 1956 p.114 & Koos 2006 pp.26-27. The first east-west crossing was made by Köhl, Fitzmaurice & von Hunefeld in Junkers W 33 WNr.2504 D-1167*Bremen* during 12-13 Apr 28, a flight of

appointment of two serving *Marinefliegeroffiziere* (Naval Aviation Officers) to the position of *Leiter der FVK: KorvKpt.*Geisler from October 1928 and *KorvKpt.*Coeler from October 1932.[25]

FIGURE 1C-9 AIRCRAFT USED BY THE FUNKVERSUCHSKOMMANDO WARNEMÜNDE FOR WIRELESS RESEARCH			
Junkers A 20	D-826	Heinkel HD 24	D-934
Junkers W 33	D-826	Heinkel HD 24	D-935
Junkers W 34	D-922	Heinkel HE 5a	D-937
LFG V 60	D-924	Heinkel HE 5b	D-938
LFG V 61	D-925	Heinkel HE 1	D-939
Rohrbach Ro VII	D-926	Udet U 13	D-945
Rohrbach Ro VII	D-927	Gebrecht W 3	D-???

Significant developments were also made in the field of heavy-oil engines, this work being co-ordinated by *Dipl-Ing.*Eisenlohr who placed contracts with the *Maschinenfabrik Augsburg-Nürnberg (MAN)* and the *Daimler-Benz AG* at Stuttgart.[26] The result was the the Daimler-Benz 750 hp diesel which was intended for long distance aircraft. A batch of 20-30 engines were built but these were used for high-performance motor boats, whilst the improved LOF 6 was eventually used as an airship engine.[27] In the meantime *Dipl-Ing.*Cornelius worked successfully with the Swiss firm of *Oerlikon* to produce a 2 cm cannon for aircraft use, this being tested on a Do R *Superwal* (See 1C5). The *Oerlikon* design was also adapted for anti-aircraft use by the *Reichsmarine* under the designation 2 cm FlaK 28 and 29.[28] Some progress was made in the development of aerial torpedoes, experiments being carried out under conditions of the greatest secrecy at the *Torpedo-Versuchs-Anstalt* (Torpedo Research Institute) at Eckernforde.[29]

---

36 hrs. - see Schmitt 1988 pp.113-119.

25   Service records for Hans Geisler & Joachim Coeler in Hildebrand 1990 pp.351-352 & 163-164. During the period Mar 30-Sep 32 Coeler had served aboard the *Linienschiffe Schleswig-Holstein* & *Hessen*. Hans Geisler was a wartime *Beobachter* with the *I.Seeflieger-Abt.*, his final position during the Great War being with the *Marine Flugchefs*. Retained by the *Reichsmarine* he served aboard minesweepers in 1921-22 before undertaking a training role with the *Schiffstammdivision der Ostsee* until 1925. He was then *Flieger-Ref.i.Stab d.Marinestation d.Ostsee*, joining the *Flotten-Abt./Marineleitung* in Apr 26. The *FVK* was responsible for the development of all types of naval communications. It was also used as a "cover" for naval flying training - see USONI *German Naval Air 1933 to 1945* in in Isby D.C. (Ed.) 2005 *The Luftwaffe and the War at Sea 1939-45: As seen by officers of the Kriegsmarine and Luftwaffe* p.24. For aircraft employed in wireless research and development - see Schliephake 1971 p.25.

26   Caspari in Caspari (Ed.) Bd.2 pp.30-31, Schliephake 1971 p.26 & Hooton 1994 pp.65-66.

27   Schliephake 1971 p.26. The LZ 127 *Graf Zeppelin* (1928) was powered by Maybach VL 2 vee 12 diesels of 420 hp. The 1928 *Daimler-Benz* diesel was further developed during the thirties to produce the massive 1,200 hp 16 cylinder DB 602 which was employed by both the LZ 129 *Hindenburg* & LZ 130 *Graf Zeppelin* - see Stroud 1966 pp.383-388, Gersdorff von K. and Grasmann K. 1985 *Die Deutsche Luftfahrt 2: Flugmotoren und Strahltriebwerke* (hereafter cited as Gersdorff and Grasmann 1985) pp.13-14 & Gunston B. 1995 *World Encyclopaedia of Aero Engines* p.48. *Schnellbooten S 10, 11, 12* & *13* (1934-35) were all powered by three-shaft *Daimler-Benz* diesel engines of a combined 3,960 hp - see Lenton H.T. 1975 *German Warships of the Second World War* p.308. *MAN* specialised in diesel engines for automotive and marine use and was an important producer of heavy lorries - see Milsom J. 1975 *German Military Transport of World War Two* p.10 & 79 and Hooton 1994 p.65.

28   Hoffschmidt E.J. 1969 *German Aircraft Guns WWI – WWII* p.113, Schliephake H. 1977 *Flugzeugbewaffnung – Die Bordwaffen der Luftwaffe von den Anfangen bis zur Gegenwart* pp.109-110 & Griehl M. 2008 *Deutsche Flugzeugbewaffnung bis 1945* p.16.

29   Schliephake 1971 p.26. However work on aerial torpedoes was not particularly rapid - see Hertel W. GenIng.a.D. *Die Beschaffung in der deutschen Luftwaffe* C/IV/6b Karlsruhe Document Collection in Suchenwirth R. Prof. 1968 *The Development of the German Air Force 1919-1939* USAF Historical Studies No.160 (hereafter cited as

NAVAL DEVELOPMENT PROGRAMMES

A. SHORE-BASED RECONAISSANCE FLOATPLANES

During the late twenties the shore-based reconnaissance floatplane was the only type of naval aircraft to be actually produced in Germany, albeit for training purposes with the *DVS*. This class of aircraft had been extensively used by all the major belligerents during the Great War and the type proved particularly effective in the coastal waters of the English Channel, the Nordsee littoral and in the Ostsee. From 1926 naval interest within Germany centred upon the progressive refinement of the Heinkel HE 1 (Hansa Brandenburg W 31) and the result was a useful general purpose seaplane that also saw considerable service as the HE 2, 5 and 8 with the naval air arms of the Sweden, Denmark and Latvia.[30]

The first aircraft type to be built for the *Reichsmarine* was the **Heinkel HE 1** (See 1C1). This twin-float cantilever monoplane was essentially an improved version of the Hansa Brandenburg W 29 *See-Jagdzweisitzer* (Two-seat Naval Fighter) powered by a 360 hp Rolls Royce Eagle IX in place of the wartime 150 Hp Benz. Ernst Heinkel had originally developed the aircraft on behalf of the *Caspar-Werke* in response to a requirement from the Swedish Navy; parts for eleven aircraft being manufactured in secret at Travemünde during 1922-23 for final assembly by the *Svenska Aero AB* at Lidingo.[31] Construction of the *Reichsmarine's* ten HE 1 floatplanes (WNr.202-211) began at *Heinkel's* new Warnemünde plant in 1923, these aircraft being put into store in Stockholm following assembly in Sweden. The HE 1 had an all-up weight of 2,400 kgs, a top speed of 183 kph and an endurance of 4.6 hours. Its service ceiling fully loaded was 3,800 metres. The HE 1 had a crew of two and in an emergency it could have been armed with fixed and flexible machine guns.[32] Following delivery to Germany in 1926 four aircraft (WNr.202, 204, 207, 208) were later re-engined with the BMW Va whilst three machines (WNr.204, 207 & 209) were ultimately fitted with the Junkers L 5.[33]

Further development of the HE 1 resulted in the **Heinkel HE 5** *See-Aufklärer* and *Langstrecken-Seeschulflugzeug* (Naval Reconnaissance and Long Range Marine Training Aircraft) of 1926, and this aircraft proved the winning design in the *Reichsmarine's Seeflug-Wettbewerb* of July.[34] The HE 5a was a three seat cantilever monoplane, powered by an imported 450 hp Napier Lion engine. It had an all-up weight of 2,500 kgs, a top speed of 209 kph and an endurance of 4.6 hrs.[35] Two HE 5c (WNr.275 & 276) and seven HE 5e floatplanes (WNr.290 & 297-302) were ordered by the *RVM* during 1927-28 for use as trainers by the *DVS*.[36] The HE 5c was powered by the 600 hp BMW VIa, whilst the HE 5e used the 750 hp BMW VI 7,3 Z engine. The loaded weight of the HE 5e was

Suchenwirth 1968) p.44.

30   Tarnstrom R.L. 1982 *Handbooks of the Armed Forces: Scandinavia* pp.22-23, 149-150 & p.183. Denmark replaced its Hansa Brandenburg W 29s within the *1.Luftflottille* with 22 HE 8 floatplanes from 1928; Sweden established a naval air arm with 16 Heinkel S 1 (HE 1) supplementing these with 13 S 2, 3 & 4 (HE 2, 3 & 4) and ultimately 26 S 5 (HE 5); Latvia replaced its Hansa Brandenburg W 33s with HE 4 floatplanes- see also Heinkel 1956 pp.73-74, Nowarra 1980 pp.88-89,98-99, 112-115 & 166-168 and Koos 2006 pp.13-25 & 30-32.

31   Heinkel 1956 pp.73-74, Turner P.St.J. 1970 *Heinkel: an aircraft album* (hereafter cited as Turner 1970) pp.9-10 & 18-21and Koos 2006 pp.13-15. The Caspar S 1 was also known as the Hansa Typ 31 & 32 and first flew on the 11 Nov 21. The Swedish machines were powered by the 260 hp Maybach Mb IVa. For further information on the Hansa Brandenburg W 29 - see Nowarra H.J. 1966 *Marine Aircraft of the 1914-1918 War* p.75.

32   Koos 2006 p.15.

33   Lange 1970 p.243 & Koos 2006 p.14.

34   Heinkel 1956 p.103. The HE 5b WNr.248 D-938 was also entered in this competition. It was powered by a 420 hp Gnome et Rhône Jupiter VI radial. Unfortunately this aircraft was lost on the 31 Jul 26.

35   Koos 2006 pp.23-25. The HE 5 was also produced in Sweden as the S 5. Two examples were exported to the USSR.

36   Ries 1970 pp.41-42.

2,900 kgs but with the extra power the aircraft's top speed was increased to 223 kph. Four similar aircraft were built for the *DVS* by *Focke Wulf* at Bremen in 1932 as the HE 5f (WNr.116-119).[37]

The final aircraft of this basic type to be built by proxy for the *Reichsmarine* was the **Heinkel HE 9** of 1929. The HE 9 differed in minor ways from the earlier HE 5e and in all Heinkel built 9 aircraft and Focke Wulf a further 3 machines mainly for use in the training role by the *DVS*.[38] The HE 9d was powered by a 700 hp BMW VI UZ engine and was capable of 260 kph with an all up weight of 3,400 kgs. The HE 9c used the 600 hp BMW VI U. The HE 9 could be armed with a single fixed and a single flexible lu.MG 08/15 machine gun.[39]

B. SHIPBOARD RECONAISSANCE AIRCRAFT

Post-war German interest in shipboard reconnaissance aircraft had been stimulated by American and in particular Japanese interest in this type of aircraft. During the Great War the major belligerents had employed seaplane tenders to deploy naval floatplanes to areas where established base facilities were lacking. To this end the *Kaiserliche Marine* had commissioned three *Flugzeugmutterschiffe* (Seaplane Tenders): the *SMS Answald* (FS I) and *Santa Elena* (FS II) in 1915 and the *SMS Oswald* (FS III) in 1918.[40] More notably the *Kleine Kreuzer* (Light Cruiser) *SMS Stuttgart* was taken in hand during 1918 for conversion as a *Flugzeugmutterschiff* capable of fleet operations although she was destined not to be used in this capacity due to the general inactivity of the *Hochseeflotte* (High Seas Fleet).[41] Later in 1925 the *Ernst Heinkel Flugzeugwerke* was approached by the Japanese naval attache with a secret contract for a shipboard reconnaissance aircraft, a request that resulted in the appearance of the Heinkel HD 25 (See 1A2). As part of this development *Heinkel* began work on a launching rail for this new aircraft, a device that would obviate the need for the floatplane to be lowered into the water using a derrick or ship's crane prior to take off.[42] From this work came the company's first compressed air catapult, the K 1 and a covert *Reichsmarine* contract for a *Bordaufklärer und Artillerie-Flugzeug* in 1926/27.[43]

37   Lange 1970 pp.243-244 & Koos 2006 pp.23-25. In the event of mobilisation extra aircraft would be needed quickly and to this end *Fertigungs GmbH* arranged for the licence production of a number of key types by other manufacturers. A good example of this policy are the orders that *Focke Wulf* received for both the HE 5 & HE 9.

38   Koos 2006 pp.33-35. In 1929 a number of world seaplane records for distance and load were achieved with the HE 9a WNr.319 D-1617. On the 10 Jun 29 a new speed record of 222.277 kph over a 1,000 km course was achieved – see Lange 1970 p.244.

39   Lange 1970 p.244 & Koos 2006 pp.33-35.

40   Jung et al 1977 pp.19-32 & 38-41 and Layman R.D. 1989 *Before the Aircraft Carrier: The Development of Aviation Vessels 1849-1922* (hereafter cited as Layman 1989) pp.21-30. Two other vessels: the *Glyndwr* & the *Adeline Hugo Stinnes 3* were also employed on naval aviation duties by the *Kaiserliche Marine*, whilst the commerce raider *Wolf* was equipped with a Friedrichshafen FF33 floatplane in 1917-18.

41   Jung et al 1977 pp.30-32 & 40-41 and Layman 1989 pp.26-27. In Oct 18 consideration was given to the conversion of two merchantmen as flight deck carriers whilst the incomplete liner *Ausonia* was another candidate for conversion as Germany's first true aircraft carrier – see Jung et al 1977 pp.33-36.

42   Heinkel 1956 pp.79-80 & 89-99. See also Nowarra 1980 pp.116-117 & Koos 2006 pp.66-67.

43   *Das Flugzeug-Katapult* in Caspari (Ed.) Bd.2 pp.171-177, Heinkel 1956 pp.105 & Koos 2006 pp.42-43. The contract was actually awarded by the *RVM* on behalf of the *Reichsmarine*. The Royal Navy began work on shipboard catapults in 1917 and the first was installed the following year. Work then ceased until 1922 when the development of both the Carey hydropneumatic and RAE multiple ram compressed air catapults was sanctioned. The first Carey catapult was installed on *HMS Vindictive* in 1925, whilst trials with the RAE catapult began in 1927 aboard *HMS Frobisher*. Catapults employing a cordite propellant were also developed, the first being installed aboard *HMS York* for use with dummy aircraft in 1930. From 1929 *HMS Ark Royal* was used for a series of trials with three new types of catapult: the Slider Type, the Extended Structure Type & the Hinged Structure Type. Catapults did not enter widespread service aboard cruisers in the RN until 1931 - Sturtivant R. & Cronin D. 1998 *Fleet Air Arm Aircraft, Units and Ships 1920 to 1939* (hereafter cited as Sturtivant and Cronin 1998) pp.15-16. In the *USN* the routine operation of compressed air catapults aboard ship commenced on the 24 May 22. Catapults were subsequently

Unlike the contemporary HE 5 monoplane floatplane the **Heinkel HD 15** *Bordaufklärer und Artillerie-Flugzeug* was a biplane flying boat. With an all up weight of 2,350 kgs the HD 15 had a maximum speed of 172 kph and endurance of 5 hours. Two machine gun positions were planned although armament was not fitted. The aircraft was powered by a single Gnome et Rhône Jupiter VI which was rated at 450 hp but with 500 hp for take off.[44] The contract also called for the development of an experimental catapult to serve for basic tests on the possibilities of the shipboard launching of seaplanes. Ernst Heinkel later recalled:

> Development work already carried out had yielded a great deal of information, on which I was now able to draw. We were quite certain about the most reliable way of enabling the catapult to be tuned round on the ship, so that the direction of launching could be into the prevailing wind. Since it had to be so rotated, the catapult had to be very small. This, in turn, required very powerful means of acceleration, so as to get the 'plane up to the take-off speed of 100 kph by the end of the catapult runway, which was scarcely 20 m long. The best way of getting it up to this speed was to pull it with a tow-rope, attached to a piston on the catapult track, which was driven forwards by compressed air. The ability of the pilot to withstand a sudden acceleration had first to be looked into. At that time no one knew exactly whether the abrupt change of velocity to which the pilot of the catapulted 'plane would be subjected would lead to impairment of health, loss of consciousness, or death. In any case the acceleration at the beginning of the catapulting had to be reduced, by allowing the compressed air to build up its full pressure behind the piston in the working cylinder gradually, and not suddenly, with a shock like the recoil of a rifle.[45]

Working in association with *Askania*, the *Ernst Heinkel Flugzeugwerke* spent much of 1928 perfecting the basic design and operation of the K 1 Katapult. Further *RVM* contracts followed for a *Katapult-Seepostflugzeug* (Catapultable Marine Mail Aircraft) for use aboard *Norddeutscher Lloyd's* new *Turbinen-Schnelldampfer Bremen* (Turbine powered Fast Freighter). Heinkel's response was the HE 12 and the more powerful *K 2 Katapult*; further development work would result in the HE 58 and its associated *K 4 Katapult* for employment aboard the *TS Europa* (See also 1E3).[46]

Although the *Referent Technik* was very interested in these developments it continued to prefer biplane designs to meet its requirement for a shipboard reconnaissance aircraft for use aboard the new *K-Klass Kleine Kreuziere* (K-Class Light Cruisers) which were expected to enter service during 1929-30.[47] The *1927-28 Bordaufklärer* requirement specified that the new design should be capable of catapult launching with recovery in sea states of up to 4-5. The aircraft should have a combat radius of 600 kms and an endurance of 2.5 hours. It was to carry a crew of two and be armed with

installed aboard battleships and then the cruiser force – see NAVAIR 00-80P-1 1970 *United States Naval Aviation 1910-1970* (hereafter cited as NAVAIR 1970) p.50.

44   Lange 1970 p.244, Nowarra 1980 pp.150-152 & Koos 2006 pp.42-43.

45   Quoted from Heinkel 1956 *He 1000* p.105 Hutchinson & Co. (Publishers) Ltd.

46   Heinkel 1956 pp.105-113. The HE 12 WNr.334 D-1717 was completed in 1929. The K 2 Katapult was capable of accelerating the 3,500 kg aircraft to 110 kph in just 20 m. The HE 58 WNr.365 D-1919 was completed in 1930. It was re-assigned to the *Bremen* in 1931 following the loss of the HE 12 - see Turner 1970 pp.27-30, Jackson R. 1983 *The Sky their Frontier: The Story of the World's Pioneer Airlines and Routes 1920-40* (hereafter cited as Jackson 1983) pp.10-11 & Koos 2006 pp38-39 & 122-123.

47   Whitley M.J. 1985 *German Cruisers of World War Two* pp.20-25. Work on a new *Kleine Kreuzer* to replace existing obsolescent vessels had begun in 1924 and three vessels were laid down in 1926 for completion in 1929-30. Space was allowed for the installation of a catapult and aircraft between the two smoke stacks, a crane being provided to allow the aircraft to be recovered from the water after landing. Neither the catapult nor the aircraft were fitted during this period.

a single fixed and two flexibly mounted machine guns. *Focke Wulf* and *Heinkel* were both given development contracts and both were powered by a single 450 hp Gnome et Rhône Jupiter VI 9 AK radial.[48]

The **Focke Wulf W 4** was unusual in being an unbraced biplane, the upper wing being supported by centre-section struts alone. Given this attempt to minimise form drag the twin floats were paradoxically heavily strutted and wire braced. The prototype which first flew in 1927 was D-1730. It had a loaded weight of 2,985 kgs, a top speed of 210 kph and a combat radius of 600 kms.[49] The **Heinkel HD 30** was a far more conventional design. The prototype, WNr.288 D-1463, also flew for the first time in 1928. It had an all up weight of 2,482 kgs, a top speed of 200 kph and a radius of action of 590 kms.[50] Re-engined with a Siemens Jupiter it was re-designated HD 30b and trials were carried out with the K 1 Katapult at Warnemünde from 1929 (See 1E3). Secret plans of November 1929 called for the production of no less than 212 HD 30 aircraft in the event of a national emergency with a further 50 to be completed as trainers, the latter being fitted with the Junkers L 5 in-line engine. A second HD 30 was built in 1932; WNr.405 D-2267 being registered to *Luftdienst* for fleet requirements work.[51]

General satisfaction with the HD 30 led to a naval development contract in 1930 for this type as the HD 60. The new aircraft was to be capable of open water operations in seas up to Sea State 5 as well as catapult operations from naval vessels. Naval tasks were to include observation *(Beobachtung)*, gunnery spotting *(Artilleriebeobachterung)* and coastal reconnaissance *(Küsten-Nahaufklärung)*.[52] The **Heinkel HD 60** was a larger and heavier aircraft powered by the 660 hp BMW VI U 6,0 Z water-cooled engine. All up weight rose to 3,400 kgs, wing span being increased by 1.1 m whilst the fuselage was 1.12 m longer. Two *Versuchsmuster* were ordered; HD 60 WNr.380 D-2157 and HD 60a WNr.381 D-2176.[53] The HD 60 first flew in August 1931 and the aircraft was subsequently evaluated at Travemünde where a top speed of 235 kph was recorded together with a range of 960 kms at a cruising speed of 207 kph. A fixed armament of two MG 17 with 1,000 rpg was installed in the forward fuselage, whilst a flexible MG 08/15 with 800 rounds was located in the rear cockpit *(B-Stand)*.[54] Unfortunately the second prototype was lost in tragic circumstances on the 16 December 1931. Test pilot Karl Wiborg lost his life at Travemünde when parts of the aircraft disintegrated due to over-stressing in a dive.[55] A third aircraft was then built to replace WNr.381. This was the HD 60b WNr.418 D-2325 which arrived at Travemünde in 1932. A small production order for 10 aircraft followed, these being He 60C WNr.431-440.[56]

Focke Wulf also produced a further floatplane to meet the new naval requirement. The **Focke Wulf W 7** was a large biplane of equal span, powered like the HD 60 by a 660 hp BMW VI 6,0 engine. First flown in 1932 the prototype, WNr.112 D-2216, was fitted with a land undercarriage and delivered to Lipetsk in the Soviet Union in the summer of that year for operational testing. Despite a top speed of 250 kph the type was not deemed suitable for either the naval *Bordaufklärer* or military *Fernaufklärer* roles and no further development was undertaken (See also 1C3).[57]

---

48   Koos 2006 p.76.
49   Lange 1970 p.222, Smith 1973 pp.20-21 & Nowarra 1980 pp.150-151.
50   Nowarra 1980 pp.170-171 & Koos 2006 pp.76-77.
51   Koos 2006 pp.76-77.
52   Koos 2006 p.126.
53   Nowarra 1980 pp.232-233 & Koos 2006 pp.126-127. This recent research differs in detail from that previously given by Lange 1970 p.249 & Green 1970 p.277.
54   Koos 2006 p.127. The only criticism appears to have been the aircraft's weight in relation to the power available from the BMW VI U 6,0 Z engine - see Green 1970 p.277.
55   Kossler in Beauvais et al 2002 p.135.
56   Koos 2006 p.126.
57   Lange 1970 p.222, Smith 1973 p.28 & Nowarra 1980 pp.204-205.

C. RECONAISSANCE FLYING BOATS

On the 6 November 1922 the revolutionary all-metal Dornier Do J freight and passenger transport flying boat flew for the first time. Allied restrictions meant that subsequent production had to take place abroad and during the twenties the type was manufactured by Dornier in Switzerland and under licence in Italy, Spain, Japan and the Netherlands. In all some 300 aircraft were completed and the type became one of the most successful production aircraft of its era.[58] Military versions were generally referred to as the Do J *Militär-Wal* and variants of this flying boat served with the Spanish, Dutch, Yugoslav, Japanese, Soviet, Argentinian and Chilean navies.[59] During the twenties several long-distance flights were made with the *Wal* including a crossing of the North Atlantic by I-DAOR in August 1924, an attempt to reach the North Pole by the famous polar explorer Amundsen in 1925, a crossing of the South Atlantic from Spain to Buenos Aires in M-MWAL in early 1926, and a flight from Casablanca to Uruguay in March 1927. These flights, together with regular airline operation by *Aero Lloyd* which flew 370,000 kms with three *Wals* during 1926-27, helped to confirm the reliability of this particular design for ocean flying in the minds of naval aviators within the *Referent Technik*.[60] However political considerations made it impossible to actually procure the *Militär-Wal* for use in Germany until 1933 when an order for six Do J IId Bis machines (WNr.247-252) was finally placed with *Dornier-Werke* at Friedrichshafen.[61]

In the meantime the *RVM* had contracted the *Ernst Heinkel Flugzeugwerke* with the development of an even larger catapult to enable the *Wal* to be launched from a new generation of specialist seaplane tenders for service on *Deutsche Luft Hansa's* trans-Atlantic route to Brazil.[62] The K 6 Katapult was far larger than the earlier K 4, the complete apparatus weighing 14 tonnes. With an operating pressure of 160 *Atu* (atmospheres) the catapult could accelerate the Dornier *Wal* to 150 kph in 1.52 seconds - an acceleration of up to 3.5 g. The K 6 was fitted to the *SS Westfalen* in 1933 and the first trial flights in the South Atlantic took place in the following year.[63] The successful recovery of large flying boats whilst the parent vessel was underway posed a further problem. This was normally achieved via a shipboard crane, the aircraft taxiing alongside the parent warship prior to be lifting aboard. To allow seaplanes to be recovered over a trailing curtain or mat *(Schleppsegel)* was developed by *Severa* using the old FF.49 WNr.1365 D-49. The *Schleppsegel* proved quite successful in that it smoothed out the wake of the vessel and enabled a more controlled recovery of the seaplane whilst the parent ship was underway.[64]

The Do J was extensively tested in Germany and this support led to the development of the type into the larger and even more capable Do R *Superwal* of 1927, several of which served with *Deutsche*

58   Stroud 1966 pp.239-243 & Dornier 1983 p.87 & 96.
59   Lange 1970 pp.195-196 & Dornier 1983 p.87 & 96.
60   Stroud 1966 pp.240-241. Wolfgang von Gronau made a number of record breaking flights in the Do J *Wal*: in 1930 he crossed the North Atlantic in Amundsen *Wal* N 25 (D-1422) with landings in the Faeroes, Iceland, Greenland Canada,& the USA; in 1931 on behalf of *DLH* he made a further flight to New York in D-2053; in 1932 he embarked on an around the world flight with stops in Greenland, Canada, the Aleutians, Japan & Indonesia where technical difficulties ended the attempt - see Lange 1970 p.196 & Hooks M. 1999 *Images of Aviation: Lufthansa* (hereafter cited as Hooks 1999) p.49. For a full listing of pioneering flights with the Dornier Wal - see & *Pionierfluge mit Dornier Wal* in Dornier 1983 p.97
61   *Table 1-C Göring's First Aircraft Production Programme (May 1933 to April 1934)* in Vajda F.A. & Dancey P.1998 *German Aircraft Industry and Production 1933-1945* (hereafter cited as Vajda & Dancey 1998) p.16. See also Dornier 1983 p.132 & Andersson 1989 p.47.
62   Jung et al 1977 p.46, Jackson 1983 pp.14-17 & Hooks 1999 pp.41-43.
63   *Das Flugzeug-Katapult* in Caspari (Ed.) Bd.2 pp.171-180 & *Die Flugsicherungsschiffe der Lufthansa* in Jung et al 1977 pp.69-74.
64   Jackson 1983 p.14 & Jung et al 1977 p.71. The Royal Navy also evaluated the Hein trailing mat in 1932 using the seaplane tender and trials vessel *HMS Ark Royal* - see Sturtivant and Cronin 1998 p.329.

Luft Hansa whilst WNr.143 D-1337 was assigned to the *SES* at Travemünde in 1928 for trials purposes.[65] *Reichsmarine* interest in the development of a large flying boat culminated with a secret contract in 1927 for a *Flugschiff* capable of trans-oceanic operations (See also 1E3).[66] The result was the Do X which was built at *Dornier's* Altenrhein plant in Switzerland and which first flew in July 1929. Although capable of carrying 150 passengers and 10 crew, the Do X was not considered to be a particularly useful design as its later rather ponderous flight across the Atlantic in 1930-31 would prove. However it did provide useful data on the construction and operation of very large aircraft and its great size was a useful propaganda tool for Germany's emerging aircraft industry.[67]

D. TORPEDO-BOMBER FLOATPLANES

During the Great War aircraft had proved themselves capable of sinking enemy vessels through the medium of aerial torpedo attack. In the case of the *Marine-Luftstreitkräfte* this had first occurred during an attack on Russian naval units in Monsund near Riga in the Ostsee on the 12 September 1917 when a destroyer was badly damaged.[68] Following the formation of a *Torpedo Versuchsverband* (Torpedo Research Unit) in 1916 three specialist *Torpedostaffeln* (Torpedo Squadrons) had been formed with twin-engine floatplanes such as the Gotha WD 14 and these units scored a number of successes in British coastal waters in 1916-17.[69]

A period of enforced idleness followed but in 1927 the *Ernst Heinkel Flugzeugwerke* completed the first new *Torpedoflugzeuge* in response to a *Referent Technik* requirement. The **Heinkel HE 7** was similar in layout to the wartime torpedo bombers, in that it was a twin-engine floatplane with separately braced pontoons.[70] Unlike wartime aircraft it was a monoplane of mixed wood and metal construction. The engines were two 450 hp Gnome et Rhône Jupiter VI 9AB radials and with a gross weight of 6,000 kgs a top speed of 200 kph was obtained with a service ceiling of 2,300m. Open gun positions were provided in the nose and in the rear fuselage. In place of the torpedo it was envisaged that a 37 mm *Kanone* could be fitted for attacks on surfaced submarines *(U-Boot Jagd)*. No less than 228 of these useful aircraft were included in the *Reichsmarine's* secret procurement programme of 1929/30. However only the prototype WNr.266, later registered

65   Kossler in Beauvais et al 2002 p.134. However the first Do J did not reach Travemünde until 1928 when two aircraft arrived at the *SES* and it is therefore difficult to see how testing in Germany contributed to the Do R unless this source is referring to evaluation of the aircraft already in commercial service - see Andersson 1989 p.43. Meanwhile a further Do R, D-1385, was used by Severa - see Stroud 1966 pp.247-248 & Andersson 1989 p.45.

66   Schliephake 1971 pp.24-25, *Anhang C Zeittafel* in Caspari H-A. (Ed.) Bd.3 p.294 & Kossler in Beauvais et al 2002 p.132.

67   Weal 1980 pp.1-10 & Dornier 1983 p.114. The Do X was initially powered by twelve 525 hp Siemens Jupiter radials mounted in pairs above the wing. Prior to the trans-Atlantic flight these were replaced by twelve 615 hp Curtiss GV-1570 Conqueror liquid cooled vee-twelves. For the key 2,324 km crossing from the Cape Verde islands to the Brazilian island of Fernando de Noronha the Do X had to be largely stripped of all internal fittings in an attempt to reduce weight. For much of this flight the aircraft skimmed the ocean at heights of just 3 m above the waves, only when fuel had been reduced and darkness fell was the Do X able to climb to 50-80 m - see also Stroud 1966, Jackson 1983 & Hooks 1999.

68   Thiele H. 2004 *Luftwaffe Aerial Torpedo Aircraft and Operations in World War Two* (hereafter cited as Thiele 2004) pp.6-7. The attack was carried out by 4 torpedo bombers acting in concert with bombers and surface forces. It is possible that the Russian destroyer was actually sunk. The British *RNAS* had recorded their first aerial torpedo success in the Sea of Marmara in Aug 15 - see also Smith P.C. 1974 *The Story of the Torpedo Bomber* p.10.

69   Thiele 2004 p.7. Three British steamers were sunk by torpedo aircraft of the *2. Torpedostaffel (I.Seeflieger-Abteilung)* operating from Zeebrugge. *Oblt.z.See* Hermann Becker was *Kap.2.Torp.St.* until the 15 Jun 17 when he was shot down to become a PoW - see also service record for Hermann Becker in Hildebrand 1990 pp.59-60. For further details on the more important German torpedo floatplanes - see Nowarra 1966 pp.40-41 (Friedrichshafen FF 41), 46-47 (Gotha WD 11), 48-49 (Gotha WD 14) & 52-53 (Hansa Brandenburg GW) and Thiele 2004 p.8.

70   Nowarra 1980 pp.150-151 & Koos 2006 pp.28-29.

D-1552, was completed and this was subsequently used for torpedo development work at the *Torpedo-Versuchsanstalt Eckernförde*.[71] At around this time the *Referent Technik* also acquired three examples of the record breaking Dornier Do D Bas *Torpedoflugzeug* these machines being powered by a single BMW VI liquid-cooled engine.[72] The streamlined all metal Do D Bas had an all up weight of 3,900 kgs and a top speed of 195 kph.[73]

However single-engine types were of limited utility and in 1930 the *Referent Technik* issued a new requirement for a large twin-engine four seat *See-Mehrzweckflugzeugs* (Naval Multi-Role Aircraft) capable of open sea operations in Sea State 2-3 and ideally 4-5. A disposable load of 1,000 kgs was also specified.[74] Two prototypes were duly ordered from the *Ernst Heinkel Flugzeugwerke*. **Heinkel HD 59a** WNr.378 D-2214 was completed in the following year, the first flight taking place in September 1931. The second aircraft **HD 59b** WNr.379 D-2215 was used for weapons trials at Lipetsk and Travemünde between the 6 July and the 2 September 1932 being fitted with a faired wheel undercarriage for this purpose.[75] Trials with a twin-float installation, presumably by D-2214, followed in January 1932.[76] Ostensibly a freight aircraft for the *RVM*, the HD 59 was powered by two 660 hp BMW VI 6,0 ZU engines with a total of 2,700 litres of fuel. Top speed was 220 kph and the operational radius was 875 kms with an all up weight of 9,000 kgs.[77] To suit its intended roles of shipping attack, mine-laying and coastal reconnaissance the aircraft could carry a single 675 kg torpedo on a single PVC 1000 rack or up to 1,000 kgs of bombs and/or mines internally in four Maga 5 C 50 magazines and externally beneath the fuselage on three chemical projector S 200 racks.[78] The He 59B was also fitted with open defensive positions in the nose *(A-Stand)*, rear fuselage *(B-Stand)* and lower fuselage *(C-Stand)* for single flexibly mounted MG 15 machine guns.[79] A third aircraft WNr.442 D-2622 was the production prototype for the planned *B-Serie* (B-Series) which were to be built from 1933 by both *Heinkel* and the *Arado Handelsgesellschaft* at Warnemünde.[80]

E. FIGHTER FLOATPLANES

It seems strange that German naval interest in the float fighter re-emerged at a time when this type of aircraft had almost totally disappeared from the inventory of the other major powers. Initially development focused on the *See-Jagdzweisitzer* (Two-seat Naval Fighter) in the tradition of the wartime Hansa Brandenburg W 29 and to this end the *Ernst Heinkel Flugzeugwerke* designed and built a single example of the HE 31 during 1927/28.[81] The **Heinkel HE 31** was a two seat monoplane

---

71   Koos 2006 pp.28-29. Secret trials were undertaken out of sight of land during the late 20s and early 30s using a modifed Junkers G 24/See and the HE 7 - an aircraft that was progressively modified to suit this role. For concealment the HE 7 was ostensibly in the employment of *Hansa Luftbild*, an aerial photographic and survey company. The G 24 was almost certainly one of two (D-954 & D-1230) operated by *Severa* - see Thiele 2004 pp.9-11.

72   Lange 1970 pp.194-195, Nowarra 1980 pp.146-147 & Thiele 2004 pp.9-10. In Jul & Aug 27 the Do D Bas gained three load, distance - speed records for seaplanes, the most relevant to naval operations being 1,000 kgs over 1,600 kms at 175.6 kph. The 3 Do D Bas were purchased using *RVM* funds - see Dornier 1983 p.92.

73   Lange 1970 p.195.

74   Koos 2006 p.124.

75   Schliephake H. *Secret Flight Testing in Lipetsk, Russia* in Beauvais et al 2002 (hereafter cited as Schliephake in Beauvais et al 2002) pp.47-49 & Kossler in Beauvais et al 2002 pp.135-137.

76   Nowarra 1980 pp.218-219 & Koos 2006 pp.124-125. There is some confusion about which aircraft flew first - it has been suggested that the D-2215 was the first to fly with a land undercarriage and that the D-2214 was fitted with a float undercarriage - see Green 1970 pp.273-274.

77   Koos 2006 p.125.

78   Hertel W. Dipl.Ing.GenIng.a.D.1955 *Procurement in the German Air Force* USAF Historical Studies No.170 p.50.

79   Green 1970 p.274 & Koos 2006 p.125.

80   Green 1970 p.274. Two He 59B were ordered from Heinkel in 1933 - see Vajda and Dancey 1998 p.10.

81   Nowarra 1966 p.75 & Imrie A. 1989 *German Naval Air Service* Nr.73-75 & 84. The RAF's Fleet Air Arm had operated a number of its Fairey Flycatcher fleet fighters on floats during the twenties although by all accounts they often found it difficult to actually take off - see Taylor H.A. 1974 *Fairey Aircraft since 1915* (hereafter cited as Taylor

of mixed construction, powered unusually by an imported 700 hp Packard 3 A 2500 5,1 twelve-cylinder liquid cooled engine. Overall weight was 3,150 kgs and the HE 31 demonstrated a top speed of 250 kph and initial climb rate of 2.5 minutes to 1,000 m. It was intended that the aircraft be armed with a single fixed machine gun together with two flexible guns on a ring mounting in the rear cockpit. HE 31 WNr.310 first flew in October 1928 and was registered to *Severa* as D-1522. Following trials at Travemünde in 1929 it was not decided to pursue this type of aircraft and the HE 31 was not included in the contingency production plan of that year. It was later re-engined with a 576 hp Napier Lion XI.[82]

In 1928, concurrently with the development of the HE 31, the *Referent Technik* placed a requirement with both the *Arado Handelsgesellschaft* and the *Ernst Heinkel Flugzeugwerke* for a catapult capable *Marine-Jagdeinsitzer* (Single-seat Naval Fighter) suitable for either land or water based operation.[83] At that time *Arado* was the preferred contractor for the *Reichsheer's Jagdeinsitzer* programme but interestingly that company's proposal for this new naval requirement bore little resemblance to the contemporary Arado SD I (See 1C3). Instead the **Arado SSD I** featured a deep central fuselage that entirely filled the gap between the braced upper and lower wings. In the case of the lower fuselage a neat ventral "channel" radiator installation for the 650 hp BMW VI water cooled engine helped to fill the gap; in the case of the upper fuselage, a slight dip in the wing centre-section allowed the fuselage to actually meet the upper wing to give the pilot an excellent view forwards and upwards.[84] The single *Versuchsmuster*, WNr.53 D-1905, was completed as a floatplane in 1929, a single centre-line float being balanced by two outriggers under the lower wing. Catapult trials began the same year. In 1930 a fixed wheel undercarriage was substituted to allow operational trials to be carried out at Lipetsk. The performance of the SSD I (Land) was considerably better than the float-based version a top speed of 280 kph being recorded with a gross weight of 2,030 kgs.[85]

Heinkel's proposal was based on his earlier work for the Soviet *VVS-RKKA*. In 1927 the Soviet authorities had commissioned the *Ernst Heinkel Flugzeugwerke* to design a new single-seat fighter. The result was the Heinkel HD 37 which first flew on the 10 July 1928 and which was subsequently accepted for service with the *VVS* as the I-7 with 131 aircraft being manufactured under licence in the USSR between 1931-34.[86] Some localised strengthening to equip the aircraft for catapult launching and floatplane operation resulted in the **Heinkel HD 38** which first flew on the 7 May 1929.[87] Compared to the earlier HD 37 the new HD 38a with a similar wheel undercarriage was 169 kgs heavier with an empty weight of 1,436 kgs. However even this increased figure was well below that of contemporary *Arado* fighters and this helps to explain the HD 38's superior performance (See 1C3). With twin floats the HD 38aW had an all-up weight of 2,046 kgs and a top speed of 285 kph and the climb to 3,000 m took 4.7 minutes; with a wheel undercarriage the HD 38aL's top speed was 292 kph and the climb to 3,000 m took 4.1 minutes.[88]

1974) pp.113-126 & Thetford O. 1977 *British Naval Aircraft since 1912* pp.118-123.

82   Nowarra 1980 pp.170-172 & Koos 2006 pp.78-79.

83   Koos 2006 p.92.

84   Kosin R. 1983 *Die Entwicklung der deutschen Jagdflugzeuge* (hereafter cited as Kosin 1983) pp.66-67. See also Kranzhoff J A 1997 *Arado: Geschichte eines Flugzeugwerks* p.29.

85   Lange 1970 p.162, Nowarra 1980 pp.180-181 & Kosin 1983 pp.66-67. See also Schliephake in Beauvais et al 2002 pp.48-49.

86   Nowarra 1980 pp.172-174, Kosin 1983 p.66 & Koos pp.90-91. The I-7 was produced as a stop gap due to delays in the appearance of the preferred I-5. Production I-7 fighters were fitted with 680 hp M-17 engines, licence built BMW VI engines - see also Nemecek V. 1986 *The History of Soviet Aircraft from 1918* pp.11-12. The HD 37 could itself trace its design pedigree back to the earlier HD 23 that had been designed to meet an *IJN* requirement for a shipboard fighter - see Nowarra 1980 pp.130 & 131 and Koos 2006 pp.60-62.

87   Nowarra 1980 pp.182-184 & Koos 2006 pp.92-94.

88   Kosin 1983 p.66 & Koos 2006 p.94.

Successful trials with the HD 38a led to the type being included in the *1929 Marineluft Fabrikationsprogramm* (Naval Air Construction Programme). An order was placed for eight HD 38b fighters (WNr.366-369 & 384) plus two to be built by the *Arado Handelsgesellschaft* (WNr.63 & 64). However in an emergency it was intended to acquire no less than 30 examples of the *Seejagdeinsitzer* together with a further 80 examples of the *Landjagdeinsitzer.*[89] The HD 38b fighters were delivered from 1931 and of these WNr.369 D-2272 was sent to Lipetsk for operational trials in July and August of that year where it was flown in mock combat with the resident Fokker D.XIII fighters and the experimental Arado Ar 64.[90] A further order was then placed for eight HD 38c fighters (WNr.385-390) with again two being completed in 1932 at *Arado's* Warnemünde plant (WNr.79 & 81) where all subsequent production of the HD 38d was to be completed (See 2C3).[91] It was intended that these aircraft be used as the initial equipment of the planned *Seejagdstaffel* (Naval Fighter Squadron).[92]

The success of the HD 38 led to Heinkel being approached by the *Referent Technik* to design a new catapult-capable single-seat fighter using the same power plant - the 750 hp BMW VI 7,3 Z. The result was the much improved Heinkel HD 49 which first flew in November 1932. The HD 49a WNr.371 D-2363 was an early manifestation of the brilliance of the newly employed Günter brothers whose talents would seen underpin much of the innovative design work at the *Ernst Heinkel Flugzeugwerke.*[93] Attention to aerodynamic detail led to a considerable improvement in performance the He 49aL having a top speed of 325 kph, whilst the He 49aW could manage a very respectable 310 kph. However climb performance was down on the smaller HD 38 at 5.9 and 6.4 minutes to 3,000 m respectively.[94] The HD 49a had a gross weight of 1,950 kgs (Land) and 1970 kgs (Water). Some directional instability led to an increase in fuselage length in the case of the He 49b that first flew in February 1933 and this was followed in the late spring by a third prototype, the He 49c, which was fitted with a BMW 6,0 ZU engine.[95]

F. DIVE BOMBERS

Unlike the preceding categories of combat aircraft the dive bomber was new to naval warfare. Throughout the twenties the shipboard torpedo bomber had been the primary strike aircraft aboard British, American and Japanese carriers.[96] However the *USN* carried out its first dive bombing exercise in December 1926 and followed this with an official study of the new tactics in May 1927. During the latter part of the decade pilots of the United States Marine Corps had begun to experiment with dive bombing attacks using their Curtiss F8C (OC-1) Falcons and the 30 June 1928 the *USN* placed its first contract with the Naval Aircraft Factory and the Glenn Martin concern for a special purpose dive bomber.[97] Senior officers within the *Marineleitung* were also

89   Koos 2006 pp.92-94.
90   Schliephake in Beauvais et al 2002 pp.48-49 & Koos 2006 93.
91   Koos 2006 pp.93-94. It is not clear what improvements were introduced in the HD 38c & d - see also Lange 1970 p.246. Arado completed 11 HD 38 fighters in 1933 - see *Table 1-B German Aircraft Production in 1933* in Vajda and Dancey 1998 p.15.
92   Kurowski F.1979 *Seekrieg aus der Luft* p.19.
93   Green 1970 p.267. Walter and his twin brother Siegfried Günter were respectively an aerodynamicist and a mathematician. At Warnemünde they worked under the direction of the Chief Engineer Karl Schwarzler. The Günter brothers had previously worked as designers for *Bäumer-Aero* at Hamburg - see Heinkel 1956 pp.129-132.
94   Nowarra 1980 pp.216-218 & Koos 2006 pp.111-112.
95   Green 1970 p.267. Further development of the HD 49 would result in the He 51 fighter.
96   Sturtivant and Cronin 1998 pp.6-11, NAVAIR p.51, *Table 7 Carrier Air Groups and squadrons (up to 1950)* in Terzibaschitsch S. 1980 *Aircraft carriers of the US Navy* pp.301-302 & Sekigawa E. 1974 *Pictorial History of Japanese Military Aviation* (hereafter cited as Sekigawa 1974) pp.23-24 & p.31.
97   NAVAIR 1970 p.45 & pp.60-61 and Smith P.C. 1981 *Impact! The Dive Bomber Pilots Speak* (hereafter cited as

aware of developments in the Far East where the Imperial Japanese Navy *(IJN)* had initiated a development programme for a shipboard dive bomber in 1931.[98] As this programme failed to produce an acceptable aircraft the *Ernst Heinkel Flugzeugwerke* was approached in 1932 with the task of designing a suitable type. The result was the **Heinkel HD 66** which, following adaptation by Aichi for carrier employment, was adopted by the *IJN* in 1934 as the Navy Type 94 Carrier Bomber or Aichi D1A1.[99]

Alive to the possibilities of this design the Referent Technik ordered two further prototypes as the **Heinkel HD 50** in December 1931. The first of these was the 380 hp Junkers L5 engined HD 50a WNr.406 D-2326, whereas the HD 50b WNr.408 D-2471 was fitted with a 504 hp Siemens Jupiter radial. Trials with the first of these robust aircraft began at Travemünde in April 1933 where the He 50aW demonstrated a top speed of 200 kph with a gross weight of 2,210 kgs.[100]

G. COMPRESSION-IGNITION ENGINES

The *Reichsmarine* was not alone in its interest in the development of heavy-oil or diesel aero-engines. In Britain Henry Tizard and David Pye, both later to become important in scientific research within aeronautics, were keen exponents of the diesel engine as they believed that the petrol engine had reached a natural power limit on account of an inherent chemical instability of the fuel.[101] In 1928 Capt.Lionel Woolson and Prof.Herman Dohner in the USA designed and built the world's first practical diesel engine for aeroplane use.[102] In 1931 this engine, the Packard DR-980 of 225 hp, set an un-refuelled endurance record of 84 hours and 32 minutes aboard a Bellanca Pacemaker thus demonstrating one of the key advantages of the diesel engine over its petrol-fuelled contemporary.[103]

The use of diesels aboard lighter-than-aircraft was commonplace. The highly successful Zeppelin LZ 127 *Graf Zeppelin* of 1928 employed five Maybach VL 2 twelve-cylinder diesel engines and sufficient fuel was carried to stay aloft for 118 hours when fully loaded with 13,411 kgs of passengers, cargo and mail.[104] During the airship's 1929 world cruise the engines ran for over 500

Smith 1981) pp.23-31. The first dedicated shipboard dive bomber to enter service with the *USN* was the Martin BM that was re-equipped VT-1S in 1932 aboard the *USS Lexington* - see also Swanborough G. and Bowers P.M. 1976 *United States Navy Aircraft since 1911* pp.314-315. The *RWM* was well aware of these developments. This was due in part to the reports of the *Ullstein* journalist Walter Kleffel who had been secretly contracted to report on the latest military developments in the *USA* during his 6 month tour of that country in 1929. Kleffel had been much impressed by the capabilities of the *USN's* Helldivers - see Ishoven van A. 1977 *The Fall of an Eagle: The Life of Fighter Ace Ernst Udet* pp.127-128.

98   Sekigawa 1974 pp.51-52. The *IJN's* first carrier dive bomber programme was a *6-Shi* requirement issued to *Yokosuka Ku-Sho* and *Nakijima*. Neither prototype was acceptable, nor indeed were the *7-Shi* replacements.

99   Green 1970 p.264 & Nowarra 1980 pp.208-210. The HD 66 was powered by a 715 hp Siemens und Halske Sh 22B radial, the Aichi D1A1 being re-engined with a Nakajima Kotobuki 2-kai-1 radial of 580 hp - see Koos 2006 pp.113-114.

100   Green 1970 pp.264-265, Nowarra 1980 pp.210-211 & Koos 2006 pp.136-137. See also Francillon R.J. 1979 *Japanese Aircraft of the Pacific War* pp.268-271 & Smith 1981 p.32.

101   Nahum A. *Propulsion* in Jarrett P. (Ed.) 1997 *Aircraft of the Second World War: The Development of the Warplane 1939-45* (hereafter cited as Nahum in Jarrett (Ed.) 1997) pp.257-258. Tizard became Chairman of the Aeronautical Research Committee, whilst Pye became Director of Scientific Research at the Air Ministry. During the twenties research in Britain and the USA had shown that the quality of crude oil stock varied widely and that in some instances the resulting refined petrol had quite poor characteristics when subject to high compression. This instability resulted in premature detonation or "knock", a potentially destructive condition in high powered petrol engines.

102   Gunston B. 1995 *World Encyclopaedia of Aero Engines* (hereafter cited as Gunston 1995) p.116.

103   Taylor M.J.H. (Ed.) 1993 *Jane's Encyclopedia of Aviation* p.149. This record was accomplished between the 25 - 28 May 31 at Jackonsville, Florida by Walter Lees & Frederic Brossy.

104   Stroud 1966 pp.383-385. In nearly 9 years of operation LZ 127 flew 17,178 hrs, 1,695,272 kms and carried 13,100 passengers. It made 590 flights with 144 ocean crossings. The Maybach VL 2 was also the engine of choice aboard the *USN's* two new airships, the ZRS-4 & 5 - see Althoff W. 1990 *Sky Ships: A History of the Airship in the United*

hours with nothing more than routine servicing setting a new standard for reliability and endurance that it was unattainable for contemporary petrol engines.[105] The key features of the airship diesel were illustrated in a contemporary document:

> In the Maybach engine the first consideration is to allow for the longest possible time between overhauls. These airship engines do not generally require a major overhaul till 2,000 to 3,000 flying hours have been accomplished. In an aeroplane engine a major overhaul is generally necessary before 500 hours, so the improvement in reliability is very great. This improvement has been brought about by great attention to details. Very prolonged running-in periods (over 200 hours) on the bench take place before the engine is issued. Roller bearings are employed practically throughout, and a special camshaft drive renders the engine reversible, a most desirable feature on an airship. The normal speed of operation is low (1,300 rpm). Special attention is paid to combustion so as to make the fuel consumption as low as possible, since weight of fuel consumed becomes a very important item over long trips. To achieve all these objects, the engine has to be made heavier than the usual aeroplane engine. The 600 hp Maybach engine weighs 3.2 kg/hp against the normal 0.91 kg/hp of the aeroplane engine. A portion of the difference is, however, made good by the reduced fuel consumption, due to a high compression ratio (7.21). The engine is designed to run either on liquid or on gaseous fuel. The combined stroke volume of the twelve cylinders (arranged in a V) is 33 litres. This corresponds to an output of 15 hp/litre, slightly less than the Liberty of 1917.[106]

Nayler J.L. and Ower E. 1930
Aviation of To-Day: Its History and Development

Clearly the advantages of the aero-diesel lay in its low fuel consumption and reliability. Associated to these points were the low cost of its fuel and its practically non-inflammable nature.[107] The latter issue was of major concern aboard airships but it was also a major cause of injury and mortality aboard aircraft equipped with petrol engines in the event of a crash or through enemy action.[108] The disadvantages of the airship diesel were its huge weight, low output and low operating speed. It was these disadvantages that the *Junkers Motorenbau* design team sought to overcome through

States Navy p.87.

105   Stern W.J. *Aircraft Engines* in Nayler J.L. and Ower E. 1930 *Aviation of To-Day: Its History and Development* (hereafter cited as Stern in Nayler and Ower 1930) p.390. This flight from Lakehurst to Los Angeles via Friedrichshafen and Tokyo took 12 days, 14 hrs and 20 mins at an average speed of 113 kph - see Stroud 1966 p.383-384. In Britain the massive Beardmore Tornado 8-Cyl. in-line engine was developed for the ill-fated R-101. The Tornado developed 585 hp at 900 rpm for a weight of 1,900 kgs - see Gunston 1995 p.23. Interestingly Vickers elected to use the proven Rolls Royce Condor III petrol engine aboard the R-100 - see Andrews C.F. 1969 *Vickers Aircraft since 1908* p.32.

106   Quoted from W.J.Stern in Nayler and Ower 1930 *Aviation of To-Day: Its History and Development* pp.390-391 Frederick Warne & Co.Ltd.

107   Grey C.G. 1943 *Luftwaffe* p.p.137-139. Grey considered the development of the diesel engine for use in aeroplanes as highly overdue. He points to the loss of life in the Great War due to fire aboard aeroplanes and suggests that the continuing emphasis on high powered petrol engines stemmed from military rather than civil funding for aero-engine development during the twenties.

108   Gersdorff and Grasmann 1985 p.14. For the new Zeppelin LZ 129 & 130 *Daimler-Benz* developed the even larger LOF 6 (later DB 602) water-cooled 16-cyl.vee diesel. This developed up to 1320 hp at 1650 rpm but weighed 2000 kgs. The compression ratio was 16:1 - see Lange 1970 p.408. The LZ 129 was completed in Dec 35 and first flew on the 4 Mar 36. Following the loss of the LZ 129 at Lakehurst on the 6 May 37, the LZ 130 was re-designed to use helium as a lifting gas and first flown on the 14 Sep 38. Two sister ships for *Deutsche Zeppelin-Reederei* were cancelled - see Stroud 1966 pp.386-388.

the development of the experimental Junkers FO 4 compression-ignition engine for use in heavier than air machines.[109]

Compression-ignition developments in other countries often made use of four-stroke air-cooled radial engine layouts. Notable examples were the American nine-cylinder Guiberson A-980 and Packard DR-980 radials and the French seven-cylinder Clerget 9A radial, whilst in Germany *BMW* sought to develop a diesel version of the highly successful BMW 132 Hornet.[110] However in-line water cooled diesel engines were also being developed. In Italy Fiat briefly toyed with the six-cylinder in-line AN.1, whilst in France Jalbert developed four and six-cylinder in-line engines under sponsorship from the French Government.[111] By contrast the Junkers team adopted a completely different approach to the problem and opted for a two-stroke cycle with opposed pistons in a single cylinder. In this way the six-cylinder in-line **Junkers FO 4** was in reality a twelve-cylinder engine.[112] Following ignition the pistons moved vertically away from each other, one uncovering the lower inlet port and the other the upper outlet port. The ports were carefully shaped to help swirl the exhaust gas from the cylinder and to assist the mixing of the oil spray as the piston nearly reached top dead centre. An engine driven blower on the rear of the engine provided high pressure air for two scavenge pumps that further facilitated the evacuation of the exhaust gases.[113]

The FO 4 was publicly displayed at the *ILA* in Berlin in 1928 and by the following year was considered to be sufficiently reliable to install in a specially modified Junkers F 24 airframe.[114] In its production form the **Jumo 4** was a six-cylinder in-line water cooled compression-ignition engine. The cylinders had a diameter of 120 mm with a stroke of 210 mm giving a total capacity of 28.6 litres. The engine weighed 750 kgs and was rated at 750 hp at 1,700 rpm.[115] This gave it a power to weight ratio of 1:1 and an output of 26:1 hp/litre, a significant improvement on the Maybach VL 2. However it remained a weighty engine being more than a third heavier than the older BMW VI U and two thirds heavier than *Junkers'* new twelve cylinder petrol engine, the 20 litre Jumo 210 (See 3C2).[116] This was in large part due to the much greater stresses associated with the diesel engine with its much higher compression ratios. The Jumo 4 had a compression ratio (Vd) of 17:1, whereas the BMW VI U and Jumo 210 had a far more modest 7.3:1.[117] The outcome was a more massive engine block than the new petrol engines.[118] A further problem, in this case peculiar to the opposed

109   Gersdorff and Grasmann 1985 pp.88-89 & Schmitt 1988 p.206-207.

110   Gunston 1995 p. 79, 116, 43 & 26 & Bingham V. 1998 *Major Piston Aero Engines of World War II* (hereafter cited as Bingham 1998) p.17. Meanwhile within Germany *Siemens* experimented with a number of radial diesels: the 4-Cyl.Sh 12 & 13 for light aeroplanes and the 9-Cyl.Sh 20 experimental motor. The diesel version of the BMW 132 was the 4-stroke BMW-Lanova 114. This interesting engine was liquid-cooled and developed 650 hp at 2,200 rpm. Work ceased in 1937 - see Gersdorff and Grasmann 1985 pp.50-52.

111   Gunston 1995 p.60 & pp.88-89.

112   Gersdorff and Grasmann 1985 p.89 & Gunston 1995 p.89. The FO 4 was based on the earlier 5-cyl. FO 3 compression-ignition engine. Junkers also tested a 6-cyl.radial diesel of 70 hp. This was test flown on a Junkers A 50 sports aeroplane in 1929 – see Schmitt 1988 p.207. However development was abandoned - see Lange 1970 p.418.

113   Stern in Nayler and Ower 1930 p.395, Bridgmann L. (Ed.) 1946 *Jane's All the World's Aircraft 1945/46* (hereafter cited as Bridgmann (Ed.) 1946) p.294 & Gunston 1995 p.89.

114   Stroud 1966 p.306 & Turner P.St.J. and Nowarra H.J. 1971 *Junkers: an aircraft album* (hereafter cited as Turner and Nowarra 1971) p.33. This aircraft had been previously operated by *UAE* in Spain. The first flight with the FO 4 was made in Feb 29 - see Lange 1970 p. & Schmitt 1988 pp.207-208.

115   Lange 1970 p.418, Gersdorff and Grasmann 1985 p.89 & Schmitt 1988 p.207. The FO 4 had developed 600 hp at 1,600 rpm, whilst the initial Jumo 4 had been rated at 720 hp at 1,700 rpm. It passed its type test (*Masterprufung*) in Mar 31.

116   Gersdorff and Grasmann 1985 p.79 & 94.

117   Lange 1970 p.419 & Gersdorff and Grasmann 1985 p.59, 79 & 94.

118   Chamberlain G. 1984 *Airships - Cardington: A history of Cardington airship station and its role in world airship development* p.123. Most diesel engines used far more rigid mountings than were possible in airships or aeroplanes. The Beardmore Torandos suffered particularly from this problem aboard the R-101 where the rated 585 hp was simply unobtainable. Nearly 100 hp per engine was lost due to the inability of the airship's structure to contain the

cylinder design, was the complicated reduction gearing for the propeller. This was driven from two crankshafts rather than the more normal single crankshaft and was therefore more susceptible to mechanical failure.

Nonetheless the general success of the flight trials led to a small order for the Jumo 204 from *DLH* which re-engined its fleet of Junkers F 24 transports with the new engine.[119] In 1934 the airline went one stage further and re-engined the massive Junkers G.38a D-2000 (D-AZUR) with four Jumo 204 diesel engines. In the following year the G.38b D-2500 (D-APIS) was also re-engined.[120]

Military interest was heavily influenced by strategic considerations.[121] The fuel consumption of a compression-ignition engine was only 75% of that of the conventional four-stroke petrol engine.[122] Therefore an aircraft with diesel engines needed only three-quarters of the fuel to fly the same distance as one with petrol engines. Diesel or heavy oil fuel was also cheaper, more readily available and easier to refine than the high octane fuels needed for high powered petrol engines. Furthermore the compression-ignition cycle would eliminate the detonation problems that were increasingly associated with high compression petrol engines. In the *Junkers'* design the low grade fuel was delivered directly to the cylinders via engine driven fuel pumps and injectors.[123] This system coupled to the compression-ignition cycle obviated the need for carburation and the sometimes troublesome magneto-ignition (See 3C2).[124] Engine controls within the cockpit were also simplified, the mixture, carburettor heat controls and ignition switches being deleted.

Given the prospect of large orders for the planned Ju 86 medium bomber/fast air transport and the Do 18 flying boat the *Junkers* team set about improving the basic Jumo 4 design. A major concern was weight and to this end cylinder size was reduced still further to a diameter of 105 mm with a stroke of 160 mm. This gave an overall capacity of 16.6 litres and weight of 520 kg. In its initial form the new **Jumo 5** developed 550 hp at 2,100 rpm but this was increased to 600 hp at 2,200 rpm in the production engine.[125] Despite output had actually increased the Jumo 4 output had actually increased to 36:1 hp/litre, whilst the power to weight ratio had improved to 1: 0.87

Completed in 1932 the Jumo 5 passed its *Masterprufung* in the following year.[126] The manufacturer's test bed was Focke Wulf A17c D-1444 (later D-UNIK), whilst *DLH* carried out proving trials with the new engine using Ju 52/3m D-AJYR during 1934.[127] In the meantime

loads exerted by these high compression engines at high power settings.

119 Stroud 1966 pp.306-307, Turner and Nowarra 1971 p.33 & Schmitt 1988 pp.105-106. One of the 5 single-engined Ju 52 transports was also re-engined with the Jumo 204 as the Ju 52do WNr.4003 – see Schmitt 1988 p.171. In 1934 consideration was also given to re-engining the Fairey Long Range Monoplane with a Jumo 4. In the end it was decided that this installation would not give the required advantage over the rival Bleriot-Zappata 110 aircraft to justify the expense - see Taylor 1974 pp.191-192 & Spec.27/33 in Meekcoms K.J. and Morgan E.B. 1994 *The British Aircraft Specifications File: British Military and Commercial Aircraft Specifications 1920-1949* p.186.

120 Turner and Nowarra 1971 pp.51-52 & Stroud J. 1984 'Die Junkers Größflugzeuge' in *Air Enthusiast* No.24 p.39 & 78. Stroud has clear memories of the black exhaust trails left by the Jumo 204 diesels during a visit to Croydon by D-APIS in 1936 - see also Schmitt 1988 p.129.

121 Suchenwirth 1968 p.22 & 126.

122 Kens K. and Nowarra H.J. 1961 *Die deutschen Flugzeuge 1933-1945: Deutschlands Luftfahrt-Entwicklungen bis ende des Zweiten Weltkrieges* pp.602-605. Fuel consumption figures (gr/hp/hr) were: Jumo 205 (170), BMW VI (225), Jumo 210 (235) & DB 600 (225).

123 Bridgmann (Ed.) 1946 p.294 & Gersdorff and Grasmann 1985 pp.170-172.

124 Stern in Nayler and Ower 1930 p.393.

125 Lange 1970 p.419, Gersdorff and Grasmann 1985 pp.90-92, Schmitt 1988 pp.208-211, Bingham 1998 pp.24-25 & Gunston 1995 pp.89-90. The original FO 3 engine of 1926 had used 5 large cylinders and had developed 830 hp at 1200 rpm.

126 Lange 1970 p.419.

127 Stroud 1966 p.329 & Turner and Nowarra 1971 p.66. D-1444 was a former *DLH* aircraft. Fin area was increased to compensate for the increased torque of the Jumo 5. A four blade airscrew was used for test purposes - see also

tooling for large scale production began in the same year although the first flight cleared engines did not become available until March 1935 when Ju 86cb D-ALAL was re-engined with the Jumo 205C.[128] Even then the supply of engines remained strictly limited and the Do 18a D-AHIS was completed in the same month with the Jumo 5. It would be the autumn before *Dornier* received any production Jumo 205C engines.[129]

Smith 1973 p.15 & Schmitt 1988 pp.209-210.

128   Vajda & Dancey 1998 p.237. Two production lines appear to have been established (presumably at Dessau & Kothen.) with WNr. in the 17000 & 30000 sequences - see Ries 1970. The Ju 86ba1 D-ABUK was completed with the Jumo 205C in Apr 35 as the first prototype for the proposed *B-Serie* transport - see Stroud 1966 pp.336-339 & Green 1970 pp.414-416.

129   Stroud 1966 pp.255-257 & Green 1970 pp.124-125. Like the Ju 86 the Do 18 had been designed from the outset to use the Jumo 205.

1C5

Ordnance Development 1918-33

A. BARRELLED ORDNANCE

In contrast to the massive improvements made in airframe and aero-engine design, the *Luftstreitkräfte* finished the war with much the same aircraft weapons with which it had begun the conflict four years earlier. The two main aircraft mounted weapons were both derivatives of the standard infantry issue Vickers-Maxim machine gun manufactured under licence by the *Deutsche Waffen und Munitionsfabriken (DWM)* in Berlin as the 7.92 mm MG Modell 08.[1] The considerable weight of this gun, 26.5 kgs together with a sled mounting of a further 32 kgs, made it impractical for aircraft use in its basic form. Furthermore the basic infantry weapon was water cooled with a relatively low rate of fire (400 rpm) and had an effective range of just 600 metres.[2] In 1913 Karl Heinemann of *DWM* produced a lightened variant of the basic weapon for use as an infantry light machine gun which featured a rifle stock with an integral pistol grip, belt feed from a drum and air cooling. By re-designing the operating mechanism Heinemann achieved a dramatic increase in the cyclic rate of fire (700 rpm), whilst the basic weight of the improved weapon was just 10 kgs.[3] The new gun was adopted by the infantry as the 7.92 mm SMG Modell 13 *(Parabellum)*, whilst in 1915 it became the first machine gun to see widespread service with the *Fliegertruppe* when it was adopted as a fixed weapon on the early German fighters.[4] However the MG 13 quickly proved far more suitable on flexible mountings and it was in this form that it was used on nearly all German multi-seat combat aircraft for the remainder of the conflict.[5] For fixed installation as pilot's guns it was replaced by a stripped down version of the basic MG 08. This was the 7.92 mm luft MG 08/15 which differed

1   Markham G. 1989 *Guns of the Reich: Firearms of the German Forces 1939-1945* (hereafter cited as Markham 1989) pp.122-128. The Maxim machine gun was widely employed. In Britain it was built by the Vickers, Sons & Maxim for the British Army. The Loewe family had substantial holdings in the British company as well as in the German manufacturer *DWM*. See also Wallace Clarke R. 1994 *British Aircraft Armament Vol.2 RAF Guns and Gunsights from 1914 to the present day* (hereafter cited as Wallace Clarke 1994) pp.24-26.

2   Hoffschmidt E.J. 1969 *German Aircraft Guns WWI - WWII* (hereafter cited as Hoffschmidt 1969) p.73 & Markham 1989 p.126. Further data was obtained from Schliephake H. 1977 *Flugzeugbewaffnung – Die Bordwaffen der Luftwaffe von den Anfangen bis zur Gegenwart* (hereafter cited as Schliephake 1977) pp.79-81 & www.wikipedia. org.de (hereafter cited as Wikipedia 2007).

3   Hoffschmidt 1969 pp.72-74. Heinemann joined *DWM* in 1911 having already made a name for himself elsewhere in the design and development of automatic weapons. He re-designed the basic Maxim operating mechanism so that individual cartridges were engaged by a feed pawl operating off the locking mechanism. This speeded up the rate of fire which was made possible by the re-positioning of the return spring to store energy more efficiently for the return stroke.

4   Lamberton W.M.1960 *Fighter Aircraft of the 1914-1918 War* (hereafter cited as Lamberton 1960) pp.177-178, Hoffschmidt 1969 pp.68-69, Schliephake 1977 pp.81-84, Markham 1989 pp.129-130 & Griehl M. 2008 *Deutsche Flugzeugbewaffnung bis 1945* (hereafter cited as Griehl 2008) pp.11-12. The *Parabellum* was initially used as a fixed pilot's weapon but its flexibility and weight made it ideally suited for ring mountings on multi-seat aircraft - see Lamberton W.M.1962 *Reconnaissance and Bomber Aircraft of the 1914-1918 War* (hereafter cited as Lamberton 1962) p.183.

5   Lamberton 1962 p.183 & Hoffschmidt 1969 p.69. Later weapons appear to have been designated MG 14/17 - see Griehl 2008 p.11.

from the basic weapon chiefly in having its water jacket replaced by a fretted sleeve, the air flow over the barrel when fitted to an aircraft being sufficient to cool the gun.[6] The lu.MG 08/15 also had a superior rate of fire, some 450 rpm, whilst later guns would boost this still further to 600 rpm through the use of a recoil booster or *Ruckstossverstarker S.*[7] However the usefulness of any fixed gun rested on its ability to fire through the propeller arc of tractor aircraft.[8] In April 1915 the Dutch designer Anthony Fokker produced just such an interrupter gear. This simple mechanism consisted of a cam plate attached to the propeller shaft which was connected to the trigger by a lever to stop the gun from firing whilst a propeller blade was in the way. As the propeller turned in excess of 1,200 rpm there was no diminution in the rate of fire and the overall result proved revolutionary as it allowed German pilots to attack for the first time an enemy machine which was directly in their path.[9] Initially a single lu.MG 08/15 was mounted immediately in front of the pilot's cockpit, later a twin mounting was adopted for all German fighter aircraft *(Jagdflugzeuge).*[10]

Air combat evolved rapidly during the last two years of the war and the need for improved types of aircraft weapon for offensive as well as defensive purposes became ever more pressing. The major requirements for fixed weapons were for improved reliability and a greater weight of fire. The latter could be achieved by either increasing the rate of fire or by increasing the calibre of the weapon so that a larger round was fired, or preferably by both means. The former required improvements in the operating mechanisms and in the quality of the ammunition. For example the Germans were the first to introduce metal disintegrating cartridge links as a replacement for the generally unsatisfactory webbing ammunition belts.[11] The overall weight of the gun was another

6   Schliephake 1977 pp.84-88 & Markham 1989. The modification of the MG 08 for infantry use as the LMG 08/15 with a rifle stock and bipod was the responsibility of *Obst.*von Merkatz of the *GPK (Geschütz Prufungs Kommission)*. The standard water cooled MG 08 was used aboard lighter than air machines such as the Zeppelins where the air speed was too low to ensure adequate cooling - see Griehl 2008 p.9. Many Lu.MG 08/15 were manufactured in Spandau, hence the Allied designation of this weapon - see Lamberton 1960 p.179. The designation Lu.MG 08/15 was applied to aircraft machine guns - see Schliephake 1977 pp.86-88 & Gander T. & Chamberlain P. 1978 *Small Arms, Artillery and Special Weapons of the Third Reich: An Encyclopedic Survey* (hereafter cited as Gander and Chamberlain 1978) p.71 & wikipedia 2007. The British followed a very similar path with the modification of the Vickers Maxim Mk.I for aerial use as the Mk.I* - see Wallace Clarke 1994 pp.26.

7   Markham 1989 p.126. The recoil booster deflected a portion of the propellant gas to increase the rearward thrust on the barrel and thus speed up the rate of fire. The contemporary 0.303 in Vickers Mk.II weapon had a 700 rpm rate of fire - see *Aircraft machine-guns in use in November 1918 and those about to be introduced* in Woodman H. *Armament Development* in Jarrett P. (Ed.) 1997 *Biplane to Monoplane: Aircraft development 1919-39* (hereafter cited as Woodman in Jarrett (Ed.) 1997) p.184 & Wallace Clarke 1994 pp.24-26.

8   Lamberton 1960 p.178 & Wallace Clarke 1994 p.27. To get around this problem both the French and the British developed a number of "pusher" aircraft whereby the crew sat in front to the engine which drove a rearward facing propeller. Such types included the Maurice Farman MF.11 (Shorthorn) & Vickers FB 5 - see also Lamberton 1962 pp.86-87, Lamberton 1960 pp.76-77 & Bowyer C. 1979 *Guns in the Sky: The Air Gunners of World War Two* (hereafter cited as Bowyer 1979) pp.5-7.

9   Hoffschmidt 1969 & Lange B. 1970 *Das Buch der deutschen Luftfahrtechnik* (hereafter cited as Lange 1970) pp.122-123. The interrupter mechanism was produced in matter of days by Fokker and his co-workers Lubbe, Heber & Leimberger of the *Luft-Verkehrs GmbH* at Berlin-Johannisthal in 1915. *Patent Nr.310396* was issued for this invention on the 6 Jul 17 by the *Kaiserliches Patentamt* - see Postma T. 1979 *Fokker: Aircraft Builders to the World* (hereafter cited as Postma 1979) p.25. However Fokker was not the first to patent such equipment. August Euler had been the first to recognise of fixing a machine gun in aircraft in such a way that by pointing the machine at the enemy the gun was also brought to bear on the target. He was awarded *Patentschrift Nr.248601* on the 24 Jul 10 for this concept. Franz Schneider, technical director of *LVG*, after examining the idea of a *Kanonenmotor* whereby a fixed gun was mounted between the cylinder banks of a Vee engine so as to fire through a hollow airscrew boss *(Patent Nr.290120,* dated 11 Jan 13), had taken out a similar patent to Fokker on the 15 Jul 13 *(Patent Nr.276396).* However Schneider's earlier ideas had evidently been forgotten in the turmoil of war - see Lamberton 1960 p.178 & Kosin R. 1983 *Die Entwicklung der deutschen Jagdflugzeuge* (hereafter cited as Kosin 1983) pp.15-19.

10   Kosin 1983 pp.18-19.

11   Wallace Clarke 1994 pp.28-29. The basic German design was initially copied and then improved for use by the RAF in 1918 as the Prideaux system of steel cartridge links. It had already proved necessary to enclose the fabric belts in

concern, particularly for flexible mountings where the gunner had to balance his weapon against the slipstream. Given the comparatively poor performance of combat aircraft during the Great War the weight of machine guns, their associated ammunition and either the interrupter gear or flexible mounting all impacted on aircraft performance and overall load carrying capability.

Wartime experience had shown that rates of fire of around 500 rpm were quite inadequate once aircraft performance had exceeded 160 kph and had effectively reduced target acquisition to a matter of seconds.[12] The German solution was the ingenious 7.92 mm Gast twin barrel machine gun which had, in its refined form, provided a combined rate of fire of 1,800 rpm. The prototype of this weapon, designed by Carl Gast, first appeared in January 1916; a successful demonstration to *Luftstreitkräfte* officials followed on the 22 August 1917. The Gast MG differed from the more conventional twin yoked MG 13 *Parabellums* in that the two barrels were actually linked by a common operating system. The recoil force from one barrel provided enough energy for a round to be loaded, fired and extracted from the other barrel which in turn provided the energy needed for the first barrel to be fired again. Ammunition feed was via two flat circular drums located on either side of the weapon. Each drum contained up to 180 rounds which were offered up to the feed mechanism by an internal spring. The overall weight of the weapon with ammunition was 27 kgs.[13] An immediate order for 3,000 weapons was placed with the *Vorwerk AG* at Barmen, the first 100 units to be delivered by the 1 June 1918. Further orders quickly followed but relatively few were delivered before the close of hostilities.[14]

The other solution to the problem of insufficient fire power was to increase the weight of the projectile. In Britain in 1918 a number of worn out Vickers machine guns were re-bored to accept the French 11 mm *Desvignes* incendiary round for anti-balloon operations.[15] Similar weapons were used by both the French and the Belgians.[16] Meanwhile in Germany the appearance on the Western Front of armoured fighting vehicles prompted the development of a heavier version of the existing MG 08. In 1917 the basic weapon was scaled up to fire a 12.7 mm 770-grain round. With a tungsten steel core these projectiles proved easily capable of penetrating the sides of captured British and French tanks at 100 metres and in 1918 the new weapon was quickly put into production for both ground and air use under the designation 12.7 mm MG Tank und Flieger *(TuF)*. Unfortunately for the *Luftstreitkräfte* none of these excellent weapons had been delivered by November 1918.[17]

Nonetheless during the latter part of the war both the *Luftstreitkräfte* and the *Marineflieger* made limited use of an even larger weapon, the 2 cm *Flugzeugkanone* (Aircraft Cannon). In response to a June 1915 requirement both Heinrich Ehrhardt and *Dr.*Reinhold Becker developed weapons in this category but it was only the latter that saw operational service being employed aboard a variety of aircraft in 1918.[18] The *Becker Kanone* employed an advanced primer ignition blow

guide trunking to avoid flapping in the slipstream.

12   Bowyer 1979 p.28. This finding is based on the performance of the 0.303 in Lewis machine gun - the standard defensive weapon used by the British air forces. Field modifications later led to 800 rpm and two weapons were then yoked together to provide 1,600 rpm.

13   Hoffschmidt 1969 pp.75-77, Schliephake 1977 pp.90-91 & Wikipedia 2007.

14   Hoffschmidt 1969 p.76 & Schliephake 1977 p.91. The Gast MG proved effective in service and a further 6,000 were ordered in the autumn of 1918.

15   Lamberton 1960 p.182 & Wallace Clarke 1994 p.29. Trials were carried out at Orfordness in Mar 18. However in service the recoil proved excessive. The USAAS ordered 900 11 mm Vickers guns.

16   Lamberton 1960 p.182.

17   Hoffschmidt 1969 p.10. A total of 4,000 *TuF* machines guns were on the point of delivery at the end of the Great War.

18   Lamberton 1962 p.187 & Hoffschmidt 1969 pp.78-79 & Schliephake 1977 pp.93-94. One further cannon design that did not reach the production stage was the 2 cm Szakats of 1918. Designed by Gabriel Szakats, a Polish engineer working for the *Fahrzeug Fabrik* of Frankfurt, this weapon had a number of novel features including a revolving feed mechanism actuated by a powerful recoil moment- see Lamberton 1960 p.183 & Hoffschmidt 1969

back mechanism to fire, eject and re-load the 2 cm projectiles, ten or fifteen of which were fed to the gun from a vertically mounted flat magazine. In the case of advanced primer ignition the cartridge was fired just before it was fully chambered, the initial recoil being used to stop the forward movement of the bolt as the projectile left the barrel.[19] This design feature had the added advantage of spreading the recoil energy over a longer period of the firing cycle thus reducing the recoil, a particularly important feature in respect of aircraft mountings. The 2 cm Becker Kanone was also a light weapon, 30 kgs plus a 5 kg 15-round magazine. It was fitted with spade grips with two triggers, one for single shots and one for automatic fire.[20]

Initial trials held in mid-1915 with the Becker Kanone aboard a Gotha G-I had been disappointing. Thereafter technical support had been provided by the *Spandau Arsenal* in Berlin and in June 1916 120 guns were ordered. Ammunition feed problems were finally overcome in November of that year although trials with drum magazines and belt feed would continue into 1918. Most production weapons were used by the *Heer*, these being manufactured by the *Maschinenfabrik Augsburg-Nürnberg. (MAN)* This firm also completed 428 of the 2 cm Flz.K. Typ 2 for the *Luftstreitkräfte*, smaller numbers being completed by the *Stahlwerke Becker* at Willich am Rhein.[21] It had been intended to arm a fighter with the 2 cm *Kanone* and to this end *Albatros* began work on the D-VI in 1917. However a major problem with advanced primer ignition was the inherent difficulty of synchronising such a weapon to fire through the propeller arc. As a result work on this design ceased in June 1918.[22] Of all the principal combatants it was only France that successfully introduced a cannon armed fighter into operational service. This was the 37 mm *Puteaux* shell-gun which was modified by the *Hispano Suiza* designer Marc Birkigt to fire through the hollow airscrew shaft of a geared *Hispano Suiza* vee-eight engine. The so-called *moteur canon* was fitted to the specially modified SPAD S.XII Ca-1 and some success was obtained by the French aces Guynemer and Fonck.[23] However the *Puteaux* shell-gun was a single shot weapon with a relatively low muzzle velocity and at this stage better results could be obtained more safely with conventional rifle-calibre machine guns.[24]

In the wake of the Treaty of Versailles, which restricted machine gun holdings to just 2,336 weapons, the newly formed *Reichsheer* did what it could to conceal a proportion of its existing

p.82. The 2 cm *Flz.K.* was used operationally aboard the Friedrichshafen G.IIIa & A.E.G. G-IVk. These aircraft appear to have been used in the ground strafing role. Ring mounted and downward firing Flz.K. were also fitted to the A.E.G. J-II & the Albatros J-II close support aircraft which appeared in the closing months of the war - see Lamberton 1962 pp.146-147,112-113 & 156-157 and Williams A.G. & Gustin E. *Flying Guns - World War 1: Development of Aircraft Guns, Ammunition and Installations 1914-32* (hereafter cited as Williams and Gustin Undated).

19   Williams and Gustin Undated, Hoffschmidt 1969 p.79 & 81 and Schliephake 1977.93. Dr.Becker had patented his design in Sep 13. Interestingly official German interest *(Artillerie Prufungs Kommission)* had favoured the Ehrhardt-Kanone which enjoyed the backing of *Rheinmetall*; the *Stahlwerke Becker AG* was considered to lack sufficient experience in weapon design and manufacture. The APK also considered the locked-breech mechanism of the Ehrhardt Kanone to be superior to the API blowback system employed by *Becker*. However the Ehrhardt Kanone was subject to greater recoil forces, vibration and more frequent jams.

20   Williams and Gustin Undated. See also Hoffschmidt 1969 p.79 & Schliephake 1977 pp.93-94.

21   Imrie A. 1971 *Pictorial History of the German Army Air Service* (hereafter cited as Imrie 1971) pp.150-151, Gander and Chamberlain 1978 p.127 & Williams and Gustin Undated.

22   Kosin 1983 pp.47-48. The Albatros D-VI first flew in Feb 18.

23   Lamberton 1960 p.183 & Gunston B. 1995 *World Encyclopaedia of Aero Engines* p.83. The SPAD S.XII was a derivative of the successful S.VII scout. It first appeared in early 1917 and 300 were eventually completed. The single Vickers gun was retained for sighting purposes. A major problem of the *Puteaux* canon was its tremendous recoil. The S.XIV was a floatplane version developed by *Becherau and Herbemont*, 40 of which were completed in 1918 - some seeing service in the Adriatic Sea – see Lamberton 1960 p.107. The British authorities expended a great deal of time of effort trying to develop a recoilless gun for aircraft use, notably the Davis & *COW* guns. A Vickers 1-pounder (37 mm) gun was used in small numbers in FE 2 aircraft for home defence purposes and for nocturnal ground attack from 1917 - see Wallace Clarke 1994 pp.32-46.

24   Lamberton 1960 p.183.

stock including its most advanced weapons (See 1A2 & 1E2).[25] More than 60 different companies had been engaged in the manufacture of components for the new 12.7 mm Maschinengewehr TuF with final assembly by *MAN*. The *Heereswaffenamt (WaA)* had issued contracts for 6,000 weapons and despite the Allied occupation the component suppliers remained under orders to complete these orders.[26] In the meantime the completed examples were initially referred to as the MG 08 SS in order to conceal their existence from the *Interallierte Militär-Kontroll-Kommission (IMKK)* but Allied intelligence quickly learned of the new machine gun and *WaA* officials had to order the destruction of most of these weapons.[27] A similar situation existed in respect of the Gast MG. On the 18 November 1921 a member of the *WaA's* secret *Flugtechnik-Referat* wrote to the directors of *Vorwerk AG* at Barmen stating:

> The *Gast* gun made by you having become of no use any more at the front, I feel obliged to state that at the present moment we still consider the gun to be of the latest type. The accuracy of the work and the firing were never, not even approximately, attained by the other hitherto existing machine gun systems.
>
> We may say that the *Gast* gun may be qualified as the ideal for aeroplane armament. We also declare that you can further continue delivering the remainder of the complete order for 3,000 guns.
>
> If, with a view to the present circumstances some doubt may have arisen as to this delivery, I certify herewith that we shall fulfil the obligations of the contract...[28]

Signed: Buffe
18 November 1921

Once again the *IMKK's* inspection teams did their best to seek out the hidden stocks of these forbidden weapons. However it would not be until 1921 that the first 25 examples, together with ammunition and manufacturer's drawings were discovered near Königsberg in Ostpreussen.[29]

Development and production of both the Becker and Ehrhardt Kanone was moved abroad in an attempt to avoid the activities of the *IMKK*. With the covert support of the *Reichsheer* Becker successfully negotiated an agreement with the Swiss firm *Seebach Maschinenbau Aktien Gesellschaft (SEMAG)* which was located near Zurich. Production of the 2 cm Flz.K. Typ 2 was re-started and in

---

25   Markham 1989 p.124. Initially the *Reichsheer* had only been permitted 1,926 machine guns. This figure did not of course include any aircraft weapons. The revised figure of 2,336 machine guns was agreed in 1921.

26   Hoffschmidt 1969 pp.10 -11 & Walter J. 2004 *Guns of the Third Reich* (hereafter cited as Walter 2004) p.23. It had been hoped that the initial order for 4,000 *TuF* would have been complete by the autumn of 1918. The supplementary order for 2,000 was placed in Oct 18. Payment was guaranteed for completed parts - even if these were seized by the Allies. Companies were directed to *"continue manufacture at all costs"*. However Allied restrictions would later see both *Mauser* and *DWM* banned from weapons production. The *HWA* was responsible for the development and service introduction of all types of military weapons, specialist equipment and munitions. Military aviation was concealed within this organisation in *Wa.Prw.6*, later *Wa.Prw.8*. The *HWA* was eventually divided into 12 numbered Ordnance Evaluation Departments: *Wa.Prw.1* (Ballistics & Ammunition), *2* (Infantry weapons), *3* (Engineering), *4* (Artillery weapons), *5* (Pioneer equipment), *6* (Motor vehicles including armoured vehicles), *7* (Signals equipment), *8* (Optical & observation equipment), *9* (Smoke & chemical weapons), *10* (Rockets - liquid propellants), *11* (Rockets - solid propellants) & *12* (Administration & personnel) - see Fleischer W. 2003 *German Air-Dropped Weapons to 1945* (hereafter cited as Fleischer 2003) p.6.

27   Hoffschmidt 1969 p.11. The US authorities finally located a *TuF* machine gun in Aug 21. This weapon was shipped to the Springfield Armory for evaluation. It was not considered to be superior to the 0.5 in Browning that was then under development for the *US* forces.

28   Quoted from Hoffschmidt 1969 *German Aircraft Guns WWI – WWII* p.77 WE Inc.

29   Hoffschmidt 1969 pp.76-77.

1921 *SEMAG* introduced an improved version with a longer barrel and more powerful cartridges. These combined to give a higher muzzle velocity, a greater effective range and increased accuracy. A number of *SEMAG* 2 cm Kanone were subsequently sold to China and Spain before the company was absorbed into *Werkzeug Maschinenfabrik Oerlikon* in the mid-twenties.[30] Meanwhile to evade the Allied inspection teams all completed Ehrhardt Kanonen, together with spare parts, patterns and drawings were secretly transferred from the *Rheinische Metallwaren und-Maschinenfabrik* at Düsseldorf-Unterluss to a warehouse in the Netherlands. As a result none of these advanced weapons fell into Allied hands. Later in 1929 *Rheinmetall* form two foreign subsidiaries for the further development and manufacture of prohibited weapons such as the Ehrhardt Kanone. Of these the *Hollandische Artillerie-Industrie en Handelmaatschappij (HAIH)* in the Netherlands proved unsuccessful, but the creation of the *Waffenfabrik Solothurn AG* in Switzerland quickly resulted in the development of the basic design into the Solothurn MK-ST-5 which was later adopted by the *Reichswehr* for shipboard and land based use as the 2 cm C/30 and 2 cm FlaK 30 respectively (See also 1E2). The MK-ST-11 was developed in parallel as an aircraft cannon.[31]

During the late twenties *Oerlikon* used the *Becker* patents and the *SEMAG* improvements to establish two separate types of automatic cannon: the Oerlikon Typ F (Becker) and Typ L (SEMAG). The Typ F was the lightest weapon of the two designs with a recoil force of some 60-70 kgs and a muzzle velocity of 550-575 m/sec. The Typ L had a longer barrel, a higher muzzle velocity (670-700 m/sec) and a higher recoil force (115-120 kgs). It was also a heavier weapon at 43 kgs in comparison to the Typ F at 30 kgs.[32] In 1931 a contract was placed by the *Reichswehr* for the supply of a number of *Oerlikon* anti-aircraft guns as the 2 cm FlaK 28 and FlaK 29 (See 1E2).[33] A small number of *Oerlikon Flugzeugkanone* were also purchased for experimental purposes, at least one being fitted to a Dornier Do R Superwal whilst another was tested at Lipetsk aboard an Albatros L 77v.[34]

Whilst the pioneering recoil-operated Becker and Ehrhardt Kanonen were both successfully developed abroad the withdrawal of the Allied inspection teams in 1926 allowed some innovative weapon development to finally take place in Germany itself. In 1929 H.F.A.Lubbe, a former designer at the *Luft-Verkehrs GmbH* at Berlin-Johannisthal and at that time senior partner of the *Arado Handelsgesellschaft* at Warnemünde, produced an experimental gas operated 2 cm *Flugzeugkanone* with a cyclic rate of fire of 360 rpm.[35] In the Lubbe Kanone the action was returned by diverting some of the propellant gas behind the projectile into a cylinder beneath the barrel. This ejected the spent cartridge, re-cocked the weapon and chambered the following round. Recoil forces were

30 Hoffschmidt 1969 p.80 & Gander and Chamberlain 1978 p.127. Under this agreement all Becker drawings and tooling was transferred to *SEMAG* and ultimately to *Oerlikon*, another Swiss firm that also enjoyed secret financial support from the Reich Government.

31 Hoffschmidt 1969 p.81, Schliephake 1977 p.95, Gander and Chamberlain 1978 p.127 & Griehl 2008 p.14.

32 Hoffschmidt 1969 p.113, Schliephake 1977 pp.109-110 & Griehl 2008 p.16. There was a third line of development - the Oerlikon Typ S which was a larger and heavier weapon altogether.

33 Müller W. 1995 *Waffen-Arsenal und Fahrzeuge der Heere und Luftstreitkräfte: 2cm Flak im Einsatz 1935-1945* p.3.

34 Nowarra H.J. 1982 *Fernaufklärer 1915-1945: Enstehung, Entwicklung, Einsatz* p.23. The weapon evaluated by the *Reichsmarine* aboard the *Superwal* would appear to be either an Oerlikon Typ L or Typ S, whilst that installed in the Albatros L 77v was probably a Typ F - see also Hoffschmidt 1969 p.113, Kosin 1983 p.68 & Schliephake H. *Secret Flight Testing in Lipetsk, Russia* in Beauvais H., Kossler K., Mayer M. and Regel C. 2002 *German Secret Flight Test Centres to 1945: Johannisthal, Lipetsk, Rechlin, Travemünde, Tarnewitz, Peenemunde-West* (hereafter cited as Schliephake in Beauvais et al 2002) p.48.

35 Kranzhoff J A 1997 *Arado: Geschichte eines Flugzeugwerks* (hereafter cited as Kranzhoff 1997) pp.10-15. Heinrich Friedrich August Lubbe was an experienced pilot, designer and business manager. He was something of an authority in the field of aircraft armament having worked with Fokker on the first successful interrupter gear. In Nov 25 he had become the senior partner within the newly established *Arado Handels Gesselschaft* at Warnemünde. Lubbe remained active in weapon development delivering 200 machine gun mechanisms to the *Reichsheer* in 1930 under conditions of the greatest security. These Lubbe weapons were tested at both Staaken and Lipetsk.

reduced and the overall weight of the weapon without the drum feed was 48.5 kgs.[36] In 1931 *Rheinmetall* became interested in the weapon and three Lubbe Kanonen were subsequently tested by the *WaA*. However the trials proved disappointing and no further development was undertaken and what was actually a very promising design.[37]

In contrast to the considerable amount of development work associated with the *Flugzeugkanone*, there was very little advancement in the design of aerial machine guns until the end of this period.[38] A considerable number of lu.MG 08/15 had been hidden away after the war and it was these weapons that were fitted to the fifty Fokker D.XIII fighters and other combat aircraft used by the *Flugzentrum Lipetsk* between 1925-33 (See 1D1).[39] In the meantime the tactical disadvantages of the heavy LMG 08/15 resulted in a post-war *Reichsheer* requirement for a lighter air-cooled machine gun for use by the *Infanterie, Kavallerie* and motorised troops. The result was the MG 13 which was manufactured by *Rheinmetall's* Sommerda subsidiary in Sweden.[40] Interestingly *Rheinmetall* pursued a separate line of development at Solothurn in Switzerland where the S2-200 was developed using a unique barrel-locked rotating bolt with locking sleeve mechanism that had been developed by Louis Stange. Although offered to the *Reichswehr* as the MG 30 the Solothurn S2-200 was not considered to be substantially better than the existing MG 13 and a production order was not forthcoming.[41] However the operating mechanism was to form the basis of the first new aerial machine gun - the Solothurn S6-200 which was offered as a replacement for the ageing lu.MG 08/15 in 1932.[42]

After satisfactory bench tests the MG 15 was initially tested as a flexibly mounted weapon aboard the Dornier Do P heavy bomber at the *Wissenschaftliche Versuchs-und Prüfanstalt für Luftfahrzeuge (Wivupal)* at Lipetsk in 1932 (See 1D1). Other types that were fitted with the MG 15 for trials during 1932-33 were the new Do F heavy night bomber and the Heinkel HD 45 long range reconnaissance aircraft. The *Drehkranz* D 30/15 was specially developed as a ring mounting for this weapon and this was adopted as standard for the new multi-seat combat aircraft then under development (See 3C4).[43]

---

36   Hoffschmidt 1969 p.83. A major advantage of the Lubbe Kanone was its simplicity, there being just 50 parts in all. See also Kranzhoff 1997 p.45.

37   Hoffschmidt 1969 p.83.

38   Woodman in Jarrett (Ed.) 1997 pp.186-188. To be fair this was also true of other nations. In the USA the 0.3 in Browning was introduced as the standard machine gun for both fixed and flexible mountings. In the early 30s a single 0.3 in supplemented by a single 0.5 in Browning became the normal armament for fighter aircraft. In Britain the RAF continued to rely on the Vickers, albeit in the Mk.II & III variants into well into the 30s whilst the Lewis gun remained the standard flexible machine gun - see Wallace Clarke 1994 p.22 & pp.30-32. In France the licence built Vickers was replaced in 1929 by the 7.5 mm Darne machine gun. This had a cyclic rate of fire of 1,200 rpm and was an advance on contemporary weapons.

39   Ries K. 1970 *Luftwaffe Bd.1 Die Maulwurfe 1919-1935* (hereafter cited as Ries 1970) p.50, Kosin 1983 pp.57-59 & Schliephake in Beauvais et al 2002 p.42.

40   Schliephake 1977 p.93, Gander and Chamberlain 1978 p.71 & 74, Markham 1989 pp.129-131 & Griehl 2008 pp.14-15. Due to Allied prohibitions on the manufacture of machine guns in Germany development of this weapon was undertaken under the out of sequence designation Gerat 13. The MG 13 was initially manufactured in Sweden before production was transferred to *Simson und Co.* in Germany in 1932. The MG 13 was not an un-qualified success: its length made it somewhat unwieldy in action, the 25 round box magazine was incapable of sustained fire, and to replace a hot barrel the gun had to be partially dismantled. Nonetheless it was a considerable improvement on the LMG 08/15.

41   Markham 1989 p.131.

42   Markham 1989 p.132 & Griehl 2008 pp.14-15. Production MG 30 weapons were sold to Austria & Hungary. Work on the MG 15 had begun in 1930. The resulting design met all the requirements for aircraft use being light and with a short barrel. However *Wa.Prüf.2* had reservations and it would take the personal intervention of *the Chef WaA* (von Brockelberg) to get the weapon into production - see Hertel W. Dipl.Ing.GenIng.a.D.1955 *Procurement in the German Air Force* USAF Historical Studies No.170 (hereafter cited as Hertel 1955) p.45.

43   Schliephake in Beauvais et al 2002 p.48. See also Hertel 1955 p.46.

B. DROP ORDNANCE

Despite the pre-occupation with the design of aircraft for reconnaissance and observation purposes the development of drop ordnance dated back to 1912 when the first prototype weapons were developed by the *Artillerie-Prüfungs-Kommission (APK)*.[44] The initial German aerial bombs were manufactured by the *Karbonit-Werke* and these together with those from a number of other manufacturers were generally of poor aerodynamic shape and small capacity.[45] To overcome the aerodynamic problems of the early weapons a new range of streamlined ordnance was introduced in 1916 following development work by *Goerz* at Berlin-Friedenau in association with the *Prüfanstalt und Werft der Fliegertruppe* evaluation centre. The resultant *PuW* ordnance was manufactured in a range of weights and sizes from 12.5 kgs to 1,000 kgs *(Photo 1C-12)*. The 12.5 kg weapon was a thick walled bomb which relied on fragmentation for its destructive effect, some 1,400 splinters being created on impact. In Germany such weapons were known as *Splitterbomben* (Anti-personnel bombs). The larger weapons were thin-walled and relied on the blast effect of their filling to cause damage to the target. These were referred to as *Sprengbomben* (Blast bombs).[46] For safety the bombs were fused so that they would not explode in the event of an accident whilst loading or in flight. The bomb's fins caused the weapon to rotate in free fall from the aircraft. This centrifugal force armed the nose mounted impact fuse.[47] The *PuW* ordnance remained effective throughout the latter stages of the Great War and as such these weapons would form the basis for post-war planning by the *WaA*.

The *Luftstreitkräfte's* widespread employment of specialist close support aircraft *(Schlachtflugzeuge)* from 1917 and particularly in the major battles of 1918 necessitated the development of a range of small anti-personnel weapons to replace the bundles of time-delayed grenades *(Stielhandgranaten)* then in use by the observers of low-flying aircraft. The result was the 1 kg-*Mause* which were dropped in clusters for maximum effect.[48]

Towards the end of the war a number of incendiary bombs were developed to supplement the high explosive ordnance already carried by the *Größflugzeuge* (heavy bombers). These *Brandbomben* included 10 kg designs by the *Karbonit, Traisen* and *Wollersdorf* concerns but a lighter 1 kg design, the B 1 E was preferred for maximum dispersal.[49] The B 1 E *Elektronbrandbombe* was designed to penetrate the roofs of domestic buildings before igniting in the attic cavities. In the final stages of the war an incendiary attack on England by *Bogohl 3* was prepared with these weapons but was ultimately forbidden by *Kaiser* Wilhelm II.[50]

With the exception of chemical warfare measures the development of new types of drop ordnance received scant attention until the late -twenties (See 5C4).[51] However from 1927 the *WaA* was engaged in joint trials of the existing *PuW* ordnance with the Swedish air force *(Flygvapnet)*. The

---

44 Fleischer 2003 p.13 & pp.16-17. Poor aerodynamic shape was also the hall mark of the early British bombs. The Bomb HE, RL 112 lb Mk.I and the improved Mk.III would remain standard weapons for many years - see MacBean J.A. and Hogben A.S. 1990 *Bombs Gone: The development and use of British air-dropped weapons from 1912 to the present day* (hereafter cited as Macbean and Hogben 1990) pp.20-22. The French used modified artillery shells - see Lamberton 1962 p.189.
45 Lamberton 1962 p.189 & Fleischer 2003 p.13.
46 Fleischer 2003 p.15 & pp.18-20.
47 Fleischer 2003 p.15.
48 Fleischer 2003 p.15 & 21.
49 Fleischer 2003 p.15, 18, 20 & 22. Other early bomb manufacturers included *Traisen, Skoda* & *Wollersdorf.*
50 Fleischer 2003 p.15.
51 MacBean and Hogben 1990 p.39. This was also true of most other air arms where stocks of wartime drop ordnance were progressively expended in a series of colonial engagements in Africa, the Middle East and India - see also *Small Wars of the 1920s and 1930s* in Hallion R.P. 1989 *Strike from the Sky: The History of Battlefield Air Attack 1911-1945* pp.55-75.

Swedish armaments firm of *AB Bofors* had a secured a manufacturing licence for these weapons in 1918 and following the formation of the *Flygvapnet* in July 1926 it was decided to modernise the existing force with a number of Nieuport NiD 29 C1 fighters and Fokker C.VE reconnaissance bombers.[52] The Swedish Fokker C.VE were powered by 730 hp Bristol Pegasus radials and as such were representative of the new types of combat aircraft then under secret development in Germany, hence the *WaA's* interest in these service trials (See C2).[53] With the assistance of German personnel from the *Deutsche Versuchsanstalt für Luftfahrt (DVL)* the *Flygvapnet's III.Fliegerkorps* carried out a series of ballistic trials between September 1927 and March 1928. In general the 50 kg *PuW* ordnance performed adequately at lower altitudes but a serious problem was encountered when the bombs were dropped above 4,500 m. The bombs simply disintegrated, only debris reaching the ground. A similar failure occurred with the 300 kg *PuW* bomb. Painstaking investigation revealed that all the bombs had broken up where the tail fins were attached to the conical projectile body. These attachments were reinforced but to no avail. Analysis revealed that torsional stress was the cause, this being induced by the exceptional high rotation of the weapon when dropped from these altitudes.[54]

Whilst these trials were under way preparations were being made at the behest of the *WaA's Waffen Prüfwesen 8F* for a further series of trials at the *Wivupal* at Lipetsk where the Junkers G 24 and Roland Ro VIII airliners were to be tested as *Behelfsbomber* in the summer of 1928 (See 1A3, 1C2 & 1D1). Three different types of *PuW* ordnance were evaluated at Lipetsk, these being 12 kg, 50 kg and 300 kg in weight.[55] For the most part they were filled with a practice material. In addition to the normal impact fuses *(Aufschlagzünder)*, a number of the smaller bombs were armed using *Rheinmetall's* newly developed electrical bomb fuses *(Elektrischer Zunder)*.[56] The Junkers A 35, which was capable of carrying six 12 kg or two 50 kg *PuW* bombs was used to evaluate the smaller ordnance, whilst the larger G 24 and Ro VIII airliners were fitted with external racks for two or three 300 kg *PuW* bombs.[57] During the 1928 test season the auxiliary night bombers each flew some 10 sorties, whilst the A 35 flew a further 8 sorties. The poor performance of the *PuW* ordnance was confirmed, particularly when dropped from heights above 3,500 metres. In 1929 an enlarged test team of twenty men carried out a further series of exhaustive tests focused on new bomb sights, modified bomb release mechanisms and improved bomb fuses. A further 1,200 practice bombs were dropped from the Ro VIII and G 24 as well as from the single engine Dornier Do B *Merkur*[58].

Although the existing *PuW* ordnance had some limited utility of dropped from below 3,500 metres and by slow moving aircraft clearly the time had come for it to be replaced by a new generation of drop ordnance.[59] In any case the *PuW* ordnance was expensive to manufacture and

52   Green W. and Fricker J. 1958 *The Air Forces of the World: Their History, Development and Present Strength* pp.266-267. Following the import of 8 of these aircraft from Fokker in the Netherlands 46 C.VE were built under licence in Sweden. The C.V was one of the most successful combat aircraft of the 20s being widely exported and built under licence in 6 countries - see also Postma 1979 p.61, 64 & pp.68-69 and Morse S. (Ed.) 1982 *The Illustrated Encylopedia of Aircraft* Vol.8 No.93 pp.1858-1859.

53   Fleischer 2003 p.25. The *RWM* paid one half of the licence fees for the manufacture of 100 50 kg *PuW* bombs, the rest being covered by *Bofors* whilst the *Flygvapnet* covered the cost of the flight trials.

54   Fleischer 2003 pp.25-27. The bombs rotated at up to 3,000 rpm when falling from heights above 4,000 m. In essence the bomb had behaved like a spinning top with the greatest forces being applied to the fins which were the weakest component of the bomb. See also Hertel 1955 p.47.

55   Schliephake in Beauvais et al 2002 p.44, 46 & 48.

56   Fleischer 2003 p.29. *Rheinmetall AG* had carried out much of the development work on the new electrical fuses at its Swedish Sommerda facility. The *Chemisch-Technische Reichsanstalt* also played an important part in bringing this equipment to service status.

57   Schliephake in Beauvais et al 2002 p.48. For further information on the Junkers A 35 – see Nowarra 1980 pp.138-139 & Schmitt G. 1988 *Hugo Junkers and his Aircraft* p.124 &157.

58   Schliephake in Beauvais et al 2002 p.48 & Fleischer 2003 p.27.

59   Fleischer 2003 p.27. A number of 12 kg *PuW* bombs had failed to explode when dropped from horizontal racks at

the great length of the larger bombs made it difficult to mount on existing aircraft types. On the 17 January 1930 the *WaA* assigned *Waffen Prüfwesen 1 (Ballistischen-und Munitions)* the following development objectives:[60]

FIGURE 1C-10 Notrüstung (EMERGENCY ARMAMENT) PROGRAMM 1930
Air-dropped *bomben*:
New cylindrical bombs of calibres 10 kg, 50 kg and 300 kg *C-Bomben*.
10 kg bombs of cast-steel fabrication.
Bomben and cylindrical tubes.
Brandbomben (Incendiary bombs).
Gasbomben (Gas Bombs) Details to be established between *Abteilungen Wa Prüf 1* and *Wa Prüf 8*)
Leuchtbomben (Illumination flares)
Fuses (Zunden):
Zeitzünder (Time fuses) for air-dropped bombs
Aufschlagzünder (Impact fuses) for air-dropped bombs
Substitute materials for various fuses.
Ideal solutions:
A 1,000 kg air-dropped bomb.

Concerns over the ballistic shape of air-dropped ordnance coincided with further thinking on the destructive effect of different types of munitions. The *WaA* called for the development of two different types of *Sprengbomben*, a small *Splitterbomb* as well as larger *Minenbomben* (High-explosive bombs).[61] It had been recognised that static targets such as buildings suffered more from blast as a result of the shock waves that emanated from the detonation of the high explosive than the explosive disintegration of the bomb itself.[62] Such a requirement favoured a short, cylindrical-shaped body which coincidentally had better ballistic properties and was easier to manufacture than the earlier *PuW* weapons. The new *Sprengbombe-Cylindrische (SC)* ordnance had a body length approximately one third of that of the earlier *PuW* weapons. Each bomb consisted on three parts: a nose portion, a cylindrical body, and a short tail end complete with stabilising fins. The early weapons were made from welded sheets of rolled steel plate. Mechanical nose fuses were employed for the SC 10 *Splitterbomben*, whilst electrical nose fuses were used for the larger SC 50 and 250 *Sprengbomben*.[63]

---

low altitude. For future use it was decided to carry these weapons vertically in internal magazines each holding 5 bombs.

60   Fleischer 2003 p.28.

61   Hertel 1955 pp.47-48 & Fleischer 2003 pp.28-29. German bomb design in the post-war period was heavily influenced by developments in the USA where the destructive effect of thin cased bombs had become apparent in the staged bombing of former capital ships. The US authorities had also adopted unstreamlined cylindrical cases which proved to have superior ballistic properties.

62   Macbean and Hogben 1990 pp.74-80 & 83-85. The British would later develop a range of High Capacity (HC) bombs to maximise blast effect in area attacks on German cities. Bombs with a similar Charge to Weight ratio (CWR) to that used in the SC ordnance were referred to as Medium Capacity bombs (MC) by the RAF. The British relied heavily on their range of General Purpose (GP) ordnance for most bombing operations despite their poor CWR of only 23-30%.

63   Fleischer 2003 pp.32-33. The British Air Ministry had in fact ordered a new range of General Purpose bombs as

In 1929 the *Truppenamt* authorised the expenditure of RM 30,000 for the development and testing of the new *C-Bomben*. Orders were placed for 200 SC 10, 100 SC 50 and 25 SC 250 weapons.[64] Following delivery the effectiveness of these weapons were evaluated at *Wivupal* under the direction of *Dipl.Ing.*Ernst Marquard, *Referat 2b* within *Wa.Prüf.8F*, in a series of trials beginning in the summer of 1930 (See 1D1).[65] Initial trials focused on the ballistic properties of the newly developed *SC* ordnance and the smooth jettisoning of these weapons from their carrier aircraft - in this case two Junkers W 33 aircraft that had been specially prepared for this role.[66] Although these trials were largely successful there were some problems with both the mechanical and electrical fuses which were later resolved. In 1931 the focus moved to low level attacks with both the SC 10 and SC 50 below a height of 100 m. using the Arado SD IV fighter and Heinkel HD 45 light reconnaissance bomber, whilst trials were also pursued with the horizontally mounted SC 250 from a greater altitude using a Junkers W 34. Finally in 1932 the oversized SC 500 Minenbomb were tested, again from horizontal racks, whilst the smaller weapons were grouped together to form cluster munitions.[67] Four SC 10 could be grouped using a GR 4 C-10 cradle, whilst 36 of the wartime B 1 E Elektronbrandbomben could be released from a Brandbomben-Schuttkasten BSK 36 canister to achieve a greater density of incendiary munitions on the target. It was also concluded that vertical suspension by the nose of the bomb would be advantageous in the case of the SC 50 and SC 250, this arrangement becoming standard aboard the Dornier Do F (Do 11) *Nachtbomber* which could be fitted with four Zwimag 5 C 50 magazines and four NHC 250 racks. Sixteen SC 10 could be stacked in an internal Sammelmagazinen Samag 16 C 10/V bomb magazine within the fuselage of the HD 45 whilst the HE 46 and Ar 65 were fitted with a double magazine for six SC 10 Splitterbomben - the Zwillingsmagazinen Zwimag 6 C 10 (See also 1C3).[68]

The later success of the *SC* ordnance can be attributed to their good ballistic properties, their highly efficient explosive filling and their novel electrical fusing system.[69] In 1926 Herbert Ruhlemann of the *Rheinmetall* concern had been assigned the task of developing the electrical fusing

early as 1921 but with little funding and no clear threat development was protracted. Limited production began in 1925 with a CWR of 23%. Later developments had a slightly higher CWR. Interestingly the British GP bomb had a streamlined shaped not unlike the PuW ordnance although the weapons were much shorter in length. The tail fins were enclosed by a ring for greater stability and overall security from accidental damage in handling - see Macbean and Hogben 1990 pp.47-48.

64   Hertel 1955 pp.47-48 & Fleischer 2003 p.32.

65   Service record for Ernst Marquard in Hildebrand K.F.1991 *Die Generale der deutschen Luftwaffe 1935-1945 Band 2 H-N* pp.356-357. A former military aviator who had completed his fighter pilot training too late to see war service, Ernst Marquard had been discharged on the 20 Jan 19. He had then studied at the *Maschinenbau-Studium* at the *Technischen-Hochschule Stuttgart* receiving his *Diplom-Ingenieur* on the 6 Jul 22. Following employment with the *Allgemeinen Vergaser-Gesellschaft* he had entered *Reichsdienst* in Oct 24 where his speciality was chemical weapons and drop ordnance. From Jun 26 he was assigned to *Wa.Prw.6F* as *Referat IIc*, whilst from Apr 27 he had been *Referat IIb* within the *WaA's Wa.Prüf.9*.

66   Schliephake in Beauvais et al 2002 p.48.

67   Kosin 1983 p.60, Fleischer 2003 pp.32-33 & Schliephake in Beauvais et al 2002 p.48. The over-sized SC 500 was intended for shipping attack - see Hertel 1955 p.47.

68   Hertel 1955 p.50, Fleischer 2003 p.33 & Koos V. 2006 *Typenbucher Deutsche Luftfahrt: Ernst Heinkel Flugzeugwerke 1922-1932* (hereafter cited as Koos 2006) p.107 & 109. A total of six SC 10 could be carried by the SD IV fighter, probably in a *Zwimag* 6 C 10 - see Kosin 1983 p.73.

69   Macbean and Hogben 1990 p.83. It would not be until the German attacks on Britain during 1940-41 that the British finally realised that the *SC* Ordnance were about twice as effective as British equivalent bombs weight for weight. This was entirely due to the superiority of the German high explosive filling. Thereafter British bombs were filled with much more powerful explosives such as RDX, Torpex, Amatex & Minol - see also *Annex 4 Bombs and Bombsights* in Webster C. and Frankland N. 1961 *The Strategic Air Offensive against Germany Vol.IV Annexes and Appendices* pp.31-34 & *App.C The Progress of Armament:Section I – H.E. Bombs – H.E.Fillings* in Harris A.T. ACM 1995 *Despatch on War Operations 23rd February 1942 to 8th May 1945* (Herafter cited as Harris 1995) p.94.

system for air-dropped weapons at Sommerda in Sweden.[70] Recent developments in electronics had resulted in the commercial availability of condensers (capacitors), devices that could be used to store an electrical charge. This allowed the fuse to be charged at the moment of release from the aircraft effectively priming the bomb for an impact detonation or for a time delay if this was desired. As the bomb dropped clear of the aircraft an electrical resistance in the fuse caused a short delay before the voltage became strong enough to arm the weapon.[71] This ensured a clean separation from the aircraft. Provided that the main switch to the aircraft's bomb arming fuse box was switched off this method also reduced the risk of accidental detonation whilst the weapons were being loaded onto their racks, whilst the aircraft was on the ground, and during take-off and flight. If necessary bombs could also be jettisoned unarmed without major risk to friendly forces.[72]

C. BOMB AND GUN SIGHTS

The major problem for all bombing operations was the accurate calculation of the time that it would take for a bomb to fall from the bombing aircraft to the ground and of the distance that the aircraft would therefore move during that same period. Clearly to achieve a direct hit on the target the observer would have to release his bombs well before the point at which the aircraft was immediately above its objective.[73] There were two different solutions to this increasingly complex problem: mechanical drift sights which were favoured by the British and optical telescopic sights that were favoured by the Germans.[74] At the end of the Great War the *Luftstreitkräfte's* bombers were equipped with either *Zeiss* or *Goerz* prismatic sights for daytime or nocturnal operations respectively. In the case of the *Zeiss* telescopic sight the observer *(Beobachter)* would start by observing how long it took a known landmark to pass through his sights. Mathematical tables were then consulted to find a sight setting when set against the known altitude of the bomber.[75] This gave the desired release point.

Great War bombers were comparatively slow and bombed from medium levels. However by the late twenties both the cruising speed of bombers and their operating altitudes had steadily increased and this required greater sophistication in terms of the bomb sighting equipment.[76] The optical instrument firm of *Goerz* continued to develop its wartime bomb sights to keep pace with these developments and a number were exported to the USSR and to Japan.[77] From 1930 four different models of the *Goerz* bomb sight were tested at Lipetsk (See also 1C3 & 1D1). These were the Goerz-Boykow Fl 213 sighting periscope which was intended for naval use aboard the HD 59 *Mehrzweckflugzeug* (Multi-Role Aircraft), the Fl.218 and 220 *Richtenfernrohr* sights which were tested aboard the HD 41b *Aufklärungsflugzeuge* (Reconnaissance Aircraft) and the Goerz Fl

---

70   Fleischer 2003 pp.32-33. The British in common with other air forces continued to use mechanical fuses or pistols. These were generally tail mounted and consisted of a wind driven vane that unwound as the bomb dropped clear of the aircraft to arm the weapon - see *App.2 British Bomb Pistols and Fuzes* in Macbean and Hogben 1990 pp.287-293 & *App.C The Progress of Armament:Section IV – Fuzes and Pistols* in Harris 1995 pp.96-97.

71   *Bombs and other missiles dropped on the U.K. 1940-1945* in Ramsey W.G. (Ed.) 1987 *The Blitz Then and Now Vol.1* pp.147-177 & *Abwurfmunition (Air-Dropped Weapons)* in Fleischer 2003 pp.137-184.

72   Fleischer 2003 p.33.

73   Odhams Press Undated *Britain's Wonderful Fighting Forces* pp.54-55.

74   Lamberton 1962 pp.190-191. In 1918 the RAF used the High Altitude Drift Sight Mk.Ia on its Handley Page 0/400 heavy night bombers. This sight consisted of a complex framework of metal slides that could be adjusted to allow for the height of the aircraft above the target, the wind velocity and the aircraft's drift when flying across the wind.

75   Lamberton 1962 p.191 & Woodman in Jarrett (Ed.) 1997 pp.191-192.

76   Hooton E. *Military Aviation - the Slow Developer* in Jarrett (Ed.) 1997 pp.61-63.

77   Woodman in Jarret (Ed.) 1997 pp.191-192.

219 mechanical sight for night bombing which was to be employed aboard the Do F *Nachtbomber* (Night Bomber).[78] The telescopic *Zeiss* Lotfernrohr 6 bomb sight was also evaluated (See 3C4).[79]

The problems of accurately taking aim at an enemy aircraft during air combat manoeuvres was largely solved by the *Luftstreitkräfte* through the adoption of the ring and bead sight.[80] Interestingly German pilots preferred the ring sight to be located at the muzzle end of the machine gun with the bead forming the back sight; the British used a ring back sight and a bead foresight.[81] The ring sight allowed an experienced pilot to allow sufficient deflection or "lead" for a target that was crossing in front of his own aircraft. For example for an enemy aircraft crossing at right angles at a speed of 160 kph (100 mph) at a range of 183 m (200 yds) the target should be placed on edge of the outer ring with the bead centred within the small ring at the centre of the sight. Bullets fired at this distance would take 0.254 seconds to reach the target by which time it would have moved forward 11.5 m.[82]

In 1917 the British began to replace its existing ring and bead sights with the new Aldis Sight.[83] Although this looked like a telescope, and was often reported as such, it was in fact a collimeter optical gun sight which magnified the view through the sighting tube and simultaneously placed an aiming mark or reticule (graticule) in the centre of the eyepiece. Once again concentric circles allowed the pilot to estimate the amount of lead required for the bullets to actually hit the target aircraft.[84] Although captured Aldis sights were much prized by German pilots who fitted them to their own machines, the collimeter sight, manufactured in Germany by *Optische Antal Oigee*, was used by the *Luftstreitkräfte* mainly in conjunction with the MG 13 Parabellum on flexible mountings.[85]

In 1918 the optical instrument makers *Oigee* of Berlin introduced the world's first operational reflector gun sight. This was an extension of the collimated sight in that the reticule or aiming mark was projected by a light source onto an inclined glass screen in front of the pilot's eyes. This had the advantage of not restricting his vision to a telescopic view of the world ahead. In later types of sight it would also allow the pilot to adjust the reticule to conform with the known wing span of the target aircraft thus informing him when the target was at the optimum range.[86] *Oigee* introduced two different sights, one for day and night use and a smaller one purely for night use. Examples of the larger sight were allocated to *Jasta 12* which was employed at a variety of points on the Western Front where they were fitted to the unit's Albatros D-Va and Fokker Dr.I *Jagdflugzeuge* for operational trials.[87]

78   Koos 2006 pp.124-125. The Goerz Fl.219 bomb sight was specifically intended for night operation - see Hertel 1955 p.48.

79   Hertel 1955 p.48 & Fleischer 2003 p.33 & 36. See also Schliephake in Beauvais et al 2002 p.48.

80   Wallace Clarke 1994. Both the German and British air arms had initially used a variant of the naval "gate" sight. This was a rectangular frame divided by a single horizontal and two vertical wires. The gap between the two vertical wires was set so that the wing span of an enemy aircraft filled it at a known range. This avoided the excessive use of ammunition when the target was out of range. The gate sight was mounted on the muzzle end of the machine gun with a bead backsight on the gun casing. Gate sights were widely used aboard the Fokker Eindecker fighters of 1915 - see also Hoffschmidt 1969.

81   Wallace Clarke 1994 pp.121-123.

82   Wallace Clarke 1994 p.122. For the evolution of air combat tactics during the Great War - see Johnson J.E. 1964 *Full Circle: The Story of Air Fighting* pp.19-99.

83   Wallace Clarke 1994 pp.129-132. The Aldis Sight had been submitted for testing in 1915 and was issued for operational trials with selected front-line squadrons in mid 1916 where it received the highest praise.

84   Wallace Clarke 1994 p.131.

85   Wallace Clarke 1994 pp.135-136. Other types of gun sight were employed by the *Luftstreitkräfte* in the closing stages of the war. One such example was the Busch ZF 12 which was again used in conjunction with the MG 14 Parabellum - see Imrie 1971 p.147.

86   Wallace Clarke 1994 pp.135-136. *Oigee's* design was based on the patented work of Sir Howard Grubb. A Vickers Mallock reflector sight was evaluated in 1915 but no further development was undertaken despite the success of the trials - see also Woodman in Jarrett (Ed.) 1997 p.191.

87   Imrie 1971 p.152 & Wallace Clarke 1994 p.136. *Jasta 12* was commanded by Lt.Hermann Becker *(23 Luftsiege)* -

Although forbidden by the Armistice to engage in aerial armament development *Oigee* did continue to improve its basic reflector gun sight during the twenties. The result was the Oigee Electrische Nivellier Instrument which was offered for export in the early thirties. The ENI sight underwent operational tests with the 17th Pursuit Group at McCook Field and it was also fitted to a number of other types. The design was considered so good that it became the basis for American Type N reflector sight which was adopted for service use as the N-2 in 1936.[88] Meanwhile in Germany the *Flugtechnik Referat* had selected an alternative design by *Zeiss* for covert production as the Reflexnivier Revi 1 reflector gun sight for use with the Fokker D.XIII fighters at Lipetsk (See 1D1).[89]

Interestingly such post-war types as the Heinkel HD 17 and Albatros L 76 not only used British Vickers-Scarff type rotatable gun mounts *(Drehkranz 29)* but also Norman vane sights in preference to the wartime German gun mounts and the Oigee Collimeter Sight.[90] The vane sight was a novel solution to the growing problem of increased air speed which made it more difficult for gunners to accurately allow for the speed of their own aircraft when shooting at an attacking fighter approaching from the beam or quarter. In 1915 Lt.G.H.Norman of the RFC had introduced a novel solution to this problem in the form of a swivelling foresight which was deflected by small vanes that reacted to the slipstream of the gunner's aircraft.[91] This concept was steadily refined and the vane sight was subsequently exported widely. Together with the reflector gun sight it would become standard equipment within the secret *Fliegertruppe* during the twenties and early thirties.

    see Franks N., Bailey F. and Duiven R. 1996 *The Jasta Pilots: Detailed listings and histories August 1916 - November 1918* pp.26-27.

88   Wallace Clarke 1994 p.141.

89   Ries 1970 p.87 & Wallace Clarke 1994 pp.139-141. However another authoritative source attributes the new reflector sights to *Oigee* - see Hertel 1955 p.46.

90   Hertel 1955 p.46. The Drehkranzes 29 was also used on early examples of the HD 45 & HE 46.

91   Kosin 1983 p.69 & Wallace Clarke 1994 pp.123-125.

1D1

The Fliegerschule Stahr and the Flugzentrum Lipetsk

Clandestine developments in the Soviet Union 1923-1933

The establishment of a military mission in the USSR during the early twenties marked the first stage in a new and productive German-Soviet relationship following the trials and tribulations of the Great War.[1] As an initial step a small number of *Reichswehr* officers under the direction of *Obst.*Otto Hasse, the newly appointed *Chef der Truppenamt (Chief of the Troop Office)*, visited the industrial and service centres of the Red Army in February 1923 as part of a secret fact-finding tour (See 1A2); the need for secrecy and deception were features that were to characterise all the intricate agreements that were to follow over a period of more than a decade.[2] Not surprisingly given the ferocity and extent of the civil war which had raged unabated from the revolution in 1917 they found a nation in disarray. The emergent *Raboche-Krestyanskogo Krasnogo Vozdushnogo Flota (RKKVF)* (Workers' and Peasants' Red Air Fleet) was in a particularly parlous state as most of its heterogeneous collection of aircraft was obsolete and the Bolsheviks had inherited very few experienced pilots from the former Imperial Russian Flying Corps.[3]

A.V.Sergeev, the Head of the *GU-RKKVF* from February 1921 until March 1923, was therefore anxious to regenerate the Soviet aircraft industry which had all but collapsed.[4] The acquisition of new

---

1   Barraclough G. (Ed.) 1978 *The Times Atlas of World History* pp.258-259. Fatally weakened by the strain of 3 years of costly and largely unsuccessful military operations the Tsarist Government effectively collapsed with the abdication of Tsar Nicholas II on the 15 Mar 17. A period of ineffective interim government followed until an abortive military coup in Sep 17 was followed by a more successful Bolshevik uprising under the general leadership of Leonid Lenin in Oct 17. Anxious to disengage in the east the return of Lenin from exile in Switzerland had been largely engineered by the Germans. A peace treaty followed at Brest-Litovsk in Mar 18 that enabled the Germans to reinforce the embattled Western Front with powerful forces from the east. This made the initially successful German offensive of Apr 18 possible. Meanwhile in Russia civil war broke out between the Bolshevik (Red) Forces and the Monarchist (White) Forces. These battles, together with British and French intervention on the White side, would continue until 1921.

2   Mason H.M. 1973 *The Rise of the Luftwaffe 1918-1940* (hereafter cited as Mason 1973) p.103, Hooton E.R. 1994 *Phoenix Triumphant: The Rise and Rise of the Luftwaffe* (hereafter cited as Hooton 1994) p.44 & Vercamer A. and Pipes J. *German Military in the Soviet Union 1918-1933* in www.feldgrau.com. (hereafter cited as Vercamer and Pipes Undated). See also Suchenwirth R. 1968 *The Development of the German Air Force 1919-1939* USAF Historical Studies No.160 (hereafter cited as Suchenwirth 1968) pp.11-13. Otto Hasse was *Chef d.Truppenamt* from Feb 23-Oct 25 and as such was mainly responsible for the establishment of German bases in the USSR. He was *Bfr.WK III* Berlin from Feb 26-Apr 29 & finally *KomGen.Gr.Kdo.1* from Apr 29-Sep 32 as a *Gen.d.Inf.* - see service record for Otto Hasse in Pipes Undated in www.axishistory.com. One of the officers who accompanied Hasse was *Hptm.*Kurt Student, the *Flugtechnikreferat* within the *HWA* - see service record for Kurt Student in Hildebrand K.F.1992 *Die Generale der deutschen Luftwaffe 1935-1945 Band 3 O-Z* (hereafter cited as Hildebrand 1992) pp.363-365.

3   Boyd A. 1977 *The Soviet Air Force since 1918* (hereafter cited as Boyd 1977) pp.5-6. By their nature most Imperial officers were monarchists and had supported the White Forces. On the 1 Oct 23 the *RKKVF* had a strength of 322 aircraft, including 36 naval machines.

4   Boyd 1977 pp.6-7. By the end of 1920 when no new aircraft or engines were actually completed, the workforce

combat aircraft was a vital component of this programme and in the short term it was acknowledged that despite the political and economic problems that such a policy would induce this equipment would have to be purchased from abroad. To begin with domestic production centred on types already in service and the R-1 reconnaissance bomber, a Soviet derivative of the Airco DH 9, was built at the state aircraft factories in Moskva (GAZ-1) and Taganrog (GAZ-10), whilst the U-1, a Soviet copy of the ubiquitous Avro 504K trainer, was produced at another factory in the capital (GAZ-5).[5] The Soviets were also anxious for the Germans to establish manufacturing facilities for both aircraft and aero-engines in the USSR, and as early as July 1921 the *Reichsheer's Sondergruppe "R"* (Special Group Russia) had opened covert negotiations with the *Junkers Flugzeugwerke GmbH* at Dessau (See 1C1).[6]

German military assistance was also provided and during 1924 seven former *Luftstreitkräfte* officers including *Hauptleute.a.D.*Schondorff and Martin Fiebig were attached to the *VVS (Voenno-vozdushnye sili)* (Soviet Air Force), whilst other former *Fliegeroffiziere* formed the staff of the air command school at Borisoglebsk.[7] Only the most promising Soviet flight students were sent to this school where formation leaders received both practical and theoretical training. From time-to-time courses in bad-weather and night flying were also held at this establishment.[8]

Meanwhile events in Germany during 1922-23 had only served to emphasise the urgent need for clandestine weapons training together with development facilities for the emergent *Reichsheer* and to handle the frustratingly protracted negotiations with the Soviet authorities Seeckt ordered the formation of the *Zentrale Moskau (Z.Mo.)* (Moscow Centre) (See 1A2).[9] The first leader of the *Zentrale* was the very experienced *Obst.i.G.*Hermann von der Lieth-Thomsen who was recalled on the basis of his proven administrative skills and his thorough knowledge of military aviation.[10] Both he, and his equally talented deputy, *Maj.i.G.*Oskar Ritter von Niedermayer from the *Sondergruppe R (Russland)*, were carried on the inactive list *(a.D.)* for their service in the Soviet Union as part of

available for aviation within the USSR totalled just 3,500 men and this figure would decline further during 1921. In 1922 Soviet production would total 43 airframes and 8 engines (*GU - Glavnoe upravlenie* - Chief Directorate).

5   Boyd 1977 pp.7-8. The U-1 was an unlicensed copy of the Avro 504K - 737 would be built at *GAZ-5 Moscow* & *GAZ-23 Leningrad* between 1923-3 (*GAZ - Gosudararstvenny aviatsionny zavod*).

6   Mason 1973 p.103 & Schmitt G. 1988 *Hugo Junkers and his Aircraft* (hereafter cited as Schmitt 1988) p.132.

7   Zeidler M. 1994 *Reichswehr und Rote Armee 1920-1933* (hereafter cited as Zeidler 1994) & Schliephake H. *Secret Flight Testing in Lipetsk, Russia* in Beauvais H., Kossler K., Mayer M. and Regel C. 2002 *German Secret Flight Test Centres to 1945: Johannisthal, Lipetsk, Rechlin, Travemünde, Tarnewitz, Peenemunde-West* (hereafter cited as Schliephake in Beauvais et al 2002) p.42. *Hptm.a.D.*Martin Fiebig is thought to have eventually become an instructor within the command faculty of the *Zhukovski* Air Force Engineering Academy in Moscow. This started a four year command programme in 1923 but was closed in 1927 - see Boyd 1977 p.11 & Corum J.S. 1997 *The Luftwaffe: Creating the Operational Air War 1918-1940* (hereafter cited as Corum 1997) p.75. Fiebig was an experienced bomber pilot. He flew with *Bogohl 3* over England and eventually commanded *Bogohl 9* - see service record for Martin Fiebig in Hildebrand K.F.1990 *Die Generale der deutschen Luftwaffe 1935-1945 Band 1 A-G* (hereafter cited as Hildebrand 1990) pp.280-281. *Hptm.*Schondorff remained with the *VVS-RKKA* until 1931 - see Hooton 1994 p.47.

8   Boyd 1977 p.24.

9   Shirer W.L. 1969 *The Collapse of the Third Republic: An Inquiry into the Fall of France in 1940* pp.146-148 & Mason 1973 p.103 & pp.120-124. This culminated in the Franco-Belgian military occupation of the Ruhr in Jan 23 to secure unpaid war reparations, an event that was quickly followed by economic meltdown and hyperinflation.

10   Suchenwirth 1968 p.13 & Hooton 1994 p.44. *Obst.i.G.*Hermann von der Lieth-Thomsen had been *GenLt.*Ernst von Hoeppner's *Chef des Generalstabs* within the wartime *Luftstreitkrafte.* An outstanding officer, he had been instrumental in the wartime success of German military aviation for which he was decorated with the *Plm* on the 8 Apr 17 - see Hoeppner von, E. W. 1921 *Germany's War in the Air: The Development and Operations of German Military Aviation in the World War* pp.34-36, 40 & 78-80 and Imrie A. 1971 *Pictorial History of the German Army Air Service* pp.26-27, 31-32 & 39-40 and Angolia J.R. and Hackney C.R. 1984 *The Pour le Mérite and Germany's First Aces* (hereafter cited as Angolia and Hackney 1984) pp.126-127 & service record for Hermann von der Lieth Thomsen in Hildebrand K.F.1991 *Die Generale der deutschen Luftwaffe 1935-1945 Band 2 H-N* (hereafter cited as Hildebrand 1991) pp.296-297. Lieth-Thomsen was appointed *Chef Z.Mo.* on the 20 Sep 23 and arrived in Moskva on the 13 Nov 23 - see Hooton 1994 p.44.

an elaborate commercial cover for their negotiations with high-ranking officers of the *GU-VVS*.[11] In fact an agreement took more than three years to reach, delayed in part by an on-going struggle for power within both the *GU-VVS* and the highest echelons of the Soviet state, and it was not until the 15 April 1925 that Lieth-Thomsen finally signed an understanding with Pyotr Ionovich Baranov, the new Head of the *GU-VVS*, and work could begin on the first of three planned secret German facilities in the east.[12] Lieth-Thomsen's contact in Berlin was *Hptm.a.D.*Veit Fischer.[13]

The site chosen for the secret air base had of necessity to be remote from major centres of population but at the same time it had to be on the main railway system and the airfield had to have access to military training areas where low-level flying could take place unnoticed by outside observers. One of the locations that met all these requirements was near to Lipetsk, a small town beside the River Voronezh, some 100 kms north of that regional centre and over 350 kms south of the capital.[14] *Maj.a.D.*Walter Stahr, the *Reichswehr's* commander designate, first visited the site in March 1924 and a development contract was signed with the Soviet authorities on the 15 April.[15] Work on extending the existing facilities occupied much of the remainder of that year and with further improvements in subsequent years the facility, which was initially given the cover-name *Fliegerschule Stahr*, soon took on the appearance of a thoroughly modern air base and test centre *(Photo 1D-1)*:

11   Suchenwirth 1968 p.13. Niedermayer was an outstanding staff officer who had been knighted for his services during the Great War. He had served briefly in the *RWM* post-war but had been retained as a civilian employee where his extensive knowledge of languages made him very useful in delicate and sensitive negotiations abroad whilst working on behalf of the Ministry. Retired officers were put on the *ausser Dienst (a.D.)*. The *Sondergruppe R* was established within the *Truppenamt* in Dec 20 with responsibility for all future contacts with the Soviet authorities. *Obst.*Walther Nicolai was *Chef Sondergruppe R*. The Treaty of Rapello which was signed on the 16 Apr 22 was the formal basis for the development of German test facilities in the USSR. These secret agreements with the Red Army had the full support of *Reichspräsident* Ebert, *Reichskanzlers* Wirth and Cuno as well as their *Reichswehrministers* - see Seaton A. 1982 *The German Army 1933-1945* p.8.

12   Boyd 1977 pp.18-21 & Hooton 1994 p.15. In addition to being Head of the Chief Directorate of the *GU-VVSRKKA*, Baranov was Head of the newly created Chief Directorate for the aircraft industry - the *GUAP*. The combination of these posts had been instigated by Trotski and had the full support of Frunze. Baranov's deputy Yakov Ivanovich Aksnis was a key player on the Soviet side of these agreements, Aksnis was a German speaker who had already visited Germany on a number of occasions on military business. In 1927 he would visit Germany to study aircraft and aero-engine developments and engineering techniques. He was also responsible for the contractual negotiations with the *Ernst Heinkel Flugzeugwerke AG* for the HD 43 fighter & HD 55 flying boat - see also Heinkel E. 1956 *He 1000* pp.115-116 & Koos V. 2006 *Typenbucher Deutsche Luftfahrt: Ernst Heinkel Flugzeugwerke 1922-1932* (hereafter cited as Koos 2006) pp.103-104 & 115-116.

13   *App. German Military Aviation, 1919-1933* in Cooper M. 1981 *The German Air Force 1933-1945: An Anatomy of Failure* p.381. Veit Fischer had been associated with the *bayerischen Fliegertruppe* from Mar 15. He was trained as an observer at Schleißheim in 1915/16 and served with *Kasta 34*, prior to being appointed *Fhr.Kasta 38*. He then specialised in wireless (FT) and saw service in Turkey with the *Fl.Abt.Pascha II & 304b*. Post war he served with the *bayerischen Luftpolizei* - see service record for Veit Fischer in Hildebrand 1990 pp.292-293.

14   Kreipe W. Gen.d.Flg.a.D. and Koester R. Obst.a.D. 1955 *Technical Training within the German Luftwaffe* USAF Historical Studies No.169 (hereafter cited as Kreipe and Koester 1955) p.14, Ries K. 1970 *Luftwaffe Bd.1 Die Maulwurfe 1919-1935* (hereafter cited as Ries 1970) p.80, Schliephake H. 1971 *The Birth of the Luftwaffe* (hereafter cited as Schliephake 1971) pp.16-17 & Mason 1973 pp.151-152. The *Reichswehr* had originally been offered a combined sea and land site near Odessa on the Black Sea coast. However as the *Reichsmarine* had already concluded a secret agreement with the Swedish Navy it had no use for test facilities in the USSR. The *Reichsheer* preferred a more remote inland site for security reasons.

15   Schliephake in Beauvais et al 2002 p.42. *Maj.a.D.*Walter Stahr was a pre-war military aviator who had served as a *Beobachter* with *Feld-Fl.Abt.2 & 25* and as *Fhr.Feld-Fl.Abt.2* prior to his appointment as *Fl.Gr.Fhr.3* (Apr 15), *KoFl AOK 7* (Feb 17) & *KoFl AOK 17* (Jan 18). In the *Reichswehr* he had been a *Flieger-Referent in T 4 Ausbildungs* (Apr 20) and a *Flieger-Referent b.Stab.3.Division* Berlin (Dec 20-Dec 22). He had been discharged with the rank of *Maj.* on the 31 Dec 22 - see service record for Walter Stahr in Hildebrand 1992 pp.341-342. Stahr was accompanied by *Lt.a.D.*Heinz Frhr.von Beaulieu-Marconnay, formerly of *Jasta 65* - see also Franks N., Bailey F. and Duiven R. 1996 *The Jasta Pilots: Detailed listings and histories August 1916 - November 1918* (hereafter cited as Franks et al 1996) p.97.

Around two runways there came into being a large complex of hangars, wharves, production and repair shops...There were administrative and living quarters, a hospital equipped with the most modern clinical apparatus, wireless and telephone installations, railway connections and so forth. The German flyers' colony was quartered in the wide area of the aerodrome, which was highly modern according to the standards of the time, camouflaged on the outside to give the impression (that the buildings belonged to) the *4th.Eskadrilya* of the *VVS*. The whole complex was sealed off and guarded by Soviet militia.[16]

*Gen.d.Flg.a.D.*Wilhelm Speidel
Flugschuler Fliegerschule Stahr 1928

*Maj.a.D.*Stahr was appointed *Kommandant* at Lipetsk in March 1925.[17] This experienced officer being responsible for the day-to-day management of the facility, overall supervision of the training courses and experimental work, and for the immediate liaison with the resident *VVS* staff.[18] It had been agreed in Moskva that Soviet personnel were to be given full access to the test programme, whilst courses were also conducted on their behalf by German instructors. Much of this work centred on the maintenance of modern airframes and aero-engines and was therefore of a technical nature, the *GU-VVS* placing considerable value on this access to the latest aviation technology. The objectives of *Flugzentrum Lipetsk* were defined as:[19]

FLUGZENTRUM LIPETSK OBJECTIVES

- Training of flying personnel to become fighter pilots and instructors *(Jagdlehrer)*
- Training of aircraft technical personnel *(Flugtechnisches Personal)*
- Conducting courses for fighter pilots *(Jagdflieger-Lehrgange)*
- Conducting courses for aircrew observers *(Beobachter-Lehrgange)*
- Conducting tactical and technical combat testing of military aircraft *(Waffen Prüfwesens - Versuchsgruppe)*
- Accumulating experience of a tactical, technical and organisational nature in all regimes

The position of Lipetsk, deep within the continental interior, also brought the permanent staff into intimate contact with the extremes of the Russian climate. Overall precipitation was low and mainly in the form of summer storms, but the temperature range was high with an annual variation of 27 C. At least three months recorded average temperatures below freezing and this effectively restricted the training programme to a six month period beginning in April each year *(Photo 1D-2)*.[20]

---

16 Quoted from Mason 1973 *The Rise of the Luftwaffe 1918-1940* p.152 with the knowledge of the Orion Publishing Group. *Rittm.*Wilhelm Speidel was a *Flugschuler* at Lipetsk from Apr 28-Jan 29. It would appear that he actually learned to fly during this period as he was not an *Alte Adler*. Speidel would travel to the USA on behalf of *T 3 Fremde Heeres* in the following year and would spend 12 months with the *USAAC* on a fact finding tour - see service record for Wilhelm Speidel in Hildebrand 1992 pp.320-322. For further details of the construction works at Lipetsk - see Suchenwirth 1968 p.27.

17 Service record for Walter Stahr in Hildebrand 1992 pp.341-342. The school was not opened until Aug 25. The selection of a combat officer with proven leadership experience as opposed to an officer with school experience indicates the emphasis placed by *Hptm.*Helmuth Wilberg's *TA (L)* on tactical training and developmental testing at Lipetsk - see Corum 1997 pp.115-118.

18 Schliephake 1971 pp.16-17.

19 Schliephake 1971 p.18 & Schliephake in Beauvais et al 2002 p.42. See also Vercamer and Pipes Undated.

20 Shackleton M.R. 1939 *Europe: A Regional Geography* pp.22-24 & p.27. During the winter months the climate of European Russia is affected by the Siberian High which reduces the impact of the winter cyclonic activity that

There was therefore some variation in the number of German personnel at Lipetsk at different times of the year:

> The German personnel consisted of a permanent party that remained at Lipetsk throughout the year, numbering about sixty men. In addition there were about fifty men making up the personnel of the military training courses, held during the summer months; and finally, there were between seventy and a hundred men engaged in technical experiments. Thus there were, on an average, about two hundred Germans always present during the summer. The VVS was represented at Lipetsk by a fairly large number of soldiers who were trained in special technical courses by German instructors, both foremen and mechanics...[21]

Gen.d.Flg.a.D. Wilhelm Speidel
Flugschuler Fliegerschule Stahr 1928

Arrangements for the delivery of the fifty Fokker D.XIII fighters were undertaken on behalf of the *Reichswehr* by the prominent Hamburg industrialist Hugo Stinnes (See 1A2).[22] The completed aircraft were disassembled for shipment by sea from the Ostsee port of Stettin to Leningrad aboard the freighter *Edmund Hugo Stinnes 4* on the 28 May 1925. On arrival in the Soviet Union the shipping crates were then placed, unopened, in sealed and guarded railway box-cars for the final 1,000 kms journey via Moskva to Lipetsk where they arrived in June.[23] Unfortunately several cases of serious damage then came to light and the repair and flight testing of the D.XIII fighters occupied the remainder of that year's flying season.[24] The multi-national nature of this important consignment did not escape comment on the part of the young students who were later to fly these advanced fighter aircraft. Wolfgang Falck would later recall that this Dutch aircraft with its British engine and Spanish instruments had been intended for an undisclosed South American customer before its acquisition by the German authorities. A truly cosmopolitan enterprise.[25]

Test flying and refresher training was carried out during the late summer of 1925 with the aim of producing sufficient instructors for the first fighter course which had been scheduled for the following year.[26] *Oblt.a.D.*Werner Junck, a former *Reichswehr* officer, had been selected as

dominates western Europe. The skies are generally cloudy but there is very little water vapour and the result is less precipitation. Remoteness from the warming influence of the Atlantic Ocean also causes far lower temperatures in winter than are experienced at points for the same latitude further west. Lipetsk (52 45 N) is almost on the same latitude as Berlin & Birmingham but during Dec, Jan & Feb mean monthly temperatures are consistently below 0 C. In Mar temperature fluctuate around 0 C but rise quickly in April to around 10 C. Thereafter remoteness from the ocean has the opposite effect. Temperatures rise to around 20 C in generally clear skies although the incidence of convectional activity increases with heavy, sometimes thundery, showers. The wettest months are July & August but overall precipitation totals c.670 mm or slightly more then Berlin.

21   Quoted from Mason 1973 *The Rise of the Luftwaffe 1918-1940* p.152 with the knowledge of the Orion Publishing Group.
22   Schliephake 1971 pp.17-18 & Mason 1973 p.151. Hugo Stinnes was an ardent nationalist whose industrial holdings were estimated at 20% of Germany's post war economy. His fortune rested primarily on cellulose, shipping and publishing. The 50 Fokker D.XIII fighters were part of a purchase for 100 fighters financed covertly on behalf of the *Reichswehr* by Stinnes in 1923 following the Franco-Belgian occupation of the Ruhr. The order for 50 Fokker D XI fighters was not taken up and these aircraft were subsequently sold to Romania - see also Mason 1973 p.126 & Postma T. 1979 *Fokker: Aircraft Builders to the World* (hereafter cited as Postma 1979) p.59 & 61.
23   Ries 1970 p.80 & Mason 1973 p.151.
24   Schliephake in Beauvais et al 2002 p.42. The aircraft were also armed at this point with the standard wartime twin lu.MG 08/15 machine gun - see Kosin 1983 p.59. Flight testing was carried out by *Ing.*Hans Leutert from *Hptm.* Kurt Student's *Wa.Prw.6F.* He had previously test flown the aircraft in the Netherlands - see Mason 1973 p.126.
25   Constable T.J. and Toliver R.F. 1968 *Horrido! Fighter Aces of the Luftwaffe* (hereafter cited as Constable and Toliver 1968) p.133. See also Ries 1970 p.80.
26   Gundelach K. Hptm.a.D., Koester R. Obst.a.D. & Kreipe W. Gen.d.Flg.a.D. *Ausbildung in der Fliegertruppe* in B/

Lehrgangsleiter for the *Fliegerschule Stahr.*[27] Other experienced members of the supervisory staff during this formative phase were *Oblt.a.D.*Carl-August von Schoenebeck, *Oblt.a.D.*Ernst Bormann and *Lt.d.Res.a.D.*Hermann Frommherz, all former fighter pilots with the wartime *Luftstreitkräfte.*[28] Prior to starting these contracts both Junck and Schoenebeck had been in South America, the latter on a *Reichswehr* contract, whilst Frommherz had been employed by the *badischen Luftverkehrs-Gesellschaft.*[29] A regular officer who joined the staff at Lipetsk was *Hptm.*Egloff Frhr.von Freyberg-Eisenberg. Although carried on the strength of *Reiter-Regiment 4* (Potsdam), Freyberg was actually *Flieger-Referent beim Stab 3.Division* (Berlin) (Aviation Advisor on the Staff of the 3rd Division) and his presence in the Ukraine was undoubtedly in connection with these duties. From April 1930 he was responsible for the supervision of the replacement pilot training programme within the *RWM.*[30] In the meantime *Hptm.*Kurt Student's covert *Waffen Prüfwesens 6 Flugzeuge (Wa.Prw.6F)* (Ordnance Test Department 6 – Aircraft) was represented at Lipetsk by *Oblt.a.D.*Hans-Joachim Rath who arrived in the Ukraine in April 1925.[31]

Understandably all the early arrivals at the *Fliegerschule* were also former wartime pilots, most of whom were sadly out of practice on any powered aircraft let alone a powerful fighter such as the Fokker D.XIII with its 450 h.p. Napier Lion 12-cylinder W engine.[32] When flown hard, for example in air combat manoeuvres, the Fokker D.XIII displayed some interesting, if not a little disturbing, handling characteristics:[33]

III/1b, Karlsruhe Document Collection (hereafter cited as Gundelach et al Undated) p.31 & Schliephake 1971 p.17.

27   Townsend P. 1970 *Duel of Eagles* (hereafter cited as Townsend 1970) p.83. *Oblt.a.D.*Ernst Udet had also been considered for the post of *Lehrgangsleiter* but his penchant for display flying and film making had resulted in him being passed over in favour of Junck who had completed 5 years post-war service with the *Reichsheer*. Werner Junck had trained at *FEA 8* in 1916 and had served with *Feld-Fl.Abt.33* before joining *Jasta 8* where he scored *5 abschusse*. He had been retained on the *Reichswehr's* secret pilot roster until Jun 23 when he was released to fly commercially in Venezuela & Colombia. He was re-engaged in a civilian capacity in Jan 25 - see also service record for Werner Junck in Hildebrand 1991 pp.142-143 & Franks et al 1996 p.175.

28   Mason 1973 p.153. Carl-August Schoenebeck had learned to fly with *FEA 3* in 1916/17 before joining *Fl.Abt.203*. His career as a *Jagdflieger* began in Jul 17 when he transferred to *JG 1*. He subsequently served with *Jasta 59* and as *Fhr.Jasta 33* - see service record for Carl August von Schoenebeck in Hildebrand 1992 pp.213-214. Ernst Bormann scored *16 abschusse* with the *Jasta Boelcke*. He had trained as a pilot at *FEA 7* in 1917 before serving with *Fl.Abt.42*. He joined the *Jasta Boelcke* in May 18 – see service record for Ernst Bormann in Hildebrand 1990 pp.106-107. Hermann Frommherz was a contemporary of Bormann who scored 10 *abschusse* with the *Jasta Boelcke* before transferring to *Jasta 27* which he led from Jul 18. He ended the war with *32 abschusse* and would have received the *Plm* if the armistice had not been signed - see service records for Hermann Frommherz in Hildebrand 1990 pp.325-326. However another useful source does not mention Frommherz - see Townsend 1970 p.83. See also Franks et al 1996.

29   Townsend 1970 p.83. Ernst Bormann's employment history between 1920-25 is not known. It is known that he was employed as a *Fluglehrer* at the *Fliegerschule Stahr* and later in Germany from Aug 25-Sep 30 - see service record for Ernst Bormann in Hildebrand 1990 p.107. All these instructors were employed on a civilian basis and paid in US dollars - see Suchenwirth 1968 p.27.

30   Schliephake in Beauvais et al 2002 p.42. Freyberg was a pre-war military aviator who had trained at Döberitz with *Flieger-Bataillon 1* during 1912-14. His wartime service had been mainly with the *Aufklärungsflieger* but it had also included a period with the *Brieftauben-Abteilung Ostende* in 1914-15. He had ended the war as *Fl.Gr.Fhr.5* within *AOK 7*. *Reichswehr* service had been with *IR 9* at Potsdam. See service record for Egloff Frhr.von Freyberg in Hildebrand 1990 pp.313-314.

31   Service record for Hans-Joachim Rath in Hildebrand 1992 pp.81-82. Hans-Joachim Rath had learned to fly at the *FEA 1* during 1915/16. His operational service included *Kogohl 5, Jasta 22* & *Schlasta 5*. However he was also assigned to the *Flugmusterei* where he was involved in the selection of new fighter aircraft for the *Luftstreitkräfte*. Postwar he had continued his work with the *Flugmusterei* as *Fhr.d.Bauaufsicht (Siemens)* and as *Adjutant*. He was discharged into civilian life at the end of 1920 and worked for *Deutschen Girozentrale* in Berlin until re-engaged by the *RWM* in a civilian capacity in Oct 24. He was assigned to *Wa.Prw.6F* within the *Insp.d.W.u.G.*

32   Kosin 1983 p.58.The Fokker D.XIII was considered to be the finest fighter aircraft in the world in the mid-twenties - see also Mombeek E, Smith J.R. and Creek E.J.1999 *Luftwaffe Colours:Jagdwaffe Vol.1 Sctn.1 Birth of the Luftwaffe Fighter Force* p.13.

33   *Flugschuler Tagbuch* in Kosin 1983 p.58-59. See also Mason 1973 p.157.

FIGURE 1D-1 FLYING CHARACTERISTICS OF THE FOKKER D.XIII FIGHTER
1. Fokker D.XIII control pressures are almost zero;
2. In steep turns it tends to drop its nose, and falls vertically when banked hard over;
3. A snap roll produces three rotations, followed by a spin;
4. Spin to the left: machine drops into a flat spin.

The first refresher course was held in 1925 but the results were not entirely satisfactory and several of the *Altmarker* (Wartime Pilots) were unable to gain an acceptable level of proficiency, a situation which was duly reported by Junck to *Maj.*Helmuth Wilberg's *T2 III (L)* (Military Aviation Office) in Berlin.[34]

At the end of 1925 Junck and Schoenebeck returned to Germany to select the students for the first full *Jagdflieger-Lehrgang* (Fighter Course) to be held at Lipetsk. A total of twelve of the most promising students from the various *Sportflug Zweigstellen* (Sportflug Branch Schools) were selected for training as instructor pilots during the 1926 season (See also 1D2).[35] The first full fighter course was then undertaken in 1927 when the new *Jungmarker* (Young Hares) made the transition from the basic flying course at the *DVS Zweigstelle Berlin-Staaken* (DVS Branch Staaken).[36] Unlike the *Altmarker* or former *Luftstreitkräfte* pilots, the *Jungmarker* were *Fahnenjunker* or officer candidates whose entry into the *Reichsheer* was delayed by a course of flying instruction at the *DVS*. The top ten or twelve students were then posted to Lipetsk for advanced flying training on the Fokker D.XIII (See 1E1).[37]

A typical training cycle would begin in October at Staaken before transfer to Lipetsk in April or May of the following year.[38] To facilitate training the *Jagdflieger-Lehrgang* was assigned sixteen Fokker D.XIII fighters, whilst a single Heinkel HD 21 and two Albatros L 69 *A2 Schulflugzeuge* (Elementary Trainers) were also assigned for continuation training and proficiency checks.[39] To prolong the life of these fighters, the only ones available to the *Reichsheer* during 1925-32, at least

34   Townsend 1970 p.84 & Mason 1973 pp.153-154. Unfortunately it has not been possible to identify the first students that were sent to Lipetsk. However the *T V (L)* staff were not convinced that young pilots with only a few hours on the A2 training aircraft as used by *Sportflug GmbH* could actually cope with such a powerful fighter. Junck was convinced that they could make the grade and he was therefore recalled to Germany to select the first group of *Jungmarker* for the fighter training programme. Wilberg was replaced as *Chef T V (L)* by *Maj.*Hugo Sperrle in Oct 27 - see service records for Hugo Sperrle & Hellmuth Wilberg in Hildebrand 1992 pp.325-326 & 513-514.

35   Townsend 1970 pp.84-85 & Mason 1973 p.154. Unfortunately the identity of these 12 instructor pilots is not known with certainty. *Rittm.*Otto Dessloch attended an air tactical course at Lipetsk in 1926 but he was an *Alte Adler* who had been trained as an observer at Schleißheim in 1914/15 and then as a pilot in 1916. In 1917 he had been *Fhr.Jasta 16 & 35* before being assigned as *Fhr.Fliegerschule 1*, later 5 in 1917-18. Following his training in Lipetsk in 1926 he was not employed as an instructor - see service record for Otto Dessloch in Hildebrand 1990 pp.186-187.

36   Ries 1970 pp.42-43, Mason 1973 p.156 & Ries K. 1988 *Deutsche Flugzeugführerschulen und ihre Maschinen 1919-1945* (hereafter cited as Ries 1988) p.10. The *Deutsche Verkehrsfliegerschule GmbH (DVS)* was established at Berlin-Staaken in Apr 27, primarily to provide flying instruction to aspiring commercial pilots and as such was financed by the RVM. The *Zweigstelle* Schleißheim was also opened in 1927 partly in response to the need to prepare pilots for the *Jagdflieger-Lehrgang* at Lipetsk – see Kreipe and Koster 1955 p.11. Unfortunately it has not been possible to positively identify any of the *Flugschuler* on the *1927 Jagdflieger Lehrgang*. This may explain why other authoritative sources suggest that the first *Jungmarker* did not reach Lipetsk until 1928 - see Kreipe and Koester 1955 p.15 & *Anhang C Zeittafel* in *Caspari* H-A. (Ed.) Undated *E-Stellen Travemünde und Tarnewitz Band 3* (hereafter cited as Caspari Undated) p.294.

37   Kreipe and Koster 1955 p.15 & Suchenwirth 1968 pp.25-27.

38   Hildebrand 1990-92. Analysis of service records. See also Falck W. 2002 *Wolfgang Falck: The Happy Falcon - An Autobiography by the Father of the Night Fighters* (hereafter cited as Falck 2002) p.16.

39   Schliephake 1971 p.17 & Andersson L. 1989 'Secret Luftwaffe: German Military Aviation Build-up between the Wars' in *Air Enthusiast* No.41 1989 (hereafter cited as Andersson 1989) p.40 & 44.

one third were always in storage, the individual aircraft being rotated into service and then back to store.[40]

FIGURE 1D-2 STUDENTS THOUGHT TO HAVE BEEN AT LIPETSK SUMMER 1928					
Oblt.	*Karl-Eduard*	*Wilke*	*31.03.28*	*15.09.29*	*Art.Rgt.1*
Hptm.	Eberhard	Fischer	01.04.28	30.11.29	Inf.Rgt.16
Oblt.	*Alexander*	*Holle*	*01.04.28*	*31.10.29*	*Inf.Rgt.16*
Oblt.	*Kurt*	*Kleinrath*	*01.04.28*	*30.11.28*	*Art.Rgt.2*
Oblt.	Rudolf	Meister	01.04.28	30.04.31	Inf.Rgt.4
Hptm.	Gottlob	Müller	01.04.28	31.08.29	Krftfr.Abt.7
Lt.	*Andreas*	*Nielsen*	*01.04.28*	*30.09.29*	*Inf.Rgt.6*
Oblt.	*Hans*	*Seidemann*	*01.04.28*	*31.10.29*	*Inf.Rgt.9*
Rittm.	*Wilhelm*	*Speidel*	*01.04.28*	*31.01.29*	*Rtr.Rgt.11*
Rittm.	Karl	Veith	01.04.28	30.09.31	Art.Rgt.7
Oblt.	*Oskar*	*Dinort*	*05.28*	*30.09.28*	*Inf.Rgt.2*
Oblt.	*Hermann*	*Plocher*	*01.05.28*	*30.04.30*	*Inf.Rgt.13*
Hptm.	Ehrenfried	Tschoeltsch	01.05.28	31.10.28	Inf.Rgt.10
Students without wartime flying experience					

At that time the training programme still resembled that of the wartime *Jagdflieger-Staffelschule*, the main difference being an increased emphasis on low-level work where the pilots learnt the specialised techniques of ground support with air-to-ground firing being practised at a training ground near Voronezh. One of the reasons for this training was the comparatively poor climb and high-altitude performance of the D.XIII, but it also reflected the pre-occupation of the *Reichsheer* with tactical air operations (See 1A3).

The course covered the following phases of fighter pilot activity:[41]

a. Practice flights to acquaint the students with the – for German students – completely unfamiliar fighter and trainer aircraft types (unfamiliar chiefly in respect to speed and horse power);
b. Practice flights designed to ensure familiarity with the new aircraft under all possible conditions;
c. Practice in formation flying, in groups of two aircraft up to Staffel strength;
d. Target location practice and artillery operation; and
e. Practice in aerial combat.

*Gen.d.Flg.a.D.*Werner Kreipe and *Obst.a.D.*Rudolf Koester
Technical Training in the German Air Force - USAF Historical Studies No.169

40   Hooton 1994 p.46.
41   Mason 1973 pp.157-158 & Corum1997 p.115.

Understandably the high point of the course, at least from the point of view of the students, remained the air-air combat training which steadily increased in complexity from singletons to *Rotte* (pair), *Kette* (flight) and ultimately *Staffel* (squadron) sized formations.[42]

In the meantime the arrival from Germany of the Heinkel HD 17 reconnaissance aircraft had allowed the establishment of a *Beobachter-Lehrgang* (Observer's Course) (See also 1C2).[43] Students for this course were not necessarily pilots and so their preparatory training in Berlin and later at the *Artillerieschule Jüterbog* where they were taught tactics, the theoretical aspects of air navigation and the practical aspects of wireless telegraphy was relatively simple to arrange.[44] The six month course in Germany was then followed by a summer at Lipetsk where theory was turned into practice and the students were also able to undertake aerial gunnery and bombing. Artillery observation and ranging was carried out in conjunction with elements of the Red Army in the Voronezh area.

The programme at Lipetsk was sub-divided into the following individual subjects:[45]

a.   Ground and air tactics, as illustrated in aerial manoeuvres;
b.   Aircraft construction, including engines and aircraft equipment;
c.   Air armament, bombs, practice in shooting airborne artillery and in dropping explosives;
d.   Aerial reconnaissance and anti-artillery techniques; adjustment fire techniques – with help of classroom instruction in radio-communication and the mountain observers course;
e.   Direction finding, aerial navigation and meteorology;
f.   Aerial photography techniques; and
g.   Russian and English language instruction.

Gen.d.Flg.a.D. Werner Kreipe and *Obst.a.D.* Rudolf Koester
Technical Training in the German Air Force - USAF Historical Studies No.169

Only six HD 17s were used at Lipetsk although these were supplemented by six Albatros L 76a during the period 1927-31.[46] Within the *Flugzentrum* (Flight Centre) these aircraft were assigned to the *Beobachter-Staffel* (2 machines) and the *Beobachter-Lehrgang* (4 machines).[47] Given their

---

42   Kreipe and Koester 1955 p.25. See also Ries 1970 pp.81-82 & Mason 1973 p.158.

43   Ries 1970 p.81, Schliephake 1971 p.17 & Hooton 1994 p.45. There is some confusion as to the date of the first course for *Artilleriebeobachteren*. Ries states that it was in 1926 and it seems likely that the HD 17s were delivered during that year. However other sources suggest that it might not have been until 1928 - see Nowarra H.J. 1981 *Nahaufklärer 1910-1945: Die Augen des Heeres* (hereafter cited as Nowarra 1981) pp.33-35 & *Anhang C Zeittafel* in Caspari Undated p.294.

44   Kreipe and Koester 1955 p.15-16 – "*Observer training, which had been rather neglected so far, was concentrated at a special training centre in Berlin, where the courses were officially designated as Tarnlehrgange (Camouflage Courses). The Tarnlehrgange were both theoretical and practical. The practical sessions were devoted to tactical training in the use of wireless communication, night observation training, artillery observation training with two-way radio (including practice in the various fire adjustment methods). In Germany in 1927 and 1928 it was impossible to carry out training of this kind in the air. Therefore a successful substitute had been devised in the form of so-called Steilbeobachterlehrgange (Mountain Observers courses). Held in the Riesengebirge or in Oberbayern. the "aircraft" radio station was located in the mountains some 1,000 m above sea level, while the artillery targets lay in the valley below, in the line of vision of the aircraft stations above.*" See also the service record for Karl von Gerlach in Hildebrand 1990 pp.357-358.

45   Kreipe and Koester 1955 p.22. See also *TA-L, Ausbildung Lehrgang L 1927 (30 November 1926)* in BA/MA RH 2/2299 in Corum 1997 p.115.

46   *App.B "Aircraft Stock of the German Air Training School at Lipezk/Russia - actual stock on October 1, 1929* in Schliephake 1971 p.62. See also *Aircraft based at Lipetsk 1925-1933* in Andersson 1989 p.44. The six HD 17 *Aufklärer* had the EHF WNr.239-244 - see Koos 2006 p.47. The six L 76a *Aufklärer* had the Albatros C/N 10102, 10103 & 10122-10125 – see Nowarra H.J. 1980 *Die Verbotenen Flugzeuge 1921-1935 – Die getarnte Luftwaffe* p.144.

47   Schliephake 1971 p.17.

few numbers these reconnaissance machines had a particularly high utilisation rate. Officers who are known to have undertaken the *Beobachter-Lehrgang* include *Oblt.*Alfred Boner (*Nachr.Abt.3* - Potsdam) who arrived in 1929 following a preparatory course in Germany that had begun the previous November and *Rittm.*Karl von Gerlach (*Rtr.Rgt.11* - Neustadt) who arrived in 1930 after preparatory training at the *Artillerieschule Jüterbog*.[48] The maintenance of an aerial photography capability was a further operational objective for the *Beobachter-Lehrgang*. Following his training *Oblt.*Karl-Eduard Wilke (*Art.Rgt.1* - Königsberg) was retained at Lipetsk in October 1928 as *Leiter der Bildstelle* for a further period of twelve months.[49] In 1929 forty six students were posted to Lipetsk, three quarters of these being serving officers on the *Beobachter-Lehrgang*.[50]

The civilian staff were increasingly supplemented by serving officers who were carried on the inactive list during their service in the Soviet Union.[51] Arrangements for the students who would only be away for a six month period were slightly different. Each officer was provided with an elaborate cover which concealed their actual whereabouts from not only their relatives but even the personnel within their parent units. Travel to Lipetsk was undertaken in civilian dress, officers being smuggled aboard passenger vessels for the passage to Leningrad before the train journey south. All letters from Germany were routed through a field post number in Berlin before being forwarded by special courier to the *Deutschen Botschaft* (Embassy) in Moskva. Even at Lipetsk uniforms were not worn, nor were pay books carried.[52]

The conditions at Lipetsk were initially quite primitive, furniture being knocked up from the packing crates that had been used to transport the D.XIII fighters to the Soviet Union in the first place. Hans-Heinrich Brustellin, *Flugschuler Lipetsk* in 1930, recalled that the food was bad but that the *Kasino* (Officers' Mess) was reasonably comfortable.[53] The permanent staff were permitted to

---

48 Service records for Alfred Boner & Karl von Gerlach in Hildebrand 1990 pp.104-105 & 357-358. Alfred Boner had joined the *Reichsheer - Nachrichten-Abt.3* at Potsdam - as an officer candidate *(Fahnenjunker)* on the 1 Jan 21. He completed courses at the *Infanterie-Schule München* (Aug 22-Jul 23), *Artillerie-Schule Jüterbog* (Aug 23-Aug 24) & *Aero Lloyd* at Berlin-Staaken (Dec 24-Apr 25). He was posted to Lipetsk in Nov 28 prior to attachment to the *Firma Lorenz Elektro* at Potsdam. Karl von Gerlach had entered the *Heer* on the 22 Mar 14 and had served with *Jäger-Btl.4* until Aug 15 and later with *Landwehr-Inf-Rgt.66*. He trained as a *Flugzeugbeobachter* with *FEA 11* in 1916 and served with *Fl.Abt.267* & *241*. Retained by the *Reichsheer* he served with *Inf.Rgt.1* at Königsberg until Dec 22 and then with *Rtr. Rgt.11* at Neustadt/Oberschlesien. He arrived at Lipetsk in 1930 and later served with the *Hauptbildstelle* until Apr 31.

49 Kiehl H. 1983 *Kampfgeschwader "Legion Condor" 53: Berichte, Erlebnisse u.Dokumente 1936-1945* p.17 - GenMaj.a.D.Karl-Eduard Wilke states:*"I was at the school from the 1.5.1928 until the 15.10.1929, initially as a student, from 1.10.1928 as Leiter der Bildstelle"* After a short period of service in the *Infanterie* in 1918 and with the *Freikorps Eulenburg* in 1919 Karl-Eduard Wilke had been reactivated in Apr 23 as a *Batterie-Offizier* within *AR 1*. He leant to fly at Königsberg between Jan-Jun 26 and was posted to Lipetsk for further flying training in Apr 28 - see service record for Karl-Eduard Wilke in Hildebrand 1992 pp.522-523.

50 Hooton 1994 p.46. In 1929 10 *Offizieranwarter* were sent to Lipetsk, presumably from Schleißheim to train as fighter pilots. Officers on the *Beobachter-Lehrgang* are thought to have included *Oblt.*Walter Boenicke, *Oblt.*Alfred Boner, *Hptm.*Karl Barlen, *Hptm.*Wolf Frhr.von Biedermann, *Hptm.*Erhard Krüger & *Hptm.*Alfred Sturm - see Hildebrand 1990-92.

51 Hooton 1994 p.46. Following the 1926 scandal it was mandatory for serving officers to be transferred to the *ausser Dienstliste* prior to a tour of duty at Lipetsk. *"The personnel groups, whether airmen or firm's representatives, travelled with genuine passports and transit visas, except that names and professional occupations were occasionally altered. For the duration of their stay in Russia, military personnel were excluded from the Active Service Lists, whilst the civilian workers were deleted from their firm's personnel lists. Correspondence was also handled via disguised addresses, mail between Lipetsk and Berlin being transported solely by courier aircraft."* See also Mason 1973 pp.155-156. However the comings and goings of *Reichsheer* officers did not go unnoticed. Sir.Horace Rumbold, the British Ambassador to Berlin, noted on the 29 Apr 31 that no less than 66 officers had inexplicably disappeared from the active list before reappearing without loss of seniority - see Hooton 1994 p.69.

52 Mason 1973 p.153.

53 Townsend 1970 pp.94-95. Officer candidate Hans-Heinrich Brustellin began his flying training with the *DVS* on the 4 Apr 29, obtained his *A-Schein* on the 13 Nov 29 and was sent to Lipetsk in the following year. He then joined *Rtr.Rgt.2* (Ostpr.) - see also Reichsverkehrsministerium 1929 *Nachrichten für Luftfahrer*.

travel in the local area, including into the town of Lipetsk itself. In the beginning the students were confined to the base which was guarded by the Soviet militia. However by the early thirties these rules had been relaxed and life had become a great deal more congenial for the flight students:

We had a wonderful life in Lipetsk, with daily flight duty, weather permitting, and daily sports as well, including shooting. It didn't matter with what: pistols, rifles, light machine guns, heavy machine guns, or shot guns at clay pigeons. We also played tennis, and were allowed to go out at night in our truck, a type of delivery van having two benches in the back. While taking walks in the park we might hear a Russian military band playing concerts, or take notice of the Soviet officers' club downtown - brightly lit, with all the windows open - and how thoroughly the officers and their wives enjoyed life.

Around the park stood a fence, and from behind it the Russian populace stood and watched in awe, staring at the miraculous sights. By comparison they had virtually nothing to eat or drink. It was terribly sad to witness the stark contrasts in the daily life of the Russians.

We were not allowed direct contact with the people, but occasionally we could talk with them. After a while we met some nice young Russian girls, a few of whom became our girlfriends. I want to make clear that the word "girlfriend" left a bad taste in German mouths, but that didn't apply to the Russians. They were fantastic girls, super companions, and joined us in everything we did. But they were absolutely taboo, as I'll explain soon. There was a boathouse *Am Fluss* from which we swam, and large boats equipped with cushioned seats in which we cruised on our days off. Behind them we would troll a bottle of champagne, cooling in the water.

I had a girlfriend whose name was Olga. Her father was a professor at the University of Kiev, where she was a student. We got on famously, although in the beginning she didn't speak a word of German. But then she began to meet me every day with a new torrent of German words, and was soon speaking ten times better German than I did Russian. One day Olga said her mother was coming along. Then and there the red warning light went on for me. The Russian girls were always trying to marry us German, to escape the hell of their own country. Some of the base personnel did get married in Lipetsk, and eventually took their Russian wives back to Germany. But Olga and I were still far too young. I had no intention of marrying, least of all to a Russian girl, so from that day on I did not dare go to the park. I only dashed through it on the way to the boathouse.[54]

Obst.a.D. Wolfgang Falck
Flugschuler Lipetsk 1932

The transfer of supplies, and in particular live ammunition and bombs, was more difficult and in the early years many of these items had to be smuggled across the Ostsee in small craft manned by *Reichswehr* personnel.[55] This somewhat risky undertaking was necessary because Soviet Customs were not party to the secret agreement between the two governments and were often

---

54   Quoted from Falck 2002 *Wolfgang Falck: The Happy Falcon – An Autobiography of the Father of Night Fighters* pp.17-18 with kind permission of Eagle Editions Ltd. However Russian female interest appears to have been reserved for the German pilots. During one of his visits *Maj.* Sperrle was asked by one of the ladies: *"Tell me, Major, do you fly or merely shoot a gun in self-defence?"* On hearing it was the latter her interest cooled - see Townsend 1970 p.84 with knowledge of the Orion Publishing Group.

55   Schliephake 1971 p.19.

suspicious and obstinate; attitudes which resulted in long delays in the delivery of urgently required spares. Fortunately this situation was later eased when the Soviet authorities established a Customs station within the base at Lipetsk where incoming goods were inspected and outgoing boxes and crates sealed for return to Germany.[56] The *PuW* bombs used for the 1928-29 trials, for example, arrived in crates marked as *Mittelpufferkupplungen* (central buffer couplings) and *Kaminaufsatze* (chimney hoods).[57] A measure of the efficiency of these procedures can be gauged by the way in which the Napier Lion engines, used by both the Fokker D.XIII and the Heinkel HD 17, were returned to Fokker at Amsterdam before being sent in good faith to the parent company in Britain for major overhaul prior to their covert return to the Soviet Union. Neither Fokker nor the British Government appear to have been aware of the true nature of these contracts nor of their invaluable assistance to the *Reichsheer's* clandestine aviation development work.[58] Nonetheless it was a convoluted and dangerous arrangement and the necessary non-metric tools were later obtained which allowed all maintenance work to be completed at Lipetsk.[59]

1928 was to prove a year of some significance to the *Reichswehr's* covert activities in the Soviet Union. In Moskva Lieth-Thomsen's degenerative eye condition had rendered him almost completely blind and he was he replaced as *Chef Z.Mo.* by *Maj.*Oskar Ritter von Niedermeyer.[60] At the same time this key office was removed from the jurisdiction of the *Chef des Heeresleitung* (Chief of the Army Command) and placed under the direction of *T 3 (Fremde Heer)* (Troop Office Branch 3 – Foreign Armies) thus emphasising its intelligence gathering role as opposed to its former administrative focus.[61] By this time *Z.Mo.* was also responsible for an even more secret *Gaskampfschule* (Chemical Warfare Establishment) near Saratov on the west bank of the Volga (See 5C4), whilst two years later in 1930 a *Kampfwagenschule* (Armoured Vehicle School) was established at Kazan, also in the central Volga region of the Ukraine.[62]

At the same time the testing and experimental side of Lipetsk's work was stepped up to meet a demand from *Maj.*Hugo Sperrle's *T 2 V (L)* (Military Aviation Office) that an evaluation be carried out to evaluate the suitability of *Deutsche Luft Hansa's* Junkers G 24 and Rohrbach Ro VIII airliners as *Behelfsnachtbomber* (Auxiliary Night Bombers)(See 1A3 & 1C2).[63] The existing *Versuchsgruppe* (Experimental Group) was reinforced to form the *Wissenschaftliche Versuchs-und Prüfanstalt für Luftfahrzeuge (Wivupal)* (Aircraft Scientific Test and Evaluation Institute) and sub-divided into three separate but related Desks or *Referate*:[64]

56   Suchenwirth 1968 p.28 & Mason 1973 pp.158-159.
57   Fleischer W. 2003 *German Air-Dropped Weapons to 1945* (hereafter cited as Fleischer 2003) p.25.
58   Schliephake 1971 p.19 & Mason 1973 p.157. The Napier Lion was a very widely used and reliable power plant. It was compact 12 cylinder water cooled engine in broad arrow or W form with three banks of four cylinders each attached to a common crank case. The exact model employed by the *Reichsheer* for their Lipetsk based machines is not known but it was probably the Mk.IIB of 1926 vintage - see Lumsden A.S.C. 1994 *British Piston Aero-Engines and their Aircraft* p.166.
59   Mason 1973 p.157.
60   Suchenwirth 1968 p.13. Niedermeyer would in turn be replaced by *Obst.*Hartmann in 1932 - see Hooton 1994 p.44 & *Anhang C Zeittafel* in Caspari Undated p.297. However a further source suggests that *Oblt.a.D.*Lothar Schuttel was the final *Chef Z.Mo.* - see Schliephake in Beauvais et al 2002 p.42. Another source suggests that Niedermayer did not replace Thomsen until 1929 - see Caspari Undated p.295.
61   Hooton 1994 p.50. In 1928 *T 3* established a liaison office in Berlin to work in conjunction with *Z.Mo.* – see Hooton 1994 p.44.
62   Mason 1973 p.159, Zeidler 1994 p.303, Hooton 1994 p.44 & Fleischer 2003 p.25 & 27.
63   Suchenwirth 1968 pp.27-28, Hooton 1994 p.47 & Schliephake in Beauvais et al 2002 pp.43-44. In 1927 *Maj.* Hellmuth Volkmann *(Wa.B.6F)* had drawn up an emergency procurement programme *(Notrustüngs-Programm)* as part of *T 2 V (L)'s* contingency planning in the event of a war with one of Germany's neighbours. The employment of commercial types such as the Do B *Merkur* & Junkers G 24 made a great deal of sense.
64   Schliephake in Beauvais et al 2002 p.42. The exact date of the establishment of *Wivupal* is yet to be confirmed. It has been suggested that it was used from the very beginning of training at Lipetsk in 1926 - see Hooton 1994 p.45.

FIGURE 1D-3 WISSENSCHAFTLICHE VERSUCHS-UND PRUFANSTALT FÜR LUFTFAHRZEUGE 1928		
Aircraft testing	-	Oblt.a.D.Carl-August von Schoenebeck
Aircraft armament and installation testing	-	Oblt.a.D.Emil Thuy
Drop ordnance and bomb release mechanism testing	-	Oblt.a.D.Dipl.Ing.Ernst Marquard

Both *Oblte.a.D.*Emil Thuy and Ernst Marquard were civilian employees of the *Heereswaffenamt (Wa.A.)* (Army Ordnance Office), but in reality members of *Wa.Prw.6F* (See 1C2). Thuy was a former *Jagdflieger* whose exploits with *Jasta 21* and *Jasta 28* had resulted in the award of the coveted *Pour le Mérite* in June 1918. Marquard had trained as a fighter pilot but had been too late for war service. Post war he had studied engineering at the *Technischen Hochschule Stuttgart* before specialising in chemical engineering with the *Allgemeinen Vergaser-Gesellschaft* in Berlin.[65] Thuy and Marquard headed a sixteen man test team from the *Wa.A.* which arrived at Lipetsk in July 1928. Single examples of the Rohrbach Ro VIII (WNr.18 D-991) and Junkers G 24 (WNr.844 D-878) were flown to the Ukraine having been modified for their new role at Berlin-Staaken.[66] Upon arrival at Lipetsk they were both fitted with their *Sonderausrüstung* (Special Equipment) in the form of *So II Abwehrwaffen* (Flexibly mounted defensive armament) and *So III Abwurfwaffen* (Bomb sights, bomb racks and bomb release mechanisms)(See 1C2).[67] To assist with the bomb trials a third aircraft, Junkers A 35 WNr.1059 D-897, was also deployed to Lipetsk. *Rittm.*Curt Pflugbeil (*Rtr.Rgt.11* - Neustadt) was one of the serving officers assigned to *Wivupal* to participate in these trials which lasted through into 1929.[68]

Marquard's team were primarily interested in evaluating the performance of the modified *Prüfanstalt und Werft (PuW) Splitter-und Sprengbomben* (Fragmentation and Explosive Bombs) of Great War vintage, these being the only readily available designs. Ballistic trials had already been conducted in conjunction with the Swedish *Flygvapnet* between September 1927 and March 1928 and the Lipetsk trials were seen to be a logical extension of this work (See 1C5).[69] The Swedish trials had indicated that the *PuW* ordnance was unsuitable for use by high performance modern aircraft with their greater speed and increased operational ceilings and it was therefore vital that these findings be confirmed so that improvements could be made.[70] To facilitate these new trials a two kilometre square bombing range (4 square kilometres) equipped with observation towers

65   Angolia and Hackney 1984 pp.218-219. Emil Thuy had trained as a military pilot at Johannisthal and Boblingen. He served with *Fl.Abt.53*, before joining *Jasta 21*. He was *Kap.Jasta 28* and was decorated with the *Plm* on the 30 Jun 18. His final score was *32 abschusse*. Post war he worked for *Siemens Schukert* in Finland before joining the *RWM*. Ernst Marquard entered *Reichsdienst* in Oct 24 where his speciality was chemical weapons and drop ordnance. From Jun 26 he was assigned to *Wa.Prw.6F* as *Referat IIc* - see service record for Ernst Marquard in Hildebrand 1991 pp.356-357.

66   Schliephake in Beauvais et al 2002 p.42. The Rohrbach Ro VIII was modified at the firm's Berlin works. Indeed the aircraft was in the works when the Allied inspectors carried out a surprise visit being quickly moved to the middle of the hangar where it was quickly covered with dust-covers, ladders, staging and bits of workshop equipment. The Allied inspectors repeatedly walked right by the modified aircraft without realising what was hidden under the sheeting – see Schliephake 1971 p.20. See also Mason 1973 p.162.

67   Schliephake in Beauvais et al 2002 p.44.

68   Service record for Curt Pflugbeil in Hildebrand 1992 pp.31-33. Curt Pflugbeil had trained as a pilot in 1915-16 and saw wartime service with the *Kampfstaffeln (Kasta 24, 27 & 23)* as well as with *Schützstaffel 9*. He was injured in Apr 18 but retained by the *Reichsheer* in *Inf.Rgt.11*. Just prior to his assignment to Lipetsk he had completed an 8 month *Ausbildungsstab des Lehrgangs für Heerestechnik*.

69   Fleischer 2003 pp.25-27. The Swedish trials had been partially funded by the *RWM* in association with *Bofors*. Both the 50 & 300 kg *PuW* ordnance had broken up in the air when dropped from heights above 4,500m. It seems likely that these trials were observed by *Rittm.*Curt Pflugbeil - see service record for Curt Pflugbeil in Hildebrand 1992 pp.30-33.

70   Fleischer 2003 p.26. The Swedes had used the Fokker C-V reconnaissance bomber as the platform for these trials.

and marked out with targets, including a 50 cm thick concrete slab for use in the planned bomb penetration studies was prepared at Lipetsk.[71]

PuW bombs weighing up to 300 kgs were evaluated at Lipetsk during 1928 and 1929. The smaller 12 kg and 50 kg bombs were dropped from a Junkers A 35, whilst the larger G 24 and Ro VIII airliners were fitted with external racks for two or three 300 kg *PuW* bombs.[72] The poor performance of the *PuW* ordnance was confirmed, particularly when dropped from heights above 3,500 metres. Nonetheless in 1929 an enlarged test team of twenty men carried out a further series of exhaustive tests which looked at new bomb sights, modified bomb release mechanisms as well as improved bomb fuses. In 1930 these trials were then repeated using two Junkers W 34 aircraft to test drop the newly developed SC *(Sprengbombe-Cylindrisch)* (Cylindrical Explosive Bombs) ordnance.[73] The smaller SC 50 and SC 250 bombs were suspended vertically inside the cabin of the W 34 whilst in 1932 trials included the larger SC 500 bombs which were carried horizontally below the fuselage centre-section. In all cases the bombs were released electrically (See 1C5). The trial flights were made by *Ing.*Hans Leutert *(Fliegerstaffel Staaken)*, von Rochow *(Flugzeugführer)*, *Oblt.a.D.*Eberhard Mohnicke *(Fliegerstaffel Rechlin)*, Hoppe *(Ref.Flugzeuge Rechlin)* and Hans von Boltenstern. Marquard *(Ref.f.Abwurfmunition Wa.Prw.9 II b)* and Pflugbeil *(RWM)* were amongst those acting as observers.[74]

In his capacity as *Chef T 2 V (L)*, *Maj.*Sperrle made regular bi-annual visits to Lipetsk.[75] However during the 1928 summer training period *GenLt.*Werner von Blomberg, the *Chef der Truppenamt*, undertook a major inspection tour of the *Reichsheer's* facilities in the USSR.[76] In addition to visiting Lipetsk, where amongst the *Flugschuleren* were Oskar Dinort, Andreas Nielsen, Hermann Plocher and Karl-Eduard Wilke, the inspection team also toured the tank school at Kazan and the chemical warfare establishment near Saratov.[77] Joint exercises were held in the Voronezh area where the D.XIII fighters and HD 17 and L 76 reconnaissance aircraft demonstrated their close support role in association with Red Army units. The Soviet authorities, who greatly valued the presence of the German centres were anxious to make a favourable impression, an aim which was certainly achieved:

> The reception of the German officers was everywhere friendly, often cordial and very hospitable. The Commissar for War, Voroshilov, had given instructions to show everything and to meet all our wishes...The value of the co-operation to the Red Army was emphasised time and again, as was the wish to hear the verdict of German officers, which is considered authoritative, about the achievements of the Red Army.[78]

*GenLt.*Werner von Blomberg
Chef der Truppenamt,
Summer 1928

---

71 Fleischer 2003 p.26. A reputable source suggests that the concrete platform was 30 cm thick and mounted on a 1.5 m stone platform – see Schliephake K. 2002 *German Secret Flight Test Centres* p.59.

72 Fleischer 2003 p.26. Initially the Ro VIII carried its offensive load of two 300 kg bombs beneath the wings, whilst up to fourteen 50 kg bombs could be carried in recesses in the cabin floor. Later ground clearance was increased to enable the type to carry three 300 kg bombs below the fuselage - see Schliephake in Beauvais et al 2000 p.44.

73 Schliephake in Beauvais et al 2002 pp.48-49. The W 34 aircraft were WNr.2589 D-1844 & WNr.2590 D-1845.

74 Service records for Ernst Marquard in Hildebrand 1991 pp.356-357& Curt Pflugbeil in Hildebrand 1992 pp.30-33 and Schliephake in Beauvais et al 2002 p.48. The other observers of the bombing trials were Holm, Koch & Peter. See also Fleischer 2003 p.32-33.

75 Townsend 1970 p.84 & Hooton 1994 p.45.

76 Mason 1973 p.159 & Mitcham S.W.1988 *Hitler's Field Marshals and their Battles* pp.21-22. Blomberg was *Chef d.Truppenant* from 1 Apr 27 - 30 Sep 29 when he was replaced with *GenLt.*Kurt Frhr.von Hammerstein-Equord. See also service record for Werner von Blomberg in www.wikipedia.org.

77 Mason 1973 p.159. This source may be in error as the *Panzerschule* Kazan was not opened until 1930.

78 Quoted from Mason 1973 *The Rise of the Luftwaffe 1918-1940* p.159 with the knowledge of the Orion Publishing Group. See also Kreipe and Koester 1955 p.27.

Schoenebeck replaced Junck as *Ausbildungsleiter Fliegerschule Stahr* in 1928 following the Junck's decision to return to Germany to take up the position of Chief Pilot at the *Albatros Flugzeugwerke GmbH*.[79] In the following year instructions were received from *Maj.*Hellmuth Felmy, the new *Chef T 2 V (L)*, for the Staff to draw up a Fighter Manual for use by the emerging *Fliegertruppe*.[80] To provide the basis for this work a *Jagdstaffel* (Fighter Squadron) was established at Lipetsk with eighteen Fokker D.XIII fighters with which the instructors could evaluate and refine their tactics.[81] The resulting manual was a truly comprehensive document which covered not only the entire training syllabus but also the tactical control and employment of fighter aircraft, formation flying, high-altitude flying, aerial combat procedures, air-to-air and air-to-ground gunnery and bombing. The use of camera guns proved particularly helpful in illustrating the concepts within the manual, whilst they also helped refine the skills of the young *Flugschuler* on the parallel *Jagdfliegerlehrgang*. Individual performance was assessed using camera gun film during flight de-briefings, a procedure which allowed each student to recognise his own strengths and weaknesses. It was also used to confirm "victories" during the major dog-fights between two opposing *Staffeln* which marked the culmination of the course.[82]

The most promising *Flugschuleren* would often return to Lipetsk as *Hilfslehrer* (Assistant Instructors). Johannes Janke, an experienced former commercial pilot with *Deutsche Luft Hansa*, was a student on the 1929 *Jagdflieger-Lehrgang*. In view of his exceptional flying skill he was permitted special privileges being allowed to go off-base within 160 kilometres to go wild-fowling, his mobility being assured via the use of a little Chevrolet truck.[83] He would return to Lipetsk in 1932 together with Hassow von Printz, Wilhelm Mackrocki and *"Krotze"* Roth.[84] Other graduates of the 1929-30 period included Nicolaus von Below, Alexander von Blomberg, Hans-Heinrich Brustellin, Paul Deichmann, Hans-Detlef Herhudt von Rohden, Wolf-Heinrich Frhr.von Houwald, Lothar von Janson, Josef Kammhuber, Günther Korten, Werner Krahl, Werner Kreipe, Georg Riecke and Hans-Bruno Schulz-Heyn.[85]

Considering the ever-present risk of collision during air combat training the number of serious accidents at Lipetsk were mercifully low. Like all flight training schools the *Fliegerschule Stahr* suffered its fair share of minor accidents, but few of these resulted in the complete loss of an aircraft *(Photo 1D-3)*. However other incidents were more serious and on the 30 August 1930 *Rittm.a.D* Amlinger was killed in an air collision, whilst in 1933 von Poelschau was another fatality when his fighter collided with that of Ernst-Siegfried Steen following a simulated attack on a HD 17 during air combat training.[86] Unfortunately the 1932 course was marred by two fatal accidents, an accident

79   Service record for Werner Junck in Hildebrand 1991 pp.142-143.
80   Gundelach et al Undated p.31. See also Suchenwirth 1968 pp.27-28 & Corum 1997 p.118. Felmy replaced Sperrle in Feb 29 - see service record for Hellmuth Felmy in Hildebrand 1990 pp.273-275.
81   Schliephake 1971 pp.17-18.
82   Gundelach et al Undated p.31. See also Suchenwirth 1968 &pp.27-28 Corum 1997 p.118. However the lack of oxygen equipment aboard the Fokker D.XIII made high altitude operations impossible - see Schliephake 1971 p.18.
83   Townsend 1970 pp.91-92. As a civilian Janke had been one of the first students to attend the new *DVS-Zweigstelle* at *Schleißheim* in 1927 where he gained his *A/B Schein*. He was awarded his *C-Schein (Land u See)* at Braunschweig & *Warnemünde* in the following year. He then flew Rohrbach Ro VIII airliners for *DLH* before transferring to the *Reichswehr* in 1929.
84   Ries 1970 p.83.
85   Hildebrand 1990-92, Hooton 1994 & deZeng H.L. and Stankey D.G. 2013 *Luftwaffe Officer Career Summaries* in *Luftwaffe 1933-1945* in www.ww2.dk . See also Townsend 1970 & Obermaier E. 1966 *Die Ritterkreuztrager der Luftwaffe Bd.I Jagdflieger 1939-1945*. *Fahnenjunker* Nikolaus von Below had been accepted by *IR 12* (Halberstadt) in Apr 28. Prior to recruit training he was sent to *DVS Schleißheim* and from there to Lipetsk in May 29. His formal service with *IR 12* began following his return from Russia in Oct 29 - see Below N. Obst.a.D.2001 *At Hitler's Side – The Memoirs of Hitler's Luftwaffe Adujtant 1937-1945* p.12.
86   Ries 1970 p.81, Mason 1973 p.158 & Schliephake in Beauvais et al 2002 p.48. With the usual secrecy Ammlinger's body was shipped back to Germany in a crate marked "spare parts". Unfortunately his pregnant wife learned of his arrival and as the ship bearing his body entered Stettin harbour she leapt to her death from a chartered aircraft

rate which was dramatically higher than that of the preceding seven years. The two incidents in 1932 both involved students although in the first it had been one of the two civilian instructors, *Rittm.a.D.*Gustav *"Bolli"*Bollmann, who had died after his aircraft had been hit by that of Frhr.von Houwald during formation flying practice (See 1E1). The other fatality occurred quite separately when Hans-Karl von Tresckow, one of the five naval students, was killed during the course of aerobatic training.[87] In order to maintain the secrecy which surrounded all the *Reichswehr's* activities in the Soviet Union the bodies of the three men were shipped home in sealed crates marked "spare parts", an undignified end to a great adventure.[88]

In 1930 *Maj.a.D.*Stahr was replaced as Kommandant by a serving officer in the form of *Maj.* Max Mohr.[89] Mohr was another pre-war military aviator having been trained at Halberstadt in 1913-14. Like his predecessor he was an *Aufklärungsflieger* with command experience, ultimately as *Fliegergruppenführer 13* during 1917-18. His *Reichsheer* service had been a *Kompaniechef in Infanterie-Regiment 7* (Oberschlesien) prior to six years as *Flieger-Referent* within the 5.*Division* at Stuttgart from October 1923. He was then "retired" and simultaneously appointed *Leiter der Wivupal.*[90] His *Ausbildungsleiter* was *Maj.*Hellmuth Bieneck, who had already served one tour in this capacity in 1929 and was also carried on the *ausser Dienstliste.* Bieneck was a former *Kampfflieger*, who had served as a *Staffelführer* with both *Kagohl 4* and *Kagohl 7* during the Great War.[91] The replacement of civilian personnel by these officers was indicative of the value of this practical experience for key personnel for the planned *Fliegertruppe* (See 1A3).[92]

The first year of Mohr's tenure was also the last full training year. The secret decision on the 30 November 1930 to covertly employ military aircraft within the frontiers of the Reich had been facilitated by the steady expansion of the *DVS* training organisation (See 1A3). As a result after the 1931 season the *Beobachter-Lehrgang* was re-located to the *DVS Braunschweig* as a means of saving some of the *RM* 3 million that was being spent annually on the *Flugzentrum.*[93] However the *Jagdflieger-Lehrgang* would continue for a further three years, it not being possible to camouflage the activities of fighter aircraft within Germany at that time.[94]

overhead. The circumstances were duly reported in the press and Carl von Ossietzky openly accused the German Government of complicity in an article in the *Die Weltbuhne* - see Townsend 1970 pp.93-94. Meanwhile at Lipetsk collateral damage from German flight activities was mercifully slight. On one occasion a number of Soviet civilians were struck by fragments from a crashing D.XIII. On another occasion a Soviet peasant farmer was killed during a ground strafing exercise. The Germans paid compensation - interestingly at over the odds for horses and relatively little for the farmer. Such was the regard for human life in Stalinist Russia - see also Falck 2002 p.18.

87   Ries 1970 p.81 & Falck 2002 p.18.

88   Schliepake 1971 p.19 & Mason 1973 p.158.

89   Schliephake in Beauvais et al 2002 p.42.

90   Service record for Max Mohr in Hildebrand 1991 pp.398-399. In 1914 Mohr was a pilot in *Fl.-Btl.2* before being assigned to *Fl-Abt.35*. From 1915 he was successively *Fhr.Fl-Abt.37, 17, 30* & *265*, being appointed acting *KoFl b.AOK 11* on two occasions during the winter of 1917. Immediately post-war he served as a *Kp.Fhr.* in the *Freikorps Görlitz*.

91   Service record for Hellmuth Bieneck in Hildebrand 1990 pp.81-82. Bieneck had trained as a military aviator at Leipzig in 1913 and in 1914 had been assigned to *Fl.-Btl.I*. His wartime service had initially been with the *Fest. Fl.-Abt.Posen* & *Feld-Fl.-Abt.36*. Post-war he had been a *Kp.Chef* in *IR 16* (Oldenburg) and as a *Fl.-Referent* in the 6.*Div.* (Münster) from Jul 25 until May 29. During the winter of 1929/30 he had been attached to Felmy's *Insp.1 (L)* as *Ltr.d.geheimen Fliegerausbildung i.RWM* (Leader of Secret Flying Training in the RWM).

92   Schliephake 1971 p.17 & Andersson 1989 p.44. Interestingly the two Fokker D.VII fighters attached to the *Fliegerschule Stahr* were supplied by the VVS in the late 20s having been bought at an earlier date from Fokker in the Netherlands - see Postma 1979 p.59 & Hooton 1994 p.47.

93   Suchenwirth 1968 p.32, Mason 1973 p.163 & Nowarra 1981 p.33. This money was found from within the *Reichswehr's* Blue Budget, a portion of the overall Defence Budget that was administered separately by the *RWM's Wehramt.* This budget was audited by a special branch of the Reich Audit Office so as to maintain secrecy. Costs had risen steadily, particularly in respect to aircraft testing. In the early years the Lipetsk operation had cost around *RM* 2 million, by 1930 the figure was *RM* 3 m - see Hooton 1994 p.74.

94   Braatz K. 2005 *Gott oder ein Flugzeug: Leben und Sterben des Jagdfliegers Günther Lützow* pp.56-84.

FIGURE 1D-4 ORGANISATION AND EQUIPMENT OF THE FLUGZENTRUM LIPETSK
1930

Stabes Gruppe	Junkers F 13 (1)
	Junkers A 20 (1)
	Junkers K 47 (3) *
	Albatros L 76 (4) *
Aufklärungsstaffel	Heinkel HD 17 (2)
Jagdstaffel	Fokker D.XIII (18)
Beobachter-Lehrgang	Heinkel HD 17 (4)
Jagdflieger-Lehrgang	Fokker D.XIII (16)
	Fokker D.VII (1)
	Heinkel HD 17 (2)
	Heinkel HD 21 (1)
	Albatros L 69 (2)

* The *Stabes-Gruppe* (HQ Group) had three aircraft attached for test purposes, these almost certainly being the Junkers K 47, whilst there were also four trainers, these probably being the Albatros L 78 as six of this type had been on-charge on the 1 Oct 29.

FIGURE 1D-5 AIRCRAFT KNOWN TO HAVE BEEN BASED AT LIPETSK
1925-1933

Aircraft Type	Qty	Aircraft Type	Qty
Fokker D.VII	2	Albatros L 76a	6
Fokker D.XIII	52	Albatros L 77v	6
Junkers F 13	1	Albatros L 78	7
Junkers A 20	2	Junkers A 48 (K 47)	3
Heinkel HD 21	1	Junkers W 34fi (K 43)	2
Heinkel HD 17	7	Junkers W 33b	1
Albatros L 68a	1	BFW M 23c	1
Albatros L 69	2		

Several new aircraft had been added during the previous year, notably the Albatros L 76a and the L 78, both of these types being employed primarily as trainers.

Photo 1A-1 Original caption: *Reichspräsidenten*
Friedrich Ebert published on the 25th anniversary of
his death on the 26 February 1925.
Bundesarchiv, Bild 102-00015/Photo: Georg Pahl

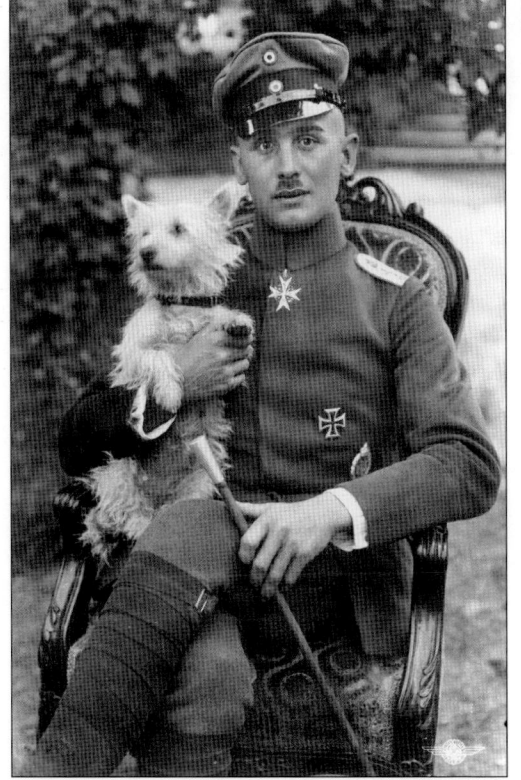

Photo 1A-2 Original caption: Portrait of Rudolf
Berthold in the uniform of a *Oberleutnant* sitting
outside with his dog, with his decorations (*Eisernes
Kreuz, Preußische Militär-Flugzeugführer-Abzeichen*).
Order of the *Pour le Mérite* (awarded on the 12
October 1916).
Bundesarchiv Bild 146-1998-009-14A Photo: o.Ang.

For the author's detailed commentaries on all photographs in this section please see page 317ff.

Photo 1A-3 Original caption: Berlin, March 1919: *Freikorps* shock troops on standby during the preliminary artillery bombardment on the Bülowplatz. General strike and armed struggles in support of the striking central German workers and for the recognition of ASR, release of all political prisoners, etc. from 3 to 12 March 1919. Through provocation *General* von Lüttwitz created the pretext for the movement of his troops into Berlin, on 6 March where they proceed with artillery against the Republican Militia. Shown here: *Freikorps Stroßtrupp* advancing in the protection of a tank on the Bülowplatz.
Bundesarchiv Bild 183-R94405 Photo: o.Ang. (Scherl Agency)

Photo 1A-4 Original caption: The German peace delegates and experts at Versailles in 1919. The members of the German delegation (l.to r.): Prof. Dr. Schücking, *Reichspostminister* Johannes Giesberts, *Reichsjustizminister* Dr. Otto Landsberg, *Reichsminister des Auswärtigen* Dr. Ulrich Graf Brockdorff-Rantzau, *Präsident der Preußischen Landesversammlung* Robert Leinert, Dr. Karl Melchior.
Bundesarchiv Bild 183-R01213 Photo: o.Ang.

Photo 1A-5 Original caption: Wismar – The *Freikorps Rossbach* during the Kapp-Putsch of 1920.
Bundesarchiv Bild 119-2815-20 Photo: o.Ang.

Photo 1A-6 Original caption: 1919. The last German *Jagdstaffel* prepares to take off from Döberitz.
Bundesarchiv Bild 183-R43291 Photo: o.Ang. Scherl Agency

Photo 1A-7 Original caption: Studio portrait of Hermann Göring, standing with medals (*Eisernes Kreuz II. and I.Klasse, Preußisches Militär-Flugzeugführer-Abzeichen, Verwundeten-Abzeichen in Schwarz, Pour le Mérite* – awarded 2 June 1918).
Bundesarchiv Bild 146-2013-0013 Photo: o.Ang.

Above: Photo 1A-8 Original caption: The creator and organiser of the *Reichswehr* [*Generaloberst* Hans von Seeckt] with his infantry students (Dresden) in the first *Reichswehr* maneuvers in 1925 in Thüringen, near Erfurt as *Chef der Heeresleitung*. Bundesarchiv Bild 146-2005-0163 Photo: Oscar Tellgmann

Right: Photo 1A-9 Original caption: Our successful fighter pilot *Leutnant* Udet - Portrait of Ernst Udet Order *Pour le Mérite* (awarded on 9 April 1918). Bundesarchiv Bild 146-1978-098-21A Photo: Postkartenvertrieb W.Sanke, Berlin N 37

Photo 1A-10 Original caption: *Deutsche Luftstreitkräfte* 1918. A *Beobachter* with a machine gun.
Bundesarchiv Bild 183-R27828 Photo: o.Ang. (Scherl)

Photo 1A-11 Original caption: A German secret enterprise behind the Iron Curtain in the steppes of the Volga
region near Volsk in the years 1928 to 1931 (Dissolved in 1933). The HD 40 our largest machine in use, is about
to depart at the airfield of the *Tomka Kampfmittel-Versuchsplatz* – a joint *Reichswehr* and the Red Army chemical
weapons-testing ground. The aircraft is fitted with the *Kampfstoffbomben* and *Kamppfstofftanken* (chemical
weapons bombs and tanks). The pilot, pictured right, gives a good indication of the size of the aircraft.
Bundesarchiv MSg 2 Bild-00782-42 Photo: o.Ang.

Above: Photo 1A-12 Original caption: Honouring the Reich Constitution in Berlin on 11 August 1923. *Reichspräsident* [Friedrich] Ebert and *Reichswehrminister* [Otto] Gessler proceed in front of the guard of honour.
Bundesarchiv Bild 102-10844 Photo: Georg Pahl

Right: Photo 1A-13 Original caption: This year's major cavalry manoeuvres in Döberitz in Berlin! *Reichswehrminister* Dr. Gessler and *General* von Seeckt were present during the manoeuvres. Subsequent to the manoeuvre a parade of troops took place. *Reichswehrminister* Dr. [Otto] Gessler (right) and *General* [Hans] von Seeckt (left) are seen in the exercise area.
Bundesarchiv Bild 102-10883 Photo: Georg Pahl

Above: Photo 1A-14 Original caption: *Reichswehrminister* Dr. Groener has resigned from his post! *Reichswehrminister* Dr. Groener with *Reichswehr* officers during an exercise. Bundesarchiv Bild 102-13484 Photo: Georg Pahl

Left: Photo 1A-15 Original caption: *General* (Kurt) Schleicher – at an event in front of the *Reichstag* in 1932. (Schleicher (left) is seen here in the company of his friend and colleague *Gen.d.Inf.* Kurt von Hammerstein-Equord, the *Chef des Heeresleitung* (right)). Bundesarchiv Bild 146-1992-018-01A Photo: Hartmann

Above: Photo 1A-16 Original caption: *Stahlhelm* – Kurt Schleicher (left), Franz von Papen (centre), Wilhelm Freiherr von Gayl (right).
Bundesarchiv Bild 146-2012-0056 Photo: o.Ang.

Right: Photo 1A-17 Original caption: On the forthcoming eightieth birthday of the *Reichspräsidenten* von Hindenburg! This was the last civil record of *Reichspräsidenten* von Hindenburg in his office at the Presidential Palace.
Bundesarchiv Bild 102-04763 Photo: o.Ang.

Above: Photo 1A-18 Original caption: The historic Potsdam Tag of 21 March 1933. *Reichspräsident* von Hindenburg, *Reichskanzler* Hitler and *Reichswehrminister* von Blomberg infront of the Garrison Church in Berlin.
Archiv Title: At the inauguration of the *Reichstag-* Paul von Hindenburg (with *Pickelhaube*), Werner von Blomberg (with *Stahlhelm*) and Adolf Hitler in front of the Garrison Church.
Bundesarchiv Bild 102-16082 Photo: Georg Pahl

Left: Photo 1B-1 Original caption: *Ministerialdirigent* Ernst Brandenburg appointed an honorary Dr. Ing! The *Technische Hochschule Braunschweig* has awarded the *Leiter der Luftfahrtabteilung im Reichsverkehrsministerium, MinDir.*Ernst Brandenburg a honorary Doctorate in Engineering in view of his services to aviation.
Bundesarchiv Bild 102-06974 Photo: o.Ang.

Photo 1B-2 Original caption: The *Reichs* Government is flying to the inauguration of the *deutschen Museums*, which will take place on the 5 May in Munchen. The two Junkers aircraft are seen shortly before take-off. (Bundesarchiv Bild 102-01371 Photo: Georg Pahl)

Photo 1B-3 Original caption: The first launch of the Ocean giant flying boat Rohrbach *"Romar"* in Travemünde! Left to right: Dr. [Adolf] Rohrbach, the builder of this flying ocean liner, the well-known commander of the ocean flying boat [Hermann] Steindorf, and *Direktor* [Otto] Merkel of *Luft Hansa* after the successful flight from Travemünde.
Bundesarchiv Bild 102-10107 Photo: Georg Pahl

Photo 1B-4 Original caption: Jubilation for an aeroplane! It is now about 10 years ago since the first Junkers aircraft of type F 13 with the registration number "1," was officially handed over to the airline. Nothing proves the vigour of this type better than the fact that the "D 1" which was built in 1919 is still in use today as a German transport.
Bundesarchiv Bild 102-07981 Photo: o.Ang.

Photo 1B-5 Original caption: The "fliegende Haus", the largest German landplane in the World! Professor Junkers, the *General-Construkteur*, with his co-workers in front of the new G.38 long range aircraft.
Bundesarchiv Bild 102-08683 Photo: Georg Pahl

Photo 1C-1 Original caption: *Flugboot* Dornier J *"Wal"* with the registration D-861 *"Hai"* photographed between 1926-30.
Bundesarchiv, Bild 102-00858/Photo: Georg Pahl

Photo 1C-2 Original caption: Germany 1928. *Junkers-Werke* in Dessau and Portrait of the founder of the works, Professor Junkers.
Bundesarchiv Bild 183-R14718 Photo: o.Ang. (Scherl)

Left: Photo 1C-3 Original caption: *Generalleutnant* Otto Hasse, *Kommandant der 3. Division*, during field manoeuvres. Bundesarchiv Bild 102-00363A Photo: Georg Pahl

Below: Photo 1C-4 Original caption: Interesting experiments with a German parachute, which allows jumps from a height of 40 m. The parachute doll is seen on the wing of the aircraft before take-off. The attendant releases the connection string height at 40 m and observes the functioning of the parachute. Bundesarchiv Bild 102-14834 Photo: Georg Pahl

Right: Photo 1C-5 Original caption: Dr.
Heinkel and Günther Plüschow, Dr. Ernst
Heinkel (r.) in the 30s *Chef der Heinkel
Flugzeugwerke* in Warnemünde with pilot
Käpitanleutnant a.D. Günther Plüschow (l.).
Bundesarchiv Bild 183-S55983 Photo: o.Ang.

Below: Photo 1C-6 Original caption: Junkers
A 48dy, *Jagdflugzeug*, used as a precursor to the
Stuka Ju 87. Werkfoto Junkers (MBB) 48/2.
Bundesarchiv Bild 146-0908-500 Photo:
o.Ang.

Photo 1C-7 Original caption: *Flugzeugkonstrukteur Dornier*, Prof.Dr.Claude Dornier with the Dornier Do K-3
aircraft (Coded D-2183; First flight August 1931).
Bundesarchiv Bild 102-03504A Photo: Georg Pahl

Photo 1C-8 Original caption: The world record flight of the long range Dornier Do X flying boat.
Bundesarchiv Bild 102-01216A Photo: Georg Pahl

Photo 1C-9 Original caption: En route landing in Berlin (Tempelhof) by oceanic flier Könnecke on his long
range flight over the Ocean in his Caspar aircraft *"Germania"*.
Bundesarchiv Bild 102-00394A/Photo Georg Pahl

Photo 1C-10 Original caption: The enormous seaworthiness of the new German flying boat Rohrbach "Romar" in Travemünde! The Rohrbach Flugboot *"Romar"* with 2,400 hp jumps out of the water at a maximum load of 20,000 kg. when starting with a speed of 150 kph.
Bundesarchiv Bild 102-07269 Photo: o.Ang.

Photo 1C-11 Original caption: Bases and installations, *Seeflugstation Travemünde* - Aerial view by the *Stabsbildabteilung beim Kommandeur der Flieger der Flotte* from 14 August 1918 - *H 102 Stabia K.d.Flieg.F. "Travemünde" 14.8.18, 4.30 pm, Hohe 200 m, Lange 25 cm (Seeflugstation).*
Bundesarchiv Bild 134-B3289 Photo: o.Ang.

Photo 1C-12 Original caption: Bombs being loaded under a large German aircraft, circa November 1917.
Bundesarchiv Bild 146-1971-045-48 Photo: o.Ang.

Photo 1D-1 Original caption: Hangars I, II and III at Lipetsk in Soviet Union.
Bundsarchiv RH 2 Bild-02292-041 Photo: o.Ang.

Photo 1D-2 Original caption: Lipetsk, Soviet Union – Fokker D.XIII aircraft (Coded 11) fitted with skis.
Bundesarchiv RH 2 Bild-02292-072 Photo: o.Ang.

Photo 1D-3 Original caption: Crash of a Fokker D.XIII with a Russian pilot – Lipetsk, Soviet Union. Wreck of a
Fokker D.XIII aircraft.
Bundesarchiv RH 2 Bild-02292-014 Photo: o.Ang.

Above: Photo 1D-4 Original caption:
During the great German autumn
gliding flights on the Rhön in the
presence of the *General* (Erich)
Ludendorff, a world record was set for a
12 km long flight by the famous glider
Marteus. A glider takes off from the
Wasserkuppe.
Bundesarchiv Bild 102-10292 Photo:
Georg Pahl

Right: Photo 1D-5 Original
caption: Friedrichshafen! A *Zeppelin-
Luftschiffhalle* in use to accommodate
aircraft.
Bundesarchiv Bild 102-00715/Photo
Georg Pahl

Photo 1D-6 Original caption: *Größflugtag* in Staaken near Berlin! On the 2nd day of Easter, a large *Flugtag* took place at Staaken near Berlin, where famous German pilots displayed their skills in front of tens of thousands of spectators. The highlight of the event was the demonstration by Bleriot who flew the original Bleriot machine across the English Channel in 1909. The best German pilots at the *Größflugtag* at Staaken were (l. to r.): the Berlin aerobatic pilot Frau Marga von Etzdorf, the well-known German pilot Ernst Udet, and pilot Fieseler, both known for their daring display flying.
Bundesarchiv Bild 102-05708 Photo: Georg Pahl

Photo 1D-7 Original caption: Studio portrait of Paul Bäumer, standing with cigarette in hand with *Eisernes Kreuz II.* and *I.Klasse, Preußischer Militär-Flugzeugführerabzeichen.*
Bundesarchiv Bild 146-2013-0012 Photo: o.Ang.

Photo 1D-8 Original caption: Award ceremony of the *Adlerplakette des Deutschen Reichausschußes für Leibesübungen* (the Reich's Committee for Physical Education's Eagle Badge) to the famous German glider pilot Günther Groenhoff! *Staatsminister a.D.*Dominicus solemnly hands over the eagle badge to the German glider pilot Günther Groenhoff.
Bundesarchiv Bild 102-13051 Photo: Georg Pahl

Photo 1D-9 Original caption: Flying students! The *Hochschule fur Leibesübungen* has established a gliding course for flight students in the heights near Berlin Gatow. Under the guidance of an experienced instructor, the students are trained gliding flight. The course takes the form of a *Flugsemester*. At the end of the semester, the main test takes place and after successful completion of this assessment, the flight student is awarded the title A-pilot. A successful take-off for the flight student. The launch team has torn down the slope to tug the glider into the air.
Bundesarchiv Bild 102-14452 Photo: Georg Pahl

Photo 1D-10 Original caption: Images from the *deutschen Rundflug*, which took place for the first time after the war with the participation of over 90 small aircraft at Tempelhof in Berlin. An early start for the fliers of the *deutschen Rundflug* at 4 o'clock in the morning.
Bundesarchiv Bild 102-01480 Photo: Georg Pahl

Photo 1D-11 Original caption: The arrival of the first European flyer at the *Zentralflughafen Berlin-Tempelhof!* Last year's winner of the *Europa-Rundfluges* Morzik on his arrival as the second German to land at the *Zentralflughafen* in Berlin, is greeted by his wife and friends. Berlin-Tempelhof, *Zentralflughafen* - arrival of the fourth placed after the race and the overall winner at the International *Europa-Rundflug* Fritz [Friedrich] Morzik in his BFW M.23c aircraft.
Bundesarchiv Bild 102-10197 Photo: Georg Pahl

Photo 1D-12 Original caption: A major international air show connected with inverted flight took place at the *Zentralflughafen* Berlin! The best German aerobatic pilot Gerhard Fieseler is seen flying inverted just 25 m above the ground.
Bundesarchiv Bild 102-13561 Photo: Georg Pahl

Photo 1D-13 Original caption: Ju 52/3m aircraft (*der Regierungsstaffel/Fliegerstaffel des Führers* (*FdF*)), Adolf Hitler's machine – possibly coded D-2600 *Immelmann*.
Bundesarchiv Bild 146-1979-106-30 Photo: o.Ang.

Photo 1D-14 Original caption: The jubilant reception of the airship *"Graf Zeppelin"* in the German capital Berlin! The landing of the *"Graf Zeppelin"* at the new mooring mast in Staaken in Berlin. The airship moored for the first time in Germany at the mooring mast in Staaken.
Bundesarchiv Bild 102-06793 Photo: Georg Pahl

Photo 1D-15 Original caption: The jubilant reception of the *"Graf Zeppelin"* at the airship port in Berlin-Staaken! The happy landing of the *"Graf Zeppelin"* in Staaken at the mooring mast. In the background a small airship can be seen.
Bundesarchiv Bild 102-09990 Photo: Georg Pahl

Photo 1E-1 Original caption: *Reichswehrmänover* in Königstein, 1930.
Bundesarchiv Bild 102-01819A Photo: Georg Pahl

Photo 1E-2 Original caption: Pontoon Bridge during the large scale pioneer exercise under the cover of artificial fog on the Elbe near Höhenwarthe! For the first time the construction of a military bridge was practiced using a chemical smoke screen. *Pioniere* are seen at work on the construction of the pontoon bridge at Höhenwarthe on the Elbe before screening.
Bundesarchiv Bild 102-1894 Photo: Georg Pahl

Above: Photo 1E-3 Original caption: The
first major exercise of this year's *Reichswehr*
autumn manoeuvres were held in Ostpreussen!
Manoeuvre images of the *1.Division* between
Goldap and Angerapp in Ostpreussen. A *leichte
Geschütz* in firing position in the exercise area.
Bundesarchiv Bild 102-11934 Photo: Georg Pahl

Right: Photo 1E-4 Original caption: Our
successful fighter pilot *Oberleutnant* Greim.
Bundesarchiv Bild 146-1969-030-18 Photo:
o.Ang. Postkartenvertrieb W.Sanke, Berlin

Photo 1E-5 Original caption: The large *Reichswehr* exercise in in the area of Königshofen in Unterfranken took place in the presence of *Reichspräsidenten von Hindenburg* and many foreign military attaches. It is the first time since the war, that such *Reichswehr* manoeuvres have taken place in western Germany in the area between Kissingen, Meiningen and Würzburg. A camouflaged heavy machine gun is seen in the exercise area.
Bundesarchiv Bild 102-10892 Photo: Georg Pahl

Photo 1E-6 Original caption: *4./Res.Feld-Art.Rgt.13*, *Feldkanone* provisionally mounted as an anti-aircraft gun on an improvised turntable, *Armeeoberkommando 7, Estfront*, France. Soldiers of *Reserve-Feldartillerie-Regiments Nr.13* use a Feldkanone 96 as a *Fliegerabwehrgeschütz*, Rangefinder to the left.
Bundesarchiv Bild 136-0635 Photo: Oscar Tellgmann

Photo 1E-7 Original caption: German Anti-Aircraft Gun on a lorry mounting. The *Fliegerabwehr* on the Italian Front in 1917.
Bundesarchiv Bild 183-S29499 Photo: o.Ang. (Scherl)

Photo 1E-8 Original caption: *Flugabwehrkanone* during the autumn manoeuvres near Bad Mergentheim in Southern Germany, September 1926.
Bundesarchiv Bild 102-03179 Photo: Georg Pahl

Photo 1E-9 Original caption: With gas masks beside the searchlight – two German soldiers with gas masks operate a searchlight of the *Flakartillerie* in 1918.
Bundesarchiv Bild 183-R27853 Photo: o.Ang. Scherl Agency

Photo 1E-10 Original caption: *Linienschiff SMS "Hannover"* - Launched September 29, 1905, decommissioned in December 1918; recommissioned February 1921 for the *Reichsmarine*, taken out of service September 1931, scrapped 1944/1946; Gunnery practice.
Bundesarchiv Bild 134-B2097 Photo: o.Ang.

Photo 1E-11 Original caption: *Großes Torpedoboot SMS "S 19"* - Launched 17 October 1912, later served with the *Reichsmarine*, decommissioned 31 March 1931, broken up 1935.
Bundesarchiv Bild 134-B0485 Photo: o.Ang.

Photo 1E-19 Original caption: The German *Kreuzer "Berlin"* out of service! The German *Kreuzer "Berlin"* in the port of Kiel, behind lies the German *Linienschiff "Hessen"*.
Bundesarchiv Bild 102-07600 Photo: o.Ang.

Photo 1E-20 Original caption: At the launching of *Panzerkreuzer* "A" in the *Germania-Werft, Kiel*, the ship was christened by *Reichspsident* von Hindenburg in the name of *"Deutschland"*. The *Panzerkreuzer Deutschland* was cheered by a crowd of many thousands as she made her way down the slips.
Bundesarchiv Bild 102-11704 Photo: Georg Pahl

Above: Photo 1E-21 Original caption: The new catapult aircraft of the German giant steamer *"Europa"*. The new aircraft catapult aboard the German giant steamer *"Europa"* has been placed into service. The catapult aircraft shortens the shuttle service of urgent mail to America by 24 hours. Bundesarchiv Bild 102-10309 Photo: o.Ang.

Right: Photo 1E-22 Original caption: *Admiral* [Erich] Raeder, the new *Chef der Marineleitung* today (4.10) takes office - Portrait of Erich Raeder sitting at his office desk. Bundesarchiv Bild 146-1987-080-30A Photo: o.Ang. (Polyphot Agency)

Photo 1E-23 Original caption: Aerial photograph of the *Hilfschiffe* (*Flugzeugmutterschiff*) *SMH "Santa Helena"*.
Launched on the 16 November 1907 as a Freighter and re-commissioned as a Seaplane Tender by July 1915.
Transferred to the USA in 1919.
Bundesarchiv Bild 134-B4228 Photo: o.Ang.

Photo 1E-24 Original caption: Aerial view of the French Aircraft Carrier *"Bearn"* – Launched 15 April 1920.
Bundesarchiv Bild 134-B1530 Photo: o.Ang.

FIGURE 1D-6 FLUGSCHULER JAGDFLIEGER-LEHRGANG LIPETSK 1931	
Hans-Jurgen Aschmann	Walter Kienzle
Max Collmann	Günther Lützow
Wolfgang Falck	Günther Radusch
Ekhart Hefter	Ralph von Rettberg
Wolfdietrich von Houwald	Hannes Trautloft

The importance of *Wivupal* as a flight test centre however increased during the first part of the new decade and the number of test and administrative personnel rose to total nearly 300 during this period.[95] The busiest year for testing was undoubtedly 1931 when the prototypes of six new military aircraft were present, these being the Arado SD IV and Heinkel HD 38 fighters, the Focke Wulf S 39 and Heinkel HD 45 and 46 reconnaissance aircraft and the Do P heavy night bomber (See 1C2 & 1C3).[96] At the same time tests were carried out using the new SC Ordnance using two Junkers W 34 aircraft, whilst an Albatros L 77v was employed for armament trials with a flexibly mounted 20 mm cannon (See 1C5).[97] Several of the trials aircraft were secretly flown, often at night over sensitive foreign stages, from Germany to Lipetsk along *Deruluft GmbH's* airline route via Ostpreussen and the Ostsee States to Moskva, the military aircraft turning south near Velikye Luki for the final leg to Lipetsk (See also 1D2).[98] During one of these clandestine flights *Dipl-Ing.*Dietrich Schwenke was obliged to make a forced landing near Vitebsk in the new HD 46 *Aufklärungsflugzeug* after experiencing engine trouble.[99] Unfortunately this was not the first time a German aircraft had been forced down whilst in transit to Lipetsk. On the 11 June 1930 Emil Thuy and his *Bordmechaniker Herr* Kunne were both killed when they attempted a take-off in their Albatros L 76a from an emergency landing field near Smolensk.[100]

For the most part flight testing of these aircraft was carried out by civilian employees of the *Reichsverband der Deutschen Luftfahrtindustrie (RdL)*, supplemented where appropriate by *Flugzentrum* personnel. These included the Rechlin based *Herrn.*Dietrich Frhr.von Massenbach *(Fhr. Gr.III)*, Hoppe *(Ref.Flugzeuge)* and Schwenke *(Ref.Ausrüstung)* together with *Herrn.*Heinz Simon *(Ltr.T 5)* and Karl Wiborg *(Flugzeugführer)* from the *E-Stelle Travemünde*; Lipetsk permanent staff pilots included *Herrn* Albert Blumensaat *(Schiesslehrer)*, Gustav Bollmann *(Fluglehrer)*, Hermann Dick *(Ausbildungsleiter)* and Schoenebeck *(Ausbildungsleiter)*; service personnel included Hans-

95   *Anhang C Zeittafel* in Caspari Undated p.296 & Schliephake in Beauvais et al 2002 p.48. During the early stages of the *Fliegerschule Stahr* the permanent staff totalled 60-70 officers and men to which some 45 students were added during the summer months - see Hooton 1994 p.46.

96   Schliephake in Beauvais et al 2002 pp.48-49. See also Nowarra 1980 pp.182-184, 190-193, 204-209 & 216-217 and Mason 1973 pp.160-161. Schoenebeck did a great deal to guide the development of the Arado fighter series being employed by the *Arado Flugzeugwerk* as chief pilot and military advisor from Jan 32 following his return from Lipetsk - see also Townsend 1970 p.116, Kosin 1983 p.75 & service record for Carl-August von Schoenebeck in Hildebrand 1992 pp.213-214.

97   Schliephake in Beauvais et al 2002 p.48. The L 77v used for armament trials has not been identified but it was built by *Heinkel* and fitted with a rotatable machine gun mount *(Drehkanz)* in the rear cockpit.

98   Schliephake 1971 p.19 & Hooton 1994 p.47. One of the earliest aircraft to fly along this "commercial" route was the twin-engine Heinkel HD 20 WNr.251 D-1157. This aircraft had been designed to meet a requirement for a long range photo-reconnaissance platform. It was registered to the *DVL* - see also Koos 2006 pp.53-54. Aircraft such as the Junkers K 47 were despatched at night to over fly the Danzig Corridor to Ostpresseun and then across Poland for a second time to reach Belorussia - see Mason 1973 pp.161-162.

99   Schliephake in Beauvais et al 2002 p.43 & Koos 2006 p.109.

100 Schliephake in Beauvais et al 2002 pp.48-49. The two men were flying Albatros L 76a WNr.10 101 D-1127.

Jurgen von Cramon-Taubadel *(Reichsheer)* and Rudolf Spies *(Ref.i.Reichsmarine Gruppe BSx)*.[101] In 1932 these pilots would collectively evaluate another batch of experimental aircraft types: the Dornier F and P bombers, the Albatros L 81, Focke Wulf W 7 and Heinkel HD 46 tactical reconnaissance aircraft and the large He 59 naval multi-role aircraft.[102]

FIGURE 1D-7 AIRCRAFT KNOWN TO HAVE UNDERGONE TEST AT LIPETSK 1928-1933			
In contemporary German documents the *Flugzentrum's* role as an experimental centre was covered by the designation *Wissenschaftliche Versuchs- und Prufanstalt für Luftfahrzeuge*, or Scientific Trial and Test Establishment for Aircraft.			
Aircraft Type	**WNr.**	**Registration**	**Function**
Albatros L 81	10164	D-2198	Two seat Reconnaissance Aircraft
Albatros L 84	10187	D-1899	Two seat Fighter
Arado SD II	??	D-2799	Single seat Fighter
Arado SD III	54	D-1973	Single seat Fighter
Arado SSD I *	53	D-1905	Single seat Naval Fighter
Arado Ar 64	65	D-2470	Single seat Fighter
Arado Ar 64	66	D-2338	Single seat Fighter
Arado Ar 65	71 ?	D-2218	Single seat Fighter
Dornier B	???	D-????	Auxiliary Bomber
Dornier P	180	D-1982	Heavy Night Bomber
Dornier F	230	D-2270	Four seat Medium Bomber
Focke Wulf W 7 *	112	D-2216	Two seat Naval Reconnaissance Aircraft
Focke Wulf S 39 *	???	D-????	Two seat Naval Reconnaissance Aircraft
Heinkel HD 38a *	369	D-2272	Single seat Naval Fighter
Heinkel HD 40 II	274	D-1180	Medium Bomber
Heinkel HD 41a	321	D-1694	Two seat Reconnaissance Aircraft
Heinkel HD 45a	364	D-2064	Two seat Reconnaissance Aircraft
Heinkel He 45b	391	D-2238	Two seat Reconnaissance Aircraft
Heinkel HD 46a	376	D-1702	Two seat Reconnaissance Aircraft
Heinkel HD 46b	377	D-1028	Two seat Reconnaissance Aircraft
Heinkel He 59b *	379	D-2215	Four seat Naval Multi-Role Aircraft
Junkers A 35	1059	D-987	Two seat Light Bomber
Junkers G 24ge	844	D-878	Auxiliary Bomber
Rohrbach Ro VIIIMb	18	D-991	Auxiliary Bomber
*Naval aircraft which were fitted with wheel undercarriages for test purposes at Lipetsk.			

101   Schliephake in Beauvais et al 2002 p.48. See also Ries 1970 p.83.
102   Andersson 1989 p.44 & Schliephake in Beauvais et al 2002 pp.48-49. See also Nowarra 1980 pp.192-193, 204-209, 212-214 & 218-219.

The *Reichswehr's* Soviet hosts profited greatly from this activity as a comprehensive exhibition of equipment marked the culmination of each trials period at the *Flugzentrum*. On these occasions technical experts from the Central Aero and Hydrodynamics Institute *(Ts.AGI)*, the Armament Test Centre at Yagi and the Scientific Test Institute *(NII-VVS)* at Monino were fully briefed on the tests, whilst the various prototypes were also made available for test-flying by Soviet pilots.[103] The Germans on the other hand learnt very little of the latest Soviet developments which were carefully concealed at other centres in the USSR.

In February 1932 Mohr was replaced as *Chef der Flugzentrum Lipetsk* by *Hptm.*Gottlob Müller and thereafter there was a progressive reduction in the *Reichswehr's* activities at Lipetsk, a trend which was particularly worrying to the Soviet authorities who brought pressure to bear in an effort to convince the Germans of the continuing value of the facility.[104] In 1932 *Marshal* Tukhachevski, the Chief of Ordnance within the Red Army, attended the *Reichsheer's* autumn manoeuvres but in his discussions with senior German officers he had been unable to influence events.[105] Further hard bargaining followed with Soviet demands for the resumption of fighter training which would necessitate the return of the instructing staff together with their new Arado SD IV fighters from Germany. There was also a high level of Soviet interest in heavy bomber operations which was coupled to a further demand for the training of German night bomber crews to be based in the USSR. This request was undoubtedly stimulated by the presence of the Dornier Do F and P bombers at Lipetsk together with the formation in the USSR of the *Aviatsiya Osobovo Naznacheniya (AON)* as the controlling formation for the increasing number of TB-3 (ANT-6) heavy bombers in Soviet service.[106]

Adolf Hitler, as the new *Reichskanzler*, was equally determined to terminate the Lipetsk arrangement and although a small fighter course was conducted at the *Flugzentrum* in 1933 and some limited testing was also undertaken, *Hptm.*Wilhelm Speidel, *Leiter Gruppe II (Organisation) Heer* within the new *Luftschützamt* (Air Defence Office), was ordered to travel to Lipetsk in the mid-summer of that year to supervise the closure of the centre.[107] All movable equipment, including the experimental aircraft, was returned to the Reich, whilst by way of compensation the *VVS* received the surviving training machines together with all the airfield infrastructure which had been built-up since 1925.[108]

Good relations with the Soviets were maintained to the very end:

103   Schliephake in Beauvais et al 2002 p.48. For example in Sep 31 a two day event was held for the Soviet Authorities. See also Boyd 1977 pp.24-25 & Suchenwirth 1968 p.31.
104   Suchenwirth 1968 p.32. *Hptm.*Müller had been a student and staff member at Lipetsk during Apr 28-Aug 29. He had seen war service as a *Jagdflieger* with *Jasta 79b* in 1918 before being retained in the *Reichsheer* as an officer within *Kraftfahr-Abt.7* München during 1920-28 - see service record for Gottlob Müller in Hildebrand 1991 pp.412-413.
105   Suchenwirth 1968 p.30 & Mason 1973 pp.163-164. During 1932 *GenMaj.*Hilmar Ritter von Mittelberger, *Insp.d.Waffenschulen*, met Yakov Alksnis, the new Chief *GU-VVS*. See also Hooton 1994 pp.78-79.
106   Suchenwirth 1968 pp.32-33, Ries 1970 p.83, Mason 1973 p.164 & Boyd 1977 p.25.
107   Schliephake in Beauvais et al 2002 pp.48-49. *Obstlt.*Hellmuth Felmy, *Chef Insp.1 (L)* proposed on the 28 Oct 32 that Lipetsk be closed - see Hooton 1994 p.78. However Hitler added a further emphasis to this decision – see Schliephake 1971 p.21. Flight testing in 1933 focused on the Ar 65 fighter, He 45 & 46 reconnaissance aircraft & the Do 11 bomber, all types that were being produced in secret for the emergent Luftwaffe - see also Vajda F.A. & Dancey P.1998 *German Aircraft Industry and Production 1933-1945* p.10. The members of the final 1933 *Jagdflieger-Lehrgang* were Wilhelm Berlin, Eberhard d'Elsa, Oskar Henrici, , Douglas Pitcairn, Dietrich Robitzsch, Joachim Schlichting & Ernst-Siegfried Steen - see Ries K. 1986 *Luftwaffe Photo-Report 1919-1945* p.19. *Hptm.* Speidel had been a student at Lipetsk in 1928. During 1929-30 he spent a year in the USA as a guest of the *USAAC* before returning to Germany where he was successively a *Referent* in *T 3 (Fremde Heer)*, *T 2 (Organisation)* & *Insp.1 (L)* - see service record for Wilhelm Speidel in Hildebrand 1992 pp.320-323.
108   *Anhang C Zeittafel* in Caspari Undated p.298 & Schliephake in Beauvais et al 2002 p.49. The Soviets were gifted the Do P bomber & 30 Fokker D.XIII fighters, whilst they acquired the Focke Wulf W 7. However another authoritative source suggests that the aircraft and buildings were sold to the Soviet authorities - see Ries 1970 p.83.

Today we had our official farewell party with Thomsen (the Russian *Kommandant* at Lipetsk) and Dandorf. We had a cold collation, eggs in mayonnaise, bouillon, chicken, pudding with fruit, and coffee, Vodka, liqueurs and strawberry-cup. Even between the various courses there were lots of toasts and speeches, and singing of the *Internationale* and the *Deutschlandlied*, with cheering and expressions of hope that "such good relations" between our two countries might continue, and to this we had to empty our full glasses over and over again.[109]

Unknown *Flugschuler Lipetsk*
16 August 1933

In all some 450 German personnel had been trained at Lipetsk between 1925-33. This figure included over 200 aircrew, 120 of which had qualified as fighter pilots.[110] The value of the base as a trials establishment during the period when the *Reichswehr* was prevented from conducting such activities in Germany was simply incalculable.

109   Quoted from Schliephake 1971 *The Birth of the Luftwaffe* p.32-33 with the kind permission of Ian Allan Publishing.
110   Mason 1973 p.164, Nowarra 1981 p.36 & Hooton 1994 p.79. Lipetsk was the only one of Seeckt's Soviet ventures to be thoroughly cost effective. Two thirds of the fighter pilots trained at Lipetsk between1927-33 were *Offizieranwarter*. One source suggests that as many technical personnel had also been trained at Lipetsk - see Hooton 1994 p.46.

1D2

Civil Aviation in the Weimar Republic 1920-1933

Wir deutschen Flieger	We German fliers
Wurden Sieger	became victorious
Durch ans allein	through ourselves alone.
Volk, flieg, Du Wieder	German people, you must fly
Und Du wirst Sieger	and you will be victorious
Durch Dich allein	through yourself alone.

Dedication on the Wasserkuppe to the glider pilots of Germany.

For two years after the enactment of the Treaty of Versailles in May 1920 Germany was prohibited, except in very limited circumstances, from exercising the privilege of powered flight (See 1B1).[1] Not surprisingly the former members of the *Luftstreitkräfte* and *Marineflieger* who sought to find a new outlet for their aeronautical skills in post-war Europe were to find this measure restriction particularly frustrating, sentiments which were eloquently expressed by *Hptm.a.D.*Hermann Steiner in his later book *The Rise and Fall of the Luftwaffe*:

> What were we going to do? Most of us were very young; in fact most of us had left school to become fliers. Now we had no place to go, nothing to do…we felt nostalgia. We looked for an object for our dreams, an object for our idealism. Most of us determined to go on flying, no matter what the peace conditions might be, no matter what would be allowed or forbidden in the future… This nostalgia for something better, for something higher, this passion for flying - which with many of us was almost a sickness - grew stronger and stronger during the next few years of revolution, inflation and unemployment, when life became all but hopeless and without point for a great part of the German people. For many of us, flying became the very meaning of life.[2]

To fulfil these dreams many former military pilots turned to un-powered flight, the only option in Weimar Germany during the early twenties.[3] Hermann Steiner was one of a group of ex-military pilots who went to University to study aeronautical engineering:

1   Quoted from Hermann 1943 *The Rise and Fall of the Luftwaffe* p.15 (hereafter cited as Hermann 1943) p.19 John Long Ltd. Hptm.a.D.Hermann Steiner was a *Kampfflieger* (Bomber Pilot) in the *Luftstreitkräfte* during the Great War. In his book he writes under the pseudonym Hptm.Hermann as he was not in sympathy with the Nazi regime of the period.
2   Quoted from Hermann 1943 *The Rise and Fall of the Luftwaffe* p.15 John Long Ltd.
3   Hermann 1943 p.17. Others would move abroad, notably *Hptm.a.D.*Hermann Göring who went to Denmark and later Sweden – see Mosley L. 1974 *The Reich Marshal: A Biography of Hermann Göring* pp.48-53. Göring gained the substantive rank of *Hptm.* by relinquishing his pension rights – see Irving D. 1989 *Göring: A Biography* pp.38-39. Although gliding had been at the forefront of early experiments with flight – witness the early achievements of Otto Lilienthal who was unfortunately killed in a gliding accident in 1896 – very little gliding had taken place in Germany following the development of powered aircraft – see Mason H.M. 1973 *The Rise of the Luftwaffe 1918-1940* (hereafter cited as Mason 1973) pp.106-107.

We looked funny enough, young former soldiers and former flyers that filled the universities of Germany. We were twenty and twenty-one and twenty-two years old, and the poor food of these past few years and, indeed, of the years to come, made most of us look thin and frail and even younger than we were. Many of us didn't have any civilian clothes to wear. We wore our old uniforms. We cut the metal buttons from the jackets - that was all. We had no goal but to study as fast and as much as we could in order to make something of ourselves. And all the time we had a dream. It was the dream of flying again.[4]

Steiner was one of many young men who joined together with other students to form a *Verein*, or Club:

This movement was born spontaneously and grew simultaneously in many parts of Germany during 1919 and 1920. I think the only explanation for this amazing fact was to be found in the attitude of the German youth in its decision to go flying - no matter what. I do not know why it happened that the Rhön mountains in central Germany became the Mecca of the new movement, though there had been some glider experiments in the Rhön even before the war. Probably the Rhön became the centre because it was in the geographical centre of Germany and thus easily reached by all the young men, who didn't have the money for long journeys. As it was, the whole glider business, cheap as it was compared with any other kind of flying, presented almost insurmountable difficulties and the greatest sacrifices for us penniless young men. But it didn't matter. Here again was chance to fly - and, incidentally, to fly without doing something illegal. The Treaty of Versailles had not restricted gliding, for the simple reason that there had been no gliding at the time of Versailles.[5]

Steiner and his contemporaries built their own gliders from whatever came to hand. This work was almost entirely carried out in the evenings after a hard day of work or study. To transport their new creations to the gliding sites required that they me easily taken apart prior to re-assembly on arrival. They could not afford to rent a room at the inn at Gersfeld, near the Wasserkuppe; they therefore slept in tents or in the packing cases beside their gliders. The weather was often bad with days of rain or even fog.[6] However this was a time for discussion and the development of that unique camaraderie that comes when a group of enthusiasts are thrown together in adversity *(Photo 1D-4)*:

Well, finally the rain stopped, the cover of fog tore open, and the atmosphere began to clear. Immediately we started to send our gliders up into the air. Among the many entries was my plane, called "Black Devil" because it was covered in black cotton. For a few minutes I was the happy holder of the world record on the "Black Devil". First, Klemperer tried and achieved a flight that lasted something like one and a half minutes. Then I came along and bettered his record by another half a minute. Then Klemperer tried again and established the unheard of world record of two and half minutes in the air, which as far as I know was not beaten until next year.[7]

---

4   Quoted from Hermann 1943 *The Rise and Fall of the Luftwaffe* p.16-17 John Long Ltd.
5   Quoted from Hermann 1943 *The Rise and Fall of the Luftwaffe* p.17 John Long Ltd. Oskar Ursinus was the force behind the Rhön glider trials in 1920 – see Grey C.G. 1943 *The Luftwaffe* (hereafter cited as Grey 1943) p.96. His periodical *Flugsport* would have promoted the event – see Ishoven van A. 1977 *The Fall of an Eagle: The Life of Fighter Ace Ernst Udet* (hereafter cited as Ishoven 1977) p.83.
6   Grey 1943 p.97. The Rhön Mountains are located 30-50 kms north of Frankfurt am Main in Hesse.
7   Quoted from Hermann 1943 *The Rise and Fall of the Luftwaffe* p.18 John Long Ltd. The Rhön Trials began in

Among those present at the Wasserkuppe were some who could afford rooms at the inn in Gersfeld. *Professors* Ludwig Prantl and Theodor von Karman took a lively interest in the experiments. Another was *Hptm.*Kurt Student who visited with his wife. As a result of his observations secret funding for some of the gliding groups was arranged via the *Reichsverkehrsministerium (RVM)* although in reality this money came from the *Reichswehr* budget (See also 1A2).[8] More overt assistance was provided by detachments of men from both the *Reichsheer* and the *Reichsmarine* who assisted with time-keeping, communications and the recovery of the gliders.[9]

The Rhön trials would continue each August throughout the twenties. In 1921 the longest flight lasted five and a half minutes and in the course of some of these longer flights a figure of eight circuit was flown. However the highlight of this year was a flight by Klemperer of nearly five kilometres from the top of the Wasserkuppe to nearby Gersfeld following the end of the competition. Klemperer had been in the air for no less than thirteen minutes.[10] In 1922 Hentzen beat this record by a huge margin when he achieved a flight of over three hours in a Hannover monoplane, whilst several other pilots achieved flights in excess of an hour. Other trials were successfully held at Rossitten in Ostpreussen where pilots made use of a sea breeze to carry out soaring flight along the coastal Kurische Haff.[11]

The creation of a Government sponsored flying training organisation was made possible by the progressive relaxation of Allied restrictions on civil aviation during 1922-23 (See 1B1).[12] The result was *Sportflug GmbH* which began operations on the 1 January 1924 and was thereafter progressively extended so that by the end of the year a network of ten flight training centres or *Zweigstellen* had been formed (See also 1A2):[13]

FIGURE 1D-8 ORGANISATION OF SPORTFLUG GmbH 1924-1926			
Berlin-Staaken	Brandenburg	Leipzig-Schkeuditz	Sachsen
Boblingen	Bad Württemberg	Osnabrück	Nord Sachsen
Hannover	Nord Sachsen	München-Schleißheim	Bayern
Königsberg	Ostpreussen	Stettin-Kreckow	Mecklenburg
Leipzig-Mockau	Sachsen	Würzburg am Main	Bayern

Fritz Siebel was the first Director of *Sportflug* in Berlin, although he was quickly succeeded in May 1924 by *Hptm.a.D.*Hermann Fricke (former *Fhr.Fl.Abt.3 LB*). Another director was *Oblt.a.D.*Theo Croneiss.[14] As limitations on aircraft performance were still in force the schools had

1920. *Dr.*Klemperer was on the staff of the *Technischen-Hochschule Aachen*. A former *Leutnant* in the *österreichischen Fliegertruppe*, his glider had been constructed by students at the *Schule* – see Lange B. 1970 *Das Buch der deutschen Luftfahrtechnik* (hereafter cited as Lange 1970) pp.155-156.

8   Hermann 1943 p.18 & Mason 1973 pp.107-108. *Hptm.*Student was *Ref.f.Flugtechnik b.d.Insp.d.Waffen u.Geräte/ HWA*. See service record for Kurt Student in Hildebrand K.F.1992 *Die Generale der deutschen Luftwaffe 1935-1945 Band 3 O-Z* (hereafter cited as Hildebrand 1992) pp.363-365.

9   Ries K. 1970 *Luftwaffe Bd.1 Die Maulwurfe 1919-1935* (hereafter cited as Ries 1970) p.24. *Reichswehr* assistance was provided annually for several years.

10   Grey 1943 p.98. In Sep 21 *Herr* Martens managed a flight of 21 mins after which he was able to land back at a point just 50 m from his take-off point and only 12 m below it in height.

11   Grey 1943 p.99.

12   Mason 1973 pp.112-113.

13   Kreipe W. Gen.d.Flg.a.D. and Koester R. Obst.a.D. 1955 *Technical Training within the German Luftwaffe* USAF Historical Studies No.169 (hereafter cited as Kreipe and Koester 1955) p.8 & Ries 1970 p.41, Mason 1973 pp.135-136 & Ries K. 1988 *Deutsche Flugzeugführerschulen und ihre Maschinen 1919-1945* (hereafter cited as Ries 1988) p.10. The assertion that training began at Warnemünde is probably incorrect, this facility was in all likelihood *Aerosport GmbH* – see Mason 1973 p.135.

14   Suchenwirth R. 1968 *The Development of the German Air Force 1919-1939* USAF Historical Studies No.160

to make do with relatively low powered machines such as the Albatros L 60 and the Dietrich DP IIa as well as wartime trainers such as the Albatros B-II and LVG B-I.[15] Training was therefore restricted to the *A1, A2* and later the *B-1* licence.[16] However the quality of instruction was extremely high and the *Sportflug* organisation and its students was well served by pilots of the calibre of Leopold Anslinger, Heinrich Benz, Alfred Brocke, Theo Cammann, Gustav Engwer, Otto Fruhner, August Heinzinger, Lenz Lorenz and Hermann Weller.[17]

There were a number of significant developments in 1925 including the formation of the *Deutschen Verkehrsfliegerschule (DVS) GmbH* on the 1 April, initially under the leadership of *Maj.a.D.*Alfred Keller (former *Kdr.Bogohl 1*) and from January 1927 from 1 January 1927 *Dr.*Günther Ziegler.[18] This commercial flying training organisation was financed by the *RVM* to provide flight training for prospective transport pilots and other flight crew.[19] Training at the *DVS* therefore concentrated on the more advanced *B 2* and *C* licences, and as such this organisation can be seen to be a natural progression from the elementary training being provided by *Sportflug*.[20] The main base of the *DVS* was the well-equipped international airport at Berlin-Staaken, but there would also be a marine offshoot at Warnemünde (See 1E3).[21] The majority of the students who passed through Staaken and Warnemünde were destined for airline service with Germany's major carriers: *Deutscher Aero Lloyd*, the *Junkers Luftverkehrs AG* and *Deruluft* prior to 1926 and *Deutsche Luft Hansa* thereafter. To meet its training requirements the *DVS* employed a wide variety of different aircraft types, most of which were financed directly by the *RVM*. Within a year of its opening the *DVS* Staaken had a fleet of sixteen aircraft: three Dietrich DP IX, two Junkers F 13, two Dornier *Komet III* and six Junkers A 20.[22]

In common with France, Great Britain and other nations, one of the earliest manifestations of commercial aviation in Germany following the cessation of hostilities had been the emergence of

(hereafter cited as Suchenwirth 1968) pp.10-11, Mason 1973 p.135 & Ries 1988 p.10. See also service record for Hermann Fricke in Hildebrand K.F.1990 *Die Generale der deutschen Luftwaffe 1935-1945 Band 1 A-G* (hereafter cited as Hildebrand 1990) pp.317-319. Theo Croneiss, a former *Jagdflieger* with 6 *LS*, was influential in helping Willy Messerschmitt develop his range of light sports planes from 1924. Croneiss also formed the *Nordbayerische Verkehrsflug AG* at around this time – see Smith J.R. 1971 *Messerschmitt: An Aircraft Album* (hereafter cited as Smith 1971) p.9 & Ishoven van A. 1975 *Messerschmitt: Aircraft Designer* (hereafter cited as Ishoven 1975) p. 27 & 29. It has suggested that Croneiss was Director of *Sportflug* – see Smith 1971 p.9 & Ries 1988 p.10.

15   Ries 1970 p.41, Lange 1970 p.61, 89, 58 & 191 and Nowarra H.J. 1980 *Die Verbotenen Flugzeuge 1921-1935 – Die getarnte Luftwaffe* (hereafter cited as Nowarra 1980) pp.64-66 & 98-99.

16   Ries 1988 p.10 & Carlsen S. and Meyer M. 1998 *Die Flugzeugführer Ausbiludung der deutschen Luftwaffe 1935-1945 Bd.I Von der Grundausbildung bis zur Blindflugschule* (hereafter cited as Carlsen and Meyer 1998) p.15.

17   Ries 1988 p.10.

18   Ries 1988 p.10 & Carlsen and Meyer 1998 p.17. Alfred Keller had been one of the wartime *Luftstreitkräfte's* leading bomber commanders (*Plm* 4 Dec 17). He was recruited by *DLR* in Dec 18 and remained with that company as *Ltr.d.Landflugdienstes* (Leader of Land Flight Services) until May 23 when he changed allegiance to *Junkers Luftreederei* – see service record for Alfred Keller in Angolia J.R. and Hackney C.R. 1984 *The Pour le Mérite and Germany's First Aces* (hereafter cited as Angolia and Hackney 1984) pp.172-173 & Hildebrand K.F.1991 *Die Generale der deutschen Luftwaffe 1935-1945 Band 2 H-N* (hereafter cited as Hildebrand 1991) p.163-164. *Lt.d.Res.* Günther Ziegler saw extensive wartime service with the *FFA d.Armee Ant.Gaede, FFA 65, Jasta 26, Armeeflugpark 4, Kampfeinsitzerstaffel 7* & *Fl.Ers.Abt.10*. He joined *Sportflug* in Jul 24 before being appointed Director *DVS (Land)* in Berlin – see Service record for Günther Ziegler in Hildebrand 1992 pp.567-568. The Director *DVS (See)* was *Oblt.z.S.a.D.*Wolfgang von Gronau who was also *Ltr.d.DVS Zweigstelle List* – see service record for Wolfgang von Gronau in Hildebrand 1990 pp.395-396.

19   Suchenwirth 1968 pp.15-16.

20   Ries 1970 pp.41-42 & Ries 1988 p.10.

21   Ries 1970 p.42 & Carlsen and Meyer 1998 p.17.

22   Ries 1970 pp.43-44. The aircraft were purchased by the *RVM* and supplied free of charge *"as material assistance"* to the *DVS* – see Hooton E.R. 1994 *Phoenix Triumphant: The Rise and Rise of the Luftwaffe* (hereafter cited as Hooton 1994) p.58. See also Lange 1970 p.191, 194 & pp.272-273 and Nowarra 1980 pp.92-95.

air transport.[23] For the most part these had begun as small scale operations, financed by the aircraft manufacturing companies, by existing transport businesses and occasionally as speculative ventures. In Germany several aircraft manufacturers established their own airlines, notably: the *Albatros-Gesellschaft, Deutsche Luft-Reederei (AEG), Lloyd Ostflug GmbH (Junkers)* and *Rumpler-Luftverkehr* in an attempt to create captive markets for their own products.[24] The *Lloyd Luftverkehr Sablatnig* represented a joint enterprise by the *Norddeutscher Lloyd* shipping line and the *Sablatnig* aircraft manufacturing company.[25]

Under the operational leadership of *Maj.a.D.*Alfred Keller *Deutsche Luft-Reederei (DLR)* had the distinction of becoming the world's first airline.[26] Although it had been established in 1917 by *AEG* it was not until the 6 January 1919 that the first commercial flights were made using ex-military aircraft such as the single-engine AEG J-II and the twin-engine AEG G-V.[27] These aircraft offered few concessions to the fare paying public and relatively few passengers were actually carried on the west German routes between Berlin and Weimar, Hamburg and the Ruhr where rival railway connections were fast, comfortable and reliable.[28] In 1921 only 320 passengers were carried on these routes together with 963 kgs of mail and 2,223 kgs of parcels and telegrams.[29] Nonetheless the company continued to expand and in the same year, with the backing of the shipping company *HAPAG* and the airship manufacturer *Luftschiffbau Zeppelin, AEG* used the *DLR* as the basis for a new airline grouping, the *Aero-Union AG*.[30]

The conditions in the east were different. Here the overland connections were less efficient and following the Treaty adjustments Ostpreussen lay geographically isolated from the rest of Germany.[31] Here the main carrier was *Lloyd Ostflug GmbH*, established on the 7 November 1920 and later transformed into the *Junkers Luftverkehr AG*.[32] In 1921 it carried 979 passengers, together with 486 kgs of mail and 4,260 kgs of parcels on the eastern routes that stretched from Berlin to Königsberg/Ostpr. and onward into the Ostsee states.[33] *Oblt.z.See a.D.*Gotthard Sachsenberg had been the driving force behind *Lloyd Ostflug*, having purchased on his own behalf a number of ex-military aircraft following the secession of hostilities in the east in 1919 (See 1A1).[34] In 1921

23   Jackson R. 1983 *The Sky their Frontier: The Story of the World's Pioneer Airlines and Routes 1920-40* (hereafter cited as Jackson 1983) p.95, 101 & pp.107-108.

24   Ries 1970 p.42, Irving D. 1973 *The Rise and Fall of the Luftwaffe: The Life of Luftwaffe Marshal Erhard Milch* (hereafter cited as Irving 1973) pp.12-13 & 15, Jackson 1983 p.101, Schmitt G. 1988 *Hugo Junkers and his Aircraft* (hereafter cited as Schmitt 1988) pp.67-85 & Seifert K-D. 1999 *Die deutsche Luftfahrt 28: Der deutsche Luftverkehr 1926-1945 – auf dem Weg zum Weltverkehr* (hereafter cited as Seifert 1999) p.9.

25   Hooks M. 1999 *Images of Aviation: Lufthansa* (hereafter cited as Hooks 1999) p.7. Across Europe many shipping companies and later railroad companies appreciated the value of air transportation during the twenties and thirties.

26   Hooks 1999 p.7. See also service record for Alfred Keller in Hildebrand 1991 pp.163-164.

27   Hermann 1943 p.44 & Irving 1973 p.12. For aircraft details – see Stroud J.1966 *European Transport Aircraft since 1910* (hereafter cited as Stroud 1966) pp.217-220.

28   Hermann 1943 p.44. The Berlin-Weimar route was opened in Feb 19. According to this source 10,000 passengers were carried by the *DLR* but this seems unlikely even for the whole period 1919-23 – see Grey 1943 p.93. For information on the *Reichsbahn* – see Naval Intelligence Division 1945 *Germany Vol.IV Ports and Communications* (hereafter cited as NID 1945) pp.215-216.

29   Grey 1943 p.93. In mid-1920 the *DLR* Fleet comprised 71 single-engine and 13 twin-engine aircraft. Nearly all were ex-military types – AEG G, J (K & N) Srs., Albatros L58, Dornier *Komet I*, Friedrichshafen G.III & FF.49, LVG C Srs., & Rumpler C Srs. - see Stroud 1966 pp.217-222, 237-239, 277-280, 347-349 & 363-364 and Jackson 1983 p.101.

30   Jackson 1983 101 & Hooks 1999 p.7.

31   *European Political Problems 1919-1934* in Barraclough G. (Ed.) 1978 *The Times Atlas of World History* pp.264-265.

32   Schmitt 1988 pp.67-69.

33   Grey 1943 p.93 & Hermann 1943 pp.44-45. See also Irving 1973 pp.12-14.

34   Hermann 1943 pp.44-45 & Ries 1970 p.13. Gotthard Sachsenberg was the *Marineluftstreitkräfte's* leading fighter pilot with 31 *LS* (*Plm* 5 Aug 18) – see Angolia and Hackney 1984 pp.228-231. At the end of the War he formed an ad hoc *Jagdgeschwader* for service in Kurland in support of the *Freikorps* and the *Reichsheer*. Following receipt

he joined forces with *Professor* Hugo Junkers to establish *Junkers Luftverkehr AG*. The outstanding success of this new company can be attributed in part to Sachsenberg's energy and *Prof.*Junkers' foresight and in part to the excellence of his company's products, initially in the form of the superb all-metal Junkers F 13 limousine (See also 1C):

> If you think about the situation of air transport soberly, quite soberly, you will arrive at the conviction that it will inevitably be at least as important as other means of transport, that is to say, the railway, the steamship and the motor car.[35]

*Prof.*Hugo Junkers
1923

In December 1921 Junkers established an air transport department - the *Abteilung Luftverkehr* - within the parent company at Dessau.[36] Sachsenberg quickly developed the route network through the involvement of like-minded pilots and entrepreneurs. One such man was *Hptm.a.D.*Erhard Milch who from 26 February 1920 had been the *Leiter der Danziger Luftpost GmbH*.[37] Starting with a solitary Rumpler C-I biplane which could carry a single passenger in an open cockpit, Milch's company accepted the first of several F 13 cabin monoplanes from Junkers in 1921.[38] In the meantime the *Junkers Luftverkehr* hired and provided further training, including engineering expertise, to former military pilots. Up to four months were spent at Dessau during which time each prospective air transport pilot was taken through all the works' departments including fuselage and wing construction and engine manufacture.[39] Each graduate of this programme was therefore fully equipped to deal with any emergency that might occur and was more than capable of making on the spot repairs that would enable his aircraft to complete its journey in the event of a problem.[40]

However in the short term manufacture of the F 13 and other new types in Germany was prohibited by the on-going restrictions of the Treaty of Versailles (See 1B1 and 1C1). This forced the existing airline companies to use relatively inefficient and expensive ex-military aircraft. By the end of 1922 the *Aero-Union* fleet had been reduced to just 45 machines and worse was to come

of the disbandment order Sachsenberg set up house at the old airfield at Königsberg/Ostpr. where many turned to agriculture as a means of survival. Sachsenberg on the other hand obtained a concession from the *RVM* to fly the Berlin-Königsberg route.

35   Quoted from *Junkers und die Weltluftfahrt, 1934* p.69 in Schmitt 1988 *Hugo Junkers and his Aircraft* p.67 VEB Verlag für Verkehrswesen. See also Hermann 1943 p.45 & Irving 1973 pp.12-13.

36   Schmitt 1988 p.69.

37   Hermann 1943 p.46, Irving 1973 pp.12-13 & Schmitt 1988 pp.69-77. Prior to forming *Danziger Luftpost*, Erhard Milch had been *Fhr.d.Polizeifliegerstaffel Königsberg*. As a pre-war career officer he had seen considerable active service in the *Feldartillerie* and *Luftstreitkräfte*. He also had the distinction of being appointed *Fhr.JG 6* as a non-pilot officer – see service record for Erhard Milch in Hildebrand 1991 pp.394-395. See also Schilling F and Rettinghaus H 1994 *Die Geschichte der Luftpolizei* pp.13-26.

38   Irving 1973 p.13. Henceforth Milch's advertising cards contained the message: *"Passengers are conveyed by the most up-to-date Junkers cabin aircraft. Special clothing like furs, goggles etc are not needed."* A flight time of 5 hrs 30 mins was claimed for the Berlin to Königsberg route with stops at Schniedemuhl (later Stettin) and Danzig. The railway journey took 14 hrs, hence the attraction of even an uncomfortable ride by air. However this operation came to a premature halt in Oct 21 due to the activities of the *ILUK* which regarded the new Junkers F13 airliners to be in breach of the Treaty Regulations. The Danzig F 13s were registered as Dz, known aircraft being Dz 4, 31, 32, 33, 35, 38, 40, 41 & 43. The aircraft were destroyed by the French authorities – see also Schmitt 1988 pp.69-70.

39   Schmitt 1988 p.78. *"It was the usual thing at Junkers that for some time all pilots had to be involved in practical work in the aircraft works. This enabled them to become familiar with material – duraluminium – with its processing and its characteristics, for at that time this was completely new in aircraft construction"* – see Loose F. *Zu Wasser, zu Lande und in der Luft* in Schmitt 1988.

40   Schmitt 1988 p.78.

as the German economy spiralled into hyper-inflation during 1923 (See 1A2).[41] Early in that year *Aero-Union* joined forces with *Lloyd Luftdienst GmbH* to form *Deutscher Aero Lloyd AG (DAL)* with its head office at newly opened airport at Berlin-Tempelhof.[42] This firm had financial backing from the *Deutsche Bank* (*Dr.*Emil-Georg von Stauss) and several shipping companies as well as from private venture capitalists. It also enjoyed considerable subsidies from the *Reichspost*.[43]

Stauss was to be the prime mover in the fortunes of *Aero Lloyd*. In addition to his commercial links he had good contacts with the *Reichspost*, the *Reichsverkehrsministerium* and the *Reichswehr*.[44] With its large pool of ex-military aircraft, *Aero Lloyd* was seen from the start by *Maj.a.D.Dr.*Ernst Brandenburg *(wartime Kdr.Kagohl 3)* of the *RVM's Abteilung Luftfahrt* (Aviation Branch) as well as by serving officers in the secret *TA (L)* as an important element in their covert strategy to re-build German military aviation (See also 1A2 & 1B1).[45] Growing commercial links with the emergent Soviet Union had been encouraged by the formation of the *Deutsche-Russische-Verkehrsgesellschaft DbH* in November 1921.[46] Within the framework provided by the *Aero-Union*, *Deruluft* began operations over Milch's defunct route from Berlin to Königsberg and then onward to Moskva via Kovno and Smolensk on the 1 May 1922. *Deruluft* was primarily equipped with the Fokker F.III.[47]

However at Dessau there was a very different philosophy toward the development of air travel. Both Sachsenberg and Junkers were visionaries.[48] For them air travel was nothing less than an extension of a brotherhood of the air as the basis for continued international development, co-operation and peaceful coexistence:

A whole world was to be conquered, or, to be precise, a whole world was to be connected and brought closer together by means of aeroplanes and airlines. We had no intention or ambition to run all these airlines ourselves. What we wanted was to build the bridges connecting the different parts of the world with each other and to leave the construction of the local airlines to the people who were living and working in the various countries.[49]

Evidence of this philosophy in practice can be seen in the Scandinavian countries where the *Nordeuropa-Union* was established encompassing airline companies in Estonia (*Aeronaut*), Finland

41   Jackson 1983 p.101.
42   Jackson 1983 p.101. Tempelhof was officially opened on the 8 Oct 23 – see Zapf J. 2001 *Flugplätze der Luftwaffe 1934-1945 und was davon ubrig blieb Bd.1 Berlin & Brandenburg* (hereafter cited as Zapf 2001) pp.54-56.
43   Hermann 1943 p.46 & Jackson 1983 p.101.
44   Hermann 1943 p.46.
45   Suchenwirth 1968 pp.9-10. Although injured in a flying accident Ernst Brandenburg had made an indelible mark on the evolution of the *Luftstreitkräfte's* bombing operations and post-war his position within the *RVM* was to be of significant help to *Maj.*Helmuth Wilberg's *TA (L)*. His appointment as *Chef d.Abt.Luftverkehr* in 1924 had been influenced by *Gen.d.Inf.*Hans Seeckt, the *Chef d.Heeresleitung* – see Rabenau von F. Gen.a.D. 1940 *Seeckt: Aus seinem Leben* p.529. See also Mason 1973 p.139, Angolia and Hackney 1984 pp.140-141 & Corum J.S. 1997 *The Luftwaffe: Creating the Operational Air War 1918-1940* (hereafter cited as Corum 1997) pp.34-36. The *DLR* fleet had been built around the AEG J II & LVG C VI but there were also a number of twin-engine AEG G V & Friedrichshafen G.III aircraft – see Stroud 1966 pp.217-220, 277-280 & 347-349.
46   Hooks 1999 p.7. *Deruluft* was jointly funded by Germany and the USSR. The German holding was via *DLR*, later *DAL* – see Jackson 1983 p.101 & 118.
47   Hooks 1999 p.7. At least 8 Fokker F III 5-seat airliners were registered to *Deruluft* – RR 1 -10 less R-5 & R-7 – see Stroud 1966 pp.459-464.
48   Hermann 1943 pp.45-46. Hugo Junkers was more of an idealist: *"The aeroplane will become a weapon of happy humanitarianism that will carry blessings to all peoples and all nations and that will bring back blessings from all people and all nations."* Hermann Steiner joined Junkers as an engineer in 1923. The following year he was assigned to the *Abteilung Luftverkehr*. As a friend and confidante of the *Professor* he is well qualified to speak of developments within the companies that collectively made up the *Junkers* Empire.
49   Quoted from Hermann 1943 *The Rise of the Luftwaffe* p.47 John Long Ltd.

(Aero OY) and Sweden *(AB Aerotransport)*. In 1924 Norway *(Aerotransport AS)* and Denmark *(Dansk Lufttransport AB)* were included and the grouping renamed the *Skandinavische Union*.[50] In each case the *Abteilung Luftverkehr* at Dessau provided financial assistance to start the company, this being followed by the supply of aircraft. In the first instance this took the form of the excellent F 13 limousine.[51]

Milch remained active within the *Junkers Luftverkehr AG*.[52] During the previous two years he had conducted the initial negotiations with aviation representatives in Switzerland *(Ad Astra AG)*, Austria *(Österreichische Luftverkehrs AG)* and Hungary *(Ungarische Aero Express AG)*, a grouping that collectively became the *Trans-Europa Union* in November 1923.[53]He also took the lead in Poland *(Polski Linia Lotnicza Aerolot)* where the Polish Government paid a handsome subsidy for each flight from Danzig through Warschau to Lvov.[54] Meanwhile in the same spirit of decentralised co-operation the *Junkers Luftverkehr* spawned a number of new airlines within Germany itself during 1924-25: the *Sachsische Luftverkehrs AG* (Dresden), the *Südwestdeutschen Luftverkehrs AG* (Frankfurt am Main), the *Schlesische Luftverkehrs AG* (Breslau), the *Oberschlesische Luftverkehrs AG* (Gleiwitz) and the *Luftverkehrsgesellschaft Ruhrgebiet AG* (Essen).[55]

The activities and aspirations of the two major companies led to increasing competition within Germany. During 1925 no less than 70 of Germany's aerodromes were served by both companies and their subsidiaries, a situation that led to a reduction in passenger revenue for each scheduled service.[56] For the most part the companies that formed the *Junkers Luftverkehr* combine enjoyed modern equipment in the form of the Junkers F 13 and to a much lesser extent the K 16, whilst *Aero Lloyd* continued to use older aircraft alongside a small number of Albatros L 58 and Dornier *Komet* aircraft and a larger number of Fokker F.II and F.III airliners *(Photo 1D-5)*.[57] The result was a decline in flight safety, profitability and overall efficiency. Using this as an excuse the *RVM* stepped in to force an amalgamation of the two companies into a single national airline (See 1B1).[58] However it can be argued that the real reason was to force *Junkers* out of the airline business entirely and concentrate all Germany's commercial air transport assets into a single company that could work more effectively with the *T 2 III (L)* in the covert development of military aviation (See also 1A2).[59]

The resulting combine was *Deutsche Luft Hansa (DLH)* which was created by the *RVM* on the 6

50   Schmitt 1988 p.71.
51   Schmitt 1988 p.67.
52   Schmitt 1988 pp.74-76. *Junkers Luftverkehr* had a starting capital of 2 m Marks.
53   Irving 1973 p.15 & Schmitt 1988 pp.76-77. The inaugural meeting of the *Trans-Europa Union* took place at München on the 22 Nov 23.
54   Irving 1973 p.15.
55   Schmitt 1988 pp.75-76.
56   *Brandenburg Letter to Prussian Ministry of Trade, 23 Nov 24* quoted in Polte W. 1956 *Uns aber gehorte der Himmel* p.145 in Irving 1973 *The Rise and Fall of the Luftwaffe: The Life of Luftwaffe Marshal Erhard Milch* p.16 with the knowledge of the Orion Publishing Group & Schmitt 1988 p.84. Nonetheless in 1925 the *Junkers Luftverkehr AG* combine was responsible for 40% of the World's air traffic – see Schmitt 1988 p.77.
57   Stroud 1966 pp.221-222, 237-239 & 459-464. *DAL* is known to have operated the Albatros L 58 D-244, 246 & 576 together with the Dornier C D-223 & 248. Some of *DAL's* 40 or so Fokker airliners were completed in the former Fokker factory at Schwerin, whilst others were completed at Berlin-Staaken as Fokker-Grulich F II & F IIIs. *Dr.Ing.*Karl Grulich was Technical Director of *DAL* – see also Postma T. 1979 *Fokker: Aircraft Builders to the World* pp.51-53 & 59. The overall importance of Fokker aircraft to the European air transport industry can be seen in a contemporary promotional document for 1925 – see *Fokker Air Traffic 1925* in Postma 1979 p.65.
58   Hermann 1943 p.58, Mason 1973 pp.144-145 & Schmitt 1988 p.85. The *RVM* forced the merger through by the simple expedient of stopping the payment of all subsidies to both companies at the end of 1925 – see Grey 1943 p.110 & Seifert 1999 p.10.
59   Seiffert 1999 pp.10-14. Milch was to cooperate fully with the *T 2 III (L)* and its successor the *T2 V (L)* in the provision of technical data and new technologies and flight procedures – see BA/MA RH 2./2187 (4 Apr 27) & BA/MA RH 2/2191 – aircraft development in Corum 1997 p.77.

January 1926.[60] *Deutscher Aero Lloyd* contributed 208 personnel, whilst *Junkers Luftwerkehr* provided 225 employees of the new company.[61] The capital of *DLH* was fixed at *RM* 25 million with the following share allocation with the Reich Government and the individual German States getting the lion's share (45%) with the balance being provided by the regional air transport companies and private investors.[62] *Junkers* got a cash settlement that enabled him to restore the solvency of the *Junkers Flugzeugwerke AG* but this did not represent the true value of his former assets within *Junkers Luftverkehr* (See 1B1).[63] *DLH* inherited 162 aircraft of numerous types from the two companies and their subsidiaries, of these 80 were Junkers designs (49%).[64] Stauss was *Präsident* of *DLH* and the three executive directors of the new airline were named as *Dr.*Otto Merkel and *Maj.a.D.*Martin Wronsky who both came from *DAL*, and Erhard Milch who was recruited from *Junkers Luftverkehr.*[65]

DLH began commercial operations in April 1926, initially over eight routes.[66] There was an early emphasis on air freight and in that month 6,940 kgs was carried; by the end of the year the total freight moved by German air carriers had reached 1,073,912 kgs. In addition 559,816 kgs of mail was carried, an increase of 48% over 1925. Total passenger numbers had also increased from 55,200 in 1925 to 84,600 in 1926 of which *DLH* carried 56,268.[67] During the course of the year the first tri-motor aircraft were introduced in the form of the all-metal Junkers G 23/24, nineteen of which were acquired.[68] The Directors of *DLH* was also keen to develop an all-weather and night flying capability and as part of this strategy *Hptm.a.D.Dr.*Robert Knauss *(former Stab KoFl 4)* was appointed *Leiter der Verkehrsabteilung DLH*, whilst Carl-August Frhr.von Gablenz *(Bogohl 7)* became Milch's *Technischer Mitarbeiter* (Technical Director) within the Air Traffic Department. Prior to this appointment Knauss had been *Leiter des Nachtflugbetriebes* (Night Flying Operations) and later *Technischer Mitarbeiter* within *Aero Lloyd.*[69] The first scheduled night passenger service

60   Suchenwirth 1968 p.14, Hooks 1999 p.7 & *Aktienbuch der Aero Hansa Aktiengesellschaft zu Berlin, 6.Januar 1926* in Seifert 1999 p.13. The majority of the *Junkers Luftverkehr's* senior personnel, including Hermann Steiner and Gotthard Sachsenberg refused to serve with *DLH* – see Hermann 1943 p.57.

61   Schmitt 1988 p.85. See also *Tabelle 2: Ubbersicht über die eingebrachten Vermogenswerte mit Stand vom 31.Dezember 1925 (in RM)* in Seifert 1999 p.18.

62   *App.I Civil Aviation* in NID 1945 p.622. This cash injection gave Brandenburg a seat on the Board of Directors, together with the Burgermeisters of the major cities such as Köln, Essen and München, bankers and leading aircraft manufacturers – see Grey 1943 p.111 & *Der Aufsichtsrat der Luft Hansa 1926* in Seifert 1999 p.29.

63   Schmitt 1988 p.86. *Junkers Luftverkehr* was valued at 30 million *RM*. The RVM used this to pay off Junkers and acquire its controlling share in *DLH*.

64   *Aircraft in Service with the Deutsche Luft Hansa AG 1926-1933* in Schmitt 1988 p.86 & *Tabelle 1: Eingebrachte Flugzeuge* in Seifert 1999 p.15.

65   Hermann 1943 p.53, Irving 1973 p.16 & Hooton 1994 p.53. Sachsenberg, Steiner et al never forgave Milch for this perceived "act of treachery". In Nov 25 Sachsenberg had stated in the presence of von Gablenz: *As a Junkers official my sole interest is to wreck the new company (DLH) and enable our company (Junkers) to regain control of Junkers Luftverkehr."* However Milch saw the formation of *DLH* as inevitable and took the view that *Prof.*Junkers should concentrate on designing and building aircraft - see Irving 1973 p.17. However he was not alone in joining *DLH*; Herr Heck, the former *Präsident* of *Junkers Luftverkehr* became the *Vizepräsident* of *DLH* – see Grey 1943 p.111.

66   Jackson 1983 p.102 & Hooks 1999 p.9. Most of the routes were inaugurated by the end of Apr 26 – see *Mitteleuropaisches Liniennetz im Sommer 1926* in Seifert 1999 p.22. The main types used by *DLH* in 1926 were: the Junkers F 13, Do *Komet III*, Do *Wal,* Fokker F II & F III and the Junkers G 24.

67   Hooks 1999 p.9. In 1926 *DLH* flew 6,141,000 kms, carrying 56,628 passengers, 257,464 kgs of freight, 385,945 kgs of packages and 301,345 kgs of post – see *Tabelle 3: Verkehrleistungen der Luft Hansa 1926 bis 1928* in Seifert 1999 p.38.

68   Grey 1943 p.120, Stroud 1966 pp.303-306 and Schmitt 1988 pp.96-102 & *Construction and employment of G 23/24 aircraft from Dessau and Limhamm 1st construction series* in Schmitt 1988 p.151. The early aircraft were built in Sweden because of Allied restrictions, whilst the use of three motors also stemmed from contemporary regulations on engine size. Two low-rate engines would simply not have provided sufficient power. However this configuration quickly became popular in other countries as it also offered greater flight safety in the event of engine failure – see also Stroud J. *The Evolution of the Transport Aircraft* in Jarrett P. (Ed.) 1997 *Biplane to Monoplane: Aircraft development 1919-39* pp.31-32.

69   Service record for Carl-August von Gablenz in Hildebrand 1990 pp.339-340 and for Robert Knauss in Hildebrand

was carried out on the 1 May 1926 between Berlin and Königsberg using a Junkers G 24.[70] From 1929 an Instrument Rating was a requirement for all *DLH* pilots.[71] By 1931 no less than eighteen *Flughäfen* had been equipped with the *Lorenz* navigational beacons *(Funkfeuer)* which permitted accurate aerial navigation by night and in bad weather.[72]

The development of *DLH* as an international carrier was facilitated by the Paris Air Agreement, signed on the 21 May 1926 (See 1B1).[73] Three days later the first air service between Berlin and Paris via Köln was flown by *DLH* and the French airline *Lignes Farman* in conjunction with the *Societe Generale des Transports Aeriens*.[74] In the same month *DLH* employed *DAL*'s four Dornier J *Wal* flying boats to initiate a more direct flight to Stockholm using Stettin as the point of departure, previously these machines had been used on the Danzig-Stockholm route.[75] Then in August 1926 no less than ten new international routes were agreed at the 16th.Conference of the International Air Traffic Association, held appropriately enough in Berlin.[76] Over the next three years further agreements would be signed with Switzerland, Great Britain, Czechoslovakia and Poland.[77]

Meanwhile Milch and his associates, were keen to extend the reach of *DLH* into both Asia and South America.[78] In July-August 1926 Dr.Robert Knauss staged a proving flight from Berlin to Peking, a distance of 10,000 kms right across Russia.[79] In November 1926 a proving flight was made using the Dornier *Wal Atlantico* between Buenos Aires and Rio de Janeiro prior to the founding of a new company, the *Syndicato Condor Ltda*. in Rio de Janeiro, to develop an air transport network along the Brazilian seaboard. The Brazilian carrier *VARIG (Empresa de Viacao Rio Grandense)* was then established within the framework offered by the *Syndicato Condor* to take responsibility for internal services within that vast nation.[80] This left *DLH* free to consider the feasibility of an aerial

1991 pp.189-190. Gablenz had previously been Technical Director at *Junkers Luftverkehr* – see also Irving 1973 p.17.

70   Jackson 1983 p.102 & Hooks 1999 p.9. This was the World's first scheduled passenger night flight. *DLH* later used its fleet of 22 *Komet IIIs* on the Berlin-Königsberg service. Mail and freight services had been flown at night prior to the 1 May 26, whilst a pioneering flight by the French Air Union airline had been made on the 27 Jan 26 between Paris and London using a Farman Goliath - see Stroud 1966 p.245 & Jackson 1983 p.98.

71   Hooton 1994 p.53.

72   Schmitt-Rops H. 1930 *Das Funkwesen in der Luftfahrt*. See also Trenkle F. 1986 *Bordfunkgerate - Vom Funksender zum Bordradar Die deutsche Luftfahrt 7* p.83 & Hooton 1994 p.53.

73   *App.I Civil Aviation* in NID 1945 p.622 & Suchenwirth 1968 p.15.

74   *App.I Civil Aviation* in NID 1945 p.622 & Jackson 1983 p.102.

75   Stroud 1966 p.240 & Jackson 1983 p.102. The Stettin-Stockholm service began on the 3 May 26. The 4 Do J were almost certainly WNr.41-44 D-861-864.

76   Jackson 1983 p.103. These resulted from a series of bilateral negotiations that had been held over the summer months.

77   *App.I Civil Aviation* in NID 1945 p.622. These agreements dated from France (1926), Switzerland (1936), Britain (1926), Czechoslovakia (1927) & Poland (1929). By the end of the twenties *DLH* operated regular services into Czechoslovakia, Denmark, France, Great Britain, Italy, Norway, Poland, Russia, Spain & Switzerland – see Jackson 1983 p.103. In 1927 & 1928 *DLH* carried more passengers than all its rivals in Britain, France & Italy combined – see Hooton 1994 p.53.

78   Irving 1973 pp.18-19. Milch's key associates in the development of *DLH* were Carl-August von Gablenz, Joachim von Schroder & Robert Knauss.

79   *Construction and employment of G 23/24 aircraft from Dessau and Limhamm 1st construction series* p.151 & *2nd series* pp.152-153 in Schmitt 1988. Two G 24 airliners (D-901 *Tyr* & D-903 *Hera*) were used in this trans-continental flight across Russia to China. The aircraft left Berlin on the 24 Jul 26 and arrived in Peking on the 30 Aug 26 before returning to Berlin on the 26 Sep 26 – see Schmitt 1988 p.pp.101-102, Hooks 1999 p.9 & Seifert 1999 pp.44-45. The round trip totalled 20,000 kms; flight time to Peking was 72 hrs. For an account of this flight - see Grey 1943 pp.118-119. Meanwhile in the Middle East in one of its final innovations *Junkers Luftverkehr* had established the *Junkers Luftverkehr Persien* in Jan 27. This resulted from earlier demonstrations and proving flights by *Junkers* personnel beginning in Apr 23 – see Schmitt 1988 p.77.

80   Schmitt 1988 pp.64-66. German interest in the development of air transport within South America originally stemmed from the formation of the *Sociedad Colombo Alemana de Transportes Aeros (SCADTA)* in Colombia in 1919 and the abortive attempt by *DAL* & *SCADTA* to establish a *Condor Syndikat* in Berlin in 1924 to look at

crossing of the South Atlantic from Africa to effect a truly inter-continental route network focused on the rapidly expanding German Berlin-Tempelhof hub. This new airport was located just 5 kms south of the city centre and as such was very accessible to the travelling public (See also 1B11).[81]

All of this activity acted as a stimulus to the progressive expansion of the *DVS* training organisation. Under Brandenburg's instigation additional *Zweigstellen* were opened at List auf Sylt and Schleißheim (1927), whilst in October 1929 the *Zweigstelle Staaken* was transferred to Braunschweig.[82]

Basic flying training up to the *B 1* Licence on landplanes was carried out at Schleißheim in Bayern, whilst multi-engine flight training up to *C 2* standard was concentrated at Braunschweig in Nord Sachsen. The *Zweigstelle Braunschweig* (Nord Sachsen) also provided flight training for wireless operators *(Bordfunkermaschinisten)* and aircraft mechanics *(Flugzeugwarten)*. This pattern of training was then replicated for seaplane types at Warnemünde (*B* Licence) and List auf Sylt (*C* Licence).[83]

However the pattern of ab initio instruction (A Licence) changed as a result of the Paris Air Agreements. *Sportflug* had been recognised as a para-military organisation and was disbanded on the 21 May 1926.[84] It was replaced by a new organisation: the *Deutsche Luftfahrt GmbH* under *Maj.a.D.*Leo Leonhardy (former *Kdr.Bogohl 6*).[85] *Luftfahrt* began operations at Berlin-Staaken, Boblingen (Gustav Engwer) and Würzburg (*Hptm.a.D.*Robert Ritter von Greim) on the 1 April 1927 and provided tuition for a small fee at *A1, A2* and *B1* standard, ostensibly to aspiring commercial pilots but principally to covert *Fliegeroffiziere* within the *Reichsheer* who attended regular three month proficiency courses at one of these centres (See 1E1).[86]

By this time there were already around twenty full-blown private flying clubs in Germany, in addition to numerous gliding clubs.[87] As economic conditions improved more and more people became involved in *Motorflugsport* as opposed to un-powered flight, an enthusiasm that was promoted by a resurgence in air displays and aerobatic competitions by the like of Paul Bäumer,

a pan-American network. Not surprisingly opposing American interests prevented this venture from becoming a commercial reality. Nonetheless *SCADTA* bought a total of 11 Junkers F 13 airliners and would go on to buy more advanced types from that company in the thirties. Elsewhere in South America the *Junkers Luftverkehr* had been active in supporting the formation of *Lloyd Aereo Bolivano (LAB)* in Bolivia; it also attempted to form an airline *(Aero Lloyd)* in Argentina but without the support of the Argentinian Government this was doomed to failure – see Jackson 1983 pp.134-136 & Hooks 1999 pp.9-10.

81   Hooks 1999 pp.57-60. Huge sums of money were spent by the *RVM* on the development of Berlin's new central airport at Tempelhof – see Zapf 2001 p.56.

82   Ries 1970 p.42, Irving 1973 p.19, Ries 1988 p.10 & Carlsen and Meyer 1998 p.17. Alfred Keller was appointed *Ltr.d.DVS Staaken* on the 1 May 25, moving with the *Schule* to Braunschweig in Oct 29 – see service record for Alfred Keller in Hildebrand 1991 pp.163-164. Following service with the *Sondergruppe R*, Albert Vierling had been a *Geschäftsführer* with the *bayerischen Sportflug GmbH*. On the 1 Apr 27 he became *Ltr.DVS Schleißheim* – see service record for Albert Vierling in Hildebrand 1992 pp.434-436. Konrad Goltz was one of the early *Marineflieger* being appointed *Kdr.d.Freiwilligen Marine-Fliegerkorps* on the 1 Aug 14. He saw extensive war service and was advisor to the Turkish Navy during 1918. Prior to Jan 27 Goltz had been *Geschäftsführer d.Firma Seeflug GmbH* at Warnemünde – see service record for Konrad Goltz in Hildebrand 1990 pp.377-378. Heinz Scheurlen learned to fly in Sep 14 and thereafter saw extensive service with the *Marineluftstreitkräfte*. He transferred to the *Luft-Polizei* in 1919 before joining *Junkers Luftverkehr* as a *Technischer Leiter* in 1923. He was active in Persia and Russia. He was appointed *Ltr.DVS List* on the 1 Mar 27 – see service record for Heinz Scheurlen in Hildebrand 1992 pp.179-180.

83   Ries 1988 p.10 & Carlsen and Meyer 1998 p.17.

84   Ries 1988 p.11 & Carlsen and Meyer 1998 p.15.

85   Ries 1988 p.11. *Hptm.a.D.*Leo Leonhardy had been the wartime *Kdr.Bogohl 6* and for his leadership of this unit he was decorated with the *Plm* on the 2 Oct 18. Unfortunately his tenure at *Luftfahrt GmbH* was cut short by his premature death through heart failure at the age of 37 yrs on the 12 Jul 28 – see Angolia and Hackney 1984 pp.248-249.

86   Suchenwirth 1968 p.15, Ries 1970 p.44, Ries 1988 p.11 & Carlsen and Myer 1998 p.15. Robert Ritter von Greim joined *Luftfahrt GmbH* on the 1 Jan 27 after 3 yrs in Canton organising military aviation in Southern China – see service record for Robert Ritter von Greim in Hildebrand 1990 pp.387-389.

87   Grey 1943 p.118. The number of flying clubs was dated at Dec 26.

Robert Weichel's *Kunstflugstaffel Weichel*, Gerhard Fieseler and Ernst Udet *(Photo 1D-6).*[88] Notable clubs included: *Aerosport*/Warnemünde, the *Fliegerschule Auffaht*/Münster Westfalen, the *Fliegerschule Dietrich-Gobiet* /Kassel-Waldau and *Bäumer-Aero*/Hamburg-Fühlsbuttel *(Photo 1D-7).*[89] A more definitive list includes.[90]

FIGURE 1D-9 ORGANISATION OF THE DEUTSCHE VERKEHRSFLIEGERSCHULE GmbH
1929

DVS GmbH Zentrale - Berlin-Staaken
Dr.Günther Ziegler

Zweigstelle Braunschweig	**Zweigstelle Schleißheim**
Ltr. - Maj.a.d.Alfred Keller	Ltr - Hptm.a.D.Albert Vierling
Fluglehrer:	Fluglehrer:
Walter Fruhner	Heinz (?) von Beaulieu
Hermann Frommherz	Pepi Deutsch
Ulrich Neckel	Otto Fruhner
Fritz Morzik	Rudolf Schonger
Hermann Steindorf	Stein
P.Stutz	Willi Stohr
	Lenz Lorenz
Zweigstelle Warnemünde	**Zweigstelle List auf Sylt**
Ltr. - KorvKap.a.D.Konrad Goltz	Ltr. - KapLt.a.D.Heinz Scheurlen
Fluglehrer:	Fluglehrer:
Festner	Walter Diele
Otto-Lutz (?) Förster	H.Loll
Gerhard Nitschke	

---

88   Ries 1970 p.45. Paul Bäumer had finished the war as a *Lt.d.Res.*, a holder of the *Plm* (2 Nov 18) and *44 LS*; Robert Weichel had been an *Uffz* with *Jasta 23b* from Jun 18; Gerhard Fieseler had been a *Lt.d.Res.* who had served with *FFA 243* & *Fl.Abt.41* prior to joining *Jasta 25* in May 17 where he accumulated19 *LS* – see Angolia and Hackney 1984 pp.268-269 & Franks N., Bailey F. and Duiven R. 1996 *The Jasta Pilots: Detailed listings and histories August 1916 - November 1918* p.291 & 135. Ernst Udet flew 17 displays in 1925, took part in 4 races and carried out advertising flights for Bavarian Films, the *Circus Krone* and Gasoline Oil. In 1926 he flew 25 displays and carried out advertising for *Trumpf* chocolates, *Weltholzer* and *Vedol-oil* amongst other firms – see Herlin H. 1958 *Udet – eines Mannes Leben* p.134 and Ishoven 1977 pp.100-103, 105-107 & 115-117. With financial help from his wartime comrade Harry von Bülow, Bäumer founded his own aircraft manufacturing company *Bäumer-Aero GmbH* in Hamburg in 1924. He was tragically killed during an aerobatic display in a Rohrbach Ro IX *Rofix* over Copenhagen on the 15 Jul 27 – see Lange 1970 pp.171-172.

89   Ries 1970 p.45. A number of private flying training schools were established in Germany during 1924 & 1925 – see Gundelach K., Koester R. Obst.aD. and Kreipe W.Gen.d.Flg.a.D.Undated *Ausbildung in der Fliegertruppe* in Suchenwirth 1968 p.11.

90   Kreipe and Koester 1955 pp.8-9 & Ries 1970 p.45.

FIGURE 1D-10 PRIVATELY OWNED GERMAN FLYING TRAINING SCHOOLS

Aero-Express Luftbetriebes GmbH	Leipzig-Mockau
Aerosport GmbH	Warnemünde
Albatros Fliegerschule GmbH	Berlin-Johannisthal
Bäumer-Aero GmbH	Hamburg-Fühlsbuttel
Bayerische Sportflug GmbH	Schleißheim
Fliegerschulen der Akademischen Fliegergruppen (Akaflieg)	Various
Fliegerschule Albert & Co.	Barmen
Fliegerschule Auffahrt GmbH	Münster/Westfalen
Fliegerschule Otto Bornemann	Berlin-Staaken
Fliegerschule Dietrich-Gobiet	Kassel-Waldau
Fliegerschule Fabeck & Gaa	Hannover
Fliegerschule Rheinland GmbH	Düsseldorf-Lohausen
Fliegerschulen des "Sturmvogel"	Various
Focke Wulf Werkfliegerschule für Kaufer	Bremen
Raab-Katzenstein Flugzeugwerk	Kassel-Bettenhausen
Raab-Katzenstein Flugzeugwerk	Bonn-Hangelar
Sportflug GmbH für Mittelfranken und Oberpfalz	Nürnberg-Fürth

Most of the privately owned powered and gliding clubs were affiliated to the *Deutscher Luftfahrtverband (DLV)*. Founded in 1902 the German Aviation Association sponsored regional and national sport flying events and acted together with the *Aero-Clubs von Deutschland* as a lobby to promote the growth of sport aviation.[91] The close links between these two organisations came in part from shared officers. The *Präsident* of the *DLV* was former *Staatsminister* Alexander Dominicus, whilst his *Vizepräsident* during 1926-28 was *Maj.a.D.*Wilhelm Haehnelt (former *KoFl AOK 2*) who was also *Vizepräsident* of the *Aero-Clubs von Deutschland* until 1935 *(Photo 1D-8)*.[92] The *Präsident* of the *Aero Clubs von Deutschland* until his death in 1929 was *Maj.a.D.*von Tuschli, a widely respected and popular figure in light aviation throughout Europe.[93] Another significant personality was *Maj.a.D.*Wilhelm Baur de Betaz *(Fl.Gr.Fhr.23)* who was general secretary of the *DLV* from October 1926, whilst Haehnelt was *Vizepräsident*.[94] The growth in club membership

---

91   Ries 1988 p.9. From the mid-20s a number of German light aircraft were designed specifically to meet the requirements of the *DLV's* regional competitions – see Lange 1970 pp.138-142. Messerschmitt designed the S 16 (1924), M 19 (1925) & M 23 (1929) specifically to enter *DLV* sponsored events or to meet *DLV* specifications – see Smith 1971 p.14, pp.18-19 & 23-26 & Ishoven 1975 pp.32-34. In common with most national aero clubs, the *Aero-Clubs von Deutschland* was affiliated to the *Federation Aeronautique Internationale (FAI)* in Paris – see Grey 1943 p.104. The *FAI* had been founded in 1905 to provide (amongst other objectives) *"by means of the international regulation of the sport of aviation, the control and judging of performances throughout the world in order to contribute to the progress of aircraft manufacture."* In Britain the Royal Aero Club – originally founded in 1901 to promote the sport of ballooning – performed the same function as the *Aero-Clubs von Deutschland* – see Desouetter D.M. Undated *All About Aircraft* pp.280-281 & 324-326.

92   Grey 1943 p.104 & Ries 1988 p.9. See also service record for Wilhelm Haehnelt in Hildebrand 1991 pp.7-8.

93   Grey 1943 p.105 & 125.

94   Service record for Wilhelm Baur de Betaz in Hildebrand 1990 pp.55-56. Wilhelm Baur de Betaz was a pre-war military pilot who had seen war service with the *Aufklärungsverbände* and had been active in flying training.

was quite marked during the latter part of the decade. The number of *Jungflieger* (Young Pilots) in the clubs affiliated to the *DLV* increased from 1,400 in 1927, through 2,500 in 1928 to 4,300 in 1929.[95]

For administrative purposes the affiliated clubs were organised into twelve geographical *DLV Gruppen*:[96]

FIGURE 1D-11 ORGANISATION OF THE DEUTSCHER Luftfahrtverband 1928	
Gruppe Ost	Königsberg/Ostpreussen
Gruppe Schlesien	Breslau
Gruppe Oberschlesien	Gleiwitz
Gruppe Pommern	Stettin
Gruppe Brandenburg und Grenzmark	Berlin
Gruppe Nordwest	Münster/Westfalen
Gruppe Bayern	München
Gruppe Mitteldeutschland	Weimar
Gruppe Sachsen	Dresden
Gruppe Südwest	Darmstadt
Gruppe West	Essen
Gruppe Württemberg	Stuttgart

The huge emphasis on, and continuing popularity in, gliding led to the establishment of seven *DLV* sponsored gliding schools *(Photo 1D-9)*:

FIGURE 1D-12 DLV GLIDING SCHOOLS 1928	
Segelfliegerschule	Annaberg/Oberschlesien
Segelfliegerschule	Dornberg bei Kassel
Segelfliegerschule	Grunau im Reisengebirge
Segelfliegerschule	Rossitten/Kurische Nehrung
Segelfliegerschule	Schwarzenberg/Sachsen
Segelfliegerschule	Wangen/Allgäu
Segelfliegerschule	Wasserkuppe/Rhön

Unlike most other flying training establishments the *DLV* gliding schools were nearly all located in mountainous areas where ridge soaring and mountain wave flying was possible. The exception was the *Segelfliegerschule Rossitten* which was on the coast of Ostpreussen.[97]

---

95   *Entwicklung der Jungfliegergruppen in DLV Statistik JA, Blatt 1, 1 IV 30* in Ries 1970 p.100.
96   Ries 1988 p.9.
97   Ries 1970 p.45 & Ries 1988 p.9. The *1.Deutschen Küstensegelflug-Wettbewerb* had been held at Rossitten between the 18-28 May 23 – see Lange 1970 p.138. Udet had hoped to fly the new U 7*Kolibri* during the second event in May 24 but this was frustrated by the lack of an engine. A third event was held in May 25 – see Ishoven 1977 p.95.

The lifting of some of the restrictions on civil aviation led to the development of gliders with small auxiliary motors. In May 1924 such machines had been included in a separate class during the *2.Deutschen Küstensegelflug-Wettbewerb* at Rossitten.[98] Immediately after this event the 140 km *Ostpreussischen Samland-Küstenflug* was held for powered aircraft. This attracted a number of entries including Ungewitter (Albatros L 60), Antonius Raab (DP IIa), Gnadig (Stahlwerk-Mark Eindecker), Zimmermann (Junkers T 19) together with Udet and Hailer (both flying the Udet U 6). Udet and Zimmermann took first and second place.[99] In August of the same year Udet entered the diminutive U 7 *Kolibri* in the ultra-light section of the annual Rhön Trials. Despite bad weather with continuous rain Udet won first prize. Other entries in this prestigious event were two powered gliders designed by Willy Messerschmitt, the S 16a and S 16b, as well as the Bäumer B I *Roter Vogel*.[100]

In addition to organising local events and competitions, in 1925 the *DLV* organised the first major national aviation event. The *Deutscher Rundflug*, which was held between the 31 May and the 9 June, was sponsored by the *Berliner Zeitung* newspaper.[101] This prestigious event attracted no less than 91 entries in three separate classes: *Gruppe A* (White) *Leichtflugzeuge* with engines up to 40 hp, *Gruppe B* (Red) *Kleinflugzeuge* with engines between 41 and 80 hp, and *Gruppe C* (Blue) *Sportflugzeuge* with engines between 81 and 120 hp. The *Gruppe A* course totalled 3,000 kms, whilst the course for the other two *Gruppen* totalled 5,000 kms.[102] Just to complete these legs would be a major achievement, especially for the ultra-lights. Winners of the three prizes were: *Gruppe A* - Hptm.a.D.Bruno Loerzer in the strange twin-engined Daimler-Klemm L 21 D-623; *Gruppe B* - Herr Hochmuth in Udet U 10 D-660; *Gruppe C* - Herr Ritter in Caspar CT 1 D-662 *(Photo 1D-10)*.[103] In all 59 different types and sub-types were represented although only 56 aircraft actually took part in the competition.[104]

Despite the success of the *Deutscher Rundflug* the following years were witness to regional rather than national events. The most significant of these was the *Sachsenrundflug* which was organised by the *DLV Gruppe Sachsen* (Dresden) and held biennially in 1925 and 1927.[105] At least two other *DLV Gruppen* also organised events: the *Gruppe Südwest* (Darmstadt) organised the *Süddeutscher Rundflug* in 1926, whilst the *Gruppe Ost* (Königsberg) organised the *Ostpreussischer Rundlflug* in 1929.[106] Theo Croneiss was particularly successful in these regional events gaining first place at Dresden in 1927 and in Königsberg in 1919. On both occasions Croneiss flew low wing monoplane designs by Willy Messerschmitt; in 1927 the M 19 D-1221 and in 1929 the new M 23b.[107]

---

98   Lange 1970 p.138.

99   Lange 1970 p.138 & Ishoven 1977 p.95. One of the Messerschmitt S 16 aircraft was flown by *Oblt.*Heinrich Seywald, a serving *Reichswehr* officer, whilst Paul Bäumer flew his own *Rotter Vogel* – see service record for Heinrich Seywald in Hildebrand 1992 pp.297-299 and also Smith 1971 p.14.

100 Lange 1970 p.138. The event was organised by *Maj.a.D.*von Linsingen of the *DLV*.

101 Lange 1970 pp.138-139.

102 Lange 1970 p.139. Bruno Loerzer had been a particularly successful fighter pilot scoring 44 *LS* and ending the war with the *Plm* (12 Feb 18) and *Kdr.JG 3*. Next to Udet he was the highest scoring *Experte* to survive the war. Post war he had gained employment as a cigar salesman – see service record for Angolia and Hackney 1984 pp.184-185 & Bruno Loerzer in Hildebrand 1991 pp.309-310. Four other holders of the *Plm* took part in the *Deutscher Rundflug* of 1925: Paul Bäumer *(Jasta Boelcke)*, Walter Blume *(Kap.Jasta 9)*, Carl Jacobs *(Kap.Jasta 7)* & Ernst Udet *(Kap.Jasta 11)* – see Angolia and Hackney 1984 pp.268-269,.244-245, 226-227 & 190-195.

103 Lange 1970 p.139. See this source for a complete list of entries for the *Deutscher Rundflug* of 1925.

104 Lange 1970 p.139.

105 Lange 1970 pp.140-141. The *1925 Sachsenrundflug* was organised in 4 classes although entries were restricted to the heavier *B, C & D Klassen*. The winning pilots were *Klass B* – Sommer (Junkers T 26), *C* – Wenke (Junkers K 16) & *D* – Kurt Student (Albatros L 69). The Junkers T 26 was unusual in that it could be configured as either a biplane or as a parasol wing monoplane, the conversion taking just 30 mins – see Schmitt 1988 pp.106-107. The victor of the *1926 Suddeutscher Rundflug* was Hermann Steindorf (Junkers A 20).

106 Lange 1970 p.140. Croneiss's M 23b may have been D-1668. This machine was flown by him in the *1929 Europa Rundflug* – see Lange 1970 pp.140-142, Smith 1971 pp.23-26 & Ishoven 1975 p.54.

107 Lange 1970 pp.140-141 & Ishoven 1975 p.34 & 54.

In 1929 the French organised *Challenge de Tourism Internationale* attracted a great deal of interest, no less than 24 German entries being recorded amongst the total of 82 participants.[108] Two aircraft manufacturers dominated the German entries: the *Leichtflugzeugbau Klemm* (Boblingen) with the L 25 (4 entries) and L 26 (2 entries), and the *Messerschmitt-Flugzeugbau GmbH* (Augsburg) with the M 23b (6 entries).[109] Beginning on the 7 August 1929 the 6,200 km route began at Paris-Orly and took in Basel, Marseille, Mailand (Milan), Agram, Bucharest, Wien, Prague, Warszawa, Poznan, Berlin, Amsterdam and Brussels before the survivors - many were forced to drop out following force landings due to weather or technical problems - reached Orly on the 20 August. The overall winner was the *DVS Fluglehrer* Fritz Morzik in M 23b D-1673, two other German pilots being placed in the top ten: Robert Lusser was fourth (Klemm L 25) and von Dungern was sixth (M 23b).[110]

Morzik's win brought the *Europa-Rundflug*, as the event was known in Germany, to Berlin in July 1930. The organisation of the event therefore fell to the *Aero-Clubs von Deutschland*, under its new *Präsident Hptm.a.D.*Gerhardt von Hoeppner, the son of the former *KoGenLuft*.[111] Once again there was large German presence with 30 entries out of a total of 60 from six nations; once again the event was dominated by *Messerschmitt* and *Klemm* with eleven and nine aircraft respectively. The 7,560 km route began at Tempelhof and took in Frankfurt/Main, Reims, St.Inglevert, London, Bristol, Paris, Madrid, Sevilla, Barcelona, Nimes, Lyon, Bern, München, Wien, Prague, Breslau, Poznan, Warszawa, Königsberg/Ostpr., Danzig and Tempelhof.[112] The event was won for a second time by Morzik, on this occasion in the enclosed cabin version of the Messerschmitt M 23, the M 23c D-1883 *(Photo 1D-11)*. Second and third places also went to German pilots: Reinhold von Poss and Notz both of whom flew in Klemm L 25E monoplanes, D-1901and D-1902.[113] All three aircraft were powered by the superb Argus As 8 *Spezial* 4-cylinder inverted inline engine which offered 95 hp at 1,900 rpm for take-off and a maximum continuous output of 80 hp at 1,400 rpm. The engine weighed just 113 kgs (See also (1C).[114]

The third *Europa-Rundflug* was not held until 1932, when once again Germany was the host nation.[115] Six nations were represented with a total of 42 entries, of which 15 were German.[116] Both Willy Messerschmitt and the Günter Brothers, Siegfried and Walter, of the *Ernst Heinkel Flugzeugwerke* developed new aircraft for this event.[117] Four M 29 racing monoplanes were ordered

108   Lange 1970 pp.141-142. The Klemm L 25 was a particularly successful two-seat low-wing monoplane, 300 examples of which were built at Boblingen between 1928-33 – see Vajda F.A. & Dancey P.1998 *German Aircraft Industry and Production 1933-1945* (hereafter cited as Vajda & Dancey 1998) p.221.

109   Lange 1970 p.142.

110   Lange 1970 p.142.

111   Grey 1943 p.125.

112   Lange 1970 p.142-144. Of the 60 entries in the *1930 Europa Rundflug*: Germany (30), Poland (12), Britain (7), France (6), Spain (3) & Switzerland (2). The remaining German types were the Arado L IIa (4), Akaflieg Darmstadt D 18 (1), Albatros L 100 (1), Albatros L 101 (1) & Junkers A 50 (3). See this source for the detailed listing of aircraft and pilots.

113   Lange 1970 pp.143-144. A fourth German was placed 5th – W.Polte in the Sh 13a radial engine Messerschmitt M 23c D-1892.

114   Gersdorff von K. and Grasmann K. 1985 *Die Deutsche Luftfahrt 2: Flugmotoren und Strahltriebwerke* (hereafter cited as Gersdorff and Grasmann 1985) pp.119-120. The new engine, designed by *Dr.*M.Christian, had become available to aircraft designers in 1929.

115   Lange 1970 pp.145-146. This was possibly due to the increasingly poor economic position throughout Europe and indeed the World. Alternatively the cost of staging the event had become sufficiently prohibitive for it to be re-scheduled as a biennual rather than annual event.

116   Lange 1970 pp.145-146. For the *1932 Europa Rundflug* there were 42 entries: Germany (15), France, (8), Poland (5), Czechoslovakia (4) & Switzerland (2). See this source for detailed listings.

117   Turner P.St.J. 1970 *Heinkel: an aircraft album* (hereafter cited as Turner 1970) pp.55-57. See also Heinkel E. 1956 *He 1000* (hereafter cited as Heinkel 1956) p.132 & Koos V. 2006 *Typenbucher Deutsche Luftfahrt: Ernst Heinkel Flugzeugwerke 1922-1932* (hereafter cited as Koos 2006) pp.133-135. Klemm produced another cabin monoplane, the L 32 for the *1932 Europa Rundflug* – see Lange 1970 p.312.

from *Messerschmitt* and Fritz Morzik, Reinhold von Poss, Kreuzkamp and Oskar Dinort were the nominated pilots. Unfortunately Kreuzkamp's aircraft (D-2308) disintegrated in the air for no apparent reason; on the following day Poss's aircraft also broke up as he came into land at Schleißheim. Poss managed to parachute to safety but his observer, Starchinsky, was killed. It was a massive blow to the German team and to Messerschmitt.[118] The cause of the accidents was probably the moving horizontal tailplane, but the authorities moved quickly to withdraw the type from the competition.[119] Morzik and Poss were both re-allocated to other aircraft and in this competition it was Heinkel's HE 64 (150 hp Argus As 8R) that stole the show; Hans Seidemann in D-2260 flew the 7,346 km course in three days rather than the six that were allowed (See also 1E1).[120] Good performances were also turned in by Fritz Morzik and Werner Junck in HE 64 D-2304 and D-2305 respectively. However the highest points total was achieved by Zwirko, a Polish pilot flying a RWD 6, with 461 points; Morzik and Poss came joint second with 458 points *(Photo 1D-12)*.[121]

Under the leadership of Hoeppner, the *Aero-Clubs von Deutschland* had resurrected the *Deutschlandflug* in August 1931 to fill the void left by the now biennual international event. However the increasingly difficult economic position led to just nineteen entrants in two different weight classes. Beginning at Berlin-Staaken on the 15 August the contestants flew north-west to Lübeck before turning south west for Münster, Duisburg, and Boblingen before turning south east to München by nightfall. On the next day the competitors flew east to Wien-Aspern, before turning north for Brünn, Breslau and finally Tempelhof. Much of Day 2 was flown over high and inhospitable ground. Oskar Dinort was the winning entrant flying a Klemm L 26 Va; Wolf Hirth, the aero engine designer, was second in a Klemm L 25bf. The *Klemm Leichtflugzeugbau* dominated the competition, the first seven places going to crews flying the L 25 or L 26. For the first time two women pilots featured in the top ten: Liesel Bach was fourth, whilst Elly Beinhorn came in seventh.[122]

The economic downturn also adversely affected *Deutsche Luft Hansa*. Under *Dr.*Merkel's management the company had accrued a large deficit (*RM* 19.8 million), a position which was then made completely untenable by the Government's decision in April 1929 to halve the annual subsidy.[123] In June the management had therefore little choice but to lay-off 35% of the company's staff. Merkel was replaced by Milch who took over as chief executive in September.[124] A series of

---

118   Smith 1971 pp.30-31 & Ishoven 1975 p.69. Willy Messerschmitt's *BFW* concern had been declared bankrupt in Jun 31 and at the time of the *Europa Rundflug* he was trading on a much reduced basis as the *Messerschmitt-Flugzeugbau GmbH* – see also Ishoven 1975 pp.65-67 & Vajda and Dancey 1998 p.170.

119   Ries 1970 p.111 & Smith 1971 p.31.

120   Turner 1970 pp.56-57 & Koos 2006 p.134. One authoritative source suggests that Hans Seidemann won the competition as a result of this feat – see Heinkel 1956 p.132.

121   Lange 1970 p.146. As a result the next event was hosted by Poland.

122   Lange 1970 p.147. Elly Beinhorn would receive the *Hindenburg-Pokal* (Hindenburg Cup) in 1932 for her world flight in a Klemm L 26. The *Hindenburg-Pokal* had been established in 1928 by the new *Reichspräsident* to honour the achievements of individual aviators. Earlier recipients were: Frhr.von Warthausen for his world flight in a 20 hp Klemm (1928), Wolf Hirth for his foreign flight over France, Britain, Italy & Czechoslovakia (1929), Heinrich Schlerf for his contribution to the training of *Motorsportflieger* (1930) & August Lauw for his long distance flight from Wilhelmshaven to North Africa (1931). The last receipient was Karl Schwabe for his Africa flights (1933) – see *Hindenburg-Pokale* in Lange p.147.

123   Irving 1973 p.21. The hand of Sachsenberg may be discerned. Certainly Junkers and Sachsenberg had been paying regular sums to certain Socialist Deputies in the Reichstag to undermine *DLH's* position – see Hermann 1943 pp.53-54 & 57-58. To counter this political pressure Milch authorised the payment in Jun 29 of *RM* 10,000 to Hermann Göring who was retained as "an expert consultant". Other sums were paid to Social Democrat Deputy Keil and the German People's Party *Dr.*Cremer – see *Milch Memoirs* & *Obstlt.a.D.*Killinger CSDIC Interrogation in Irving 1973 p.21. However cuts were inevitable as the Government sought to reduce its expenditure in the face of a world-wide economic recession. The *RVM* spent *RM* 55.5 million in 1928, but this fell to *RM* 42.8 million in 1929 – see Hooton 1994 p.53.

124   Irving 1973 p.22. Karl Grulich was another casualty. He was replaced by Dr.Stussel & Dr.Schatzki.

cost cutting measures quickly followed.[125] These included the concentration of spare parts and maintenance at Berlin-Staaken where all major overhauls of *DLH* aircraft were undertaken. A further problem was the diverse fleet, a result of a deliberate policy: *"We are prepared to accept the extraordinary diversity of aircraft and engine types, in order to give the entire German industry involved a means of surviving"*.[126] In 1929 this amounted to 160 aircraft of 15 different types, a situation that could no longer be sustained:[127]

FIGURE 1D-13 DEUTSCHE LUFT HANSA AIRCRAFT FLEET 1929			
BFW M 20	2	Focke Wulf A 38 Möwe	12
Caspar C.35	2	Junkers F 13	43
Dornier B Merkur	26	Junkers F 24ko	9
Dornier J Wal	7	Junkers G 24	8
Dornier R Superwal	3	Junkers G 31	3
Fokker-Grulich F.II	16	Junkers W 33	4
Fokker-Grulich F.III	8	Rohrbach Roland	16
		Rohrbach Romar	1

There were also four *DLH* subsidiaries: the *Nordbayerische Verkehrsflug AG*, the *Luftverkehrsgesellschaft mbH*, the *Luftverkehrs AG Westfalen "WELU"* and the *Hamburgische Luftverkehrs GmbH* with a further 32 aircraft of 9 different types.[128]

Passenger numbers fell quite noticeably from 120,700 in 1928 to only 96,800 during the succeeding year, a decline that would then continue into 1930 when just 93,700 passengers were flown; freight services also declined slightly during this period, although air mail was already recovering from an earlier slump *(Table I-1)*.[129] This led to more redundancies in September 1931 when Milch personally informed his maintenance staff at Staaken that a further 1,200 employees would have to go.[130] It was a desperate time. By December there would be 5.66 million unemployed in Germany.[131]

Nonetheless *DLH* continued to prosper. It also continued to exert considerable economic muscle within the aircraft industry; contracts for new equipment during 1930 totalling RM 8.6 million.[132] Milch was keen to adopt the new Ju 52 as the company's new standard airliner. However he wanted a more powerful three-engined design, a proposal that was flatly rejected by Professor Junkers.[133]

---

125   Irving 1973 pp.22-23. Milch successfully converted the massive short term debt into long term loans, repayable to the banks at a rate of RM 2 million per year.

126   Quoted form *Milch Lecture, Berlin, 23 Apr 28 Technical Problems of Lufthansa* in *Nachrichtenblatt des Reichsverbändes der deutschen Luftfahrtindustrie* in Irving 1973 *The Rise and Fall of the Luftwaffe: The Life of Luftwaffe Marshal Erhard Milch* p.23 with the knowledge of the Orion Publishing Group.

127   Ries 1970 p.46.

128   Ries 1970 p.46.

129   *App.I Civil Aviation* in NID 1945 p.623. The peak year was 1927 when 151,100 passengers, 2,326 tons of freight and 627 tons of mail were transported by air. The main operating economies were a reduction in the number of short haul routes – see also *Tabelle 3: Verkehrsleistungen der Luft Hansa 1926 bis 1929* in Seifert 1999 p.38. *DLH* flew 111,115 passengers and carried 1,891 tons of freight and 317 tons of mail in 1928.

130   Irving 1973 p.26. However the workers did appreciate that the Director had taken the trouble to go to Staaken in person. He arranged for some compensation. Many would be re-engaged later in the decade.

131   Meinck G. 1959 *Hitler und die deutsche Aufrusting 1933-1937* p.16.

132   Irving 1973 p.25.

133   Irving 1973 p.25. The J 52 had been designed by *Dipl.Ing.*Ernst Zindel as a freighter for use in undeveloped parts of the world such as Persia and New Guinea – see Stroud 1966 pp.322-325 & Nowarra H.J. 1987 *Aircraft & Legend:*

It was at this point that *BMW* secured a manufacturing licence for the Pratt and Whitney Hornet radial and Milch had his own engineer, *Dr.*Schatzki, re-design the Ju 52 with three licence built Hornet engines.[134] The prevailing economic crisis added weight to Milch's requirements. Given his increasingly parlous financial position Junkers had little option but to agree to Milch's demands and the result was the Ju 52/3m which first entered service with *DLH* in May 1932 *(Photo 1D-13).*[135]

Milch was also interested in the acquisition of much larger transport aircraft, although in these notable cases his business acumen saved the company from any major financial embarrassment.[136] In 1933, following its protracted and much criticised trans-Atlantic flights, the airline was assigned the Dornier Do X *Flugschiff* D-1929 (See 1E3). However *DLH* appears to have had little use for this particular giant and in September the Do X was briefly transferred to the *Deutsche Versuchsanstalt für Luftfahrt (DVL)* prior to entering a museum in 1934.[137]

In the meantime the Junkers G.38 flying wing *(Größraumflugel)* had made its first flight on the 6 November 1929.[138] Capable of carrying nineteen passengers, six of these occupying wing root accommodation, the G.38 WNr.3301 D-2000 was used to break a series of speed and endurance records for an aircraft carrying a 5,000 kg payload during March and April 1930. Initially contracted to the *RVM* the machine was then used for a number of demonstration and proving flights before making a 9,000 km European tour in October-November 1930 when it visited Prague, Wien, Budapest, Belgrade, Bucharest, Constanza, Constantinople, Athens, Rome, Marseilles, Barcelona, Madrid, Lisbon, Bordeaux, Paris and Köln before returning to Dessau.[139] With accommodation increased to 30 passengers, the D-2000 was re-engined over the winter months with the more powerful Junkers L 88a in the outboard as well as inboard positions before joining *DLH* on the 7 May 1931 for use on the Amsterdam to London route.[140] A second aircraft, G.38 WNr.3302 D-2500 with a capacity for 34 passengers, was delivered to the airline in 1932 beginning operations from Berlin on the 1 July. This aircraft cost the *DLH* RM 1.5 million.[141]

1932 also saw the entry into scheduled service of the large 112,000 cu m airship LZ 127 *Graf*

Junkers Ju 52 (hereafter cited as Nowarra 1987) pp.17-25. Powered by a single 800 hp Junkers L 88 the J 52 WNr.4001 D-1974 first flew on the 11 Sep 30. It was later re-engined with a 690 hp BMW VIIau. However Milch was not alone in wanting a three engine version of the basic J 52 – see Schmitt 1988 pp.170-171 & Nowarra 1987 p.26.

134   Irving 1973 p.25. See also Gersdorff and Grasmann 1985 p.53 & Gunston B. 1995 *World Encyclopaedia of Aero Engines* pp.26-27.

135   Irving 1973 p.25 & Schmitt 1988 p.172. This was Ju 52/3m WNr.4013 D-2201. However the first Ju 52/3m to be delivered went to the President of the *FAI* – Ju 52/3m WNr.4016 CV-FAI, in itself a sale of some international significance. Junkers had lost money on the development of the giant G.38 and on the construction of the A 50 *Sportsflugzeug. Prof.*Junkers had a predilection for emphasising scientific and technical innovation at the expense of good business practice – see Schmitt 1988 p.162.

136   Irving 1973 p.22. The Do X was covertly financed, at least in part, by the *Reichsmarine* – see Schliephake H. 1971 *The Birth of the Luftwaffe* pp.24-25 & Beauvais et al 2002 p.132.

137   Weal J. 1980 'Dr Dornier's Great White Wal' in *Air Enthusiast* No.13 (hereafter cited as Weal 1980) p.12 & Hooks 1999 p.41.

138   Stroud J. 1984 'Die Junkers Größflugzeuge' in *Air Enthusiast* No.24 (hereafter cited as Stroud 1984) pp.31-34. *Prof.* Junkers had been fascinated by the concept of the flying-wing and in particular its application to outsize aircraft. His first design essay appeared in 1919 – the Junkers JG 1. This was followed by a twin boom proiect in 1921 and a massive canard design, the J 1000 in 1923-24. Work on the G.38 began in 1928 - see also Schmitt 1988 pp.88-90.

139   Stroud 1984 pp.34-36 & Schmitt 1988 pp.125-129. It would appear that the design and construction of the G.38 was entirely financed by *Junkers* - an investment that would contribute to the company's financial problems in 1931.

140   Stroud 1984 p.39 & Schmitt 1988 p.129. The G.38 had originally been fitted with Junkers L 8 units in the outboard positions and L 55 engines inboard.

141   Stroud 1984 p.36-39 & Schmitt 1988 p.129. This order appears to ha been placed following the high demand for seats on the original machine. The G 38b was originally powered by a mix of L 8 & L 88 engines, but it was re-engined with four L 88 engines prior to service with *DLH*. There was a certain novelty value in flying in such a large aircraft. However its cruising speed of 185 kph did not make it a very fast airliner.

Zeppelin (Photo 1D-14).[142] LZ 127 could carry twenty passengers in unheard of luxury over great distances and was successfully operated over the Friedrichshafen-Recife route and from the autumn onward the Friedrichshafen to Rio de Janeiro route by the parent company, *Luftschiffbau Zeppelin*. Nine return flights were made in 1932 and a further nine in 1933.[143] In 1929 under the command of Hugo Eckener, it had made a record breaking round the world flight (34,200 kms) in 12 days 14 hours and 20 minutes: Lakehurst (USA), Friedrichshafen (Germany), Tokyo (Japan) and Los Angeles (USA) before returning to Lakehurst carrying 20 passengers, a crew of forty-one and 400 kgs of mail and freight *(Photo 1D-15)*.[144] It was one of the greatest achievements in the history of air travel and it had been made just three years after the lifting of the final restrictions on German commercial aeronautical activity.

142   Stroud 1966 pp.383-385. Earlier airship services by LZ 120 *Bodensee* had come to a premature close at the end of the 1919 season when the *ILUK* insisted that that airship and its sister, the LZ 121*Nordstern*, be handed over to the French and Italian authorities as war reparations – see Stroud 1966 p.382. During 1922-24 the *Luftschiffbau Zeppelin* had been contracted to design, build and supply a commercial airship for the *USN*. The result was the LZ 126 which effectively became the prototype for the LZ 127 *Graf Zeppelin* - see Althoff W.F. 1990 *Sky Ships: A History of the Airship in the United States Navy* pp.51-52.
143   Stroud 1966 pp.383-384 & Jackson 1983 pp.8-9. Completed in Sep 28 the LZ 127 had initially been used for a series of record breaking flights and for scientific survey work - trans-Atlantic to the USA (Oct 28), Egypt (Mar 29), trans-Atlantic to Brazil (May 30) & an Arctic cruise (Sum 31).
144   Jackson 1983 p.9.

GERMAN COMMERICIAL AIR TRAFFIC STATISTICS 1919-34								
1 Year	2 Number of Aircraft	3 Distance flown	4 Passengers Carried	5 Passengers Distance	6 Freight Goods	7 Freight Mail	8 Freight Distance	Key Events
1919		576	2.0					
1920	27	477	4.0		5.7	6.4		Start of Allied restrictions
1921	34	1660	6.8					
1922	50	1197	7.7		37	32		
1923	72	714	8.5	2.1	39	5	9	
1924	107	1574	13.4	3.3	71	22	41	
1925	142	4922	55.2	10.6	521	287	178	
1926	168	6504	84.6	14.6	1057	551	311	End of Allied restrictions
1927	194	9912	151.1	27.0	2326	627	681	
1928	200	11384	120.7	28.7	2164	350	873	
1929	177	10358	96.8	23.8	2070	385	915	World recesion begins
1930	181	10798	93.7	23.8	2176	481	1006	
1931	166	10278	98.2	25.7	2231	406	1076	
1932	170	9213	98.5	28.2	2119	384	1037	
1933	174	10483	123.0	38.3	2520	467	1269	Hitler appointed Reichskanzler
1934	174	14181	165.8	62.7	3218	772	1897	

Notes:

Units	Distances (kms), Weights (tons)
2	Includes airships from 1934 - NB aircraft became larger and flew further as time went by
3	Distances in thousand kms
4	Passengers in thousands; from 1928 passengers who broke their journey were no longer counted twice
5	Distances in millions kms
6 & 7	Newspapers were counted in "Mail" until 1928, thereafter in "Goods"
5 & 8	These are the best measures of "work done" by the airlines

Adapted from Statistisches Jahrbuch für das Deutsche Reich (Berlin)

I-1   German civil air transport – passengers, freight and mail carried 1919-34

German Military Aviation - The Years of Secrecy 1920-1933

High quality personnel were the key to *Gen.d.Inf.*Hans von Seeckt's objective to create a professionally superior army within the Treaty limitations of just 100,000 officers and men.[1] Only the very best would be selected for service with the *"Führerheer"* (Leadership Army) and in this respect the newly created *Heeres-Personalamt (HPA)* (Army Personnel Office) had an abundance of riches from which to choose, for example no less than 226,000 officers had held regular or reserve commissions in the *Feldheer* (Field Army) of 1918 and the *Reichsheer* was limited to just 4,000 commissioned ranks.[2] Competition for the top jobs was even more intense and of the 164 applicants for a single place in the *Truppenamt (TA)* (Troop Office) only 20 reached the training stage and the single successful candidate only emerged as a general staff officer three years later.[3] To offset the shortage of officers Seeckt sought to exploit an oversight on the part of the Allied powers appointing no less than 40,000 non-commissioned officers *(Unteroffiziere)*.[4] In most contemporary armies these men would have been suitable for commissions and in the same way the calibre of the ordinary rank and file *(Mannschaften)* was of a surprisingly high standard. These men were quite capable of becoming *Unteroffiziere* when the need or opportunity allowed.[5] Not surprisingly, given this breadth of excellence, the relationship between the officers and their men had to radically change and one of Seeckt's earliest reforms was to have the old army penal code, the *Militärstrafgesetzbuch (H.Dv.3)*, re-written.[6]

1   *App.XXI Peace Treaty of Versailles: Military Clauses* in Edmonds J.E. 1944 *History of the Great War: The Occupation of the Rhineland 1918-1929* (hereafter cited as Edmonds 1944) pp.396-401. Also known as the *"Führertruppe"* - see Keßelring A. GFM.a.D. 1974 *The Memoirs of Field-Marshal Keßelring* p.19.
2   Mason H.M. 1973 *The Rise of the Luftwaffe 1918-1940* (hereafter cited as Mason 1973) p.37, Seaton A. 1982 *The German Army 1933-1945* (hereafter cited as Seaton 1982) p.4 & Corum J.S. 1997 *The Luftwaffe: Creating the Operational Air War 1918-1940* (hereafter cited as Corum 1997) p.49 & 66. Seaton has described the *Reichsheer's* Officer Corps as *"monarchic and strongly opposed to the new republic, to socialism and to parliamentary control, and had good cause to remember the treatment meted out to officers by socialists and liberals and the street rabble that these had aroused at the time of the revolution"* - see Seaton 1982 p.11. In this respect Seeckt did not serve the *Reichsheer* well. *GenLt.a.D.*Moritz von Faber du Faur, whose 40 yrs service encompassed the Imperial, Republican and Nazi periods, was of the opinion that Seeckt tried to turn back the wheel of progress, at least in social terms - see Seaton 1982 p.10. There were in addition 3,040 *Beamte* (Uniformed officials), 300 *Sanitäts* (Medical) and 200 *Veterinar* (Veterinary) *Offiziere*. The importance of the veterinary officers should not be under-estimated given the importance of the horse within the *Reichsheer*, whilst the employment of *Beamte* allowed the *Truppenamt* to allocate the supervision of all non-combat tasks within the *Reichsheer* to uniformed officials or to civilian personnel. The number of *Beamte* was restricted by *Artikel 161* of the Treaty of Versailles to 10% of the 1913 figure - see *App.XXI Peace Treaty of Versailles: Military Clauses* in Edmonds 1944 p.397.
3   Mason 1973 p.93. Although the term *Offiziere im Generalstab* was not used in accordance with allied sensibilities.
4   Mason 1973 pp.93-94. There were eight times as many non-commissioned officers as required by the official establishment.
5   Seaton 1982 p.12.
6   Mason 1973 pp.91-94 & Seaton 1982 p.13. Physical abuse by officers and NCOs had been widespread in the Imperial Army - even by the hard standards of armies worldwide. The chasm that existed between the officers and their men had been a contributory cause to the revolution of 1918.

Despite opposition from more conservative quarters Seeckt also insisted on the inclusion of 180 former *Luftstreitkräfte* (Air Service) officers in the *Reichsheer's* officer corps, these men reverting to their former arm of service until a way could be found to circumvent the Treaty of Versailles.[7] In addition to the handful of key aviation personnel within the *Truppenamt*, Seeckt's concealed general staff (See 1A2), a small number of former *Luftstreitkräfte* officers were appointed to the command staffs of each of the *Wehrkreise* or military districts *(Map I-3)* as *Offiziere zbV*, also known as *Referenten zur besonderen Verwendung* (Staff Advisors for special employment).[8] Their task was to advise the *Kommandierenden General* (Commanding General) on aviation matters and to ensure that the troops on the ground did not lose sight of the vertical dimension, a feature which had become progressively more important as the Great War had progressed.[9] The first *Flieger-Referate* were appointed in 1920, together with a second officer who acted as the *Bild-Offizier* (Photographic Officer). In *Wehrkreis I* (Ostpreussen) *Hptm.*Waldemar Klepke (former *Kdr.Flieger-Gruppe 16*) was the new *Flieger-Referent*, whilst *Oblt.*Günther Lohmann (*Beobachter in Fl.Abt.233*) occupied the post of *Bild-Offizier*. The duties of the *Flieger-Referate* were:[10]

FIGURE 1E-1 DUTIES OF THE FLIEGER-REFERATE z.b.V.

- The maintenance of an up to date *Fliegerliste* (Officers with prior flying experience and those living within the *Wehrkreis* who would be subject to mobilisation)

- The creation of a cadre of replacement flying personnel comprising young *Reichsheer Offiziere* and prospective *Fahnriche*

- The inspection of civilian *Fliegerschulen* within the *Wehrkreis* in respect of the professional training of *Reichsheer* personnel

- The continuing theoretical training of *Reichsheer Offiziere* on the *geheime Fliegerliste* in the fields of ground and air tactics including war games and practice flights

- Supervision of the *Wehrkreis-Bildstelle* which provided photographic prints for training purposes, the training of *Flugzeug-Beobachteren* in aerial photographic techniques and the technical training of photographic personnel.

Weimar Germany was divided into seven *Wehrkreise*, geographical areas within which would be found the *Reichsheer's* garrisons, depots and installations. Each *Wehrkreis* formed the basis for an *Infanterie-Division* (Infantry Division), each nominally of some 12,000 officers and men.[11] These

---

7   Mason 1973 pp.90-91 & Hooton E.R. 1994 *Phoenix Triumphant: The Rise and Rise of the Luftwaffe* (hereafter cited as Hooton 1994) p.28. There were many in the *HPA* that thought that officers from the *Infanterie, Kavallerie* or *Artillerie* would have been more valuable to the *Reichsheer*. The *Fliegeroffiziere* represented 5.5% of the peacetime officer corps. However another source suggests that by 1920 the number of former *Fliegeroffiziere* had dropped to just 120 which if true gives a revised figure of just 3% - see Jung D., Wenzel B. and Abendroth A. 1977 *Die Schiffe und Boote der deutschen Seeflieger 1912-1976* p.43.

8   Kreipe W. Gen.d.Flg.a.D. and Koester R. Obst.a.D. 1955 *Technical Training within the German Luftwaffe* USAF Historical Studies No.169 (hereafter cited as Kreipe and Koester 1955) p.3. See also Hooton 1994 p.28.

9   Hoeppner von, E. W. Gen.d.Kav.a.D. 1921 *Germany's War in the Air: The Development and Operations of German Military Aviation in the World War* p.40 & 84. These positions were similar to those first created in1915 and then expanded to become *Kommandeur der Flieger der AOK... (KoFl.)* from 1916. The post war positions were advisory as military air units were no longer permitted.

10   Kreipe and Koester 1955 p.5. Waldemar Klepke was *Fl.Ref.b.WK I* between 9 May 20 - 30 Jun 23 when he was re-assigned to the *Stab Inf.Rgt.1* at Königsberg. Between 21 Jan 24 - 31 Jan 27 he was a *Kp.Chef i.Inf.Rgt.1*. Günther Lohmann was *Bild-Offz.b.WK I* between 5 May 20 - 31 Dec 20 when he was re-assigned as a *Battr.Offz.i.Art.Rgt.1* – see service records for Waldemar Klepke & Günther Lohmann in Hildebrand K.F.1991 *Die Generale der deutschen Luftwaffe 1935-1945 Band 2 H-N* (hereafter cited as Hildebrand 1991) pp.185-186 & 313-314.

11   Seaton 1982 pp.6-7 & Mitcham S.W. *1985 Hitler's Legions: The German Army Order of Battle, World War II* p.27.

divisionen comprised three *Infanterie-Regimenter*, a single *Artillerie-Regiment* (Artillery Regiment) together with individual *Nachrichten* (Signals), *Pionier* (Engineer), *Fahr* (Transport) and *Sanitäts* (Medical) *Bataillonen* or *Abteilungen*.[12] There were in addition three *Kavallerie-Divisionen* (Cavalry Divisions), each of which fielded six *Reiter-Regimenter* (Cavalry Regiments) with a few supporting arms. The *Kavallerie-Division* therefore comprised some 6,000 officers and men *(Photo 1E-1)*:[13]

FIGURE 1E-2 ORGANISATION OF THE REICHSHEER			
JUNE 1920			
Wehrkreis I	Königsberg/Ostpr.	1.Division	Gen.d.Inf.Johannes von Dassel
Wehrkreis II	Stettin/Pommern	2.Division	Gen.d.Art.Richard von Berendt
Wehrkreis III	Berlin/Brandenburg	3.Division	Gen.d.Art.Hermann Rumschottel
Wehrkreis IV	Dresden/Sachsen	4.Division	Gen.d.Inf.Paulus von Stolzmann
Wehrkreis V	Stuttgart/Bad Wurttemburg	5.Division	Gen.d.Inf.Walther Reinhardt
Wehrkreis VI	Münster/NdRhein-Wstfn	6.Division	Gen.d.Art.Friedrich von Campe
Wehrkreis VII	München/Bayern	7.Division	Gen.d.Inf.Arnold Ritter von Mohl
(Wehrkreis III)	Frankfurt an der Oder	1.Kavallerie-Div.	Gen.d.Kav.Rudolf von Horn
(Wehrkreis IV)	Breslau	2.Kavallerie-Div.	GenLt.Otto von Preinitzer
(Wehrkreis V)	Weimar	3.Kavallerie-Div.	GenLt.Johannes Koch

In choosing *Fliegeroffiziere* for the regular army, the officers of the *HPA* were guided by the need to retain officers with command or staff experience whilst establishing a pool of younger combat officers with leadership potential.[14] It was notable that none of the *Luftstreitkräfte's* surviving highly decorated leading *Experten* (Aces) were selected: *Oblt.*Ernst Udet (62 *LS*), *Lt.*Paul Bäumer (43 *LS*), *Hptm.*Bruno Loerzer (41 *LS*), *Lt.*Josef Jacobs (41 *LS*), *Oblt.*Lothar Frhr.von Richthofen (40 *LS*), *Lt.*Karl Menckhoff (39 *LS*), *Lt.*Julius Buckler (35 *LS*), *Lt.*Gustav Dorr (35 *LS*), *Hptm.*Eduard Ritter von Schleich (35 *LS*), *Lt.*Josef Veltjens (34 *LS*), *Lt.*Otto Könnecke (33 *LS*) and *Lt.*Heinrich Bongartz (33 *LS*).[15] Instead it was officers such as *Hpte.*Friedrich Cranz *(Ltr.d.Offiziers-Bildschule b.d.Insp.d.Lichtbildwesens)*, Eduard Dransfeld *(Kdr.d.physischen Abteilung d.Flugzeug-musterie)*, Friedrich Fahnert *(Kdr.d.Fliegerfunker-Abteilungen b.d.Insp.d.Fliegertruppe)*, Egloff Frhr.von Freyberg *(Grufl.AOK 7)*, Max Mohr *(Fl. Gr.Fhr.3)*, Karl Schweickhard *(Fl.Gr.Fhr.1)*, Hugo Sperrle *(KoFl.AOK 7)*, Helmuth Wilberg *(KoFl. AOK 4)* and Wilhelm Wimmer *(Stab bayerischen Luftstreitkräfte)* together with *Oblte.*Ludwig Keiper *(KoFl.3.ostmanischen Armee)* and Bruno Maaß *(Referent i.Insp.d.Fliegertruppe)* who were offered

The *Wehrkreise* were the very foundations of the *Reichsheer*.

12 Pipes J. *Reichswehr - The German Armed Forces 1919-1935* in www.feldgrau.com . (hereafter cited as Pipes Reichswehr).

13 Seaton 1982 pp.7-8 & Pipes Reichswehr. There were therefore 18 *Reiter-Rgtr.* alongside 21 *Infanterie-Rgtr.* & 7 *Artillerie-Rgtr.* The ranks shown in the table of organisation may not be accurate for Jun 20. The pre-ponderance of cavalry regiments led to a number of officers and men from other arms being re-assigned to these units. In this way Seeckt retained more infantry and artillery personnel than were permitted under the *Versailles Diktat*.

14 Hooton 1994 p.28.

15 *App.II German Victory Scores of aces of the 1914-1918 War* in Robertson B. (Ed.) 1959 *Air Aces of the 1914-1918 War* pp.196-197. The fact that many of these officers were on the *Reserveliste* may also be pertinent. It is also fair to say that many combat officers had no wish to enter post-war regular military service - see Degelow C. (Trans.Kilduff P.) 1979 *Germany's Last Knight of the Air: The Memoirs of Major Carl Degelow* pp.185-188. Degelow did fight in the *Freikorps* post-war. All but Gustav Dorr were decorated with the *Pour le Mérite* - see Angolia J.R. and Hackney C.R. 1984 *The Pour le Mérite and Germany's First Aces* (Angolia and Hackney 1984) pp.190-195 (Udet), 268-269 (Bäumer), 184-185 (Loerzer), 226-227 (Jacobs), 136-137 (Richthofen), 78 (Menckhoff), 166-167 (Buckler), 168-171 (Schleich), 234-235 (Veltjens), 242-243 (Könnecke) & 178-179 (Bongartz) and Hooton 1994 pp.28-29.

permanent commissions in the *Reichsheer*. Around half of the 180 retained officers were of a younger generation, a considerable proportion of this group being commissioned in either 1914 or 1915. For example *Oblte.*Ernst Bonatz *(Fhr.Schlasta 18)*, Karl Drum *(Fhr.Reihenbildzuges 3)*, Hans-Eberhard Gandert *(Fhr.JGr.6)*, Hans Poetsch *(BO Fl.Abt.46)* and Paul Schultheiss *(Fl.Abt.206)* together with *Lte.* Gerhard Bassenge *(Jasta Boelcke)*, Hans Jeschonnek *(Jasta 40)*, Johann Raithel *(TO Kurierfliegerstation Bamberg)*, Günther Schroth *(Fhr.d.Flieger-Depots Damaskus)*, Günter Schwartzkopff *(Fl.Abt.13)* and Georg Weiner *(Jasta 3) (See App.1B)*.[16] Personnel matters insofar as aviation training and postings were concerned was the responsibility of *Herr* von Meyern-Hohenberg who was Wilberg's Adjutant within the secret *TA I.* (Army Air Office).[17]

In order to create his professional elite Seeckt encouraged his officers to improve their capabilities through sustained education and training.[18] The minimum educational standard for commissioning was the *Arbitur* (University Matriculation Certificate) and therefore all officers were expected to be competent in at least one foreign language.[19] Overall standards were then raised still further by a new regulation that required all *Oberleutnante* and *Hauptleute* to pass the general staff examination to remain in the *Reichsheer*. This required several years of preparation and it became the duty of Regimental *Kommandeure* to organise a regular pattern of seminars, lectures and reading groups for junior officers in their commands. In accordance with *H.Dv.487 Führung und Gefecht der Verbundenen Waffen, 1921* (Leadership and Combat with Combined Arms) this required a thorough knowledge of military tactics and operations up to the level of a reinforced *Regiment* (British Brigade Battle Group). In this respect it is pertinent to note the emphasis placed by *Abteilung T 4 (Ausbildungs)* on: *"the most important goal is to create a full comprehension of the co-operation of all arms in successfully conducting operations"*.[20]

Analysis of the German conduct of the Great War had revealed a weakness on the part of many staff officers to fully appreciate the impact of new technology on the conduct of operations. This led to an emphasis on modern weaponry and technology within the general staff curriculum. Military aviation formed a key component of this focus and in July 1922 *T 4 Ausbildungs* directed that during the first year of the general staff course there should be at least one hour of lectures per week on military aviation together with one written essay or paper every two months. This pattern would then continue, albeit in a slightly different form during the second and third years of the course.[21] Education in the impact of air power was already a feature of all officer training in the *Waffenschulen - Infanterieschule Dresden, Artillerieschule Jüterbog, Kavallerieschule Hannover* and *Pionierschule München* where *"the importance of air defence is to be emphasised by all faculties in all military history subjects" (Photo 1E-2)*.[22] To achieve this goal selected *Fliegeroffiziere* were assigned

---

16   Analysis of service records within Hildebrand K.F.1990-92 *Die Generale der deutschen Luftwaffe 1935-1945 Band 1-3* (hereafter cited as Hildebrand 1990-92).

17   *App.2 Air Force Agencies in 1921-28 (Integration within the Reichswehr)* in Hertel W. Dipl.Ing.GenIng.a.D.1955 *Procurement in the German Air Force* USAF Historical Studies No.170 p.269.

18   Corum 1997 pp.65-66. This reform of military education was the most profound since that of *Gen.*Scharnhorst a century before.

19   Corum 1997 p.66. Prior to the Great War most regular officers had passed their *Arbitur*. As the decade unfolded standards would increase - see *Letter from von Seeckt to Waffenschulen, 8 Nov 24 in BA/MA RH 12-12/22* in Corum 1997 p.66.

20   *Truppenamt T 4 "Ausbildung der aus Führergehilfen im Aussicht genommenen Offiziere" 31 Juli 1922 in BA/MA 12-21/94, 4* (hereafter cited as *Truppenamt 1922* in Corum 1997) p.67. Each candidate was given the anonymity of a number and his papers were marked by several examiners - the paper's final mark being awarded on the basis of the average of all the marks. From these results only the very best officers were selected for further training as *Führergehilfen* - see Seaton 1982 p.6.

21   *Truppenamt 1922* in Corum 1997 p.67. In the second year at least 2 hrs of lectures on aviation were to be provided per month, whilst in the third year at least 90 minutes of seminars had to be held weekly.

22   *Truppenamt T 4 Directive to the Waffenschulen, 1920 in BA/MA RH 12-2/54, 9* in Corum 1997 p.66. See also

to all the *Waffenschulen* as instructors *(Lehrer)* in air tactics and operations. One such officer was *Hptm.*Walter Somme who was attached to the *Infanterieschule Döberitz* as a *Lehrer für Luftaktik* (Air Tactics Instructor) during 1925-32.[23]

Seeckt's emphasis on a high level of technical competency extended to both the *Truppenamt* and the *Heereswaffenamt (HWA)* (Army Ordnance Office) as well as the *Waffen-Inspektion* (Arms Inspectors) where officers were required to attend two or more seminars on military technology subjects each month. These included foreign weaponry, engine technology, industrial processes as well as developments in military aviation.[24] Seeckt encouraged higher professional study by encouraging up to twelve officers per year to attend civilian universities where they followed the *Diplom-Ingenieur* (Engineering Diploma) course.[25] During the twenties and early thirties a number of *Fliegeroffiziere* followed this path including *Oblt.*Gerhard Bassenge (*Technischen Hochschule Hannover* 1922-27), *Rittm.*Josef Hilgers (*Technischen Hochshule Hannover* 1923-28) and *Hptm.* August-Albert Ploch (*Technischen Hochschule Charlottenburg* 1921-28).[26] In 1923 on the basis of his recently acquired *Dipl.Ing.* at the *Technischen Hochschule Hannover*, *Oblt.a.D.*Wolfram Frhr. von Richthofen, a former *Jagdflieger*, was encouraged to join the *Reichsheer* by no less than Seeckt himself who was a friend of Wolfram's father.[27] In 1929 *Hptm.*Frhr.von Richthofen was awarded a *Dr.Ing.* (Doctorate in Engineering) following further successful study.[28]

The *Reichswehr* also organised and funded overseas study tours for selected serving officers for between one to four months. These had numerous advantages, notably: it developed links between the military of different nations; it allowed *Reichswehr* officers to observe at first hand the latest developments in proscribed weapons such as tanks and aircraft; it enabled an assessment to be made of the capabilities of foreign armies and air arms.[29] The emphasis on good linguistic skills greatly facilitated such visits and poular destinations were the Soviet Union and the USA. On their return the officers were required to write an extensive reports which was then forwarded to *T 3 (Fremde Heer)* (Foreign Armies) and in the case of *Fliegeroffiziere* to *TA (L)'s Fremde Luftstreitkräfte-Referat* (Foreign Air Services Desk), later *Referat VI* within the later *T 2 V (L)* (See 1A2).[30] *Fliegeroffiziere*

Matuschka E. 1983 *Organisation des Reichsheeres* in *Handbuch zur deutschen Militärgeschichte 1648-1939.*

23   Service record for Walter Somme in Hildebrand K.F.1992 *Die Generale der deutschen Luftwaffe 1935-1945 Band 3 O-Z* (hereafter cited as Hildebrand 1992) pp.311-312.

24   *Hans von Seeckt - Letter to the Waffenamt and Branch Inspectorates, 24 Jan 1924 in BA/MA RH 12-2/21* in Corum 1997 p.68.

25   Renz von O.GenLt.a.D. 1958 *The Development of German Anti-Aircraft Weapons and Equipment of all types up to 1945* USAF Historical Studies No.194 (hereafter cited as Renz 1958) pp.60-63 & Corum 1997 p.68. The acquisition of a *Dipl.Ing.* could take the place of general staff training. The German universities did not offer degree courses in the same way as Britain - for example the M.Sc. was not available and even equivalents to the Bachelor's degree was restricted to certain specialist fields.

26   Hildebrand 1990-92. Other officers included *Hptm.*Wilhelm Becker (Charlottenburg 29-33), *Hptm.*Johann Raithel (29-31), *Rittm.*Eduard Riesch (Muchen 23-28) & *Rittm.*Georg Weiner (Dresden 25-32). As part of Seeckt's manpower economies military, technical and experimental development had been centred on the *Technischen Hochschule Charlottenburg* - see Gordon H.J. 1957 *The Reichswehr and the German Republic 1919-26.*

27   *Interview between Frhr.Gotz von Richthofen (Wolfram's son) and James Corum, 4 Sep 93* in Corum 1997 p.68. See also Corum J.S. 2008 *Wolfram von Richthofen – Master of the German Air War* (hereafter cited as Corum 2008) pp.83-84.

28   Service record for Wolfram Frhr.von Richthofen in Hildebrand 1992 pp.107-108 & Corum 2008 pp.92-93. Richthofen's wartime service had culminated with 8 months in *Jasta 11* within *JG 1* where he scored 8 *Luftsiege* - see Franks N., Bailey F. and Duiven R. 1996 *The Jasta Pilots: Detailed listings and histories August 1916 - November 1918* (hereafter cited as Franks et al 1996) p.241 & Corum 2008 pp.58-70.

29   Corum 1997 p.70.

30   *Army Aviation Organisation 1st March 1920 to 31st March 1927* & *Army Aviation Organisation 1st April 1927 to 30th September 1929* in Beauvais H., Kossler K., Mayer M. and Regel C. 2002 *German Secret Flight Test Centres to 1945: Johannisthal, Lipetsk, Rechlin, Travemünde, Tarnewitz, Peenemunde-West* (hereafter cited as Beauvais et al 2002) p.50.

who are known to have undertaken such tours include *Rittm.*Curt Pflugbeil who visited the USSR, Sweden and Italy between April 1928 and April 1931, and *Hptm.*Frhr.von Richthofen who was attached to the *Deutschen Botschaft Rom* (German Embassy in Rome) between April 1929 and October 1932 during which time he made a detailed study of the *Regia Aeronautica* (See also 1A3).[31]

Volunteers for the few available commissions were initially taken into the *Regimenter* as other ranks. After fifteen months satisfactory service, the officer candidate took a *Fahnenjunker* (Junior Ensign)'s examination and if successful was promoted to the rank of *Fahnenjunker-Gefreiter.* Regardless of his arm of service he would then attend the *Unteroffizier-Lehrgang* (NCO Training Course) at the *Infanterieschule Dresden* prior to taking his officer's examination. Successful candidates were then promoted to the rank of *Oberfahnrich* (Senior Ensign) and permitted to join the officer's mess under approval. The rigid mess discipline was then such that he could only speak if spoken to by a commissioned officer. Finally, subject to the vote of the officers of the regiment, plus the approval of his commanding officer the *Oberfahnrich* was accepted for commissioned rank as a *Leutnant.* By this time he had already completed between four and five years of his twenty five years of military service.[32] A good example of this process is provided by Sigismund Frhr.von Falkenstein who was enlisted in *Reiter-Regiment 16* at Erfurt on the 1 October 1922. Two years later on the 15 September 1924, he was promoted to the rank of *Fahnrich*, becoming an *Oberfahnrich* one year later. He was formally commissioned as a *Leutnant* on the 1 December 1925, just over three years after his original engagement.[33]

The recruiting of other ranks from unmarried German nationals aged between 17 and 21 years took place twice a year. The acceptance standards were high and candidates had to produce good documentary evidence of their educational standards and employment history. Good medical fitness was mandatory; a criminal record or involvement in illegal political activity led to immediate rejection.[34] Recruitment was organised by each *Wehrkreis* but the actual process of selection was delegated to the individual units. Under the terms of the Treaty of Versailles other ranks were required to sign-on for a minimum period of twelve years although it would seem that this was not always the case with enlisted men being re-engaged on an annual or even six monthly basis.[35] Both officers and men would see out most of their *Reichsheer* service with their parent *Regiment.* On his eighteenth birthday *Fahnenjunker* Werner Kreipe was enlisted into *Artillerie-Regiment 6* at Minden on the 1 April 1922, being promoted to *Fahnrich* on the 1 October 1924. He became an *Oberfahnrich* on the 1 August 1925 and was finally commissioned into his *Regiment* on the 1 December 1925. He was to serve as a *Batterieoffizier* within the *Artillerie-Regiment 6* until February 1931 when as an *Oberleutnant* he became the *Fursorge-Offizier* (Welfare Officer) in the *IV.(Reitenden) Abteilung* (4th Mounted Batallion) of the *Regiment*. His seniority as a *Hauptmann*

---

31   Service records for Curt Pflugbeil & Wolfram Frh.von Richthofen in Hildebrand 1992 pp.31-33 & 107-108. See also Corum 2008 pp.94-97.

32   Seaton 1982 p.12. Prior to the Great War graduates from the *Kadettenanstalt* or *Schulen* were commissioned directly into their parent regiment. Direct entrants from school or university had followed an abbreviated *Fahnenjunker* route which saw their officer training being conducted at a Kriegsschule.

33   Service record for Sigismund Frhr.von Falkenstein in Hildebrand K.F.1990 *Die Generale der deutschen Luftwaffe 1935-1945 Band 1 A-G* (hereafter cited as Hildebrand 1990) pp.265-266.

34   Mason 1973 pp.94-95. Seeckt and Heye, as well as successive *Reichswehrministers*, sought to maintain the *Reichswehr's* apolitical stance. The most celebrated incident in this respect was the court martial of Lt.Scheringer (*Art.Rgt.5*) on a charge of conspiracy to commit high treason following his attempts to recruit other junior officers in his regiment into a movement that would have supported a *NSDAP* coup - see Shirer W.L. 1963 *The Rise and Fall of the Third Reich: A History of Nazi Germany* pp.139-142 & Seaton 1982 p.19.

35   Mason 1973 pp.94-95. As evidenced by Col.John Morgan in his inspection reports to the *IKK*. Trained personnel were being released to form a "Black Reserve" with some being recruited by the *Staatspolizei*. New personnel were then being trained in their place. Morgan also discovered that *Gefreiter* were being paid as *Unteroffiziere*.

took effect from the 1 April 1934, twelve years after his original enlistment as an officer candidate *(Photo 1E-3)*.[36]

Promotion for all ranks was agonisingly slow. By the end of the decade stagnation had set in and the monotony imposed by peacetime soldiering within an artificially constrained force structure had become a serious issue:

Soldiers turned into officials, officers became candidates for pensions. What remains is a *Polizeitruppe* (Police Force). People know nothing of the tragedy of the four words: Twelve years as subalterns.[37]

*Lt.*Scheringer
Artillerie-Regiment 5

On the plus side foreign military observers had noted that the relationship between officers and men was good and far closer professionally than was the case in many contemporary armies. The quality of the *Unteroffizier-Korps* was also uniformly good. Following Seeckt's reforms discipline was strict, but generally fair with far less bullying than had been the case in Imperial days. Great stress was placed on the development of initiative at all levels and intensive training was to produce a first rate cadre of drill, weapon training and tactics instructors. From its junior officers would come some of the finest tacticians in any army of the Twentieth Century.[38] However there was also a down side. The former status of the *Offizierkorps* had been progressively eroded by the Republican Government and as economic prosperity had improved in the late twenties enlisted men had increasingly felt that they were second-class citizens; to all intents and purposes a poor and unwanted relation. Not surprisingly the suicide rate fluctuated at between four and five times the rate for remainder of the population.[39]

The lure of covert flight training has to be seen in this light. Given Allied restrictions initially this had to take the form of glider training at one of the new gliding sites in the Rhön Mountains or on the coastal sand dunes of Rossitten in Ostpreussen (See also 1D2).[40] The young *Lt.*Oskar Dinort *(Inf.Rgt.2* Allenstein) was one of the select few to take advantage of this type of training. He undertook *Segelflug-Lehrgange* (Glider Courses) at both of these sites during the early twenties and continued to further his gliding expertise as a *Sportflieger* (Sport Flier). On the 20 October 1929 he made a world record breaking endurance flight of 14 hours and 43 minutes over the Ostsee, some of this being carried out at night under the light of the moon.[41] *Lt.*Heinrich Seywald *(Kraftfahr-Abt.7)* was another officer who benefited from this training, although in his case he was already an accomplished and experienced fighter pilot. He attended a *Segelflug-Lehrgang* on the Rhön in June and July 1923.[42]

36 Service record for Werner Kreipe in Hildebrand 1991 pp.234-235. Kreipe had been born in Hannover where the barracks of the *III./Art.Rgt.6* was located - see www.lexikon-der-wehrmacht.de/Wehrmachtbis39/ Reichswehr 1932.

37 Quoted from the *Volkischer Beobachter* in Mason 1973 *The Rise of the Luftwaffe 1918-1940* p.166 with the knowledge of the Orion Publishing Group.

38 Seaton 1982 pp.12-13.

39 Mason 1973 p.166.

40 Hermann 1943 *The Rise and Fall of the Luftwaffe* pp.17-19, Grey C.G. 1943 *The Luftwaffe* p.96, Suchenwirth R. 1968 *The Development of the German Air Force 1919-1939* USAF Historical Studies No.160 (hereafter cited as Suchenwirth 1968) p. 10, Ries K. 1970 *Luftwaffe Bd.1 Die Maulwurfe 1919-1935* (hereafter cited as Ries 1970) p.24, Mason 1973 pp.107-108 & Hooton 1994 p.35.

41 Service records for Oskar Dinort in Brutting G. 1976 *Das waren die deutschen Stuka-Asse 1939-1945* (hereafter cited as Brutting 1976) pp.136-137 & Obermaier E. 1976 *Die Ritterkreuztrager der Luftwaffe Bd.II Stuka- und Schlachtflieger 1939-1945* (hereafter cited as Obermaier 1976) p.39.

42 Service record for Heinrich Seywald in Hildebrand 1992 pp.297-299. Seywald had trained as a *Beobachter* with

Although of limited military application the ability to fly unpowered aircraft was of use to the *Reichsheer* as it helped to retain existing aircrew. Nonetheless by the mid-twenties the number of officers on the *Reichsheer's Geheime Fliegerliste* (Secret Pilot Roster) had fallen due to retirements, early discharges and accidents to around 100 from the 180 that had been originally retained in 1920.[43] Examples included *Hptm.*Walther Grosch and *Rittm.*Hans Poetsch who both retired on the 31 March 1920 after a very short period of post-war service, whilst *Hptm.*Wolfgang Weese left on the 9 October 1920 and *Maj.*Wilhelm Haehnelt and *Rittm.*Hermann Fahrig were both discharged on the 31 December 1920.[44] Thereafter the haemorrhage weakened but notable losses in the early twenties included *Hptm.*Walter Stahr, *Oblt.*Werner Junck, *Oblt.*Carl-August von Schoenebeck and *Hptm.*Albert Müller-Kahle.[45]

After 1920 it had become almost impossible to obtain an early discharge as the *Interallierten Militär-Kontroll-Kommission (IMKK)* construed this as a means of circumventing the Treaty Regulations whereby a trained soldier would be replaced by another who would then be trained to the same standard.[46] The *TA (L)* was in any case desperate to hold on to the experienced flying officers it still had at its disposal. It was therefore only after a considerable struggle with his friend *Maj.*Helmuth Wilberg of the *TA (L)* that Junck whad been able to secure his early discharge in 1923:

"I've got the chance to fly again. Nothing else interests me, so please fix my discharge."
"Impossible," replied Wilberg, "the regulations only allow discharge on grounds of physical or mental deficiency."
"Well I'm physically deficient," argued Junck, "I was wounded three times, and if I go much longer in the *Reichsheer* I shall certainly qualify on mental grounds."[47]

*Lt.*Werner Junck
Btl.-Adjutant im Inf.Rgt.18

---

the *bayerischen Fliegertruppe* in 1916, seeing service with *Kampfstaffel 33, Fl.-Abt.274* & the *bay.Fl.-Abt.48*, before training as a pilot in 1917. He completed his war service with *Jasta 23,* which he led from Jun 18. He had *6 Luftsiege* - see Franks et al 1996 p.267.

43   Suchenwirth 1968 p.5 & Hooton 1994 p.57.

44   Hildebrand 1990-92. *Hptm.*Grosch was re-engaged on the 1 May 25, whilst *Rittm.*Poetsch returned to the *Reichsheer* as a civilian photographic specialist on the 1 Jul 26. *Hptm.a.D.*Weese was active in civil aviation from May 25 - Aug 33 whereas *Maj.a.D.*Haehnelt became the *Vizepräsident des Aero-Clubs von Deutschland* and from 1926 *Vizepräsident des Deutschen Luftsport-Verbändes* (1D2). *Maj.a.D.*Fahrig was re-engaged on the 1 Sep 27 as a *Hilfs-Referent b.WK IV Dresden.* See service records for Hermann Fahrig & Walther Grosch in Hildebrand 1990 pp.263-264 & 397-398, Wilhelm Haehnelt in Hildebrand 1991 pp.7-8 and Hans Poetsch & Wolfgang Weese in Hildebrand 1992 pp.48-50 & 482-483.

45   See service records for Werner Junck & Albert Müller-Kahle in Hildebrand 1991 pp.142-143 & 420-421 and for Carl-August von Schoenebeck & Walter Stahr in Hildebrand 1992 pp.213-214 & 341-342. Junck who was *Adj. II./IR 18* Münster secured employment in South America where new airlines were being developed. Schoenebeck was serving with *Kraftfahr Abt.5* at Bad Cannstatt when he left the *Reichsheer.* After a short period in industry, Schoenebeck also went to South America - in his case on behalf of the *RWM.* Both Junck and Schoenebeck would be re-employed by the *Reichsheer* as civilian instructors at Lipetsk from 1925. Müller-Kahle was a *Battr.Offz.i.AR 6* in 1923. Little is known of his civilian life. However he joined the Nationalist veterans' *Stahlhelm* organisation where he became *Fhr.d.Jung-Stahlhelms Niedersachsen* in 1928. Stahr may well have been discharged on the 31 Dec 22 as part of the *Sondergruppe R/Moskau Zentrale's* arrangements for the new establishment at Lipetsk. He was appointed head of the *Fliegerschule* and associated *Versuchsgruppe* from Mar 25.

46   Seaton 1982 p.4. There was a 5% restriction on replacements for those officers who were discharged for reasons other than death, sickness or dishonour. As this prevented a one-for one replacement the Reichswehr simply could not afford to have its already small officer corps eroded still further.

47   Quoted from Townsend P. 1970 *Duel of Eagles* (hereafter cited as Townsend 1970) p.79 with the knowledge of the Orion Publishing Group.

As there was a very real concern within the *TA (L)* that there would be insufficient junior officers to man the number of aircraft then planned in the event of mobilisation, Wilberg supported the establishment of *Sportflug GmbH* in March 1924 (See also 1A2 & 1D2).[48] Arrangements were secretly concluded with the *RVM* (Reichs Transport Ministry) that sixty men would be selected annually for an eighteen month programme of covert flying training. The first year of this training would be based in Germany, it being expected that the final six months would be carried out at the *Reichsheer's* new secret air base at Lipetsk in the Soviet Union once this became fully operational (See 1D1).[49] Each contingent would consist of thirty serving officers, of who up to one in three had no previous flying experience. The remaining thirty flight students were to be *Fahnenjunker* or officer candidates who had yet to join their *Regimenter*.[50] Technically these men were civilians, although it was clearly a very fine line.

Within the *Reichswehr* former *Luftstreitkräfte* officers or those who had trained at their own expense were now known as *Altmarker*, whilst a young pilot with no prior military experience was deemed to be a *Jungmarker*. *Jungmarker* first appeared in 1925 (See 1A2 & 1D2).[51] The young *Lt.*Dinort (*Inf.Rgt.2* Allenstein) was an early *Flugschuler* (Flight Student) who gained his *Flugführerschein-Land A* (Pilot's Licence "A" Single-Engine Land-Based Aircraft) between September 1925 and February 1926, whilst other early *Flugschuleren* included *Lt.*Alfred Boner (*Nachr.Abt.3* Potsdam), *Oblt.*Kurt Kleinrath (*Art.Rgt.2* Schwerin), *Lt.*Friedrich-Karl Knust (*Reiter-Rgt.3* Rathenow), *Lt.*Hermann Plocher (*Inf.Rgt.13* Ludwigsburg), *Oblt.*Richard Schimpf (*Inf. Rgt.21* Nürnberg) and *Lt.*Karl-Eduard Wilke (*Art.Rgt.1* Königsberg).[52]

A measure of the importance of *Sportflug* to the *Reichsheer* can be gauged by the level of its secret financial support. At this time no less than half of the overall covert aviation budget was devoted to covering the costs of airframes, engines, maintenance and even rudimentary air raid precautions.[53] The balance of the budget, some 5 million *RM* in 1925, was allocated to support the various activities of the *Sondergruppe "R"* (Special Group Russia) (See 1D1). The location of *Sportflug's* ten

48   Kreipe and Koester 1955 pp.7-8. *"On 1 January 1924, Sporflug GmbH with its headquarters in Berlin was established with government funds and under the invisible but nevertheless powerful aegis of the Reichswehrministerium. The Company maintained a chain of seven pilot training schools (one in each Wehrkreis) equipped with sport aircraft which met the criteria imposed by the Allied "definitions" for trainers. These schools held refresher courses as well as a complete programme for beginners. A great many air force fliers took advantage of the refresher course to renew their Great War pilot's licences, regardless of whether they were in the Reichswehr or in civilian life. The beginner group was recruited from a number of different sources."* See also Suchenwirth 1968 pp.10-11.

49   Ries 1970 p.41, Mason 1973 pp.135-136 & Ries K. 1988 *Deutsche Flugzeugführerschulen und ihre Maschinen 1919-1945* (hereafter cited as Ries 1988) p.10.

50   Suchenwirth 1968 p.26 & Mason 1973 p.136. As only six serving officers could be legally trained under the conditions imposed by the Paris Air Agreements it was decided to train potential officer pilots prior to their official acceptance into the *Reichsheer* and during 1924 some thirty *Fahnenjunker* (Officer Candidates) completed their *ab initio* flight training under this scheme. The training course for the *A 1* Licence took 2 mnths after which the *A 2* Licence could be obtained in a further 3 mnths – see Kreipe and Koester 1955 p.10.

51   Kreipe ad Koester 1955 p.9, Suchenwirth 1968 & Ries 1970. The terms *Altmarker* and *Jungmarker* were introduced in 1927. Interestingly some officers did receive flying training in powered aircraft prior to 1924. One such recipient was *Lt.*Otto Hoffmann von Waldau (*RR 8* Brieg) who was trained in Switzerland on two occasions between 1920-23 - see service record for Otto Hoffmann von Waldau in Hildebrand 1991 pp.113-114.

52   Hildebrand 1990-92. *Lt.*Boner learned to fly with *Aero Lloyd* at Berlin-Staaken between Dec 24-Apr 25 - see service record for Alfred Boner in Hildebrand 1990 pp.104-105; *Oblt.*Kleinrath had been reactivated in the *Reichsheer* in Nov 22. He was secretly trained as a pilot during Oct 24-May 25 - see service record for Kurt Kleinrath in Hildebrand 1991 pp.181-182; *Oblt.*Schmipf trained with the *Fluguberwachung Bayern-Nord* at Fürthin 1925, *Lt.*Plocher trained with *Sportflug* during 1925 & *Lt.*Wilke was trained at *Sportflug's Königsberg Zweigstelle* between Jan 26-Jun 26 - see service records for Hermann Plocher, Richard Schimpf & Karl-Eduard Wilke in Hildebrand 1992 pp.46-47, 185-186 & 522-523. *Lt.*Friedrich-Karl Knust was trained at *Sportflug's Zweigstelle Stettin-Kreckow* in 1925 - see Kaiser J. 2010 *Der Ritterkreuztrager der Kampfflieger Bd.I* pp.248-249.

53   Mason 1973 pp.135-136.

Zweigstellen (Branches) was also governed by strategic considerations and each *Wehrkreis* had at least one training centre so that the wartime pilots hidden within the military establishment could at last undergo refresher training:[54]

FIGURE 1E-3 THE LINK BETWEEN SPORTFLUG AND THE WEHRKREISE 1924-26			
Königsberg	Wehrkreis I	Boblingen	Wehrkreis V
Stettin-Kreckow	Wehrkreis II	Hannover	Wehrkreis VI
Berlin-Staaken	Wehrkreis III	Osnabrück	Wehrkreis VI
Leipzig-Mockau	Wehrkreis IV	München-Schleißheim	Wehrkreis VII
Leipzig-Schkeuditz	Wehrkreis IV	Würzburg am Main	Wehrkreis VII

Although the *RVM* was eventually forced by the Allied Powers to agree to the closure of *Sportflug GmbH* a useful bonus of the 1926 Paris settlement was an agreement that flight training for up to 72 serving officers could be carried out on an annual basis, provided that the expenses incurred were borne by the participants and not the *Reichsheer* (See also 1B1).[55] This was an important concession and one that the *Truppenamt's* aviation group, now designated *Gruppe T 2 V* (L), was determined to exploit. A comprehensive pilot training programme was therefore planned which provided for the annual training of forty officer-candidates to the *Führerscheins Land C* (Pilot's Licence "C" multi-engine land-based aircraft) standard prior to their formal entry into the *Reichsheer*, together with refresher training for former pilots already within the *Reichsheer* establishment. The first *Jungmarker* to begin their flight training under this extended scheme reported to the newly established *Deutsche Verkehrsfliegerschule (DVS)* (German Commercial Flying School) on the 1 April 1927.[56]

At this stage serving officers destined for further flight training at Lipetsk attended a four to five month *Flugzeugführer-Vorbereitungs-Lehrgang* at Staaken, examples included *Oblt.*Otto Dessloch (*Rtr.Rgt.17*) from April 1926, *Oblt.*Oskar Dinort (*Inf.Rgt.2*) from February 1927, *Oblt.*Paul Deichmann (*Inf.Rgt.3*) from November 1928 and *Oblt.*Hans-Detlef Herhudt von Rohden (*Fahr. Abt.6*) from November 1929.[57]

As it was no longer necessary to conceal this programme from the *ILUK* a new branch of the *DVS* was opened at Schleißheim, near München in 1927 specifically for the training of new military pilots.[58] Commander of the new facility was *Hptm.a.D.*Albert Vierling and the instructors represented some of Germany's finest pilots including Heinz von Beaulieu-Marconnay, Joseph *"Pepi"* Deutsch, Otto Fruhner, Rudolf Schonger, Stein, Willi Stör and Lenz Lorenz.[59] Each course

54   Kreipe and Koester 1955 p.8, Ries 1970 p.41 & Ries 1988 p.10.
55   Kreipe and Koester 1955 p.13 & Suchenwirth 1968 p.15. In effect the *RWM* had to agree to a trade off between their covert financial support for *Sportflug* and a more open system of flying training for serving officers. By 1926 there was more to be gained from the overt strategy for flying training and *Sportflug* was duly closed on the 21 May 26 - see Ries 1988 p.10.
56   Kreipe and Koester 1955 p.11 & 14, and Suchenwirth 1968 p.15. See also *Anhang C Zeittafel* in Caspari H-A. (Ed.) Undated *E-Stellen Travemünde und Tarnewitz Band 3* (hereafter cited as Caspari Undated) p.294.
57   Service records for Paul Deichmann, Otto Dessloch and Oskar Dinort in Hildebrand 1990 pp.182-183, 186-187 & 198-199 and for Hans-Detlef Herhudt von Rohden in Hildebrand 1991 pp.68-69.
58   Kreipe and Koester 1955 pp.11-12, Ries 1970 pp.42-43 & Ries 1988 p.10. Schleißheim took over the *B 2-Land* training from the *DVS Zweigstelle Staaken* which thereafter focused on the *C 2-Land* programme. The *B 1* course took 2 mnths and the *B 2* course a further 3 mnths; the *C 1* course took 2 mnths whilst the *C 2* programme took 5 mnths – see Kreipe and Koester 1955 p.10.
59   Ries 1970 p.43. Albert Vierling had learned to fly in 1911 at the *Militär-Fliegerschule Döberitz*. Wounded on the 17 Jul 15 he spent the remainder of the war in a number of staff positions with the *bayerischen Luftstreitkräfte*. In

consisted of thirty student pilots who were allocated in groups of five to each of the instructors. Given the calibre of the students progress was invariably rapid but it still took a year before the *Jungmarker* were ready to take their final tests for the *B-Schein* (Pilot's Licence "B" Single-Engine Land-Based Aircraft). Examination of the 1929 *Nachrichten für Luftfahrer* shows that Gotthardt Handrick, Fritz Godejohann, Kurt-Ekkhard Allolio, Gerhard Klanke, Heinz Fischer, Axel von Fiedler and Werner Andres all obtained their *Führerscheins Land-A* at Schleißheim on the 18 December 1928, whilst Ernst-Günther Moeller, Klaus Hinkelbein, Walter Brede and Martin Schumann were awarded their *Führerscheins Land-A* at Schleißheim on the 29 October 1929. In the meantime Handrick, Godejohann, Klanke, Fiedler and Otto Pilger obtained their *B-Schein* after further flight training at Schleißheim in May 1929.[60]

FIGURE 1E-4 REICHSWEHR OFFIZIERE KNOWN TO HAVE UNDERGONE GEHEIMER FLIEGERAUSBILDUNG IN THE USSR 1925-28					
Rittm.	Otto	Dessloch	26.04.26	28.02.27	Rtr.Rgt.17
Maj.	Waldemar	Klepke	01.02.27	31.05.27	Inf.Rgt.1
Maj.	Gustav	Kastner-Kirdorf	01.08.27	30.09.30	Reactivated
Rittm.	Franz	Biwer	01.10.27	30.09.28	Rtr.Rgt.15
Ritt.	Herbert	Pfeiffer	01.10.27	31.10.29	Fahr.Abt. 6
Maj.	Erich	Quade	01.10.27	30.04.29	Inf.Rgt.2
Oblt.	Günther	Wieland	01.10.27	30.09.29	Inf.Rgt.5
Oblt.	Karl-Eduard	Wilke	31.03.28	15.09.29	Art.Rgt.1
Hptm.	Eberhard	Fischer	01.04.28	30.11.29	Inf.Rgt.16
Oblt.	Alexander	Holle	01.04.28	31.10.29	Inf.Rgt.16
Oblt.	Kurt	Kleinrath	01.04.28	30.11.28	Art.Rgt.2
Lt.	Friedrich-Karl	Knust	01.04.28		(Rtr.Rgt.3)
Oblt.	Rudolf	Meister	01.04.28	30.04.31	Inf.Rgt.4
Hptm.	Gottlob	Müller	01.04.28	31.08.29	Krftfr.Abt.7
Lt.	Andreas	Nielsen	01.04.28	30.09.29	Inf.Rgt.6
Rittm.	Curt	Pflugbeil	01.08.28		Rtr.Rgt.11
Oblt.	Hans	Seidemann	01.04.28	31.10.29	Inf.Rgt.9
Rittm.	Wilhelm	Speidel	01.04.28	31.01.29	Rtr.Rgt.11
Maj.	Hugo	Sperrle	28	28	T2 V (L)
Rittm.	Karl	Veith	01.04.28	30.09.31	Art.Rgt.7
Oblt.	Hans-Hugo	Witt	01.04.28	31.10.29	Inf.Rgt.5
Oblt.	Oskar	Dinort	05.28	30.09.28	Inf.Rgt.2
Oblt.	Hermann	Plocher	01.05.28	30.04.30	Inf.Rgt.13
Hptm.	Ehrenfried	Tschoeltsch	01.05.28	31.10.28	Inf.Rgt.10
Periods detached for *geheimer Flieger Ausbildungs* (Secret Flying Training) may include preliminary training in Germany and in some instances a period with the permanent staff thereafter.					

1925 he was appointed *Geschäftsführer* of the *bayerischen Sportflug GmbH* and on the 1 Apr 27 became the *Ltr.DVS Schleißheim* - see service record for Albert Vierling in Hildebrand 1992 pp.434-436.

60   Reichsverkehrsministerium 1929 *Nachrichten für Luftfahrer*. These entries have been checked against known service histories. The status of Fritz Godejohann, Gerhard Klanke & Axel von Fiedler has yet to be established.

By the end of the decade the selection procedures for future flying officers at Schleißheim had settled into a specific pattern which assessed candidates' physical fitness, technical skills and problem solving skills:

A gentleman in civilian clothes was present during all of the tests, a very good looking man who did nothing, said nothing, and only observed us. At lunch one day he asked me to sit next to him, and so we talked. On the second day, the last test was some kind of technical examination. I was called into the testing room by a fellow wearing a white coat, made to sit down at a table with a building set - a type of erector set - and was told to construct something on the bottom so that something else would turn at the top...

When I left the room, the handsome gentleman in civilian clothes approached and said: "Tell me, *Herr* Falck, are you interested in air sports?" Something clicked in me. There had been rumours circulating that the *Reichswehr* was going to train a few young officer cadets each year to fly aeroplanes, that some would even be trained in Russia - and that there would be casualties. I thought: "For heaven's sake, does this guy want to make me a flyer?" But I managed to answer: "Oh, yes." We talked some more, and he asked me if I might have some free time tomorrow. I did have time, as I didn't have to go to school the next day. So I was interviewed for another twenty-four hours, for the whole day, and that was it.

At the time it was customary for *Regimenter* to receive the test results and then decide which officer cadets they wanted to recruit. They reported their decisions to the *Ministerium*, which in turn recorded their names and controlled the acceptance by the *Regimenter*, saying: "You can have this one and that one, but the other one you won't get right away. You can enrol him, but he won't go to your *Regimenter* just yet. First he is going to learn to fly."

The Ministry recruiters were not very popular with the regiments, because the *Regimenter* had to establish their plans but were being deprived of an officer cadet who would become a platoon *(Zugführer)* or company commander *(Kompaniechef)*.

One fortuitous day I received a letter from *Infanterie-Regiment 7*, stating they would accept me. Shortly after that, my father received a letter ordering him to appear at the *Reichswehrministerium*, where it became clear that, yes, I had been selected to become a pilot. I urged father to approve of it, to give it his blessing, and when he returned he said he had granted his approval. Now I was destined to become an aviator.[61]

Obst.i.G.a.D. Wolfgang Falck

Falck reported for training at Schleißheim in April 1931:

In the barracks six men were quartered to a large room with wardrobes, so that we had combined living and sleeping areas. My room mates were named Trautloft, Mors, Schickel, von Janson and von Rettberg. All immediately developed great relationships with the others.

---

61   Quoted from Falck W. 2002 *Wolfgang Falck: The Happy Falcon - An Autobiography by the Father of the Night Fighters* p.13 (hereafter cited as Falck 2002) with the kind permission of Eagle Editions Ltd. Falck had initially attended for interview and physical testing at the *IR 7's* Schweidntiz HQ. Due to an injury he was re-tested at the *IR 9* HQ at Postdam before going on to Berlin for pyscho-technical testing where these observations were made. During the *Reichswehr* period pilot recruitment was handled in each of the seven *Wehrkreise* by a *Sachbearbeiter für Flieger-Angelegenheiten*. In Jul 25 *Hptm.a.D.* Rudolf Roesch was employed in a civilian capacity for this task within *WK VII* München. Roesch had served the *Koniglich Bayerische Fliegertruppe* throughout the Great War, initially as a pilot with *bay.Fl.Abt.2 & 5* and later as a fighter pilot with the Fokker E Srs in *AOK 3*. He was *Fhr.Fl.Schule 3* in 1916-17 before joining the *Stab KoGenLuft* in Dec 17. See service record for Rudolf Roesch in Hildebrand 1992 pp.129-130.

Soon we were given initial instructions and divided into groups of five students. The *Lehrgangs-Leiter* was a former *Rittmeister* named Bolle. Under him, numerous experienced fliers did the actual instructing. I was put into the group led by *Fluglehrer "Pepi" Deutsch*.

As it was a test year, groups were being trained to fly in different types of aircraft. Some students were assigned to *"Flamingo"* biplanes, others to Albatros *Hochdecker* L 101s. My group was assigned to the Klemm L 26A. After a number of classroom lectures, and flying with instructors, we made solo sorties. Then the real training began. On passing the *A 2* phase we trained on *B 1* aircraft, cumbersome planes with a single heavy motor. After I made a mistake in the air one day my instructor in the *B 1* said: "Falck, you will never be able to fly faster and heavier planes." Thank God he was wrong!

Following the completion of those phases we moved on to aerobatics lessons in Flamingo planes under the watchful eye of the well-known and outstanding instructor named Stor, German *Kunstflugmeister* (National Aerobatic Champion). Most of us thought aerobatics was the ultimate type of flying, especially after driving the lumbering *B 1* around the skies. That part of the course we truly enjoyed.

Once we had passed the aerobatics, the last phase of the training was formation flying. At first we flew in flights of three machines and later with nine machines in a *Staffel*. That was something new for us. We flew with passion while really "rubbing shoulders." It too was great fun, and created feelings of personal satisfaction and camaraderie among the students.

Then came our final flight examinations. For that occasion, high ranking officers from Berlin arrived. We did not know who they were, but figured they must be leading decision makers from *Reichswehrministerium*. In the meantime, we had heard by way of rumours that twenty of us were to be sent back to the *Regimenter* and only ten would be dispatched to Russia for fighter pilot training. The big question, of course, was which of us would have the skill and luck to become a *Jagdflieger*, because that was our ultimate dream.

The flight examinations went well. We were told nothing, the gentlemen from Berlin left, we were dismissed and took leave. I went skiing with fellow student Bernd von Brauchitsch down through the Austrian Alps. From Innsbruck we boarded a southbound train and went sightseeing in Verona and on to Venice.

After our return we leave we found out which of us had been selected to go to Lipetsk, Russia for advanced flight training. Again I was fortunate, as my name was one of ten on the list which included Hannes Trautloft, Günther Lützow, Günther Radusch and Collmann too. One man, poor von Brauchitsch, broke down and cried of despair, as did many of the others who had not been chosen. We, the lucky ones, tried to hold back our joy and not let it show obviously, wishing to spare our friends even more sadness.[62]

*Obst.a.D.*Wolfgang Falck
Flugschuler Schleißheim 1932

Falck's course at Schleißheim was completed in March 1932. In April he would arrive at Lipetsk in the Ukraine where he would train for six months on the Fokker D.XIII fighter under the

---

62   Quoted from Falck 2002 *Wolfgang Falck: The Happy Falcon – An Autobiography of the Father of Night Fighters* pp.15-16 with the kind permission of Eagle Editions Ltd. *Rittm.a.D.*Carl Bolle learned to fly in 1916 and flew with *Jasta 4 & 28* before being appointed *Fhr.Jasta Boelcke* in Feb 18. He scored *36 Luftsiege* and was decorated with the *Plm* on the 28 Aug 18 - see Angolia and Hackney 1984 pp.236-237. Otto-Harald Mors later trained with *DLH* and the *KFS Tutow* before transferring to the *Fallschirmtruppe* reaching the rank of *Maj.i.G.* 01.04.42 (195) - see Patzwall K.D. 1986 *Luftwaffen-Rangliste 1945* p.94 & service history for Otto-Harald Mors in Zeng IV de, H.L., and Stankey D.G *Luftwaffe Officer Career Summaries* in www.ww2.dk. (hereafter cited as Luftwaffe Officer Career Summaries).

experienced eyes of *Lehrsgangleiter* (Course Leader) Hermann Dick and his *Fluglehreren* (Qualified Flying Instructors) Gustav *"Bolli"* Bollmann and Kneese. However much of the actual instruction was carried out by former graduates of the *Lipetsk Jagdfliegerschule: Flughilfslehreren* (Assistant Flying Instructors) Hassow von Printz, Johannes *"Yankee"* Janke, Wilhelm Makrocki, *"Krotze"* Roth and *Schiesslehrer* (Gunnery Instructor) Albert Blumensaat:[63]

FIGURE 1E-5 JAGDFLIEGER-LEHRGANG LIPETSK
1932
Kdr.Fliegerschule - Hptm.Gottlob Müller
Lehrgangsleiter - Herr Hermann Dick
Flugschuler

Hans-Jurgen Aschmann	Walter Kienzle
Max Collmann	Günther Lützow
Wolfgang Falck	Günther Radusch
Ekhart Hefter	Ralph von Rettberg
Wolfdietrich von Houwald	Hannes Trautloft

The flying programme at Lipetsk followed the comprehensive and demanding syllabus that had been devised by the *1929 Lehrstab* at Lipetsk (Instructing Staff):

Our training programme was excellent. My instructor, Bollmann, was a great guy. We students shot at air targets, at ground targets, and practiced one-on-one air combat known as dog-fighting. Later we flew *Rot* (Pair) against *Rot, Kette* (Flight) against *Kette*, and *Staffel* (Squadron) against *Staffel*.

One day we were flying *Rot* practice, and suddenly my machine strick an "enemy" aircraft. There was a terrible noise in my plane, a horrible jolt, and the upper part flew off around my ears. I instinctively banked away, regained my wits, and looked around. The motor was still running, but in front of me the canopy was missing, the engine cooling radiator tank was gone and the wing supports were bent. I felt an instinctive urge to bail out. Yet, on seeing that the plane was holding together I stayed in and landed, all the while remembering the motto *"a captain does not abandon his ship."*

But apparently I had got the wrong idea, because once back on the ground the commander raced over in a car and reprimanded me, yelling at the top of his voice, *"Idiot, why didn't you jump ?"* In the condition it was in the aeroplane might have collapsed during the landing approach, and both it and I would have been destroyed. The machine could be replaced; pilots could not.

My opponent in the air had been Ekhart Hefter. After our collision his plane was missing five feet of wing, but at least we were both alive and intact. It was a miracle, especially in hindsight, that everything went so smoothly. My plane's propeller was undamaged, and I was undamaged, but between me and the propeller everything was smashed or gone. As for the missing five feet of wing on Hefter's plane, he must have sailed right through me. Afterward we celebrated our good fortune. That afternoon in the *Kasino* (Officer's Mess) we sat arm-in-arm, surrounded by our fellow *Flugschuler*, drinking champagne and singing:

63   Ries 1970 p.83.

"On the seventh of the seventh month, 1932, forever undivided."

On another day we were again flying rot-against-rot practice. Bollmann was *Rotführer*; I flew as his wingman. But that day Bollmann's aircraft was involved in a terrible collision with a fellow student named von Houwald. Our instructor's plane spiralled out of control. I followed him down, hoping that he would jump. But no such thing happened, and Bollmann dove straight into the ground. He was our first fatality.[64]

*Obst.a.D.*Wolfgang Falck
Flugschuler Lipetsk 1932

Meanwhile in October 1929 the former *DVS Zweigstelle* at Berlin-Staaken had been transferred to Braunschweig-Broitzem on account of the increasing pressure at the former airfield.[65] A degree of specialisation then took place with Schleißheim concentrating on elementary and basic instruction *(A/B-Schein)*, whilst at Braunschweig the students were trained on larger and more complex aircraft with a view to obtaining their *Führerscheins C*. As time went by the *DVS Braunschweig* also provided specialist training for *Bordfunkermachinisten* (Wireless Operator/Mechanics), *Flugzeugwarten* (Ground Crew Technicians) and *Beobachteren* (Aerial Observers).[66] *Maj.a.D.*Alfred Keller's leadership of the *Zweigstelle Braunschweig* was also indicative of the school's specialism given Keller's wartime experience as *Kommandeur* of *Bogohl Nr.1*, a unit which had flown the large Friedrichshafen G.III night bombers over France during 1917-18.[67] Instructors at the school included Walter Fruhner, Hermann Frommherz, Ulrich Neckel, Fritz Morzik, Hermann Steindorf and P.Stutz:[68]

FIGURE 1E-6 REICHSHEER PERSONNEL TRAINED AT THE DVS-ZWEIGSTELLE BRAUNSCHWEIG EARLY 1931		
Altvater, Georg-Friedrich	Falck, Wolfgang	Neumann von,
Alvensleben von,	Groddeck von, Robert-Heinrich	Radusch, Günther
Aschmann, Hans-Jurgen	Hefter, Eckhart	Rettberg von, Ralph
Bisle,	Houwald von, Wolfdietrich	Riedinger,
Brauchitsch von, Bernd	Janson von, Lothar	Rottberg von,
Carganico,	Kienzle, Walter	Sayn-Wittgenstein Prinz, Heinrich
Cohenhausen von,	Krohmann,	Schieckel, Gerhard
Collmann, Max	Lützow, Günther	Trautloft, Hannes
Dahms, Hans-Jochen	Moreau von, Rudloph	Willigmann, Joachim
Ditfurth von, Franz-Dietrich	Mors, Otto-Harald	

---

64   Quoted from Falck 2002 *Wolfgang Falck: The Happy Falcon – An Autobiography of the Father of Night Fighters* p.18 with the kind permission of Eagle Editions Ltd. Falck evidently confused Collmann, a fellow student, and Bollmann, an instructor in his account. In this version I have substituted Bollmann for Collmann throughout as it makes more sense - see also Ries 1970 p.81 which confirms that Bollmann was killed as a result of a collision with Houwald in 1932. *Lt.d.Res.a.D.*Gustav Bollmann had seen service with *Jasta 26* during 1918 - see Franks et al 1996 p.108.
65   Kreipe and Koester 1955 p.16 & Ries 1988 p.10. See also service record for Alfred Keller in Hildebrand 1991 pp.163-164.
66   Kreipe and Koester 1955 p.12, Ries 1988 p.10 & Hooton 1994 p.59.
67   Service record for Alfred Keller in Hildebrand 1991 pp.163-164.
68   Ries 1970 p.42, Ries 1988 p.10, Hildebrand 1990-92 & Carlsen S. and Meyer M. 1998 *Die Flugzeugführer Ausbiludung der deutschen Luftwaffe 1935-1945 Bd.I Von der Grundausbildung bis zur Blindflugschule* p.17.

In effect a two stream system evolved within the *DVS* with the top ten students from each course at Schleißheim being passed to Lipetsk for advanced training on the *Flugzentrum's* Fokker D.XIII fighters, whilst those pilots earmarked for heavier aircraft moved on to Braunschweig.[69] One of the pilots who received further flight training at both Schleißheim and Braunschweig at intervals during 1928-34 was *Lt.*Clemens Graf von Schonborn-Wiesentheid.[70]

Meanwhile a new organisation was created on the 1 April 1927 to cater specifically for the needs of existing pilots within the *Reichsheer*, this being the *Deutsche Luftfahrt GmbH* under the leadership of *Maj.a.D.*Leo Leonhardy.[71] Three to four week refresher courses were conducted on an annual basis for serving officers at one of three *Zweigstellen*, these being located at the former *Sportflug* centres at Staaken, Würzburg and Boblingen.[72] *Oblt.*Dinort attended the *Zweigstelle Würzburg* on two occasions during 1927 and 1930, with *Oblt.*Boner being a course participant on the latter occasion, whilst *Oblt.*Herhudt von Rohden attended a proficiency course at Boblingen in the same year.[73] The fact that *Hptm.a.D.*Robert Ritter von Greim, a *Pour le Mérite* holder with 28 *Luftsiege* (Confirmed Victories), was *Leiter der Fliegerschule Würzburg* was certainly not a mere coincidence *(Photo 1E-4)*. Such heroes from the Great War were splendid role models for the new generation of combat pilots.[74]

However flight training was just one aspect of developing a capability and awareness of military aviation within the *Reichsheer*. Under *Gen.d.Inf.*Wilhelm Heye, the *Chef des Heeresleitung* (chief of the Army Command) from 1926-30, annual manoeuvres and war games continued to provide the *Reichsheer* with further opportunities to refine its tactical doctrine, including the use and effect of air power.[75] The *Divisional Flieger-Referate* would introduce hypothetical air attacks into these exercises and troops were expected to undertake air defence precautions including the camouflaging of their equipment and positions from aerial observation. They would also practice anti-aircraft drills, principally with the MG 08/15 machine gun *(Photo 1E-5)*.[76]

In the same way during staff exercises unit commanders were expected to make use of air support in the same way as they might request assistance from the artillery or from the engineers. The *Offiziere zbV* were also responsible for contingency arrangements with the various civilian air agencies to provide emergency air patrols in the event of an invasion. In 1928 *Flieger-Referate* were also added to the staffs of the three *Kavallerie-Divisionen*. One such officer was *Oblt.*Kurt Kleinrath who was appointed *Referent zbV* to *GenLt.*Ulrich von Henning auf Schonhoff's *1.Kavallerie-Division* at Frankfurt an der Oder following his return from *Beobachter* training in the USSR:

---

69   Hooton 1994 p.74. The first *Beobachterlehrgang* at Lipetsk was conducted during the summer of 1928, whilst in the same year a *Beobachterlehrgang* was also conducted at Voronezh. The first *Jagdfliegerlehrgang* for *Jungmarker* was held at Lipetsk in 1928 - see *Anhang C Zeittafel* in Caspari Undated p.294.

70   Service record for Clemens Graf von Schonborn in Obermaier 1976 p.140.

71   Kreipe and Koester 1955 pp.13-14 & Ries 1988 p.11. *Hptm.*Leonhardy had been the wartime *Kdr.Bogohl 6* and for his leadership he was decorated with the *Plm* on the 2 Oct 18. His tenure at *Luftfahrt GmbH* was tragically cut short by his premature death through heart failure at the age of 37 yrs on the 12 Jul 28 - see Angolia and Hackney 1984 pp.248-249.

72   Ries 1988 p.11. The *Sportflug Zweigstellen* at Königsberg, Stettin, Leipzig-Schkeuditz, Hannover & Osnabrück were all disbanded. There was an expectation that every *Reichsheer* officer holding a pilot's licence would complete at least 15-20 flying hours annually – see Kreipe and Koester 1955 p.18.

73   Service records for Alfred Boner & Oskar Dinort in Hildebrand 1990 pp.104-105 & 198-199 and for Hans-Detlef Herhudt von Rohden in Hildebrand 1991 pp.68-69.

74   Service record for Robert Ritter von Greim in Hildebrand 1990 pp.387-389. Greim had trained as a pilot in 1915 and had seen service with *Fl.-Abt.3b* & *A 204* before being trained as a fighter pilot at *bay.FEA 1 Schleißheim*. He then served with *Fl-Abt.46* & *Jasta 34* where he scored *28 Luftsiege*. As *Fhr.Jasta 34* he was also *Kdr.i.V.JGr.10* & *JGr.Greim* during the battles of 1918 - see also Angolia and Hackney 1984 pp.250-251.

75   Corum 1997 p.85 & pp.107-109. See *Seeckt Bemerkungen des Chefs der Heeresleitung (1923)* in NARA File T-177, *Roll 25, Stuck 133, para 15* in Corum 1997 p.108.

76   Corum 1997 p.108. See also Pipes Reichswehr & Hildebrand 1990-92.

The assumption of the presence of both friendly and hostile air forces was made in very maneuver witnessed during the year, which assumption the umpire has never failed to bring home to the commanders of every grade by constantly giving them an assumed air situation - the presence of friendly or hostile observation, combat, artillery or bombing planes in the air overhead. These were sometimes represented by balloons, various colours representing different types of planes, but often merely assumed and not represented. In any case, the first consideration of every officer and man throughout was concealment from overhead observation by cover, camouflage and, when this was not possible, by the dispersion of men and material in such a manner as not to offer an effective target either for air bombing or for artillery fire directed by air observers.[77]

Report of Fall Maneuvers of the German Army
13-21 September 1926

FIGURE 1E-7 FLIEGER-REFERATE BEIM WEHRKREISE 1929		
Wehrkreis I - 1.Division	Gen.d.Inf.Friedrich von Estorff	Hptm.Friedrich-Carl Hanesse
Wehrkreis II - 2.Division	Gen.d.Inf.Joachim von Amsberg	Not known
Wehrkreis III - 3.Division	Gen.d.Inf.Otto Hasse	Maj.Egloff Frhr.von Freyberg
Wehrkreis IV - 4.Division	Gen.d.Inf.Erich Wollfourth	Hptm.Egon Doerstling
Wehrkreis V - 5.Division	Gen.d.Inf.Hermann Reinicke	Maj.Max Mohr
Wehrkreis VI - 6.Division	Gen.d.Inf.Leopold Frhr.von Ledebur	Hptm.Hellmuth Bieneck
Wehrkreis VII - 7.Division	Gen.d.Art.Friedrich Frhr.Kress v.Kressenstein	Hptm.Otto Dessloch

Following the 1930 manoeuvres *Reichswehrminister GenLt.a.D.*Wilhelm Groener had expressed concerns about the realism of such simulated aerial activity.[78] This led to the decision to establish three *Reklamestaffeln* on the 1 October 1930, ostensibly as publicity units towing banners, but in reality as a nucleus around which future military air units could be formed.[79] The three *Reklamestaffeln* were strategically based at Königsberg im Ostpreussen *(Wehrkreis I)*, Berlin-Staaken *(Wehrkreis III)* and Nürnberg *(Wehkreis VII)*. From 1931 the *Reklamestaffeln* participated in army exercises and manoeuvres where they were able to simulate the activities of friendly as well as enemy aircraft. Each unit was assigned four Albatros L 75a or L 82 trainers and had a personnel strength of just 11 men. The senior pilots, namely *Oblt.*Friedrich-Karl Knust later Lothar von Janson (Königsberg), *Oblt.*Edgar Petersen later Axel von Blomberg (Staaken) and *Oblt.*Gerhard Ulbricht (Furth), were drawn from former instructors at the Lipetsk.[80] The *Reklamestaffeln* came under the overall direction of *Obstlt.*Hellmuth Felmy's *Inspektion 1 (L)* in Berlin:

77   Quoted from American Military Attache to Germany 1926 *Report on Fall Maneuvers of the German Army, 13-21 September 1926* in Corum 1997 *The Luftwaffe: Creating the Operational Air War 1918-1940* p.108 with the kind permission of the University Press of Kansas. Kurt Kleinrath was an *Artillerieoffizier*, previously on the strength of *AR 2* (Schwerin). He had been one of the first officers without flying experience to be secretly trained as a pilot during Oct 24 - May 25 (location unknown). He underwent observer training in the *USSR* between Apr - Oct 28 - see service record for Kurt Kleinrath in Hildebrand 1991 pp.181-182.

78   Suchenwirth 1968 p.32 & Mason 1973 p.163.

79   Schliephake H. 1971 *The Birth of the Luftwaffe* (hereafter cited as Schliephake 1971) p.29.

80   Hooton 1994 p.69. The genesis of these units lay in the planned *Fliegerkurierstaffeln* which would have been mobilised in the event of hostilities. See also Luftwaffe Officer Career Summaries.

I was born on the 15 February 1913 at Niederbayern near Neustadt an der Donau. The only thing I remember of the First World War was my father's absence - he fought on the Rumanian Front. As early as 1931 I volunteered for the *Reichsheer* and was sent to Regensburg (Rendsburg). I had to sign a 12 year contract, becoming one of the 100,000 men officially allowed by the Treaty of Versailles. I then underwent a series of technical courses to become a mechanic. Having success with these I was chosen, with a number of comrades, to serve with the *Reklamestaffel Mitteldeutschland* at Berlin-Döberitz. In fact its name was merely a screen to hide a unit with a totally military structure and goal. I don't remember our aircraft ever being painted with publicity messages to show them over Berlin or its suburbs.[81]

Lt.a.D. Georg Keil
Former *Flugtechnischenpersonal Reklamestaffel Mittedeutschalnd*

The need to train a considerable number of non-commissioned ground personnel had been recognised in the *Truppenamt's* revised *A-Plan* of 1929 which gave further impetus to the technical training (See also 1A3).[82] In October 1931 *Rittm.*Curt Pflugbeil was given command of *Fahr-Abteilung 2* at Rendsburg with the task of arranging for the training of non-commissioned aircrew and technical ground personnel (See also 1E2).[83] To achieve this task the existing *Fahr-Abteilung* was used as the basis for a new *Fliegerstammabteilung* with a headquarters and two training *Kompanien*. The *1.Kompanie* (Rendsburg) trained *Bordfunker-und Bordschutze* (Wireless Operators and Air Gunners), whilst the *2.Kompanie* (Stettin-Altdamm) was responsible for *Bordmechaniker-und Fliegerbodenpersonal* (Flight Mechanics and Ground Technical Personnel).[84] By August 1932 *Fahr-Abteilung 2* and its predecessors had completed the training of 809 other ranks including 79 non-commissioned aircrew.[85]

At the other end of the training spectrum was the professional development of general staff officers, the *Reichsheer's* future policy makers and commanders. As all general staff training had been banned under the Treaty of Versailles such activities had to be carried out surreptitiously within the headquarters staffs of the individual *Divisionen*.[86] Officers under training were known simply as *Führergehilfen* (Command Assistants). Quite a number of *Fliegeroffiziere* were so trained during this period:[87]

81   Quoted from Keil G. Lt.a.D. *Our Jagdgeschwader was an elite unit* in Mombeek E, Smith J.R. and Creek E.J.1999 *Luftwaffe Colours:Jagdwaffe Vol.1 Sctn.1 Birth of the Luftwaffe Fighter Force* p.29 with the kind permission of Chevron Publishing. The terms of reference for the *Reklamestaffeln* was later defined (in 1934) as: *The Reklamestaffel is an offshoot of the Deutscher Luftsportverband eV directed by its Präsident Bruno Loerzer. Members of the DLV are to conduct themselves as political combattants of the Third Reich and are expected to maintain high levels of fitness, intellect and flying ability. The Reklamestaffel and the DLV must fulfil their missions to encourage sports flying by making propaganda flights throughout Germany. Advertising and sky-writing are also key assignments. The Reklamestaffel will train its personnel at a specialist Schule to be created in Gotha*" – quoted from Mombeeck E. and Roba J-L. Undated *In the Skies of France – A Chronicle of JG 2 Richthofen Vol.1: 1934-1940* p.13 with the kind permission of Erik Mombeeck.
82   Hooton 1994 p.64. It was decided to assign the *Fahrabteilung 2* as a *Stammtruppenteil* (cadre) for the *Fliegertruppe* on the 29 Jan 30 - see *Anhang C Zeittafel* in Caspari Undated p.295.
83   Schliephake 1971 p.29. Curt Pflugbeil had spent two years abroad in the USSR, Sweden and Italy from Apr 28 examining technical training issues in foreign air arms. He was attached to the *Stab 3.Div.* in Berlin for five months in 1931, presumably to write up his findings, before taking command of *Fahr.Abt.2* at Rendsburg in Oct 31 - see service record for Curt Pflugbeil in Hildebrand 1992 pp.31-33.
84   Pipes Reichswehr. In 1931 the *Truppenamt (T 2 Organisation)* utilised the existing seven *Fahr-Abetilungen* to secretly create a range of specialist artillery, anti-aircraft artillery and technical units.
85   Hooton 1994 p.64.
86   *Article 160 of the Versailles Treaty* - see *App.XXI Peace Treaty of Versailles: Military Clauses* in Edmonds 1944 pp.396-397. For methods of selection, particularly for those officers who were to undergo a degree of technical training at the *Hochschulen* - see Renz 1958 pp.62-63.
87   Service records in Hildebrand 1990-92.

FIGURE 1E-8 SECRET GENERAL STAFF OFFICER TRAINING - FLIEGEROFFIZIERE 1920-33			
Oblt.Wolf Frhr.von Biedermann	Stab Gr.Kdos.2	Oct 20 - Sep 21	Flying training Oct 28 - May 30
Oblt.Heinz-Hellmuth von Wuhlisch	Stab 2.Division	Jan 23 - Sep 25	Altmarker
Lt.Rudolf Meister	Not known	Sep 23 - Jun 25	Flying training Apr 28 - Apr 31
Oblt.Karl Drum	Wehrkreis V	Oct 23 - Sep 24	Altmarker
Oblt.Walter Schwabedissen	Stab 5.Division	Oct 23 - Sep 24	Altmarker
Oblt.Günther Schroth	Stab 2.Division	Oct 24 - Feb 27	Altmarker
Lt.Dietrich Volkmann	Stab 4.Division	Oct 24 - Jun 25	Flying training Nov 29 - Sep 31
Oblt.Richard Schimpf	Wehrkreis VII	Sep 25 - Mar 26	Flying training Apr 25 - Sep 25
Lt.Josef Kammhuber	Stab 2.Division	Oct 26 - Sep 28	See below
Hptm.Wilhelm Speidel	Truppenamt (T 2)	Oct 26 - Jun 27	Flying training Apr 28 - Jan 29
Oblt.Wolfgang von Chamier-Glisczinski	Wehrkreis III	Oct 27 - Dec 28	Altmarker
Oblt.Walter Schwabedissen	RWM	Oct 27 - Sep 28	Altmarker
Oblt.Josef Kammhuber	Truppenamt	Oct 28 - Sep 29	Flying training May 30 - Sep 30
Oblt.Otto Hoffmann von Waldau	Stab 3.Division	Oct 28 - Sep 30	Flying training 20 - 23
Oblt.Fritz Reinshagen	Stab 2.Division	Oct 28 -Nov 30	Altmarker
Oblt.Günter Schwartzkopf	Stab 2.Division	Oct 28 - Sep 30	Altmarker
Oblt.Otto Hoffmann von Waldau	Stab 7.Division	Oct 30 - Sep 31	Flying training 20 - 23
Oblt.Paul Deichmann	Stab 1.Division	Oct 31 - Sep 33	Altmarker

Beginning in October 1931 some officers were selected for a different style of general staff training under the auspices of the *Stab Gruppen-Kommandos 1's "Reinhardt-Lehrgang"* (HQ Army Group Command 1 – Reinhardt Instructional Course) in Berlin.[88] The first *Fliegeroffizier* to be enrolled was *Hptm.*Walter Schwabedissen who had already been trained as a *Führergehilfen* within the *Stab 5.Division*. In October 1932 *Maj.*Egon Doerstling was posted to the *Reinhardt-Kurs* whilst he was also studying at the University of Berlin. He had previously spent five years in Münster as *Flieger-Referent* with the *4.Division*.[89]

By this time the growing autonomy of German military aviation was becoming increasingly evident. As part of of a cost cutting measure the *Beobachter-Lehrgang* (Aerial Observer Course) previously conducted at Lipetsk was transferred to Braunschweig-Broitzem in 1931 where it was

---

88   Service records in Hildebrand 1990-92. Reinhardt was spelt with and without the "t". The exact nature of this training is unclear at present.

89   Service record for Walter Schwabedissen in Hildebrand 1992 pp.271-272. This posting followed his assignment as *Referat I Taktik Ausbildung (Fliegerführung u.Flieger-Ausbildung)* within Felmy's *Inspektion 1 (L)*. See also service record for Egon Doerstling in Hildebrand 1990 p.207-208.

quietly absorbed into the daily activities of the resident *DVS-Zweigstelle* (See also 1D1).[90] A number of serving officers joined the *Schule's* staff to provide the specialist military instruction that was required. *Hptm.* Heinrich Aschenbrenner who had been an instructor for wireless communications, night flying operations and bombing at Lipetsk for three years from October 1926, joined the *Lehrstab* at Braunschweig in October 1931.[91]

In the meantime the German public had become increasingly aware of the flying capability of certain officers through their participation, albeit as private individuals, in such events as the *Europa-Rundflug* (See 1D2). In the *1930 Europa-Rundflug* at least three serving *Reichswehr* officers were competitors: *Oblt.* Oskar Dinort *(Inf.Rgt.2)*, *Maj.* Egloff Frhr.von Freyberg *(RWM)* and *Oblt.* Otto Hoffmann von Waldau *(Reiter-Rgt.)*.[92] In the 1932 Competition a third of the Government sponsored German team was made up by serving officers: *Oblte.* Hans-Jurgen von Cramon-Taubadel *(Reiter-Rgt.7)* and Hans Seidemann *(Inf.Rgt.9)*, whilst Walter Marienfeld flew the Akaflieg Darmstadt D 22a biplane.[93] Seidemann turned in a particularly commendable performance in one of the all red Heinkel HE 64 racing monoplanes, flying the 7,346 km course in three days rather than the six that were allowed.[94] In between these two events *Oblt.* Dinort won the *1931 Deutschlandflug* flying a Klemm L 26 monoplane.[95]

Of course these successes were merely the outward manifestation of the *Reichsheer's* considerable aviation capacity, at least in terms of its flying personnel by the close of the Weimar Republic. The annual training of between forty and sixty officers as pilots had since 1927 resulted in the addition of at least 300 trained pilots by the beginning of 1933. Lipetsk had graduated 120 fighter pilots and approximately 100 observers during the period 1925-33.[96] Of equal importance was the overall influence that the *Fliegeroffiziere* of the older generation had exerted on the policy and tactics of the *Reichsheer* (See 1A2 & 1A3). By the beginning of the new decade officers of the new generation were in positions of importance throughout the *Truppen-und Waffenämter*. Within the *Truppenamt Hptm.* Josef Kammhuber was the *Flieger-Referent* within *T 1 Führungs* (Lipetsk Graduate 1931), *Hptm.* Wilhelm Speidel was *Flieger-Referent* within *T 2 (Organisation)* (Lipetsk Graduate 1928), *Hptm.* Gerd von Massow was *Flieger-Referent* within *T 3 (Fremde Heeres)* (Trained USA 1931), whilst within the *HWA Rittm.Dipl.Ing.* Josef Hilgers was a *Referent* within *Wa.Prw.8* and *Oblt.a.D.* Hans-Joachim Rath was a *Sachbearbeiter im Wa.Prw.8 (Wivupal Lipetsk 1925-28)*.[97] Clearly all that was now required was the political will to provide the necessary hardware for this air arm in-being to flourish.

90   Suchenwirth 1968 p.32 & Hooton 1994 p.74.
91   Service record for Heinrich Aschenbrenner in Hildebrand 1990 pp.27-28.
92   *Europa-Rundflug 1930, Berlin* in Lange B. 1970 *Das Buch der deutschen Luftfahrtechnik* (hereafter cited as Lange 1970) pp.142-144. Dinort & Gravenreuth both flew the Klemm L 25, whilst Freyberg & Waldau flew the Messerschmitt M 23c.
93   *Europa-Rundflug 1932, Berlin* in Lange 1970 pp.145-146. Future *Luftwaffe* officers included Dietrich von Massenbach (He 64), Werner Junck (He 64), Theodor Osterkamp (Kl 32) and Georg Pasewaldt (Kl 32).
94   Heinkel E. 1956 *He 1000* p.132.
95   *Deutschlandflug 1931* in Lange 1970 pp.144-145 & service record for Oskar Dinort in Obermaier 1976 p.39. Dinort also set a number of world endurance records of 31 and 32 hours over Sylt and finally of 36 hours for a new world glider record - see Brutting 1976 p.136.
96   Speidel W. Gen.d.Fl.a.D. 'Reichswehr und Rote Armee' in *Vierteljahrshefte für Zeitgeschichte* Vol.1 Jan 1953 pp.24-30. See also Suchenwirth 1968 p.28.
97   Service records in Hildebrand 1990-92.

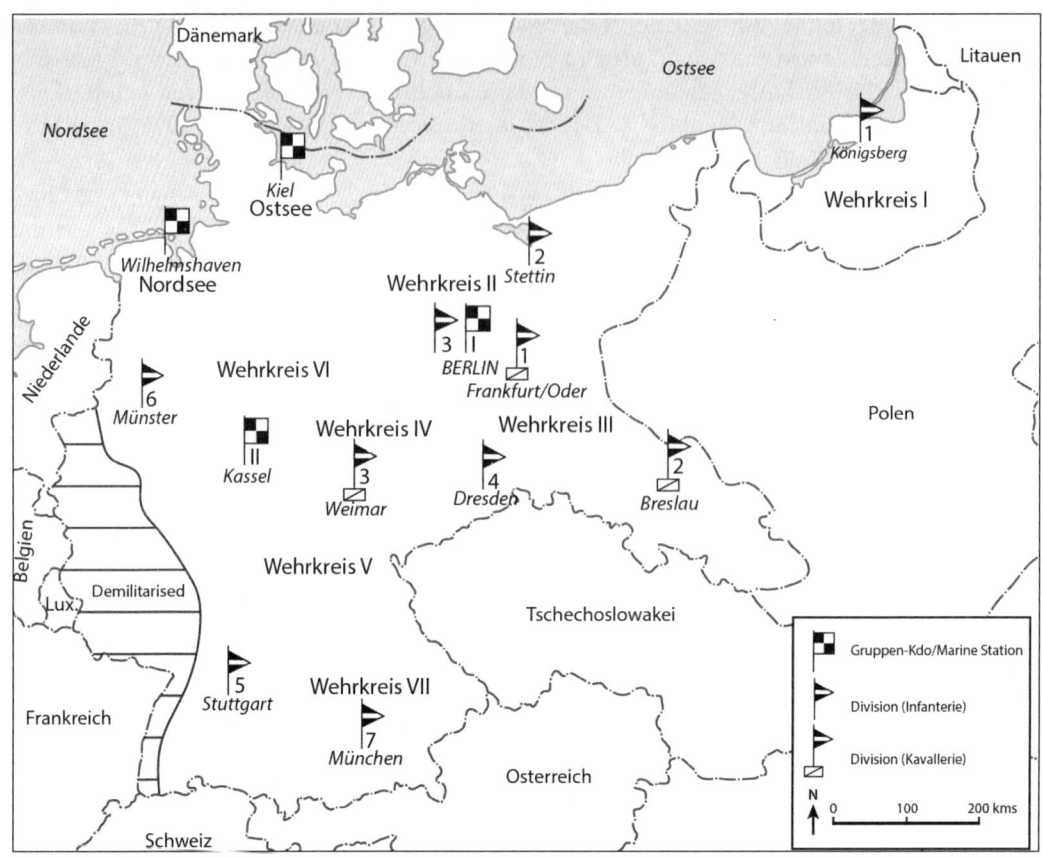

I-3   Territorial organisation of the *Reichswehr* 1920-1933

1E2

The Development of the Flakartillerie 1920-1933

Not surprisingly the rapid development of aircraft as weapons of war during the first two decades of the twentieth century acted as a stimulus for the development of ground based air defences by all the major powers.[1] Nowhere was this more true than in Germany where *Ballonabwehrkanone (BAK)* had been developed from 1906 to counter the menace posed by lighter-than-air machines.[2] From a modest beginning German ground based air defences made rapid progress to include a system of early warning and tracking *(Flugmeldedienst)* from 1915 and the centralised control of all anti-aircraft artillery under the *Kommandierenden General der Luftstreitkräfte (KoGenLuft)* from 1916 *(Photo 1E-6)*.[3] The efficiency and effectiveness of the new *Flugabwehrkanonen (FlaK)* was enhanced by the improved computation of the "lead" required for targets travelling at different heights, the better use of improved 90 cm and 110 cm searchlights and sound locators for nocturnal operations and through the introduction in 1917 of a better range finder *(Entfernungmessgerät)*. By the close of hostilities the first rudimentary fire directors were ready for service use in the form of the *Schoenlein Kommandogerate*.[4] From that year the earlier heterogeneous collection of purpose built *BAK* and modified captured guns of French and Russian origin was supplemented by the arrival of the purpose built Krupp 8.8 cm FlaK Modell L/45 which offered an increased muzzle velocity and a more rapid

1   Hogg I.V. 1978 *Anti-Aircraft: A History of Air Defence* (hereafter cited as Hogg 1978) pp.28-63.
2   Renz von O.GenLt.a.D. 1958 *The Development of German Anti-Aircraft Weapons and Equipment of all types up to 1945* USAF Historical Studies No.194 (hereafter cited as Renz 1958) pp.1-9. Development of anti-balloon guns dated back to the Franco-Prussian War of 1870-71 when 37 mm pivot-mounted guns were mounted on 4-wheeled wagons for use against French observation balloons. A second phase of development was initiated in 1906 when the *Artillerie-Prüfungs-Kommission* began an investigation into the possibility of modifying existing field and foot artillery weapons into anti-airship and aircraft weapons, trials being carried out from Mar 07. At the 1909 Frankfurt International Exhibition two German manufacturers exhibited a total of four different designs of anti-balloon gun. *Krupp* produced two designs suitable for field use, a 6.5 cm high angle gun on a field carriage and a 7.5 cm high angle gun on a motorised carriage. The 7.5 cm gun could be deployed by road at speeds up to 45 kph and then brought into action extremely quickly across the path of a reported enemy aircraft. With 75 degrees of elevation this gun could fire a 5.5 kg shell to a height of 7,000 metres. *Rheinische Metallwaren-und Maschinenfabrik* offered two alternative mobile mountings for the 5 cm *Ehrhardt* high angle gun. One of these was fully armoured whilst the other was simply mounted on an armoured lorry - see also Hogg 1978 pp.15-17.
3   Westermann E.B. 2001 *Flak: German Anti-aircraft Defenses 1914-1945* (hereafter cited as Westermann 2001) pp.16-27. In Aug 14 the German army had only six motorised high-angle equipments in the form of three *Krupp* and three *Ehrhardt* anti-balloon guns. These were in fact the company demonstrators from the 1909 Exhibition and these accompanied the advancing troops westwards in 1914. There were also a dozen horse-drawn 7.7 cm guns of various makes which were deployed along the Rhein with 2,000 rounds per gun as Germany's first home defence anti-aircraft system. In 1916 the 400 heavy naval FlaK which protected the *Kaiserliche Marine's* naval bases and installations were integrated into the homeland air defence system. For a more detailed account of German ground based air defence during the Great War -see Hoeppner von, E. W. 1921 *Germany's War in the Air: The Development and Operations of German Military Aviation in the World War* (hereafter cited as Hoeppner 1921) pp.28-33, 58-66, 77, 124-131, 159-161 & 171-172 and Renz 1958 pp.14-57.
4   Westermann 2001 pp.22-23. See also Renz 1958 pp.30-39. The number of shells fired for each aircraft brought down reduced steadily from 11,500 in 1914 to just 5,040 in 1918 - see Boog H., Rahn W., Stumpf R. and Wegner B. 1990 *Die Deutsche Reich und die zweite Weltkrieg Vol.6 Der globale Krieg* p.438.

rate of fire than its predecessors.[5] At the same time the mobility of German anti-aircraft guns at the Front was enhanced by the formation of *Kraftwagenflak (K-FlaK)*, motorised *FlaK* units equipped with 7.7 cm Modell L/27 guns mounted on the bed of an open truck; these units being specifically tasked with the destruction of low-flying aircraft over the *Hauptkampflinie (HKL)(Photo 1E-7)*.[6] The number of enemy aircraft destroyed by the ground based defences steadily increased during the course of the conflict; in 1916 322 Allied aircraft were destroyed by *FlaK*, in 1917 467 machines were brought down, whilst in the last ten months of the war 748 enemy aircraft were destroyed.[7] In total 1,588 enemy aircraft were destroyed during the Great War, an impressive figure when compared to that obtained by the French (500), British (c.300) and Italians (129).[8] By the end of hostilities the *Flakartillerie* was a truly powerful force with 2,770 guns and 718 searchlights manned by 2,800 officers and 55,000 other ranks. In addition many tens of thousands of men manned the *Flugmeldedienst* and co-ordinated the efforts of the ground defences through an elaborate command and control network.[9] Its wartime success was later acknowledged by the *KoGenLuft*:

A comparison between the rapid development of anti-aircraft and its ever increasing list of victories is its best claim to glory, and it showed that its technical development and tactical employment were based on sound principles. Its success is due chiefly to the devotion of its officers, non-commissioned officers and men in the performance of a task that was difficult and unfamiliar. It is due to them that anti-aircraft grew from small beginnings to what was at the end of the war – the best means of ground defence against aerial attacks.[10]

*GenLt.*Ernst-Wilhelm von Hoeppner
Kommandierenden General der Luftstreitkräfte

However in 1919 the whole of this elaborate organisation was swept away by the Treaty of Versailles which limited the number of artillery weapons that the *Vorläufige Reichsheer* was permitted

5   Renz 1958 pp.39-43. To make up for the shortfall in indigenous production the German Artillery made extensive use of the substantial number of Russian Putilov 3inch M1903 field guns which had been captured in the 1914-15 Campaign. These were subsequently converted to pedestal mountings as the 7.62 cm *Russische Sockel Fliegerabwehrkanone*, a similar procedure being applied to captured French 75 mm M1897 field guns which were re-bored to form the 7.7 cm *Franz* - see Hogg 1978 pp.41-42 & Westermann 2001 p.23. See also Corum J.S. 1997 *The Luftwaffe: Creating the Operational Air War 1918-1940* (hereafter cited as Corum 1997) pp.41-43.

6   Budingen E. (Ed.) 1938 *Kriegsgeschichtliche Einzelschriften der Luftwaffe Vol.1 Entwicklung und Einsatz der deutschen Flakwaffe und des Luftschützes im Weltkriege* p.189 & 195. By the end of the war there would be 800 motorised *FlaK*. Both *Krupp* & *Rheinmetall* produced 8.8 cm and 10.5 cm *FlaK* in response to the *Heer's* 1915 requirement. However the 10.5 cm weapons proved too heavy and cumbersome for field use and were confined to railway and static emplacements. *Henschel* produced a 7.62 cm *FlaK* in the last year of the war - see Renz 1958 pp.40-42 & Quarrie B. 1989 *Encyclopaedia of the German Army in the 20th Century* (hereafter cited as Quarrie 1989) p.47.

7   Lange von C. 1941 *Flakartillerie greift an: Tatsachenberichte in Wort und Bild* p.127.

8   Hogg 1978 p.67 & Corum 1997 p.43. Success rates for the *FlaK* by year were: 1914-15 (52), 1916 (323), 1917 (467) & 1918 (748) – see Neumann G. (Ed.) 1921 *Die Deutschen Luftstreitkräfte im Weltkriege* (hereafter cited as Neumann 1921) p.590 & Renz 1958 pp.56-57. In contrast German aircraft accounted for 6,811 enemy aircraft during 1914-18, a kill ratio of 4.3:1 in favour of aircraft compared to that achieved by the *FlaK*. However during 1918 *FlaK* had accounted for 47% of all enemy aircraft losses - see Westermann 2001 p.27.

9   Eberhard von W. (Ed.) 1930 *Unsere Luftstreitkräfte 1914-1918: Ein Denkmal deutschen Heldentums* p.459. At the close of hostilities there were 715 searchlights in service: 60 cm (70), 90 cm (155), 110 cm (465) & 200 cm (25). In all 51 enemy aircraft were brought down during the Great War by German units acting with searchlight support - see Renz 1958 pp.52-55. Another authoritative source states that by Nov 18 the *Luftstreitkräfte* had a force of 2,558 FlaK – see Kriegswissenschaftliche Abt.d.Lw. 1938 *Entwicklung und Einsatz der deutschen Flakwaffe und des Luftschützes im Weltkrieg* p.115.

10   Quoted from Hoeppner 1921 *Germany's War in the Air: The Development and Operations of German Military Aviation in the World War* pp.160-161 with the knowledge of the Battery Press.

to just 288 guns of all sizes; anti-aircraft artillery of all types was prohibited (See also 1A1).[11] Ultimately German military representation to these restrictions was to result in March 1920 to the *Reichsheer* being allowed to maintain a fixed *Flakbatterie* of sixteen obsolete *FlaK* as part of the fortifications at Königsberg in Ostpreussen.[12] In the meanwhile as part of *GenLt*.Hans von Seeckt's vision of a highly mobile professional army it was decided to retain seven *Kraftwagenflak-Batterien* within the *Reichsheer's* permanent order of battle as a basis for further experimentation with motorised artillery.[13] To meet with the terms of the Treaty the 7.62 cm and 7.7 cm FlaK with which these *Batterien* were equipped were converted to the status of *leichte Feldkanone* (Light Field Guns) by the simple expedient of having their anti-aircraft sights removed and their elevation capability reduced.[14] In this form the *Kraftwagengeschütz-Batterien* were incorporated into the establishment of each of the seven new *Artillerie-Regimenter* in March 1920, in most cases as the Regiment's *9.(Kraftwagen) Batterie* within the *III.Artillerie-Abteilung (Photo 1E-8)*:[15]

FIGURE 1E-9 THE REICHSHEER'S KRAFTWAGENGESCHÜTZ-BATTERIEN MARCH 1920	
6.(Kraftwagen) Batterie/Preußische Artillerie-Regiment Nr.1	Königsberg/Ospreussen
1.(Kraftwagen) Batterie/Preußische Artillerie-Regiment Nr.2	Stettin
9.(Kraftwagen) Batterie/Preußische Artillerie-Regiment Nr.3	Jüterbog (Lehrabteilung)
9.(Kraftwagen) Batterie/Artillerie-Regiment Nr.4	Dresden
9.(Kraftwagen) Batterie/Artillerie-Regiment Nr.5	Ludwigsburg
9.(Kraftwagen) Batterie/Preußische Artillerie-Regiment Nr.6	Hannover
9.(Kraftwagen) Batterie/Bayerische Artillerie-Regiment Nr.7	Nürnberg, possibly Furth

11   *App.XX I Peace Treaty of Versailles: Military Clauses in Edmonds J.E. 1944 History of the Great War: The Occupation of the Rhineland 1918-1929* (hereafter cited as Edmonds 1944) pp.396-401. Table III to this document specified the number and size of artillery weapons that were allowed. See also Renz 1958 pp.58-59. & Westermann 2001 p.29. The anti-aircraft organisations of the remaining major powers also quickly disappeared in the absence of any real threat to justify their retention. In Britain a single Regular AA Brigade was retained. However even this was grossly under strength with just 20 officers and 100 men to meet its planned establishment of 30 officers and 500 men in 1920. It was intended that home defence would be an entirely Territorial Army responsibility but the first TA AA Brigades were not formed until 1922 when four Brigades were created to defend London from air attack. All four London Brigades and the few extra formations created elsewhere thereafter remained grossly under-strength well into the thirties - see Collier B. 1957 *The Defence of the United Kingdom* pp.5-6 &15-18, Robertson B. 1981 *The Army and Aviation: A Pictorial History* p.74 & Dobinson C. 2001 *AA Command: Britain's anti-aircraft defences of World War II* (hereafter cited as Dobinson 2001) pp.59-72.

12   App.XXI in Edmonds 1944 p.401. Whilst all fortifications along the western frontier had to be dismantled the *Reichsheer* was permitted under Article 180 to maintain the fortified works in the southern and eastern areas of the country in their existing state – See also Westermann 2001 p.29.

13   Renz 1958 p.58. For Seeckt's thinking on the future form of the *Reichsheer* - see Messenger C. 1991 *The Art of Blitzkrieg* pp.57-59, Corum 1997 pp.51-52 & Delaney J. 2000 *The Blitzkreig Campaigns: Germany's Lightning War Strategy in Action* pp.21-22.

14   Renz 1958 p.58 & Hogg 1978 p.68. The standard equipment of the *Reichsheer's Artillerie-Regimenter* was provided by the 7.7 cm Feldkanone 16 & the 10.5 cm leichte Feldhaubitze 16. A small number of 15 cm schwere Feldhaubitze 13 & 15 cm schwere Kanone 16 were permitted together with the larger 21 cm Morser - see Gander T. & Chamberlain P. 1978 *Small Arms, Artillery and Special Weapons of the Third Reich: An Encyclopedic Survey* (hereafter cited as Gander and Chamberlain 1978) p.170 & 194. The elevation of the lorry mounted guns was limited to 70 degrees with a graduated arc of some 35 degrees being possible in traverse; all anti-aircraft rangefinders had to be handed into the Allied authorities - see Renz 1958 p.58.

15   *Anlage 7 Übersicht der als Fahrabteilungen getarnten Flakabteilungen, Stand: 1.November 1933* in Volker K-H. 1967 *Die deutsche Luftwaffe 1933-1939: Aufbau, Führung und Rüstung der Luftwaffe sowie die Entwicklung der deutschen Luftkriegstheori (hereafter cited as Volker 1967) p.232. See also Gliederung und Standorte der Reichswehr 1932* in www.lexikon-der-wehrmacht.de (hereafter cited Lexikon der Wehrmacht).

Understandably very few specialist *Flakartillerie* personnel were retained by the *Reichsheer* to man this small force of twenty eight guns. Amongst those that were offered commissions in the 4,000 officer *Führerheer* (Leader's Army) were *Lt.*Georg Neuffer *(Fhr.d.schw.bay.Flak Batt.146)*, *Oblt.*Richard Reimann *(Ass.b.Art.Pruf.Kom.)*, *Oblt.*Otto Wilhelm von Renz *(Ass.b.Art.Pruf.Kom.)* and *Oblt.*Wolfgang Rüter *(Adj.KoFlak b.AOK 17).*[16] Prior to their appointments within the *Artillerie-Prüfungs-Kommission* both Reimann and Renz had seen operational service with the anti-aircraft artillery: Reimann with the *Kraftwagenschutz* and as *Führer der Kanonen-Flak 89*; Renz as *Führer des Ballonabwehr-Kanonenzuges 104.*[17] Of the more experienced staff officers retained by the *Reichsheer Hptm.*Philipp Hinkelbein had been *Stabs-Offizier Flak beim Stab AOK 3* and 2 in 1916 before being appointed successively *Kommandeur der Flak beim AOK 1, 14* and *17* during 1916-18. Promoted to *Major* in December 1920, Hinkelbein was assigned to the *Stab Artillerie-Führers V* in Stuttgart.[18] *Hptm.*Günther Rüdel had been *Kommandeur der Ballon-Abwehrkanonen-Schule Ostende* from October 1915 until the end of hostilities. He was assigned as a *Referent* (Staff Advisor) to the *Reichswehrministerium (RWM)* in Berlin.[19]

However the most important *Flak* specialist to see service with the *Reichsheer* was *Maj.*Hugo Grimme. As an experienced *Artillerieoffizier*, Grimme had been appointed *Inspekteur der Ballon-Abwehr-Kanonen* in July 1915 where he was responsible for the assignment of personnel and deployment of anti-aircraft guns and equipment throughout the *Feldheer* (Field Army).[20] He wrote the first air defence regulations and was instrumental in raising the standards of training of anti-aircraft artillery personnel.[21] Following the establishment of the *Luftstreitkräfte* in October 1916 *GenLt.*Ernst-Wilhelm von Hoeppner, the *Kommandierenden General*, retained Grimme as his principal advisor *(Chef der Abteilung Flugabwehr b.KoGenLuft)* in all matters to do with ground based air defence for the remainder of the war.[22] Promoted to *Oberstleutnant* in December 1920 Grimme was initially assigned as a *Stabs-Offizier beim Stab Artillerie-Schule Jüterbog*, before being re-assigned to the *Ausbildungsstab der Inspektion der Artillerie* (Training Headquarters in the Artillery Inspectorate) in April 1921.[23]

Meanwhile during 1919-20, in common with the other branches of the *Reichsheer*, the *Flakartillerie* was subject to a thorough evaluation of its organisation, tactics and equipment (See also 1A2).[24] As part of this programme of reflection and review no less than three committees studied various aspects of air defence including the contribution made by the ground based air defence organisation.[25] Their findings were varied and reflected the inherent difficulties of

16　Hildebrand K.F.1990-92 *Die Generale der deutschen Luftwaffe 1935-1945 Band 1-3* (hereafter cited as Hildebrand 1990-92).

17　Service records for Richard Reimann & Otto Wilhelm von Renz in Hildebrand K.F.1992 *Die Generale der deutschen Luftwaffe 1935-1945 Band 3 O-Z* (hereafter cited as Hildebrand 1992) pp.95-96 & 99-100.

18　Service record for Philipp Hinkelbein in Hildebrand K.F.1991 *Die Generale der deutschen Luftwaffe 1935-1945 Band 2 H-N* (hereafter cited as Hildebrand 1991) pp.90-91.

19　Service record for Günther Rüdel in Hildebrand 1992 pp.146-147.

20　Service record for Hugo Grimme in Hildebrand K.F.1990 *Die Generale der deutschen Luftwaffe 1935-1945 Band 1 A-G* (hereafter cited as Hildebrand 1990) pp.393-394. Hugo Grimme entered the *Heer* in Mar 1891 as a *Fahnenjunker* in *Feldartillerie-Regt.26*. He later served with *Feld-Art.Rgt.62* and as a *Lehrer d.Feldart.Schule*. His initial war service was in the field of munitions supply in Berlin and with *AOK 4*.

21　Westermann 2001 pp.18-19.

22　Hoeppner 1921 p.58 & Renz 1958 p.29.

23　Service record for Hugo Grimme in Hildebrand 1990 pp.393-394.

24　Corum 1997 pp.59-60 & Westermann 2001 pp.31-32. *"It is absolutely necessary to put the experiences of the war in a broad light, and to collect this experience while the impressions won on the battlefield are still fresh, and the major proportion of the experienced officers are still in leading positions"* - Hans von Seeckt, letter to the Truppenamt et al, 1 Dezember 1919 in BA/MA 2/2275 in Corum 1997 p.59.

25　Corum J.S. 1992 *The Roots of Blitzkrieg: Hans von Seeckt and German Military Reform between the World Wars* pp.144-145.

bringing down bombing machines that were capable of rapid movement in all three dimensions. *Obstlt.a.D.*von Keller, the former *Inspekteur der HeimatLuftschütz* (Inspector of Home-based Anti-Aircraft Artillery), and therefore an officer with first hand experience of the problems of providing an effective air defence against enemy bombers attacking targets of an economic, military and infrastructure nature in Germany, was to argue that given the rapid improvements in aircraft design and performance during 1918 that the anti-aircraft artillery was in danger of being out-stripped by the attacking aircraft.[26] At that time the greatest single threat to the homeland was that posed by the *RAF* Independent Force with its powerful Handley Page 0/400 heavy night bombers and fast De Havilland DH 9A and DH 10 day bombers which was based in the area around Nancy in eastern France.[27] To help counter these attacks the *KoGenLuft* had authorised the formation of a number of *Kampfeinsitzerstaffeln (Kest)* (Single-seat Battle Squadrons) which were equipped with fighters with a good rate of climb and it was these formations that Keller had in mind when he declared that fighter aircraft must remain the primary instrument of air defence for the homeland.[28]

Keller's argument was seated in a different interpretation of the statistics. Whilst it could not be denied that when compared to the number of "kills" by fighter aircraft the anti-aircraft artillery had enjoyed its greatest level of success during the last two months of the war this was in part due to the severe fuel shortages that had restricted German air activity.[29] Indeed when expressed in terms of the number of Allied sorties flown over the Western Front in 1918 the performance of the *Flakwaffe* (Anti-Aircraft Artillery Arm) had been disappointing.[30] Nor was the *Flakwaffe* as efficient as its Allied contemporaries who were presented with far fewer targets. In 1918 the average number of shells fired per enemy aircraft destroyed was 5,040, whereas the equivalent figures for the Allied powers were: France 3,225, Britain 1,800 and America 1,055.[31]

Although this debate was useful it was nonetheless academic and the twenties were to be a period of stable peace time soldiering by the officers and men of the new *Reichsheer*. For the *Artillerie* this meant parade drills, skill at arms, horsemanship, gun drills, live firing exercises, *Batterie and Abteilung* exercises and annual manoeuvres as part of the parent division.[32] *Artillerie* personnel could

26   Keller von Obstlt.a.D. 1929 *Die heutige Wehrlosigkeit Deutschalnds im Lichte seiner Verteidigung gegen die Fliegerangriffe im Kriege 1914/18* (hereafter cited as Keller 1929) p.39. However it is not clear whether Keller contributed to the *Reichsheer's* official post-war studies.

27   *App.26 The 41st Wing RFC/RAF and the Independent Wing RAF* in Moyes P.J.R. 1964 *Bomber Squadrons of the RAF and their aircraft* (hereafter cited as Moyes 1964) pp.314-317 & Roberston B. 1978 *The RAF: A Pictorial History* pp.26-27. Beginning in Oct 17 the British made a series of day and night attacks against targets in the Mittelrhein area of western Germany. The French made comparatively few attacks on German targets behind the front - concentrating mainly on railway communications and airfields - see Christienne C. and Lissarague P.1980 *A History of French Military Aviation* pp.83-90, 100-106, 116, 118 & 134. There were in total 1,154 air attacks on German targets during the Great War: 1914 (8), 1915 (37), 1916 (96), 1917 (376) & 1918 (637). Of these totals 446 had been executed at night: 1915 (7), 1916 (75), 1917 (130) & 1918 (234). By 1918 c.900 *FlaK* were deployed in the *Heimat* - see Renz 1958 p.56.

28   Keller 1929 p.39. Nine *Kampfeinsitzerstaffeln (Kest)* were formed from Jul 16 and the original *Staffeln* were later split to form two *Ketten* eg *Kest 4a & 4b* - see Hogg 1978 p.65 & Franks N., Bailey F. and Duiven R. 1996 *The Jasta Pilots: Detailed listings and histories August 1916 - November 1918* pp.81-84.

29   Hoeppner 1921 p.160. In Sep 18 the *Flak* had shot down 132 Allied aircraft with a further 129 in Oct 18 - see Neumann 1921 p.590.

30   *Statistics of Work of the Independent Force, including casualties, Jun.-Nov.1918* in Moyes 1964 p.316.

31   Renz 1958 pp.56-57 & Hogg 1978 p.67. The effectiveness of German *FlaK* had increased steadily during the war. The number or rounds required to bring down an enemy aircraft decreased steadily: 1914-15 (11,585), 1916 (9,889), 1917 (7,418) & 1918 (5,040). American anti-aircraft personnel were trained at Fort Monroe, the Coast Artillery School, by a cadre of 25 young officers who had earlier been trained in France.

32   Knappe S. and Brusaw E. 1993 *Soldat – Reflections of a German Soldier 1936-1949* pp.88-101 & 111-126. *Maj.i.G.a.D.*Siegfried Knappe trained and saw his initial service with the *Art.Rgt.24* at Jena and Plauen. However his experiences would have been very similar to those of the *Reichsheer's Artillerie* personnel. On active service one *Art-Abt.* was nominally available to support each of the *Division's Inf.Rgtr*. However to support an attack or

be distinguished from the officers and men of other arms of service by the use of *Hochrot* (Bright Red) *Waffenfarbe* on their uniforms.[33] Numerically the *Artillerie* was the third most important arm of the *Reichsheer*, coming behind the *Infanterie* (21 *Regimenter*) and Kavallerie (18 Regimenter).[34] An *Artillerie-Regiment* of three *Abteilungen* formed part of each of the seven *Divisionen*, whilst a further three *Reitend Artillerie-Abteilungen* (Mounted Artillery Battalions) were maintained to support the three *Kavallerie-Divisionen*.[35] *Obst.*Hugo Grimme was *Kommandeur IV.(Reitenden)/Art. Rgt.6* at Verden during 1924-25.[36]

FIGURE 1E-10 ORGANISATION OF A REICHSHEER ARTILLERIE-REGIMENT 1920-33			
Stab with Nachrichtenzug (later a Stabsbatterie (mot.)			
Stab I.Abteilung	Stab II.Abteilung	Stab III.Abteilung	Ausbildungs-Battr.
1.-3.Batterien	4.-6.Batterien	7.-9.Batterien	

Each *Artillerie-Abteilung* was nominally equipped with two *Batterien* of 7.7 cm le.FK 16 field guns and one *Batterie* of 10.5 cm le.FH 16 field howitzers. However the *3.Batterie* of each *Regiment* was equipped with the 7.7 cm FK 96/16 for infantry support and one *Batterie* in each *Regiment* was equipped with 7.7 cm Luftkanone *Kraftwagengeschütze* as previously shown. Each *Batterie* had an establishment of four guns giving each *Artillerie-Abteilung* a force of twelve guns and the *Regiment* a total of thirty-six guns, twelve of which were 10.5 cm le.FH 16s.[37]

In accordance with established military tradition officers and men were recruited by, trained and deployed within their parent *Regiment* (See also 1E1). Initial military training for both officer candidates *(Offiziersanwärter)* and other ranks took place in the Regimental *Ausbildungs-Batterie*. *Fahnenjunker* would then attend specialist courses at an *Infanterieschule* and later the *Artillerieschule Jüterbog* prior to gaining further experience as a *Batterie-Offizier* with their parent *Regiment*. *Offiziersanwärter* Günther Sachs joined the *6.Preußisches Artillerie-Regiment* at Minden in March 1921 being assigned to the *8.(Beobachtungs-Batterie)* at Hannover in May 1922. In September he was posted to prior to the *Infanterieschule München* for an eleven month *Unteroffizier-Lehrgang* before spending a further eleven months at the *Artillerieschule Jüterbog*. As an *Oberfähnrich* he was assigned to the *3./Art.Rgt.6* at Münster in October 1924 and was finally commissioned as a *Leutnant* on the

---

to provide for more effective defence it was conceivable that the whole *Art.Rgt.* could be directed by the *Stab Art. Rgt.* - a common practice on the static fronts during the Great War. However prolonged "barrages" by hundreds of guns were a thing of the past for the *Reichsheer*. Gunners were trained in indirect fire using observers *(Beobachteren)*, counter-battery work and the use of direct fire in more fluid tactical situations – see also Hogg I.V. 1970 *Barrage: The Guns in Action* (hereafter cited as Hogg 1970). With the exception of the *Kraftwagengeschütz-Batterie* all guns were horse drawn, hence the pre-occupation with horsemanship. As a skilled horseman *Hptm.*Walter Feyerabend, a *Batterie-Chef in AR 1*, would represent his country in the 1928 Olympiad in Amsterdam in 1928 - see service record for Walter Feyerabend in Hildebrand 1990 pp.276-277.

33   Davis B.L. 1971 *German Army Uniforms and Insignia 1933-1945* (hereafter cited as Davis 1971) pp.16-19. The *Waffenfarbe* was used as a background colour for shoulder straps and as collar piping on the uniform jacket. The *Infanterie* and *Kavallerie* respectively used *Weiss* (White) and *Goldgelb* (Gold Yellow) *Waffenafarbe*.

34   *Gliederung und Standorte der Reichswehr 1932* in Lexikon der Wehrmacht.

35   *Gliederung und Standorte der Reichswehr 1932* in Lexikon der Wehrmacht. For equipment and training the 3 *Reitend Art-Abtn.* - the *IV.*(Potsdam) & *V.*(Sagan) */AR 3* and *IV.*(Verden)/AR 6 - formed part of their parent *Art-Rgtr*. See also Seaton A. *1982 The German Army 1933-1945* (hereafter cited as Seaton 1982) p.7.

36   Service record for Hugo Grimme in Hildebrand 1990 pp.393-394. Despite his wealth of experience Grimme was not employed by the *Reichsheer* in connection with the covert *Flakwaffe*. Prior to this posting he had been *Art.Stabsoffz.b.Gr. Kdo.I* (Berlin) during 1923. From Jan 26 he was *Kdr.Art.Rgt.5* (Ulm) until Jul 27 when he completed his military service as *Art.Fhr.VI* (Münster). He was retired on the 30 Sep 29 with the honorary *(charakter)* rank of *GenLt.*

37   Quarrie 1989 pp.47-48.

24 December 1924 - *RDA* 1.12.24 (19) - three and a half years after first joining his *Regiment*. As a young *Batterie-Offizier* he attended three further specialist courses during 1925: a *Beobachtungskursus* at the *Bildstelle* of the *6.Division* at Münster in March, a *Lehrgang zur Schulung im Beobachtungsdienst* in June and *Ausbildung im Wetterdienst* at the *Schiessplatz Jüterbog* in December. From May 1925 *Lt.*Sachs was a *Batterie-Offizier* with the *6./Art.Rgt.6* at Minden where he remained until October 1929. Further courses followed: a *Lehrgang im Artillerie-Zielbau* at Jüterbog (October 1927), a *Lehrgang A für Ausbildung im Gasschutzdienst* in Berlin (November 1927) and a *Kraftfahr-Lehrgang für Artillerie* in Jüterbog (October-November 1928). Promoted to *Oberleutnant* in April 1928 - *RDA* 1.4.28 (7) - he was re-assigned to the *9.(Kraftwagen)/Art.Rgt.6* at Hannover in October 1929 and was immediately posted to Königsberg/Pillau in Ostpreussen for a five week specialist *(Flak) Artillerie-Lehrgang*, a course which was repeated in August-September 1930.[38]

The training and deployment of non-commissioned personnel followed a very similar path. *Kanonier* Theodor Triebe was enlisted in the *Ausbildungsbatterie/Artillerie-Regiment 4* at Dresden on the 20 November 1923. Following initial training he was assigned to the *9.(Kraftwagen) Batterie/Art.Rgt.4* (Dresden) on the 1 April 1924 before being re-assigned to the *Stab III./Art.Rgt.4* on the 1 August 1925 where he was promoted to *Oberkanonier* on the 1 December of that year. He returned to the *9.(Kw.)/Art.Rgt.4* in October 1927 and became a *Gefreiter* two months later. Triebe was selected as an *Unteroffizier-Anwärter* on the 14 August 1928, nearly five years after joining his *Regiment*. After attending an *Unteroffizier-Lehrgang* he was confirmed in this rank on the 1 October 1929, becoming an *Unterwachtmeister* two years later on the 1 October 1931. Throughout this period he served with the specialist *Kraftwagengeschütz-Batterie*.[39]

The systematic training of *Artillerie* personnel in anti-aircraft gunnery appears to have begun in 1923.[40] In addition to the *Ortsfesten-Flakartillerie* (Fortress Anti-Aircraft Artillery) at Königsberg extensive use was made of the *Reichsmarine's* specialist facilities at the *Schiffsartillerieschule Kiel-Wik* and the *Küstenartillerieschule Wilhelmshaven* where students had access to aerial targets in the form of seaplanes operated by *Severa GmbH* (See 1E3).[41] In April 1922 *Oblt.*Ernst Buffa, an experienced wartime officer with *Fussartillerie-Regiment 5*, was assigned to the *9.(Kw.)/Art.Rgt.3* at Jüterbog. As he lacked practical experience of anti-aircraft gunnery he was sent on a four week *Flak-Ausbildungs-Lehrgang für Land-Marineteile* (Anti-Aircraft Artillery Training Course for Land-based Naval Elements) in June 1923. Virtually the whole of the following year was then spent with the *Reichsmarine*, initially on a *Lehrgang für Artillerie-Offizier kleiner Schiffe* (Training course for Gunnery Officers – small Ships) at Kiel-Wik (February-June 1924) and a *Flaklehrgang* (Anti-Aircraft Artillery Training Course) at Wilhelmshaven (August 1924) prior to his assignment as an instructor at the *Küstenartillerieschule (Flak)* (Coastal Artillery School – Anti-Aircraft Artillery) from October 1924. Following his re-assignment to the *9.(Kw.)/Art.Rgt.4* at Dresden in September 1925 *Hptm.*Buffa was detached to the *Ortsfesten-Flak* at Königsberg as an instructor during the autumnal exercise period.[42] Other *Artillerieoffiziere* that began their formal anti-aircraft gunnery training during 1924-25 included *Lt.*Max Schaller *(Art.Rgt.4)* and *Oblt.*Walter von Axthelm *(Art. Rgt.7)*. Following his *Land-Flak-Kurs* at Wilhelmshaven in May 1925 Axthelm was re-assigned as *Führer 9.(Kw)/Art.Rgt.7*. His further specialist training included a *Kraftfahrtechnischen Lehrgang*

38   Service record for Günther Sachs in Thomas F. and Wegmann G.1991 *Die Ritterkreuztrager der Flugabwehrtruppen Bd.2* (hereafter cited as Thomas and Wegmann 1991 Bd.2) pp.161-164.
39   Service record for Theodor Triebe in Thomas and Wegmann 1991 Bd.2 pp.252-253.
40   Thomas F. and Wegmann G.1991 *Die Ritterkreuztrager der Flugabwehrtruppen Bd.1* (hereafter cited as Thomas and Wegmann 1991 Bd.1) p.68.
41   Mallmann Showell J.P. 1979 *The German Navy in World War Two: A Reference Guide to the Kriegsmarine 1935-1945* pp.56-57.
42   Service record for Ernst Buffa in Thomas and Wegmann 1991 Bd.1 pp.67-70.

(Motor Vehicle Technology Training Course) in 1926 and a *Kraftfahr-Lehrgang für Kraftfahrlehrer* (Motor Vehicle Training Course for Motor Vehicle Instructors) in 1927. In October 1927 *Hptm.* von Axthelm was confirmed as *Batterie-Chef 9.(Kw.)/Art.Rgt.7* at Nürnberg.[43]

The development of new anti-aircraft guns, range finders, predictors and fire control equipment did not end with the prohibitions of the Versailles Treaty. In 1921 Krupp negotiated an agreement with the Swedish firm *AB Bofors* which allowed the German company to establish a small design team in Sweden in return for the manufacturing rights for existing Krupp guns.[44] Within a year this work was being covertly financed by the *RWM* and the team began work on an advanced 7.5 cm anti-aircraft gun in response to a secret *Heereswaffenamt (WaA)* requirement.[45] Prototypes of the Bofors-Krupp 7.5 cm FlaK L/60 had been completed by 1928 and these, together with a competing design by *Rheinmetall Borsig AG* at Düsseldorf, were tested by the *Reichswehr* from 1930. However there were problems with the mountings and the time taken to bring the gun into action, whilst their performance was considered to be inadequate in the face of the rapid improvements that were being made in the field of aircraft performance, particularly air speed and operating ceiling, and it was decided to re-design the gun around a more powerful 8.8 cm projectile (See 1C4).[46] The choice of the 8.8 cm round with a weight of 9 kgs was a compromise between the desired hitting power and the ease of hand loading the weapon in the field.[47] From February 1929 *Hptm.*Hermann Mertitsch was *Referent für Entwicklung der schweren Artillerie-Waffen und Flugabwehrkanonen im Heereswaffenamt (Waffen Prüfwesens 4)* (Staff Advisor for heavy artillery and anti-aircraft gun development in the Army Ordnance Office) and as such was responsible for overseeing the development of the 8.8 cm FlaK.[48]

43   Service records for Walter von Axthelm and Max Schaller in Hildebrand 1990 pp.31-32 & Hildebrand 1992 pp.169-170. Axthelm's wartime service had been with the *8.Bay.Feld-Art.Rgt.* where he had ended the war as a *Batterieführer*. In the *Reichsheer* he had been assigned to AR 7 as *Adjutant III./AR 7*. As a *Batterie-Offizier* with *Feld.Art.Rgt.48* Schaller had been badly wounded in Aug 17. He returned to action in Apr 18 and was again badly wounded in Jul 18. In the *Reichsheer* he served as a *Nachrichten-Offz.*, later *Adjutant* with *II./AR 4*. From Jul 26 he underwent *Führergehilfen-Ausbildung* with *IR 16*, later *Stab 4.Div*. See also Thomas and Wegmann 1991 Bd.1 pp.9-12.

44   Gander and Chamberlain 1978 p.147. Wartime planning had called for much greater standardisation in the production of *FlaK* from 1919 - the 7.62 cm KWK, the 8.8 cm heavy gun for field employment and the 10.5 cm heavy gun for rear areas and the *Heimat*. However all post-war development work of anti-aircraft artillery equipment in Germany was banned under the terms of the Treaty of Versailles - see Hogg 1978 pp.67-68 & Renz 1958 pp.59-60.

45   Renz 1958 p.69 & pp.93-94. In 1925 as a successor to the *Inspektion für Waffen und Gerat*, the *Heereswaffenamt (HWA)* was established with a Procurement Office and a Weapons Proving Department *(Abteilung-Prüfwesen)*. However this *Amter* did not have a *Referate* for anti-aircraft artillery matters. Initially this responsibility was assigned to the *Referent für Entwicklung der schwere Artillerie-Waffen und Flugabwehrkanonen (Motorisiert) im Wa.Prüf.4* under *Hptm.*Hermann Mertitsch Feb 29 - Mar 35 - see Service record for Hermann Mertitsch in Hildebrand 1991 pp.385-386. The development of optical instruments for the secret *Flakverbände* was handled by *Wa.Prüf.8*, searchlights by *Wa.Prüf.5*, whilst ammunition and ballistics was the responsibility of *Wa.Prüf.1* — see Renz 1958 pp.91-92.

46   Chamberlain 1978 p.147. The weight of the 7.5 cm weapon caused difficulties for its crew, a problem that was not solved until the design and introduction of an outrigger-type mounting *(Kreuz-lafette)* - see Renz 1958 pp.94-95. For details of improved aircraft design by the early thirties - see Hooton E.R. *Military Aviation – the Slow Developer* in *Jarrett* P. (Ed.) 1997 *Biplane to Monoplane: Aircraft development 1919-39* pp.55-73. By the late 20s the speed of bomber aircraft had increased to 240 kph and that of fighter aircraft to 430 kph. Operating heights had increased to 5,000 m and to 8,000 m respectively. The Krupp 7.5 cm L/60 had a ceiling of 10,000 m. First deliveries to the *Reichsheer* were made in 1932 - see Renz 1958 p.95.

47   *Entwicklungsprogramm 13.12.30 RL 4 Chef des Ausbildungswesens/General der Fliegerausbildungs und Luftwaffen-Inspektion/Waffengerate Folder 257, BA/MA* in Westermann 2001 p.44. In 1930 *Obstlt.*Rüdel would make a strong case for the acquisition of an 8.8 cm FlaK as the smallest calibre that would be effective for the planned *schwere Flakbatterien* - see Westermann 2001 p.45 & Renz 1958 p.96.

48   Service record for Hermann Mertitsch in Hildebrand 1991 pp.385-386. Prior to this posting Mertitsch had been a *Batterie-Offizier* and *Batterie-Chef* within *AR 3*.

Design work at *Bofors* began immediately with the 7.5 cm gun as a starting point for the new heavier weapon. The prototype was constructed at Essen from 1931 and testing began the year after. Outwardly the 8.8 cm L/56 FlaK was very similar to its smaller ancestor. A cruciform platform *(Kreuz-lafette)* permitted full 360 degree traverse, whilst the pillar type mounting allowed a vertical field of +85 to -5 degrees.[49] With a muzzle velocity of 820 m/sec. an absolute ceiling of 10,000 m could be achieved although the maximum altitude at which an aerial target could be engaged with any reasonable prospect of success proved to be 6,100 m.[50] The single piece inner barrel was enclosed in a jacket with a detachable breech. As the gun fired the barrel moved back against the recoil brake prior to moving forwards by the pneumatic reciprocator to its original position. This action simultaneously opened the self-setting shearing-handle lock to eject the spent shell case and compress the spring for the next cycle. However one feature that did not work particularly well in service was the loading tray and rammer and this was often removed, a well trained gun crew being capable of a higher rate of fire with hand loading - between 15 and 25 rounds per minute being achieved.[51]

The gun was linked to the *Batterie's Kommandogerate* (Predictor) by a 108 strand data transmission cable, command information for the desired elevation and traverse being displayed by means of light signals at the *Emfanger A (Hohe)* and *B (Seite)* on the right hand side of the gun. Fuse setting data was transferred to the *Zunderstellmaschine* which was located on the left side of the weapon.[52] The electrical transmission of data to all four guns in the *Batterie* was a major advance in gunnery technique as it enabled concentrated fire to be brought on a fast moving target. To make the whole equipment, weighing 5.15 tonnes transportable a special two part trailer - the Sonderanhanger 202 - was devised to lift the weapon off the ground and then allow it be towed behind a wheeled tractor. Total weight of the 8.8 cm FlaK 18 when travelling was 6.861 tonnes.[53]

Quicker progress was made with the design of smaller quick firing anti-aircraft guns for use against low flying enemy aircraft, chiefly because there was a pressing demand for a weapon of this type for the *Reichsmarine*.[54] Many of these were based on earlier aircraft weapons and the development of both types often proceeded in parallel (See also 1C5).[55] By the late twenties two Swiss based concerns: the *Werkzeug Maschinenfabrik Oerlikon* and the *Solothurn AG* had produced efficient 2 cm aircraft and anti-aircraft guns based on the earlier work of the German designers Reinhold Becker and Heinrich Ehrhardt (See 1C5).[56] In 1931 the *Reichsmarine* bought a number of Oerlikon 2 cm weapons which were also available for air defence duties with the *Küstenartillerie* and the *Reichsheer* as the 2 cm FlaK 28 and FlaK 29.[57] Of more significance was the Solothurn MK-ST-5 which was purchased by the *Reichsmarine* in the same year for installation on naval vessels as the 2 cm C/30 on pedestal mount SL/30L. The ST-5 had a cyclic rate of fire of 280 rpm although a

49   Gander and Chamberlain 1978 p.147 & 154 and Müller W. 1990 *The Heavy Flak Guns 1933-1945* (hereafter cited as Müller 1990) pp.5-11. Another source gives the elevation data as -3 to +85 degrees - see Renz 1958 p.103.

50   Renz 1958 p.105.

51   Renz 1958 pp.103-104 & Müller 1990 p.5 & pp.10-11. Unfortunately the loading tray and rammer was often subject to mechanical failure and this was another reason why hand loading was preferred.

52   Müller 1990 p.7. The *Zunderstellmaschine* was mounted separately and had to be hand serviced with the individual lateral data received from the predictor - see Renz 1958 p.103.

53   Gander and Chamberlain 1978 p.154 & Müller 1990 pp.7-9.

54   Renz 1958 p.96.

55   Hoffschmidt E.J. 1969 *German Aircraft Guns WWI - WWII* (hereafter cited as Hoffschmidt 1968) p.79 & 81.

56   Hoffschmidt 1968 p.79 & 81 and Gander and Chamberlain 1978 p.127. *Solothurn* was wholly owned by *Rheinmetall-Borsig AG*. Work on the *Ehrhardt* cannon had earlier been carried out in the Netherlands but *Rheinmetall's* attempts to form a Dutch subsidiary had been unsuccessful and *Rheinmetall* decided to acquire the *Solothurn* concern instead.

57   Gander and Chamberlain 1978 p.127 & pp.139-140 and Müller W. 1995 *German 20 mm Flak in World War II* (hereafter cited as Müller 1995) pp.3-4.

more practical 120 rpm was in fact possible, the naval weapons being provided with 98 round drum magazines.[58] The maximum horizontal range was 4,900 m and vertical range 3,700 m. The S 5-100 was adapted for military use as the 2 cm Flak 30. The most significant difference between the two weapons was the gun carriage which took the form of a triangular bottom mount with a bracket for attachment to the single-axle Sonderanhanger 51 trailer. The Kanonier Nr. 1 used the Linealvisier 21 gun sight to engage aerial targets whilst other members of the crew fed the gun with 20 round box magazines. The 2 cm Flak 30 entered service with the *Reichsheer* in 1931 and was allocated to the *Fahrabteilungen* and the *Flugabwehr-Maschinengewehr-Bataillonen*.[59]

The hitting power of the 2 cm FlaK 30 round was just 0.33 kgs and although in its high explosive form this could cause considerable damage it was recognised that several hits would be required to actually bring down a hostile aircraft.[60] The need for a more effective light anti-aircraft gun was therefore met by adopting a 3.7 cm projectile with a shot weight of 0.685 kgs. Development of the new gun, essentially a scaled-up version of the ST 5 began in 1930. The resulting Solothurn ST-10-100 was accepted in 1935 for naval use as the 3.7 cm SK C/30 in *Einheitslafette* (single pedestal mount) and for military use as the 3.7 cm FlaK 18.[61] Like the earlier 2 cm weapon, the 3.7 cm FlaK 18 could be fitted with wheels in which form it could be towed behind a tractor or limber for use with the field forces. In its static firing position the 3.7 cm FlaK used a cruciform mounting similar to that adopted by the larger 7.5 cm and 8.8 cm weapons. The 3.7 cm FlaK 18 had a similar muzzle velocity to the smaller 2 cm FlaK 30 but a slower rate of fire from clips of 6 rounds - in practical terms 70-80 rpm. The 3.7 cm FlaK 18 had an effective ceiling of 2,000 m and was issued to a *Versuchsbatterie* for operational trials in 1933/34.[62]

The use of the Modell 18 designation for both the 3.7 cm and 8.8 cm weapons was a continued attempt by the *WaA* to deceive Allied observers about the true ancestry of these new anti-aircraft guns.[63] However it is highly unlikely that this subterfuge actually fooled either the French or the British military authorities.

Of equal importance to the new guns was the design and acquisition of a more effective predictor. The lighter weapons could track their low-flying targets manually with the range data being provided by a shoulder mounted range finder - the *1 metre Entfernungmessgerät* - whilst the gunner was provided with an early form of reflector sight, the Reflexvizier 33, to improve accuracy whilst engaging aerial targets.[64] However the task of engaging fast-moving high-altitude targets was far more complex.[65] Even conventional artillery units had to have an accurate knowledge of air

58   Gander and Chamberlain 1978 p.127, *App.5 Destroyer and Torpedo Boat Armament* in Whitley M.J. 1991 *German Destroyers of World War Two* (hereafter cited as Whitley 1991) p.215 & Müller 1995 p.5. Despite the popularity of the *Oerlikon* design amongst foreign navies, the *Reichsmarine* preferred the *Rheinmetall-Solothurn* weapon - see Renz 1958 p.96.

59   Gander and Chamberlain 1978 p.132 & Müller 1995 pp.6-7. The service entry date of 1931 is that given in Renz 1958 p.97. Elevation of the 2 cm FlaK 30 was -15 to +85 degrees. Its effective range was 1,600 m and in addition to a Linealvisier 21 anti-aircraft sight a telescopic sight was provided for ground engagements - see Renz 1958 pp.97-98.

60   Renz 1958 pp.108-109.

61   Gander and Chamberlain 1978 p.136 & *App.5 Destroyer and Torpedo Boat Armament* in Whitley 1991 pp.214-215.

62   Gander and Chamberlain 1978 p.136. For anti-tank operations the 3.7 cm FlaK 18 could fire a slightly heavier armour piercing round at a higher muzzle velocity of 780 m/sec - see Renz 1958 p.109.

63   Renz 1958 p.102. *"The designation digits "18" at the time were given to all newly developed artillery items of equipment for security reasons and did not imply, as is quite commonly assumed, that they were identical with the items in use at the end of World War I."*

64   Renz 1958 pp.127-128. The Revi 33 could be set for target speeds of 0 to 150 m/sec whilst range information from the 1 metre rangefinder could be set for 300 to 3,000 m. As data on the direction of flight was also required constant training was need to retain accuracy and efficiency of the crew. A similar reflector sight was also developed for use with the 2 cm FlaK 30. Telescopic sights with a magnification of 3x8 were used to engage ground targets.

65   *App.1 Performance of Anti-Aircraft Guns/First World War & App.2 Performance of Bomber Aircraft/First World War* Hogg 1978 p.165 & 166. See also pp.75-77. In the Great War a typical German 7.7 cm Ballon-Abwehr-Kanone

density, air temperature, barometric pressure and wind velocity to accurately engage remote targets using plunging fire from field howitzers *(Feldhaubitze)*.[66] The problem for anti-aircraft artillery was even greater as wind speeds generally increased with altitude and wind direction would change. Air density decreased but none of this was uniform and it constantly changed as weather systems moved through an area. All of this data, which would affect the path of the shell through the atmosphere, then had to be set against the actual movement of the target in relation to the guns on the ground. Although most bomber formations actually moved in only two dimensions individual aircraft could move in three and by changing height could evade otherwise accurate fire.[67]

In 1925 the Jena based firm of *Carl Zeiss*, a specialist instrument manufacturer, was given a development contract for a new director for the *Reichswehr*, further technical and theoretical support being provided by *Geheimrat* Pschorr of the *Technischen Hochschule Charlottenburg*.[68] Prototype testing was carried out in association with the *Reichsmarine* which had a similar requirement for a new fire director for ship-to-ship gunnery and live fire field tests were carried out using towed targets off the German coast. The success of these trials led to an order in 1928 for ten Zeiss Kommandogerat P 27 directors for use by the *Kraftwagengeschütz-Batterien* and the *Ortsfesten-Flakbatterie* at Königsberg.[69] Once delivered these units would use the new directors to control the fire of the 7.5 cm FlaK L/60 guns that were being secretly obtained from Sweden.[70] However earlier plans to provide each *Flakbatterie* with two P 27 Kommandogerate had to be abandoned on grounds of expense.[71] In the meantime *Zeiss* continued work on a considerably more complex automatic fire control system called "Tabulator". Tabulator was the brain child of *Maj.* Karabetz, formerly of the *österreichische Armee*, and this system underwent testing from 1932 with

had a muzzle velocity of 1,675 fps. and an effective ceiling of 6,000 metres. This velocity would steadily decrease as the shell lost its impetus so that it might take 18 seconds to reach 5,000 metres. A typical single-engine night bomber such as the Voison 8 Bn.2 of 1916 had a speed of 105 kph at 4,300 metres and thus allowing for the fact that the aircraft was rarely directly overhead the gun when it was fired a time of 18 seconds is a useful example in this case. During this time the bomber would itself have travelled 525 metres which meant that the gun would have to aim this far ahead of the bomber if it was to stand any chance of hitting it. In real terms this meant a sight displacement of some 7.5 degrees.

66   Hogg 1970 p.48. For this purpose artillery units had specialised detachments to obtain this data and some officers were given specialist training in *Wetterdienst* - see service record Günther Sachs in Thomas and Wegmann 1991 Bd.2 p.162.

67   Hogg 1978 p.76. Other factors included the drift of shells on account of the gun's rifling - this induced spin and therefore stability but it also induced drift which in the case of German weapons was always to the left, whereas British shells drifted to the right. As a barrel became worn accuracy would also reduce due to changes in muzzle velocity - see Odhams Undated *Britain's Wonderful Fighting Forces* p.356.

68   Renz 1958 pp. 98-99. The development and testing of optical instruments was carried out by *Wa.Prüf.9* under *Dr.*Lechner. The development of range finding and fire control equipment was greatly facilitated by parallel work carried out legitimately on behalf of the *Reichsmarine*. The Kommandogerat P-27 appeared in prototype form in 1927. The first field tests with live firing were executed at Pillau in Ostpreussen in 1928. In Britain this equipment was referred to as "predictors", in the USA as "directors" and In Germany as *"Kommandogerate"* - see Hogg 1978 pp.76-77.

69   Renz 1958 p.90 & 99. From 1928 the *KWK-Batterien* were also involved in firing tests with the new directors although the limitations of their equipment resulted in generally unsatisfactory results. The *Reichsmarine* chose not to acquire the P 27 as naval personnel were more used to operating on the angle velocity indicator principle. The British also introduced a new predictor in 1927 - the Vickers Predictor AA No.1. Like all predictors or directors of this period the Vickers Predictor was *"a clockwork-powered mechanical computer which performed the calculations necessary to determine the bearing, elevation and fuse-length for the guns on the basis of the target's motion through the air, tracked through the gun-layer's optical sights. Resolving the necessary formulae continuously, the device fed data to the guns electrically by cable connections, enabling the crews to lay their weapons in unison (by following a pointer on a dial) under control from the site command post* - see Dobinson 2001 p.73. See also Westermann 2001 p.39.

70   Hogg 1978 p.75. The Bofors-Krupp 7.5 cm FlaK L/60 were being built for export to countries such as Spain & South America but in addition a number of guns were diverted to the *Reichsheer* via a suitably convoluted supply chain - see also Gander and Chamberlain 1978 p.147.

71   Westermann 2001 p.39.

an improved version appearing two years later. However results were disappointing and the whole programme was subsequently abandoned.[72]

The height or altitude a shell would detonate was also an issue of vital importance. In 1916 *Krupp-Tiel* had designed a clockwork fuse mechanism for general artillery use although it was not adopted by the *Flakwaffe* on account of the immense number that would have been needed.[73] Both German and British anti-aircraft gunners continued to rely on powder-burning fuses which were affected by air density, humidity and temperature. The standard powder fuse had an accuracy of 2% which meant that a shell moving at 610 metres per second would detonate at some point between 120 m short and 120 m over the target. The accuracy of the mechanical fuse was far superior being in the realm of 0.5% but even this would be on the very edge of what was required to successfully destroy an enemy aircraft.[74] New fuses of this type were introduced for use with the 7.5 and 8.8 cm *FlaK* in the early thirties.

Coincident with the design of new guns and directors was the decision in September 1930 to begin a planned period of rearmament in Germany. Under the leadership of *GenLt.*Kurt Frhr. von Hammerstein-Equord, the *Truppenamt* envisaged the acquisition of powerful *Flak* forces to work with and in support of an enlarged *Feldheer* of 21 *Divisionen* (See also 1A3).[75] The planned tactical *Flakwaffe* would comprise 28 *leichte Flakbatterien*, each with six 2 cm or 3.7 cm *FlaK*, and 27 *schwere Flakbatterien*, each with four 7.5 cm or 8.8 cm *FlaK*.[76] Meanwhile to meet the needs of home defence a further 132 *Maschinengewehr-Kompanien*, 15 *Flakzuge* with 3.7 cm *FlaK*, and 32 *schwere Flakbatterien* with 7.5 cm (six *Batterien*), 8.8 cm (24 *Batterien*) and 10.5 cm (2 *Batterien*) *FlaK* were planned. This massive force would consist of 792 *schwere MG*, 30 3.7 cm, 24 7.5 cm, 48 8.8 cm and 4 10.5 cm *FlaK* for home defence together' with 168 2 cm and 3.7 cm *FlaK* and 108 7.5 cm and 8.8 cm *FlaK* for the field forces.[77] In addition considerable sums of money were also allocated for passive air defence measures - in particular for the vital munitions and military equipment factories.[78] In the same year *GenOb.*Wilhelm Heye, the *Chef der Heersleitung*, authorised the covert re-establishment of the *Flakartillerie* with effect from 1933.[79]

Clearly the fulfilment of such a grandiose plan would take many years and a huge amount of money. As a start an anti-aircraft artillery training staff was established within the *Artillerie-Inspektion* and *Obstlt.*Rüdel was assigned as *Kommandeur des Ausbildungstabes III* with effect from the 1 February 1930.[80] This position was concerned with the co-ordination and detailed

---

72   Renz 1958 p.100 & *Interrogation Report of Gen.d.Flak.Walter von Axthelm "Part I AA Program 1930-31" Appendix C in 519.601A-12 AFHRA* in Westermann 2001 p.40. Work began on *Tabulator* in 1927-28.

73   Renz 1958 p.48. The firm of *Junghans* had also produced a mechanical fuse that employed the centrifugal force and the revolutions of the spinning shell in flight. The *Krupp* and *Junghans* fuses were used by the 8.8 cm & 10.5 cm *FlaK* only. See Renz 1958 pp.77 & Hogg 1978 pp.78-79.

74   Hogg 1978 pp.78-79. The British Army experimented with a mechanical fuse from 1925 but only 1,000 were manufactured and they were used solely for demonstrations and trials. Wartime experience would show that 8.8 cm shells had to detonate within 9 m of an aircraft to cause lethal damage.

75   *Heeresausbildungsabteilung Denkschrift, 29 Nov 1926 Heeresmotorisierung und Kriegsgliederung einer motorisierte Division in BA/MA RH 8/b 923* in Corum 1997 p.119. This document proposed the allocation a *Flak-Batterie* to each of the Division's Infanterie-Rgtr. and a *Flak-Abteilung* to the Art.Rgt. On this basis by the late 20s the *Truppenamt* had decided that between 40-50 *FlaK* would be required for each of the *Reichsheer's* seven authorised *Divisionen.*

76   Müller-Hildebrand B. 1954 *Das Heer bis zum Kriegsbeginn* (hereafter cited as Müller-Hildebrand 1954) p.20. See also Corum 1997 pp.121-122.

77   Geyer M. 1975 'Das Zweite Rüstungsprogramm (1930-1934)' in *Militärgeschichtliche Mitteilungen*, 1 p.125 & pp.145-146 in Westermann 2001 p.43.

78   Müller-Hildebrand 1954 pp.19-20 & Corum 1997 p.121.

79   Corum 1997. *GenLt.*Hammerstein-Equord replaced Heye as *Chef d.Heeresleitung* on the 31 Oct 30 - see www.wikipedia.org . & Seaton 1982 p.18.

80   Westermann 2001 p.44. Prior to this appointment Rüdel has served on the staff of the *7.Division* (München) Oct

planning of the secret organisation, equipment and training of the planned *Flakwaffe*. In his secret *Entwicklungsprogramm* (Development Plan) of the 13 December 1930 Rüdel identified six specific tasks which he considered to be "particularly important and urgent":[81]

FIGURE 1E-11 ENTWICKLUNGSPROGRAMM DER FLUGABWEHR-WAFFEN   1930
Completion of an automatic *Flugabwehrkanon* for battle against low-level aircraft (the Solthurn ST 5-100 as the 2 cm FlaK 30);
Completion of a new 8.8 cm *Flugawehrkanon* or the improved 8.8 cm FlaK 18;
Creation of an auxiliary director for remote control aiming (the *Kommando-Hilfs-Gerat*);
Creation of a new instrument for location and firing by sound;
Creation of an efficient sound-locator (the Goerz-Richtungshorer);
A Speed computer for range-finding garrisons.

Notwithstanding the *Truppenamt's* long term ambitions Rüdel's *Entwicklungprogramm* represented a very pragmatic approach to an immense task. No doubt influenced by his own work as *Referent Nachschub* (Staff Advisor for Supply) within the *Truppenamt*, Rüdel recognised the importance of keeping within the constraints of the delegated budget.[82] Only the most essential equipment could be acquired and in this respect it is useful to recognise that Rüdel foresaw *"the combat of night bomber attacks (as) the most important task of the air defence".*[83] Given this vision of the future it is peculiar that he did not attach any immediate importance to the development of a more powerful searchlight, even though he recognised that the existing 110 cm Flak-Scheinwerfer lacked the effective range to support even the interim 7.5 cm FlaK L/60 let alone the new 8.8 cm FlaK 18 *(Photo 1E-9).*[84]

With development programmes underway and international restrictions slowly evaporating it was possible to put the anti-aircraft gunnery training of the *Kraftwagengeschütz-Batterien* on a more formal footing. In the following year the *Ausbildungsstab III* issued *Richtlinien für die Gefechts- und Schiessübungen der Kw.Batterien 1931* (Guidelines for the Battle and Gunnery Training of the Motorised Batteries).[85] This led in turn to a fourteen day live-firing training and exercise period at either the *Truppen-Übungsplatzes Döberitz-Elsgrund* in Brandenburg or *Pillau* in Ostpreussen where *Hptm.*Reimann was *Fhr.der Übungs-Batterie beim Kw.-Lehrgang Pillau.*[86] *"Exactness before speed"*

22-Sep 24, as *Maj.b.Stabe Art.Rgt.7* Oct 24-Dec 26, *Stab Art.Fhr.VII* Jan 27-Sep 28 & in the *Truppenamt* thereafter - see service record for Günther Rüdel in Hildebrand 1992 pp.146-147.

81 *Entwicklungsprogramm 13.12.30 RL 4 Chef des Ausbildungswesens/General der Fliegerausbildungs und Luftwaffen-Inspektion/Waffengerate* in Folder 257, BA/MA in Westermann 2001 p.44-45.

82 *Entwicklungsprogramm 13.12.30 RL 4 Chef des Ausbildungswesens/General der Fliegerausbildungs und Luftwaffen-Inspektion/Waffengerate* in Folder 257, BA/MA in Westermann 2001 p.44. *Maj.*Rüdel was the *Referent für Naschschub* (Supply) in the *Truppenamt* during Oct 28 -Jan 30. He was promoted to *Obstlt.* on the 01.02.29 - see service record for Günther Rüdel in Hildebrand 1992 pp.146-147.

83 Quoted from *Interrogation Report of Gen.d.Flak.Walter von Axthelm Part I AA Program 1930-31 App.C* in Westermann 2001 *Flak: German Anti-aircraft Defenses 1914-1945* p.45 with the kind permission of the University Press of Kansas.

84 Renz 1958 p.100. *"No important preparatory work was done for a future anti-aircraft artillery searchlight prior to 1932"*. However it was found later during field exercises by *Fahr-Abt.3* that the effective range of the 110 cm FSW had been under-estimated - see *Horchlehrgang der KAS (July 1, 1933)"* T-4-5/Reel 1/Frames 4827867-68, NARA in Westermann p.52.

85 *Richtlinien für die Gefechts-und Schiessübungen der Kw.Batterien 1931* T-405/Reel 1/Frames 4827245-47, NARA in Westermann 2001 p.48.

86 Service record for Richard Reimann in Thomas and Wegmann 1991 Bd.2 pp.134-138. In Oct 21 *Oblt.*Reimann

was the watch phrase of the day and the 1931 *Richtlinien* stressed the importance of the correct use of the P 27 Kommandogerate in the firing drills.[87] Further live firing exercises would follow on the Schilling Peninsula near Wilhelmshaven during the summer and autumn of 1932.[88]

To help define the operational role and therefore the equipment and training needs of the emerging *Flakwaffe, Obst.*Rüdel published the *Entwicklungsprogramm der Flugabwehr-Waffen des Heeres* on the 12 June 1932.[89] With a clear emphasis on tactical support for the *Feldheer*, this document listed four major tasks for the *Flakwaffe*:

FLAKWAFFE TASKS
1932

- The reduction of hostile air reconnaissance of any sort;
- Prevention of hostile artillery range finding with air observation;
- Defence against air raids on ground targets, and;
- Support of our own air forces in the accomplishment of their tasks.[90]

Like Keller before him, Rüdel acknowledged the importance of a combined-arms approach to the complex problems of providing an effective air defence:

Flak has the task either alone or in co-operation with the *Fliegertruppe* to protect all vital installations for the protection of the *Heimat* as well as to protect the troops in the field from attacks from the air.[91]

*Obst.*Günther Rüdel
Kdr.d.Lehrstabes d.Flakartillerie/Art.Insp.d.H.

The destruction as opposed to the mere hampering of enemy aircraft was considered to be the primary objective although it was recognised that strong "barrage" fire had a major deterrent effect.[92] Equipment priorities were confirmed as the 8.8 cm *FlaK*, the 2 cm *FlaK* and 3.7 cm *FlaK* weapons, together with searchlights, radio locators including listening devices, barrage rockets,

---

had been assigned as a *Batt.Chef i.III./AR 3* where he remained until Jun 29 when he was re-assigned to Ostpreussen as *Chef.9./AR 1*. He was an instructor on the *Flak-Lehrgang Königsberg* in Aut 29 & Sum 30.

87   Hogg 1978 pp.77-78 & Westermann 2001 p.48.

88   Westermann 2001 p.48.

89   *Entwicklungsprogramm der Flugabwehr-Waffen des Heeres June 12, 1932 RL 4/Folder 257, BA-MA* in Westermann 2001 p.46. Rüdel was promoted to *Obst.* on the 01.12.31 - see service record Günther Rüdel in Hildebrand 1992 pp.146-147. *Obst.*Rüdel & *Maj.*Hubert Weise were the main authors of this document - see Renz 1958 p.100.

90   *Entwicklungsprogramm der Flugabwehr-Waffen des Heeres June 12, 1932 RL 4/Folder 257, BA-MA* in Westermann 2001 pp.46-47.

91   Quoted from *Entwicklungsprogramm der Flugabwehr-Waffen des Heeres June 12, 1932 RL 4/Folder 257, BA-MA* in Westermann 2001 *Flak: German Anti-aircraft Defenses 1914-1945* p.46 with the kind permission of the University Press of Kansas.

92   *Entwicklungsprogramm der Flugabwehr-Waffen des Heeres June 12, 1932 RL 4/Folder 257, BA-MA* in Westermann 2001 pp.46-47. Interestingly British thinking on air defence priorities followed very similar lines. In 1934 a Committee was set up under Sir Robert Brooke-Popham (AOC-in-C ADGB) to look at how best to counter the emerging air threat from Germany. The Committee considered that within an integrated air defence system the Anti-Aircraft Artillery should have the following roles: (1) to destroy hostile aircraft; (2) to co-operate with fighter aircraft by disorganising enemy formations so that (friendly) fighters might engage them with the best possible chance of success; and (3) to deny to hostile aircraft opportunities of detailed observation and accurate bombing by forcing them to fly high and later course at critical moments – see Pile F. 1949 *Ack-Ack: Britain's Defence against air attack during the Second World War* pp.58-59.

Kommandogerate and infra-red tracking. The provision of *Sperrballonen* (Barrage Balloons) was also considered to be an important. The development of remote-controlled *FlaK* and of larger 10.5 cm *FlaK* was considered less urgent, the latter on account of its weight in action which would require either static mountings *(Ortfesten)* or railway mountings *(Eisenbahn)*.[93] The interest in infra-red tracking and the development of barrage rockets both reflected contemporary scientific and technological advances.[94] From October 1931 *Hptm.*von Axthelm played a key role in drawing up the requirements for new equipment as *Referent für Waffen, Geräte und Munition in Ausbildungsstab III* (Staff Advisor for Weapons, Equipment and Munitions in Training Staff III).[95] The actual testing and development work remained the responsibility of the *WaA*, this being fragmented between *Wa.Prüf.1* where *Hptm.*Richard Reimann had a particular responsibility for Ballistics and Munitions and *Wa.Prüf.4* where *Hptm.*Mertitsch was still concerned with the development of *schwere FlaK*.[96]

Whilst the seven *Kraftwagengeschütz-Batterien* formed the basis of the planned *Flakabteilungen*, further resources and personnel would be required to "flesh out" these new units. To this end selected *Eskadronen* of the *Fahrtruppe* were ear-marked for conversion to this new role.[97] The *Fahrtruppe* had been originally been retained by the *Reichsheer* as a trained reserve without guns for the seven *Artillerie-Regimenter* and as such were administratively and operationally subordinate to the *Divisional Artillerie-Führer*.[98] Its role was to support each *Division* with horse-drawn transport, primarily as a means of providing cross-country ammunition support for the *Artillerie-Batterien* in an era when existing motorised transport was largely restricted to good quality tracks and roadways.[99] As a result the *Fahrtruppe* became the acknowledged experts in off-road horse driving and horsemanship and were responsible for training the driving instructors of all other arms at the *Kavallerieschule Hannover*.[100] Each *Fahrabteilung* consisted of seventeen officers and four hundred other ranks who were distinguished from other artillery personnel by the use of *Hellblau* (Light Blue) *Waffenfarbe*.[101]

Early in 1933 the first covert *Flak-Batterien* were formed from within the *Fahrtruppen*. In all four *Flak-Batterien (motorisiert)* were created together with a single *Scheinwerfer-Batterie (mot.)*:[102]

93   *Entwicklungsprogramm der Flugabwehr-Waffen des Heeres June 12, 1932 RL 4/Folder 257, BA-MA* in Westermann 2001 p.47.
94   Renz 1958 pp.157-159. Rocket development was not restricted by the terms of the Versailles Treaty but neither industry nor the universities showed much interest in its development. However the *WaA* began experimental work at Kummersdorf, nr.Zossen, Berlin in 1929. An early development was the RZ (Rauchzylinder) 73 which was developed as an anti-aircraft rocket at Kummersdorf-West. See also Gander and Chamberlain 1978 p.321 & Westermann 2001 p.47. Details of the infra-red tracking work are unfortunately sketchy at best – see Renz 1958 p.176 & Pritchard D. 1989 *The Radar War: Germany's Pioneering Achievement 1904-1945* p.176 & Westermann 2001 p.70.
95   Service record for Walter von Axthelm in Thomas and Wegmann 1991 Bd.1 pp.9-12. Just prior to this appointment Axthelm spent a month in Sweden as a guest of the Royal Swedish Army.
96   Service record for Richard Reimann in Thomas and Wegmann 1991 Bd.2 p.136.
97   *Gliederung und Standorte der Reichswehr 1932* in Lexikon der Wehrmacht, Renz 1958 p.101, Seaton 1982 p.73 & Westermann 2001 pp.49-50. Other *Schwadronen* were used as cadres for new *schwere Art.Abtn.* (Heavy Artillery Abt.), *Stabsbatterien für Art.Rgtr.*(Art.Rgt.HQ Battery), *Schallmess-Bttr.*(Sound Ranging Bttr.), *Beobachters-Abt.* (Observation Abt.) and even a *Gas u. Nebel-Versuchs-Bttr.*(Gas & Chemical Warfare Research Bttr.), *Funk-Kp.* (Signals Kp.), *Kradschutzen-Kp* (Armoured Car Kp.) & *Kampfwagen-Abwehr-Kp.*(Anti-Tank Kp.). The *Stab, 1. u.2.Kp.Fahr.Abt.2* formed a *Fliegerstammabteilung* under *Maj.*Pflugbeil at Rendsburg & Stettin-Altdamm - see Schliephake H. 1971 *The Birth of the Luftwaffe* p.29.
98   *Gliederung und Standorte der Reichswehr 1932* in Lexikon der Wehrmacht.
99   *Gliederung und Standorte der Reichswehr 1932* in Lexikon der Wehrmacht. Each *Division* also had a *Kraftfahrabteilung* equipped with motorised transport for Divisional supply tasks. These units later formed the basis for the *Panzer-Regimenter* - See also Diest W. 1981 *The Wehrmacht and German Rearmament* pp.28-29 & Seaton 1982 p.62 & pp.64-65.
100   Davis 1971 p.22 & Seaton 1982 p.59.
101   *Gliederung und Standorte der Reichswehr 1932* in Lexikon der Wehrmacht. *Fahr-Abt.3* was seen as an experimental *Flakabteilung* and as such was equipped with the new 7.5 cm L/60 and 2 cm FlaK 30 - see Renz 1958 p.98 & 101 & Westermann 2001 p.50.
102   *Anlage 7 Ubersicht der als Fahrabteilungen getarnten Flakabteilungen, Stand: 1.November 1933* in Volker 1967 p.232.

FIGURE 1E-12 CONVERSION OF SELECTED FAHRVERBÄNDE INTO FLAK-EINHEITEN 1933			
2.Fahr-Abteilung	Rendsburg	Hptm.Friedrich-W.Deutsch ?	Flakbatterie (mot.)
3.Fahr-Abteilung	Berlin-Lankwitz	Obstlt.Hubert Weise	Stab Flak-Abteilung (mot.)
		Rittm.Heino von Rantzau ?	Flak-Batterie (mot.)
			Scheinwerfer-Batterie (mot.)
5.Fahr-Abteilung	Ludwigsburg	Rittm.Georg Neuffer ?	Flakbatterie (mot.)
6.Fahr-Abteilung	Hannover	Hptm.Heinrich Burchard ?	Flakbatterie (mot.)

These units then joined the existing *Kraftwagengeschützen-Batterien* during the early part of 1933 to form the first covert *Flak-Abteilungen*, the *Kw.-Batterien* taking the place of those elements that had been re-organised and trained as other specialist units:[103]

FIGURE 1E-13 THE FIRST COVERT FLAKABTEILUNGEN 1 NOVEMBER 1933			
Fahr-Abteilung 1	Königsberg	6.(Kw.)/Art.Rgt.1	
		Flak-Batt./Fahr-Abt.1	- Oct 33
Fahr-Abteilung 2	Rendsburg	1.(Kw.)/Art.Rgt.2	
		Flak-Batt./Fahr-Abt.1	- Dec 32
Fahr-Abteilung 3	Berlin-Lankwitz	Stab/Fahr-Abt.3	- Dec 32
		9.(Kw.)/Art.Rgt.3	
		SW.-Batt./Fahr-Abt.3	- Dec 32
		Flak-Batt./Fahr-Abt.3	- Oct 33
		Flak-Batt./Fahr-Abt.3	- Oct 33
Fahr-Abteilung 4	Dresden	9.(Kw.)/Art.Rgt.4	
		Flak-Batt./Fahr-Abt.4	- Oct 33
Fahr-Abteilung 5	Ludwigsburg	9.(Kw.)/Art.Rgt.5	
		Flak-Batt./Fahr-Abt.5	- Dec 32
Fahr-Abteilung 6	Hannover	9.(Kw.)/Art.Rgt.6	
		Flak-Batt./Fahr-Abt.6	- Dec 32
Fahr-Abteilung 7	München	9.(Kw.)/Art.Rgt.7	
		Flak-Batt./Fahr-Abt.7	- Oct 33

For reasons of political expediency these units continued to be referred to as *Fahr-Abteilungen*. Only *Fahr-Abteilung 3* at Berlin-Lankwitz was truly of *Abteilung* status and it was this unit that was initially equipped with the 7.5 cm L/60 FlaK.[104] In March 1933 it reported a strength of

See also Renz 1958 p.101.
103   Renz 1958 p.101 & Volker 1967 pp.17-18. The *6.(Kw.)/Art.Rgt.1* at Königsberg was also equipped with the 7.5 cm L/60 FlaK.
104   Solltau G. 1989 *Die Flakabteilung I./12: Geschichte und Schicksal 1914-1945* (hereafter cited as Solltau 1989) p.13.

27 *Offiziere* and *Offiziersanwarteren*, 3 *Beamte* and 429 *Unteroffiziere* and *Mannschaften*. At that point it was organised into an *Abteilungsstab*, a *Scheinwerfer-Batterie* and a single *Flak-Batterie*. In October 1933 a further two *Flak-Batterien* were added to give the *Abteilung* a total of six 110cm FSW, four 7.5 cm FlaK L/60 and eight 8.8 cm FlaK 18.[105] The remaining *Fahr-Abteilungen* were re-organised during the course of the year around two *Flak-Batterien* so that by November 1933 a total of 15 *Flak-Batterien* and a single *Flak-Scheinwerfer-Batterie* were in existence.[106]

In the meantime Rüdel pushed ahead with an accelerated training programme for his new units. Key areas for attention included the training of optical range-finding personnel where there was wide disparity in efficiency between units, the need for more effective leadership by the *Batterie-Chef*, and an emphasis on live firing drills - especially at night.[107] Unfortunately with so few searchlights it was virtually impossible to achieve any level of proficiency in night firing exercises, a point underlined by *Obstlt.*Hubert Weise, the *Kommandeur Fahr-Abteilung 3* at Berlin-Lankwitz, who pushed hard for each of his three *Flak-Scheinwerfer-Zuge* to be assigned four rather than two lights and for each *FSW-Zuge* to be allocated a motorised signals section to facilitate mobile operations.[108] In his evaluation of the summer's searchlight training Weise concluded that *"even more than the Flak-Batterien, the Scheinwerfer-Batterien require a realistic training target"*.[109] This reference to the single-engine light aircraft of the *Reklamestaffel Mitteldeutschland* high-lighted the limitations of such slow and low-flying light aircraft in the effective training of the *Flakartillerie* (See also 1A3).

In the meantime the training of the heavy gun crews had continued apace. In March 1933 *Fahr-Abteilung 3* had received orders to conduct field trials three times each week in exercises which combined the use of searchlights and sound locators. From April these drills were conducted under simulated battlefield conditions, whilst in May these exercises were supplemented by a two-week live-firing trial at the Schillig Reede.[110] During the autumn and winter months of 1933/34 Weise carried out two large-scale planning exercises: the first in December being focused on the problems associated with defending the capital from enemy air attack; the second in February being concerned with the deployment of the *Flakartillerie* in support of the *Feldheer*.[111] During this period his officers were also expected to research and present seminars on a range of issues.[112]

Weise was typical of a new generation of *Flakoffiziere*. His wartime service had been with the *Feld-Artillerie*; his immediate post-war service with *Artillerie-Regiment 4* where he had been a *Batterie-Chef* at Bautzen (*6./Art.Rgt.4*) prior to his assignment to the *Inspektion der Artillerie* in Berlin in February 1927 (*Ausbildungs-Referent* and *Adjutant*). His first contact with the *Flakartillerie* had been in May 1929 when he attended a *Marine Flak-Lehrgang* on the island of Wangerooge prior to joining the *Stab I./Art.Rgt.3* at Schweidnitz. In October 1931 he was posted to Lankwitz as *Kommandeur Fahr-Abteilung 3*.[113] The majority of the new *Flak-Abteilung Kommandeure* had

---

105   Solltau 1989 pp.13-15.

106   *Anlage 7 Ubersicht der als Fahrabteilungen getarnten Flakabteilungen, Stand: 1.November 1933* in Volker 1967 p.232.

107   *Bemerkungen zur Ausbildung 1933 T-405 German Air Force Records: Luftgaukommandos, Flak, Deutsche Luftwaffenmission in Rumanien Reel 1/Frames 4827259-65, NARA* in Westermann 2001 p.51.

108   *3.(Preuss.) Fahabteilung, Berlin-Lankwitz, den 21.8.33 T-405/Reel 1/Frames 4827931-32, NARA* in Westermann 2001 p.52.

109   Quoted from *3.(Preuss.) Fahabteilung, Berlin-Lankwitz, den 21.8.33" T-405/Reel 1/Frames 4827931-32, NARA* in Westermann 2001 *Flak: German Anti-aircraft Defenses 1914-1945* p.52 with the kind permission of the University Press of Kansas.

110   *Ausbildung der Schw.Battr. in den Monaten Marz, April u.Mai (February 12, 1933) T-405/Reel 1/Frames 4927962-63, NARA* in Westermann 2001 p.51. See also Volker 1967 p.17.

111   *Taktische Ausbildung der Offiziere im Winter 1933/34 (October 10, 1933)" T-405/Reel 1/Frames 4827952, NARA* in Westermann 2001 p.53.

112   *Ausbildungsplan für das Winterhalbjahr 1.11.33 bis 31.3.34 (September 20, 1933)* T-405/reel 1/Frames 4827776-77, 4827784-85, NARA in Westermann 2001 p.53.

113   Service record for Hubert Weise in Thomas and Wegmann 1991 Bd.2 pp.270-272.

similar backgrounds. Most had joined one of the pre-war *Artillerie-Regimenter* as a *Fahnenjunker.* Their early employment had been characterised by active service as *Batterie-Offiziere*, mostly on the static Western Front where the *Artillerie* had assumed ever great importance in providing counter-battery, indirect and barrage fire in support of the *Infanterie*.[114] For much of their careers in the *Reichsheer* they had been employed as *Batterie-Chef* or as *Adjutante*, this service being interrupted from time to time by specialist *Lehrgange* or periods of service with operational or administrative staffs. A few officers had seen extensive service with the *Fahrtruppe*, for example Heinrich Burchard *(Fahr-Abt.6)* and Heino von Rantzau *(Fahr-Abt.2)*.[115] The remainder had spent most of the twenties in their parent *Regimenter*: Walter Feyerabend *(Art.Rgt.1)*, Helmut Richter and Wolfgang Rüter *(Art.Rgt.3)*, Ernst Buffa and Rudolf Eibenstein *(Art.Rgt.4)*, Otto Wilhelm von Renz *(Art.Rgt.5)*, Oskar Bertram *(Art.Rgt.6)* and Friedrich Heilingbrunner *(Art.Rgt.7)*.[116]

FIGURE 1E-14 PROFESSIONAL SEMINARS BY OFFIZIERE FAHR-ABTEILUNG 3 WINTER 1933-34
• Thoughts on the conduct of modern air warfare
• Defence in low-level attacks by dive bombers
• What is the minimum number of guns and searchlights for *Flak-Batterien* ?
• Smoke production in air defence
• Flak-Measuring instruments and their importance in firing operations
• Activities of air forces and air defences in the Sino-Japanese war

One of the few exceptions was *Maj.*Theodor Spiess. Spiess was a *Pionier-Offizier* who had seen post-war service with *Inf.Rgt.6* (Lübeck), *Inf.Rgt.12* (Halberstadt) and *Inf.Rgt.16* (Oldenburg). In January 1932 he had been re-assigned to the *Stab des Infanterie-Führers I* (Allenstein) where he attended a *Flak-Lehrgang* with the *II.Marine-Artillerie-Abteilung*. In October 1934 he was the appointed *Kommandeur* of the new *Flugabwehr-Maschinen-gewehr-Abteilung (Fla-MG-Abt.)* at Brandenburg.[117] This unit differed from the remaining *Flak-Abteilungen* in essentially being a *leichte Flak-Abteilung* equipped with the Oerlikon 2 cm FlaK 28 and the new Rheinmetall-Borsig 2 cm FlaK 30. The *Abteilung* was organised along *Infanterie* lines with three *Fla-MG-Kompanien*, these being formed from personnel provided by the *Inf.Rgtr.2* (Allenstein), *9* (Potsdam) and *12* (Halberstadt).[118]

October 1934 saw a further expansion in the covert *Flakverbände*. In addition to the *Fla-MG-Abt.*, three more *Flak-Abteilungen* were created at Seerappen, Döberitz and Wurzen. At the same time all *Fahr-Abteilungen* dropped their numerical designations in favour of the name of their

114   Thomas and Wegmann 1991 Bd.1 & 2. See also Hogg 1970 pp.8-33
115   Service records for Heinrich Burchard in Thomas and Wegmann 1991 Bd.1 pp.76-78 and Heino von Rantzau in Thomas and Wegmann 1991 Bd.2 pp.123-125. After a very short period of service with *AR 6* Heinrich Burchard had been posted to *Fahr-Abt.6* (Sep 23) and then *Fahr-Abt.4* (Apr 24) until re-assigned to *AR 6* (Mar 27). On the 1 Apr 32 he was posted to *Fahr-Abt.3 (Flak)* at Lankwitz as *Chef 3.Eskadron* where he remained until Nov 32 when he became *Chef 1.Esk./Fahr-Abt.6*. Heino von Rantzau joined *Fahr-Abt.2* in Oct 26 after service with *AR 2*. From Jan 28 he was an *Eskadron Chef Fahr-Abt.2* until he assumed command of *Fahr-Abt.3* in Oct 34.
116   Hildebrand 1990-92 & Thomas and Wegmann 1991 Bd.1 & Bd.2.
117   Service record for Theodor Spiess in Hildebrand 1992 pp.332-333.
118   Volker 1967 p.49. See also service record for Walter von Hippel in Thomas and Wegmann 1991 Bd.1 pp.240-245. *Rittm.*Hippel (IR 9) was *Chef 1.Kp.(2 cm Flak 30)/Fla-MG-Abt.* From 1 Oct 34, whilst *Hptm.*Wolfgang Freytag (IR 12) was also a *Schwadron-Chef* from Oct 34 – see service record for Wolfgang Freytag in Hildebrand 1990 pp.315-316.

garrison towns.[119] Production of weapons and equipment was channelled to the new units together with key personnel from the existing *Fahr-Abteilungen*.[120] However there was a general shortage of trained personnel and in August 1934 Rüdel authorised the creation of 150 *Offiziersanwarter* positions for the *Flakartillerie* and a further 70 for the *Flugmeldedienst*.[121] During this period the *Reichsheer* was secretly doubling in size from its authorised establishment of 100,000 to a new figure of 240,000 officers and men and in the year before conscription was formally introduced this expansion had to be sustained by the recruitment of volunteers and by transfers from the *Landespolizei*.[122]

FIGURE 1E-15 THE COVERT FLAK-ABTEILUNGEN OCTOBER 1934			
Flak-Abteilung	Königsberg	Maj.Walter Feyerabend	(Fahr-Abt.1)
Flak-Abteilung	Seerappen	Maj.Rudolf Eibenstein	(Fahr-Abt.1)
Flak-Abteilung	Stettin	Maj.Wolfgang Rüter	(Fahr-Abt.2)
Flak-Abteilung	Berlin-Lankwitz	Maj.Heino von Rantzau	(Fahr-Abt.3)
Flak-Abteilung	Döberitz	Maj.Otto Wilhelm von Renz	(Fahr-Abt.3)
Flak-Abteilung	Dresden	Maj.Oskar Bertram	(Fahr-Abt.4)
Flak-Abteilung	Wurzen	Maj.Ernst Buffa	(Fahr-Abt.4,5 u.6)
Flak-Abteilung	Ludwigsburg	Maj.Helmut Richter	(Fahr-Abt.5)
Flak-Abteilung	Hamburg-Wolfenbüttel	Maj.Heinrich Burchard	(Fahr-Abt.6)
Flak-Abteilung	Furth	Maj.Friedrich Heilingbrunner	(Fahr-Abt.7)
Flak-MG-Abteilung	Brandenburg	Maj.Theodor Spiess	(Inf.Rgt.2, 9 u.12)
Flak-Lehr-Abt.	Döberitz	Obstlt.Kurt Steudemann	(Flak.Kdo.Döberitz)

On the same date GenMaj.Rüdel was made *Inspekteur der Flakartillerie* and *Chef des Luftschützamtes* within the *RWM* and Obst.Weise was assigned as his *Chef des Stabes*.[123] In the following month Rüdel published his annual assessment of the effectiveness of training for the emergent *Flakverbände*. In his *Bemerkungen zur Ausbildung 1934* he acknowledged the progress that had been made in gunnery drills and the improved efficiency of the range finding crews although there was still an urgent need for these to be practised under operational conditions. As defence in depth was not yet possible he asked for a new emphasis on *"the highest level of speed"* for every task.[124] It must have seemed ironic that the rapidly improving performance of new combat aircraft

119   *Anlage 7 Ubersicht der als Fahrabteilungen getarnten Flakabteilungen, Stand: 1.November 1933* in Volker 1967 p.232. See also Volker 1967 p.49 & Westermann 2001 p.54.
120   Seaton 1982 p.60 & Westermann 2001 p.54.
121   *Werbung von Offizieranwartern (August 15, 1934)" T-405/Reel 1/Frame 4828531* in Westermann 2001 p.54. Many of these positions would be filled by the commissioning of suitable enlisted personnel from within the *Reichsheer*.
122   Seaton 1982 p.56. The existing 7 Divisional staffs were to become Corps Staffs and a further 11 Corps (*Generalkommandos*) were to be created. The 7 existing *Divisionen* were to be divided to form a total of 14 *Divisionen*, the Staffs of the new formations to be provided by the 7 *Infanterie* & 7 *Artillerie-Führeren*. The creation of 11 *Flak-Abteilungen* can be seen to be quite modest in this context. Most of the personnel for enlarged *Reichsheer* were drawn from the *Landespoliziei* and those members of the *NSDAP's SA (Sturmabteilung)* who had seen war service.
123   Service records for Günther Rüdel & Hubert Weise in Hildebrand 1992 pp.146-147 & 496-497. Weise had been promoted to *Obst.* on the 1 Apr 34 whilst Rüdel was promoted to *GenMaj.* on the 1 Oct 34.
124   *Bemerkungen zur Ausbildung (November 1934)" T-405/Reel 1/Frames 4827276-81, NARA* in Westermann 2001 pp.54-55.

was threatening to neutralise the ground defences at the very moment that a major expansion in those defences had become politically acceptable.[125]

To further improve the efficiency of the *Flakwaffe*, the existing practice facility at Döberitz-Elsgrund was expanded in October 1934 into a full blown *Flakschule* under the command of *Obstlt.*Alfred Haubold.[126] Further facilities existed for survey troops *(Messtruppen)* and *schwere FlaK* at Wustrow on the Mecklenburgische coast and over the winter months the whole school was transferred to this remote and more secure location where it was formally established as the *Flakartillerie-Schule Wustrow* on the 1 April 1935.[127] Training at the *Flakschule* was organised into three *Lehrgange: Schiessausbildung* (Gunnery Training), *Horch und Scheinwerfereinsatz* (Sound Locator and Searchlight Operations) and *Flugabwehrmesswesen* (Air Defence Survey Services).[128] *Maj.*Ludwig Schillfarth was *Leiter der Ausbildungsstab* (Training Staff) and the instructors included *Hptm.*Wolfgang Pickert and *Rittm.*Georg Neuffer.[129] Coincident with the formation of the *Flakschule* a *Flak-Lehrabteilung* with three *Lehrbatterien* was formed at Döberitz under *Obstlt. Kurt Steudemann.* Prior to his appointment Steudemann had spent a year at Lankwitz with Weise's *Fahr-Abteilung 3* and as such had been personally involved in the practical training of the emergent *Flakwaffe.*[130] The *Lehrabteilung* had the key task of demonstrating drills and procedures to *Flakpersonnel* who were under-going specialist *Lehrgange* at the *Flakschule*, whilst helping to evaluate new equipment and tactics. As such the members of this unit were amongst the most proficient in the *Flakwaffe* and set the standard that was expected from all *Flak-Abteilungen.*

In the meantime preparations for the formal transfer of the entire *Flakartillerie* organisation to the newly formed *Luftwaffe* were under way. As early as the 16 September 1933 *Reichwehrminister* Werner von Blomberg had agreed to Rüdel becoming responsible to *Reichskommissar für die Luftfahrt* Hermann Göring on all matters concerning the organisation, training, augmentation and equipping of air defence forces (See 2A1). Rüdel's primary duty was described as *"the standardised co-ordination of all military and civil preparedness measures for air defence in the field and in the homeland as well as the systematic continued development of air defence tactics and technical matters".*[131]

125   Seaton 1982 p.55.

126   Volker 1967 p.49. The earliest use of the Döberitz-Elsgrund facilities for *Flak* training appears to have been Mar 30 when *Oblt.*Max Schaller was detached from *AR 4* to supervise the creation of a *Flak* training facility at Döberitz - see service record for Max Schaller in Hildebrand 1992 pp.169-170. In Apr 31 *Oblt.*Fritz Krause *(2./AR 2)* attended a *Flakleiter-Lehrgang* prior to a posting to the *2./FA 3* at Lankwitz as an *Eskadron-Offizier* in Oct 31 - see service record for Fritz Krause in Thomas and Wegmann 1991 Bd.1 pp.319-321. *Obstlt.*Haubold was a former *Batterie-Offizier, Batterie-Chef* and member of the *Stab/AR 4.* He spent two years with the *Kdtr.Artillerie-Schiessplatzes Jüterbog* before a 3 year posting with the *Kdtr.Berlin.* Immediately prior to his assignment at Döberitz he had been a *Referent* at the *RWM* - see service record for Alfred Haubold in Hildebrand 1991 pp.41-42.

127   Service record for Ernst Herrmann in Thomas and Wegmann 1991 Bd.1 pp.227-229. *Hptm.*Herrmann was appointed *Kdr.d.Mess-Schule Wustrow* on the 1 Apr 34. The *Messtruppen* were an important element of any artillery organisation being responsible for the detailed mapping of *Batterie* positions so that all the fire of all the weapons could be properly co-ordinated for directed fire purposes - in the case of the *Flakartillerie* by the *Batterie Kommandogerat.* Herrmann had previously been a *Batterie-Offz.* in *6.(Kw.)/AR 1.*

128   Volker 1967 p.49.

129   Hildebrand 1990-92. Unlike many of his contemporaries *Maj.*Schillfarth was an *Infanterie-Offizier* from *IR 21* (Nürnberg) where he had been *Chef 12.(MG)/IR 21* from Mar 31 - see service record for Ludwig Schillfarth in Hildebrand 1992 pp.183-184; *Hptm.*Pickert had been a *Batterie-Offz., Batterie-Chef* & *Abt.Adj.i.AR 1.* He had been selected for *Führergehilfen-Ausbildung b.Stab 1.Div.* during 1924-26 - see service record for Wolfgang Pickert in Thomas and Wegmann 1991 Bd.2 pp.91-95; *Rittm.*Neuffer had been a *Batterie-Offz.* in *9.(Kw.)/AR 7* during 1921-24 before joining the *5./AR 7* and under-going *Führergehilfen-Ausbildung* in 1924-25.He had then served with *1./AR 7* and as *Adj.III./AR 7* before being appointed *Chef 3./AR 7* in Oct 29. In Sep 31 he was transferred to *FA 5* and during 1931-32 he participated in a number of tactical exercises for *Kw.-Geschützen, Luftschützen & Kw.-Batterien* - see service record for Georg Neuffer in Thomas and Wegmann 1991 Bd.2 pp.69-72.

130   Service record for Kurt Steudemann in Hildebrand 1992 pp.357-358. See also Volker 1967 p.49.

131   Quoted from *Unterstellung der Luftschütztruppen (September 16, 1933)* in *T-405/Reel 1/Frames 4828144-46,*

Over the following eighteen months ever closer ties would be forged between the *Luftkommandoamt (LA)* and the expanding *Flakwaffe* (See 2A3). However it would not be until the 1 April 1935 that the formal transfer took place and from that date the development and operational control of the *Flakartillerie* ceased to be a formal *Reichsheer* responsibility (See 3B5).[132]

NARA in Westermann 2001 *Flak: German Anti-aircraft Defenses 1914-1945* p.56 with the kind permission of the University Press of Kansas.

132   Volker 1967 pp.49-50 & Westermann 2001 pp.55-56.

1E3

The Development of German Naval Aviation 1920-1933

Although the neutralisation of the threat posed by the German Army had been the major focus for the victorious allied powers, the British and the French were also concerned with the post-war size and strength of the former *Kaiserliche Marine* (Imperial Navy). Article 181 of the Treaty of Versailles was therefore employed to massively reduce the fighting capacity of their former enemy at sea whilst Article 190 was written to effectively prevent any resurgence of German naval power.[1] The result was a small force of obsolete and ageing vessels which were of limited fighting value.[2] It was therefore understandable that the senior naval officers within the *Marineleitung* (Naval High Command) saw the role of the newly formed *Reichsmarine* to be no more than that of a coastal defence force, the aims of which were specified in a memorandum by *KonAdm.*William Michaelis in September 1920:[3]

1. The imposition of authority and the laws of the state in coastal areas;
2. The control of territorial waters along the German coast;
3. The prevention of piracy in German waters;
4. The defence of the coasts against annexation by other coastal states nearby;

1   Moore J. (Ed.) 2001 *Jane's Fighting Ships of World War I* (hereafter cited as Moore (Ed.) 2001) pp.101-109 & Bekker C. 1972 *The German Navy 1939-1945* (hereafter cited as Bekker 1972) p.8. At the outbreak of of hostilities in Aug 14 the *Kaiserliche Marine's Hochsee Flotte* possessed 13 *Linienschiffe* (9 with 30.5 cm SK & 4 with 28 cm SK as their primary armament) as well as 5 *Linienschiff Kreuziere* (30.5 cm SK). New construction would add a further 6 *Linienschiffe* (2 with 38 cm SK & 4 with 30.5 cm SK) and 3 *Linienschiff Kreuziere* (30.5 cm SK). Ignoring pre-Dreadnought vessels the *Kaiserliche Marine* lost only one of its modern capital ships during the Great War – the *Linienschiff Kreuzer Lützow* at Jutland in 1916 – see also Preston A. and Batchelor J. *1977 Battleships 1856-1919* Phoebus History of the World Wars Special (hereafter cited as Preston and Batchelor 1977) pp.38-45 & 48-56, Whitley M.J. 1989 *German Capital Ships of World War Two* (hereafter cited as Whitley 1989) pp.7-13 & Campbell N.J.M. and Sieche E. *Germany* in Sturton I. (Ed.) 2008 *Conway's Battleships: The Definitive Guide to the World's all-big-gun ships* (hereafter cited as Campbell and Sieche in Sturton (Ed.) 2008) pp.43-59.

2   Bekker 1972 p.8. Article 181 restricted the *Reichsmarine* to no more than 6 armoured ships (pre-Dreadnought *Linienschiffe*), 6 cruisers, 12 destroyers, 12 torpedo boats or the same number of replacement vessels. Replacement of existing vessels was regulated by Article 190: *Linienschiffe* and *Kreuziere* could not be replaced until they had seen at least 20 yrs service, whilst *Größe Torpedoboote* & *Torpedoboote* had to be at least 15 yrs old. New construction was limited by displacement to 10,000 BRT for *Linienschiffe*, 6,000 BRT for *kleine Kreuziere*, 800 BRT for *Größe Torrpedoboote* and 200 BRT for *Torpedoboote*. Submarines were forbidden. As nearly all modern vessels had been interned at the British Fleet anchorage at Scapa Flow following the Armistice the *Reichsmarine* was forced to re-commission older vessels of pre-war vintage as the basis for the new navy.

3   Sieche E. *Germany* in Gardiner R. and Chesneau R. (Ed.) 1980 *Conway's All the World's Fighting Ships 1922-1946* (hereafter cited as Sieche in Gardiner and Chesneau (Ed.) 1980) p.218. The post-Versailles navy would of necessity be a coast defence force and its development with an emphasis on destroyers and mine warfare vessels was very much in keeping with the French *"jeune ecole"* philosophy of the 1880s when *Adm.*Theopile Aube (French Naval Minister 1886-87) advocated the aggressive use of torpedo craft to effectively close the English Channel to British shipping – see Reynolds C.G. 1974 *Command of the Sea: The History and Strategy of Maritime Empires* (hereafter cited as Reynolds 1974) pp.407-408.

5. The control of coastal sea lanes, especially those to Ostpreussen;
6. The carrying out of courtesy visits overseas "to demonstrate the standards of efficiency and the attitudes of the whole nation";
7. The provision of security against a blockade by smaller Baltic countries;
8. The carrying out of "cultural duties" such as hydrographic survey, fishery protection and oceanography.

During the political and social turmoil of the immediate post-war years a significant number of demobilised naval personnel had joined the *Freikorps* (Volunteer Corps), principally as members of either the *Brigade Loewenfeld* or *Brigade Rode* (See 1A1).[4] Both these *Brigades* were later disbanded and the naval personnel concentrated in the *Brigade Ehrhardt* which marched on Berlin during the abortive nationalist *Kapp-Lüttwitz Putsch* of March 1920. Such overt action led to the replacement of *VizeAdm.*Adolph von Trotha as *Chef der Admiralitat* (*Chef der Marineleitung* from the 15 September 1920) in the aftermath of the Putsch and his temporary replacement by Michaelis.[5] Michaelis was in turn replaced by *Adm.*Paul Behncke who adopted a more apolitical stance and sought to re-build the *Vorläufige Reichsmarine* (Provisional Navy) as a credible force.[6] The new *Reichswehr* was formally established on the 31 March 1921, the provisional Navy being simply named the *Reichsmarine* from that date.[7] The *Reichsmarine's* new ensign was first flown on the 11 April, whilst that of the *Kaiserliche Marine* was lowered for the last time on the 31 December 1921.[8]

The organisation of the *Reichsmarine* was of necessity governed by geo-political considerations. The long coastline of northern Germany was effectively divided into two by the Jutland Peninsula (Map I-3). To the west lay the coast of Nord Sachsen together with the offshore island chain of the Ostfriesische Inseln which bordered the Deutsche Bucht, whilst in the east lay the coast of

---

4   Mason H.M. 1973 *The Rise of the Luftwaffe 1918-1940* (hereafter cited as Mason 1973) p.42 & Sieche in Gardiner and Chesneau (Ed.) 1980 p.218. The *Brigade Loewenfeld* and *Brigade Rode* (named after their commanding officers) formed the *Marinefreikorps* – a conservative military force largely opposed to the Socialist Weimar Republic and in particular the communists – see Padfield P. 1984 *Donitz: The Last Führer* (hereafter cited as Padfield 1984) pp.116-121. *KptLt.d.Res.*Friedrich Christiansen was one of those who fought in the *Marinefreikorps*. He was *Staffelführer b.Brigade Loewenfeld (III.Marine-Brigade)* from Apr 19 – Jan 20 – see service record for Friedrich Christiansen in Hildebrand K.F.1990 *Die Generale der deutschen Luftwaffe 1935-1945 Band 1 A-G* (hereafter cited as Hildebrand 1990) pp.157-158 & Angolia J.R. and Hackney C.R. 1984 *The Pour le Mérite and Germany's First Aces* (hereafter cited as Angolia and Hackney 1984) pp.174-177. *KptLt.*Rudolf Wenninger was a *Kp.Fhr.* in the same brigade between Jan-May 20 – see service record for Rudolf Wenninger in Hildebrardt K.F.1992 *Die Generale der deutschen Luftwaffe 1935-1945 Band 3 O-Z* (hereafter cited Hildebrand 1992) pp.502-504. *KorvKpt.*Rudolf Lahs was *Fhr.Eiserne Torpedobootsflottille* within the *Marinefreikorps* – see Tessin G. 1974 *Deutsche Verbände und Truppen 1918-1939.*
5   Padfield 1984 pp.121-122, Pipes J. *Reichswehr Reichsheer* in www.feldgrau.com (hereafter cited as Pipes Reichswehr) & service record for Adolf von Trotha in www.wikipedia.org (hereafter cited as Wikipedia.de). Adolph von Trotha had joined the *Kaiserliche Marine* in 1883. He quickly impressed his superiors and was a *Stabsoffz.* within the *Reichsmarineamt* under *GrAdm.*Alfred von Tirpitz between 1901-06 and was *Adj.* to the *Kaiser* in 1909 and again as a *KonAdm.* in the final years of the Great War. He was *Kdt. SMS Kaiser* from 1913 and *C.d.S.Hochseeflotte* in 1916 in time for the *Skagerrakschlacht* (Battle of Jutland) in May. In 1918 he was *Chef d.Personalamts* before being appointed *Chef d.Admiralitat* on the 26 Mar 19. It was Trotha that ordered the scuttling of the interned German Fleet at Scapa Flow on the 21 Jun 19 as a final act of defiance. However the terms of the Treaty of Versailles in respect of the *Reichsmarine* were all the more harsh in response. Following the *Kapp Putsch*, *Reichswehrminister* Gustav Noske ordered the disbandment of the *Marinefreikorps*.
6   Sieche in Gardiner and Chesnaeu (Ed.) 1980 p.218. Paul Behncke was the first *Chef d.Marineleitung*, a position that was created upon his appointment in Sep 20. He had occupied several influential positions within the *Kaiserliche Marine* and had seen action during the *Skagerrakschlacht* in May 16 as commander of the *3.Geschwaders d.Hochseeflotte*. He retired in Sep 24 having served his country for over 40 yrs – see Mallmann Showell J.P. 1979 *The German Navy in World War Two: A Reference Guide to the Kriegsmarine 1935-1945* (hereafter cited as Mallmann Showell 1979) pp.6-10 & p.174 and service record for Paul Behncke in www.wikipedia.org.
7   Mallmann Showell 1979 p.6 & Pipes Reichswehr.
8   Mallmann Showell 1979 pp.6-10.

Mecklenburg and Pommern which had been separated from that of Ostpreussen by the Treaty of Versailles. Between Pommern and Ostpreussen now lay the narrow Danzig Corridor which had been created to give the new nation state of Poland an outlet to the sea. These geographical and political realties resulted in the *Reichsmarine* being divided operationally and administratively into the *Marinestation der Nordsee* (North Sea Naval Station) in the west with its headquarters at Wilhelmshaven and the *Marinestation der Ostsee* (Baltic Sea Naval Station) in the east with its headquarters at Kiel.[9] The completion of the strategically important *Kaiser Wilhelm Kanal* in 1895 had permitted all types of warship to move freely between these two operational areas without having to transit the narrow and potentially dangerous waters between the Jutland Peninsula and the southern Scandinavia peninsula.[10]

The Treaty of Versailles, the naval clauses of which came into effect in January 1920, restricted the *Reichsmarine* to just 15,000 men. However this figure included 1,500 officers (10% of the total), a much higher proportion than had been allowed in the case of the *Reichsheer* (See 1A2 & 1E1). Only a token naval force was permitted. The maximum figures were to be 6 *Linienschiff* (pre-Dreadnought Battleships) of the obsolete *Braunschweig* (1906-08) and *Deutschland* (1904-06) *Klassen*, 6 *Kleine Kreuziere* (Light Cruisers) of the even older *Gazelle* (1899-1900) and *Hamburg* (1903-04) *Klassen*, 12 *Größer Torpedoboote* (1911-12), 12 *Torpedoboote* (1906-11) and 38 *Minensuchboote* (1916-19) (Large Torpedo Boats, Torpedo Boats and Minesweepers).[11] With the exception of the more modern light vessels many of the larger warships had already been decommissioned at the end of the Great War and some had even been disarmed.[12] The modernisation and refurbishment of these warships would take time and in 1922 *Adm.*Behncke had just 2 *Linienschiffe* and 5 *Kleine Kreuziere* in service with a number of *Torpedoboote (Photos 1E-10 & 1E-11).*[13]

Existing officers were obliged to serve until at least the age of 45 years.[14] This meant that there would be very few opportunities for new officers to enter the *Reichsmarine* before the mid-to late twenties. Eckhard Christian, an eighteen year old Berliner, was one of the few considered good enough to be selected for training as a prospective *Seeoffizier* (Naval Officer) in April 1926. His service training was to be long and thorough. Seven months of initial naval training at the *Schiffsstammdivision der Ostsee* (Baltic Naval Recruit Training Division) was followed by sea training aboard the *Reichsmarine's* newly commissioned *Segelschulschiff Niobe* (Sail Training Ship) in October before five months aboard the

9   Mallmann Showell 1979 pp.56-57 & 1999 pp.195-200. Of course the same geo-political realities had shaped the development and organisation of the *Kaiserliche Marine* but during that period the emphasis had been upon the Nordsee with main *Hochseeflotte* base being at Wilhelmshaven.

10   Naval Intelligence Division 1945 *Germany Vol.IV Ports and Communications* pp.108-111. Construction of the 85 km *Kaiser Wilhelm Kanal* began in 1887 with the aim of creating a sea level passage from Kiel in the east to Brunsbuttelkoog in the west. Large sea locks at either end prevented tidal influences from affecting vessels in the canal. The *Kanal* was used extensively by commercial traffic as it saved 680 kms on the sea route from Hamburg to Kiel. Following the commissioning in Britain of *HMS Dreadnought* in Dec 06 it became necessary to design a new class of *Linienschiff* and the *Kanal* had to be upgraded to accommodate these larger vessels – see Preston and Batchelor 1977 p.38, Reynolds 1974 p.411, Mallmann Showell 1999 p.199-200 & Moore (Ed.) 2001 pp.25-26.

11   Bekker 1972 p.8, Mallmann Showell 1979 p.10 & Sieche in Gardiner and Chesneau (Ed.) 1980 p.218. See also Padfield 1984 pp.116-117 & Mallmann Showell 1999 pp.10-12.

12   Sieche in Gardiner and Chesneau (Ed.) 1980 p.218 & 222 and Moore (Ed.) 2001 p.109 & 115. *Preussen & Lothringen (Braunschweig Klass)* were already in reserve by 1918 and employed as *F-Boote* tenders. Neither were re-commissioned. *Elsass & Hessen* would be re-commissioned in 1924 & 1925 respectively. *Schleswig-Holstein (Deutschland Klass)* would commission early but her sister *Schlesien* was taken in hand for modernisation and not re-commissioned until 1927. *Arcona & Medusa (Gazelle Klass)* were both in use as tenders for motor minesweepers, whilst *Niobe, Amazone & Thetis* had been disarmed, the latter being paid off.

13   Mallmann Showell 1979 pp.9-10. Ostensibly the prefix SMS *(Seine Majestats Schiff)* had been replaced by RMS *(Reichsmarine Schiff)* in 1920 but in reality the new prefix was not employed. Instead the ship's name was usually prefixed by its type, eg.*Linienschiff* (Ship of the Line - Battleship) & *kleine Kreuzer* (Light Cruiser).

14   Mallmann Showell 1979 p.10.

<table>
<tr><td colspan="3" align="center">FIGURE 1E-16 ORGANISATION OF THE REICHSMARINE
1922</td></tr>
</table>

	Chef der Marineleitung - Adm.Paul Behncke	
	Chef der **Marinestation Ostsee** (Kiel) - VizeAdm.Ernst Frhr.von Gagern	
Naval Forces Ostsee	Linienschiff	*Hannover*
	Kleine Kreuzer	*Berlin*
		Medusa
		Thetis
	Vermessungsschiff	*Panther*
		I.(Torpedoboots) Flottille
		5.Torpedosboots-Halbflottille
Land Forces Ostsee	Küstenwehr-Abteilung	I
		III
		V
Schiffstammdivision der Ostsee		
	Chef der **Marinestation Nordsee** (Wilhelmshaven) - VizeAdm.Hans Zenker	
Naval Forces Nordsee	Linienschiff	*Braunschweig*
	Kleine Kreuzer	*Arcona*
		Hamburg
		II. (Torpedoboots) Flottille
		11.Torpedosboots-Halbflottille
Land Forces Ostsee	Küstenwehr-Abteilung	II
		IV
		VI
Schiffsstammdivision der Nordsee		

modern *Kleine Kreuzer Emden* during the course of a world cruise *(Photo 1E-12)*. From March 1928 he attended a year-long *Fahnrichs-Lehrgang* (Officer Candidate Course) at the *Marineschule Murwik* (Flensburg) (Naval School) during which he spent two spells of training aboard the *Vermessungsschiff Meteor* (Survey Ship). He then began his operational training with a succession of four specialist *Waffen-Lehrgange* (Weapons Courses) at the *Torpedo-und Nachrichtenschule* (Torpedo and Signals School) (March 1929), the *Sperrschule* (Minewarfare School)(July 1929), an *Infanterie-Lehrgang II./ Schiffsstammdivision Stralsund* (Infantry Course) (August 1929) and finally an *Artillerie-Lehrgang* (Gunnery Course) at the *Schiffsartillerieschule* (Naval Gunnery School)(October 1929). By February 1930 *Fahnrich zur See* Christian was considered sufficiently competent to be assigned for a year's further operational training as an Ensign aboard the *Linienschiffen Elsass* and *Schleswig-Holstein*. He was finally commissioned on the 1 October 1930. During this period he also attended a *Flak-Maschinenwaffen-Lehrgang* (Light Anti-Aircraft Artillery Course)(July 1930) before being returned to the *Torpedo-und Nachrichtenschule* for a three month *Funk-Lehrgang* (Wireless Course) from January 1931. Just under five years after entering the *Reichsmarine Lt.z.See* Christian was finally ready for his first service posting: on the 29 March 1931 he returned to the *Schleswig-Holstein* as that vessel's *III.Funk-und Horch-Offizier* (3rd.Wireless Intercept Officer).[15]

Competition for places as non-commissioned personnel: *Matrosen* (Seamen) with possible advancement to *Maat* and *Obermaat, Bootsmann* and *Oberbootsmann (Unteroffiziere)*, was just as fierce. In 1926 there were 51,391 applicants for a total of 1,200 places; a success rate for those who were accepted of just 2.8 %.[16] Initial training at one of the two *Schiffsstamm-Divisionen* was followed by a specialist *Lehrgang* (Training Course) in such trades as *Schutze* (Gunner), *Maschinist* (Mechanician), *Sperrmechaniker* (Mine Artificer), *Torpedomechaniker* (Torpedo Artificer), *Artilleriemechaniker* (Armourer), *Fernschreiber* (Telegraphist) or *Funker* (Wireless Operator). *Matrosen-Bootsmann* (Ordinary Seamen) were trained as deck ratings.[17] Under the terms of the Treaty of Versailles it was expected that enlisted personnel would serve for twelve years, whilst officers served a twenty-five year engagement. No reserves were permitted, nor could merchant seamen be given naval training.[18]

Unlike their contemporaries in the *Reichsheer*, naval personnel were not permanently assigned to a unit or base. This reflected the vagaries of naval operations as well as the need to crew a wide range of different types of vessel. Assignments were deliberately varied and of necessity of much shorter duration than was found in military units. The post war service career of *Oblt.z.See* Carl Köchy, a former wartime pilot with the *II.Seeflieger-Abteilung* at Norderney and Wilhelmshaven, illustrates this pattern of employment with sea duty interspersed with shore-based assignments.[19] In August 1920 he was assigned for twelve months of sea duty as *Wach-Offizier* (Officer of the Watch) with the *8.Minensuch-Halbflottille* (8th Minesweeper Half-Flotilla) before undertaking a three month *Sport-Lehrgang* (Sports Course) at the *Marinestation der Nordsee*. In December 1921 he was assigned to the crew of the *Linienschiff Braunschweig* as *Sport-und Zug-Offizier* (Sport and Platoon Officer) where he served until re-assignment as *Wach-Offizier* aboard the *Größer Torpedoboot W 2 (II.Torpedoboots-Flottille)* in October 1922. After a further two years' sea duty Köchy was posted to *Küstenwehr-Abteilung II* (Coastal Defence Batallion) as *Chef 3.(Artillerie) Kompanie*, this unit becoming the *3.(Flak) Kompanie* of the *Marine-Artillerie-Abteilung II* (Naval Artillery Batallion) in October 1926. Further sea duty followed between September 1927 and September 1929 as *Wach-Offizier* with the rank of *KptLt.* aboard the modernised *Linienschiff Schlesien*. During this period he also attended a *Lehrgang* at the *Schiffsartillerie-Schule* and a *Flak-Lehrgang* (Anti-Aircraft Artillery Course) at the *Küstenartillerie-Schule* (Coastal Artillery School) before becoming *Bild-Offizier* (Photographic Officer) with the *Stab der Marinestation Ostsee*. During 1931/32 he was on the staff of the *Flotten-Kommandos* (Fleet Command). Finally in September 1932 *KptLt.*Köchy was

---

15   Service record for Eckhard Christian in Hildebrand 1990 pp.155-156. See also *Chronolgy* in Mallmann Showell J.P. 1999 *German Navy Handbook 1939-1945* (hereafter cited as Mallmann Showell 1999) p.viii.

16   Ostertag R. 1986 *Deutsche Minensucher: 80 Jahre Seeminenabwehr* (hereafter cited as Ostertag 1986) p.51.

17   Mallmann Showell 1979 p.147 & 1999 p.227. Other trades included: *Sanitäts* (Medical Personnel), *Marineartillerie* (Coastal Gunnery), *Kraftfahrer* (Driver), *Verwaltungs* (Administrative Personnel), *Signal* (Signalmen), *Musik* (Bandsmen), *Flugmelder* (Aircraft Spotter) & *Zimmer* (Carpenter). For equivalent trades in the Royal Navy – see Golding H. (Ed.) Undated *The Wonder Book of the Navy* pp.70-71.

18   Mallmann Showell 1979 p.10.

19   Service record for Carl Köchy in Hildebrand K.F.1991 *Die Generale der deutschen Luftwaffe 1935-1945 Band 2 H-N* (hereafter cited as Hildebrand 1991) pp.196-197. Köchy began his service with the *Kaiersliche Marine* in Aug 14 and was trained as a naval officer prior to pilot training at Wilhelmshaven from Sep 17. Following the Armistice he continued to fly with the *vorläufige Reichsmarine* being attached to the *Seeflugstation Wilhelmshaven* & *List auf Sylt* until Aug 20.

assigned to the *Linienschiff Hessen* as *II.Artillerie-Offizier* (2nd Gunnery Officer).[20]

Comparatively few former *Fliegeroffiziere* were given permanent commissions in the *Reichsmarine* and unlike their counterparts in the *Reichsheer* they were for the most part young officers without command experience. None of the *Marine-Luftstreitkräfte* (Naval Air Arm)'s four surviving holders of the *Pour le Mérite* were retained: KptLt.Horst Treusch von Buttlar-Brandenfels *(Marine-Luftschiffverbände)*, *Oblt.z.See* Gotthardt Sachsenburg *(Kdr.Marine-Jagdgeschwader)*, KptLt.d.Res. Friedrich Christiansen *(Ltr.Seeflugstation Zeebrugge)* and Lt.d.Res.Theodor Osterkamp *(Fhr. II.Marine- Feldjagdstaffel)*.[21] Nor were the *Marine-Luftstreitkräfte's* more senior personnel retained by the *Reichsmarine: Kpt.z.See* Otto Kranzbuhler *(Marineflugchef)* was discharged as a *KonAdm.* on the 29 November 1919, whilst *Kpt.z.See* Hans Herr *(Kdr.d.Luftfahrwesens des Marinekorps* until November 1917) was discharged on the 26 January 1920 also with the rank of *KonAdm.*[22] In all just 20 former *Seefliegeroffiziere* were retained.[23]

In the immediate post war years the *vorläufige Reichsmarine* had focused its efforts and resources on mine clearance in both the Deutsche Bucht where defensive barrages had been laid to prevent incursions by the Royal Navy, whilst in the Ostsee defensive barrages protected a number of coastal shipping lanes and had helped to secure the entrance to the Finnischen Meerbusen thus neutralising the Russian Fleet anchored at Kronstadt near St.Petersburg.[24] In early 1919 27,000 officers and men in a total of four *Minensuch-Flottillen* (Minesweeping Flotillas) were operating in the Nordsee together with a further five *Flottillen* in the Ostsee with a total of 266 *Minensuchbooten*, *A-und F-Booten, Torpedobooten* and requisitioned fishing vessels. The scale and importance of this dangerous task can be seen by the fact that as late as November 1920 there were still five *Minensuch-Flottillen* in operation with 33 *Minensuch-Booten* and 19 *Torpedobooten (Photo 1E-13)*.[25] The *Marineluftsreitkrafte* played a supportive role in the aerial spotting role, continuing to operate as many as 100 *Seeflugzeuge* (Seaplanes) up to August 1920 from a number of naval air stations including Wilhelmshaven, Norderney, List auf Sylt and Kiel-Holtenau.[26]

---

20   Service record for Carl Köchy in Hildebrand 1991 pp.156-157. During the 148 months between Aug 20 – Dec 32, Köchy spent 47% on sea duty, 48% on land & 5% on training courses.

21   Angolia and Hackney 1984 pp.174-177 (Christiansen), 188-189 (Buttlar-Brandenfels), 228-231 (Sachsenberg) & 238-239 (Osterkamp). The fifth *Seeflieger* to be awarded the *Plm* was FregKpt.Peter Strasser, the *Fhr.d.Luftschiffe*, who was killed in action aboard the *L 70* on the 5 Mar 18 – see Angolia and Hackney 1984 pp.148-151 & Cole C. and Cheesman E.F. 1984 *The Air Defence of Great Britain 1914-1918* p.15 & pp.437-440. The decision not to retain these men can be attributed in part of the *Reserve* status of two of the four officers. *Oblt.z.See* Gotthard Sachsenberg was directed by the *Kaiserliche Marine's Verwaltungs-Amt* in 1919 to establish a combat unit to support the *Freikorps* fighting against Bolshevik forces in the eastern territories. Lt.d.Res.Theo Osterkamp & *Lt.z.See* Brockhoff were *Staffelkäpitane* within the *Geschwader Sachsenberg* – see Ries K. 1970 *Luftwaffe Bd.1 Die Maulwurfe 1919-1935* (hereafter cited as Ries 1970) pp.13-14 & Hooton E.R. 1994 *Phoenix Triumphant: The Rise and Rise of the Luftwaffe* (hereafter cited as Hooton 1994) pp.22-23.

22   Jung D., Wenzel B. and Abendroth A. 1977 *Die Schiffe und Boote der deutschen Seeflieger 1912-1976* (hereafter cited as Jung et al 1977) pp.393-394.

23   Jung et al 1977 p.43, Hildebrand K.F.1990-92 *Die Generale der deutschen Luftwaffe 1935-1945" Band 1-3* (hereafter cited as Hildebrand 1990-92) & Hooton 1994 p.29. It has been suggested elsewhere that by 1921 the Reichsmarine had just 15 naval aviators – see Corum J.S. 1997 *The Luftwaffe: Creating the Operational Air War 1918-1940* (hereafter cited as Corum 1997) p.79.

24   Ostertag 1986 pp.45-50.

25   Thienemann E. 'Der deutsche Minenraumdienst' in *Marine Rundschau* Vol.I Feb 1961 in Suchenwirth R. Prof. 1968 *The Development of the German Air Force 1919-1939* USAF Historical Studies No.160 (hereafter cited as Suchenwirth 1968) p.41 & Ostertag 1986 p.52. Such was the scale of this work that all *Minensuchbooten* had been withdrawn from the front line by 1922 for refurbishment and in the case of the older vessels for diposal. The first *Minensuchhalbflottille* to be formed by the *Reichsmarine* appears to have been established in Oct 24 under *KorvKpt.* Hugo Schmidt at Kiel with just 4 minesweepers: *M 113, M 122, M 136 & M 145.* See service record for Hugo Schmidt in Hildebrand 1992 pp.207-208.

26   Suchenwirth 1968 p.41, Kurowski F.1979 *Seekrieg aus der Luft* (hereafter cited as Kurowski 1979) p.17 & Hooton 1994 p.29. *Lt.z.See* Carl Köchy was a *FF* and *Schrifts-Offz.*(Records Officer) at Wilhelmshaven Oct-Nov 19, List

FIGURE 1E-17 KNOWN SEEFLIEGEROFFIZIERE IN THE REICHSMARINE	
Oblt.z.See Fried.Arnauld de la Periere	Ltr.Seeflugstation Zeebrugge (PoW 17 Dec 15)
Oblt.z.See Hermann Bruch	FF.i.Marine Flieger Abteilung
Oblt.z.See Busse ?	*Not known*
Oblt.z.See Joachim Coeler	FF.i.I.See-Flieger-Abteilung
Lt.z.See Hans-Arnim Czech	FF.i.Seeflugstation Norderney
KptLt. Walther Faber	Adjutant u.Referent i.Marine-Flugchefs
Oblt.z.See Frankenberg u.Proschlitz	*Not known*
Oblt.z.See Hans Geisler	Stab Marine-Flugchefs
Oblt.z.See Werner Goette ?	*Not known*
Oblt. z.See Günther Horstmann	Wach.Offz.Luftschiff L63
Lt.z.See Ulrich Kessler	FF.i.II.See-Flieger-Abteilung
Lt.z.See Carl Köchy	FF.i.II.See-Flieger-Abteilung
Oblt.z.See Otto Krueger	Ltr.Seeflugstation Reval
Oblt.z.See Walther Lech	Fhr.Reisenflugzeug-Kommandos Norderney
Lt.z.See Hans Metzner	FF.i.Kommando der Hochseeflotte
Oblt.z.See Hans Ritter	2.Adjutant I.See-Flieger-Abteilung
Lt.z.See Ernst-August Roth	FF.i.II.See-Flieger-Abteilung
Oblt.z.See Ernst Schirlitz	Wach.Offz.Luftschiff L33 (PoW 24 Sep 16)
Oblt.z.See Schuz ?	*Not known*
Oblt.z.See Hans Siburg	FF i.Seeflieger-Versuchs-Kdo

Despite the Allied prohibition the contribution to naval operations provided by the wartime *Marine-Fliegerverbände* had been fully acknowledged and Trotha had quickly established a *Referent für Seeflugwesen (Referent A II 1)* (Staff Advisor for Naval Aviation) within the *Flotten-Abteilung* of the *Marineleitung*.[27] *KptLt.*Walther Faber was appointed to this post in February 1920.[28] Faber was the most senior serving *Marinefliegeroffizier* and one of Germany's earliest naval

Nov 19 – Jan 20 & Wilhelmshaven Jan-Aug 20 before being re-assigned to the *8.Minensuch-Halbflottille* in the Nordsee as *Wach-Offz.* – see service record for Carl Köchy in Hildebrand 1991 pp.196-197. Another source suggests that the use of aircraft was authorised until Oct 19 – see Ries 1970 p.14.

27 Hooton 1994 p.29 & Corum 1997 p.79. At the close of hostilities the *Marine-Fliegerverbände* had a strength of 16,122 officers and men of whom 2,116 were aircrew. In all there were 1,478 aircraft on charge of which 673 were first line and 334 were training floatplanes. The *Marine-Fliegerverbände* was deployed geographically under the operational command of the: *KoFl.d.Hochseestreitkräfte* (List/Sylt, Helgoland, Norderney & Borkum); *KoFl.b.Festungs Gouvernement Wilhelmshaven* (Tondern, Nordholz, Barge, Wangerooge & Hage); *KdFl.d.Ostseestreitkräfte* (Apenrade, Flensburg, Holtenau, Warnemünde & Putzig); *KoFl.b.Befehlshaber d.Balitischen Gewasser* (Libau & Windau plus the tender *Glydwr*); *KoFl.b.Marine Corps Flandern* (Zeebrugge & Ostende); *Fhr.d.Luftschiffe* (Nordholz, Ahlhorn, Duren, Fühlsbuttel, Hage, Jüterbog, Kiel, Seddin, Seerappen, Tondern, Wainoden & Wildeshausen). Naval air stations and facilities were also established at Chanak in the Dardanelles, Kawak on the Bosphrous, Xanthi in Greece, Varna & Zupuldak in Bulgaria and at Constanta & Duingi in Romania – see Nowarra H.J. 1966 *Marine Aircraft of the 1914-1918 War* (hereafter cited as Nowarra 1966) pp.13-14 & Thompson A. 2013 *Küstenflieger: The Operational History of the German Coastal Air Service 1935-1944* (hereafter cited as Thompson 2013) pp.13-14.

28 Service record for Walther Faber in Axis Biographical Research in www.reocities.com (hereafter cited as ABR in Reocities) & Thompson 2013 p.18. Faber was a member of the *Reichsmarineamt* Mar-Jul 19 and the *Admiralitat* Jul 19-Sep 20. He served with the *Friedenskommission* (Armistice Commission) as part of the *Gruppe Marineluftfahrt*

aviators having completed his flying training in May 1913. His wartime service had included a period as *Leiter der Seeflugstation List auf Sylt* in 1915/16, service with *See-Flieger-Abteilung I* in the east during 1916 and as *Adjutant und Referent (Flieger-Ausbildungs)* with the *Marineflugchef* during 1917/19.[29] Initially Faber worked alone to draw lessons from the recently concluded conflict, whilst attempting to preserve the spirit of naval aviation during this difficult period.[30] In one respect the *Reichsmarine* was more fortunate than the Reichsheer as the Allied powers accepted that it was reasonable for the *Reichsmarine* to maintain an anti-aircraft capability, both within the context of its coastal fortifications and also at sea aboard its operational warships.[31] Of course the maintenance of such a capability required regular and realistic training and to this end *Oblt.z.See* Hans Ritter was authorised to purchase six war-surplus Friedrichshafen FF.49 *Seeflugzeuge* for the sum of 6,000 marks for the aircraft and their 200 hp Benz engines.[32] These reliable two-seat floatplanes had already proved admirable aircraft for coastal patrol duties having a range of 690 kms as well as an ability to alight in comparatively rough waters.[33] Clearly the FF 49s could not be overtly connected to the *Reichsmarine* and the commercial firm of *Deutscher Aero Lloyd AG* was therefore contracted from 1924 to fly and maintain the aircraft (See also 1D2).[34]

Faber remained as *Referent für Seeflugwesen* (Staff Advisor for Naval Aviation) until the end of March 1923 when he was re-assigned as *Navigations-Offizier* (Navigating Officer) aboard the *Kleine Kreuzer Medusa*. He would not return to further the cause of naval aviation.[35] His successor within the *Flotten-Abteilung* as *Referent für Flugwesen und Luftschütz* (Staff Advisor for Naval

---

Feb-Sep 20. By which time he had also been appointed to the *Marineleitung* (Feb 20) – see *Anhang C Zeittafel* in Caspari H.A. Dr. (Ed.) Undated *E-Stellen Travemünde und Tarnewitz 3.Band – Die Geschichte der Seeflugzeug-Eprobungsstelle Travemünde und daraus hervorgegangenen E-Stelle für Flugzeugbewaffnung Tarnewitz* (hereafter cited as Caspari (Ed.) Bd.3) p.291 & Kossler K. *The E-Stelle Travemünde* in Beauvais H., Kossler K., Mayer M. and Regel C. 2002 *German Secret Flight Test Centres to 1945: Johannisthal, Lipetsk, Rechlin, Travemünde, Tarnewitz, Peenemunde-West* (hereafter cited as Kossler in Beauvais et al 2002) p.131. See also Hooton 1994 p.29.

29   Service record for Walther Faber in ABR in Reocities. However Faber was not *Marineflugchef* as suggested by one source – see Thompson 2013 p.18. See also Kilduff P. 1991 *Germany's First Air Force 1914-1918* (hereafter cited as Kilduff 1991) p.88.

30   Hooton 1994 p.29. Neither the *vorlaufuge Reichsmarine* nor its permanent successor seems to have taken aviation as seriously as the *Reichsheer*. A comprehensive review of the performance of the *Marine-Fliegerverbände* does not appear to have taken place. However the *Marineleitung* was keen for the *Reichsmarine* to preserve the skills and technology for the operation of naval aircraft including floatplanes and airships against the time when such aircraft could once again be employed – see Corum 1997 pp.78-79.

31   Hooton 1994 p.29.

32   Schliephake H. 1971 *The Birth of the Luftwaffe* (hereafter cited as Schliephake 1971) p.15. *Oblt.z.See* Ritter had been *Stationsleiter der Kampffliegerschule Langfuhr* (Danzig), later *Stationsleiter List auf Sylt, Helgoland* & *Norderney* during the period Jan 19 – Sep 20. See service record for Hans Ritter in Hildebrand 1992 pp.116-117. The six FF.49 floatplanes were purchased in Jan 23 – see Ries 1970 p.41.

33   Nowarra 1966 pp.30-31. A total of 240 Friedrichshafen FF.49 *Seeflugzeuge* had been built for the *Marinefliegerverbände* during 1917-18. They were employed in coastal reconnaissance and *U-Boot* escort duties, chiefly in the Nordsee area of operations where their good water characteristics were a particular advantage.

34   Schliephake 1971 pp.15-16. This contract was important to *DAL* which was formed during the early part of 1923 as part of a further rationalisation of Germany's post-war air transport operators. The effects of the 1923 economic crash were beginning to bite. It is thought that the six FF.49 aircraft used for naval support duties were D-40, 45, 47, 49, 85 & 86. Certainly D-40, 47, 49 & 85 were all registered to *Aerosport* prior to their use with *Severa* – see *Aircraft used by the German Navy and registered to Severa/Luftdienst, RDL E-Stelle Travemünde and DVS 1925-1933* in Andersson L. 1989 'Secret Luftwaffe: German Military Aviation Build-up between the Wars' in *Air Enthusiast* No.41 1989 (hereafter cited as Andersson 1989) p.48 & Stroud J.1966 *European Transport Aircraft since 1910* (hereafter cited as Stroud 1966) pp.278-280.

35   Service record for Walther Faber in ABR Reocities. From this point Faber's career took a different course. In Jun 24 he became a *Referent* with the *Insp.d.Torpedo-u.Minenwesen*, in Jun 28 *1.Offz.*on the *kleine Kreuzer Emden* during a World cruise before being detached to the *Technische Hochschule Berlin* Jan 30 – Mar 32. He was then *C.d.S.u.Insp.i.V.i.Insp.d.Torpedo- u.Minenwesen* Mar 32 – Oct 34 with the rank of *Kpt.z.See* before joining the *TVK Eckernförde* Oct 34 – Sep 35. See also Mallmann Showell 1999 p.viii.

Aviation and Air Defence) was *KptLt.*Ritter. Ritter had just completed five months as *Kommandant Artillerieschulboot Drache*, a support vessel attached to the *Schiffsartillerie-Schule* at Kiel-Wik. Ritter had learned to fly in 1916 and had initially been assigned to the *Seeflugstation Angernsee* in Kurland. In March 1917 he had attended a *Lehrgang* at the *Kampfeinsitzer-Schule Danzig* before joining the *Seefliegerstaffel Flandern* where he flew single seat fighters over Belgium. As an *Oblt.z.See* he was *2.Adjutant I.Seeflieger-Abteilung* from March 1918 until January 1919.[36]

In 1924 Ritter was successful in gaining funds to establish the *Seeflugzeug-Versuchsabteilung (Severa GmbH)* at Warnemünde, ostensibly as a successor to the *Deutscher Aero Lloyd* operation whose FF.49 floatplanes had provided targets for naval gunnery practice, but in reality as a training and experimental establishment for the development of German naval aviation *(Photo 1E-14).*[37] With its head office in Berlin and its operating bases at the former *Seeflugstationen* at Norderney in the central Ost Friesische Inseln and at Kiel-Holtenau in Schleswig-Holstein, this overtly civilian concern was provided with an ever increasing annual budget. By 1928 this had reached RM 1,350,000.[38] Under the direction of Theo Osterkamp and Hans von Schiller, *Severa* soon attracted the services of several former *Marineflieger* in the form of Eberhard Cranz, Gerhard Hubrich, von Roques, Theodor Rowehl and Rudolf Stark.[39]

With great difficulty Ritter also completed arrangements for the ab initio flight training of serving naval officers. Under the terms of the Paris Aviation Convention only six officers could receive flight training annually, these numbers being closely monitored by the *Interalliierte Luftfahrt-Überwachungs-Kommission (ILUK).*[40] In 1924 *Oblte.z.See* Alex von Blessingh and Georg-Hermann Edert became the first *Reichsmarine* officers to be trained as pilots, this being carried out at the *Aerosport GmbH* at Warnemünde where former naval pilot Walter Bachmann proved especially sympathetic to the *Reichsmarine's* needs.[41] Other training was covertly carried out by *Severa* at Norderney and Holtenau, including that of technical personnel and *Beobachteren* (observers).[42]

Of equal importance was the covert acquisition of modern naval aircraft. The *Ruhr Krise* (Ruhr Crisis) of January 1923 had provided the political imperative for such action and *Kpt.z.See* Günther Lohmann, the *Chef des Seetransport-Abteilung* (Chief of the Naval Transport Department) within the *Allgemeine-Marineamt* (General Naval Office), was authorised to secretly provide the funding for ten Heinkel HE 1 *Seeflugzeuge* (See also 1A2 & 1C4).[43] Heinkel was no stranger to naval

---

36   Thompson 2013 p.21. This source suggests that Faber was replaced by briefly by *Oblt.z.See* Werner Goette and then by *Oblt.z.See* Wolfgang Cesar although this is not substantiated elsewhere and these officers were of junior rank. On the 8 Nov 17 *Lt.z.See* Ritter was shot down unharmed to the west of Dunkerque. He did not score any *Luftsiege* as a *Marine-Jagdflieger* – see service record for Hans Ritter in Hildebrand 1992 pp.116-117 & Franks N., Bailey F. and Duiven R. 1996 *The Jasta Pilots: Detailed listings and histories August 1916 - November 1918* (hereafter cited as Franks el al 1996) p.314.

37   Suchenwirth 1968 p.42, Ries 1970 p.41, Schliephake 1971 p.16, Mason 1973 p.145 & Kurowski 1979 p.17. See also Corum 1997 p.80.

38   Hooton 1994 p.61.

39   Kurowski 1979 p.17. *Lt.d.Res.a.D.*Osterkamp was *Stationsleiter Holtenau* between 1926-31 before occupying a similar position at Norderney – see service record for Theodor Osterkamp in Hildebrand 1992 pp.12-13. Hans von Schiller may then have been *Stationsleiter Holtenau.*

40   Schliephake 1971 p.16.

41   Jung et al 1977 p.44, Kurowski 1979 p.18, Andersson 1989 p.43 & Carlsen S. and Meyer M. 1998 *Die Flugzeugführer Ausbildung der deutschen Luftwaffe 1935-1945 Bd.I Von der Grundausbildung bis zur Blindflugschule* (hereafter cited as Carlsen and Meyer 1998) p.56. Walter Bachmann was the *Direktor* of *Aerosport GmbH* at Warnemünde – see Lange B. 1970 *Das Buch der deutschen Luftfahrtechnik* (hereafter cited as Lange 1970) p.171. *Lt.d.Res.*Bachmann was a former naval pilot with *Seefrontstaffel II* – se Franks et al 1996 p.307.

42   Kurowski 1979 p.18, Andersson 1989 p.43 & Thompson 2013 p.24.

43   Jung et al 1977 p.44 & Andersson 1989 p.43. Although subordinate to the *Flotten-Abteilung*, the *Referent für Flugwesen und Luftschütz* was actually concealed within the *Allgemeinesamt* (General Office) as *Ref A II 1*. See also Siehe in Gardiner and Chesneau (Ed.) 1980 p.219.

aviation having been chief designer at the *Hansa Brandenburgische Flugzeugwerke* between 1914 and 1919 after earlier employment in both the *Albatros* and *LVG* concerns. He had been personally responsible for the highly successful W 29 and W 33 fighter floatplanes which had been used with great effectiveness against the British during 1917-18 by *KptLt.d.Res.*Friedrich Christiansen's *IC Staffel* at Zeebrugge and it was an improved version of the W 29 that Ritter sought to obtain for the *Reichsmarine (Photo 1E-15)*.[44] As the S 1 this aircraft was already in production with the *Svenska Aero AB* at Lidingo for the Swedish Navy.[45] The contract for the German machines was placed by *KptLt.a.D.*Walter Hormel, a *Direktor* of the *Hugo Stinnes* concern.[46] The aircraft were constructed in secret at Heinkel's Warnemünde works and the components were then shipped across the Baltic to Sweden where the aircraft were assembled and tested before being placed in store in a warehouse in Stockholm harbour (See also 1C1).[47]

Ernst Heinkel's relationship with *Svenska Aero* was mirrored by that of Hugo Junkers whose Dessau based *Junkers Flugzeug-und Motorenwerke AG* had secretly financed the establishment of *AB Flygindustri* at Limhamn near Malmo in Sweden in 1925.[48] In addition to assembling commercial aircraft such as the Junkers F 13 and G 23/24 this works was involved in the modification of these types for military and naval purposes, initially in support of Junkers' contracts to supply the *VVS-RKKA* (Soviet Air Force) with combat aircraft (See 1C1).[49] As a result of both of these arrangements the *Marineleitung* did not consider it to be useful to become involved in the establishment of covert testing and training installations in Russia despite the offer of a combined land and sea base near Odessa on the Black Sea coast (See 1D1).[50]

Whilst the acquisition of the HE 1 floatplanes can be seen to be a contingency measure similar to that of the *Reichsheer's* purchase of the Fokker D.XIII fighters, Lohmann was also anxious to support aircraft design and development within Germany itself (See 1A2 & 1C4). To this end he became interested in the fortunes of the *Caspar-Werke GmbH* at Lübeck-Travemünde.[51] Secret financial support for Heinkel, Caspar and other companies such as the *LFG* at Stralsund and the Berlin based *Rohrbach Metall-Flugzeugbau GmbH* was to result in the design and construction of several naval prototypes during the early to mid-twenties when it was still impossible to manufacture warplanes in series.[52] At Travemünde these took the form of the Caspar CJ 14 *Jagdflugzeug* (Fighter Aircraft) and the CS 14 *Marine-Aufklärungsflugzeug* (Naval reconnaissance Aircraft), whilst at

44 Heinkel E. 1956 *He 1000* (hereafter cited as Heinkel 1956) pp.48-67. & Kilduff 1991 pp.97-100. For details of the Brandenburg W 29 & W 33 – see Nowarra 1966 p.75. As *Ltr.d.Seeflugstation Zeebrugge, Oblt.d.Res.*Christiansen had been decorated with the *Plm* on the 11 Dec 17 – see Angolia and Hackney 1984 pp.174-177.

45 Heinkel 1956 pp.72-74. To circumvent the activities of the *ILUK*, Heinkel had entered into an agreement with the Swedish *Svenska Aero AB* to manufacture his designs. This arrangement had been greatly facilitated by the good offices of *Oblt.z.See a.D.*Carl Clemens Bucker, then resident in Sweden. See also Koos V. 2006 *Typenbucher Deutsche Luftfahrt: Ernst Heinkel Flugzeugwerke 1922-1932* (hereafter cited as Koos 2006) pp.13-15.

46 Koos 2006 p.13. Walter Hormel was an early naval aviator (DLV Licence Nr.100, 24 Aug 11) who had been *Stationsleiter Warnemünde* during the Great War - see Angolia and Hackney 1984 p.15.

47 Koos 2006 p.13. With the WNr.202-211 the ten HE 1 floatplanes were assembled in Sweden, the first being tested by Carl Bucker on the 7 Nov 23.

48 Schmitt G. 1988 *Hugo Junkers and his Aircraft* (hereafter cited as Schmitt 1988) p.146.

49 Schmitt 1988 p.147 & pp.153-159. Modifications were made at Limhamm to the Junkers A 20 Srs (R 02) and also to the G 23 Srs (R 42) to make them suitable for naval employment – see also Andersson 1989 p.45.

50 Jung et al 1977 p.45 & Kossler in Beauvais et al 2002 p.131.

51 Lange 1970 p.181 & Kossler in Beauvais et al 2002 p.131. *Dr.jur.*Karl Caspar had been an aircraft constructor since 1911. In 1918 he established his own company at Priwall on the Travemünde.

52 Lange 1970 pp.350-351. Rohrbach's Danish subsidiary was also known as *Dansk Aero*. Caspar designed naval prototype aircraft included the U1/U2 *Bordflugzeug für Unterseeboote* (1921), S 1 & S 2 (HE 1 & HE 2) *Mehrzweckflugzegug* (1922-23) CJ 14 & CS 14 *Jagdeinsitzer* (1924), C 27 *Marine-Seeflugzeug* (1926), C 30 *Nahaufklärer* (1926), C 33 *Jagd-Schulzweisitzer* (1928) & C 36 *Mehrzweckflugzeug* (1928) - see Lange 1970 pp.181-183 & Nowarra H.J. 1980 *Die Verbotenen Flugzeuge 1921-1935 – Die getarnte Luftwaffe* pp.86-87, 88-89, 98-99, 102-104, 124-127 & 164-165.

Copenhagen the innovative all-metal Rohrbach Ro II *Flugboot* (Flying Boat) was completed in 1923. Although not recognised by the *FAI*, no doubt on account of its "illegal" pedigree, the Ro II went on to achieve no less than seven international speed and range records.[53] Meanwhile at Warnemünde the HE 1 was further developed into the HE 4 and 5, the latter being the first "complex" type to be manufactured in series following the lifting of restrictions in 1926.[54]

However the wider activities of *Kpt.z.See* Lohmann were to be of even greater long term significance for this officer had been tasked with sponsoring the clandestine development of both submarines and naval aircraft on behalf of the *Reichsmarine*.[55] Using money from the sale of surplus naval equipment as well as that provided from German industrial interests via the *Ruhrfond* (Ruhr Fund), Lohmann was able to subsidise a variety of ventures at both home and abroad to the long term benefit of the *Reichsmarine* (See 1A2). In the Netherlands he subsidised the Dutch firm of *NV Ingenieurskantoor voor Scheepsbouw* in their construction of submarines for other naval powers and in so doing kept German naval architects abreast of the latest thinking and constructional techniques.[56] In Germany he placed orders for experimental coastal motor boats which would be capable of torpedo attacks with the *Travemünde Yachthafen AG*. During 1923-26 six former *Kaiserliche Marine LM Unterseeboote-Zerstörer* (Submarine Destroyer) motor boats were re-commissioned to which further experimental craft were added including the *Narwal*, a motor torpedo boat capable of 34.8 knts, which was built by the *Caspar-Werke* at Travemünde.[57]

The re-establishment of the *Reichsmarine's* fighting capability continued under *Adm.*Hans Zenker who succeeded *Adm.*Behncke on the 1 October 1924 *(Photo 1E-16)*.[58] The refurbishment of the *Linienschiff* resulted in the re-commissioning of the *Elsass* (1924) and *Hessen* (1925). The existing units *Braunschweig* and *Hannover* were de-commissioned in 1926-27 and replaced by *Schlesien* and *Schleswig-Holstein*.[59] In the meantime the de-commissioning and sale of the *Kleine Kreuzer Niobe* in 1925 permitted the commissioning of the *Reichsmarine's* first new major warship, the *Kleine Kreuzer Emden*. Her construction had been delayed by the economic crisis of 1923 but

---

53   Lange 1970 p.182 & 351, Nowarra 1980 pp.96-98 & Haagen R. and Caspari H.A.Dr. *Rohrbach-Flugboote* in Caspari Undated Bd.3 pp.68-82.

54   Heinkel 1956 pp.103-104 & Koos 2006 pp.21-25. In all 17 HE 5 floatplanes were manufactured by *Heinkel* at Warnemünde, mainly for use by the *DVS*. Two examples were sold to the USSR, the rest were entered on the German civil register. A further 22 S 5A aircraft were completed in Sweden for military use.

55   Sieche in Gardiner and Chesneau (Ed.) 1980 p.219. *Kpt.z.See* Günther Lohmann was an astute and knowledgeable officer with a sound economic background. Through his contacts with industry and the shipping companies he was able to build up a network of fictitious firms across Europe that enabled the *Reichsmarine* to profit from prohibited weapons development including aircraft and submarines.

56   Sieche in Gardiner and Chesneau (Ed.) 1980 p.219. The *IvS* was managed by *Dr.Ing.*Hans Techel & *KorvKpt.a.D.*Hans Blum. The wartime UB III & UC III boats were further developed. Two smaller *U-Booten* were then built for Turkey, these being delivered in 1928, whilst three *U-Booten* were built for Finland and delivered in 1930. All five submarines were tested by former German naval submariners. A further boat was designed to meet a Spanish order but the vessel was eventually sold to Turkey. The final project was a small 250 ton coastal submarine for Finland that became the forerunner of the German Typ IIA Klas. An *Unterseeboot Referent* had secretly been established within the *Insp.d.Torpedo-u.Minenwesen* – see Padfield 1984 pp.124-125, 127, 134-136 & 140-142.

57   Sieche in Gardiner and Chesneau (Ed.) 1980 p.248. Although not specifically banned by the Treaty of Versailles the MTB was developed secretly in Germany as a cost effective way of providing an effective coastal defence force. During the 20s the *Vegesack* firm of Lurssen worked closely with the *Reichsmarine's K-Amt* to refine the design. This led to the UZ-16, later S 1, which was completed in 1930 and to the first production craft – the S 2 group of four boats in 1932 – see Mason 1973 p.145.

58   Service record for Hans Zenker in www.wikipedia.org Zenker had entered the *Kaiserliche Marine* in 1889 and was *Kdt.*of the *kleine Kreuzer Lübeck* (1911) & *Cöln* (1912/13) before becoming *Kdt.d.Linien Kreuzer von der Tann* (1916/17) – the latter during the *Skagerrakschlacht* of May 16. Thereafter he had been *Abt.Chef i.Admiralitat* (1917), *Bfr.d.Sicherung der Nordsee* (1918), *Insp.d.Marineartillerie* (1920) and *Chef d.Marinestation Nordsee* (1920-23).

59   Sieche in Gardiner and Chesneau (ed.) 1980 p.222.

she proved a worthy addition to the Fleet *(Photo 1E-17)*.[60] In October 1926 the first of six new *Größe Torpedobooten* was launched at Wilhelmshaven. The Typ 23 *Raubvogel Größe Torpedobooten* displaced 1,130 tons full load and were armed with three 10.5 cm L/45 and six 50 cm torpedoes in two triple launchers. They were capable of 32-34 knts and had a crew of 120 officers and men. These vessels would be followed by six Typ 24 *Raubtier Größe Torpedobooten* from October 1928, the last being completed in August 1929 *(Photo 1E-18)*.[61] In terms of seamanship training the pre-war practice of foreign training cruises had been re-introduced from January 1924. Each year one of the Reichsmarine's *kleine Kreuziere* would embark a class of *Fahnriche* for such a voyage which enabled the *Reichsmarine's* future *Offiziere* to learn their trade at sea, to visit foreign ports and show the Flag for Weimar Germany *(Photo 1E-19)*.[62]

In 1926 Zenker also authorised the upgrading of the *Referent für Flugwesen und Luftschütz* to the status of a covert *Gruppe* within the *Seetransport-Abteilung*. The first *Chef der Gruppe BSx (B-Amt Seetransportabteilung Gruppe x)* was *Kpt.z.See* Rudolf Lahs who took up his new post in June of that year.[63] The enlarged staff was divided into four *Referate* (Advisors/Desks) with specific responsibility for naval staff matters, training, technical matters and administration:[64]

FIGURE 1E-18 ORGANISATION OF THE GRUPPE BSx			
JUNE 1926			
Chef Gruppe BSx - Kpt.z.See Rudolf Lahs			
Führungs	**Ausbildungs**	**Technik**	**Verwaltungs**
KptLt.Hans Geisler	Oblt.z.See a.D.Wolfgang von Gronau	KptLt.Joachim Coeler	Not known

The key naval personnel in this new organisation were *KptLte.*Hans Geisler and Joachim Coeler. Geisler had just completed five months staff training *(Führergehilfen-Ausbildung)* following a short period of service as *Flieger-Referent im Stab der Marinestation der Ostsee*.[65] He would be

---

60 Siehe in Gardiner and Chesneau (Ed.) 1980 p.222 & 229. In addition the *kleine Kreuzer Nymphe* & *Amazone* were reconstructed in the early 20s before being returned to service. The *Emden* was laid down in Dec 21 but not completed until Oct 25. Despite being a new ship she did not represent any advance on Great War thinking being based on the *Cöln Klas* of 1918 with single shielded mountings (MPL) for her 8 x 15 cm SK L/45 guns – see Whitley M.J. 1985 *German Cruisers of World War Two* (hereafter cited as Whitley 1985) pp.16-19.

61 Whitley M.J. 1991 *German Destroyers of World War Two* pp.45-47.

62 Mallmann Showell 1999 pp.vii-viii. The cadet training cruises began in Jan 24 when the *kleine Kreuzer Berlin* visited the Azores, Canaries, Madeira and Spain. This was repeated in Oct 24 and Sep 25 (to South America), whilst *Emden* departed for a world cruise in Nov 26 before *Berlin* toured Australia and the Far East from Dec 27. *Emden* conducted a second world cruise from Dec 28 which was followed immediately on its return in May 29 by the newly commissioned *Karlsruhe* which sailed for the Mediterranean and S.Africa. *Emden* sailed for Africa and the Far East in Dec 30 which was followed by *Karlsruhe's* voyage to South America and Alaska from Nov 31. For details of such a training cruise – see Mahlke H. Obstlt.i.G.a.D. *Memoirs of a Stuka Pilot* (hereafter cited as Mahlke 2013) pp.21-32. *Fhn.*Mahlke was aboard the *kleine Kreuzer Köln* during a cruise to Spain, Egypt, Australia, the South Seas, Japan, China, India, the Netherlands East Indies, Ceylon, Egypt, Crete, Corfu, Italy and Spain between Dec 32 – Dec 33.

63 Andersson 1989 p.43 & Hooton 1994 p.59. Rudolf Lahs entered the *Kaiserliche Marine* in 1899 and by 1917 was *Chef 12.Torpedo-Halbflottille* as a *KorvKpt*. Post war he was *Kdr.d.Eiserne Torpedoboot-Flottille* in support of the *Marinefreikorps* prior to staff appointments in the *Flottenkdo.* & *Wehrkreis VI*. Following a period as *Kdr.Marine-Abt.Stralsund* he undertook a 2 yr cruise around Africa aboard the freighter *Adolf Woermann* in preparation for a posting as *Ltr.d.Abt. Flotten-u.Seetransport*. On the 1 Apr 28 he was re-assigned as *Ref.A II 1/Chef Gruppe BSx* and learned to fly at Lipetsk – see service record for Rudolf Lahs in www.wikipedia.org.

64 Jung et al 1977 p.45, Hooton 1994 p.59 & Kossler in Beauvais et al 2002 p.131. There was also an Intelligence Desk headed by *Lt.z.See* Werner Bartz later *KorvKpt.*Beelitz – see Thompson 2013.

65 Service record for Hans Geisler in Hildebrand 1990 pp.351-352. These had been Geisler's first aviation related posting since Sep 20. For a period in 1921 he had seen sea duty with the *6.Minensuch-Halbflottille* before becoming *Kdt.Minensuchboot M 82* from Nov 21. During Sep 22 – Mar 25 he was a *Kp.Fhr.b.d.Schiffstammdivision d.Ostsee*.

responsible for staff matters including policy formulation. Coeler had followed a very different path being trained in the employment of anti-aircraft artillery during 1923 before a posting as *Kompanie-Führer bei der Küstenwehr-Abteilung II* in 1924-25. He had than been the *Marine-Nachrichtenoffizier Wilhelmshaven* before joining the *Gruppe BSx*.[66] He would be responsible for all technical developments within the sphere of naval aviation, a particularly important post following the relaxation of Allied restrictions. Five civil engineers *(Diplom Ingenieure)* were employed to assist Coeler in the development of naval aircraft and their associated equipment.[67]

The shortage of serving *Marine-Fliegeroffiziere* necessitated the employment of a significant number of former naval aircrew and officials *(Beamten)*. One such officer was *Oblt.z.See a.D.* Wolfgang von Gronau who had seen war service with the *II.Seefliegerabteilung* in the Nordsee in 1915 and in 1917 and had carried out experimental work with the *Seeflieger- Versuchskommando Warnemünde*.[68] He was employed in a civilian capacity by the *Reichsmarine* from October 1925 to co-ordinate the expanding training programme for naval personnel. This included lectures on the employment of naval aviation within *Fahnrich-Lehrgange* at the two *Schiffstammdivisionen* as well as the provision of additional flight training places at *Seeflug GmbH* at Warnemünde.[69] During 1926 Georg Kolbe, Hans-Karl von Tresckow and Karl Wiborg were amongst those undertaking initial flight training at *Seeflug*.[70]

Fortunately the situation was then eased when a *Zweigstelle* or branch of the *Deustchen Verkehrsfliegerschule (DVS)* was established at Warnemünde in January 1927 under the direction of *KorvKpt.a.D.* Konrad Goltz (See also 1D2).[71] Under the terms of the 1926 Paris Air Agreement a limited number of naval officers were permitted to receive instruction for their *A 2, B 2* and *C-See Flugführerscheinen* (Flight Licences) alongside bona fide students from those German airlines that operated floatplanes and flying boats.[72] Within months a further *DVS Zweigstelle* was opened at the former *Seeflugstation List* on the island of Sylt under the leadership of *KptLt.a.D.* Heinz Scheurlen.[73]

---

66   Service record for Joachim Coeler in Hildebrand 1990 pp.163-164. Following the end of the war Coeler had been a *Kp.Fhr.i.d.Schiffstammdivision d.Nordsee* (Oct 20 – Feb 22) including a period aboard the *Linienschiff Braunschweig*.

67   Hildebrand 1990-92. Eisenlohr was appointed on the 1 Jan 26, Spies on the 16 Mar 27. Spies had previously been a *Hilfsreferent* within the *Reichsheer's T 2 (V) L*. He took part in the *1926 Seeflug-Bewerbe* being placed third overall in Heinkel HD 24 WNr.250 D-935 – see also Heinkel 1956 pp.103-104, Lange 1970 pp.140-141, Schliphake 1971 p.24 & Koos 2006 pp.63-65.

68   Service record for Wolfgang von Gronau in Hildebrand 1990 pp.395-396. Groener's wartime service had culminated with a posting as *1.Adj.i.Stab d.Kdrs.d.Flg.d.Hochseeflotte* in 1918. Following a brief period as *Ltr.d.Seeflugstation Wilhelmshaven*, Gronau had left the *Marine* in Nov 19 to find employment in civil aviation.

69   Siburg H. Gen.d.Flg.a.D. *Vorbereitende Massnahmen der Marineleitung auf dem Gebeits des Seeflugwesens in den Jahren 1920-1933* in A/V/1, Karlsruhe Document Collection in Suchenwirth 1968 pp.42-43. *Seeflug GmbH* was formed in Jun 25 under *KorvKpt.a.D.Konrad Goltz*. Goltz had been a leading *Marineflieger* being the *Kdr.d.Freiwilligen Marine-Fliegerkorps* and its successor the *Marine-Landflieger-Abt.* from Apr 14. In 1916/17 he had been responsible for the training and development of the *Kaiserliche Marine's* first *Torpedostaffeln* as *Fhr.SSK Flensburg*, from Jul 17 he had been *Kdr.d.Seefliger in Turkei* – see service record for Konrad Goltz in Hildebrand 1990 pp.377-378 & Thiele H. 2004 *Luftwaffe Aerial Torpedo Aircraft and Operations in World War Two* (hereafter cited as Thiele 2004) p.6. *Seeflug* also operated a *Zweigstelle* at Stettin-Altdamm – see Suchenwirth 1968 p.43. See also Kurowski 1979 p.18 & Carlsen and Meyer 1998 p.56.

70   Schack von Wittenau Graf S. 1961 *Pionierfluge eines Lufthansa-Käpitans 1926-1945* pp.33-41. Other early *Flugschuler* included: Ackermann, Dolling, Eichele, Grutering, von Lielienfeld, Lohmeyer & Palm.

71   Ries K. 1988 *Deutsche Flugzeugführerschulen und ihre Maschinen 1919-1945* (hereafter cited as Ries 1988) p.10. This source suggests that the *DVS Zweigstelle Warnemünde* was opened in 1926. However see service record for Konrad Goltz in Hildebrand 1990 p.378 & Carlsen and Meyer 1998 p.56.

72   Townsend P. 1970 *Duel of Eagles* pp.91-92. Johannes Janke, son of a *Reichsmarine Admiral*, was awarded his *C-Schein (Land u.See)* at Braunschweig & Warnemünde in 1928 prior to joining *DLH* as a commercial pilot.

73   Ries 1988 p.10. Heinz Scheurlen had been trained as a naval pilot with the *FMF* at Berlin-Johannisthal (Sep-Dec 14) before seeing service at Warnemünde, Holtenau & Libau (14-16). He was of Germany's first torpedo attack pilots from May 16 and in Mar 18 was *Fhr.d.Torpedoflugzegstaffel Zeebrugge* on the Channel coast – see Thiele 2004 p.6. He resigned from the *Reichsmarine* in Nov 19 to join the *Luft-Polizei* in Kiel. He later worked for *Junkers*

Fluglehreren (Flight Instructors) at the two *Zweigstellen* included Festner, Otto-Lutz Förster, Gerhard Nitschke, Walter Diele and H.Loll. The two *Deutschen Verkehrsfliegerschulen-See* were equipped with a range of aircraft types including the Arado W II, Dornier Do E and J, Heinkel HE 1, HE 5, HE 9 and HD 24 and the Junkers F 13, G 24 and W 33.[74] Training for *Beobachteren* began at Warnemünde on the 1 October 1928 when the *K-Gruppe* was established under the leadership of *Lt.d.Res.a.D.*Fritz Koehler, an experienced wartime observer and fighter pilot. Under the designation *Seeadler* a two year programme of instruction trained a total of 25 *Reichsmarine Offiziere* as *Flugzeugbeobachteren* in naval air tactics, aerial reconnaissance in co-operation with surface units of the *Reichsmarine*, ship identification, over-water navigation (including wireless navigation techniques), spotting for ship's guns, meteorology and the dropping of bombs and torpedoes.[75]

There was considerable interest at this time in the development of flying boats for future naval employment. The most obvious candidate was the Dornier Do J *Wal*, a type that prior to 1926 had been manufactured in quantity in Italy, but which from that date could also be built at the *Dornier-Werke GmbH's* main plant at Friedrichshafen in southern Germany.[76] During the early twenties several long-distance flights had been made with the *Wal* and given its significant load-carrying capability it was obvious that the aircraft was also suitable for the maritime reconnaissance role (See 1C4).[77] The *Reichsmarine* secretly carried out extensive tests with the *Wal* and this support led to the development of the Do R *Superwal* in 1926, six of which served with *Deutsche Luft Hansa* on its Ostsee services whilst WNr.148 D-1385 was employed by *Severa* from 1928 (See 1C4).[78] Continued naval interest in the large flying boat culminated with a secret contract in 1927 for a *Flugschiff* (Flying Ship) capable of trans-oceanic operations; long range maritime reconnaissance, mine-laying and torpedo bombing.[79] The result was the incredible Do X D-1929 which was built at *Dornier's* Altenrhein plant in Switzerland and which first flew in July 1929.[80]

The *Dornier* flying boats fitted in well with the *Marineleitung's* prevailing view on the operational employment of naval aviation in any future conflict. In April 1928 the *Marineleitung* published a paper entitled *"Guidelines for the use of our Sea-Striking Force in a Future War"* in which the principal missions for the *Reichsmarine* were stated to be:[81]

Flugwerkehr & *DLH* before being appointed *Ltr.d.DVS Zweigstelle List* in Mar 27 – see service record for Heinz Scheurlen in Hildebrand 1992 pp.179-180.

74   Ries 1970 p.42 & Ries 1988 p.10.

75   Kreipe and Koester 1955 pp.22-23, Suchenwirth 1968 p.43 & *Anhang C Zeittafel* in Caspari Undated Bd.3 p.294. Unlike most former servicemen associated with naval aviation Fritz Koehler was an ex-*Luftstreitkräfte* officer who had been trained as *Flugzeugbeobachter* Apr-Aug 16 before serving with *Fl.Abt.48*. During Aug-Dec 17 he trained as a pilot and later served with *Jasta 25, 28* & *Kampfeinsitzerstaffel 9* scoring *1 LS*. He saw service with *Freikorps Haas* from Jan 19 – see service record for Fritz Koehler in Hildebrand 1991 pp.198-199.

76   Lange 1970 pp.195-198, Schliephake 1971 p.24, Nowarra 1980 pp.90-9 & *Dornier GmbH 1983 Dornier: Die Chronik des altesten deutschen Flugwerks* (hereafter cited as Dornier 1983) p.96.

77   Lange 1970 pp.195-196 & *Pionierfluge mit Dornier Wal* in Dornier 1983 p.97.

78   Stroud 1966 pp.247-248, Nowarra 1980 pp.128-129 & 148-149 and Dornier 1983 pp.100-101. In Germany the Do J had entered service with *Aero Lloyd* who it is thought operated D-861 – 864. In 1926 these aircraft passed to *DLH*. In fact Dornier did not build the Do J at Friedrichshafen until 1932 when it constructed a batch for *DLH* for use on the South Atlantic service – see Hooks M. 1999 *Images of Aviation: Lufthansa* p.11.

79   Schliephake 1971 p.25, Jung et al 1977 p.45, Hooton 1994 p.65, Seifert K-D. 1999 *Die deutsche Luftfahrt 28: Der deutsche Luftverkehr 1926-1945 – auf dem Weg zum Weltverkehr* (hereafter cited as Seifert 1999) p.129 & 141 and Kossler in Beauvais et al 2002 p.132. However another authoritative source suggests that the *Reichsmarine* was never very interested in this project – see Weal J. 1980 'Dr.Dornier's Great White Wal' in *Air Enthusiast* No.13 (hereafter cited as Weal 1980) p.3.

80   Stroud 1966 pp.249-252, Weal 1980 p.6 & Dornier 1983 p.111. It was planned that the Do X carry up to 4 torpedoes and be armed with two 3.7 cm cannon and 5 machine guns in its naval reconnaissance role – see *Arbeitsprogramm BS x b 1928* in Seifert 1999 p.141.

81   Rahn W. 1976 *Reichsmarine und Landesverteidigung, 1919-28 Konzeption und Führung der Marine in der Weimar Republik* (hereafter cited as Rahn 1976) pp.274-276.

PRINCIPAL MISSIONS OF THE REICHSMARINE IN A FUTURE WAR
APRIL 1928

- to protect German maritime trade and at the same time attack that of the enemy;
- to protect essential military sea transport;
- to protect the German coast against enemy attack, including amphibious landings; and
- to support amphibious operations on the part of German forces.

Given the cordial relations that existed with the Soviet Union, the principal enemy was considered to be France. The French *Marine* (Navy) was a large but somewhat dated force which of political necessity had to be divided into an Atlantic Fleet (Brest), a Mediterranean Fleet (Marseilles-Toulon) and smaller forces spread world-wide in support of France's extensive colonial interests in the Caribbean, Africa and Indo-China.[82] In 1928 the core of the French *Marine* was its six Dreadnought Battleships *(Cuirasses de 1ere rang)* which had been completed during 1914-16. Three of these warships had been modernised in 1919-20, whilst the remaining vessels were being taken in hand for modernisation from 1926.[83] There were relatively few modern cruisers *(Croiseurs)*, most of the surviving wartime vessels being outdated armoured cruisers *(Croiseurs Cuirasses)* which were progressively withdrawn. By 1928 new construction had added five modern light cruisers and two heavy cruisers to this ageing force.[84] Naval aviation was supported by the recently completed aircraft carrier *Bearn* to which the specially designed Seaplane Tender *(Transport d'Hydravions) Commandant Teste* which be added in 1929.[85]

To confront these forces which could conceivably be deployed in the Nordsee or even into the Ostsee via the Skagerrak, the *Reichsmarine* needed to replace its obsolete *Linienschiffe* with modern capital ships. The optimum design of these new vessels was debated endlessly during the twenties but in April 1928 Zenker finally authorised the detailed design of Panzerschiff "A", a new class of warship capable of oceanic operation against enemy cruisers and maritime trade in the manner of the *Guerre de Course* as advocated by French naval strategists.[86] The concept was unique as it combined

82 *European Colonial Empires 1815-1914* in Barraclough G. (Ed.) 1978 *The Times Atlas of World History* pp.244-245. The extent of French overseas interests in fact required a larger navy than she could really afford. *Adm.*Raoul Castex, a historical strategist, would later advocate the abandonment of North Africa, the Middle East (where France was already dependent on the British) and Indo-China, but this was clearly unacceptable politically. New naval construction in the twenties therefore centred on cruisers, destroyers, torpedo boats and submarines, vessels that were suited to the coastal defence of France and of worldwide employment in support of her colonial possessions. To secure her position in the western Mediterranean in the face of Italian aspirations, France would later build a new naval base at Mers-el-Kebir in Algeria – see Reynolds 1974 pp.487-488. See also Roberts J. *France* in Gardiner and Chesneau (Ed.) 1980 p.255.

83 Masson le H.1969 *Navies of the Second World War: The French Navy Vol.1* (hereafter cited as Masson 1969) pp. 5-7 & 64-68. Four older pre-Dreadnought battleships were still in service for training duties – see Roberts J. in Gardiner and Chesneau (Ed.) 1980 p.257 & Smigielski A. and Hervieux P. in Sturton 2008 pp.30-33.

84 Masson 1969 pp.89-95. These were the *Duguay-Trouin Class* (3 light cruisers) completed 1923-24, the *Duquesne Class* (2 heavy cruisers) completed 1925-26 and the *Suffren Class* (2 light cruisers) completed 1927-28 with a further 2 vessels to be completed 1929-30. In addition to these warships the French *Marine* had commissioned 4 ex-*Kaiserliche Marine Kleine Kreuziere* from four different classes – see Roberts J. in Gardiner and Chesneau (Ed.) 1980 p.257.

85 Masson 1969 pp.82-83 & 88-89. Authorised in 1922 the *Bearn* was commissioned in 1927. It could operate 40 aircraft. Authorised in 1925 the *Commandant Teste* was not commissioned until 1929. This large vessel was designed with operations in colonial waters in mind where permanent shore based installations and facilities might be lacking – see also Chesneau R. 1984 *Aircraft Carriers of the World 1914 to the Present: An Illustrated Encyclopedia* (hereafter cited as Chesneau 1984) pp.63-66.

86 Sieche in Gardiner and Chesneau (Ed.) 1980 p.219, Whitley 1989 pp.15-19 & Mallmann Showell 1999 p.5. The debate over a future capital ship for the *Reichsmarine* had been lengthy beginning in 1920 under *Adm.*Behncke. The *Panzerschiff* concept was very much in the spirit of the French *Marine's jeune ecole* thinking of the 1880s which

the 28 cm primary armament of the pre-war capital ship with the 10,000 ton displacement limit for new cruiser construction as agreed by the signatories of the Washington Naval Treaty of 1922. The result was a warship that could easily outgun the most modern heavy cruisers, for example France's *Duquesne Class* of 1925-26, but was also fast enough to outrun any opposing battleship which was powerful enough to sink it.[87] *Ersatz Preussen* was laid down in February 1929 at the *Deutsche Werke* in Kiel, her sister *Ersatz Lothringen*, would follow at Wilhelmshaven in June 1931 *(Photo 1E-20)*.[88]

However of more immediate consequence to the *Reichsmarine* were the first three new *Kleine Kreuziere* which were commissioned between April 1929 and January 1930.[89] The *K-Klass* was a significant improvement over the earlier *Emden* and were armed with nine 15 cm SK C/25 guns in three triple turrets. They were better protected than the French *Duguay-Trouin Class* of 1923-24 and were also fast with a maximum speed of 32.5 knts which suited the ships for their intended scouting role.[90] *Oblt.z.See* Hans Metzner, former naval aviator, would serve as *Wach und 2.Artillerie-Offizier* aboard the *Kleine Kreuzer Karlsruhe* during her first commission and shakedown cruise through the Mediterranean to South Africa between October 1929 and September 1931, whilst the young *Lt.z.See* Christian was *2.Adjutant* and *Signal-Offizier* on the same vessel from the time of Metzner's departure.[91]

Although the new warships were built without the equipment to operate floatplanes, the *Marineleitung* was well aware of the advantages of such a capability for the scouting role and for the planned war against enemy commercial shipping. Fortunately the expertise was already available within the *Ernst Heinkel Flugzeugwerke* who had completed the HD 25 and HD 26 for the Imperial Japanese Navy *(IJN)* in 1925-26 (See 1C1).[92] In the following year the *RVM* in conjunction with *Gruppe BSx* placed a contract with *Heinkel* for an experimental catapult to serve for basic tests on

had sought to neutralise Britain's maritime dominance through cruiser operations against Britain's maritime trade. For the *Reichsmarine* this was a clear break with tradition as the *Kaiserliche Marine* had sought to confront Britain's naval dominance in a major fleet engagement. However the inability of the *Hochseeflotte* to break the Royal Navy's blockade of the Nordsee in 1916 required a new approach and it was within this context that *VizAdm.*Wolfgang Wegener's thinking on the future form of *Reichsmarine* strategy, doctrine and equipment evolved – see also Reynolds 1974 p.489.

87   Reynolds 1974 pp.479-481, Mallmann Showell 1979 pp.10-12 & Whitley 1989 pp.17-18. Following the Great War there were several well-meant attempts to limit naval rearmament. In 1922 the major maritime powers, but not Germany, had signed the Washington Naval Treaty which limited the overall tonnage available for warship construction for each of the signatories – essentially to preserve the status quo and restrict the maximum size of primary armament to 16 inches (40.6 cm) for battleships and to 8 inches (20.3 cm) for cruisers. The *Duquesne Class* were armed with 8 x 20.3 cm guns in twin turrets – see Masson 1969 p.6 & pp.91-92.

88   Whitley 1989 p.20 & 25. As replacements for the two de-commissioned *Linienschiffe* the first two *Panzerschiffe* were initially named *Ersatz Preussen* & *Erstaz Lothringen*. They would be commissioned as the *Deutschland* and *Admiral Scheer*.

89   Whitley 1985 pp.20-25.

90   Whitley 1985 pp.22-24. However the issue of protection had been addressed in the *Suffren Class* of 1927-30. These were true contemporaries of the German *K-Klass* – see Masson 1969 pp.93-95. The pre-Great War *kleine Kreuziere Thetis, Arcona, Medusa, Nymphe* & *Amazone* were all de-commissioned in and around 1929. Most were deleted in Mar 31 but in several cases their hulls would find further employment – see Siecehe in Gardiner and Chesneau (Ed.) 1980 p.222.

91   Service record for Hans Metzner in Hildebrand 1991 pp.389-391. Prior to this assignment Metzner, who had been re-engaged in Jul 23 after a period of higher education, had been *Wach-Offz.* in *T 146, T 139* & *T 190* and *1.Adj. I.Torpedoboots-Halbflottille* during 1923-26, *Marine-Nachr-Offz.Kiel* in 1926-27 and *Bild-Offz.b.Kdo.d. Marinestation d.Ostsee* 1927-29. The final position would have made use of his expertise in aerial reconnaissance from the Great War. There is a slight discrepancy between the dates shown for *Karlsruhe's* shakedown cruise in Mallmann Showell 1999 p.viii and that shown in *App.II Construction, Commanders and Fates* in Whitley 1985 p.169. See also service record for Eckhard Christian in Hildebrand 1990 pp.155-156.

92   Heinkel 1956 pp.89-99, Nowarra 1980 pp.116-117 & Koos 2006 pp.66-69. Shipboard floatplanes were already in service with the Pacific navies and with the Royal Navy – see Larkins W.T. 1996 *Battleship and Cruiser Aircraft of the United States Navy 1910-1949* pp.11-13, Navair 00-80P-1 1970 *United States Naval Aviation 1910-1970* pp.49-50, Sekigawa E.1974 *Pictorial History of Japanese Military Aviation* p.31. & Sturtivant R. and Cronin D. 1998 *Fleet Air Arm Aircraft, Units and Ships 1920 to 1939* (hereafter cited as Sturtivant and Cronin 1998) pp.15-17.

the possibilities of shipboard launching of seaplanes (See 1C4). The result was the K 1 (Katapult 1) and in the same year Heinkel produced the HD 15 a small three seat flying boat for trials purposes.[93] The success of these experiments quickly led to an *RVM* contract in 1928 for a larger catapult and a *Katapult-Seepostflugzeug* for use aboard the *Norddeutschen-Lloyd's* new turbine powered liner *TS Bremen*. *Norddeutscher Lloyd* had its eyes on the Blue Riband for the fastest crossing of the Atlantic Ocean, whilst the *RVM* sought to improve on even this time by forwarding the post by air whilst the ship was still 24 hours out from New York. The new K 2 Katapult was fitted to the *Bremen* in 1929 and the specially designed HE 12 WNr.334 D-1717 was embarked for trials on the North Atlantic route.[94] Later in 1930 a sister ship, the *TS Europa*, was equipped with the even more powerful K 4 Katapult and embarked the larger HE 58 WNr.365 D-1919 *(Photo 1E-21)*. Although a strictly commercial operation with these aircraft and their Ju 46 replacements being operated by *Deutsche Luft Hansa* personnel, the ships also carried naval personnel in mufti during a series of cruises in the Mediterranean and in northern waters (See also 1D2).[95] In the meantime three ocean freighters belonging to *HAPAG* and *Norddeustcher Lloyd* were fitted with the new *Heinkel* catapults: the *Colombus*, *Oceana* and *Lützow*, and from 1929 *Severa* crews flew the smaller Junkers F 13 floatplanes from these vessels as a means of gaining operational experience in catapult operations.[96] From that year the training of naval pilots in catapult operations was enhanced by the delivery of the *Schleuderprahm Sch.Pr.11*: a *Heinkel* catapult mounted on a barge or lighter.[97]

At the end of September 1929 Rudolf Lahs retired with the honorary rank of *KonAdm.* to take up a new position as *Präsident der Reichsverbände der Deutschen Luftfahrt (RDL)*.[98] His successor was *Kpt.z.See* Konrad Zander who took up post on the 20 September 1929. Like his predecessor Zander was not a *Marineflieger*; his considerable operational experience had been with the *Torpedobooten* where he had been successively *Chef der I.Torpedoboots-Flottille* (1923-26), *Chef des Stabes der Inspektion des Torpedo-und Minenwesens* (1926-28) and *Chef des Stabes der Marinestation Ostsee* (1928-29).[99] Under Zander the *Gruppe BSx* was transformed into the *Luftschützgruppe* (Air Defence Group) on the 1 October 1929, initially within the *Allgemeine Amt* but from 1932 under the direct authority of *Adm.* Erich Raeder, the new *Chef der Marineleitung (Photo E-22)*.[100]

93   Heinkel 1956 p.105. *Das Flugzeug-Katapult* in Caspari (Ed.) Undated Bd.2 pp.172-180 & Koos 2006 pp.42-43.
94   Heinkel 1956 p.106, Jung et al 1977 p.46 & Koos 2006 pp.38-39.
95   Heinkel 1956 pp.113-114, Schmidt 1988 pp.163-165 & Koos 2006 pp.122-123.
96   Jung et al 1977 pp.66-67 & Nowarra H.J. 1982 *Fernaufklärer 1915-1945: Enstehung, Entwicklung, Einsatz* pp.38-41. *Severa* used six Junkers F 13 aircraft from 1926: D-298, 354, 837, 883, 1378 & 1382. D-298 & 883 are known to have been embarked for these secret reconnaissance missions using catapult equipment – see also Andersson 1989 p.43 & 48.
97   Jung et al 1977 pp.46-47& Ries 1988 p.71. The *Sch.Pr.11* was initially deployed at Warnemünde.
98   Hooton 1994 p.59. From 9 Jun -22 Sep 29 *KptLt.* Coeler had been *Chef i.V.Gruppe BSx* – see service record for Joachim Coeler in Hildebrand 1990 p.164. Lahs retired on the 30 Sep 29 – see service record for Rudolf Lahs in www.wikipedia.org He went on to become *Präsident d.Reichsverbändes der deutschen Luftfahrt-Industrie* during 1929-52.
99   Service record for Konrad Zander in Hildebrand 1992 pp.558-559. Zander had entered the *Kaiserliche Marine* in Apr 01 and had seen war service as *Kdt.Torpedoboote V 181* & *V 183* in the *15.Torpedoboots-Halbflottille* (1914-15), as *Kdt. V 47* in the *Zerstörer-Flottille Flandern* (1915-17) and as *Chef 2.Zerstörer-Halbflottille Flandern* (1917-18). Post-war he had been *Chef d.I.Minensuchflottille* (1919-20) before joining the staff of the *Marineschule Murwik* (1920-23). For the organisation of the *Ls-Gruppe* – see *Vorgeschichte der deutschen Seefliegerei nach dem 1.Weltkrieg* Caspari H.A. Dr. (Ed.) Undated *E-Stellen Travemünde und Tarnewitz 2.Band – Die Geschichte der Seeflugzeug-Eprobungsstelle Travemünde und daraus hervorgegangenen E-Stelle für Flugzeugbewaffnung Tarnewitz* (hereafter cited as Caspari (Ed.) Undated Bd.2) p.34.
100 Jung et al 1977 pp.45-46, Hooton 1994 p.59 & *Anhang C Zeittafel* in Caspari (Ed.) Undated Bd.3 p.295. *VizAdm.* Raeder replaced *Adm.* Zenker as *Chef d.Marineleitung* on the 24 Sep 28. Prior to this he had been *Chef d.Marinestation d.Ostee* (1925-28). Raeder was considered to be one of the most able young officers of the *Kaiserliche Marine* and his war service had been almost entirely with the operational staff as *1.Admiralstaboffizier*, later *C.d.S. b.Stab.d.Bfr.d. Aufklärungsschiffe* (1912-18). A short period of sea duty had followed as *Kdt.kleine Kreuzer Cöln* in 1918 – see

FIGURE 1E-19 ORGANISATION OF THE LUFTSCHÜTZGRUPPE 1929-33		
Referat a	**Referat b**	**Referat c**
Militärische Angelegenheiten (Naval Matters and Policy)	Taktik, Organisation und Bereitschaft (Tactics, Organisation and Readiness)	Personal und Ausbildung (Personnel and Training)

When Zander took over the *Gruppe BSx's* covert training programme was turning out just a dozen qualified pilots and observers a year – ostensibly to meet the needs of *Severa*. Initial training was carried out at the *Yachtclub Neustadt* near Lübeck before suitable personnel were sent to the *DVS Zweigstelle Warnemünde* and ultimately to the *Zweigstelle List* to train for their professional licences.[101] Operational training and further proficiency training was *Severa's* preserve. For example in 1929 Walter Rubensdörffer obtained his *A-Schein*, Paul Achilles and Johannes Gentzen both obtained their *Flugführerschein B-Land* and *See*, whilst Georg Kolbe and Hans-Karl Tresckow completed their *C-See Lehrgange*.[102] Through *KorvKpt.*Hermann Bruch, his *Referent für Fliegerausbildung (Referat c)*, Zander sought to improve both the quantity and quality of flight training with longer courses for student pilots at Warnemünde, whilst *Severa* was transformed in 1929 into the *Luftdienst GmbH* (Air Services Ltd.). Its activities were simultaneously increased to include the training of *Bordfunkeren* (Wireless operators), *Beobachtern* (Observers) and *Flugmechaniker* (Flight Engineers) alongside its traditional target-towing, personnel transport and naval liaison tasks.[103] In August 1929 the *RWM* informed the *Marineleitung* that a contract had been arranged with *Luftdienst* to provide the *Reichsmarine* with 3,000 flying hours per year, this figure being sub-divided into the *Marinestation der Nordsee* (1,550 hrs), the *Flottenkommando* (500 hrs) and the *Marinestation der Ostsee* (950 hrs).[104] From the summer of 1930 the *Reichsmarine* followed the *Reichsheer's* lead in providing flight training for selected training officer candidates prior to their "official" induction

Service record for Erich Raeder in ABR in Reocities.

101   Kreipe W. Gen.d.Flg.a.D. and Koester R. Obst.a.D. 1955 *Technical Training within the German Luftwaffe* USAF Historical Studies No.169 (hereafter cited as Kreipe and Koester 1955) pp.12-13, Suchenwirth 1968 p.43, Hooton 1994 p.58, Carlsen and Meyer 1998 p.17 & Thompson 2013 p.23. The DVS Warnemünde focused on the *A-B 1* syllabus, whilst *DVS Zweigstelle List* met the requirments of the more advanced *B 2* & *C-Flugführerschein*. The main *A 2* trainer was the Heinkel HD 24, the type that had been placed third overall in the *1926 Seeflug-Wettbewerbe*. Two aircraft of this type were delivered to Warnemünde in 1926 and a further 16 in 1927 – see Koos 2006 pp.63-65. For details of *A/B* flight training at the *DVS Warnemünde* during1932 – see Mahlke 2013 pp.7-17. Mahlke trained on the U 12 *Flamingo* and the HD 24 prior to basic officer training at Stralsund between Aug-Nov 32 – see Mahlke 2013 pp.18-20.

102   Reichsverkehrsministerium 1929 *Nachrichten für Luftfahrer*. Interestingly Theo Osterkamp, *Stationsleiter Holtenau*, re-qualified for his *B-Land u.See Flugführerschein* on the 4 Jun 29, whilst Heinz Scheurlen, *Ltr.d.DVS List*, re-qualified for his *Land u.See C Flugführerschein* on the 10 Apr 29. See also Suchenwirth 1968 p.43 & Hooton 1994 p.60.

103   Schliephake 1971 p.26 & Hooton 1994 p.59. In Feb 29 *Severa* was briefly known as the *Abteilung Küstenflug der Deutsche Luft Hansa* before objections from that airline resulted in it being re-titled – *GmbH* in Jul 29 – see Hooton 1994 p.61. Hermann Bruch had undergone wartime flying training prior to deployment aboard the *Flugzeugmutterschiff* (Seaplane Tender) *Santa Elena* – see Jung et al 1977 pp.21-24. Post war he had served as a *Minensuchboot-Kdt.* (1919-22) before becoming the *Flieger Referent b.Marinestation d.Nordsee* (1922-25). He had then served as *Wach-Offz.* aboard the *kleine Kreuzer Amazone* (1925-27) and as *Kp.Fhr.b.d. Marine-Artillerie-Abt.II* (1927-28) before returning to naval aviation duties as *Flieger Refrent b.Mainestation Ostsee* (1928-29) – see service record for Hermann Bruch in Hildebrand 1990 pp.119-120. Earlier *Referate (Ausbildungs)/Gruppe BSx* had been Wolfgang von Gronau & Ulrich Kessler – see Hooton 1994 p.59 & Thompson 2013 p.22..

104   US Office of Naval Intelligence 1947 *German Naval Air 1933 to 1945: A Report based on German Naval Staff Documents* in Isby D.C. (Ed.) 2005 *The Luftwaffe and the War at Sea 1939-45: As seen by officers of the Kriegsmarine and Luftwaffe* (hereafter cited as USONI in Isby (Ed.) 2005). These 3,000 contracted hours were costed at 453 RM per hr., a total of 1,359,000 RM per annum during the period 1929-31 p.25. See also Thompson 2013 p.24.

FIGURE 1E-20 LISTE DER MARINEOFFIZIERE MIT "SONDERAUSBILDUNG" (FLIEGEROFFIZIERE)
1 NOVEMBER 1930

Kap.z.See Konrad Zander	01.10.28 (1)	Marineleitung
FregKap.Walther Faber	01.10.30 (4)	z.V.d.Chefs d.Marineleitung
KorvKap.Hans Geisler	01.01.28 (1)	z.V.d.Chefs d.Marineleitung
KorvKap.Schuz	01.01.28 (4)	Schiffsstammdivision Ostsee
Korv.Kap.Otto Krueger	01.10.29 (2)	Schiffsstammdivision Nordsee
KorvKap.Busse	01.10.29 (3)	Marinedepotinspektion
KorvKap.Hans Siburg	01.07.30 (2)	Marineleitung
KorvKap.Walther Lech	01.10.30 (7)	Kommandantur Borkum
KorvKap.Hermann Bruch	01.11.30 (1)	Marineleitung
KapLt.Ernst Schirlitz	01.04.23 (3)	Marineleitung
KapLt.Joachim Coeler	01.01.24 (1)	Linienschiff Schleswig-Holstein
KapLt.Egbert von Frankenberg u.P.	01.02.25 (2)	Marinestation d.Nordsee
KapLt.Günther Horstmann	01.04.25 (6)	Insp.d.Torpedo-u.Minenwesens
KapLt.Werner Goette	01.01.28 (3)	Kreuzer Köln
KapLt.Carl Köchy	01.10.28 (5)	Marinestation d.Ostsee
KapLt.Hans-Armin Czech	01.12.28 (2)	Torpedoboot Jaguar
Oblt.z.See Otto Schroeder-Zollinger	01.04.25 (5)	Marinestation d.Ostsee
Oblt.z.See Hans Geisse	01.04.25 (12)	z.V.Chef d.Marinestation d.Ostsee
Oblt.z.See Klaus Ferber	01.04.25 (16)	z.V.Chefs d.Marinestation d.Ostsee
Oblt.z.See Axel von Blessingh	01.04.25 (17)	z.V.Chefs d.Marinestation d.Ostsee
Oblt.z.See Heinz-Ludwig von Holleben	01.04.25 (23)	Torpedoboot T 190
Oblt.z.See Hans Metzner	01.04.25 (26)	Kreuzer Karlsruhe
Oblt.z.See Georg-Hermann Edert	01.07.25 (7)	z.V.Chefs Marinestation d.Nordsee
Oblt.z.See Hermann Jordan	01.07.25 (10)	Marinestation d.Nordsee
Oblt.z.See Eugen Bischoff	01.07.25 (11)	Kreuzer Emden
Oblt.z.See Hugo Pahl	01.07.25 (12)	Marineschule Flensburg-Murwik
Oblt.z.See Martin Mettig	01.07.28 (2)	z.V.Chefs Marinestation d.Nordsee
Oblt.Heinrich Minner	01.07.28 (18)	Marinestation d.Nordsee
Oblt.z.See Hermann Busch	01.07.29 (15)	Marinestation d.Ostsee

into the Navy.[105] In the meantime the decision to procure a small number of fighter seaplanes for the *Reichsmarine* necessitated more specialised training than was politically expedient in Germany.

105   USONI in Isby (Ed.) 2005 p.25. On the 31 Jan 30 both the French and British Ambassadors in Berlin formally protested to the German Government that the *Reichswehr* had secretly trained 100 more serving officers than had been permitted under the 1926 Paris Air Agreement. As of that date 458 officers had recived flying training as pilots. The Ambassadors also protested the use by *Luftdienst* of aircraft to lay smoke screens for the *Reichsmarine's* warships during combined exercises. The *RWM's* response was: *Marineflugzeuge gibt es nicht* (Naval aircraft do not exist).

From 1930 naval aviators were attached to the *Lipetsk Jagdflieger-Lehrgang* and *Oblt.z.See* Georg-Hermann Edert would have almost certainly been one of the first to go to the Ukraine.[106] In 1932 Johannsen, Rodig, Johannes Gentzen, Walter Rubensdörffer and Hans-Karl von Tresckow were all posted to Lipetsk for training as fighter pilots (See also 1D1 & 1E1).[107]

Under Lahs' leadership there had already been a great deal of progress in the development of new naval aviation technology (See 1C4). This extended beyond the development of new aircraft to include wireless telegraphy, compression-ignition engines and weapons.[108] The increasing emphasis on wireless telegraphy led to the successive appointment of two *Marinefliegeroffiziere* to the position of *Leiter der Funk-Versuchs-Kommando (FVK)* (Wireless Research Command) at Warnemünde *KorvKpt.*Geisler from October 1928 and *KorvKpt.*Coeler from October 1932.[109]

Despite on-going Treaty limitations both Zenker and Raeder favoured the development of a blue-water navy in the tradition of the former *Kaiserliche Marine*.[110] The advantages of big-gun warships was continually emphasised in contemporary *Marineleitung* policy documents and papers and such thinking was certainly behind the development of the *Panzerschiffe*, up to six of which could be legitimately commissioned in place of the obsolescent *Linienschiffe*.[111] However contemporary German naval thinking was confused on the whole notion of air power: *"The influence of the air force on the conduct of future war is difficult to determine because this weapon and defensive measures against it is still in a state of constant development and flux" (Photo 1E-23).*[112] It has to be accepted that the *Marineleitung* was not alone in this respect and the naval staffs of Britain, Japan and the USA all had the big-gun lobbies despite the fact that each nation was simultaneously engaged in

---

106 Schliephake 1971 p.26, Jung et al 1977 pp.47-48 & Hooton 1994 p.59. In 1931 6 naval aviatorsattended the *Jagdfliegerlehrgang* at Lipetsk: Behrend, Brix, Mauke, Nitschke, Restemeyer, Wiborg & Woldenga – see *Vorgeschichte der deutschen Seefliegerei nach dem 1.Weltkrieg* in Caspari (Ed.) Undated Bd.2 p.32.

107 Ries 1970 p.83.

108 Schliephake 1971 p.25 & Hooton 1994 pp.65-66. The *FVK* was responsible for the development of all types of naval communications. It was also used as a cover for naval flying training – see USONI in Isby (Ed.) 2005 p.24. For developments in diesel engines – see Gersdorff von K. and Grasmann K. 1985 *Die Deutsche Luftfahrt 2: Flugmotoren und Strahltriebwerke* pp.13-15 & 88-92 and Gunston B. 1995 *World Encyclopaedia of Aero Engines* p.49 & 89. The *LZ 127 Graf Zeppelin* (1928) was powered by Maybach VL 2 vee-twelve diesel engines of 420 hp. The 1928 *Daimler-Benz* diesel was further developed during the thirties to produce the massive DB 602 16-cylinder engine of 1,200 hp which was employed on both the *LZ 129 Hindenburg* and *LZ 130 Graf Zeppelin*, whilst *Schnellbooten S 10, 11, 12 & 13* (1934-35) were all powered by three shaft *Daimler-Benz* diesel engines of a combined 3,960 hp – see Lenton H.T. 1975 *German Warships of the Second World War* p.309. For developments in aircraft weapons, particularly *Flugzeug-Kanone* – see Hoffschmidt E.J. 1969 *German Aircraft Guns WWI – WWII* pp.112-115, Schliephake H. 1977 *Flugzeugbewaffnung – Die Bordwaffen der Luftwaffe von den Anfangen bis zur Gegenwart* pp.109-110 & Hertel W. Dipl.Ing.GenIng.a.D.1955 *Procurement in the German Air Force* USAF Historical Studies No.170 pp.45-51. However work on aerial torpedoes was not particularly rapid and experimental work at the *SES* and *TVA* focused on trials with new types such as the Do D Bas, G 24/See & HE 7 with existing torpedoes– see Thiele 2004 pp.10-11.

109 Service records for Hans Geisler & Joachim Coeler in Hildebrand 1990 pp.351-352 & 163-164. See also Trenkle F. 1986 *Bordfunkgerate - Vom Funksender zum Bordradar Die deutsche Luftfahrt 7* pp.23-30 & 83-85 & Andersson 1989 p.43.

110 *Letter Adm.Zenker to VizAdm.Raeder 1927* in Mallmann Showell 1999 p.5. The only true "blue-water" navies at this time were the *RN & USN*. The term was coined to describe navies capable of worldwide oceanic operations. As such the emphasis was on the design and construction of powerful battleships supported by fast armoured cruisers to act as scouts for the main battle fleet or of independent action in the defence of friendly commerce or offence in the case of enemy shipping. This term first came into use in the 1880s when its leading exponent was the British Royal Navy - see Reynolds 1974 p.407 & pp.485-486. Witness also the *Reichsmarine's* policy of annual foreign cruises from 1924 to acquaint its personnel with oceanic operations – see Mallmann Showell 1999 p.vii-viii.

111 *Marineleitung Denkschrift, Mai 1929 Braucht Deutschland größe Kriegsschiffe?* in Rahn 1976 p.281-286 (hereafter cited *as Denkschrift 1929* in Rahn 1976). See also Bekker 1972 pp.14-19, Mallmann Showell 1979 p.12 & Sieche in Gardiner and Chesneau (Ed.) 1980 p.219.

112 Sourced from *Drenkschift 1929* in Rahn 1976 *Reichsmarine und Landesverteidigung, 1919-28 Konzeption und Führung der Marine in der Weimar Republik* p.282 Bernard und Graefe Verlag.

the development of shipboard strike aviation.[113] Japan and the USA were at the forefront of such developments with the construction of four large aircraft carriers: the Japanese *Akagi* (1927) and *Kaga* (1928) and the American *Lexington* (1925) and *Saratoga* (1927). Each of these powerful warships could operate 60 or more combat aircraft including fighters, bombers and scouts *(Photo E-24)*.[114] Germany was fortunate that she enjoyed good relations with the *IJN* via Ernst Heinkel's commercial contacts and this ensured that Zander's *Luftschützgruppe* was kept abreast of the latest thinking in the development of shipboard combat aircraft.[115]

In 1930 the *Referent Technik* (Aviation Technology Desk) issued two important development contracts for new naval aircraft.[116] The first called for the refinement of the existing Heinkel HD 30 *Bordaufklärer* (Shipboard Reconnaissance Floatplane) into the HD 60 *Seeaufklärer* and the second for the design of a new type, the shore based *See-Mehrzweckflugzeug* (Coastal Multi-role Aircraft)(See 1C4). The latter was to be a large twin-engined floatplane capable of torpedo attack, bombing, mine-laying and reconnaissance duties. Heinkel's response was the HD 59 which first flew in September 1931.[117] The HD 60 on the otherhand was a much smaller, single-engined design the prototype of which first flew in late 1931.[118] These two types, together with the HD 38 *See-Jagdflugzeuge* (Floatplane Fighter) and the Dornier Do J IId Bis *Militär-Wal Aufklärungs-Flugboot* (Reconnaissance Flying Boat) were all to be powered by the BMW VI liquid-cooled engine thus simplifying engine supply and maintenance requirements.[119]

It has been suggested that neither Zenker nor Raeder fully appreciated the importance of naval aviation.[120] However given Germany's geo-political situation at that time their policies were both balanced and realistic. Naval aviation had certainly not been ignored. Indeed both naval operations and training continued to be informed by a succession of former *Marine-Fliegeroffiziere* who occupied the post of *Flieger Referent beim Marinestation* at both Wilhelmshaven and Kiel. *Oblt.z.See* Hermann Bruch (1922-25), *Oblt.z.See* Ernst-August Roth (1924-26) and *KptLt.*Otto Krueger (1926-29) were all *Flieger Referent beim Marinestation der Nordsee*, whilst *Oblt.z.See* Hans-Armin Czech (1924-25), *KptLt.*Hans Geisler (1925), *KptLt.*Hans Siburg (1926-28) *KptLt.*Bruch (1928-29) and *KorvKpt.*Krueger (1931-34) were all *Flieger Referent beim Marinestation der Ostsee*.[121] Beginning with *KptLt.*Ritter in October 1928, a *Referent für Flugwesen* (Naval Aviation Advisor)

113   Reynolds 1974 p.486 & 495. Although battleship development was effectively prevented by the Washington Naval Agreements this was largely due to the accepted dominance of this type of warship in naval thinking. The aircraft carrier had simply not come of age – see Chesneau 1984 pp.32-36.

114   Chesneau 1984 pp.89-99, 157-162 & 198-201. British aircraft carriers of this period were all conversions of existing warship hulls. In comparison to their American and Japanese contemporaries they were smaller and embarked far fewer aircraft – see also Friedman N. 1988 *British Carrier Aviation – The Evolution of the Ships and their Aircraft* pp.90-107.

115   Heinkel 1956 pp.89-91 & p.179 and Corum 1997 p.112. Heinkel had designed a succession of aircraft for the IJN from 1925: HD 25, HD 26, HD 28, HD 56, HD 62 & HD 66. See also Koos 2006 pp.66-69, 72-73,117-118, 129-130 & 136-137.

116   Kens K. and Nowarra H.J. 1961 *Die deutschen Flugzeuge 1933-1945: Deutschlands Luftfahrt-Entwicklungen bis ende des Zweiten Weltkrieges* (hereafter cited as Kens and Nowarra 1961) pp.259-260 & Green W. 1970 *The War Planes of the Third Reich* (hereafter cited as Green 1970) p.273 & 277.

117   Green 1970 p.273 & Koos 2006 pp.124-125.

118   Green 1970 p.277 & Koos 2006 pp.126-127.

119   Andersson 1989 p.44-45 & p.48 and Vajda and Dancey 1998 p.10 & 233.

120   Corum 1997 p.109. Indeed Raeder would be a strong proponent of a naval air arm once this became a reality –see USONI in Isby (Ed.) 2005 pp.28-30.

121   Kreipe and Koester 1955 p.4. The *Flieger Referent b.Marinestationen* performed the same role as their opposite numbers in the *Wehrkreise*. They were also refered to as *Referent zbV – Luftschütz*. In addition the position of *Bild-Offz.b.Marinestation* was often held by a *Marinefliegeroffizier*. See also service records in Hildebrand 1990-92. The suggestion that *KptLt.*Walther Lech was the first *Ref.b.Marinestation d.Ostsee* in 1923 (Thompson 2013 p.21) is not substantiated by his service record – see Hildebrand 191 pp.286-287. KptLt.Lech was *Marine-Nachrichten Offz.Kiel* during Oct 22 – Sep 24.

was also established within the *Flotten-Abteilung/Marineleitung* and this post became the basis for the *5.Admiralstabs-Offizier (Flugwesen)* (5th Admiral Staff Officer – Aviation) in April 1931 when the position was briefly held by *KptLt.*Ulrich Kessler.[122]

A further commitment to the restoration of naval air power can be seen in Zander's decision to renovate and refurbish many of the *Kaiserliche Marine's* former *Seeflugstationen*. The existing facilities at Norderney, List, Kiel, Travemünde and Warnemünde were improved, whilst former facilities at Wangerooge, Wilhelmshaven, Mariensel and Bug auf Rügen were secretly renovated. Finally work on new installations was begun at Helgoland, Nest and Pillau so as to provide a string of naval air stations that stretched from Norderney in the Ost Friesische Inseln to Pillau in Ostpreussen *(Map I-3)*.[123]

On the 1 October 1932 Zander was succeeded by *FregKpt.*Rudolf Wenninger, an officer who, given the pace of political change in Germany at that time, would have very different priorities to his predecessor (See also 1A3).[124] Wenninger was the third non-*Marineflieger* to take charge of the development of naval aviation. As a highly decorated *U-Boot* officer from the Great War (*Pour le Mérite* 30 March 1918) he had been employed by the *Reichsmarine* in mine clearance operations in the Ostsee (1920-22), aboard the *Kleine Kreuziere Thetis* and *Berlin* – the latter in Far Eastern waters (1922-24 & 1927-29) and as a staff officer im *Stab der Marinestation der Ostsee* (1924-27). In April 1929 he had been briefly posted as *Leiter des Luftschützgruppe* but in September had returned to Kiel for special duties with the *Chefs der Marinestation* and later with the *Marineleitung*. He had been re-assigned to the *Luftschützgruppe* as a *Referent* in September 1931.[125] Given the shortage of *Marinefliegeroffiziere* Wenninger was not alone in being a non-aviator within the *Luftschützgruppe*: *KptLt.*Wilhelm Meendsen-Bohlken was a *Referent* from the 1 April 1931, whilst in October 1932 *KorvKpt.*Wolfgang Weigand was assigned to this staff.[126] Other non-aviation officers would include *KorvKpt.*Heinz Degenhardt and *KptLt.*Paul Ascher.[127]

---

122   Service record for Hans Ritter in Hildebrand 1992 pp.116-117. Promoted to *KorvKpt.* in May 30 Ritter would hold this influential position until Sep 35. Kessler had trained as a *Marineflieger* in 1917 prior to postings at the *Seefliegerstationen Helgoland, Zeebrugge* & *Norderney*. In 1918 he was *Fhr.* of a *Riesenflugzeuges* (Giant Aircraft). His post-war service mirrored that of other former *Marineflieger* with duty as a *Wach-Offz. b.d.II.Torpedoboots-Flottille* (1921-23), as *Adj.d.Schiffstamm-Division d.Nordsee* (1923-25) and as *Wach-Offz.* & *Adj.* aboard the *kleine Kreuzer Hamburg* (1925-27). He was *Gr.Ltr.Marineflugwesen i.d.Marineleitung* (1927-29) before under-going *Führergehilfen-Ausbildung* (Staff Officer Training) (1929-31). He was *5.Adm.StOffz. i.Stab.d.Flottenkommandos* during 1 Apr 31 – 30 Sep 31 – see service record for Ulrich Kessler in Hildebrand 1991 pp.168-169.

123   Schliephake 1971 p.26 & Jung et al 1977 pp.47-48.

124   Hooton 1994 p.76. On the 1 Oct 32 Zander was promoted to *KonAdm.* and simultaneously appointed *Insp.d.Torpedo-u.Minenwesens* – see service record for Konrad Zander in Hildebrand 1992 pp.558-559.

125   Service record for Rudolf Wenninger in Hildebrand 1992 pp.502-504. Wenninger had been *Kdt.UB 17* (May 15 – Jul 16), *UC 17* (Jul 16 – Jun 17) & *UB 55* (Jun 17 – Apr 18). He was captured by the British on the 22 Apr 18. In the *Reichsmarine* he had been *Chef d.6.Ostsee Minensuch-Halbflottille, Chef i.V.d.5.Ostsee Minensuch-Halbflottille, Navigations-Offz.kleine Kreuzer Thetis* & *I.Offz. kleine Kreuzer Berlin*. See also Mallmann Showell 1999 p.viii.

126   Service record for Wilhelm Meendsen-Bohlken in ABR in www.reocities.com Meendsen-Bohlken was another former submariner whose *Reichsmarine* service had been with the *I.Ostsee-Minensuch-Flottille* (1920-23), *Flotten-Adj.* (1923), *Navigations-Offz. Swinemünde* (1923-24), *Adj.Küstenwehr-Abt.I* (1924-26) & *Wach-u.Div.Offz. & Boot Kdt.* aboard the *Torpedobooten Seeadler* & *Wolf i.II.Torpedoboots-Flottille* (1926-29). He then attended *Führergehilfen-Ausbildung* (1929-31) before assignment to the *Luftschützgruppe*. Wolfgang Weigand's war service had been primarily aboard the *Linienschiff Thüringen* with which he saw action in the *Skagerrakschlacht* (May 16). In the *Reichsmarine* he had been *Kp.Fhr.Küstenwehr-Abt. Pillau* (1920-23), *Adj.Kdtr.Pillau* (1923-24), *2.Adm. StOffz.b. Marinestation d.Ostsee* (1924-25), *Artillerie-Offz.kleine Kreuzer Amazone* (1925-27), *Adj.Kdtr. Kiel* (1927-28), *Kdr.d.I.Abt.d.Schiffstammdivision d.Nordsee* (1928-29) & *Marine-Verbindungs- Offz.b.Wehrkreis VI Münster* (1929-32) – see service record for Wolfgang Weigand in Hildebrand 1992 pp.490-491.

127   *Anlage 5 Verzeichnis der aktiven und inaktiven Flieger-und Flugabwehr (Luftschütz)-Offiziere im Reichsluftfahrtministerium, Stand: 1.Juni 1933* in Volker K-H. 1967 *Die deutsche Luftwaffe 1933-1939: Aufbau, Führung und Rüstung der Luftwaffe sowie die Entwicklung der deutschen Luftkriegstheorie* pp.229-230. See also ABR in www.reocities.com & Hildebrand 1990-92. It has not been possible to identify who occupied the other key *Flieger-Referent (Flieger-Ausbildung)*. *KptLt.*Eugen Bischoff is a possible candidate although his appointment as

Wenninger's main objective was not the continued development of naval aviation in Germany, nor indeed its acceptance as an integral force by the *Marineleitung* within the *Reichsmarine*. Indeed Zander's legacy was such that in 1933 a *Marineleitung* policy paper on the role of naval aviation stated:

> The aircraft is one of the most important weapons in the conduct of naval warfare. Its ability to scout for naval forces over a wide area lessens the chance of surprise attack; because it can deliver swift counter attacks it has become an invaluable offensive and defensive weapon; it can no longer be regarded as only suitable for ancillary functions; it has become an integral force in naval warfare.[128]

Wenninger's concern was far more fundamental, specifically the very survival of the emerging *Marineluftstreitkräfte* as an independent force within the overall organisation of the *Reichsmarine*. One of the consequences of the 1928 Phoebus Affair that led directly and indirectly to the retirement of both Lohmann and Zenker had been the replacement of the pro-*Reichsmarine Reichswehrminister* Otto Gessler by *GenLt.a.D.* Wilhelm Groener (See also 1A3).[129] Groener quickly sought to establish Government control over the clandestine rearmament programmes. A particular area of concern was the parallel development of both fighters and bombers by the *Reichsmarine* and the *Reichsheer*, a situation that became even less sustainable as the strength of the German economy began to fail in the face of the worldwide economic depression of the early thirties (See 1C2).[130] Clearly economies could be achieved in the development and production of new aircraft technology but in the knowledge that this had all happened during the Great War both the *Marineleitung* and the *Luftschützgruppe* were reluctant to subordinate their position to the more powerful *Reichsheer* lobby.[131] Some senior *Reichsmarine* officers were in fact concerned that the very future of their service was in jeopardy as there were some Socialist politicians that questioned the usefulness of such a small force at a time of increasing economic stringency. To co-operate too closely with the *Reichsheer* could only weaken the *Reichsmarine's* independence and this was a further powerful reason to maintain a cool distance at this juncture.[132]

However by 1932 the economic position, particularly in the light of the *Reichsmarine's* massive

---

Kdr.d.Erprobungsstelle Travemünde in Dec 33 would suggest a technical rather than a training specialism. Another candidate is *KptLt.* Lorenz. *KptLt.* Kessler was *Ref.Flieger-Ausbildung* until the 30 Sep 29 when he was re-assigned for *Führergehilfen-Ausbildung* – see service record for Ulrich Kessler in Hildebrand 1991 pp.168-169 & Thompson 2013 p.22.

128   Quoted from Gaul W. Obst.i.G.a.D. *The German Naval Air Force 1933 – September 1939* in Isby (Ed.) 2005 *The Luftwaffe and the War at Sea 1939-45: As seen by officers of the Kriegsmarine and Luftwaffe* p.80 with the kind permission of Lionel Leventhal Ltd./Greenhill Books. See also Schliephake 1971 p.30 & Hooton 1994 p.66.

129   Sieche in Gardiner and Chesneau (Ed.) 1980 p.219. The collapse of the *Phoebus AG*, one of Germany's largest companies, in 1927 had led to a media exposure of Lohmann's involvement in illegal naval developments. The affair acutely embarrassed the *Reichswehr* and led to the resignation of the *Reichswehrminister, Dr.* Gessler, and somewhat later in Sep 28 to *Adm.* Zenker who had accepted a degree of responsibility for Lohmann's activities. Zenker had been replaced by *VizAdm.* Erich Raeder as *Chef d.Marineleitung*. Inevitably Lohmann was also a casualty. He retired from naval service and died soon after in 1928 - see also Seaton A. 1982 *The German Army 1933-1945* p.16 & Hooton 1994 p.61.

130   Hooton 1994 p.66 & Corum 1997 pp.110-111. It was eventually agreed that landplane development would be the responsibility of the *Reichsheer* whilst seaplanes would remain a *Reichsmarine* responsibility.

131   *RWM to Marineamt – Vorschlage für die Entwicklung der Luftfahrtindustrie, 11 Januar 1927* in BA/MA RH2/2187 in Corum 1997 p.111. The *Luftstreitkräfte* had assumed responsibility for all airframe and aero-engine production during the Great War and in 1927 the *Reichsheer's Abt.T 1* had suggested a joint army-naval aircraft development programme. The *Marineleitung's* response to this proposal had been luke-warm – see *Marineamt to TA 1* in BA/MA RH2/2187 in Corum 1997 p.111.

132   Corum 1997 p.111. However the *Marineleitung* did involve itself with the *Heeresleitung* in *Kriegspiel* (Wargames) and military manoeuvres.

expenditure on the *Panzerschiff-Programm*, eventually demanded some flexibility on the part of the *Marineleitung*.[133] In November 1932 Raeder finally indicated his readiness, albeit with certain reservations, to co-operation with the *Reichsheer* on the formation of a centralised command structure for military aviation.[134] Detailed discussions followed and on the 8 February 1933 the new *Reichswehrminister, Gen.d.Inf.* Werner von Blomberg, ordered the establishment of an independent *Luftschützamt* (Air Defence Office) within the *RWM*.[135] Although led by *Obst.*Eberhard Bohnstedt, a *Reichsheer* nominee, Wenninger was appointed *Chef des Stabes* (Chief of Staff) in a new structure that was formally established on the 1 April 1933 (See 1A3). Within the new *Luftschützamt* both services were given equal status *(LA-I Heer & LA-I Marine)* each with three parallel *gruppen* covering *Gruppe I -Taktik, Gruppe II - Organisation* and *Gruppe III - Ausbildudungs (III)*.[136] The three Marinegruppen were led by *KorvKpt.*Kessler (?) *(Taktik), FregKpt.*Weigand *(Organisation)* and *FregKpt.*Geisler *(Ausbiludungs)*.[137]

This structure allowed the *Marineleitung* to retain control over its own air operations, equipment and specialised training at a time when the appointment of Hermann Göring as *Reichskommissar für die Luftfahrt* (Reichs Commissioner for Aviation) threatened a total loss of executive control to the *Reichswehr's* new political masters.[138] This concern was voiced retrospectively by *KorvKpt.*Hans Siburg:

> Both the *Reichsheer* and the *Reichsmarine* were well aware of the fact that Göring would not be content to restrict himself to civilian aviation. Neither branch of service, and this applied particularly to the *Reichsmarine*, felt it could afford to get along without an air service of its own. In order to confront Göring's desire for power with a united front, the *Reichsheer*, whose most important officers were in the *Inspektion der Flieger* (Military Aviation Inspectorate), the majority of which were in favour of an independent air arm, considered it advisable to concentrate at least the development of all air equipment in the *Heereswaffenamt* (Army Ordnance Office). The *Reichsmarine* agreed to the proposal in an attempt to salvage what it could. Thus, shortly after the National Socialists had come to power, the *Referent Technisches-Entwicklung* (Technical Development Desk), including the *Erprobungsstelle Travemünde* (Travemünde Testing Station), was transferred from the *Allgemeinen Amt (BS)* to *Wa.Prw.8F* (Weapons Testing Department 8F) of the *Heereswaffenamt*.[139]

133   Sieche in Gardiner and Chesneau (Ed.) 1980 p.219. The *SPD* had actually campaigned under the slogan *"Food not Panzerkreuzer"* during the 1928 national elections for the *Reichstag*. In the years that followed the *Panzerschiffsfrage* (Panzerschiff Quarrel) became one of the most controversial issues of German domestic policy. *The Panzerschiff Deutschland* cost £3.75 m – see Preston A. (Ed.) 1989 *Jane's Fighting Ships of World War II* p.145. See also Hooton 1994 p.66 & Corum 1997 p.110.

134   *RWM Befehl Nr.401/33, Geheim, dated 21 Marz 1933* in (Author Unknown) *Geschichte des deutschen Generalstabs* in Suchenwirth 1968 p.46 & Maass B. 1955 *The Organisation of the German Air Force High Command and Higher Echelon Headquarters within the German Air Force* USAF Historical Studies No.190 (hereafter cited as Maass 1955) p.15. Suchenwirth gives the *LS-Amt* a different organisational structure. See also Schliephake 1971 p.30.

135   Suchenwirth 1968 p.46 & Jung et al 1977 p.48. The *Luftschützamt* brought together the formerly distinct and separate aviation offices of the *Reichsheer Inspektion 1 (L)* and the *Reichsmarine's Marine-Luftschützgruppe*. At the outset it was intended that the position of the *Chef d.LS-Amt* would be rotated between officers nominated by the two services. In a remarkable turn-about neither of the two senior officers in the new *LS-Amt* were military aviators – see service record for Rudolf Wenninger in Hildebrand 1992 pp.502-504& for Eberhard Bohnstedt in ABR in www.reocities.com.

136   Suchenwirth 1968 p.47. See also Maass 1955 p.15.

137   Service records for Hans Geisler, Ulrich Kessler & Wolfgang Weigand in Hildebrand 1990-92.

138   Suchenwirth 1968 pp.46-47. *"The Luftschützamt was to represent both the Heeres-und Marineleitung in dealing with all questions within its area of responsibility... All tactical-technical requirements were to be first approved by the Heeres-und Marineleitung."*

139   Quoted from Siburg H. Gen.d.Flg.a.D. *Vorbereitende Massnahmen der Marineleitung auf dem Gebiete des Seeflugwesens in den Jahren 1920-133* in A/V/1, Karlsruhe Document Collection in Suchenwirth 1968 *The Development of the*

Unfortunately for the *Reichsmarine* this arrangement proved very short-lived. Just three months on the 15 May 1933 the combined *Luftschützamt* was formally transferred from the *RWM* to the newly formed *RLM* (Air Ministry) where it came under Göring's direct political control (See 2A3). The battle for operational control of the *Reichsmarine's* embryonic air force would now enter a new and altogether more controversial phase.

MAPS

I-3 Territorial organisation of the *Reichswehr* 1920-1933 (See Page 270)

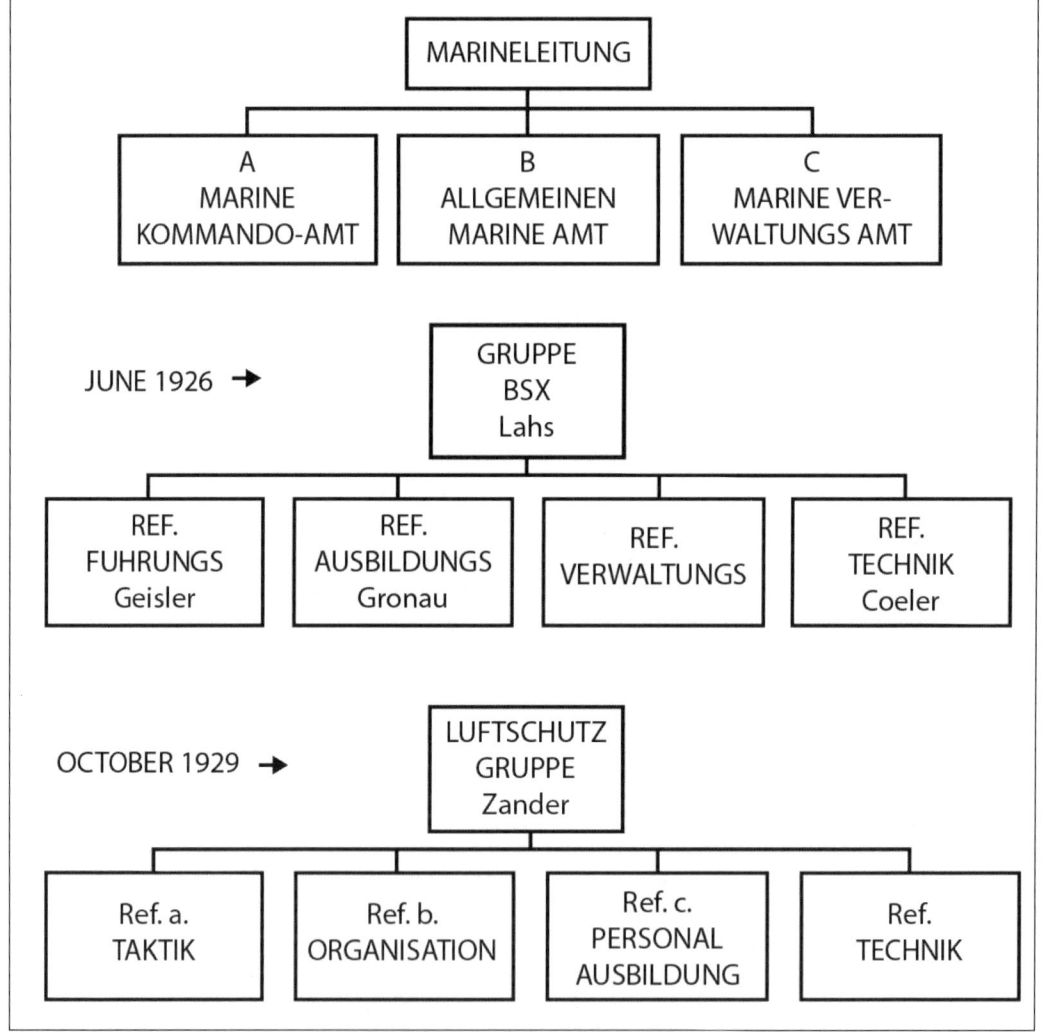

I-7   Organisation of the *Gruppe BSx* and the *Luftschützgruppe*, June 1926 – March 1933

German Air Force 1919-1939 USAF Historical Studies No.160 p.46. Hans Siburg had seen wartime service aboard the *Kaiserliche Marine's Flugzeugmutterschiff* (Seaplane Tender) *Oswald – see* Jung et al 1977 pp.24-26. Within the *Reichsmarine* his initial service had been as *Wach-Offz.* aboard the *Vermessungsschiffe* (Survery Vessels) *Tritin, Panther* & *Meteor* – the latter in Antarctica - and the *kleine Kreuzer Berlin* during a S.American cruise (1920-26). He had then been the *Fl.Ref.b.Marinestation d.Ostsee* (1926-28) before a short period at sea as a *Wach-Offz.* aboard the *Linienschiff Hessen* (1928-29) – see service record for Hans Siburg in Hildebrand 1992 pp.302-304.

Part 1 - Photo Commentaries

Photo 1A-1 Original caption: *Reichspräsidenten* **Friedrich Ebert published on the 25th anniversary of his death on the 26 February 1925.**

Bundesarchiv, Bild 102-00015/Photo: Georg Pahl

Friedrich Ebert was the first *Präsident* of a democratic Germany. He had been born in Heidelberg on the 4 Feb 1871 and entered politics in 1889 becoming leader of the *SPD* in 1913. He was elected as *Präsident* on the 11 February 1919 and died in office on the 28 February 1925. This photograph, taken on the 15 February 1925, was the last taken before his death to sceptic shock fourteen days later.

A moderate social democrat, Ebert played a pivotal role in the transformation of Germany from an Imperial monarchy to a democratic Republic during 1918-19. During the post-war internal struggles he allied himself with the conservative and nationalistic right including the *Freikorps* to crush the revolutionary left. He was opposed to the terms of the Treaty of Versailles which he regarded as *"unrealisable and unbearable"* but realised that Germany would have to accept or face military occupation by the Allies. His time as *Präsident* was also marked by the pressures of war reparations which led inexorably to a period of hyper-inflation, economic crisis and the French occupation of the Ruhr in 1923.

It was during this period that the first steps were taken by the Weimar Government to secretly acquire military aircraft and to negotiate the use of clandestine bases in the Soviet Union for the development of proscribed weapons and the covert training of *Reichswehr* personnel, decisions that were undoubtedly authorised by Ebert and his *Reichswehrminister* Otto Gessler.

The survival of the Weimar Republic during this particularly turbulent period can be largely attributed to his ability to balance the disparate political forces within Germany, whilst maintaining a degree of national independence in the face of sustained and highly intrusive Allied restrictions.

Photo 1A-2 Original caption: Portrait of Rudolf Berthold in the uniform of a *Oberleutnant* sitting outside with his dog, with his decorations (Eisernes Kreuz, *Preußische Militär-Flugzeugführer-Abzeichen*). Order of the *Pour le Mérite* (awarded on the 12 October 1916).

Bundesarchiv Bild 146-1998-009-14A Photo: o.Ang.

Born on the 24 March 1891 at Ditterswind, bei Bamberg, Rudolf Berthold was a pre-war regular officer with *Infanterie-Rgt.20 "Graf Tauentzein"* who transferred to the *Fliegertruppe* just before the beginning of hostilities. As a pilot he went to war with *Feld FA 23* with which he survived being shot down on the 15 September 1915. In January 1916 he transferred to *Kampfeinsitzer-Kdo.V* where he flew one of the new Fokker E.III monoplanes and soon scored his first *Luftsiege* although he was himself shot down and badly wounded after his sixth *LS*. He returned to combat in September with *Jasta 4* in the *AOK 2* sector and was soon awarded the *Pour le Mérite* for his eighth *LS* before being appointed *Fhr.Jasta 14* in support of *AOK 5*.

Thereafter Berthold enjoyed relatively little personal success, scoring just 4 victories with *Jasta 14* before a transfer to the *AOK 4* sector in August 1917 as *Fhr.Jasta 18*. Hard fighting now became the norm and Berthold would achieve 16 *LS* in just three months before being shot down by a British fighter. His right arm was torn apart by machine gun fire and would become withered and useless. Nonetheless, promoted to *Hauptmann*, he again returned to combat in March 1918 as *Kdr. Jagdgeschwader II (Jasta 12, 13, 15 & 19)* flying a specially modified aircraft to allow for his disability. His devotion to duty was unstinting. His right arm became infected and he often flew in extreme pain. Nevertheless he scored a further 16 *LS* before the 10 August 1918 when he was shot down from an altitude of 4,500 metres and crashed into a house. He was hospitalised for the remainder of the war.

Appalled by the chaos into which Germany collapsed following the armistice, *Hptm.*Berthold was one of those who took it upon themselves to fight the communist revolutionaries. He founded the 1,200 strong *Eiserne Schar Berthold* but was murdered in Hamburg on the 15 March 1920. Despite a locally agreed truce in which his men had laid down their weapons, *Spartakists* set about him, battering his body with rifle butts before strangling him with the ribbon of his own *Pour le Mérite*. It was tragic end to a true nationalist and patriot whose gravestone is inscribed: *"Honoured by his enemies – slain by his German brethren".*

Photo 1A-3 Original caption: Berlin, March 1919: *Freikorps* **shock troops on standby during the preliminary artillery bombardment on the Bülowplatz. General strike and armed struggles in support of the striking central German workers and for the recognition of ASR, release of all political prisoners, etc. from 3 to 12 March 1919. Through provocation** *General* **von Lüttwitz created the pretext for the movement of his troops into Berlin, on 6 March where they proceed with artillery against the Republican Militia. Shown here:** *Freikorps Stroßtrupp* **advancing in the protection of a tank on the Bülowplatz.**

Bundesarchiv Bild 183-R94405 Photo: o.Ang. (Scherl Agency)

The nine months following the end of hostilities were a period of extreme unrest and political division within post-Imperial Germany. With the abdication and exile of *Kaiser* Wilhelm II the old order had been swept away but it was certainly not clear as what would become the nature of the new Germany.

During this revolutionary period there were three distinct processes at work: (1) in the wake of the Kiel Mutiny, the appearance of sailor's and worker's councils across Germany demanding peace and access to food, supplies and services and a national congress in Berlin in December 1918; (2) the emergence of the extreme left who saw Germany's immediate post-war situation as an ideal opportunity to establish a Marxist state, pressures that would result in the establishment of a Republic in Bayern, the appearance of the *Spartakist League* and the creation of the German Communist Party (*KPD*) in January 1919; and (3) constitutional reform by more conservative elements that would eventually result in the formation of the democratic elected Weimar Republic in June 1919.

Predictably the revolutionary pressures exerted by the left quickly resulted in counter-pressures from the right as the monarchists, land owners and industrialists sought to maintain the status quo. In this struggle they had the support of the *Offizierkorps* and large segments of the disbanding *Feldheer*. These highly trained and well-equipped combat veterans formed the *Freiwilligen Korps* that sprung up across Germany in January 1919. Eventually numbering several hundred thousand men, a significant number were deployed in the eastern territories where they fought against Bolshevik forces in the Ostsee region and the Poles in Ostpreussen and Schlesien, whilst within Germany other units fought in the streets against the *Spartakists* and Communists.

In these pitch battles the *Frei Korps* were usually victorious. The *Bayerische Republik* was quashed and a Marxist Revolution averted. Many left-wing leaders were murdered including Karl Liebnecht and Rosa Luxemburg in Berlin and Kurt Eisner in Bayern. In this image the cameraman has captured the scale of the fighting in the German capital in March 1919 when various heavily armed *Frei Korps* detachments sought to finally clear Berlin of left wing revolutionaries.

Many members of the *Luftstreitkräfte* joined the *Frei Korps*. *Hptle.*Ulrich Grauert and Victor Krocker led air units in the defence of Berlin, whilst *Hptm.*Bruno Loerzer and *Oblte.*Oskar Frhr. von Boenigk and Gotthard Sachsenberg were active in the East and in Kurland.

Photo 1A-4 Original caption: The German peace delegates and experts at Versailles in 1919. The members of the German delegation (l.to r.): Prof. Dr. Schücking, *Reichspostminister* **Johannes Giesberts,** *Reichsjustizminister* **Dr. Otto Landsberg,** *Reichsminister des Auswärtigen* **Dr. Ulrich Graf Brockdorff-Rantzau,** *Präsident der Preußischen Landesversammlung* **Robert Leinert, Dr. Karl Melchior.**

Bundesarchiv Bild 183-R01213 Photo: o.Ang.

The terms of the Treaty of Versailles were deeply distasteful to the new German Government and to the wider German people. Referring to the Treaty as a *Diktat*, Philipp Schiedemann, Germany's first democratically elected *Ministerpräsident*, resigned rather than sign the Treaty. His successor Gustav Bauer informed the Allies that he would sign if certain clauses – notably Articles 227 (surrender of the Kaiser Wilhelm II for trial), 230 (co-operation with the Allies in the prosecution of war crimes) and 231 (acceptance of national war guilt) were withdrawn. However when faced with a threatened Allied occupation of Germany, *Reichspräsident* Friedrich Ebert and the *Ministerpräsident* had no option but to authorise their delegates in Paris to sign the Treaty on the 28 June 1919.

The terms of the Treaty were far reaching in respect of the payment of war reparations, assessed in 1921 at 132 billion Marks ($31.4 billion or £6.6 billion), the loss of all overseas territories together with large sections of German territory and finally massive restrictions on the future size and capability of the German armed forces. The loss of Elsass and Lothringen in the west, parts of Schleswig-Holstein in the north, and the Memelland, Westpreussen, the Wartheland and Oberschlesien in the east were keenly felt leaving many ethnic Germans in unsympathetic foreign lands. In addition the Rheinland was to be demilitarised and was subject to partial occupation by the Allies.

The restrictions to the embryonic *Reichswehr* saw the *Reichsheer* reduced in size to 100,000 and the *Reichsmarine* to 15,000 officers and men with strict terms of engagement. The retention, development and manufacture of heavy artillery, tanks, poison gas, aircraft and submarines were all prohibited. All modern warships had to be surrendered and the *Reichsmarine* was only permitted to retain strictly limited numbers of obsolete pre-war warships the replacement of which was also time limited.

In respect of military and naval aviation Article 198 stated: *"The armed forces of Germany must not include any military or naval air forces. Germany may, during a period not extending beyond October 1, 1919, maintain a maximum number of one hundred seaplanes or flying boats, which shall be exclusively employed in searching for submarine mines, shall be furnished with the necessary equipment for this purpose, and shall in no case carry arms, munitions or bombs of any nature whatever. In addition to the engines installed in the seaplanes or flying boats above mentioned, one spare engine may be provided for each engine of each of these craft. No dirigible shall be kept."*

Photo 1A-5 Original caption: Wismar–The *Freikorps Rossbach* **during the Kapp-Putsch of 1920.**

Bundesarchiv Bild 119-2815-20 Photo: o.Ang.

The existence of large numbers of independently led well-trained and heavily armed troops through much of Germany presented the Weimar Government with something of a problem once the immediate communist threat had been removed following the battles of 1919. Under the terms of the Treaty of Versailles the existing *vorläufige Reichsheer* of 400,000 officers and men now had to be reduced by three quarters whilst the various *Frei Korps* had to be disbanded in their entirety.

On the 29 February 1920 *Reichswehrminister* Gustav Noske ordered the dissolution of the *Marinebrigaden Loewenfeld* and *Ehrhardt* which were quartered in the vicinity of Berlin but both commanders refused to comply with this instruction. This in turn triggered off a military coup against Gustav Bauer's elected Government. During the early hours of the 13 March a mixture of regular troops and *Frei Korps* soldiers occupied a number of Government buildings in the capital with the open support of *Gen.d.Inf.*Walther von Lüttwitz, the *Oberbefehlshaber des Reichswehr-Gruppenkommando 1*, and de facto commander of all regular troops in Berlin, Ostpreussen, Pommern, Brandenburg and Schlesien. *GenLt.*Hans von Seeckt, the *Chef des Heeresleitung*, declined to act against such a sizeable element of the *Reichsheer* stating: *"Troops do not fire on troops."*

With such open defiance on the part of the *Reichsheer* and lacking the support of many monarchists, land-owners and industrialists the Government had little option but to flee to Dresden and ultimately Stuttgart in the south of Germany. *Reichspräsident* Ebert supported by the *SPD* members of his *Kabinett* called upon the working classes to foil the coup through a general strike. In the meantime Wolfgang Kapp, a Preussen civil servant, declared himself *Reichskanzler* and von Lüttwitz became the new *Reichswehrminister.*

The strike began on the 14 March and by the 15 March it had effectively spread throughout Germany with nearly twelve million workers refusing to co-operate with the new Government. In Berlin gas, water and electricity supplies were cut off and the newspapers were shut down. Unable to govern the *Putschists* elected to surrender. Bloodshed had been minimal and in keeping with this low key approach both Kapp and von Lüttwitz were required to resign their positions before leaving for exile in Sweden and Hungary respectively. In the meantime encouraged by events in Berlin where the workers had effectively brought down a right wing *Putsch*, communist factions in the Ruhr had risen in rebellion. On this occasion the *Reichsheer* acted in support of the elected Government and the rising was quickly and brutally quashed by the *Freikorps*.

Photo 1A-6 Original caption: 1919. The last German *Jagdstaffel* prepares to take off from Döberitz.
Bundesarchiv Bild 183-R43291 Photo: o.Ang. Scherl Agency

Located 25 kms to the west of the centre of Berlin, Döberitz was the *Koniglich-Preußische Fliegertruppe's* first *Flugplatze* and is therefore widely regarded as the birth place of German military aviation. The airfield was developed on open ground within the existing *Truppenübungsplatz* and it was used by the *Luftschiffertruppe* from 1901 until the establishment of the *Provisorische Militärfliegerschule Döberitz* (*Hptm.*de le Roi) in May 1910; the soldiers were housed under canvas until shortly before the war when hutted accommodation was finally provided. In May 1913 the *Fliegerstation* was commanded by *Maj.*Richard Roethe and together with *Hptlte.*Felix Wagenführ and Wilhelm Grade there were just seven other regular *Fliegeroffiziere* at Döberitz including *Lte.*Alexander von Scheele, Helmuth Förster and Alfred Mahncke. By this stage training had been supplemented by the formation of the *Lehr-und Versuchsanstalt für Militärflugwesen*, whilst in 1914 *Flieger-Bataillon Nr.1* was established at Döberitz with two *kompanien*, the third being located at Größenhain.

Following mobilisation in August 1914 the *Flugstation Döberitz's* main task was the training of replacement flight personnel, *Flieger-Ersatz-Abteilung Nr.2* being created from the existing *Militärfliegerschule* on the 1 August 1914. A year later the replacement unit was transferred to the *Albatros Flugzeugwerke* at Schniedemuhl/Pommern and thereafter the training of the *Luftstreitkräfte's Fliegerfunkpersonal* was focused at Döberitz.

This photograph from 1919 shows one of the *Luftstreitkräfte's Jagdstaffeln* shortly after *GenLt.*Ernst von Hoeppner's announcement of the disbandment of his position as *Kommandierender General der Luftstreitkräfte (KoGen-Luft)* on the 21 January 1919 but before the complete disbandment of the *Luftstreitkräfte* on the 8 May 1920. Closest to the camera are two of the new Fokker D.VIII *Jagdflugzeuge* which had reached the Front in small numbers in the final months of the war to serve alongside the existing Fokker D.VII as seen here. The Fokker D.VII was widely regarded as the finest single-seat fighter of the war. Its exceptional manoeuvrability at high altitudes and its high power-to-weight ratio gave its pilots an edge over most Allied fighters and as a result it was widely used from May 1918. In a measure to rapidly increase production, the Fokker D.VII was built under licence by the *Albatros Werke* and the *Ostdeutsche Albatros Werke*, whilst all three firms employed both the 185 hp *BMW* and 160/180 hp *Mercedes* engines to produce in excess of 3,000 examples of this fighter. On the 11 November 1918 there were 775 of these aircraft at the Front serving with 46 *Jagdstaffeln* and the surrender of all Fokker D.VII *Jagdflugzeuge* was an unusual but specific requirement of the Allies' Armistice Terms.

Photo 1A-7 Original caption: Studio portrait of Hermann Göring, standing with medals (*Eisernes Kreuz II. and I.Klasse, Preußisches Militär-Flugzeugführer-Abzeichen, Verwundeten-abzeichen in Schwarz, Pour le Mérite* – awarded 2 June 1918).
Bundesarchiv Bild 146-2013-0013 Photo: o.Ang.

This image taken in June or July 1918 shows *Oblt*.Göring at about the time he was appointed *Kdr.des Jagdgeschwaders I "Richthofen"* following the death of *Hptm*.Wilhelm Reinhardt in an accident at Berlin-Adlershof on the 3 July.

Born on the 12 January 1893 at Rosenheim, Göring was admitted as an officer candidate to *Inf. Rgt.112* at Mulhouse in 1912, receiving his commission on the 20 January 1914. Convinced by Bruno Loerzer, a brother officer in *Inf.Rgt.112*, that he should join the *Fliegertruppe*, Göring trained as an observer at *FEA 3* and joined Loerzer in *Feld FA 25* in October 1914. In the summer of 1915 he trained as a pilot at Freiburg and thereafter served with *Feld FA 25*, where he scored 2 *Luftsiege*, and *Art.FA 203* until the summer of 1916 when he transferred to the *Kampfeinsitzer-Kdo.Metz* and added another victory to his score. He served briefly with *Jasta 7* and *Jasta 5* during the autumn before he was wounded in a one-sided fight with a superior force of British fighters on the 2 November. His aircraft was hit 60 times, whilst he was wounded in the leg and hip. He was hospitalised and did not return to the Front until February 1917 when he was posted to Loerzer's *Jasta 26*. Over the next three months he gained four more *LS* and on the 17 May he was appointed *Fhr.Jasta 27*. He was promoted to *Oberleutnant* on the 18 August and a week later he became the first pilot in his *Jasta* to reach five victories when he scored his twelfth *LS*. Flying over the *AOK 4* sector in Belgium he once again came under Loerzer's command in February 1918 when *Jasta 27* joined the *Jasta Boelcke, Jasta 26* and *36* to form *Jagdgeschwaders III*. In May *JG III* moved south to support *AOK 7* on the Somme and by June Göring's score had reached 20 *LS* and he was decorated with the *Pour le Mérite*.

As *Kdr.JG I* Göring remained in action against the British to the north of the Somme until the 27 September when the *Geschwader* was re-deployed to support *Heeresabteilung C* near St.Mihiel before transferring to *AOK 5* to the north of Verdun on the 8 October. His final score was 22 *LS*, whilst that of *JG I* between June 1917 and November 1918 was 644 *LS* for the loss of 56 pilots and a further 52 wounded.

JG I consisted of *Jasta 4, 6, 10 & 11* and Göring's loyalty to many of his former colleagues in arms would eventually result in their appointment to positions in the new *Luftwaffe - Oblt*.Karl Bodenschatz (*Adjutant JG I*), *Oblt*.Ernst Udet (*Fhr.Jasta 4*), *Lt*.Arthur Laumann (*Fhr.Jasta 10*), *Lt*.Wolfram Frhr.von Richthofen (*Fhr.Jasta 11*) and *Oblt*.Erich Rüdiger von Wedel (*Fhr.Jasta 11*). Other pilots of note from this period who survived the war included: *Lt*.Alfred Gerstenberg (*Jasta 11*), *Vfw*.Alois Heldmann (*Jasta 10*), *Lt*.Hans Klein (*Jasta 4*) and *Lt*.Lothar von Richthofen (*Jasta 11* + 24 Jul 22).

Photo 1A-8 Original caption: The creator and organiser of the *Reichswehr* [*Generaloberst* Hans von Seeckt] with his infantry students (Dresden) in the first *Reichswehr* maneuvers in 1925 in Thüringen, near Erfurt as *Chef der Heeresleitung*.
Bundesarchiv Bild 146-2005-0163 Photo: Oscar Tellgmann

GenLt.Hans von Seeckt was appointed to the post of *Chef des Heeresleitung* within the

Reichswehrministerium in March 1920 following the removal of *GenMaj.*Walter Reinhardt in the wake of the abortive *Kapp Putsch*. Denied heavy artillery, tanks and aircraft Seeckt focused on the one asset he could transform, the personnel of the 100,000 man Reichsheer which he turned into a highly trained professional army which was without equal in the World. The *Offizierkorps* were well trained and educated and in the fullness of time would produce tacticians of the highest order. Foreign military observers noted that the relationship between the officers and enlisted personnel was particularly good and a far cry from the class ridden Imperial army. The enlisted personnel were also of a very high quality and competition for the limited number of places available each year was fierce. Perhaps the only problem with *Reichsheer's* personnel was their overwhelmingly conservative outlook, the officers in particular were monarchic and strongly opposed to the new Republic. Nonetheless Seeckt demanded a totally apolitical stance from his officers and offenders those who broke this rigid code were summarily discharged.

Seeckt was progressive in his thinking and fully appreciated the importance of armour, mobility and air power to the army of the future. To this end he supported a rapprochement with the Soviet Union which saw the joint development of secret bases deep in the USSR where tanks, artillery, chemical warfare and military aviation could all be developed. He provided strong support for *Maj.* Helmuth Wilberg as his first *Chef der Luftschützgruppe,* a covert air staff that was variously known as the *TA (L),* the *T 2 III (L)* and the *T 2 V (L).* He was also influential in the secret acquisition of 50 Fokker D.XIII fighters in the wake of the *Ruhrkrise* of 1923. These would later find their way to Lipetsk in the Soviet Union where the *Reichsheer's* new generation of military pilots would receive their operational training. Meanwhile in Germany, Seeckt's ready acceptance of the importance of military air power led to the incorporation of a good deal of air doctrine into *H.Dv.487 Führung und Gefecht der Verbundenen Waffen* (Leadership and Battle with Combined Arms) which was first published in 1922-23.

In this photograph of 1925 *Gen.d.Inf.*von Seeckt is seen with a new generation of young *Leutnante,* officers under training at the *Infanterieschule Dresden*. Similar schools existed for the other major arms: the *Artillerieschule Jüterbog, Kavallerieschule Hannover* and the *Pionierschule München*.

Photo 1A-9 Original caption: Our successful fighter pilot *Leutnant* Udet - Portrait of Ernst Udet Order *Pour le Mérite* (awarded on 9 April 1918).

Bundesarchiv Bild 146-1978-098-21A Photo: Postkartenvertrieb W.Sanke, Berlin N 37

Following the death of Richthofen, Ernst Udet was Germany's leading surviving *Experte* from the Great War with 62 *Luftsiege* and as such his views on air fighting had been sought as part of *Maj.* Helmuth Wilberg (*Luftschütz-Referent*)'s post-war evaluation of the recently concluded air war.

Born on the 26 April 1896 he volunteered for military service in August 1914, was rejected on account of his age, and thereafter served as a volunteer motorcyclist before training as military pilot in 1915 with a posting to the Elsass sector in August as a pilot within *Art.FA 206* later *Feld-FA 68*. During the latter part of 1916 he served in the Champagne sector as a member of *Jasta 15* and on the 22 January 1917 he was commissioned as a *Leutnant der Reserve*. He became *Jasta 15's* first *Experte* in May 1917. At his request he transferred to *Jasta 37* in the summer and quickly became that *Staffel's* first *Experte*. He was appointed *Führer Jasta 37* in support of *AOK 6* on the 7 November 1917 and continued to score steadily reaching 19 *LS* by March 1918. At this point he was recruited by *Rittm.*Manfred von Richthofen and transferred the *Jagdgeschwader Richthofen* as acting *Fhr.Jasta 11* on the 23 March before being confirmed as *Fhr.Jasta 4* in May. Air combat was now increasingly intense and on the 29 June Udet was shot down in flames, saving himself with one of the newly issued parachutes. Following a period of convalescence he was promoted to *Oberleutnant der Reserve* and returned to the Front in September as *Fhr.Jasta 4* in support of *Armee-Abt.C* and later *AOK 5*. Having scored 39 *LS* with *Jasta 4*, with 20 *LS* during 3-25 August 1918 at the time of the final German offensive, *Oblt.*Udet was posted to the *Inspektion des Flugwesens* in Berlin in October where he remained until discharged on the 10 January 1919.

Photo 1A-10 Original caption: *Deutsche Luftstreitkräfte* 1918. A *Beobachter* with a machine gun.
Bundesarchiv Bild 183-R27828 Photo: o.Ang. (Scherl)

The *Infanterieflieger* as a concept first came into being in 1916 during the fighting in and around Verdun. Initially the *Flieger Abteilungen* employed standard armed *"C"* category aircraft, these being protected from enemy fighters by similar machines flown by the newly formed *Schützstaffeln*. However by 1917 it was clear that a smaller more agile aircraft was required for low-level operations over the *Hauptkampflinie (HKL)* and the *"CL"* category appeared. These specially designed two-seat aircraft were supposed to have an empty weight of just 360 kgs, be powered by a 160/180 hp engine, be armed with a fixed and a flexible machine gun, and equipped with wireless and camera. The successful designs came from the *Halberstadter Flugzeugwerke* and the *Hannoverische Waggonfabrik* and both were produced in quantity during 1917-18. Not surprisingly both models were considerably heavier than expected at around 750 kgs empty and 1,100 kgs fully loaded. However they did prove to be remarkably agile and were considered to be especially dangerous opponents by the Allied scout pilots of 1918.

In 1918 the new Halberstadt and Hannover CL-Serie were assigned to the *Schützstaffeln* which in March 1918 were re-designated *Schlachtstaffeln* or *Schlasta*. Of the 38 available units in March, many were grouped together to form powerful *Schlachtgruppen* and even *Schlachtgeschwadern* to support the *Feldheer* in the planned spring offensive in the West - the three attacking armies were assigned 27 *Schlasta* as well as 42 *Jasta*, 55 *Flieger Abteilungen* and 4 *Bombengeschwadern*. Initially total air superiority over the *HKL* was achieved but by the third day of the offensive the *Schlasta* had started to suffer increasingly heavy losses to enemy anti-aircraft fire.

The *Beobachter* of Halberstadt CL-II *Flugzeug Nr.2 "Brunhilde"* inspects his *Deutschen Waffen- und Munitionsfabriken* le.MG 14/17 more commonly known as the *Parabellum-Maschinengewehr*. This 7.92 mm machine gun was the standard *Luftstreitkräfte* defensive weapon for use on flexible mountings as seen here. Like the pilot's 7.92 mm lu.MG 08/15 on a fixed mounting, the le.MG 14 was air cooled and belt fed, the 100 round belt being contained within a *grosser Munitionstrommel*. The weapon was recoil operated with a cyclic rate of fire of 700 rounds per minute. Fitted with a shoulder butt, the gun was aimed using a *Zielfernrohr* (telescopic sight) and ring foresight and proved highly satisfactory in service. In addition to his duties as observer and rear gunner, the *Beobachter* of a CL machine was also provided with *Stielhandgranate* in a wooden rack on the side of the fuselage and coloured flares in webbing on the fuselage top decking. Later in 1918 the 1 kg *Mause Splitterbombe* would become available and proved highly effective against troops caught in the open.

The tactical and *Staffel* markings are of note. A *Schlasta* of 1918 had an establishment of six *CL* machines and in this case they have each been numbered on the front fuselage, whilst a girl's name in white capital letters has been painted on the rear fuselage.

Photo 1A-11 Original caption: A German secret enterprise behind the Iron Curtain in the steppes of the Volga region near Volsk in the years 1928 to 1931 (Dissolved in 1933). The HD 40 our largest machine in use, is about to depart at the airfield of the *Tomka Kampfmittel-Versuchsplatz* – a joint *Reichswehr* and the Red Army chemical weapons-testing ground. The aircraft is fitted with the *Kampfstoffbomben* and *Kamppfstofftanken* (chemical weapons

bombs and tanks). The pilot, pictured right, gives a good indication of the size of the aircraft.
Bundesarchiv MSg 2 Bild-00782-42 Photo: o.Ang.

A great deal of secrecy surrounded the activities of the *Reichsheer* at the *Tomka Kampfmittel-Versuchsplatz*. In agreeing to the secret military clauses of the Treaty of Rapello, the Red Army had hoped in part to benefit from the expertise of the *Reichsheer's* gas warfare personnel. To this end a joint facility was established at Podosinki, near Moscow in 1926. Under the leadership of Hans Hackmack aerial dispersal trials with the new *Kampfstoffbehalter Typ G-125* were carried out using a Junkers F 13 and a Junkers A 20. When fire destroyed this initial facility a new test centre was established in 1928 by *Obst.a.D.*Wilhelm Trepper, previously *Chef des Stabes der Inspektion der Artillerie,* near Saratov some 750 kms south-east of the Soviet capital. Once again aircraft, including the Heinkel HD 40, were employed to test the effectiveness of the aerial application of a number of poison gases including *Senfgas* (Mustard Gas), *Perstoff* (Chlorine Gas) and *Blaukreuzkampfstoffen* (Blue Cross agents - Adamsite).

Secrecy extends to the exact identity of the aircraft seen in this image. Identified in the original caption as a Heinkel HD 40, this aircraft was developed in 1927 from the earlier HD 39 *Zeitungsflugzeug* (WNr.238 D-889). Both machines were employed by the *Ullstein AG* publishing group to transport copies of the *Berliner Zeitung* newspaper swiftly around Germany. Two aircraft were completed for *Ullstein* these being HD 40/I WNr.267 and WNr.268 but it appears that the second aircraft was actually with the *DVL* at Berlin-Adlershof when it crashed on the 19 May 1927.

As it is known HD 40/I WNr.267 D-1200 also crashed near Stettin on the 27 July 1927, it can only have been a third aircraft, the HD 40/II WNr.274 D-1180, that was subject to the *Deutsche Versuchsanstalt für Luftfahrt's Abteilung M (Militärische)'s* instruction that "various changes" be made to a HD 40 at the *Heinkel-Werke* between 19-27 August 1927 prior to its deployment to the newly established *Versuchsgruppe* at Lipetsk in 1928. Unfortunately WNr.274 crashed en route to Lipetsk and had to be returned to Germany for repair. More than a year later on the December 2, 1929 the *Heereswaffenamt's Waffenprüfwesen 8* (*Maj.*Wilhelm Wimmer) requested that a HD 40 be made available for testing new target and ordnance dropping devices as part of the *1930 Arbeitsplan* for Lipetsk. Following these tests WNr.274 was transferred to *Tomka* where it is known from Russian sources that a HD 40 was involved in the testing of chemical warfare agents at the *Tomka Kampfmittel-Versuchsplatz* and this is confirmed by this photograph of an unmarked aircraft. Following the completion of this programme the HD 40 was then disassembled for return to Germany by ground transport in 1931. It was subsequently withdrawn from use in September 1933. On the basis of this information this photograph is believed to date from 1931.

Photo 1A-12 Original caption: Honouring the Reich Constitution in Berlin on 11 August 1923. *Reichspräsident* [Friedrich] Ebert and *Reichswehrminister* [Otto] Gessler proceed in front of the guard of honour.
Bundesarchiv Bild 102-10844 Photo: Georg Pahl

The *Verfassungsfeier* – Anniversary - of the new Weimar Republic took place in Berlin on the 11 August 1923 against a backcloth of deepening economic disaster, partial foreign occupation and internal political division.

The root cause of these problems was the difficulty that successive Governments had encountered in trying to transform the country from a command-based war economy to a peacetime economy based on free enterprise with relatively little public expenditure. Reluctant to raise taxes to finance Government spending, Governments had survived by printing more money. As a result the value of the Mark had fallen remorselessly from one tenth of its pre-war value in 1920 to one hundredth of its value in 1922 and this rate of decline was accelerating. By the beginning of 1923 the value of the mark had fallen to just two thousand five hundredth of the earlier gold mark.

These extreme financial difficulties were compounded by the burden of the war debt. On the 27 April 1921 the Allied Reparations Commission had fixed Germany's liability at 132 billion gold marks of which 2 billion was to be paid annually together with 25% of the value of her exports. The French in particular wanted payment in full and on time. On the 9 January 1923 the Allies declared that the German authorities had defaulted on the required deliveries of coal, timber and telegraph poles. In the course of the following week French and Belgian troops began their occupation of the Ruhr precipitating a major political crisis.

With the *Reichswehr* powerless to prevent the military occupation – *Gen.d.Inf.*von Seeckt wisely resisted all pressure to initiate a military response – a policy of passive resistance to the occupation began. Industrialists were instructed not to hand over coal stocks. A general strike was declared within the Ruhr but this only served to accelerate the rate of inflation as tax revenues and export earnings fell. By August the German currency had collapsed although hyper-inflation would not peak for a further three months. Confidence in the Weimar Government evaporated and into this power vacuum came the extremists from both the left and right of the political divide. There was a communist rising in Hamburg, tension through much of the country and an attempted coup in München by Adolf Hitler and his fledgling *NSDAP*, supported by right wing nationalists such as *Gen.d.Inf.*Otto Ludendorff.

Three individuals effectively saved the Republic. Gustav Stresemann took power as *Reichskanzler*, Hans von Seeckt was given the authority to put down the rebellions and restore order, and Hjalmar Schacht, the *Präsident des Reichsbank*, would become the architect of economic recovery with the introduction of the *Rentenmark*, a new currency fixed against the US Dollar. Passive resistance was called off on the 26 September but the real victims of the crisis were the German people. Germany would be turned into a nation of high prices, low wages and high unemployment. Personal savings had been wiped out and the middle classes in particular were thereafter more inclined to support more extreme political parties.

Photo 1A-13 Original caption: This year's major cavalry manoeuvres in Döberitz in Berlin! *Reichswehrminister* Dr. Gessler and *General* von Seeckt were present during the manoeuvres. Subsequent to the manoeuvre a parade of troops took place. *Reichswehrminister* Dr. [Otto] Gessler (right) and *General* [Hans] von Seeckt (left) are seen in the exercise area.

Bundesarchiv Bild 102-10883 Photo: Georg Pahl

This image from August 1926 reveals little of the growing antipathy between *GenOb.*Hans von Seeckt as *Chef des Heeresleitung* and his nominal superior *Reichswehrminister Dr.*Otto Gessler. However within three months von Seeckt would have been forced to resign over the scandal that had arisen over the presence at these manoeuvres of *Prinz* Wilhelm von Preussen (*Inf.Rgt.9*) in the pre-war uniform of the *1.Garde-Regiment zu Fuss*. Such an outward manifestation of the Imperial past had resulted in a public outcry which both Gessler and the new *Reichspräsident* used as an excuse to rid themselves of von Seeckt who they independently considered to be both increasingly arrogant and haughty. Hindenburg had said privately that *"von Seeckt's insufferable conceit was ruining the Reichsheer"*. Seeckt was replaced by *Gen.d.Inf.*Wilhelm Heye, the *Befehlshaber der Wehrkreis I*.

The talented Gessler who had done so much to ensure the survival of the *Reichswehr* would also be gone in little more than a year. Again a victim of public disquiet; on this occasion the covert activities of the *Sondergruppe R* and the "misuse" of service funds in the wake of *Kpt.z.S.*Lohmann's activities in the Phoebus Affair. Gessler was replaced as *Reichswehrminister* by *GenLt.a.D.*Wilhelm Groener.

Using "black" funds obtained from the sale of warships, the *Reichsmarine's* share of the *Ruhrfond* plus smaller sums diverted from other sources, Walter Lohmann had been responsible for the financing of nearly all the *Reichsmarine's* clandestine and semi-clandestine projects during 1923-27. These projects included the further development of submarines as well as naval aircraft. The firms of *Dornier, Heinkel* and *Rohrbach* all enjoyed naval patronage whilst Lohmann later bought out right the assets of the *Caspar-Werke* at Travemünde. The naval flight facilities firm *Severa* was another Lohmann financed enterprise. However it was Lohmann's attempts to generate further unofficial funds for the *Reichsmarine* through a variety of non-naval enterprises that would bring his covert work into the public domain and ultimately cause both his downfall as well as those of Gessler and *Adm.*Hans Zenker, the *Chef des Marineleitung*.

Photo 1A-14 Original caption: *Reichswehrminister* Dr. Groener has resigned from his post! *Reichswehrminister* Dr. Groener with *Reichswehr* officers during an exercise.

Bundesarchiv Bild 102-13484 Photo: Georg Pahl

Wilhelm Groener enjoyed a long and successful career, initially as a professional soldier and thereafter as a leading politician in the Weimar Republic. He was born into a military family on the 22 November 1867 in Ludwigsburg. He entered the *3.Wurttemburgische Infanterie Regiment Nr.121* in 1884 and finished top of his class at the *Kriegschule Berlin*. He was appointed to the *Generalstabes* in 1899 as a *Hauptmann*. Thereafter he gained an excellent reputation for his thorough staff work and excellent organisational skills. He served in the newly formed *Kriegsnahrungsministerium* (War Food Ministry) from December 1915 and he was *Chef der Kriegsamt* from November 1916 until August 1917.

After a period at the Front in France and in the Ukraine, he was appointed *1.Oberquartiermeister* under *GFM.*Paul von Hindenburg in October 1918. As such he oversaw the withdrawal of the *Feldheer* from France and Belgium and its later demobilisation, he personally advised the *Kaiser* that he should abdicate, and secretly made a pact with the newly elected *Reichspräsident* Friedrich Ebert that secured the *Reichsheer's* future as a pillar of the state in return for military involvement in the internal struggle against the communist revolution. Groener supported German acceptance of the Versailles settlement, he started the re-organisation of the *Reichswehr* and he recommended that Hans von Seeckt become *Chef des Heeresleitung*. As some of these measures were deeply unpopular amongst senior officers, Groener chose to retire from the *Heer* on the 30 September 1919.

Over the next decade Groener moved in and out of politics. At Ebert's request he served as *Reichsverkehrsminister* during 1920-23 and as such oversaw the nationalisation of the German railway network into the highly successful *Deutsche Reichsbahn*. Then on the 20 January 1928, *Reichspräsident* Hindenburg brought him out of retirement to replace Otto Gessler as *Reichswehrminister*. This was a period of financial retrenchment but simultaneously a period of significant rearmament, particularly in the *Reichsmarine* with the arrival of a new class of *kleine Kreuzer* and the launching of the *Panzerschiffe*. Steps were also taken to finalise the design of modern combat aircraft for both branches of the *Reichswehr* as well as to begin their covert production and stockpiling. The debate on the future form of the military air arm also reached a head with the decision on the 24 February 1932 to secretly create an independent *Reichsluftwaffe*. In the meantime it had been Groener that had pushed for the creation of the *Reklamestaffeln*, the *Reichsheer's* first air units, on the 29 November 1930.

Groener was concerned about the growing power of the *NSDAP's Sturmabteilung (SA)* which clearly had ambitions for pre-eminence within Germany's military. On the 8 October 1931 he additionally became acting *Reichsminister des Innern* and as a result the issue of the *SA* became even more difficult for him to resolve. As *RMI* he was in favour of banning the *SA*, whilst as *RWM* he could appreciate the advantages of being able to call upon a paramilitary force akin to the earlier *Frei Korps*. In the end he supported *Reichskanzler* Bruning and the *SA* and the *SS* were outlawed, actions that would eventually topple him from power. His opponent was Kurt von Schleicher, a man who saw an alliance with the *NSDAP* to be to his personal advantage. Schleicher's standing with the *Präsident* had improved whereas Groener had fallen from favour in the wake of his second marriage and the early birth of his son. Increasingly isolated in the *Reichstag* and in the *Reichswehr*, Groener decided to resign his posts on the 30 May 1932. He retired to Potsdam and died in Bornstedt on the 3 May 1939.

He is seen here in happier times in the company of an Allied general and two *Reichsheer* officers.

Photo 1A-15 Original caption: *General* (Kurt) Schleicher – at an event in front of the *Reichstag* in 1932. (Schleicher (left) is seen here in the company of his friend and colleague *Gen.d.Inf.* Kurt von Hammerstein-Equord, the *Chef des Heeresleitung* (right)).

Bundesarchiv Bild 146-1992-018-01A Photo: Hartmann

GenLt. Kurt Schleicher had played an important, at times pivotal role, in the fortunes of the Weimar Republic. As *GenLt.* Wilhelm Groener's protégé within the wartime *Oberste Heeresleitung*, he had emerged onto the political stage to play a key role in the negotiations that led to the Groener-Ebert Pact of 1919. He was also instrumental in establishing the *Frei Korps* which proved so successful in quashing the *Spartakists*. With *Gen.d.Inf.* Hans von Seeckt's patronage Schleicher became a leading light in the highly secret *Sondergruppe Russland* where he helped to finalise the financial and technical aspects of German support for the Red Army in return for Soviet support for clandestine German activities in the USSR. He was also involved in the murderous activities of the so-called *Schwarz Reichswehr* which sought to eliminate those Germans who co-operated with the Allied Control Commission.

By the mid-twenties Schleicher was already accustomed to secret wheeling and dealing and it was he who leaked the information that led to Seeckt's downfall in 1926, whilst he simultaneously promoted his own cause as a member of *Reichspräsident* Hindenburg's inner circle. The appointment of his former mentor Groener as the new *Reichswehrminister* led to Schleicher's appointment in 1929 as the *Chef der Ministeramt* within the *RWM*. This was a position of considerable influence and Schleicher was able to secure the *Reichsmarine's* threatened *Panzerschiff Programm* despite the opposition of the majority Social Democrats. His ability to secure the necessary votes for successive *Reichswehr* budgets at a time of increasing economic difficulty confirmed his position as the *Reichswehr's* chief fixer.

Gen.d.Inf. Kurt von Hammerstein-Equord had replaced *GenOb.* Wilhelm Heye as *Chef der Heeresleitung* on the 1 November 1930 after a period as *Chef des Truppenamt*. Hammerstein was a man of strong views which were often expressed without thought. He was not in favour of an independent air arm and instead favoured a traditional subordination of military air power to the needs of the *Feldheer,* a stance in which he enjoyed the support of *GenMaj.* Wilhelm Adam, the new *Chef des Truppenamt,* as well as both *Obst.* Hermann Geyer and *Obstlt.* Wilhelm Keitel, his former *Abteilungschef* in the *TA*. In this respect his thinking followed that in the USSR, USA and Japan, but was in contrast to that found in Britain and France.

Although Hammerstein and Schleicher were friends, the *Chef der Heeresleitung* was utterly opposed to Hitler and the *NSDAP*. During 1932 he repeatedly warned the *Reichspräsident* of the danger posed by the National Socialists who he referred to as criminals and perverts. Hindenburg assured him that he would not allow Hitler to become *Reichskanzler*.

Photo 1A-16 Original caption: *Stahlhelm* – **Kurt Schleicher (left), Franz von Papen (centre), Wilhelm Freiherr von Gayl (right).**

Bundesarchiv Bild 146-2012-0056 Photo: o.Ang.

Taken at some point after the 1 June 1932 this image shows: *Reichskanzler* Franz von Papen, *Reichswehrminister* Kurt von Schleicher, and *Reichsminister des Innern* Wilhelm Friedrich Frhr.von Gayl.

By the late twenties *GenLt.*Schleicher's interests had become increasingly political. No less than eleven Governments had come and gone during 1919-28, and he was certainly no friend of the democratic process. Instead he advocated a more active Presidential role in which the *Reichskanzler* would be responsible to the *Präsident* rather than to the *Reichstag.* As part of this policy he actively undermined the existing coalition Government which led to the fall of *Reichskanzler* Hermann Müller in January 1930 and his replacement by the amenable Heinrich Bruning. Despite their majority in the *Reichstag* all Social Democrats were removed from ministerial office. The ground was being prepared for a far more dictatorial approach to the government of Germany.

Schleicher was also concerned that the *Reichswehr's* reserve of trained personnel was rapidly dwindling as a result of the Treaty limitations on military service and in March 1931 he entered into a secret pact with Ernst Röhm, the *Chef SA*, which recognised the *NSDAP's* para-military force as an official militia in time of national emergency. His admiration for the *NSDAP* also led to ever closer relations with other senior National Socialists, although Göring was one of those who were aware of Schleicher's track record for duplicity. This trait duly re-surfaced in 1932 when he used his influence with the *Reichspräsident* to oust both Groener and Bruning when they attempted to outlaw the *SA.* As a result of these manoeuvres Schleicher was appointed *Reichswehrminister* in the new von Papen Government of June 1932.

At Schleicher's instigation, Hindenburg selected Franz von Papen as Bruning's successor. Papen was a former member of the *Größer Generalstab*, Ambassador to the USA and confirmed monarchist. As a long term member of the *Zentrum Partei* he had gone against his colleagues in 1925 in supporting Hindenburg for the post of *Reichspräsident* and in replacing Bruning he broke a pledge to his Party Chairman to not accept the position of *Reichskanzler.* He was however merely a figurehead in the new Government as it was Schleicher that chose the new members of the *Kabinett.* Papen had virtually no support in the *Reichstag* either and in an attempt to strengthen his position he called for national elections in July. The result was unexpected as the *NSDAP* secured 123 seats to become the largest party in the *Reichstag* but without a clear majority. In an attempt to resolve this situation another election was held in November but it too was inconclusive. In the face of growing discord between the *NSDAP* and the communist *KPD* and lacking the support of the *Reichspräsident*, Papen was forced to step down to be replaced by Hindenburg's preferred candidate. Schleicher was appointed *Reichskanzler* on the 3 December 1932.

Photo 1A-17 Original caption: On the forthcoming eightieth birthday of the *Reichspräsidenten* von Hindenburg! This was the last civil record of *Reichspräsidenten* von Hindenburg in his office at the Presidential Palace.

Bundesarchiv Bild 102-04763 Photo: o.Ang.

Following the unexpected death in office of Friedrich Ebert in February 1925 a presidential vacuum existed until May of that year. Initial elections failed to produce a candidate with a sufficient majority and concern over the likely outcome led to *Grossadmiral* Alfred von Tirpitz, the former *Staatssekretär der Reichsmarineamt*, urging Hindenburg to stand as an independent non-party candidate. Largely because of the support of the *BVP*, the large female vote and his status as Germany's greatest war hero, Hindenburg won the second round of elections and took office on the 12 May 1925.

Initially Hindenburg took little part in the daily round of politics and instead performed the republican equivalent of a constitutional monarch being the figure head of the German state. However this position would slowly change as Germany descended into a new round of economic problems and social discord in the early thirties. Heavily influenced by an inner circle (*Kamarilla*), which consisted of Wilhelm Groener, Kurt von Schleicher, Otto Meissner and his son Oskar who acted as his father's *ADC*, Hindenburg moved increasingly toward a more Presidental style of Government in which he appointed the *Reichskanzler* who was responsible thereafter to the *Reichspräsident* and not the *Reichstag*. By April 1930 this stance had already resulted in the collapse of the Hermann Müller led-coalition Government and his replacement by the first of five Hindenburg nominees: Heinrich Bruning (Mar 30 – May 32), Franz von Papen (Jun – Dec 32), Kurt Schleicher (Dec 32 – Jan 33) and Adolf Hitler (from Jan 33).

This formal portrait photograph of *GFM.a.D.*Paul von Hindenburg was taken in September 1927. His military career had begun in 1866 and he had seen action in both the Austro-Prussian War (1866) and the Franco-Prussian War (1870-71) being decorated for bravery. He had thereafter risen through the ranks to reach *General der Infanterie* in 1903 as a *Kommandierenden General des Armeekorps*. He retired in 1911 but was re-activated in 1914 by von Moltke, the *Chef des Größe Generalstab*. Hindenburg took command of *AOK 8* in Ostpreussen and soon after won the decisive Battles of Tannenberg and the Masurian Lakes which effectively removed the Russian threat to Germany's eastern borders. Taking the offensive in the east *GFM.*Hindenburg's armies won a series of victories during 1914-16 before he was appointed *Chef des Oberste Heeresleitung* in August 1916. For the remainder of the war he was de facto head of the *Heer* and he played an important part in Germany's defensive successes on the Western Front and ultimately Germany's 1918 offensive against the western Allies. With the Allied advance toward Germany in the autumn of 1918, he played a decisive role in persuading *Kaiser* Wilhelm II to abdicate and thus bring the Great War to a close. He retired from military service in July 1919.

Photo 1A-18 Original caption: The historic Potsdam Tag of 21 March 1933. *Reichspräsident* von Hindenburg, *Reichskanzler* Hitler and *Reichswehrminister* von Blomberg infront of the Garrison Church in Berlin.

Archiv Title: At the inauguration of the *Reichstag*- Paul von Hindenburg (with *Pickelhaube*), Werner von Blomberg (with *Stahlhelm*) and Adolf Hitler in front of the Garrison Church.

Bundesarchiv Bild 102-16082 Photo: Georg Pahl

Reichspräsident Hindenburg's choice of Kurt von Schleicher as *Reichskanzler* in December 1932 had represented one final attempt to keep Hitler from securing that position. At that time it appeared that divisions within the *NSDAP* might give Schleicher an opportunity to reach an accommodation between the left wing of the *NSDAP* and the Trade Unionists within both the *SDP* and Christian Democrats. However he had not counted on the unpopularity of his Government and his own position in the face of political manoeuvres by the deposed Franz von Papen and the ambitious Adolf Hitler. Through his own indiscretions he quickly lost the support of Hindenburg and his influential inner-circle, whilst the clear need to effectively control the activities of the rival political groups within Germany increasingly pushed the *Reichspräsident* to consider a new approach. On the 30 January 1933 he appointed Hitler as the new *Reichskanzler*; Franz von Papen was to serve as *Vizekanzler*, whilst *Gen.d.Inf.*Werner von Blomberg was re-assigned as *Reichswehrminister*.

Hindenburg had first met Hitler in a highly charged meeting in October 1931 and thereafter there was never any love between these two men. Hitler regarded Hindenburg to be a "reactionary old fool" whilst Hindenburg referred to Hitler, inaccurately as it turned out, as that "Bohemian Corporal". Hitler had then stood unsuccessfully against Hindenburg in the 1932 Presidential Elections, whilst in August Hindenburg had rejected Hitler's demands for the position of *Reichskanzler* following the NSDAP's success in the national elections. Forced by circumstance in January 1933, Hindenburg still thought he could control Hitler. There were only two other *NSDAP* members of the *Kabinett*: Hermann Göring and Wilhelm Frick, whilst his former protégé Papen occupied a position of considerable power. Nonetheless he agreed 27 February. He also supported Hitler's demands for powers to restrict the freedom of the press and the suspension of civil liberties.

This image commemorates the opening of the new *Reichstag* on the 21 March 1933. In a carefully orchestrated event Hitler skilfully linked the emerging *NSDAP* state with existing Prussian-German traditions. Hindenburg gave Hitler his own vote of confidence with the words: *"May the old spirit of this celebrated shrine permeate the generation of today, may it liberate us from selfishness and party strife and bring us together in national self-consciousness to bless a proud and free Germany, united in herself."*

Photo 1B-1 Original caption: *Ministerialdirigent* **Ernst Brandenburg appointed an honorary Dr. Ing! The** *Technische Hochschule Braunschweig* **has awarded the** *Leiter der Luftfahrtabteilung im Reichsverkehrsministerium, MinDir.***Ernst Brandenburg a honorary Doctorate in Engineering in view of his services to aviation.**

Bundesarchiv Bild 102-06974 Photo: o.Ang.

Ernst Brandenburg played a highly significant role in the development of civil aviation during the Weimar period. A highly decorated (*Pour le Mérite* 14 Jun 17) bomber pilot and *Kdr.BoGOHL 3 – the England Geschwader* – he was invalided out of the *Luftstreitkräfte* with the rank of *Major* after losing a leg in an accident.

Post war he joined the civil service and served in the *Reichsverkehrsministerium* becoming the *Leiter der Abteilung für Luft-und Kraftfahrwesen* later *Ltr.d.Luftfahrtabteilung* from April 1924. Thereafter his energy, foresight and organisational ability enabled him to take a leading role in the formation of the *Deutsche Verkehrsfliegerschule* in 1925, the amalgamation of the competing *Deutscher Aero Lloyd* and *Junkers Luftverkehr* concerns to form *Deutsche Luft Hansa* in 1926, and in the general development of aviation within Germany following the lifting of Allied restrictions on commercial aviation in the same year. The growth of the *Deutsche Luftfahrtverband* and the resurgence of the *Luftschiffbau Zeppelin* can also be attributed in part to his encouragement and support.

As Germany's economic position worsened in the early thirties he was able to provide substantial financial support to key development programmes and firms thus ensuring the eventual success of the *Reichswehr's* covert air armament programmes. In 1928 he was awarded an honorary Doctorate in recognition of his on-going contribution to the cause of German aviation. Although he did not transfer to Göring's *Reichsluftfahrtministerium* in 1933, preferring to remain in the *RVM* as *Leiter der Kraftfahr-und Landstrassenwesen,* he was later honoured with the honorary rank of *Oberst* on the 27 August 1939.

Photo 1B-2 Original caption: The *Reichs* **Government is flying to the inauguration of the** *deutschen Museums,* **which will take place on the 5 May in München. The two Junkers aircraft are seen shortly before take-off.**

(Bundesarchiv Bild 102-01371 Photo: Georg Pahl)

This image was taken by Georg Pahl at Germany's new national air transport hub at Berlin-Tempelhof early in May 1925. The two Junkers G 23 air transports are painted in the livery of *Ad Astra Aero*, the Swiss carrier, which had ordered four aircraft in February 1925. They are almost certainly WNr.832 CH-132 and WNr.834 CH 133 which were manufactured at Junkers' Dessau plant in 1924 before being shipped to *AB Flygindustri's* Limhamm plant in Sweden for assembly to avoid the restrictive practices of the *Interalliierte Luftfahrt-Überwachungs-Kommission (ILUK)* within Germany. Powered by wing mounted 160 hp Mercedes D IIIa in-line engines and a nose mounted Junkers L 2 of 195 hp the G 23 was under-powered and following the lifting of restrictions in 1926 it was replaced in production at Dessau by the externally similar G 24 with three Junkers L 2 motors. The G 24 featured an enclosed cockpit for the crew and a toilet for the passengers.

The Junkers G 23/G 24 series of air transports were of great significance to the development of commercial aviation in the mid-to late twenties offering all metal construction, three engine safety and greater capacity with nine passenger seats. The crew of three included two pilots and a wireless operator whose role became increasingly important as night and all weather operations became more frequent. The first scheduled night service in the world, from Berlin to Königsberg/Ostpreussen, was flown using a G 24 on the 1 May 1926. *Deutsche Luft Hansa* had a European Fleet of 18 G 23/G 24 aircraft in 1926 and the G 24 remained in full service on the Airline's international routes until as late as 1934.

Following the completion of around 60 G 23/G 24 *Verkehrsflugzeuge* at Limhamm and Dessau, the Junkers design team turned their attention to the larger and heavier G 31. This aircraft was optimised for passenger comfort, particularly on night flights when sleeping berths were provided in place of the normal 15 seat day configuration. *DLH* acquired seven G 31 airliners which were employed on the Hamburg-London, Berlin-Königsberg, Berlin-Wien and Berlin-Paris routes from 1928. Six other G 31s were built for foreign operators and three of these saw service in the heavy freight role in New Guinea.

Photo 1B-3 Original caption: The first launch of the Ocean giant flying boat Rohrbach *"Romar"* in Travemünde! Left to right: Dr. [Adolf] Rohrbach, the builder of this flying ocean liner, the well-known commander of the ocean flying boat [Hermann] Steindorf, and *Direktor* [Otto] Merkel of *Luft Hansa* after the successful flight from Travemünde.

Bundesarchiv Bild 102-10107 Photo: Georg Pahl

Born in Gotha on the 28 March 1889, Adolf Rohrbach had worked in the design department of *Zeppelin's Abteilung Flugzeugbau* from 1914 where he was engaged in the development of very large multi-engine aircraft. The futuristic Staaken E.4/20 commercial transport was without doubt a world beater when it appeared but in 1920 ILUK ordered that it be dismantled. Undeterred he studied for qualification as a *Dr.-Ing.* at the prestigious *Technische Hochschule* at Berlin-Charlottenburg before branching out on his own, establishing the *Rohrbach Metall-Flugzeugbau GmbH* in Berlin in 1922. Like Hugo Junkers and Claude Dornier, *Dr-Ing.*Rohrbach was a proponent of all-metal construction but unlike these compatriots Rohrbach increasingly cultivated military contracts to finance his work. Due to Allied restrictions many of his early designs including the Ro II, Ro III and Ro IV flying boats were built in Denmark at the *Rohrbach-Metal-Aeroplan Co.A/S* but from 1926 manufacturing was concentrated in Berlin where the company finally enjoyed commercial success with the three engine monoplane Ro VIII *Roland*, eighteen of which were bought for *Deutsche Luft Hansa*.

Unfortunately Rohrbach enjoyed less success with his other designs. The loss of the advanced Ro IX *Rofix* in a crash near Copenhagen on the 15 July 1927 with the death of its test pilot Paul Bäumer was a cause of official unease in his designs even though the cause was almost certainly pilot error. Nor were his flying boats more successful. The Ro V *Rocco* (1927) did not perform satisfactorily and despite its promise the later Ro X *Romar* (1928) was incapable of performing the trans-Atlantic operations for which it had been designed. Following the completion of three aircraft for *DLH* and one for the French *Aeronavale* (part of Germany's on-going war reparations) Rohrbach found it impossible to gain any further Government contracts and in the absence of any other work the bankrupt the *Rohrbach* concern was finally bought out by the newly established *Weser Flugzeugbau GmbH* in 1934. *Weser* retained Adolf Rohrbach as *Chefkonstrukteur* of the new Lemwerder plant at Bremen. By this stage his fertile brain had turned to the challenge of vertical flight, thoughts which would lead to *Dipl.Ing.*Simon's WP 1003 of 1938 which utilised tilt rotor technology. Adolf Rohrbach died in 1939.

This photograph is dated August 1928. The Ro X first took to the air in the hands of Hermann Steindorf on the 7 August and he is seen here after the successful completion of that flight in the company of Adolf Rohrbach and Otto Merkel. Steindorf (Lizenz Nr.335 23 Nov 12) had previously been *Chefpilot* at the *DVS-Zweigstelle Braunschweig*, whilst Otto Merkel had originally been a Director of *Deutscher Aero Lloyd* before becoming Chief Executive of *DLH* in 1926. By June 1929 *DLH's* financial position had become untenable and Merkel was replaced by Erhard Milch.

Photo 1B-4 Original caption: Jubilation for an aeroplane! It is now about 10 years ago since the first Junkers aircraft of type F 13 with the registration number "1," was officially handed over to the airline. Nothing proves the vigour of this type better than the fact that the "D 1" which was built in 1919 is still in use today as a German transport.

Bundesarchiv Bild 102-07981 Photo: o.Ang.

According to Junkers records, F 13 WNr.531 was one of the first three aircraft of this new type to be completed at Dessau in June 1919. Originally referred to as the J 13/3, this machine made its trial flights during the period 26 June to 16 July 1919. It was then given the temporary registration D-183 for the transfer flight to Berlin-Adlershof where it was officially entered on to the *Luftfahrzeugrolle* as D-1. The temporary registration was then removed. Assigned to *Junkers Luftverkehr* and given the fleet name *"Herta"* which was later replaced by *"Nachtigall"* it is possible that the aircraft was briefly confiscated by the *ILUK* in 1920 as the type's performance and payload exceeded the restrictions set by the Allied Control Commission. In 1920 WNr.531's registration was confirmed as D-1 on the new *Luftfahrzeugrolle B* and on the 13 April 1922 ownership was transferred to the *Bayerische Luft Lloyd*. Four years later she was transferred to the newly formed *Deutsche Luft Hansa* as part of that airline's initial fleet of 48 F 13 airliners. *DLH* employed the D-1 on the Berlin-Dresden and Berlin-Stettin routes and it is in connection with these services that she is seen in this image from June 1929.

D-1 became D-OJOP on the new *Luftfahrzeugrolle* of 1934 but continued in *DLH* use until the end of the decade thus marking twenty years of commercial employment – a remarkable achievement for an aircraft of this period. She was briefly utilised by *Hansa Flug Dienst* from 1938 but it seems likely that with the outbreak of hostilities she was transferred to the *Luftwaffe* where her civil codes were replaced by the *Stammkennzeichen* TV+OO in 1940. F 13 WNr.531 was finally withdrawn from use after suffering storm damage in November 1940 and passed to the *Deutsche Luftfahrtsammlung* in Berlin-Moabit for preservation. Unfortunately this historic aircraft was later destroyed in an Allied bombing raid on the German capital in January 1943.

Although few F 13 transports would survive in service as long as the D-1, this pioneering *Junkers'* design was one of aviation's true great aircraft. With its advanced cantilever monoplane layout, all-metal construction and fully enclosed cabin for four passengers the F 13 offered its operators good performance, reliability and economy. There were numerous variants of the basic design, mainly in respect of its engine installation that varied from the original 160/170 hp Daimler

D.IIIa through the standard BMW IIIa of 185 hp to the BMW Va of 360 hp as well as many foreign engines. Production continued to as late as 1932 with 322 aircraft being manufactured at Dessau. Of these just over 100 were completed in the period 1919-22 when production was restricted by *ILUK* and the airlines had access to large numbers of war surplus aircraft which were cheaper to acquire and operate. Thereafter production quickly rose to one per week during 1923-24 and in 1923 *Junkers Luftverkehr* had 60 aircraft of this type in service. By 1926 the company had flown 281,748 passengers over 15 million kilometres. The F 13 was used by airlines all over Europe, the Middle East as well as in North and South America.

Photo 1B-5 Original caption: The "fliegende Haus", the largest German landplane in the World! Professor Junkers, the *General-Construkteur*, with his co-workers in front of the new G.38 long range aircraft.
Bundesarchiv Bild 102-08683 Photo: Georg Pahl
"We must use aircraft to bring the peoples of the world closer to each other. My greatest aim is to contribute to that fruitful struggle which is for the benefit and cultural progress of mankind." Prof.Hugo Junkers, Dessau, 14 August 1927.

In creating the Junkers F 13, G 23/24, G 31, W 33 & W 34 Hugo Junkers had gone a long way to fulfilling this deep seated ambition. By the late twenties his aircraft were in use throughout the world making air transport of mail, goods and people a reality and helping to open up previously under-developed regions. His other ambition was to construct a very large commercial air transport, a goal that he had set himself as early as 1914 when he foresaw the eventual development of a 100 seat, and perhaps even a 1,000 seat aircraft. The construction of a range of all-metal aircraft had followed and in 1922 he took a further step along this road with the creation of the *Junkers Flugversuchsgruppe* within the *Forschungsamt Professor Junkers*. This group of experienced pilots were given a set a clear goals which in effect resulted in a scientific-technological approach to aircraft research and development. By 1924 drawings for the projected J 1000 had been created where 100 passengers, baggage, engines, fuel and 10 crew were all accommodated in a massive flying wing.

As an intermediate step work began on the very large, but considerably less ambitious, *Größflugzeuge* G.38 in 1928 with financial support being provided by the *RVM*. This aircraft would house its four engines and some of its payload in a large wing but in other respects it was more conventional and in its final form 26 of the 30 passengers were accommodated in three fuselage cabins. G.38 WNr.3301, which was completed with two Junkers L 55 engines of 600 hp and two Junkers L 8 of 400 hp at Dessau in the following October first flew on the 6 November 1929. This image almost certainly dates from the 10 November when the international press were given an opportunity to inspect the aircraft. Thereafter a series of record-breaking and long distance proving flights were made and by the 18 November 1930 c.1,000 passengers had been carried in the course of 30 flights, whilst some 20,000 people had visited the giant machine on the ground. Following a major overhaul, which included the replacement of the inner L 55 engines with L 88 engines of 800 hp, the G.38 was assigned to *Deutsche Luft Hansa* on the 7 May 1931. Over the following two and a half months the aircraft flew a further 35,000 kms, mainly on the Amsterdam to London route.

Although a second G.38 was later completed (WNr.3302 D-2500) in September 1931 with accommodation for 34 passengers, the two aircraft were not financially viable. They were however extremely popular and had caused quite a stir both in Germany and abroad. In a large military ceremony on the 29 April 1933 D-2500 was named *Generalfeldmarschall von Hindenburg*, whilst at some unknown date the D-2000 was named *Deutschland* thus forever linking this prestigious design with the emerging National Socialist State.

Unfortunately Hugo Junkers was treated far less well by successive German administrations.

He was driven to the verge of bankruptcy in 1925 by the *Reichswehr* sponsored Fili Affair in the Soviet Union which resulted in him having to hand over *Junkers Luftverkehr* to the *RVM* sponsored *DLH* in 1926. Ultimately he was even forced to relinquish control of the *Junkers Flugzeug-und Motorenwerke* to the newly formed *RLM* in 1933 who installed *Dr.*Heinrich Koppenberg as Managing Director.

Photo 1C-1 Original caption: *Flugboot* **Dornier J** *"Wal"* **with the registration D-861** *"Hai"* **photographed between 1926-30.**
    Bundesarchiv, Bild 102-00858/Photo: Georg Pahl
    To circumvent the restrictive activities of the *ILUK* Claude Dornier established the *Construzioni Meccaniche Aeronautiche SA (CMASA)* at the Marine di Pisa in Italy in 1922 and eventually more than 150 of the superb Do *Wal* flying boats would be built in Italy for both worldwide commercial and military employment.
    The Wal was one of the World's true great aircraft and apart from the twenty world records that were achieved in February 1925 by Dornier pilots Richard Wagner and Guido Guidi, it was to make a number of pioneering long distance flights including a return flight from Spain to the Canary Islands (4,500 kms) in 1924, the first east to west crossing of the South Atlantic from Spain to Buenos Aires (10,270 kms) in 1926, a formation flight from the Netherlands to the Dutch East Indies (15,600 kms) in 1929, an east-west flight across the North Atlantic (6,800 kms) in 1930 and an around the world flight (44,000 kms) in 1932.
    Do J *Wal* (Rolls Royce Eagle IX) C/Nr.24/41 was constructed at Pisa and was initially registered as I-DAAR before being bought by *Deutscher Aero Lloyd (DAL)* as one of a batch of four aircraft for use on its Danzig to Stockholm route. Re-registered as D-861 this aircraft could accommodate 8-10 passengers in an enclosed cabin in the bow with a flight crew of two in an open cockpit located immediately beneath the lead engine. It would subsequently see service with *Deutsche Luft Hansa* as seen in this image before being passed to the *Deutsche Verkehrsfliegerschule (DVS)* in 1929. It was finally sold to *Nordiska Flygrederiet* at Danzig with whom it suffered an accident on the 6 October 1931. In this photograph two passengers are being helped by one of the two crew members to enter the cabin whilst the rear engine is running to provide steerage.
    Eventually quite a number of Do J *Flugboote* would appear on the German register, mainly for use with the *DVS Zweigstellen* at List auf Sylt and Warnemünde. In 1932 a small batch were ordered by the *RWM* from *Dornier-Friedrichshafen* for use by the *Marineflieger* thus confirming the continued excellence of this more than decade old design. These *Militär-Wal 33* boats used 750 hp BMW VI engines and could be armed with machine guns in three flexible mountings in both the bow and rear fuselage whilst up to 200 kgs of ordnance could be carried beneath the wings on external racks. Officially the *Militär-Wal 33* or *10-tonne Wal* were referred to as Do 15 *Seeflugzeuge* and the first examples were delivered to the *DVS* for training in the last part of 1933.

Photo 1C-2 Original caption: **Germany 1928.** *Junkers-Werke* **in Dessau and Portrait of the founder of the works, Professor Junkers.**
    Bundesarchiv Bild 183-R14718 Photo: o.Ang. (Scherl)
    At the instigation of the *Inspektion der Fliegertruppe* the *Junkers-Fokker AG (JFA)* was established at *Prof.*Junkers existing works at Dessau on the 20 October 1917, largely to produce the revolutionary armoured Junkers J-I *Infanterieflugzeug* which was used for contact patrol work over the Western Front during the last year of the war. This early collaboration did not survive the war and in June 1919 the *Junkers Flugzeugwerke GmbH* was formed to produce a range of all-metal aircraft for the

civil market. The most important of these early models was without doubt the F 13 which was to establish Junkers as the World's leading exponent of all-metal construction for aircraft. However initial production of this small airliner was initially frustrated by the activities of the *ILUK* and it would not be until 1923 that output of this type increased significantly to average one per week. In due course Junkers would follow the F 13 with a number of far larger *Größflugzeuge*. The G 23 *Verkehrsflugzeug* was quickly followed by the refined G 24 and the even larger capacity G 31. Once again initial production of these large multi-engine types was frustrated by *ILUK* but following the signing of the Paris Air Agreement in 1926 un-restricted production of civil types could proceed at Dessau. With the F 13 supplanted in production by the W 33 and later W 34, output at Dessau had easily outstripped that of any other aircraft plant in Germany by the time of this photograph in 1928. Junkers' 1,000th aircraft was a G 31 completed on the 24 May 1928.

Having designed and built a range of marine and aero diesel engines during the Great War, Junkers decided in 1923 to establish the *Junkers Motorenbau* on the Dessau site. Initially this focused on the production of conventional carburettor petrol engines starting with the 80 hp L 1. However the most successful model was the 310 hp L 5 of which 1,000 would be built in the period up to 1933. From 1924 the development of heavy oil compression ignition (diesel) engines was resumed and this was to result in the 520 hp Jumo FO 4 which found increasing favour with *Deutsche Luft Hansa* from 1932 when at least six of the existing single-engine F 24 *Verkehrsflugzeuge* were modified to take the new power plant.

Junkers' success can be attributed to his foresight, expertise and driving ambition to make aviation a peaceful force for change in the years following the Great War. He was also a sound businessman and the creation of his own airline, the *Junkers Luftverkehr AG,* in 1924 was not only a commercial success in its own right but it secured a reliable market for the products of the Junkers manufacturing combine at Dessau.

Photo 1C-3 Original caption: *Generalleutnant* Otto Hasse, Kommandant der 3. Division, during field manoeuvres.

Bundesarchiv Bild 102-00363A Photo: Georg Pahl

Despite the excellence of his designs *Prof.*Hugo Junkers had found himself in serious financial difficulties by 1921. His salvation came in the form of *Obst.*Otto Hasse who as part of his work on behalf of the top secret *Sondergruppe R* visited Dessau with the proposal that Junkers open an aircraft and engine factory in the Soviet Union. The deal included $35 million of covert *Reichswehr* funding and Hasse indicated that thereafter there would be the promise of regular production contracts for *Junkers* designed aircraft from the *RKKVF*. This was just one of several covert projects that would be agreed between *Reichswehr* representatives and the *Luftfahrtindustrie* over the decade which was to establish the military-industrial basis for aerial re-armament in the thirties.

Born on the 21 June 1871 in Schlawe, Otto Hasse had enlisted in *Infanterie-Rgt. "Graf Kirchbach" (1.Niederschlesisches) Nr.46* in Posen on the 27 September 1890. During the Great War he had been a member of the *Größen Generalstab* and had served with several operational staffs as well as with the *Inspektion des Militärischen Verkehrswesens.* On the 12 May 1918 he was decorated with the *Eichenlaub* to his *Pour le Mérite* for his work as *Chef des Generalstabes* in the *X.Reserve-Korps* in the Battle of Kemmel. He finished the war as *Chef des Stabes der AOK 1.*

Hasse would become one of the *Reichsheer's* leading generals. As an *Obstlt.* he became the first *Chef T 1 (Heeres)* before being appointed *Chef des Truppenamtes* in April 1922. In the following year he had been central to the negotiations that under-pinned the secret military clauses of the Treaty of Rapello which enabled the *Reichswehr* to establish a number of covert bases inside the

Soviet Union. These included the *Flugzentrum Lipetsk* (1925), *Panzerschule Kasan* (1926) and the *Kampfmittel-Versuchsplatz Tomka* (1928). Military and technical assistance was also provided to the Red Army through the secondment of *Reichsheer* experts to the major Soviet military academies. Promoted to *Generalleutnant* on the 1 February 1926 he then succeeded *GenLt.*Rudolf von Horn as *Kdr.der 3.Division* in Berlin and this photograph dates from his time with that formation. Promoted to *General der Infanterie* on the 1 February 1929 he was appointed *Oberbefehlshaber vom Gruppenkommando 1* in April of that year with responsibility for the defence of Germany's eastern frontier. The *HrGrKdo.1* in Berlin controlled the *1.Division* (Königsberg/Ostpr.), *2.Division* (Stettin), *3.Division* (Berlin) and *4.Division* (Dresden) as well as the *1.Kavallerie-Division* (Frankfurt/ Oder) and *2.Kavallerie-Division* (Breslau) and as such was the more important of the *Reichsheer's* two operational commands. He was retired from the *Reichsheer* on the 30 September 1932 after 42 years of distinguished service.

Photo 1C-4 Original caption: Interesting experiments with a German parachute, which allows jumps from a height of 40 m. The parachute doll is seen on the wing of the aircraft before take-off. The attendant releases the connection string height at 40 m and observes the functioning of the parachute.

Bundesarchiv Bild 102-14834 Photo: Georg Pahl

In common with the other major combatants the *Luftstreitkräfte* had made use of parachutes for its balloon based observers from 1916 and in so doing had greatly reduced their mortality rate. Unlike the other combatants the *Luftstreitkräfte* had introduced parachutes for its aircrew in the closing months of the conflict and in so doing had saved many lives including that of Ernst Udet (28 June 1918) and Paul Bäumer (14 September 1918). This seat-type static-line parachute was designed by *Uffz.*Otto Heinecke of *Feldluftschiffer Abteilung 23* and had been successful on about two thirds of the 70 times it was employed during the war.

Although not widely used by either sport or commercial aviators during the post-war years, parachutes continued to be developed most notably by Leslie Irvin's Irving Air Chute Company of Buffalo, NY. The Irving Type A-1 Chute of 1919 incorporated a back pack rather than the earlier seat pack, a manually operated rip cord which allowed the operator to fall free from the aircraft and a small drogue chute to draw the main canopy from the pack.

From 1930 the *Deutsche Versuchsanstalt für Luftfahrt (DVL)* at Berlin-Adlershof was engaged in a large scale parachute research and development programme. Under the leadership of *Dipl.Ing.* Friedrich Hoffmann a team that included *Ing.*von Stryk and Herbert Klar had conducted a series of tests with weighted dummies of 100 kg which were parachuted to the ground from heights of 80 and 100 metres from aircraft moving at speeds from 250 to 400 kph. The stresses on the dummies were recorded using a special instrument and by 1933 all major German and foreign parachutes had been evaluated scientifically. In this trial from February 1931 Junkers A 35 WNr.1064 D-1010 being used to drop one of the test dummies. The A 35 of 1926 was an enlarged and more powerful derivative of the earlier A 20, and a number were converted from the earlier type – hence the inaccurate caption. The A 35 had been preceded by the three-seat A 32 but it reverted to a two-seat layout. Most aircraft were fitted with the 280/310 hp Junkers L 5 engine although a few had the BMW IV. This aircraft was manufactured in military guise by *AB Flygindustri* in Sweden as the R 53. Junkers A 35 D-1010 was withdrawn from use in May 1932.

Under the successive leadership of *Dr.*Friedrich Bendemann (1915), *Dr.Ing.*Wilhelm Hoff (1919), *Dr.Ing.*Georg Madelung (1926) and Ottfried von Dewitz (1931) the *DVL* carried out a huge amount of very useful theoretical and practical development work on behalf of the German aviation industry. It was also a test centre for new types and to help with the testing of the new military aircraft that were being developed in secret in the mid-twenties *Hptm.*Kurt Student was responsible for the creation of the *Abteilung M (Militärische Erpobung)* within the *DVL* to oversee developments at a new site at Rechlin in Mecklenburg. The initial personnel engaged in this secret work were *Dipl.Ing.*Wilhelm Degen, *Dr.*Karl Genthe, *Ing.*Bruno Gollhammer and *Dipl.Ing.* Schaper. From 1929 this responsibility passed to the *Albatros Flugzeugwerke GmbH*. Meanwhile at Adlershof the *DVL* continued to grow in importance. In 1932 it employed 480 scientific officers, technicians and administrators in five major departments: *Aerodynamische Abt.* (*Dr.Ing.*Seewald), *Statische Abt.* (*Prof.Dr.Ing.*Thalau), *Motoren-Abt.*(*Dipl.Ing.*Kurtz), *Abt.d.Elektrotechnik u.Funkwesen* (*Prof.Dr.phil.*Fassbender) & the *Pruf-Abt.*(*Dipl.Ing.*Thelen).

Photo 1C-5 Original caption: Dr. Heinkel and Günther Plüschow, Dr. Ernst Heinkel (r.) in the 30s *Chef der Heinkel Flugzeugwerke* in Warnemünde with pilot *Käpitanleutnant a.D.* Günther Plüschow (l.).

Bundesarchiv Bild 183-S55983 Photo: o.Ang.

By 1929 when this photograph was taken Ernst Heinkel was the constructor of choice for both the *Reichsmarine* and the *Reichsheer* as the two services pursued a series of clandestine aviation programmes. Heinkel had begun his design career before the Great War with short spells at Berlin-Johannisthal with both the *Luftverkehrsgesellschaft (LVG)* (Sep 11) and the *Albatros-Werke GmbH* (Spr 13) before joining the newly formed *Brandenburgische Flugzeugwerke,* later *Hansa und Brandenburgische Flugzeugwerke GmbH* at Briest bei Brandenburg. Following the end of hostilities he had joined the *Caspar-Werke AG* at Travemünde where he was responsible for the S 1 *Seeflugzeuge* which was manufactured in Sweden but following a dispute over the rights to this design he left Caspar to establish his own company – the *Ernst Heinkel Flugzeugwerke GmbH* at Warnemünde – in December 1922.

Over the following seven years he became a prolific designer with a succession of seaplanes which were for the most part manufactured abroad due to Allied restrictions on the construction of military types within Germany. Most notable was the HE 1 family which was continuously improved throughout the decade to include the HE 9 of 1929. His expertise in naval seaplanes led to a series of contracts to supply the Imperial Japanese Navy, the Soviet Navy and the navies of the Baltic States. He also designed a series of military landplanes for the *Reichsheer* and the Soviet Air Force and it was this expertise that would place his company in an excellent position to benefit from the placing of production contracts by the *Reichswehr* in 1932. At that point the following types were under development or on order: *Reichsmarine* – HD 38, HD 42, He 59 & He 60, and for the *Reichsheer* – He 45, He 46 & He 50.

Günther Pluschow was a celebrity of note when this image was taken having just returned from the Argentine where he had carried out the first aerial survey of Patagonia in Heinkel HD 24W WNr.271 D-1313 *"Tsingtau"*, exploits which had been publicised through his book *"Silberkondor über Feuerland"* and a documentary film. Known as the *"Fliegers von Tsingtau"* Pluschow had first gained fame in the opening stages of the Great War when as a naval aviator he had carried out a number of operations in China against the Japanese. He had then executed an enterprising escape back to Germany via the USA and Italy only to be detained by the British at Gibraltar. Following his escape from a PoW camp in England he managed to return to Germany via the Netherlands. For the remainder of the war he was *Stationsleiter Libau*. Pluschow returned to Patagonia in 1930 only to be tragically killed in a crash on the 28 January 1931.

Photo 1C-6 Original caption: Junkers A 48dy, *Jagdflugzeug*, used as a precursor to the *Stuka* Ju 87. Werkfoto Junkers (MBB) 48/2.
Bundesarchiv Bild 146-0908-500 Photo: o.Ang.

The Junkers A 48, which appeared in 1927, was the latest in a line of radical two-seat single-engine, low wing, all-metal aeroplanes that had first appeared with the Junkers J 8 and its production successor the Junkers CL.I close support aircraft of 1918. These had been followed by the A 20 (1923), A 25 (1925) and A 35 (1926) all of which had obvious military applications and for which reason were further developed outside of Germany in the USSR and Sweden. Thus the A 20 was known as the Ju 20 when produced at Fili for the Soviet Navy and the R 02 when modified at Limhamm for other possible military customers, whilst the A 25 and A 35 became the R 41 and R 53 in Sweden and were successfully exported abroad to a number of military air arms.

The civil A 48 as designed by *Dipl.Ing.*Karl Plauth and *Dipl.Ing.*Hermann Pohlmann at Dessau was a two seat training and experimental aircraft. Seven aircraft would eventually appear on the *deutsche Luftfahrzeugrolle*: A 48b (600 hp Bristol Jupiter VII) D-2248, D-2284 & D-2532; A 48da (550 hp BMW Hornet) D-ITOR – possibly a disarmed K 47 that was returned to Dessau; A 48dy (540 hp Siemens Sh 20) D-2012; A 48fi (510 hp Siemens Jupiter VI) D-1057 & D-2185.

There were in addition a further seven aircraft that were delivered to Limhamm for modification to a military standard (K 47). These were A 48b (600 hp Bristol Jupiter VII) and A 48ba (550 hp BMW Hornet). In this version a gun position occupied the rear cockpit so that the pilot and gunner effectively sat back-to-back. Despite demonstrations in several countries sales were restricted to China and the USSR with the two Soviet examples being employed for test purposes by the *NII-VVS* in 1930. A year later in 1931 three A 48fi machines WNr.3361, 3362 (D-1057) & 3363 (D-2532) were deployed to Lipetsk where they were evaluated in the two-seat fighter and fighter bomber roles with considerable success being very popular with the pilots. More examples were requested but the type had not gained favour with *Wa.Prüf.8* presumably because of its all-metal construction and higher costs. These aircraft appear to have been modified to a single tail layout.

It is known that A 48dy WNr.3365 D-2012 (see above at Dessau) was also tested a Lipetsk before being passed to the *DVL* in June 1931. It was thereafter used for research purposes at Berlin-Adlershof and later re-registered D-IRES.

Photo 1C-7 Original caption: *Flugzeugkonstrukteur Dornier*, Prof.Dr.Claude Dornier with the Dornier Do K-3 aircraft (Coded D-2183; First flight August 1931).
Bundesarchiv Bild 102-03504A Photo: Georg Pahl

Despite the world economic downturn, the first part of the thirties was a time of great design productivity at *Prof.Dr.*Dornier's *Dornier-Metallbauten GmbH*; in 1931 alone the Do C2 *See-Kampfzweisitzer,* Do C3 *Seeaufklärer,* Do C4 *Jagdzweisitzer,* Do Y *Bomber* and Do K3 *Verkehrsflugzeug* would all make their debut, whilst larger versions of the tried and tested Do *Wal Flugboot* also appeared. In 1932 these would be followed by the Do F *Bomber* and Do 12 *Libelle III leichtes Amphibienflugzeug*, the former being selected for series production by the *Reichswehr* as its first dedicated medium-range night bomber.

Born in Kempten on the 14 May 1884, Claude Dornier entered the new and exciting world of aviation in 1910 when he joined the *Luftschiffbau Zeppelin*. He soon became a specialist in the design of light metal structures and in 1914 was selected by Graf Zeppelin to lead a seaplane design team. Initially based at Lindau-Reutin on the Bodensee the team was re-located to Seemoos, near Friedrichshafen in 1916 where Dornier designed a series of advanced metal stressed skin landplanes. Following the armistice Dornier turned to the design of commercial sea and landplanes at Manzell and in the twenties the newly formed *Dornier Metallbauten GmbH* prospered with the series manufacture of the *Delphin Verkehrsflugboot*, the *Libelle Kleinflugboot*, and the *Komet* and *Merkur Verkehrsflugzeuge*. However his most successful design the *Wal Verkehrsflugboot* had to be manufactured abroad from 1922 because of allied restrictions.

Following a decision to establish a manufacturing facility (*AG für Dornier-Flugzeuge*) at Altenrhein on the Swiss side of the Bodensee in 1926, Dornier became progressively more involved in the design of large military aircraft with the two-engine Do N of 1926 which was built under licence in Japan, the four-engine Do P of 1930 which was tested at Lipetsk and the three-engine Do Y which was ultimately sold to Yugoslavia. The Do Y and Do F bombers both made use of a new wing planform that was first introduced on the Do K 3.

From 1932 manufacturing was once more focused on Friedrichshafen with construction of the new 8.5 tonne *Wal* being followed by that of the Do F (Do 11).

Photo 1C-8 Original caption: The world record flight of the long range Dornier Do X flying boat.
Bundesarchiv Bild 102-01216A Photo: Georg Pahl

Members of the crew together with some of the 159 passengers that were aboard the Do X for its record breaking flight on the 21 October 1929. The aircraft still carried enough fuel for a journey of 1,200 kms but the flight was limited to a tour of the Bodensee at just under 400 metres. In all there had been 10 crew, 150 passengers and 9 stowaways aboard. The *Flugschiff's* all up weight for this record-breaking flight was 52 tonnes. The Do X was initially powered by twelve Siemens Jupiter air-cooled radials arranged in pairs atop the mainplane. Nominally capable of producing 400 hp apiece the Jupiters' output actually was more in the order of 310 hp and following cooling problems with the aft facing engines it was decided to replace the complete installation with twelve Curtiss GV-1570 Conqueror liquid-cooled engines of 615 hp apiece. Unfortunately the anticipated improvement in power output was largely offset by the weight of the new installation which added 1.09 tonnes to the all up weight.

Flown for the first time on the 12 July 1929 the Do X had been designed at Manzell but built at *Dornier's* new manufacturing facility at Altenrhein on the southern shore of the Bodensee in a period of eighteen months beginning in December 1927. Notable as the largest aircraft in the world at that time the Do X was to prove something of a disappointment in terms of its performance. For the trans-Atlantic flight to Brazil, the USA and ultimately back to Germany during 1930-32 the *Flugschiff* was only able to sustain a cruising speed of 169 kph over a distance of 3,218 kms without a commercial payload. Indeed to extend its range the aircraft was actually flown as low as 3 metres over the sea to maximise the lift available from its enormous 48 metre wing. The *Kommandant* for much of the overseas venture was *KptLt.d.Res.* Friedrich Christiansen, whilst *Flugkäpitan* Horst Merz was first pilot and the *Reichsverkehrsministerium's* representative on board in Christiansen's absence.

Reichsmarine interest had centred on the possible use of the Do X as a long range maritime reconnaissance torpedo bomber with a crew of ten, five defensive machine gun positions, two fixed 3.7 cm cannon and racks for four aerial torpedoes. However the *Gruppe BSx's* interest evaporated as it became clear that the type's poor performance precluded a useful payload and no further aircraft of this type were constructed for German use. Two aircraft were completed during 1931-32 to meet an Italian order for a commercial flying boat but they were little used. Do X D-1929 was briefly registered to *Deutsche Luft Hansa* in 1933 before being re-assigned to the *DVL*. In 1934 *Dornier's* premier *Flugschiff* was transferred to the *Luftfahrtmuseum* in Berlin where she continued to attract a level of attention from the public which far outweighed her actual utility.

Photo 1C-9 Original caption: En route landing in Berlin (Tempelhof) by oceanic flier Könnecke on his long range flight over the Ocean in his Caspar aircraft *"Germania"*.
Bundesarchiv Bild 102-00394A/Photo Georg Pahl

In 1921 Karl Caspar established the *Caspar-Werke AG* at Lübeck-Travemünde to build seaplanes, his first product being the diminutive U 1/U 2 *U-Boot Flugzeug* for the US and Japanese Navies. Thereafter Allied restrictions forced *Caspar* to focus on the design of low-powered *Sportflugzeuge* until covert naval contracts were received for the CJ 14 and CS 14 combat aircraft, prototypes of which were completed by *Dansk Aero* in Copenhagen. Further designs followed but *Caspar* was destined not to achieve any form of lasting commercial success and from the mid-twenties the firm became increasingly dependent on *Reichswehr* subsidies.

The Caspar C 32 *Streuflugzeug* was one of Caspar's final designs. Otto Könnecke's WNr.7010 D-1145 was the fourth of four aircraft to be built and was purchased by Graf Solms-Laubach who named it *"Germania"*. The first aircraft WNr.7006 D-1142 was employed by the *Biologische Reichsanstalt für Land-und Forstwirtschaft* in Berlin before being acquired by the *DVS* in 1933. The *DVS* had already purchased the remaining two machines (WNr.7008 D-1143 & WNr.7009 D-1144) in 1928.

The twenties and thirties was a time of great aerial endeavour with record breaking flights being made on an annual basis. For many the crossing of the Atlantic Ocean was the greatest goal and the years 1919-28 were to see a flurry of activity from both sides of the Pond. Charles Lindbergh made the first successful non-stop west to east crossing of the Atlantic on the 20-21 May 1927 between Roosevelt Field, New York to Le Bourget, Paris in his purpose built Ryan NYP Monoplane *"The Spirit of St.Louis"*. He covered 5,809 kms in 33.5 hours. In the same year Otto Könnecke, a highly decorated (Plm 26 Sep 18) and successful *Jagdflieger* from the Great War with 35 *Luftsiege*, planned to complete the more difficult east-west crossing in his specially modified Caspar C 32 D-1145 *"Germania"* which had an endurance of 50 hours. However his intention to fly across the Atlantic from Köln to Newfoundland was thwarted by a storm system over the North Atlantic. In a change of plan he then left Germany on the 20 Sep 27 to fly east around the world to the USA in stages via India and Japan to the west coast of the USA before flying east to New York and from there back to Germany. His first leg was to Calcutta routing over Hungary, Romania, Turkey and Persia. Unfortunately problems with the crew and the aircraft prevented any further progress.

The first successful east to west crossing against the prevailing winds was then made on the 23-24 April 1928 by a Germano-Irish crew (Hermann Köhl, James Fitzmaurice & Ehrenfried Frhr.von Hunefeld) who flew Junkers W 33 (Junkers L5) WNr.2504 D-1167 *"Bremen"* from Baldonnel in the Irish Republic to Greenly Island off Labrador covering c.3,600 kms in 36 hours.

Photo 1C-10 Original caption: The enormous seaworthiness of the new German flying boat Rohrbach *"Romar"* in Travemünde! The Rohrbach Flugboot "Romar" with 2,400 hp jumps out of the water at a maximum load of 20,000 kg. when starting with a speed of 150 kph.
Bundesarchiv Bild 102-07269 Photo: o.Ang.

One of the most spectacular images of a flying boat ever taken was this one of *Rohrbach Metall Fugzeugbau GmbH's* Ro X *Romar* c/n 29 in December 1928 and published in February 1929 – although the statistics quoted in the original caption proved to be rather misleading !

Intended for trans-Atlantic operation the design range of the *Romar* was 4,000 kms with a 1,100 kg payload and on this basis three aircraft were ordered by *Deutsche Luft Hansa* in 1928. In its passenger configuration the *Romar* had two cabins in the hull for four and eight passengers respectively. Powered by three BMW VIU engines of 650 hp it first flew at Travemünde on the 7

August 1928 and was officially unveiled at the *II.Internationale Luftfahrtausstellung (ILA) Berlin* in October of that year. The third machine was powered by three 750 hp BMW VIuz engines and had room for sixteen passengers being designated *Romar II*.

Testing of the prototype *Romar* by the *SES Travemünde* culminated in sea trials in the open waters of the Lübecker Bucht between the 11 and 13 December 1928. Carrying a payload of 3,100 kgs the 14.5 tonne *Romar* performed well in front of representatives from the *DLH*, the *DVL* and *RVM* in seas up to Sea State 5 as this spectacular image shows with the flying boat being thrown 8 to 10 m into the air. However on the fourth landing in a cross sea the starboard stabilising float was buckled and caused the boat to lean heavily before the boat was stabilised by the bow design. Nonetheless the excellence of the design received favourable content in the 11 July's edition of the *"Flight"* magazine. On the 17 April 1929 *Rohrbach's* test pilot Hermann Steindorf set a new seaplane record with the *Romar* lifting a payload of 5,000 kgs to 2,000 m., whilst on the 20 August he took off from Travemünde, flew west and north down the Dutch and English coasts to Oslo in Norway and then returned – a total distance of 2,600 kms.

Despite their seaworthiness the *Romar* lacked the range for trans-oceanic operations and as a result *DLH* confined the operations of their three aircraft to the Ostsee during 1929-33. With the exception of a single aircraft that was delivered to the *Marine nationale Francaise's CEPA* at Frejus-St.Raphael no other orders were forthcoming. This proved a fatal blow to the fortunes of *Dr.Adolf Rohrbach's* firm which urgently need work following the completion of the final batch of *Roland II Verkehrsflugzeuge* in 1929. Whilst continuing to seek further *RVM* contracts, Rohrbach looked for work abroad and during 1931-32 he carried out design work on behalf of the Czech *Avia* aircraft company at Prague-Katovice. Of three projects, the A 42 transport reaching the prototype stage but the A 46 *Roterra* three-engine monoplane bomber remained a design study, its complexity being beyond the resources of most air arms to buy and operate.

The writing was now well and truly on the wall. The complexity of Rohrbach's designs taken together with his arrogance, extravagant life style and lack of sympathy for the emerging *NSDAP* regime meant that he failed to find favour with *DLH*, the *RVM* or the *RWM*. In February 1933 Erhard Milch recommended that he file for bankruptcy. Soon afterwards the shipbuilding firm of *AG Weser* sought his expertise to help with the sub-contract work that they had received for the Do 11 from the newly formed *RLM*. The *Weser Flugzeugbau GmbH* was duly created on the 14 April 1934, this new enterprise taking over Rohrbach's remaining assets, his debts and in return giving him the position of *Chefkonstrukteur*.

Photo 1C-11 Original caption: Bases and installations, *Seeflugstation Travemünde* - Aerial view by the *Stabsbildabteilung beim Kommandeur der Flieger der Flotte* from 14 August 1918 - *H 102 Stabia K.d.Flieg.F. "Travemünde" 14.8.18, 4.30 pm, Hohe 200 m, Lange 25 cm (Seeflugstation).*
Bundesarchiv Bild 134-B3289 Photo: o.Ang.

The *Seeflugstation Travemünde* was of special significance to the covert development of naval aviation during the post-war period being the site of the *See-Erprobungsstelle (SES)* from its creation in April 1928. Prior to that it had been employed by Karl Caspar's *Caspar-Werke AG* for the design of a number of naval aircraft prototypes including the C 30 (1926) and C 36 (1927-28) two-seat *Aufklärungsflugzeuge*.

Meanwhile the facilities at Priwall on the Travemünde were greatly enhanced from late 1926 when *Deutsche Luft Hansa* erected a large 60m x 60m *Seeflugzeughalle* and is associated hard standings and slipways – these being located between the buildings and the slip by the water's edge on the photograph. At the same time the *Flenderwerke* (Lübeck) was commissioned to deliver a similarly dimensioned floating dock – both of these facilities being sufficiently large to accommodate the giant Do X *Flugschiff* which by that time was under construction at *Dornier's* new factory at Altenrhein in southern Germany. In the meantime Lübeck-Travemünde was *DLH's* main operating base for its water based aircraft flying routes in the western Ostsee and Skagerrak. For the most part these were carried out by the Dornier Do J *Wal* four of which had been inherited from *Deutscher Aero Lloyd*.

By the beginning of 1928 the *Caspar-Werke* was in severe financial difficulties and its assets were then used by *Kpt.z.S.*Walter Lohmann of the *Reichsmarine's Seetransportabteilung* to create the *SES*. The *SES* was nominally part of the *Reichsverband der deutschen Luftfahrtindustrie (RdL)* but in reality was a fully functioning covert naval aviation testing facility. *KptLt.a.D.*Hermann Moll was appointed the *Geschäftführer der SES* and under his leadership the facility was further expanded and modernised, whilst *KptLt.*Ernst-August Roth was released from the *Reichsmarine* on the 1 April 1928 to take up the post of *Chefpilot*. From that date the *SES* played a vital part in supporting the *Gruppe BSx's* covert *Arbeitsprogramm* of 1928-30 which included the development of no less than 11 combat types including the *Größflugboot* Do X, *Fernaufklärer* Do R *Superwal* and Ro V *Rocco*, *Dreizweckeflugzeug* HE 7, *Seejagdzweisitzer* HE 31, *Seeaufklärer* C 36, *Flottenerkunder* HD 30 and W 4, and the *Artillerieflugboot* HD 15. Further contracts for a *Seejagdeinsitzer* and an additional *Fernerkunder* were also to be placed.

To help cope with the sheer volume of this development work additional personnel were recruited including Karl Wiborg, Gerhard Hubrich, Hugo Dobberthien and Erich Gundermann. The *Leiter Gruppe F (*Flugerprobung*)* was *Ing.*Wilhelm Huth. Test flying was sometimes very hazardous and the *SES's* first fatality was Karl Wiborg who died on the 16 December 1931 when He 60a WNr.381 D-2176 broke up during a dive and crashed directly in front of the *Flugleitung*.

Photo 1C-12 Original caption: Bombs being loaded under a large German aircraft, circa November 1917.

Bundesarchiv Bild 146-1971-045-48 Photo: o.Ang.

In the early stages of the Great War the *Fliegertruppe* had employed a variety of small, aerodynamically inefficient *Artillerieprüfungskommission (APK)* and *Karbonit AG* bombs in attacks using airships and aeroplanes. From 1916 these early examples of *Abwurfmunition* were progressively replaced by a new series of bombs that were developed by the *Fliegertruppe's Prüfanstalt und Werft (PuW)* in association with the *Firma Goerz* at Berlin-Friedenau. The new *PuW* ordnance was characterised by their long aerodynamic finned bodies which could be slung on steel cables horizontally beneath the fuselage and/ or wings of bomber-reconnaissance aircraft. With the exception of the small 12.5 kg *PuW* bomb which was in effect a fragmentation weapon, the *PuW* ordnance was thin-walled with a proportionally greater explosive charge relying on its pressure wave or blast effect to inflict damage on the target. Impact fuses with centrifugal force arming were fitted as standard, the rotation of the falling bomb arming the weapon. This meant the bombs were very safe to handle on the ground with little if any risk of premature detonation. In this image armourers are loading a mix of 50 and 100 kg *PuW* ordnance to the underside of a Gotha G-V *Größflugzeug* – in all 450 kgs. The forward steel cable can be seen on the two larger weapons. In addition to that shown much larger 300 kg and 1,000 kg *PuW* ordnance was produced.

The *Gotha Waggonfabrik* produced a number of *Größflugzeuge* for both land and marine use during the Great War. The *Gotha G-Serie* were all twin-engine biplane bombers with defensive ring mounted le.MG 14 *"Parabellum"* machine guns in the nose and rear fuselage and a ventral gun tunnel allowing the rear gunner to fire backwards below the tail. The two 200/220 hp Benz engines were installed between the wings as "pusher" units, the propellers being behind the wing trailing edge giving the G-IV a maximum speed of 140 kph. Sufficient fuel was carried for up to seven hours flight, the maximum bomb load being 450 kgs over shorter distances. Based in Belgium, *KaGOHL 3* was equipped with thirty Gotha G-IV *Größflugzeuge* for attacks on England. The first such attack was carried out on the 22 May 1917 and was led by *Hptm.*Ernst Brandenburg. On the 13 June fourteen *Größflugzeuge* attacked London in daylight inflicting more damage than all the earlier airship raids combined and causing a degree of civil panic. From July these raids were carried out by night and continued until May 1918. The remaining *KaGOHL*, re-titled *BoGOHL* from 18 December 1917, were equipped with fifteen *G-Serie* aircraft and employed over the Western Front where attacks were made on Paris from January 1918. Five *Bomberkommandeure* were decorated with the *Pour le Mérite*: *Hptm.*Brandenburg (*KaGOHL 3* - 14 Jun 17), *Hptm.*Rudolf Kleine (*KaGOHL 3* – 3 Oct 17), *Hptm.*Alfred Keller (*KaGOHL 1* - 4 Dec 17), *Hptm.*Hermann Köhl (*BoGOHL 7* – 21 May 18) & *Maj.*Leo Leonhardy (*BoGOHL 6* – 2 Oct 18).

In the absence of better drop ordnance, *PuW* bombs re-appeared at Lipetsk in 1928-29 when the newly formed *Versuchsgruppe* undertook a series of trials to ascertain their suitability aboard converted Rohrbach Ro VIII *Roland* and Junkers G 23 *Verkehrsflugzeuge*. Although problems were encountered when drops above 3,000 m were made, these trials were adjudged to be a partial success and arrangements were therefore made for *Sonderausrüstung So III (Abwurfwaffen)* sets to be manufactured and stored at Berlin-Staaken for use by *DLH's* Junkers G 23/24 airliners in a national emergency. Responsibility for this overall programme had rested with *Oblt.a.D.Dipl.Ing.* Ernst Marquard from the *Heereswaffenamt's Wa.Prüf.6F*.

Photo 1D-1 Original caption: Hangars I, II and III at Lipetsk in Soviet Union.

Bundsarchiv RH 2 Bild-02292-041 Photo: o.Ang.

Newcomers to the *Flugzentrum Lipetsk* were met by a message which stated: *"Herzlich Willkommen am Arsch der Welt"* or politely translated as *"Welcome to the middle of nowhere"*. Certainly this training and test facility was well concealed by its remoteness 1,750 kms east of Berlin and 360 kms south-south-east of Moscow. The nearest town of consequence was Voronezh 110 kms away to the south by fair weather road, or further by rail. The airfield itself lay north of Lipetsk, a small iron making town, and close to the River Voronezh. The surrounding countryside was intensively farmed, the agricultural collectives making good use of the rich black earths that underlie the region to grow wheat and keep livestock. The general elevation the airfield was just under 200 m above sea level.

The three main *Halle* lay on the edge of the grass surfaced flying ground with stores and workshops close by. Under the terms of the Germano-Soviet agreement of 15 April 1924 the Soviet authorities were responsible for providing the manual labour and materials to expand the site from its original single hangar, a workshop and old factory building. The *VVS-RKKA* also provided technicians to service and maintain the *Reichsheer's* aircraft, the whole enterprise being camouflaged from outside eyes by the presence of a regular *VVS* reconnaissance unit on the other side of the airfield. To further explain the presence of German personnel, this unit was equipped with the Junkers H 21 a two-seat reconnaissance aircraft which had been built at Fili in the *USSR* with the help of designers and technicians from the *Junkers* concern.

This photograph dates from 1926-28 by which time the *Fliegerschule Stahr* was in full operation training the *Reichsheer's* next generation of military aviators using the Fokker D.XIII *Jagdflugzeug* and the Heinkel HD 17 *Aufklärungsflugzeug*. Frontline testing of new combat aircraft began in 1928, the test unit being referred to as the *Wissenschaftliche Versuchs-und Prüfanstalt für Luftfahrzeuge (Wivupal)*. The initial 16 man *Versuchstelle* arrived in 1928 under the leadership of Emil Thuy and Ernst Marquard, respectively the *Referente für Waffen und Bomben* the *Heereswaffenamt's Waffen Prüfwesens*

6F. The initial programme focused on the need to ascertain the suitability of *Deutsche Luft Hansa's* Junkers G 24 (WNr.844 D-844 Coded 78) and Rohrbach Ro VIII *Roland* (WNr.18 D-991 Coded 91) airliners as emergency bombers. To this end both types had been modified with *Sonderausrüstung* (Special Equipment) *So II* and *III* these being defensive gun positions and bomb carrying equipment respectively. Initially this took the form of ring mountings for the air cooled MG 08/15 machine gun and bomb racks for the 300 kg PuW drop ordnance. A large 2 km square bombing range equipped with observation towers and simulated targets were constructed for the trials.

Each type flew 10 sorties in September 1928 whilst the smaller two-seat Junkers A 35 (WNr.1059 D-987 Coded 9) made 8 sorties carrying smaller ordnance. The Great War vintage *PuW* ordnance quickly showed that it was unsuitable for attacks above 3,000 metres. In other respects it was recognised that further testing of the G 24 and Ro VIII was required and both types therefore returned to Lipetsk in 1929. From 1930 the first of the *Reichswehr's* new combat aircraft were tested by the *Wivupal,* these being the Arado SD III and SSD I *Jagdflugzeuge* whilst two modified Junkers W 34 were used for the initial trials of the new *SC-Abwurfwaffen.* In 1931 there were nearly 200 men attached to the *Versuchsgruppe* and aircraft tested in that year included the Ar 64 and HD 38 *Jagdflugzeuge* and the Albatros L 77v and Junkers K 47 (A 48) *Jagdzweisitzer;* bomb trials continued with the W 34. Test personnel in that year were Albert Blumensaat, Gustav Bollmann, Hans-Jurgen von Cramon, Hermann Dick, Hoppe, Knaser, Dietrich von Massenbach, Carl-August von Schoenebeck, Dietrich Schwenke, Heinz Simon, Rudolf Spies and Karl Wiborg.

Photo 1D-2 Original caption: Lipetsk, Soviet Union – Fokker D.XIII aircraft (Coded 11) fitted with skis.

Bundesarchiv RH 2 Bild-02292-072 Photo: o.Ang.

Whilst activity at Lipetsk always reached a peak during the summer months, a permanent staff of around sixty officers was to be found at the base throughout the winter and some students actually arrived in the Soviet Union in October or November of each year. Two such were *Rittm.* Franz Biwer, an *Eskadron-Fhr.* in *Reiter-Rgt.15* and *Maj.* Erich Quade from the *Stab/HrGrKdo.2* who both arrived in October 1927. *Maj.* Quade who had earlier spent five years as a *Lehrer für Lufttaktik* at *the Infanterieschule München* would remain at Lipetsk for eighteen months before returning to the *Infanterie-Rgt.2* as a *Bataillons-Kommandeur.* Another autumnal arrival was *Hptm.* Heinrich Seywald who was detached from *Kraftfahr-Abt.7* in November 1928. He like many who would be posted to Lipetsk for refresher training or for a period on the permanent staff was a highly experienced combat airman with wartime service as an observer in *Kasta 33, Flieger-Abteilungen 274* and *48* and as a pilot and *Fhr.Jasta 23.* Since then his service with the *Reichsheer's Kraftfahrtruppe* had been broken once before when he attended a month long *Segel-Lehrgang* on the Rhön in 1923.

Oblt.a.D. Werner Junck was the first *Lehrgangsleiter* of the *Fliegerschule Stahr* and he occupied this post from January 1925 until his return to Germany as *Chef-Pilot der Firma Albatros-Flugzeugwerke* at Berlin-Johannisthal in 1927. The former *Fhr.Jasta 8,* his task was to oversee the test flying of the newly arrived Fokker D.XIII *Jagdflugzeuge* in June 1925, the writing of a training syllabus and the training of instructors prior to the arrival of the first *Jagdflieger-Lehrgang* in April 1926. This initial group of former *Luftstreitkräfte* pilots found the step up to the 450 hp Napier Lion powered Fokker D.XIII a challenge and as a result in the winter of that year Junck and *Oblt.a.D.* Carl-August von Schoenebeck returned to Germany to select the most promising of *Sportflug's* current *Flugschuler* for additional training at the *DVS Zweigstelle Berlin-Staaken* and thereafter at Lipetsk from April 1927.

Of the fifty Fokker D.XIII *Jagdflugzeuge* based at Lipetsk only around sixteen were actually in service at any given time, the remaining machines being subject to major overhauls prior to storage.

A ski undercarriage could be fitted to the D.XIII as was indeed the case with training aircraft in Germany where the winters were much colder than in Britain or France. Unlike the wartime Fokker D.VII, two of which were also based at Lipetsk, the new D.XIII was a sesquiplane with a long span upper wing which was braced to a smaller span lower wing. Ailerons were fitted to the upper wing only and were of unusually long span. The British Napier Lion II twelve-cylinder broad-arrow engine was a very compact and powerful engine and conferred a top speed of 270 kph on this aircraft. The initial rate of climb was 1.7 minutes to 1,000 metres and the aircraft was armed with two belt-fed lu.MG 08/15 machine guns in the same way as its Great War predecessors. The fuel tanks were in the centre section of the upper wing as can be seen in this photograph.

Photo 1D-3 Original caption: Crash of a Fokker D.XIII with a Russian pilot – Lipetsk, Soviet Union. Wreck of a Fokker D.XIII aircraft.

Bundesarchiv RH 2 Bild-02292-014 Photo: o.Ang.

The *Fliegerschule Stahr* was allocated all fifty of the Fokker D.XIII *Jagdflugzeuge* that had been secretly obtained by the *Reichswehr* using Black Funding. In common with all types of aircraft engaged in flying training attrition was relatively high and it is estimated that seven aircraft were written off in the first three years of the *Fliegerschule's* activities. However actual fatalities during the period 1926-30 appear to have been restricted to *Rittm.a.D.*Amlinger who died in a collision during air combat training. As the *Fliegerschule* specialised in the teaching of air combat manoeuvres it was not surprising that the risk of collision was high. For this reason all *Flugschuler* were required to wear parachutes and Wolfgang Falck would later recall that they were expected to use them after he was reprimanded for not abandoning his aircraft following a mid-air collision with Ekhart Hefter in July 1932. In this incident Hefter lost five feet from his upper wing when he effectively rammed Falck's aircraft. The damage to Falck's Fokker D.XIII had been restricted to the loss of his radiator tank and windshield together with bent inter-plane struts. They were both lucky to survive.

The repatriation of Amlinger's body had a tragic postscript when his pregnant wife managed to jump to her death from a *Deutsche Luft Hansa* aircraft over Stettin at the time that the ship bearing his remains entered the port. Widely reported in the press, including the London *Times*, this incident had the undesired effect of publicising the *Reichsheer's* clandestine activities in the USSR. However the authorities maintained that *Rittmeister ausser Dienst* Amlinger had died in a riding accident and was in any case a private individual and therefore of no concern of the *Reichsheer.*

The presence of *VVS* personnel at the *Fliegerschule* formed part of the original agreement between Germany and the Soviet Union. The *RKKVVS* was keen to profit from German combat expertise and technology and Soviet personnel therefore formed an integral part of the overall operation. It is not known whether the Soviet pilot died in this incident which dates from the period 1926-28.

On the 1 October 1929 there were still 43 Fokker D.XIII on charge at the *Fliegerschule Lipetsk* – Serial Numbers: 4599-4601, 4603-4610, 4625, 4627, 4687-4690, 4692-4696, 4698, 4702-4706 & 4865.

Photo 1D-4 Original caption: During the great German autumn gliding flights on the Rhön in the presence of the *General* (Erich) Ludendorff, a world record was set for a 12 km long flight by the famous glider Marteus. A glider takes off from the Wasserkuppe.

Bundesarchiv Bild 102-10292 Photo: Georg Pahl

The restrictions on German aviation imposed by the Allies following the end of hostilities had one unexpected outcome – the massive growth in gliding as a sport both for the former aviators of the *Luftstreitkräfte* and for a rising generation of air enthusiasts that were enthused by the achievements of the Great War airmen. *Hptm.a.D.*Hermann Steiner, a former bomber pilot, later recalled:

"*This movement was born spontaneously and grew simultaneously in many parts of Germany during 1919 and 1920. I think the only explanation for this amazing fact was to be found in the attitude of the German youth in its decision to go flying – no matter what. I do not know why it happened in the Rhön mountains in central Germany became the Mecca of the new movement, though there had been some glider experiments in the Rhön even before the war. Probably the Rhön became the centre because it was in the geographical centre of Germany and thus easily reached by all the young men, who didn't have the money for long journeys. As it was the whole glider business, cheap as it was compared with any other kind of flying, presented almost insurmountable difficulties and the greatest sacrifices for us penniless young men. But it didn't matter. Here again was a chance to fly – and, incidentally, to fly without doing something illegal. The Treaty of Versailles had not restricted gliding, for the simple reason that there had been no gliding at the time of Versailles.*"

Meanwhile the potential provided by the gliding movement did not go unnoticed or indeed unobserved by the covert aviation agencies of the new *Reichswehr*. *Hptm.*Kurt Student, a former *Jagdflieger* and *Kdr.Jagdgruppe AOK 3*, was a frequent visitor to the Rhön. The young glider enthusiasts were oblivious to his true role as *Referent für Flugtechnik bei der Inspektion für Waffen und Geräte* in the *Reichswehrministerium*. The presence at these events of such notaries as *Gen.d.Inf.a.D.*Erich Ludendorff and *Prinz* Heinrich von Preussen, the deposed *Kaiser's* brother and former *GrößAdm.* and *Oberbefehlshaber der Ostsee*, did much to generate public interest in aviation.

This image dates from August 1923 and shows the method used to catapult these home-built gliders into the air. Initially only flights of one to two minutes had been achieved but by 1923 quite respectable flights were possible. This aircraft was designed by the *Akademische Fliegergruppe Dresden* and was *Baunummer 7*.

Photo 1D-5 Original caption: Friedrichshafen! A *Zeppelin-Luftschiffhalle* in use to accommodate aircraft.

Bundesarchiv Bild 102-00715/Photo Georg Pahl

The *Zeppelinhalle* near Friedrichshafen am Bodensee was used to build the first German post-war commercial airship – the *Luftschiff* LZ 120 *"Bodensee"* - which entered service with the *Deutsche Luftschiffahrts AG (Delag)* in August 1919 on its Friedrichshafen to Berlin service. However in 1920 the *ILUK* informed the German Government that no further flights would be allowed and the LZ 120 was transferred to the *Regia Marine* (Royal Italian Navy) in July 1921. Unlike many other *Zeppelinhalle* this particular example survived enforced demolition.

The aircraft in the foreground is Dornier *Komet II* (BMW IV/Rolls Royce Falcon) C/Nr.52 D-396 which was registered to the *Dornier Metallbauten GmbH* in 1923. It is seen here at Friedrichshafen in September 1924 possibly in connection with tests into a four blade propeller installation which was to be employed in the larger *Komet III* (Rolls Royce Eagle IX) which first flew in December of that year. The fuselage of this particular machine was later used by the *Technische Hochschule Aachen* during 1926-27 for strength and torsion tests.

Constructed at the former *Zeppelin-Werke Lindau*, a small number of these four-seat cabin monoplanes served successively with the *Deutsche Luft-Reederei (DLR)* and *the Deutscher Aero Lloyd (DAL)* before being transferred to the *Deutsche Luft Hansa (DLH)* in 1926. They were representative of the small *Verkehrsflugzeuge* which appeared following the Allied imposition of the *Begriffsbestimmungen für den deutschen Luftfahrzeugbau* of May 1922. These restrictions effectively limited aircraft manufactured in Germany to a ceiling of 4,000 m (Rule 4), a maximum speed of 170 kph at 2,000 m (Rule 5) and a maximum payload including crew, instruments, fuel and oil of just 600 kgs (Rule 7).

Photo 1D-6 Original caption: *Größflugtag* **in Staaken near Berlin! On the 2nd day of Easter, a large** *Flugtag* **took place at Staaken near Berlin, where famous German pilots displayed their skills in front of tens of thousands of spectators. The highlight of the event was the demonstration by Bleriot who flew the original Bleriot machine across the English Channel in 1909. The best German pilots at the** *Größflugtag* **at Staaken were (l. to r.): the Berlin aerobatic pilot Frau Marga von Etzdorf, the well-known German pilot Ernst Udet, and pilot Fieseler, both known for their daring display flying.**

Bundesarchiv Bild 102-05708 Photo: Georg Pahl

An informal but undoubtedly staged photograph of three of Germany's most celebrated *Sportflieger*: Marga von Etzdorf, Ernst Udet and Gerhard Fieseler at the *Größflugtag* at Berlin-Staaken in April 1928.

Following on from the *1925 Deutscher Rundflug Oblt.a.D.*Ernst Udet quickly became Germany's best known and arguably most glamorous stunt pilot giving numerous flying displays, publicity flights and demonstrations in addition to taking part in air races. Overseas flights and film appearances would follow but in April 1928 it was the prospect that Udet was planning a trans-Atlantic flight to New York later that month with Thea Rasche, Germany's first female pilot since the war, that excited the press. Udet is seen here in the cockpit of his distinctive red and silver Udet U 12 *Flamingo* c/n 269 D-822 which was emblazoned with his name on the side of the fuselage.

Like Udet, Gerhard Fieseler had been a Great War *Jagdflieger* and post-war aerobatic display pilot. His wartime service had been in the east where he ended the war as Germany's highest scoring *Experte* to survive the conflict with 19 *Luftsiege*. He resumed flying in 1926 when he joined the *Raab-Katzenstein GmbH* as a flying instructor.

Marga von Etzdorf was twenty years old when this photo was taken and had only recently completed her flying training at the *Fliegerschule Bornemann* at Staaken. However she was a rising star and she would become the first woman in the world to fly commercially for an airline joining *Deutsche Luft Hansa* to fly the Junkers F 13 later that year. After a number of European flights she would become internationally famous for her solo flight from Berlin to Tokyo in 1931 in her Junkers A 50ce *Junior* D-1811 *"Kiek in die Welt"* before tragically taking her own life at Aleppo in Syria during an abortive flight to Australia in May 1933.

Photo 1D-7 Original caption: Studio portrait of Paul Bäumer, standing with cigarette in hand with *Eisernes Kreuz II.* **and** *I.Klasse, Preußischer Militär-Flugzeugführerabzeichen.*

Bundesarchiv Bild 146-2013-0012 Photo: o.Ang.

Paul Bäumer was born in the Rheinland on the 11 May 1896 and although his aspiration had been to train as a dentist he underwent flying training at his own expense in 1914. Despite trying to join a flying unit he would serve in *Inf.Rgt.70* in France and Russia before being transferred to the *Fliegertruppe* as a dental assistant. As a result he did not reach the Front as a pilot until May 1917 when he eventually reached *Jasta 5* where he quickly distinguished himself and earned a transfer in July to the prestigious *Jasta Boelcke*. An exceptionally courageous pilot he was repeatedly decorated and in in March 1918 he was commissioned as a *Leutnant der Reserve*. He received the *Pour le Mérite* on the 2 November 1918 for 43 *Luftsiege* just days before the close of hostilities. His exploits had earned him the unofficial title *"Der Eiserne Adler"*.

Following his discharge he returned to dentistry but retained an active interest in aviation as a *Sportflieger,* his expertise being recognised as second only to Udet. He established a *Fliegerschule* and in 1924 *Bäumer-Aero GmbH* in Hamburg to construct a range of *Sportflugzeuge* to his own design and to those of the two talented Günter Brothers. The best design to appear from this new *Büro* was the B IV *Sausewind* (65 hp Wright). Using the B IV D-1158 Bäumer set a new world altitude record of 6,782 metres on the 8 July 1927.

By this time Bäumer was also carrying out work as a test pilot on behalf of the *Rohrbach Metall-Flugzeugbau GmbH* and it was whilst carrying out a series of spinning exercises during an aerobatic demonstration in the experimental Rohrbach Ro IX *Rofix* single-seat fighter that he crashed to his death 2 kms from the coast of the Oresund in Denmark on the 15 July 1927. Although later ruled as pilot error this incident would call into question the structural integrity of *Dr.*Adolf Rohrbach's all-metal aircraft and as a result he was not favoured with any further development contracts from the *Reichsheer.*

Photo 1D-8 Original caption: Award ceremony of the *Adlerplakette des Deutschen Reichausschusses für Leibesübungen* (the Reich's Committee for Physical Education's Eagle Badge) to the famous German glider pilot Günther Groenhoff! *Staatsminister a.D.*Dominicus solemnly hands over the eagle badge to the German glider pilot Günther Groenhoff.

Bundesarchiv Bild 102-13051 Photo: Georg Pahl

After a period of distinguished public service during which he introduced social reforms in the city of Strasbourg (1902-10), as *Oberburgermeister der Berlin-Schoneberg* (1911-21) and ultimately *preußischer Innenminister* (1921), Alexander Dominicus played an important role in the post-war development of sport aviation as *Präsident* of the *Deutsche Luftfahrtverband eV (DLV)* during 1926-33. He is seen here in January 1932 at an awards ceremony.

The *DLV* was founded in 1902 and acted as an umbrella organisation for the various clubs and associations that appeared both before the Great War and in its aftermath. Other influential bodies in this sphere included the *Aero-Club von Deutschlands* (previously the *Kaiserlicher Deutscher Aero-Club*) founded in 1907 and the post-war *Ring der Flieger* from 1920. With the growth of the gliding movement in Germany there was a need to support the work of the clubs and associations through a nationally recognised system of licensing and competition. By 1928 *DLV* sponsored *Segelflugschulen* had been established at Annaberg/Oberschlesien, Dornberg/Kassel, Grunau/Riesengebirge, Schwarzenberg/Sachsen and Wangen/Allgäu. Following the re-appearance of flying training schools and flying clubs in the mid-to late twenties this work had been extended to include all aspects of German sport aviation at both the national and international level and an important aspect of the *DLV's* work was the organisation of annual air shows at the larger German towns and cities. By the end of the decade a total of twelve geographical *DLV-Landesgruppen* had been formed which reported to the organisation's headquarters in Bremen. These were: 1 – *Ost* (Königsberg/Ospr.), 2 – *Schlesien* (Breslau), 3 – *Oberschlesien* (Gleiwitz), 4 – *Pommern* (Stettin), 5 – *Brandenburg u.Grenzmark* (Berlin), 6 – *Nordwest* (Münster/Westf.), 7 – *Bayern* (München), 8 – *Mitteldeutschland* (Weimar), 9 – *Sachsen* (Dresden), 10 – *Südwest* (Darmstadt), 11 – *West* (Essen) and 12 – *Württemberg* (Stuttgart). In 1931 there were approximately 50,000 members of the *DLV*.

Following the *NSDAP* accession to power and the appointment of Hermann Göring to the position of *Reichskommissar für die Luftfahrt* in February 1933 the *Deutsche Luftfahrtverband eV* was disbanded on the 25 March of the same year and re-established as the para-military *Deutschen Luftsportverbände eV (DLV).*

Photo 1D-9 Original caption: Flying students! The *Hochschule für Leibesübungen* has established a gliding course for flight students in the heights near Berlin Gatow. Under the guidance of an experienced instructor, the students are trained gliding flight. The course takes the form of a *Flugsemester*. At the end of the semester, the main test takes place and after successful

completion of this assessment, the flight student is awarded the title A-pilot. A successful take-off for the flight student. The launch team has torn down the slope to tug the glider into the air.

Bundesarchiv Bild 102-14452 Photo: Georg Pahl

With the windsock showing that the glider has been accurately launched down the slope into a steady breeze, the student pilot feels the full effect of his primary controls. Small fore and aft movements of the control column are required to keep the glider safely in the air, whilst the low airspeed requires larger movements from left to right to keep the wings level. The feet control the rudder to keep the aircraft in balance. Flights such as these were normally straight forward hops in a straight line. Much more height was required if a turn was to be successfully concluded. The glider is a *Zogling* which was usually launched using an elastic cable or bungee.

In the mid-twenties the *Rhön-Rossitten Gesellschaft* and the *Deutschen Modell-und Segelflug Verbände* established the requirements for the "A" and "B" Gliding Certificates as a flight of either 300 metres or 30 seconds (A), and two flights of 45 seconds in straight lines plus one of 60 seconds during which an "S" pattern was followed thus demonstrating the ability to make continuous turns in alternate directions (B). Later as glider performance increased flights of five or more minutes would qualify the glider pilot for the C Certificate.

The *Rhön-Rossitten Gesellschaft (RRG)* had been formed as a national gliding organisation in 1924 by Dr.Ernst Brandenburg, the *Leiter der Abteilung der Luft-und Kraftfahrwesen* within the *Reichsverkehrsministerium*, following lobbying by *Rhonvater* Oskar Ursinus. The *RRG* quickly became extremely influential in the development of gliding within Germany. In addition to managing the *Segelflugschulen* at Rossitten in Ospreussen and on the Wasserkuppe it designed and built new gliders in its own workshops. In 1925 Ursinus appointed Alexander Lippisch to lead the *RRG's Technische Abteilung* whose work included the development of *motorsegler* such as the *Liliput* and *Hummel* together with the *Storch* family of tailless gliders. From 1926 the *RRG* developed winch-launching and aero-tows using powered aircraft which allowed gliders to be flown in areas which lacked suitable natural topography for successful unpowered flight. With the additional support of the *Deutsche-Luftfahrtverband eV, Segelflugschulen* had been established at Annaberg/Oberschlesien, Dornberg bei Kassel, Grunau in the Reisengebirge, Schwarzenberg/Sachsen and Wangen/Allgäu by the end of 1928.

The pre-eminence of Germany in terms of gliding led to the founding of the *Internationale Studienkommission für motorlosen Flug (ISTUS)* in Frankfurt on the 13 June 1930 with the task of recording international gliding achievements. The founding nations were Germany, Belgium, France, the Netherlands, Italy and the USA. At that point the German system of glider certification was adopted and eventually formalised for use worldwide by the *Federation Aeronautique Internationale (FAI)* in Paris.

Photo 1D-10 Original caption: Images from the *deutschen Rundflug*, which took place for the first time after the war with the participation of over 90 small aircraft at Tempelhof in Berlin. An early start for the fliers of the *deutschen Rundflug* at 4 o'clock in the morning.

Bundesarchiv Bild 102-01480 Photo: Georg Pahl

Organised by *Maj.a.D.*Lothar von Linsingen (Pilot's Licence Nr.307 9 Oct 12) on behalf of the *Aeroclub von Deutschland* the 1925 *Deutscher Rundflug* was the first major sport aviation event to be held in Weimar Germany. The *BZ-Preis der Lufte (Berliner Zeitung "BZ-Am Mittag")* attracted a staggering 91 entries with thee 57 different aircraft models being organised into three classes: *Gruppe A (Weiss)* aircraft under 40 hp, *Gruppe B (Rot)* those between 41 – 80 hp and *Gruppe C (Blau)* for those between 81 -120 hp. The low power of all these types reflected the restrictions imposed on German civil aviation by the *Begriffsbestimmungen für den deutschen Luftfahrzeugbau* (Definitions of Categories of German Aircraft Construction) of May 1922, restrictions that would not be removed until the Paris Air Agreement was signed on the 21 May 1926.

Held over a ten period from the 31 May to the 9 June 1925 *Gruppe A* aircraft followed a 3,000 km course, whilst those in the other two *Gruppen* flew a route of 5,000 kms, all routes beginning and ending at Berlin-Tempelhof. Combined the routes covered much of Germany with visits being made to 34 towns so as to enable as many people as possible to engage with light aviation. Winning entries were *Hptm.a.D.*Bruno Loerzer (Plm 12 Feb 18) in Klemm L 21 D-623 (*Gruppe A*), Karl Hochmuth in Udet U-10 D-660 (*Gruppe B*) and *KptLt.*Hans Ritter in Caspar CT 1 D-662 (*Gruppe C*). Hans Ritter was a serving *Reichsmarine* officer who held the position of *Referent für Flugwesen und Luftschütz* in the *Flotten-Abteilung/Marineleitung* at that time. In addition to Loerzer a number of *Pour le Mérite* pilots took part in this prestigious event thus connecting Germany's recent aviation past with the aviation of the present: Paul Bäumer (2 Nov 18), Walter Blume (30 Sep 18), Carl Jacobs (18 Jul 18) and Ernst Udet (9 Apr 18).

The photograph captures Hochmuth's Udet U 10 (70 hp Siemens Sh 10) D-660 at the moment of departure – a member of the *Luftpolizei* holds the green and white starting flag on the right of the image. Also visible is Junkers T 26E (80 hp Junkers L 1a) D-656 which was an unusual aircraft in that it could be flown as a parasol monoplane as seen here or as a biplane - the T 26 marked the *Junkers Flugzeugwerke's* largely unsuccessful attempt to enter the highly competitive German light aircraft market - and the Udet U-8a (100 hp Bristol Lucifer) D-670 which was a three passenger light transport. The D-670 was utilised by *Deutsche Luft Hansa* until it crashed on the 29 July 1926. It was later re-built and allocated to the *Deutsche Verkehrsfliegerschule* for training duties.

The *1925 Deutscher Rundflug* and the *1926 Seeflug-Wettbewerb Warnemünde* were the first visible manifestations of the rapid growth in confidence and capability within civil aviation in Weimar Germany. First, second and third places in the Warnemünde competition for seaplanes went to the Heinkel HE 5a D-937 (Wolfgang von Gronau), Junkers W 33 D-921 (William Langanke) and Heinkel HD 24 D-935 (Rudolf Spies).

Photo 1D-11 Original caption: The arrival of the first European flyer at the *Zentralflughafen Berlin-Tempelhof*! Last year's winner of the *Europa-Rundfluges* Morzik on his arrival as the second German to land at the *Zentralflughafen* in Berlin, is greeted by his wife and friends. Berlin-Tempelhof, *Zentralflughafen* - arrival of the fourth placed after the race and the overall winner at the International *Europa-Rundflug* Fritz [Friedrich] Morzik in his BFW M.23c aircraft.

Bundesarchiv Bild 102-10197 Photo: Georg Pahl

Sponsored by the *Aeroclub von Deutschland* the *1930 Europa-Rundflug* was based in Berlin following Fritz Morzik's success in Paris the previous year. On this occasion there were no less than 30 individual entries by German pilots, the next largest contingents coming from Poland (12), England (7) and France (6) out of a total of 60 participants. Once again Morzik was flying a Messerschmitt M 23, although on this occasion it was M 23c D-1883 which was fitted with the new Argus As 8 4-cylinder inverted in-line *Sportflugmotor* which was rated at 95 hp @ 1,600 rpm and 80 hp @ 1,400 rpm. Ten other German pilots also flew the M 23, five with the As 8 motor, 4 with the Sh 14a radial and 1 with a BMW X radial. Of these the Sh 14a powered aircraft were the fastest with a top speed of 220 kph, whilst the As 8 aircraft could only achieve 175 kph. Despite this handicap Morzik was once again judged to be the overall winner over a challenging route of 7,650 kms that reached out from Berlin to Frankfurt am Main, Reims, St.Inglevert, Calais, London, Bristol, Paris, Madrid, Sevilla, Barcelona, Nimes, Lyon, Bern, München, Wien, Prag,

Breslau, Poznan, Warszawa, Königsberg/Ostpr., Danzig and finally back to Berlin. In addition to commercial pilots and the *Sportflieger* a number of serving *Reichswehr* officers were participants including *Oblt.*Oskar Dinort (*Inf.Rgt.2*) in Klemm L 25E D-1900 and *Oblt.*Hoffmann von Waldau (undergoing general staff training with the *3.Division*) in M 23c D-1891.

Friedrich-Wilhelm (Fritz) Morzik was a *Fluglehrer* and *Flugleiter* at the *DVS-Zweigstelle Braunschweig* at that time having previously been employed as a commercial pilot by the *Junkers-Flugzeugwerke* (from 1923) and by *Deutscher Aero Lloyd* (from 1921). He had enlisted in *Grenadier-Rgt.5* at Danzig before the Great War where he had served as an *Unteroffizier*. He had trained as a *Beobachter* with *Flieger-Bataillon 2* in 1914 and thereafter served with *Feld FA 17* during the opening stages of the conflict before training as a pilot in 1915. After spending some time with *Versuchspark West* he had been assigned as a pilot with *FA 300* as part of the *Pascha I* expedition into Palestine from February 1916. Following his return to Germany in 1917 he retrained as a fighter pilot and served briefly with *Jasta 26* before being posted to *FEA 1 & 2*. During 1918 he served with *Kampfeinsitzer-Staffeln 5* and 8. In September 1919 he was transferred as an *Offz.Stellvertreter* to the *Luftpolizei* and served as a *Zugwachtmeister* at Breslau until March 1921.

The various *Rundflüge, Flugtage* and other competitive events were a valuable stimulus to aircraft design and development. Certainly designers such as Siegfried and Walter Günter, Willy Messerschmitt, Gerhard Fieseler and Hanns Klemm all developed their skills whilst making high performance aircraft to meet the needs of these events and it was these skills that would become the basis for the remarkably successful military aircraft programmes of the thirties.

Photo 1D-12 Original caption: A major international air show connected with inverted flight took place at the *Zentralflughafen* Berlin! The best German aerobatic pilot Gerhard Fieseler is seen flying inverted just 25 m above the ground.

Bundesarchiv Bild 102-13561 Photo: Georg Pahl

Gerhard Fieseler passes the crowd at Berlin-Tempelhof in inverted flight in his new Fieseler F2 *Tiger* c/n 140 D-2200 in 1932. Fitted with a 340 hp Walter Pollux 2 radial with an inverted oil and fuel system the F 2 featured symmetrical aerofoils on both wings and was stressed to plus and minus 12 g (gravities) – an unheard of degree of aerodynamic strength which made it possible for him to fly a whole series of complex negative manoeuvres.

Fieseler is widely regarded to be the father of modern competition aerobatics. Beginning at Zurich-Dubendorf in 1927 he introduced the negative loop, triple slow roll, 360 degree negative-g turn, figure of 8 negative-g turn, vertical 8 and horizontal 8 into his freestyle sequence whilst flying his own F 1 *Tiger-Schwalbe* D-1212 with the 300 hp Walter Pollux radial. He then went on to become *Deutscher Kunstflugmeister* in 1928, 1929, 1930, 1932 & 1933 and in 1928 was in such demand to fly at airshows that he commanded fees of 3,000-5,000 RM in Germany and up to 10,000 RM for shows abroad. In July 1934 he was invited to participate in the *Coup Mondiale d'Acrobatie Aerienne* at Paris-Vincennes and in a keenly contested international competition he became the World's first aerobatic champion (*Weltmeister*).

Fieseler had worked as an instructor and designer for the *Raab-Katzenstein Flugzeugwerke GmbH* at Kassel-Ihringhausen from 1926 until that company succumbed to the economic downturn in 1930. In the same year he acquired the *Segel-Flugzeugbau Kassel* as the basis for the *Fieseler Flugzeugbau* which initially focused on the construction of high performance sailplanes. His first commercially successful powered project was the F 5 *Sportflugzeug* (65/80 hp Hirth HM 60) which appeared in time for the *Deutschlandflug* of August 1933. His membership of the *NSDAP* would thereafter bring him considerable commercial advantages with orders in for the licence construction of the He 72 and He 46.

The aircraft in the foreground is Klemm L 25b WNr.318 D-2146. Hanns Klemm's range of *Leichtsportflugzeuge* first appeared in 1924 and by the late twenties had matured around the L 25 series which thereafter were in great demand for the many aero clubs and private owners. This particular example belongs to the *Deutsche Luftfahrt GmbH* ab initio training organisation which had replaced the government sponsored *Sportflug GmbH* which had been forced to close in November 1926. Led by *Maj.a.D.*Leo Leonhardy (*Plm* 2 Oct 18) *Luftfahrt* had three *Zweigstellen; Berlin-Staaken, Boblingen* and *Würzburg* where the training of up to 72 *Reichswehr* personnel as pilots was permitted at their own expense. The emblem of *Deutsche Luftfahrt*, and indeed that of its predecessor *Sportflug*, can be seen on the fin. The top hat worn by the pilot of D-2146 is indicative of the showmanship which characterised the events of the post-war period.

Photo 1D-13 Original caption: Ju 52/3m aircraft (*der Regierungsstaffel/Fliegerstaffel des Führers (FdF)*), Adolf Hitler's machine – possibly coded D-2600 *Immelmann*.

Bundesarchiv Bild 146-1979-106-30 Photo: o.Ang.

By the end of the twenties *Dr.*Ernst Zindel's design team at Dessau were looking to build on the success of the W 33 and W 34 which had been widely employed in the freight role in under-developed parts of the world. What was needed was an aircraft with a much larger capacity and to this end the Ju 52 was created: *"With the moderate wing load that was adopted the Ju 52 had very good, fool proof flying qualities. The box fuselage, in the style of a van with its large side panels, took the machine through the air like a rail bus, whilst the Doppelflugel (double wing) allowed a slow landing speed for small and uneven airfields."* Powered by a single nose mounted 800 hp Junkers L 88 engine Ju 52ba WNr.4001 D-1974 first flew on the 13 October 1930. Four more examples of this type followed, all with different engines, but there was insufficient demand for further production.

From the outset a three-engine version had been contemplated as it was felt that such a layout would provide greater flight safety for passenger operations. Certainly *Junkers* had plenty of experience of such a configuration with their successful G 23/24 and G 31 airliners. Erhard Milch, the *Leitender Mitarbeiter der Deutsche Luft Hansa*, was to later claim that he had been the inspiration behind this re-design but in reality both Colombia and Bolivia had already requested such a machine and WNr.4008-4012, all of which had been laid down as single-engine Ju 52s, were completed with three engines and delivered in 1932 to the *Lloyd Aereo Boliviano* (2) and Colombia's *Escuela de Aviacion* (3). *DLH* received the first dedicated Ju 52/3m ce airframe WNr.4013 which was named *Boelcke* and registered to the airline as D-2201 in May 1932. In all a further five Ju 52/3m ce were completed with un-cowled 525 hp Pratt and Whitney Hornet A2 radials of which *DLH* received WNr.4015 *Richthofen* D-2202 and WNr.4019 D-2468. The others were sold abroad together with Ju 52/3m ba WNr.4016 which was powered by three Hispano Suiza 12 engines and registered to the President of the *Federation Aeronautique Internationale* as CV-FAI.

It is hard to be positive about the identity of the aircraft in the photograph. In the light of the caption it is likely that it is *DLH's* D-2202 which had been chartered to the *NSDAP* for Hitler's unsuccessful Presidential Campaign Tour of October 1932. The pilot for these flights was *DLH's Flugkäpitan* Hans Baur who became the *Führer's* personal pilot in February 1933. At that point *DLH* assigned both the D-2201, which had been under repair following a mid-air collision, and D-2202 for Hitler's personal use. By this time the repaired D-2201 had been fitted with low drag engine cowlings and wheel spats which significantly improved its performance. During 1933 both aircraft were used intensively by Hitler and other high-ranking *NSDAP* officials including *Dr.*Josef Goebbels, *Reichsluftfahrtminister* Hermann Göring and *Stellvertreter des Führers* Rudolf Hess. In April Baur and his crew were inducted into the re-organised *DLV* for the planned visit to Italy whilst in October they were enlisted into the *SS* in recognition of the important role they played to the Führer's security.

The Ju 52/3m ce carried a crew of three plus seventeen passengers. Its cruising speed (cowled variant) was 222 kph at 900 metres with a maximum speed of 271 kph; take off distance was 340 m, landing distance 245 m; range with full payload was 950 kms. The Ju 52/3m went on to become one of the most important transport aircraft in Europe, whilst its excellent flying qualities and large payload made it an ideal military aircraft.

Photo 1D-14 Original caption: The jubilant reception of the airship *"Graf Zeppelin"* in the German capital Berlin! The landing of the *"Graf Zeppelin"* at the new mooring mast in Staaken in Berlin. The airship moored for the first time in Germany at the mooring mast in Staaken.

Bundesarchiv Bild 102-06793 Photo: Georg Pahl

Funded to a large extent by public subscription the giant LZ 127 *"Graf Zeppelin"* was completed at Friedrichshafen in July 1928. It completed its first flight – a 36 hour air test – on the 18 September and less than a month later embarked on its first trans-Atlantic flight to Lakehurst, New Jersey where she docked on the 15 October. On this first non-stop flight on behalf of the *Luftschiffbau Zeppelin* it carried 10 fare paying passengers and 10 guests as well as its crew of 37. It also carried 62,000 letters and 100 specially franked postcards. The return flight to Friedrichshafen with 24 passengers and 100,000 items of mail began on the 29 October and lasted until the 1 November. Quite severe weather was encountered on the selected northern route yet the crossing was made in 71 hours and 7 minutes. Shortly after the LZ 127 made the short flight north of Berlin where this photograph was taken later in November 1928.

At this point in history there was considerable confidence in the rigid airship as the future for long haul air travel. The LZ 127 could carry 24 passengers in considerable comfort with an on-board dining room, sleeping berths for twenty passengers and an extensive viewing platform. Her five Maybach VL II heavy-oil (diesel) engines produced 550 hp apiece and gave the streamlined airship a cruising speed of 115 kph with an endurance of 118 hours. *Luftschiffbau Zeppelin* invested in a new *Zeppelinhalle* at Friedrichshafen to construct the much larger LZ 129 and LZ 130. These could carry as many as 150 day passengers or 50 trans-oceanic passengers with sleeping accommodation.

The Junkers G.38, Dornier Do X and the LZ 127 were the giants of the air in the late twenties. Together they illustrated the huge leap that had been made by a fledgling aircraft industry that had been effectively emasculated until just a few years previously. The technologies they employed in terms of light alloy metals, aerodynamics, high powered petrol and diesel engines and wireless telegraphy were rightly regarded as world class. C.G.Grey, Editor of the *"Aeroplane"* would later write: *"German aeroplanes were up the standard of other countries and better than most. German engines, as usual, were reliable, and German pilots were of high quality."* He also noted: *"that by about 1930 the scientific importance of aviation was being taught in nearly all German higher technical schools and universities. These courses took in aircraft and aero-engine design and construction, aero-dynamics, aerology, meteorology, navigation instruments and air law."*

Photo 1D-15 Original caption: The jubilant reception of the *"Graf Zeppelin"* at the airship port in Berlin-Staaken! The happy landing of the *"Graf Zeppelin"* in Staaken at the mooring mast. In the background a small airship can be seen.

Bundesarchiv Bild 102-09990 Photo: Georg Pahl

In June 1930 the LZ 127 *Graf Zeppelin* returned to Berlin after yet another of Hugo Eckener's prestige flights. She had left Friedrichshafen on the 18 May for her first flight to South America via Seville in Spain to Pernambuco (Recife) and ultimately Rio de Janeiro in Brazil which was reached on the 24 May. Four days later she retraced her route to Pernambuco before flying north to Lakehurst, New Jersey to pick up the prevailing westerly winds for a return flight across the North Atlantic to Seville and Friedrichshafen.

However the previous year had seen her circumnavigate the World in an odyssey that had taken the airship from Lakehurst to Friedrichshafen, Tokyo and Los Angeles with 20 passengers, 400 kg of mail and freight and a crew of 41. This momentous flight had taken 12 days, 14 hours and 20 minutes and had covered 34,200 kms at an average speed of 113 kph. In all respects the LZ 127 was a trailblazer for the *Luftschiffbau Zeppelin*. In 1931 she would even undertake a cruise into the Arctic flying as far north as Franz Josef Land inside 80 degrees north on the edge of the permanent ice cap. Regular passenger and mail services between Friedrichshafen and Pernambuco began in March 1932 with four return flights in the spring and a further five in the autumn, with the last three going all the way to Rio de Janeiro. This pattern then continued with 9 flights in 1933, 12 in 1934 and 16 in 1935.

The LZ 127 was the World's most successful commercial airship flying 1,695,272 kms and carrying 13,100 passengers in a total of 590 flights which included 144 ocean crossings. It was withdrawn from service following the *Hindenburg* disaster in 1937 and broken up in 1940.

A small non-rigid airship or "blimp" can be seen in the background. Such airships were used for advertising purposes – in this case for *"Trumpf Chokolade"*. It was almost certainly a product of the Goodyear Tire and Rubber Company of Akron, Ohio.

Photo 1E-1 Original caption: *Reichswehrmänover* in Königstein, 1930.
Bundesarchiv Bild 102-01819A Photo: Georg Pahl

A horse-drawn *Feldartillerie-Batterie* passes the review stand in Königstein in Sachische Schweiz within *Wehrkreis IV*, probably at the close of the annual autumnal manoeuvres, witness the review personnel on the left of the image and the formal nature of the *Batterie* personnel. The *Bundesarchiv's* classification of this image indicates a *Kavallerie* connection which if true would suggest that this *Batterie* forms part of the *V.(Reitend)/Artillerie-Regiment 3* which was garrisoned at Sagan and Sprottau in support of the *2.Kavallerie-Division* (*GenLt.*Gerd von Rundstedt). The *Reichsheer's* three dedicated *Reitend-Artillerieabteilungen* each comprised of three *Artilleriebatterien* equipped with the 7.7 cm le.FK 16 field gun.

In this image the *Batterie-Offiziere* ride alongside the lead gun teams each of which consists of six horses towing the gun limber complete with crew and ammunition and a 7.7 cm le.FK 16 field gun of Great War vintage. A gun crew consisted of a gun leader (*Unterwachtmeister*), five gunners (*Kanoniere*) and three horsemen (*Fahrern*). Four gun crews comprised a *Batterie* which was commanded by a *Batterie-Chef* (*Hauptmann*) and supported by two other officers, one of whom was trained as an artillery observer. Within the largely non-motorised *Reichswehr Artillerie-Regimenter* almost as much time was spent training personnel in equine skills as was devoted to gunnery practice.

Given the traditions of the pre-war *Kavallerie-Regimenter* it is not surprising that a large number of the *Reichsheer's* secret *Fliegeroffiziere* were *Kavallerie-Offiziere*. The 1930 *geheime Fliegerliste* lists: *Rittm.*Johannes Fink & *Oblt.*Wilhelm Becker (*RR 1*), *Rittm.*Plaschke, *Rittm.*Paul Schultheiss & *Oblt.*von Detten (*RR 3*), *Oblt.*Helmuth von Hoffmann & *Oblt.*Hans-Georg Schmidt von Altenstadt (*RR 4*), *Rittm.*Heinz-Hellmuth von Wuhlisch (*RR 5*), *Oblt.*Otto-Friedrich Frhr.von Houwald & *Oblt.*Hans Jeschonnek (*RR 6*), *Rittm.*Ernst Bonatz, *Rittm.*Walter Somme & *Oblt.* Hans-Jurgen von Cramon-Taubadel (*RR 7*), *Maj.*Theodor Schubert & *Rittm.*Gaze (*RR 8*), *Rittm.* Karl von Gerlach, *Rittm.*Curt Pflugbeil, *Rittm.*Günther Schroth, *Oblt.*Hans von Koppelow, *Oblt.* von Oheimb & *Oblt.*Frhr.von Wichtingen (RR 11), *Maj.*Hellmuth Bieneck, *Maj.*Friedrich Cranz,

*Maj.*Gebhard von Kotze & *Lt.*Helmut Kuster (*RR 14*), *Rittm.*Franz Biwer & *Rittm.*Wolfgang von Chamier-Glisczinski (*RR 16*), *Rittm.*Otto Dessloch (*RR 17*) and *Maj.*Max Mohr & *Rittm.*Karl Barlen (*RR 18*). In addition *Rittm.*Hermann (?) Martini was serving with the *Kavallerie-Schule*.

Photo 1E-2 Original caption: Pontoon Bridge during the large scale pioneer exercise under the cover of artificial fog on the Elbe near Höhenwarthe! For the first time the construction of a military bridge was practiced using a chemical smoke screen. *Pioniere* are seen at work on the construction of the pontoon bridge at Höhenwarthe on the Elbe before screening.
Bundesarchiv Bild 102-1894 Photo: Georg Pahl
The great rivers of Europe presented formidable barriers to any advancing army effectively restricting its movement and channelling it along expected routes which could then be blocked by lines of fortifications. The *Pioniere* were therefore central to the *Reichsheer's* ability to move cross country along routes of its own choice and to achieve this aim each of the *Reichsheer's* seven peacetime *Divisionen* was assigned a *Pionierebataillon* which were located at Königsberg/Ostpr. (1), Stettin (2), Küstrin (3), Magdeburg (4), Ulm (5), Minden (6) and München (7). The *Pionierschule* was also located at München within *Wehrkreis VII*.

The smaller rivers could be bridged using wooden braced structures but for wider rivers such as the Elbe a pontoon bridge was required. Pontoon bridges were flexible wooden roadways which rested on a series of small floating pontoons which were anchored to the river banks by a network of steel hawsers. Depending on the strength of the river flow this type of bridge could be extended over considerable distances to span even the largest river. The *Reichsheer* employed the *Brückengerät C*, a wooden pontoon and trestle equipment which had a load capacity of up to 5.3 tonnes. This was sufficient for a largely un-motorised force which was not equipped with armoured vehicles.

In addition to bridging, the *Pioniere* were trained in the construction of field infrastructure and fortifications, the laying and removal of mines and in general explosive demolition work. Each *Pionierbataillon* consisted of a *Stab* (HQ), two *Pionierkompanien*, a *Brückenkolonne C* and a *Pionierkolonne*. The *Brückenkolonne* consisted of two *Pontonzuge* each with 8 *Halb-Pontons* and a *M-Boot*.

In this image the *M-Boot* can be seen in the right foreground whilst additional *pontons* are being rowed into position in the middle of the river. The foot of the bridge has been anchored to the bank with the help of a wooden pile. *Pioniere* on the opposite bank, presumably from the *Bataillon's* other *Pontonzug*, are also building a pontoon bridge outward to join up in mid-stream. The reference in the title to smoke screening was an important element of the exercise if there was any likelihood of enemy artillery fire being directed at the bridge.

A number of *Fliegeroffiziere* were assigned to the *Pioniere* in 1930: *Hptm.*Robert Pistorius (*Kp. Chef/Pi.Btl.2*), *Oblte.*Günther Korten (*Bildstelle Berlin*) and Platz (*Pi.Btl.4*), *Hptm.*Fritz Löb (*Kp. Chef/Pi.Btl.6*) and *Oblt.*Max Ibel (*Pi.Btl.7 - Lipetsk*).

Photo 1E-3 Original caption: The first major exercise of this year's *Reichswehr* autumn manoeuvres were held in Ostpreussen! Manoeuvre images of the *1.Division* between Goldap and Angerapp in Ostpreussen. A *leichte Geschütz* in firing position in the exercise area.
Bundesarchiv Bild 102-11934 Photo: Georg Pahl
Kanoniere of *Artillerie-Regiment Nr.1* prepare to fire their 7.7 cm leichte Feldkanone 16 during the *Reichsheer's* annual manoeuvres in August 1928. The 7.7 cm le.FK 16 had a weight in action of 1.325 tonnes, a shell weight of 6.1 kgs and a maximum range of 10,300 metres at an elevation of 40 degrees from the horizontal. Muzzle velocity was 600 mps. In the light of recent combat experience

it was known that the weapon was not particularly effective against well designed earthworks and concrete fortifications. The only heavier artillery weapon permitted under the terms of the Treaty of Versailles was the low velocity 10.5 cm leichte Feldhaubitz 16 which could project a 14.8 kg shell over a range of 9,225 metres at high angles. This weapon weighed 1.45 tonnes in action. All heavy artillery had been banned.

Each of the *Reichswehr's* seven *Artillerie-Regimenter* consisted of a *Stab* with a *Nachrichtenzug*, eventually this would become the *Stabsbatterie (mot)*, plus three *Abteilungen* each with three *Batterien* – two with the 7.7 cm le.FK 16 and one with the 10.5 cm le.FH 16 - and an *Ausbildungsbatterie*, which also provided a *Wetterzug*. Within this overall structure each *Regiment* had one *Batterie* – usually the *3.Batterie* – equipped with the 7.7 cm leichte Feldkanone 96/16 to provide a dedicated infantry support capability, whilst another *Batterie* – usually the *9.Batterie* – was equipped with the lorry mounted 7.5 cm FlaK L/60 (*Kraftwagengeschütz*).

The *Stab, II.* and *Ausbildungsbattr./Artillerie-Rgt.1* were all garrisoned at Königsberg/Ostpreussen, whilst the *I.Abt.*was located at Insterburg and the *III.Abt.* at Gumbinnen. By the end of the twenties the *1.Kp.(Kraftwagenversuchs)/Fahrabteilung 1* at Königsberg was also covertly acting as a cadre for the proscribed heavy artillery on behalf of *GrKdo.1*. A similar function was performed by the *1.Kp./Kraftfahrabteilung 5* at Ulm within *GrKdo.2*.

In 1930 *Hptm.*Friedrich-Carl Hanesse (*Art.Rgt.6*) (*Flg.Referent 1.Division* 1 Oct 27 – 31 Oct 31), *Hptm.*Günther Lohmann (*Lehrer a.d.Artillerie-Schule Jüterbog*) and *Oblt.*Theodor Macht (Lipetsk 1 May 30 – 30 Sep 30) were all carried on *Art.Rgt.1's* books as *Offiziere* with *geheime Fliegerausbildungs*.

Photo 1E-4 Original caption: Our successful fighter pilot *Oberleutnant* Greim.
Bundesarchiv Bild 146-1969-030-18 Photo: o.Ang. Postkartenvertrieb W.Sanke, Berlin

Robert Greim was born in Bayreuth on the 22 June 1892. Following cadet training he joined the *bayerischen Eisenbahn-Batallion* as a *Fahnenjunker* and was commissioned on the 25 October 1913 as a *Batterie-Offz. in bayerischen Feldartillerie-Rgt.8*. In the early fighting of 1914-15 he distinguished himself during the *Schlacht am Lothringen*, at Nancy-Epinal, at St.Mihiel and in the assault on the Camp des Romains.

He transferred to the *Fliegertruppe* in August 1915 and trained as a *Beobachter* seeing service with *FA 3b* and *Feld FA A 204*. While flying with *Lt.*Hempel he scored his first *Luftsiege* alongside more routine artillery shoots, aerial photography flights, bombing raids and patrols. He trained as a pilot at Schleißheim over the winter of 1916-17 and was promoted to *Oberleutnant* on the 17 January 1917 before serving briefly in *FA 46*. In April he transferred to fighters becoming *Fhr. bayerische Jasta 34* on the 19 June. Initially deployed in support of *Heeresabteilung C* at St.Mihiel, *Jasta 34b* moved to *AOK 5* on the Verdun Front in September where it largely remained until March 1918. Thereafter it supported *AOK 2* on the Somme and *Oblt.*Greim took on the additional role as *Kdr.Jagdgruppe 10,* later *Jagdgruppe Greim* in the fierce fighting associated with the German Spring Offensive through to August. During this period his forces were in a continuous state of flux but for the most part consisted of *Jasta 34b* and *Jasta 37*. His own score reached 21 *LS* on the 27 August 1918 and he was decorated with the *Ritterkreuz des koniglichen Hausordens von Hohenzollern* to which the *Pour le Mérite* was added on the 8 October with the *bayerischer Militär-Max-Josef-Orden* on the 25 October. The latter award brought the addition of nobility and henceforth he was known as Robert Ritter von Greim. His final score was 28 *LS*.

He was discharged at the end of March 1920 but on the 15 February 1921 was given the honorary rank of *Hauptmann* back-dated to the end of his service. By this time he was often appearing with Ernst Udet at air shows where the pair would re-enact dogfights from the Great

War, whilst professionally he took his banking examinations and worked as a Bank Clerk. The lure of flying then took him to China where he became a military aviation advisor to *Gen.*Chaing Kai-Shek in Canton between 1924-27. He then returned home to take up the position of *Leiter der Deutsche Luftfahrt, Zweigstelle Würzburg* where he came back into contact with a new generation of aspiring young military pilots whilst also running refresher training for former colleagues and members of the wartime *Luftstreitkräfte*.

Photo 1E-5 Original caption: The large *Reichswehr* exercise in in the area of Königshofen in Unterfranken took place in the presence of *Reichspräsidenten von Hindenburg* and many foreign military attaches. It is the first time since the war, that such *Reichswehr* manoeuvres have taken place in western Germany in the area between Kissingen, Meiningen and Würzburg. A camouflaged heavy machine gun is seen in the exercise area.
Bundesarchiv Bild 102-10892 Photo: Georg Pahl

This employment of the *Reichswehr's* standard heavy machine gun in the air defence or indirect fire role in September 1930 is indicative of the training in the vertical dimension that had continued throughout the post-war period. As a result of the *Feldheer's* experience in the Great War *Gen.d.Inf.* Hans von Seeckt, the first *Chef der Heeresleitung*, had insisted that the importance of military aviation to future military operations be recognised in *Heeresdienstvorschrift Nr.487 Führung und Gefecht der Verbundenen Waffen* (Leadership and Battle with Combined Arms) which appeared in two parts in 1921 and 1923. As a result the *Reichsheer* took air power far more seriously than did other European armies. Although denied actual aircraft, the *Reichsheer's geheime Fliegeroffiziere* played a major role in all *Reichswehr* exercises and large scale manoeuvres where both friendly and hostile aircraft were assumed to be present. The vital importance of overhead camouflage was endlessly reinforced and practiced and troop and vehicle dispersal also reflected this reality.

The Divisional staff included a *Flieger-Referent* (*Referent zbV*) and a *Bild-Offizier*, both of whom were former *Luftstreitkräfte Offiziere* with command and/or operational experience. In 1930 the *Referate zbV* were: *Hptm.*Hanesse (*1.Div.*), *Hptm.*Putzier (*2.Div.*), *Hptm.*Zoch (*3.Div.*), *Hptm.* Doerstling (*4.Div.*), *Rittm.*Barlen (*5.Div.*), *Rittm.*Somme (*6.Div.*), *Rittm.*Dessloch (*7.Div.*), *Rittm.* Plaschke (*1.Kav.Div.*), *Rittm.*Bonatz (*2.Kav.Div.*) & *Rittm.*Biwer (*3.Kav.Div.*), whilst the *Bild-Offiziere* were: *Oblt.*Korten (*1.Div.*), *Oblt.*Berger (*2.Div.*), *Rittm.*von Chamier-Glisczinski (*3.Div.*), *Oblt.*Cartun (*4.Div.*), *Oblt.*Krüger (*5.Div.*), *Rittm.*Gaze (*6.Div.*) & *Oblt.*Pregler (*7.Div.*).

Each winter the *RWM's Truppenamt* conducted *Kriegspielen* in which the covert air staff were required to play a full and active part. The 1927 *Kriegspiel* used the scenario of a Polish attack on Germany's eastern frontier during the course of which air attacks were made against German towns and cities. Officers attending covert general staff training as *Führergehilfen* were required to complete a thorough study of air doctrine, theory and technology.

In this image a *schwere maschinengewehr Model 08/15* crew in full *Feldanzug* (field order) with side arms, entrenching tools, bayonets, water bottles, map cases and binoculars, prepare to engage low flying hostile aircraft. They are wearing coloured rubber bands around their *Stahlhelm* – *Rot* or *Blau* for the two opposing sides in the field exercise, whilst the supervising staff and umpires wore *Weiss* bands. The stencilling on the side of the heavy metal tripod indicates that these men form part of *Infanterie Regiment Nr.13's MG Kompanie* at Ludwigsburg which had an establishment of 12 water cooled MG 08/15 heavy machine guns. *Inf.Rgt.13* formed part of the *5.Division* (*Gen.d.Inf.*Hans Frhr. Suetter von Lotzen) at Stuttgart in south-west Germany and was garrisoned at Ludwigsburg, Stuttgart, Ulm and Schwäbisch-Gmund. *Oblt.*Hermann Plocher, a *Zugführer*, is the only known *Fliegeroffizier* to have been attached to the *Inf.Rgt.13* in 1930.

Photo 1E-6 Original caption: *4./Res.Feld-Art.Rgt.13, Feldkanone* **provisionally mounted as an anti-aircraft gun on an improvised turntable,** *Armeeoberkommando 7, Estfront,* **France. Soldiers of** *Reserve-Feldartillerie-Regiments Nr.13* **use a Feldkanone 96 as a** *Fliegerabwehrgeschütz,* **Rangefinder to the left.**

Bundesarchiv Bild 136-0635 Photo: Oscar Tellgmann

In the early part of the war the lack of dedicated *Flakgeschützen* led to a number of improvised solutions to deal with the growing problem presented by enemy reconnaissance and bombing aircraft. This photograph is of interest as it shows just such a mounting in a wooden revetment on the edge of a wood. A standard 7.7 cm FK 96 artillery piece complete with splinter shield has been mounted on a rotatable wooden frame with metal runners on top of a concrete plinth. The railway lines in the foreground show how the weapon was moved on to the turntable in the first place. The maximum elevation of the gun has been significantly increased from the 14 degrees previously obtained on its fixed carriage. However its low muzzle velocity of 465 m/sec with its associated long flight times and the low rate of fire in this particular installation would have made it a largely ineffective anti-aircraft gun. In mid-1915 the *Feldheer* had just 175 of these improvised anti-aircraft guns available for use along the entire length of the Front and *Gen.d.Inf.*Erich von Falkenhayn, the *Chef des Oberste Heeresleitung,* observed on the 26 May that *"the combat of enemy aircraft by artillery has been up to this point generally accompanied by only very limited success, even with large expenditures of ammunition".*

The one metre range finder (*Entfernungsmesser*) was an essential part of the gun's fire control as the distance of the target had to be known with accuracy to ensure the correct elevation to compensate for the fall of the shot. Much needed to be learned about the science of anti-aircraft gunnery during this period and a training school for officers of the *Ballon-Abwehr-Kanone Verbände* was also established at Ostende in Belgium in 1915 where a two week *BAK-Lehrgang* was conducted to give theoretical and practical instruction Meanwhile on the 10 July 1915 *Maj.*Hugo Grimme was appointed to the new position of *Inspekteur der Ballon-Abwehr-Kanone,* whilst each *Stab/AOK* were assigned a dedicated *BAK-Offizier.*

At the beginning of the war the *Deutsches Heer,* the combined forces of the *Preußische, Bayerische, Wurttemburgische & Sachsische Heer,* underwent a general mobilisation that massively increased their size to total 30,037 *Offiziere,* 106,477 *Unteroffiziere* and 647,811 *Mannschaften.* To preserve the pre-war regular units of the *Heer,* mobilised units were generally referred to as *Reserveverbände* as was the case with *Reserve-Feldartillerie-Regiment Nr.13* although of course all units had a sprinkling of regular personnel whilst regular units were restored to full strength through the addition of reserve personnel. Following the advance to the River Marne in 1914 and the subsequent stabilisation of the Western Front during the autumn the western *Feldheer* took up positions that stretched from the sea at Nieuport in Belgium to Pfetterhouse on the border with Switzerland. *Armeeoberkommando 7 (GenOb.*Josias von Heeringen until 28 August 1916) consisting of three *Armeekorps* faced the French in the Aisne Sector near Soissons in Northern France.

Photo 1E-7 Original caption: German Anti-Aircraft Gun on a lorry mounting. The *Fliegerabwehr* **on the Italian Front in 1917.**

Bundesarchiv Bild 183-S29499 Photo: o.Ang. (Scherl)

The *Luftstreitkräfte's Kraftwagenflak* had its origins in the lorry mounted *Ballon-Abwehr-Kanone* that had first appeared in 1909 in response to an earlier request from the *Artillerie-Prüfungs-Kommission* for conversions of existing artillery weapons for use against an emerging threat from increasingly capable lighter-than-air craft such as Graf Zeppelin's rigid airships. *Krupp* had proposed a motorised carriage for the 7.5 cm Kanon which could be deployed by road at speeds of up to 45 kph before being brought into action extremely quickly across the path of a reported enemy aircraft. With 75 degrees of elevation this gun could fire a 5.5 kg shell to a height of 7,000 metres. As an alternative the *Rheinische Metallwaren-und Maschinenfabrik* had offered two different mobile mountings for the 5 cm *Ehrhardt* high angle gun; one fully armoured whilst the other was simply mounted on an armoured lorry. The *Krupp* prototype was then evaluated in the annual manoeuvres of the following year when it was found that the recoil caused damage to the lorry chassis, that the working space around the gun was too restricted and that some form of accurate range finding was urgently required. Thereafter progress in developing an effective *BAK* was slow and the outbreak of hostilities found the *Feldheer* equipped with just 6 motorised and 12 horse drawn *BAK* despite the fact that it had already been recognised that each *Felddivision* should have a *BAK-Batterie* with additional *Batterien* at both *Korps* and *Armee* level.

Following the brief period of mobile operations during the autumn of 1914 the opposing forces took up increasingly static positions and lines, a deployment that favoured the static emplacement of the few available *BAK* and it would not be until the autumn of 1917 that the *Kraftwagenflak* would begin to appear in numbers at the Front. For reasons of weight the favoured weapon was the 2.5 tonne 7.7 cm BAK despite its known deficiencies against high flying targets and the most popular platform was the Ehrhardt Platform oder BAK-Wagen Typ E-V/4 Kraftwagen 14 although the example in this photograph may equally be a Krupp or Daimler chassis. On the Western Front these weapons were largely employed in counter-acting low-flying enemy aircraft near the *Hauptkampflinie (HKL)*.

In this scene members of the gun crew are seen lowering the sides of the vehicle to increase the working area on the truck bed. Camouflage in the form of foliage has been discarded and the side lockers are being opened to access the ready use ammunition. The 7.7 cm BAK had a muzzle velocity of 510 m/sec. and a rate of fire of up to 8 rounds per minute. Maximum elevation was 70 degrees above the horizontal. The vehicle is armoured around the cab and engine. The radiator louvres are open which suggests that the vehicle has recently arrived in this position.

Motorised *BAK* also became progressively more important in the defence of the *Heimat* (Homeland). By the end of 1917 104 heavy and 112 light motorised guns were deployed inside Germany together with 998 horse drawn or emplaced weapons with key industrial facilities and transportation hubs being amongst the best protected locations. The importance of the ground based air defences in the *Heimat* increased still further in the last year of the war as the British Independent Air Force became more active in its attacks on Germany by both day and night.

Photo 1E-8 Original caption: *Flugabwehrkanone* during the autumn manoeuvres near Bad Mergentheim in Southern Germany, September 1926.
Bundesarchiv Bild 102-03179 Photo: Georg Pahl
Under the terms of the Treaty of Versailles the newly formed *Vorläufige Reichsheer* was denied the retention of *Flakartillerie* with the exception of sixteen obsolete weapons in the fortress at Königsberg in Ostpreussen. *GenLt.*Hans von Seeckt's response was to create a single motorised *Artilleriebatterie* within each of the seven regular *Artillerie-Regimenter*. These units were to carry on the traditions and expertise of the wartime *Kraftwagen-Flakartillerie* but to conform with the Treaty regulations the truck mounted 7.7 cm *Luftkanone* had their anti-aircraft sights removed and their elevation capability reduced to a maximum of 70 degrees from the horizontal. To its regret the *Reichsheer* was denied the use of the more effective and preferred wartime 8.8 cm *Flugabwehrkanone* which had seen extensive service during 1917-18.

This photograph was taken in the rolling hills of the Main-Tauber District of Baden Württemberg within *Wehrkreis V* in September 1926 and shows a *Kraftwagen-Flak* unit of *the 9.(Kfw.)/Artillerie-Regiment 6* from Hannover. The 7.7 cm *leichte Feldkanone* is seen in the indirect fire role with a moderate level of elevation. In accordance with its "declared" role the crew enjoy the protection of a splinter shield which was not fitted to anti-aircraft weapons. The number in the crew also appears to have been reduced from the ten *Kanoniere* that was the norm in the *Kraftwagenflak*. The officer on the right with the white arm band is an umpire who will judge the crew's performance as well as their vulnerability to "enemy" action during the field manoeuvres. The original caption to this photograph alludes to the crew's covert role in the maintenance of an anti-aircraft artillery capability within the *Reichsheer*.

The overall weight of the vehicle when in action was in the order of 8-tonnes which taken together with its solid rubber tyres and a 80 hp petrol engine gave the vehicle a limited cross country capability over firm ground. The maximum road speed was in the order of 45 kph.

Photo 1E-9 Original caption: With gas masks beside the searchlight – two German soldiers with gas masks operate a searchlight of the *Flakartillerie* in 1918.

Bundesarchiv Bild 183-R27853 Photo: o.Ang. Scherl Agency

Experiments with the use of searchlights had begun in Germany as early as 1912 when they were found to be useful in blinding the pilot of an attacking aircraft whilst exposing his machine to anti-aircraft fire. In response to a number of Allied night attacks a number of improved searchlights were brought into service in 1915, their effectiveness being enhanced through sound location. Thereafter the number of searchlights steadily increased from 132 in June 1916 to 718 by November 1918. Improved types based on those already in use aboard warships of the *Kaiserliche Marine* were also introduced and the 110 cm and 200 cm Flakscheinwerfer of 1918 had an effective ceiling of 4,000 and 5,500 metres respectively. Searchlights proved highly effective against the slow moving aircraft of the Great War and greatly increased the probability of effective disabling fire by ground based defences, thus saving valuable ammunition which would have otherwise been expended in un-aimed barrage fire.

During the Great War the *Flak Scheinwerfer* units were normally deployed as *Heeres* and *Korpstruppen* under the *Kommandeur der Flakartillerie beim Armee Oberkommando*. For example searchlight units assigned to *AOK 18* for *Unternehmen Michael* on the 21 March 1918 consisted of *Flak Scheinwerfer Zuge* 240, 403, 405 and 729, whilst *AK.III* deployed *Flak SW Zuge* 207 and 698, *AK.IX* the *Flak SW Zug* 726 and *AK.XVII* the *Flak SW Zuge* 180 and 181. *Unternehmen Michael* was the final German Spring Offensive in the West which very nearly reached Paris before leading to a progressive collapse of the German Western Front and the end of the war.

Despite the fact that *Obstlt.*Günther Rüdel, the *Kdr. des Ausbildungstabes III* within the *Inspektion der Artillerie*, recognised that *"the combat of night bomber attacks (would be) the most important task of the air defence"* in 1930, the replacement of the 110 cm Flakscheinwerfer by a more capable design was not considered a priority in his *Entwicklungsprogramm der Flugabwehr-Waffen* of that year.

Photo 1E-10 Original caption: *Linienschiff SMS "Hannover"* - Launched September 29, 1905, decommissioned in December 1918; recommissioned February 1921 for the *Reichsmarine*, taken out of service September 1931, scrapped 1944/1946; Gunnery practice.

Bundesarchiv Bild 134-B2097 Photo: o.Ang.

Backbone of the *Reichsmarine's* naval forces in the twenties were the six *Linienschiffe* that had been authorised under the terms of *Artikel 181* of the Treaty of Versailles. In all eight units were retained and although six could be operational at any given time, manning considerations effectively limited this number to just four ships – each vessel required c.35 officers and 708 enlisted men. All of these vessels had been made obsolete in their planned fleet role following the arrival of the all big-gun Dreadnought-style *Großlinienschiffe* which had first been commissioned into the *Kaiserliche Marine* in 1908. As a result none of the retained units saw much action during the Great War being too slow and under-gunned to be risked outside coastal waters. The exceptions were the three *Deutschland-Klass* vessels that formed the *II. Geschwader* of the *Hochseeflotte* and saw action in the *Skagerrak Schlacht* (Battle of Jutland) of May 1916.

Two of the older *Braunschweig-Klass* ships, which had already been disarmed, were promptly converted into *F-Boot* tenders. Of the remainder *Hannover* and *Braunschweig* were the only two *Linienschiffe* to be re-commissioned in the immediate post-war years. *Hannover* was a *Deutschland-Klass Linienschiff* with slightly better internal protection than the *Braunschweig-Klass*. She had been refitted in 1920-21 and fitted with a pair of twin torpedo tubes before being assigned to the *Marinestation der Ostsee* at Kiel. She served until 1927 before being taken in hand for a further refit in 1929-30 when she received a tubular fighting mast with a heavy foretop as well as a new bridge structure. She was finally de-commissioned in 1935, disarmed and used for shock test work in connection with magnetic seabed mines. The remaining vessels were taken into the yards at yearly intervals from 1923 before being re-commissioned. *Elsass* served 1924-30, *Hessen* 1925-34, *Schleswig-Holstein* 1926-32 and *Schlesien* 1927-34. Braunschweig was decommissioned in 1926 and together with *Elsass* was stricken in 1931. *Hessen* was converted into a radio-controlled target vessel in 1935-36, whilst *Schleswig-Holstein* and *Schlesien* were modified as *Schulschiffe* in 1932 and 1936 respectively.

The *Reichsmarine's Linienschiffe* displaced around 13,200 tonnes (14,218 tonnes full load) and were armed with four 28 cm SK L/40 in two twin turrets with a secondary armament of ten 15 cm SK L/45 in place of the original 17 cm SK L/40 guns originally installed in single casemate mountings on the beam. Most of the 8.8 cm FlaK were landed. Initially coal fired, the triple expansion machinery could propel them at speeds of up to 18 knts although the more normal cruising speed was just 10 knts.

Photo 1E-11 Original caption: *Großes Torpedoboot SMS "S 19"* - Launched 17 October 1912, later served with the *Reichsmarine*, decommissioned 31 March 1931, broken up 1935.

Bundesarchiv Bild 134-B0485 Photo: o.Ang.

Although classed as a *Große Torpedoboot*, the *S 19* was one of the *Kaiserliche Marine's* first group (*Große Torpedoboot 1911*) of ocean going *Zerstörern* (Destroyers). Built by *Schichau-Werke* of Elbing the *S 19* displaced 650 tonnes and was armed with two 8.8 cm T/K L 45 on open mounts and four single 45 cm torpedo tubes and had a crew of c.80 officers and men. As such these small and very fast vessels (37 knts) were seen by the World's navies as force multipliers as it was thought that torpedo attacks by such relatively inexpensive vessels could neutralise if not sink vastly superior and expensive capital ships.

As successive *Große Torpedobooten Klassen* during the Great War had nearly doubled in size with upgraded armament, the *Reichsmarine* rightly regarded the *S 19* and her eleven sisters as *Torpedoboote* and had them re-armed with two 10.5 cm L/45 guns and re-boilered during 1921-23. As such the *S 19* served the *Reichsmarine* well until stricken in 1931.

During this period the *I. Torpedoboots Flottille* and *5. Torpedoboots Halbflottille* reported to the *Marinestation der Nordsee* at Wilhelmshaven whilst the *II. Torpedoboots Flottille* and *11. Torpedoboots Halbflottille* came under the *Marinestation der Ostsee* at Kiel.

A number of naval *Fliegeroffiziere* served aboard the *Reichsmarine's Torpedoboote* including *Oblt.z.S.* Carl Köchy who served as *Wach-Offz.* aboard *W 2* in 1922-24, these small warships being considered ideal postings for young officers to gain valuable sea experience. After seeing immediate post-war service in mine clearance operations as *Chef der I. Nordsee-Minensuchflottille* during 1919-20, *FregKpt.* Konrad Zander, the future *Leiter der Luftschützgruppe/Marineleitung*, was *Chef der I. Torpedoboots-Flottille* from March 1923 to September 1926.

Photo 1E-12 Original caption: Special vessel (Sail Training Ship) *"Niobe"* **- Launched in 1913 applied and collected 1916/1917 (name:** *Aldebaran, Niobe, Schwalbe / Swan***), 1922 by the** *Reichsmarine* **as** *"Niobe"* **converted into a three-masted barque, July 1932 capsized in the Fehmarnbelt; See here after conversion, under full sail.**

Bundesarchiv Bild 134-B0391 Photo: o.Ang.

Although the *Kaiserliche Marine* had abandoned sail training in 1910 because it was considered outmoded in an era of steam powered armoured warships, it was appreciated that sail training had many advantages, not least that it encouraged high standards of seamanship and the value of teamwork. It was therefore decided to reintroduce sail training for the *Reichsmarine's* aspiring officer cadets and in 1922 the Danish built four-masted gaff-sail schooner *Schwalbe* (formerly *Niobe, Aldebaran* & *Morten Jensen*) was purchased and taken in hand for conversion to a three-masted barque. The *Segelschulschiff Niobe* (645 tonnes) re-commissioned on the 19 December 1923 with a crew of 7 officers and 27 ratings and accommodation for up to 64 midshipmen. She was assigned to the *Marinestation der Nordsee* with Wilhelmshaven as her home port. *Matrose* Eckhard Christian, later to train as a naval aviator, was trained aboard the *Niobe* during July – October 1926.

There had always been concerns that the *Niobe* was still top heavy and tragically these fears were realised on the 26 July 1932 when the ship capsized in a freak summer storm off the Island of Fehmarn in the Ostsee. In all 69 died including the majority of that year's class of officer cadets. Amongst the 40 survivors was naval aviator Werner Klumper. The loss of so many cadets was nothing short of a crisis for the *Reichsmarine* which immediately called upon its reserve intake pool to bridge the gap. Also affected were the 12 office candidates who were undergoing flight training at the *DVS Zweigstelle Warnemünde*. Their training to *B 1 (See)* standard was immediately accelerated so that they could begin their basic naval training at Stralsund in September. These twelve naval aviators were (Paul) Bohn, Hans Brockmann, (Ludwig) Fehling, Hannibal Gude, (Karl-Ferdinand) Hielscher, Robert Kowalewski, Kuppers, Luckhardt, Helmut Mahlke, (Rudolf) Rucker, (Joachim) Sander and (Siegfried) Storp.

The wreck of the *Niobe* was later raised, the bodies removed for interment and then the vessel was ceremonially sunk on the 18 September 1933 by the *Torpedoboot Jaguar* with much of the small *Reichsmarine* in attendance. A memorial to this maritime disaster survives to this day on the island of Fehmarn.

Photo 1E-13 Original caption: *Minensuchboot SMS M 78* **- Launched 26 September 1917.**

Bundesarchiv Bild 134-B0665 Photo: o.Ang.

Article 193 of the Treaty of Versailles required the German Government to clear the huge number of mines that had been laid in the Deutsche Bucht and Western Ostsee so that unimpeded mercantile trade could be resumed. The main task of the *vorläufige Reichsmarine* during 1919-22 was therefore mine clearance and to this end in 1919 the *Minensuchverband der Nordsee* deployed 88 *M-Boote*, 43 *A-Boote* and 27 *F-Boote* in four *Flottillen*, whilst a further 2 *M-Boote*, 55 *T-Boote*, 26 *F-Boote* and 25 converted fishing vessels were deployed in the five *Flottillen* of the *Minensuchverband der Ostsee*. These figures were steadily reduced with the release of the fishing vessels and the progressive retirement of the *A* and *F-Booten* but the mine sweeping programme continued until the 8 August 1922 when the *Leiter des Minensuch-Aussendienstes* was disbanded.

Post-1922 the *Minensuchverbände* remained an important element of the *Reichsmarine* with 38 *Minensucher* of modern design remaining in the inventory. Many were subsequently converted into auxiliary vessels of different types but a *Minensuchhalbflottille* was maintained within each *Marinestation* – that in the Nordsee being based at Cuxhaven whilst that in the Ostsee was located at Kiel. Initially each *Halbflottille* consisted of just 4 *M-Boote* but from 1932 this number was increased to 8 Minensucher. Meanwhile followjng the development of the magnetic mine by the *Sperrversuchskommando (SVK)* a new wooden class of motor minesweeper were introduced – these being the small *R-Boote* of 60 tonnes which were brought into service after 1927. The *R-Boote* formed the *1.Raumsboothalbflottille* from 1933. On the 1 October 1933 the growing importance of the *Reichsmarine's* minewarfare units led to the creation of the position of *Führer der Minensuchboote* under *FregKpt.*Kurt Ramien.

The *M 78* was a member of the *M 57-96* group of steam-powered *Minensucher* of late war construction. Displacing 515 tonnes (690 tonnes full load), she was armed with two 8.8 cm L/45 Schiffskanone and could make 16 knts. With a crew of c.40 the *M 78* served with both the *Kaiserliche Marine* and the *Reichsmarine* although there is no record of her employment after 1922. The bow post seen in the photograph is part of the mounting structure for the *Scherbrettminenraumer* equipment, a new mine anchor cutting equipment that was first introduced in the Nordsee in April 1918 by the *IV.Minensuchflottille* (*KorvKpt.*Krah). Unlike the more usual paravane cutting equipment that was streamed from the stern, the *Scherbrettminenraumer* was towed from the minesweeper's bow which enabled single vessel sweeps to be carried out thus increasing the overall safety of a number of *Minensucher* working together in a minefield.

Photo 1E-14 Original caption: *Kaiserliche Marine, Fliegerei – Schwimmerflugzeug Nr.1673, Type Friedrichsafhen FF 49C; pilot and seamen beside the aircraft on the 25 April 1918.*
Bundesarchiv Bild 134-B3024 hoto: o.Ang.

A total of 240 Friedrichshafen FF.49 *Seeflugzeuge* were built for the *Kaiserliche Marine's Marineflieger* during 1917-18. Initially delivered in the *BFT* category of an unarmed wireless transmitter equipped seaplane, the heavier FF 49C was a *CHFT* aircraft with one machine gun and full wireless transmitter and receiving equipment which became the main variant from September 1917. The final thirty FF 49C of 1918 were armed with two machine guns as well as carrying full wireless equipment. FF 49C Nr.1673 was a CHFT category aircraft ordered by the *Reichs Marine Amt* in July 1917.

Extract from the *See-Versuchskommando (SVK)* report on Friedrichshafen FF 49C Nr.1699 – ordered on the 27 August 1917, delivered 20 September 1917 and accepted for service on the 19 December 1917. Marine Designation: *CHFT*. Two-seat twin-float reconnaissance biplane manufactured by the *Flugzeugbau Friedrichshafen GmbH*. Dimensions: Wingspan 17.8 m, Length 11.65 m, Height 4.45 m. Weights: Empty 1,515 kgs, Loaded 2,147 kgs. Engine: 200 hp six-cylinder water-cooled Benz. Endurance: 5.75 hrs. Speeds: Take-off 83 kph, Climb 118 kph, Cruise 140 kph. Rate of climb: To 800 m 6.2 mins, to 1,000 m 8 mins, to 1,500 m 13.2 mins.

Initially the *Kaiserliche Marine* had employed the *Zeppelins* of its *Marine-Luftschiff-Abteilung* to investigate merchant shipping en route through in the southern part of the Nordsee, prize crews being carried to take control of any vessels found in prohibited areas or those carrying war materials for the enemy. Quite quickly this task was passed to the *C-Typ Seeflugzeuge* that were assigned to the *Seeflugstationen* at Zeebrugge, Ostend, Bochum, Norderney, Helgoland and List auf Sylt and from the latter half of 1917 the most important type used for this work was the FF.49. Its excellent seakeeping allowed the crew of one seaplane to land near to suspicious vessels to conduct a close inspection whilst a second aircraft kept station overhead. Vessels not cooperating could then be attacked. Post-war these same characteristics led to the retention of many of these aircraft as part of a force of 100 *Seeflugzeuge* that were permitted for mine-spotting duties by the *vorläufige Reichsmarine* until October 1919.

Later in 1923 *KptLt.*Hans Ritter, the new *Referent für Flugwesen und Luftschütz*, was able to purchase six war-surplus FF 49C *Seeflugzeuge* for fleet requirements duties. These aircraft were initially operated on behalf of the *Reichsmarine* by *Deutscher Aero Lloyd* before being passed to *Aerosport GmbH* at Warnemünde for training purposes. It seems likely that these machines were entered on the *Luftfahrzeugrolle* as D-40, D-45, D-47, D-49, D-85 & D-86. These last examples of the type were employed by the *Seeflugzeug-Versuchsabteilung (Severa) GmbH* which flew the aircraft from the former *Seeflugstationen* at Norderney and Kiel-Holtenau for target towing, aerial photography, and naval co-operation tasks as well as for the covert operational training of the *Reichsmarine's* new generation of naval aviators.

Photo 1E-15 Original caption: *Kaiserliche Marine, Fliegerei* – 1918 aerial view of a *Rotte* from the *"C" Staffel*, monoplane fighter type "Hansa-Brandenburg W.29" Marine-Nr.2532.
Bundesarchiv Bild 134-B3332 Photo: o.Ang.

The appearance of the Hansa Brandenburg W 29 over the waters of the Nordsee in May 1918 gave the aggressive pilots of the *Seejagdstaffeln* a real advantage over their RAF prey. Designed by Ernst Heinkel the W 29 was a true two-seat fighter with the pilot having two fixed lu.MG 08/15 machine guns firing though the propeller arc whilst the observer had a single Parabellum on a flexible mounting in the rear cockpit. Powered by a 195 hp Benz in-line engine the W 29 was capable of 175 kph, 15 kph faster than the earlier W 12, and it became virtually impossible for British flying boats to escape once they had been spotted by the patrolling *Marineflieger*.

Extract from the *See-Versuchskommando (SVK)* report on Hansa Brandenburg W 29 Nr.2204 – ordered on the 17 January 1918, delivered 4 April 1918 and accepted for service on the 5 April 1918. Marine Designation: C3MG. Two-seat twin-float monoplane fighter manufactured by the *Hansa Brandenburgische Flugzeugwerke AG*. Dimensions: Wingspan 13.5 m, Length 9.35 m, Height 3.1 m. Weights: Empty 1,000 kgs, Loaded 1,463 kgs. Engine: 150 hp six-cylinder water-cooled Benz. Endurance: 4 hrs. Speeds: Take-off 98 kph, Climb 118 kph, Cruise 168 kph. Rate of climb: To 1,000 m 5.9 mins, to 1,500 m 10.4 mins, to 2,000 m 15.8 mins.

The W 29 was built in three batches totalling 78 machines during the course of 1918. Nr.2201-2206 were in the C3MG category as described above, whilst Nr.2507-2536, 2501-2506 and 2564-2583 were classified as C2MG/HFT with the 150 hp Benz, one fixed and one flexibly mounted machine gun and the important but heavy wireless transmitter. Finally Nr.2507-2536 were 150 hp Benz powered C3MG aircraft. A further batch, Nr.2584-2587 in the C3MG category, were under construction at the end of the war.

*Oblt.d.Res.*Friedrich Christiansen, the *Stationsleiter Zeebrugge,* and his crews collected the first five C2MG/FHT aircraft from Kiel-Holtenau and flew them back to Belgium on the 1 July 1918. They went into action on the very next day. Five days later the *Staffel* caught *HM Submarine* C 25 on the surface off the British coast and so damage her superstructure with machine gun fire that she was unable to dive, she was later attacked again with bombs and machine gun fire whilst under tow. Part of the *Marineflieger's* success can be attributed to their decision to patrol in formations of three, five or seven machines. Such formations could easily overwhelm single or pairs of enemy patrol aircraft and flying boats from the Royal Naval Air Station at Great Yarmouth were frequently attacked close to the English coast. The position of enemy vessels could also be reported by wireless and suitable vessels attacked with light bombs and machine gun fire. In addition to the W 29s based at Zeebrugge, the *Marineflieger* flew the type with success over the Deutsche Bucht from Borkum and Norderney. The W 29 *Seejagdzweisitzer* seen in the photograph were based at the *Seeflugstation Borkum* in the Ostfriesische Inseln.

In the post-war period the W 29 provided Heinkel with the basis for the new Caspar S 1 – later Heinkel HE 1 - which became the first naval combat aircraft to be ordered in any quantity by the *Reichsmarine*.

Photo 1E-16 Original caption: *Admiral* Zenker, the former chief of the *Marineleitung* has died at the age of 62 years! *Admiral* Hans Zenker, especially distinguished himself in the war at the *Schlacht am Skagerrak* (Battle of Jutland) on the *Schlachtkreuzer "Von der Tann"*. From 1924-1928 he led the development of the German *Reichsmarine*.
Bundesarchiv Bild 102-13764 Photo: Georg Pahl

*Adm.*Hans Zenker succeeded *Adm.*Paul Behncke as *Chef der Marineleitung* in October 1924 and for the next four years he concentrated on building the *Reichsmarine* into an increasingly effective force with the construction of the *kleiner Kreuzer Emden* and two *Klassen* of new *Torpedobooten*. He was also central to the design debate that would result in the new *Panzerschiffe* that were planned to replace the *Reichsmarine's* obsolete *Linienschiff* and in the plans for a new class of *kleiner Kreuzer* to replace the ageing *Gazelle* and *Bremen-Klassen*. Covertly he oversaw the continued development of submarines and naval aircraft and it was his implicit involvement in the Lohmann Affair that would eventually result in him tendering his resignation in October 1928.

Hans Zenker had entered the *Kaiserliche Marine* in April 1889 and by 1914 had been *Kommandant* of the *kleinen Kreuziere SMS Lübeck* and *SMS Cöln*. He was *Kommandant* of the powerful *SMS Von der Tann* in 1916-17 and fought his ship with distinction against the British Grand Fleet in the *Skagerrak Schlacht*. A spell in the *Admiralstab* in Berlin followed before he was appointed *Befehlshaber der Sicherung der Nordsee* in 1918 with responsibility for escort vessels and mine warfare in the Nordsee before he became *Inspekteur der Marineartillerie* in the newly formed *Reichsmarine*. From 1920-23 he was *Chef der Marinestation der Nordsee*.

*Adm.*Hans Zenker died at Göttingen on the 14 August 1932.

Photo 1E-17 Original caption: *Leichter Kreuzer "Emden III"* – launched 7 January 1925, sunk 3 May 1945 in the Heikendorfer Bucht.
Bundesarchiv Bild 134-C0135 Photo: o.Ang.

The *Emden* was the first major warship to be completed for the *Reichsmarine*. Built at the *Reichsmarinewerft*, Wilhelmshaven between November 1921 and October 1925 she was of conventional Great War design and as such she incorporated outdated features such as single mountings for her eight 15 cm L/45 Schiffskanone, rudimentary fire control arrangements, and relatively inefficient mixed coal-oil propulsion – features which were in part the result of Allied restrictions, whilst her protracted construction reflected the increasingly dire economic situation facing the Weimar Republic between 1922-24. The result was a *leichte Kreuzer* replacement for the *Gazelle-Klasse* vessel *Niobe* which was sold to Yugoslavia in 1925. *Emden* commissioned on the 15 October of that year under the command of *Kpt.z.S.*Kurt Foerster. She displaced 5,689 tonnes (7,102 t full load) had a secondary armament of two 8.8 cm FlaK and four 50 cm torpedo tubes in two pairs. Capable of 29.4 knts her economical cruising speed was 14 knts. Her crew consisted of 19 officers and 464 enlisted men.

She spent most of her first commission as a *Schulschiff* with a crew of 29 officers and 445 enlisted men together with 162 *Seekadette*. Her first cruise lasted from the 14 November 1926 until the 14 March 1928 and routed through the Atlantic Ocean to Cape Town, the Indian Ocean to the Cocos Islands and then on to Japan, Alaska and down the western seaboard of North and South America around Cape Horn to Rio de Janeiro and then back across the Atlantic to the Azores and Spain.

During this period of extended operation in quite challenging conditions she proved to be a good sea boat. She was then taken in hand for a refit and consideration was given to replacing her single gun mountings with turrets during 1928. However given the arrival of the *K-Klass* and probably due to the costs involved she re-commissioned as a *Schulschiff* and carried out three more overseas cruises before the end of 1931 when she was de-commissioned for boiler work to be carried out.

She is seen here soon after her commissioning in the winter of 1925/26. She was then modified with a reduced main mast with a flying bridge at its base and with a taller second funnel before embarking on her first world cruise. *Seekadett* Eckhard Christian, a future naval aviator, underwent training aboard the *Emden* during 1926-28. He was eventually commissioned as a *Leutnant zur See* on the 1 October 1930 after four and a half years officer training.

Photo 1E-18 Original caption: *Torpedoboote Typ 24 "Raubtier-Klasse" – "Leopard" (LP)* at sea. View of the starboard side.

DVM 10 Bild 23-63-27 Photo: o.Ang.

By the mid-twenties a number of the *Reichsmarine's* small number of ageing *Zerstörer* and *Torpedobooten* were simply worn out and it became imperative that they be replaced with more modern vessels. Work on the six units of the *Typ 23 Raubvogel Klasse* began in 1925, these being small warships by international standards and certainly not comparable to the British *Amazon* or French *Bourrasque* destroyers. Their design was effectively obsolete being based on that of the *Kaiserliche Marine's S 113* and *B 114* designs. The *Typ 23* displaced 938 tonnes (1,310 t full load) and was armed with three 10.5 cm L/45 guns in single shielded mounts plus six 50 cm torpedo tubes in two triple mountings. With a crew of 120 officers and men the oil fired Typ 23 could steam at up to 34 kts and had a range of 1,800 miles at 17 kts.

Initially classified as *Zerstörern,* the six new ships were commissioned in 1926-28: *Möwe* (Oct 26), *Greif* & *Seeadler* (Mar 27), *Albatros* (May 28), *Falke* & *Kondor* (Jul 28) and were followed by the six units of the similar *Typ 24 Raubtier-Klasse* at 948 tonnes (1,319 t full load). It had been intended to arm these ships with three 12.7 cm guns but in the end modernised 10.5 cm weapons were fitted. The six *Typ 24* were commissioned in 1928-29: *Iltis* (Oct 28), *Wolff* (Nov 28), *Tiger* (Jan 29), *Luchs* (Apr 29), *Leopard* (Jun 29) & *Jaguar* (Aug 29). The arrival of these new warships allowed most of the existing *Zerstörer* and *Torpedobooten* to be de-commissioned, sold or converted for other tasks.

Leopard and her sisters were all built at the *Reichsmarinewerft* at Wilhelmshaven. From 1931 both the *Typ 23* and *24* were rearmed with the new 53.3 cm torpedo.

Photo 1E-19 Original caption: The German *Kreuzer "Berlin"* out of service! The German *Kreuzer "Berlin"* in the port of Kiel, behind lies the German *Linienschiff "Hessen"*.

Bundesarchiv Bild 102-07600 Photo: o.Ang.

The Treaty of Versailles had permitted the *Reichsmarine* to retain up to six *leichte Kreuziere* from a pool of eight such vessels from the pre-war *Gazelle* and *Bremen Klassen* which were modernised in the twenties to extend their useful lives; *Berlin* and her sister *Hamburg* were re-armed with eight to ten 10.5 cm L/45 Schiffskanone in single mounts in 1920, whilst *Berlin* was modernised in 1921-22 and fitted with a new bow in place of the earlier ram-bow.

Thereafter *Berlin* was largely employed as an ocean going *Schulschiff für Seekadet* and as such was attached to the *Inspekteur für Bildwesens der Marine* along with the *Segelschulschiff Niobe*. Following a cruise in Norwegian waters in November 1923, she departed Kiel in January 1924 for a two month Atlantic cruise to the Azores, Canaries, Madeira and Spain. A second overseas cruise followed in October thus establishing a pattern which would then continue for much of the decade. In 1925 the *Berlin* would visit South America, whilst in 1927/28 she would tour the Far East visiting Australia. With the arrival of the new *leichte Kreuzerie* of the *Köln-Klasse* it was finally possible to dispose of the older vessels. *Berlin* was de-commissioned in April 1929 and was later used as an accommodation vessel at Kiel.

SMS Berlin (3,792 tonnes, 4,180 t full load) had been ordered from the *Kaiser-Werft, Danzig* in 1902 and was commissioned into the *Kaiserliche Marine's Hochseeflotte* on the 4 April 1905. Coal burning with a top speed of 22 knts, she was manned by a crew of 14 officers and 274-287 enlisted men. *Berlin* was deployed to foreign stations during 1911-12 and 1913-14 before modification in 1915 as a minelayer. She was disarmed in 1917 and used for coastal defence duties until the end of the war.

There is some confusion as to the correct title for this image as the *Bundesarchiv* provides two alternatives, that used above and *"The German Hochseeflotte leaves for Spain! The German Hochseeflotte has started a spring trip to Spain to sustain the friendly relations between the two countries. Led by the Linienschiffe Schleswig-Holstein, Elsass and Hessen, and the Kreuzer Amazone, Berlin and Nymphe the same have already left Kiel. This image shows the German Hochseeflotte in Kiel during the departure to Spain. The grosse Kreuzer Berlin, behind the Linienschiffe Hessen and the Schleswig-Holstein leave Kiel. March 1927."* [Bild 102-04036, März 1927]

Photo 1E-20 Original caption: At the launching of *Panzerkreuzer* "A" in the *Germania-Werft, Kiel*, the ship was christened by *Reichspsident* von Hindenburg in the name of "*Deutschland*". The *Panzerkreuzer Deutschland* was cheered by a crowd of many thousands as she made her way down the slips.

Bundesarchiv Bild 102-11704 Photo: Georg Pahl

19 May 1931, twelve years after the ignominy of the Versailles Accord which had placed such crippling restrictions on the size and capability of the newly formed *Reichsmarine*, a modern capital ship finally slid into the water at Kiel as the future flagship and pride of a properly modernised navy. To the rest of the World's navies the *Panzerschiff Deutschland* represented a new class of warship, a heavily armed and well protected vessel that could outgun any vessel that could catch her, whilst she was faster than any vessel that could actually sink her.

The *Panzerschiff* concept had taken more than six years to finalise. The only constant had been a hull displacement of 10,000 tonnes this being the maximum allowed by the Allies as a replacement for the existing *Linienschiffe*. Within this constraint, questions of firepower, protection and propulsion had been debated endlessly by the *Reichsmarine's* senior officers under the successive leadership of *Admirals* Behncke and Zenker. Proposals had ranged from a heavily armed and protected coastal monitor suitable for operations in the Kattegat and Ostsee against the Polish and French navies, to a heavily armed heavy cruiser where protection was sacrificed for speed and endurance. Such a vessel would be optimised for oceanic operations. Zenker was firmly in favour of a capital ship solution with a main armament of 30.5 cm guns even though the tonnage permissible for each vessel was less than half that enjoyed by other navies. However other officers felt that a 28 cm armament was more appropriate to the displacement constraints. By June 1927 three proposals had emerged: *Typ A* four 38 cm, 250 mm protection, 18 kts; *Typ B* six 30.5 cm, 250 mm protection, 18 kts; *Typ C* six 28 cm, 100 mm protection, 26-27 kts. Of these *Typ C* was the most favoured although all concerned knew that it was a compromise. Zenker finally signed off the *Typ Sketch* on the 11 April 1928 and full drawings were completed on the 28 December. *Ersatz Preussen (Panzerschiff A)* was finally laid down as *Bau-Nr.219* at the *Deutsche Werke,* Kiel on the 9 February 1929.

The *Deutschland* was commissioned into the *Reichsmarine* on the 1 April 1933 after four years in the yards. Displacing 11,700 tonnes (15,200 t full load) she was armed with six 28 cm SK C/28 guns in two triple turrets, eight 15 cm SK C/28 in single turrets together with a *FlaK* outfit of three 8.8 cm L/45 supported by 2 cm MG C/30 and MG 08/15 weapons. There were also two quadruple 53.3 cm torpedo tubes and provision for a catapult and one, later two, aircraft although due to the Treaty restrictions this was not fitted during her first commission. Her diesel engines gave her a range of 18,650 kms at 15 kts and a maximum speed of 26 kts. Under the command of *Kpt.z.S.*Hermann von Fischel *Deutschland* undertook her shake-down cruise in the western Atlantic before entering Wilhelmshaven and thence to the Ostsee where she spent much of the following year undertaking further trials and training.

Photo 1E-21 Original caption: The new catapult aircraft of the German giant steamer "*Europa*". The new aircraft catapult aboard the German giant steamer "*Europa*" has been placed into service. The catapult aircraft shortens the shuttle service of urgent mail to America by 24 hours.

Bundesarchiv Bild 102-10309 Photo: o.Ang.

The story behind this photograph in reality began five years earlier in June 1925 when Ernst Heinkel was approached by *Capt.*Kojima, the Japanese Naval Attache, to secretly develop and build two different types of shipboard floatplane (HD 25 & HD 26) with a launching rail for installation aboard the *Nagato,* the Imperial Japanese Navy's newest battleship. This successful venture was then followed in 1926 by a covert *Reichsmarine* contract for a three seat *Bordaufklärer und Artillerie-Flugzeug* (HD 15) together with a rotatable compressed air catapult for shipboard employment. The Katapult K-1 appeared in 1928 and quickly proved capable of accelerating the small flying boat to 100 kph over a distance of just 20 metres. Then in the same year came the *RVM* contract for a small mail carrying floatplane (HE 12) for use aboard the *Norddeutscher Lloyd's (NDL)* 51,656 tonne *Turbinen-Schnelldampfer Bremen* and a more powerful catapult. The K 2 was installed aboard the *Bremen* in June 1929 and was found to be capable of accelerating a 3,500 kg aircraft to 110 kph in 20 m, a performance well in excess of what was actually required for the HE 12.

Without any testing from a moving vessel the He 12 WNr.334 D-1717 was launched from the *Bremen* whilst the vessel was 180 nautical miles from New York on the 22 July 1929 – it had been intended to launch at 400 nm but the *NDL* was determined to take the *Blue Riband* for the fastest crossing of the Atlantic Ocean on this maiden voyage and nothing was allowed to get in the way of achieving that prestigious goal. On the return voyage the HE 12 was launched 500 nm from Bremerhaven on the 1 August and landed a good day earlier than the ship made port. The success of this venture immediately resulted in a further *RVM* contract for a new catapult and a larger mailplane (HE 58) for the *TS Europa* (49,746 tonne). The K 4 was installed aboard the *Europa* between the 31 July – 7 August 1930 and the first catapult start for the HE 58 WNr.365 D-1919 duly took place off the USA on the 28 August. The He 58 was then transferred to the *TS Bremen,* whilst the new Junkers Ju 46 was taken aboard the *Europa* for continued operations on the Atlantic mail route.

In the meantime *Heinkel* had been given the challenge of designing a far more powerful catapult for *Deutsche Luft Hansa's* planned trans-ocean flying boat service to South America. The K 6 could launch a 14-tonne *Seeflugzeuge* to 150 kph in just 1.52 seconds and was first installed aboard the *SS Westfalen,* a 5,637 tonne freighter that had been converted into a *Flugsicherungsschiff* by the *Deutsche Schiff-und Maschinenbau AG* at Bremen. The K 6 was used for the first experimental launch of Dornier Do J *Wal* IIa Bos WNr.210 D-2069 *Monsun* in the South Atlantic in May 1933. The similar but more powerful K-7 was installed aboard *DLH's* second *Flugsicherungsschiff,* the *MS*

Schwabenland, in 1933 and *Heinkel* received further contracts for the larger K-9 (15 tonne) and K-10 (18-tonne) catapults soon after.

The archive title for this image is interestingly "the *Turbinenschiff "Bremen"- Wasserflugzeug Heinkel HE 58 D-1919 "Bremen"* hanging on the crane" which may suggest that this photo actually dates from after the loss of the HE 12 off New Scotland on the 5/6 October 1931 and before the introduction of the Ju 46 on that vessel later in 1932.

Photo 1E-22 Original caption: *Admiral* [Erich] Raeder, the new *Chef der Marineleitung* today (4.10) takes office - Portrait of Erich Raeder sitting at his office desk.
Bundesarchiv Bild 146-1987-080-30A Photo: o.Ang. (Polyphot Agency)

*Adm.*Erich Raeder became the *Chef des Marineleitung* on the 1 October 1928. His earlier appointments within the *Reichsmarine* had been *Chef der Zentralabteilung/Reichsmarineamtes* (15 Jul 19), *Abt.Chef Marinearchiv/Marineleitung* (1 Jul 20), *Inspekteur der Bildungswesens der Marine* (20 Jul 22), *Befehlshaber der leichten Seestreitkräfte der Nordsee* (19 Sep 24) and *Chef der Marinestation der Ostsee* (10 Jan 25).

Erich Raeder had been born on the 24 April 1876 in Wandsbek bei Hamburg. He had entered the *Kaiserliche Marine* in April 1894 and had reached the rank of *KorvKpt.* by the outbreak of hostilities. Having undergone training as a staff officer at the *Marineakademie* in 1903-04 and 1904-05 he spent much of the war on the staff of the *Befehlshaber der Aufklarüngsstreitkräfte der Hochseeflotte,* initially as *1.ASO* and from 14 June 1917 as *Chef des Stabes.* As a result he did not get his own command until the 17 January 1918 when he was appointed *Kdt.kleine Kreuzer Cöln.*

Raeder's thinking on the nature and employment of sea power was heavily influenced by the ideas of *GrossAdm.*Alfred Tirpitz with whom he worked in 1906-08 and *VizAdm.*Franz von Hipper on whose staff he served from 1912-17. As such he favoured the creation of a balanced fleet centred on the battleship which would enable Germany to gain parity with the Royal Navy. During the Great War Raeder opposed the alternative strategy of *"guerre de course"* as proposed by his contemporary *FregKpt.*Wolfgang Wegener. Wegener argued that Germany lacked the industrial capacity to create a Fleet which was powerful enough to successfully oppose the British in a traditional naval battle. Instead he recommended an emphasis on cruisers and submarines which could attack Britain's mercantile trade. It was a debate that Raeder would be forced to re-open at a later date.

In the meantime it came as no surprise that Raeder was a strong supporter of the *Panzerschiff Programm,* although by the late twenties it was clear that such vessels would have to be employed in attacks on enemy merchant shipping in the event of war. Despite these realities Raeder continued to aspire to the notion of a balanced fleet and was also keen to retain operational control over the emergent *Marineluftstreitkräfte.* In this respect he was initially successful in his early arguments with Hermann Göring and in July 1934 a separate *Höheren Luftamtes* was created at Kiel solely to deal with naval aviation.

Photo 1E-23 Original caption: Aerial photograph of the *Hilfschiffe* (*Flugzeugmutterschiff*) SMH "Santa Helena". Launched on the 16 November 1907 as a Freighter and re-commissioned as a Seaplane Tender by July 1915. Transferred to the USA in 1919.
Bundesarchiv Bild 134-B4228 Photo: o.Ang.

The concept of aircraft carrying warships was explored by both the French and British navies in the years preceding the Great War. Following the outbreak of hostilities the *Kaiserliche Marine* began the conversion of two freighters into seaplane tenders for the *Marineluftsreitkrafte,* whilst a further vessel, the *SMH Glyndwr,* was employed with minimal alterations as a seaplane training vessel.

Meanwhile initial sea trials with the *SMH Answald* and *SMH Santa Elena* quickly indicated that these slow vessels were unsuitable for operations in the Nordsee and following further modification they were finally commissioned in July 1915 and assigned to the *Führer der Aufklärungsschiffe* for operations against Imperial Russian forces in the eastern Ostsee.

The *SMH Santa Elena (FMS II)* had originally been built by *Blohm und Voss, Hamburg* (*Bau-Art.196*) in 1907 as a freighter for the *Hamburg-Sudamerikanischen Dampfschifffahrt-gesellschaft*. She was modified for new role with capacity for three, later four, *Seeflugzeuge* by the *Kaiserlichen Werft Danzig* from August 1914 and she was actually the first such vessel to commission on the 2 July 1915. Based at Libau the *Santa Elena's* aircraft carried out reconnaissance and bombing operations against Russian naval air stations, shipping and shore installations in the Riga Bucht from August 1915 until November 1917. Too slow for operations with other naval vessels she was generally employed as a floating *Seeflugstation* for her *Seeflugzeuge*. For the Oesel operation in October 1917 she acted as the mother ship for 16 *Seeflugzeuge* which were moored to a boom and to buoys around the ship. Following the capture of that island she was transferred to the Oresund for neutrality patrol duties in the Kattegat before moving further west to Wilhelmshaven in February 1918. Here she was employed in support of mine laying and sweeping operations in the Deutsche Bucht.

This image dates from 18 May 1918 when the *SMH Santa Elena* was attached to the *Kommandeur der Flieger der Hochseestreitkräfte* at Wilhelmshaven for mine warfare duties. The four hangars, protected to the sides by canvas curtains, were arranged in pairs either side of the existing superstructure with stores being held in the holds beneath. In common with the other *Flugzeugmutterschiffen* she generally carried *Seeflugzeuge* of the Friedrichshafen FF series, these having good sea-keeping qualities. For defensive purposes she is armed with two 8.8 cm L/45 FlaK on single mounts near the stern of the vessel. The *Santa Elena* displaced 7,415 BRT and was steam powered with a speed of c.11 knts. She had a crew of 7 officers and 115 ratings.

A further *Flugzeugmutterschiff* was commissioned on the 17 July 1918 as the *SMH Oswald (FMS III)*. She was operational in the Kattegat on submarine escort duties. Her *Flugstationsleiter* was *Oblt.z.S.*Hans Siburg.

Photo 1E-24 Original caption: Aerial view of the French Aircraft Carrier *"Bearn"* – Launched 15 April 1920.

Bundesarchiv Bild 134-B1530 Photo: o.Ang.

The *Marine nationale francaise* was the first naval power to commission an aircraft carrying warship, the *croiseur porte-avions Foudre,* in 1913. Converted merchant vessels followed for use as *transports d'hydravions* during the Great War and following the armistice active consideration was given to the conversion of the fifth planned *Normandie-Classe cuirasse* (authorised in November 1913 and work suspended in 1915) into the *Marine nationale's* first dedicated *porte-avions* for landplanes.

Work on the new *porte-avions* did not begin until August 1923 and took a further four years to complete. Her design was heavily influenced by that of *HMS Eagle* (1924), a contemporary conversion of a dreadnought hull for aviation use with a single uninterrupted flight deck dominated by a large island structure to starboard containing the bridge and a single funnel. Like the *Eagle*, the *Bearn* was a high sided vessel, the 180 m. flight deck being 15.4 m. above the water line above a pair of 124 m. long hangars which were in turn superimposed on workshops and storage spaces for dismantled aircraft. Three electrically powered lifts moved aircraft and stores to and from the hangar deck to the flight deck, whilst a single 12-tonne gooseneck crane was situated aft of the island was capable of moving seaplanes on and off the ship. Part of the *cuirasse's* planned secondary armament was retained for defensive purposes, this taking the form of eight 155mm/55 calibre guns in single casemate mountings as seen. Her anti-aircraft guns consisted of six 75 mm/50 calibre and eight 37 mm weapons.

With an overall displacement of 22,501 tonnes (28,900 t full load), the *Bearn* was capable of operating 40 aircraft. Commissioned as an experimental *porte-avions* in May 1927 she joined the Fleet in May 1928 after extensive trials. Her mixed turbine/reciprocating propulsion machinery was able to drive the vessel at up to 21.5 kts which was adequate for the biplanes of the period but ultimately proved too slow for more advanced monoplanes. An advanced *Schneider*-designed aircraft arrester system was installed on the flight deck. The *Flottille d'aviation du Bearn* (*Flottille 7*) consisted of 12 *avions de bombardement et torpillage* (Levasseur PL.4 R3b (1927) later PL.7 T3 (1930) *Esc 7B1*), 12 *avions de reconnaissance et surveillance* (Levasseur PL.4 R3b (1927) later PL.10 R3b & PL.101 R3b (1933) *Esc.7S1*) and 8 *avions de chasse* (Dewoitine D.1 C1 (1927) later Wibault 74 C1 (1929) and ultimately Dewoitine D.376 C1 (1938) *Esc.7C1*)

Minor improvements were incorporated during the early thirties when a downward sloping flight deck was installed in the bow and in the mid-thirties when anti-aircraft machine guns were added. Never regarded as more than an experimental vessel to gain experience in the operation of shipboard aircraft it had been anticipated that the *Bearn* would be replaced by two more advanced *porte-avions* (*Joffre-Classe*) in the late thirties. This was certainly overdue as the *Bearn* had been overtaken by developments abroad, most notably by Britain which had commissioned three more capable aircraft carriers, whilst the two Pacific navies had taken shipboard aviation to a totally new level with the construction of the *USS Lexington* (1925) and *Saratoga* (1927) and the *IJN's Akagi* (1927) and *Kaga* (1928).

Part 1 Appendices

Appendix A

Weimar Republic Ministeries and Officials

1A. REICHSPRÄSIDENT			
Friedrich Ebert	SDP	11 Feb 19	28 Feb 25 +
Hans Luther	acting	28 Feb 25	12 Mar 25
Walter Simons	acting	12 Mar 25	12 May 25
Paul von Hindenburg	GFM	12 May 25	2 Aug 34 +

1B. REICHSKANZLER			

The position of *Reichskanzler* was preceded by that of *Ministerpräsident* until 1920.

Philipp Scheidemann	SPD	13 Feb 19	20 Jun 19
Gustav Bauer	SPD	21 Jun 19	26 Mar 20
Hermann Müller	SPD	27 Mar 20	8 Jun 20
Constantin Fehrenbach	Zentrum	25 Jun 20	4 May 21
Joseph Wirth	Zentrum	10 May 21	14 Nov 22
Wilhelm Cuno		22 Nov 22	12 Aug 23
Gustav Stresemann	DVP	13 Aug 23	23 Nov 23
Wilhelm Marx	Zentrum	30 Nov 23	15 Jan 25
Hans Luther		15 Jan 25	16 May 26
Wilhelm Marx	Zentrum	16 May 26	28 Jun 28
Hermann Müller	SPD	28 Jun 28	30 Mar 30
Heinrich Bruning	Zentrum	30 Mar 30	31 May 32
Franz von Papen	(Zentrum)	1 Jun 32	1 Dec 32
Kurt von Schleicher	GenLt.	3 Dec 32	28 Jan 33
Adolf Hitler	NSDAP	30 Jan 33	

REICHSWEHRMINISTERIUM

The *Reichswehrministerium* was established in Oct 19 from the *preußische Kriegsministerium* and the *Reichsmarineamt*. The *RWM* consisted of the *Heeresleitung* and the *Marineleitung* to which a *Ministeramt* was added in 1929. The *Reichsheer* and *Reichsmarine* were collectively referred to as the *Reichswehr*.

2A. REICHSWEHRMINISTER

Gustav Noske	SPD	13 Feb 19	22 Mar 20
Otto Gessler	DDP	27 Mar 20	19 Jan 28
Wilhelm Groener	GenLt.a.D.	20 Jan 28	30 May 32
Kurt von Schleicher	GenLt.	1 Jun 32	28 Jan 33
Werner von Blomberg	(GFM)	30 Jan 33	(26 Jan 38)

2B. CHEF DER HEERESLEITUNG

Walther Reinhardt	GenMaj.	13 Sep 19	19 Mar 20
Hans von Seeckt	GenOb.	Mar 20	Oct 26
Wilhelm Heye	GenOb.	Oct 26	31 Oct 30
Kurt von Hammerstein-Equord	Gen.d.Inf.	1 Nov 30	27 Dec 33
Werner von Fritsch	Gen.d.Art.	1 Jan 34	1 Jun 35

2C. CHEF DER MARINELEITUNG

Adolf von Trotha	VizAdm.	Sep 19	Mar 20
William Michaelis	KonAdm.	Mar 20	Sep 20
Paul Behncke	Adm.	1 Sep 20	30 Sep 24
Hans Zenker	Adm.	1 Oct 24	30 Sep 28
Erich Raeder	Adm.	1 Oct 28	1 Jun 35

2D. MINISTERAMT

Kurt von Schleicher	GenLt.	1 Feb 29	1 Jun 32
Ferdinand von Bredow	GenMaj.	1 Jun 32	30 Jan 33
Walter von Reichenau	Obst.	1 Feb 33	1 Feb 34

3. REICHSHEER

The *vorläufige Reichsheer* (provisional Army) was established on the 6 Mar 19. It was re-structured on the 1 Oct 19 as the *Ubergangsheer* (transitional Army) before being reduced in size to 200,000 officers and men in May 20 and to 100,000 men of all ranks in Oct 20. It was retitled the *Reichsheer* on the 1 Jan 21 and remained largely unchanged until the 20 May 35.

The *Chef der Heeresleitung* included five *Amter* (Offices): the *Truppenamt (TA)*, *Heereswaffenamt (WaA)*, *Heerespersonalamt (PA)*, *Heeresverwaltungsamt (VA)* and the *Allgemeine Heeresamt (AHA)* with a strength of c.200 officers, mostly former *Generalstabsoffiziere*, of whom c.60 were to be found in each of the *TA* and *WaA*. The other departments of significance were the *Waffen-Inspektion für Schulen: Infanterie, Kavallerie, Artillerie, Pioniere u.Festungen, Kraftfahrtruppen* and *Nachrichtentruppen*.

The *Truppenamt* was the cover designation for the proscribed *Generalstabes des Heeres*. It initially consisted of seven *Abteilungen* (Branches): *T1* (*Heeresabt.* – cover provided by the *Abt. Landesverteidigung*), *T2* (*Organisationabt.*), *T3* (*Fremde Heeres* – cover provided by *Heeresstatistische Abt.*), *T4* (*Lehr* later *Heeresausbildungsabt.*), *T5* (*Wehrabt.*), *T6* (*Abt.f.Erziehungs-u.Bildungswesen*) & *T7* (*Transportabt.*). However in Jun 21 it was reduced in size to *T1-4* & *T7*.

3A. TRUPPENAMT (TA)

Hans von Seeckt	GenMaj.	11 Oct 19	26 Mar 20
Wilhelm Heye	GenLt.	26 Mar 20	Feb 23
Otto Hasse	GenMaj.	Feb 23	Oct 25
Georg Wetzell	GenMaj.	Oct 25	27 Jan 27
Werner von Blomberg	GenMaj.	27 Jan 27	30 Sep 29
Kurt von Hammerstein-Equord	GenLt.	30 Sep 29	31 Oct 30
Wilhelm Adam	GenLt.	31 Oct 30	30 Sep 33
Ludwig Beck	GenMaj.	1 Oct 33	1 Jul 35

3B. COVERT LUFTSCHÜTZ

Initially a covert *Luftschütz-Referat* was created within the *Truppenamt* as the *TA(L)*, whilst a *Fremde-Luftstreitkräfte Referat* was lodged within *T3*. In 1925 the *TA(L)* was expanded and re-organised into four later six *Referate*.In Jan 25 it briefly became *Gruppe T2 III (L)* in the *Truppenamt's Organisationabteilung* before being "dissolved" following Allied concerns over the *Reichsheer's* covert military aviation activities. From the Aut 25 it was again referred to as the *TA(L)* before becoming the *T2 V (L)* in Apr 27. It seems probable that during this period that the previously separate *Fremde-Luftstreitkräfte Refeat* was transferred to the *TA(L)* as *Ref.VI Fremde Luftstreitkräfte*. In Jul 29 *T2 V (L)* was transferred from the *Truppenamt* to the *Insp.d.Waffenschulen* where it became the *Inspektion 1 (L)* thus coming under the direction of the *Chef d.Heeresleitung*. It was expanded to a total of nine *Referate*. It remained in this form until the 24 Jan 33 when it was transferred to the *RWM* prior to being amalgamated with the *Reichsmarine's Luftschützgruppe* on the 1 Apr 33 to form the *Luftschützamt (LS Amt)*. It briefly consisted of an *Abteilung 1L (Heer)* and an *Abteilung 1L (Marine)* each with three *Gruppen* before being reorganised in Jun 33 with six *abteilungen*. Transferred to the *RLM* on the 15 May 33 it was re-designated the *Luftkommandoamt (LA)* on the 1 Apr 34.

Helmuth Wilberg	Maj.	1 Oct 19	30 Sep 27	
Hugo Sperrle	Maj.	1 Oct 27	31 Jan 29	
Hellmuth Felmy	Obstlt.	1 Feb 29	31 Mar 33	
Hellmuth Volkmann	Obstlt.	1 Apr 33	Jun 33	(1L Heer)
Eberhard Bohnstedt	Obst.i.G.	1 Apr 33	31 Aug 33	(LS Amt)
Walther Wever	(GenMaj.)	1 Sep 33	(28 Feb 35)	

3C. HEERESWAFFENAMT (WaA)

The *WaA* dealt with all matters of equipment and weapons development and procurement. It was divided into nine numbered *Waffen Prüfwesens Abteilungen*: *Wa Prüf 1 Ballistiche und Munions, 2 Infanterie, 3 Pionier, 4 Artillerie, 5 Pionier, 6 Kraftfahrwesen, 7 Nachrichten, 8 Optik, Messwesen, Wetter, Feuerleitung und Kartendruck, 9 Gasschutz.*

Max Ludwig	GenLt.	1 Mar 26	31 May 29
Alfred von Vollard-Bockelberg	GenLt.	1 Jun 29	31 Dec 33
Kurt Liese	GenMaj.	1 Dec 33	(28 Feb 38)

3D. COVERT LUFTTECHNIK

Initially a covert *Flugtechnik Referat* was established within the *Inspektion für Waffen und Great (WaA)*, whilst a *Fliegerrüstungwirtschaftliches Referat* was created within the *WaA* as the *Wa Wi L*. Concealed within the *Abt.Kraftfahrwesens* the *Flugtechnik Referat* was known as the *Insp.WG 6F*. From Oct 25 an enlarged *Flugtechnik Referat* was incorporated into the *WaA's Wa Prüf 6 (Kraftfahrwesen)* as the *Wa Prüf 6F*, whilst a parallel *Beschaffungs-Referat* was created in the same *Abteilung* as the *Wa B 6F*. On the 1 Feb 28 both *Referate* together with the previously separate *Wa Wi L* were amalgamated to form the *Gruppe Wa (L)* within the *WaA* and then enlarged with the formation of three *Gruppen*. Expansion to five *Gruppen* in 1929 led to a further transformation as the *Wa Prüf 8F* within the *Abteilung Optik, Messwesen, Wetter, Feuerleitung und Kartendruck*. The *Wa Prüf 8F* remained within the *WaA* until May 33 when it was transferred to the *RLM* as *LB II Technik*. In Oct 33 *LB II* was upgraded to form the *Technisches Amt (LC)* within the *RLM*.

Kurt Student	Hptm.	1 Apr 20	31 Oct 28
Hellmuth Volkmann	Maj.	1 Nov 28	30 Sep 29
Wilhelm Wimmer	(Obst.)	1 Oct 29	(31 May 36)

3E. HEERESPERSONALAMT (HPA)

Wilhelm Heye	GenLt.	1 Apr 22	31 Oct 23
Hermann Reinicke	GenLt.	1 Oct 23	31 Jan 27
Joachim von Stulpnagel	GenMaj.	1 Feb 27	31 Oct 29
Erich Frhr.von Bussche-Ippenburg	GenLt.	1 Nov 30	30 Sep 33

3F. HEERESVERWALTUNGSAMT (VA)

Friedrich Karmann	(Gen.d.Inf.)	1 Mar 34	15 Sep 39 +

3G. ALLEGEMEINE HEERESAMT (AHA)

Alfred Bohm-Tettelbach	GenLt.	1 Nov 30	31 Jan 33 Wehramt
Friedrich Fromm	(Gen.d.Art.)	1 Feb 33	15 Feb 40

4. REICHSMARINE

The *vorläufige Reichsmarine* (provisional Navy) was created on the 16 Apr 19 from the *Kaiserliche Marine*. From the 31 Mar 21 it was re-titled the *Reichsmarine* which remained unchanged until the 21 May 35. The *Reichsmarine* was limited to 15,000 officers and men (the *Kaiserliche Marine* had c.80,000 men of all ranks).

Overall command of the *Reichsmarine* rested with the *Admiralitat* until the 15 Sep 20 when the *Chef der Marineleitung* was created within the *RWM*. The *Chef der Marineleitung* included three *Amter* (Offices): the *Marinekommandoamt (A)*, the *Allgemeine Marineamt (B)* and the *Marineverwaltungsamt (C)*. Territorially the *Reichsmarine* was divided into two *Marinestationen:* the *Marinestation der Nordsee* at Wilhelmshaven and the *Marinestation der Ostsee* at Kiel. Operational control of the Fleet rested with the *Flotten-Abteilung*, later, *Flottenkommando*.

4A. FLOTTENKOMMANDO			
Conrad Mommsen	VizAdm.	1 Apr 25	29 Sep 27
Iwan Oldekop	VizAdm.	30 Sep 27	30 Sep 31
Walter Gladisch	VizAdm.	1 Oct 31	30 Sep 33
Richard Foerster	(Adm.)	22 Sep 33	(20 Dec 36)

4B. COVERT LUFTSCHÜTZ

Following the creation of the *Reichsmarine* a *Referate für Seeflugwesen (Ref.A II 1)* was established within the *Flotten-Abteilung/Marinekommandoamt*. This position was later re-titled *Referate für Flugwesen und Luftschütz* before being expanded and reorganised in Jun 26. From that date the *Gruppe BSx* with four *Referate* was formed within the cover provided by the *Seetransportabteilung/ Allgemeine-Marineamt*. The *Gruppe BSx* became the *Luftschützgruppe* on the 1 Oct 29 and in 1932 was transferred from the *B-Amt* to the direct supervision of the *Chef d.Marineleitung*. In Apr 33 it was amalgamated with the *Reichsheer's Inspektion 1 (L)* to form the *Luftschützamt/RWM*. The *Abteilung 1 L (Marine)* only survived until Jun 33 when its responsibilities were transferred to the various *Luftamter/RLM*.

Walther Faber	KptLt.	1 Feb 20	31 Mar 23	
Hans Ritter	KptLt.	1 Apr 23	Jun 26	
Rudolf Lahs	Kpt.z.See	Jun 26	30 Sep 29	
Konrad Zander	Kpt.z.See	20 Sep 29	30 Sep 32	
Rudolf (Ralph) Wenninger	FregKpt.	1 Oct 32	31 Mar 33	
Rudolf (Ralph) Wenninger	FregKpt.	1 Apr 33	Jun 33	(1L Marine)

5. REICHSVERKEHRSMINISTERIUM

The *RVM* was created in Berlin in 1919 to oversee the development of transport services within Germany. Its most significant achievement was the nationalisation of the railways during 1920-24 within the structure provided by the *Deutsche Reichsbahn-Gesellschaft*. In 1932 the *RVM* consisted of five *Abteilungen: Luftfahrt (L), Kraftfahr und Schifffahrt (K), Wasserbautechnik (W), Eisenbahn-Verwaltungs (E I) & Eisenbahntechnische (E II)*.

5A. REICHSVERKEHRSMINISTER			
Johannes Bell	Zentrum	13 Feb 19	1 May 20
Gustav Bauer	SPD	2 May 20	21 Jun 20
Wilhelm Groener	GenLt.a.D.	25 Jun 20	12 Aug 23
Rudolf Oeser	DDP	13 Aug 23	11 Oct 24
Rudolf Krohne	DVP	12 Oct 24	17 Dec 26
Wilhelm Koch	DNVP	28 Jan 27	11 Jun 28
Theodor von Guerard	Zentrum	27 Jun 28	6 Feb 29
Georg Schatzel	BVP	7 Feb 29	12 Apr 29
Adam Stegerwald	Zentrum	13 Apr 29	27 Mar 30
Theodor von Guerard	Zentrum	30 Mar 30	7 Oct 31
Gottfried Treviranus	KVP	9 Oct 31	30 May 32
Paul Frhr.von Eltz-Rübenach		1 Jun 32	2 Feb 37

Civil aviation was initially the responsibility of the *Reichsministerium des Inneren* until 8 Jan 20 when it was transferred to the *Reichsverkehrsministerium*. On the 30 Jan 33 it was re-assigned to the *Reichskommissar für die Luftfahrt*, which in turn became the *Reichsluftfahrtministerium* on the 1 May 33. During this period the Branch was itself re-titled and re-structured on several occasions:

Reichsluftamt	4 Dec 18	30 Sep 19
Reichsamt für Luft-und Kraftfahrwesen	1 Oct 19	31 Mar 21
Abteilung für Luft-und Kraftfahrwesen	1 Apr 21	31 Dec 25
Luftfahrtabteilung	1 Jan 26	29 Jan 33
Abteilung I Luftverkehr	30 Jan 33	19 Apr 34

5B. LEITER DER LUFTFAHRTABTEILUNG			
August Euler		4 Dec 18	28 Feb 21
Traugott Bredow		1 Mar 21	31 Mar 24
Ernst Brandenburg	Maj.a.D.	1 Apr 24	29 Jan 33
Willy Fisch		30 Jan 33	19 Apr 34

Appendix B

Known Fliegeroffiziere Retained by the Reichsheer

1920

1. STABSOFFIZIERE (51)		
Oblt.Karl Barlen	Stab Insp.d.Fliegertruppe	Inf.Rgt.15
Oblt.Feorg Behrla	*Not known*	*Inf.Rgt.*
Hptm.Hellmuth Bieneck	Fhr.Fl.Abt.301	Inf.Rgt.16
Hptm.Friedrich Cranz	Ltr.d.Offiziers-Bildschule/ Insp.d.Lichtbildwesens	Bild.Offz.WK VI
Oblt.Otto Dessloch	Fhr.Fliegerschule 5	Inf.Rgt.21
Hptm.Egon Doerstling	Fhr.i.Bogohl 5	Inf.Rgt.10
Hptm.Eduard Dransfeld	Kdr.d.phys.Abt.d.Insp.d.Fliegertruppe	Kraftfahr.Abt.7
Hptm.Friedrich Fahnert	Grufl.AOK 7	Nachr.Abt.19
Rittm.Hermann Fahrig	Stab turkischen AOK 8	Kraftfahr.Abt.12
Hptm.Hellmuth Felmy	Fhr.Fl.Abt. A 256	Kraftfahr.Abt.5
Oblt.Hans-Eberhard Gandert	Fhr.JGr.6	Inf.Rgt.7
Hptm.Ulrich Grauert	Fhr.Fl.Abt.17	Art.Rgt.7
Maj.Wilhelm Haehnelt	Sonderkommando b.d. Insp.d.Fliegertruppen	Ref.zbV.WK III
Hptm.Oskar von dem Hagen	Fl.Gr.Fhr.1	Unknown
Oblt.Friedrich-Carl Hanesse	Kdr.Schlachtgruppe III	Art.Rgt.7
Oblt.Hartmann	*Not known*	*Art.Rgt.4*
Hptm.Holdermann	*Not known*	*Inf.Rgt.2*
Hptm.Hermann Hoth	Stab KoGenLuft	Inf.Rgt.18
Oblt.Paul Jeschonnek	Ia KoFl.AOK 4	Unknown
Oblt.Ludwig Keiper	KoFl.3.ostmanischen Armee	Inf.Rgt.15
Oblt.Maximilian Kieffer	Nachr.Offz.b.Stab KoFL AOK 6	Art.Rgt.7
Hptm.Waldemar Klepke	Fl.Gr.Kdr.16	Ref.zbV.WK I
Hptm.Victor Krocker	Kdr.Fl.Abt. A 211	Stab.6.Div.
Oblt.Erhard Krüger	Fhr.d.Stabs Bild Abt.A	Inf.Rgt.1
Hptm.Bernhard Kühl	Stab KoFl.AK VII	Inf.Rgt.4
Oblt.Walter Lackner	Stab KoFl.Heim 7	Inf.Rgt.1
Oblt.Heinrich Lorenz	Ltr.d.Fliegerschule d.Armeeflugpark 4	Inf.Rgt.2

Oblt.Bruno Maaß	Ref.i.Insp.d.Fliegertruppe	Reiter Rgt.9
Rittm.Hermann ? Martini	Fhr.Jasta 58	*Reiter Rgt.*
Hptm.Max Mohr	Fl.Gr.Fhr.3	Inf.Rgt.11
Oblt.Richard Putzier	Fhr.Fl.Abt.250	Art.Rgt.3
Hptm.Erich Quade	Kdr.Beobachterschule Thorn	Inf.Sch.München
Hptm.Theodor Schubert	Stab KoFl.Heimat I	Nachr.Abt.1
Hptm.Julius Schulz	Kdr.Fliegerschule Krefeld	Kraftfahr.Abt.1
Hptm.Karl Schweickhard	Fl.Gr.Fhr.I	Inf.Rgt.14
Hptm.Eduard Seldner	Fhr.Jasta 31	Inf.Rgt.14
Hptm.Walter Somme	Fhr.Kasta ?	Inf.Rgt.3
Oblt.Helmut Sonnenburg	Fhr.Feld Fl.Abt.250	Inf.Rgt.20
Hptm.Hugo Sperrle	KoFl.AOK 7	Ref.zbV.5.Div.
Hptm.Walter Stahr	KoFl.AOK 17	Ref.zbV.3.Div.
Hptm.Friedrich Starke	Technische Offz.Bogohl 4	Kraftfahr.Abt.3
Maj.Alfred Streccius	Ko.Fl.AOK 5	Inf.Rgt.11
Hptm.Kurt Student	Ltr.d.Abt.d.Vers.u.Wiss.Adlershorst	Insp.WaG/HWA
Oblt.Karl Veith	Bild-Offz.b.Kdr.d.Flg. Armee Abt.C	Art.Rgt.7
Hptm.Wilhelm Vogt	Unknown	Unknown
Hptm.Hellmuth Volkmann	Fhr.Fl.Abt. A 211	Inf.Rgt.14
Hptm.Wolfgang Weese	Bogohl 3	T3/RWM
Hptm.Helmuth Wilberg	KoFl.AOK 4	TA (L)/RWM
Hptm.Wilhelm Wimmer	Stab bayerischen Luftstreitkräfte	Inf.Rgt.20
Oblt.Heinz-Hellmuth von Wuhlisch	Stab AK XIV	Reiter Rgt.5
Oblt.Philipp Zoch	Stab KoFl.AOK 18	Inf.Rgt.5

2. OTHER OFFICERS (49)		
Lt.Otto Abernetty	Fhr.Schlasta 13	Inf.Rgt.1
Lt.Heinrich Aschenbrenner	Kogohl 2	Inf.Rgt.3
Oblt.Adolf Baeumker	Beobachter, Luftschiffertruppe	Reiter Rgt.4
Lt.Eberhard Baier	Jasta 18	Fahr.Abt.3
Lt.Gerhard Bassenge	Jasta Boelcke	Inf.Rgt.3
Lt.Wilhelm Becker	Lehrer Beobachterschule Thorn	Inf.Rgt.17
Oblt.Franz Biwer	Art.Fl.Abt.224	Reiter Rgt.15
Oblt.Ernst Bonatz	Fhr.Schlasta 18	Reiter Rgt.3
Lt.Ulrich Buchholz	Jasta 20	Inf.Rgt.8
Lt.Wolfgang v.Chamier-Glisczinski	Beobachter Fl.Abt.23	Inf.Rgt.16
Lt.Paul Deichmann	Beobachter Fl.Abt.8	Inf.Rgt.3

Lt.Karl Deinhardt	Kampfeinsitzer-Staffel 1a	Inf.Rgt.14
Oblt.Karl Drum	Fhr.Reihenbildzuges 3	Inf.Rgt.14
Lt.Eberhard Fischer	Adj.Fl.Ers.Abt.11	Inf.Rgt.16
Oblt.Heinz Funcke	Fhr.Schlasta 3	Inf.Rgt.18
Lt.Karl von Gerlach	Offz.z..b.V.Fl.Abt.241	Inf.Rgt.1
Hptm.Walther Grosch	Flugzeugführer JG 1	a.D.
Oblt.von Harbou	*Not known*	*Inf.Rgt.2*
Lt.Rudiger von Heyking	Kagohl 2	Kraftfahr.Abt.4
Lt.Hermann Hiller	Fl.Ers.Abt.10	Art.Rgt.5
Lt.Hans Jeschonnek	Jasta 40	Reiter Rgt.11
Lt.Otto Jordan	Fhr.Gr.Bildstelle 191	Art.Rgt.5
Lt.Werner Junck	Fhr.Jasta 8	Inf.Rgt.18
Lt.Günther Lohmann	Beobachter Fl.Abt.233	Bild.Offz.WK I
Lt.Josef Mai	Jasta 5	*Not known*
Lt.Rudolph Meister	Beobachter Fl.Abt.285	Inf.Rgt.4
Oblt.Angelo Müller	*Not known*	*Not known*
Lt.Gottlob Müller	Jasta 79	Kraftfahr.Abt.7
Oblt.Kurt Müller	*Not known*	*Not known*
Oblt.Albert Müller-Kahle	Fhr.Fl.Abt.6	Bild.Offz.WK II
Lt.Herbert Pfeiffer	Feld Fl.Abt.226	Fahr.Abt.3
Oblt.Curt Pflugbeil	Armeeflugpark 11	Inf.Rgt.11
Lt.Robert Pistorius	Beobachter	Pioneer Bn.2
Lt.August-Albert Ploch	Fl.Ers.Abt.5	Art.Rgt.6
Oblt.Hans Poetsch	Beobachter Fl.Abt.46	a.D.
Lt.Johann Raithel	TO Kurierfliegerstaffel Bamberg	Inf.Rgt.20
Lt.Fritz Reinshagen	Beobachter Fl.Abt.39 (L)	Inf.Rgt.14
Lt.Georg Rieke	Beobachter Bogohl 4	Inf.Rgt.16
Lt.Eduard Riesch	Fhr.d.Fliegerschule b.Armeeflugpark 6	Inf.Rgt.19
Hptm.Erwin von Romer	Beobachter	Inf.Rgt.10
Lt.Xaver Sattler	Bild Offz.Fl.Ers.Abt.19	Reiter Rgt.13
Lt.Heinrich Seywald	Fhr.Jasta 23	Kraftfahr.Abt.7
Oblt.Carl-August von Schoenebeck	Fhr.Jasta 33	Kraftfahr.Abt.5
Lt.Günther Schroth	Fhr.d.Flieger-Depots Damaskus	Reiter Rgt.5
Oblt.Paul Schultheiss	Fl.Abt.206	Reiter Rgt.18
Lt.Günter Schwartzkopff	Fl.Abt.13	Inf.Rgt.6
Lt.Ehrenfried Tschoeltsch	Fl.Abt.219	Inf.Rgt.11
Lt.Georg Weiner	Jasta 3	Kraftfahr.Abt.4
Lt.Günther Wieland	Offz.zbV Fl.Abt. A 273	Inf.Rgt.3

Appendix C

Military Aircraft Developments during the Reichswehr Period

1919-1932

It is very difficult to correctly assign certain designs to the categories below as the records are incomplete and in some cases shrouded in secrecy. Even the designations applied to these types can be misleading. In the case of the *Junkers Flugzeugwerke* the design work for military versions of their civil aircraft was carried out at Dessau whilst the civil machines were modified by *AB Flygindustri* in Sweden. At this point a new designation was applied eg. the Junkers A 25 in its military form was known by the Deassu design team as the K 45 whilst Swedish aircraft were referred to as the R 41. Nonetheless the listing below shows the extent of the German Aviation Industry's covert involvement in military aircraft design and manufacture during the period when this activity was effectively banned in Germany.

1. TO MEET REICHSHEER REQUIREMENTS			
Heinkel HD 17	Two seat short range reconnaissance aircraft	8	1924 450 hp Lion
Albatros L 68	Single seat fighter	4	1925 100 hp Lucifer
Heinkel HD 33	Two seat long range reconnaissance aircraft	1	1925 485 hp BMW VI
Caspar C 30	Two seat short range reconnaissance aircraft		1926 500 hp HS
Albatros L 76	Two seat short range reconnaissance aircraft	6	1927 600 hp BMW VI
Albatros L 77v	Two seat fighter	5	1928 600 hp BMW VI
Albatros L 78	Two seat short range reconnaissance aircraft	13	1928 600 hp BMW VI
Arado SD I	Single seat fighter	1	1928 425 hp Jupiter
Arado SD II/III	Single seat fighter	2	1929 530/490 Jupiter
BFW M 22	Multi-seat bomber	1	1929 500 hp Jupiter
Heinkel HD 41	Two seat short range reconnaissance aircraft	3	1929 Various
Arado SD IV	Single seat fighter	27	1930 Various
Dornier Do P	Multi-seat heavy bomber	2	1930 525 hp Jupiter
Arado SD V	Single seat fighter	80	1931 750 hp BMW VI
Focke Wulf S 39	Two seat short range reconnaissance aircraft	1	1931 510 hp Jupiter
Heinkel HD 46	Two seat short range reconnaissance aircraft	1	1931 Jupiter
Heinkel HE 46	Two seat short range reconnaissance aircraft		1932 Sh 22
Focke Wulf S 40	Two seat short range reconnaissance aircraft	1	1932 510 hp Jupiter
Dornier Do F	Multi-seat bomber		1932 550 hp Jupiter

Heinkel HE 45	Two seat reconnaissance bomber			1932 600 hp BMW VI

2. TO MEET REICHSMARINE REQUIRMENTS

Caspar U 1	Single seat submarine-borne floatplane		1	1921 50 hp Sh
Heinkel HE 1	Two seat coastal floatplane		10	1922 240 hp Eagle
LFG V 19	Single seat reconnaissance floatplane		1	1922 110 hp Oberursel
Heinkel HD 14	Multi-seat torpedo bomber floatplane		1	1925 600 hp Fiat
Caspar C 29	Two seat reconnaissance floatplane			1926 400 hp HS
Dornier Do R Wal	Multi-seat reconnaissance flying boat			1926/27 Various
Heinkel HD 24	Two seat training aircraft (floatplane)		20	1926 230 hp BMW IV
Focke Wulf W 4	Two seat reconnaissance floatplane		1	1927 480 hp Jupiter
Heinkel HD 15	Multi-seat shipboard reconnaissance flying boat		1	1927 450 hp Jupiter
Heinkel HE 9	Two/Three seat reconnaissance floatplane		11	1928 750 hp BMW VI
Heinkel HD 19	Two seat reconnaissance aircraft (floatplane)			1928 410 hp Jupiter
Arado SSD I	Single seat catapultable fighter floatplane		1	1929 650 hp BMW VI
Arado W II	Two seat multi-role floatplane		1	1929 96 hp Sh 12
Heinkel HD 38	Single seat catapultable fighter floatplane		12	1929 750 hp BMW VI
Focke Wulf W 7	Two seat reconnaissance floatplane		1	1931 650 hp BMW VI
Heinkel HD 42	Two seat training floatplane			1931
Heinkel HD 49	Single seat fighter floatplane		1	1932 BMW VI
Heinkel He 59	Multi-seat combat floatplane			1932 60 hp BMW VI

3. TO MEET FOREIGN MILITARY REQUIREMENTS

Caspar U 1	Single seat submarine-borne floatplane	USA	2	1921 50 hp Sh
Caspar U 2	Single seat submarine-borne floatplane	Japan	2	1921 50 hp Sh
Dornier A Libelle	Three seat flying boat	USA	1	1921 100 hp Lucifer
Dornier Cs II Delphin	Multi-seat Transport Flying Boat	USA	1	1921 260 hp Falcon
Caspar S 1 (HE 1)	Two seat coastal floatplane	Sweden		1922 240 hp AS
Dornier Do H Falke	Single seat fighter	USA	1	1922 325 hp Wright
Dornier Seefalke	Single seat fighter	Japan	1	1922 350 hp BMW IV
Junkers A 20 (R 2)	Two seat reconnaissance floatplane	USSR	40	1923 185 hp BMW III
Junkers T 21 (H 21)	Two seat reconnaissance aircraft	USSR	122	1923 240 hp BMW IV

Junkers T 22 (H 22)	Single seat fighter	USSR	1	1923
Rohrbach Ro II	Multi-seat reconnaissance flying boat	Japan		1922 340 hp Eagle
Caspar S 2 (HE 2)	Two seat coastal floatplane	Sweden		1923 360 hp Eagle
Junkers A 35 (K 53)	Two seat reconnaissance aircraft	USSR		1924 310 hp Ju L 5
Albatros L 65	Two seat reconnaissance aircraft	Lithuania		1925 450 hp Lion
Heinkel HE 4	Three seat coastal floatplane	Sweden		1925 360 hp Eagle
Heinkel HE 5	Two seat coastal floatplane	Sweden		1925-28 Various
Heinkel HD 25	Two seat shipboard reconnaissance floatplane	Japan		1925 450 hp Lion
Heinkel HD 26	Single seat shipboard floatplane	Japan		1925 300 hp HS
Junkers K 30 (R 42)	Multi seat bomber	USSR		1925 310 hp Ju L5
Rohrbach Rodra	Multi seat reconnaissance flying boat	Turkey	2	1925 450 hp L-D
Rohrbach Ro IV	Multi seat flying boat	Britain	1	1925 450 hp Lion
Rohrbach Ro IX	Singe seat fighter	Japan	1	1926 550 hp BMW VI
Dornier Do N	Multi seat bomber	Japan		1927 500 hp BMW VI
Heinkel HD 28	Three seat reconnaissance floatplane	Japan	1	1927 650 hp LD
Rohrbach Ro VI	Multi-seat heavy bomber	Britain	1	1927 650 hp Condor
Heinkel HE 8	Three seat reconnaissance floatplane	Denmark	22	1928 450 hp Jaguar
Heinkel HD 16	Multi-seat Torpedo Bomber	Sweden	2	1928 675 hp Leopard
Heinkel HD 37	Single seat fighter	USSR		1928 750 hp BMW VI
Heinkel HD 55	Multi-seat catapultable flying boat	USSR	30	1930 Jupiter
Dornier Do Y	Multi-seat bomber	Yugoslavia	2	1931 625 hp GR
Heinkel He 50	Two seat dive shipboard bomber	Japan		1931 Various

4. PRIVATE VENTURE DESIGNS

Caspar Cl 14	Single seat fighter		1	1924 325 hp Jaguar
Caspar CS 14	Single seat fighter		1	1924 450 hp Lion
Dornier Do E	Multi-seat reconnaissance flying boat	Various	5	1924 360 hp Eagle
Junkers A 20 (R 02)	Two seat combat aircraft	Turkey	64	1925 Daimler D IIIa
Junkers A 25 (K 41)	Two seat combat aircraft			1926
Dornier Do J Wal	Multi-seat Reconnaissance flying boat	Various		1926 Various
Junkers A 32 (K 39)	Three seat combat aircraft			1926 550 hpBMW VI
Junkers A 35 (K 53)	Two seat reconnaissance aircraft	Various		1926 310 hp Ju L 5

Junkers W 34 (K 43)	Multi-seat combat aircraft	Various		1926 Various
Albatros L 74	Two seat reconnaissance aircraft		2	1927 320 hp BMW IV
Dornier Do D Bas	Multi-seat torpedo bomber floatplane		3	1927 500 hp BMW VI
Heinkel HE 7	Multi-seat torpedo bomber floatplane		1	1927 450 hp Jupiter
Junkers S 36 (K 37)	Multi-seat combat aircraft	Japan		1927 480 hp Jupiter
Caspar C 33	Single seat fighter trainer		1	1928 80 hp Sh 11
Caspar C 36	Two seat combat aircraft (floatplane)		1	1928 600 hp BMW VI
Heinkel HD 30	Two seat catapultable floatplane		1	1928 450 hp Jupiter
Heinkel HE 31	Two seat reconnaissance floatplane		1	1928 800 hp Packard
Heinkel HD 34	Multi-seat bomber		1	1928 750 hp BMW VI
Junkers A 48 (K 47)	Two seat fighter	Various		1928 Various
Junkers G.38 (K 51)	Multi-seat heavy bomber	Japan	6	1929 800 hp Ju L 88
Albatros L 84	Two seat fighter		2	1931 660 hp BMW VI
Dornier Do C 1	Two seat fighter		2	1931 710 hp BMW VI
Dornier Do C 2	Two seat combat floatplane	Bolivia		1931 740 hp HS
Heinkel HD 43	Single seat fighter		2	1931 750 hp BMW VI
Albatros L 81	Two seat short range reconnaissance aircraft		1	1932 360 hp BMW IV
Junkers Ju 52 (K 54)	Multi-seat torpedo bomber		1	1932

Appendix D

Civil Flying Training Organisations providing Tuition to Reichswehr Personnel

1. SPORTFLUG GmbH

Sportflug GmbH was established in Jun 24 with financial assistance from both the *RVM* and *RWM* to provide ab initio (*A1 & A2*) and basic flying (*B1*) training to *Reichsheer* sponsored officers as well as private individuals including former members of the *Luftstreitkräfte*. The *Leiter d.Sportflug GmbH* from May 24 was *Hptm.a.D.*Hermann Fricke (*Plm* 23 Dec 17) with a HQ in Berlin. There were seven later ten *Zweigstellen* located throughout Germany so as to provide coverage for the *Reichsheer's Wehrkreise.*

Berlin-Staaken/Brandenburg	Wehrkreis III	
Boblingen/Bad Württemberg	Wehrkreis V	
Furth-Atzenhof/Bayern	Wehrkreis VII	Eberhard von Conta/Theo Croneiss
Hannover-Vahrenheide/Nord Sachsen	Wehrkreis VI	Martin Zander
Königsberg-Devau/Ostpreussen	Wehrkreis I	
Leipzig-Mockau/Sachsen	Wehrkreis IV	
Leipzig-Schkeuditz (1924 only)	Wehrkreis IV	
München-Schleißheim/Bayern	Wehrkreis VII	Albert Vierling
Stettin-Krecow/Pommern	Wehrkreis II	
Würzburg/Bayern	Wehrkreis VII	Nopitsch

Sportflug was dissolved on the 1 Nov 26 following the *Pariser Luftfahrtabkommens* (Paris Air Agreements) signed on the 22 May 26.

2. AEROSPORT GmbH

Aerosport GmbH was formed in Jun 24 with financial assistance from both the *RVM* and *RWM* to provide ab initio (*A1 & A2*) and basic flying (*B1*) training to private individuals including those from the *Reichsmarine*. It was based at Warnemünde under the direction of Walter Bachmann.

3. SEVERA GmbH

The *Seeflugzeugversuchsabteilung GmbH* was established at Berlin-Staaken with operating bases at Norderney (Horst von Schiller) and Kiel-Holtenau (Theodor Osterkamp) in 1924 to provide target facilities aircraft for the *Reichsmarine's* warships, coastal and shipboard anti-aircraft artillery as well as the clandestine training of both *Seebeobachtern* and *Flugzeugführern* on behalf of the *Reichsmarine*. Later *Bordfunker* and *Bordmonteure* were trained, ostensibly for *DLH*. Flight training

386

took place at Warnemünde under the auspices of *Seeflug GmbH* (*KorvKpt.a.D.*Konrad Goltz) from Jul 25 to Dec 26 when the training function was passed to the newly formed *DVS Zweigstelle Warnemünde*.

In Feb 29 *Severa* was briefly re-designated the *Abt.Küstenflug der DLH* before being rebranded in Jul 29 as *Luftdienst GmbH*. At this point its remit was expanded to include the training of *Bordfunkern, Beobachtern* & *Flugmechaniker* and the number of contracted flight hours increased.

4. DEUTSCHE LUFTFAHRT GmbH

Following the dissolution of *Sportflug GmbH* the *Deutschen Luftfahrt GmbH* was established on the 1 Apr 27 with private finance but employing much of *Sportflug's* equipment and facilities. The *Leiter* was *Maj.a.D.*Leo Leonhardy (*Plm* 2 Oct 18) who was succeeded by *Hptm.a.D.*Robert Ritter von Greim (*Plm* 14 Oct 18) from 1 Oct 27. Under the *Pariser Luftfahrtabkommens* (Paris Air Agreements) a total of 72 *Reichsheer* officers were permitted to undertake ab initio (*A1 & A2*) and basic flying (*B1*) training annually provided it was at their own expense.

Berlin-Staaken/Brandenburg		Wehrkreis III
Boblingen/Bad Württemberg	Oblt.a.D.Rudolf Trautvetter (31/33)	Wehrkreis V
Würzburg/Bayern	Hptm.a.D.Robert Ritter von Greim	Wehrkreis V

An additional *Zweigstelle* at Königsberg-Devau/Ostpreussen (*Wehrkreis I*) appears to have only existed for short period in1927.

The *Deutschen Luftfahrt GmbH* was dissolved in Dec 33, its assets being distributed amongst the *DVS* & *DLV* including the *Abt.Reklame d.DLV*.

5. DEUTSCHE VERKEHRSFLIEGERSCHULE GmbH (DVS)

The growth of commercial aviation in Germany during the 20s led to the need for a commercial flying training organisation to train aircrew for the airlines. As a result the *DVS GmbH* was established at Berlin-Staaken on the 1 Apr 25. The *Direktor* of the *DVS* was *Maj.a.D.*Alfred Keller (*Plm* 4 Dec 17). Following the creation of the *DLH* in 1926 the *DVS* was partly financed by that airline and additional *Zweigstellen* were added at List auf Sylt, Schleißheim and Warnemünde in 1927 whilst the Staaken facility was transferred to Braunschweig in 1928. The *Direktor DVS-See* at Warnemünde was *Oblt.z.S.a.D.*Wolfgang von Gronau. *DVS Zentrale* remained at Staaken until 1929 when it moved to Braunschweig-Broitzem. *Dr.*Günther Ziegler replaced *Maj.*Keller as *Direktor DVS-Land* on the 1 Jan 27.

The covert flight training of military personnel was also provided by the *DVS*, a degree of specialisation taking place by which basic (*B2*) pilot training took place at Schleißheim, whilst advanced (*C2*) pilot training and the training of military *Beobachtern* and other flight crew categories took place at Braunschweig. Later, continuation fighter pilot training for graduates of the Lipetsk facility was provided at Schleißheim. Naval pilot (*B1 & C2*) training and the training of naval *Beobachtern* took place at both Warnemünde and List.

Following the creation of the *RLM* in1933 further expansion took place with the establishment of additional *Zweigstellen* at Boblingen, Cottbus, Stettin and Würzburg, whilst the *Zweigstelle* List was transferred to Travemünde. Refresher training for re-activated *Luftstreitkräfte* pilots was provided at Würzburg. In 1934 the *DVS* was used as a cover for purely military flying training schools at Neuruppin and Prenzlau, the *Technischeschule* at Jüterbog and covert military air units at Seerappen.

Berlin-Staaken later Braunschweig	Maj.a.D.Alfred Keller	Apr 25
Schleißheim/Bayern	Hptm.a.D.Albert Vierling	Jan 27
Warnemünde/Mecklenburg	KorvKpt.a.D.Konrad Goltz	Jan 27
List auf Sylt	Oblt.z.S.a.D.Heinz Scheurlen	Mar 27
Boblingen/Bad Württemberg	Dipl.Ing.Hermann Huppenbauer	Apr 33
Würzburg/Bayern	Hptm.a.D.Robert Ritter von Greim	Dec 33
Cottbus/Brandenburg	Maj.Otto Dessloch	Feb 34
Stettin-Altdamm/Pommern	Dr.Georg Pasewaldt	Apr 34

The *DVS Zweigstellen* were progressively converted into *Luftwaffe Fliegerschulen* over the period Oct 33 – Apr 36:

Schleißheim	Jagdfliegerschule Schleißheim	1 Oct 33
Cottbus	Fliegerschule Cottbus	1 Feb 34
Braunschweig	Aufklärungsfliegerschule Braunschweig	1 Jul 34
Würzburg	Fliegerschule Kitzingen	1 Oct 34
Boblingen	Fliegerübungsstelle d.DVL Boblingen	Nov 34
Warnemünde	Flugzeugführerschule (See) Warnemünde	1 May 35
	Fliegerwaffenlehrgang (See) Warnemünde	Dec 33
Travemünde	Flugzeugführerschule (See) Travemünde	1 Jan 36
Stettin	Flugzeugführerschule (See) Stettin	1 Apr 36

6. DEUTSCHEN LUFTSPORT-VERBAND eV

Following the formation of the *RLM* in 1933 the existing *Deutschen Luftfahrtverband (DLV)* was dissolved and in its place the *Deutschen Luftsport-Verband eV (DLV)* was created on the 25 Mar 33 to control all aspects of sport aviation within the Reich. The first *Präsident des DLV* and *Reichsluftsportführer* was *Hptm.a.D.*Bruno Loerzer (*Plm* 14 Feb 18). As a uniformed para-military organisation the new *DLV* was ideally placed to provide clandestine military flight training on behalf of the emerging *Luftwaffe* and from Jan 34 *Flieger-Ausbildungs* and *Übungstellen* were established within the sixteen *Fliegerlandesgruppen* to provide ab initio *A2* pilot training and refresher training for qualified flight personnel (this listing dates from 1 Oct 35).

Boblingen	Bad Wuttemberg	Übungs.	Luftkreis V	Nov 34
Braunschweig-Waggum	Nord Sachsen	Übungs.	Luftkreis IV	
Breslau-Gandau	Schlesien	Übungs.	Luftkreis III	
Darmstadt	Hessen	Übungs.	Luftkreis IV	
Diepholz	Nord Sachsen	Ausb.	Luftkreis IV	
Dortmund-Brackel	Nordrhein-Westfalen	Übungs.	Luftkreis IV	34
Dresden-Rahnitz	Sachsen	Übungs.	Luftkreis III	34
Düsseldorf-Lohausen	Nordrhein-Westfalen	Übungs.	Luftkreis IV	Jan 34
Erfurt-Bindersleben	Thüringen	Übungs.	Luftkreis III	34
Essen-Mülheim	Nordrhein-Westfalen	Übungs.	Luftkreis IV	Jan 34
Frankfurt/Oder	Brandenburg	Übungs.	Luftkreis II	Jan 34
Freiburg	Bad Württemberg	Übungs.	Luftkreis V	35
Halberstadt	Anhorn	Ausb.	Luftkreis II	Aug 35
Hannover-Vahrenheide	Nord Sachsen	Übungs.	Luftkreis IV	35
Hennigsdorf	Brandenburg	Ausb.	Luftkreis II	
Herzogenaurach	Bayern	Ausb.	Luftkreis V	
Kaufbeuren	Bayern	Ausb.	Luftkreis V	Sep 35
Königsberg-Devau	Ostpreussen	Übungs.	Luftkreis I	35
Leipzig-Mockau	Sachsen	Übungs.	Luftkreis III	35
Mannheim-Stadt	Bad Württemberg	Übungs.	Luftkreis V	35
München-Oberweisenfeld	Bayern	Übungs.	Luftkreis V	35
Neukuhren	Ostpreussen	Ausb.	Luftkreis I	35
Nürnberg	Bayern	Übungs.	Luftkreis V	
Quakenbruck	Nord Sachsen	Ausb.	Luftkreis IV	
Stettin	Pommern	Übungs.	Luftkreis II	
Weimar-Nohra	Thüringen	Ausb.	Luftkreis III	35

Appendix E

Aircraft Purchased by the RVM for the Government Sponsored Fliegerschulen

This is not an exhaustive listing particularly in respect of acquisitions for the summer of 1933 to July 1934 in the register range D-2500 to D-3400. Although registrations were generally issued sequentially by the *RVM* this was not always the case. Relatively few of the original 500 aircraft registered in the *LFR-A* sequence (1919-20) survived *ILUK's* disarmament activities to be re-registered in the *LFR-B* sequence (1920-34) - on the 31 Mar 21 *ILUK* noted that there were 136 civil aircraft in Germany registered to 20 operators. New registrations had reached D-500 to 700 by 1925, D-1000 to 1400 in 1928, D-1780 to 1980 in 1930, D-2200 to 2371 in 1932 and to D-2700 to 3463 in 1934. Care also needs to be exercised in those cases where aircraft were re-registered to the *Fliegerschulen*. Aircraft often passed through several hands and this was particularly true of the *DLH* machines that were passed to the *DVS* following their replacement in airline service. Good examples are the Rohrbach *Roland I* airliners which served with *DLH* from 1926-34 when three of the survivors were passed to the *DVS*.

Where known the transfer of *LFR-B* numbered aircraft to the new *LFR* lettered sequence from March 1934 is shown, however this listing is far from complete.

The high level of attrition in this listing shows the dangers inherent in flying training in the twenties and thirties.

LVG C VI	4587	D-12	Sportflug Ex-DAL		
Friedrichshafen FF 71a	3077	D-40	Seeflug Ex-DAL		
Friedrichshafen FF.49	1368	D-85	Aerosport Ex-Lloyd LV to DVS		
Friedrichshafen FF.49	223	D-86	DVS Ex-Lloyd LV Sablatnig		Destroyed Aug 28
Friedrichshafen FF.49	1364	D-146	DVS Ex-DLR		Cancelled Jul 28
LFG V 13	85	D-160	Aerosport		To Norway Feb 29
Junkers F 13 f1e	717	D-354	DVS Ex-Severa		
Junkers F 13 ce	721	D-358	Unterfrankische Sportflug to DVS		
Junkers F 13 ce	722	D-359	DVS Ex-DLH		Crashed Jun 31
Dietrich DP IIa	111	D-363	Sportflug/Berlin		Cancelled Feb 32
Junkers F 13 de	728	D-370	DVS Ex-DVL		Destroyed Jun 34
LFG V 13	91	D-402	DVS		Withdrawn Mar 32
Sablatnig P III	265	D-415	DVS		
Junkers F 13 f1e	695	D-419	DVS Ex-DLH	(D-OLEF)	Cancelled Jun 38
Fokker-Grulich F II	1596	D-423	DVS		

Junkers F 13 f1e	703	D-425	DVS Ex-DLH	(D-OBON)	
Junkers F 13 f1e	704	D-426	DVS Ex-OLAG	(D-OJAL)	
Junkers F 13 f1e	707	D-429	DVS Ex-DLH	(D-OHUN)	
Junkers F 13 f1e	743	D-433	DVS Ex-Österreichische LV	(D-OKAX)	
Udet U 12		D-449	Deutsche Luftfahrt		Destroyed May 27
Junkers F 13	547	D-454	DVS Ex-DLH	(D-OMIZ)	
Junkers F 13	761	D-466	DVS Ex-DLH	(D-OSAF)	Cancelled Mar 38
Albatros L 30	10025	D-501	Deutsche Luftfahrt		Cancelled Mar 32
Junkers A 20/A 35	1038	D-510	DVS Ex-Severa		
Albatros L 30	10029	D-511	Deutsche Luftfahrt		Cancelled Mar 32
Albatros L 30	10028	D-512	Deutsche Luftfahrt		To Wurtt.Luftfahrt
Junkers F 13 bi	748	D-557	DVS Ex-DLH	(D-OGEX)	Cancelled Jun 37
Junkers F 13 fi	681	D-561	DVS Ex-DLH	(D-OZYR)	Cancelled Jun 37
Dornier Merkur	71	D-562	DVS Ex-DLH		Destroyed 35
Junkers F 13 bi	687	D-565	DVS Ex-DLH	(D-OGIT)	
Junkers F 13	701	D-567	DVS Ex-RVM		Crashed Nov 28
Albatros L 30	10024	D-568	Unterfrankische Sportflug/Würzburg		Destroyed Apr 29
Junkers F 13 ci	719	D-579	DVS Ex-RVM		Crashed Jun 34
Dornier Komet III	74	D-580	DVS Ex-DLH		Cancelled Aug 33
Junkers F 13 f1e	706	D-582	DVS Ex-DLH	(D-OLAS)	
Dietrich DS I	162	D-595	Mittelfranken u.Oberpfalz Sportflug Ex-Nordbayerischer VF		
Albatros L 68	10040	D-651	DVS		Destroyed Mar 32
LFG V 39 c	101	D-668	Deutsche Luftfahrt/Berlin		Cancelled Mar 32
Heinkel HD 21	4	D-676	Süd-Dt.Sportflug/Boblingen to Dt.Luftfahrt		Cancelled Apr 32
Heinkel HD 21	220	D-680	Sportflug to DVS		Destroyed May 29
Heinkel HD 21	2	D-685	Stettiner Sportflug to Dt.Luftfahrt/ Berlin		
Heinkel HD 21	1	D-686	Stettiner Sportflug to Dt.Luftfahrt/ Berlin To G.Friedrich		
Heinkel HD 21	3	D-691	Stettiner Sportflug		
Junkers A 20a	865	D-704	DVS Ex-DLH		To RLM
Junkers A 20	868	D-708	DVS Ex-DVL		To RLM
Junkers A 20	864	D-713	Deutsche Luftfahrt Ex-RDL/Staaken		Cancelled Mar 34
Heinkel HD 21	5	D-722	Stettiner Sportflug to Dt.Luftfahrt		Destroyed Mar 32
Heinkel HD 32	233	D-746	DVS		To DLV

Junkers A 20	876	D-748	DVS			Scrapped Apr 31
Junkers A 20	877	D-749	DVS			Scrapped Apr 31
LVG B III	397	D-760	Sportflug/Würzburg to Dt.Luftfahrt			Destroyed Jun 28
Heinkel HD 21	9	D-762	Sportflug to Dt.Luftfahrt			To Brazil May 31
Dietrich DS I	148	D-769	Mittelfranken u.Oberpfalz Sportflug/ Furth			
Dornier Merkur	83	D-774	DVS			
Focke Wulf A 16a	13	D-776	DVS			Crashed Dec 25
BFW M 17	25	D-779	Sportflug/FürthEx-Nordbayerischer VF			Preserved
Udet U-12	252	D-787	Deutschen Luftfahrt/Berlin			Destroyed Mar 30
LVG B III	420	D-793	Unterfrankische Sportflug/Würzburg			Destroyed Aug 28
Dietrich DS I	179	D-799	Bayrische Sportflug/Würzburg Ex-DLV			Exported Apr 30
Dietrich DP IX	153	D-802	DVS			Cancelled Feb 33
Udet U 12	259	D-813	Deutsche Luftfahrt			Burnt Nov 28
Dornier B III	80	D-815	DVS			Scrapped May 30
Dietrich DS I	177	D-825	Unterfrankischer Sportflug/Würzburg			To DVL/Adlershof
Udet U-11	243	D-828	DVS Ex-DLH not accepted			Crashed 31
Caspar S 1	5010	D-830	DVS Ex-Luftdienst			
Junkers F 13 co	781	D-831	DVS Ex-Ju to DVL RDL & Dt.Luftfahrt			To Poland
Junkers F 13 f1e	799	D-833	DVS Ex-Luftdienst			
Junkers F 13 d1e	790	D-838	DVS	(D-ONIQ)		To DLV
Udet U-8b		D-839	DVS Ex-Nordbayerische VF			
Heinkel HD 32	16	D-840	DVS Staaken			
Heinkel HD 32	17	D-841	DVS Staaken			
Heinkel HD 32	18	D-842	DVS			To DVL
Heinkel HD 32	19	D-843	DVS			To DVL
LFG V 60	114	D-850	DVS			Destroyed Sep 28
LVG B III	364	D-852	Unterfrankischer Sportflug/Würzburg			Export Sep 29
Dornier Do J Wal	24/41	D-861	DVS Ex-DLH			Accident Oct 31
Dornier Do J Wal	26/43	D-863	DVS Ex-DLH			To Nordiska Flyg.
Dornier Do J Wal	27/44	D-864	DVS Ex-DLH			To Nordiska Flyg.
Udet U 12	272	D-865	Deutsche Luftfahrt to DVS			Destroyed Feb 33
Udet U 12	273	D-867	Deutsche Luftfahrt			Destroyed Sep 30
Junkers F 13	793	D-870	DVS			Crashed Jun 34
Junkers G 24 ge	902	D-879	DVS Ex-DLH	(D-ABIP)		

Junkers G 24 ge	908	D-880	DVS Ex-DLH to DLH to DVS	(D-ADIL)	
Junkers A 20	1054	D-882	DVS		Scrapped Jun 30
Udet U 12	278	D-883	Deutsche Luftfahrt		Destroyed Oct 29
Heinkel HD 39	238	D-889	Deutsche Luftfahrt Ex-Ullstein		Cancelled Jun 32
Junkers A 20	1055	D-898	DVS Ex-Deutsche Seewarte		To RLM
Junkers A 20	1053	D-900	DVS Ex-RRG		To RLM
Udet U 12	279	D-905	Deutsche Luftfahrt		Destroyed Dec 28
Udet U 12	280	D-909	Deutsche Luftfahrt		Destroyed Aug 30
Focke Wulf A 16c	20	D-914	DVS/Staaken		Destroyed Apr 29
Junkers G 24	841	D-915	DVS Ex-DVL		Scrapped
Heinkel HE 1	207	D-939	DVS Ex-Luftdienst		Destroyed Feb 34
Junkers G 24 ge	922	D-954	DVS Ex-Luftdienst		
Junkers A 20	1046	D-955	DVS		To DVL
Junkers A 20	1048	D-957	DVS		Withdrawn May 32
Junkers A 20	1049	D-958	DVS		Scrapped Aug 31
Arado SC I	23	D-965	Fliegerschule Staaken		
Focke Wulf S 1	27	D-966	DVS		Destroyed Sep 33
Dornier B Merkur	97	D-971	DVS Ex-DLH		Cancelled Apr 32
Dornier B Merkur	99	D-973	DVS		Dismantled Nov 31
Daimler L 20 B I	6	D-978	Deutsche Luftfahrt		Destroyed Apr 28
Daimler L 20 B I	7	D-979	Deutsche Luftfahrt		Destroyed Sep 30
Junkers A 35	1063	D-986	DVS Ex-DVL		Destroyed Sep 30
Junkers A 35	1059	D-987	DVS Ex-RDL Staaken		To Flugsicherung
Junkers A 35	1062	D-989	DVS		Destroyed 34
Junkers A 35	1061	D-990	DVS Ex-DVL		Destroyed May 30
Focke Wulf S 1	21	D-994	Deutsche Luftfahrt		To H.Jensen
Junkers G 24 ce	950	D-1000	DVS Ex-DVL		
Junkers F 13 de	796	D-1001	DVS Ex-DVL	(D-OBAX)	Destroyed Apr 37
Albatros L 68a	10090	D-1002	DVS		To DVL
Albatros L 68a	10091	D-1003	DVS		Destroyed Feb 31
Heinkel HD 45A (HD 41c)	363	D-1011	DVS Ex-RDL Staaken		
Daimler L 20 B I	40	D-1013	Deutsche Luftfahrt		Export Nov 32
Arado SC I	24	D-1015	DVS		Destroyed Apr 32
Arado SC I	25	D-1021	DVS		Destroyed Apr 31
Daimler L 20 B I	41	D-1022	Deutsche Luftfahrt		
Caspar C 27	7004	D-1023	DVS		Withdrawn Mar 32
Albatros L 68a	10088	D-1030	DVS		Destroyed Feb 33

Arado SC I	27	D-1035	DVS/Schleißheim Ex-DVL		Destroyed Nov 32
Junkers F 13 ci	532	D-1036	DVS Ex-DLH		
Arado Ar 64D	67	D-1039	DVS/Schleißheim		
LFG V 60	121	D-1040	DVS		
Junkers W 33 b1	2500	D-1048	DVS Ex-Luftdienst		
Udet U 12	312	D-1053	DVS		Destroyed Nov 28
Udet U 12	314	D-1055	DVS	`	Destroyed Sep 28
Focke Wulf S 1b	29	D-1056	DVS		To Flugwiss.Gr.TH
Junkers G 24 ge	933	D-1062	DVS Ex-DLH		
Junkers G 24 ge	939	D-1063	DVS		
Junkers W 33 bi	2501	D-1064	DVS Ex-Luftdienst		
Focke Wulf GL 18a	30	D-1066	DVS		
Dornier Do B Merkur	157	D-1083	DVS Ex-DLH	(D-UHAS)	
Dornier Do B Merkur	158	D-1084	DVS Ex-DLH	(D-UVIZ)	
Dornier Do B-Jal Merkur	161	D-1087	DVS Ex-DLH	(D-UGAP)	
Junkers G 24 ge	941	D-1088	DVS Ex-DLH		
Junkers G 24 ge	927	D-1089	DVS Ex-DLH	(D-ADOX)	
Junkers G 24 ge	846	D-1091	DVS Ex-DLH	(D-AQOL)	
Junkers G 24 ge	912	D-1092	DVS Ex-DLH		
Udet U 12	317	D-1094	DVS		Destroyed Aug 33
Udet U 12	318	D-1095	DVS		Cancelled Mar 28
Heinkel HD 22	252	D-1096	DVS	(D-IQIL)	
Focke Wulf GL 18c	31	D-1097	DVS/Staaken		Stored Mar 32
Heinkel HD 24	255	D-1098	DVS		Cancelled Mar 28
Heinkel HD 24	256	D-1099	DVS		Destroyed Nov 29
Arado SC I	29	D-1104	Bay.Sportflug/Würzburg to Dt.Luftfahrt		Withdrawn Dec 33
Albtaros L 74	10096	D-1110	DVS to DVL to DVS to Dt.Luftfahrt		
Albatros L 76	10115	D-1113	DVS		Destroyed Jun 31
Dornier Do R Superwal R2	118	D-1115	DVS Ex-Severa		
Udet U 12	354	D-1116	DVS		
Udet U 12	355	D-1117	DVS		Scrapped Aug 29
Fokker D.VII	8510	D-1123	Unterfrankische Sportflug/Würzburg		Export May 29
Junkers F 13	2001	D-1126	DVS Ex-Junkers		(D-OHAS)
Albatros L 76a	10104	D-1128	DVS ex E-Stelle Staaken		Withdrawn Oct 31
Albatros L 76a	10107	D-1130	DVS ex E-Stelle Staaken		Withdrawn Oct 31
Heinkel HE 1	202	D-1134	DVS Ex-Severa		

Udet U 12	319	D-1135	DVS		Destroyed Aug 28
Udet U 12	320	D-1136	DVS		Destroyed Sep 33
Aero Sport S 1	111	D-1141	Aerosport		Withdrawn Mar 32
Caspar C 32	7006	D-1142	DVS Ex-Biologische Reichsanstalt		
Caspar C 32	7008	D-1143	DVS		Withdrawn Apr 33
Caspar C 32	7009	D-1144	DVS Ex-DVL to DVL to DVS		Museum May 32
LVG B III	375	D-1148	Unterfrankische Sportflug/Würzburg		Destroyed Apr 29
Heinkel HD 24	262	D-1160	DVS		Destroyed Apr 31
Daimler L 20 B I	15	D-1161	Deutsche Luftfahrt		To P.Wehrmaan
Daimler L 20 B I	16	D-1162	Deutsche Luftfahrt		To Kleist & Co.
Daimler L 20 B I	17	D-1163	Deutsche Luftfahrt		To Akaflieg Stuttgart
Heinkel HE 5c	275	D-1164	DVS		Cancelled Jun 32
Heinkel HD 24	263	D-1165	DVS		Cancelled May 29
Heinkel HD 22	258	D-1168	DVS Ex-DVL		
Heinkel HD 24	260	D-1174	DVS		Destroyed Feb 32
Heinkel HD 24	261	D-1175	DVS		Destroyed Jun 28
Udet U 12	392	D-1178	DVS		Destroyed Jul 31
Junkers F 13 JL6 f1e	569	D-1183	DVS Ex-DLH	(D-OLOF)	
Udet U 12	323	D-1184	DVS/Schleißheim		Withdrawn Jul 28
Udet U 12	329	D-1187	DVS		Destroyed Oct 32
Udet U 12	330	D-1188	DVS		Destroyed Feb 33
Udet U 12	331	D-1189	DVS		To Braunsch.Instit.
Raab-Katzenstein RK IIa	58	D-1190	Fliegerschule Staaken		Export Jul 29
Arado SC I	30	D-1191	DVS to DVL to DVS		
Arado SC I	32	D-1192	DVS		Destroyed 31
Udet U 12	332	D-1202	DVS		Destroyed Dec 30
Junkers F 13 fe	2003	D-1203	Deutsche Luftfahrt Ex-UAE to DVS		Destroyed Mar 34
Arado SC I	33	D-1204	DVS		Destroyed May 32
Daimler L 20 B I	22	D-1207	DVS Ex-Aero Express		To Aero Express
Daimler L 20 B I	18	D-1217	Deutsche Luftfahrt		
Daimler L 20 B I	19	D-1218	Deutsche Luftfahrt		Export Jan 33
Raab-Katzenstein RK IIa	60	D-1222	Fliegerschule Staaken		Withdrawn Apr 32
Udet U-12b	334	D-1229	DVS/Berlin to DVL to DVS/ Braunschweig To DLV		
Junkers W 33 b	2507	D-1231	DVS		

Dornier Do B Bal 2 Merkur	166	D-1232	DVS		
Arado SC I	35	D-1241	DVS/Schleißheim Ex-DVL		Destroyed Oct 31
Udet U 12	333	D-1242	DVS		Destroyed Jul 33
Udet U 12	335	D-1243	DVS		Destroyed Dec 33
Heinkel HD 24	269	D-1245	DVS		Destroyed Aug 30
Junkers W 33 b	2508	D-1248	DVS Ex-Luftdienst		
Junkers W 33 b	2509	D-1249	DVS		
Arado SC I	36	D-1251	DVS		Destroyed May 28
Klemm L 20 B I	29	D-1256	Deutsche Luftfahrt		Export Aug 32
Udet U 12	336	D-1257	DVS		Destroyed Sep 30
Udet U 12	337	D-1258	DVS		
Udet U 12	338	D-1259	DVS		Destroyed Jul 32
Heinkel HD 24	270	D-1267	DVS		Cancelled Jun 28
Heinkel HE 5c	276	D-1268	DVS		Destroyed Apr 28
Udet U 12	342	D-1274	Unterfrankische Sportflug/Würzburg		
Udet U 12	345	D-1275	Unterfrankische Sportflug/Würzburg		
Caspar C 27	7001	D-1276	DVS		
Rohrbach Ro VIII Roland I	35	D-1280	DVS Ex-DLH	(D-AGUN)	
Udet U-12b	350	D-1284	DVS		
Heinkel HD 24	272	D-1286	DVS		Destroyed Jul 28
Albatros L 76	10116	D-1289	DVS		
Udet U 12	356	D-1295	DVS		
Udet U 12	357	D-1296	DVS		Collision Jul 32
Rohrbach Ro VIII Roland I	37	D-1297	DVS Ex-DLH	(D-AKIL)	
Daimler L 20 B I	45	D-1299	Deutsche Luftfahrt		Destroyed Sep 32
Daimler L 20 B I	46	D-1300	Deutsche Luftfahrt		To L.Beyer
Udet U 12	361	D-1302	DVS		Destroyed Sep 33
Udet U 12	359	D-1303	DVS		Scrapped Apr 36
Udet U 12	362	D-1305	DVS		Destroyed Jul 29
Daimler L 20 B I	51	D-1307	Deutsche Luftfahrt		Destroyed Mar 30
Heinkel HD 24	271	D-1313	DVS		Destroyed Jan 31
BFW 1 Sperber a	351	D-1315	DVS		To A.v.Bismarck
Udet U 12	372	D-1317	DVS		Destroyed Apr 34
Udet U 12	373	D-1318	DVS		
Udet U 12	363	D-1321	DVS to Unterfr.Sportflug to DVS		Destroyed May 32

Udet U 12	370	D-1323	DVS		To Aero Express
Udet U 12	374	D-1324	DVS		To Aero Express
Rohrbach Ro VIII Roland Ia	39	D-1327	DVS Ex-DLH		
Raab-Katzenstein RK IIc	33	D-1332	Fliegerschule Staaken		To Flugwiss.Gr.TH
Junkers G 24	831	D-1335	DVS Ex-DLH		Scrapped Jun 30
Heinkel HE 5e	290	D-1336	DVS		(D-OKUT)
Heinkel HE 5e	298	D-1341	DVS		
Focke Wulf A 17a	42	D-1342	DVS Ex-DLH		
Focke Wulf A 17a	38	D-1345	DVS Ex-Albatros		
Heinkel HE 5e	297	D-1346	DVS		
Albatros L 75	10117	D-1348	DVS		Destroyed Oct 28
Focke Wulf GL 22	37	D-1349	DVS		Stored Jun 30
Udet U 12	375	D-1354	DVS		Destroyed Jul 33
Focke Wulf A 17a	43	D-1358	DVS Ex-DLH		
Udet U 12	377	D-1361	DVS		
Heinkel HE 5e	299	D-1362	DVS		Destroyed Jun 33
Focke Wulf A 17a	44	D-1367	DVS Ex-DLH		
Udet U 12	378	D-1368	DVS		
Udet U 12	383	D-1369	DVS		Dismantled Apr 31
Udet U 12	384	D-1370	DVS		Destroyed Sep 33
Udet U 12	385	D-1371	DVS		(D-EEGO)
Udet U 12	386	D-1372	DVS		Destroyed Sep 31
Junkers F 13 fe	2022	D-1374	DVS Ex-DLH		
Focke Wulf GL 22	379	D-1375	DVS/Staaken		Stored Jun 30
Udet U 12	387	D-1376	DVS		Destroyed Aug 28
Junkers F 13 h1e	2015	D-1378	DVS Ex-Luftdienst	(D-OBIV)	
Focke Wulf A 17a	45	D-1380	DVS Ex-DLH		
Junkers F 13 f1e	2016	D-1382	DVS Ex-DVL	(D-ONUS)	
Junkers W 33 b1	2517	D-1384	DVS Ex-Lufttdienst		
Heinkel HE 5e	300	D-1386	DVS	(D-OXAX)	
Albatros L 68	10120	D-1387	Deutsche Luftfahrt Ex-Albatros		Withdrawn Dec 36
Arado SC II	41	D-1390	DVS		Destroyed Sep 29
Arado SC II	42	D-1398	DVS		Destroyed Mar 31
Udet U 12	388	D-1400	DVS		To DVL
Udet U 12	389	D-1401	DVS to DVL to DVS		Destroyed Apr 34
Heinkel HE 5e	301	D-1404	DVS		Cancelled Jun 30
Udet U 12	390	D-1406	DVS		

Arado SC II	43	D-1409	DVS		Destroyed Jan 33
Arado W 2	38	D-1412	DVS/List & Warnemünde		Crashed 35
Raab-Katzenstein RK IIc	72	D-1413	DVS		Cancelled Jun 29
Raab-Katzenstein RK IIa	32	D-1415	DVS		Destroyed Dec 28
Focke Wulf A 17a	48	D-1416	DVS Ex-DLH		
Focke Wulf GL 22	40	D-1418	DVS/Staaken		Crashed Dec 28
Raab Katzenstein RK 9	319	D-1419	Fliegerschule Staaken		To Vereinzur-Ford.
Dornier Do J Wal	37	D-1422	DVS Ex-G-EBQO		Museum Mar 32
Junkers W 33 b	2021	D-1424	DVS Ex-Luftdienst		To Luftdienst
Udet U 12	395	D-1435	DVS		
Arado SC II	44	D-1436	DVS		
Udet U 12	396	D-1448	DVS		
Junkers W 33 b	2522	D-1459	DS Ex-Luftdienst		
Udet U 12	397	D-1460	DVS		Destroyed Feb 30
Udet U 12	398	D-1461	DVS		To Sturmvogel
Focke Wulf GL 22	41	D-1462	DVS/Staaken		Crashed Nov 28
Heinkel HD 30a	288	D-1463	DVS Ex-Luftdienst		
Raab Katzenstein Kl Ic	74	D-1464	Sportflug/Würzburg to Dt.Luftfahrt		Withdrawn Dec 33
Heinkel HD 24b	281	D-1468	DVS		Cancelled Sep 33
Heinkel HD 24b	278	D-1470	DVS		Destroyed Nov 28
Heinkel HD 24b	280	D-1471	DVS		Destroyed Apr 32
Heinkel HE 1	204	D-1474	DVS Ex-Luftdienst		Cancelled Jun 37
Heinkel HD 24b	279	D-1477	DVS		Destroyed Nov 28
Arado SC II	48	D-1478	DVS		Cancelled Jun 37
Klemm L 25	85	D-1481	Deutsche Luftfahrt		To Fhr.v.Hunefeld
Focke Wulf A 17a	51	D-1484	DVS Ex-DLH		Withdrawn Apr 32
Udet U 12	401	D-1486	DVS		
Udet U 12	402	D-1487	DVS		Destroyed May 32
Udet U 12	399	D-1493	DVS Ex-DVL		
Udet U 12	400	D-1494	DVS Ex-DVL		
Alabtros L 75a	10127	D-1495	DVS		
Klemm L 20 B I	104	D-1498	Deutsche Luftfahrt		To R.Klein
Albatros L 75a	10128	D-1499	DVS		Destroyed Mar 32
Junkers W 33 bl	2521	D-1501	DVS		
Udet U 12	404	D-1506	DVS		Destroyed Aug 33
Udet U 12	405	D-1507	DVS		Destroyed May 34

Albatros L 75a	10129	D-1509	DVS		Destroyed Aug 29
Udet U 12	406	D-1512	DVS to Sturmvogel to DVL to DVS	To DLV	
Albatros L 75a	10126	D-1514	DVS		Destroyed Jun 34
Raab Katzenstein RK IIa	78	D-1517	Deutsche Luftfahrt		Destroyed Nov 36
Heinkel HD 24b	282	D-1526	DVS		Destroyed Aug 29
Udet U 12	410	D-1528	DVS		(D-ELEF)
Albatros L 75b	10131	D-1529	DVS		Destroyed Jun 34
Heinkel HD 24b	283	D-1530	DVS		Destroyed Jun 31
Heinkel HD 24b	284	D-1531	DVS		Destroyed Oct 31
Albatros L 75b	10132	D-1532	DVS		Destroyed Jun 34
Albatros L 75b	10133	D-1536	DVS		Destroyed Jun 34
Udet U 12	412	D-1538	DVS		Destroyed Aug 33
Arado SC II	45	D-1542	DVS		
Albatros L 75b	10135	D-1543	DVS		To Flugsicherung
Arado W 2	48	D-1544	DVS/List & Warnemünde		Withdrawn Jun 37
Udet U 12	423	D-1545	DVS		Crashed May 29
Albatros L 77 v	10136	D-1546	DVS Ex-E Stelle Staaken		Withdrawn Oct 31
Albatros L 77 v	10138	D-1548	DVS Ex-E Stelle Staaken		Withdrawn Oct 31
Albatros L 77 v	10139	D-1549	DVS Ex-E Stelle Staaken		Withdrawn Oct 31
Albatros L 75b	10130	D-1550	DVS		Dismantled Apr 31
Albatros L 75b	10141	D-1551	DVS		
Udet U 12	424	D-1554	DVS		
Arado SC II	50	D-1557	DVS		
Heinkel HD 24b	324	D-1558	DVS		Destroyed Oct 31
Klemm L 20 B I	133	D-1559	Deutsche Luftfahrt		To H.Gruse
Udet U 12	425	D-1560	DVS		Destroyed Jun 34
Arado SC II	50	D-1562	DVS		
BFW M 21a	417	D-1566	DVS		Destroyed Sep 33
BFW M 21b	416	D-1568	DVS		To DVL/Adlershof
Albatros L 77 v	304	D-1574	DVS Ex-E Stelle Staaken		Withdrawn Oct 31
Albatros L 75a	10142	D-1584	DVS		
Albatros L 75a	10143	D-1585	DVS		Destroyed Jun 33
DLFW II	5	D-1586	Sportflug/Würzburg to Dt.Luftfahrt		Withdrawn Dec 33
Raab Katzenstein Kl Ic	75	D-1587	DVS		
Junkers W 33 b	2526	D-1590	DVS Ex-DLH		
Albatros L 75a	10144	D-1591	DVS		
Albatros L 75a	10145	D-1593	DVS		Destroyed Jun 30

Dornier Do D Bas	187	D-1597	DVS		Dismantled Sep 31
Dornier Do D Bas	188	D-1598	DVS		Destroyed Oct 33
Albatros L 75a	10146	D-1602	DVS		
Focke Wulf S 24	85	D-1607	DVS		Destroyed Jun 32
Focke Wulf S 24	86	D-1621	Sportflug/Würzburg to Dt.Luftfahrt		Dbf Apr 32
Heinkel HE 9b	325	D-1625	DVS Ex-Heinkel		
Junkers W 33 c	2535	D-1630	DVS Ex-Junkers		
Udet U 12	278a	D-1650	Deutsche Luftfahrt		Destroyed Mar 30
Klemm L 25 Ia	160	D-1654	Dt.Luftfahrt Ex-Fhr.v.Gravenreuth		Destroyed Jan 37
Heinkel HE 10	317	D-1662	DVS		
BFW M 23 b	465	D-1673	DVS		To DVL/Adlershof
Albatros L 75c	10134	D-1680	DVS Ex-DVL		Destroyed Dec 30
Heinkel HE 9c	329	D-1689	DVS		Cancelled Jun 31
Heinkel HE 9c	330	D-1690	DVS		Destroyed Apr 34
Heinkel HE 9c	321	D-1691	DVS to Luftdienst		
Albatros L 82a	10158	D-1704	DVS		To DVL
Albatros L 82b	10162	D-1706	DVS Ex-Albatros		To Ostpr.Flugsport
Klemm L 26	140	D-1715	Deutsche Luftfahrt		To Denmark Jun 31
Junkers W 33 d	2558	D-1732	DVS	(D-OMEN)	
Junkers W 33 d	2559	D-1740	DVS Ex-Luftdienst		
Junkers W 33 d gao d2ao	2562	D-1741	DVS Ex-Luftdienst		
Albatros L 75a	10148	D-1749	DVS		
Rohrbach Ro VIII Roland II	50	D-1756	DVS Ex-DLH	(D-ANAX)	
Focke Wulf A 29b	61	D-1757	DVS Ex-DLH		
Udet U 12	431	D-1759	DVS		Destroyed Mar 30
Udet U 12	437	D-1760	DVS		Destroyed Sep 30
Dornier Do R Superwal R4	190	D-1761	DVS Ex-DLH		Destroyed Jan 37
Udet U 12	427	D-1764	DVS		
Udet U 12	428	D-1765	DVS		Destroyed Jun 34
Udet U 12	429	D-1766	DVS		
BFW M 23a	432	D-1769	Sportflug f.Mittelfr'n u.Oberpfalz Furth	To DLV	
Albatros L 75a	10159	D-1777	DVS	(D-IBOF)	
BFW M 23b	473	D-1780	Sportflug f.Mittelfr'n u.Oberpfalz Furth		Destroyed Feb 32
Heinkel HD 42a	333	D-1793	DVS	(D-IPYL)	

Klemm L 26a II	199	D-1808	Deutsche Luftfahrt		Destroyed Jul 32
Klemm L 26a II	200	D-1809	Deutsche Luftfahrt to DVS		
Klemm L 26a II	202	D-1817	Dt. Luftfahrt to DVS	(D-EJAS)	
Klemm L 26a II	201	D-1825	Deutsche Luftfahrt to DVS		
Klemm L 26a II	207	D-1834	Deutsche Luftfahrt to DVS		
Junkers W 34 f1y	2596	D-1852	DVS Ex-Luftdienst		
Albatros L 82c	10163	D-1878	Deutsche Luftfahrt		To Reklame-Abt.
Albatros L 101	10180	D-1895	DVS	(D-ENIS)	
Arado SSD I	53	D-1905	DVS Ex-Luftdienst		Crashed 33
Junkers W 33 c3eL	2542	D-1925	DVS Ex-Junkers	(D-OVYL)	
Albatros L 82c	10166	D-1926	Deutsche Luftfahrt		Destroyed Jul 31
Albatros L 82c	10167	D-1927	Deutsche Luftfahrt		To Reklame-Abt.
BFW M 20b	443	D-1930	DVS		Crashed Oct 30
Albatros L 82c	10168	D-1932	Deutsche Luftfahrt		To Reklame-Abt.
Albatros L 82c	10169	D-1933	Deutsche Luftfahrt		To Reklame-Abt.
Albatros L 82c	10170	D-1934	Deutsche Luftfahrt		To Reklame-Abt.
Albatros L 82c	10171	D-1935	Deutsche Luftfahrt		To Reklame-Abt.
Albatros L 82c	10172	D-1938	Deutsche Luftfahrt		To Reklame-Abt.
Albatros L 82c	10173	D-1940	Deutsche Luftfahrt		To Reklame-Abt.
Heinkel HE 9d	360	D-1941	DVS		To RDL
Albatros L 82c	10174	D-1945	Deutsche Luftfahrt		To Reklame-Abt.
Albatros L 82c	10175	D-1946	Deutsche Luftfahrt		To Reklame-Abt.
Heinkel HE 9d	361	D-1947	DVS Travemünde Ex-RDL		
Heinkel HE 9d	362	D-1950	DVS		To RDL
Albatros L 82c	10177	D-1951	Deutsche Luftfahrt		To Reklame-Abt.
Albatros L 82c	10176	D-1952	Deutsche Luftfahrt		Destroyed May 33
Albatros L 82c	10178	D-1953	Deutsche Luftfahrt		Destroyed Jun 33
Junkers F 13 he	2058	D-1954	DVS		
Junkers F 13 he	2059	D-1955	DVS		
Junkers W 33 d	2565	D-1956	DVS	(D-ONAP)	
Junkers W 33 f	2578	D-1957	DVS		
Junkers F 13 he	2056	D-1959	DVS to RDL to Flugsich'g to DVS	(D-OHAT)	Cancelled Aug 38
Junkers F 13 ke	2077	D-1961	DVS to RDL to Flugsich'g to DVS	(D-OKEF)	
Heinkel HD 41a	321	D-1964	Deutsche Luftfahrt		Destroyed Sep 31
Heinkel HE 9	103	D-1966	DVS	(D-IXOX)	
Dornier Do S Has	183	D-1967	DVS/List Ex-Test		Accident 35
Klemm L 26 Va	233	D-1969	DVS		

Klemm L 26 Va	234	D-1971	DVS		
Klemm L 26 Va	235	D-1972	DVS		Destroyed Sep 32
Klemm L 26 Va	249	D-1981	DVS		Destroyed Jun 34
Arado SC II	62	D-1984	Deutsche Luftfahrt Ex-DVL		Cancelled Jun 37
Klemm L 26 Va	256	D-1996	DVS		
Focke Wulf A 32	104	D-1997	DVS		Destroyed Jun 34
Albatros L 101	10184	D-2001	DVS		
Albatros L 101	10185	D-2002	DVS		
Heinkel HE 9d	101	D-2003	DVS	(D-IPYV)	
Junkers W 33 f	2579	D-2008	DVS Ex-DLH		
Junkers A 50 ci	3577	D-2010	DVS Ex-DLH		
BFW M 23 b1	538	D-2020	DVS Ex-DVL/Adlershof		
Heinkel HD 42b	372	D-2032	DVS/Braunschweig		
Heinkel HD 42b	373	D-2033	DVS/Braunschweig	(D-IBIV)	
Heinkel HD 42b	374	D-2034	DVS/Braunschweig		Destroyed Aug 33
Heinkel HD 42b	375	D-2035	DVS/Braunschweig		Destroyed Aug 32
Dornier Do J Wal IIb Bos	223	D-2053	DVS	(D-AMAX)	Destroyed Nov 34
Heinkel HD 41	364	D-2064	DVS Ex-E Stelle Staaken	(D-ILEU)	
Heinkel HE 57	343	D-2067	DVS Ex-Heinkel Warnemünde	(D-OJAS)	
Dornier Do J Wal IIa K Bos	185	D-2068	DVS Ex-DLH		Accident Oct 31
Dornier Do J Wal IIa K Bos	210	D-2069	DVS Ex-DLH	(D-ABIR)	
Focke Wulf A 38b	108	D-2073	DVS Ex-DLH		
Arado Ar 64D	70	D-2075	DVS/Schleißheim Ex-E Stelle Staaken		
Focke Wulf A 38b	109	D-2082	DVS Ex-DLH	(D-UPIN)	
Albatros L 78	10151	D-2093	DVS Ex-Albatros		
Albatros L 78	10152	D-2094	DVS Ex-Albatros		
Klemm L 26 a II	273	D-2097	Deutsche Luftfahrt Ex-Klemm		
Albatros L 78	10153	D-2098	DVS Ex-Albatros		Destroyed Apr 34
Albatros L 78	10154	D-2099	DVS		
Focke Wulf A 38b	110	D-2107	DVS Ex-DLH		
Focke Wulf A 32	113	D-2129	DVS		Destroyed Jun 34
Albatros L 78	10188	D-2131	DVS		
Albatros L 78	10189	D-2132	DVS		
Junkers W 33 d	2569	D-2134	DVS		Crashed Jun 34
Junkers W 33 d	2570	D-2135	DVS		

Junkers W 34 f1ao	2712	D-2136	DVS		
Klemm L 25 b VIII	337	D-2137	Deutsche Luftfahrt		
Klemm L 25 b	318	D-2146	Deutsche Luftfahrt		
Klemm L 25 b	319	D-2147	Deutsche Luftfahrt		Cancelled Aug 36
Klemm L 25 b VII	335	D-2148	Deutsche Luftfahrt		
Heinkel HE 9d	383	D-2158	DVS		
Dornier Do J Wal IIc Sas	224	D-2159	DVS	(D-AGUS)	
Klemm L 26 Va	341	D-2160	DVS		
Klemm L 26 Va	342	D-2161	DVS		Destroyed Jan 32
Klemm L 26 Va	343	D-2162	DVS		
Klemm L 26 Va	344	D-2163	DVS		
Klemm L 26 Va	346	D-2165	Deutsche Luftfahrt Ex-DVL		Destroyed Oct 32
Albatros L 78	106	D-2173	DVS		
Albatros L 78	107	D-2174	DVS		
Focke Wulf A 29	114	D-2178	DVS		
Klemm L 26 Va	353	D-2180	DVS Ex-DVL		
Albatros L 75	10191	D-2190	DVS		
Albatros L 75	10192	D-2191	DVS		Destroyed Jun 34
Albatros L 75	10194	D-2193	DVS		Destroyed Jun 32
Albatros L 75	10196	D-2194	DVS		
Albatros L 75	10193	D-2195	DVS Ex-DVL		
Albatros L 75	10195	D-2196	DVS Ex-DVL		
Junkers Ju 52/3mce	4013	D-2201	DVS Ex-DLH	(D-ADOM)	To Flugber.RLM
Junkers Ju 52/3mce	4015	D-2202	DVS Ex-DLH	(D-ADYL)	To Flugber.RLM
Albatros L 75 DSB	10197	D-2205	DVS		
Albatros L 75 DSB	10198	D-2206	DVS		
Albatros L 75 DSB	10199	D-2207	DVS		Destroyed Jun 34
Albatros L 83	10186	D-2111	DVS		
Heinkel He 63A	401	D-2219	DVS	(D-IKIT)	
Heinkel He 5f	116	D-2221	DVS	(D-OLUQ)	
Heinkel He 5f	117	D-2231	DVS	(D-OMIP)	
Heinkel He 5f	119	D-2236	DVS	(D-ODIX)	
Heinkel He 45B	391	D-2238	DVS Ex-Heinkel		
Junkers W 34 f1ue	2714	D-2239	DVS Ex-Luftdienst	(D-ONAZ)	To Hansa Luftbild
Heinkel He 45B	393	D-2245	DVS	(D-IKIX)	
Klemm L 26 Va	395	D-2246	DVS		
Klemm L 26 Va	396	D-2247	DVS		
Heinkel He 45B	394	D-2251	DVS		To E-Stelle Staaken

Albatros L 75 DSB	125	D-2254	DVS		
Heinkel He 64A	404	D-2258	DVS		Crashed Apr 32
BFW M29 a	601	D-2259	DVS		Crashed Aug 32
Heinkel He 64B	409	D-2260	DVS Ex-Aero Club von Deutschland		
Heinkel He 45B	400	D-2262	DVS Ex-E Stelle Staaken	(D-IQAZ)	
Heinkel He 63	402	D-2263	DVS		
Klemm VL26 sf V	397	D-2265	DVS		
Klemm VL26 sf V	398	D-2266	DVS		Destroyed Sep 32
Arado Ar 64D	68	D-2277	DVS Ex-E Stelle Staaken		
Arado Ar 64D	69	D-2278	DVS Ex-E Stelle Staaken		
Arado Ar 64E	72	D-2279	DVS Ex-E Stelle Staaken		
Arado Ar 64E	73	D-2280	DVS Ex-E Stelle Staaken	(D-IPEF)	
Arado Ar 64E	75	D-2281	DVS Ex-E Stelle Staaken		Destroyed Jun 34
Heinkel He 45B	396	D-2287	DVS Ex-Heinkel		
Dornier Do J Wal IId Bis	219	D-2294	DVS		
Heinkel He 64C	426	D-2302	DVS		To Italy Apr 34
Heinkel He 64C	424	D-2304	DVS Ex-Heinkel		
Klemm Kl 32 XIV	403	D-2310	DVS Ex-Aero Club von Deutschland	(D-ERNY)	
Klemm Kl 32 V	405	D-2311	DVS Ex-Aero Club von Deutschland		
Junkers F 13 ke	2068	D-2313	DVS		
Junkers F 13 ke	2076	D-2315	DVS		
Junkers F 13 ko	2079	D-2316	Deutsche Luftfahrt		To Reklame-Abt.
Junkers Ju 52/1mce (K45c)	4004	D-2317	DVS to AB Flygindustri to Luftdienst	(D-UBES)	
Junkers W 33 d	2566	D-2318	DVS Ex-DVL		
Klemm Kl 32 XII	407	D-2328	DVS		
Albatros L 75 DSB	150	D-2331	DVS		
Albatros L 75 DSB	151	D-2332	DVS		
Albatros L 75 DSB	149	D-2337	DVS		
Albatros L 75 DSB	152	D-2342	DVS		
Albatros L 75 DSB	153	D-2343	DVS		Destroyed Dec 32
Heinkel HE 42C	419	D-2346	DVS	(D-IZYS)	
Junkers W 34 fei	2709	D-2350	DVS Ex-Luftdienst		
Heinkel HE 42C	420	D-2351	DVS		Destroyed Aug 33
Heinkel HE 42C	421	D-2353	DVS		Destroyed Jul 34
Heinkel HE 42C	422	D-2354	DVS		Destroyed Jan 34
Arado Ar 64E	82	D-2355	DVS		

DH 82A Tiger Moth	3142	D-2357	DVS	(D-EVYN)	
Heinkel He 45B	398	D-2368	DVS Ex-E Stelle Staaken	(D-IPIM)	
Heinkel He 45B	399	D-2369	DVS Ex-E Stelle Staaken		
Heinkel HE 42C	428	D-2370	DVS	(D-IGUV)	
Albatros L 101c	142	D-2372	DVS		
Albatros L 101c	143	D-2373	DVS	(D-EHEK)	
Albatros L 101c	144	D-2374	DVS		Dbf May 33
Albatros L 101c	145	D-2375	DVS		
Albatros L 101c	146	D-2376	DVS		
Albatros L 101c	147	D-2377	DVS		Destroyed 34
Klemm L 26 Vc	425	D-2381	DVS	(D-ELYP)	
Klemm L 26 Vc	426	D-2382	DVS		Destroyed Aug 33
Klemm L 26 Vc	427	D-2383	DVS		
Klemm L 26 Vc	428	D-2384	DVS		
Klemm L 26 Vc	429	D-2385	DVS		
Klemm L 26 Vc	423	D-2387	DVS		
Klemm L 26 Vc	421	D-2388	DVS		Destroyed Jun 33
Klemm L 26 Vc	380	D-2389	DVS	(D-EJIL)	
Klemm L 26 Vc	422	D-2391	DVS		
Klemm L 26 sfc V	431	D-2401	DVS		Destroyed Apr 34
Klemm L 26 sfc V	432	D-2402	DVS		
Klemm L 26 sfc V	433	D-2403	DVS		
Klemm L 26 sfc V	434	D-2404	DVS		
Klemm L 26 sfc V	435	D-2405	DVS		
Heinkel He 45B	395	D-2406	DVS Ex-E Stelle Staaken	(D-IGUT)	
Heinkel He 45B	397	D-2407	DVS Ex-E Stelle Staaken	(D-ILYM)	
Klemm L 25 VIIc	467	D-2429	Deutsche Luftfahrt		
Klemm L 25 VIIc	468	D-2430	Deutsche Luftfahrt		Destroyed Jul 33
Klemm L 25 VIIc	469	D-2431	Deutsche Luftfahrt		
BFW M 27b	614	D-2461	DVS Ex-DLV	(D-ESYR)	
Albatros L 78	10155	D-2467	DVS		
Arado Ar 64A	65	D-2470	DVS/Schleißheim Ex-Lipetsk		
Albatros L 78	10156	D-2487	DVS		
Dornier Do J Wal IIe Bos	236	D-2488	DVS	(D-AGAF)	
Junkers A 48 fi	3363	D-2532	DVS Ex- Lipetsk	(D-IPOS)	Crashed Jul 35
Heinkel He 42D	443	D-2543	DVS		
Heinkel He 42D	444	D-2544	DVS		
Heinkel He 42D	445	D-2545	DVS		

Heinkel He 42D	446	D-2546	DVS		Destroyed May 34
Heinkel He 42D	447	D-2547	DVS		
Heinkel He 42D	448	D-2548	DVS		Destroyed May 34
Heinkel He 42D	449	D-2549	DVS		
Heinkel He 42D	450	D-2550	DVS		
Heinkel He 42D	451	D-2551	DVS		
Heinkel He 42D	452	D-2552	DVS		
Heinkel He 42D	453	D-2553	DVS		
Heinkel He 42D	455	D-2555	DVS		
Heinkel He 42D	456	D-2556	DVS		
Albatros L 101D	184	D-2576	DVS		
Albatros L 101D	185	D-2577	DVS		
Albatros L 101D	186	D-2578	DVS		
Albatros L 101D	187	D-2579	DVS		
Albatros L 101D	188	D-2580	DVS		
Albatros L 101D	189	D-2581	DVS		Crashed May 34
Albatros L 101D	190	D-2582	DVS		
Albatros L 101D	191	D-2583	DVS		
Albatros L 101D	192	D-2584	DVS		
Klemm Kl 32 XIVa	601	D-2597	DVS		
Klemm Kl 32 XIVa	602	D-2598	DVS		
Klemm Kl 32 XIVa	603	D-2599	DVS		
Focke Wulf Fw 44 V3 b	156	D-2613	DVS	(D-ESYK)	
Focke Wulf Fw 44B	157	D-2614	DVS	(D-ENEF)	
Focke Wulf Fw 44B	158	D-2615	DVS	(D-ELEL)	
Focke Wulf Fw 44B	159	D-2616	DVS		
Focke Wulf Fw 44B	160	D-2617	DVS		
Focke Wulf Fw 44B	161	D-2618	DVS		Destroyed 35
Focke Wulf Fw 44B	162	D-2619	DVS		
Focke Wulf Fw 44B	163	D-2620	DVS	(D-EMEH)	
Focke Wulf Fw 44C	164	D-2621	DVS	(D-EGEF)	
Albatros L 101D	193	D-2651	DVS	(D-EGEK)	
Albatros L 101D	194	D-2652	DVS		Crashed Feb 34
Albatros L 101D	194	D-2653	DVS		
Albatros L 101D	195	D-2654	DVS	(D-ERYN)	
Albatros L 101D	196	D-2655	DVS	(D-EXUK)	
Albatros L 101D	197	D-2656	DVS		
Albatros L 101D	198	D-2657	DVS		

Albatros L 101D	199	D-2658	DVS		
Albatros L 101D	200	D-2659	DVS		
Albatros L 101D	201	D-2660	DVS	(D-EVOV)	
Klemm Kl 32 XIVa	604	D-2671	DVS		
Klemm Kl 32 XIVa	610	D-2677	DVS		
Junkers W 33 he	2752	D-2689	DVS Ex-DLH		
Albatros L 101B	178	D-2705	DVS		
Albatros L 101B	179	D-2706	DVS		
Albatros L 101B	180	D-2707	DVS		
Albatros L 101B	181	D-2708	DVS	(D-IDUQ)	
Albatros L 101B	182	D-2709	DVS	(D-IDEV)	
Albatros L 101D	203	D-2714	DVS		
Albatros L 101D	204	D-2715	DVS		
Albatros L 101D	205	D-2716	DVS		
Albatros L 101D	206	D-2717	DVS		
Albatros L 101D	207	D-2718	DVS	(D-ERUZ)	
Albatros L 101D	208	D-2719	DVS	(D-EHOQ)	
Albatros L 101D	209	D-2720	DVS		
Albatros L 101D	210	D-2721	DVS	(D-EQOH)	
Albatros L 101D	211	D-2722	DVS		
Albatros L 101D	212	D-2723	DVS	(D-EPOZ)	
Albatros L 101D	213	D-2744	DVS		
Albatros L 101D	214	D-2745	DVS		
Albatros L 101D	215	D-2746	DVS	(D-EMAK)	
Albatros L 101D	216	D-2747	DVS		
Albatros L 101D	217	D-2748	DVS	(D-ELOQ)	
Albatros L 101D	218	D-2749	DVS		
Albatros L 101D	219	D-2750	DVS		
Albatros L 101D	220	D-2751	DVS		
Albatros L 101D	221	D-2752	DVS		
Albatros L 101D	222	D-2753	DVS		
Junkers W 33 he	2748	D-2756	DVS	(D-OHIP)	
Junkers W 33 he	2749	D-2757	DVS	(D-OPAZ)	
Junkers W 33 he	2750	D-2758	DVS		
Junkers Ju 52/3m fe	4031	D-2759	DVS		
Heinkel HD 38 c	388	D-2770	Aero Sport		Cancelled Jun 34
Arado Ar 66C	120	D-2777	DVS		
Arado Ar 66C	121	D-2778	DVS		
Arado Ar 66C	122	D-2779	DVS		

Arado Ar 66C	123	D-2780	DVS		
Arado Ar 66C	124	D-2781	DVS		
Arado Ar 66C	125	D-2782	DVS		
Arado Ar 66C	126	D-2783	DVS		
Arado Ar 66C	127	D-2784	DVS		
Arado Ar 66C	128	D-2785	DVS		
Arado Ar 66C	129	D-2786	DVS		
Arado Ar 66C	130	D-2787	DVS	(D-IJER)	
Arado Ar 66C	131	D-2788	DVS		
Arado Ar 66C	132	D-2789	DVS	(D-IMIX)	
Arado Ar 66C	133	D-2790	DVS		
Arado Ar 66C	134	D-2791	DVS		
Arado Ar 66C	135	D-2792	DVS	(D-IZOR)	
Albatros L 101D	223	D-2793	DVS		
Albatros L 101D	224	D-2794	DVS		Destroyed 34
Albatros L 101D	225	D-2795	DVS		Destroyed 34
Albatros L 101D	226	D-2796	DVS		
Albatros L 101D	227	D-2797	DVS		
Albatros L 101D	228	D-2798	DVS		
Arado Ar 64E	83	D-2799	DVS/Schleißheim		
Focke Wulf AL 101D		D-2808	DVS/Cottbus	(D-ETYZ)	
Focke Wulf Fw 44D	266	D-2951	DVS	(D-EXEP)	
Focke Wulf Fw 44D	267	D-2952	DVS		
Focke Wulf Fw 44D	268	D-2953	DVS		
Focke Wulf Fw 44D	269	D-2954	DVS		
Focke Wulf Fw 44D	270	D-2955	DVS		
Junkers Ju 52/3m f1e	4033	D-3012	DVS Ex-DLH	(D-AFYS)	To DVL
Junkers W 33 he	2753	D-3013	DVS		
Junkers W 33 he	2754	D-3014	DVS		
Junkers W 33 b	2510	D-3016	DVS		
Dornier Do J Wal IId Bis	248	D-3019	DVS Ex-E Stelle Travemünde	(D-ABER)	
Dornier Do J Wal IId Bis	296	D-3024	DVS	(D-ADOR)	
Junkers W 34 d2i	2568	D-3046	DVS		
Junkers W 33 he		D-3054	DVS		
Albatros L 101D	281	D-3122	DVS		
Albatros L 101D	282	D-3126	DVS	(D-EQIS)	
Albatros L 101D	283	D-3130	DVS		

Albatros L 101D	284	D-3135	DVS	(D-EZAZ)	
Albatros L 101D	285	D-3139	DVS		
Albatros L 101D	286	D-3143	DVS		
Junkers W 33 he	2758	D-3145	DVS		
Albatros L 101D	287	D-3147	DVS	(D-EVYK)	
Albatros L 101D	288	D-3152	DVS	(D-EXUH)	
Junkers W 33 he	2760	D-3154	DVS		
Focke Wulf Fw 44D	338	D-3155	DVS	(D-ETIK)	
Albatros L 101D	289	D-3157	DVS		
Focke Wulf Fw 44D	339	D-3163	DVS	(D-EPYL)	
Albatros L 101D	291	D-3166	DVS		
Albatros L 101D	292	D-3169	DVS	(D-EVYZ)	
Albatros L 101D	293	D-3172	DVS		
Focke Wulf Fw 44E	340	D-3174	DVS		
Albatros L 101D	294	D-3176	DVS		
Albatros L 101D	295	D-3180	DVS		
Focke Wulf Fw 44E	345	D-3196	DVS		
Focke Wulf Fw 44E	347	D-3205	DVS		
Focke Wulf Fw 44E	348	D-3209	DVS		
Focke Wulf Fw 44E	349	D-3213	DVS		
Focke Wulf Fw 44E	350	D-3217	DVS		
Junkers W 33 he	2767	D-3329	DVS		
Heinkel He 72D		D-3331	DVS		
Junkers W 33 he	2768	D-3333	DVS		
Junkers W 34	2766	D-3342	DVS Ex-Luftdienst	(D-UBAS)	To Eurasia
BFW M 23b	626	D-3420	DVS		

Appendix F

Aircraft Registered to Severa, DLH Küstenabteilung & Luftdienst

LVG C VI	5071	D-35	Severa Ex-DLR		To DLH
Friedrichshafen FF 49C		D-40	Severa		
Friedrichshafen FF 49C		D-45	Severa Ex-DAL		
Friedrichshafen FF 49C		D-47	Severa		
Friedrichshafen FF 71a	1365	D-49	Severa Ex-DAL		Cancelled Nov 33
Friedrichshafen FF 49C	1368	D-85	Severa Ex-Aerosport		
Friedrichshafen FF 49C	223	D-86	Severa Ex-Sabltanig LV		
Junkers F 13 f1e	717	D-354	Severa Ex-Bayerische LV		To DVS
Junkers A 20/A 35	1038	D-510	Severa		To DVS
Junkers A 35	1044	D-826	Severa to Luftdienst		
Caspar S 1	5010	D-830	Severa to Luftdienst		To DVS
Junkers F 13 f1e	799	D-833	Severa to Luftdienst		To DVS
Junkers F 13 d1e	789	D-837	Severa		
Heinkel HE 5a	247	D-937	Severa		
Heinkel HE 1	205	D-938	Severa to Luftdienst		Destroyed Apr 30
Heinkel HE 1	207	D-939	Severa to Luftdienst		To DVS
Heinkel HE 1	208	D-945	Severa to Luftdienst		Destroyed Sep 29
Junkers G 24 ge	922	D-954	Severa to Luftdienst		To DVS
Heinkel HE 1	203	D-1045	Severa to Luftdienst		Withdrawn Oct 33
Heinkel HE 1	206	D-1046	Severa		
Heinkel HE 1	211	D-1047	Severa to Luftdienst		Withdrawn Oct 33
Junkers A 35	1069	D-1058	Severa		Crashed Sep 28
Junkers W 33 bi	2501	D-1064	Severa to Luftdienst		To DVS
Dornier Do R Superwal R2	118	D-1115	Severa		To DVS
Heinkel Heinkel HE 1	202	D-1134	Severa		To DVS
Heinkel HE 1	209	D-1199	Severa to Luftdienst		
Junkers G 24 hle	923	D-1230	Severa		To Sweden
Heinkel HD 15	265	D-1237	Severa		To E-St.Trave'de
Junkers W 33 b	2508	D-1248	Severa to Luftdienst		To DVS
Rohrbach Ro V	26	D-1261	Severa		Withdrawn Jan 32

Heinkel HE 1	210	D-1282	Severa		Destroyed Apr 29
Junkers F 13 h1e	2015	D-1378	Severa to Luftdienst		To DVS
Junkers F 13 f1e	2016	D-1382	Severa to Luftdienst		To DVL
Junkers W 33	2515	D-1383	Severa		Crashed Dec 28
Junkers W 33 b1	2517	D-1384	Severa to Luftdienst to DVL to Luftdienst To DVS		
Dornier Do R Superwal R2	148	D-1385	Severa		Cancelled Nov 36
Junkers W 33 b	2519	D-1423	Severa to Luftdienst	(D-OJEH)	To Sweden
Junkers W 33 b	2021	D-1424	Severa to Luftdienst to DVS to Luftdienst		
Junkers W 33 b	2522	D-1459	Severa to Luftdienst		To DVS
Heinkel HD 30a	288	D-1463	Luftdienst ex-DVL		To DVS
Heinkel HE 1	204	D-1474	Severa to Luftdienst		To DVS
Heinkel HE 5e	302	D-1511	Severa		To DVL
Heinkel HE 31	310	D-1522	Severa		To DVL
Udet U 12	426	D-1582	(Severa)		To DVL
BFW M 23 b	462	D-1670	Luftdienst Ex-Eli Beinhorn		To H.Müller
Heinkel HE 9c	321	D-1691	Luftdienst Ex-DVS		
Klemm L 25 Ia	173	D-1713	Luftdienst Ex-Siebel		Destroyed Feb 32
Junkers W 33 d	2559	D-1740	Luftdienst Ex-DVL		To DVS
Junkers W 33 d gao d2ao	2562	D-1741	Luftdienst Ex-Junkers		To DVS
Junkers W 34 f1y	2596	D-1852	Luftdienst		To DVS
Klemm L 25e	242	D-1901	Luftdienst		
Arado SSD I	53	D-1905	Luftdienst		To DVS
Junkers Ju 52/1do	4001	D-1974	Luftdienst Ex-Air Express	(D-UZYP)	
Heinkel HE 9d	382	D-2095	Luftdienst	(D-IXAV)	
Junkers W 34 f1ue	2714	D-2239	Luftdienst		To DVS
Heinkel HE 30b	405	D-2267	Luftdienst	(D-IKIK)	
Klemm Kl 32 V	406	D-2312	Luftdienst	(D-EKIQ)	
Junkers Ju 52/1mce (K45c)	4004	D-2317	Luftdienst Ex-DVS	(D-UBES)	
Junkers W 34 fei	2709	D-2350	Luftdienst		To DVS
Junkers W 34	2766	D-3342	Luftdienst Ex-DLH		To DVS

Appendix G

Reichswehr Personnel known to have Trained at the DVS

1925 -34

1. REICHSHEER PERSONNEL – ZWEIGSTELLE UNKNOWN

Kurt-Eckhard von Allolio Apr 28 – Mar 29	Walter Oesau (FF) 34 –
Axel von Blomberg Apr 27 – Mar 28	Robert Olejnik (FF) Oct 33 –
Hans-Jochen Dahms	Hans-Joachim Osterroht Apr 28 – Mar 29
Friedrich Dreyer (FF) Jul 27 – Mar 28	Edgar Petersen (FF) Aug 26 – 27
Jobst-Heinrich von Heydebreck (FF) Apr 28 – Mar 29	D.Gf .v.Pfeil u.Klein-E'guth (FF) Apr 27 – Mar 28
Karl-Heinrich Heyse (FF) Apr 27 – Mar 28	Sigmund Frhr.von Rotberg Apr 31 – Mar 32
Claus Hinkelbein (FF) Apr 29 – Mar 30	Walter Rubensdörffer (FF) Apr 28 – Mar 32
Walter Kienitz (FF)	Fritz Schaffer Nov 29 – Jan 34
Hans-Günther von Kornatzki (FF) Apr 27 – Mar 28	Wolfgang Schellmann (FF) Apr 30 – Sep 31
Hubert Kroeck (FF) Apr 32 - Mar 33	Hermann Schubert Jul 30 – 32
Siegfried Mahrenholtz (FF) Apr 27 – Apr 29	Otto Stams (FF) Jan 27 –
Günther Maltzahn (FF) Apr 30 – Mar 31	Klaus Uebe (FF/BO) Jun 31 – Sep 32
Otto-Harald Mors (FF) Apr 31 – Mar 32	J-F.Graf Vitzthum von Eckstadt Apr 30 – Sep 31

2. REICHSMARINE PERSONNEL – ZWEIGSTELLE UNKNOWN

Helmuth Bode	Gerd Stein (FF) Oct 27 – Mar 28
Bernhard Jope	Otto-Friedrich Werner Apr 30 – Mar 31
Martin Mettig (FF) Aug – Dec 27	

3. DVS ZWEIGSTELLE BERLIN-STAAKEN
Maj.a.D.Alfred Keller 1 May 25 – 28

Edmund Daser (FF)	Gerhard Ulbricht (FF) Oct 25 – Sep 26
Oskar Dinort (FF) Feb – Jun 27	

4. DVS ZWEIGSTELLE BRAUNSCHWEIG
Maj.a.D.Alfred Keller 28 – 31 Dec 33

Friedrich Alberti (BO) Mar – Sep 34	Ortwin Giesse (FF/BO) 31- 33
Kurt-Ekhard Allolio (FF) Nov 33 – Mar 34	Robert-Heinrich von Groddeck 31

Georg-Fridrich Altvater 31

von Alvensleben 31

Hans-Jurgen Aschmann 31

Franz von Benda Mar – Oct 34

Bisle 31

Carganico 31

von Cohenhausen 31

Max Collmann

Hans-Jochen Dahms 31

Edmund Daser (FF)

Ulrich Diesing (FF) Apr 31 – Sep 32

Oskar Dinort (FF) Sep 27 – May 28

Franz-Dietrich von Ditfurth 31

Heinrich Eichhorn (BO) Dec 34 – Jun 35

Johannes Fink (FF) Oct 33 – Mar 34

Adolf Galland (FF)

D.Heisterman zon Ziehlberg (FF) Oct 33-Mar 34

Karl-Heinrich Heyse (FF) Nov 33 – Feb 34

Wolfdietrich von Houwald 31

Walter Kienzle 31

Peter Kogl (FF)

Krohmann 31

Arthur Menke (BO) Apr 32 – Jun 33

von Neumann 31

Günther Radusch 31

Ralph von Rettberg 31

Riedinger 31

Heinrich Schlosser (FF) 31 - 32

Hermann Schmidt (FF) Apr 31 –

Otto Weiss (FF) Mar – Jun 33 & Jun – Sep 34

Joachim Willigmann 31

5. DVS ZWEIGSTELLE SCHLEISSHEIM
Hptm.a.D.Albert Vierling 1 Apr 27 – 31 Dec 33

Nicolaus von Below (FF) Apr 28 – May 29

Rudolf Braun (FF) Sep 34 –

Bernd von Brauchitsch (FF) Apr 31 -

Hans Busolt (FF) Mar 29 – Mar 30

Edmund Daser (FF)

Fritz Doench (FF) Oct 30 –Sep 31

Heinrich Eichhorn (FF) Dec 33 – Jan 34

Siegfried von Eschwege (FF) Apr 27 – Mar 28

Wolfgang Falck (FF) Apr 31 - & 33

Waldemar von Glassow (FF) 31 –

Ernst Hechler (FF) May 28 –

D.Heistermann zon Ziehlberg (FF) Apr 28 – Mar 29

Karl Hentschel (FF) Jun 28 – Sep 34 & Oct 34

Hubertus Hitschold (FF) Oct 31 –

Lothar von Janson (FF) Apr 31 -

Peter Kogl (FF) Dec 33 -

Siegfried Lehmann (FF) Apr 28 –

Günther Lützow (FF) Apr 31 – Feb 32

Rudolf Mayr (FF) Oct 31 – 33

Otto-Harald Mors (FF) Apr 31 -

Rudolf Frhr von Moreau (FF)

Otto Pilger (FF) Apr 28 – Mar 29

Helmut Pohle (FF) Oct 30 – Feb 33

von Rotberg (FF) Apr 31 -

Gerhard Schieckel (FF) Apr 31 -

Heinrich Schlosser (FF) 31 -

Hermann Schmidt (FF)

Hans-Hermann Schroth (FF) Apr 30 –

Heinrich Seeliger (FF) Apr – Jun 34

Erich von Selle (FF) Apr 29 – Mar 30

Henning Strumpell (FF) 34 –

Botho von Stuckrad (FF) Apr 30 – Mar 31

Hannes Trautloft (FF) Apr 31 – Oct 32

H.Frhr.v.Treusch v.Buttlar (FF) Apr 30 – Mar 32

Walther Wadehn Sep – Oct 34

Otto Winterer (FF) Apr 29 – Mar 30

6. DVS ZWEIGSTELLE WARNEMÜNDE

KorvKpt.a.D.Konrad Goltz 1 Juan 27 – 31 Dec 29

Maj.Hermann Becker 1 Jan 30 – 31 Jul 34

Obstlt.Joachim Coeler 1 Aug 34 – 30 Sep 34

Wolfgang Buhring (BO) Oct 33 – Oct 34	Hermann Schmidt (FF)
Hans-Armin Czech (FF) May 29 –	Wilhelm Schmitter (BM) Dec 34 – Sep 35
Waldemar von Glassow (FF)	Wilhelm Schwengers (FF) Apr 28 – Mar 29
Eugen Gries May 34 –	Heinrich Seeliger (FF) Oct 33 – Mar 34
Ernst Hechler (FF) – Mar 29	Gerd Stein (FF) Oct 33– Oct 34
Arno Kleyenstuber Apr 30 – Mar 31	Walter Storp (FF) 33-34
Werner Klumper 31 – Mar 32	Walter Weygoldt (FF/BO) Oct 30 – Sep 32
Hans Kriependorf (FF) Apr 29 – Mar 30	Lienhart Wiesand (BO) Apr 29 – Mar 30
Karl-Hermann Lion (FF) May 34 – 35	Günther Zetzsche (FF) Apr 30 – Mar 31
Helmut Mahlke Apr – Aug 32 & May 35 – Mar 36	

7. DVS ZWEIGSTELLE LIST later TRAVEMÜNDE

KorvKpt.Heinz Scheurlen 1 Mar 27 – 30 Sep 34

Waldemar von Glassow (FF)	Gerd Müller-Trimbusch (FF) – Oct 36
Wilhelm Kern (FF) Jan - Mar 35	Wilhelm Schwengers (FF) – Apr 35

8. DVS ZWEIGSTELLE COTTBUS

Maj.Oskar Frhr.von Boenigk 1 Jul 34 – 21 Sep 34

Obstlt.Otto Dessloch 1 Dec 33 – 31 Mar 35

Heinz Cramer (FF) 34 –	Henning Strumpell (FF) 32 - 34
Hans Keppler (FF) 34 – Mar 35	Joachim Poetter Mar 34 --
Arthur Menke Jun – Sep 31	Hans Sauer – Jul 34
Werner Molders (FF) Feb – Dec 34	

9. DVS ZWEIGSTELLE STETTIN

Georg Pasewaldt 1 Jul 34 – 36

Gerhard Gieke (FF) Jun 35 – Oct 36	Johannes Polzin Apr 35 – Oct 36
Peter Kogl (FF)	

Appendix H

Reichswehr Staffs and Facilities in the Soviet Union

1921-33

---

1. SONDERGRUPPE R (RUSSLAND)

Gruppenleiter
Obst.Walter Nicolai 21 -24
Maj.Herbert Fischer (Frank) 24-28

Offiziere
Maj.a.D.Dr.Oskar Ritter von Niedermayer (Neumann)
Maj.Friedrich Tschunke (Teichmann)
Obstlt.a.D.Wilhelm Schubert – Firma Junkers

---

2. ZENTRALE MOSKAU (Z.MO.)

Gruppenleiter
Obst.Hermann von der Lieth-Thomsen 23-28
Maj.a.D.Dr.Oskar Ritter von Niedermayer 28-31
Maj.a.D.Lothar Schuttel 31-33

Adjutant
Oblt.a.D.Hans-Joachim Rath

Offiziere
Hptm.Alfred Gerstenberg 26-32

---

3. GESELLSCHAFT FÜR FORDERUNG GEWERBLICHER UNTERNEHMUNGEN GmbH (Gefu)
Moskau, Khlebny pereulok, 28

Maj.Friedrich Tschunke (Chairman)
Direktor T.Eckhardt
Obstlt.Wolfgang Mentzel (Chair of Supervisory Council)

Gefu was established in 1921 to support the development of a Soviet armaments industry whilst providing the *Reichswehr* with an opportunity to continue with weapons developments that had been banned within Germany. *Gefu* was financed to the tune of 75 m Goldmark ($18 m). The main areas of activity were the *Junkerswerk* airframe and aero-engine factory at Fili, the *Bersol AG* chemical factory near Ivashchenkovo/Samara which produced *Bersol, Phosgen* and *Lost* (explosives and poison gases), assistance by *Krupp* in the manufacture of artillery ammunition at Zlatoust, Tula, Petrograd & Petrokrepost.

415

4. JUNKERSWERK FILI

Junkers financed the establishment of a manufacturing facility at Fili nr.Moscow in 1923. The *Direktor* was *Obstlt.a.D.*Wilhelm Schubert, *Techn.Leiter* was Hans Hackmack and the *Flugleiter* was Kurt Bauerhin, later Reinhold Poss. *Junkers* withdrew from the enterprise in 1927.

5. GRUPPEN SCHROEDER & FIEBIG

In response to Soviet requests for military and technical assistance for the emergent *RKK-VVS* a small number of experienced ex-*Luftstreitkräfte* officers were contracted to work in the USSR between Aug 24 –Apr 26. These included J.Schroeder, *Hptm.*Martin Fiebig, *Lt.*H.Johannesson, Rudolf Hasenohr, Droste and *Oblt.a.D.*Hans Joachim Rath.

6. FLUGZENTRUM LIPETSK
15 Apr 1925 – 15 Sep 1933

Initially the *Flugzentrum* operated as a *Fliegerschule* for advanced flying training and refresher training for selected *Reichsheer offiziere*. In 1925 there were only 7 German and c.20 Soviet personnel but the total quickly rose to c.200. With the beginning of flight testing in 1930 more officers and technicians were deployed so that by 1932 there were 43 Germans, 26 Soviet pilots and 234 Soviet workers and technicians at the base.

Leiter der Fliegerschule

Maj.a.D.Walter Stahr Jun 25 – 1 Dec 29
Maj.Max Mohr 1 Dec 29 – 28 Feb 32 ?
Hptm.Gottlob Müller 1 Feb 32 ? – 30 Sep 33

The *Fliegerschule* consisted of a *Jagdfliegerlehrgang* and a *Beobachterlehrgang*. *Oblt.a.D.* Carl August von Schoenebeck, was *Leiter d.Jagdfliegerlehrgang* until Dec 31, whilst *Jagdlehrer* included *Oblt.a.D.*Werner Junck until 1927 and possibly *Oblt.a.D.* Ernst Bormann until Sep 30. Thereafter selected Lipetsk graduates returned as *Hilfslehrer* including Edgar Petersen from Jun 29, Hans-Jurgen von Cramon-Taubadel in 1931, Max Ibel in 32-33 & Johannes Janke. Other instructional personnel included *Oblt.*Heinrich Aschenbrenner (Wireless Oct 26-Sep 29) & *Lt.*H.Johannesson (Photography 25-30), and may have included *Hptm.a.D.*Ulrich Buchholz, *Hptm.*Otto Dessloch, *Maj.a.D.*Erich Quade & *Hptm.a.D.*Georg Rieke. *Technischer-Leiter* was Gottfried Reidenbach (Apr 27-Sep 32).

7. PANZERSCHULE KASAN (KAMA)
2 Oct 26 – 20 Jul 33

The *Panzerschule* consisted of a *Lehrgang, Versuchsabteilung, Technische Abteilung* & a *Buchhaltung*. Successive *Direktors* were *Obstlt.a.D.*Mahlbrand (29/30 - *Markart*), *Obst.*Ludwig Ritter von Radlmaier (30/31 - *Raabe*) and *Maj.*Josef Harpe (31/33 - *Hacker*). The *Lehrgang* provided seconded personnel with opportunities to conduct live artillery shoots, weapons training, tactical communications and cross-country driving.

8. VERSUCHSPLATZ PODOSINKI

A German *Versuchsgruppe* (*Gruppe Amberg*) conducted joint German-Soviet aero-chemical tests at Podosinki, nr.Moscow from Sep 26. *Leiter* was Hans Hackmack (*Amberg*). These followed earlier experiments at the Kurische Nehrung in Ostpreussen using agricultural chemicals and Junkers F 13 and W 33 aircraft. Trials in the USSR included the use of Typ G-125 Kampfstoffbehalter (toxic chemical containers) using a Junkers F 13 and A 20 aircraft.

9. GASTESTGELANDE BEI VOLSK (TOMKA)
1928 – 15 Aug 33

Following the destruction by fire of the Podosinki testing station in winter 26/27 a new chemical warfare testing facility was established near Prichernavaskaya, nr Saratov under the leadership of *Obst.a.D.*Wilhelm Trepper, later *Dr-Ing.*Leopold von Sicherer an expert chemist. By 1929 there were 33 Germans in residence, for the most part chemists. Aircraft were again provided to test the aerial application of poison gases.

Appendix I

Lipetsk Graduates

1926-1933

Name	Date	Name	Date
Aschmann, Hans-Jurgen	31	Kusserow, Ernst	32
Below, Nicolaus von	May 29 – Sep 29	Lehmann, Siegfried	-Sep 29
Berchtenbreiter, Anton	29-32	Leonhardy, Kurt	Oct 32 – Jun 33
Biwer, Franz	Oct 27 – Sep 28	Loytved-Hardegg, Rudolf	Oct 32 – May 33
Blomberg, Alexander von		Lützow, Günther	May 32 – Sep 32
Boenicke, Walter	Nov 28 – Apr 31	Macht, Theodor	May 30 – Sep 30
Boner, Alfred (BO)	Nov 28	Mahrenholtz, Siegfried	May 29 – Oct 30
Brustellin, Hans-Heinrich	32	Meister, Rudolf	Mar 28 – May 31
		Moricke, Friedrich	Jun 31 – Oct 32
Deichmann, Paul		Müller, Gottlob	Apr 28 – Aug 29
Dessloch, Otto	Apr 26 – Feb 27	Nielsen, Andreas	Apr 28 – Sep 29
Dinort, Oskar	May 28 – Sep 28	Pape, Horst	Apr 30 –
Doench, Fritz (BO)	Nov 29 – Sep 30	Pasquay, Frithjof	Oct 32 – May 33
Dreyer, Friedrich	May 29 – Oct 30	Pflugbeil, Curt	Apr 28 -
Georg-Hermann Edert	30 ?		
Elsa, Eberhard Trutzschler d'	- Aug 33	Pitcairn, Douglas	- Sep 33
Falck, Wolfgang	31	Ploch, August	- 32
Fischer, Eberhard	Apr 28 – Nov 29	Plocher, Hermann	May 28 – Apr 30
Fütterer, Kuno Heribert (BO?)	Prager, Friedrich	Oct 32 – May 33	
Johannes Gentzen	32		
Gerlach, Karl von (BO)	30	Printz, Hasso von	32
Greiff, Kurt von	Apr 29 – Sep 29	Quade, Erich	Oct 27 – Sep 27
Heidemeyer, Hans	Nov 29 – Apr 31	Radusch, Günther	31
Heistermann v.Ziehlberg D.	May 29 – Sep 29		
Herhudt v.Rohden, Hans-D	- Jan 31	Rettberg, Ralph von	31
Hessel, Friedrich	Nov 29 – Jan 33	Rieke, Georg	Aug 29 –
		Rodig	32
Hill, Walter	May 30 – Sep 30	Rubensdörffer, Walter	Apr 32 – Oct 32
Hitschold, Hubertus	32	Schenk zu Schweinsberg, G	Oct 32 – May 33
Hoffmann, Helmuth von	May 30 – Sep 30	Schimpf, Richard (BO)	- Sep 30
Holle, Alexander	Mar 28 – Oct 29	Schroth, Hans-Hermann	- Sep 31

Houwald, Otto-Friedrich		Schubert, Hermann	32
Houwald, Wolfdietrich von	31	Schulz-Heyn, Bruno	
Ibel, Max	Aug 28 – Oct 31	Seidemann, Hans	Apr 28 – Oct 29
Janson, Lothar von		Seywald, Heinrich	Nov 28 – Mar 30
Johannsen	32		
Jordan, Otto	Nov 28 – Apr 30	Speidel, Wilhelm (BO)	Apr 28–Jan 29 & 31-33
Kammhuber, Josef	30 -31	Sperrle, Hugo (BO)	28
Kienzle, Walter	31	Sturm, Alfred	Nov 28 – Jul 30
Kleinrath, Kurt (BO)	Apr 28 – Nov 28	Tamm, Reinhold	Jun 31 – Sep 32
Kless, Maximilian	Feb 33 – Sep 33	Trautloft, Hannes	32
Kleye, Otto	Oct 32 – May 33	Trettner, Heinrich	Oct 32 -
Klitzing, Heinrich von	Oct 32 – May 33	Tschoeltsch, Ehrenfried	May 28 – Oct 28
Knust, Friedrich-Karl	Mar 28 –	Veith, Karl	Apr 28 – Oct 29
Koppelow, Hans von	- 33	Wechmar, Karl Frhr.von	
Korten, Günther		Wilke, Karl-Eduard	Mar 28 – Sep 29
Krafft von Del., Erhart	Jun 31 – Oct 32	Winterer, Otto	May 30 – Sep 30
Krahl, Werner		Witt, Hans-Hugo	Apr 28 – Oct 29
Kreipe, Werner			

Appendix J

Reichsheer Geheime Fliegerliste

1 NOVEMBER 1930

GenMaj.Hilmar Ritter von Mittelberger	01.03.30 (1)	RWM
GenMaj.Alfred Streccius	01.02.30 (1)	Inf.Rgt.17
Obst.Helmuth Wilberg	01.10.29 (13)	Kdtr.Breslau
Obstlt.Hermann Hoth	01.02.29 (26)	Stab Gr.Kdo.1
Obstlt.Erich Quade	01.04.30 (9)	Inf.Rgt.2
Obstlt.Karl-Friedrich Schweickhard	01.11.30 (16)	Inf.Rgt.14
Maj.Waldemar Klepke	01.07.26 (4)	Inf.Rgt.15
Maj.Hugo Sperrle	01.10.26 (7)	Inf.Rgt.8
Maj.Hellmuth Felmy	01.01.27 (7)	RWM
Maj.Max Mohr	01.02.27 (26)	Reiter Rgt.18
Maj.Bernhard Kühl	01.04.27 (6)	Inf.Rgt.1
Maj.Egloff Frhr.von Freyberg-Allmendingen	01.05.27 (4)	Kdtr.Döberitz
Maj.Holdermann	01.02.28 (8)	Inf.Rgt.2
Maj.Ulrich Grauert	01.02.28 (23a)	RWM
Maj.Hellmuth Volkmann	01.02.28 (28b)	Art.Fhr.II
Maj.Wilhelm Wimmer	01.02.28 (38a)	RWM
Maj.Hellmuth Bieneck	01.04.29 (3)	Reiter Rgt.14
Maj.Gebhard von Kotze	01.11.29	Inf.Schule
Maj.Kurt Student	01.01.30 (1)	Inf.Rgt.2
Maj.Theodor Schubert	01.02.30	Reiter Rgt.8
Maj.Friedrich Cranz	01.04.30 (11)	Reiter Rgt.14
Maj.Waldemar Reinecke	vorl.Pat.	RWM
Hptm.Victor Krocker	16.09.17 (2)	Kdtr.Breslau
Hptm.Egon Doerstling	20.06.18 (5)	Inf.Rgt.10
Hptm.Erdmann	15.07.18 (14)	Nachr.Abt.6
Hptm.Eduard Seldner	18.08.18 (8)	RWM

Rittm.Curt Pflugbeil	18.08.18 (25)	Reiter Rgt.11
Hptm.Erich Koch	18.10.18 (5)	Inf.Rgt.18
Rittm.Walter Somme	18.10.18 (6)	Reiter Rgt.7
Rittm.Otto Dessloch	18.10.18 (45)	Reiter Rgt.17
Hptm.Hartmann	01.12.21 (1)	Art.Rgt.4
Hptm.Feorg Behrla	01.01.22 (9)	Stab Gr.Kdo.2
Rittm.Hermann ? Martini	01.06.22 (3)	Kav.Schule
Hptm.Richard Putzier	01.06.22 (7)	Art.Rgt.2
Rittm.Karl Barlen	01.10.22 (2)	Reiter Rgt.18
Rittm.Maximilian Kieffer	01.12.22 (10)	Fahr.Abt.7
Hptm.Kurt Müller	01.01.23 (1)	RWM
Rittm.Angelo Müller	01.02.23 (7)	Fahr.Abt.7
Hptm.Hans-Eberhard Gandert	01.08.23 (1)	Inf.Rgt.1
Hptm.Heinrich Lorenz	01.11.23 (4)	Inf.Rgt.17
Hptm.Philipp Zoch	01.12.23 (2)	Kdtr.Döberitz
Hptm.Friedrich-Carl Hanesse	01.01.24 (5)	Art.Rgt.1
Rittm.Heinz-Hellmuth von Wuhlisch	01.02.24 (2)	Reiter Rgt.5
Hptm.Maximilian Ritter von Pohl	01.06.24 (12)	Art.Rgt.5
Rittm.Paul Schultheiss	01.11.24 (5)	Reiter Rgt.3
Hptm.Erhard Krüger	01.11.24 (6)	Inf.Rgt.1
Hptm.Ludwig Keiper	01.11.24 (8)	Inf.Rgt.16
Rittm.Dipl.Ing.Josef Hilgers	01.02.25 (17)	Fahr.Abt.2
Rittm.Joachim Sperling	01.02.25 (18)	Fahr.Abt.5
Hptm.Wolf Frhr.von Biedermann	01.02.25 (19)	Inf.Rgt.10
Hptm.von Harbou	01.04.25 (10)	Inf.Rgt.2
Hptm.Baumbach	01.05.25 (2)	Art.Rgt.2
Rittm.Ernst Bonatz	01.02.26 (10)	Reiter Rgt.7
Hptm.Fritz Lob	01.02.26 (33)	Pion.Btl.6
Hptm.Alfred Sturm	01.03.26 (7)	Inf.Rgt.8
Hptm.Schlager	01.04.26 (11)	Art.Rgt.6
Hptm.Wilhelm Speidel	01.04.26 (18)	RWM
Hptm.Karl Drum	01.04.26 (19)	RWM
Rittm.Günther Schroth	01.02.27 (8)	Reiter Rgt.11
Hptm.Josef Mai	01.02.27 (28)	Kraftfahr.Abt.5
Rittm.Franz Biwer	01.04.27 (7)	Reiter Rgt.16
Hptm.Eberhard Fischer	01.02.28 (32)	Inf.Rgt.2
Hptm.Heinz Funcke	01.02.28 (33)	Inf.Rgt.18

Hptm.Johannes Fink	01.02.28 (43)	Reiter Rgt.1
Hptm.Karl Veith	01.02.28 (50)	Art.Rgt.7
Hptm.Walter Schwabedissen	01.03.28 (2)	RWM
Hptm.Friedel	01.03.28 (4)	Inf.Rgt.15
Hptm.Dipl.Ing.Eduard Riesch	01.04.28 (14)	RWM
Hptm.Ehrenfried Tschoeltsch	01.04.28 (15)	Inf.Rgt.10
Hptm.Dipl.Ing.August Ploch	01.04.28 (31)	RWM
Hptm.Heinrich Seywald	01.04.28 (43)	Kraftfahr.Abt.4
Hptm.Gottlob Müller	01.05.28 (5a)	Kraftfahr.Abt.7
Rittm.Wolfgang von Chamier-Glisczinski	01.01.29 (1a)	Reiter Rgt.16
Hptm.Kuno Heribert Futterer	01.01.29 (2a)	Inf.Rgt.17
Hptm.Rudiger von Heyking	01.01.29 (5)	Stab 4.Div.
Rittm.Herbert Pfeiffer	01.02.29 (24a)	Fahr.Abt.6
Hptm.Otto Abernetty	01.02.29 (33a)	Inf.Rgt.5
Hptm.Xaver Sattler	01.02.29 (35)	Kdtr.Küstrin
Hptm.Stapelberg	01.02.29 (40a)	Inf.Rgt.15
Hptm.Ulrich Buchholz	01.02.29 (42)	Inf.Rgt.8
Hptm.Wolfram Frhr.von Richthofen	01.02.29 (43)	Art.Rgt.5
Hptm.Robert Pistorius	01.04.29 (9a)	Pion.Btl.2
Rittm.Karl von Gerlach	01.04.29 (12)	Reiter Rgt.11
Hptm.Kurt Malzer	01.07.29 (1)	Art.Rgt.4
Hptm.Georg Rieke	31.07.29 (Char)	Inf.Rgt.16
Rittm.Plaschke	01.10.29 (14a)	Reiter Rgt.3
Hptm.Gerhard Conrad	01.02.30 (17)	Inf.Rgt.6
Hptm.Robert Fuchs	01.02.30 (22)	Kdtr.Berlin
Hptm.Heinrich Aschenbrenner	01.02.30 (32)	Kdtr.Küstrin
Hptm.Eberhard Baier	01.02.30	Art.Rgt.3
Hptm.Georg Weiner	01.02.30 (39)	Kraftfahr.Abt.2
Hptm.Günther Lohmann	01.04.30 (5)	Art.Rgt.1
Rittm.Gaze	01.04.30 (13)	Reiter Rgt.8
Oblt.Kurt Berger	01.04.25 (175)	Inf.Rgt.4
Oblt.Josef Kammhuber	01.04.25 (180)	RWM
Oblt.Gerd von Massow	01.04.25	Inf.Rgt.9
Oblt.Fritz Reinshagen	01.04.25 (218)	Inf.Rgt.5
Oblt.Johann Raithel	01.04.25 (226)	Inf.Rgt.20
Oblt.Rudolf Meister	01.04.25 (250)	Inf.Rgt.4

Oblt.Dietrich Volkmann	01.04.25 (256)	Inf.Rgt.10
Oblt.Günther Korten	01.04.25 (280)	Pion.Btl.4
Oblt.Ernst Weber	01.04.25 (281)	Inf.Rgt.14
Oblt.Wilhelm Becker	01.04.25 (289)	Reiter Rgt.1
Oblt.Günter Schwartzkopff	01.04.25 (308)	Inf.Rgt.6
Oblt.Dipl.Ing.Gerhard Bassenge	01.04.25 (310)	Inf.Rgt.6
Oblt.Günther Wieland	01.04.25 (325)	Inf.Rgt.5
Oblt.Cartun	01.04.25 (327)	Inf.Rgt.7
Oblt.von Oheimb	01.04.25 (354)	Reiter Rgt.11
Oblt.Otto Jordan	01.04.25 (360)	Art.Rgt.5
Oblt.Richard Schimpf	01.04.25 (373)	Inf.Rgt.21
Oblt.Wilhelm Meyer	01.04.25 (380)	Inf.Rgt.5
Oblt.Hans Jeschonnek	01.04.25 (386)	Reiter Rgt.6
Oblt.Heusinger	01.04.25 (417)	Stab Inf.Fhr.II
Oblt.Max Ibel	01.04.25 (436)	Pion.Btl.7
Oblt.Pregler	01.04.25 (463)	Art.Rgt.7
Oblt.Alexander Holle	01.04.25 (477)	Inf.Rgt.16
Oblt.Otto Hoffmann von Waldau	01.04.25 (487)	Stab.7.Div.
Oblt.Paul Deichmann	01.04.25 (524)	Inf.Rgt.3
Oblt.Notz	01.04.25 (589)	Inf.Rgt.20
Oblt.Adolf-Friedrich Krüger	01.04.25 (616)	Inf.Rgt.4
Oblt.Theodor Macht	01.04.25 (656)	Art.Rgt.1
Oblt.Walter Boenicke	01.07.25 (2)	Fahr.Abt.5
Oblt.Hans-Detlef Herhudt von Rohden	01.11.25 (1)	Fahr.Abt.6
Oblt.Kosters	01.02.26 (12)	Inf.Rgt.6
Oblt.Kurt Kleinrath	01.02.26 (22)	Art.Rgt.2
Oblt.Otto-Friedrich Frhr.von Houwald	01.02.26 (41)	Reiter Rgt.6
Oblt.Max (?) Kriesche	01.03.26 (3)	Art.Rgt.2
Oblt.von Scheel	01.04.26 (8)	Inf.Rgt.11
Oblt.Rudolf Koester	01.04.27 (1)	Stab 2.Div.
Oblt.Frhr.von Wichtingen	01.05.27 (4)	Reiter Rgt.11
Oblt.Arno de Salengre-Drabbe	01.05.27 (6)	Inf.Rgt.12
Oblt.Ernst Emminghaus	01.06.27 (9)	Stab 5.Div.
Oblt.Hermann Plocher	01.08.27 (3)	Inf.Rgt.13
Oblt.Hans Seidemann	01.08.27 (4)	Inf.Rgt.9
Oblt.Hans-Jurgen von Cramon-Taubadel	01.11.27 (11)	Reiter Rgt.7
Oblt.Lothar von Wurmb	01.01.28 (1)	Inf.Rgt.7

Oblt.Schnarrenberger	01.01.28 (7)	Inf.Rgt.14
Oblt.Hans Hugo Witt	01.01.28 (8)	Inf.Rgt.5
Oblt.Karl Mehnert	01.01.28 (10)	Inf.Rgt.11
Oblt.Hans-Bruno Schulz-Heyn	01.01.28 (13)	Inf.Rgt.2
Oblt.Hans Meyer	01.02.28 (17)	Inf.Rgt.1
Oblt.Werner Krahl	01.02.28 (25)	Inf.Rgt.10
Oblt.Hans Korte	01.02.28 (51)	Inf.Rgt.14
Oblt.Berchtenbreiter	01.04.28 (20)	Inf.Rgt.20
Oblt.Andreas Nielsen	01.04.28 (52a)	Inf.Rgt.6
Oblt.Alfred Boner	01.04.28 (62)	Nachr.Abt.3
Oblt.Pusinelli	01.04.28 (75)	Inf.Rgt.10
Oblt.Friedrich Hessel	01.08.28 (14)	Inf.Rgt.21
Oblt.Walter Hill	01.08.28 (15)	Inf.Rgt.3
Oblt.Werner Kreipe	01.09.28 (6)	Art.Rgt.6
Oblt.von Detten	01.11.28 (21)	Reiter Rgt.3
Oblt.Hellmuth Petzold	01.11.28 (26)	Inf.Rgt.4
Oblt.Hans Georg Schmidt von Altenstadt	01.02.29 (37)	Reiter Rgt.4
Oblt.Helmuth von Hoffmann	01.04.29 (30)	Reiter Rgt.4
Oblt.Dybwad	01.07.29 (6)	Art.Rgt.2
Oblt.Fritz Doench	01.08.29 (2)	Art.Rgt.3
Oblt.Günther Borner		Art.Rgt.4
Oblt.Hans von Koppelow		Reiter Rgt.11
Oblt.Waldemar Lerche	01.04.30 (5)	Inf.Rgt.157 ?
Lt.Helmut Kuster	01.04.29 (3)	Reiter Rgt.14
Lt.Meinecke	01.09.29 (2)	Art.Rgt.3
ObArzt.Diringshofen	01.02.29 (1)	Stab 7.Div.

Part 2

The Rise of Hitler 1933-1934

2A1

Further thinking on a Strategy for Air Power 1933-34

Strategy, or the art of deployment of a nation's resources so as to obtain a political and/or military advantage over neighbouring states, must of necessity reflect the geo-political and technological realities of its time.[1] This was certainly true of the later strategic deployment of the *Luftwaffe* and in any discussion of its performance it is necessary to take account of the specific factors that shaped its birth during the early to mid-thirties.

The creation of a military air arm in Germany from 1933 resulted from a political desire for national resurgence based on the existing secret foundations provided by the *Reichswehr* in the years following the Great War (See1A2 & 1A3). As the new leader of Germany Hitler had great plans for the future of Germany, plans that included the recovery of territories lost as a result of the Treaty of Versailles at home and overseas, as well as the possible expansion of the new *Reich* to the east.[2] Such plans would, of necessity, bring Germany into direct conflict with both Poland and France, two nations which would undoubtedly see co-operation against Germany to be in their mutual interest.[3]

German strategy was of necessity continental in its outlook. Her dominance of Europe during the latter part of the nineteenth century had come in part from her strategically advantageous position in the centre of the European land mass and in part from her industrial power bases in the coal and steel producing Ruhr district of Nordrhein-Westfalen and the chemical and textiles centres of Sachsen.[4] Versailles had sought to largely neutralise German heavy industry, but paradoxically the various Paris treaties of 1919 had equally fragmented Germany's former eastern neighbour to produce a far more favourable geo-political situation for incremental conquest once her military machine had been rebuilt.[5]

---

1   Cooper M. 1981 *The German Air Force 1933-1945: An Anatomy of Failure* (hereafter cited as Cooper 1981) p.34. This author suggests that strategy consists of three elements: Policy, Means and Application. Of these policy is arguable the most important but a nation must still have the means to implement its chosen policy and at this crucial time in German history the economic means to successfully rearm was largely absent.

2   Hitler A. 1927 *Mein Kampf: 4 ½ Jahre Kampf gegen Luge, Dummbeit und Seigbeit*. Regarded inside Germany as the bible for National Socialism it was also an accurate blueprint of what Hitler intended to do in the future. In economic terms he was a proponent of national self-sufficiency and economic independence. To achieve these goals territorial expansion was an inevitable by-product of National Socialism – see Shirer W.L. 1963 *The Rise and Fall of the Third Reich: A History of Nazi Germany* (hereafter cited as Shirer 1963) pp.21-28 & Snyder L.L. 1976 *Encyclopaedia of the Third Reich* (hereafter cited as Snyder 1976) pp.224-226.

3   Shirer W.L. 1969 *The Collapse of the Third Republic: An Inquiry into the Fall of France in 1940* (hereafter cited as Shirer 1969) pp.256-265 & p.464. However in the wake of Hitler's Non-Aggression Pact with Poland in 1934 there was a period of uncertainty in France as to Poland's position in the event of a Franco-German conflict. On the 4 Jun 36 *Gen.* Aplhonse Georges declared that *"There was complete uncertainty about Poland"* – see *Evenements, Rapport* in Shirer 1969.

4   Barraclough G. (Ed.) 1978 *The Times Atlas of World History* (hereafter cited as Barraclough (Ed.) 1978). See in particular *Population Growth and Movements 1815-1914* pp.208-209, *The Industrial Revolution in Europe 1815-1870* pp.210-211, *The Industrial Revolution in Europe 1870-1914* pp.212-213 & *Germany and Italy: the struggles for unification 1815-1871* pp.216-217. See also Shackleton M.R. 1939 *Europe: A Regional Geography* (hereafter cited as Shackleton 1939) pp.252-256 & 263-264.

5   *European Political Problems 1919-1934* in Barraclough (Ed.) 1978 pp.264-265.

Following Versailles Germany was even more dependent on her European neighbours for the raw materials that were the basis of military power. She still had abundant supplies of good quality coal, but the exhaustion of all but the relatively insignificant Siegerland iron ore deposits together with the loss of the previously important iron ore fields in Lothringen (Lorraine) had made Germany especially dependent on foreign supplies for her planned rearmament programme.[6] In a world that was rapidly becoming dependent on the internal combustion engine, Hitler's Germany was also cruelly dependent on imported oil, only having very small natural resources of her own.[7] Within Europe the closest significant source of supply was Romania but rail transport through the notoriously unstable Balkan nations was fraught with political difficulty. Imports from further afield were equally tenuous, at least in time of war, and therefore it was not in Germany's strategic interests to become dependent on oceanic trade.[8]

These geo-political realities shaped German foreign policy *(Map 1-1)*. To west and east lay potential enemies both of whom had incorporated significant industrial resources of the former Reich. The mutual isolation of these two nations was therefore an important strategic goal, both from each other, so avoiding the nightmare of the two-front war, and from their potential allies such as the Soviet Union in the east and Great Britain in the west.[9] The strategic position of the British Isles athwart German maritime communications was an added factor which favoured the prosecution of harmonious relations with this island nation.[10] To the north and south lay smaller and less important states. None were a potential threat to even a weakened Germany but they were, nonetheless, useful as sources of industrial raw materials and agricultural products.[11] German foreign policy was therefore directed at the isolation of hostile neighbours, a good example of this being the negotiation of a non-aggression pact with Poland in January 1934, and the maintenance of the status quo amongst her smaller neighbours, particularly in the volatile Balkan region where unfavourable *coup d'etats* were not unknown.[12]

6   Blanchard W.O. and Visher S.S. 1931 *Economic Geography of Europe* (hereafter cited as Blanchard and Visher 1931) p.67, 110 & pp.250-251 & Shackleton 1939 p.134 & 254. In 1929, the last year of full production prior to the World economic down-turn, Germany had consumed 21.28 m tons of iron ore with just over a quarter (25.8%) coming from domestic ore fields. By 1933 consumption had fallen to 7.37 m tons with domestic ores contributing 27.5%. Germany's chief source of iron ore was Sweden which supplied 35.4% of the total – see *Table 4 German Sources of iron ore 1929-35* in Overy R.J. 1984 *Goering: The Iron Man* (hereafter cited as Overy 1984) p. 63. Nor did the decline in industrial activity augur well for rapid rearmament – see Murray W. 1985 *Luftwaffe: Strategy for Defeat 1933-45* (hereafter cited as Murray 1985) p.3.

7   Blanchard and Visher 1931 p.73 & 254. In 1926 Germany had produced just 0.7 m barrels of petroleum. By comparison Romanian output had reached 30 m barrels by 1928. This unfavourable position put against a background of increasing demand arising from the motorisation of the armed forces had encouraged the development of the hydrogenation process through which 150 kilos of Benzine and 200 kilos of Diesel could be obtained from 1,000 kgs of Lignite (US Dept. of Commerce) for which Germany had reserves calculated at 13 b tons. See also Murray 1985 p.3 & Girbig W. 1980 *…mit Kurs auf Leuna: Die Luftoffensive gegen die Triebstoffindustrie und der deutsche Abwehreinsatze 1944-1945* pp.9-10.

8   Blanchard and Visher 1931 p.79, 126 & 129. Nonetheless as a leading industrial nation Germany still accounted for 16% of the World's exports of manufactured goods in 1928, whilst it's foreign trade was second only to Britain. In 1929 its Merchant Marine totalled in excess of 4 m gross metric tonnes (France in excess of 3 m & Britain in excess of 20 m tonnes). Not surprisingly economic blockade of Germany had been a major feature of British naval strategy during the Great War. Confined within its pre-war borders this had eventually led to the economic collapse of Germany – see Murray 1985 p.2.

9   Shirer 1963 pp.212-213. A further lesson from the Great War: German victory in the West had nearly been achieved in 1918 following a political solution in the East.

10   Irving D. 1978 *The War Path: Hitler's Germany 1933-1939* (hereafter cited as Irving 1978) p.xx, xxiv & 56. Hitler regarded Britain as a future partner in his plans for a new World order; he admired the British people, their Empire and the Royal Navy.

11   *Table II Mineral Production in Europe 1913* & 1928 in Blanchard and Visher 1931 p.67 & pp.322-324. Scandinavia was a particularly important source of minerals, whilst the Balkans could offer agricultural products and oil.

12   Shirer 1963 pp.210-213. Following a meeting between Hitler and Josef Liski, the Polish Ambassador in Nov 33 a

Predictably Germany's strategic interests shaped the organisation, structure and equipment of its armed forces. As a continental power Germany possessed the opportunity of directly threatening its neighbours by means of a land offensive.[13] It was also vulnerable in its weakened state to similar attention on the part of both France and Poland. A strong army was clearly vital in both these scenarios.[14] It was also recognised that the *Heer* should be capable of quickly moving from one front to another, a capability which demanded good internal communications. For the most part these would be based on the existing extensive rail network largely united under the *Deutsche Reichsbahn* (c.55,000 kms), but alive to the technologies of the time the *Heeresleitung* also looked to the development of motorised forces.[15] Nor was it a coincidence that one of the first programmes of public works to be initiated by the *NSDAP* on assuming power in Germany was the construction of a national *autobahn* system.[16]

Germany's maritime interests were of less consequence to the formulation of a national strategy. It was accepted that the protection of her large merchant marine was an important objective, but the loss of her overseas colonies in Africa and the Pacific had largely confined Germany's strategic interests to that of the European continent.[17] Moreover her experience in the Great War, when Germany possessed a vastly more effective fleet, had nonetheless revealed just how easy it was for the British to blockade her ports.[18] The maintenance of good relations with Britain was therefore an important foreign policy objective and whilst Hitler sympathised with the *Marineleitung's* desire to see the return of a Blue Water Navy, he was astute enough to realise that the *Reichsmarine* must not be allowed to threaten the power of the British Royal Navy *(Photo 2A-1).*[19] Naval rearmament

joint communique had been issued in which the two Governments agreed to *deal with the questions touching both countries by means of direct negotiations and to renounce all application of force in their relations with each other for the consolidation of European peace.* A 10 year *Non-Aggression Pact* would follow on the 26 Jan 34. It was a diplomatic master stroke coming so soon after Hitler's decision to withdraw from the League of Nations and the *European Disarmament Conferences.* In signing the Pact Hitler effectively divided Poland from France, whilst re-assuring other European nations such as Britain that his intentions were peaceful. Poland's reasons for signing the Pact came from unease over Soviet intentions – see Shirer 1969 p.258.

13   Cooper M. 1978 *The German Army 1933-1945: It's Political and Military Failure* (hereafter cited as Cooper 1978) p.133 & Seaton A. 1982 *The German Army 1933-1945* (hereafter cited as Seaton 1982) p.xxi. Germany had long borders with Poland in the east, Czechoslovakia and Austria in the south and France and the Low Countries in the west. The advantages of interior lines of communication to move forces from one front to another had been successfully demonstrated in the Great War.

14   Shirer 1963 p.281 & Seaton 1982 pp.55-57. In Feb 33 Hitler instructed *Gen.d.Art.*Werner von Fritsch, the new *Chef d.Heeresleitung,* to increase the size of the *Reichsheer* from 100,000 to 300,000 men by the 1 Oct 34. The number of *Infanterie Divisionen* was to increase from 7 to 21, the balance being made up by the 3 *Reiter Divisionen* plus supporting arms.

15   *Statistique internationale des chemins de fer, 1938* in Naval Intelligence Division 1945 *BR 529C Geographical Handbook Series: Germany Vol.IV Ports and Communications* (hereafter cited as NID 1945) pp.192-193, p.215 & 227. Germany had a greater track mileage than any other European country, whilst track density was second only to Britain. As part of the reparations arrangements the railway network had been nationalised in 1924 under a national operating authority – the *Deutsche Reichsbahn Gesellschaft.* In 1937 there were 20,166 steam and 543 electric locomotives plus 700 high-speed diesel-electric railcars.

16   NID 1945 pp.449-450. The *Reichsautobahn Gesellschaft* was established on the 25 Aug 33 as a subsidiary of the *Reichsbahn.* The initial project envisaged 7,250 kms of highway and the first route to be opened for traffic was Frankfurt-Darmstadt-Heidelberg. Dr.Fritz Todt was appointed *Generalinspekteur für da Deutsche Strassenwesen* on the 28 Jun 33 – see service record for Fritz Todt in Hildebrand K.F.1992 *Die Generale der deutschen Luftwaffe 1935-1945 Band 3 O-Z* (hereafter cited as Hildebrand 1992) pp.403-404. See also Snyder 1976 p.284 & pp.348-349.

17   Sieche E. *Germany* in Gardiner R. and Chesneau R. (Ed.) 1980 *Conway's All the World's Fighting Ships 1922-1946* (hereafter cited as Sieche in Gardiner and Chesneau (Ed.) 1980) p.218.

18   Preston A. and Batchelor J. 1977 *Battleships 1856-1919* Phoebus History of the World Wars Special pp.46-47.

19   Shirer 1963 pp.287-289. Hitler would move to an early understanding with Britain over the question of naval rearmament. The Anglo-German Naval Agreement was signed on the 18 Jun 35. This permitted Germany to construct new warships up to 35% of the strength of the Royal Navy (420,000 tons) – see Mallmann Showell J.P. 1979 *The German Navy in World War Two: A Reference Guide to the Kriegsmarine 1935-1945* (hereafter cited as

would therefore be restricted to the neutralisation of the French *Marine* (Navy), a policy which in itself would still require a substantial naval construction programme.[20] Given this scenario it was envisaged that naval warfare would be largely restricted to European coastal waters, the Ostsee and the Nordsee, and German warship design was therefore strongly influenced by such a requirement in the initial stages of national rearmament.[21] Not surprisingly an amphibious capability in support of the *Reichsheer* was not considered an important option.

The role of air power in any future conflict was still very much the subject of debate in international circles during the early thirties. Experience in the Great War had shown aircraft to be of considerable tactical value to both the army and the navy in their combat operations and predictably the development of military aviation during the *Reichswehr* period had continued along these lines (See 1E1 & IE3).[22] However there was the possibility of a more fundamental and independent role in the conduct of national strategy, a stance that had been adopted by *Maj.*Helmuth Wilberg, *Chef TA (L)*, in his *Richtlinien für die Führung des operativen Luftkrieges* (Directives for the leadership of the operational air war) of 1926 and which then had formed the basis for further independent thinking on the part of *Maj.*Hellmuth Felmy, *Chef Inspektion 1 (L)*, in the later *Richtlinien für die Ausbildung in der Reichswehr auf dem Gebiet der Luftstreitkräfte* (Principles for the Employment of Air Forces within the German Armed Forces) of 1930 *(Photo 2A-2)*.[23] Both papers foresaw a major role for the bomber in any future conflict with a clear emphasis on independent action against the sources of an enemy's political, economic and military power and in February 1932 Felmy called for an eighty *Staffel* air arm to be created by 1938.[24] No less than half of these units were to be *Bomberstaffeln* whose primary task in the event of hostilities was the destruction of the enemy air force prior to further strategic bombing operations against the enemy homeland.[25] However Felmy was opposed to the notion of "terror" attacks as espoused by the Italian theoretician Giulio Douhet. Instead the secret air staff within the *Inspektion 1 (L)* had favoured precision attacks on key targets, specifically an enemy's command and control systems, factories, power stations, ports and lines of communication (See 1A2 & 1A3). The result was the peculiarly German doctrine of *operative Luftkrieg* (operational air war), a concept that would become the basis for *Luftwaffe* operations in the years to come.

Although Felmy's *80-Staffel* plan had failed to gain the approval of *Gen.d.Inf.*Kurt Frhr.von Hammerstein-Equord's conservative *Heeresleitung*, such thinking coincided favourably with that

Mallmann Showell 1979) pp.12-17.

20 Masson le H.1969 *Navies of the Second World War: The French Navy Vol.1* pp.8-9, 15-16, p.66 & 69. The French *Marine* had two classes of 3 battleships in service although by 1932 the 3 vessels of the more modern *Bretagne* Class were all under-going major reconstruction. Two new fast battleships had been ordered, the first in 1931 and the second in 1934 as answers to the new German *Panzerschiffe*. However for the most part French naval expenditure following the Great War had concentrated on its modernisation (renovation) of the large force of cruisers (14), flotilla leaders (25), destroyers (21) & submarines (55) – work that was carried out during1925-32. See also Roberts J. *France* in Gardiner and Chesneau (Ed.) 1980 p.255.

21 Whitley M.J. 1989 *German Capital Ships of World War Two* pp.15-30, Whitley M.J. 1985 *German Cruisers of World War Two* pp.16-27 & Whitley M.J. 1991 *German Destroyers of World War Two* pp.15-25 & 45-47. With the exception of the 3 *Panzerschiffe* that had been ordered for the express purpose of oceanic mercantile warfare, the majority of the *Reichsmarine's* new warships were best suited by their design and propulsion to the more sheltered waters of the Nordsee and Ostsee.

22 *Studie eines Offizieres über die Fliegerwaffe und ihre Verwendung* (1925) in Corum J.S. 1997 *The Luftwaffe: Creating the Operational Air War 1918-1940* (hereafter cited as Corum 1997) pp.72-74.

23 *Truppenamt T-Luft Richtlinien für die Führung des operativen Luftkrieges& Grundstaze für den Einstaz der Luftstreitkräfte 1930* in BA/MA RL 2/II 364 Entwurf in Corum 1997 pp.81-83.

24 Homze E.L.1976 *Arming the Luftwaffe: The Reich Air Ministry and the German Aircraft Industry 1919-1939* (hereafter cited as Homze 1976) pp.34-35.

25 Corum 1997 p.122. By 1938 this force would total 6 long-range reconnaissance squadrons, 14 short-range reconnaissance squadrons, 18 fighter squadrons and 42 bomber squadrons. The bomber squadrons would have 370 aircraft plus 126 in reserve.

of Adolf Hitler and Hermann Göring who both were influenced in Douhet's theories as basis for a new strategy of deterrence during the critical period of initial German re-armament:

Hitler then (28 April 1932) spoke at length on the ideas of General Douhet. As early as this he was principally interested in bombing warfare as the best means of deterring an aggressor. He talked of the importance of powerful armed forces, in which he saw the air force as occupying a position equal to the army's; this was the only way for Germany to rid herself of the shackles of Versailles short of war itself.[26]

*GFM.a.D.*Erhard Milch
Letter to David Irving - 22 June 1969

Following his appointment as *Staatssekretär der Luftfahrt*, Erhard Milch had been despatched to Rome in April 1933 to discuss his own plans for a strategic air arm with Italian officers. However he discovered that the *Regia Aeronautica*, unfettered by international restrictions and with a very different geo-political situation, had adopted a blend of aerial doctrines. Aspects of Douhetian theory had resulted in a strong bomber force but the Italians were equally concerned with the development of strong maritime forces and the evolution of assault aviation.[27] In a real sense of disappointment Milch noted that: *Nowhere was the strategy of air warfare less heeded than in the native land of General Douhet.*[28] Undeterred Milch commissioned a study of a strategic concept for the new air force from his former colleague at *Deutsche Luft Hansa, Dr.*Robert Knauss an airman of considerable intellect, insight and experience.[29]

In his *Eine geheime Denkschrift zur Luftkriegskonzeption Hitler-Deutschlands von Mai 1933* (A secret memorandum of May 1933 on an air war concept for Hitler's Germany) Knauss argued that modern states were particularly susceptible to dislocation and disruption by air bombardment and that carefully planned attacks on industrial and urban targets would interrupt the enemy's war production and possibly result in civilian pressure against further hostilities.[30] His study was based on major elements of Douhet's earlier work as well as concepts that have since been incorporated into military thinking under the heading of *"deterrence theory"*. Accepting the possibility of a pre-emptive attack by France and/or Poland he proposed the construction of a force of some 400 bombers as a deterrent shield behind which rearmament could take place. He argued that this

---

26   Quoted from Irving D. 1973 *The Rise and Fall of the Luftwaffe: The Life of Luftwaffe Marshal Erhard Milch* (hereafter cited as Irving 1973) p. 27 with the knowledge of the Orion Publishing Group.

27   Corum 1997 p.146. In Italy Douhet's views were challenged by *Capt.*Amadeo Mecozzi, a key proponent of assault aviation and in this stance he had the support of *Gen.*Italo Balbo. *The Regia Aeronautica* organised its first *Stormo Assalto* in 1931 under the command of *Col.*Mecozzi – see Emiliani A., Ghergo G.E. and Vigna A. 1975 *Regia Aeronautica: perido prebellico e fronti occidentali* (hereafter cited as Emiliani et al 1975) photos 2-4 & Hallion R.P. 1989 *Strike from the Sky: The History of Battlefield Air Attack 1911-1945* p.82.

28   Quoted from *Milch Diary, 11 Apr 33* in Irving 1973 *The Rise and Fall of the Luftwaffe: The Life of Luftwaffe Marshal Erhard Milch* p.31 with the knowledge of the Orion Publishing Group. Mussolini agreed with the thinking behind a predominantly bomber force; *Gen.*Italo Balbo did not. He advocated a mixed or combined force of fighter and reconnaissance aircraft. Milch's observation is overly harsh. The *Regia Aeronautica* actually possessed a sizable bomber force and was actively engaged in the process of equipping it with the most modern aircraft – see Emiliani et al 1975 photos 37-40 & 42.

29   Knauss R. 1933 'Eine geheime Denkschrift zur Luftkriegskonzeption Hitler-Deutschlands von Mai 1933' in Heinemann B. Maj. and Schuncke J. Maj. (Ed.) 1964 *Zeitschrift für Militärgeschichte* Nr.1 pp.72-86. See also Volker K.H. 1968 *Dokumente und Documentarfotos zue Geschichte der deutschen Luftwaffe* (hereafter cited as Volker 1968) p.29f & 34, Irving 1973 p.31 & Corum 1997 pp.131-133.

30   Cooper 1981 p.35. Knauss would later publish his theories in *Luftkrieg 1936: Der Zertrummerung von Paris* in which he set out his thinking within the context of an imaginary air attack by the *RAF* on Paris. Other German writers from this period include Hermann F. *Der Erde* im *Flammen* and Ohlinger E. *Bomben auf Kohlenstadt.*

force could be created relatively quickly and that it was cost effective, being equal at *RM* 80 million for example to the cost of building two battleships or to that of raising five field divisions. In this situation he regarded the alternative strategy of a defensive air force based on fighters to be quite inadequate.[31] Offence was simply the best means of defence.

The concept found immediate favour with Milch who coined the phrase *Risiko Flotte* (Risk Fleet) for the new force structure after the earlier use of the term by *Grossadmiral* Alfred von Tirpitz.[32] Milch in turn had no difficulty in gaining the support of his political superiors who realised the potential diplomatic benefits from the threat posed by German air power. Discussions with *Obst.* Walther von Reichenau, the *Chef des Wehrmachtamtes* (Chief of the Armed Forces Office) at the *RWM*, followed in June and the new organisational plan was finally ratified by *Reichsminister* Hermann Göring and *Reichswehrminister Gen.d.Inf.* Werner von Blomberg on the 27 June 1933.[33] A total of 600 combat aircraft were to be built for the still secret *Luftwaffe* by the end of 1935, a force which would include 400 bombers of a design capable of attacking key urban-industrial targets in both France and Poland.[34] The Dornier Do F (Do 11) was considered suitable for this role although its serious lack of range when fully loaded would preclude attacks on Paris and the industrial Nord without recourse to airfields in the de-militarised Rheinland.[35] The Junkers Ju 52/3m g3e was also considered suitable for emergency use as a *Behelfsnachtbomber* (Auxiliary Night Bomber) even though its bomb load was restricted to just 500 kgs (See 3C3).[36] Both types would have been highly vulnerable to fighter attack.

Predictably the primacy of the strategic bomber was immediately threatened by inter-service rivalry. Knauss had envisaged the expansion of the *Luftwaffe* at the expense of the other branches of the *Reichswehr*. Not surprisingly this was actively resisted. *Obst.i.G.* Konrad von Gossler, *Chef der Operationsstabes (T 2)* within the *Truppenamt* (Troop Office), questioned the validity of an independent air strategy, whilst his superior *Gen.d.Inf.* Wilhelm Adam, the *Chef d. Truppenamt* and a known opponent of an independent air arm, reiterated old arguments for a larger share of Germany's new air power to be placed under the direct control of the *Reichsheer*. He demanded sixteen rather than the twelve planned *Aufklärungsstaffeln* and that all six of the planned *Jagdstaffeln*

31   Hooton E.R. 1994 *Phoenix Triumphant: The Rise and Rise of the Luftwaffe* (hereafter cited as Hooton 1994) p.101. Knauss was aware that the French were in the process of expanding the size and capability of their bomber force. He was also familiar with the achievements of the *Regia Aeronautica* in this respect. Knauss stated: *a Panzerschiff like the Deutschland costs RM 80 million. For the expense of building two Panzerschiffe, an air fleet of four hundred heavy bombers can be built* – quoted from 'Eine geheime Denkschrift zur Luftkriegskonzeption Hitler-Deutschlands von Mai 1933' in Heinemann B. Maj. and Schuncke J. Maj. (Ed.) 1964 *Zeitschrift für Militärgeschichte* Nr.1 p.79.

32   Irving 1973. *In accordance with the plans in effect in 1933, the trial fleet was to be based on the bomber arm, in order that Germany might have a defensive force at her disposal in case the western powers should attempt to threaten her armament activity* – see GFM.a.D. Erhard Milch *Hauptgrunde für den Zusammenbruch der deutschen Luftwaffe im Weltkrieg II* in Maass B. GenLt.a.D. 1955 *The Organisation of the German Air Force High Command and Higher Echelon Headquarters within the German Air Force* USAF Historical Studies No.190 p.24.

33   *LA Nr.1305/33 g.Kdos. A 2 I, vom 29 Jun 33* in Hooton 1994 p.102. See also Cooper 1981 p.35.

34   Cooper 1981 p.35. At this point *Obst.* Bohnstedt, the *Chef LS*, proposed a mixed force of just 200 aircraft including 12 bombers. Sadly out of touch with the new political realities he was retired on the 31 Aug 33. His replacement was *Obst.i.G.* Walther Wever, one of the *Reichsheer's* most capable young staff officers – see Irving 1973 p.33 & 35.

35   Green W. 1970 *The War Planes of the Third Reich* (hereafter cited as Green 1970) pp. 110-112 & Corum 1997 p.123. The Do 11 had not been included in the initial aircraft production programme – *Table 1-C Göring's First Aircraft Production Programme (May 1933 to April 1934)* in Vajda F.A. & Dancey P.1998 *German Aircraft Industry and Production 1933-1945* (hereafter cited as Vajda & Dancey 1998) p.16 – but during the latter part of the year Milch placed large orders for the type. These orders were formalised in the *Rheinland Programm* which began in the New Year. This aimed to provide the secret Luftwaffe with 372 Dornier bombers by the 30 Sep 35 – see *Table 1-D The Rhineland Programme, 1 January 1934 – 30 September 1935* in Vajda and Dancey 1998 p.16.

36   Green 1970 pp.405-406 & Corum 1997 p.123. Problems with the Do 11 resulted in an increased order for the Ju 52/3m g3e with an order of 450 machines within the *Rheinland Programm* – see *Table 1-D The Rhineland Programme, 1 January 1934 – 30 September 1935* in Vajda and Dancey 1998 p.16.

should be directly attached to the field armies.[37] A further concern was revealed during the first *Winterkriegspiel* (Winter War Games) which indicated that the bomber fleet projected by Knauss was too small to be effective, even in the destruction of the enemy air force at the start of hostilities.[38] The technology available was simply inadequate to support the grandiose claims of the air theorists, a point that appeared to vindicate Gossler's arguments.[39]

Nor was opposition confined to the *Reichsheer*. *Adm.*Erich Raeder, *Chef der Marineleitung*, had been angered by Milch and Reichenau's joint opposition to the allocation of fighter and bomber aircraft to the *Reichsmarine* and in December 1933 Raeder called for a joint conference to resolve these concerns.[40] Although the *Marineleitung* accepted the need for an autonomous *Reichsluftwaffe* it was simply not prepared to surrender the embryonic *Marinefliegerverbände* (Naval Air Arm) or forgo those units planned for the Fleet. The *Marineleitung's* position on naval air power was clear:[41]

- A single command for all the forces employed would provide the most efficient means of conducting naval warfare;
- The success of naval operations is in large measure dependent on an air arm, experienced in conditions at sea and trained in the art of naval warfare;
- The aircraft is one of the most important weapons in the conduct of naval warfare. Its ability to scout for naval forces over a wide area lessens the chances of surprise attack; because it can deliver swift counter attacks it has become an invaluable offensive and defensive weapon; it can no longer be regarded as only suitable for ancillary functions, it has become an integral force in naval warfare.

Although no agreement was reached in December the *Marineleitung* followed up the discussion with a memorandum to Göring and the *RLM* on the 22 January 1934 (See also 2E3).[42] Preoccupied with the creation of a land based bomber force Göring and Milch were prepared to accede to these demands and on the 1 April 1934 a separate functional command was therefore established to co-ordinate the development of naval air power; the *Höheren Luftamt Kiel* was established under *KonAdm.a.D.*Konrad Zander.[43]

In the meantime it was left to *Obst.i.G.*Walther Wever, the new *Chef des Luftkommando Amt (LA)* (Chief of the Air Command Office), to accommodate the demands of the *Reichsheer* for tactical air units, whilst preserving the ambitions of Göring, Milch, Knauss and the *Alte Adler* (Old Eagles) for the new *Luftwaffe* to have an independent strategic role.[44] Given his non-aviation

---

37   Corum 1997 p.134. Apart from expressing his concern that the *Luftwaffe's* emerging air doctrine would inevitably place civilians in the front line Gossler argued that the supporters of Douhet were blinded by un-validated enthusiasm for a new and untried weapon of war. Adam's earlier 1932 plan for 12 reconnaissance squadrons had been approved by von Schleicher for completion in 1936. Adam also wanted a further 9 fighter squadrons by 1938, with a *Jagdgeschwader* to be attached to each of the four *Heeresgruppenkommandos* whilst the last squadron was to be at the disposal of the *Heeresleitung* – see Seaton 1982 p.26.

38   *Anlagen zum Winterkriegspiel 1934-35* in BA/MA RL 2 II/77 in Corum p.153.

39   Corum 1997 p.134.

40   US Office of Naval Intelligence 1947 *German Naval Air 1933-1945: A Report based on German Naval Staff Documents* in Isby D.C. (Ed.) 2005 *The Luftwaffe and the War at Sea 1939-45: As seen by officers of the Kriegsmarine and Luftwaffe* (hereafter cited as USONI in Isby (Ed.) 2005) p.26 & pp.28-30.

41   Quoted from Gaul W. Obst.i.G.a.D. *The German Naval Air Force, 1933-September 1939* in Isby (Ed.) 2005 *The Luftwaffe and the War at Sea 1939-45: As seen by officers of the Kriegsmarine and Luftwaffe* p.80 with the kind permission of Lionel Leventhal Ltd./Greenhill Books.

42   USONI in Isby (Ed.) 2005 p.29.

43   Suchenwirth R. 1968 *The Development of the German Air Force 1919-1939* USAF Historical Studies No.160 p.66 (hereafter cited as Suchenwirth 1968). The remaining five *Höheren Luftamter* would all be concerned with land based air power. See also service record for Konrad Zander in Hildebrand 1992 pp.558-559.

44   Suchenwirth R. 1969 *Command and Leadership in the German Air Force* USAF Historical Studies No.174 pp.1-4 &

background Wever arrived at the Behrenstrasse in September 1933 with a rather traditionalist view on the employment of military aviation. Thereafter his views on the structure and employment of air power steadily metamorphosed to include the independent employment of heavy bombers. He would later state in November 1935, that the planned *Luftwaffe* would have two principal roles:

> One, home defence, to which all the services and the whole population will contribute, and two - the second, more important and decisive task - the defeat of the enemy threatening us. Command of the air is the condition upon which both these tasks depend if they are to be carried out with complete success.[45]

GenMaj.Walther Wever
Chef des Luftkommando Amt

The *Luftwaffe's* ability to meet these objectives was put to the test a year later, when Wever held the second *Winterkriegspiel* at the Behrenstrasse in November 1934.[46] A French advance into south-west Germany between Luxembourg and Colmar with the intention of disrupting Germany's rearmament plans provided the scenario. For the first two days of the games Wever deployed his forces, which included 3 *Nahaufklärungsstaffeln* (Short Range Reconnaissance Squadrons), 1 *Sturzkampfgeschwader* (Dive-Bomber Wing) and 2 *Jagdgeschwadern* (Fighter Wings), tactically in support of the slowly retreating German ground forces through attacks on the Rhein bridges and night intruder operations against French airfields.[47] On the third day the bomber force, which comprised five *Kampfgeschwadern* (Bomber Wings), 1 *Behelfskampfgeschwader* (Auxiliary Bomber Wing) and 10 *Fernaufklärungsstaffeln* (Long-range Reconnaissance Squadrons), was unleashed against the French Army's rear areas and lines of communication. The bombers also acted independently of the ground war in attacks against political and economic targets including Paris:

> During the course of the *Kriegspiel*, the *Kampfverbände* were employed deep in the heart of enemy territory. At that time most of these units were equipped with provisionally armed Ju 52/3ms, which were completely inferior to the French fighters. Officers in charge of the manoeuvre suggested to *General* Wever that he assume a loss of 80% for the bomber force, but Wever refused brusquely with the words: *"That would deprive me of my confidence in*

Hooton 1994 pp.98-100. Wever was one of the *Reichsheer's* rising stars and if he had remained in the *Heer* he would almost certainly have been promoted to be *ObdH* in the fullness of time – see Irving 1973 p.35. The *Alte Adler* were the wartime *Luftstreitkräfte* officers who had remained in the *Reichsheer* as an air staff in being. They included Hugo Sperrle, Hellmuth Felmy, Hellmuth Volkmann & Wilhelm Wimmer.

45   Quoted from *Vortrag des Generalmajors Wever bei Eröffnung der Luftkriegsakademie und Lufttechnischen Akademie in Berlin-Gatow am 1.November 1935* in Corum 1997 *The Luftwaffe: Creating the Operational Air War 1918-1940* p.137 with the kind permission of the University Press of Kansas. See also Murray 1985 pp.9-10. Although these views were articulated in 1935, Wever had already substantially changed his position with respect to the employment of military air power by late 1933 as evidenced by the procurement schedule within the *Rheinland Programm* – see *Table 1-D The Rhineland Programme, 1 January 1934 – 30 September 1935* in Vajda and Dancey 1998 p.16.

46   Volker K-H. 1967 *Die deutsche Luftwaffe 1933-1939: Aufbau, Führung und Rüstung der Luftwaffe sowie die Entwicklung der deutschen Luftkriegstheorie* (hereafter cited as Volker 1967) pp. 31-33. Held on the 6, 13, 20 & 27 Nov 34 these games were observed by members of the *Truppenamt*: specifically *GenLt.*Beck (*Chef d.Truppenamtes u.C.d.GS.d.H.*), *GenMaj.*von Wietersheim, *Obstlt.i.G.*Jodl (*Operations-Abt.*), *Obst.i.G.*von Sodenstern (*Organisation-Abt.*), *Obst.i.G.*Reinhardt (*Ausbildungs-Abt.*) & *Obstlt.*Fellgiebel (*Insp.d. Nachrichtentruppe*). See also Suchenwirth 1968 pp.172-173.

47   Rieckhoff H.J. GenLt.a.D.1945 *Trumpf oder Bluff? 12 Jahre deutsche Luftwaffe* p.85. Due to the politico-military realities of 1934/35 the *Kriegsspiel* had the characteristics of a defensive operation. This led to some commentators to state, erroneously, that Wever's thinking was primarily defensive – see also Goerlitz W. 1951 *Der Zweite Weltkrieg 1939-1945 Bd.V* p.422.

strategic air operations!" Although the manoeuvre leaders pointed out that the percentage of losses would presumably be that high only in this particular instance, i.e., until the *Luftwaffe* had more modern bombers at its disposal, Wever insisted upon a lower percentage.[48]

*Gen.d.Flg.a.D.*Paul Deichmann
Conversation with Prof.Suchenwirth - 1968.

These concerns together with the realisation, at least on Milch's part, that a much larger emphasis had to be placed on training during the early stages of rearmament, combined to change the planned force structure. The result was the *Rheinland Programm* of January 1934 which called for no less than 3,715 aircraft to be delivered by the end of the following year.[49] In July 1934 this requirement was increased still further to total 4,021 aircraft, all of which were to be completed in a shorter time span, specifically by the 30 September 1935. Of this figure 86% were for military employment, primarily by the *Fliegerschulen* including the *DLV* (German Sport Aviation) which would receive 2,168 aircraft. In contrast the covert operational *Staffeln* (Squadrons) would be allocated just 1,085 (See also 2D1, 2E2 & 2E3).[50]

In addition to meeting the demands of the *Reichsheer* far more fighters and reconnaissance aircraft were to be produced than in the original plan. Despite these considerations the *Kampfverbände* (Bomber Command) remained pre-dominant throughout this formative period:[51]

FIGURE 2A-1 AIRCRAFT DISTRIBUTION PLAN JULY 1934					
Operational Units	1,085	Lufthansa	115	Research	138
Training Schools	2,168	Flying Clubs	33	Miscellaneous	80
Airfields	156	Reichsbahn	12	Wastage	171
Target Towing	48	NSDAP	10		
A.A. Schools	5				
Total	**3,462**	**Total**	**170**	**Total**	**389**

FIGURE 2A-2 PLANNED PRODUCTION BY TYPE JULY 1934			
Bombers	822	Naval Aircraft	149
Dive Bombers	51	Trainers	1,760
Fighters	251	Communications	89
Reconnaissance	590	Other Types	309

48   Quoted from a *Commentary by Gen.d.Flg.a.D.Paul Deichmann to Richard Suchenwirth* in Suchenwirth 1968 *The Development of the German Air Force 1919-1939* USAF Historical Studies No.160 pp.172-173. In Oct 34 *Hptm.i.G.*Deichmann had just been appointed to the *Luftkommandoamt (LA)* – see service record for Paul Deichmann in Hildebrand K.F.1990 *Die Generale der deutschen Luftwaffe 1935-1945 Band 1 A-G* pp.182-183.

49   *Table 1-D The Rhineland Programme, 1 January 1934 – 30 September 1935* in Vajda and Dancey 1998 p.16.

50   Irving 1973 p.31. *Table 1-D The Rhineland Programme, 1 January 1934 – 30 September 1935* in Vajda and Dancey 1998 p.16.

51   *Table 1-D The Rhineland Programme, 1 January 1934 – 30 September 1935* in Vajda and Dancey 1998 p.16.

Some sources have suggested that the change in force structure was enforced by known inadequacies within the German aircraft industry (See 2C3).[52] Whilst it must be accepted that this was a potential constraint, the available evidence in fact shows that in each successive plan the overall demands of the *RLM* were increased not just in terms of numbers but in overall airframe structural weight and the number of aero-engines. Thus from the very first plan in June 1933, Milch increased the overall order to 1,000 machines in September 1933, and via the *Rheinland Programm* to an eventual total of 4,021 aircraft in July 1934.[53] During the same period employment in the aircraft industry rose swiftly from the January 1933 figure of 3,988 employees to total 39,567 employees by July 1934.[54] Milch's expectations were not therefore unrealistic and by the 28 February 1935 the German Aircraft Industry had delivered 259 Ju 52/3m g3e *Behelfsbomber*. Production of the Do 11 *mittlere Nachtbomber* (Medium Night Bomber) on the other hand was still disappointing being restricted by a lack of flight ready Sh 22B radial engines and inherent design deficiencies in the airframe.[55]

Although rumour belied reality the perception of growing German air power caused increasing disquiet amongst Germany's neighbours. If anything Milch's earlier order of the 25 July 1933 *to make it impossible for foreign powers from deriving any clear picture of the rate of growth, or of the actual size and organisation of the Luftwaffe we are founding* had magnified the true impact of the embryonic *Luftwaffe* on the European stage.[56] In July 1934, the British Government, alarmed by the large sums that the *RLM* had publicly announced for the expansion of aviation in the Reich, requested clarification from the German authorities only to be told that the sum was required to overhaul and modernise *Deutsche Luft Hansa's* fleet of airliners.[57] Neither the French nor the British were really deceived by this explanation but at the same time neither government was keen to take overt action against Germany.[58] Nonetheless these developments coupled with Hitler's decision to withdraw Germany from both the League of Nations and the Geneva Disarmament Conference in October 1933 encouraged these reluctant governments to take the first, albeit faltering steps, to redress the perceived imbalance (See also 2E1).[59]

Under pressure from Britain to allow Germany military parity the French Government informed their erstwhile ally on the 17 April 1934 that France *refused to legalise German rearmament* contrary to the Treaty of Versailles and that henceforth *France will assure her security by her own means.*[60]

52   Hooton 1994 p.104 & *Table 1-A Growth of German Aviation Industry, 1933/34* in Vjada and Dancey 1998 p.11.
53   *Table 1-D The Rhineland Programme, 1 January 1934 – 30 September 1935* in Vajda and Dancey 1998 p.16.
54   *Table 1-A Growth of German Aviation Industry, 1933/34* in Vjada and Dancey 1998 p.11.
55   Hooton 1994 p.103 & 105. The aero-engine plants were the Achilles' Heel of the *Rheinland Programm*. Shortages of raw materials were another concern.
56   *Order on camouflage of Luftwaffe, 25 Juli 1933 Dokumente Nr.71* in Volker 1968 p.183. See also Irving 1973 p.33.
57   Irving 1973 pp.38-39. See also Hooton 1994 pp.112-113.
58   Shirer 1969 p.257 & 264. From 1932 the British Government had been a prime mover behind the World Disarmament Conferences in Geneva – see Terraine J. 1974 *The Mighty Continent* (hereafter cited as Terraine 1974) p.139. French politics was already torn by dissension between the Far Right and the Far Left. Following the signing of the Germano-Polish Non-Aggression Pact, France's only counterpoint in the East was the Soviet Union and an alliance with this revolutionary country was not acceptable to either the middle or right wing politicians – see Shirer 1969 pp.256-257. Nonetheless military staff talks did take place between the two nations. In 1933 a French military mission observed a series of air-ground exercises in the USSR – see Haute van A. 1974 *Pictorial History of the French Air Force 1909-1940* (hereafter cited as Haute 1974 p.84). Interestingly France was more interested in an understanding with Fascist Italy at this time to provide a counter-point to German interests in Austria/. The Rome Pact was duly signed on the 7 Jan 35 – see Shirer 1969 p.260.
59   *Phipps Papers, I 1/14* in Overy 1984 p.37 & 248. *Göring was one of the influences on Hitler in his rejection of any serious attempt at disarmament, particularly in the air. Not only did Göring reject plans for a reduction of air forces or the international renunciation of bombing, but he pressed Hitler in the summer of 1935 for a further doubling of air strength.* See Letter from Phipps to Simon, dated 17.4.1935 on Göring's influence on Hitler on the disarmament issue & Letter from Neurath to Phipps on Göring's demands for a doubling of air strength.
60   Quoted from Shirer 1969 *The Collapse of the Third Republic: An Inquiry into the Fall of France in 1940* p.257 Secker & Warburg Ltd. This was effectively the death blow for the Geneva Disarmament Conferences.

Thus German re-armament, especially in the air, was already beginning to drive a wedge between two allies. Work on the *Maginot Line* was accelerated, whilst the *Aviation Militaire* (French Military Air Arm) was finally made an autonomous arm as the *Armée de l'Air* (French Air Force).[61] The French also began a limited air modernisation programme (*Plan I*) with the introduction of new supercharged fighter aircraft together with new medium and heavy night bombers.[62] In Britain a similarly cautious government finally agreed to undertake a significant expansion of the *RAF*.[63] Under Expansion Scheme "A", agreed by the Cabinet on the 18 July 1934, the overall strength of the Metropolitan *RAF* would be increased from 488 combat aircraft to a total of 1,252 in the front-line by March 1939.[64] However the inherent inadequacies of this initial scheme were only too apparent to British politicians such as Winston Churchill who raised the issue in the House of Commons on the 20 July 1934.[65]

These concerns lend weight to the argument that even at this early stage the *Luftwaffe* had a significant deterrent capability on the international stage. Certainly it had caused a great deal of alarm in Britain, a nation which knew itself to be secure from land and sea attack but at the same time to be peculiarly vulnerable to a strike from the air:

> I think it is well also for the man in the street to realise that there is no power on earth that can prevent him from being bombed. Whatever people may tell him, the bomber will always get through. The only defence is offence, which means you have to kill more women and children more quickly than the enemy if you want to save yourselves.[66]

Stanley Baldwin
Parliamentary Speech - 10 November 1932

In the event of hostilities in Europe, the British would not rush to support France in a land campaign against Germany as they had done in 1914. This attitude therefore largely neutralised

---

61   Shirer 1969 pp.256-257 & Christienne C. and Lissarague P.1980 *A History of French Military Aviation* (hereafter cited as Christienne and Lissarague 1980) pp.250-252. This reorganisation had been initiated in Oct 33 and was officially promulgated on the 2 Jul 34.

62   Christienne and Lissarague 1980 pp.261-264. *Plan I*, also known as the *Plan des 1,010 Avions* consisted of a balanced force of 350 fighters, 350 bombers & 310 reconnaissance aircraft. The total was later increased to 1,343 aircraft. It was due for completion within 3 years. Types procured under *Plan I* included the Dewoitine D.500 C1 fighter, the Amiot 143 M4 & Potez 540 M4 *multiplace de combat* (*BCR*) & the Bloch MB.200 BN4 night bomber. For the *BCR* concept - see Christienne and Lissarague 1980 pp.259-260. See also Haute 1974.

63   Terraine J. 1985 *The Right of the Line: The Royal Air Force in the European War 1939-1945* (hereafter cited as Terraine 1985) pp 24-25. The earlier 52-Squadron Scheme of 1923 had still not been fulfilled. By 1932 the Metropolitan *RAF* comprised just 42 squadrons and due to the Disarmament Conferences and the adverse economic situation no more were formed during the following two financial years – see Collier B. 1957 *The Defence of the United Kingdom* (hereafter cited as Collier 1957) p.19.

64   Collier 1957 pp.27-28. Expansion was prompted by intelligence estimates that Germany intended to have a first-line strength of 576 aircraft backed by reserves and a substantial force of training aircraft by the 1 Oct 35. A further German expansion to 1,368 aircraft was expected by the 1 Oct 36. Scheme A would provide the Metropolitan *RAF* with 80 heavy bombers, 96 medium bombers, 300 light bombers, 24 torpedo bombers, 336 fighters & 124 reconnaissance aircraft – 960 machines in total. Adopted in Jul 34 the Plan was to be completed in 5 years.

65   Churchill W.S. 1948 *The Second World War Vol.1 The Gathering Storm* p.92.

66   Quoted from Collier 1957 *Defence of the United Kingdom* p.29 with the kind permission of the IWM: 51498 (Held at the Department of Collections Access, the Imperial War Museum). See also Dean M. 1979 *The RAF and the Two World Wars* p.59. This speech, widely reported in the media of the time, had a considerable effect on the public psyche, reinforcing existing public attitudes and concerns. Baldwin told the House of Commons that the first-line strength of the *RAF* was 880 machines of which 560 constituted the Metropolitan Air Force. He suggested that Germany probably had between 600 and 1,000 aircraft of all types, mostly training machines.

the French military threat to Hitler's Germany because the French were not prepared to act alone.[67] In this respect the air threat posed by the secret and therefore intangible *Luftwaffe* can be seen to have fulfilled Knauss's original intention, not in the damage that it could have actually inflicted, but in the threat that it posed to an already sensitised public influenced by such publications as Southwold's *"The Gas War of 1940"* published in 1931.[68] This fact together with Hitler's astute move to remove Poland from the French sphere of influence, had effectively isolated France from both of her immediate allies thus securing for Germany a breathing space during which rearmament to be undertaken without interruption.

MAPS

I-1 Changes to the territorial boundaries of the German *Reich* following the peace treaties of 1919 (See Page 69)

---

67   Shirer 1969 pp.264-265. See also Terraine 1974.
68   Cooper 1981 pp.37-39, Terraine 1985 pp.12-13 & Corum 1997 pp.101-104. Southwold, writing under the pseudonym Miles, wrote: *Poland was attacked from the air, and its bloody ruins occupied by tanks. Alsace and Lorraine were invaded after punishment from a German air fleet that left alive a mere handful of their people* – quoted from Clarke I.F. 1966 *Voices Prophesying War 1763-1984* p.102 Oxford University Press. Military theorists were also well known to a wider public. These included Fuller & Liddell Hart in Britain, Mitchell & Seversky in the USA and Rougeron in France.

2A2

Command and Leadership

The Roles of Göring and Milch

Unlike his opposite numbers in the *Reichsheer* and the *Reichsmarine, Reichskommissar für die Luftfahrt* (Reichs Commissioner for Aviation) Hermann Göring was first and foremost a political appointment.[1] Nonetheless he had significant military experience and he had begun his adult life as a *Kompanie-Offizier* in the *4.badischen Infanterie-Regiment* in January 1914. He was one of the first officers to transfer to the *Luftstreitkräfte (Military Air Service)* under-going training as a *Beobachter* (Observer) in October of that year before joining *Feldflieger-Abteilung 25* in the Verdun sector. Here he flew with *Lt.*Bruno Loerzer against the French. Training as a pilot followed in the summer of 1915. He then returned to his original unit where he scored his first victory, a Farman biplane, on the 16 November of that year. A more belligerent role followed in 1916 when he started flying single-seat scouts. During the autumn he flew as a pilot with the *Kampfstaffel Metz* as well as with *Jasta 7* and *Jasta 5*. He was wounded in combat on the 2 November 1916 and spent four months in hospital. In February 1917 he joined *Oblt.*Loerzer's *Jasta 26* in Elsass where he flew an Albatros D-III. He was given his own squadron - *Jasta 27* - on the 17 May and soon after both he and Loerzer were based in the Ypres sector where they fought the British. Göring was promoted to *Oberleutnant* on the 18 August 1917; by November he had *15 Abschusse* and he received the *Pour le Mérite* on the 2 June 1918 with a score of *18 Luftsiege* (Aerial victories). Following the death of *Hptm.*Wilhelm Reinhard he was appointed *Kommandeur Jagdgeschwader 1 "Freiherr von Richthofen"* on the 17 July and his *Adjutant* was *Oblt.*Karl Bodenschatz. During the final months of hostilities Göring brought his overall score to 22 *Luftsiege*.[2]

Increasingly disillusioned by the revolutionary nature of German politics and unwilling to serve in new *Reichsheer* he resigned on the 11 March 1920 with the honorary rank of *Hauptmann* (See also 1A1). For a short period Göring gained some employment by flying in Denmark and Sweden. He returned to Germany in 1922 where he first met Adolf Hitler. Göring willingly joined the *NSDAP* and Hitler gave him charge of the *Sturmabteilung (SA)*, a motley rabble of some 2,000 thugs. A year later - 8 November 1923 - he was with Hitler in München at the time of ill-fated *Putsch*. Badly wounded in the engagement Göring fled abroad to avoid imprisonment moving first to the Tirol, then Rome and finally Stockholm. He did not return to Germany until 1927 where he

1   Suchenwirth R. Dr.1959 *Historical Turning Points in the German Air Force War Effort* USAF Historical Studies No.189 (hereafter referred to as Suchenwirth 1959) p.3. In Feb 33 the *Reichswehr's* most senior officers were *GenLt.* Kurt von Schleicher (*RWM*), *Gen.d.Inf.*Curt Frhr.von Hammerstein-Equord (*Reichsheer*) & *Adm.*Erich Raeder (*Reichsmarine*) - see Cooper M. 1978 *The German Army 1933-1945: It's Political and Military Failure* pp.10-12 & Mallmann Showell J.P. 1979 *The German Navy in World War Two: A Reference Guide to the Kriegsmarine 1935-1945* p.178.

2   Service record for Hermann Göring in Hildebrand K.F.1990 *Die Generale der deutschen Luftwaffe 1935-1945 Band 1 A-G* (hereafter cited as Hildebrand 1990) pp.369-370. See also Mason H.M. 1973 *The Rise of the Luftwaffe 1918-1940* pp.10-15, Angolia J.R. and Hackney C.R. 1984 *The Pour le Mérite and Germany's First Aces* pp.202-204 & Irving D. 1989 *Göring: A Biography* (hereafter cited as Irving 1989) pp.32-37.

became one of the first twelve National Socialist deputies to be elected to the *Reichstag (Photo 2A-3)*. In the years that followed he worked tirelessly to promote the Party's cause and his contribution was duly recognised in August 1932 when he was elected *Präsident des Deutschen Reichstags* (President of the German Parliament). In January 1933 he was appointed *preußischer Innenminister* (Prussian Minister of the Interior) and simultaneously *Reichsminister* without portfolio. Göring's final role in bringing Hitler to power was to help rig the outcome of the national elections in March 1933; the German Communist Party (*KPD*) was outlawed and this effectively excluded the 81 communist deputies from the *Reichstag* giving the *NSDAP* the two thirds majority that was required to form a new government.[3]

Göring's reward was to be appointed *Reichskommissar für die Luftfahrt* with the task of restoring Germany's military air power.[4] He immediately set about gathering together key individuals, men who included Karl Bodenschatz, Bruno Loerzer and Erhard Milch. Bodenschatz later recalled a conversation with Göring at the *Reichskommissar's* Kaiserdamm apartment:

> I am *Reichskommissar für die Luftfahrt* but in reality the first *Reichsminister der Luftfahrt* since the war. What I have promised when we parted in Aschaffenburg in 1918 I shall carry out - we shall have a German Air Force again. Not a military affair as yet ...you understand! The Treaty of Versailles is still in force. But as soon as the *Führer* has completed the political preparations to do away with Treaty, I want to be ready. I need a reliable friend to work with me - will you be my *Adjutant* again?[5]

On the 5 May 1933 his position was upgraded as *Reichsminister der Luftfahrt*.[6] As *RdL* it might have been expected that Göring would take the dominant role in the development of German aviation. Certainly he acted as a figure head and as early as the 30 January he addressed a large gathering of pilots and industrialists at the *Deutscher Aero-Club* in Berlin. After informing them that substantial credits would be made available to order new aircraft he stated:

> You will need workers but you can take your pick from six million unemployed. We shall put them to work building new aerodromes, factories, aircraft and engines. We shall pay men to take up flying and we shall bring experienced *Unteroffiziere* from the *Reichswehr* to discipline them. Even if they are not allowed to wear the uniform of airmen, they must be trained like real soldiers.[7]

3   Shirer W.L. 1963 *The Rise and Fall of the Third Reich: A History of Nazi Germany* (hereafter cited as Shirer 1963) pp.68-69, 73-75, 162, 170-171, 196, 184, 191-194, 200, 203-204 & 216, Mosley L. 1974 *The Reich Marshal: A Biography of Hermann Göring* (hereafter cited as Mosley 1974) pp.48-154, Irving 1989 pp.44-120 & Service record for Hermann Göring in Hildebrand 1990 pp.369-370.

4   Suchenwirth R. 1968 *The Development of the German Air Force 1919-1939* USAF Historical Studies No.160 (hereafter cited as Suchenwirth 1968) p.53 & 57.

5   Quoted from Mosley 1974 *The Reich Marshal: A Biography of Hermann Göring* p.167 with the knowledge of the Orion Publishing Group. *Maj.*Bodenschatz was still a serving officer with the *Reichsheer*. He was transferred to the still secret *Luftwaffe* as Göring's principal adjutant on the 1 Apr 33 - see service record for Karl Bodenschatz in Hildebrand 1990 pp.89-90. Loerzer was given the post of *Kommissar der Luftschiffe* - see Irving 1989 p.130.

6   Suchenwirth R. 1969 *Command and Leadership in the German Air Force* USAF Historical Studies No.174 (hereafter cited as Suchenwirth 1969 p.122, Mosley 1974 p.166, Irving 1989 p.130 & service record for Hermann Göring in Hildebrand 1990 pp.369-370.

7   Quoted from Moseley 1974 *The Reich Marshal: A Biography of Hermann Göring* p.169 with the knowledge of the Orion Publishing Group. This gathering was to mark the 25th Anniversary of the *Deutscher Aero-Club*. See also Lee A. 1972 *Goering; Air Leader* (hereafter cited as Lee 1972) p.40. In 1934 2 million workers were already engaged in construction projects associated with the emerging *Luftwaffe* - see Irving D. 1973 *The Rise and Fall of the Luftwaffe: The Life of Luftwaffe Marshal Erhard Milch* (hereafter cited as Irving 1973) pp.34-35.

He was also a strong proponent of the strategic use of air power and took great personal satisfaction from being associated with the most modern and arguably the most spectacular of the armed forces of the new *Reich* (See 2A1).[8] However despite his strong personal interest in aeronautics his other political commitments and responsibilities left little time and energy for this new role and he was an infrequent visitor to the Ministry.[9] Erhard Milch, his *Staatssekretär*, dutifully renovated the old boardroom at the Behrenstrasse for Göring's use but he was to officiate their on just two occasions:[10]

FIGURE 2A-3 POSITIONS OF STATE HELD BY HERMANN GÖRING 1932-35	
30 Aug 32	Präsidenten des Deutschen Reichstags
30 Jan 33	Reichsminister ohne Geschaftsbereich
30 Jan 33	Preußischen Minister des Innern
2 Feb 33	Reichskommissar für die Luftfahrt
11 Apr 33	Preußischen Ministerpräsidenten
21 Apr 33	Reichsminister des Innern
5 May 33	Reichsminister der Luftfahrt
8 Jul 33	Präsidenten des Preussichen Staatsrates
3 Jul 34	Reichsforstmeister und Reichsjägermeister
30 Jan 35	Reichsstatthalters in Preussen
1 Mar 35	Chef der Reichsluftwaffe
1 Jun 35	Oberbefehlshaber der Luftwaffe

Göring's interests were primarily political and it was the pursuit of personal power that had always been his major pre-occupation *(Photo 2A-4)*.[11] This was particularly true of the early years of *Nazi* Germany when the *NSDAP's* hold on the nation was comparatively tenuous and whilst there were still powerful factions for dissent within the *Reich*. These forces were of a disparate nature and included the communists, the military, the trade unions and even the church, whilst the emergence of the *SA* as a distinct force within the Party became progressively more worrying.[12]

8   Overy R.J. 1984 *Goering: The Iron Man* (hereafter cited as Overy 1984) p.33. This author suggests: *"The air force served the purpose of identifying the Nazi movement, and Göring in particular, with the most spectacular and modern of the three services. The glamour of aviation served a specific propaganda purpose. Moreover Göring believed that a future war might be won by air power alone, thus making the older services redundant."* In answer to Blomberg's concerns about the huge expenditure associated with the establishment of the Luftwaffe Göring was able to defend his position: *"Strategic air warfare was a cheaper, faster and ultimately more 'national-socialist' way of solving Germany's military problems."* Quoted from Overy R.J. 1984 *Goering: The Iron Man* p.33 Routledge & Kegan Paul plc.

9   Suchenwirth 1969 p.123, Lee 1972 p.40 & Irving 1989 p.131. However one of his first visits after being appointed *RdL* was to the *E-Stelle* Rechlin on the 29 Mar 33. He was visibly impressed: *"I had no idea that you are so advanced..."* Quoted from Volker K-H. 1962 *Die Entwicklung der militärischen Luftfahrt in Deutschland 1920-1933* Deutsche Verlags-Anstalt. Also present were *Gen.d.Inf.*von Blomberg, & *Adm.*Raeder. See also Irving 1973 p.31.

10   Irving 1973 p.30. Göring preferred to use his main office at the *Preußischen Ministerium des Innern* in the Unter der Linden and later another office adjacent to his official Berlin residence in Leipziger Platz 7a. See also Suchenwirth 1969 p.123, Mosley 1974 pp.177-178 & *Kurzbiographien des Reichsmarschalls und der Generalfeldmarschalle der deutschen Luftwaffe Göring* in Absolon R. (Ed.) 1984 *Rangliste der Generale der deutschen Luftwaffe nach dem stand vom 20.April 1945* pp.105-106.

11   Suchenwirth 1969 pp.121-123, Mosley 1974 pp.109-118 & Irving 1989 pp.92-94 & 170.

12   Shirer 1963 p.190 & Overy 1984 pp.26-27.

Göring played a crucial role in the establishment of a unified nation under the leadership of Adolf Hitler, his most important contributions being his acceptance by the higher echelons of German society, his control of the *Forschungsamt* (Wireless Intercept Office) and the *Geheime Staatspolizeiamt* (Office of the Secret State Police).[13] Technically part of the *RLM*, but in reality nothing to do with the Air Ministry, the *Forschungsamt* was created by Göring in April 1933 to tap telephones, intercept diplomatic, commercial and media radio messages and to break codes.[14] Funded by the *Preussichen Staatsrates* (Prussian State Department), the *Forschungsamt* began work with just four code-breakers but it expanded rapidly under the leadership of *KorvKap.a.D.*Hans Schimpf to eventually embrace all aspects of communication inside the *Reich*.[15] It was an invaluable source of intelligence on individuals, groups and even foreign powers and Göring was to use this power ruthlessly to further his own interests and those of his *Führer*.[16] The *Geheime Staatspolizeiamt* or *Gestapo* was also created by Göring in April 1933, ostensibly to combat the communists, but in reality with a wider brief which extended to all Göring's political opponents including those inside the Party.[17] The *Gestapo* was hidden within the *Preussichen Innern-Ministerium* (Prussian Interior Ministry) and was initially under the control of Rudolf Diels, another Göring appointee.[18]

His position within the Party as Hitler's confidant and within the Government as a *Reichsminister* put Göring at the centre of a succession of internal struggles.[19] These intrigues included the *Reichstag* fire of the 27 February 1933, the purge of the dissidents and their incarceration in the first concentration camps from May 1933, the subsequent control of the more militant elements of the *SA* during the summer of 1933, and perhaps most significantly the purging of the *SA's* leaders on the 30 June 1934.[20] Some 84 activists and unfortunates were murdered during the *Die Nacht der langen Messer* (Night of the Long Knives), most of whom were members of the *SA*, but in the orgy of killing both Göring and Himmler, the *Reichsführer-SS*, took the opportunity to settle some

13   Kahn D. 1978 *Hitler's Spies: German Military Intelligence in the World War II* (hereafter cited as Kahn 1978) pp.55-56 & Irving 1989 pp.123-126. See also Overy 1984 pp.26-27 & 35.
14   Kahn 1978 pp.178-179. The *Forschungsamt* was the brainchild of Gottfried Schapper, a *Nazi* Party member and employee of the *RWM* where he was a cryptanalyst. The *Forschungsamt* was initially concealed in the attic of the *RLM* in the Behrenstrasse before it moved into a hotel and finally in 1934/35 into a converted housing complex, the Schiller Colonades at Schillerstrasse 116-124. By Jul 33 there were c.20 wireless operators, telephone technicians, cryptanalysts and evaluators.
15   Kahn 1978 pp.179-180. Göring's authority was needed for all wire taps. Reports were typed on light brown paper and were sent to Göring who used them to advance himself and Hitler. Valuable economic, political, diplomatic and military intelligence was gained by the *Forschungsamt*.
16   Mosley 1974 pp.187-188. Göring's first job each day was to read the intercepts of the previous 24 hours.
17   Snyder L.L. 1976 *Encyclopaedia of the Third Reich* (hereafter cited as Snyder 1976) pp.113-114. The basis of the *Gestapo* was the Prussian Political Police which Göring had transferred to the *Preußischen Ministerium des Innern* in a move to protect *Adm.*Magnus von Levetzow, the Chief of Police in Berlin, from the increasingly belligerent activities of the *SA*. Göring also saw this force as the basis for a personal army that would be utterly loyal to him alone.
18   Overy 1984 pp.26-27 & Irving 1989 pp.121-122. Under Göring & Diels the *Gestapo*, staffed primarily by lawyers and intellectuals, became a major weapon in the Party's on-going struggle with political dissidents and in particular the German communists. Göring lost control of the *Gestapo* to an emerging political rival in the form of Heinrich Himmler on the 20 Apr 34 although he retained control of *Pol-GenMaj.*Walther Wecke's *Landespolizeigruppe "General Göring"* - see Bender R.J. and Petersen G.A. 1975 *Hermann Göring from Regiment to Fallschirmpanzerkorps* pp.7-9, Otte A. 1988 *Die Weissen Spiegel: Vom Regiment zum Fallschirmpanzerkorps* pp.5-6 & Kurowski F. 1995 *The History of the Fallschirmpanzerkorps Hermann Göring: Soldiers of the Reichsmarschall* pp.1-2. In 1939 the *Gestapo* was incorporated into the *Reichssicherheitshauptamt (RSHA)* as its *IV.Amt*.
19   Overy 1984 pp.25-27.
20   Mosley 1974 pp.157-161 & 173-177, Overy 1984 pp.28-31 & Irving 1989 pp.115-119. Göring did himself great disservice in the trial that followed the *Reichstag Fire*. There were many who believed that Göring had personally stage managed the whole incident. He maintained that this was not the case and he saw the trial in Nov 33 as a means of clearing his name as well as finally discrediting the communists. All bar one of the defendants were acquitted and Göring publicly lost a great deal of his political prestige in his judicial contest with Georgi Dimitrov, one of the five accused - see also Snyder 1976 pp.288-289.

personal scores *(Photo 2A-5)*.[21] With his pivotal role acknowledged by *Reichspräsident GFM.a.D.*Paul von Hindenburg, Göring was publicly portrayed as the hero of the hour. These events served to emphasise his earlier political standing within the emerging *Third Reich*.[22] Increasingly he was seen as Hitler's right hand man, emissary and ultimately his deputy.[23]

Ironically his success in internal affairs led to a progressive weakening of his ministerial power-base with the loss of his responsibilities in Prussia as power became more centralised, whilst the virtual suspension of the *Reichstag* in the mid-thirties led to a further loss of influence in the Government.[24] To offset this trend Göring sought to extend his interest into economic and foreign affairs and in the wake of three official visits to Italy during 1933 he visited Poland in March 1934 before undertaking a ten-day tour of the Balkans in May of that year.[25] Unfortunately his performance in Rome was less than helpful and he ultimately earned the enmity of Benito Mussolini who even refused to deal with him in matters of negotiation between Italy and Germany *(Photo 2A-6)*.[26] In Poland he was more successful and he was able to develop a personal relationship with Jozef Lipski, the new Polish Ambassador in Berlin, which over the years encouraged the Poles to progressively distance themselves from the French.[27] He also made a favourable impression in Yugoslavia in October 1934 when he arrived at Belgrade in the new Junkers G.38 on the occasion of state funeral of the murdered king.[28] Indeed the Balkan nations found Germany's interest in

---

21   Shirer 1963 pp.219-224, Mosley 1974 pp.187-196, Snyder 1976 pp.31-33 & Irving 1989 pp.145-149 . Whilst Hitler and his assassins travelled to München to deal with Roehm and his immediate associates, Göring co-ordinated the killings in Berlin. In this he was assisted by Himmler, Korner & *Obst.i.G.*Walther Reichenau *(C.d.S.d.RWM)*, in a remarkable partnership that reflected the shared concerns of the Party and the *Reichsheer* in the increasing power of the *SA* - see Hohne H. 1972 *The Order of the Death's Head* (hereafter cited as Hohne 1972)p.97 & Seaton A. 1982 *The German Army 1933-1945* (hereafter cited as Seaton 1982) pp.45-49. Most of the executions were carried out by Himmler's *SS* although *Pol-GenMaj.*Walther Wecke's *Landespolizeigruppe "General Göring"* had a hand in rounding up the unfortunates on Göring's lists – see Hohne 1972 p.96, 102 & pp.106-109 & 110-119.Gotthard Sachsenberg narrowly escaped with his life. He was actually arrested and put on a truck bound for the Lichterfelde to be shot when the truck was stopped and he was imprisoned instead. Göring certainly had no love of the man, it was perhaps Milch that saved him - see Hermann 1943 *The Rise and Fall of the Luftwaffe* (hereafter cited as Hermann 1943) p.58. Kurt Schleicher was one of those who were murdered: *"Göring had sent his Landespolizei to deal with the General - but an unidentified "hit squad" of five assassins had beaten the green-uniformed police to it. They burst into the general's Babelsberg villa at midday and shot the general to death in a hail of bullets - seven bullet wounds were found, and five cartridge cases. They had slain the general's wife as well. Unabashed, Göring instructed his staff to describe the killing as suicide." -* Quoted from Irving 1989 *Göring: A Biography* p.147 with the knowledge of the Orion Publishing Group. Milch arranged for 800 men from the *Fl.Tech.Schule Jüterbog (Obstlt.*Student) to secure the *RLM* and Berlin's airfields, 400 of these men later formed an honour guard for Hitler when he returned to Berlin from Munch - see Irving 1973 p.41. The *Reichsheer* had been placed on standby - see Seaton 1982 p.47.

22   *Telegram 088/Teleg.4012 from Hindenburg* in Mosley 1974 p.195: *"Accept my approval and gratitude for your successful action in suppressing the high treason. With comradely thanks and greetings"* (Signed) Hindenburg. See also Shirer 1963 p.225, Suchenwirth 1969 p.136 & Irving 1989 p.150.

23   Mosley 1974 p.196 & Irving 1989 p.153. On the 7 Dec 34 Hitler secretly nominated Göring as his deputy and simultaneously specified him as his successor. In fact Rudolf Hess held that position, having been named Deputy Führer on the 21 Apr 33 - see Suchenwirth 1969 p.140 & Snyder 1976 pp.142-143. It has been suggested that Göring's position within the *Nazi* hierarchy was still precarious in 1934 – see Overy 1984 p.31 – although this source confirms the strength of Göring's personal relationship with the *Führer* during this key period – see Overy 1984 p.34.

24   Overy 1984 pp.31-32.

25   Suchenwirth 1969 p.141, Overy 1984 p.32 & Irving 1989 pp.152-153.

26   Mosley 1974 pp.172-173, Overy 1984 p.32 & Irving 1989 pp.122-123. On the 11 Oct 33 Mussolini remarked to the British Ambassador that Göring was *"a former inmate of an asylum"*. Göring's last discussions with Mussolini took place on the 6 & 7 Nov 33 when the *Reichsminister* attempted to re-assure *Il Duce* that Hitler had no designs on Austria. Mussolini was not deceived and in Mar 34 he signed the Roman Protocols with both Austria and Hungary thus guaranteeing the former's sovereignty - at least for the time being.

27   Shirer 1963 pp.212-213 & Irving 1989 p.142. Göring was to visit the Polish State Hunting Ground at Bialowieza annually during 1934-38.

28   Irving 1989 pp.142-143 & 152-153. However this was not Göring's first visit. On the 15 May 34 accompanied by

the region to be a useful counter-weight to that of Mussolini's Italy which had its own territorial ambitions in south-eastern Europe.[29]

In many ways Göring's contribution to the development of German aviation has to be seen in this light. He liked to be centre-stage, to be at the focus of power, and to be seen as a source of that power. He delighted in the trappings of government and the possession of titled-positions and one of his first actions on being appointed *Reichsminister der Luftfahrt* was to personally design his own standard.[30] In a related vein he proposed to the Cabinet on the 7 April 1933 that the *Reich* should re-introduce honours and distinctions.[31] Not surprisingly he also had a major hand in the design of the new ceremonial uniforms for the *Deutsche Luftsportverband (DLV)*, uniforms that would later be adopted by the *Luftwaffe* (see 2D2).[32] These designs, which were modelled on the 4 October 1933, included the wearing by all ranks of the *Fliegermesser* or pilot's knife, replaced at a later date by the *Fliegerdolch* or pilot's dagger.[33] In addition to his support for these rather archaic embellishments for what was otherwise a modern service, Göring took a particular interest in his own uniforms and those of his generals.[34] As early as the 31 August 1933 he had been accorded the honorary rank of *General der Infanterie* by the personal order of *Präsident* Hindenburg, a title which he had been actively seeking for some time.[35]

Aside from his interest in the trappings of power Göring's position as an independent minister of state within the *Kabinett* (Cabinet) gave him equality with Hjalmar Schacht, the finance minister, and with Blomberg who was technically his superior within the *Reichswehr*.[36] Moreover his refusal

Milch, Korner, Kerrl & Prinz Philipp of Hesse (and rather scandalously his girlfriend Emmy Sonnemann) Göring had made a ten day tour of the Balkans beginning in Rome before moving on to Budapest, Belgrade and south to Greece. The tour was a calculated affront to Mussolini and Italian pretensions in this key mineral rich area. It was rumoured that Italian Fascists had been responsible for the King's assassination in Marseilles. Foreign observers in Belgrade conceded that Göring had "stolen the show" and this particular visit was instrumental in establishing closer links between Yugoslavia and Germany.

29   Overy 1984 p.32 & Irving 1989 p.153. The fact that the French saw Yugoslavia, Czechoslovakia and Romania as valuable eastern allies would not have escaped Hitler or Göring. Between 1929-37 the French sponsored regular military conferences with these states - see Shirer W.L. 1969 *The Collapse of the Third Republic: An Inquiry into the Fall of France in 1940* p.184 & 346 & Palmer A. *Operation Punishment* in Liddell Hart B.H. & Pitt B. (Ed.) *History of the Second World War Vol.1* pp.374-375.

30   Suchenwirth 1959 p.3 & Suchenwirth 1969 p.134 . Göring personally designed the Command Flag (Standard) for the *RdL* which was introduced on the 5 May 33. Prior to this he had used the Command Flag for the *Preußischen Ministarpräsident* - see Davis B.L. 1975 *Flags and Standards of the Third Reich: Army, Navy and Air Force* pp.134-136.

31   Irving 1989 p.156. Göring was of the opinion that the paucity of honours was one of the reasons for the failure of Weimar Republic.

32   Bender R.J. 1972 *Air Organisations of the Third Reich: The Luftwaffe* (hereafter cited as Bender 1972) pp.8-14 & Davis B.L. 1991 *Uniforms and Insignia of the Luftwaffe Vol.1: 1933-1940* (hereafter cited as Davis 1991) pp.13-27. The *DLV* was reorganised on the 25 Mar 33 as a state sponsored and controlled organisation - see also Ries K. 1970 *Luftwaffe Bd.1 Die Maulwurfe 1919-1935* pp.45-46.

33   Davis 1991 p.14. Göring took a personal hand in the design of the new uniform. The date the uniforms were introduced has not been recorded, although from Sep 33 all officers assigned to the secret *Luftwaffe* had been issued with the *DLV* uniform for use on specified occasions. The first time Hitler witnessed the use of the uniform en masse was on his return to Berlin from München on the occasion of the purge of the *SA*. He commented; *"This the first welcome sight today. The men have been well chosen for their race!"* - see Irving 1973 p.41 & Irving 1989 pp.156-157.

34   Irving 1989 p.157. It became normal practice for Göring to present each *General* with a fine sword, signed by himself.

35   Service record for Hermann Göring in Hildebrand 1990 pp.369-370. See also *Die deutsche Luftfahrt – Jahrbuch 1936* p.15 in Maass B. 1955 *The Organisation of the German Air Force High Command and Higher Echelon Headquarters within the German Air Force* USAF Historical Studies No.190 (hereafter cited as Maass 1955) p.18, Suchenwirth 1968 p.52, Suchenwirth 1969 p.123 & Irving 1989 p.134. Having a *General's* rank gave Göring some standing amongst his contemporaries in the *Reichswehr*.

36   Suchenwirth 1969 p.131 & Snyder 1976 pp.307-308 & 29-30.Schacht had helped the *NSDAP's* rise to power by arranging financial support from wealthy Rheinland industrialists. He was rewarded in Mar 33 when he was named *Präsident d.Reichsbank*. In Aug 34 he was made *Reichsminister*. Blomberg was promoted to *GenOb.* by Hindenburg on the 31 Aug 33. Göring refused to acknowledge that he was subordinate to anybody other than Hitler - see also

to acknowledge the authority of anyone but Hitler was to be particularly advantageous to the *Luftwaffe* as he was able to secure very generous funding for its development.[37] Blomberg's ministry often tried to put a block on the *Luftwaffe's* demands for more money. When that happened Göring would intervene, saying:

"Give that stuff to me!" before returning from an audience with Hitler with the words: *"Here it is. The Führer is surprised that we're so modest. He expected us to ask for a lot more. Incidentally, once and for all, money is no object! Remember that!"*[38]

Göring was committed to a high level of rearmament both as a means of restoring Germany's freedom of action on the international stage and as a way of re-energising the economy in the wake of the world economic downturn.[39] Even at this stage he was a major consumer of the *Reich's* resources and in the fiscal year 1934/35 the *Luftwaffe* spent *RM* 642 million out of a total *Reichswehr* budget of *RM* 1,953 million (32.9%).[40] It was a major employer of civilian labour, both in the rapidly expanding aero-industry and also in the plethora of construction projects associated with the ground organisation (See also 3B3). At the same time it was a major consumer of scarce raw materials.[41]

Göring's political position also allowed him to successfully out-manoeuvre *Gen.d.Inf.* Freiherr Kurt von Hammerstein-Equord and his successor *Gen.d.Art.* Werner Frhr.von Fritsch as *Chef der Heeresleitung*.[42] Good examples are provided by Göring's acquisition of the *Reichsheer's* residual aviation interests during the late summer of 1933 and Fritsch's agreement to administrative control by the *RLM* over the *Reichsheer's* embryonic anti-aircraft force, the *Fahrtruppen-Flak*, in April 1934 (See 2A3, 2B1 & 2C1).[43] The issue of control over the *Flakartillerie* had been the subject of considerable debate with the *Reichsheer* being anxious to maintain an air defence capability on the battlefield (See also 1A3).[44] On the other hand Göring had successfully argued that the air defence of the Reich was clearly a *Luftwaffe* responsibility and that an integrated air defence system of fighter aircraft and anti-aircraft artillery was in the best interests of the nation's security. Something of a compromise was reached with operational control of the *Fahrtruppe (Flak)* remaining with the

Maass 1955 p.24.

37 Maass 1955 p.24 & Irving 1973 pp.32-33. Schacht was responsible for financing the rearmament programme: *"an old skeleton company - eventually the Metal Research Company "Mefo" was chosen - should be guaranteed by the Reichsbank and used to cover the financing of industry with its own bills of exchange, of nominal validity of three months, automatically extended each time. These Reich-backed "Mefo-Bills" could be discounted at the Reichsbank at any time, and would go to selected big industrial concerns as payment. Milch and Schacht were directors of the company. It was a neat economic trick, but not al illicit one"*. See also Suchenwirth 1969 p.131.

38 Quoted from Suchenwirth 1969 *Command and Leadership in the German Air Force* USAF Historical Studies No.174 p.131.

39 Overy 1984 p.37.

40 *Table 1 German military expenditure 1934/5 - 1937/8 (billion RM)* in Overy 1984 p.38.

41 Mosley 1974 p.169 & pp.203-204 and Overy 1984 pp.37-38.

42 Seaton 1982 pp.30-32. The *Heeresleitung* was opposed to the creation of a separate air arm. Following the establishment of the *RLM* on the 27 Apr 33 it demanded the return of all flying and anti-aircraft artillery units that were earmarked for operations with the *Feldheer* – see Hooton E.R. 1994 *Phoenix Triumphant: The Rise and Rise of the Luftwaffe* pp.71-73 & p.99. The *Marineleitung* was determined to retain operational control over those units assigned to naval air operations - see USONI 1947 *German Naval Air 1933 to 1945 – A Report based on German Naval Staff Documents* & Gaul W. Obst.i.G.a.D. *The German Naval Air Force, 1933 – September 1939* in Isby D.C. (Ed.) 2005 *The Luftwaffe and the War at Sea 1939-45: As seen by officers of the Kriegsmarine and Luftwaffe* p.26 & 80.

43 Hermann 1943 p.65, Maass 1955 pp.14-19.& Overy 1984 pp.32-33. It had taken political pressure from Hitler to obtain Blomberg's agreement to the transfer of the *Luftschützamt* to the *RLM* on the 15 May 33. Blomberg had established the *LS-Amt* on the 21 Feb 33 under his personal direction. It was transferred to *RLM* control on the 15 May 33, and physically to the Behrenstrasse on the 1 Sep 33.

44 Seaton 1982 pp.73-74.

Reichsheer, being disguised as *Ausbildungsstab 3* within *Inspektion Nr.4 (Artillerie)*, until such time as the *Luftwaffe* was publicly revealed as an independent service.[45]

Despite these successes at ministerial level Göring was never comfortable with routine administrative tasks and he found it increasingly difficult to discipline himself to hard, continuous work *(Photo 2A-7)*.[46] In the light of these observations it has been suggested that his main contribution to the development of the *Luftwaffe "lay in the domineering force of his personality and its impact upon associates and subordinates"*.[47] Certainly Albert Keßelring, the *Luftwaffe's Chef LD* (Administrative Chief) later recalled: *"He was always at his best under pressure…when the rest of us were completely exhausted, (he) was still able to go on"*, whilst Hans-Jurgen Stumpff, who was *Chef LP* (Chief of Personnel) from June 1933, also remembered his significant impact: *"You left every conference with him, boosted to an extra thousand rpm."*.[48]

The *"Iron Man"* was clearly an imposing individual with his impressive bearing, portly frame, his startling blue eyes, and an array of high decorations resting upon the most splendid of uniforms. His powerful voice had a great effect upon all listeners, and he learned to make it an instrument of clarity and persuasion. He was inordinately optimistic, and seemed not to know the meaning of the word impossible. One word from him and countless ambitious minds and industrious hands in a number of fields went earnestly to work, each vying with the other to report new successes to the Commander.

One of his greatest strengths was his recognition of his own inadequacies and he was not slow to appoint other men to positions which he could not fill himself.[49] Unfortunately his choice was not always wise and often he would allow his heart to rule his mind with the appointment of old friends to key government positions. This was done partly out of loyalty to former comrades and partly due to his distrust of the professionals whose strength lay in their knowledge and expertise, attributes which he knew he lacked.[50] Key appointments during this period included *Hptm.a.D.*Bruno Loerzer who was quickly appointed *Präsident Deutsche Luftsport-Verband e.V. (DLV)* (President of German Sport Aviation), *Maj.*Karl Bodenschatz who became his *Chef Adjutant* and Paul Korner, a former officer who had joined the Göring household in 1928 as an informal chauffeur and who was later elevated as *Staatssekretär des Preussichen Staatsrates* (Prussian State Secretary) where he had a supervisory role over the *Forschungsamt*.[51]

---

45   Westermann E.B. 2001 *Flak: German Anti-aircraft Defenses 1914-1945* pp.54-57. On the 16 Sep 33 Blomberg created the position *of Inspekteur der Flakartillerie und Chef des Luftschützes* within the overall authority of the *RWM*. However the *RLM* had responsibility for the organisation, training, expansion and equipment of ground-based air defence forces from the 1 Apr 34 – see *Contribution by Gen.d.Flg.a.D.Hellmuth Felmy* in Maass 1955 p.25. GenMaj. Günther Rüdel was appointed as *Insp.d.Flak.u.Chef.d.Luftschützes/RWM* on the 1 Oct 34 - see service record for Günther Rüdel in Hildebrand K.F.1992 *Die Generale der deutschen Luftwaffe 1935-1945 Band 3 O-Z* pp.146-147. See also *Contributions by Gen.d.Flg.a.D.Rudolf Bogatsch & Gen.d.Flak.a.D.Walther von Axthelm* in Maass 1955 p.20.

46   Suchenwirth 1959 p.3, 1968 p.54 & 1969 pp.142-143.

47   Quoted from *Keßelring A. GFM.a.D.* in Suchenwirth 1969 *Command and Leadership in the German Air Force* p.131.

48   Quoted from *Interview with GFM.a.D.Albert Keßelring & Prof.Suchenwirth, 30 Jan 56* in Karlsruhe Document Collection D/II/1 in Suchenwirth 1969 *Command and Leadership in the German Air Force* USAF Historical Studies No.174 p.131. See also Irving 1989 p.131.

49   Suchenwirth 1969 p.129 & Cooper M. 1981 *The German Air Force 1933-1945: An Anatomy of Failure* (hereafter cited as Cooper 1981) p.8-9.

50   Suchenwirth 1969 p.128. Göring made a point of recruiting nearly all of the former *Luftstreitkräfte's* holders of the *Pour le Mérite* for the new *Luftwaffe*. In most cases such men received accelerated promotion to equal that of officers who had remained in military service after the war – see Suchenwirth 1969 p.54, Lee 1972 p.40 & Angolia and Hackney 1984..

51   Service record for Karl Bodenschatz in Hildebrand 1990 pp.89-90 & Bruno Loerzer in Hildebrand K.F.1991

Without doubt one of Göring's most inspired appointments was that of Erhard Milch as *Staatssekretär für die Luftfahrt* (State Secretary for Aviation).[52] Unlike Loerzer and Bodenschatz he was not a wartime comrade, in fact he was not even a pilot although he had seen war-service as an observer in the *Luftstreitkräfte's* reconnaissance forces.[53] Nor did Milch particularly want the post, being concerned amongst other things of Göring's earlier morphine addiction (See 1A3). He was finally won around by Hitler:

I may not have known you very long; but you are an expert in your own field and we have nobody in the Party who knows as much about aviation as you. You must accept! It is not the Party calling you, it is Germany - Germany needs you in this office![54]

Conversation between Hitler and Milch
31 January 1933

Milch became *Staatssekretär* on the 22 February 1933.[55] Milch and Göring were never to form a close friendship and at times their relationship could only be described as tempestuous.[56] Nonetheless Milch proved an admirable choice as *Staatssekretär* where his unbroken association with the development of German commercial aviation had given him an excellent knowledge of the aviation industry and in particular its capabilities and its personalities (See also 1D2). He also had excellent connections with the Party and was held in high esteem by the *Führer*.[57]

On a personal level Milch was a first-class administrator and a superb organiser. Like Göring he was an optimist and very ambitious. He too coveted military rank being appointed a honorary *Oberst* on the 28 October 1933 and a honorary *Generalmajor* on the 24 March 1934, but whilst these honours undoubtedly gave him a great deal of personal satisfaction he saw them primarily as a means to an end *(Photo 2A-8)*.[58] As a civilian in an increasingly militaristic organisation it was essential for him to have this seniority over his office chiefs and equality with his opposite numbers in the *RWM*. Equally he understood the importance of good personnel management and as a sensitive individual

Die Generale der deutschen Luftwaffe 1935-1945 Band 2 H-N (hereafter cited as Hildebrand 1991) pp.309-310, Suchenwirth 1969 pp.133-134 & Irving 1989 p.123 & 130.

52 Suchenwirth 1969 p.19 & pp.127- 128. Milch was not keen to accept the post being more than content with his role at Lufthansa. He suggested *KonAdm.a.D.*Rudolf Lahs, the *Präsident d.Reichsverband der deutschen Luftfahrtindustrie*, or Ernst Brandenburg , the *Chef Abt.Luftverkehr /RVM*, as alternative candidates. Göring preferred Lahs but the *Admiral* had been unenthusiastic - see Heinkel E. 1956 *He 1000* p.154. Brandenburg, a man of great experience, versatility and talent, would have been a major asset to the emerging *Luftwaffe* - see Irving 1973 p.29.
53 Service record for Erhard Milch in Hildebrand 1991 pp.394-395. See also Suchenwirth 1969 p.128.
54 Quoted from *Milch Diary, 31 Jan 1933 & MCH, 11 Mar 47* p.1776 in Irving 1973 *The Rise and Fall of the Luftwaffe: initially The Life of Luftwaffe Marshal Erhard Milch* p.29 with the knowledge of the Orion Publishing Group. Göring had become addicted following his wounding in the *München Putsch* of 1923 - see Mosley 1974 pp.77-86 & Irving 1989 pp.54-67. Göring was still addicted in 1933 although he assured Milch that he was no longer a user - *Interrogation of Erhard Milch, 11 Mar 47*, MCH in Irving 1973 p.29. Hitler was well disposed toward Milch who had arranged for *DLH* aircraft to put at his disposal during election battles in 1932 - see Herrmann 1943 pp.54-55, Suchenwirth 1969 p.19 & Sweeting C.G. 2001 *Hitler's Squadron: The Führer's Personal Aircraft and Transport Unit 1933-45* p.14.
55 *Dokumente Nr.40* in Volker K.H. 1968 *Dokumente und Documentarfotos zue Geschichte der deutschen Luftwaffe* p.131. Milch joined the *NSDAP* with an artificially low membership number (123,685) after the Party's election victory of Mar 33 – See Irving 1973 p.356. See also Suchenwirth 1969 p.19.
56 Suchenwirth 1969 & Irving 1973 p.42.
57 Suchenwirth 1969 p.25.
58 Suchenwirth 1969 p.19 & Service record for Erhard Milch in Hildebrand 1991 pp.394-395. Milch saw himself as a soldier, whilst his military contemporaries regarded him as a civilian - a captain of industry - see Suchenwirth 1969 pp.24-25.

he was able to generate loyalty from his immediate staff.[59] Nonetheless he could also be utterly ruthless, as was shown in his removal of *Professor* Junkers from control of the *Junkers Flugzeug- und Motorenwerke* in October 1933 (See 2C3), and his abrupt manner and caustic tongue when dealing with men he perceived as threats to his position were to later earn him many enemies.[60]

It has already been shown that Milch was not only a guiding light in the administrative aspects of the development of the *Luftwaffe* but also in many aspects of its strategic doctrine and future equipment (See 2A1 & 2C2). On the 27 August 1933 Milch inspected the blueprints for a new Heinkel twin-engine monoplane which had potential as a second generation medium bomber for the *Luftwaffe*, development contracts for this and a similar design from *Junkers* being placed early in 1934 (See 3C2).[61] Also in 1933 strategic thinking had led to thoughts of an even larger four-engine long range bomber, a machine which Milch felt should *"be able to fly right round Britain under combat conditions"*, an aircraft which could truly dominate the European skies (See 3C2).[62] However such a concept was still well into the future and development contracts were not issued until 1935. In the meantime Milch had become interested in the concept of the dive bomber and orders were issued on the 12 October 1933 for the formation of a *Sturzkampfgruppe* (Dive Bomber Group) at Schwerin (See 2E2 & 3C2).[63] At that time the United States Navy and Marine Corps were probably the leading authorities on this form of attack and Göring supplied his friend Ernst Udet with sufficient funding to purchase two Curtiss Hawk II biplanes, an export version of the standard F11C/BFC Goshawk shipboard single-seat fighter-bomber which had entered American service in February 1933.[64] Officials within the *RLM's Technisches Amt* (Technical Office) were not particularly impressed with the Hawk but on the 16 December 1933 Milch had Udet demonstrate the machine's capabilities to him at Berlin-Tempelhof *(Photo 2A-9)*. He was sufficiently impressed to ask Udet to attend all future conferences on dive bombing at the Ministry.[65]

In Göring's absence it was Milch that signed most of the important orders.[66] He even had to deal with the contingency planning associated with the threat of foreign intervention following the Führer's decision to withdraw from Geneva in October 1933 (See 2E1). At that critical point Göring was in Sweden visiting the grave of his wife Carin and therefore Blomberg instructed Milch to take

---

59   Suchenwirth 1969 p.21 & 25. *"(Milch was) a man of indomitable health and energy, stubborn but alert in his work, tremendously ambitious, efficient, without the polish of a diplomat but pleasant and congenial as long as no one tried to usurp his position as deputy to Göring, he was obviously of great help to the officers who were recruited from the Reichsheer and were unfamiliar with the Luftwaffe"* – quoted from *Keßelring A.GFM.a.D.* in Suchenwirth 1968 *Command and Leadership in the German Air Force* USAF Historical Studies No.174 p.58.

60   Herrmann 1943 pp.56-58. He had *Prof.*Hugo Junkers replaced by his son Klaus Junkers, whilst Heinrich Koppenberg was appointed General Manager of *JFM*. A major expansion of the Dessau site quickly followed - see Irving 1973 pp.34-35 & Cooper 1981 p.11.

61   *Milch Diary, 25 Aug 33* in Irving 1973 p.35.

62   Irving 1973 p.35. Wever saw this as a *"Ural Bomber"*, a long range weapon for use in the inevitable conflict with Communist Russia; Milch appears to have appreciated its maritime potential for a possible war with Britain. See Suchenwirth 1969 pp.5-6.

63   Ishoven van A. 1977 *The Fall of an Eagle: The Life of Fighter Ace Ernst Udet* (hereafter cited as Ishoven 1977) p.147. Milch was not alone in seeing the potential of dive bombing. In *H.Dv.300 "Die Truppenführung" 1933* a whole section was devoted to the dive bomber which was seen as a long range artillery weapon for destroying point targets behind the *HKL* - see *H.Dv.300 1933* in Corum J.S. 1997 *The Luftwaffe: Creating the Operational Air War 1918-1940* p.129.

64   Ishoven 1977 pp.141-142. Each aircraft cost between $ 11,825 - $ 15,700 less engines - see Bowers P.M. 1979 *Curtiss Aircraft 1907-1947* p.281-282

65   Suchenwirth 1969 pp.59-61 & Ishoven 1977 pp.146-147. Göring issued orders to proceed with the dive bomber on the 31 Jan 34.

66   *Milch Diary, 20, 23 & 24 Oct 33* in Irving 1973 p.36. *"The directive for the event of sanctions"* was issued on the 25 Oct 33 - see Irving 1973 p.360. Göring's capacity for work suffered from the fact that he tired very easily, possibly from the narcotics addiction which he overcame for only short periods. In any case lacked the talent and inclination to devote himself to steady routine style work - see Suchenwirth 1969 pp.143-144.

what precautions he could to protect the Reich from air attack.[67] It was a time of considerable tension and with only the three *Reklamestaffeln* (Publicity Squadrons) it is difficult to see just what could have been achieved if the French had used this incident as an excuse to nip German rearmament in the bud. Even before this incident Milch had taken the threat of French air attack seriously and in August 1933 he had authorised a programme of air raid precautions in Berlin.[68]

However Milch's increasingly high profile, which included talks with the *Reichspräsident* during 1934, had begun to annoy Göring who saw himself to be the true architect of the new *Luftwaffe*.[69] Evidence of this strained relationship was evident at a high level conference at Bayreuth between Hitler, Göring, Milch and Walther Wever, the new *Chef der Luftkommando Amt*, on the 31 July 1934 when Göring supported the *Führer's* plan for an even more rapid expansion in production and openly insulted his *Staatssekretär* when he opposed the plan (See 2C1).[70] In fact it was Milch that had a more realistic appreciation of the position at that time. He appreciated the futility of greater production when existing designs and models were already out-classed by those in existence elsewhere. He regarded it as essential that aircraft production was linked to a parallel programme of aircrew training and infrastructure development.[71] A few days later Milch was again snubbed when Göring told him that he would not be required at a further meeting with the *Führer* at Berchtesgaden in August, although on this occasion the *Reichsminister* was over-ruled by Hitler.[72]

Fortunately such tensions were still short-lived and on the very next day Göring apologised to Milch and informed him that he had asked Hitler to name Milch as the next *Reichsminister der Luftfahrt* in the event of his incapacitation.[73] Göring also sought to protect his *Staatssekretär* from the gossip that had begun to circulate in respect of Milch's ancestry. Theo Croneiss, the celebrated sports flier and aviation entrepreneur, had no love for Milch and in revenge for past disagreements he had built up a dossier on the *Staatssekretär* which showed Milch to be a Jew by his father, Anton Milch *(Photo 2A-10)*. When appraised of the accusation Milch took the matter up with his mother who provided him with a signed letter from her which established that Milch was in fact the product of an incestuous relationship with her brother. Göring and Hitler were both content with this explanation but other versions of this story continued to circulate for many years amongst Milch's enemies.[74] Croneiss, by this time an *Oberführer* in the SA, was reprimanded by Göring in October 1933 for the slander and he was lucky to survive the purge of 1934 when several personal enemies of the leadership were summarily executed.[75]

---

67   Irving 1973 p.36 & 38. In 1934 he was actively considering smoke screens for the Ruhr - still de-militarised at that time, whilst Hitler had already expressed an interest in the construction of Flak Towers in selected cities.

68   *Telegram, Newton to Simon, 31 Aug 1933* & *Milch Notes, 1934* in Irving 1973 p.38.

69   *Milch Diary, 24 & 28 Mar, 1 & 5 Apr 1934* in Irving 1973 p.39. Early in 1934 Hindenburg summoned Milch and asked him to explain the emerging air doctrine of strategic bombing. Following a 7 minute presentation the *Präsident* commented positively on the concept: *"I now understand it perfectly. Your ideas are well founded, even if somewhat unfamiliar to me at first. Keep on the same track even if others should not agree with you."*

70   *Milch Diary 31 Jul 34* in Irving 1973 p.42. Wever had encouraged Milch to resist Hitler's unrealistic demands.

71   *Pre-Trial Interrogation, 25 Oct 1946* in Irving 1973 p.42. Hitler and Göring wanted a propaganda air force as a deterrent to outside intervention, Milch wanted the real thing. *"Göring was impatient because Hitler was impatient. Hitler wanted to see results. Hitler wanted and demanded in the shortest possible time and in no uncertain terms an air force impressive enough to be used as a political weapons, not to defeat another air force"* - see Hermann 1943 p.64.

72   *Milch Diary several entries for Aug-Sep 34* in Irving 1973 p.42.

73   *Milch Diary several entries for Aug-Sep 34* in Irving 1973 p.42.

74   Irving 1989 pp.131-132. Milch had been shocked by these allegations into his own ancestry. The truth of this complex matter is unclear - however the ramifications for Milch personally of Jewish heritage could have been terminal.

75   Irving 1989 p.151. Göring actually protected Croneiss from the death squads. He was permitted to keep his position at the *Bayerische Flugzeugwerke AG*.

2A3

The Development of a Command Apparatus

The contribution of Wever

Although subordinate to the *RLM* (Air Ministry) from the 15 May 1933, the newly formed *Luftschützamt* (Air Defence Office) was initially concealed within the *RWM* (War Ministry) where it continued to work alongside the *Heeresleitung* (Army High Command) and *Marineleitung* (Naval High Command) on a day to day basis.[1] However a new unified structure was adopted in place of the earlier parallel organisation based on the specific interests of each of the more senior services. Due to the preponderance of *Heeresoffiziere* (Army Officers) within the Office, the *Reichsmarine* (Navy) arranged for a small naval staff to be included in each of its six branches *(Chart II-1)*:[2]

FIGURE 2A-4 ORGANISATION OF THE LUFTSCHÜTZAMT		
JUNE 1933		
Amtschef: Obst.i.G.Eberhard Bohnstedt		
Chef des Stabes: FregKpt.Rudolf Wenninger		
Adjutant: Rittm.Plaschke		
Büro-Offizier: Maj.a.D.von Holwede		
LA 1 Fliegerführungsabteilung	Air Command Branch	Obstlt.Bernhard Kühl
LA 2 Fliegerorganisationsabteilung	Air Organisation Branch	Obstlt.Hellmuth Volkmann
LA 3 Fliegerausbildungsabteilung	Air Training Branch	FregKpt.Hans Geisler
LA 4 Luftschützabteilung	Air Defence Branch	Obstlt.Rudolf Bogatsch
Personalabteilung	Personnel Branch	Maj.Paul Schultheiss
Allgemeine-Abteilung	General Branch	Maj.Egon Doerstling
Nachschub-Gruppe	Supply Group	Hptm.a.D.Walther Grosch
Fliegergerate-Inspizient	Air Equipment	Inspectorate Maj.Eduard Seldner
Insp.d.Luftschütztruppen	Air Defence Troops	Inspectorate Obst.Günther Rüdel
Hauptbildstelle, Bildabteilung	Main Photographic Branch	Maj.Friedrich Cranz

1   Unknown *Geschichte des deutschen Generalstabs* (hereafter cited as Geschichte des deutschen Generalstabes) & *LA.Nr.617/33 g.Kdos.L 1 (H) II A Bildung des Luftministeriums 10 Mai 33* in Maass B. 1955 *The Organisation of the German Air Force High Command and Higher Echelon Headquarters within the German Air Force* USAF Historical Studies No.190 (hereafter cited as Maass 1955) p.15. See also Suchenwirth R. 1968 *The Development of the German Air Force 1919-1939* USAF Historical Studies No.160 (hereafter cited as Suchenwirth 1968) p.46 & Seaton A. 1982 *The German Army 1933-1945* (hereafter cited as Seaton 1982) p.32.

2   *Anlage 4 Besetzung der wichtigsten miltarischen Planstellen im Reichsluftfahrtministerium, Stand: 1.Juni 1933* in Volker K-H. 1967 *Die deutsche Luftwaffe 1933-1939: Aufbau, Führung und Rüstung der Luftwaffe sowie die Entwicklung der deutschen Luftkriegstheorie* (hereafter cited as Volker 1967) p.228. See also *Geschichte des deutschen Generalstabes* in Maass 1955 p.15. *Abt. L2 (Technik)* was transferred to the *Allgemeines Luftamt* as *LB II* - see Beauvais H., Kossler K., Mayer M. and Regel C. 2002 *German Secret Flight Test Centres to 1945: Johannisthal, Lipetsk, Rechlin, Travemünde, Tarnewitz, Peenemunde-West.*

Overall responsibility for military aviation remained with *Obst.*Eberhard Bohnstedt and it was under his auspices that the first secret organisation plan was formulated on the basis of the earlier work of the *Inspektion 1 (L)*.

The planned force structure was dominated by the needs of the *Reichsheer* (Army), a tactical concept of the use of air power which was clearly out of sympathy with the quite separate strategic thinking of Milch and Knauss or indeed the concept of *operativer Luftkrieg* (operational Air War) as espoused by Felmy and Wimmer (See 1A2, 1A3 & 2A1). Bohnstedt's restricted vision for the future of the new *Luftwaffe* was finally confirmed in a meeting with *Staatssekretär* (State Secretary) Erhard Milch in the summer of 1933 when the *Chef LS* submitted his own plan for the new air arm's requirements, a force that comprised just 144 fighters, 12 bombers and around 50 reconnaissance aircraft:[3]

FIGURE 2A-5 PLANNED FORCE STRUCTURE	
MAY 1933	
Aufklärungsstaffel 1	Königsberg/Ostpr.
Aufklärungsstaffel 2	Döberitz
Aufklärungsstaffel 3	Größenhain
Aufklärungsstaffel 4	Boblingen
Jagdgeschwader 1	Leipzig
Bombengeschwader 1	Nürnberg-Fürth
Flugzeugführerschule (S)	Schleißheim
Beobachterschule	Braunschweig
Reserve Beobachterschule	Hildesheim
Technische Schule	Döberitz

Bohnstedt was staggered to learn of Milch's own plans for some 600 first-line aircraft and in November 1934 he was transferred thus leaving the way open for a more suitable candidate to work with Milch within the *RLM* (See 2A3).[4]

In response to his request for a new *Chef LS, Reichsminister* Hermann Göring was offered a choice between *Obstn.i.G.*Erich Frhr.von Manstein and Walther Wever.[5] Blomberg considered both men to be outstanding staff officers but it was Wever who was favoured by *Obst.i.G.*Hans-Jurgen Stumpff, the new *Chef der Personalabteilung* (Chief of the Personnel Branch), for the post of *Chef der Luftschützamt (Photo 2A-11)*:

3   Ries K. 1970 *Luftwaffe Bd.1 Die Maulwurfe 1919-1935* (hereafter cited as Ries 1970) p.114 & Irving D. 1973 *The Rise and Fall of the Luftwaffe: The Life of Luftwaffe Marshal Erhard Milch* (hereafter cited as Irving 1973) pp.31-32. Bohnstedt's response to Milch's revelations was: *"But this is terrible! Poor Germany!"*

4   Service record for Eberhard Bohnstedt in AxisBiographicalResearch in www.reocities.com . He was transferred to Schweidnitz as *Kdr.Inf.Rgt.7* on the 1 Nov 34 and retired 8 months later with the rank of *GenMaj.(char)*.

5   Suchenwirth R. 1969 *Command and Leadership in the German Air Force* USAF Historical Studies No.174 (hereafter cited as Suchenwirth 1969) p.3. Mansterin was appointed *Chef T 1 (Operations)* in the *Truppenamt* in 1935; Wever was *Chef T 4 (Ausbildung)* in the *Truppenamt* - see Seaton 1982 p.299. Manstein, then *C.d.GS.i.Wehrkreis III Berlin*, was considered to be somewhat old fashioned, hostile to technological advance and no admirer of aviation - see Irving 1973 p.35 & Mitcham S.W.1988 *Hitler's Field Marshals and their Battles* p.242. According to Milch both Stumpff and Wever's Personnel Files were endorsed with *"Suitable for a later Oberbefehlshaber des Heeres"* - see Irving 1973 p.359.

"I had known Wever ever since World War I. At that time I was assigned to the *Personalamt der Oberste Heeresleitung* and Wever was *Ia* in the *Operations-Abteilung (T1)*. Later I became acquainted with the work he had done on the staffs of *(GenOb*.Hans) von Seeckt and *(Gen.d.Inf*.Wilhelm) Heye, and finally as *Personal Chef* in charge of *Offiziere i.G.* He was an outstanding military man in the *Heeresleitung*, even then. In the 100,000 man *Reichsheer*, he and Manstein were the most outstanding personalities amongst the younger officers. I considered both of them to be "coming men" for the *Truppenamt*. When I was transferred to the *Luftwaffe* on the 1 July 1933, I immediately suggested to Göring that a number of men be recruited from the *Reichsheer*. Wever, I thought, was the better choice for the *Luftkommando Amt*, since I felt Manstein was too stubborn. Göring gladly accepted my recommendations and requested Wever's transfer from *(Gen.d.Inf*.Kurt Frhr.von) Hammerstein (*Chef d.Heeresleitung*). Wever decided to accept during a trip with me up the Rhein."[6]

*GenOb.a.D.*Hans-Jurgen Stumpff

Wever's arrival on the 1 September 1933 coincided with the physical transfer of the *Luftschützamt* to the *RLM's* offices at the Behrenstrasse. Here it formed one of five major *Amter* (Offices) within the overall Ministry.[7] At this time the designation *Luftschützamt* was retained as part of the elaborate camouflage ordered by *Staatssekretär* Erhard Milch on the 25 July 1933 when he signed orders *"to make it impossible for foreign powers to prove actual violations of our existing foreign commitments* and *to prevent foreign powers from deriving any clear picture of the rate of growth, or of the actual size and organisation of the Luftwaffe we are founding"*.[8] These considerations were to remain in force until the *Luftwaffe* was officially unveiled some nineteen months later.

However the *Luftschützamt*, to be renamed the *Luftkommandoamt (LA)* (Air Command Office) in the following year, then underwent further modification with the loss of the personnel function, this being elevated to form a separate *Amt* within the new *RLM* structure (See 2B2).[9] The role of the *Ausbildungsabteilung (LA III)* (Training Branch) was also modified with the creation of the *Kommando der Fliegerschulen* (Flying Schools Command), an organisation that was itself retitled the *Inspektion der Fliegerschulen* (Flying Schools Inspectorate) on the 1 November 1933 (See 2D1). *FregKpt.*Hans Geisler was the first *Leiter LA III*.[10] His branch consisted of four *Gruppen* (Departments). These covered the overall supervision of *Luftwaffe* training *(LA III,1)*, the organisation of training programmes at troop level *(LA III,2)*, the preparation of training directives *(LA III,3)* and budgetary affairs *(LA III,4)*.[11] Due to the limited scope of the training programme together with the continuing need for secrecy Geisler later admitted that his branch had been

6   Quoted from *Interview between GenOb.a.D.Hans-Jurgen Stumpff & Prof.Richard Suchenwirth, 22 Nov 54* in Karlsruhe Document Collection, D /II/1 in Suchenwirth 1969 *Command and Leadership in the German Air Force* USAF Historical Studies No.174 pp.2-3.

7   *Information from GenLt.a.D.Bruno Maaß and Gen.d.Flg.a.D.Josef Kammhuber* in Maass 1955 p.18. Both officers formed part of the *LS-Amt* in Sep 33.

8   *Dokument Nr.71 Order on camouflage of Luftwaffe, 25 Jul 33* in Volker K.H. 1968 *Dokumente und Documentarfotos zue Geschichte der deutschen Luftwaffe* p.183. See also Maass 1955 p.29.

9   Maass 1955 p.36 & Volker 1967 p.33. The *Luftschütz-Abt.* (Bogatsch) was transferred to the jurisdiction of the *Insp.d.Luftschütztruppen*. The *Lw.Offizier-Korps* was created on the 1 Oct 33 – see Maass 1955 p.22.

10 *Information from Gen.d.Flg.a.D.Hans Geisler* in Maass 1955 p.36. Geisler had just completed a short period of sea duty as *1.Offizier* aboard the *Linienschiff Schleswig-Holstein*. He was appointed *Ltr.LA III* on the 3 Apr 33 & transferred to the *Lw.* on the 1 Sep 33 - see service record for Hans Geisler in Hildebrand K.F.1990 *Die Generale der deutschen Luftwaffe 1935-1945 Band 1 A-G* (hereafter cited as Hildebrand 1990) pp.351-352.

11 *Information from Gen.d.Flg.a.D.Hans Geisler* in Maass 1955 pp.36-37.

unable to become fully effective during 1933/34.[12]

In the meantime the increasing flow of combat aircraft from the factories and trained personnel from the *Fliegerschulen* had finally allowed the *Organisations-Abteilung (LA II)* to activate the first operational units in line with the established plan:[13]

FIGURE 2A-6 INITIAL FORCE STRUCTURE 1 APRIL 1934	
5 Aufklärungsstaffeln	Reconnaissance Squadrons
5 Kampfstaffeln	Bomber Squadrons
2 Behelfskampfgruppen *	Auxiliary Bomber Groups
3 Jagdstaffeln	Fighter Squadrons
1 Seeaufklärungsstaffel	Naval Reconnaissance Squadron
1 SeejagdstaffelNaval	Naval Fighter Squadron
1 Seemehrzweckstaffel	Naval Multi-Purpose Suadron
1 Luftdienstschleppstaffel	Fleet Requirements Squadron
*To be provided by DLH following mobilisation.	

Instructions to form the first operational units were issued on the 1 April 1934 (See 2E2). These units were the *Jagdgruppe Döberitz* (Fighter Group Döberitz) which was created from the *Reklamestaffeln Mittel-und Süddeutschland* (Propaganda Squadrons), and the *Aufklärungsstaffel Neuhausen* (Reconnaissance Squadron Neuhausen) which grew out of the *Reklamestaffel Ostdeutschland.*[14] However it would be several months before these units reached full strength and the lack of equipment and trained personnel effectively delayed the formation of the other planned units, for example the *Seeaufklärungsstaffel* (Naval Reconnaissance Squadron) was not activated until the 1 September 1934 (See 2E3). In accordance with Milch's directive none of these units were publicly referred to by their functional designations, their former titles remaining in force. However far more ambitious plans were already in place. The *Rheinland Programm* (Rhineland Programme) in its initial form (January 1934) envisaged the production of 3,715 aircraft by the close of the following year, whilst in its definitive form (July 1934) no less than 4,021 aircraft were to be delivered by the end of September 1935.[15] No fewer than 1,954 of these were combat aircraft. The *Luftkommandoamt* anticipated that these aircraft would permit a major expansion of the *Luftwaffe's* front line by the autumn of 1936. The planned force structure by this date was *(Map II-1)*:[16]

---

12   *Information from Gen.d.Flg.a.D.Hans Geisler* in Maass 1955 p.36.

13   Ries 1970 p.115 & Schliephake H. 1971 *The Birth of the Luftwaffe* (hereafter cited as Schliephake 1971) p.32.

14   Volker 1967 pp.45-46 & Ries K. 1974 *Luftwaffen-Story 1935-1939* (hereafter cited as Ries 1974) p.16.

15   *Table 6-F RLM Plans* in Vajda F.A. & Dancey P.1998 *German Aircraft Industry and Production 1933-1945* (hereafter cited as Vajda & Dancey 1998) pp.113-114. For the definitive schedule - see *Table 1-D The Rhineland Programme, 1 January 1934 - 30 September 1935* in Vajda and Dancey 1998 pp.16-17.

16   Ries 1974 pp.18-19.

FIGURE 2A-7 PLANNED FORCE STRUCTURE BY OCTOBER 1936 25 APRIL 1934		
Kampfregiment Greifswald	(KG 152)	Greifswald
	(KG 352)	Tutow
Neubrandenburg *		
Kampfregiment Merseburg	(KG 153)	Merseburg
	(KG 553)	Finsterwalde
		Brandis *
Kampfregiment Gotha	(KG 253)	Gotha
	(KG 753)	Erfurt *
		Nordhausen
Kampfregiment Bielefeld	(KG 154)	Bielefeld Area
		Fassberg
		Wunstorf
Kampfregiment Ulm	(KG 155)	Ulm
	(KG 455)	Giebelstadt
		Gersthofen *
Sturzkampfregiment Schwerin	(KG 162)	Schwerin
Lübeck-Blankenses		Kitzingen
Jagdregiment Döberitz	(JG 132)	Döberitz
Jüterbog-Damm		Zerbst Area
Jagdregiment Hamm	(JG 134)	Hamm Area
		Unna Area
		Hamm Area
1 (F) Aufklärungsstaffel	121	Neuhausen
Stab & 3 (F) Aufklärungsstaffeln	122	Angermunde/
		Eberswalde
Stab & 2 (F) Aufklärungsstaffeln	123	Größenhain
Stab & 2 (F) Aufklärungsstaffeln	124	Kassel
Stab & 3 (F) Aufklärungsstaffeln	125	Würzburg
1 (H) Aufklärungsstaffel	111	Neuhausen
Stab & 2 (H) Aufklärungsstaffeln	112	Stargard Area
Stab & 2 (H) Aufklärungsstaffeln	212	Cottbus
Stab & 3 (H) Aufklärungsstaffeln	114	Münster

Stab & 2 (H) Aufklärungsstaffeln	115	Goppingen
Geschwader (See)	116	Kiel-Holtenau Stralsund
Geschwader (See)	216	Norderny List auf Sylt Wilhelmshaven
Kreisflugpark		Seerappen Stendal Liegnitz

The numerical designations were those to be adopted following the official unveiling of the Luftwaffe in Mar 35

* Initially established as a Kriesflugpark

Although relatively few units were to be activated during the first year of this programme it was deemed necessary on the 1 April 1934 to establish the first command organisations.[17]

Chief amongst these were the five territorial *gehobene Luftamter* (Higher Air Offices), each of which was responsible for a specific geographical area within the *Reich (Map II-2)*.[18] These air administrative offices performed a similar role to that of the *Reichsheer's* seven *Wehrkreise* (Military Districts) although, for the most part, they did not share mutual boundaries.[19] Furthermore given the continuing need for secrecy the *gehobene Luftamter* had to be overtly civilian organisations. They were therefore led by former officers *(Offiziere a.D.)* who held the title *Präsident der Luftamt* (Air Office President).[20] On the 1 July 1934 a sixth *gehobene Luftamt* was formed to deal specifically with the needs of naval aviation (See also 2E3).[21]

As the *gehobene Luftamter* were not considered to be executive commands it was necessary to establish a parallel operational command structure in the event of war. At this stage only two autonomous commands were established to meet this requirement, the most important of which was the *1.Fliegerdivision* with its headquarters in Berlin.[22]

---

17   Maass 1955 p.27. As the force expanded it was no longer possible, or indeed appropriate, for the *RLM* to continue the day-to-day administration of the individual schools, operational units and ground facilities.

18   *Anlage 11 Die territoriale Einteilung der Luftwaffe in Luftkreise, Stand: 1.April 1934* in Volker 1967 p.236. See also Volker 1967 p.36.

19   *The Wehrkreis System* in Mitcham S.W. 1985 *Hitler's Legions: The German Army Order of Battle, World War II* pp.27-28. The *Reichsheer* comprised just 7 *Wehrkreise*: *I* (Königsberg), *II* (Stettin), *III* (Berlin), *IV* (Dresden), *V* (Stuttgart), *VI* (Münster) & *VII* (München). Each *Wehrkreis* had been associated with a single *Infanterie-Division* that bore the same number as its parent. The *Wehrkreis* was a territorial organisation which in time of war would provide higher level headquarters and act as the basis for new formations. The three *Kavallerie-Divn.* were located at Frankfurt an der Oder (*WK III*), Breslau (*WK IV*) & Weimar (*WK IV*) - see also Seaton 1982 p.7.

20   Nielsen A. GenLt.a.D. 1959 *The German Air Force General Staff* USAF Historical Studies No.173 (hereafter cited as Nielsen 1959) p.43 & Cooper M. 1981 *The German Air Force 1933-1945: An Anatomy of Failure* (hereafter cited as Cooper 1981) p.7. See also Hildebrand K.F.1990-92 *Die Generale der deutschen Luftwaffe 1935-1945 Band 1-3* (hereafter cited as Hildebrand 1990-92).

21   *Anlage 12 Besetzung der leitenden Stellen in den Kommandobehorden und Schulen der Luftwaffe, Stand: 1.April 1934* in Volker 1967 p.237.

22   Maass 1955 pp.53-54. See also *Anlage 12 Besetzung der leitenden Stellen in den Kommandobehorden und Schulen der Luftwaffe, Stand: 1.April 1934* in Volker 1967 p.237. Other officers associated with the *Stab/Fl-Div.1* were: *Maj.* Hein-Hellmuth von Wuhlisch (Ia), *Hptm.*Alexander Holle (*Ia op*) & *Maj.*Helmut Sonnenburg (*Adj.*) with Hptm. Günther Wieland (zV) & Oblt.Klaus Uebe (zV) - see service records in Hildebrand 1990-92 Bd. 1-3.

FIGURE 2A-8 THE GEHOBENE LUFTAMTER
1934-35

Standort	Präsident	Chef des Stabes
Königsberg/Ostpr.	GenLt.Edmund Wachenfeld	Obstlt.Helmuth Förster
Berlin	GenLt.Leonhard Kaupisch	Obstlt.Ernst Müller
Dresden	GenMaj.Karl Schweickhard	Obst.Heinrich Danckelmann
Münster	GenLt.Hans Halm	Obstlt.Erich Musshoff
München	GenLt.Karl Eberth	Obstlt.Ludwig Wolff
Kiel	KonAdm.Konrad Zander	FregKap.Rudolf Stark

FIGURE 2A-9 ORGANISATION OF THE 1. FLIEGERDIVISION
1934-1935

Kdr. - Obst.Hugo Sperrle

Ia - Maj.i.G.Heinz-Hellmuth von Wuhlisch

One Jagdgruppe	Fighter Group
Two Kampfgruppen	Bomber Groups
Three Aufklärungsstaffeln (F)	Long Range Reconnaissance Squadrons

*Obst.*Hugo Sperrle was appointed *Kommandeur der 1.Fliegerdivision* with effect from the 1 April 1934 and he simultaneously occupied the post of *Kommandeur der Heeresflieger* (Commander of Army Aviation), an additional position that effectively placed all of the secret Luftwaffe's land based operational units under his command.[23] Unlike the *1.Fl.-Div.* which could have been deployed independently in accordance with the Luftwaffe's emerging doctrine of *operativer Luftkrieg*, the *Kdo.d.Heeresflieger*, which consisted of just two *Aufklärungsstaffeln (H)* (Army Reconnaissance Squadrons), would have been deployed in the direct support of the ground forces (See 2A1).[24] In the event of hostilities Sperrle would also have been able to count on the mobilisable reserve provided by *Luft Hansa* (See 2D2). Milch had arranged with *Dr.*Robert Knauss that under these circumstances the airline would provide a total of five *Behelfskampfstaffeln* (Auxiliary Bomber Squadrons), each of 18 aircraft, a force which would effectively double the *Luftwaffe's* striking power. These *Staffeln* were nominally under the command of the *Flugkommando Berlin* (Berlin Air Command).[25]

The only forces not under Sperrle's command were those associated with naval aviation. The *Führers der Marineluftstreitkräftes (FdL)* (Commander of Naval Air Services) was established at Kiel under the command of *FregKpt.*Hermann Bruch on the 1 July 1934.[26] By the end of the year Bruch

---

23   Maass 1955 p.54. Prior to this appointment *Obst.*Sperrle had been assigned to the *RLM* as an *Offizier zbV* - see service record for Hugo Sperrle in Hildebrand 1992 pp.325-326

24   Seaton1982 p.30. It was envisaged that a *Heeresaufklärungsstaffel* would have been attached to each of the two *Heeresgruppenkommandos: I* Berlin (Rundstedt)& *II* Kassel (Leeb).

25   Ries 1974 pp.19-20. *Hptm.*Kuno-Heribert Fütterer was assigned to the *Flugkommando Berlin* as military liaison for *Dr.*Knauss - see service record for Kuno-Heribert Fütterer in Hildebrand 1990 pp.331-332.

26   *LA Nr.500/34 g.Kdos. La II ZA v. 10.2.34* in Jung D., Wenzel B. and Abendroth A.1977 *Die Schiffe und Boote der deutschen Seeflieger 1912-1976* p.57. See also US Office of Naval Intelligence 1947 *German Naval Air 1933 to 1945: A Report based on German Naval Staff Documents* in Isby D.C. (Ed.) 2005 *The Luftwaffe and the War at Sea 1939-45:*

would have a balanced force of three *Staffeln* available at the naval air stations of Kiel-Holtenau and List auf Sylt (See 2E3).[27] Unlike the *Luftwaffe's* remaining operational units the *FdL* came under the operational direction of the *Marineleitung/Reichsmarine*, not the *Luftkommandoamt*.[28]

Whilst Sperrle would exercise immediate control over land-based air units, overall direction in time of war would rest with *GenMaj.* Wever and in particular *Obst.* Bernhard Kühl's *Führungsabteilung* (LA I) (Air Leadership Branch) within the *Luftkommando-Amt* in Berlin.[29] Following its reorganisation in October 1933 the *Luftkommando Amt* had assumed the character of a covert *Generalstabes* (General Staff) with an organisation that reflected those of the *Heeresleitung* and *Marineleitung*.[30] This high level status was also reflected by the fact that the chiefs of the operations, organisation and training branches, namely *Obstltn.* Kühl, Volkmann and Geisler, as well as the heads of many of the subordinate groups and staffs, were all *Generalstabsoffiziere (Offiziere i.G.)* (General Staff Officers).[31]

Initially the most important branches were *LA I, LA II* and *LA III.* Kühl, an *Aufklärungsflieger* (Reconnaissance Pilot) from the Great War, had previously served with *T 2 V (L)* during 1923-26 before being re-assigned as *Leiter Führungsabteilung (LA I)* in January 1933.[32] His role was to co-ordinate the work of the *LA I, 1 Operations* (Operations), *LA I/Qu. Nachschub* (Supply) and *LA I/Fremde Luftmachte* (Intelligence).[33] Clearly in wartime *LA I,1* would have assumed a command role, but in the interim this staff was mainly concerned with the development of strategic and tactical doctrine together with contingency planning, the determination of requirements for new aircraft, weapons and equipment in association with the *LC* (Technical Office), and co-ordinating the planned growth of the Luftwaffe with *LA II*.[34] *LA I /Qu.* (Quartermaster) was formed on the 1 May 1934 under *Maj.i.G.* Hans-Georg von Seidel to develop an effective supply system for the new air arm, to make recommendations for new supply organisations and to issue instructions and directives pertaining to all supply operations.[35] *LA I/Fr.L.* under *Obstlt.(E)* Hilmer Frhr.von Bülow continued the important role of the *Inspektion 1 (L)'s Referent VI Fremde Luftstreitkräfte* of monitoring and evaluating foreign air forces and providing *LA I,1* with an accurate digest of the war potential and likely impact of the air power of neighbouring nations.[36]

As seen by officers of the Kriegsmarine and Luftwaffe (hereafter cited as USONI in Isby (Ed.) 2005) pp.29-30. Like Geisler, *FregKpt.* Bruch had also just completed a tour of sea duty - in his case as *1. Offizier* aboard the *Kleiner Kreuzer Köln* - see service record for Hermann Bruch in Hildebrand 1990 pp.119-120.

27   Kurowski F.1979 *Seekrieg aus der Luft* p.19 & Ries 1974 p.158 & 163.

28   USONI in Isby (Ed.) 2005 p.29 & Gaul W. Obst.i.G.a.D. *The German Naval Air Force, 1933 - September 1939* in Isby (Ed.) 2005 pp.80-81.

29   Maass 1955 p.34. Wever was promoted to *GenMaj.* on 1 Oct 34 - see service record for Walther Wever in Hildebrand 1992 pp.507-508.

30   Cooper 1981 p.17.

31   Nielsen 1959 pp.44-45.

32   Service record for Bernhard Kühl in Hildebrand 1991 pp.265-266. Kühl had received *Flugzeugführer u.Beobachter* training at Döberitz in Jul 14 before seeing wartime service with *Fest-Fl.Abt.7 (37)* during 1914-16. He then successively commanded *Fl.Abt.26 (A 259)*, *Feldfl.Abt.45* & *Fl.Abt.A 202* during 1916-18 before joining the staff of *AK VII.* At the end of the war he was *Kdr.d.Versuchs-Abt.d. Insp.d.Lichtbildwesens*. He was promoted to *Obst.* on the 1 Apr 34.

33   *Information from Gen.d.Fl.a.D.Hans-Georg Seidel & GenLt.a.D. Josef Schmid in Maass 1955 pp.33-35*. Both these officers were assigned to the *LA* in 1934.

34   *Information from Gen.d.Fl.a.D.Hans-Georg Seidel & GenLt.a.D..Josef Schmid in Maass 1955 p.34* Following the completion of his *Generalstabs-Ausbildung* at the *Reichswehr-Akademie*, *Hptm.i.G.* Deichmann was a *Referent* in *LA I* from the 1 Oct 34 - see service record for Paul Deichmann in Hildebrand 1990 pp.182-183.

35   *Information from Gen.d.Fl.a.D.Hans-Georg Seidel & GenLt.a.D. Josef Schmid in Maass 1955 p.34*. *Maj.i.G.* von Seidel was appointed on the 1 May 34 - see service record for Hans-Georg von Seidel in Hildebrand 1992 pp.287-288. Interestingly Seidel had not been a career officer with the *Reichsheer* or a Great War pilot/observer. He re-joined the *Reichsheer* on the 1 May 34, immediately transferring to the *Luftwaffe*.

36   *Information from Gen.d.Fl.a.D.Hans-Georg Seidel & GenLt.a.D.Josef Schmid in Maass 1955 pp.34-35*. *Maj.(E)* von Bülow had been promoted to *Obstlt.(E)* on his transfer to the *Luftwaffe* on the 1 Jun 34 - see service record

FIGURE 2A-10 ORGANISATION OF THE LUFTKOMMANDO AMT 1 APRIL 1934		
LA I	Führungsabteilung	Operations
LA II	Organisationsabteilung	Organisation
LA III	Ausbildungsabteilung	Training
LA IV	Starke-u.Ausrüstungsnachweisung	Strength and Equipment
LA V	Nachschubabteilung	Supply
LA/NVW	Abt.Nachrichtenverbindungswesens	Signals
LA/ZL	Abt.Zivilen Luftschütz	Civil Air Defence

The *Organisations-Abteilung (LA II)* under *Obst.i.G.*Hellmuth Volkmann had an important role to play in the establishment of the new air arm. *LA II* consisted of five, later four, *Gruppen* of which *LA II,1* was concerned with general organisational planning at the policy-making level, *LA II,2* was responsible for unit activation, mobilisation planning and unit organisation, *LA II,3* prepared strength and equipment authorisation tables and *LA II,4* looked after the ground organisation.[37] *LA II,5* had a rather unique role in that it was concerned with the organisation of the *Fahrtruppen (Flak)*, an organisation which was still nominally part of the *Reichsheer*.[38] During the course of 1934 *Gruppe LA II,3* under *Maj.(E)* Hans Graf von Hachenburg was upgraded to form *LA IV* within the *Luftkommando Amt* where it assumed responsibility for the unit roster, or *Liste der Einheiten*, in addition to its primary function.[39]

The principal task of the *Luftkommando Amt* was to translate political decisions into functional directives and then to exercise an overall level of supervision over their implementation. Wever therefore played an important and influential role in the formulation of Germany's air strategy and tactical doctrine.[40] He learnt to fly, a qualification which would later become indispensable for all *Luftwaffe* officers of high rank, and he read Douhet's *Command of the Air* as well as Hitler's *Mein Kampf*.[41] The latter was of particular significance as Wever realised, more accurately than either Göring or Milch, that the Führer would eventually confront his ideological enemy in the east in a clash which would require the development of a *Langstrecken-Grossbomber* (Long Range Heavy Bomber)(See 3C2). Thus, whilst Milch thought in terms of a four-engine aircraft for maritime

for Hilmer von Bülow in Hildebrand 1990 pp.127-128. *"In 1933 the Abteilung Fremde Luftstreitkräfte was again assigned additional personnel in the course of the creation of the Reichsluftfahrtministerium and was redesignated the Abteilung Fremde Luftmachte. More and more emphasis was placed on military matters. A Target Section was attached to this Abteilung, and contact was established with the Amt Ausland/Abwehr, which meant the beginning of a shift in functions until the Abteilung was integrated into the Luftwaffen Generalstabes at the beginning of 1938 and redesignated the 5.Abteilung"* - quoted from Bülow Frhr. von H. GenLt.a.D. Undated *Die Abteilung Fremde Luftmachte im Reichswehr-und Reichsluftfahrtministerium 1927-1937* Karlsruhe Document Collection.

37   Maass 1955 pp.35-36. *Rittm.*, later *Maj.i.G.*Bruno Maaß, was a *Gruppenleiter* in *LA II* - see service record for Bruno Maaß in Hildebrand 1991 pp.333-334. *LA II, 2* did not have any responsibility for the *Flakartillerie*. Volkmann was promoted to *Obst.i.G.* on the 1 Jul 34 - see service record for Hellmuth Volkmann in Hildebrand 1992 pp.450-452.

38   Maass 1955 p.36. Of necessity *LA II,5* worked closely with *Maj.*Walther von Axthelm's *Ausbildungsstab 3 Insp.4 (Artillerie)* within the *Reichsheer* - see also service record for Walther von Axthelm in Hildebrand 1990 pp.31-32.

39   *Information provided by GenLt.a.D.Johannes Graf von Hachenburg* in Maass 1955 pp.37-38. See also service record for Johannes Ludwig Graf von Hachenburg in Hildebrand 1991 pp.5-6.

40   Corum J.S. 1997 *The Luftwaffe: Creating the Operational Air War 1918-1940* (hereafter cited as Corum 1997) pp.127-128.

41   Suchenwirth 1969 pp.5-6.

warfare in the west, Wever saw the potential of such an aircraft for attacks on the Soviet Union's industrial heartland. For him the new strategic bomber had to be a *"Ural-Bomber"*, an aircraft with an operational radius of 2,400 kms., which would permit attacks on the Don Basin, Moskva and Leningrad from bases in Ostpreussen and Schlesien.[42]

Wever also differed from both Göring and Milch in being a professional soldier with a wealth of experience in staff work:

> Walther Wever was born on the 11 November 1887 in Wilhelmsort, in Bromberg... In 1905 he joined an infantry regiment as an *Frahnich*, being promoted the following year to *Leutnant*. After a number of years of *Truppendienst* he was promoted in 1914 to *Oberleutnant*. He served on the Western Front during World War I, rising in 1915 to the rank of *Hauptmann* and to a position on the *Generalstabes*. In October 1917 he was transferred to the staff of *Generalfeldmarschall* Paul von Hindenburg and *Generaloberst* Erich Ludendorff, where he established a reputation as a keen and thorough *Offizier i.G.* He served in several significant staff positions during the closing months of the war, always applying himself to the tasks at hand with great industry and freshness of mind.
>
> After the fall of the Monarchy in 1918, Wever remained on active duty in the *Reichswehr* as a member of the *Truppenamt*. On the 1 February 1926 he was promoted to *Major i.G.* in *Abteilung T.1 (Operations)* of the *Truppenamt*, all of which came under the command of *Generalmajor* Werner von Blomberg. It was during a staff trip with this Branch that Wever became the first German officer to suggest the proper utilisation of armour in warfare (1927-28)...In 1930 Wever was an *Oberstleutnant i.G.*, and two years later became an *Oberst i.G.* and *Abteilungsleiter* in the *Truppenamt*. Ultimately Wever assumed command of *Abteilung T.4 (Ausbildungs)* as the successor to *Generalmajor* Walther von Brauchitsch.[43]
>
> *Gen.d.Flg.a.D.*Hellmuth Felmy
> Interview with Prof. Richard Suchenwirth - 25 June 1954

Fortunately Wever got on well with both Göring and Milch and this period was therefore marked by a commendable level of harmony at the highest levels of command.[44] This was in large part due to Wever's willingness to stay in the background, but he also possessed a very high level of tact. Milch would later testify:

> He was the most significant of the officers taken over from the *Reichsheer*. If he had remained in the *Heer* he would have reached the highest positions there as well. He possessed not only tremendous professional ability, but also great personal qualities. He was the only General Staff Chief since the end of the Great War who came close to Moltke.[45]

Wever's personal attributes were appreciated by junior officers throughout the *Luftwaffe*: Greeting his new assignment with enthusiasm, Wever devoted his full attention to the

---

42   Suchenwirth 1969 p.6, Faber H. (Ed.) 1979 *Luftwaffe: An Analysis by former Luftwaffe Generals* p.160 & Hooton E.R. 1994 *Phoenix Triumphant: The Rise and Rise of the Luftwaffe* (hereafter cited as Hooton 1994) p.108.

43   Quoted from *Interview with Gen.d.Flg.a.D.Hellmuth Felmy, 25 Jun 54* in D/II/1, Karlsruhe Document Collection in Suchenwirth 1969 *Command and Leadership in the German Air Force* USAF Historical Studies No.174 pp.1-2.

44   Suchenwirth 1969 p.14.

45   Quoted from an *Interview between GFM.a.D.Erhard Milch and Prof.Richard Suchenwirth, 29 September 1954* in D/I/2, Karlsruhe Document Collection in Suchenwirth 1969 *Command and Leadership in the German Air Force* USAF Historical Studies No.174 p.5.

new mission with typical zeal. His quick intelligence, his remarkable receptiveness towards the developments of modern technology, and his vast store of military experience soon enabled him to grasp the fundamental concepts of his mission. He worked untiringly to exploit the unusually favourable circumstances provided by the time in order to create a military instrument equal to the other *Reichswehr* branches for the defence of the nation. He was quick to realise that the chance given him was a unique one, and that he might take advantage of all the available national and economic resources in creating a new and unique force. He himself learned to fly at the age of 46, and soon became one of the most enthusiastic pilots in the *Luftwaffe*; in this, as in other fields, he set a challenging example to young and old.[46]

Wever was a consummate "people" manager. Whenever he appeared, his colleagues redoubled their efforts because he had made them aware of their common goals and they knew that he supported and appreciated their work:

Wever, a medium-sized man with graying hair, a sharply chiselled nose and chin, was capable of turning from deep seriousness to mercurial liveliness and humour. His colleagues were invariably captivated when the critical sternness of his face was relieved by the smile they knew so well, a smile expressing marvellous self-assurance and superiority, but with the warmest kindness. Wever was a fatherly supervisor, but his mind was extraordinarily keen and told him instantly whether his discussion partner was trying to cloak superficial knowledge with a flow of words or was standing on an uncertain ground. He was fond of testing the capabilities of his staff members, but never in a pedantic or discouraging fashion. He would sit across the desk from an officer, present a situation, and force the man to collect his thoughts. In the course of the conversation he would frequently interrupt his partner to present arguments of his own, thereby forcing the man to consider the matter in all of its aspects. Wever's method threw his colleague onto the defensive, and he kept after the officer until all the pros and cons had been thrashed out and the problem lay clearly crystallised before them. Often after such a session he let his subordinate go without giving a final solution. The decision in the matter would then be delivered the next morning.[47]

Of necessity Wever had to work closely with the other *Amt-Chef* within the *RLM*, namely *Obstn.*Hans-Jurgen Stumpff (Personnel), Albert Keßelring (Administration), and Wilhelm Wimmer (Technical Office)(See 2B1). There would always be a particularly close link between the *Luftkommando Amt* which was responsible for deciding the air arm's future requirements and the *Technisches Amt* (Technical Office) which was responsible for translating those requirements into operational hardware (See 2C1). There has already been reference to Wever's role in the evolution of a long range heavy bomber, but of more immediate concern was a second generation of combat aircraft which would be suitable for a conflict with France (See 2A1). Earlier requirements were revised by *LA I,1* in 1934, to include *Rüstungsflugzeug* (Re-Armament Aircraft) *I (Kampfflugzeug)*, *II (Sturzkampfflugzeug)*, *III (Jagdflugzeug)* & *IV (Flugzeugzerstörer)* (See 3C2).[48] Great store was placed

---

46 Quoted from Nielsen 1959 *The German Air Force General Staff* USAH Historical Studies No.173 pp.28-29.

47 Quoted from a *joint interview with Gen.d.Flg.a.D.Paul Deichmann & Gen.d.Flg.a.D.Wilhlem Speidel, 1954* in Suchenwirth 1969 *Command and Leadership in the German Air Force* USAF Historical Studies No.174 p.9. Deichmann & Speidel were both *Referate* in the *LA* at this time - see service records for Paul Deichmann in Hildebrand 1990 pp.182-183 and Wilhelm Speidel in Hildebrand 1992 pp.320-322.

48 Green W. 1970 *The War Planes of the Third Reich* (hereafter cited as Green 1970), Kosin R. 1983 *Die Entwicklung der deutschen Jagdflugzeuge* (hereafter cited as Kosin 1983) pp.79-83, Hooton 1994 pp.108-109. & Corum

on the successful development of a fast twin-engine medium bomber to replace the unsatisfactory Do 11 (See 2A1 & 2C3). It was also acknowledged that there was a need for a long range fighter, a machine capable of escorting and protecting the *Luftwaffe's* new medium bombers in their deep penetration raids over enemy territory. These concerns resulted in the concept of a *Kampfzerstörer*, or twin-engine multi-role aircraft (See 4C2).[49]

The *Reichswehr's* pre-occupation with France as the probable enemy continued to be re-affirmed throughout this period as confirmed in Blomberg's comments to *Gen.d.Art.*Werner Frhr.von Fritsch, *Adm.*Erich Raeder and *Gen.d.Inf.*Hermann Göring at a secret conference on the 9 October 1934.[50] The political and therefore strategic role of Germany's emerging air power continued to be one of deterrence although its actual capability was usefully camouflaged by an increasing emphasis on numerical strength.[51] It was agreed that air parity with France should be the immediate objective, although it was accepted that this would not be easily attained as the newly reorganised *Armée de l'Air* (French Air Force) was still Europe's largest air force and it was known that a modernisation programme had been initiated.[52] Predictably this led to a re-appraisal of the still incomplete *Rheinland Program* and notwithstanding Milch's earlier concerns a new production plan was agreed on the 1 January 1935 which would provide a revised total of 9,853 aircraft by the 1 October 1936 (See 2C3).[53]

1997 pp.165-166 The following types were developed: *Rüstungsflugzeug I (Kampfflugzeug)* He 111/Ju 86, *II (Sturzkampfflugzeug)* Ar 81/Ha 137/He 118/Hs 123/Ju 87, *III (Jagdflugzeug)* Ar 80/Bf 109/Fw 159/He 112 & *IV (Flugzeugzerstörer)* Bf 110/Fw 57/Hs 124. See also Mankau H. and Petrick P. 2001 *Messerschmitt Bf 110 - Me 210 - Me 410: Die Messerschmitt-Zerstörer und ihre Konkurrenten* (hereafter cited as Mankau and Petrick 2001) p.13.

49   *Luftdienstvorschrift L.Dv.10 Der Kampfflugzeug, 1934.* The modern fighter was seen as the most dangerous opponent of the bomber and much of *L.Dv.10* dealt with tactics for fighting and avoiding enemy fighters. An escort fighter was therefore seen as a vital adjunct to the bomber force. See also Green 1970 pp.573-575, Kosin 1983 pp.89-91 & Mankau and Petrick 2001 pp.13-14.

50   *Milch Diary, 9 Oct 34* in Irving 1973 p.42.

51   *Flugzeugbeschaffungsprogramm vom 1.7.1934, Stand vom Dezember 1934 in DZ/MGFA, Akte L II 1296* in Volker 1967 p.57. On the 1 Mar 34 the *Luftwaffe* had just 77 combat aircraft including 27 bombers and 12 fighters; by the end of the year it had received an additional 77 Do 11 & 193 Ju 52/3m bombers, 19 Ar 64 & 80 Ar 65 fighters, 4 He 70, 150 He 45 & 84 He 46 reconnaissance aircraft, and 27 He 60, 16 Do 15, 12 HD 38 & 14 He 49 seaplanes. In total 676 first line combat aircraft – see also *App.G Activation Schedule of the Operational Flying Units of the Luftwaffe 1933, 1934 & 28 Mar 35* in Schliephake 1971 pp.70-74. The size of the *Rheinland Programm* tended to conceal the fact the majority of the new aircraft were trainers – see *Table 1-D The Rhineland Programme, 1 January 1934 – 30 September 1935* in Vajda and Dancey 1998 pp.16-17.

52   Haute van A. 1974 *Pictorial History of the French Air Force 1909-1940* & Christienne C. and Lissarague P.1980 *A History of French Military Aviation* pp.243-247 & 250-256. The *Armée de l'Air* was formed on the 1 Apr 33. Following the passing of the Organisation Law on the 2 Jul 34 the *Armée de l'Air* was re-organised into territorial air regions instead of functional air divisions. The process of replacing the earlier *Regimental* structure with *Escadres* had already begun in 1932. In their initial form most *Escadres* equated to an Italian *Stormo* and to a Luftwaffe *Gruppe*. *Plan I* was adopted in Jul 34. It envisaged the procurement of 1,010 new combat aircraft for the *Armée de l'Air*. The bombing arm, neglected for many years, would be modernised and expanded with 350 new aircraft, mainly of the Bloch MB 200 BN4 type.

53   *Table 1-I Production Plan No.1 (up to 1 April 1937)* in Vajda and Dancey 1998 p.21. In Oct 35 Milch would extend this *Plan* still further to Apr 37 with an additional 1,305 aircraft including 270 of the planned He 111 & Ju 86 medium bombers.

FIGURE 2A-11 ORGANISATION OF THE METROPOLITAN ARMEE DE L'AIR
1 JULY 1934

1ere REGION AERIENNE - METZ

2eme Brigade Aerienne	8eme Brigade Aerienne	11eme Brigade Aerienne
7 Escadre de Chasse	38eme Demi-Brigade A'ne	21ere Demi-Brigade A'ne
32 Escadre d'Observation	38 Escadre d'Observation	21 Escadre de Bombardement
52 Escadre de Reconnaissance	BA 138 Metz-Thionville	33 Escadre d'Observation
BA 102 Dijon	BA 121 Nancy	

51ere Demi-Brigade Aerienne

1st Battalion d'Aerostatieres – Metz

2nd Battalion d'Aerostatieres – Epinay

BA 151 Metz

2eme REGION AERIENNE - PARIS

4oze Brigade Aerienne	12eme Brigade Aerienne
1 Escadre de Chasse	*12eme Demi-Brigade Aerienne*
34 Escadre d'Observation	6 Escadre de Chasse
54 Escadre de Reconnaissance	12 Escadre de Chasse
BA 104 Dugny	BA 112 Rheims
52eme Demi-Brigade Aerienne	**22eme Demi-Brigade Aerienne**
1st Battalion d'Aerostatieres – Compiegne	22 Escadre de Bombardement
2nd Battalion d'Aerostatieres – Compiegne	42 Escadre Mixte
BA 152 Compiegne	BA 122 Chartres

3eme REGION AERIENNE - TOURS

1ere Brigade Aerienne	3eme Brigade Aerienne
36eme Demi-Brigade Aerienne	**3eme Demi-Brigade Aerienne**
36 Escadre d'Observation	3 Escadre de Chasse
BA 136 Pau	BA 103 Chateauroux
53eme Demi-Brigade Aerienne	**31eme Demi-Brigade Aerienne**
1st Battalion d'Aerostatieres – Toulouse	2 Escadre de Chasse
2nd Battalion d'Aerostatieres – Toulouse	31 Escadre d'Observation
BA 153 Toulouse	BA 131 Tours

4oze REGION AERIENNE – LYONS

5eme Brigade Aerienne

5 Escadre de Chasse

35 Escadre d'Observation

55 Escadre de Reconnaissance

BA 105 Lyons-Bron

An Escadre usually consisted of 2 Groupes each of 2 Escadrilles (each of 9 aircraft)

However some Escadres de Chasse had 3 Groupes, whilst some Groupes had 3 Escadrilles

The Battalions d'Aerostatieres were Observation Balloon units

Source: Christienne C. and Lissarague P.1980 *A History of French Military Aviation* p.257.

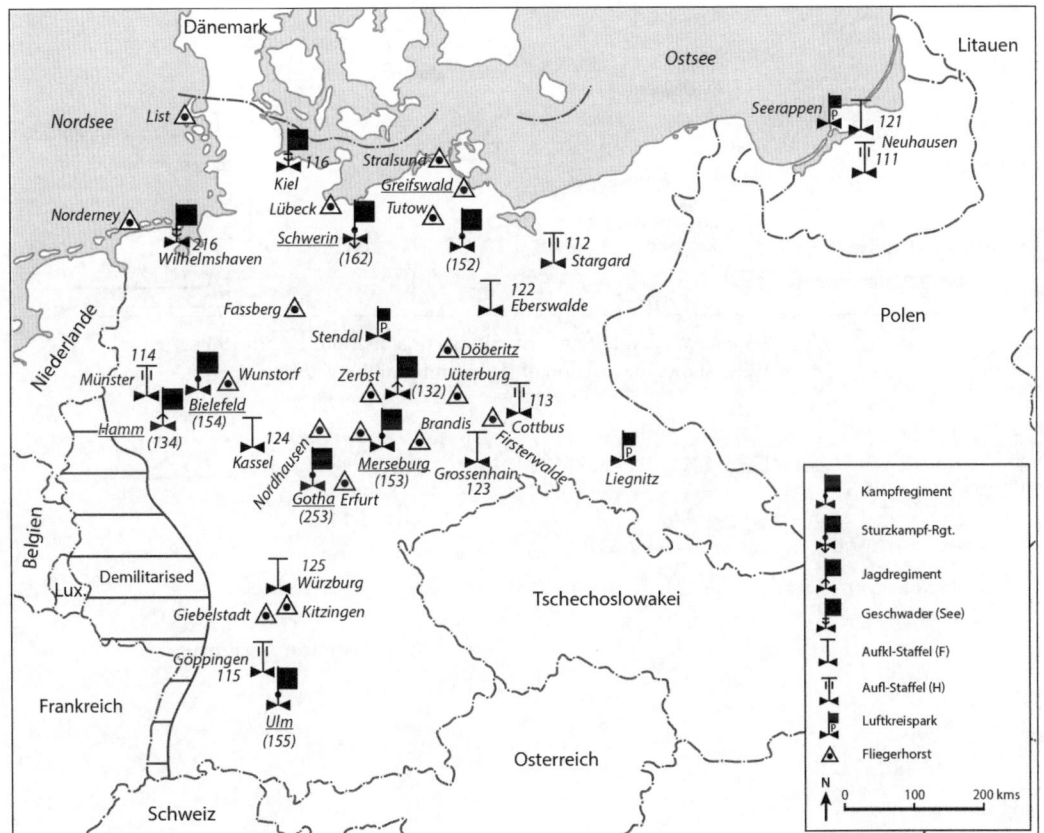

II-1   Planned territorial deployment of the secret *Reichsluftwaffe*, Date: 1 April 1934

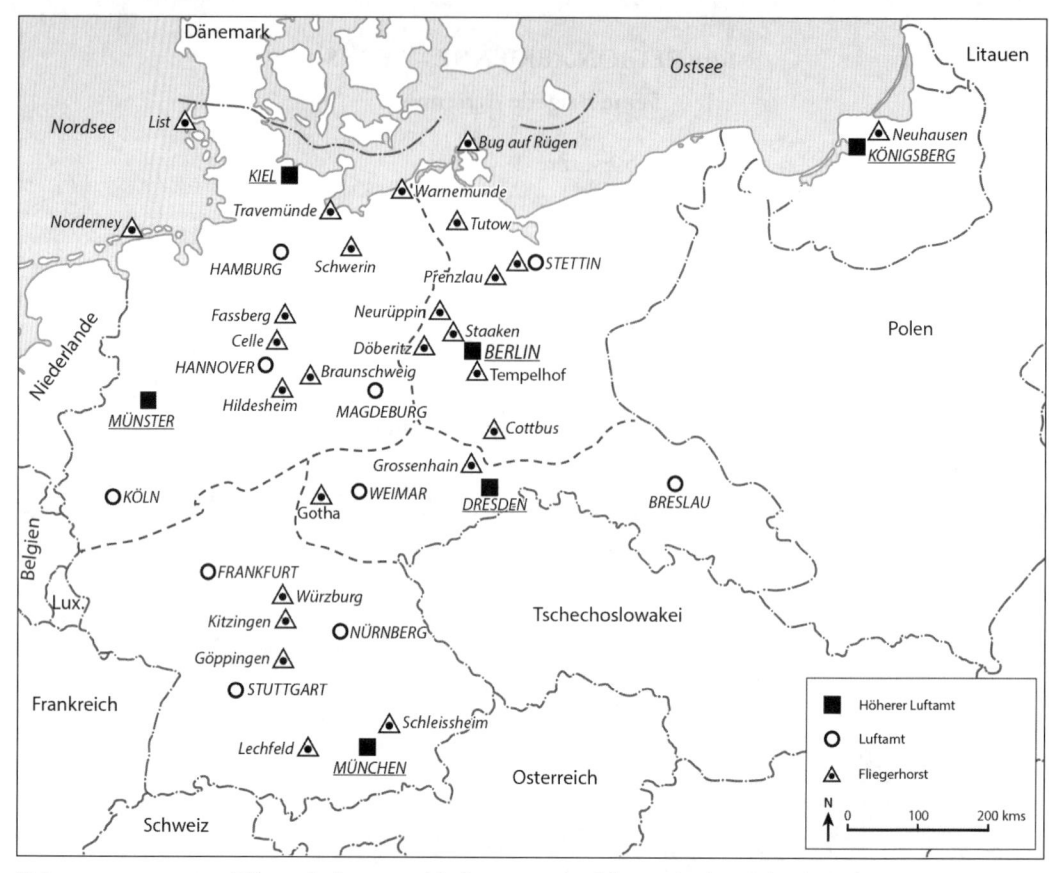

II-2   *Höheren Luftamter* and Luftamter territorial organisation: 1 April 1934.
                       The map also shows the location of the existing "military" *Flugplatze*.

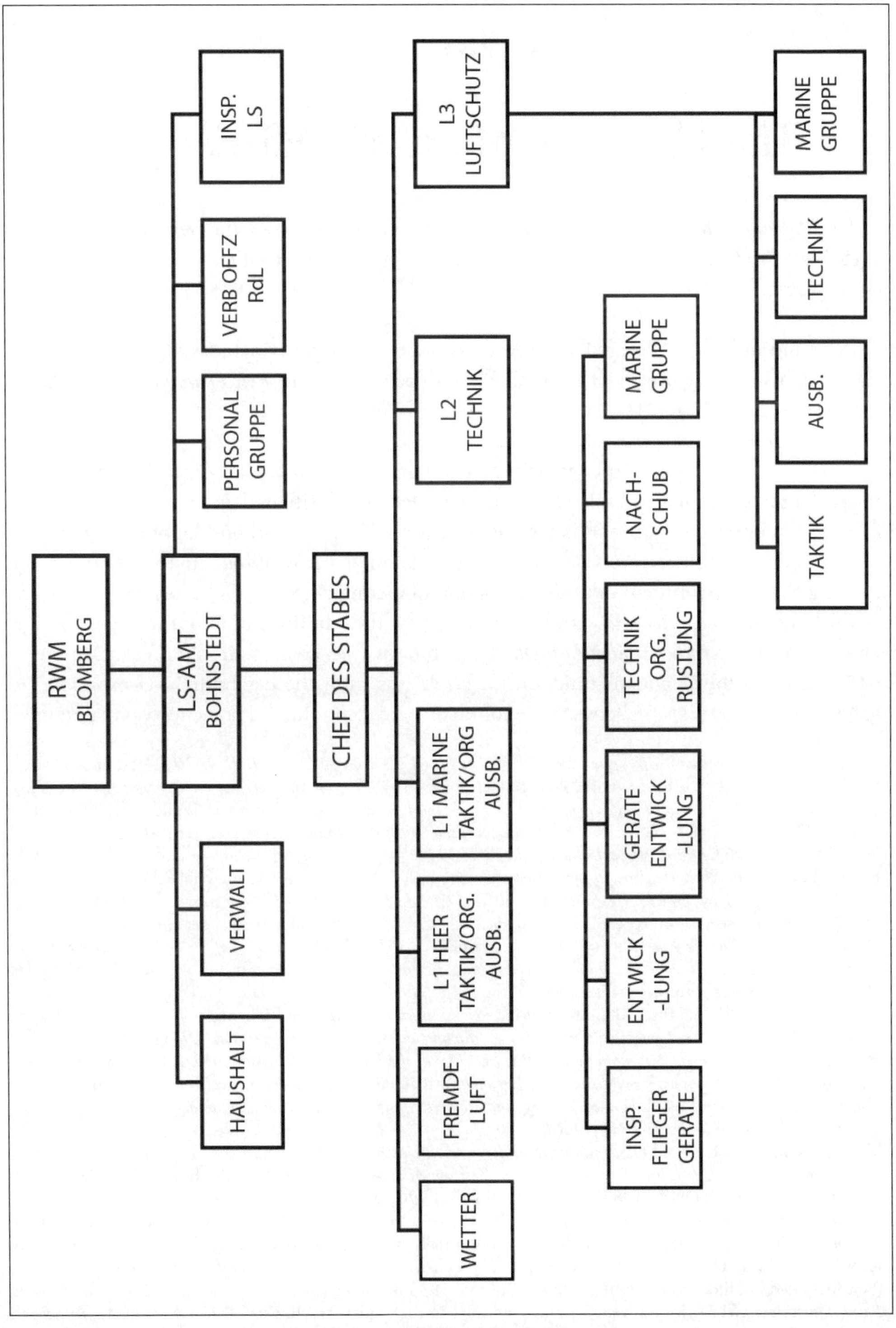

II-1 Organisation of the *Luftschütz-Amt (RWM)*, 1 April 1933

2B1

The Creation of an Air Ministry

The *Reichsluftfahrtministerium (RLM)* was established as an official organ of the German Government on the 15 May 1933 *(Chart II-2)*.[1] Its first and as later events were to dictate, only minister, was Hermann Göring:

> The scope and authority delegated to the *Reichsminister der Luftfahrt* includes all ramifications of aviation within the Reich. The missions and powers of the *Reichskommissars für die Luftfahrt* are herewith transferred to the *Reichsminister der Luftfahrt*.[2]

The former civilian departments associated with the *Reichskommissars für die Luftfahrt* were then moved into provisional premises, the former *Danatbank* situated in the Behrenstrasse in Berlin.[3] The most important part of this organisation at this time was without doubt the *Allgemeines Luftamt* which dealt with all aspects of commercial aviation and it was this activity that did much to conceal the illicit development of military aviation in Germany (See 2B5).[4] However there were, in addition, a *Verwaltungsabteilung* with responsibility for the administration of the overall budget for aviation and an *Abteilung Zivilen Luftschütz* which dealt with civilian air raid precautions.[5]

Despite its ostensibly "civilian" function the *RLM* was from the beginning a *Generalstabes* in waiting.[6] The traditional division between the command and technological branches was maintained.

1   *Reichsverteidigungsminister u.Bfr.d.gesamten Wehrmacht Nr.617/33, Geheim, I, (H) II A, 10.5.1933* in Unknown *Geschichte des deutschen Generalstabs* in Maass B. GenLt.a.D. 1955 *The Organisation of the German Air Force High Command and Higher Echelon Headquarters within the German Air Force* USAF Historical Studies No.190 (hereafter cited as Maass 1955) p.17 & *Reichsverteidigungsminister u.Bfr.d.gesamten Wehrmacht Nr.1007/33 , 15.5.1933* in Volker K-H. 1967 *Die deutsche Luftwaffe 1933-1939: Aufbau, Führung und Rüstung der Luftwaffe sowie die Entwicklung der deutschen Luftkriegstheorie* (hereafter cited as Volker 1967) p.12. The establishment of the *RLM* had been authorised by *Präsident* Hindenburg on the 27 Apr 33. He envisaged the *RLM* as subordinate to the Blomberg's *RWM* - see Seaton A. 1982 *The German Army 1933-1945* (hereafter cited as Seaton 1982) p.31.

2   Quoted from *Die deutsche Luftfahrt - Jahrbuch 1936* in Maass 1955 *The Organisation of the German Air Force High Command and Higher Echelon Headquarters within the German Air Force* USAF Historical Studies No.180 p.16. This Directive dealing with the establishment of the *Reichsluftfahrtministerium*, dated 5 May 1933, was to go into effect as of 1 March 1933. Hitler appointed Göring *Reichsminister der Luftfahrt (RdL)* on the 5 May 33 - see Absolon R. (Ed.) 1984 *Rangliste der Generale der deutschen Luftwaffe nach dem stand vom 20.April 1945* p.106.

3   Hooton E.R. 1994 *Phoenix Triumphant: The Rise and Rise of the Luftwaffe* (hereafter cited as Hooton 1994) p.94. The primary civilian department was the *Abt.I Luftverkehr* that had been formed on the 30 Jan 33 from the *RVM's Luftfahrtabteilung* – see Vogt E. Dr. *Zulassung und Kennzeichnung der deutschen Zivilflugzeuge 1914-1945 4.Die deutsche Luftfahrzeugrolle 1920-1934 (LFR B)*.

4   Maass B. GenLt.a.D. Undated *Organisation der Fliegerstellen 1920-1933*, A/I/2, Karlsruhe Document Collection in Suchenwirth R. Prof. 1968 *The Development of the German Air Force 1919-1939* USAF Historical Studies No.160 (hereafter cited as Suchenwirth 1968) p.57. See also Volker 1967 p.13.

5   *Information provided by Min.Dir.a.D.Willy Fisch* in Maass 1955 p.18. Willy Fisch was *Chef des Allgemeinen Luftamtes (LB)* in the *RLM* from the 3 Mar 33 – essentially he was Ernst Brandenburg's successor – see service record for Willy Fisch in Hildebrand K.F.1990 *Die Generale der deutschen Luftwaffe 1935-1945 Band 1 A-G* (hereafter cited as Hildebrand 1990) pp.286-287. From 1933 *Min.Dir.*Brandenburg was *Ltr.d.Abt.K (Kraftfahr-u. Landstrassenwesen)/RVM* (Motor Vehicles and Highways in the Transport Ministry)(Paul Frhr.von Eltz-Rübenach later Julius Dorpmuller) – see career notes for Ernst Brandenburg in Wikipedia.de.

6   Unknown *Geschichte des deutschen Generalstabs* in Maass 1955 p.17 & Volker 1967 p.14. Although physically

The important *Wa.Prw.8*, which had been transferred to Göring's control prior to May 1933, was temporarily incorporated into the *Allgemeines Luftamt* prior to its elevation as a distinct office within the Ministry during the autumn.[7] In fact by the late summer Göring had managed to consolidate his hold over all aeronautical matters by having the *Luftschützamt* relocated to the Behrensstrasse together with the *RWM's* remaining aviation sections, the *Fliegerbestaendeverwaltung (Wa.N.1)* and the *Hauptbildstelle*. Formerly part of the *Reichsheer's Waffenamt (WaA)* the former *Wa.N 1* dealt with air supply issues, whilst the *Hauptbildstelle* was concerned with aerial photography.[8] Both of these were also incorporated into the *Allgemeines Luftamt*. Following this transfer the *Luftschützamt* was re-titled the *Luftkommandoamt (LA)* and the remaining *Amter* were also re-categorised as the *Allgemeines Luftamt (LB)*, *Technisches Amt (LC)* and *Verwaltungsamt (LD)(Chart II-3)*.[9]

FIGURE 2B-1 ORGANISATION OF THE RLM 1 OCTOBER 1933		
Staatssekretär Erhard Milch		
Zentralabteilung	(ZA) Central Branch	Kpt.z.S. Rudolf Wenninger
Luftschützamt	(LA) Air Defence Office	Obst.i.G.Walther Wever
Allgemeines Luftamt	(LB) General Air Office	Min.Dir.Willy Fisch
Technisches Amt	(LC) Technical Office	Obst.Wilhelm Wimmer
Verwaltungsamt	(LD) Administrative Office	Obst.Albert Keßelring
Personalamt	(LP) Personnel Office	Obst.Hans-Jurgen Stumpff
Kdo.d.Fliegerschulen	Flying School Command	Obst.Friedrich Christiansen
Abt.für Zivilen Luftschütz	Civil Air Defence Branch	Min.Dir.Kurt Knipfer

In its organisation and its personnel the *RLM* had of necessity to remain a civilian organisation if Germany was to comply with the clauses of the Versailles Treaty and to this end many of its officials were drawn from the civil service. Both Göring and Erhard Milch, his *Staatssekretär für die Luftfahrt*, were civilians although they were soon accorded honorary military rank: on the 31 August 1933 Göring was given the honorary rank of *General der Infanterie* by *Reichspräsident Generalfeldmarschall a.D.* Paul Hindenburg, whilst Milch was given the honorary rank of *Oberst* on the 2 October 1933.[10] Those officers who were transferred from the *Reichswehr* to the *RLM*

separate until the summer Göring contrived to have the *Luftschützamt/RWM* made subordinate to the *RLM*. Blomberg ordered that the *LS Amt* be transferred to *RLM* control on the 10 May 33 - see Seaton 1982 p.31. The *RLM's* military function was kept secret until Mar 35 - see also Schliephake H. 1971 *The Birth of the Luftwaffe* (hereafter cited as Schliephake 1971) p.31.

7   Maass 1955 pp.17-18. In its new form *Wa.Prüf 8* was initially referred to as the *Gruppe Technik*. See also *Gen.d.Flg.a.D.Hans Siburg* in Maass 1955 p.21. Siburg was then a *Referent* in the *Gruppe Technik* – see service record for Hans Siburg in Hildebrand K.F.1992 *Die Generale der deutschen Luftwaffe 1935-1945 Band 3 O-Z* pp.302-304.

8   *Information provided by GenLt.a.D.Maass & Gen.d.Flg.a.D.Kammhuber* in Maass 1955 p.18. The *Luftschützamt* was relocated from the Bendlerstrasse to the Behrensstrasse on the 1 Sep 33. The *Fliegerbestaendeverwaltung* was re-titled the *Nachschub Gruppe* - see Hertel W. Dipl.Ing.GenIng.a.D.1955 *Procurement in the German Air Force* USAF Historical Studies No.170 p.108 & *information provided by GenLt.a.D.Walther Grosch* in Maass 1955 p.19. Grosch was the former *Gr.Ltr.Nachschub*.

9   Volker 1967 p.14 & 33, Suchenwirth 1968 p.58 & Schliephake 1971 p.31.

10   Service record for Hermann Göring in Hildebrand 1990 pp.369-370. On the 31 Aug 33 Göring was given the honorary rank of *Gen.d.Inf.* by *Reichspräsident GFM.a.D.* von Hindenburg - see also Davis B.L. 1995 *Uniforms and*

normally wore civilian attire whilst on duty, although the wearing of *DLV* uniforms for formal occasions was also permitted (See 2B2).[11]

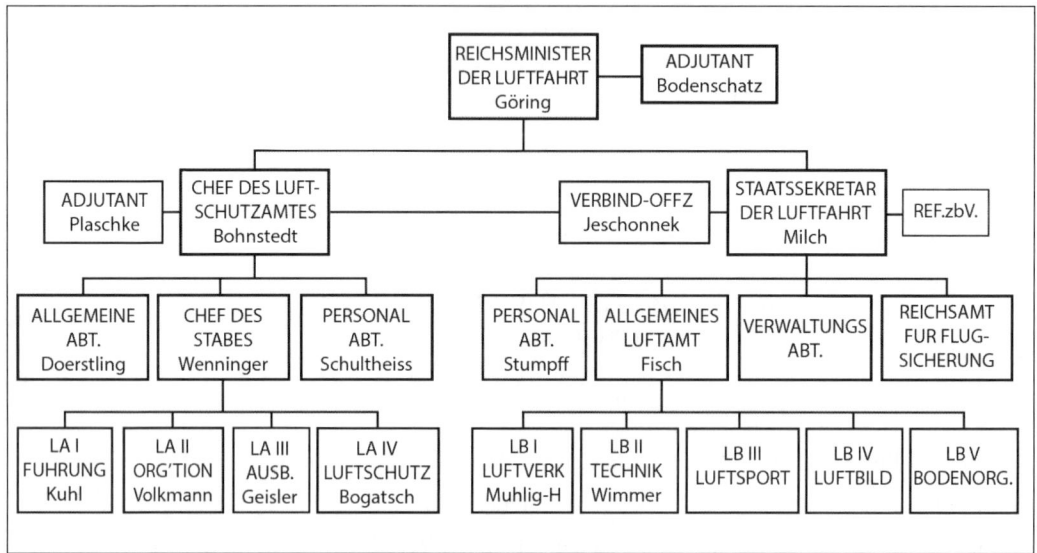

II-2   Organisation of the *Reichsluftfahrtministerium*, 1 June 1933

Insignia of the Luftwaffe Vol.2: 1940-1945 p.263 & *Die deutsche Luftfahrt - Jahrbuch 1936* p.15; Milch was given the honorary rank of *Obst.* on the 28 Oct 33 - see service record for Erhard Milch in Hildebrand K.F.1991 *Die Generale der deutschen Luftwaffe 1935-1945 Band 2 H-N* pp.394-395. See also Hooton 1994 p.95. Milch had not been Göring's first choice as *SS.d.L.* He had hoped to appoint *KonAdm.a.D.*Rudolf Lahs, the *Präsident d.Reichsverband der deutschen Luftfahrtindustrie* and former *Chef* of the *Reichsmarine's Gruppe BSx*, but Lahs had been unenthusiastic - see Heinkel E. 1956 He 1000 (hereafter cited as Heinkel 1956) p.154.

11   Maass B. Undated *Organisation der Fliegerstellen im RWM 1920-1933* in A/I/2, Karlsruhe Document Collection. All *RLM* personnel wore civilian attire whilst on duty. See also Volker 1967 pp.20-21.

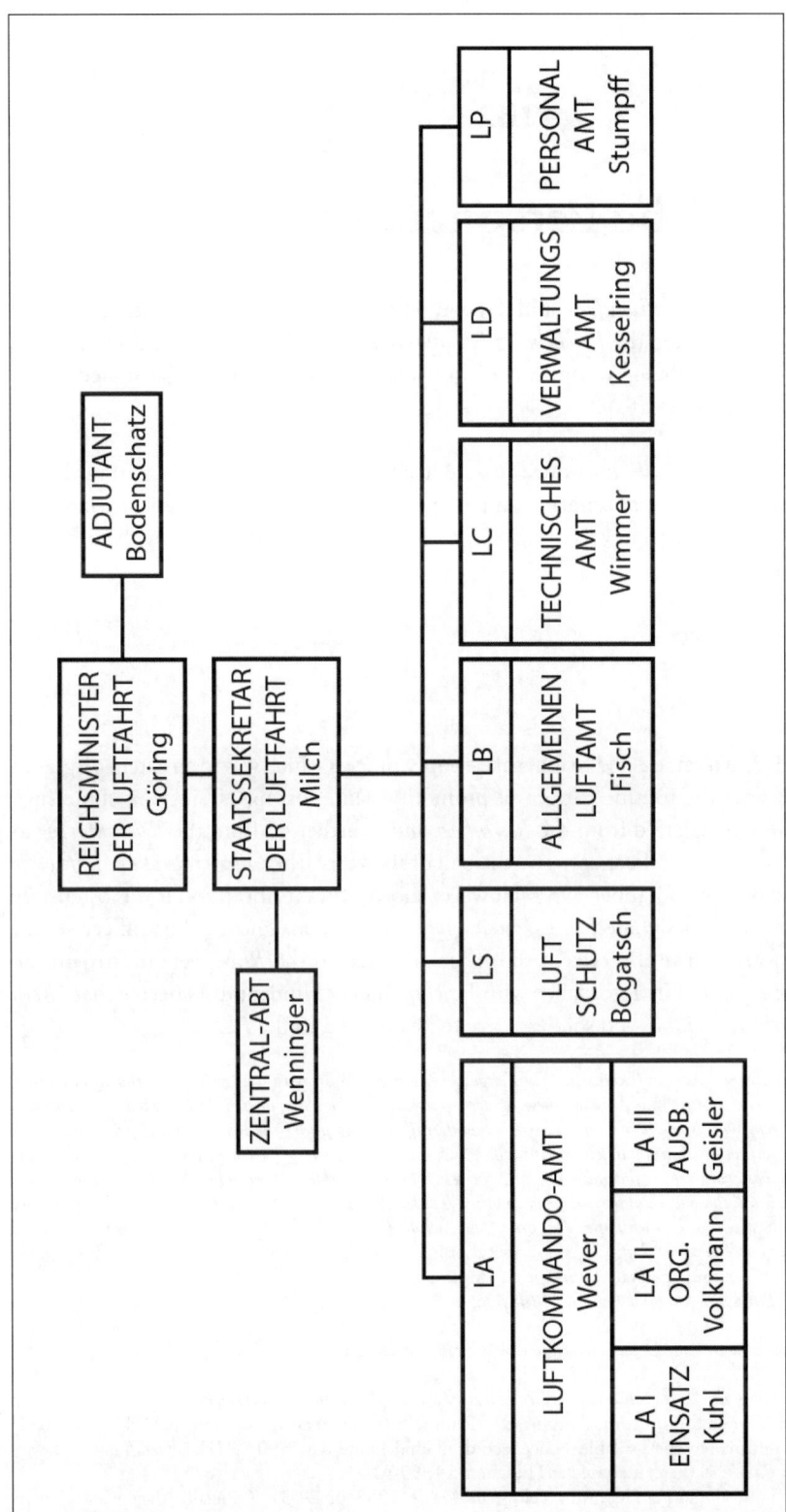

II-3 Organisation of the *Reichsluftfahrtministerium*, 1 September 1933

2B2

The Personalamt

The ultimate success of the new *Luftwaffe* would depend on the quality of its personnel and it is to Blomberg's credit that he instructed the *Reichsheer's Personalamt* (Army Personnel Office) to transfer officers of the highest calibre to the new arm, some forty general staff officers being assigned to the *RLM* on the 10 May 1933 *(Photo 2B-1)*.[1]

> Over the next few years the *Reichswehr* must devote itself wholly to the task of creating the reserves denied us until now. A panzer army and an air force are to be established. It will be necessary to give it preference over everything else, and this must be understood by the other branches of the *Reichswehr*.

*GenOb.*Werner von Blomberg
Reichswehrminister
1 June 1933

Other key personnel were then selected to join this group, a process which was to an extent disguised by timing their transfer with the routine pattern of promotions and postings. Using this subterfuge a total of 182 officers were transferred from the *Reichsheer* and a further 42 from the *Reichsmarine* to form the nucleus of the *Luftwaffe's* officer corps by the end of the year.[2] The *Offizierkorps der Luftwaffe* was officially established on the 1 October 1933. However shortly after its inception it was ostensibly disbanded and its members re-designated as *Ergänzungsoffiziere* or re-assigned to line officer status, presumably with their former arm of service.[3] All officers assigned to the *RLM* were overtly on the inactive list *(ausser Dienst or a.D.)* in accordance with R*eichspräsident* Hindenburg's decree that *"Kein Soldat ins Reichsluftfahrtministerium"* - no soldiers were to be assigned to the *RLM*.[4]

1 Quoted from *The Liebmann Papers* in the *Institut für Zeitgeschichte ED 1*. Blomberg made this remarks at a meeting at Bad Wildungen on the 1 Jun 33. *"Most of these officers, particularly the older ones, had occupied Generalstabes positions during the Great War. Some had received their General Staff training under the Reichswehr. A few of the latter group had come to the Luftwaffe from the Reichsmarine where they had received similar training for General Staff service. The selection of officers was arbitrary. At the order of the Reichswehrminister, all those officers whose names appeared on the so-called "pilot roster", ie. all those who, at some time or another, had seen service as pilots or had completed flight training, were automatically transferred to the Luftwaffe. This order also included Generalstabsoffiziere. "*- see See also Nielsen A. 1959 *The German Air Force General Staff* USAF Historical Studies No.173 (hereafter cited as Nielsen 1959) p.41. For Blomberg's support for the emergent *Luftwaffe* & *Panzerwaffe* – see Irving D. 1973 *The Rise and Fall of the Luftwaffe: The Life of Luftwaffe Marshal Erhard Milch* p.32 & Mitcham S.W.1988 *Hitler's Field Marshals and their Battles* pp.32-33.
2 Volker K.H. 1968 *Dokumente und Documentarfotos zue Geschichte der deutschen Luftwaffe* p.16 & Irving D. 1989 *Göring: A Biography* p.131.
3 Maass B. GenLt.a.D. 1955 *The Organisation of the German Air Force High Command and Higher Echelon Headquarters within the German Air Force* USAF Historical Studies No.190 (hereafter cited as Maass 1955) p.22. However their revised status is not confirmed by the available service records in Hildebrand K.F.1990-92 *Die Generale der deutschen Luftwaffe 1935-1945 Band 1-3* (hereafter cited as Hildebrand 1990-92).
4 Information provided by Gen.d.Flg.Hellmuth Felmy in Maass 1955 pp.29-31. Officially they were civilian employees of the ministry and as such wore civilian clothing whilst at work. On more formal occasions officials wore

Not surprisingly there was resentment from some of those officers who had been arbitrarily selected for service with the *Luftwaffe*, this being shown by the documented case of *Obst*. Albert Keßelring who was at that time the *Kommandeur* of the *III./Artillerie Regiment Nr.4* at Dresden:

> When, in September 1933, *Oberst* Stumpff sought me out during a day-and-night exercise at manoeuvres with the object of interesting me in the appointment of *Chef der Verwaltungsamt* of the future *Luftwaffe* he got a very lukewarm response. I wanted to stay with the *Reichsheer* and recommended that the administrative work of the *Luftfahrt*, and later that of the *Luftwaffe*, should be taken over by the *Reichsheer*. The matter was settled that evening at a mess dinner, however, at which the foreign military attaches and the *Chef des Heeresleitung* were our guests. When I presented myself to *GenLt*.Freiherr von Hammerstein the following conversation ensued.

> "Has Stumpff told you about your future employment ?"
> "Yes."
> "Well, are you satisfied about it ?"

> When I said no and proceeded to summarise my reasons he cut me short with:

> "You are a soldier and have to obey orders."[5]

> *GFM.a.D.*Albert Keßelring
> Former *Chef des Verwaltungsamtes (LD)*

Of these early officers Hans-Jurgen Stumpff was to play a particularly important role in shaping the new *Luftwaffe*. Born in 1889 he had entered the *Heer* in 1907 and by 1916 he had been singled out for general staff training, ending the Great War as a *Hauptmann im Generalstabe*. His subsequent career in the *Reichsheer* had been competent but his appointment as head of the *Personalabteilung* (Personnel Branch) on the 1 June 1933 was a stroke of brilliance.[6] He personally advised Göring on the selection of key personnel and in this way the *Luftwaffe* gained the services of Walther Wever, Albert Keßelring and Karl Kitzinger, officers who would more than complement the military aviation experts from the pilot roster (See 1E1).[7] Indeed given the needs of the flying units for experienced personnel relatively few former pilots were assigned to the *RLM* at this formative stage and of the four *Amt-Chef* (Office Chiefs) only *Obst*.Wilhelm Wimmer was an *Alte Adler* (Old Eagle).[8]

During the course of 1933 the *Personalabteilung* absorbed the personnel management assets of the *Luftschützamt* and was transformed into the *Luftwaffen Personalamt*:[9]

the *DLV* uniform - see Suchenwirth R. 1968 *The Development of the German Air Force 1919-1939* USAF Historical Studies No.160 pp.57-58.

5   Quoted from Keßelring A. GFM.a.D. 1974 *The Memoirs of Field-Marshal Keßelring* p.25 William Kimber and Co.Ltd.

6   Service record for Hans-Jurgen Stumpff in Hildebrand K.F.1992 *Die Generale der deutschen Luftwaffe 1935-1945 Band 3 O-Z* pp.369-370. Stumpff was a recognised authority in questions pertaining to military personnel administration - see Nielsen 1959 p.25.

7   Nielsen 1959 p.42. *"Since the number of Reichsheer GSO taken over by the Luftwaffe was still not sufficient - especially in point of older officers - to fill the top posts of the RLM, the Reichswehrminister, with the concurrence of the Heeresleitung, authorised the assignment to the Luftwaffe of several outstanding officers from the latter agency who had never had anything to do with flying, but who seemed to be eminently well-qualified for the posts they were to fill."*

8   Nielsen 1959 pp.42-43. *Obst.Wimmer was the only office chief who was not a member of the Generalstabes. His qualifications for the job were excellent (Chef LC), however. In the Waffenamt he had been in charge of all matters pertaining to aeronautical developments, and his new office merely required him to continue his work on a larger scale. A specialist in his field, Wimmer did an outstanding job.*

9   *Information provided by GenLt.a.D.Andreas Nielsen & Obst.a.D.Rudolf Koester in Maass 1955 pp.48-49.*

FIGURE 2B-2 ORGANISATION OF THE PERSONALAMT			
1934			
Amtschef - Obst.i.G.Hans-Jurgen Stumpff			
Adjutant -	Adjutant	Administration	
LP I -	Offiziers	Officer Personnel	Obstlt.Ulrich Grauert
LP II -	Mannschaft	Enlisted Personnel	Obstlt.Karl-Siegfried Gossrau
LP III -	Zivil	Civilian Employees	RegRat.Wilhelm Sander
LP IV -	Allgemeine	General Matters	GenLt.Bodo von Witzendorff
LP V -	Erg.Offiziers	Auxiliary Personnel	Obst.Peter Hermann

The *Personalamt* (Personnel Office) consisted of five *Abteilungen* (Branches), each of which was further sub-divided into *Gruppen* (Departments) and *Referate* (Desks) which performed specific functions.[10] Not surprisingly the most important *Abteilungen* were *LP I* and *II* which dealt respectively with the assignment, evaluation and promotion of officers and enlisted men. These branches were also responsible for the development of training programmes, disciplinary guidelines and leave regulations. They also had some specialist functions, *LP I* being responsible for the assignment of all flying personnel regardless of rank, whilst *LP II* dealt with conscription procedures. However there were anomalies and the assignment of *Generalstabesoffiziere* (General Staff Officers) did not come under the jurisdiction of *LP I*, being instead a function of the *Adjutant's* branch (See also 3A7).[11]

By the 1 April 1934 *LP III* had been transferred to the *Verwaltungsamt* where it formed the basis for *LD II* (See 2B3), but the remaining two branches continued to play an increasingly important role as the *Luftwaffe* expanded, disciplinary matters for officers for example being handled by *LP IV*. This branch also dealt with legal matters, welfare funds and the administration of military orders and awards, a function which would become particularly important in time of war.[12]

Ultimately the *Personalamt* would be responsible for co-ordinating recruitment but in the early years the Luftwaffe remained dependent on the *Reichsheer* and *Reichsmarine* for not only its manpower but also its general personnel administration. For example, the promotion of officers and the conduct of courts martial were not fully delegated until after 1935.[13] Personnel were selected after the completion of their basic military training on the basis for their suitability for further training as aircrew, or as ground specialists, for example as signals and transportation troops. Examples of officer transfers to the secret air arm during 1933/34 include Hans-Henning Freiherr von Beust, Albert Bock, Walter Bradel, Wolfgang von Chamier-Glisczinki, Heinz Cramer, Arved Cruger, Claus Hinkelbein, Heinrich Hofer, Lothar Lau, Walter Lehwess-Litzmann, Günther Lützow, Dietrich Frhr.von Massenbach, Werner Molders, Joachim Poetter, Alfons Orthofer and

Hptm.i.G.Nielsen was a *GSO* in the *LP* from 1 Jul 35 - 31 Jul 36 - see service record for Andreas Nielsen in Hildebrand K.F.1991 *Die Generale der deutschen Luftwaffe 1935-1945 Band 2 H-N* pp.448-449. See also Ries K. 1974 *Luftwaffen-Story 1935-1939* (hereafter cited as Ries 1974) p.11.

10   *Information provided by GenLt.a.D.Andreas Nielsen & Obst.a.D.Rudolf Koester* in Maass 1955 pp.48-49. The *Adjutantur* also dealt with the general administration of the *LP* and the issuance of criteria for performance evaluations; *LP I* was additionally responsible for the reactivation of retired officer personnel; *LP II* had a supervisory function in terms of the supply of personnel.

11   *Information provided by GenLt.a.D.Andreas Nielsen & Obst.a.D.Rudolf Koester* in Maass 1955 p.49. *LP IV* also handled questions concerning the military code of honour and advised the *LD* on payroll issues; *LP V* was responsible for the personnel administration of all *Erg-Offiziere, Offiziere z.b.V. & Reserve-Offiziere* - a particularly important function at this early stage in the *Luftwaffe's* growth.

12   Maass 1955 p.49.

13   Maass 1955 p.23.

Martin Vetter all of whom came from the *Reichsheer*, whilst Hans Emig, Martin Harlinghausen, Carl Schumacher, Walter Storp and Willi Viertel were former naval officers.[14]

FIGURE 2B-3 RLM OFFICER ROSTER 1 JUNE 1933	
1. STAFF OFFICERS (OFFIZIERE i.G.)	
Maj.i.G.Egon Doerstling	KorvKpt.Hans Ritter
FregKpt.Hans-Ferdinand Geisler	Hptm.i.G.Walter Schwabedissen
Hptm.i.G.Hans Jeschonnek	Hptm.i.G.Wilhelm Speidel
Hptm.i.G.Josef Kammhuber	Obstlt.i.G.Hellmuth Volkmann
Hptm.i.G.Rudolf Meister	KorvKpt.Wolfgang Weigand
Maj.i.G.Maximilian Ritter von Pohl	FregKpt.Rudolf Wenninger
2. OTHER ACTIVE OFFICERS FROM THE REICHSWEHR	
Oblt.z.S.Paul Achilles	KorvKpt.Ulrich Kessler
KptLt.Paul Ascher	KptLt.Wilhelm Meendsen-Bohlken
KptLt.Eugen Bischoff	KorvKpt.Hans Siburg
KorvKpt.Heinz Degenhardt	Oblt.z.S.Walter Weygolt
Hptm.Walter von Axthelm	Hptm.Gerd von Massow
Maj.Karl Bodenschatz	Maj.Kurt Müller
Obstlt.Rudolf Bogatsch	Rittm.Plaschke
Obst.Eberhard Bohnstedt	Hptm.August Ploch
Oblt.von der Burg	Hptm.Werner Prellberg
Maj.Friedrich Cranz	Maj.Waldemar Reinecke
Hptm.Karl Drum	Obst.Günther Rüdel
Hptm.Johannes Fink	Hptm.Schnepper
Hptm.Dr.von Harbou	Maj.Paul Schultheiss
Maj.Alfred Haubold	Hptm.Werner Schwartzkopf
Hptm.Joseph Hilgers	Maj.Eduard Seldner
Oblt.Werner Knublauch	Maj.Kurt Wagner
Obstlt.Bernhard Kühl	Obstlt.Wilhelm Wimmer
Hptm.Walter (?) Lorenz	

14   *Anlage 5 Verzeichnis der aktiven und inaktiven Flieger-und Flugabwehr (Luftschütz)-Offiziere im Reichsluftfahrtministerium, Stand: 1.Juni 1933* in Volker K-H. 1967 *Die deutsche Luftwaffe 1933-1939: Aufbau, Führung und Rüstung der Luftwaffe sowie die Entwicklung der deutschen Luftkriegstheorie* (hereafter cited as Volker 1967) pp.229-230. See also individual service records in Obermaier E. 1966 *Die Ritterkreuztrager der Luftwaffe Bd.I Jagdflieger 1939-1945*, Obermaier E. 1976 *Die Ritterkreuztrager der Luftwaffe Bd.II Stuka- und Schlachtflieger 1939-1945* & Kaiser J. 2010-11 *Der Ritterkreuztrager der Kampfflieger Bd.I & II*. See also, Brutting G. 1976 *Das waren die deutschen Stuka-Asse 1939-1945* & Brutting G. 1986 *Das waren die deutschen Kampfflieger-Asse 1939-1945*.

3. INACTIVE OFFICERS (OFFIZIERE a.D.)	
Oblt.a.D.Alexander (?) Andrae	Maj.a.D.von Holwede
Hptm.a.D.Hans-Jochen von Arnim	Hptm.a.D.Hans-von Karmainsky
Oblt.a.D.Werner Bartz	Oblt.z.S.a.D.Korn
Oblt.z.S.a.D.von Bentheim	Hptm.a.D.Walter Lackner
Oblt.z.S.a.D.Erich Boenisch	Oblt.z.S.a.D.Otto Leo
Maj.a.D.Hilmer Freiherr von Bülow	Lt.a.D.Nikolaus Graf von Luckner
KptLt.a.D.Frege	Rittm.a.D.Bruno Maaß
Oblt.z.S.a.D.Freymadl	Hptm.a.D. Georg-Adolf (?) Mentzel
Hptm.a.D.Geerkens	Hptm.a.D.Morell
Lt.d.R.a.D.Helmuth Giesler	Hptm.a.D.von der Osten
Lt.z.S.a.D.Grader	Hptm.a.D.Heinrich Seywald
Hptm.a.D.Walther Grosch	Hptm.a.D.Silber
Oblt.a.D.Herrmann	Lt.z.S.a.D.Wachsmuth
Oblt.a.D.Hess	Oblt.a.D. Wandel

As the covert *Luftwaffe* lacked its own staff college Blomberg instructed the *Reichsheer* and the *Reichsmarine* to transfer staff officers of suitable quality to the air arm.[15] The employment of these men was to result in the evolution of the *Luftwaffe* along traditional military lines, a *Regimental* structure being proposed initially although this was replaced by *Geschwadern* in the *Fliegertruppe* in accordance with Great War traditions.[16] Relatively few staff officers were assigned to the rapidly expanding *RLM* and in June 1933 this group made up just 16% of the total.[17] Nor was the *Reichsmarine* able to spare enough experienced officers of high rank to safeguard its interests and in June 1933 only 25% of all officers in the *RLM* had a naval background.[18] A significant proportion of officials were in fact former officers who had been directly recruited from civilian life.[19]

To meet the needs of the flying units the *Personalamt* had to rely mainly on the officers from the *Reichswehr's* pilot roster, men who for the most part had been trained at Lipetsk and at the *DVS Zweigstellen* at Schleißheim, Braunschweig, List and Warnemünde.[20] However the secret *Luftwaffe* also gained the services of several influential aviators from civilian life, including Friedrich Christiansen, Robert Ritter von Greim Alfred Keller, Joachim-Friedrich Huth, Werner Junck, Carl-August von Schoenebeck and Theo Osterkamp *(Photo 2B-2)*.[21] These aviators from the Great War were employed as the air arm's first generation of unit commanders seeing service in the flying schools and the covert operational units from the 1 April 1934 (See 2D3).[22]

15   Nielsen 1959 pp.44-45. The *Reichswehr* had not been permitted a war academy under the Treaty of Versailles. However suitable officers had received training as *Führergehilfen* (Command Assistants) in the post-war period. The *Kriegsakademie* in Berlin was reopened on the 18 Oct 35 under *Gen.d.Inf.*Curt Liebmann – see Mitcham 1988 p.32.
16   Ries 1974 pp.18-19.
17   Analysis of material in *Anlage 5 Verzeichnis der Aktiven und inaktiven Flieger- und Flugabwehr (Luftschütz)-Offiziere im Reichsluftfahrtministerium, Stand: 1.Juni 1933* in Volker 1967 pp.229-230.
18   Analysis of material in *Anlage 5 Verzeichnis der Aktiven und inaktiven Flieger- und Flugabwehr (Luftschütz)-Offiziere im Reichsluftfahrtministerium, Stand: 1.Juni 1933* in Volker 1967 pp.229-230.
19   Analysis of material in *Anlage 5 Verzeichnis der Aktiven und inaktiven Flieger- und Flugabwehr (Luftschütz)-Offiziere im Reichsluftfahrtministerium, Stand: 1.Juni 1933* in Volker 1967 pp.229-230.
20   Maass 1955 p.19 & Ries K. 1988 *Deutsche Flugzeugführerschulen und ihre Maschinen 1919-1945* pp.10-11 & 53-54.
21   Individual service records in Hildebrand 1990-92.
22   Individual service records in Hildebrand 1990-92. See also Volker 1967 p.20 & Hooton 1994 p.110.

2B3

The Verwaltungsamt

Whilst Stumpff co-ordinated the activities of the *Personalamt* (Personnel Office) at the Behrensstrasse, Keßelring brought his formidable administrative skills to bear on the newly formed *Verwaltungsamt* (Administrative Office).[1] Overtly this office was responsible for the administration of German civil aviation, however it was the needs of a rapidly expanding *Luftwaffe* that absorbed the lion's share of the aviation budget:[2]

\multicolumn{4}{c}{**FIGURE 2B-4 ORGANISATION OF THE VERWALTUNGSAMT**}

\multicolumn{4}{c}{**FIGURE 2B-4 ORGANISATION OF THE VERWALTUNGSAMT** 1 APRIL 1934}			
\multicolumn{4}{c}{Amtschef - Obst.i.G.Albert Keßelring}			
LD I	Haushalts-und Wirtschaftsabteilung	Budget and Economics	MinRat.Dr.Wolfgang Höfeld
LD II	Beamten-und Besoldungsabteilung	State Servants and Payrolls	ObRegRat.Dr.Wilhelm Sander
LD III	Liegenschafts-und Unterkunftswesen	Real Estate and Housing	MinRat.Dr.Wilhelm Untriesser
LD IV	Verpflegung und Bekleidung	Food and Clothing	Obstlt.Hans Sommer

Unlike the *Personalamt* this office was primarily staffed by ministerial officials (*Beamte*) and its principal functions were the administration of the huge budget for aviation, the *Luftwaffe's* burgeoning construction programme and the provision of food and clothing for this new arm of the *Reichswehr*.[3]

LD I (Haushalts und Wirtschaftsabteilung) (Budget and Economics) grew out of the slightly earlier *Verwaltungsabteilung* which had been established in March 1933 to service the *Reichskommissioner für die Luftfahrt*.[4] *ObRegRat Dr.*Wolfgang Höfeld, a former *Marine-Reserve Offizier* who had undergone flight training at Zeebrugge in 1916-17 before serving in the *Marine-Infanterie*, had been recruited from financial service in the *Finanzamt Berlin-Alexanderplatz* to head up this new Branch.[5] He would now become Keßelring's financial expert in the administration of quite incredible sums when compared to the *Reichswehr* budget of the twenties, some 210 million *RM*

---

1   Keßelring A. GFM.a.D. 1974 *The Memoirs of Field-Marshal Keßelring* (hereafter cited as Keßelring 1974) pp.32-33. See also service record for Albert Keßelring in Hildebrand K.F.1991 *Die Generale der deutschen Luftwaffe 1935-1945 Band 2 H-N* pp.165-167.

2   *Anlage 10 Besetzung der Amter und Abteilungen des Reichsluftministeriums, Stand: 1.April 1934* in Volker K-H. 1967 *Die deutsche Luftwaffe 1933-1939: Aufbau, Führung und Rüstung der Luftwaffe sowie die Entwicklung der deutschen Luftkriegstheorie* p.235. See also Ries K. 1974 *Luftwaffen-Story 1935-1939* pp.10-11.

3   Maass B. GenLt.a.D. 1955 *The Organisation of the German Air Force High Command and Higher Echelon Headquarters within the German Air Force* USAF Historical Studies No.190 (hereafter cited as Maass 1955) p.48.

4   *Information provided by MinDir.Willy Fisch* in Maass 1955 p.18.

5   Service record for Wolfgang Höfeld in Hildebrand 1991 pp.103-104. Following service in the *Reichsfinanzministerium* in 1921-22, Höfeld had worked in a succession of *Finanzamter* in the Berlin area.

being publicly admitted for the fiscal year 1934/35.[6] In fact the true sum was far larger - RM 642 million[7] - but the habits of austerity were still very much in evidence and the selection of Keßelring as *Amt-Chef* ensured that the *Luftwaffe* received value for money at this critical stage:

> With the benefit of my experience in retrenchment, I set to work helped by men who were grand fellows as well as talented experts. The first task was to lay the foundations for our budget. In a few months we had completed our estimates in practical form for ministry and service expenditure. The *Luftwaffe* has been accused of exorbitance in its demands and appropriations, but no one who followed the scrupulous examination of every single budget item is likely to make this charge. I was only a spendthrift with bare necessities. I constantly showed our plans, both psychological and material, to the competent authorities by means of circular flying trips, and so awakened their sympathies for air force requirements. These three-to-four day flights helped one to forget the frustrations of office work and internal bickerings and drew us closer together without too much palaver. This method of working I made a guiding principle.[8]

GFM.a.D.Albert Keßelring
Former *Chef des Verwaltungsamtes (LD)*

The significance of his contribution was undoubted:

> The infrastructure of the *Luftwaffe* was part and parcel of the extravagance of *Nazidom* and Keßelring spent the money well, and at a colossal pace. He swept everybody along by a torrent of instructions and saw everything for himself. If some fell by the wayside he was apparently inexhaustible. The high morale of the *Luftwaffe*, that priceless asset in battle, was to be the product of his high standards.[9]

Kenneth Macksey
1978

Much of this was of course channelled into aircraft construction – the remit of *Obstlt.*Wilhelm Wimmer's *Technische Amtes (LC)* (See 2C1). During May 1933 Milch commissioned studies for a 1,000 aircraft programme for the secret *Luftwaffe,* an objective that was subsequently agreed by Hitler in June (See 2A1).[10] The necessity for secrecy together with the actual problem of raising the estimated RM 30 billion for the overall rearmament programme resulted in an innovative strategy on the part of *Dr.* Hjalmar Schacht, the *Präsident des Reichsbank*:

---

6   *Reichsgesetzblatt, 26 Mar 1934* in Irving D. 1973 *The Rise and Fall of the Luftwaffe: The Life of Luftwaffe Marshall Erhard Milch* (hereafter cited as Irving 1973) p.38 & 361. This compared to *RM* 78.3 m in 1933/34. See also Overy R.J. 1984 *Goering: The Iron Man* (hereafter cited as Overy 1984) pp.37-38.
7   *Table 1 German Military Expenditure 1934/5 - 1937/8* in Overy R.J. 1979 'The German Motorosierung and Rearmament: a Reply' in *Economic History Review* Vol.32 (hereafter cited as Overy 1979) p.113. In 1934/35 the overall military budget had been *RM* 1,953 m.
8   Quoted from Keßelring 1974 *The Memoirs of Field-Marshal Keßelring* p.32 William Kimber and Co.Ltd.
9   Quoted from Macksey K. 1978 *Keßelring: The Making of the Luftwaffe* p.46 with the kind permission of Pavilion Books – copyright Batsford 1978. This commentator also states: *"...it can be claimed that it was he who was the heart and brain behind the sudden and yet relatively smooth emergence of a new factor in the European balance of power in 1935".*
10   *Milch Diary, 13 May 1933* in Irving 1973 p.31 *"Major technical conference on thousand-aircraft programme".*

An old skeleton company - eventually the Metal Research Company *"Mefo"* was chosen - should be guaranteed by the *Reichsbank* and used to cover the financing of industry with its own bills of exchange, of nominal validity of three months, automatically extended each time. These *Reich*-backed *"Mefo-bills"* could be discounted at the *Reichsbank* at any time, and would go to selected big industrial concerns as payment. Milch and Schacht were the directors of the company. It was neat economic trick, but not an illicit one.[11]

Huge sums were therefore spent on the development of the aircraft and aero-engine industries and on procurement. However of equal importance was the construction of airfields and factories which by the end of 1933 was occupying two million civilian workers, whilst in 1934 work began on a vast new complex for the *RLM* in the Leipzigerstrasse in Berlin together with an underground operations centre at Potsdam (See 3B4).[12] The introduction of the *Rheinland Programm* in April then necessitated a further major round year of airfield construction. Unlike their predecessors which were generally former military airfields from the Great War several of these new airfields were on greenfield sites, a situation which required a more extensive works programme.[13]

FIGURE 2B-5 AIRFIELDS DESIGNATED FOR COVERT MILITARY USE JUNE 1933		
Braunschweig-Broitzem	Kiel-Holtenau	Prenzlau
Cottbus	Kitzingen	Rechlin
Döberitz (Plan I)	Königsberg-Neuhausen	Schleißheim
Fassberg	Lechfeld	Seerappen
Gotha	List/Sylt	Tutow
Hildesheim	Neuruppin	Warnemünde
Jüterbog-Damm	Nürnberg-Fürth	

FIGURE 2B-6 ADDITIONAL AIRFIELDS TO BE DEVELOPED FOR MILITARY USE APRIL 1934		
Angermunde	Greifswald	Nordhausen
Bielefeld	Größenhain	Schwerin
Brandis	Hamm	Stargard
Eberswalde	Kassel	Stendal
Erfurt	Liegnitz	Stralsund
Fassberg	Lübeck-Blankensee	Ulm
Finsterwalde	Merseburg	Unna
Gersthofen	Münster	Wilhelmshaven
Giebelstadt	Neubrandenburg	Wunstorf
Goppingen	Norderney	Würzburg
		Zerbst

11   Quoted from Irving 1973 *The Rise and Fall of the Luftwaffe: The Life of Luftwaffe Marshal Erhard Milch* pp.32-33 with the knowledge of the Orion Publishing Group. However it has been suggested that Schacht insisted on an orthodox and conservative approach to financing re-armament during 1934-35 – see Overy 1984 p.38.
12   Irving 1973 pp.38-39.
13   Ries K. 1974 *Luftwaffen-Story 1935-1939* pp.18-19.

Not surprisingly the *Luftwaffe's* share of the secret rearmament budget in the financial year 1934/35 was 32.9%; in 1935/36 it would rise to 37.4% when *RM* 1,036 million was authorised.[14]

In October 1933 Höfeld's *Verwaltungsabteilung* had been absorbed into the newly formed *RLM* and simultaneously upgraded to form the *Verwaltungsamtes (LD)* under *Obst.*Keßelring.[15] Branch *LD III (Liegenschafts-und Unterkunftswesen)* (Estates and Accommodation) was created under *Dr.*Wilhelm Untrieser with specific responsibility for the rapidly expanding physical infrastructure.[16] The covert Luftwaffe's construction expert was *ObReg-Baurat Dipl.Ing.*Karl Gallwitz who was appointed *Leiter LD III-Bau* on the 16 May 1933 after a period of *Reichsheer* service in *Wehrkreis III* Berlin.[17] In his new role Gallwitz was destined to be an extremely busy man and the quality of the emerging Luftwaffe's *Friedensstandorte* (Peace Time Garrisons) can be directly attributed to the supervisory work of his team (See 3B4).

As *Leiter LD IV (Verpflegung-und Bekleidung)* (Food and Clothing) *Obstlt.*Hans Sommer was the only regular officer to be appointed to Keßelring's senior team.[18] *LD IV* was formed in December 1933 to provide the rapidly expanding *Luftwaffe* with its uniforms, specialist protective clothing and rations. At that time the responsibility for clothing extended to the whole of the *Deutsche Luftsport-Verband eV (DLV)* whose uniform was worn by covert members of the new air arm whose units were concealed within the wider ranks of this now para-military organisation (See 2D2).[19]

The creation of the *Verwaltungsamtes* also marked the transfer of responsibility for the personnel administration and remuneration of salaried officials and clerical employees from the *Personalamt*. Thus *RegRat.Dr.*Wilhelm Sander's *LP III* was transformed into *LD II (Beamten-und Besoldungsabteilung)* and came under Keßelring's overall jurisdiction.[20] Sander had been transferred to the *RLM* from the *Höheren Heeres-Verwaltungsdienst* (Army Administrative Service) in October 1933 and was the only one of Keßelring's four *Abteilungsleiter* not to have seen war service.[21]

14   *Table 1 German Military Expenditure 1934/5 - 1937/8* in Overy 1979 p.113.
15   *Information provided by Gen.d.Flg.a.D.Hans Siburg* in Maass 1955 p.21. Keßelring was appointed as *Chef LD* on the 1 Oct 33 – see service record for Albert Keßelring in Hildebrand 1991 pp.165-167.
16   Service record for Wilhelm Unterieser in Hildebrand K.F.1992 *Die Generale der deutschen Luftwaffe 1935-1945 Band 3 O-Z* pp.428-429. Untrieser's war service had been as a *Beamte* in the *Infanterie*. Post war he had been retained by the *Reichsheer* seeing service in *Wehrkreis VI* Münster and *the RWM*.
17   Service record for Karl Gallwitz in Hildebrand K.F.1990 *Die Generale der deutschen Luftwaffe 1935-1945 Band 1 A-G* pp.343-344. Gallwitz had seen action in the *Infanterie* during the Great War being promoted to *Hptm.d.Res*. After returning to State Service in his construction speciality, he had joined the *Reichsheer* in Apr 27.
18   Service record for Hans Sommer in Hildebrand 1992 pp.313-314. Sommer was a pre-war *Infanterie-Offizier* who had been captured by the British following the Campaign in German South-West Africa (Namibia). His *Reichsheer* service had been with *Inf.Rgt.16, 15 & 6*.
19   Ries K. 1970 *Luftwaffe Bd.1 Die Maulwurfe 1919-1935* pp.94-96. The *DLV* was formed out of the earlier *Deutsche Luftfahrtverband (DLV)* on the 25 Mar 33. Göring appointed his wartime colleague *Hptm.a.D.*Bruno Loerzer as *Präsident d.DLV* and *Reichsluftsportführer* – see service record for Bruno Loerzer in Hildebrand 1991 pp.309-310. With c.50,000 members in 1931 the transformation of the previously civilian *DLV* into a uniformed para-military organisation was an immense undertaking. Bender R.J. 1972 *Air Organisations of the Third Reich: The Luftwaffe* pp.8-14 & Davis B.L. 1991 *Uniforms and Insignia of the Luftwaffe Vol.1: 1933-1940* pp.13-27.
20   Maass 1955 p.21 & 49. The date of this transfer is not known with certainty but was after Oct 33 and before the 1 Apr 34. *LD II* did not deal with the personnel administration of aero-technical personnel.
21   Service record for Wilhelm Sander in Hildebrand 1992 pp.160-161. Sander had entered the *Reichsheer* as a *Beamte* on the 18 Feb 25.

2B4

The Zentralabteilung

The *Zentralabteilung (ZA)* (Central Branch) was established in October 1933 to control and co-ordinate the work of several of the smaller central service departments within the newly created *RLM*.[1] *Leiter* of this *Abteilung*, from April 1934 was *Kpt.z.S.*Rudolf Wenninger, the former *Chef des Stabes* within the *Luftschützamt (Photo 2B-3)*.[2]

FIGURE 2B-7 ORGANISATION OF THE ZENTRALABTEILUNG APRIL 1934		
Abtschef - Kpt.z.See Rudolf Wenninger		
Adjutantur	-	Adjutant
Kommandant des RLM	-	RLM Headquarters Command
Buerodirektor des RLM	-	RLM Secretariat
Attachegruppe	-	Air Attaches
Abwehrgruppe	-	Passive Air Defence
Gruppe Rechtswesen	-	Legal Affairs
Gruppe Politische Angelegenheiten	-	Political Affairs
Gruppe Sanitätswesen	-	Medical Affairs
Pressegruppe	-	Public Relations

The *Adjutantur* (Adjutant) performed a similar function for *Staatssekretär* Milch as *Maj.*Karl Bodenschatz provided for *Reichsminister* Göring.[3] *Hptm.i.G.*Hans Jeschonnek was assigned as Milch's *Führungsoffizier* and *Verbindungsoffizier* (Leadership and Liaison Officer) with the *RWM* in September 1933. From October 1934 he took over as *Adjutant*, whilst *Hptm.i.G.*Günther Korten assumed his former position as Milch's *Generalstabsoffizier*.[4]

1   *Information provided by GenLt.a.D.Hermann Bruch* in Maass B. GenLt.a.D. 1955 *The Organisation of the German Air Force High Command and Higher Echelon Headquarters within the German Air Force* USAF Historical Studies No.190 (hereafter cited as Maass 1955) pp.32-33.
2   Service record for Rudolf Wenninger in Hildebrand K.F.1992 *Die Generale der deutschen Luftwaffe 1935-1945 Band 3 O-Z* (hereafter cited as Hildebrand 1992) pp.502-504. Known as Ralph within his own family, Wenninger was one of the few naval officers to attain high rank within the *Luftwaffe* during the thirties. Interestingly in this respect was his lack of aviation experience. During the Great War he had served in the *U-Boot* arm and was captured by the British in Apr 18. He enjoyed a varied post-war career with the *Reichsmarine* before being appointed *Ltr.d.Marine-Luftschützgruppe/Marineleitung* in Oct 32. He was formally transferred to the *Luftwaffe* in Oct 34 with the rank of *Obst.i.G.* Bruch, another naval officer, replaced Wenninger in Apr 35 as *Chef ZA* - see service record for Hermann Bruch in Hildebrand K.F.1990 *Die Generale der deutschen Luftwaffe 1935-1945 Band 1 A-G* (hereafter cited as Hildebrand 1990) pp.119-120.
3   *Information provided by GenLt.a.D.Hermann Bruch* in Maass 1955 p.32.
4   Service records for Hans Jeschonnek & Günther Korten in Hildebrand K.F.1991 *Die Generale der deutschen Luftwaffe 1935-1945 Band 2 H-N* (hereafter cited as Hildebrand 1991) pp.138-139 & 217-218.

However the core function of the *Zentralabteilung* was the handling of the Luftwaffe's external relationships with political and diplomatic agencies at both home and abroad. To this end the *Adjutanter/ZA* dealt directly with the *Reichswehr, Reichsheer, Reichsmarine* and *Auswaertiges Amt* (Foreign Office), whilst the *Attachegruppe* supervised the work of the German air attaches abroad and those of foreign powers inside Germany (See 4A3).[5] Similar liaison functions were provided by the *Gruppe Politische Angelegenheiten* which provided a link with the various *NSDAP* agencies, and the *Pressegruppe* which handled the release of ministerial information to the media.[6] Denied *Attaches* under the Treaty of Versailles, the first military and naval attaches were not appointed until the 1 April 1933 when 7 *Reichsheer* and 4 *Reichsmarine* officers were assigned to cover a total of fourteen different countries.[7]

More wide-ranging were the activities of the *Gruppe Sanitätswesen*. Originally it had been envisaged that the air arm's medical affairs would be handled by the *Heeressanitäts-Inspektion* (Army Medical Inspectorate) within the *RWM* and indeed until 1939 all air medical officer personnel continued to be trained at the *Militärarztliche Akademie des Heeres* (Army Medical Academy). Notwithstanding this arrangement it was decided to form the *Gruppe Sanitätswesen* (Medical Services Group) in 1933 as the supervisory authority for all aero-medical affairs.[8] The *Gruppe's* area of jurisdiction was extensive and included the supervision of medical facilities attached to the various units, the establishment and operation of aircrew medical examinations and the supervision of research into flight medicine (See 9D1).

Another *Gruppe* with wide-ranging responsibilities was the *Abwehrgruppe* which determined the air defence requirements for industrial installations, issues of camouflage and, in conjunction with the *Technisches Amt* (Technical Office) and the *Reichswirtschaftsministerium* (Economics Ministry), the regulation of export licences for all air armament equipment. The *Leiter der Abwehrstelle Luft/ZA* from May 1933 was *Oblt.a.D.*Hans-Joachim Rath.[9]

The *RLM's* increasingly complex legal affairs were the responsibility of the *Gruppe Rechtswesen* which provided legal guidance and if necessary counsel and representation to the various *RLM Amter* and *Abteilungen* in their dealings with other branches of the *Reichswehr*, the civilian authorities and the many diverse commercial organisations (See 8D1).[10] Much of the basic legislation controlling

5   *Information provided by GenLt.a.D.Hermann Bruch* in Maass 1955 p.32. The first *Chef des Attachegruppe/ZA* was *Maj.i.G.*Friedrich Hanesse (Apr 35) - see service record for Friedrich Hanesse in Hildebrand 1991 pp.28-29. Hanesse was an *Alte Adler* whose war service had been with *Feld-FA A 225* and as *Fhr.d.Schutzstaffel 9* & *Schlachtstaffel 2.* He had served in *Art.Rgt.6* during the *Reichsheer* period.

6   *Information provided by GenLt.a.D.Hermann Bruch* in Maass 1955 p.33.

7   Kahn D. 1978 *Hitler's Spies: German Military Intelligence in the World War II* (hereafter cited as Kahn 1978) p.73. The first *Luftwaffe* attaches were not appointed until 1935: in Jan 35 *Maj.*Paul Schultheiss (Budapest - Hungary) & Apr 35 *Hptm.i.G.*Otto Hoffmann von Waldau (Rom - Italy) - see service record for Hoffmann von Waldau in Hildebrand 1991 pp.113-114 & service record for Paul Schultheiss in Hildebrand 1992 pp.254-255.

8   *Information provided by GenObStArzt.a.D.Prof.Dr.med.Oskar Schroeder* in Maass 1955 pp.32-33. Prior to 1935 all applicants for medical posts in the *Luftwaffe* were selected by the *Heeressanitätsinspektion.* The decision to take control of medical affairs within the *Luftwaffe* was undoubtedly a further manifestation of Göring's desire for complete control over all aspects of German aviation activity.

9   *Information provided by GenLt.a.D.Hermann Bruch* in Maass 1955 p.32. In this respect the *Gruppe Abwehr* had no connection with the *Abwehr/RWM* which focused on military and naval intelligence and counter-intelligence activities - see Kahn 1978 pp.223-226. *Maj.(Char)* Hans Busch was *Gruppenleiter (Abwehr)* from Apr 34 - see service record for Hans Busch in Hildebrand 1990 pp.140-141. Busch was a pre-war military aviator who had served with the *Aufklärungsflieger* and on the staff of the *KoGenLuft.* He joined the covert *Luftwaffe* in Jul 33. See also service record for Hans-Joachim Rath in Hildebrand 1992 pp.81-82. Discharged from military service in Dec 20, Rath had served in a civilian technical capacity from Oct 24 with *Wa Prüf 6F, WaA (L)* & *Wa Prüf 8.* He was in the USSR during 1925-28. His war service with the *Luftstreitkräfte* had been diverse: *KaGOHL 5, Jasta 22, Flugmusterei, Schlasta 5* & the *Bauaufsicht Siemens* (Construction Supervision).

10   *Information provided by GenLt.a.D.Hermann Bruch* in Maass 1955 p.32. See also *Teil VIII Rechtswesen* in Westarp Graf von E.J. Obstlt. (Ed.) 1941 *Westarpscher Taschenkalender 1941/42 für die Luftwaffe sowie für Luftschütz,*

Luftwaffe activity was taken over unaltered from the *Reichsheer*, for example the Code of Military Justice (*Militärstrafgesetzbuch*), the Obligations of the Soldier (*Die Pflichten des Soldaten vom 25.5.1934*), the Criminal Records Regulation (*Strafregisterverordnung vom 17.2.1934*), regulations over the execution of imprisonment (*Strafvollstreckungsvorschrift für die Reichswehr vom 27.11.1933*) and complaint procedures (*Beschwerdeordnung*). All of these directives, regulations and procedures were incorporated into the *L.Dv.3 Militärstrafgesetzbuch* which was subject to periodic update and amendment.[11]

Security and the overall supervision of *RLM* personnel rested with the *Kommandantur* (*RLM* Commandant); the *Stabschef im RLM* being *Maj.*Willibald Spang.[12] A separate *Flugbereitschaft des RLM* (*RLM* Flight Readiness Section) under *Obstlt.*Gustav Kastner-Kirdorf was maintained at Berlin-Staaken to provide air transport facilities for senior officers and officials throughout the Reich.[13] The embryonic *Regierungsstaffel* (Government Squadron) also formed part of this overall organisation. However this was not a military organisation and as such was commanded by *Flugkäpitan* Hans Baur, a *SS-Standartenfuherer*, and Hitler's personal pilot. At this time it consisted of four Ju 52/3m airliners that had been specially modified for VIP transportation.[14]

Luftverkehr und Luftsport pp.290-362.

11   *Luftdienstvorschrift L.Dv.3 Militärstrafgesetzbuch. L.Dv.3* was a large publication with 14 separate *Teilen* (Parts). The equivalent *Reichsheer* publication was *H.Dv.3*, whilst in the *Reichsmarine* this legislation was principally covered by *M.Dv.124*.

12   *Information provided by GenLt.a.D.Hermann Bruch* in Maass 1955 p.32. See also service record for Willibald Spang in Hildebrand 1992 pp.317-319. Spang was a highly decorated member of the wartime *Luftstreitkräfte* (*RK I.Klasse d.koniglich-württembergischen Friedrichs-Orden mit Schwerten* – 31 Aug 17 & *RK d.koniglich- württembergischen Albrechts-Ordens mit Schwerten* – 4 Jan 18) who was re-engaged as a *Hptm.a.D.* on the 1 Apr 33.

13   *App.G Activation Survey of the Operational Flying Units of the Luftwaffe* in Schliephake H. 1971 *The Birth of the Luftwaffe* p.70. This unit was also later known as the *Flugbereitschaft Ob.d.L.* See also the service record for Gustav Kastner-Kirdorf in Hildebrand 1991 pp.153-154. *Maj.a.D.*Kastner-Kirdorf had previously been the *Ltr.d.Reklame-Abt.d.DLV* – a cover for the *Reichsheer's* first air units – see Ries K. 1970 *Luftwaffe Bd.1 Die Maulwurfe 1919-1935* p.113 & Hooton E.R. 1994 *Phoenix Triumphant: The Rise and Rise of the Luftwaffe* p.69. The *Flugbereitschaft d.RLM* was subordinate to the *Insp.d.Fliegerschulen* - see *Information provided by Obst..a.D.Alois Heldmann* in Maass 1955 p.51.

14   Sweeting C.G. 2001 *Hitler's Squadron: The Führer's personal aircraft and transport unit 1933-45* pp.19-20. The Ju 52/3m aircraft on charge in 1934 were WNr.4013 D-ADOM (D-2201) *Oswald Boelcke*, WNr.4015 D-AYDL (D-2202) *Richthofen*, WNr.4019 D-AFIR (D-2468) *Joachim von Schroeder* & WNr.4021 D-2600 (D-AHUT) *Immelmann*. The first three aircraft were delivered to *DLH* in 1932 as that Airline's first examples of the new Ju 52/3m - see Hooks M. 1999 *Images of Aviation: Lufthansa* p.81.

2B5

The Allgemeines Luftamt

Civil aviation was the responsibility of the *Allgemeines Luftamt* (General Air Office), a department which was initially organised into six separate but related *Abteilungen* (Branches): *Luftverkehr* (Commercial Aviation), *Luftaufsicht* (Air Traffic Control Service), *Bodenorganisation und Flugsicherung* (Ground Organisation and Flight Safety), *Fliegerbestaendeverwaltung* (Air Supply), *Luftbildwesen* (Aerial Photography Service) and *Wetterdienst* (Meteorological Service).[1]

In keeping with the other major *Amter* there was a degree of re-organisation during the winter of 1933/34 and it would not be until July 1934 that a definitive organisation appeared. Unlike the other *Amter* the *Allgemeines Luftamt* was led by a civilian official, *Ministerialdirektor* Willy Fisch, and all of his office heads were also civilians.[2] Fisch was no stranger to civil aviation having been employed in Ernst Brandenburg's *Abteilung Luftfahrt* within the *Reichsverkehrsministerium* from its inception in 1919. As part of these duties he had represented German air interests with the *interalliierten Luftfahrtgarantie-Komitee* and in a number of internal aviation conferences including the important Paris Air Agreement of 1926.[3]

Abteilungen LB I and *LB II* were effectively responsible for the regulation of all air traffic within the frontiers of the Reich and whilst *LB I* dealt with the wider political, administrative and legal matters that pertained to civil aviation, *LB II* was responsible for the granting of licences for both aircraft, engineers and aircrew and the supervision of meetings and conferences held by the various civilian aviation associations.[4] As acknowledged experts within their respective fields both *MinRat.* Albert Mühlig-Hofmann and *ObRegRat.* Hermann Dahlmann continued their earlier work from the *Abteilung Luftfahrt/Reichsverkehrsministerium* (Aviation Branch of the Transport Ministry) as

---

1   *Information provided by MinDir.a.D. Willy Fisch* in Maass B. GenLt.a.D. 1955 *The Organisation of the German Air Force High Command and Higher Echelon Headquarters within the German Air Force* USAF Historical Studies No.190 (hereafter cited as Maass 1955) p.20. The initial organisation: LB I (*Luftverkehr*), LB II (*Technik*), LB III (*Luftsport u.Ausbildung*), LB IV (*Luftbildwesen*) & LB V (*Bodenorganisation*) - see *Anlage 3 Gliederung des Reichsluftfahrtministeriums (RLM) Stand: 1.Juni 1933* in Volker K-H. 1967 *Die deutsche Luftwaffe 1933-1939: Aufbau, Führung und Rüstung der Luftwaffe sowie die Entwicklung der deutschen Luftkriegstheorie* (hereafter cited as Volker 1967) p.227. LB II (*Technik*) had been *Abt.L2 (Technik)* within the *LS-Amt* and prior to that had been *Wa.Prfw.8* within the *WaA*. In Oct 33 it was elevated to become a separate Office, the *LC Technisches Amt* - see *information provided by Gen.d.Flg.a.D.Hans Siburg* in Maass 1955 p.21, Hertel W. Dipl.Ing.GenIng.a.D.1955 *Procurement in the German Air Force* USAF Historical Studies No.170 p.111 & Beauvais H., Kossler K., Mayer M. and Regel C. 2002 *German Secret Flight Test Centres to 1945: Johannisthal, Lipetsk, Rechlin, Travemünde, Tarnewitz, Peenemunde-West* p.38.

2   Ries K. 1974 *Luftwaffen-Story 1935-1939* (hereafter cited as Ries 1974) p.10. See also the service record for Willy Fisch in Hildebrand K.F.1990 *Die Generale der deutschen Luftwaffe 1935-1945 Band 1 A-G* (hereafter cited as Hildebrand 1990) pp.286-287.

3   Suchenwirth R. Prof. 1968 *The Development of the German Air Force 1919-1939* USAF Historical Studies No.160 pp.14-15. Willy Fisch had been a pre-war regular officer serving in railway and telegraph units before becoming involved in the development of military aviation in 1911. After further service with the *Telegraphen-Truppe*, Fisch was posted as a pilot to *FA 29* on the outbreak of war. Thereafter he was involved in the development of aerial wireless telegraphy before serving as *1.Adj.d.Insp.d.Fliegertruppen* (1916/17) and as a *Referent in the Kriegsministerium* (1917/19). He was discharged as a *Maj.(Char.)* – see Service record for Willy Fisch in Hildebrand 1990 pp.286-287.

4   *Information provided by MinDir.a.D. Willy Fisch* in Maass 1955 p.43.

Chef LB I and *LB II* respectively.[5]

FIGURE 2B-8 ORGANISATION OF THE ALLGEMEINES LUFTAMT JULY 1934		
Amtschef - Min.-Dirigent Willy Fisch		
LB I	Abteilung Luftverkehr	Commercial Aviation
LB II	Abteilung Luftoheit	Air Sovereignty
LB III	Abteilung Wetterdienst	Meteorological Service
LB IV	Abteilung Luftbildwesen	Aerial Photography
LB V	Abteilung Bodenorganisation u.-Flugsicherung	Ground organisation and Flight Safety

In March 1934 *LB II* introduced new nationality marks and aircraft registrations for all German registered aircraft. Henceforth all German aircraft would carry the *NSDAP Hakenkreuz* (Swastika) on the port side of the vertical tailplane. The black *Hakenkreuz* in a white disc was centred on a red chord-wise band across the centre of the fin and rudder. The starboard side was marked with three horizontal bands in the national colours of black, white and red. In-line with international practice the earlier numerical sequence of aircraft registrations was replaced with a four letter registration with a D-prefix.[6] Aircraft registration was governed by aircraft weight, the first letter in the four character sequence being the class indicator:[7]

FIGURE 2B-9 NEW SYSTEM OF AIRCRAFT REGISTRATION 20 MARCH 1934				
Class	Registration	Descriptor	Landplanes	Seaplanes
A1	D-Y...	1 person	up to 500 kgs	up to 600 kgs
A2	D-E...	1 to 3 persons	500 to 1,000 kgs	600 to 2,200 kgs
B1	D-J...	1 to 4 persons	1,000 to 2,500 kgs	
B2	D-O...	1 to 8 persons	2,500 to 5,000 kgs	2,200 to 5,000 kgs
C	D-U...	Single engine	over 5,000 kgs	over 5,500 kgs
	D-A...	Multi-engine	over 5,000 kgs	over 5,500 kgs

Thereafter the remaining three letters were allocated in alphabetical sequence, beginning with AAA and ending with ZZZ. One exception to this new system was the D.I... sequence. This was reserved for experimental aircraft but in reality many "military" types used registrations in this

5   Service record for Albert Mühlig-Hofmann in Hildebrand K.F.1991 *Die Generale der deutschen Luftwaffe 1935-1945 Band 2 H-N* pp.406-407 & service record for Hermann Dahlmann in Hildebrand 1990 pp.178-179. Both men had served in the *Luftstreitkräfte* as pilots during the war and thereafter as *Referate* within the *Abt.Luftverkehr*. Albert Mühlig-Hofmann was a pre-war military aviator with extensive front line experience as an *Aufklarer*. He underwent refresher training with *AGr.122* in Jun 37 prior to commissioning as a *Maj.d.Res.* in Oct 37. Hermann Dahlmann had trained as a *Beobachter* & *Flugzeugführer* in 1915 and saw service with *Feld-FA 63, FA A 252, Jasta 29* & as *Kdr.d.Fliegerschule Graudenz*. He ended the war as *Adj.JG 3* (Bruno Loerzer). He was promoted to *MinRat.* on the 28 Jul 34 and would transfer to the *Luftwaffe* on the 1 Aug 39 as an *Obst.* RDA 01.01.39.

6   Ries K. 1970 *Luftwaffe Bd.1 Die Maulwurfe 1919-1935* p.112. This policy effectively ended the international community's ability to monitor German aircraft production and ownership.

7   Merrick K.A. 1977 *German Aircraft Markings 1939-1945* (hereafter cited as Merrick 1977) pp.10-13. See also Ullmann M. 2002 *Luftwaffe Colours 1935-1945* pp.145-146.

particular sequence (See also App.H D-UBAF to UHAR).[8]

By this time Germany was without doubt the most air-minded nation in Europe, a situation which Göring was quick to exploit for the future benefit of German military aviation. Since 1926 commercial air transport had been centralised under the auspices of *Deutsche Luft Hansa (DLH)* and by the early thirties Berlin had become the hub for Europe's largest and most efficient airline system.[9] The commercial success of *DLH* depended on good equipment, well-trained personnel and an integrated and efficient ground organisation and in this the airline had the total and unreserved backing of the *Allgemeines Luftamt*.

LB V, the *Abteilung Bodenorganisation und Flugsicherung*, was responsible for the planning of new aviation facilities and for flight safety in general.[10] *Hptm.*Ernst-August Roth, a naval officer, headed the *Referent für Bodenorganisation Land und See* from January 1934. His task was to handle all aspects associated with the rapidly expanding ground infrastructure for military as well as commercial aviation.[11] In October 1934 *Obstlt.(E)* Martin Nitzsche, a communications specialist and another former naval officer, took over the *Flugsicherungs-Referent* with the task of planning the development of radio direction finding as an aid to flight navigation in poor weather and at night (See also 4D4).[12]

In the meantime to support *DLH's* extensive airline operations and those of the two main flying training organisations, the *Deutsche Verkehrsfliegerschule (DVS)* and *Deutsche Luftfahrt GmbH* it was decided in October 1933 to divide Germany into fifteen separate air regional offices or *Luftämter (Map II-2)*. These geographical commands were in turn subordinate to the *Gehobene Luftämter* as that organisation's *Gruppe V* (See 2A3).[13] Their internal organisation reflected that of the *Allgemeines Luftamt* and as such they were responsible for the day-to-day administrative activity including liaison with the municipal and local police authorities for their specific geographical region. They were administered by the *Luftpolizei* and led by an officer in the *Luftwaffen Reserve*.[14]

Flughäfenleitungen, or airport control groups, and *Luftaufsichtwachen*, or air traffic observation stations, were established to carry out routine administrative duties in connection with air sovereignty, signals communications and the provision of meteorological services at each of the principal *Flughäfen* (Airports) and Berlin-Tempelhof, the *Reich's Zentralflughafen*.[15] Around these facilities a 1.5 km radius circle of controlled airspace was established, whilst aircraft entering a further circle of 10 km radius had to be in wireless communication with the resident *Luftaufsichtwachen*.[16] The 61

8   Merrick 1977 p.12. However the suggestion by this author that the registrations were issued in strict alphabetical sequence does not appear to have been followed – see *Golden Years of Aviation* in www.airhistory.org.uk

9   Jackson R. 1983 *The Sky their Frontier: The Story of the World's Pioneer Airlines and Routes 1920-40* pp.101-105, Hooks M. 1999 *Images of Aviation: Lufthansa* pp.9-11 & Seifert K-D. 1999 *Die deutsche Luftfahrt 28: Der deutsche Luftverkehr 1926-1945 – auf dem Weg zum Weltverkehr* pp.15-144.

10   *Information provided by MinDir.a.D.Willy Fisch* in Maass 1955 p.45.

11   Service record for Ernst-August Roth in Hildebrand K.F.1992 *Die Generale der deutschen Luftwaffe 1935-1945 Band 3 O-Z* pp.138-139. *KptLt.(Char.)* Ernst-August Roth had been discharged from the *Reichsmarine* on the 31 Mar 28 and immediately re-employed in a civilian capacity as *Chef-Pilot* and *Ltr.i.V.d.E-Stelle Travemünde d.RdL*. From the 16 Nov 31 he was a *Referent* in the *LS-Amt/Marineleitung*.

12   Service record for Martin Nitzsche in Hildebrand 1991 pp.450-451. A former *U-Boot Kommandant* from the Great War, Nitzsche re-entered military service when he joined the *Luftwaffe* as an *Ergänzungsoffizier* in Oct 34.

13   *Information provided by MinDir.a.D.Willy Fisch* in Maass 1955 p.45. See also *Teil VI Reichsluftfahrtverwaltung* in Westarp Graf von E.J. Obstlt. (Ed.) 1941 *Westarpscher Taschenkalender 1941/42 für die Luftwaffe sowie für Luftschütz, Luftverkehr und Luftsport* (hereafter cited as Westarp (Ed.) 1941) pp.232-273 & *Anlage 11 Die territoriale Einteilung der Luftwaffe in Luftkreise, Stand: 1.April 1934* in Volker 1967 p.237.

14   *Information provided by MinDir.a.D.Willy Fisch* in Maass 1955 p.45. See also *Achte Verordnung über den Aufbau der Reichsluftfahrtverwaltung vom 28.April 1939* in Westarp 1941 pp.232-235.

15   Ries K. and Dierich W. 1993 *Fliegerhorste und Einsatzhafen der Luftwaffe: Planskizzen 1935-1945* (hereafter cited as Ries and Dierich 1993) pp.10-11.

16   *Teil VI Reichsluftfahrtverwaltung* in Westarp (Ed.) 1941 pp.236-238.

civil airports were classified into two categories depending on the level of facilities provided for air traffic. There were in addition numerous commercial landing grounds - *Verkehrslandeplätzen*:[17]

FIGURE 2B-10 THE AIR REGIONAL OFFICES - LUFTAMTER 1933-1935			
Königsberg	Not known	Halle/Saale	Not known
Stettin	Obstlt.Claus Hempel (Jun 34)	Weimar	Obstlt.Walter Heling (Oct 34)
Kiel	Maj.Konrad Pueschel (Oct 33)	Hannover	Maj.Erich Homburg (Jun 34)
Hamburg	Not known	Münster	Obstlt.Karl-A.Mensching (Jul 35)
Berlin	Obstlt.Gustav Nordt (Jun 34)	Frankfurt/Main	Obstlt.Hubert Hartog (Apr 35)
Magdeburg	Obstlt.Job-H.von Dewall (Jul 34)	Köln	Obstlt.Franz Walz (Dec 33)
Breslau	Not known	Nürnberg	Not known
Dresden	Not known	München	Maj.Karl Angerstein (Oct 34)
Stuttgart	Obstlt.Hermann Muggenthaler (Oct 35)		

FIGURE 2B-11 TASKS AND DUTIES OF THE LUFTAMT 1933-1938	
The granting of permission to establish airports	The supervision and guidance of commercial air activity
The licensing of pilots	
The granting of permission to hold aviation events	Air Traffic Control
The determination of prohibited flying areas	The supervision of flight safety programmes
The issuance of landing prohibitions	The maintenance of meteorological services

FIGURE 2B-12 PRINCIPAL FLUGHÄFEN (I.ORDNUNG) 1934		
Berlin-Tempelhof/Brdbg.	Frankfurt-Rhein-Main/Hess.	Mannheim-Stadt/Bad Wttbg.
Breslau-Gandau/Schles.	Hamburg-Fühlsbuttel/Nd.Sachs.	Norderney/Nd.Sachs.
Cottbus/Brdbg.	Köln-Butzweilerhof/Nordrh.-Westf.	Nürnberg/Bay.(1935)
Dresden-Klotzsche/Sachs.	Königsberg-Devau/Ostpr.	Travemünde/Schlesw.-Holst.
Essen-Mülheim/Nordrh.-Westf.	Leipzig-Schkeuditz/Sachs.	Weimar-Nohra/Thur.
		Weser-See/Nd.Sachs.

17   Ries and Dierich 1993 pp.23-63. This listing is based on the 1932 register of *Flughäfen I u II.Ordnung*.

FLUGHÄFEN (II.ORDNUNG) 1934		
Aachen-Merzbruck/Nordrh.-Westf.	Gleiwitz/Schles.	Osnabrück/Nd.Sachs.
Allenstein-Deuthen/Ostpr.	Görlitz/Schles.	Plauen/Vogtl.
Bremen-Neulanderfeld/Nd.Sachs.	Goslar/Nd.Sachs	Quedlinburg/Anh.
Bremer'hvnWesermunde/Nd.Sachs.	Guben/Nd.Lausitz	Bad Reichenhall/Bay.
Darmstadt-Griesheim/Hess.	Halberstadt/Anh.	Schwarza-Rudolstadt/Thur.
Dessau/Anh.	Hall-Nietleben/Anh.	Schwerin-Gorries/Mecklbg.
Dresden-Heller/Sachs.	Karlsruhe/Bad Wttbg.	Sellin a.Rugen (See)
Düsseldorf-Lohausen/Nordrh.-Wtf.	Kiel-Holtenau/Schlesw.Holst.	Stolp-Reitz/Pomm.
Frankfurt-Rebstock/Hess.	Konstanz/Bad Wttbg.	Wangerooge/Nd.Sachs.
Frankfurt a.d.Oder/Brdbg.	Langeoog/Ostfries.	Wernigerode/Anh.
Freiburg-Breisgau/Bad Wttbg.	Leipzig-Mockau/Nd.Sachs.	Westerland a.Sylt/Schlesw.Holst.
Friedrich'hfn-Löwenthal/Bad Wttbg.	Marineburg/Ostpr.	Wiesbaden-Erbenheim/Hess.
Gelsenkirchen-Buer/Nordrh.-Westf.	Meiningen/Thur.	Würzburg-Gaglenburg/Bay.
Gera/Thur.	Monchen Gladbach-Rheydt/Ndrh.-Wfl.	Wyk a.Fohr/Schlesw.Holst.
Giessen/Hess.	München-Oberweisenfeld/Bay.	Zwickau/Sachs.

In 1934 those men serving in the air traffic control service or *Reichsluftaufsichtdienst* were re-designated *Luftpolizei* and became a nominal branch of the *DLV*.[18]

In addition to its major responsibilities the *Allgemeines Luftamt* was also responsible for the *Abteilung Luftbildwesen (LB IV)*, the Reich's central agency for aerial photography.[19] This branch had been one of the last to be transferred from the *RWM* where it had been responsible for the secret work at Lipetsk and Braunschweig (See 1D1). Much of the work of the *Abteilung* had obvious military applications, for example the procurement of aerial photographs for use in the planning of strategic air operations as directed by *LA I (Führung)* (See 2A3). The *Abteilung Luftbildwesens* was also responsible for the training of aerial photography specialists, this work being carried out at the *Luftbildschule Hildesheim* (Aerial Photography School).[20] Following the formation of the first *Aufklärungsstaffeln* (Reconnaissance Squadrons), *LB IV* was also responsible for the evaluation and further improvement of the tactical use of aerial photography and the branch produced training films for use by the new units.[21] For this purpose a central film archive and lending library, the *Hauptbildstelle* was established under the command of *Maj.*Friedrich Cranz.[22]

Although the secret air arm was by far the most important user of aerial photography equipment

18   Bender R.J. 1972 *Air Organisations of the Third Reich: The Luftwaffe* p.15 & Davis B.L. 1991 *Uniforms and Insignia of the Luftwaffe Vol.1: 1933-1940* pp.27-28. See also *Entwicklung der Luftpolizei nach der Auflosung der Polizeifliegerstaffeln* in Schilling F. and Rettinghaus H. 1994 *Die Geschichte der Luftpolizei* pp.27-34.

19   *Information provided by MinDir.a.D.Willy Fisch* in Maass 1955. It was tasked with the supervision of the technical aspects of aerial photography including the development of cameras and their associated equipment.

20   *Information provided by MinDir.a.D.Willy Fisch* in Maass 1955 p.44. The *Luftbildschule* was directly subordinate to the *Ltr d.Abteilung Luftbildwesen.*

21   *Information provided by MinDir.a.D.Willy Fisch* in Maass 1955 pp.44-45. *LB IV* controlled the licensing or all aerial photography and its approval was required by any civilian agency wishing to take aerial photographs. Furthermore it controlled the publication of all aerial photographs.

22   Service record for Friedrich Cranz in Hildebrand 1990 pp.171-172. An aerial photographic specialist from the Great War and career officer with the *Reichsheer*, Cranz was appointed *Ltr.d.LB IV* on the 17 May 33. From Nov 28 he had been *Ltr.d.Hauptbildstelle/RWM.*

LB IV also openly supported the work of civilian agencies whose products were still inevitably of military value. The *Hansa Luftbild GmbH* for example used a specially modified Focke Wulf A 21 for aerial photography. The *Photo-Möwe* was in fact nothing short of a flying photographic laboratory with the fuselage cabin being divided into a photographic area behind which was a dark-room.[23] The *RLM* placed contracts with such firms for topographic surveys, the resultant images being used for cartographic purposes, land use surveys, and government planning before finding their way into the *Hauptbildstelle*.[24]

MAPS

II-2   *Höheren Luftamter* and *Luftamter* territorial organisation: 1 April 1934. The map also shows the location of the existing *Flughäfen* (See Page 467)

23   Nowarra H.J. 1981 *Nahaufklärer 1910-1945: Die Augen des Heeres* pp.135-137. A development of the A 17 *Möwe*, only one example of the A 21 was completed in 1927. It was registered D-1738 - see also Lange B. 1970 *Das Buch der deutschen Luftfahrtechnik* p.223 & Smith J.R. 1973 *Focke Wulf: An Aircraft Album* p.19.

24   *Information provided by MinDir.a.D. Willy Fisch* in Maass 1955 pp.44-45. Wilhelm Gessner was Head of *Hansa Luftbild* from 1923-1945 – see Smith J.R., Creek E.J. and Petrick P. 2003 *On Special Missions: The Luftwaffe's Research and Experimental Squadrons 1923-1945* pp.6-7.

2C1

The Technisches Amt

The *Technisches Amt (LC)* (Technical Office) was a direct descendant of the *Heereswaffenamt's (WaA) Waffen Prüfwesens Abteilung 8 Flugzeuge* (Army Ordnance Office's Weapons Development and Testing Branch 8 - Aircraft) (See 1C2).[1] In May 1933 this office had been transferred to the *Allgemeines Luftamt* (General Office) as its *Gruppe Technik (LB II)* (Technical Group) before being elevated to the status of an independent department within the *RLM* in October of that year.[2] In addition to aircraft design and manufacture the *C-Amt* took on wider responsibilities for related aviation equipment. For example wireless telegraphy was absorbed from *Wa.Prüf 7* and photographic equipment from *Wa.Prüf.8*.[3]

The core missions of the *Technisches Amtes* were to provide the *Luftwaffe* with equipment superior to that produced abroad and to supply this equipment to the service in adequate quantities at the right time.[4] To execute these missions the *LC's* constituent *Abteilungen* (Branches) were responsible for the development, testing and procurement of all aviation equipment in conformance with requirements and instructions from the *Luftkommandoamt (LA)*(Air Command Office) (See 2A). Initially this necessitated the covert acquisition of military aircraft and armament for the still secret *Luftwaffe*, an objective which required the *C-Amt* to work closely with the *Heereswaffenamt (WaA)*, the *Deutsche Versuchsanstalt für Luftfahrt (DVL)* (German Research Institute for Aviation) and the emerging air armaments industry.[5] The *Technisches Amt* inherited its effective vertical organisation from the *WaA* and the smooth-running of this office can be attributed to its *Amt-Chef*, its sound organisational base and to the quality of the officers who were assigned to its two major branches.

1 Maass B. GenLt.a.D. 1955 *The Organisation of the German Air Force High Command and Higher Echelon Headquarters within the German Air Force* USAF Historical Studies No.190 (hereafter cited as Maass 1955) p.14. See also Unknown *Geschichte des deutschen Generalstabes* in Maass 1955 p.15.

2 *Information provided by MinDir.a.D.Willy Fisch* in Maass 1955 p.18 & Gen.d.Flg.a.D.Hans Siburg in Maass 1955 p.21. The *Gruppe Technik* formed the original *LB II* in the *Allgemeines Luftamt* (May 33) - see Volker K-H. 1967 *Die deutsche Luftwaffe 1933-1939: Aufbau, Führung und Rüstung der Luftwaffe sowie die Entwicklung der deutschen Luftkriegstheorie* (hereafter cited as Volker 1967) p.13 & Beauvais H., Kossler K., Mayer M. and Regel C. 2002 *German Secret Flight Test Centres to 1945: Johannisthal, Lipetsk, Rechlin, Travemünde, Tarnewitz, Peenemunde-West* (hereafter cited as Beauvais et al 2002) p.38.

3 *App.10 German Air Force Organisation Chart 1933-36* in Hertel W. Dipl.Ing.GenIng.a.D. 1955 *Procurement in the German Air Force* USAF Historical Studies No.170 (hereafter cited as Hertel 1955) pp.281-282. Hertel identifies these as *Wa.Prw.1 & 2* respectively but this is believed to be incorrect – see Hertel 1955 p.117 & W. 2003 *German Air-Dropped Weapons to 1945* (hereafter cited as Fleischer 2003) p.6.

4 Hertel 1955 p.113. Prior to 1934 all aeronautical research had been controlled by the *RVM*. However much of the research had been hypothetical and not always of direct interest to the aircraft manufacturing concerns – see Hertel 1955 p.111 & 116.

5 *Information provided by GenIng.a.D.Walter Hertel* in Maass 1955 pp.46-47. Hertel was *Gr.Ltr.Flugzeugbeschaffung i.LC III* from the 1 Apr 34 - see service record for Walter Hertel in Hildebrand K.F.1991 *Die Generale der deutschen Luftwaffe 1935-1945 Band 2 H-N* (hereafter cited as Hildebrand 1991) pp.73-74. During this period *LC III* was not concerned with the development and procurement of anti-aircraft weapons and munitions - see also Hertel 1955 p.120 & Westermann E.B. 2001 *Flak: German Anti-aircraft Defenses 1914-1945* p.56.

FIGURE 2C-1 ORGANISATION OF THE TECHNISCHES AMT			
1 APRIL 1934			
Amt Chef - Obst.Wilhelm Wimmer			
Chef-Ing. - Roluf Lucht			
Chef-Personal – Not known			
Adj. - Rittm.Max Pendele			
LC I	**Abteilung Forschung**	**Research**	**MinRat.Adolf Baeumker**
LC II	**Abteilung Entwicklung**	**Development**	**Maj.Wolfram Frhr.von Richthofen**
LC II, 1	Flugzeuge	Airframes	Huebner
LC II, 2	Motoren	Engines	Sachse
LC II, 3	Bordausrüstung	Aircraft equipment	Welle
LC II, 4	FT	Wireless	Schwartz
LC II, 5	Bomben u.Waffen	Weapons	Marquard
LC II, 6	Fertigung	Manufacturing	Bauer
LC III	**Abteilung Beschaffung**	**Procurement**	**Maj.i.G.Fritz Lob**
LC III, 1	Flugzeuge	Airframes	Hertel
LC III, 2	Motoren	Engines	Bullinger
LC III, 3	Rüstung	Equipment	Maaschaft
LC III, 4	Bau-Aufsicht	Construction	Schwarz
LC III, 5	Wirtschaft Inspektion	Economics	Witting
	Flakverbindungsstelle	Flak liaison	Aderholt
LC IV	**Abteilung Haushalt**	**Budget**	**ObRegRat Fritz Müller (from 1 Jan 35)**

The *LC* was the only one of the *RLM's* new *Amter* to be led by an *Alte Adler* (Old Eagle). *Obstlt.* Wilhelm Wimmer had been the *Referent Technik* in *T2 V (L)* from October 1926, *Leiter Wa.Prüf 8* from October 1929 and *Leiter LB II (Flugtechnik)* prior to the creation of the *C-Amt*.[6] This was therefore a period of considerable continuity. He was ably assisted in the development and acquisition of new equipment by *Majore* Wolfram Frhr.von Richthofen and Fritz Löb who were appointed to lead *LC II* and *LC III* respectively.[7] *LC II* was responsible for the assignment of industrial firms to the design and development of specific projects in response to the requirements and directives of the *Luftkommandoamt*.[8] The development of new ammunition, bombs and weapons was also

6   Service record for Wilhelm Wimmer in Hildebrand K.F.1992 *Die Generale der deutschen Luftwaffe 1935-1945 Band 3 O-Z* (hereafter cited as Hildebrand 1992) pp.526-527. Richthofen thought very highly of Wimmer who he regarded as *"the best technical mind in the Luftwaffe"* - see Corum J.S. 2008 *Wolfram von Richthofen – Master of the German Air War* (hereafter cited as Corum 2008) p.103. The basis for the *Luftwaffe's* technical superiority was laid by Wimmer and his team – see Hooton E.R. 1994 *Phoenix Triumphant: The Rise and Rise of the Luftwaffe* (hereafter cited as Hooton 1994) p.97 & 151 & Corum J.S. 1997 *The Luftwaffe: Creating the Operational Air War 1918-1940* pp.165-166.

7   Service record for Wolfram Frhr.von Richthofen in Hildebrand 1992 pp.107-108 & for Fritz Löb in Hildebrand 1991 pp.300-301. *Maj.*Richthofen had recently returned from three years with the German Embassy in Rome. Following the Great War he had served in the cavalry and motor vehicle units of the *Reichsheer* – see also Corum 2008 pp.80-105. *Maj.i.G.*Lob was a career *Pioneeroffizier* who had seen *RWM* service with the *Truppenamt's T2 (Organisation)* & *T5 (Transport)* during 1925-30.

8   *Information provided by GenIng.a.D.Walter Hertel in Maass 1955 p.46.*

handled by *LC II* although in these cases it also worked closely with the *WaA* who had similar interests.[9] For example both the *Reichsheer* and the secret air arm were both in the market for a new air-cooled light machine gun to replace the MG 08/15 and it was appreciated that collaboration and the sharing of developmental information would be of mutual benefit. In the end the two services were destined to differ with the selection by the *Reichsheer* of the *Rheinische Metallwaren- und Maschinenfabrik* MG 13 in 1932, whilst the *Technisches Amt* recommended the procurement of an alternative *Rheinmetall* design as the MG 15 for both fixed and flexible installation aboard combat aircraft (See 3C4).[10] However both weapons used the standard 7.92 mm military cartridge.

The important standardisation and simplification work previously carried out by *Fertigung GmbH* was transferred to *LC II* where the inclusion of standardised components and equipment could be ensured at the design stage of new types.[11] As a result the *Technische Amt* was able to inherit the sophisticated component catalogue that had been built-up over the preceding years. *GenIng.a.D.*Walter Hertel claimed that this *system dispensed with the necessity to give the individual items spare part and storage numbers and , when properly applied, insured against mistakes.*[12]

Standardised parts were also categorised by their appropriate *DIN-L* or *Deutsche Industrienorm – Luftwaffe* (German Industrial Standards – Air Force).[13]

The first major test of *Fertigung's* endeavour was the *ABC Programm* which saw the *Junkers Flugzeugwerke AG* lead a team of four non-aircraft firms in the production of 179 Ju 52/3m *Behelfsbomber* together with 45 W 33 and W 34 *Flugzeuge*. Planned by Klaus Junkers as a means of training personnel in these new factories in the intricacies of aircraft manufacture, a total of seven separate sub-assembly divisions were established to produce sub-assemblies and parts for the main *Junkers'* production line at Dessau. Such a programme could only be successful if total part standardisation had been achieved.[14]

9   Fleischer 2003 pp.34-36. Drop ordnance remained a *WaA* responsibility for a while longer – see Hertel 1955 p.117. See also Heitman H. 1955 *The Planning and Development of Bombs for the German Air Force 1925-1945* USAF Historical Studies No.192 pp.108-111.

10   Hoffschmidt E.J. 1969 *German Aircraft Guns WWI - WWII* pp.90-92, Schliephake H. 1977 *Flugzeugbewaffnung – Die Bordwaffen der Luftwaffe von den Anfangen bis zur Gegenwart* pp.97-102, Markham G. 1989 *Guns of the Reich: Firearms of the German Forces 1939-1945* pp.129-131 & Griehl M. 2008 *Deutsche Flugzeugbewaffnung bis 1945* (hereafter cited as Griehl 2008) pp.14-16 & 47-48.

11   Hertel 1955 pp.117-118. *Fertigung* had been formed within *Wa.Prüf.6B* in 1926 and had moved via the *Wa.L.* to *Wa.Prüf.8*. With the transformation of *Wa.Prüf 8* into *LB II* in Apr 33 *Fertigungs* was transferred from *Gruppe 4 Beschaffung* to *Gruppe 2 Entwicklung* – see also Regel C. *Organisation and Responsibility for Development and Testing 1920-1945* in Beauvais et al 2002 p.38.

12   Quoted from Hertel 1955 *Procurement in the German Air Force* p.70 USAF Historical Studies No.170. The catalogue shows the overall ranges for aircraft parts and components. Each sub-component could be identified by its unique numerical designator. This national system avoided duplication within the Industry and also facilitated licence production. See *App.6 Assemblies and Subassemblies used in Aircraft Construction* in Hertel 1955 pp.275-277. "*The numbering system was designed to identify unmistakably the various items of equipment and part-assemblies of which they consisted, as well as the individual parts of which the part-assemblies consisted. Each item of equipment, each part-assembly, and each individual part, with the exception of standard items, received a catalogue number. Construction drawings were not required for each individual part, so that drawing or blueprint numbering was not necessary, but each part had to have its catalogue number*" - Hertel 1955 p.70 USAF Historical Studies No.170.

13   Hertel 1955 p.71.

14   Vajda F.A. & Dancey P.1998 *German Aircraft Industry and Production 1933-1945* (hereafter cited as Vajda & Dancey 1998) p.11 & 213. These subsidiaries were *ATG, Blohm und Voss, Henschel* & the *Dessauer Wagonfabrik*. See also Irving D. 1973 *The Rise and Fall of the Luftwaffe: The Life of Luftwaffe Marshall Erhard Milch* p.35 & pp.37-38, Nowarra H.J. 1987 *Aircraft & Legend: Junkers Ju 52* pp.36-39 & Hooton 1994 p.103.

FIGURE 2C-2 ASSEMBLIES AND SUB-ASSEMBLIES USED IN AIRCRAFT CONSTRUCTION		
Assembly Group	**Sub-Assemblies**	**Catalogue Nr.**
Airframe		
Fuselage	Nose/Centre piece/Rear part/Shell	10-19 (100-199)
Undercarriage	Undercarriage/Tail skid/ Brake assembly/Floats	20-29 (200-299)
Control surfaces	Horizontal stabiliser/Elevator/Vertical stabiliser/Rudder/Ailerons/Flaps	30-39 (300-399)
Control system	Controls in airframe/in wings/Elevator trim/Rudder trim/Hyd. Controls	40-49 (400-499)
Supporting sfces	Upper wings/Lower wings/Struts and Bracing wires	50-59 (500-599)
Engine installation	Aircraft engine/Engine mountings/Engine cowlings	60-69 (600-699)
Engine controls	Engine controls/Pipework/Coolant/Lubrication/Fuel systems	70-79 (700-799)
Equipment	Fixed weapons/Flexible weapons/Bombs/Photographic equipment	80-89 (800-899)
Operating equip.	Electrical installations – airframe/ - wings/Radio equipment/Oxygen	90-99 (900-999)
Engines		
Crank case	Top/Bottom	100-199
Crank gear	Crank shaft/Connecting Rods/Pistons	200-299
Cylinders	Left cylinder/Right cylinder	300-399
Cam gears	Valve cams – right/-left/Cam drive	400-499
Auxiliary Drives	For Ignition magneto/Lubrication/fuel pumps/Tachometer/Generator	500-599
Auxiliary inst.	Carburettor/Ignition/Fuel/Lubrication/Cooling systems	600-799
Suppl.items	Engine mountings/Cowlings/Exhaust syst./Electrical inst./Controls	800-899
Special equipment	Special tools/Tool /Parts containers/Shipping cases/Packing	900-999

Once a type had been selected for production it then fell to Loeb's *LC III* to supervise the actual procurement programmes, a process that involved the branch in industrial planning and the inspection of manufacturing facilities and personnel, the latter task being the responsibility of the *Büros für Industriearbeiter* (Industrial Personnel Bureau) under *Obstlt.(E)* Otto Mooyer.[15] Mooyer had a key task in helping Industry meet the *LA's* increasingly ambitious targets for new equipment. Due to the small size of the aircraft industry, just 3,200 employees in 1932, there were insufficient trained factory workers for the planned new factories. New personnel from other areas of the economy therefore had to be trained, whilst existing industrial personnel had in some cases to be upskilled.[16] Meanwhile in common with all offices within the *Technisches Amt*, *LC III* dealt with all items of air equipment including airframes, engines, propellers, undercarriage assemblies, instrumentation, wireless equipment, and weapons and munitions, these being dealt

15 *Information provided by GenIng.a.D.Walter Hertel* in Maass 1955 p.47. The office of the *Beauftrager für Industriepersonal* actually lay outside the *RLM* but was subordinate to the *LC*. Otto Mooyer was one of the older pre-war officers who had left the *Heer* following the war. He was engaged as a personnel specialist in Jun 34 – see service record for Otto Mooyer in Hildebrand 1991 pp.402-403. Individual offices were assigned on a geographical basis - the *Beauftrager für Industriepersonal* in Bayern was *Maj.*Hanns Frhr.von Crailsheim who covered *BMW* and the *Bayerische Flugzeugbau* - see service record for Hanns Frhr.von Crailsheim in Hildebrand K.F.1990 *Die Generale der deutschen Luftwaffe 1935-1945 Band 1 A-G* pp.169-170.

16 Hertel 1955 p.122. The domestic aircraft industry had been hard hit by the economic downturn of the early 30s and overall employment of trained industrial workers had fallen – see Hertel 1955 p.76 & Vajda and Dancey 1998 p.10.

with by separate numbered *Referente* (Desks) within the respective *Abteilungen*.[17]

The remaining two branches supported the primary work of *LC II* and *LC III* with the *Abteilung Haushalt* (Budget Administration Branch) being responsible for the formal preparation of orders to the air armament industry and for ultimately overall budgetary administration within the C-Amt, whilst the *Abteilung Forschung* (Research Branch) was responsible for the allocation of research projects to the various research institutes, for example the *Aerodynamische Versuchsanstalt (AVA)* (Aerodynamic Research Institute) at Göttingen, the *Deutsche Forschungsanstalt für Segelflug (DFS)* (German Sailplane Research Institute) at Darmstadt-Griesheim and the *Deutsche Versuchsanstalt für Luftfahrt eV (DVL)* at Berlin-Adlershof.[18] In 1932 the *DVL* had a workforce of 480 employees but this figure would be more than trebled by 1937. The establishment was organised into four *Direktionen* (Directorates): *Flugwerk* (Airframes), *Triebwerk* (Engines), *Ausrüstung* (Equipment) and *Verwaltung* (Administration). On the 1 April 1933 a *Prüfstelle für Luftfahrzeuge* (Aircraft Testing Station) was established within the *DVL* to carry out experimental flight testing.[19] The data and findings of the various research programmes were then made available to the various design bureaux throughout the industry.[20]

The *Technisches Amt* was also responsible for the testing of equipment prior to its release for front-line service. It therefore took over control of the existing *Eprobungsstellen der Luftfahrt* (Aviation Testing Stations) at Rechlin and Travemünde. The *E-Stelle Rechlin* was organised in a very similar way to both the *DVL* and the *LC* with separate *Gruppen* (Departments) for *Flugwerk (T1)*, *Triebwerke (T2)* and *Ausrüstung (T3)* plus *Bewaffnung (T5)* (Weapons) *and Betrieb (B)*(Works). At Rechlin a special *Abteilung M* (Military Branch) was responsible for the secret flight testing of military prototypes (See 4C4).[21]

MINISTERIAL REGULATION

The *RLM's* ambition to rigorously control the industry can be further seen in the introduction during 1933 of an entirely new and standardised system of product designation whereby each design was allocated a number from a numerical series based on that already in use by the *Heereswaffenamt (WaA)*:[22]

---

17   *App. 10 German Air Force Organisation Chart 1933-36* in Hertel 1955 pp.281-282. Hertel was in charge of *LC III/1 Flugzeugbeschaffung* (Aircraft Procurement) from Feb 33 to Mar 34 - see service record for Walter Hertel in Hildebrand 1991 pp.73-74. In another example *Oblt.d.Res.* Ernst Marquard was in charge of *Ref.LC II/5b Abwurfmunition* - see service record for Ernst Marquard in Hildebrand 1991 pp.356-357. See also Griehl 2008 p.17

18   *Information provided by GenIng.a.D. Walter Hertel* in Maass 1955 pp.46-47. Initially *LC IV* concerned itself solely with the issuing of contracts to the Luftwaffe's suppliers. The *C-Amt's* administrative workload was serviced by the *LD* – see Hertel 1955 p.121.

19   Lange B. 1970 *Das Buch der deutschen Luftfahrtechnik* (hereafter cited as Lange 1970) pp.188-191& Vajda and Dancey p.105 & 107.

20   *Information provided by GenIng.a.D. Walter Hertel* in Maass 1955 p.46. This took the form of papers and reports as well as periodic seminars or symposiums where engineers were given the opportunity to ask questions and provide the theoreticians with the benefit of their practical experience - see Spate W. 1989 *Top Secret Bird: The Luftwaffe's Me 163 Comet.*

21   *Organisation of the E-Stelle Rechlin 1928 to 1945* in Beauvais et al 2002 p.127. From Jul 34 the *Kdr.d.Fl.Erp.Stellen* was *Obstlt.*Walter Stahr. Previously Stahr had been the *Militärischer Leiter* at the *DVL* - see service record for Walter Stahr in Hildebrand 1992 pp.341-342.

22   *App.7 Materials Categories Numbering System for Air Force Equipment and Ammunition* in Hertel 1955 p.277-278 & *Annex B Die Typenliste des RLM Generalluftzeugmeisters Abteilung C 1933-45* in Vajda and Dancey 1998 pp.283-290. See also *App.1 The "8" Series Type Numbers* in Smith J.R. and Kay A. 1972 *German Aircraft of the Second World War* (hereafter cited as Smith and Kay 1972) pp.715-726.

FIGURE 2C-3 THE TYPENLISTE DES RLM (GERATEMAPP)		
8	-	Powered aircraft and Missiles
9	-	Piston engines
10	-	Rescue and safety equipment
11	-	Nautical aircraft equipment
13	-	Ammunition (WaA)
18	-	Bomb release equipment
19	-	Aircraft electrical supply equipment
102	-	Machine guns, mounts and appliances
106	-	Aircraft cannon and equipment
108	-	Un-powered aircraft
109	-	Turbojet and Rocket engines
112	-	Water surface craft
113	-	Ammunition (RLM) and drop containers
121	-	Surface motor vehicles
124	-	Telephone, radio and flash signal equipment
125	-	Searchlight equipment
126	-	Aircraft lighting equipment and electrical installations
127	-	Observation and surveying equipment
130	-	Engineer equipment
132	-	Camouflage equipment and materials
133	-	Fire-fighting equipment
134	-	Ordnance equipment
135	-	Photographic equipment
139	-	Housekeeping equipment
140	-	Workshop and artisan's tools and equipment, power plants and machinery

An early example of this system was the new *Arado* basic trainer, the 8-66 which began to reach the *Fliegerschulen* in 1933. In practice the 8-prefix was not used by service units and the design number was usually prefixed by the manufacturer's two-letter abbreviation, in this case Ar for *Arado*. The numbers in each series were usually allocated in blocks to each of the major manufacturers and *Arado's* initial allocation was from 8-64 to 8-69:[23]

---

23   *Annex B Die Typenliste des RLM Generalluftzeugmeisters Abteilung C 1933-45* in Vajda and Dancey 1998 pp.284-285. See also *App.1 The "8" Series Type Numbers* in Smith and Kay 1972 p.717.

FIGURE 2C-4 ARADO FLUGZEUGWERKE GMBH		
Initial Block Allocation of RLM 8-Typennummern		
Ar 64	-	Single seat fighter
Ar 65	-	Single seat fighter
Ar 66	-	Two seat basic trainer
Ar 67	-	Single seat home defence fighter
Ar 68	-	Single seat fighter
Ar 69	-	Two seat primary trainer

It was relatively straightforward to apply the system to new designs and in those instances where a particular manufacturer had employed a numerical sequence which had not been used elsewhere. For example *Dornier* had reverted to a numerical system in the early thirties after using up the alphabetical range and as a result its products used low numerical designations.[24] The *RLM* therefore allocated *Dornier* a block from 8-10 through to 8-29. By contrast *Heinkel* had used a sequential numerical system from 1922 and its new designs were typified by the designations HD 45, HE 46, HD 50, HD 59 and HD 60. However it was not possible to simply allocate the entire block from 8-45 to 8-60 to *Heinkel* as both *Junkers* and *Focke Wulf* had numerical designations in this sequence.[25] Predictably the result was somewhat chaotic with existing designs being simply prefixed by the new standardised manufacturer's abbreviations:[26]

FIGURE 2C-5 AIRFRAME MANUFACTURERS			
Examples of un-blocked use of the RLM 8-Typennummern			
Former Designation	**8-Typ**	**Former Designation**	**8-Typ**
Heinkel HD 42	He 42	Heinkel	He 51*
Focke Wulf A 43	Fw 43	Junkers F 52	Ju 52
Focke Wulf S 44	Fw 44	Focke Wulf	Fw 55*
Heinkel HD 45	He 45	Focke Wulf	Fw 56*
Heinkel HE 46	He 46	Focke Wulf	Fw 57*
Focke Wulf A 47	Fw 47	Focke Wulf	Fw 58*
Heinkel HD 49	He 49	Heinkel HD 59	He 59
Junkers A 49	Ju 49	Heinkel HD 60	He 60
Heinkel HD 50	He 50		

* These were new designs allocated under the RLM 8-Series.

24   Lange 1970 pp.193-207. See also Dornier GmbH 1983 *Dornier: Die Chronik des ältesten deutschen Flugwerks* pp.81-143.
25   Lange 1970 pp.243-249. See also Koos V. 2006 *Typenbucher Deutsche Luftfahrt: Ernst Heinkel Flugzeugwerke 1922-1932.*
26   *Annex B Die Typenliste des RLM Generalluftzeugmeisters Abteilung C 1933-45* in Vajda and Dancey 1998 p.284. See also *App.1 The "8" Series Type Numbers* in Smith and Kay 1972 pp.716-717.

FIGURE 2C-6 AIRFRAME MANUFACTURERS			
Initial block allocations of RLM 8-Typennummern			
Dornier	8- 10 to 29	Albatros	8-101 to 103
Klemm	8- 31 to 36	Klemm	8-104 to 107
Focke Wulf	8- 55 to 58	BFW	8-108 to 110
Arado	8- 64 to 69	Heinkel	8-111 to 120
Heinkel	8- 70 to 74	Henschel	8-121 to 130
Arado	8- 75 to 81	Bucker	8-131 to 134
Junkers	8- 84 to 90	Hansa	8-135 to 144
Fieseler	8- 97 to 99	Gotha	8-145 to 150

In the case of the engine manufacturers the allocation was more straightforward and the seven major firms were each allocated a single block of one hundred numbers in the *9-Typnummern Serie*. Interestingly the new system was not always applied retrospectively and existing types often retained their original designations, good examples being the Argus As 10 and the BMW VI although the Siemens-Halske Sh 22 was re-designated the SAM 322 in 1934 following the restructuring of the parent company.[27] Once again manufacturer's abbreviations were utilised:[28]

FIGURE 2C-7 AERO-ENGINE MANUFACTURERS	
Allocation of the RLM 9-Typennummern	
BMW Flugmotorenbau GmbH	100-199
Junkers Flugzeug- und Motorenwerke A.G.	200-299
Siemens Apparate & Maschinen GmbH	300-399
Argus Motoren GmbH	400-499
Hirth-Motoren GmbH	500-599
Daimler-Benz A.G.	600-699
Deutz-Werke Köln	700-799

27   Vajda and Dancey 1998 p.234 The BMW VI was actually allocated the *Type Nummern* 9-106 but this was not often used – see Lange 1970 p.398.
28   Vajda and Dancey 1998 p.154. See also *9-RLM-Typnummern* in Lange 1970 p.392.

2C2

New Equipment Programmes

The first two years of the *Technisches Amt* (Technical Office) were destined to be amongst the most significant in terms of the *Luftwaffe's* future equipment in that many of its wartime combat aircraft, engines and associated equipment were the result of operational requirements that were issued by *LA I,1* and thereafter developed by *LC II* during 1933-35 (See also 2A3):[1]

FIGURE 2C-8 AIRCRAFT DEVELOPMENT PROGRAMMES 1933-1934		
1933	**Heimatschützjäger**	**Home Defence Fighter**
1933	**Nahaufklärungsflugzeug**	**Tactical Reconnaissance Aircraft**
1933	**Schulflugzeuge**	**Primary Training Aircraft**
1933	Sturzkampfflugzeug	Dive Bomber
1934	Kampf-Verkehrsflugzeug	Bomber/Transport aircraft
1934	Jagdflugzeug	Day Fighter aircraft
1934	Kampfzerstörer	Heavy Fighter aircraft
1934	Fernaufklärungsflugboot	Long Range Reconnaissance Flying Boat
1934	Hochseefahiger-Fernaufklärungsflugboot	Oceanic Reconnaissance Flying Boat

The first *Chef LC II* was *KorvKap.*Hans Siburg who had previously been *Referent Prüfwesen* within the *LS-Amt.*[2] In June 1934 he was replaced by *Maj.*Wolfram Frhr.von Richthofen, an *Alte Adler* from the *Jagdgeschwader Nr.1 Richthofen* and more recently a *Referent* within *LA III (Ausbildungs).*[3] Aircraft development *(Referent für Flugzeugentwicklung)* was under the supervision of *Dipl.Ing.*Gerbert Hubner, who had previously worked as an engineer with *BFW, Focke Wulf* and *Henschel.*[4]

Despite the *Luftkommando Amt* (Air Command Office)'s general pre-occupation with the development of offensive air power the more astute planners within *LA I, 1* realised that during the early stages of the *Rheinland Programm* there was very real risk of a pre-emptive French air and

1   Cooper M. 1981 *The German Air Force 1933-1945: An Anatomy of Failure* pp.29-30,Corum J.S. 1997 *The Luftwaffe: Creating the Operational Air War 1918-1940* pp.165-166 & Cescotti R. 2001 *Bombers and Reconnaissance Aircraft: 1935 to the Present* pp.14-16 & 31-32.

2   Service record for Hans Siburg in Hildebrand K.F.1992 *Die Generale der deutschen Luftwaffe 1935-1945 Band 3 O-Z* (hereafter cited as Hildebrand 1992) pp.302-304. He moved to *the Inspekteurs der Schulen* on the 1 Jun 34 as *a FlVizeKdre.* See also *Organisation of the RLM Technisches Amt (B.II) as of 15.06.1933* in BA/MA Freiburg, RL 3/2220.

3   Service record for Wolfram Frhr.von Richthofen in Hildebrand 1992 pp.107-108. *Lt.*Richthofen, a cousin of *Rittm.* Manfred Frhr.von Richthofen served with *Jasta 11* from the 4 Apr 18 until the end of the war. He scored 8 *Abschusse* - see Corum J.S. 2008 *Wolfram von Richthofen – Master of the German Air War* pp.58-70.

4   Service record for Gerbert Hübner in Hildebrand K.F.1991 *Die Generale der deutschen Luftwaffe 1935-1945 Band 2 H-N* (hereafter cited as Hildebrand 1991) pp.125-126.

land offensive against objectives in western Germany, a scenario that required the acquisition of new tactical and defensive types which could be placed in production with the minimum of delay. During the course of 1933 three requirements were therefore issued to the Industry, these being for a *Heimatschützjäger* (Home Defence Fighter), a *Nahaufklärungsfluggzeug* (Tactical Reconnaissance Aircraft) and a *Sturzkampfflugzeug* (Dive Bomber).

The extension of ministerial control over the industry was also intended to cover the nature of experimental work although in this instance Milch never successfully enforced complete authority over the design bureaux. It had been his intention to progressively reduce competition within the industry by restricting the number of firms involved in any particular project.[5] This kind of control tended to reinforce existing strengths at the expense of innovation, for example *RLM* officials expected either *Arado* or *Heinkel* to produce the next fighter aircraft for the secret air arm because of their proven record of successful design in this area; similarly *Junkers* and *Dornier* were considered to be the natural sources for the next generation of bomber aircraft due to their earlier work with the Ju 52/3m and the Do 11.[6]

However Milch soon found that the various design bureaux continued to produce a variety of designs to meet a whole range of different specifications and that this diversity was in fact a source of strength. A good example of this practice was the way in which Messerschmitt successfully tendered for the new fighter contract despite being positively shunned by the Ministry in the early stages of the competition *(Photo 2C-1)*.[7] Milch also found that several of the new aircraft manufacturers wanted to become involved in aircraft design and within a year design bureaux had been established at the *AGO Flugzweugwerke GmbH* (Oscherlseben), *Hamburger Flugzeugbau* (Hamburg), *Gothaer Waggonfabrik, Abteilung Flugzeugbau* (Gotha) and the *Henschel-Flugzeugwerke AG* (Berlin). Interestingly some of these bureaux then became the most innovative, a good example being provided by that of *Dr.-Ing.Richard Vogt at the *Hamburger Flugzeugbau*.[8]

Innovative airframe design was well within the capabilities of the aircraft industry. However this seemed to be less true in the case of high powered aero-engines.[9] By 1933 the BMW VI had clearly reached the end of its design potential. It was simply too heavy with a weight to power ratio of 0.73:1 (Kg/HP). Although it would become the *Luftwaffe's* standard power plant for the rearmament period new designs were required for the next generation of combat aircraft.[10] To this

5   Green W. 1970 *The War Planes of the Third Reich* (hereafter cited as Green 1970) p.10 & Hooton E.R. 1994 *Phoenix Triumphant: The Rise and Rise of the Luftwaffe* (hereafter cited as Hooton 1994) p.104.
6   Green 1970 p.32, 414 & 524.
7   Irving 1973 p. & Hooton 1994 p.104. Milch's enmity for Willy Messerschmitt went back to his days as Managing Director of *DLH* when he cancelled the order for the M 20 *Verkehrsflugzeug* following the crash of two of these aircraft in 1931. The order was however later re-instated and the type gave good service. Suspicion over the poor structural integrity of Messerschmitt's designs was reinforced following the loss of two of the five M 29 *Sportflugzeuge* in 1932. In allowing Messerschmitt to tender for the fighter contract Milch almost certainly bowed to political pressure from Rudolf Hess (Deputy Führer) and Göring. Theo Croneiss was a *BFW* Director and Hess had strong links with the company. Both would have lobbied Göring for Messerschmitt to be included in the design contest - see Ishoven van A. 1975 *Messerschmitt: Aircraft Designer* p.67 & pp.73-75, Nowarra H.J. 1963 *The Messerschmitt 109: A Famous German Fighter* p.11, Smith J.R. 1971 *Messerschmitt: An Aircraft Album* (hereafter cited as Smith 1971) pp.9-10, 20-21 & 30-31, Kosin R. 1983 *Die Entwicklung der deutschen Jagdflugzeuge* (hereafter cited as Kosin 1983) p.94 & Hooton 1994 p.97.
8   Green 1970 p.69, 246 & 374, Lange B. 1970 *Das Buch der deutschen Luftfahrtechnik* (hereafter cited as Lange 1970) p.155, 173, 239 & 264 & Vajda and Dancey 1998 p.154, 171, pp.199-201 & p.209.
9   Hooton 1994 p.103 & Vajda and Dancey 1998 p.13. Aero-engine design and production was considered to be the *Achilles' Heel* of the aircraft industry – see also Hertel W. Dipl.Ing.GenIng.a.D.1955 *Procurement in the German Air Force* USAF Historical Studies No.170 (hereafter cited as Hertel 1955) pp.78-79.
10   Gersdorff von K. and Grasmann K. 1985 *Die Deutsche Luftfahrt 2: Flugmotoren und Strahltriebwerke* (hereafter cited as Gersdorff and Grasmann 1985) pp.58-61. The BMW VI dated from 1925. However it would power the Ar 65, Ar 68F, Do 15, Do 17E/F, Do 23, He 45, He 51, He 59 & He 60.

end *LC II* continued the development of new high-powered liquid cooled engines in both the 20 and 30 litre categories (See also 1C3).[11] The French *Hispano Suiza* company was a leading exponent of the liquid cooled vee twelve aero-engine.[12] Initially rated at 650-800 hp the 35.74 litre HS 12Y was introduced in 1933 and in the following year a licence production agreement was signed with the Soviet Union where it was manufactured as the M-100.[13] Spurred on by the Schneider Trophy races designers in both Britain and Italy had also made great strides in developing high performance aero-engines. Fiat had produced the 1,050 hp AS 5 for the 1929 race, whilst in 1931 Rolls Royce engineers managed to increase the basic output of its 1929 racing engine from 1,900 hp to a staggering 2,350 hp using a specially blended fuel.[14] Although neither of these hand built engines were suitable for general service use their evolution had given their design teams a considerable edge over contemporary German practice.

The *Technische Amtes* was also interested in the continued development of the *Junkers Motorenbau* compression-ignition heavy oil engines (See 1C2). The superior fuel economy offered by these engines coupled to the low fire risk of diesel fuel made them highly attractive for use in bomber aircraft as well as long range airliners and flying boats.[15] During the course of 1932 the existing Jumo 4 was down-sized from 28.6 to just 16.6 litres by reducing the size of the cylinders to produce the Jumo 5. At the same time engine speed was increased from 1,600 to over 2,200 rpm to produce 600 hp. This was a weight to power ratio of 1.18:1 (Kg/HP) and this engine was earmarked for use in the proposed Ju 86 medium bomber/ airliner (See 4C2).[16]

Other areas of endeavour included aircraft instruments, flying clothing, rescue and safety equipment, photographic equipment, wireless communications, aircraft armament and drop ordnance (See 7B3, 8D4, 6C6, 4D4 & 1C5). The need for more sophisticated instrumentation had emerged in the mid-twenties when *Aero Lloyd* and in particular its successor *DLH* had begun night operations.[17] This activities required more sophisticated instrumentation than had hitherto been provided and this trend was further stimulated by the demands of all-weather operations when they began in the late twenties (See 1D2).[18] The military advantages of all-weather air operations

11   Hertel 1955 p.444, Gersdorff and Grasmann 1985 pp.74-80, 95-96 & p.99 and Bingham V. 1998 *Major Piston Aero Engines of World War II* (hereafter cited as Bingham 1998) pp.77-78 & 85-87. For general trends at this time – see Nahum A. *Propulsion* in Jarrett P. (Ed.) 1997 *Aircraft of the Second World War: The Development of the Warplane 1939-45* (hereafter cited as Nahum in Jarrett (Ed.) 1997) pp.251-252.

12   Gunston B. 1995 *World Encyclopaedia of Aero Engines* (hereafter cited as Gunston 1995) p.83. During the twenties *Hispano Suiza* had produced a number of liquid cooled V-12 (390-600 hp), W-12 (535-635 hp) and even W-18 (1125-1680 hp) engines - see Smith H. 1981 *Aircraft Piston Engines: From the Manly Balzer to the Continental Tiara* (hereafter cited as Smith 1981) pp.77-79 & Bingham 1998 pp.157-163.

13   Smith 1981 p.92 & Gunston 1995 p.93. Ultimately *Klimov* would obtain 1,600 hp from the 34 litre VK-107 - the highest rating of any HS 12Y development – see Bingham 1998 pp.170-173.

14   Gunston 1995 p.60 & 142. For high octane fuels - see Nahum in Jarrett (Ed.) 1997 p.257-258

15   Gersdorff and Grasmann 1985 pp.89-92 & Gunston 1995 pp.89-90. The engines employed vertically opposed pistons working in a single cylinder barrel. This gave the engine an extremely small frontal area which greatly reduced form drag.

16   Gersdorff and Grasmann 1985 p.94 & Schmitt G. 1988 *Hugo Junkers and his Aircraft* pp.207-208.

17   Jackson R. 1983 *The Sky their Frontier: The Story of the World's Pioneer Airlines and Routes 1920-40* p.102 & 105 & Seifert K-D. 1999 *Die deutsche Luftfahrt 28: Der deutsche Luftverkehr 1926-1945 – auf dem Weg zum Weltverkehr* p.21, 27 & 91. The Directors of *DLH* were keen to develop an all-weather and night flying capability and as part of this strategy *Hptm.a.D.Dr.*Robert Knauss, previously *Leiter des Nachtflugbetriebes* (Night Flying Operations) and later *Technischer Mitarbeiter* within *Aero Lloyd*, was appointed *Leiter der Verkehrsabteilung DLH*, whilst Carl-August Frhr.von Gablenz became *Technischer Mitarbeiter* (Technical Director) – see service records for Robert Knauss in Hildebrand 1991 pp.189-190 and for Carl-August Frhr.von Gablenz in Hildebrand K.F.1990 *Die Generale der deutschen Luftwaffe 1935-1945 Band 1 A-G* pp.339-340.

18   Hertel 1955 pp.34-35. For what has been referred to as "intuitive" flight the pilot needs few instruments and these were purely for reference rather than for direction. To this end an air speed indicator (ASI), altimeter, magnetic compass, oil (and water) temperature gauge and tachometer were all that were required. These were little changed

were not lost on *LC II* and its predecessor the *Wa.Prüf.8F*. The *DVL* at Berlin-Adlershof purchased examples of foreign flight instruments which were subject to detailed examination with reports being freely distributed to interested German firms. Simultaneously *Referent 1c*, later *LC II, 3 (Bordausrüstung)* issued guidelines on the basic principles to which all new instrumentation and aircraft equipment should adhere, namely: manufacture, testing, acceptance, external markings, standard fastenings and dimensions:[19]

FIGURE 2C-9 BORDAUSRÜSTUNG ITEMS	
Engine control instruments	Airborne electrical instruments and installations
Flight control instruments	Airborne intercommunications facilities
Autopilot controls	Medical equipment
Navigational instruments	Flying clothing
Altimeters	Take-off and landing equipment
Rescue and safety instruments and equipment	

The design and manufacture of an effective and reliable artificial horizon or attitude indicator *(Fluglagegerät)* proved to be the most difficult task. An indigenous design by *Gyrorector GmbH* was tested by *DLH* but was considered too bulky for all but large multi-engine aircraft. Instead *Askania* acquired a production licence for the already proven suction driven *Sperry* attitude indicator from the USA and further work at *Gyrorector* was halted.[20] Suction driven gryoscopes were also utilised for the directional compass, although work continued at *Siemens Apparate und Maschinen GmbH* on electrically driven alternatives which it was felt would be both smaller and more accurate.(See also 9C4)[21]

LC II (Prüfwesen) was responsible for all aircraft, engine and equipment testing, a function executed by the *Kommando der Fliegererprobungsstelle (KdE)* that was formed under *FlKdre.*Walter Stahr on the 1 July 1934.[22] At that time the *KdE* controlled the main *E-Stellen* at Rechlin (*Dipl. Ing.* Dietrich Frhr. von Massenbach) and Travemünde (*FregKap.a.D.* Hermann Moll) together with residual interests at Berlin-Staaken.[23] In anticipation of greatly increased testing activity a significant building and expansion programme was already underway at the two *E-Stellen* with new administrative buildings at Travemünde, whilst a large new hangar, Halle 105, was erected on the north side of the Rechlin facility.[24] During 1933 the focus at Rechlin was upon existing types such as the Albatros L 76 and L 78, the Arado Ar 65, Heinkel He 45 and He 46 and the unfortunate Do

---

from the instrumentation that was fitted to aircraft during the Great War.

19 Hertel 1955 pp.36-37.
20 Hertel 1955 pp.38-39.
21 Hertel 1955 pp.39-40. Although most flight and engine instrumentation could be carried over from commercial operations, the design of some items specifically required by the military had to begin from scratch.
22 Beauvais H., Kossler K., Mayer M. and Regel C. 2002 *German Secret Flight Test Centres to 1945: Johannisthal, Lipetsk, Rechlin, Travemünde, Tarnewitz, Peenemunde-West* (hereafter cited as Beauvais et al 2002) p.38. Stahr had previously been *Militärischer Leiter d.DVL* at Berlin-Adlershof and prior to that *Kdr.d.Fliegerschule Lipetsk*. He became *Kdr.E-Stelle Rechlin* in Feb 34 - see service record for Walter Stahr in Hildebrand 1992 pp.341-342. See also BA/MA Freiburg, RL 3/2234.
23 Beauvais et al 2002 p.127 & 138. Dietrich Frhr.von Massenbach had previously been *Fl.H.Kdt.Staaken* – see Zweng IV de H.L. and Stankey D.G. 2013 *Luftwaffe Officer Career Summaries*. A former *Geschäftsführer d.Seeflugzeug-Eprobungsstelle (SES)* Hermann Moll entered the *Lw.* as an *Erg.Offizier* on the 1 Oct 33 as *Ltr.d.E-Stelle Travemünde* - see service record for Hermann Moll in Hildebrand 1991 pp.400-401.
24 Beauvais et al 2002 pp.60-64 & p.138. Dual civilian use of Travemünde ceased on the 14 Jul 34 – see Beauvais et al 2002 p.139.

11 (See 2C3). The emphasis on the *Behelfsbomber* programme necessitated a considerable amount of experimental work with such types as the Dornier Merkur, the Junkers G 24 and Ju 52/3m and the Rohrbach Ro VIII.[25] Meanwhile at Travemünde prototypes of the new He 59 and He 60 floatplanes had arrived during 1932/33 and the testing and preparation of these types for service with the *Marineflieger* occupied a great deal of time an effort.[26]

A. THE HEIMATSCHÜTZJÄGER PROGRAMM

This 1933 requirement envisaged the acquisition of a relatively unsophisticated single-seat fighter which would be suitable for use by the proposed auxiliary home-defence fighter units *(Behelfsheimatschützjagdstaffeln)* and as an *Übungsflugzeug* (Proficiency Trainer) by the *Jagdfliegerschulen* (Fighter Schools). Use of the 240 hp AS 10 engine was specified together with a fixed armament of one MG 17 machine gun. A monoplane configuration was preferred.[27] Four firms were invited to tender for the competition, these being *Arado* and *Heinkel*, both of which had current expertise with fighter aircraft, together with *Focke Wulf* and *Henschel*.[28] The urgency of the programme resulted in contracts for three prototypes from each manufacturer, competitive trials being scheduled for the Ar 76, He 74, Fw 56 and Hs 121 in the spring or early summer of 1935.[29] By this time a certain amount of re-design had become necessary following a decision by *LC II* to double the fixed armament and add an internal bomb magazine for three vertically mounted light bombs.[30]

Interestingly the *Heinkel* team opted for a biplane layout, the Günter brothers scaling down their earlier work on the He 51 to produce an extremely small and compact single-bay biplane.[31] The remaining designs were all monoplanes, the Ar 76 and Fw 56 being of the preferred parasol configuration in the manner of the latest French fighters, whilst the design of the Hs 121 was influenced by contemporary practice in Poland.[32] Not surprisingly the *LC II* favoured the Ar 76 and the Fw 56 and it was the latter that was the first of the four contenders to fly in November 1933. The remaining two prototypes were also completed in short order and during the course of 1934 these machines were the subject of intensive flight testing at Johannisthal, Adlershof and Rechlin. The loss of the first prototype led to additional wire bracing of the interplane struts and in its modified form the Fw 56A-0 was found to have exceptionally good diving characteristics, recovery

25   Beauvais et al 2002 p.65.
26   Beauvais et al 2002 pp.135-136. He 59 D-2215 was first tested in Sep 31 with a wheel undercarriage. Initially designated He 59b it seems to have been referred to as the He 59a, at least in its landplane form. The He 60a D-2325 began flight testing early in 1933 - see also Koos V. 2006 *Typenbucher Deutsche Luftfahrt: Ernst Heinkel Flugzeugwerke 1922-1932* (hereafter cited as Koos 2006) pp.124-127.
27   Green 1970 p.31 & Kosin 1983 p.85.
28   Green 1970 p.31, 173, 285 & 375. It is not entirely clear as to whether *Heinkel* was one of the original contenders or whether the firm intended to compete with its own independently designed type. An initial proposal by Robert Lusser appears to pre-date the requirement; Lusser designed a cantilever low-wing monoplane with a retractable undercarriage but he then left *Heinkel* for the *Klemm Leichtflugzeugbau* in 1932. A compact biplane was then put forward by the Günter Brothers - see Kosin 1983 p.88.
29   *Annex B Die Typenliste des RLM Generalluftzeugmeisters Abteilung C 1933-45* in Vajda and Dancey 1998 pp.285-286.
30   Green 1970 p.173.
31   Kens K. and Nowarra H.J. 1961 *Die deutschen Flugzeuge 1933-1945: Deutschlands Luftfahrt-Entwicklungen bis ende des Zweiten Weltkrieges* (hereafter cited as Kens and Nowarra 1961) p.266 & Green 1970 p.285.
32   Green 1970 p.375 & 384 and Kosin 1983 p.87. The Hs 121a first flew on the 4 Jan 34. It was not a success and the aircraft was immediately re-designed around a low cantilever wing layout as the Hs 125. Although this aircraft possessed good flying characteristics *LC II* had already found in favour of the Fw 56 and no production contract was forthcoming - see also Kens and Nowarra 1961 & Kranzhoff J A 1997 *Arado: Geschichte eines Flugzeugwerks* (hereafter cited as Kranzhoff 1997) p.56. For comparative data – see Wagner W. 1980 Kurt Tank - *Konstrukteur und Testpilot bei Focke Wulf Die deutsche Luftfahrt 1* (hereafter cited as Wagner 1980) p.54.

from a terminal velocity dive for example being a simple affair.[33] Interestingly the Ar 76a D-ISEN was also lost at an early stage in the test programme, and in this case the subsequent modifications were made to the tail assembly. The *Arado* fighter was in fact the last of the competing designs to fly, *Dipl.Ing.*Walter Blume's design team being preoccupied with parallel work on the Ar 67 and 68 fighters which the firm hoped would be adopted as a replacement for the He 51A. The revised Ar 76b was therefore not completed until the spring of 1935 by which time a decision had already been made in favour of the rival Fw 56.[34] Despite its outstanding qualities the He 74B was not favoured by *LC II* on account of its biplane layout.[35]

B. NAHAUFKLÄRUNGSFLUGZEUG

Unlike the *Heimatschützjagdflugzeug* requirement which sought to produce a new type of combat aircraft, the *Nahaufklärungsflugzeug* requirement was for a replacement machine for the He 46 which had not even reached service units in 1933 (See 2C3). Nonetheless such a procedure was quite normal given the time that was often required for a paper design to be satisfactorily translated into an effective service machine and in the case of a replacement for the He 46 this process was to take no less than five years.

Just one design was selected by *LC II* for prototype construction, this being the Henschel Hs 122.[36] Another product of the prolific Nicolaus bureau the Hs 122 followed contemporary practice in the design of tactical reconnaissance aircraft in being a parasol-wing monoplane, a configuration which gave both pilot and observer a wide field of view. The wing was fitted with large hydraulically operated trailing edge flaps which, when extended, changed the overall camber of the wing to improve lift and thus the aircraft's low speed handling characteristics. The Hs 122 also featured a robust oleo-sprung main undercarriage which would suit rough-field operations, an important capability for all such aircraft. All-metal construction also suited the new aircraft to field operations away from established base facilities.[37]

Although designed around the 660 hp Sh 22B radial the first prototype was fitted with a Rolls Royce Kestrel XI.[38] This prototype was followed by the Hs 122b D-UDIZ and the V3 D-UBAV which were both powered by the nine-cylinder Siemens und Halske Sh 22B radial. Service trials were carried out during the summer and autumn of 1935 at Fassberg on the Lüneburger Heide. These showed the Hs 122B to have excellent handling characteristics and superior low speed and short field capabilities to that required by *LC II*. However in other respects it was felt that the aircraft did not offer a sufficiently superior performance over the existing He 46 and the contract

---

33 Kens and Nowarra 1961 pp.197-198 & Green 1970 pp.173-176. The Fw 56 was subject to minor revisions to improve the airflow around the engine, to give the pilot better rearward visibility and to damp out some undercarriage problems. See also Smith J.R. 1973 *Focke Wulf: An Aircraft Album* (hereafter cited as Smith 1973) pp.35-37 & Wagner 1980 pp.49-53. An early decision was made to order the type in quantity - see *Table 1-J Early German Production Plans* in Vajda and Dancey 1998 p.22.

34 Kens and Nowarra 1961 p.46, Green 1970 pp.31-32 & Kosin 1983 p.85. The Ar 76 possessed outstanding handling with excellent spin recovery characteristics. It was also directionally very stable and would have made an excellent gun platform. An order for 182 Ar 76 was subsequently placed as confirmed in *Lieferplan Nr.2* - see *Table 2-A Extract from Lieferplan Nr.2 for Arado (situation 30 Apr 36)* in Vajda and Dancey 1998 p.23.

35 Green 1970 p.286.

36 Green 1970 p.376. It is not clear why only *Henschel*, a new company to aircraft design and construction, was given a contract by the *RLM* for this important type.

37 Kens and Nowarra 1961 pp.313-314 & Green 1970 p.376.

38 Green 1970 p.376. This was probably due to the problems *Siemens* was having with meeting the existing production contract for engines for the Do 11 & He 46. Some consideration may have been made to using the new Jumo 210 but this would not be available in quantity until 1937 at the earliest. Another source suggests that the Hs 122a was fitted with a 640 hp Rolls Royce Kestrel V - see Lange 1970 p.264.

for 55 machines, placed in January 1935, was later reduced (See 3C3).[39]

C. SCHULFLUGZEUGE

Prior to 1929 the tactical and technical agencies of both the *Reichsheer* and the *Reichsmarine* had not taken any steps to influence the design of aircraft for flying training duties.[40] Given the emphasis on training aircraft within the *Rheinland Programm*, arguably the most important of the early requirements was for a primary trainer *(A2/Land Schulflugzeug)*. Fortunately once again commercial derived designs were again available at this critical juncture. The *Focke Wulf Flugzeugbau*, under the leadership of its new technical director Kurt Tank, had begun development of its new A 44 *Stieglitz Sportflugzeug* in 1931. The A 44a D-2409 first flew in the late summer of the following year, but exhibited several poor handling characteristics which were only ironed out after exhaustive testing by Tank.[41] However these had been resolved by 1933 when the *RLM* requirement was issued and the company was well placed to win the subsequent competition with *Arado* and *Heinkel* which had both produced designs to meet the official specification.[42]

The Arado Ar 69 appears not to have been favoured. It initially appeared powered by a 105 hp Hirth HM 504A four-cylinder in-line engine, but the Ar 69b D-EPYT of 1934 had been modified to take the 150 hp seven-cylinder Siemens und Halske Sh 14A radial. An aerobatic version was designated Ar 69d.[43] The use of both the 135 hp 4 cylinder inverted in-line Argus AS 8 and the 150 hp Sh 14A radial appears to have been specified by *LC II* as both *Focke Wulf* and *Heinkel* produced two variants of their basic design. The Fw 44C and He 72A both used the AS 8, whilst the Fw 44B and He 72B had the Sh 14A.[44] The He 72 *Kadett* appeared in 1933 and together with the Fw 44 it was ordered into quantity production by *LC III* during the course of that year.[45]

At the same time as production contracts were being finalised for both the Fw 44 and He 72, *LC II* placed a development contract with the newly established firm of *Bucker* at Berlin-Rangsdorf for a new primary trainer with superior aerobatic qualities for use by the *DLV*.[46] The Bu 131 was a

39   Green 1970 pp.376-377 & *Table 1-J Early German Production Plans* in Vajda and Dancey 1998 p.22.

40   Hertel 1955 p.11. During the period 1926-33 the main training types were: *A-Schein* – Heinkel HD 21, Udet U 12, Albatros L 68 & L 101; *B-Schein* – Arado SC I/II & L 75, Heinkel HD 22 & HD 42, Junkers F 13, W 33 & W 34; *C-Schein* – Junkers G 24 & Dornier *Wal* – see Ries K. 1970 *Luftwaffe Bd.1 Die Maulwurfe 1919-1935* pp.55-65, Ries K. 1988 *Deutsche Flugzeugführerschulen und ihre Maschinen 1919-1945* pp.25-53 & Carlsen S. and Meyer M. 1998 *Die Flugzeugführer Ausbildung der deutschen Luftwaffe 1935-1945 Bd.I Von der Grundausbildung bis zur Blindflugschule* pp.19-33.

41   Conradis H. 1960 *Design for Flight: The Kurt Tank Story* pp.48-50 & Smith 1973 pp.29-32. See also Wagner 1980 pp.44-47.

42   Turner P.St.J. 1970 *Heinkel: an aircraft album* pp.70-72. See also *Table 1-B German Aircraft Production in 1933* in Vajda and Dancey 1998 p.15. Thirteen examples of the Fw 44A/B were completed by *Focke Wulf* in 1933 including D-2613-2620 & probably the Fw 44D D-2910, 2911 & 2913-2916 - see Lange 1970 pp.224-225. The Fw 44 would later be built in quantity for export - see Smith 1973 pp.31-32 & Vajda and Dancey 1998 pp.254-256.

43   Kens and Nowarra 1961 pp.45-46 & Lange 1970 p.163. Known Ar 69a aircraft were D-2821, 2822, D-EFYX & ENOS, whilst examples of the Ar 69b/d included D-2827, ETAN & EPYT. A production order may not have been forthcoming because the Ar 69 did not appear until 1934 by which time orders had been placed for the Fw 44 & He 72. It was also possible that *Arado's* existing commitments with the Ar 64 & 65 fighters and Ar 66 *B2 Schulflugzeug* made additional orders impractical - see also Kranzhoff 1997 pp.55-56 which states that just 7 Ar 69 *Schulflugzeuge* had been built when production finished on the 30 Apr 36.

44   Kens and Nowarra 1961 p.195 & 265 and Smith J.R. and Kay A. 1972 *German Aircraft of the Second World War* (hereafter cited as Smith and Kay 1972) p.156 & 236. An authoritative source indicates that the Fw 44A, B, D & F all used the Sh 14A radial engine whilst the Fw 44C & E employed the AS 8. The Fw 44F was equipped for night flying - see Lange 1970 pp.224-225 & Smith 1973 pp.30-31.

45   Lange 1970 p.251. Two He 72 aircraft were completed in 1933 - see *Table 9-M Heinkel Rostock Production* in Vajda and Dancey 1998 p.208. The Fw 44D was licence built by *Bucker* & *Siebel* - see Lange 1970 p.225.

46   Lange 1970 p.180 & Smith and Kay 1972 p.91. The *Bucker Flugzeugbau GmbH* was a new firm, established by Carl

slightly smaller aircraft at the lower end of the *A2/Land* category and as such was powered by the 80 hp Hirth HM 60R inverted four-cylinder in-line engine. Bu 131 D-3150 first flew on the 27 April 1934 and in the same year the type entered limited production at Berlin-Rangsdorf.[47]

Simultaneously the *Arado Flugzeugwerke* was given a contract for a basic trainer in the heavier *B1/Land* category. Work on this aircraft had begun as a private venture in 1930 with a number of project designs but lack of finance delayed the aircraft's completion until September 1932 when Ar 66a D-2335 was flown.[48] Flight testing followed at the *Erprobungsstelle Staaken* and the improved Ar 66c featured an improved undercarriage with oil-damped spring struts, wheel brakes and low-pressure tires as well as counter-balanced ailerons on all four wings. The Argus As 10C-2 engined Ar 66C was ordered into production in 1933.[49]

D. DROP ORDNANCE

In terms of drop ordnance there were three major tasks facing the newly created *Technisches Amtes* in 1933:[50]

1. Assign contracts to industry for improved drop ordnance and supervise these developments;
2. Complete the operational testing of existing drop ordnance with the new aircraft coming into service, and;
3. Organise the large scale production of drop ordnance and associated fuses (see 2C3).

The earlier work by the *Heereswaffenamt (WaA)* (Army Ordnance Office) had resulted in the development of a new generation of *Sprengbombe-Cylindrische (SC)* (High Explosive Cylindrical Bombs) weapons; these comprised the SC 10 and SC 50 *Splitterbomben* (Fragmentation Bombs) together with the SC 250 *Minenbombe* (Demolition Bomb). Trials were also underway for the SC 500 *Minenbombe*, in reality an "over-dimensioned" SC 250.[51] The only other type of bomb within the *Luftwaffe's* new inventory was the *Elektronbrandbombe* (Elektron Incendiary Bomb), a small incendiary device that dated from the Great War (See also 1C3).

The main objectives of the trials programme for the period 1933/34 were:[52]

1. Ballistic measurement of vertically jettisoned SC 250 *Minenbomben*;
2. The correct determination of the fuse time delay for the release of *Minenbomben*;
3. Development of a practical *Brandbombe*. It needed to be determined whether the existing B 1 E *Elektronbrandbombe* was still capable of fulfilling the latest demands and whether it could be adopted for service in an unaltered form.

The need to examine the ballistic properties of vertically jettisoned ordnance stemmed in part

---

Clemens Bucker in Oct 33 at Berlin-Rangsdorf. Anders Andersson was the Chief Designer - see Kens and Nowarra 1961 p.119 & Vajda and Dancey 1998 p.184.

47   Kens and Nowarra 1961 p.119 & Smith and Kay 1972 p.91. A total of 25 Bu 131A were built at Rangsdorf in 1934/35.
48   Kranzhoff 1997 p.54.
49   Kranzhoff 1997 p.54. The first contract was for 320 Ar 66 aircraft; 10 examples of the float equipped Ar 66B were also completed. See also Kens and Nowarra 1961 pp.42-43 & Smith and Kay 1972 pp.17-18.
50   Fleischer W. 2003 *German Air-Dropped Weapons to 1945* (hereafter cited as Fleischer 2003) p.34 & 36.
51   Hertel 1955 pp.47-48. This work had been secretly co-ordinated by *Gr.2 Wa.Prw.8*.
52   Fleischer 2003 p.33.

from the adoption of the Ju 52/3m g3e *Behelfsbomber* (Auxiliary Bomber) (See 2C3). The fuselage structure of this aircraft prevented the horizontal stowage of bombs within the aircraft's cabin and the solution was to develop the *Electrische Senkrecht Aufhangung für Cylindrischebombe* (Electrical Vertical Suspension Magazine for Cylindrical Bombs) or ESAC 250 bomb magazine in which the ordnance was suspended vertically (See also 3C4).[53] Unlike contemporary American practice the bombs were suspended by the nose rather than the tail end. It was found that following release the airflow acting on the bomb's fins pushed the weapon away rearwards before allowing the nose to drop into a downward trajectory. This prevented the bomb from somersaulting or oscillating in a pendulum fashion during the early stages of the drop which improved bombing accuracy.[54] These trials became protracted due to the lack of bombing ranges and the need to preserve secrecy. Prior to 1935 live bomb releases could only be carried out at the *Artillerieschiessplatz Jüterbog* (Artillery Range Jüterbog), where the detonations were concealed by simultaneous artillery shoots. For practical purposes it was only possible to conduct these trials for one to two weeks per quarter during 1933/34.[55]

The trials associated with ascertaining the most effective time delay for the new electrical fuses (*elektrischen Zünder*) occupied several years beginning in 1933. Patented by *Rheinmetall-Borsig* the electrical fuse had been selected by the WaA in 1932 for all *Minenbomben* larger than the SC 10 (See 1E1). There were several advantages of electrical fusing, compared to the more traditional mechanical or impact systems:[56]

1. Provided that the fuse was not connected to an electrical supply there was no possibility of detonation during transport or handling;
2. Provided that the aircraft's main bomb arming box was switched off there was no danger of premature detonation in the event of a bomb being dropped from an aircraft during loading, taxying or take off;
3. Once the storage condenser was loaded the time delay inherent in the design of the fuse ensured that the fuse did not become fully active until after the bomb had left the aircraft thus ensuring safe release;
4. In the event of an in-flight emergency the bombs could be jettisoned inert by not arming the fuses;
5. It was easy to set a variety of time delay settings using a range of different fuses.

For medium level horizontal attacks the initial setting of 0.1 second from the time the bomb hit the target to detonation was found to be too long. Trials at the *Artillerieschiessplatz Jüterbog*, where a simulated armaments factory had been erected, eventually indicated that a 0.08 second time delay for the Zünder 15 El.AZC 50 fuse was the most effective setting. However for low level attacks a much greater delay was required and the initial 5 second delay virtually coinciding with the passage of the aircraft above the target. Trials indicated a 14 second delay to be more effective.[57] Fuses were

---

53   Heitman H. 1955 *The Planning and Development of Bombs for the German Air Force 1925-1945* USAF Historical Studies No.192 (hereafter cited as Heitman 1955) pp.62-63 & Nowarra H.J. 1987 *Aircraft & Legend: Junkers Ju 52* p.36 & 40. Vertical stowage was also a feature of both the He 111 & Ju 86 - see Green 1970 p.287 & 41.
54   Heitman 1955 p.65 & Fleischer 2003 p.29.
55   Fleischer 2003 p.34. In this respect the loss of the testing facilities at Lipetsk was a major constraint. Fortunately most of the trials needed for the new drop ordnance had already been completed.
56   Fleischer 2003 p.33.
57   Fleischer 2003 p.33. *Luftwaffe* regulations and service instructions for all fuses associated with air dropped munitions were initially covered in *L.Dv.152 Zundervorschrift (Nur für Abwurfmunition) 1936*. See also *Bombs and other Missiles dropped on the UK 1940-45* in Ramsey W.G. (Ed.) 1987 *The Blitz Then and Now Vol.1* pp.153-156.

referred to as *o. V.* (*ohne Verzogerung* - without delay), *m. V.* (*mit Verzogerung* - with delay) or *VZ* (*Verzugszundung* - safety time delay).[58]

In addition to the old B 1 E there were also two other *Brandbomben* available for testing. These were the smaller B 0.2 E which weighed just 200 gm. and the heavier B 4 E of 4 kgs. in weight.[59] The B 4 E resembled the SC 10 in shape and like the B 1 E was fitted with an AZ (3) impact fuse. It was dropped in clusters of four from the standard GR 4 C-10 cradle. The B 0.2 E was too small for independent loading and 200 of these bomblets could be packed into the box-like Brandbomben-Schuttkasten 36 (BSK 36) drop container.[60] Trials were carried out during the early part of 1934 over the evacuated Gut Leppin estate at the *E-Stelle Rechlin*.[61] The B 4 E was quickly discarded as it failed to produce an satisfactory concentration at the target impact point.[62] The B 0.2 E proved much more effective as collectively it produced fires which proved very difficult to extinguish under realistic conditions. Furthermore the fuses fitted to the B 0.2 E made the device much safer than the B 1 E during transport.[63]

58   Fleischer 2003 p.37.
59   Fleischer 2003 p.139 & 143.
60   Fleischer 2003 pp.37-38. When loaded the sheet aluminium BSK 36 weighed between 42-46 kgs and was designed for loading onto the Trager Schloss 50 or into the ESAC 250 vertical magazine.
61   Fleischer 2003 p.38. This was made possible by the need to expand the *E-Stelle Rechlin*. Neighbouring farms and villages were evacuated and then used for bomb trials - see Beauvais et al 2002 pp.62-63.
62   Fleischer 2003 p.37. An order for 200 B 4 E *Brandbomben* had been placed for trials purposes.
63   Fleischer 2003 p.37.

2C3

Production

A. EXPANDING THE INDUSTRIAL BASE

The need to rapidly expand the air armament industry was reinforced by the delicate international situation following Germany's withdrawal from the Geneva Disarmament Conference in mid-October 1933.[1] Within days *Staatssekretär* Erhard Milch had issued the first firm contracts for purely military aircraft.[2] On the 20 October Milch called all the leading industrialists to a meeting at the Behrenstrasse:

> In addition to the Ministry's top officials I saw not only aircraft and engine factory chiefs but also senior directors of the industry producing light-weight and heavy raw materials. The assembly was presided over by *Staatssekretär* Milch. He appealed to the dependability, loyalty, ardour and patriotism of those present, and indicated that for Germany the hour had struck for the construction of a new air force. The climax of the meeting was when Hermann Göring entered, silently greeted by all present with arms raised in salute. He announced that the *Führer* has ordered him to establish Germany as an air power within one year.[3]

Göring and Milch's grandiose plans for a new military air arm rested on the ability of the German aircraft industry to deliver aircraft in large numbers to the new units which were to be created from the 1 April 1934.[4] This was undoubtedly Milch's greatest challenge for the effects of the recent economic depression coupled to the years of enforced international restrictions had reduced the industry to a workforce of 3,988 employees of whom 2,813 worked in the airframe plants and 1,175 were employed in the engine works as at the 31 January 1933 (See also 1C).[5] This

---

1   Irving D. 1973 *The Rise and Fall of the Luftwaffe: The Life of Luftwaffe Marshal Erhard Milch* (hereafter cited as Irving 1973) p.36. In the wake of the national elections Hitler was faced with five major challenges: holding on to power; resolving the tensions that existed between the *SA* and the *Heer;* revitalising the still stagnant economy; accelerating the pace of rearmament; and achieving equality visavis the other European powers at the Geneva Disarmament Conference. In an attempt to deceive the European Governments, Hitler delivered a celebrated *"Peace Speech"* in the *Reichstag* on the 17 May 33. The Allied powers reluctance to accord Germany armaments parity led to Hitler's first gamble in foreign affairs – his withdrawal from the Geneva Conference and the League of Nations on the 14 Oct 33 – see Shirer W.L. 1963 *The Rise and Fall of the Third Reich: A History of Nazi Germany* p.204 & pp.209-210. Hitler had informed the British that he wanted a 300,000 man army without tanks, heavy artillery or bombers – see *Telegram Phipps to Simon, 24 Oct* 1933 in DBFP (3) Vol.V in Irving 1973 p.36.
2   Volker K-H. 1962 *Die Entwicklung der militärischen Luftfhart in Deutschland 1920-1933* (hereafter cited as Volker 1962) pp.212. However another source suggests that the first military orders may have actually been placed in May 33 - see *Table 1-C Göring's First Aircraft Production Programme* (May 1933 to April 1934) in Vajda F.A. and Dancey P.1998 *German Aircraft Industry and Production 1933-1945* (hereafter cited as Vajda and Dancey 1998) p.16.
3   Quoted from Koppenberg H. 1935 *The Development of Dessau during 1934* in Irving 1973 *The Rise and Fall of the Luftwaffe: The Life of Luftwaffe Marshal Erhard Milch* p.36 with the knowledge of the Orion Publishing Group. Dr.Koppenberg had just been appointed Director General at the *Junkers Flugzeug-und Motorenwerke* AG at Dessau.
4   Hertel W. Dipl.Ing.GenIng.a.D.1955 *Procurement in the German Air Force* USAF Historical Studies No.170 (hereafter cited as Hertel 1955) p.309. See also Irving 1973 p.36.
5   *Table 1-A Growth of the German Aviation Industry, 1933/34* in Vajda and Dancey 1998 p.11. See also Irving 1973

state of affairs was underlined by an *Inspektion 1 (L)* (Army Air Inspectorate) report, dated 4 April 1933, which stated that even after nine months of mobilisation it would still be impossible for the industry to produce more than 100 machines per month.[6]

For Milch and his political masters industrial expansion implied a high level of ministerial control and the *Staatssekretär* moved swiftly to bring the industry under the overall direction of the *RLM*. In June 1933 *Obst.*Albert Keßelring (*Chef Verwaltungsabteilung /RLM*) visited the *Ernst Heinkel AG* where he inspected the restricted facilities at Warnemünde. In any case these were now required by the *Reichsmarine* and Heinkel readily agreed to the Ministry's proposal that a major new manufacturing complex be established at Rostock-Marienehe where the aircraft to meet new government contracts would be built.[7] This pattern was then progressively replicated across the rest of the air armament industry and the majority of manufacturers were quick to appreciate this new reality.[8] In fact they had little choice for the *RLM* effectively controlled the entire national market for aircraft. Similar agreements were therefore signed with Claudius Dornier for a thousand Do F (Do 11) bombers which allowed the *Dornier-Werke GmbH* to expand its manufacturing base at Friedrichshafen with further facilities at Löwenthal and Allmansweiler, whilst massive Government funding for the *Arado* concern at Warnemünde effectively brought this company under ministerial control from the 4 March 1933 with an agreement that a large new factory was to be built in Brandenburg.[9]

However despite these political and economic realties Milch was to experience rather less success with *Prof.*Hugo Junkers who resolutely resisted state control and who persistently refused to sign over his personal patents to the *Junkers Flugzeugwerke*.[10] However as Dessau was one of the only two large scale manufacturing facilities, Milch could not possibly afford to leave the important *Junkers* concern in unsympathetic private hands. Acting on Göring's instructions he adopted drastic measures via the state controlled judiciary to force *Prof.*Junkers to comply with his demands, measures which even included the arrest of several of Junkers' senior colleagues in

      p.33 & Hooton E.R. 1994 *Phoenix Triumphant: The Rise and Rise of the Luftwaffe* (hereafter cited as Hooton 1994) p.102.

6   Hooton 1994 p.77.

7   Heinkel E. 1956 *He 1000* (hereafter cited as Heinkel 1956) pp.157-158 & Vajda and Dancey 1998 p.11. Marienehe would employ 3,000 workers. A further advantage of this site was the River Warnow which would allow seaplanes to be tested. *Heinkel* had only produced 228 aircraft at Warnemünde during 1923-32 – see Vajda and Dancey 1998 p.203. See also *Milch Diary 1 Jul 33* in Irving 1973 p.34.

8   Hooton 1994 p.102. However this did not at first include Claudius Dornier, nor the pacifist democrat *Prof.*Hugo Junkers - see Schmitt G. 1988 *Hugo Junkers and his Aircraft* (hereafter cited as Schmitt 1988) pp.212-213. To help overcome the inertia which inevitably resulted from normal bureaucratic channels (planning authorities, building controls, passive air defence agencies etc) the *C-Amt* appointed its own representatives to each of the major plants (BMW-Allach & Eisenach, Dornier-Friedrichsahfen & Oberpfaffenhofen, Heinkel-Warnemünde, Rostock & Marienehe and Arado-Warnemünde) as its local industrial executives. Their *mission was to establish the closest possible cooperation between the factories and the Technische Amt, the mission assigning agency, to accelerate the execution of sub-contracts and to bring about the speediest possible settlement of all formal details with the local authorities... In addition ...the industrial executives were to organise within the individual firms the Mobilisation Planning offices, which were to be responsible for the maintenance of the factories at a level adequate to meet the requirements of any possible mobilisation, and were to train factory personnel for their missions.* – quoted from Hertel 1955 *Procurement in the German Air Force* pp.318-319 USAF Historical Studies No.170.

9   Hertel 1955 p.315, Irving 1973 p.35 and Vajda and Dancey 1998 pp.158-159 & p.190. By Jul 35 Dornier would employ 7,080 employees. The *Arado Flugzeugwerke GmbH* was formed on the 4 Mar 33. The new site at Neuendorf was purchased on the 6 Sep 34. In Jul 35 *Arado* employed 3,749 workers - see also Kranzhoff J A 1997 *Arado: Geschichte eines Flugzeugwerks* (hereafter cited as Kranzhoff 1997) pp.51-53.

10   Hermann Hptm. 1943 *The Rise and Fall of the Luftwaffe* (hereafter cited as Hermann 1943) pp.56-57 & Schmitt 1988 p.213. Hermann was an employee of the *Junkers Flugzeugwerk*. The *Junkers-Flugzeugwerk AG* and *Junkers-Mototrenbau GmbH* were in fact in dire need of state funding at that time. *Prof.*Junkers personally held some 350 German registered patents for his own designs and those of his collaborators.

March 1933 as risks to the security of the new regime.[11] Confined to Dessau from April 1933 and denied all contracts for his two companies the *Professor* had little option but to finally co-operate with the *RLM*. In October he was successfully blackmailed through the threat of a stage trial into relinquishing all personal influence over his companies.[12] Finally following his possibly premature death on the 5 February 1935 his wife was in turn forced to sell all her holdings in the Dessau plants to the *RLM* for *RM* 27.12 million - a fraction of the real worth of the combined airframe and engine facilities.[13] In the meantime in August 1933 the *Junkers-Flugzeugwerk AG* had been given an order for around 1,000 Ju 52/3m bomber-transports plus a number of older W 33 and W 34 aircraft to be employed as training aircraft.[14]

However ministerial control over the existing manufacturers was only a partial solution and Milch knew that to meet the ever more ambitious production plans it would be necessary to mobilise as much industrial capacity as possible.[15] He therefore brought the smaller airframe manufacturers into the overall scheme through the issue of contracts for the licence production of key types. In this way the *Focke Wulf Flugzeugbau AG* at Bremen became involved in the He 45 Programme, whilst the resurgent *Bayerische Flugzeugwerke AG* at Augsburg was also given small contracts for both the He 45 and the Do 11.[16] Finally in an attempt to increase overall capacity Milch introduced a number of new manufacturers into the industry and following a series of negotiations in 1933-34 several firms began to diversify their product lines to include aircraft, instrumentation and engine components.[17] This scheme resulted in the re-appearance of traditional airframe manufacturers such as the *Gotha Waggonfabrik AG* and the *Aktiengesellschaft Gustav Otto (AGO)* who had both successfully built a range of aircraft for the *Luftstreitkräfte* in the Great War, as well as the integration of a number of established firms such as the *Blohm und Voss Schiffswerft, Henschel und Sohn GmbH* and the *Erla Maschinenwerk* for whom aircraft construction was a new venture. In some cases this decision reflected commercial realities, for example *Blohm und Voss* who had traditionally built oceanic liners appreciated the potential of aircraft for inter-continental travel, whilst in other cases

---

11 Schmitt 1988 p.214 & Irving D. 1989 *Göring: A Biography* p.135. In this the *RLM* were assisted by dissension within the *Junkers* board. *Prof.*Junkers had always been more interested in scientific research and technological invention than in making a profit. This was partly the cause of the firm's financial difficulties at this crucial moment. On the 2 Jun 33 Junkers transferred the patents and other registered protective rights over to the *RLM*. See also Irving 1973 p.34.

12 Schmitt 1988 p.214. In addition to the judiciary, pressure had come from the *LD* in the form of Keßelring, *Dr.*Wolfgang Höfeld (*Chef LD I*) and von Hellingrath to force Junkers to resign from the chairman's position of both firms on the 24 November. Following the 18 Oct 33 Junkers was effectively confined to his country estate at Bayrischzell. Even family visitors had to be escorted by plain clothes policemen. The telephone line to his house was severed. See also Irving 1973 pp.36-37

13 Schmitt 1988 p.218. *Frau* Junkers eventually received a further *RM* 3.5 million for the patent rights.

14 'Junkers Diary, 24 Aug 1933' in *Junkers Nachrichten*, 1962 in Irving 1973 p.35. Conversation between Klaus Junkers and Erhard Milch on the 22 Aug 33. *Junkers* would only complete 41 aircraft in 1933. It manufactured 238 in the following year.

15 *Table 1-C Göring's First Aircraft Production Programme (May 1933-April 1934)* in Vajda and Dancey 1998 p.16. Göring's first plan for the secret *Luftwaffe* was 295 military aircraft to be procured between May 33 and Apr 34. By May 33 Milch was already planning for 1,000 aircraft - see Irving 1973 pp.33-34. However in Aug 33 he was thinking in terms of 4,021 machines to be delivered under the *Rheinland Programm* - see *Table 1-D The Rheinland Programme, 1 January 1934 - 30 September 1935* in Vajda and Dancey 1998 pp.16-17.

16 Vajda and Dancey 1998 pp.16-17 & p.197. *Focke Wulf* would construct no less than 174 He 45 *Aufklärer* under licence. Milch had hoped to order a small number of M 34 bombers from *BFW* but this firm only emerged from bankruptcy on the 27 Apr 33. This situation together with the inherent obsolescence of the design led to this project being cancelled. Instead *BFW* received orders for 30 Do 11 and 24 He 45 aircraft and in 1934 turnover increased to *RM* 2,616,000 (1933 *RM* 166,000) – see Ishoven van A. 1975 *Messerschmitt: Aircraft Designer* (hereafter cited as Ishoven 1975) p.90. It has been suggested that *BFW* suffered from Milch's personal animosity toward Willy Messerschmitt - see Ishoven 1975 p.79 & Vajda and Dancey 1998 p.170.

17 Irving 1973 p.34 & Vajda and Dancey 1998 p.10.

it reflected a desire to return to a field of production that had been denied to Germany since 1919. Undoubtedly all these new firms were attracted by the generous financial incentives offered by the *RLM*.[18]

FIGURE 2C-10 NEW AIRCRAFT MANUFACTURERS 1933-1935		
AGO-Flugzeugwerke GmbH	Oschersleben	1934
ATG-Maschinen GmbH	Leipzig-Mockau	1934
Bachmann, von Blumenthal and Co.	Furth	1933
Blohm und Voss Schiffswerft	Hamburg-Finkenwerder	1933
Bucker Flugzeugbau GmbH	Berlin-Rangsdorf	1933
Erla Maschinenwerk GmbH	Leipzig-Mockau	1934
Flettner-Flugzeugbau	Berlin-Johannisthal	1935
Flugzeugbau Kiel GmbH	Kiel	1935
Gotha Waggonfabrik AG	Gotha	1933
Flugzeugbau Halle GmbH	Halle	1934
Henschel Flugzeug-Werke AG	Berlin-Schonefeld	1933
Muhlenbau und Industrie AG	Braunschweig-Waggum	1934
Weser Flugzeugbau GmbH	Bremen	1934

Of equal, if not greater importance, were plans to expand the diminutive aero-engine industry. Once again existing plant was expanded in size, additional branch factories were opened, whilst other firms were enlisted to produce aero-engines under licence.[19]

Inevitably the size and experience of these firms varied considerably and it had been Milch's intention that the new entrants should participate in the expansion of the industry as component suppliers or in some cases as licence manufacturers of products belonging to the established design bureaux. Understandably it was the smaller firms that tended to fall into the first category and companies such as *Bachmann* entered the industry as component suppliers within the He 45 and He 46 *Aufklärer* Programmes.[20] In the case of the larger firms such as *Erla* and *ATG* new factories were built to accommodate separate assembly lines for key types such as the He 51 and the Ju 52/3m.[21] To meet the demand for greatly increased Ju 52/3m production *Junkers* adopted the *ABC Programm* in August 1933 by which *ATG, Henschel* and the *Hamburger Flugzeugbau* were completely integrated into a co-ordinated manufacturing Programme which was projected to deliver 4,845 Ju 52/3m, 199 W 33 and 1,191 W 34 aircraft by the 1 October 1935. The working week at Dessau was immediately increased to 48 hours with the prospect of more to follow, whilst labour was re-organised along para-military lines with workers being marched in columns to a compulsory roll call prior to the start of each shift.[22]

18   Hertel 1955 p.315, Irving 1973 pp.34-35 and Vajda and Dancey 1998 p.10.
19   Hertel 1955 p.316 and Vajda and Dancey 1998 p.209 & pp.231-242.
20   Vajda and Dancey 1998 p.17. Production of the He 45 would eventually total 426 machines: BFW (94), Fw (174), Go (68) and He (88), whilst 424 He 46 were completed: Ao (50), Fi (12), Go (60), Ha (129), He (198) and MIAG (83).
21   Vajda and Dancey 1998 pp.166-167 & 192-194.
22   Vajda and Dancey 1998 p.11, pp.166-167 & p.209. *ATG* at Leipzig-Lindenthal had been purchased by Friedrich Flick's

FIGURE 2C-11 AERO-ENGINE PLANTS		
Bayerische Flugmotorenbau	München-Allach	HQ
	Eisenach	Existing
Junkers Motorenwerke	Dessau	HQ
	Kothen	New
	Magdeburg	New
Daimler-Benz	Stuttgart-Unterturkheim	HQ
	Berlin-Marienfelde	Existing
	Berlin-Genshagen	New
Siemens Apparate-u.Maschinen	Berlin-Spandau	HQ
	Berlin-Basdorf	New
Hirth Motorenwerke	Stuttgart-Zuffenhausen	HQ
	Berlin-Waltersdorf	New
Argus Motorenwerke	Berlin-Reinickendorf	HQ
Henschel Flugmotorenwerke	Kassel-Altenbauna	New - DB
Mitteldeutsche Motorenwerke	Leipzig-Taucha	New - Ju
Niedersachsische Werke	Braunschweig-Querum	New – DB
Pommerische Motorenwerke	Stettin-Arnimswalde	New – Ju

Once *Prof.*Junkers had been removed in October 1933, Milch approved the appointment of *Dr.*Heinrich Koppenberg, the former technical director of the *Mitteldeutsche Stahlwerke AG*, as the Director General of the combined *Junkers Flugzeug-und Motorenwerke AG*.[23] The first measures to expand and at the same time de-centralise the manufacturing process were taken the day after his appointment. In November a former railway locomotive repair plant in the southern part of Dessau was rented for the production of Ju 52/3m fuselages, whilst in December the decision was taken to build a completely new factory next to the old one in the western suburbs. Work began in February 1934 and by the summer the buildings were complete and production had begun to meet the first *RLM* contract for 450 Ju 52/3m auxiliary bombers *(Behelfsbomber)*.[24]

Urged on by Koppenberg, who was very much in favour of American-style mass-production techniques, the works management team at Dessau under Klaus Junkers and *Oberingenieur* Thiedemann introduced a new manufacturing process in which the overall process was broken down into a number of sequential stages. In turn each stage consisted of a series of separate but related jobs which could on occasion be performed in geographically distinct factories.[25] Thus for the Ju 52/3m wing fabrication was ultimately sub-contracted to *Weserflug* at Nordenham, whilst the main fuselage and tail assembly were built at Dessau by the parent company. The finished sub-

---

Mitteldeutsche Stahlwerke in 1933. It would build the Ju 52/3m, a new plant at Leipzig-Mockau being commissioned in 1935. *Henschel* at Berlin-Johannisthal was the main contractor for the W 33 (139) and W 34 (759). It too would commission new plant at Berlin-Schonefeld in 1935. The *ABC Programm* may date from the 19 Dec 33.

23   Irving 1973 pp.37-38 & Vajda and Dancey 1998 p.215. Born on the 15 Mar 90 Koppenberg was *"a choleric, bull-necked technocrat with no aviation background"* - see Hooton 1994 p.103.

24   Vajda and Dancey 1998 p.213.

25   Nowarra H.J. 1987 *Aircraft and Legend: Junkers Ju 52* (hereafter cited as Nowarra 1987) p.36.

assemblies were then brought together at the new factory at Dessau for erection and testing.[26] Such a process increased efficiency through specialisation but at the same time it was utterly dependent on effective co-ordination between the sub-assembly plants and their component suppliers and these plants with the final assembly point.[27] Evidence of the efficiency of the new system was the delivery of no less than 179 Ju 52/3m aircraft during 1934; *Junkers* had completed just 17 machines of this type during the previous year.[28]

Quality control was also a vital issue and following the introduction of this method of production the industry began to move towards a standardised system of assembly tooling whereby the parent firm constructed a "master jig" from which a set of production jigs were then fabricated for use by each of the licensees or sub-assembly manufacturers. A duplicate master jig was also supplied which allowed each manufacturer to test the accuracy of the production jigs at regular intervals, a process which was then replicated at regular intervals with the master jigs being returned to the parent firm to ensure that an acceptable level of tolerance was maintained. With the exception of the *Dornier Flugzeugwerke* which persevered with its own individualised system, there was also a high degree of commonality between the assembly tooling employed by the various major manufacturers. The assembly tools were constructed from heavy steel members that were bolted together, check points being included to ensure the accuracy of the fabrication process. This universal system also permitted quite substantial changes to be made to the final shape of each component part, a facility which allowed new variants to be rapidly introduced on to the production line. The system was to later also prove particularly resilient to bombing as damaged sections could be simply replaced by new parts which were quickly bolted into place. Furthermore the individual jigs were rarely set into the concrete floors and this allowed them to be moved about the factory or replaced by new tooling as and when the need arose.[29]

Output in the aero-engine plants was also increased. By May 1934 BMW was producing 80 BMW VI and 80 BMW 132 engines per month at Allach, whilst a further 50 BMW 132 radials were completed at Eisenach with each plant working two standard shifts of 40 hours per week.[30] This output was supported in part by component manufacture for the BMW 132 by *Daimler-Benz* at both Stuttgart-Unterturkheim and Marienfelde from late 1934 and early 1935 respectively.[31] New entrants to the industry would be assigned to the licence production of the new 30 litre high-powered engines once their development was complete in the middle of the decade. For example the *Henschel Flugmotorenwerke GmbH* was established in August 1936 to support the output of the existing *Daimler-Benz* factories.[32]

The licence production of approved types was a significant strategy in training new work forces in aircraft manufacturing techniques. It was also useful in boosting production through the use of

26 Koppenberg H. 1934 *Plan for expansion of Junkers concern, Dessau, 6 July 1934* in Irving 1973 p.38. Milch confirmed Koppenberg's plans for a new factory on the Dessau site. Production began in Jun 34 with the target of assembling 200 aircraft and 1,000 engines per month. See also Vajda and Dancey 1998 pp.213-214.

27 Nowarra 1987 p.36. New production and assembly halls were erected at Dessau totalling 67,000 m2 of floor space – see Vajda and Dancey 1998 p.213.

28 *Table 1-B German Aircraft Production in 1933 & Table 1-F German Aircraft Production in 1934* in Vajda and Dancey 1998 p.15 & 18.

29 Green W. 1970 *The War Planes of the Third Reich* (hereafter cited as Green 1970) p.11.

30 Vajda and Dancey 1998 p.233. *BMW* had acquired the *Eisenacher Fahrzeugwerke* in 1929 for the production of its range of motor-cycles – see Lange 1970 p.395.

31 Vajda and Dancey 1998 p.235. *Daimler-Benz's* plants at Unterturkheim and Marienfelde were under-employed at this time and were engaged in repair work for the Argus AS 8, BMW VI and Junkers L5.

32 Lange 1970 p.403 & Vajda and Dancey 1998 p.209. The *Henschel Flugmotorenwerke, Niedersachische Motorenwerke & Pommerische Motorenwerke* would all produce the DB 601, whilst the *Mitteldeutsche Motorenwerke & Pommerische Motorenwerke* would be engaged in the Jumo 211 programme – see www.technikmuseum-magdeburg.de

multiple production lines for each type:[33]

FIGURE 2C-12 LICENCE PRODUCTION OF COMBAT TYPES 1933-1936	
Arado Ar 65	AGO and Erla
Dornier Do 11	BFW
Heinkel He 45	Focke Wulf, Gotha and BFW
Heinkel He 46	MIAG., Halle, Gotha and Fieseler
Heinkel He 50	Arado and BFW
Heinkel He 51	Arado, Erla, AGO and Fieseler
Heinkel He 59	Arado
Heinkel He 60	Arado and Weser
Junkers Ju 52/3m	ATG

Some attempt was also made at this time to disperse the industry away from its traditional centres in the north-west, south and east *(Map II-3)*, one example of this policy being the establishment of the *Arado Flugzeugwerke-Zweigstelle Brandenburg-Neuendorf* in December 1934.[34] Milch was also concerned about the vulnerability of the *Leichtflugzeugbau Klemm GmbH* at Boblingen, a factory which lay close to the French border on the Rhein and government contracts were therefore made conditional on the fact that a new factory would be built in the Leipzig area.[35] The result of this agreement was the establishment of a subsidiary firm, the *Klemm Flugzeugbau Halle-Saale GmbH*, in 1934 and the new firm was promptly given contracts to build the Fw 44 primary trainer and the He 46.[36] Similar concerns in respect of *Daimler-Benz's* Stuttgart-Unterturkheim and *Hirth's* Stuttgart-Zuffenhausen facilities. In the case of the former transfer of manufacturing to a new plant at Marienfelde was already underway, whilst a much larger facility would later open at Genshagen in 1937.[37] Many of Germany's new aero-engine factories would be located in the vicinity of Berlin where labour, power supplies and component suppliers were plentiful. In the context of the mid-thirties this was a sound distribution but it would later prove to be a less successful concentration once the range of enemy bombers increased.

Nonetheless great care was exercised in the location and actual construction of all new factory accommodation. The new sites were all to be found in open country away from centres of population and the size of individual buildings was restricted with a few exceptions to 4,000 square metres. Buildings were mostly of steel frame construction so that bomb damage would be limited to immediate cratering and blast damage to nearby cladding. The design also produced

33   Green 1970 p.10 & Vajda and Dancey 1998 p.18. It was *RLM* policy for each major combat type and each type of engine to be produced by at least two physically separate factories so as to maintain output in the event of hostile action – see Hertel 1955 p.314.

34   Hertel 1955 pp.310-311 & Green 1970 p.10. New factories were only permitted in an area of central Germany bordered: *on the west by an almost straight line, one the east by a line east of Stettin to west of Breslau, and in the northwest by a line from west of Bremen to Kassel to east of Friedrichshafen* – quoted from Hertel 1955 *Procurement in the German Air Force* p.310 USAF Historical Studies No.170. The only exception was the Ruhr. See also Vajda and Dancey 1998 p.159.

35   Irving 1973 .

36   Vajda and Dancey 1998 p.225.

37   Hertel 1955 p.316 & Vajda and Dancey 1998 pp.235-236. Production of the DB 600 was planned for a new plant – probably Genshagen. Thereafter *Daimler-Benz* activity at Unterturkheim was largely restricted to design and development work.

Above: Photo 2A-1 Original caption:
"*Deutschland*" 1934: Accompanied
by the *Reichskriegsminister, General*
von Blomberg (2nd from right)
and the *Chefs der Marineleitung,
Admiral Raeder* (2nd from left) Adolf
Hitler takes a voyage on board the
"*Deutschland*" in the North Sea.
Bundesarchiv Bild 146-1984-030-03
Photo: o.Ang. Scherl Agency

Right: Photo 2A-2 Original caption:
Portrait of Hellmuth Felmy in the
uniform of a *Luftwaffe Oberst*.
Bundesarchiv Bild 183-1998-0720-
501 Photo: o.Ang.

For the author's detailed commentaries on all photographs in this section please see page 565ff.

Photo 2A-3 Original caption: The battle for the Young-Plan in the *Reichstag* in Berlin! This significant meeting was attended by representatives of all political parties. As a leader of the National Socialists in the *Reichstag*, *Hauptmann* Hermann Göring goes to the reading of the Young-Plan in the *Reichstag*.
Bundesarchiv Bild 102-01908A Photo Georg Pahl

Photo 2A-4 Original caption: In Fascist Germany 1934. Berlin: Leading Nazis at the *Presseball* at the *Festsalen im Zoologischen Garten: Reichspropagandaminister* J.Goebbels (left), *Ministerpräsident* H.Göring (centre), *Reichswehrminister* W.von Blomberg (right) with ladies.
Bundesarchiv Bild 183-M0921-500 Photo: o.Ang. AND-ZB/Archiv

Photo 2A-5 Original caption: Adolf Hitler discusses the government crisis with his staff! From right to left, Hitler's *Stabschef Hautpmann* Röhm, talks excitedly to an intent Adolf Hitler - left in the picture, in the middle - *Reichstag Präsident Hauptmann* Göring. (*Zentralflughafen* Berlin-Tempelhof, 30 November 1932).
Bundesarchiv Bild 102-14081 Photo: Georg Pahl

Photo 2A-6 Original caption: The *preußischer Ministerpräsident* Hermann Göring with (to his right) the Italian *Korporativ-Minister* Bottai, and left the vice-secretary of the Italian Fascist Party Professor, his Excellence, Marcipati at the *NSDAP Parteitag* in Nürnberg on the 3 September 1933.
Bundesarchiv Bild 102-02912A Photo: Georg Pahl

Photo 2A-7 Original caption: The inauguration of the new bison enclosure by the *preußische Ministerpräsident* General Hermann Göring in the State Nature Reserve Schorfheide on Werbelin lake in the Mark! The *preußische Ministerpräsident* and his guests during the visit to the Schorfheide. From left to right: *Reichsfinanzminister* von Schwerin Krossik, *Vizekanzler* [Franz] von Papen, *Staatssekretär* [Hans-Heinrich] Lammers, the *preussiche Justizminister* [Hanns] Kerrl, Hermann Göring and the Italian Ambassador in Berlin [Vittorio] Cerutti.
Bundesarchiv Bild 102-15927 Photo: Georg Pahl

Photo 2A-8 Original caption: In honour of the German participants of the *Europa-Rundflug* 1934 at the *Flugverbandshaus* (in Berlin). From left to right: *Staatssekretär* Milch, *Hauptmann* Seidemann and *Major* von Kehler. Berlin - Speech by *Staatssekretär* Erhard Milch (standing), Hans Seidemann, Richard von Kehler (left to right).
Bundesarchiv Bild 183-2005-0103-517 Photo: o.Ang.Scherl Agency

Photo 2A-9 Original caption: *Kronprinz* Wilhelm and Enst Udet at the *Volksflugtag* in Berlin on the 1 April 1934. Berlin – Ernst Udet and Wilhelm von Preussen beside an aircraft at the *Volksflugtag* at the Tempelhofer Field.
Bundesarchiv Bild 102-01779 Photo: Georg Pahl

Photo 2A-10 Original caption: The famous *Ozeanflieger Hauptmann* Köhl at the *Nordbayerischen Verkehrs-Flug-Gesellschaft!* Our picture shows the famous *Ozeanflieger Hauptmann* Köhl (center) with his wife (left) and *Direktor* Croneiss of the *Nordbayerischen Verkehrs-Flug-Gesellschaft* having taken over the ocean flyer's hat - From left to right: *Frau* Köhl, Hermann Köhl, not known, Theo Croneiss, Children.
Bundesarchiv Bild 102-09801 Photo: Georg Pahl

Photo 2A-11 Original caption: *Generalleutnant* Walther Wever. Born 11.11.1887. Photographed 1.4.1930 as *Kdr.d.II./IR 12*. 1921 *Hauptmann im Generalstab d.Gr.Kdos.I, Hptm.i.Generalstab des Chefs des Generalstabes des Feldheeres*. Died 3.June 1936 in Dresden.
Bundesarchiv Bild 146-1976-026-04A Photo: o.Ang.

Photo 2B-1 Original caption: *Gen.d.Inf.* Gerd von Rundstedt, *Gen.d.Art.* Werner Frhr.von Fritsch and *GenOb.*
Werner von Blomberg at the *Ehrenmal* in the Unter den Linden, 1934.
Bundesarchiv Bild 146-1973-023-07 Photo: Georg Pahl

Photo 2B-2 Original caption: The *Deutschlandflug* 1933. Pilot (Theodor) Osterkamp visits his aircraft with his bride. Aviatrix Gudrun Pagge and Theodor Osterkamp.
Bundesarchiv Bild 183-2008-1016-504 Photo: o.Ang.Scherl Agency

Photo 2B-3 Original caption: Social evening by leading members of the *Reichswehr* and the *SS* in the former *militärarztlichen Akademie* at Invalidenstrasse 48, Berlin. Clockwise around the table: *Fliegerchef* Karl Eberth, *Käpitan zur See* Wilhelm Canaris, *SS-Gruppenführer* and *Chef der SD* Reinhard Heydrich, the *Chef des Heeresverwaltungsamtes Generalmajor* Friedrich Karmann, the *Kommandeur der Kriegsakademie Generalleutnant* Curt Liebmann and *Fliegerkommodore* (Ralph) Wenninger. Bundesarchiv Bild 183-H26899 Photo: o.Ang.

Photo 2C-1 Original caption: Heavy plane crash near Dresden. The aircraft on the Berlin-Wien route, departed the *Zentralflughafen Tempelhof* and crashed shortly before landing in Dresden, all 8 occupants were killed. [06/10/1930]. Our picture shows the *Messerschmitt-Type*, which includes the crashed airliner D-1930 which was flown by pilot Erich Pust. Bundesarchiv Bild 183-R08592 Photo o.Ang. (Scherl)

Photo 2D-1 Original caption: Our successful *Seekampfflieger Oberleutnant* Christiansen – A studio portrait of Friedrich Christiansen with medals (including the *Pour le Mérite*, awarded on 11 December 1917). Bundesarchiv Bild 146-2013-0006 Photo: o.Ang. Postenkartenvertrieb W.Sanke, Berlin

Photo 2D-2 Original caption: The *Fest der Flieger*, 1934 in the *Festsalen im Zoologischen Garten*. The following aviation pioniers were honoured: (from left to right): Thelen, Mackenthun, *GehRat.*Schutte, Bruno Loerzer (*Präsident des DLV*), *Staatssekretär* Milch, Prof.von Parseval and Hans Grade.
Bundesarchiv Bild 183-2008-0414-300 Photo: o.Ang. Scherl Agency

Photo 2D-3 Original caption: The first *Nazi Flugtag* in Staaken near Berlin on 9 April 1933. *National Sozialisten* in preparation for the take-off of a new self-built glider at Staaken. *Flieger SA*.
Bundesarchiv Bild 102-14501 Photo: Georg Pahl

Photo 2E-1 Original caption: Opening of the *Winterhilfswerkes* 1934-1935 by the leader in the *Reichstag* on the 9 October 1934. Berlin, *Reichstag* (Kroll Opera House) Adolf Hitler speech, from the left on the government benches Wilhelm Frick, Hermann Göring, Joseph Goebbels, behind Eltz of Rübenach, Richard Walther Darré, Franz Seldte, Hjalmar Schacht and Werner von Blomberg.
Bundesarchiv Bild 102-04121 Photo: Georg Pahl

Photo 2E-2 Original caption: Labour service men visited the *Jagdstaffel "Richthofen"* at Döberitz in Berlin for the first time on 3 August 1935. *Flugplatz Döberitz* - members of the *Reichsarbeitsdienstes* with *Jagdgeschwader "Richthofen"* help push a *Schulflugzeugs* Heinkel He 72 *Kadett* (Registered. D-ELIF, with the legend *Reklame-Staffel Mitteldeutschland des DLV* on the rear fuselage).
Bundesarchiv Bild 102-04676A Photo: Georg Pahl

Photo 2E-3 Original caption: Junkers Ju 52 named *"Hermann Göring"* (Registered D-AJIM) of the *Regierungsstaffel*, later the *Fliegerstaffel des Führers*.
Bundesarchiv Bild 146-1989-014-30 Photo: o.Ang.

Photo 2E-4 Original caption: *Panzerschiff Deutschland* – launched 19 May 1931, change of name to *Lützow* on the 15 November 1939, wrecked 4 May 1945, sunk in 1947; in the *Kaiser Wilhelm Kanal* passing the *Levensauer Hochbrücke*.
Bundesarchiv Bild 134-C0095 Photo: o.Ang.

Photo 2E-5 Original caption: *Leichter Kreuzer "Karlsruhe"* - Launched 20 August 1927, sunk off Kristiansand 9
April 1940.
Bundesarchiv Bild 134-B0309 Photo: o.Ang.

large uninterrupted floor areas, whilst the steel frames facilitated the installation of overhead cranes and monorail systems. Large doors of the hangar type were a feature of the main assembly halls which could be up to 6,000 square metres in size. Each site occupied some 12 to 16 hectares with individual buildings being widely dispersed to minimise bomb damage. An elaborate air-raid precautions system was also installed and underground shelters were provided for the workforce as a matter of course.[38] To more thoroughly understand the effect of contemporary drop ordnance on buildings of different types trials were carried out from 1934 on the former Gut Leppin estate adjacent to the *Erprobungsstelle Rechlin*.[39]

Overall aircraft production during 1933 was just 368 machines; in 1934 it totalled 1,968 aircraft of which 840 were military types. The emphasis had been on the production of training aircraft with 1,278 machines.[40] However production rates continued to vary considerably from month to month:[41]

FIGURE 2C-13 ESTIMATED AIRCRAFT MONTHLY PRODUCTION FIGURES 1934			
January	45	July	182
February	87	August	273
March	137	September	216
April	140	October	232
May	147	November	220
June	128	December	161

This had been accomplished by the consistent expansion of the industry so that by the 31 January 1935 overall employment had risen to 53,865 and floor area had increased to 200,000 square metres.[42]

B. EARLY PRODUCTION PROGRAMMES

Soon after his appointment as *Reichsminister für die Luftfahrt*, Göring authorised the Third Reich's first official aeronautical production Programme. Dated May 1933 this Programme envisaged the procurement of 295 existing types as the basis for the *Luftwaffe's* first military units. The emphasis

38 Hertel 1955 p.317 & Green 1970 p.10. Buildings *were to be spaced at least twice the width of the structure concerned apart. The individual structures were placed so as to minimise the risks of being hit in stick-bombing runs. Roofs were designed to avoid reflecting the sunlight, and the colours of roofs and walls were to match the surrounding terrain as closely as possible. Arrangements were also to be provided for blackouts and for protection and action against fire and explosions* – quoted from Hertel 1955 *Procurement in the German Air Force* p.317 USAF Historical Studies No.170.
39 Fleischer W. 2003 *German Air-Dropped Weapons to 1945* (hereafter cited as Fleischer 2003) pp.37-38. These trials were conducted from 1934 and included the dropping of high explosive and incendiary bombs.
40 *Table 1-B German Aircraft Production in 1933 & Table 1-F German Aircraft Production in 1934* in Vajda and Dancey 1998 p.15 & 18. However according to the *FlugzeugbeschaffungsProgramm vom 1.7.1934, Stand vom Dezember 1934* in DZ/MGFA, Akte L II 1296 in Volker K-H. 1967 *Die deutsche Luftwaffe 1933-1939: Aufbau, Führung und Rüstung der Luftwaffe sowie die Entwicklung der deutschen Luftkriegstheorie* (hereafter cited as Volker 1967) p.57 the *Luftwaffe* had received 2,090 aircraft of which 676 were combat types by the 31 Dec 34: 77 Do 11 & 193 Ju 52/3m bombers, 19 Ar 64 & 80 Ar 65 fighters, 4 He 70, 150 He 45 & 84 He 46 reconnaissance aircraft, and 27 He 60, 16 Do 15, 12 HD 38 & 14 He 59 floatplanes.
41 *Monthly German Aircraft Production January 1934 to December 1941 Inclusive* in Green 1970 fp.
42 *Table 1-A Growth of German Aviation Industry 1933-34* in Vajda and Dancey 1998 p.11. Employment comprised 37,869 (Airframe) and 15,996 (Engine). On the 31 Oct 34 a further 2,600 men were employed in the equipment plants.

was placed on tactical reconnaissance aircraft (80 He 45B), fighters (60 Ar 64D) and a very limited force of bombers (10 Do Y, 36 Ju 52/3m & 10 M 34). The *Marineflieger* (Naval Air Arm) were to be given a small force of seaplanes (6 Do Wal & 20 He 60). The whole force was to be under-pinned by a number of training aircraft (19 Fw 44B, 8 L 100/L 102B & 46 L 101D).[43]

Göring had hoped that his initial Programme would be complete by April 1934 and for the most part this was achieved *(Table 2-I)*.[44] In the interim the *RLM* tried to purchase military equipment from abroad. In this they were largely unsuccessful. Plans to equip the projected *Jagdgeschwader 1* at Rechlin with the Fiat CR.30 fighter came to naught.[45] Export licences for British warplanes were also refused by the British Government, however a small number of Rolls Royce Kestrel and Buzzard supercharged engines and the Armstrong Siddeley Panther radial engine were supplied and these were later used to power some of the *Luftwaffe's* new combat aircraft prototypes.[46]

Milch's far more ambitious plans finally saw reality with the *Rheinland-Programm (Flugzeug Beschaffungs Programm 1934)* which envisaged the procurement of no less than 4,021 aircraft between the 1 January 1934 and 30 September 1935:[47]

43   *Table 1-C Göring's First Aircraft Production Programme (May 1933 to April 1934)* in Vajda and Dancey 1998 p.16.

44   *Table 1-B German Aircraft Production in 1933* & *Table 1-C Göring's First Aircraft Production Programme (May 1933 to April 1934)* in Vajda and Dancey 1998 pp.15-16. A copy of this plan was reproduced photographically in Woodman D. 1934 *Hitler Rearms: An Exposure of Germany's War Plans.*

45   *Milch Memoirs and Diary 11 Apr 33* in Irving 1973 p.31. Göring and Milch met Mussolini during a visit to Italy in Apr 33. It was also agreed that the *Regia Aeronautica* would provide refresher training for German pilots and observers - see 2D1. Following on from the success of his earlier Fiat CR 20 series, Celestino Rosatelli designed the new CR 30 which first flew in Mar 32. A total of 121 were built during 1932-25 for the *Regia Aeronautica* – see Morse S. (Ed.) 1982 *The Illustrated Encyclopedia of Aircraft* (hereafter cited as Morse (Ed.) 1982) Vol.8 p.1794.

46   Heinkel 1956 pp.142-144. In 1933 Rolls Royce wanted to buy an example of the He 70 as an engine test bed for their new Kestrel V. Ernst Heinkel went further and proposed that the *RLM* obtain the manufacturing rights for the Kestrel in return for British rights for his new He 70 *Verkehrsflugzeug*. However the *RLM* would not agree to the exchange although Rolls Royce did obtain He 70G-1 WNr.1692 D-UBOF in 1935 which was re-registered as G-ADZF – see Turner P.St.J. 1970 *Heinkel: an aircraft album* (hereafter cited as Turner 1970) p.67 & www. airhistory.org.uk . The small number of Kestrel engines that were supplied proved very useful in the development of new warplanes for the *Luftwaffe*. The prototypes of the Ar 80, Bf 109, Ha 137, He 112 & Ju 87 were all powered by this high powered engine prior to the appearance of the indigenous Jumo 210. The Buzzard was used on the Fw 57 prior to the delivery of the DB 600 - see Kosin R. 1983 *Die Entwicklung der deutschen Jagdflugzeuge* (hereafter cited as Kosin 1983) p.90 although this view is not substantiated elsewhere – see Smith J.R. 1973 *Focke Wulf: An Aircraft Album* pp.37-38 & Green 1970 p.177. A small batch of He 46E/F *Nahaufklärer* were built from 1935 with the Panther engine - see Green 1970 p.263 & Ries K. 1974 *Luftwaffen-Story 1935-1939* (hereafter cited as Ries 1974) p.77. The order for 85 Panther engines came directly from Hitler who was hoping to win over the influential Cliveden Set by cultivating Sir John Siddeley who he invited to Germany. The *RLM* were not consulted and there was no obvious use of these engines - see Hermann 1943 p.69. For further information on the Kestrel V & Buzzard – see Lumsden A.S.C. 1994 *British Piston Aero-Engines and their Aircraft* p.195 & 198.

47   Irving 1973 p.34, Hooton 1994 p.104 & Vajda and Dancey 1998. Milch's first Programme for 1,000 aircraft was drawn up at the *RLM* in just 3 days in May 33 - see Volker 1967 p.27 & Hooton 1994 p.102. Although not formalised this plan appears to have been the basis for initial conversations with Heinkel and Junkers and served to precipitate the removal of *Prof.*Junkers from Dessau. For details of the *Rheinland Programm* see - *Table 1-D The Rhineland Programme, 1 January 1934 - 30 September 1935* in Vajda and Dancey 1998 pp.16-17. However there appears to have been two versions of this Programme, the first dated 19 Jan 34 for 3,715 aircraft by the 31 Dec 35, and the second dated 1 Jul 34 for 4,021 aircraft for completion by the 30 Sep 35 - see *Table 6-F RLM Plans* in Vajda and Dancey 1998 pp.112-113. Most sources choose the latter to be the definitive *Rheinland Programm* - see Air Ministry 1948 *The Rise and Fall of the German Air Force 1933-1945* (hereafter cited as Air Ministry 1948) p.8, Volker 1967 p.56 & Schliephake H. 1971 *The Birth of the Luftwaffe* p.33.

FIGURE 2C-14 FLUGZEUGBESCHAFFUNGSPROGRAMM 1934 - THE RHEINLAND PROGRAMM JULY 1934			
Reconnaissance - Total 662			
Heinkel He 45	320	Heinkel He 70	72
Heinkel He 46	270		
Fighters - Total 245			
Arado Ar 64	19	Heinkel He 51	141
Arado Ar 65	85		
Bombers - Total 894			
Dornier Do 11	150	Dornier Do 17+	9
Dornier Do 13/23	222	Heinkel He 111+	9
Heinkel He 50	51	Junkers Ju 86+	3
Junkers Ju 52/3m	450		
Naval Aircraft - Total 153			
Dornier Do 15	21	Heinkel He 59	21
Heinkel He 38	12	Heinkel He 60	81
Heinkel He 51W	14	Dornier Do 18+	4
Overall Total - 1,954 combat aircraft			
+ Pre-production series of new types. The remaining 2,067 aircraft comprised 1,760 trainers, 89 communications aircraft and 218 miscellaneous types.			

The *Rheinland Programm* was a realistic and balanced approach to the key issue of aircraft procurement. It recognised the Industry's embryonic state and the need for the firms new to aircraft manufacture to "cut their teeth" on a range of simple designs such as the Ar 66, Fw 44, He 45 and He 46. It also recognised the *Luftwaffe's* pressing need for training aircraft (44% of the total) compared to combat types (49%). In accordance with Milch's preference for a deterrent force or *Risikoflotte*, the bulk of the combat types would be bombers - 46% of all combat aircraft being in this category (See 2A1).[48] The dedicated type was the Dornier Do 11, although concerns with this design had already led to extensive modification as the Do 13. A larger number of Ju 52/3m g3e *Behelfsbomber* were ordered as a back-up and by February 1935 the monthly production of this important type had reached 64 machines.[49]

The *Rheinland Programm* was ambitious but attainable. However Hitler wanted more and in July 1934 he met Göring, Milch and *Obst.*Walther Wever *(Chef LA)* at Bayreuth. Göring, who was already out of touch with the reality of industrial expansion, was only too happy to comply but

48   Irving 1973 p., Volker 1967 p.27, Hooton 1994 p.101 & Corum J.S. 1997 *The Luftwaffe: Creating the Operational Air War 1918-1940* p.162.

49   *Table 1-E Aircraft Orders and Deliveries RLM LA/LC Nr.1/35 g.Kdos. LA 11 2C vom 1.1.35* in Vajda and Dancey 1998 p.17. By contrast no examples of the Do 11 nor the Do 13 were delivered in Feb 35.

Milch knew better.[50] Nonetheless the *LA* and *LC* came up with a new joint procurement plan for the 1 January 1935. Total orders were increased to 9,853 aircraft of which 2,105 had already been delivered under the existing *Rheinland Programm (Table 2-II)*.[51]

C. AIRFRAME PRODUCTION

1. RECONAISSANCE AIRCRAFT

In terms of potential combat aircraft, production of the dual role He 45 *Fernaufklärer* (Long Range Reconnaissance Aircraft) was second in importance only to the Ju 52/3m g3e. However due to other commitments relatively few were built by the *Heinkel Flugzeugwerke* at Warnemünde and most of the production was carried out by *Gotha* and *Focke Wulf* who both built the **He 45C** and the *Bayersiche Flugzeugbau* who completed twelve *C-Reihe* before switching to the **He 45D**.[52] The major difference between the *C/D-Reihe* and the earlier *A/B-Reihe* was the installation of the more powerful 750 hp BMW VI 7,3 engine. The He 45C/D also had reinforced tail skids, slightly bigger rudders and cables in place of rods between the ailerons. The *C/D-Reihe* differed only in equipment installation. For drop ordnance the He 45 was fitted with two Zwimag 6 C 10 magazines internally and two ETC 50 racks under the fuselage. A small number of aircraft were equipped with the Lotfe 6 tachometric bombsight as lead aircraft.[53]

The rapidity with which deliveries increased during 1934 was testimony to the relatively unsophisticated nature of the aircraft structure and systems. A similar situation existed with respect to the He 46C, 84 of which were completed by the beginning of 1935, the majority of these being manufactured at Warnemünde.[54] However unlike the He 45C/D which proved trouble-free in service the **He 46C** suffered from an uncomfortably high level of vibration at cruising speed, a phenomenon which at full power could reach alarming levels. Investigation of this problem revealed the engine to be at fault. Mass-production of the Siemens und Halske Sh 22 radial had proved difficult and had caused delays in the more important Do 11 Programme. Under pressure to boost deliveries the manufacturers had cut corners and quality had inevitably suffered, a situation that had then led to rough-running and in some instances engine failure. In the case of the He 46 this was disturbing but the type was robust and could land easily in confined spaces. The same circumstances in the Do 11 were often fatal.[55] The He 46C was fitted with two Zwimag 6 C

---

50   *Milch Diary 31 Jul 34* in Irving 1973 p.42. Unfortunately the extent of Hitler's demands are not entirely clear. One source suggests that an additional 2,000 aircraft was proposed - see Hooton 1994 p.104. Wever sided with Göring although he later admitted to Milch that he knew such demands were impossible and apologised for his lack of support.

51   Air Ministry 1948 p.7. This was just 216 aircraft short of that planned for 31 Dec 34. A remarkable achievement for the industry. A total of 1,968 aircraft were built in 1934 - see *App.5 Aircraft Production, 1933-1939* in Hooton 1994 p.279 & *Table 1-F German Aircraft Production in 1934* in Vajda and Dancey 1998 p.18.

52   *Table 1-B German Aircraft Production in 1933* in Vajda and Dancey 1998 p.15. Only 8 He 45B aircraft were delivered by *Heinkel* in 1933. Taken together the *Bayersiche Flugzeugbau*, *Gotha* and the parent company delivered 142 in 1934 by which time *Focke Wulf* had also completed tooling for this type - see *Table 1-F German Aircraft Production in 1934* in Vajda and Dancey 1998 p.18.

53   Hertel 1955 p.50 & Green 1970 pp.259-261. *Heinkel* completed only 69 He 45A/B aircraft including a small number for export to China as the He 61 - see Turner 1970 pp.41-43.

54   *Table 1-B German Aircraft Production in 1933 & Table 1-F German Aircraft Production in 1934* in Vajda and Dancey 1998 p.15 & 18. *Heinkel* only delivered one aircraft in 1933. Tooling by *Fieseler, Gotha* and *MIAG* was largely complete by the end of the following year. Both *Fieseler* and *MIAG* had been awarded contracts for 150 He 46 aircraft.

55   Green 1970 pp.261-264. The vibration was so bad that the pilot found it difficult to read his cockpit instrumentation. In an effort to alleviate the problem the engine bearers were modified, whilst other damping measures were evaluated - all to no avail.

10 internal bomb magazines and a Goerz Fl.219 bomb sight.[56] In addition to the standard He 46C *Nahaufklärer, Heinkel* completed seven examples of the unarmed **He 46D** during 1934 for demonstration purposes by the *DLV*.[57]

First flown in 1933 the spectacular performance of the new Heinkel He 70 high speed transport for *DLH* quickly caught the imagination of both the German public and the planners within the *RLM*, the latter being particularly interested in a modified version for the *Fernaufklärer* role.[58] Work on this version began early in 1934 when the third and fourth prototypes, the He 70c D-UHYS and He 70d D-UKOL, was returned to Warnemünde where the decking aft of the pilot's cockpit was raised to provide a faired dorsal gun position. Further re-design led to this fairing being more extensively glazed and at the same time centralised atop the fuselage. A bomb-bay was also incorporated into the lower centre section which could accommodate six SC 50 bombs (*E-Reihe*) or an additional fuel tank and vertically mounted camera (*F-Reihe*). Following trials both variants were ordered into production in the autumn of 1934 as the **He 70E** light bomber and the **He 70F** reconnaissance machine with an initial order for 72 machines.[59]

2. FIGHTER AIRCRAFT

Relatively few fighters were ordered in the *RLM's* early production programmes. Earlier thinking had crystallised in orders for sixty **Ar 64D** single seat fighters in May 1933.[60] These were slightly improved variants of the Arado SD III but the parent company produced only one fighter in that year, and nineteen production machines in the first three months of 1934 before manufacture ceased in favour of the much improved **Ar 65E**.[61] The new fighter introduced the much more powerful BMW VI 7,3 Z 12-cylinder vee engine which was mated to a longer, deeper fuselage which was fitted with a larger fin. These modifications combined to produce an aircraft with docile handling characteristics which proved easy to fly and an ideal machine for the *Reklamestaffeln* (Propaganda Squadrons) (See 2E1). The later **Ar 65F** had a superior equipment fit that increased overall weight by 40 kgs.[62]

Prior to the formation of the *RLM* the *Reichswehr's Gruppe Technik* (Armed Forces Aero-Technical Group) had shown a keen interest in the new HD 49b that was under test at Warnemünde.[63] This

---

56   Hertel 1955 p.50.
57   Green 1970 pp.262-263. The prototype He 46D was the D-3258 which was followed in due course by D-IJIA, ITEU, ITAI, ILOU, IXUI & IRAN.
58   Green 1970 pp.280-281. He 70a WNr.403 D-2537 was delivered to *DLH* for trials in Mar 33. It quickly established 8 international speed records with loads of 500 to 1,000 kgs in Mar-Apr 33. The prototype demonstrated that an average speed of 355 kph with a payload of 1,000 kgs could be maintained over a measured 100 km course. The *RAF's* fastest service fighter, the Hawker Fury I, had a maximum speed of only 345 kph - see Thetford O. 1976 *Aircraft of the Royal Air Force since 1918* (hereafter cited as Thetford 1976) pp.322-323. The technical documentation for the He 70F was later covered by *L.Dv.316 He 70F Flugzeughandbuch 1937* & *L.Dv.317 He 70F Flugzeugbeschreibung 1937*.
59   *Table 1-J Early German Production Plans* in Vajda and Dancey 1998 p.22.
60   *Table 1-C Göring's First Aircraft Production Programme (May 1933 to April 1934)* in Vajda and Dancey 1998 p.16.
61   Kosin 1983 p.75. *Arado* records confirm a total production run of 19 Ar 64 aircraft, despite initial expectations of 27 aircraft pre month from 1932 - see Kranzhoff 1997 p.47.
62   Morse (Ed.) 1982 Vol.2 pp.259-260. There were 6 different models of the basic Ar 65. The first 2 aircraft had been completed in Apr 32 but production capacity at Warnemünde was so limited that 12 of the early aircraft were built by *Erla*. *Arado* records indicate a planned production run of 157 units - see Kranzhoff 1997 p.48. The technical documentation for the Ar 65F was covered in 1935 by the issue of *L.Dv.307 Flugzeughandbuch, L.Dv.308 Bauschreibung* (construction specification) & *L.Dv.309 Reparaturanleitung* (workshop manual). The fuel system for the aircraft was the subject of *L.Dv.328 Beschreibung, Einbau- und Behandlunsvorschrift für die geschützte Betriebsstoffbehälteranlage*.
63   Green 1970 p.267. Originally designed to meet a *Reichsmarine* requirement the He 49a had flown in Nov 32, being

was subsequently refined as the HD 51a D-ILGY and it was this version that was ordered into production by the *C-Amt* in the closing months of 1933. Nine pre-production **He 51A-0** aircraft were ordered and in July 1934 the first of these reached the *DLV Reklamestaffel Mitteldeutschland* at Döberitz for trials. Unfortunately this process was not without incident and there were several accidents for which the aircrew had blamed the flying characteristics of the new fighter. However on this occasion it was the training techniques that were at fault rather than the basic design of the aircraft and these were subsequently modified to take account of the He 51's higher wing loading.[64] There were also concerns about the limited capacity of *Heinkel's* Warnemünde plant and it was decided that both *Arado* and the *Erla Maschinenwerk GmbH* should build the type. An initial order for 141 machines was included in the *Rheinland Programm*.[65] Even so initial deliveries of the **He 51A-1** did not begin until April 1935 which served to delay the introduction of the type. It would take several more months for production to wind up. Like the earlier Ar 65, production He 51A fighters could be fitted with an internal Zwimag 6 C 10 for ground attack missions.[66]

3. BOMBER AIRCRAFT

Preparation for the series production of the Do F had begun at Friedrichshafen late in 1932.[67] Initial deliveries were made the following autumn when the *Deutsche Reichsbahn* (German National Railways) initiated an air freight service with the type on the 1 November 1933 (See 2D2).[68] However it did not take long for worrying structural problems to appear. The Do F (**Do 11C**) suffered from dangerous wing flexing with associated vibration under certain flight conditions which required turns to be limited to 45 degrees of bank, whilst poor directional stability had quickly resulted in the redesign of the vertical tail surfaces, small auxiliary fins being added beneath the horizontal tailplane.[69] To alleviate the wing flexing it was agreed to reduce overall span by more than a metre and reduce the taper on the wing leading edge. In this form the aircraft was known as the **Do 11D** and existing aircraft were modified retrospectively.[70]

In this new form the aircraft was finally considered acceptable for service use as a dedicated *Nachtbomber (Land)* (Land-based Night Bomber) although it was subject to various flight

followed by the He 49b in Feb 33. The He 49c followed in the Spr 33 - see Koos V. 2006 *Typenbucher Deutsche Luftfahrt: Ernst Heinkel Flugzeugwerke 1922-1932* (hereafter cited as Koos 2006) pp.111-112.

64   Green 1970 pp.267-269. In this respect the He 51A compared unfavourably with the docile Ar 65 with its lower wing loading. The pre-production aircraft were all given non-sequential civilian registrations D-IQEE (A-01), IHAO (A-02), ITIU (A-03), IJAY (A-04), IDIE (A-05), IREI (A-06), IMIP (A-07), IZER (A-08) & IROL (A-09). See also Kosin 1983 pp.75-76.

65   *Table 1-D The Rhineland Programme, 1 January 1934 - 30 September 1935* in Vajda and Dancey 1998 pp.16-17. See also Grabmann W. GenMaj.a.D. 1956 *German Air Force Air Defence Operations Vol.I 1933-41* USAF Historical Studies No.164 p.26.

66   Green 1970 p.270. See also Hertel 1955 p.50.

67   Green 1970 p.110. This contract had been placed by the *RWM*.

68   Stroud J. 1966 *European Transport Aircraft since 1910* (hereafter cited as Stroud 1966) pp.253-254 & Dornier 1983 *Dornier: Die Chronik des ältesten deutschen Flugzeugwerks* (hereafter cited as Dornier 1983) p.124. At least 16 Do F aircraft were registered commercially, 10 with *DLH*. Modified aircraft were designated Do 11Da. Each aircraft was delivered with an assortment of wooden crates in which were inter-changeable nose sections, machine gun mountings, bomb racks etc. These were marked as spare parts - see Green 1970 p.111.

69   Green 1970 p.111 & Hooton 1994 p.105.

70   Green 1970 p.111 & *LC BB.Nr.1850/35 0 1 g.Kdos., Kennblatt des Technischen Amtes im RLM für das Flugzeugmuster Do 11A 1935* in Dierich W. 1973 *Kampfgeschwader 51 "Edelweiss": Eine Chronik aus Dokumenten und Berichten 1937-1945* (hereafter cited as Dierich 1973) pp.320-322. The Do 11 could carry 1,000 kgs of bombs for 1,200 km or 1,500 kgs for 690 kms. For details of the armament of the Do 11 - see *L.Dv.221 Do 11 Bedienungsvorschrift So, 1935*. The fuel system was covered by *L.Dv.321 Beschreibung, Einbau-und Behandlungsvorschrift für die geschützte Betriebsstoffbehälteranlage Do 11D, 1935*.

restrictions which were still the subject of concern. This included an unreliable electro-mechanical undercarriage retraction system which was eventually permanently locked down, and unsatisfactory engines in the form of the Siemens und Halske Sh 22B.[71] The seriousness of this situation was finally underlined on the 19 December 1934 when *Obst.*Wilhelm Wimmer *(Chef LC)* and *Maj.*Wolfram Frhr.von Richthofen *(Chef LC II)* held a key meeting with *Obst.*Hugo Sperrle *(Kdr.Fliegerdivision Nr.1)* and *Obst.*Alfred Keller *(Kdr.Fliegergruppe Fassberg)* following which it was decided to halt production of the Do 11D in favour of the slightly improved Do 13C.[72] By this time some 77 Dornier bombers had been accepted but training attrition was so high that the type had been dubbed the *"Fliegender Sarg"* (Flying Coffin) by its unfortunate crews.[73]

The **Do 13C** had a fixed spatted undercarriage, Junkers-type "double-wing" flaps and BMW VI engines in place of the troublesome Sh 22B units. Unfortunately it too suffered from structural problems, whilst there were also engine cooling problems with the liquid cooled vee twelves.[74] Flush radiators in the lower part of the engine nacelles would eventually cure the latter problem but it would take a completely re-stressed airframe as well as further wing modifications to produce an acceptable solution to the more major structural problems. The *Dornier* team substantially strengthened the fuselage with additional supporting frames and internal cross-bracing. The double-wing trailing-edge flaps were retained to improve lift and overall control whilst the variant was also fitted with the enlarged tail surface area of the Do 11D. In this modified form the **Do 13e** C/Nr.350 first flew on the 1 September 1934 and was subject to extensive testing during the autumn. The *Technisches Amt* (Technical Office) then elected to switch the remaining contracts for the Do 11/13 to this new variant which was to be re-designated the Do 23 from 1935.[75]

In view of the on-going problems with the dedicated *Dornier* bombers, the conversion of the reliable **Ju 52/3m g3e** to the auxiliary bomber *(Behelfsbomber)* role became increasingly vital to the *Luftwaffe's* ability to successfully prosecute an air war. In fact the type was not suitable for such duties, a point made by officers from the *Heereswaffenamt* (Army Ordnance Office) prior to 1933, as the wing centre section cross members effectively prevented the horizontal stowage of even small bombs within the fuselage.[76] The solution was to develop the MWN ESAC 250/IX bomb magazine in which either 1 SC 250, 4 SC 50 or 4 BSK 36 could be carried and released vertically through the small holes in the fuselage floor of the Ju 52/3m (See also 3C4).[77] Defensive stations

71   Green 1970 p.111 & Dornier 1983 p.127. Problems and delays in the output of the Sh 22 severely restricted the delivery of the Do 11 throughout 1933-34.

72   *Besprechungsprotokolle LCII, LC-Besprechungen (Akte E 20): 19.12.1934 Besprechung zwischen Kommodore Sperrle, Keller und Amtschef LC über Sachlage Do 11* in DZ/MGFA, Akte E 1635 in Volker 1967 p.58. See also Nowarra 1987 pp.36-37 & Hooton 1994 p.105. However this was not the first time Sperrle had voiced his concerns - see *Aktennotiz vom 18.7.1934 betr. Telefongespräch Oberst Sperrle/Geerdts in DZ/MGFA Akte E 1635* in Volker 1967 p.58. Three Do 13B-D prototypes were built at Friedrichshafen with C/Nr.293-294 - see *Table D-C Dornier Construction Numbers* in Vajda and Dancey 1998 pp.307-308.

73   *Table 1-F German Aircraft Production in 1934* in Vajda and Dancey 1998 p.18. *Dornier-Friedrichshafen* built two batches of Do 11 bombers: C/Nr.261-292 (32) & C/Nr.301-349 (49) before Do 11 production was switched to *Dornier-Wismar* - see *Table D-C Dornier Construction Numbers* in Vajda and Dancey 1998 pp.307-308. See also Hooton 1994 p.105.

74   Green 1970 p.111. The simplified Do 13A was manufactured with the Siemens Jupiter radial but converted to the more powerful and reliable BMW VI prior to delivery - see Dornier 1983 p.126.

75   Green 1970 pp.111-112 & p.130. It appears that only 4 Do 13 *Kampfflugzeuge* were delivered: Do 13b, c, d & e - see Dornier 1983 p.126.

76   Nowarra 1987 p.35.

77   Hertel 1955 p.50, Heitman H. 1955 *The Planning and Development of Bombs for the German Air Force 1925-1945* USAF Historical Studies No.192 (hereafter cited as Heitman 1955) pp.62-63, Nowarra 1987 pp.35-36 & 40-41 and Fleischer 2003 p.30. The Ju 52/3m could carry 900 kgs of bombs for 1,200 km or 1,500 kgs for 750 kms - see *LC BB.Nr.2763/33 0 1 g.Kdos., Kennblatt des Technischen Amtes im RLM für das Flugzeugmuster Ju 52 1933* in Dierich 1973 pp.318-320. The first two bomber conversions were completed in 1933. These were WNr.4032 &

were also incorporated above and below the fuselage. The *B-Stand* (Dorsal Position) consisted of a MG 15 on a D 30 Drehkranz ring mount, whilst the *C-Stand* (Ventral Position) was more complex as it had to incorporate the bombing station with the Goerz Fl 219b sight as well as the ventral gun position. The D 52 Drehkranz was a purpose built retractable gondola located between the fixed undercarriage legs of the aircraft.[78] In its *Behelfsbomber* guise the machine was designated the Ju 52/3m g3e and it was manufactured in quantity for the *Kampfverbände* (Bomber Arm) from 1934.[79]

4. DIVE BOMBER AIRCRAFT

Further examples of the **He 50A** were ordered in 1934 to provide an interim aircraft for the planned *Sturzkampfverbände* (Dive Bomber Arm).[80] These sturdy biplanes of mixed construction could carry a 500 kg bomb on an external PVC 500 rack when flown solo, but with the addition of a *Beobachter* (Observer) plus a defensive machine gun on a D 30 Drehkanz the type could also be used as a reconnaissance bomber.[81] The Sh 22B radial was fitted with a two-pitch three-blade metal propeller which allowed the pilot to coarsen the blade pitch prior to a dive attack.[82]

5. NAVAL AIRCRAFT

The *Heinkel* design bureau was the most important source of aircraft for naval employment although due to pressure of other work production contracts for the HD 38, He 59 and He 60 were placed with other manufacturers. Thus *Arado* completed 11 **HD 38D** floatplane fighters in 1933 before it started to tool up for the series production of both the He 59B and He 60C.[83] To meet the needs of the *DVS Zweigstellen* (See) (DVS Marine Branches) *Heinkel* produced 28 **He 42E** *See-Schulflugzeuge* (Floatplane Training Aircraft) during 1934. The He 42E was fitted with an up-rated Junkers L 5G engine of 425 hp which enhanced the type's performance at altitude. The *E Reihe* was catapultable and could be armed with a flexible MG 15 machine gun for armament training.[84]

In the summer of 1934 the *Marineflieger* took delivery of the first production **He 59B-1** *Mehrzweckflugzeug* (Naval Multi-Role Aircraft), these being assigned to the *DVS Zweigstelle List*. Thirteen of these large but capable biplanes were delivered by the end of the year. The He 59B could carry a wide variety of ordnance both internally and externally beneath the fuselage and wings. It

---

4034.

78   *LC BB.Nr.2763/33 0 1 g.Kdos., Kennblatt des Technischen Amtes im RLM für das Flugzeugmuster Ju 52 1933* in Dierich 1973 pp.318-320. See also Green 1970 pp.405-406. The armament installation is covered by *L.Dv.212 Ju 52/3m Beschreibung, Einbau-und Prüfvorschrift für So, 1935.*

79   *Table 1-C Göring's First Aircraft Production Programme (May 1933 to April 1934)* in Vajda and Dancey 1998 p.16.

80   *Table 1-D The Rhineland Programme, 1 January 1934 - 30 September 1935* in Vajda and Dancey 1998 pp.16-17. Twelve examples were also produced for export in 1934 as the He 66aCh. These were powered by the Siemens Jupiter VI, not the Sh 22B which was in short supply at that time - see Green 1970 pp.264-265 & Turner 1970 p.49. The He 66 was also built under licence in Japan as the Aichi D1A1 shipboard dive bomber - see Francillon R.J. 1979 *Japanese Aircraft of the Pacific War* pp.268-271.

81   Green 1970 p.265. The rear cockpit was faired over when the aircraft was employed as a dive bomber. The pilot had a single fixed machine gun firing forward for which a *Revi* (Reflector) sight was provided, this also being used for dive bombing - see Hertel 1955 p.50. For technical documentation see *L.Dv.313 He 50 Flugzeughandbuch* & *L.Dv.314 He 50 Flugzeugbeschreibung.*

82   Green 1970 p.265.

83   *Table 1-F German Aircraft Production in 1934* in Vajda and Dancey 1998 p.18.

84   Lange 1970 p.247, Turner 1970 p.41 & Koos 2006 pp.101-102. *Heinkel* completed 14 He 42D at Warnemünde in 1933 and then began series production of the improved *E-Reihe* in 1934. Some sources suggest that the He 42E was re-designated He 42C at some point. The earlier *D-Reihe* were re-designated He 42B. Technical documentation was covered by *L.Dv.359 He 42E Flugzeughandbuch* & *L.Dv.360 He 42E Flugzeugbeschreibung.*

carried a crew of four and was powered by two BMW VI 6,0 ZU engines.[85] During the same year *Dornier-Friedrichshafen* delivered a similar number of **Do 15** flying boats. However the Do 15 was not a new design being based on the earlier *8-Tonnen Wal* of 1931, a variant which in its civilian guise had already seen considerable service with *DLH* (See 2D2).[86] To suit the aircraft for its role as a long range reconnaissance aircraft the Do 15 was armed with a flexible MG 15 machine gun on a D 30 ring mount in the bow and two more defensive guns on D 30 mounts in the fuselage aft of the wing trailing edge. Like most naval aircraft of this period the Do 15 was powered by the BMW VI, two of these engines being mounted back to back on the wing centre-section.[87]

Small scale production of the **He 60A-0** and **B-0** coastal reconnaissance floatplane took place during 1933/34, ten examples of the *A-Reihe* being on charge with the *DVS* for training by the 1 March 1934 (See also 2C2).[88] The He 60B introduced minor equipment changes including provision for a defensive MG 15 in the rear cockpit together with some structural improvements but was in other respects indistinguishable from its immediate predecessor. The first two **He 60C-0**, D-ILRO and D-IXES, commenced trials in the late autumn of 1934 and entered production over the winter. The *C-Reihe* was fitted with catapult launching points for shipboard operation and was powered by the BMW VI 6,0 ZU engine. It carried its 140 kg ordnance load on a single S 125 chemical projector rack.[89]

The final naval type to enter production during this period was the **He 51W** floatplane fighter. During 1933 the He 49c D-2727 was re-built to He 51A standard and fitted with two single-step light metal floats. This aircraft was followed by He 51A-2 D-IFTI which became the production prototype for the naval fighter, fourteen examples of which were delivered during 1934 as a replacement for the HD 38D.[90]

6. TRAINING AIRCRAFT

In the meantime the bulk of the aircraft delivered during 1933-34 were of the trainer or sports category, these being delivered in large numbers to the new *Fliegerschulen* (Flying Schools) and the various *DLV Ausbildungs-und Übungsstellen* (Air Sport Training and Proficiency Centres).[91] Production of these relatively simple types was also sub-contracted throughout the industry with the Ar 66C being built under licence by *Gotha* and the Fw 44 being the first product of the

85   Green 1970 pp.273-274. Technical documentation was covered by *L.Dv.304 He 59 Flugzeughandbuch 1935* & *L.Dv.305 He 59 Baubeschreibung 1935*, whilst drop ordnance was covered by *L.Dv.224 He 59 Beschreibung, Einbau-und Prüfvorschrift der So 3 1935*.

86   Green 1970 pp.112-113 & Dornier 1983 p.132. An alternative designation was for the Do 15 was the Do J IId *Militär-Wal*, whilst training aircraft for the *DVS* were designated Do J IId16a Bis – see Lange 1970 p.198.

87   Green 1970 p.113 & Dornier 1983 p.132.

88   Green 1970 pp.277-279. Fourteen examples of the He 60A-0 were built - see Smith J.R. and Kay A. 1972 *German Aircraft of the Second World War* (hereafter cited as Smith and Kay 1972) p.230. These aircraft may have been designated He 60A-1 & B-1 - see Lange 1970 p.249.

89   Hertel 1955 p.50, Green 1970 pp.278-279 & Smith and Kay 1972 pp.230-231. Technical documentation was covered by *L.Dv.365 He 60E Flugzeughandbuch*, whilst the fuel system was covered by *L.Dv.327 Beschreibung, Einbau-und Behandlungsvorschrift für die geschützte Betriebsstoffbehälteranlge He 60* and for the armament installation by *L.Dv.232 He 60 Beschreibung, Einbau-und Prüfvorschrift für So* & *L.Dv.233 He 60 Bedienungsvorschrift für So 1 1936*.

90   Kens K. and Nowarra H.J. 1961 *Die deutschen Flugzeuge 1933-1945: Deutschlands Luftfahrt-Entwicklungen bis ende des Zweiten Weltkrieges* (hereafter cited as Kens and Nowarra 1961) p.259 & Green 1970 p.270. Although Green suggests that the initial batch of 8 He 51W were not completed until 1936 by which time they were designated He 51B-2, production of 14 He 51W during 1934 is confirmed by *Table 1-F German Aircraft Production in 1934* in Vajda and Dancey 1998 p.18.

91   Ries 1974 pp.26-39 & *Table 1-D The Rhineland Programme, 1 January 1934 – 30 September 1935* in Vajda and Dancey 1998 p.17.

Flugzeugbau Halle.[92] The introduction of new aircraft in this category also continued and whilst the **He 72A/B**, **Fw 44A/B** and **Ar 66C** became the standard *A/B Schulflugzeuge* of the period these were joined in late 1934 by the first examples of the **Bu 131A** which was ordered for use by the *DLV* (See 2C2).[93]

Interestingly the largest single order for an aircraft type within the *1934 Flugzeug-beschaffungs Programm* was for the Junkers **W 34**. In all 1,191 of these rugged, adaptable aircraft were ordered by *LC III* for advanced pilot training, the training of observers, wireless operators and gunners, and as a light transport and communications type.[94]

7. COMMUNICATIONS AIRCRAFT

The *RLM* placed substantial orders with the *Leichtflugzeugbau Klemm* at Boblingen. Whilst the majority of these were for the **L 25**, **L 26** and **L 27** two seat monoplanes which were employed as trainers and sports planes by the *DLV*, a small number of three and four seat **Kl 31** and **Kl 32** cabin monoplanes were also purchased as communications types.[95]

In the meantime *BFW* had continued to construct a range of light aircraft which included the **M 31** and **M 35**, both of which appeared in 1933.[96] The latter design was of some consequence to the development of the company as the success of this aircraft and its successor the M 37 in the various sporting events of 1934-35 did much to restore the firm's fortunes with the *RLM*.[97] The M 37, which became the **Bf 108A** under the new *RLM* system, was one of three types especially commissioned by the *Technisches Amt* for employment by the national team for the 1934 *Europa-Rundflug* (also known as the *Challenge de Tourisme Internationale*), the others being the Fieseler **Fi 97** and the Klemm **Kl 36** (See 2D2).[98] The prototype Bf 108A D-ILIT, which first flew in June 1934, was a beautifully proportioned enclosed cabin, low-wing monoplane of all metal-construction. It was unusual, for a machine of its type, to be fitted with a retractable undercarriage.[99] It was powered by a 240 hp Hirth HM 8U eight-cylinder inverted-vee engine, whilst other high performance sports aircraft used in the *Europa-Rundflug* made use of the 225 hp Argus As 17 6-Cylinder in-line engine of 225 hp.[100] Seven Bf 108A were built under Government contract, six of these being delivered in 1934.[101]

92   Vajda and Dancey 1998 p.201 & 225. For details of the Ar 66 – see Kranzhoff 1997 pp.54-55. See also *L.Dv.347 Flugzeughandbuch* & *L.Dv.348 Bauschreibung.*
93   Kens and Nowarra 1961 pp.119-120, 195-196 & 265-26, Smith and Kay 1972 pp.91-92, 155-157 & 236-238, Wagner W. 1980 *Kurt Tank - Konstrukteur und Testpilot bei Focke Wulf" Die deutsche Luftfahrt 1* pp.44-47. The technical documentation for these trainers was covered by: Fw 44 - *L.Dv.371 Flugzeughandbuch & L.Dv.372 Flugzeugbeschreibung;* He 72 - *L.Dv.368 Flugzeughandbuch & L.Dv.369 Flugzeugbeschreibung.*
94   *Table 1-J Early German Production Plans* in Vajda and Dancey 1998 p.22. Initially *Junkers* and *Henschel* were the main contractors for the W 34 but several other firms would later be engaged in this Programme.
95   Kens and Nowarra 1961 pp.402-404, Lange 1970 pp.309-312 & Smith and Kay 1972 pp.459-461.
96   *Table 1-F German Aircraft Production in 1934* in Vajda and Dancey 1998 p.18. Six M 35 *Sportflugzeuge* were built in 1934. See also Smith J.R. 1971 *Messerschmitt: An Aircraft Album* (hereafter cited as Smith 1971) pp.33-34 & Ishoven 1975 p.77.
97   Lange 1970 p.322 and Ishoven 1975 p.77 & 79. *Prof.*Willy Messerschmitt's friendship with *Reichsleiter* Rudolf Hess was a further major factor in this reversal of fortune - see Smith 1971 p.10.
98   Lange 1970 pp.148-149 & Smith 1971 p.35. The Fi 97 & Kl 36 were also powered by either the Hirth HM 8U or the AS 17 – see Lange 1970 p.216 & 313.
99   Smith 1971 pp.35-36, Kens and Nowarra 1961 pp.413-414 & Smith and Kay 1972 pp.464-465.
100   Gersdorff von K. and Grasmann K. 1985 *Die Deutsche Luftfahrt 2: Flugmotoren und Strahltriebwerke* (hereafter cited as Gersdorff and Grasmann 1985) p.122 & pp.126-127.
101   Smith 1971 p.36 & *Table 1-F German Aircraft Production in 1934* in Vajda and Dancey 1998 p.18.

D. ENGINE PRODUCTION

Difficulties in the aero-engine plants were Milch's biggest worry. Co-operation between the prime contractors, *BMW, Daimler-Benz, Junkers* and *Siemens und Halske*, and their sub-contractors was poor. There was a general lack of skilled labour, as well as shortages of raw materials and in the early stages of expansion of the necessary capital.[102] During 1933-35 the aircraft industry was highly dependent for its combat aircraft on just three basic engine designs, these being the BMW 132 and Siemens und Halske Sh 22 air cooled radials and the ageing BMW VI liquid cooled vee-twelve.

Of these the BMW VI was by far the most important. Production of the existing 750 hp **BMW VI U 6,0 Z** continued for naval applications and for use on large aircraft such as the Do 13, but for the new fighter aircraft and high performance transports the **BMW VI 7,3 Z** was developed with direct fuel injection.[103] In this engine the compression ratio was increased to boost take off performance to 800 hp at 1,755 rpm. The earlier *BMW* carburettor was replaced by a *Zenith* unit.[104] The BMW VI was manufactured at München-Allach but output from this one facility proved insufficient during the first half of 1934 and this restricted the service entry of both the He 45 and He 60.[105] *BMW* was also responsible for the production of the BMW 132. This engine was a progressive development of the Pratt and Whitney Hornet which the company had been building under licence from 1929.[106] The **BMW 132A** was a nine-cylinder radial engine fitted with a *Pallas-Stromberg* carburettor and initially rated at 660 hp. Introduced in 1933 it was a little under-powered for use in twin-engine service aircraft but when installed as a triple engine layout in the Ju 52/3m g3e it proved highly effective and reliable.[107] The BMW 132A was manufactured at *BMW's* Allach and Eisenach plants, whilst parts for this increasingly important engine were also made under contract by *Daimler-Benz* at Stuttgart-Unterturkheim and from January 1935 the new plant at Berlin-Marienfelde.[108]

For its new generation of twin-engine combat aircraft, principally the Do F (Do 11), and the He 46 the *RVM* had pinned its hopes on a new engine then under development at *Siemens und Halske*. The earlier large 31.5 litre Sh 20B radial had not proved a success, delivering just 540 hp at 1,840 rpm.[109] The company had therefore re-designed the engine to run at 2,500 rpm but with a reduced stroke of 160 mm in comparison to the Sh20's longer 188 mm. Cylinder bore was unchanged at 154 mm. The new engine had a smaller capacity (26.8 litres) but a higher power output (650 hp).[110] The **Siemens und Halske Sh 22B** entered production in 1932 and the *RLM* put the company under considerable pressure to increase its production at Berlin-Spandau to meet the need for large numbers of these engines. Unfortunately this led to many problems and the company was unable to meet the agreed delivery schedules for these engines.[111] Unfortunately the engine was highly prone

---

102 Hooton 1994 p.103 & Vajda and Dancey 1998 p.13. The sub-contractors in particular found it very difficult to change from low volume piece work to high volume mass production of components. Poor decision making on the part of the *RLM* and the engine companies also contributed to lower than expected production.

103 Lange 1970 p.397 & Gersdorff and Grasmann 1985 p.58 & 61. The BMW VI 7,3 Z was officially referred to as the BMW 106A but in practice this designation was rarely used - see Vajda and Dancey 1998 p.233.

104 Lange 1970 p.397. The propeller reduction gear was also removed making the slow revving BMW VI 7,3 Z a direct drive power plant.

105 Vajda and Dancey 1998 p.13.

106 Gersdorff and Grasmann 1985 p.53.

107 Gersdorff and Grasmann 1985 p.53 & 56. The BMW 132 was considerably more powerful than the basic 525-550 hp BMW Hornet - see L.B. (Ed.) 1946 *Jane's All the World's Aircraft 1946* pp.288-289, Lange 1970 pp.398-399 & Gunston B. 1995 *World Encyclopaedia of Aero Engines* (hereafter cited as Gunston 1995) pp.26-27 & p.120.

108 Vajda and Dancey 1998 p.233 & 235.

109 Gersdorff and Grasmann 1985 p.47 & 49 and Gunston 1995 pp.30-31.

110 Gunston 1995 p.31.

111 Hooton 1994 p.103. Only a handful of pre-production Sh 22B radial engines were delivered to *Dornier* during

to un-damped vibration and this together with poor quality control led to frequent engine failures in service.[112] In 1934 *Siemens und Halske* was renamed the *Siemens Apparate and Maschinen GmbH* and the Sh 22B was re-designated SAM 22B.[113]

The only production engine in the 300-425 hp category was the ageing Junkers L 5. By increasing the compression ratio from 5.5:1 to 7:1 the power available for take off was increased substantially from 300 to 425 hp. In this form the engine was manufactured in limited numbers at Dessau as the **Junkers L 5G** for use with the He 42 floatplane and the W 33 he.[114]

The most significant new engine to appear in the lower power categories was the Argus As 10 of 1930 which entered quantity production as the **Argus As 10C** at Berlin-Reinickendorf in 1934.[115] A natural outgrowth of the earlier in-line As 8 this 12.7 litre inverted vee-eight air-cooled engine used eight rather than four 120 x 140 mm cylinders to develop 240 hp at 2,000 rpm. It was selected for such types as the Ar 66C, the Bf 108A and the various candidates for the *Heimatschützjäger Competition* (See also 2C2). Hirth also built a small number of engines in this power category. The 250 hp **Hirth HM 8a** was an eight cylinder inverted-vee engine developed specifically for the *1934 Europa Rundflug*. However it was not adopted for service employment.[116]

The three most important engines for light aircraft and trainers remained the **Argus AS 8**, the **Siemens und Halske Sh 14A** and the **Hirth HM 60R**. These were all manufactured in quantity and often employed in different variants of the same machine. For example both the Fw 44 and He 72 in their various forms would eventually be powered by both the As 8 and the Sh 14 (See 2C2).[117]

E. WEAPONS AND DROP ORDNANCE

To maintain secrecy during 1933/34 first line types were delivered to the clandestine units without their intended armament, such equipment being held in store. This led to all such equipment being designated *Sonderausrüstung* (Special Equipment) In the technical publications of the period.[118] Specifically: *Sonderausrüstung 1* (Fixed weapons); *Sonderausrüstung 2* (Flexible weapons) & *Sonderausrüstung 3* (Drop Ordnance) (See 3C4).

The *Luftwaffe* inherited the *Reichswehr's* clandestine stock of 640 elderly *Flugzeugmaschinengewehr* **lu.MG 08/15** (Aircraft Machine Guns), these being available for installation as fixed weapons *(Flugzeug-machinengewehr für starren Einbau)* on such types as the Ar 65 fighter and the He 45 reconnaissance aircraft.[119] Production of the new Rheinmetall Borsig **MG 15** had also begun for

1933.

112 Green 1970 p.261. As a result of these problems the decision was made to re-engine the Do 11 with the reliable and more readily available BMW VI. In its new form it was designated Do 13 – see Green 1970 p.111.
113 Lange 1970 p.425, Gersdorff and Grasmann 1985 p.48 & Vajda and Dancey 1998 p.234.
114 Lange 1970 p.416 & Gersdorff and Grasmann 1985 p.74.
115 Gersdorff and Grasmann 1985 pp.120-122 & p.124, Gunston 1995 p.16 & Vajda and Dancey 1998 p.231.
116 Lange 1970 p.413 & Gersdorff and Grasmann 1985 p.127.
117 Lange 1970 p.393, 413 & pp.424-425 and Gersdorff and Grasmann 1985 pp.46-47, 119-120 & p.126. The Sh 14A was preferred for service use in the Fw 44 & He 72 as it more closely mimicked the characteristics of larger and more powerful engines on advanced types. A similar practice was adopted by the RAF which adopted the Avro Tutor in 1932 as a replacement for its ageing fleet of Avro 504N trainers. This aircraft was powered by the 215-240 hp Armstrong Siddeley Lynx 7 cylinder radial - see Thetford 1976 pp.50-51.
118 *Archiv für technische Dokumente 1900-1945: Luftwaffen-Dienstvorschriften* in www.superborg.de 2005.
119 Volker 1967 p.59. In its conventional form the Maxim MG 08/15 had remained in service with the *Reichsheer* as a heavy machine gun during the twenties - see Walter J. 2004 *Guns of the Third Reich* p.22 & pp.29-30. The installation and use of the MG 08/15 in combat aircraft was later covered by *L.Dv.109 Einbau-und Bedienungsvorschrift für des Flugzeug - MG.08/15 starre, mit Nockenabzug 1935, L.Dv.132 Beschreibung der MG.Steuerung für das starre Flugzeug-MG.08/15 F 1935,* & *L.Dv.133 Einbau-und Einstellvorschrift der MG.-Steuerung für starre Flugzeug-MG.08/15 1935.* At the end of 1934 there were c.565 first line aircraft requiring machine guns - see Volker 1967 p.59.

flexible mounting in defensive positions *(Flugzeugmaschinengewehr für beweglichen Einbau)*; 957 examples had been delivered by the end of 1934 for use aboard such types as the Do 11, He 45, He 46, He 59, He 60 and Ju 52/3m g3e.[120]

In 1933 orders were placed by *LC III* with the *Rheinmetall-Borsig AG* for the series production of **SC 50**, **SC 250** and **SC 500** *Sprengbomben* (High Explosive Bomb) casings using the compression and extension method of manufacture. The smaller **SC 10** *Splitterbombe* (Fragmentation Bomb) was produced by the *Vereinigte Oberschlesien Huttenwerke*, whilst the **B 1 E** incendiary bomb series were manufactured by *Hagenuk* at Kiel.[121] Prior to this date casings for the new bombs were made covertly in small quantities by the smaller engineering plants, whilst filling was carried out secretly at the *Kummersdorf Versuchsschiessplatz* (Experimental Gunnery Range Kummersdorf).[122] The sophisticated **El.AZC** electrical fuzes continued to be manufactured by *Rheinmetall Borsig* at Sommerda in Sweden.[123] The scale of manufacture was governed by the *Luftkommando Amt's* overall requirement that by 1935 for sufficient ordnance to be stock-piled in the new *Munitionsanstalten* (Munitions Dumps) for the planned 1,000 bombers of the *Risiko-Flotte* to each execute 20 sorties.[124] (See App.2I Production Summary - January 1933 - December 1934)

120   Volker 1967 p.59. The MG 15 was developed from the earlier MG 30 light machine gun - see Schliephake H. 1977 *Flugzeugbewaffnung – Die Bordwaffen der Luftwaffe von den Anfangen bis zur Gegenwart* pp.97-102 & Griehl M. 2008 *Deutsche Flugzeugbewaffnung bis 1945* pp.47-48.
121   Heitman 1955 p.85 & Fleischer W. 2003 *German Air-Dropped Weapons to 1945* (hereafter cited as Fleischer 2003) p.36. The main *Rheinmetall Borsig* plant was in Düsseldorf where the original 3-piece *SC* casings were re-designed for manufacture in 1-piece using the stamp and draw process developed for the manufacture of artillery shells by *Prof.*Erhard. Interestingly both *Krupp* and *Bofors* declined the opportunity to become engaged in bomb manufacture in 1933; *Krupp* was too heavily engaged on projects for the *Reichseer* and *Reichsmarine*, whilst *Bofors* may have declined for political reasons. Limited production of *SC* ordnance for developmental purposes had been initiated in 1929 – see Heitman 1955 p.68 & Fleischer 2003 p.32.
122   Heitman 1955 p.85.
123   Heitman 1955 p.84 & Fleischer 2003 p.36.
124   Fleischer 2003 p.36. The so-called *1020 Programm*. See also Volker 1967 p.59.

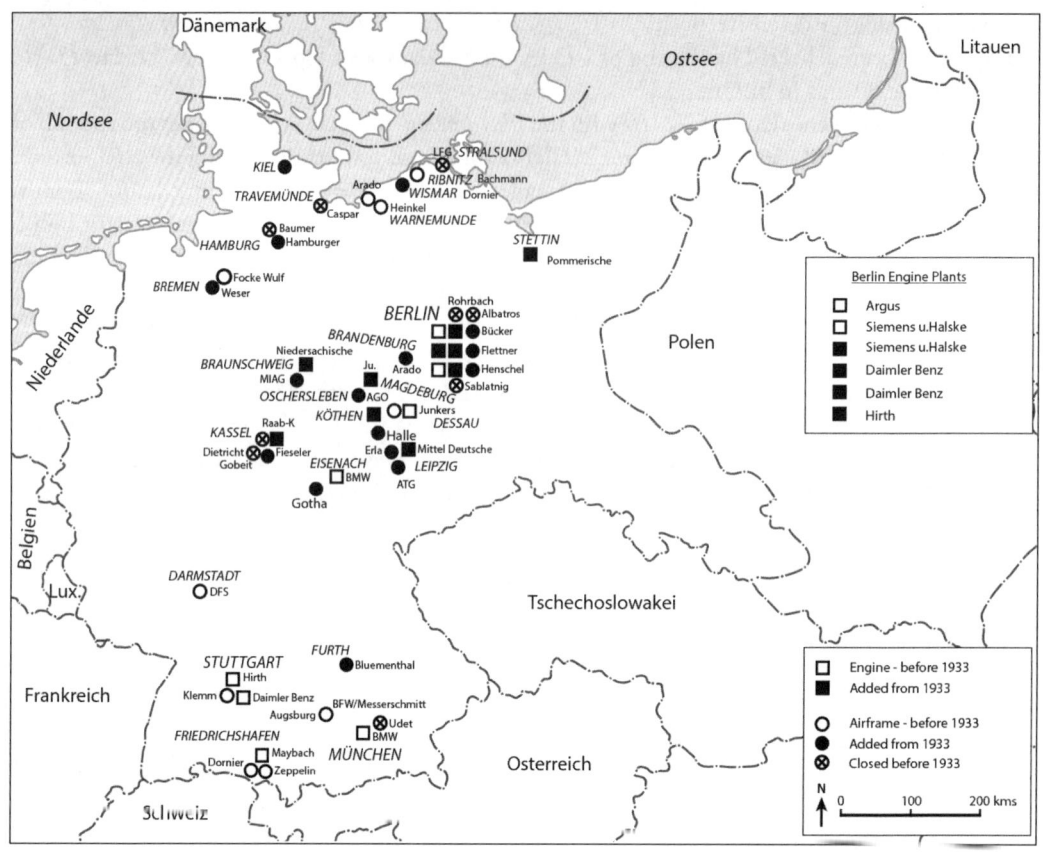

II-3   The geographical location of the German Aeronautical Industry 1920-35.

TABLE II-1
GÖRING-PROGRAMM - MAY 1933 TO APRIL 1934

Constructor	Model	Order	1933	1934	Built
Heinkel	HD 61/He 45	80	9	18+	27+
Arado	SD IV/Ar 64	60	1	19	20
Dornier	Do Y	10			5
Junkers	Ju 52/3m	36	15		
BFW	M 34	10			0
Dornier	Mil-Wal/Do 15	6		6	6
Heinkel	HD 60/He 60	20	8		
Albatros	L 100/L 102	8	8		8
Albatros	L 101	46	46		46
Focke Wulf	Fw 44	19	13		
Total		**295**			

Notes: Known construction is for May-Dec 1933 & Jan-Mar 1934 only

Adapted from Vajda F.A. & Dancey P.1998 German Aircraft Industry and Production 1933-1945 Table 1-C p.16

II-1 Göring's First Aircraft Production Programme (May 1933 to April 1934)

TABLE II-2

AIRCRAFT PROCUREMENT PLANS - SELECTED TYPES

Type	Jan-34	Jan-35
He 45	320	441
He 46	270	370
Hs 122	0	55
He 70	72	126
Ar 64	19	0
Ar 65	85	0
He 51	141	?
Do 11	150	150
Do 13	222	222
Ju 52/3m	450	762
Do 17	9	9
He 111	9	42
Ju 86	3	564
Ju 89	3	3
He 50	51	100
Ha 137	0	343
Ju 87	0	118
Do 15	21	0
Do 18	4	0
HD 38	12	0
He 51W	14	0
He 59	21	0
He 60	81	0
W 33	199	196
W 34	1191	960
Ar 76	?	?
Fw 56	180	240
Total	**2937**	**3835**
All types	**3524**	**6052**

Adapted from Vajda F.A. & Dancey P.1998 German Aircraft Industry and Production 1933-1945 Table 1-J p.22

2D1

The Inspektion der Fliegerschulen

Not surprisingly the emphasis during 1933-34 was on training, a task which was co-ordinated by the *Kommando der Fliegerschulen,* (Flying Training Command) a newly formed headquarters establishment within the *RLM.* In the light of Milch's directive regarding secrecy it was appropriate for a civilian to lead the new organisation and *Kpt.z.See.a.D.*Friedrich Christiansen was appointed to this key post with *Obst.i.G.*Hellmuth Felmy as his chief of staff *(Photo 2D-1).*[1] On the 1 November 1933 the *Kommando* was renamed the *Inspektion der Fliegerschulen* (Flight Schools Inspectorate).[2]

The main task of the *Inspektion der Fliegerschulen* was the planning and supervision of the training programme for aircrew and technical ground personnel, this function being co-ordinated by five *Gruppen* (Groups) or *Abteilungen* (Branches) each of which had a specific role.[3]

The *Inspektion* received activation orders and training guidelines from *Obst.i.G.*Walther Wever's *Luftkommando Amt* (Air Command Office) via *LA II (Organisation)* and *LA III (Ausbildung)* (Training Branch), these being translated into instructions by the appropriate *Gruppe* (See 2A3). The most important elements within the *Inspektion der Fliegerschulen* were the *Gruppe Ausbildung,* the *Gruppe Technik und Gerat,* and the *Abteilung Technische Schulen.* The *Gruppe Ausbildung* (*Hptm.i.G.*Rudolf Meister) was responsible for the processing of training guidelines, the issuance of instructions pertaining to the training of aircrew, the development of flying training schedules and general advisory functions.[4] The *Gruppe Technik und Gerat* was responsible for the supply of

---

1   Kreipe W. Gen.d.Flg.a.D. and Koester R. Obst.a.D. 1955 *Technical Training within the German Luftwaffe* USAF Historical Studies No.169 (hereafter cited as Kreipe and Koester 1955) p.29. *The leaders of the new Wehrmacht branch, including Oberst Wever (who was most impressed by the preliminary contributions of the Truppenamt and the Inspektion Nr.1 (L)), were fully aware that a strong Luftwaffe could only be developed only on a basis of a broadly conceived and smoothly functioning training programme. This conviction, coupled with the realisation that the planned strength in air units would be totally inadequate in the event of a rapid increase in Reichsheer strength from seven to twenty-one divisions, was instrumental in determining the first training programme. For the Reichsluftfahrtministerium could not begin to think of setting up new flying units until the framework for an adequate pilot training programme had been created."* As an initial measure the *Kdo.d.Fliegerschulen W* had been created within the *RWM* in Feb 33 to co-ordinate the training of military and naval flight personnel at the *DVS Zweigstellen* Braunschweig, Schleißheim, List & Warnemünde. The *Kdo.d.Fliegerschulen W* was transferred to the newly formed *RLM* on the 15 May 33 – see Kreipe and Koester 1955 pp.31-32.

2   Kreipe and Koester 1955 p.32. Carlsen S. and Meyer M. 1998 *Die Flugzeugführer Ausbiludung der deutschen Luftwaffe 1935-1945 Bd.I Von der Grundausbildung bis zur Blindflugschule* (hereafter cited as Carlsen and Meyer 1998) p.91. Christiansen had been appointed to the newly formed *RLM* on the 3 Mar 33 as a *MinRat.* He was appointed to his new role as *Inspekteur der Schulen* on on the 3 Jan 34 in succession to *FregKap.*Hans Geisler - see Ries K. 1988 *Deutsche Flugzeugführerschulen und ihre Maschinen 1919-1945* (hereafter cited as Ries 1988) p.54. Felmy was appointed *C.d.S.* on the 1 Dec 33 and simultaneously *Kdr.d.Fligerwaffenschulen* in succession to *Obstlt.* Ulrich Grauert who held this post briefly during Sep-Oct 33 prior to a posting to the *Personalamt* - see service records for Friedrich Christiansen, Hellmuth Felmy & Ulrich Grauert in Hildebrand K.F.1990 *Die Generale der deutschen Luftwaffe 1935-1945* Band 1 A-G (hereafter cited as Hildebrand 1990) pp.157-158, 273-275 & 385-386.

3   Obst.a.D.Alois Heldmann in Maass B. GenLt.a.D. 1955 *The Organisation of the German Air Force High Command and Higher Echelon Headquarters within the German Air Force* USAF Historical Studies No.190 (hereafter cited as Maass 1955) p.50. Alois Heldmann had been assigned to the *Insp.d.Schulen* at that time. See also Kreipe and Koester 1955 pp.30-31.

4   Gen.d.Flg.a.D.Hellmuth Felmy in Maass 1955 pp.36-37 & Obst.a.D.Alois Heldmann in Maass 1955 pp.50-51. In view of his later service it is thought that *Hptm.i.G.*Meister was *Ltr.Gruppe Ausbildung* between Sep 33 & Mar

aircraft, equipment, weapons, motor vehicles etc., the development of training aids and all technical matters. The *Abteilung Technische Schulen*, led by *FlgVizeKdre.*Hellmuth Bieneck, provided a parallel service to that of the *Gruppe Ausbildung* but for the technical schools where the new arm's technical ground personnel were trained.[5]

FIGURE 2D-1 ORGANISATION OF THE INSPEKTION DER FLIEGERSCHULEN
April 1934

Inspekteur - Kpt.z.See a.D.Friedrich Christiansen

C.d.S. - Obst.i.G.Hellmuth Felmy

Gruppe Organisation	-	Organisation Department
Gruppe Ausbildung	-	Training Department
Abteilung Technische Schulen	-	Technical Schools Branch
Gruppe Technik und Gerat	-	Equipment Department
Gruppe Verwaltungs	-	Administrative Department
Flugbereitschaft des RLM	-	Ministerial flight readiness section

---

The first *Technische Schule der Luftwaffe* (Luftwaffe Technical School) was established at the historic military airfield of Döberitz on the 1 October 1933 under the command of *Maj.* Kurt Student.[6] This facility was subsequently consolidated at Jüterbog-Altes Lager following an initial building programme on that site.[7] Thereafter the *Technischen Schule Jüterbog* would grow progressively in size to finally accommodate 1,500 students and as such it would be the source of most of the *Luftwaffe's* technical personnel for the remainder of the decade.[8] Tasked with providing

35 - see service record for Rudolf Meister in Hildebrand K.F.1991 *Die Generale der deutschen Luftwaffe 1935-1945 Band 2 H-N* pp.374-376 See also Zweng IV de H.L. and Stankey D.G. 2013 *Luftwaffe Officer Career Summaries.*

5   Obst.a.D.Alois Heldmann in Maass 1955 p.51. Helmuth Bieneck, the former *Ltr.d.Gruppe V* at the *DVS Braunschweig*, was appointed to this post on the 1 Apr 34 - see service record for Helmuth Bieneck in Hildebrand 1990 pp.81-82.

6   Kreipe and Koster 1955 p.40. Planning had begun in Feb 33. Döberitz was one of the *Luftstreitkräfte's* earliest air stations with employment from 1910 – see Zapf J. 2001 *Flugplatze der Luftwaffe 1934-1945 und was davon ubrig blieb Bd.1 Berlin & Brandenburg* (hereafter cited as Zapf 2001) p.102. Student was promoted to *Obstlt.* on the 1 Jan 34 - see service record for Kurt Student in Hildebrand K.F.1992 *Die Generale der deutschen Luftwaffe 1935-1945 Band 3 O-Z* (hereafter cited as Hildebrand 1992) pp.363-365. The new *Technischeschule* superseded the covert training that had been provided previously by *Fahrabteilung 2* at Rendsburg under *Maj.*Curt Pflugbeil – see Kreipe and Koester 1955 p.30.

7   Volker K-H. 1967 *Die deutsche Luftwaffe 1933-1939: Aufbau, Führung und Rüstung der Luftwaffe sowie die Entwicklung der deutschen Luftkriegstheorie* (hereafter cited as Volker 1967) pp.16-17 & Zapf 2001 p.187. The establishment of a new *Technische Schule* at Jüterbog had been ordered by the *RdL* on the 14 Aug 33. The *Schule* was opened on the 1 Sep 34 when the first personnel arrived from Döberitz. In 34/35 Student's staff included *Hptm.*Hermann Hiller (*Adj.*), *Maj.*Joachim Kortum (*Ltr.*) & *Maj.*Werner Zech (*Ltr.Kfz.Gr.*) – see Hildebrand K.F.1990-1992 *Die Generale der deutschen Luftwaffe 1935-1945 Band 1-3* (hereafter cited as Hildebrand 1990-92). Experienced instructors were drawn from Industry, *DLH*, the former *Flugzentrum Lipetsk* and former Great War personnel – see Kreipe and Koester 1955 p.45.

8   Volker 1967 p.16. An additional 1,000 *Schuler* per annum were trained by the aircraft and engine manufacturers – see Kreipe and Koester 1955 p.40. On the 1 Jan 34 the *RAF* had 1,794 apprentices under training. These were boy entrants who underwent a 3 yr course at No.1 School of Technical Training (Boys) at Halton prior to 7 yrs active service plus 2 yrs in the Reserve – see Adkin F.J. 1983 *From the Ground Up* (hereafter cited as Adkin 1983) pp.103-115 & 172-173, Roberston B. 1978 *The RAF: A Pictorial History* (hereafter cited as Robertson 1978) pp.40-41 & Rogers W.G. *The Vital Role of Maintenance: The Early Days* in Ross A. (Ed.) 1993 *75 Eventful Years: A Tribute to the*

basic technical or trade training for the large numbers of *Grundschuler* (Technical Students), it also provided *Unteroffizier-Lehrgange* (Junior NCO Instructional Courses) and *Feldwebel-Lehrgange* (Senior NCO Instructional Courses) for supervisory personnel:[9]

FIGURE 2D-2 PRINCIPAL LUFTWAFFE TECHNICAL TRADES	
Flugzeugmechaniker	Aircraft Mechanic
Flugmotorenschlosser	Engine Mechanic
Flugzeugfeinmechaniker und Elektriker	Aircraft Instrument Mechanic & Electrician
Fallschirm und Sicherheitswarte	Parachute Packer and Safety Equipment
Flugzeughandwerker	Aircraft Craftsman
Flugzeug-Geräteverwalter	Aircraft Equipment Administrator

The *Flugzeughandwerker* trade-group was sub-divided to cover *Flugzeugklempner* (sheet metal worker - aircraft), *Flugzeugmaler* (painter - aircraft), *Flugzeugsattler* (leather worker - aircraft) and *Flugzeugtischler* (carpenter - aircraft).[10] At this early stage in the *Luftwaffe's* expansion there was a greater demand for wood workers than there was for metal workers. However this balance would change as the decade advanced and aircraft became more sophisticated. To supplement the work of the main *Technische Schule* a *Zweigstelle* (Branch) was established in July 1934 at Berlin-Adlershof under *Rittm.Dipl.Ing.*Eduard Riesch.[11] This facility would also have a capacity of 1,500 *Grundschuler* and would later formed the basis for the separate *Hohere Flieger Technische Schule Berlin-Adlershof* (Higher Air Technical School).[12]

Given the clandestine nature of military aviation during this period the *Reichswehr* was obliged to continue its earlier reliance on the *DVS* (German Commercial Flying School) organisation for the bulk of its training.[13] Not surprisingly more schools were required and in addition to those already operational at Braunschweig, Schleißheim, List and Warnemünde, further facilities were activated at Boblingen, Würzburg, Cottbus and Stettin during 1933-34:[14]

Royal Air Force 1918-1993 pp.220-224.

9 Vogt H. 1994 *Schlachtfeld Luftfahrzeug: Der Einsatz der schwarzen Manner im II.Weltkrieg* (hereafter cited as Vogt 1994) pp.147-150.

10 Vogt 1994 p.156. In 1934 the *RAF* introduced three new Grade Trades: Fitter's Mate, Flight Rigger & Flight Mechanic to supplement those already in existence: Fitter Aero Engine, Fitter Driver Petrol & Fitter Armourer – see Robertson 1978 p.94 & Adkin 1983 p.173.

11 Ries K. 1974 *Luftwaffen-Story 1935-1939* (hereafter cited as Ries 1974) p.45 & service record for Eduard Riesch in Hildebrand 1992 pp.114-115. Riesch had been appointed to Student's staff at Döberitz on the 1 Oct 33. He transferred to Jüterbog as a *Lehrer* (Instructor) in Oct 35. *Hptm.*Robert Fuchs was a *Lehrer* at the *Hoh.Fl.Tech.Sch.* during 1 Oct 34 – 31 Mar 35 – see service record for Robert Fuchs in Hildebrand 1990 pp.329-330. The airfield at Berlin-Adlershof was also known as Berlin-Johannisthal – see Zapf 2001 pp.36-39.

12 Kreipe and Koester 1955 p.40 & Carlsen and Meyer 1998 p.91.

13 Ries 1988 p.54 & Carlsen and Meyer 1998 pp.17-18.

14 Ries 1988 p.54 & www.ww2.dk. Although this listing is dated Dec 33, the *DVS Zweigstellen Boblingen* (Apr 33) and *Würzburg* (Dec 33) were already in existence. That at Würzburg was based on the earlier *Deutsche Luftfahrt GmbH Zweigstelle Würzburg* which had been created in Jan 27, whilst the formation of the *FFS Cottbus* was ordered on the 31 Jan 34 and came into beginning of Feb 34 as the *Fl.Ub.Stelle Cottbus d.DLV, DVS Cottbus* – see Carlsen and Meyer 1998 p.44, 57 & pp.371-372 and Zapf 2001 p.88. The *DVS Zweigstelle* Stettin was opened on the 1 Apr 34 to provide both *Land/See* training up to *C-Schein* standard – see Ries 1988 p.180. For postings and seniority – see Hildebrand 1990-92.

FIGURE 2D-3 DVS ZWEIGSTELLEN December 1933		
Braunschweig	-	Maj.a.D.Alfred Keller
Schleißheim	-	Hptm.a.D.Josef Mai
Boblingen	-	Dipl.Ing.Hermann Huppenbauer
Würzburg	-	Hptm.a.D.Robert Ritter von Greim
Cottbus	-	Maj.Otto Dessloch
Warnemünde	-	KorvKap.Joachim Coeler
List/Sylt.	-	Oblt.z.S.a.D.Heinz Scheurlen
Stettin	-	Dr.Georg Pasewaldt

The proficiency training of existing flight personnel was an early priority. In the Spring of 1933 *FhJu-Gfr.*Wolfgang Falck, a cadet with the *10.//R 7* at Breslau-Carlowitz, was ordered by the RWM to report to Berlin for refresher training:

On arriving in the capital I promptly reported to the department within the *Ministerium* that was covertly conducting fighter pilot training. There I received orders to return to Schleißheim for a specified amount of time to take a refresher course. I will never forget my introduction to the *Lehrgangsleiter* of our so called *Sportsverbände - Hptm.*Bayer. He was standing on the station platform welcoming us youngsters attired in our civilian clothes. Bayer greeted each of us cordially, took our bags, packed them into his car, and drove us to our quarters. Again we were treated as human beings, and even as gentlemen.

The four or six weeks we spent at Schleißheim were too short and immensely enjoyable. We flew the Arado 64, the first German built fighter plane with radial engine. It had a very strong torque movement and was totally dependent on British oil. Once a tanker carrying the oil could not reach Germany in time due to bad weather, so we didn't fly for three or four days. Otherwise we flew our old routine: air combat practice, formation flights, aerobatics, and everything else. It was a wonderful time and we immensely enjoyed it.[15]

*Obst.i.G.a.D.*Wolfgang Falck

A deal was also brokered between Göring and Mussolinio in April 1933 for the covert training of fighter pilots and observers in Italy.[16] In all 49 pilots and 98 observers were sent to a number of *Regia Aeronautica* (Royal Italian Air Force) facilities for further instruction. One of the members of the experienced group which was sent to the fighter school at Grottaglie in southern Italy was Adolf Galland, a graduate of the *DVS Zweigstellen* Braunschweig and Schleißheim and an aspiring airline pilot with *DLH*. He later recalled that the training did not entirely go according to plan:

---

15   Quoted from Falck W. Obst.i.G.a.D. 2002 *Wolfgang Falck: The Happy Falcon - An Autobiography by the Father of the Night Fighters* (hereafter cited as Falck 2002) p.23 with the kind permission of Eagle Editions Ltd. Wolfgang Falck had undergone fighter pilot training at Lipetsk in 1931.

16   *Milch Diary 11 Apr 33* in Irving D. 1973 *The Rise and Fall of the Luftwaffe: The Life of Luftwaffe Marshal Erhard Milch* p.31. Mussolini and Balbo also agreed to supply Germany with fighter aircraft but this part of the agreement was not honoured. The German Party was led by *Maj.a.D.*Curt Pflugbeil. This officer had re-enlisted in the *Reichsheer* in Apr 31 only to be discharged in Jun 33 to lead this training detachment – see service record for Curt Pflugbeil in Hildebrand 1992 pp.31-33 & Hooton E.R. 1994 *Phoenix Triumphant: The Rise and Rise of the Luftwaffe* p.111.

Aglow with enthusiasm, in July we started packing. Unrecognisable in our disguise, we went by train via Frankfurt to southern Italy, and another group was despatched to Udine in northern Italy. At the Brenner frontier we were ostensibly a batch of Süd-Tirolische recruits going on manoeuvres.

In Bari were collected by buses which were unmistakably Army transport, despite their civilian registration numbers, and we travelled in them to Grottaglie, an Italian airship base during the First World War. On the way we stopped in an isolated olive grove, where the drivers exchanged the civil registration numbers for military ones. The men disappeared together with our Italian escort, all of whom had worn civvies. I remember in particular a little, wiry man with a jet-black Balbo beard. After a while they all returned, having transformed themselves into officers of the *Regia Aeronautica*; the man with the pointed beard turned out to be the Major and commander of the air base, and was in charge of the training course.

In Grottaglie, we were shown to our quarters, after being fed and then taken up the Quartermaster, who issued us with Italian airmen's uniforms. We were now disguised as the *Duce's avieri*. It was a strange sensation to find oneself a recruit outside a barracks, and what is more, in a foreign country. The thought struck me that I could have experienced the same at the *Infanterie Regiment 18* in Paderborn without going to all this trouble.

We soon started to curse our disguise and did not mince our words, hoping that our Italian instructors would understand them as little as we understood their commands. After the order *"Rompere le rige"* we had to shout *"Viva il re!"* and our trainers wondered why they could not break us of our habit of following this exclamation with some juicy expression or other. We did not intend this as a slight on Victor Emmanuel, with whom we had no quarrel, but were simply giving vent to our disappointment over the rather inefficient organisation and our dissatisfaction with the barrack drill, for which we did not blame the Italians, but Göring.

Obviously something had gone wrong. Here they presumed we were absolute novices and acted accordingly; we, on the other hand, had completed our full training, and a pretty good one at that. We were only interested in the latest fighter aircraft and in shooting practice. What good were these little trainer planes to us? We wanted to fly the fastest fighters in the world of which Göring had spoken. I suppose he should have discussed this matter a bit more with Balbo.

Recently an Italian pilot had set up a new world record for upside-down flying - incidentally, a thoroughly pointless achievement. We "beginners" were very little impressed by it. When my turn came to perform aerobatics I put the Breda on her back and flew placidly to and fro between Taranto and Grottaglie. The Italians looked on with displeasure and after half an hour grew visibly restless. Somebody had disregarded their "world record". I was given an unmistakable order to land after forty minutes.

The misunderstanding about our position with regard to training was shortly cleared up, and we went over to combat training. In contrast to the Italian personnel we enjoyed shooting very much and, while firing at balloons held on strings by Italian soldiers in trenches, were eager to shoot them almost out of their hands before they released them. Ground-shooting practice, when the "Süd Tirolische" were flying, became the most unpopular duty for the crews of the Grottaglie aerodrome.[17]

GenLt.a.D. Adolf Galland
Former *Flugschuler Grottaglie, Italia*

17   Quoted from Galland A. GenLt.a.D. 1953 *Die Ersten und die Letzen* p.17-18 Cerebus Publishing Limited. In the abridged edition Galland states: *"We had the opportunity to fly all the modern types of Italian aircraft, plus a lot of aerobatics, gunnery and shooting practice that we could not have obtained in Germany."* The results achieved in Italy proved disappointing and the agreement was cancelled in 1934 – see Kreipe and Koster 1955 p.30.

In all some 1,753 flying hours were amassed in Italy during the period 1933-34 and on their return to Germany in 1934 a number of these experienced aviators were appointed instructors at the various *Fliegerwaffenschulen*, a notable example being Schleißheim where all covert fighter training was carried out:

Again we returned to Schleißheim, to the *Deutsche Verkehrsfliegerschule*, now operating secretly as a *Jagdfliegerschule*. Commanding the *Schule* was *Major* Mai. My *Lehrgangsleiter* was *Lt.*Teetzmann; other instructors were *Leutnante* Graf Stillfried, von Heynitz and Pantke. In addition four of us became *Jagdlehren* - Lützow, Trautloft, Radusch and I - and we always had five or six students working as *Untergruppenlehrer*. Students came from the *Luftsportsverband*, or from the *Reichsheer*.

As officer quarters had not yet been built at Schleißheim, we were quartered in Schloss Mittenheim, a few kilometres distant. Franz Lützow and I shared a large room in the castle, which we transformed into a nice living room and joint bedroom by moving wardrobes around. Our Casino also occupied part of the castle at first.

The course lasted, so far as I can remember, three months. Being a *Jagdlehrer* was a fabulous job. We developed, supervised and guided the programme, and flew daily, often two or three sorties. Prior to going aloft we discussed the details of each upcoming flight with the other students, and afterward we'd conduct a debriefing.

We also decided who would be fighter pilots and who would be dismissed. The demands placed on the students were extremely high, and we had a large number of candidates who were disqualified, not for human reasons or character, but because they lacked sufficient flying skills. *Prinz* Louis-Ferdinand von Preussen and his brother, *Prinz* Hubertus, sons of the Crown Prince, were among my students. I had to teach both of them basic infantry skills, which proved very funny, marching arm-in-arm at double time. I also gave the brothers flight training, but ultimately had to disqualify Prinz Louis-Ferdinand. He was a good pilot, but simply not suitable as a fighter pilot. On the other hand, *Prinz* Hubertus succeeded in qualifying as a fighter pilot, but only after great effort.

Again we had a grand time in Schleißheim. The town was a suburb of München, and we thoroughly enjoyed visits to the capital of Bayern. For us it was a time of self-confirmation after all we had been through. Finally, our life in the *Reichsheer* was good, and just then, at least, we were living in a sane world.

Yet we experienced personnel losses, especially in the refresher courses. One time, Walter Kienzle started taxying an Arado SC I and ran full speed into the side of a metal hangar. Thank God he was unharmed. However, while flying Arado 64s two fellow cadets named Aschmann and Collmann collided during take-off. Both were burned alive.

Concurrent with the fighter pilot training was blind flying (instrument) training for the staff, namely the *Lehrgangsleiteren* and *Jagdlehreren*. Again we suffered heavy losses training in the Ju 52 and with the W 34. We suffered another bad day when *Oblt.*Graf Stillfried and *Oblt.*von Heynitz crashed. Those were cruel reminders of what could happen to us.[18]

*Obst.a.D.*Wolfgang Falck
Former *Untergruppelehrer DVS Schleißheim*

---

18   Quoted from Falck 2002 *Wolfgang Falck: The Happy Falcon - An Autobiography by the Father of the Night Fighters* (hereafter cited as Falck 2002) pp.26-27 with the kind permission of Eagle Editions Ltd.

Up to the spring of 1934 the old pattern of flying training continued with primary and basic instruction being carried out at Cottbus, Würzburg, Schleißheim and Warnemünde for the *A/B* Licence, whilst advanced flying training was provided at Braunschweig and List for the *C* Licence:

> In 1931 I joined my Grandfather's regiment as an 18 year old *Fahnenjunker* and quickly volunteered to become a pilot. It was a goal that I had not much chance of attaining: the Treaty of Versailles having forbidden Germany to have an air force. We knew, however, that a *Luftwaffe* had been created secretly. In spite of some eye problems (that I could more or less hide), I was accepted in the *Deutsche Luftsportverband* at Cottbus. It was here that I met the great Udet, an *Experte* from the Great War. I learned to fly in an aircraft which his company produced (U-12 Flamingo). I flew the Heinkel *Kadett*, the Focke Wulf *Stieglitz* and Junkers W 34. My unit was not political but we still regarded Hitler with some hope: he was the only man who could save Germany from her miserable situation. But, we were very suspicious of the troops of the *SA*.[19]

*Obstlt.a.D.*Hennig Strumpell
Former *Flugschuler DVS Zweigstelle Cottbus*

In terms of their equipment all the *Fliegerschulen* continued to employ a wide variety of different aircraft types:[20]

FIGURE 2D-4 AIRCRAFT TYPES EMPLOYED FOR TRAINING PURPOSES 1933-1934	
Albatros	L 75, L 78, L 101, L 102
Arado	SC I, SC II, Ar 65, Ar 66
BFW	U 12, M 18, M 23, M 27
Bucker	Bu 131
Dornier	Do B
Focke Wulf	GL 18, A 20, A 28, Fw 44
Heinkel	HD 32, HD 45, He 72
Junkers	F 13, W 33, W 34, Ju 52/3m
Klemm	L 20, L 25, L 26, Kl 31

However the expansion of flying training and the needs of the *Fliegergruppen* (Air Groups) required a more sophisticated structure which began to appear in the first half of 1934 with the formation of six *Fliegerwaffenschulen* (Aerial Weapons Schools).[21] These were specialised operational training units at which the newly qualified aircrew from the *Fliegerschulen* could receive instruction on the latest types of combat aircraft, albeit still under the camouflage of overtly civilian flying organisations:[22]

19   Quoted from Strumpell H. Obstlt.a.D. *"Our best fighter of the time…"* in Mombeek E, Smith J.R. and Creek E.J. 1999 *Luftwaffe Colours:Jagdwaffe Vol.1 Sctn.1 Birth of the Luftwaffe Fighter Force* p.36 with the kind permission of Erik Mombeeck via Chevron Publishing.

20   Listing from Ries 1974 p.48. See also *Anlage III Flugzeugpark der Deutschen Verkehrsfliegerschule GmbH Warneumde b) Seeflugzeuge (Stichtag: 7.Juni 1934)* in Ries 1970 p.148.

21   *RdL. LA Nr.1941/159/33 g.Kdos. A II 2 A, 14 August 1933 Ersten Aufstellungsabschnitt der Fliegerwaffenschulen* in Zapf 2001 p.260.

22   Ries 1974 pp.64-71, Carlsen S. and Meyer M. 2000 *Die Flugzeugführer Ausbildung der deutschen Luftwaffe 1935-*

FIGURE 2D-5 FLOATPLANES ON CHARGE AT THE DVS WARNEMÜNDE 7 JUNE 1934	
Arado Ar 66	D-INAP
Heinkel HE 5	D-OKOF, D-OMIP
Heinkel HE 9	D-IPYF
Heinkel He 42	D-INEV, D-IZYS, D-IBOQ, D-INAS, D-IJOQ, D-2544, D-2545, D-2549, D-2550, D-2554 & D-2555
Heinkel He 60	D-IPOP

FIGURE 2D-6 FLIEGERWAFFENSCHULEN 1934-1935			
Lechfeld	Kampffliegerschule	Obstlt.Curt Pflugbeil	Mar 34
Schleißheim	Jagdfliegerschule	Maj.Josef Mai	Apr 34
Braunschweig	Aufklärungsfliegerschule	Obstlt.Walter Somme	Jul 34
Hildesheim	Aufklärungsfliegerschule	Obstlt.Waldemar Reinicke	Jul 34
Prenzlau	Kampffliegerschule	Not known	Jul 34
Warnemünde	Fliegerwaffenschule (See)	Obstlt.i.G.Ulrich Kessler	Oct 34

A *Fliegerwaffenlehrgang (See)* was also created at Bug auf Rügen on the 5 April 1934 under *Hptm.*Otto Schroeder-Zollinger, whilst a *Fliegerschützenlehrgang* (Aerial Gunnery Instructional Course) existed at Schleißheim until the 31 Dec 34 under *Hptm.*Gottlob Müller.

Felmy was responsible for the covertly military aspects of these *Schulen* being appointed *Kommandeur der Fliegerwaffenschulen* alongside his other duties. Great care was exercised in concealing the true purpose of these facilities, the loading of aircraft with operational equipment for example being undertaken behind closed doors. Formation flying was also restricted to a maximum of nine aircraft.[23]

Three of these schools were derived from the original *DVS* organisation and additional *A/B* and *C Schulen* were therefore created during the course of 1934. The new *Fliegerschulen* were usually offshoots of existing organisations. In April 1934 two facilities were created to provide flight training to *A2* standard: the *Fliegerschule Kitzingen* (*Maj.*Heinrich Lorenz) which was an offshoot of the *DVS Zweigstelle Würzburg* and the *Fliegerschule Magdeburg* (*Maj.*Alfred Sturm – Jan 35) was derived from the *DVS Zweigstelle Cottbus*. Others would follow over the summer: the *Fliegerschule Celle* (*B2*) in April 1934 (*Maj.*Heinz Benz) and in July 1934 two *C-Schulen*: the *Fliegerschulen Gotha* (*Maj.*Albert Vierling) and Neuruppin (*FlgKdt.*Hermann Steindorf).[24] To co-ordinate the activities of this larger group of schools the position of *Kommandeur der Fliegerschulen (Land)* was created on the 1 July 1934 at *Neuruppin* under the former *Kommandeur der Fliegerschulen der Deutschen Verkehrsfliegerschulen*, *Maj.Dr.*Günther Ziegler.[25] In October a similar position was

1945 Bd.II Fliegerwaffenschulen und Ergänzungsgruppen (hereafter cited as Carlsen and Meyer 2000) p.8, 356, 480 & 516 and www.ww2.dk . For postings – see Hildebrand 1990-92. The *FFS Neuruppin* was an offshoot of the *DVS Zweigstelle Braunschweig* – see Zapf 2001 p.227.

23   Ries 1974 p.45, Carlsen and Meyer 1998 p.91 & www.ww2.dk . See also service record for Hellmuth Felmy in Hildebrand 1990 pp.273-275.

24   Ries 1974 p.48 & Carlsen and Meyer 1998 pp.44-57.

25   Kreipe and Koester 1955 p.34, Ries 1974 p.48 & Carlsen and Meyer 1998 p.91. Günther Ziegler had been

created at Warnemünde as the *Kommandeur der Fliegerschulen (See)*.[26] By this time naval *A/B* training was being carried out at Warnemünde and the former *DVS Zweigstelle Stettin*, whilst *Flugzeugführerlehrgangen (See) C* were held at Warnemünde and at Travemünde.[27]

appointed *Kdr.d.Fl.Schulen d.DVS* in Feb 34. He was a true *Alte Adler* having seen service with *Luftschiffer-Bataillon 1* before training as a military pilot in Aug-Dec 14 and seeing wartime service as an *Aufklärer* and *Jagdflieger*. He had joined the *SA* in 1931 and was thereafter involved in the evolution of the *NS-Fliegerkorps* – see service record for Günther Ziegler in Hildebrand 1992 pp.567-568.

26   Ries 1974 pp.48-49 & Carlsen and Meyer 1998 p.91. Although another reputable source states that the *Stab* was located at Kiel – see Kreipe and Koester 1955 p.34. It is thought that *Obstlt.*Hans Siburg was *Kdr.d.Fliegerschulen (See)* – see service record for Hans Siburg in Hildebrand 1992 pp.302-304. During the summer of 1934 Siburg toured the USA where he studied American flight training methods.

27   Ries 1974 p.48, Ries 1988 p.180 & Carlsen and Meyer 2000 p.516.

2D2

The Role of Civil Aviation in the Re-Establishment of the Military Air Arm

Civil aviation played a significant role in the establishment of a military air capability in Germany up to 1935. This took a number of forms:

- Support for technical advances in aircraft and aircraft equipment;
- The development of sophisticated ground facilities together with an integrated, co-ordinated ground organisation (See 2B5);
- Flight training facilities for elementary (*A/B*) advanced (*C*) and instrument flying (*BF*) training;
- The provision of a mobilisable reserve of auxiliary bombing aircraft in the event of an international crisis;
- Opportunities to promote the superiority of German aviation and aviators on the national and international stage;
- A camouflage under which the newly formed military air units and facilities could be secretly developed.

During the lean period of the world economic recession orders from *Deutsche Luft Hansa* had been instrumental in the very survival of the German aircraft industry (See 1C). During the first half of the new decade the airline would also be responsible for further technological innovation in the face of growing competition from imported American designs.[1] The Airline's immediate response was to order the development of the He 70 and Ju 160 single-engine light transport aircraft.[2] The record breaking He 70 heralded a new era in high speed air transport and like many

1   Stroud J. *The Evolution of the Transport Aircraft* in Jarrett P. (Ed.) 1997 *Biplane to Monoplane: Aircraft development 1919-39* (hereafter cited as Stroud in Jarret (Ed.) 1997) pp.35-43. The immediate spur to German development was the Lockheed Orion, two examples of which were purchased by *Swissair* for use on its Zurich-München-Wien services in 1932 – see also Francillon R.J. 1982 *Lockheed Aircraft since 1913* (hereafter cited as Francillon 1982) pp.106-113. However of more concern was the arrival of the Douglas DC-2 which entered airline service with *TWA* in 1934 and which was purchased by both *KLM* and Swissair – see also Francillon R.J. 1979 *McDonnell Douglas Aircraft since 1920* pp.178-191. As early as Jan 34 Fokker had bought the rights to manufacture the DC-2 in the Netherlands, although in reality only airframe assembly took place – see also Postma T. 1979 *Fokker: Aircraft Builders to the World* p.93. The Lockheed 10A Electra was also introduced in 1934 and this modern design would find much favour with European operators beginning with LOT in Nov 35 – see Francillon 1982 pp.116-127. In 1934 *Luft Hansa* bought two Boeing 247 10-seat airliners. These were registered as D-AGAR (c/n 1944) & D-AKIN (c/n 1945) – see Bowers P.M. 1966 *Boeing Aircraft since 1916* pp.182-187 & Seifert K-D. 1999 *Die deutsche Luftfahrt 28: Der deutsche Luftverkehr 1926-1945 – auf dem Weg zum Weltverkehr* (hereafter cited as Seifert 1999) pp.330-331. Of these two machines D-AKIN spent its entire life at the *E-Stelle Rechlin* where it was used as a flying test bed for automatic course controls – see Beauvais H., Kossler K., Mayer M. and Regel C. 2002 *German Secret Flight Test Centres to 1945: Johannisthal, Lipetsk, Rechlin, Travemünde, Tarnewitz, Peenemunde-West* (hereafter cited as Beauvais et al 2002) p.73.
2   Stroud J.1966 *European Transport Aircraft since 1910* (hereafter cited as Stroud 1966) pp.286-289 & 333-335, Heinkel E. 1956 *He 1000* (hereafter cited as Heinkel 1956) pp.136-140, Turner P.St.J. 1970 *Heinkel: an aircraft*

modern civil aircraft was superior in many respects to contemporary military designs.[3] As such it was ordered in a modified form for the secret *Luftwaffe* (See 2C3).[4] *Luft Hansa* also joined with the *Luftwaffe* in planning a new generation of fast twin-engine monoplanes which would be of equal use as transports and medium bombers (See 3C2). In 1934 these would appear as the He 111 and Ju 86.[5] The latter providing further evidence of *Luft Hansa's* continued interest in the development and use of the Jumo 5 (later 205) compression-ignition heavy oil engine (See 3C2).[6] The use of this engine was also favoured by the Airline aboard the trans-Atlantic seaplanes then on order.[7] At the same time the Airline supported the development of a twin-engine high speed mailplane, an aircraft that would eventually appear in a rather different form as the Do 17 *Schnellbomber* (See 3C2).[8]

A distinctive feature of its commercial services was *Luft Hansa's* ability to operate by night and in poor weather conditions, a capability which was dependent on efficient air and ground communications and modern navigational equipment (See also 4D4).[9] By 1933 the airline had introduced two different wireless communication systems within its growing fleet, these were the standard 20 W-DLH-Station for short-haul operations and the 70/100 W-LW-Station for long-haul flights.[10] Radio direction-finding (*QDM/QDR*) was also possible with a developing system of ground based non-directional beacons (*NDB*) together with the airborne LW-Peilempfanger Spez.173 N and this equipment was further developed by *Telefunken* to provide a let-down procedure (*QGH*) in poor weather conditions.[11]

In the meantime *Lorenz* had pioneered a beam approach system which enabled *DLH's* airliners to make *QGA* instrument approaches to land at suitably equipped airfields in poor weather conditions.[12] The ground based elements of this system included a powerful 500W-UKW-

	album (hereafter cited as Turner 1970) pp.62-69, Schmitt G. 1988 *Hugo Junkers and his Aircraft* (hereafter cited as Schmitt 1988) pp.174-175, Seifert 1999 pp.320-321 & 308-310 & Hooks M. 1999 *Images of Aviation: Luft Hansa* (hereafter cited as Hooks 1999) p.85-92.
3	Heinkel 1956 pp.140-141 & Turner 1970 p.68. Between the 14 Mar – 28 Apr 33 *DLH's Flugkäpitan* Untucht established 8 international speed records over 100 – 2,000 kms with loads of 1,000 – 2,000 kgs – see also Green W. 1970 *The War Planes of the Third Reich* (hereafter cited as Green 1970) pp.280-281.
4	Green 1970 p.281. & Cescotti R. 2001 *The History of German Aviation: Bombers and Reconnaissance Aircraft 1935 to the Present* (hereafter cited as Cescotti 2001) p.95.
5	Stroud 1966 pp.289-291 & 336-339, Seifert 1999 pp.310-311 & 321-322 and Hooks 1999 pp.93-96. See also Heinkel 1956 pp.166-168, Turner P.St.J. and Nowarra H.J. 1971 *Junkers: an aircraft album* pp.78-83, Nowarra H.J. 1980 *Heinkel He 111 – A Documentary History* pp.26-43. For military developments – see Green 1970 pp.287-288 & 414-416 and Cescotti 2001 pp.52-66.
6	Gersdorff von K. and Grasmann K. 1985 *Die Deutsche Luftfahrt 2: Flugmotoren und Strahltriebwerke* pp.90-91 & Gunston B. 1995 *World Encyclopaedia of Aero Engines* pp.89-90. From 1932 at least six *Luft Hansa* F 24 transports were re-engined with the Jumo 4 (204) heavy oil engine – see Stroud 1966 pp.306-307 & Schmitt 1988 pp.105-106 & 209-211. *DLH* were attracted to the fuel economy and enhanced safety offered by the Jumo 4 & 5 engines and would employ this power plant on the Ju 86, Do 18 & Ha 139 – see Seifert 1999 p.279, pp.293-294 & 321-322.
7	Stroud 1966 p.226-229 & 255-257 & Hooks 1999 pp.46-47 & 50-51.
8	Green 1970 pp.113-115 & Cescotti 2001 pp.66-68.
9	Jackson R. 1983 *The Sky their Frontier: The Story of the World's Pioneer Airlines and Routes 1920-40* (hereafter cited as Jackson 1983) p.105 & Seifert 1999 pp144-157. Arguably *Luft Hansa* was the most modern airline in Europe, if not the World, at that time.
10	Trenkle F. 1986 *Die deutsche Luftfahrt 7: Bordfunkgerate - Vom Funksender zum Bordradar* (hereafter cited as Trenkle 1986) pp.26-30. The 20 W-DLH-Kleinstation - SEZ 26 248 (300-510 KHz) was provided by *Lorenz* and the Spez.378 F/Stat.285 F (323-564 KHz). See also Hirst M. *Sophisticated Systems* in Jarrett (Ed.) 1997 p.163.
11	Trenkle 1986 pp.83-85. First developed and employed in the USA as the Radio Range System, these radio "lighthouses" had relatively short range and could be adversely affected by topography, the coastline and by diurnal changes. However they were particularly useful for homing to an airfield and they would become more efficient as the decade progressed – see also Hirst in Jarrett (Ed.) 1997 pp.160-163.
12	Trenkle 1986 pp.97-99. Work on this system was carried out in 1932/33. It employed a 500 W ground transmitter which operated within the 30.3 – 33.3 MHz waveband. The airborne equipment could interpret these signals as either a Morse E (Dot) or T (Dash). When the two signals overlapped a continuous tone was heard in the pilot's

Ansteuerungsfunkfeuer (*AFF*) (30.0-33.3 mc/s) wireless beacon that was located at the upwind end of the active runway, and low-powered beacons, that were located 300 m from the airfield boundary - the 5W-UKW/MW-Haupt-Einflugzeichensenders (38 mc/s/700 kc/s)(*HEZ*) and 3000m from the boundary - the 5W-UKW/GW-Vor-Einflugzeichensenders (38 mc/s/1700 kc/s) (*VEZ*) under the approach path. The *AFF* transmitted a single focused energy beam (*Leitstrahl*) that was modulated to give a *Morse E* (dot) to the left of the optimal approach path and a *Morse T* (dash) to the right of the path. Where the two over-lapped a steady tone or equi-signal would be heard. The outer (*VEZ*) and inner (*HEZ*) markers transmitted a vertical beam to give an aural tone.[13]

The aircraft based elements of the system consisted of a special receiver which was tuned to the frequencies in use: 30-33.3 mc/s for the main beam, 38 mc/s for the outer and inner markers and to 700 and 1700 kc/s for the approach markers. The pilot would manoeuvre his aircraft to intercept the approach beam at a range of 20-30 kms from the airfield. As he passed over the outer marker (*VEZ*) at a height of 200m he would reduce power and begin a controlled rate of descent to intercept the inner marker (*HEZ*) at around 30 m maintaining his course by reference to the aural tone in his headphones. If this tone changed to dots he was left of the approach path, if he heard dashes he was to right of the path. Unlike later systems he was entirely reliant on his altimeter and vertical speed indicator for height information and if the runway was not visible he would go-around by making a controlled climb on instruments.[14]

The high standard of crew proficiency required for regular commercial operations provided an ideal environment for the advanced training of military aviators who were covertly assigned to Berlin-Staaken where they joined genuine airline crews.[15] Possibly to avoid disclosure in the event of an accident crew training was performed by a specially created division of the *Deutsche Reichsbahn* (German State Railways), whilst all military personnel wore *DLH* uniforms whilst on duty. Initially three *Staffeln* were formed in November 1933 ostensibly for the rapid delivery of priority freight cargoes.[16] However their real purpose was to provide realistic training for the *Fernauklarer* and the *Kampfflieger*, whilst in time of war the civilian staff and their aircraft would be

headset which indicated that he was lined up with the runway. A controlled rate of descent was initiated on passing overhead the outer marker (*Vorsignal*) at 3,000 m from the runway threshold. The aircraft's proximity to the airfield was indicated by passing over the inner marker (*Hauptsignal*) at 300 m from the airfield's perimeter.

13   Trenkle 1986 pp.98-99.

14   Trenkle 1986 p.98, Coombs L.F.E. 1997 *The Lion has Wings: The race to prepare the RAF for World War II 1935-1940* pp.71-72 & Wakefield K. 1999 *Pfadfinder: Luftwaffe Pathfinder Operations over Britain, 1940-44* p.5. The original *DLH* equipment of 1933 was known as the *Typ EB 1*. The airline also used the improved *EB 2* from 1935. The first equipment to be installed in Britain was a London-Croydon in 1935. See also *AP 1751 Blind Approach Pilot's Handbook* in Johnson B. 1978 *The Secret War*.

15   Nowarra H.J. 1987 *Aircraft & Legend: Junkers Ju 52* (hereafter cited as Nowarra 1987) pp.34-35 The training included pilots (*FF*), wireless operators (*BF*) & flight engineers (*BM*). Pilot training included precision landings, high speed flights, night landings, beacon-guided approaches, navigational flying, blind flying and proficiency flying. Radio operators focused on radio navigation, whilst flight engineers called for system management and the handling of emergencies – see Ries K. 1974 *Luftwaffen-Story 1935-1939* (hereafter cited as Ries 1974) pp.58-64. Amongst those at the *Streckenschule Berlin* at this time was former *Infanterie-Offz.* Heinrich Graf von Stillfried und Rattonitz who was trained at the *DVS Braunschweig* & *Fliegergruppe Lechfeld* before joining the *Streckenschule* for two months from Oct 34 – see Zweng IV de H.L. and Stankey D.G. 2013 *Luftwaffe Officer Career Summaries* (hereafter cited as Zweng and Stankey 2013).

16   Kreipe W. Gen.d.Flg.a.D. and Koester R. Obst.a.D. 1955 *Technical Training within the German Luftwaffe* USAF Historical Studies No.169 (hereafter cited as Kreipe and Koester 1955) p.42 & Seifert 1999 p.157. Following initial discussions in Feb 33 an agreement was reached between *Staatssekretär* Milch and *Dr.* Julius Dorpmuller (*Generaldirektor Deutschen Reichsbahn Gesellschaft*) on the 21 Jul 33 for the formation of the *Reichsbahnstrecken*. *DLH* would supply the aircraft and *RM* 650,000 would be set aside in 1934 to finance the new *Fluggesellschaft*. The first *Reichsbahnstrecke* (Berlin-Königsberg) was flown on the night of the 1 Nov 33 by Ju 52/3m D-2624 *Rudolf Berthold*. On the 24 Mar 34 a further secret order authorised the creation of a further two *RB-Streckenstaffeln*. The original three *Reichsbahnstrecken* were then re-numbered - see Ries 1974 p.63.

assigned to *Bombengeschwader I* as part of the *Flugkommando Berlin* (Air Command Berlin). To this end the individual *Staffeln* were commanded by military officers on the inactive list (*a.D.*), whilst the instructing staff also included experienced military personnel alongside those from *DLH*. From October 1933 *Hptm.*Kuno Heribert Fütterer was the first *Leiter der Streckenschule Berlin-Tempelhof*, whilst *Rittm.a.D.*Georg Rieke was *Käpitan Streckenstaffel 1* (Berlin-Königsberg), later *Streckenstaffel 2* (Berlin-Breslau)(See 2E2).[17] Each *Staffel* was equipped with two Dornier Do F aircraft as well as a single Junkers Ju 52/3m and was allocated a different route from the central hub at Berlin:[18]

FIGURE 2D-7 THE REICHSBAHN-STRECKENSTAFFELN AUGUST 1934		
Kdr.Streckenschule Berlin - Maj.Kuno-Heribert Futterer		
Reichsbahnstrecke 1	Berlin - Königsberg	Streckenstaffel 1
Reichsbahnstrecke 2	Berlin - Breslau	Streckenstaffel 2
Reichsbahnstrecke 3	Berlin - Hamburg, later Münster	Streckenstaffel 3
Reichsbahnstrecke 4	Berlin - München	Streckenstaffel 4
Reichsbahnstrecke 5	Berlin - Frankfurt/Main, later Stuttgart	Streckenstaffel 5
RB-Streckenstaffeln 4 and 5 were activated by a secret order dated 24 March 1934.		

FIGURE 2D-8 AIRCRAFT USED BY THE REICHSBAHN-STRECKENSTAFFELN	
Do 11da (10)	D-ABEL, ABOS, ADAN, ADUL, AFEZ, AFOT, AGIF, AGYM, AHER, AJOL & AZUN
Ju 52/3m (12)	D-ABAT, ADIH, ADYL, AFIR, AJUP, ANUT, APYX, AQAM, ARES, ATOL, AVES & AVIR
AIRCRAFT USED BY THE REICHSBAHN-STRECKENSCHULE	
Ju 52/3m	D-ABON, ADES, ADIF, ADIH, ADYA, AFEH, AHYR, ANUT, APEH, APUS & ATOL

17   Ries 1974 p.58 & 63. Service record for Kuno Heribert Fütterer in Hildebrand K.F.1990 *Die Generale der deutschen Luftwaffe 1935-1945 Band 1 A-G* pp.331-332.Kuno Fütterer was an *Alte Adler* who had received his flight training in 1915 before serving as a *BO* (Observer) in *Feld-FA 45* in 1916/17. By the close of hostilities he was *Adj.BoGohl 6*. Post-war he had remained in the *Reichsheer* within *IR 17* (Braunschweig). He would be promoted to *Maj.* on the 1 Oct 34. Georg Rieke had undergone secret flying training at Lipetsk (29/31) and in Italy (Jul-Sep 33). He had then been attached to the *Insp.d.Schulen* as the *Offz.bV* before moving to Tempelhof where according to this source he was *Ltr.d.Streckenschule Berlin* from Oct 33 – see service record for Georg Rieke in Hildebrand K.F.1992 *Die Generale der deutschen Luftwaffe 1935-1945 Band 3 O-Z* (hereafter cited as Hildebrand 1992) pp.112-113.. Other officers associated with the *Reichsbahn* were *Rittm.*Hans Poetsch who took over as *Fhr.d.Streckenstaffel 1* on the 1 Jun 34 before going to the *Fliegergruppe Tutow* – see service record for Hans Poetsch in Hildebrand 1992 pp.48-49 and ; Karl Frhr.von Wechmar who had trained at Lipetsk and Grottaglie before serving at the *Streckenschule* between Oct 33 – Feb 35 – see Zweng and Stankey 2013. However it has been suggested that the *Streckenschule Berlin* was not opened until the 1 Apr 36 – see Ries 1974 p.63 & Carlsen and Meyer 1998 p.34.

18   Ries 1974 pp.63-64. The new routes were introduced on the 1 Oct 34 although Münster proved to be inaccessible in bad weather. Dortmund was designated as an alternate destination. At least 7 Do 11Da aircraft were registered to the *Deutsche Reichsbahngesellschaft*, whilst a further 5 were registered to *DLH* – see Stroud 1966 p.254. In addition 12 Ju 52/3m aircraft were allocated to the *Deutsche Reichsbahn* including Ju 52/3m ce D-ADOM (D-2201) WNr.4015, Ju 52/3m ce D-ADYL (D-2202) WNr.4109 & Ju 52/3m D-AFIR (D-2468) WNr.5065 which were transferred from *DLH* – see Nowarra 1987 p.34. More recent research has shown there to be as many as 20 Ju 52/3m aircraft registered to the *Deutsche Reichsbahn* or the *Streckenschule Berlin*. In addition Ju 52/3m WN.4053 which was variously registered as D-AXAN/D-2600/D-AHIT/D-ANAO & Ju 52/3m D-AVAN were registered to the *Deutsche Reichsbahn* – see www.airhistory.org.uk The commercial value to *DLH* of the *Reichsbahnstrecken* was considerable rising to 17.3% of all takings for the Airline's European routes in 1935 when 2,883,452 kms were flown – see *Tabelle 33 Leistungen auf den Reichsbahnstrecken* in Seifert 1999 p.158.

The *Streckenschule Berlin* eventually had an establishment of 130 *Flugschuler* (Flight Students) of whom 70 were pilots, 30 wireless operators and 30 were flight engineers. It proved an invaluable advanced training resource for the covert *Luftwaffe* in the period prior to the establishment of its own *Blindflugschulen*.[19]

By the end of 1934 *Luft Hansa* had a total of 41 of its efficient and adaptable Ju 52/3m airliners in service, within a total fleet of 144 aircraft.[20] In an emergency this resource would provide the secret *Luftwaffe* with a valuable reserve of auxiliary bombers (*Behelfsbomber*)(See 2A3). Based on the earlier experimental work at Lipetsk, armament conversion kits (*Sonderausrüstung 2* and *3*) were produced and placed in store so that these aircraft could be rapidly re-fitted for the bombing role and on the 27 October 1933 Göring ordered the formation of the *Stab/Bombengeschwader I* from the *Verkehrinspektion der DLH* (*DLH* Transport Inspectorate)(See 2C3 & 3C4).[21] In June 1934 the auxiliary reserve was re-organised into two separate mobilisable *Kampfgeschwadern* (Bomber Wings): the *Behelfskampfgeschwader 172* at Berlin-Tempelhof and Tutow and the *Behelfskampfgeschwader 274* at Tempelhof and Fassberg.[22] However in the short term both units remained at *Kampfgruppe* (Bomber Group) strength and ultimately plans for the *BKG 274* was abandoned, this formation being absorbed into *BKG 172* as the *II./BKG 172*.[23] Operational control of the *Luft Hansa* reserve was in the hands of the Airline's Traffic Manager, *Dr.*Robert Knauss, an acknowledged and influential theoretician on the employment of offensive air power (See 2A1).[24] His military liaison was provided by *Hptm.*Kuno-Heribert Fütterer as *Offiziere zbV* in the *Stab/Behelfskampfgeschwader* and *Kommandeur der Langenstreckenschule Berlin*.[25]

Its new aircraft and operating procedures enabled *Luft Hansa* to intensify its activity on its already extensive network of European routes, whilst further developing its overseas connections.[26] A particular area of interest was the establishment of a mail service to Brazil where *Luft Hansa* already had a substantial interest via the *Syndicato Condor Ltda.* (See 1D2). In 1932 *DLH* chartered the *SS Westfalen* (5,367 BRT) and had the vessel modified with a 15 tonne crane and Heinkel K 6 catapult to launch and recover its Dornier Do J II *Wal* flying boats.[27] After initial proving trials at Bremerhaven the *Westfalen* sailed for a point in the Atlantic Ocean 1,500 kms west of Bathurst in West Africa. On the 6 June 1933 *Flugkapitan* Blankenburg's crew aboard D-2069 *Monsun* successfully located the *Westfalen* using radio location, landed alongside the ship where the aircraft was lifted aboard for refuelling. On the following day the *Wal* was catapulted off the *Westfalen* and successfully returned to the Bathurst. In October 1933 a successful crossing to Natal

---

19   Ries 1974 p.63.
20   *Tabelle 31: Die Lufthansa-Flotte 1932 und 1934* in Seifert 1999 p.155. Other machines such as the W 34, of which 10 were on charge by Dec 34, could also have been converted as *Behelfsbomber* in an emergency – see Ries 1974 p.114.
21   Seifert 1999 p.159 & Ries 1974 p.112 & 115. *So 2 (II)* covered defensive weapons, whilst *So 3 (III)* was air drop ordnance – see Beauvais et al 2002 p.44. The *Sonderausrüstung* were almost certainly kept at *Luft Hansa's* major maintenance facility at Berlin-Staaken which had come under military control from the 1 Jul 34 – see service record for Gustav Kastner-Kirdorf in Hildebrand K.F.1991 *Die Generale der deutschen Luftwaffe 1935-1945 Band 2 H-N* (hereafter cited ass Hildebrand 1991) & Hooks 1999.
22   Ries 1974 p.112 & 115. The newly formed covert *Kampfgruppen* were based at Tutow & Fassberg and it is likely that the emergency *Gruppen* would have been subordinate to these formations if war had broken out during 1934/35.
23   Ries 1974 p.115.
24   Irving D. 1973 *The Rise and Fall of the Luftwaffe: The Life of Luftwaffe Marshal Erhard Milch* p.33 & Murray W. 1985 *Luftwaffe: Strategy for Defeat 1933-45* p.8. See also service record for Robert Knauss in Hildebrand 1991 pp.189-190.
25   Service record for Kuno-Heribert Fütterer in Hildebrand 1990 pp.331-332.
26   Jung D., Wenzel B. and Abendroth A. 1977 *Die Schiffe und Boote der deutschen Seeflieger 1912-1976* (hereafter cited as Jung et al 1977) pp.66-69 See also *Streckennetz der deutschen Lufthansa und ihr nahestehender Gesellschaften 1935* in Seifert 1999 p.160.
27   Jung et al 1977 pp.70-71 & Jackson 1983 pp.137-138. The time for the Atlantic crossing was 14 hrs 5 mins.

was achieved with one *Wal* flying mail out to the *Westfalen* where it was placed aboard a second *Wal* which was then launched by catapult for the onward flight to Brazil.[28] The first scheduled crossing took place in February 1934 when a He 70 flew 47 kgs of mail from Berlin to Seville via Stuttgart and Marseille, where a Ju 52/3m g3e flew it on to Bathurst via Las Palmas. The mail then went aboard the *Westfalen* which sailed for a point in the Atlantic from where the *Wal* could be launched for Natal. Finally a W 34/See flew the mail on to Rio de Janeiro where a further connection was made for Buenos Aires in Argentina.[29] During that year *Luft Hansa* completed 47 scheduled flights to and from Brazil carrying 3,900 kgs of mail westbound and 2,740 kgs eastbound.[30]

In 1934 *Luft Hansa* purchased the *MS Schwarzenfels* which was modified to operate the Do R *Superwal* as the *MS Schwabenland* (8,188 BRT). Using the new equipment a night service to Brazil was initiated in the following year, the overall transit time being reduced to three days.[31] In 1936 the reliable but ageing Do *Wal* flying boats were finally replaced on the South Atlantic route by the new Do 18E.[32] Such operations gained considerable international prestige for *Luft Hansa* and for Germany whilst these pioneering operations would prove highly informative for the covert *Luftwaffe* and in particular the *Marineflieger* (Naval Air Arm) which also operated the Dornier *Wal* from 1934 (See 2E3 & 4E7).[33]

In the meantime the intense public interest in flying and aviation in general had resulted in a plethora of private gliding and flying clubs throughout Germany. In 1933 some 300 of these were already affiliated to the *Deutsche Luftfahrtverband (DLV)*, a voluntary organisation which had been very successful in promoting private flying and sports aviation (See 1D2).[34] Not surprisingly *Reichskommissar der Luftfahrt* Hermann Göring quickly realised the para-military potential of such an organisation and even before the formation of the *RLM* he had dissolved the original *Deutsche Luftfahrtverband (DLV)* in favour of the officially sponsored *Deutsche Luftsportverband (DLV)*.[35]

The new *DLV* was established on the 25 March 1933 with *Hptm.a.D.* Bruno Loerzer as its first *Präsident (Photo 2D-2)*.[36] All the formerly independent clubs were obliged to join the new

---

28   Jung et al 1977 p.72, Jackson 1983 pp.15-16 & Seifert 1999 pp.152-154.

29   Jackson 1983 p.17. The operating conditions were quite primitive. Prior to the laying of steel matting Bathurst proved unusable by landplanes in the rainy season; accommodation was rudimentary as passengers were not carried on these flights; the wireless direction finding apparatus was not always reliable; there were delays in re-stocking the various bases with supplies and spare parts.

30   Jackson 1983 p.17 & Seifert 1999 p.154. In addition to the 10 tonne Do J *Wal* II *DLH* had 6 Do R *Superwal Flugbooten* which were used on the Ostsee services – see Stroud 1966 pp.247-248.

31   Jung et al 1977 pp.75-77 & Jackson 1983 pp.16-17. The first flight was made on the 30 Mar 35. In Jul 35 *Luft Hansa* joined forces with *Air France* to introduce a twice weekly mail service to South America.

32   Hooks 1999 pp.41-43. *Luft Hansa* employed the 10-tonne Do J Wal II f bos WNr.299 D-ADYS *Tornado*, WNr.298 D-AGAT *Boreas*, WNr.237 (D-2399) D-AKER *Taifun*, Do J Wal II C Bos WNr.676 D-AKYM *Mistral* & Do J Wal II F WNr.300 D-ALOX *Passat* on the South Atlantic service. Together they made 328 crossings – see Stroud 1966 pp.242-243. *Luft Hansa* purchased 5 Do 18E *Flugbooten* and orders were also placed for two four-engine designs for trans-Atlantic operation: the Ha 139 & Do 26 – see Stroud 1966 p.226-229, 255-257 & 258-259.

33   *Table 1-C Göring's First Aircraft Procurement Programme (May 1933 to April 1934)* in Vajda F.A. & Dancey P.1998 *German Aircraft Industry and Production 1933-1945* (hereafter cited as Vajda & Dancey 1998) p.16. The *Marineflieger* took delivery of the first of 21 Do *Wal Flugbooten* ordered under the *Rheinland Programm* in Feb 34 – see *Table 1-D The Rhineland Programme 1 January 1934 – 30 September 1935* in Vajda and Dancey 1998 pp.16-17.

34   Ries K. 1970 *Luftwaffe Bd.1 Die Maulwurfe 1919-1935* (hereafter cited as Ries 1970) p.94 & Ries K. 1988 *Deutsche Flugzeugführerschulen und ihre Maschinen 1919-1945* (hereafter cited as Ries 1988) p.9.

35   *Information provided by Gr.Ltr.Kehrberg* in Kreipe and Koester 1955 p.47 & Ries 1970 p.94. In 1931 the "old" *DLV* had some c.50,000 members.

36   Ries 1970 p.94 & Ries 1988 p.53. Loerzer owed his position to his close friendship with Göring that went back to their days together in the *Luftstreitkräfte*. Loerzer had been *Kdr.JGr.3* from Dec 17. From 1930 he had been *Ltr.d.Reichsverbändes der deutschen Luftfahrzeug-Halter* – see service record for Bruno Loerzer in Hildebrand 1991 pp.309-310. The former *Präsident d.DLV, Staatsminister* a.D.Alexander Dominicus, resigned. The *Aeroclub von Deutschland* was also disbanded although it would later be resurrected within the new political framework – see Kreipe and Koester 1955 p.47.

organisation which also incorporated the *Sturmvogel*, the *Akademischen Fliegergruppen*, the *Ring Deutscher Flieger* and from September 1933 the former *NSDAP* air units – the *SA* and *SS Fliegersturme (Photo 2D-3).*[37] Although not publicly revealed Loerzer's other status as *Inspekteur der Reserveflieger* was indicative of the para-military nature of the *DLV*, a stance which was soon confirmed by the introduction of uniforms, ranks and drill.[38]

As *Reichsminister der Luftfahrt*, Göring established the following objectives for the re-organised *DLV*:[39]

- Promotion of flying and aviation amongst the German people;
- Training of pilots and technical personnel for future integration into the planned *Luftwaffe*;
- Proficiency training for pilots and technical personnel of the former *Luftstreitkräfte, Marineflieger* and personnel of the aircraft industry;
- Supervision of all sport aviation in Germany together with its representation in international events.

Uniforms were introduced into the *DLV* during the course of 1933. Four uniform dress orders were prescribed of which the Walking-Out Dress (*Strassenanzug*) was the most commonly worn by *DLV* members for both off-duty and working hours. Ceremonial occasions were marked by the wearing of Service Dress (*Dienstanzug*) and Informal Full-Dress (*Kleiner Gesellschaftsanzug*). For evening wear Formal Full-Dress (*Grosser Gesellschaftsanzug*) would be worn, for example at dining-in nights. The uniform was also adopted in September 1933 by *RLM* officials and *DVS* personnel.[40] The officers of the secret *Luftwaffe Offizierkorps* could be distinguished from the main membership of the *DLV* by the wearing of paired shoulder cords as opposed to the single cord worn on the right shoulder.[41] Different coloured collar patches (*Kragenspiegel*) were used to denote the different categories of personnel.[42]

To facilitate central control from *DLV* Headquarters in Berlin the various aviation centres were organised into sixteen geographical *Fliegerlandesgruppen*.[43]

---

37   Ries 1970 pp.94-96 & Ries 1988 p.53. The *SA-SS Fliegersturm* had been created in Jul 33 from a number of earlier units; it was incorporated into the *DLV* in Sep 33 thus ending any aspirations the *SA* had in forming an independent air arm. However these men would be influential in politicising the new organisation - see Davis B.L. 1991 *Uniforms and Insignia of the Luftwaffe Vol.1: 1933-1940* (hereafter cited as Davis 1991) pp.13-14. *Maj. (char.)* Eduard Ritter von Schleich was a prominent member of the *SA-SS Fliegersturm* as *Fhr.d.SS-Fliegerstaffel Süd* from Oct 31. The *Schwarzer-Ritter* (Black Knight) was a holder of the *Pour le Mérite* (4 Dec 17) for his exploits in the *bayerischen Luftstreitkräfte* where he scored 35 *Luftsiege* – see Angolia J.R. and Hackney C.R. 1984 *The Pour le Mérite and Germany's First Aces* pp.168-171. From Dec 34 he was *Fhr.d.Landesgruppe XI (Thüringen) d.DLV* - see service record for Eduard Ritter von Schleich in Hildebrand 1992 pp.187-189. After a period as *Referent b.Stab d.Obersten SA-Führung* (from Apr 31), *Dr.*Günther Ziegler had been appointed *Fhr.i.V.d.NS-Fliegerkorps* and later *Geschaftsführer d.NSFK* until the 31 Dec 33 – see service record for Günther Ziegler in Hildebrand 1992 pp.567-568.

38   *Der Reichsverteidigungsminister und Befehlshaber der gesamten Wehrmacht LP Nr.1555/33 g.kdos.II, Berlin, den 5.12.1933* in DZ/MGFA, Akte II L 49 in Volker 1967 p.21. See also *Information provided by Gr.Ltr.Kehrberg* in Kreipe and Koester 1955 p.48a, Ries 1970 p.94 & Ries 1988 p.54 & 76.

39   *Information provided by Gr.Ltr.Kehrberg* in Kreipe and Koester 1955 pp.47-48.

40   Davis 1991 pp.14-18.

41   Davis 1991 p.14.

42   Ries 1970 p.96 & Davis 1991 p.21.

43   Ries 1970 p.95. In 1935 the *Fliegerlandesgruppen* would broadly correspond to the new territorial *Luftgaue* – see *Anlage 11 Die territoriale Einteilung der Luftwaffe in Luftkreis, Stand: 1.April 1934* in Volker K-H. 1967 *Die deutsche Luftwaffe 1933-1939: Aufbau, Führung und Rüstung der Luftwaffe sowie die Entwicklung der deutschen Luftkriegstheorie* (hereafter cited as Volker 1967) p.236. The *Fliegerlandesgruppen* were sub-divided into *Untergruppen (Regimenter), Ortsgruppen (Abteilungen) & Fliegersturme (Kompanien)* – see *Gr.Ltr.Kehrberg* in Kreipe and Koester

FIGURE 2D-9 DLV COLLAR PATCH COLOURS		
Weiss	White	Reichsminister & Staatssekretär
Schwarz	Black	All other officers and personnel assigned to the RLM
Gelb	Yellow	Flying personnel of the covert units
Blau	Blue	All other DLV personnel
Grun	Green	Luftpolizei (Reichsluftaufsicht)

FIGURE 2D-10 DLV FLIEGERLANDESGRUPPEN		
I	Ostpreussen	Königsberg
II	Pommern	Stettin
III	Nordmark	Hamburg
IV	Niedersachsen	Hannover
V	Westfalen	Essen
VI	Rheinland	Essen
VII	Südwest	Darmstadt
VIII	Baden	Mannheim
IX	Wurttemburg	Stuttgart
X	Bayern	München
XI	Thüringen	Weimar
XII	Sachsen	Dresden
XIII	Provinz Sachsen	Magdeburg
XIV	Brandenburg-Grenzmark	Berlin
XV	Schlesien	Breslau
XVI	Danzig	Danzig

For the 30,000 members flying training naturally formed the focus for *DLV* activity and during the course of 1933-34 the first *Segelflugabteilungen* (Glider Detachments), *Fliegerübungs- und Fliegerausbildungsstellen* (Flight Proficiency and Flight Training Centres) were established.[44] A youth wing (*Fliegerjugend*) with a further 30,000 members was formed, which in its junior echelon concentrated on the building and flying of model aircraft, whilst the members of its senior section were able to progress to glider training at a *Segelflugabteilung*. Powered flying was provided by the *Fliegerübungsstellen* which concentrated on proficiency training for qualified pilots and by the *Fliegerausbildungsstellen* which provided primary or training to *A*-standard for student pilots:

By 1933 I had the opportunity to fly in gliders which I really enjoyed. The following year I joined a private aviation club which soon became incorporated into the *Deutsche Luftsportverband (DLV)* formed at that time to promote public interest in aeromodelling, gliding, balloons and powered aircraft as to form the basis for the new *Luftwaffe*. As a

1955 p.48.

44   *Information provided by Gr.Ltr.Krehberg* in Kreipe and Koester 1955 p.48. See also Ries 1970 pp.104-105 & Ries 1988 p.62.

member of this club and with financial assistance from my father, I had the opportunity to win my *A1* and *A2* Certificates, the latter allowing me to pilot single-engine aircraft to carry a passenger.

As we were still civilians, we normally flew the Klemm L 25. This aircraft was so light and slow that we were not authorised to take off if the weather was too windy![45]

Winfried Schmidt
Former *DLV Flugschuler*

In accordance with its predecessor the new *DLV* continued to sponsor and organise major aviation events both at regional and national level, the most important of these being the *Deutschlandflug* and the *Europa-Rundflug*.[46] The *Deutschlandflug* was an annual event in which the better pilots from the various *Fliegerlandesgruppen* competed over a series of timed stages. In 1934 the event was held in June when no less than 107 aircraft from 23 *Gruppen* took part in the four day event which covered a total of 4,700 kilometres. The winner was the *DLV Fliegerlandesgruppe Niedersachsen* whose three Klemm L 25d VIIR monoplanes gained a total of 1,361 points.[47] The *Europa-Rundflug* (also known as the *Challenge de Tourism Internationale*) on the other hand was a biennual international competition which had been won in 1932 by the Polish team from which another strong entry was expected in 1934. With national prestige at stake the *Deutschen Aero-Club* and the *DLV* prepared a formidable national team under the leadership of Theo Osterkamp which would employ three new sports types especially designed for the competition:[48]

FIGURE 2D-11 THE NATIONAL TEAM FOR THE EUROPA-RUNDFLUG SEPTEMBER 1934				
12	Brindlinger	Bf 108	HM 8U	D-IZAN
14	Theo Osterkamp	Bf 108	HM 8U	D-IMUT
15	Carl Francke	Bf 108	As 17	D-IGAK
16	Werner Junck	Bf 108	HM 8U	D-IJES
17	Wolfgang Hirth	Fi 97	HM 8U	D-IVIF
18	Bayer	Fi 97	As 17	D-IBYR
19	Hans Seidemann	Fi 97	As 17	D-IPUS
21	Hubrich	Fi 97	HM 8U	D-IZUH
22	Georg Pasewaldt	Fi 97	HM 8U	D-IDAH
23	Eberhard	Kl 36	As 17	D-IJIP
24	Stein	Kl 36	HM 8U	D-IHEK
25	Krüger	Kl 36	As 17	D-IDIR
26	Fritz Morzik	Kl 36	HM 8U	D-IBAV

45   Quoted from Schmidt W. *The thing that mattered above all else was that I could fly...* in Mombeek E, Smith J.R. and Creek E.J.1999 *Luftwaffe Colours:Jagdwaffe Vol.1 Sctn.1 Birth of the Luftwaffe Fighter Force* p.70 with the kind permission of Erik Mombeeck via Chevron Publishing. See also Information provided by *Gr.Ltr.Krehberg* in Kreipe and Koester 1955 pp.48-48a, Ries 1974 p.32 & Ries 1988 p.54.
46   Lange B. 1970 *Das Buch der deutschen Luftfahrtechnik* (hereafter cited as Lange 1970) pp.147-149.
47   *Deutschlandflug 1934* in Lange 1970 pp.147-148 & Ries 1988 pp.60-61.
48   *Europa-Rundflug 1934, Warschau* in Lange 1970 pp.148-149.

There were several good individual performances over certain stages of the 9,500 kilometre route, for example Carl Francke being the first into Berlin on the 7th September, whilst he and Werner Junck were the first to arrive in Paris. However, despite this good start the Poles were ultimately victorious with Plonczynski gaining a total of 1,896 points. The best German entrant was Hans Seidemann who achieved 1,846 points in his Fieseler Fi 97 to gain third place, whilst Osterkamp and Junck were placed fifth and sixth respectively.[49]

The various establishments and facilities controlled by *Luft Hansa,* the *DVS* and the *DLV* also provided excellent cover for the covert military units which were formed from April 1934. For example the *Jagdgruppe Döberitz* continued to be known as the *Reklamestaffel Mitteldeutschland* (Central Germany Propaganda Squadron), whilst the *Mehrzweckstaffel* (Naval Multi-Role Squadron) at List was known openly as the *DVS Zweigstelle List auf Sylt* (See 2E2 & 2E3). In some cases more than one military facility existed under a single cover, examples being the *Reklame-Abteilungschule* at Gotha which concealed both an *Aufklärungsstaffel (H)* (Tactical Reconnaissance Squadron) and a *Flugzeugführerschule* (Pilot Training School), whilst a similar arrangement existed at Kitzingen under the cover provided by the *Deutsche Versuchsanstalt für Luftfahrt* (German Aviation Research Institute)(See 2D1). However as the rate of expansion increased it became necessary to actually create some fictitious civilian organisations to cover the activities of the resident military unit. Good examples of this include the *Funkpeilversuchsinstitut des Reichsstandes der Industrie, Gr.9,* or (Group 9 of the German Industry's Wireless Research Institute), which concealed the *Kampfgruppe Tutow* (Bomber Group Tutow), and the *Depot der Luftverkehrs AG Niedersachsen* (Depot of the Lower Saxony Air Transport Co.Ltd.), at Erfurt where a *Luftpark* (Air Depot) was established (See 2D3).[50]

---

49   *Europa-Rundflug 1934, Warschau* in Lange 1970 pp.148-149. *Hptm.*Hans Seidemann was just completing his covert general staff officer's training as an *Offz.zbV.d.Chef d.Heeresleitung* at the time of the *Europa-Rundflug.* In Oct 34 he was posted to the *RLM* as a *Referent* – see service record for Hans Seidemann in Hildebrand 1992 pp.289-290.

50   *App.C Code-Designations of the Luftwaffen units during the activation period (April 12 1934)* in Schliephake H. 1971 *The Birth of the Luftwaffe* pp.63-64. See also Volker 1967 & Ries 1970 p.115.

2D3

Secret Military Aviation Facilities
(Partial Listing)

1934-1935

Cover Provided by	Location	Designated Unit Jun 33
Reperaturwerkstatt u. Ersatzteillager d. RB	Brandenburg	Kreisflugpark
Deutsche Verkehrs- Fliegerschule (DVS)	Braunschweig	Aufklärungschule
Nautische Vermessungsabteilung	Bug auf Rugen	
Erprobungsstelle d. DVL	Celle	
Deutsche Versuchsanstalt f.Luftfahrt (DVL)	Cottbus	Flugzeugführerschule
Reklamestaffel Mitteldeutschland	Döberitz	Jagdfliegergruppe
Depot d.Luftverkehrs AG Niedersachsen	Erfurt	Kreisflugpark
Hanseatische Fliegerschule	Fassberg	Kampffliegergruppe
Reklamestaffel Süddeutschland	Furth	Jagdfliegergruppe
Suddeutsche Lufthansa GmbH. (Gebirgsschule)	Gersthofen	Kreisflugpark
Luftbildvermessung	Goppingen	
Reklame-Abteilungschule	Gotha	Flugzeugführerschule u.Aufklärungsstaffel
Deutsche Luftfahrt GmbH.	Hildesheim	Fliegerbildschule
Lager d. Suddeutschen Lufthansa AG	Ingolstadt	
Technische Schule u.-Ersatzteillager d.DVS	Jüterbog	Fliegertechnische Schule u.Luftzeugamt
Luftbildlandesvermessung Westdeutschland	Kassel	
Luftdienst e.V. und Luftverkehr Schleswig-Holstein GmbH.	Kiel-Holtenau	Seefliegerstaffel u.Luftpark (See)
Deutsche Versuchsanstallt f.Luftfahrt (DVL)	Kitzingen	Fluzeugführerschule u.Aufklärungsstaffel
Lager d. Luftverkehr Ostpreussen GmbH.	Königsberg	
Hohenflugzentrale d.Deutschen Flugwetterdienstes	Lechfeld	Kampffliegerschule
Depot d.Schlesichen Luftverkehrs AG	Liegnitz	Kreisflugpark

Deutsche Verkehrs- Fliegerschule (DVS)	List auf Sylt	Seefliegerstaffel
Reichsbahnfrachtflugzentrale (RB)	Magdeburg	
Flugwetterdienst Westdeutschland	Münster	
Lager d. Luftverkehr Pommern GmbH.	Neubrandenburg	Kreisflugpark
Reklamestaffel Ostdeutschland	Königsberg-Neuhausen	Aufklärungsstaffel
Deutsche Verkehrs- Fliegerschule (DVS)	Neuruppin	Flugzeugführerschule
Luftdienst e.V.	Norderney	
Reklamestaffel Süddeutschland	Nürnberg-Fürth	Jagdfliegergruppe
Depot d. Luftverkehrs AG Niedersachsen	Pattensen	
Forst-u.Landwirtschaftliches Flugversuchs-Institut	Prenzlau	Kampfbeobachter Schule u.Aufklärungsstaffel
Lufttransportzentrale d. RB	Querfurt	
Fliegerlager d.Freiwilligen Arbeitsdienstes	Quedlinberg	
Erprobungsstelle d. R.d.L.	Rechlin	Jagdfliegergruppe
Deutsche Verkehrs-Fliegerschule (DVS)	Schleißheim	Jagdfliegerschule
Deutsche Verkehrs- Fliegerschule (DVS)	Seerappen	Aufklärungsstaffel u.Kreisflugpark
Deutsche Versuchsanstallt f.Luftfahrt (DVL)	Seligenstadt	
Depot d. Luftverkehrs- gesellschaft Brandenburg	Stendal	Kreisflugpark
Küstenwetterdienstzentrale Ostsee	Stralsund	
Funkpeilversuchsinstitut d.Reichsstandes d.Industrie Gr.9	Tutow	Kampffliegergruppe
Lager d. Suddeutschen Lufthansa AG	Ulm	Kreisflugpark
Deutsche Verkehrs-Fliegerschule (DVS)	Warnemünde	Seefliegerschule
Küstenwetterdienstzentrale Nordsee	Wilhelmshaven	
Deutsche Luftfahrt GmbH.	Würzburg	Flugzeugführerschule
Truppenübungsplatz	Wustrow	Flakartillerieschule

Liste der Tarnbezeichnungen der aufzustellenden Verbände der Luftwaffe LC Nr.1594/34 zbV. geh. Kdos. 12.4.1934

2E1

The First Crisis

Hitler withdraws Germany from the Geneva Disarmament Conference

The rise to power of the *Nationalsozialistische deutsche Arbeiterpartei (NSDAP)* in Germany had been accomplished at a time when the other European powers had been concerned with the issue of international disarmament.[1] Following the 1928 Pact of Paris which had renounced war as an instrument of national policy, the vast majority of European nations had agreed to a major disarmament conference at Geneva, beginning in February 1932.[2] Initially the delegates had been given a relatively wide brief aimed at the progressive reduction and ultimate elimination of weapons specified in the Treaty of Versailles. However given the growing public concern with aerial bombardment discussion had swung progressively towards this aspect of warfare at the virtual expense of all the remaining issues.[3]

Predictably Hitler's interest in the Geneva Conference centred less on disarmament and more on military parity. Following his well publicised "Peace Speech" in the *Reichstag* (German Parliament) during May 1933 he had instructed his Geneva delegates, including *Maj.a.D.*Waldemar Reinicke of the *Allgemeines Luftamt (LB)*, to offer German co operation In the limitation of air armament and the prohibition of bombing.[4] *(Photo 2E-1)* Failing international agreement in these areas he

1   Terraine J. 1985 *The Right of the Line: The Royal Air Force in the European War 1939-1945* (hereafter cited as Terraine 1985) p.8.

2   Terraine J. 1974 *The Mighty Continent: A View of Europe in the Twentieth Century* p.139. *"Disarmament - the "general limitation of the armaments of all nations" envisaged in the Treaty of Versailles - became the great quest of the post war years and nowhere was it pursued more wholeheartedly than Britain, where dread of military commitment was linked to dread of military expenditure, and both were excused by constant reference to the "futility of War".* The Pact of Paris (also called the Kellogg Pact) had been signed by the representatives of 15 nations, including Germany, Britain, France, Italy, Japan and the USA on the 27 Aug 28 - see Terraine 1985 p.7. Some 60 nations, including non-members of the League of Nations such as the *USA* and the *USSR*, attended the Geneva conferences that were held at intervals between Feb 32 - Nov 34 - Snyder L.L. 1976 *Encyclopaedia of the Third Reich* (hereafter cited as Snyder 1976) p.68.

3   Terraine 1985 p.8. The worry over aerial bombardment reflected the popular mood in much of Europe and in particular Britain, the only nation to have suffered sustained aerial attack during the Great War. Just days before the Conference opened in Feb 32 Japanese warplanes had bombed Shanghai. In his famous speech in the House of Commons on the 10 Nov 32 Stanley Baldwin stated: *"I think it is well also for the man in the street to realise that there is no power on earth that can prevent him from being bombed. Whatever people may tell him, the bomber will always get through"* – quoted from Collier B. 1957 *The Defence of the United Kingdom* p.29 with the kind permission of the IWM: 51498 (Held at the Department of Collections Access, the Imperial War Museum). See also Dean M. 1979 *The RAF and the Two World Wars* p.59. At this stage in these negotiations there were some in the British Government who were prepared to sacrifice the RAF in order to secure an international disarmament agreement. Expenditure on the RAF had already been reduced in the Estimates of 1932-33 - see Grey C.G. 1940 *A History of the Air Ministry* pp.221-224.

4   Shirer W.L. 1963 *The Rise and Fall of the Third Reich: A History of Nazi Germany* (hereafter cited as Shirer 1963) pp.209-210. Hitler delivered this speech to the *Reichstag* on the 17 May 33. Hitler cleverly embraced President Roosevelt's call for peace and international disarmament made on the preceding day. Hitler stated: *"Germany is entirely ready to renounce all offensive weapons if the armed nations, on their side, will destroy their offensive weapons... Germany would also be perfectly ready to disband her entire military establishment and the destroy the small amount of arms remaining to her, if the neighbouring countries will do the same...Germany is prepared to agree to any solemn pact on non-aggression, because she does not think of attacking but only of acquiring security"* - sourced from Shirer 1963 *The*

declared that as an alternative Germany must be accorded military parity with her neighbours. A threefold expansion of the *Reichsheer* was then proposed, albeit with the suggestion that tanks, poison gas and heavy artillery would still be prohibited.[5] These proposals were all rejected by the British and French governments and on the 14 October 1933 Hitler formally withdrew Germany from the Disarmament Conference.[6] In making this decision he had *Präsident* Hindenburg's full confidence.[7]

Several weeks of uncertainty followed. Foreign intervention was expected to prevent Germany from rearming in contravention of the Versailles Treaty. Hitler decided to stand firm in such an eventuality and he instructed *Gen.d.Inf.*Werner von Blomberg, the newly appointed *Reichswehrminister*, to issue secret directives to the *Reichswehr* that any military sanctions would be met by force.[8] The *Führer's* brinkmanship proved worrying to many, both in the *Reichstag* and the *Reichswehr*. *Staatssekretär* Erhard Milch noted that Göring was deeply depressed at this time although this could be attributed to the anniversary of his wife's death.[9] Predictably the crisis did not prevent Göring from visiting his wife's grave in Sweden in late October and therefore the responsibility for aerial defensive measures devolved to his *Staatssekretär*.[10]

Tasked with the aerial defence of the capital and the central German industrial centres Milch knew that he could only offer token resistance with the three *Staffeln* (Squadrons) of the *Reklamesabteilung (Propaganda Branch)*.[11] Following earlier discussions in Italy with Mussolini and

Rise and Fall of the Third Reich: A History of Nazi Germany p.210 Secker & Warburg Ltd.

5   *Milich Diary, 25 May 1933* in Irving D. 1973 *The Rise and Fall of the Luftwaffe: The Life of Luftwaffe Marshal Erhard Milch* (hereafter cited as Irving 1973) p.32. In the absence of any meaningful concessions by the major European Powers Reinicke had requested that Germany be permitted a force of 500 fighter and reconnaissance aircraft. See also *Abschrift einer Aktionnotiz des Ministerialdirektors Fisch (RLM) vom 22.5.1933 zur Vorlage für Staatssekretär Milch über ein am Vormittag gefuhrtes Telefongesprach mit Major Reinicke (LB-Amt)* in Volker K-H. 1967 *Die deutsche Luftwaffe 1933-1939: Aufbau, Führung und Rüstung der Luftwaffe sowie die Entwicklung der deutschen Luftkriegstheorie* p.26. Privately little of advantage to Germany was expected from the Geneva Conference. On 1 Jun 33 *Gen.d.Inf.*Blomberg *(RWM)* informed his commanders: *"Over the next few years the Wehrmacht must devote itself wholly to the task of creating the reserves denied us until now. A Panzerarmee and a Luftwaffe are to be established. The Offizierkorps of the latter is to be an elite, fired only by a will to win. It will be necessary to give it preference over everything else, and this must be understood by the other branches of the Wehrmacht"* – quoted from *The Liebmann Papers* in the *Institut für Zeitgeschichte ED 1 (GenLt.*C.Liebmann's unpublished memoranda on Hitler's and Blomberg's principal speeches and conferences) in Irving 1973 *The Rise and Fall of the Luftwaffe: The Life of Luftwaffe Marshal Erhard Milch* p.32 with the knowledge of the Orion Publishing Group.

6   Shirer 1963 p.210 & Irving 1973 p.36. By Oct 33 it had become clear that the major European Powers would not agree to immediate disarmament - eight years being proposed as a transition period. Germany's withdrawal from the Disarmament Conference was not the only reason for its failure. The French were insistent that their security be guaranteed prior to any agreement on disarmament - see Shirer W.L. 1969 *The Collapse of the Third Republic: An Inquiry into the Fall of France in 1940* pp.257-258 & Snyder 1976 p.68.

7   Irving D. 1978 *The War Path: Hitler's Germany 1933-1939* (hereafter cited as Irving 1978) p.32. Hitler sent Walther Funk to collect the *Präsident* from Ostpreussen to sign the necessary authorisation. Hindenburg's approval was unconditional: *"At last a man with the courage of his convictions!"*

8   *Blomberg's Directive*, TMWC, XXXIV pp.487-491 in Shirer 1963 p.210. On the 30 Jan 33 Blomberg, *Bfr.Wehrkreis I*, had acted decisively in support of the new regime – Schleicher, Hammerstein & Reichenau all appear to have had doubts. On that day Hindenburg appointed him to succeed Schleicher as *Reichswehrminister*, whilst Hitler had already succeeded Schleicher as *Reichskanzler* - see Seaton A. 1982 *The German Army 1933-1945* p.33, & 35 and Mitcham S.W.1988 *Hitler's Field Marshals and their Battles* pp.18-20. *GenOb.*von Blomberg issued a Directive to the *Reichswehr* on the 14 Oct 33 concerning the defence of the Reich. Item 5 assigned the following mission to the *Reichsluftwaffe*: *"Defence in the air over Berlin and the industrial region of Mitteldeutschland, with main emphasis on Berlin"* - quoted from Grabmann W. GenMaj.a.D. 1956 *German Air Force Air Defence Operations Vol.I 1933-41* USAF Historical Studies No.164 (hereafter cited as Grabmann 1956) p.25.

9   *Milch Diary, 12 Oct 33* in Irving 1973 p.36.

10   Irving 1973 p.36. See also Irving D. 1989 *Göring: A Biography* p.135. Although fighters and anti-aircraft guns were in short supply, the *Luftwaffe* did possess a viable aircraft reporting system and the authority to order passive air defence measures - see Grabmann 1956 p.25.

11   *Milch Diary, 20, 23 & 24 May 1933* in Irving 1973 p.36. In Göring's absence Milch discussed plans for the last

Balbo, it had been hoped to re-equip these units with the new Fiat CR.30 fighter but as these had aircraft had not materialised this had left Germany dependent on the indigenous Arado Ar 64 despite its known handling problems.[12] Nor would resistance have been prolonged on the ground. Defence lines were drawn but none had been fortified and the *Reichsheer* would have been too weak to hold off a determined military offensive.[13]

FIGURE 2E-1 COVERT OPERATIONAL UNITS 1 OCTOBER 1933	
Reklamestaffel Ostdeutschland	Königsberg-Neuhausen
Reklamestaffel Mitteldeutschland	Berlin-Staaken
Reklamestaffel Süddeutschland	Nürnberg-Fürth
Seeübungsstaffel	Warnemünde
Severa (Luftdienst eV)	Kiel-Holtenau

Fortunately for Germany Hitler's gamble paid off. He had correctly judged the political and public mood in both France and Britain and within a month he had consolidated his own political position within Germany through national elections for a single party state and a referendum on his decision to withdraw from Geneva. Both were overwhelming in favour of the *NSDAP* and its *Führer*.[14]

ditch defence of Germany with Blomberg.

12   Irving 1973 p.31. For the Ar 64's shortcomings - see Kosin R. 1983 *Die Entwicklung der deutschen Jagdflugzeug* p.75.
13   *Blomberg's Directive*, TMWC, XXXIV pp.487-491 in Shirer 1963 p.211. Blomberg's secret directive to the *Reichsheer* and *Reichsmarine* envisaged a holding operation in the west against France, in the south against Czechosolvakia and in the east against Poland - see also *Milch Diary, 25 Oct 33* in Irving 1973 p.36.
14   Shirer 1963 pp.211-212 & Irving 1978 p.32. With Hindenburg's full support Hitler called for national elections on the 12 Nov 33 for a new single party (*NSDAP*) State and a Plebiscite on his policy at Geneva. In a remarkable turn out 96% of the electorate voted with 95% approval for Hitler's decision to withdraw from the Disarmament Conference. The vote for the single party state was 92%. An overwhelming declaration of public approval for Hitler and the *NSDAP*.

2E2

The Formation of Covert Military Units 1934

On the 1 April 1934 the first combat units were created from cadres provided by the three *Reklamestaffeln* (Propaganda Squadrons) and the *Seeübungsstaffel* (Naval Proficiency Squadron) (See 2E3).[1] The *Fliegergruppe Döberitz* (Döberitz Air Group) was the first major unit with a *Stab* (Headquarters) being established on the 1 May, whilst the component *Staffeln* were activated from the 1 July 1934 with personnel and equipment from the *Reklamestaffeln Mittel-und Süddeutschland* (Photo 2E-2).[2] Initially this *Gruppe*, and those that followed in 1934/35 were formed on the basis of about half the planned war establishment. Most of the pilots assigned to the *Fliegergruppe Döberitz* were graduates of Lipetsk and Schleißheim and the initial equipment was the Arado Ar 65E/F to which a few examples of the new He 51A-0 were added for evaluation in the summer of 1934.[3]

As initially equipped the *Jagdgruppe Döberitz* had only a very limited operational capability. The short range of both the Ar 65E/F and the later He 51A effectively restricted the *Gruppe* to an area bounded by a line from Schwerin in the north, to Braunschweig in the west, to Leipzig and Görlitz in the south and east. Furthermore following any operation at that distance from base the defending fighters would be obliged to land to refuel and rearm.[4]

In the meantime the *Reklamestaffel Ostdeutschland* at Neuhausen/Ostpr. was transformed into the first *Fernaufklärungsstaffel* (Long Range Reconnaissance Squadron) (*Hptm.i.G.*Fritz Reinshagen), whilst another *Staffel* was formed on the same date at Prenzlau/Brandenburg.[5] Both these units were

1   *RdL LP Nr.1860/34 g.Kdos. II 2, Berlin, den 8.3.1934* in DZ/MGFA, Akte II L 49, Teil 2 in Volker K-H. 1967 *Die deutsche Luftwaffe 1933-1939: Aufbau, Führung und Rüstung der Luftwaffe sowie die Entwicklung der deutschen Luftkriegstheorie* (hereafter cited as Volker 1967) p.45. This order (*Befehl*) assigned personnel to the new *Fliegergruppen*. The three *Reklamestaffeln* were known collectively as the *Reklameabteilung* by this time.

2   Volker 1967 p.46, Schliephake H. 1971 *The Birth of the Luftwaffe* (hereafter cited as Schliephake 1971) p.32 & Ries K. 1974 *Luftwaffen-Story 1935-1939* (hereafter cited as Ries 1974) pp.89-90. See also *RdL LA Nr.1090/34 g.Kdos. L.A.II 2 A, Berlin, 20.April 1934 Aufstellung des Jagdgeschwaders 132 in Döberitz* in Mombeeck E. and Roba J-L. Undated *In the Skies of France – A Chronicle of JG 2 Richthofen Vol.1: 1934-1940* p.12-13.

3   *Aus der alteren Geschichte der neuen Luftwaffe* in Priller J. 1980 *JG 26: Geschichte eines Jagdgeschwaders. Das JG 26 (Schlageter) 1937-1945* pp.369-370 & Prien J., Stemmer G., Rodeike P. and Bock W. 2000 *Die Jagdfliegerverbände der Deutschen Luftwaffe 1934 bis 1945 Teil 1 Vorkriegszeit und Einsatz über Polen - 1934 bis 1939* (cited hereafter as Prien et al 2000) p.111 & 122. As *Ltr.DVS Zweigstelle Würzburg Hptm.a.D.*Robert Ritter von Greim re-enlisted in the *Reichsheer* with the rank of *Maj.* on the 1 Jan 34. He formally transferred to the secret *Luftwaffe* on the 1 Apr 34. Although not a career officer, von Greim's war record of *25 Luftsiege* with a *Plm* on th 8 Oct 18 and his continued association with aviation from 1924 made him a natural choice as commander of the *Luftwaffe's* first *Jagdgruppe* - see Angolia J.R. and Hackney C.R. 1984 *The Pour le Mérite and Germany's First Aces*(hereafter cited as Angolia and Hackney 1984) pp.250-251 and service record for Robert Ritter von Greim in Hildebrand K.F.1990 *Die Generale der deutschen Luftwaffe 1935-1945 Band 1 A-G* pp.387-389.

4   Grabmann W. GenMaj.a.D. 1956 *German Air Force Air Defence Operations Vol.I 1933-41* USAF Historical Studies No.164 p.26. The fighter defence of München could be provided from Schleißheim but it would be impossible for fighters based in southern Bayern to intervene effectively over central Germany.

5   *RdL LP Nr.1860/34 g.Kdos. II 2, Berlin, den 8.3.1934* in DZ/MGFA, Akte II L 49, Teil 2 in Volker 1967 p.46. This *Staffel* was expected to reach its nominal strength between Jul-Oct 34 - see Ries 1974 p.80 & 85. *Hptm.i.G.*Reinshagen was a career officer who had seen brief wartime service as a *Beobachter* with *Fl-Abtn. A 277 &*

intended to fulfil the strategic or long range reconnaissance function although given their primary equipment, the Heinkel He 45C, it is hard to see just what they could have actually achieved on active service (See 2C3).[6] On the 20 April 1934 orders were issued for a third *Fernaufklärungsstaffel* to be formed at Celle/Nord Sachsen (*Hptm.*Günther Wieland) as part of the resident *Fliegerschule* (Flying School) and this too received the He 45C/D during the period July to November 1934; on the 29 November this Staffel was instructed to re-locate to Größenhain/Sachsen.[7]

FIGURE 2E-2 OFFICER PERSONNEL ASSIGNED TO THE FLIEGERGRUPPE DÖBERITZ SUMMER 1934		
Kommandeur -	Maj.Robert Ritter von Greim	
Adjutant -	Oblt.Hans-Günter von Kornatzki	
Hauptmann beim Stabe -	Hptm.Oskar Dinort	
Chef der Stabskompanie -	Hptm.Heinz von Beaulieu-Marconnay	
Käpitan 1.Staffel -	Hptm.Johann Raithel	
Käpitan 2.Staffel -	Hptm.Hans-Hugo Witt	
Käpitan 3.Staffel -	Hptm.Hans-Jurgen von Cramon-Taubadel	
Staffeloffiziere		
Werner Andres	Siegfried von Eschwege	Erich Noack
Nicolaus von Below	Gotthardt Handrick	Ralph von Rettberg
Alexander von Blomberg	Ekkehard Hefter	Walter Rubensdorffer
Erich Bode	Lothar von Janson	Wehrmann
Hans-Heinrich Brustellin	Walter Kienzle	Otto-Hans Winterer
Hans Busolt	Siegfried Lehmann	

The first bomber units were also formed as a result of the 20 April order with *Kampfgruppen* (Bomber Groups) being activated at both Fassberg (*Obst.*Alfred Keller) and Tutow (*Maj.*August Ploch) on the 1 June 1934.[8] In both cases a *Stab* and two *Staffeln* were initially established, the third

39 (L) in 1918 - see service record for Fritz Reinshagen in Hildebrand K.F.1992 *Die Generale der deutschen Luftwaffe 1935-1945 Band 3 O-Z* (hereafter cited as Hildebrand 1992) pp.97-98.

6 Nowarra H.J. 1982 *Fernaufklärer 1915-1945: Enstehung, Entwicklung, Einsatz* p.26.

7 Ries 1974 p.85. See also Volker 1967 p.46 & Nowarra 1982 p.26. *Hptm.*Wieland was a career officer who had seen wartime service as a *Beobachter* with *FA A 273* & *FA 428*. He had undergone refresher training at Lipetsk during 27/29. Transferred to the *Lw.* on the 1 May 34 his first posting was to *Fl-Div.1* - see service record for Günther Wieland in Hildebrand 1992 pp.511-512.

8 *RdL LP Nr.1860/34 g.Kdos. II 2, Berlin, den 8.3.1934 in DZ/MGFA, Akte II L 49, Teil 2* in Volker 1967 p.46 & Ries 1974 p.115. *Bombenkeller,* the former *Kdr.BoGohl 1* and *Plm* (4 Dec 17) was something of a legend in wartime German military aviation. Active in civil aviation throughout the 20s he had been *Ltr.d.DVS Staaken* later *Braunschweig* from 1 May 25, he was another natural choice as one of the *Luftwaffe's* first operational commanders – see Angolia and Hackney 1984 pp.172-173 and service record for Alfred Keller in Hildebrand K.F.1991 *Die Generale der deutschen Luftwaffe 1935-1945 Band 2 H-N* (hereafter cited as Hildebrand 1991) pp.165-166. August Ploch was a career *Artillerie-Offz.* who had served in *FA 202* in 1917-18. He may have been *Kdr.I./KG 252* although he has also been listed as a *Staffelkäpitan* – see service record for August Ploch in Hilderand 1992 pp.44-45 & Zweng IV de H.L. and Stankey D.G. 2013 *Luftwaffe Officer Career Summaries.* The suggestion that *Maj.*Paul

Staffel being activated at a later date.[9] Primary equipment was the Junkers Ju 52/3m g3e although both *Fliegergruppen* were expected to quickly re-equip with the dedicated Dornier Do 11D (Photo 2E-3).[10]

FIGURE 2E-3 COMMAND PERSONNEL OF THE FLIEGERGRUPPE FASSBERG SUMMER 1934		
Kommandeur	-	Obst.Alfred Keller
Adjutant	-	Hptm.Klaus Uebe
Käpitan 1.Staffel	-	Maj.Georg Rieke
Käpitan 2.Staffel	-	Hptm.Arno Salenge de Drappe
Käpitan 3.Staffel	-	Maj.Egbert Frhr. von Althaus

Operationally all of these these units came under the command of *Obst.*Hugo Sperrle whose *Fliegerdivision 1* (1st Air Division) would be reinforced in an emergency by *Hptm.a.D.*Robert Knauss's *Deutsche Luft Hansa* component, the *Bombengeschwader 1* (Bomber Wing 1) (See 2A3 & 2C2).[11] During this formative phase Sperrle was also the designated *Kommandeur der Heeresflieger* (Commander of Army Aviation) despite the very different demands of this position.[12] Initially just two *Heeresaufklärungsstaffeln* (Army Reconnaissance Squadrons) were formed, these being offshoots of the *Fliegerschulen* at Cottbus and Gotha (See 2D1).[13] Initially these units were equipped with the Albatros L 78 and He 45C.[14] In the event of war the *Cottbus Staffel* would have been attached to *GenOb.*Gerd von Rundstedt's *Gruppenkommando I* (Army Group I) at Berlin, whilst the *Gotha Staffel* would have supported *GenOb.*Wilhelm Ritter von Leeb's *Gruppenkommando II* (Army Group II) at Kassel.[15] Later in 1934 the new He 46 was introduced into both *Staffeln*.[16]

It inevitably took some time for the new *Fliegergruppen* to reach their full establishment of men and machines and it was not to be until the autumn that it was possible to activate the

---

Schultheiss may have been *Kdr.Fl.Gr.Tutow* during 1 Apr 34 – 31 Mar 35 – see Zeng IV de, H.L., and Stankey D.G. 2008 *Bomber Units of the Luftwaffe 1933-1945: A Reference Source* Vol.2 p.311 - is unlikely as he is known to have been *Chef.Pers.Abt.* in the *LS-Amt* until the 30 Sep 34 when he formally transferred to the *Luftwaffe*. Three months later on the 1 Jan 35 he was appointed *Luftattache* in Budapest – see service record for Paul Schultheiss in Hildebrand 1992 pp.254-255.

9   Ries 1974 p.115. In the case of the *Fliegergruppe Tutow* the *Stab* was activated on the 1 Jun 34 and the *1.u.2.Kampfstaffel* on the 1 Jul 34. The *3.Staffel* was not established until the 1 Apr 35.

10   Green W. 1970 *The War Planes of the Third Reich* (hereafter cited as Green 1970) pp.110-112. On-going problems with the Do 11C/D curtailed these plans. Although 77 examples were delivered during 1934 very few were assigned to Fassberg and Tutow - see *Table 1-F German Aircraft Production in 1934* in Vajda F.A. & Dancey P.1998 *German Aircraft Industry and Production 1933-1945* p.18.

11   Ries 1974 p.112-115. *Bombengeschwader 1* was in fact the first unit to be established. In Jun 34 the *BG 1* provided the nucleus for the *BKG 172* & *274*. Nominally based in Berlin these unit's war stations were Tutow and Fassberg respectively where they would reinforce the two regular *Kampfgruppen*. *Hptm.a.D.*Knauss was *Leiter der Verkehrsabteilung der Lufthansa* - see service record for Robert Knauss in Hildebrand 1991 pp.189-190.

12   Maass B. 1955 *The Organisation of the German Air Force High Command and Higher Echelon Headquarters within the German Air Force* USAF Historical Studies No.190 p.54.

13   *RdL LP Nr.1860/34 g.Kdos. II 2, Berlin, den 8.3.1934* in DZ/MGFA, Akte II L 49, Teil 2 in Volker 1967 p.46. See also Ries 1974 p.72 & 75. This source gives Münster as the base for *Gr.Kdo.II H-Staffel*.

14   Ries 1974 p.75.

15   Seaton A. 1982 *The German Army 1933-1945* p.7 & Mitcham S.W.1988 *Hitler's Field Marshals and their Battles* p.129 & 284.

16   Green 1970 p.262, Ries 1974 p.75 & Nowarra H.J. 1981 *Nahaufklärer 1910-1945: Die Augen des Heeres* p.40.

Sturzkampfgruppe (Dive Bomber Group) that had been planned as far back as October 1933.[17] However training in dive attacks had not been neglected and during this formative period von Greim's *Fliegergruppe Döberitz* had used both the Ar 65E/F and the Heinkel He 50A for experimental work in this area.[18] Aircraft of both these types would later be transferred to Schwerin in where a new *Fliegergruppe* was established, initially with a strength of just one *Staffel*.[19]

In response to Milch's earlier order for the secrecy the *RLM* went to considerable lengths to preserve the anonymity of the covert *Fliegergruppen*.[20] It was quite possible for even senior civilian managers to be unaware of the true nature of the extent of this deception. For example Milch's adjutant, Hans-Karl von Winterfeld, recorded in his unpublished memoirs that *Deutsche Luft Hansa's* Commercial Manager almost collapsed when he received a massive bill to cover the operating costs of the *Süddeustche Lufthansa GmbH*.[21] This almost defunct subsidiary had only ever operated a handful of obsolescent aircraft on local routes, but in 1934 it was employed by the *RLM* as cover for a Kreisflugpark (Military Air Depot) which was developed in secret at Augsburg-Gersthofen.[22]

17   Schliephake 1971 p.32.
18   Green 1970 p.27 & 266 and Schliephake 1971 p.32.
19   Ries K. 1970 *Luftwaffe Bd.1 Die Maulwurfe 1919-1935* (hereafter cited as Ries 1970) p.116 & Nauroth H. 1988 *Stukageschwader 2 Immelmann: Eine Dokumentation über das erfolgreichste deutsche Stukageschwader* p.21. There is a great deal of confusion regarding the exact formation date for the *Fliegergruppe Schwerin*. Whilst many authors cite Oct 34, one authoritative source indicates 1 Oct 35 - see Ries 1974 p.139 and this is backed by the fact that the I./JG 132 did not transfer its 24 He 50 *Sturzbomber* to Schwerin until this date – see Prien et al 2000 p.111, whilst the earliest known postings were on the 1 Jul 35 – see de Zeng H.L. and Stankey D.G. *Luftwaffe Officer Career Summaries*. However given the fact that the *Fliegergruppe* was awarded the Honour Title *"Immelmann"* on the 3 Apr 35 - see *Luftwaffen-Verordnungsblatt Nr.12, 29.5.1935* p.80 in Davis B.L. 1991 *Uniforms and Insignia of the Luftwaffe Vol.1: 1933-1940* p.185 – the earlier date of Oct 34 may be correct insofar as a cadre or nucleus is concerned.
20   *Order on Camouflage of Luftwaffe, Signed Milch, 19 Jun 33* in Volker K.H. 1968 *"Dokumente und Documentarfotos zue Geschichte der deutschen Luftwaffe"* p.183.
21   *Hans-Karl von Winterfeld (DLH Verkehrs-Inspektion), unpublished memoirs* in Irving D. 1973 *The Rise and Fall of the Luftwaffe: The Life of Luftwaffe Marshal Erhard Milch* p.33.
22   *App. C Code-Designations of the Luftwaffen units during the activation period (April 12 1934)* in Schliephake 1971 pp.63-64. See also Volker 1967 p.64 & Ries 1970 pp.115.

2E3

The Development of Naval Aviation 1933-1935

The initial covert naval unit to be formed was the *Seeübungsstaffel* (Naval Proficiency Squadron) which was established within the *DVS Zweigstelle (See)* at Warnemünde on the 1 October 1933. Equipped with the first He 60A floatplanes it was under the command of *Oblt.z.See* Martin Harlinghausen.[1] A considerable expansion was then planned and in February 1934 LA II *(Organisation)* issued activation orders for a *Führer der Marineluftstreitkräfte* and three operational *Staffeln* within the structure provided by the *Gehobene Luftamtes Kiel*:[2]

FIGURE 2E-4 ACTIVATION OF THE MARINELUFTSREITKRAFTE
1 JULY 1934

"...Gem.o.a.Verfugung (LA Nr.500/34 g.Kdos. LA II ZA v. 10.2.34)

with effect from the 1.7.34 the Headquarters of the Führer der Marineluftstreitkräfte (F.d.Luft) is to be formed at Kiel.

From this day the F.d.Luft will undertake the formation of:

I)	Stab and Geschw.(See) Fl.G./116 Holtenau
II)	1.Aufklärungsstaffel (See) Fl.1/116 at Holtenau
III)	1.Jagdstaffel (See) Fl.1/136 at Holtenau
IV)	1.Mehrzweckstaffel (See) Fl.1./286 at List/Sylt
V)	Fliegerhorsttrupp Holtenau with kleine Bildstelle
VI)	Fliegerhorsttrupp List with kleine Bildstelle

F.d.Luft comes under the L.K.VI (See) from 6.7.34..."

The *Gehobene Luftamtes Kiel* was the first command structure to be established this being the naval equivalent of the territorial *Gehobene Luftamter* (See 2A3). The *Präsident des Gehobene*

---

1   Jung D., Wenzel B. and Abendroth A.1977 *Die Schiffe und Boote der deutschen Seeflieger 1912-1976* p.49 (hereafter cited as Jung et al 1977) p.48 & Kurowski F.1979 *Seekrieg aus der Luft* (hereafter cited as Kurowski 1979) p.19. The last *Lehrgang* held by the *DVS* at Warnemünde for the secret *Luftwaffe* was held between Oct 33 - Sep 34. Harlinghausen had just completed his flight training as a pilot and observer whilst nominally at the disposal of the *Chef des Marinestation der Ostsee* - see service record for Martin Harlinghusen in Hildebrand K.F.1991 *Die Generale der deutschen Luftwaffe 1935-1945 Band 2 H-N* (hereafter cited as Hildebrand 1991) pp.32-33. He 60 *Seeflugzeuge* known to have been assigned to the *Seeübungsstaffel* include He 60C D-2507 and He 60D D-2511 & 2512 – see www.airhistory.org.uk

2   *LA Nr.500/34 g.Kdos. LA II ZA v. 10.2.34* in Jung et al 1977 p.49. Author's translation.

Luftamtes Kiel was *KonAdm.a.D.*Konrad Zander, the former *Chef der Luftschützgruppe*, and his first chief of staff was *FregKpt.*Rudolf Stark.[3] Although the *Gehobene Luftamtes Kiel* had a similar structure to the other *Luftamter* it did differ in that its territorial responsibilities were of necessity confined to a narrow coastal band in north-western and north-eastern Germany together with the coastal districts of Ostpreussen (See 2E4). It also had an unusual degree of functionality being only concerned with naval aviation. This independence was formally expressed in the following memorandum issued by the *Marineleitung* and accepted by the *RLM* on the 22 January 1934:

> The operational air force *(Luftwaffe)* is under the authority and control of the *Reichsluftfahrtministerium.*
>
> The *Marinefliegerverbände* are under the command of the *Führer der Marine-luftstreitkräfte (F.d.Luft).* They represent an indivisible part of the Fleet *(Flottenkommando).* Material and personnel are provided by the *Reichsminister der Luftfahrt.*
>
> The *Führer der Marineluftstreitkräfte* is a commanding officer designated by the *Reichsminister der Luftfahrt.* In taking over his naval command, he and all air forces under his command are transferred to the *Flottenkommando* with regard to all matters of a strategic, tactical or disciplinary nature. He is responsible for the preservation and development of the Naval, aeronautical and technical training of personnel and for the tactical readiness of the units under his command.
>
> The aircraft of the *Marineluftstreitkräfte*, their equipment and weapons will be supplied by the *Reichsminister der Luftfahrt.* The aircraft and personnel provided by the *Reichsminister der Luftfahrt* will be assigned to the *Führer der Marineluftstreitkräfte.* Thereby they will be transferred to the authority of the *Flottenkommando.*"[4]

To help maintain its authority and influence over the development of naval aviation the *Reichsmarine* transferred between 60 and 80 naval officers to fill command positions and provide the nucleus for the planned *Marinefliegerverbände*. In addition Naval officers on the reserve and retired lists *(d.Res. & a.D.)* were recalled to take up administrative and other positions within the *Gehobene Luftamtes Kiel* and its developing ground organisation:[5]

---

3   *RdL LD III, LD Nr.8177/34 gKdos., Berlin, den 28.3.1934* in DZ/MGFA, Akte II L 49, Teil 2 in Volker K-H. 1967 *Die deutsche Luftwaffe 1933-1939: Aufbau, Führung und Rüstung der Luftwaffe sowie die Entwicklung der deutschen Luftkriegstheorie* (hereafter cited as Volker 1967) p.36 & Jung et al 1977 p.49. The *Gehobene Luftamtes Kiel* is not to be confused with the *Luftamt Kiel* which was formed in Oct 33 to regulate civil aviation within the *Gehobene Luftamtes. Präsident d.Luftamt Kiel* was *Maj.*Konrad Pueschel - see Hildebrand K.F.1992 *Die Generale der deutschen Luftwaffe 1935-1945 Band 3 O-Z* (hereafter cited as Hildebrand 1992) pp.64-65. Zander's previous posting had been as *Inspekteur des Torpedo-und Minenwesens* - see service record for Konrad Zander in Hildebrand 1992 pp.558-559.

4   Quoted from US Office of Naval Intelligence 1947 *German Naval Air 1933 to 1945: A Report based on German Naval Staff Documents* in Isby D.C.(Ed.) 2005 *The Luftwaffe and the War at Sea 1939-45: As seen by officers of the Kriegsmarine and Luftwaffe* (Cited hereafter as USONI in Isby (Ed.) 2005) pp.29-30 with the kind permission of Lionel Leventhal Ltd./Greenhill Books. The *Marineleitung* was the *Reichsmarine's* Supreme Naval Command - see Mallmann Showell J.P. 1979 *The German Navy in World War Two: A Reference Guide to the Kriegsmarine 1935-1945* (hereafter cited as Mallmann Showell 1979) p.56 & Mallmann Showell J.P. 1999 *German Navy Handbook 1939-1945* pp.219-221. The memorandum followed a key conference held between officers from the *RLM* and the *Marineleitung* on the 2 Dec 33 which sought to answer the question: *"What is the position of the Kommandierenden Admiral (Luftstreitkräfte) (B.d.Luft)? He holds a position similar to the Kommandierenden General, Heeresflieger (Kdr.d.Heeresflieger). Both are and will remain under the command of the Reichsluftfahrtministerium in every regard"* – see USONI in Isby (Ed.) 2005 p.29.

5   Gaul W. Obst.i.G.a.D. *The German Naval Air Force, 1933 - September 1939* in Isby D.C. (Ed.) 2005 (hereafter cited as Gaul in Isby (Ed.) 2005) p.84. See also Hildebrand K.F.1990-92 *Die Generale der deutschen Luftwaffe 1935-1945 Band 1-3.*

FIGURE 2E-5 KNOWN COMMAND POSITIONS WITHIN THE GEHOBENE LUFTAMTES KIEL 1 OCTOBER 1934	
Präsident	KonAdm.Konrad Zander
CdS	FregKpt.Rudolf Stark
Ia	FregKpt.Volkswirt Weigand
I Wetter	ObRegRat.Rudolf Benkendorf (15 Oct 34)
IIa	KorvKpt.Theopil Gautier
IVb (San)	ObStArzt.Dr.med.Martin Sabersky-Mussigbrodt

To protect the interests of the *Reichsmarine* within the *Luftwaffe* as a whole, some officers were assigned to the *Organisations Abteilung (LA II)* (Air Command Office – Organisation Branch), the *Personalamt (LP)* (*Luftwaffe* Personnel Office) and the *Nachschub-Gruppe* (Supply Group) within the *RLM*, for example *KorvKpt.*Ulrich Kessler was a *Gruppenleiter* in the *LA*, *KorvKpt.*Hans Siburg was an *Abteilungsleiter LC II* (Technical Office – Development Branch) and *FregKpt.*Volkswirt Weigand was a *Referent* (Desk Officer) in the Organisations-Abteilung *LA II*.[6] To represent the interests of naval aviation within the *Reichsmarine*, *KorvKpt.*Hans Ritter was assigned to the *Marineleitung* on the 1 October 1933 as the *5.Admiralstabs-Offizier* (5th Admiralty Staff Officer) with specific responsibility for naval air operations *(Flugwesen)*.[7]

The first units, necessarily covert, were formed in July 1934 (See also 2E2). Within the cover provided by the "civilian" *Luftdienst GmbH* the *Stab Fliegergeschwader (See) 116* was established at Kiel-Holtenau on the 1 July together with the He 60B equipped *Seeaufklärungsstaffel (M 1 later 1.(M)/116)*, the latter being created from Harlinghausen's *Seeübungsstaffel* which was then disbanded.[8] Two weeks later on the 15 July 1934 the *Seejagdstaffel (J 1, later 1./JG 136)* was also established at Kiel-Holtenau with a dozen Heinkel HD 38a fighters under the command of *KptLt.* Georg-Hermann Edert.[9] Finally on the 1 August the *Mehrzweckstaffel (Mz 1 later 1.(Mz.)/286)* was

6   Hildebrand 1990-92 & Gaul in Isby (Ed.) 2005 p.84. Walter Gaul had joined the *Reichsmarine* on the 31 Mar 24. He transferred to the *Lw.* on the 1 Oct 34 and was posted to the *Fl.Schule Warnemünde* prior to assignment of the *Fl.Staffel (M) Norderney* – see service record for Walter Gaul in Zweng IV de H.L. and Stankey D.G. 2013 *Luftwaffe Officer Career Summaries* (hereafter cited as Zweng and Stankey 2013). Other serving naval officers assigned to the *RLM* in Jun 33 were: *KorvKpt.*Heinz Degenhardt, *KptLt.*Paul Ascher, Eugen Bischoff, Erich (??) Lorenz and Wilhelm Meendsen-Bohlke & *Oblt.z.S.*Walter Weygoldt - see *Anlage 5 Verzeichnis der aktiven und inaktiven Flieger-und Flugabwehr (Luftschütz)-Offiziere im Reichlsuftfahrtministerium, Stand: 1.Juni 1933* in Volker 1967 pp.229-230. Following these postings both Ascher & Meendsen-Bohlke would revert to *Reichsmarine* service; As *FregKpt.* Paul Ascher would serve as *Art.Offz.* aboard the *Panzerschiff Graf Spee* (scuttled 17 Dec 39) and as *Kpt.z.S.* and *1.Adm.Stabs-Offz., Flotten-Kdo.*aboard the *Schlachtschiff Bismarck* (sunk 27 May 41) where he was *Gefallen*; Wilhelm Meendsen-Bohlke would enjoy a distinguished naval career finishing the war as *VizeAdm.* and *Flottenchef-Flottenkdo.* – see service record for Wilhelm Meendsen-Bohlke in Axis Biographical Research – Kriegsmarine in www.reocities.com

7   Service record for Hans Ritter in Hildebrand 1992 pp.116-117. Prior to this posting he had led the *Ref.f.Flugwesen in der Flottenkommando/Marineleitung.*

8   *RdL LP Nr.1860/34 gKdos. II 2, Berlin, den 8.3.1934* in DZ/MGFA, Akte II L 49, Teil 2 in Volker 1967 p.47 & Ries K. 1974 *Luftwaffen-Story 1935-1939* (hereafter cited as Ries 1974) p.163. The *Seeaufklärungsstaffel* was officially referred to as the *1.(M)/116*. Initial personnel included Wolfgang Buhring *(BO)*, Herbert Hartwig *(FF/TO)* & Werner-Ernst Hoffmann *(BO)* – see Zweng and Stankey 2013, The *Kdr.d.Fl.G.(See) 116* is unknown.

9   *RdL LP Nr.1860/34 gKdos. II 2, Berlin, den 8.3.1934* in DZ/MGFA, Akte II L 49, Teil 2 in Volker 1967 p.47 & Kurowski 1979 p.19. Initial personnel included: Georg-Hermann Edert (*Käpitan*), Richard Brunner, Helmut Goedert, Gerhard Kadow, Fritz Kube, Hermann Roth, Schoppe, Erich Schwering, Heinrich Seeliger, Wismar & Albrecht Wolter - see Ries K. 1988 *Deutsche Flugzeugführerschulen und ihre Maschinen 1919-1945* p.73, Prien J. 1992 *Einsatz des Jagdgeschwaders 77 von 1939 bis 1945: Ein Kriegstagebuch nach Dokumenten, Berichten*

created with the Heinkel He 59B and a handful of Dornier Do 15 flying boats at List auf Sylt under *KorvKpt.*Max Schöne.[10] On the 1 September the *Seeaufklärungsstaffel* was re-deployed to Norderney in the Ostfriesische Inseln with its Heinkel He 60A/B coastal reconnaissance aircraft where it could better support the *Reichsmarine's* warships based at Wilhelmshaven.[11] Its new *Käpitan* from October was *KorvKpt.*Herbert Olbrich.[12]

The resurgence of the German naval aviation came at a time of cautious optimism within the *Reichsmarine*. The first of the new *Panzerschiffe*, the *Deutschland*, had commissioned on the 1 April 1933 and almost a year later it took *Reichskanzler* Adolf Hitler and his party on a short cruise into Norwegian waters (Photo 2E-4).[13] The four modern *leichte Kreuziere* were all in active service with the *Befehlshaber der Aufklärungsstreitkräfte (BdA)*, the *Königsberg* and *Leipzig* both visiting the Royal Navy's Fleet base at Portsmouth in July 1934, whilst the *Karlsruhe* began a Far East cruise in October of that year (Photo 2E-5).[14] All eleven modern *Torpedoboote* of the Typ 23 and Typ 24 Klassen were in service, principally with the *2.Torpedo-Boote Flottille*, whilst on the 7 July 1934 the first examples of the new Typ 34 Zerstörer had been ordered from the yards.[15] Of equal importance was the decision to finally confine the older pre-Dreadnought *Linienschiffe* to training and support duties or to strike them totally from the *inactive* list.[16]

It had always been planned to equip the *Reichsmarine's* larger warships with catapult capable reconnaissance aircraft once international restrictions on naval aviation could be ignored (See 1E3). The new He 60 single-engine floatplane was therefore designed with this requirement in mind and in 1934 training in catapult take-off technique became a feature of the syllabus at Kiel-Holtenau (See 2C2).[17]

und Erinnerungen Teil 1 1934 bis Mai 1941 p.27 & Prien J., Stemmer G., Rodeike P. and Bock W. 2000 *Die Jagdfliegerverbände der Deutschen Luftwaffe 1934 bis 1945 Teil 1 Vorkriegszeit und Einsatz über Polen - 1934 bis 1939* p.275. Georg-Hermann Edert had joined the *Reichsmarine* on the 28 Nov 19 and had undergone pilot training at Warnemünde and elsewhere from Aug 28. He transferred to the *Lw.* on the 1 Oct 33 and underwent further training at Warnemünde & Schleißheim. He formed the *Vorkommando Fliegerstaffel (J) See 1* on the 1 Jul 34 – see service record for Hermann Edert in Zweng and Stankey 2013. The *Seejagdstaffel* was officially known as the *1.(J)/136* - see Ries 1974 p.94.

10   *RdL LP Nr.1860/34 gKdos. II 2, Berlin, den 8.3.1934* in DZ/MGFA, Akte II L 49, Teil 2 in Volker 1967 p.47, Ries K. 1970 *Luftwaffe Bd.1 Die Maulwurfe 1919-1935* p.117 & Kurowski 1979 p.19. An alternative formation date of the 1 Oct 34 is provide by Ries 1974 p.163. This *Staffel* was officially referred to as the *1.(Mz)/286*, later re-designated *1.(Mz)/186*. Initial personnel included Eberhard Roeger *(FF)* & Friedrich Meissner *(BO)* – see de Zweng and Stankey 2013.

11   Kurowski 1979 p.19. *Hptm.i.G.*Harlinghausen was posted to *LA III* as a *Referent* and later *Gruppenleiter* concerned with training - see service record for Martin Harlinghausen in Hildebrand 1991 pp.32-33 See also Mallmann Showell 1979 p.57.

12   Kurowski 1979 p.19. Herbert Olbrich had joined the *Kaiserliche Marine* on the 3 Oct 16, had been discharged on the 12 Dec 18 but had then re-engaged in the *Reichsmarine* as a *Ltz.See* from 10 Jan 20. He was *Oblt.z.S.* from 1 Apr 22 & *KptLt.* from 1 Oct 29. He transferred to the *Lw.* on the 1 Oct 33 and underwent flight training at Warnemünde prior to his appointment as *Kap.Fl.Staffel M 1* – see service record for Herbert Olbrich in Zweng and Stankey 2013.

13   Whitley M.J. 1989 *German Capital Ships of World War Two* (hereafter cited as Whitley 1989) p.83. The *Deutschland* then exercised with other fleet elements during May & Jun 34 before a deployment into the Atlantic for ocean gunnery trials. The second *Panzerschiff*, the *Admiral Scheer*, would commission on the 12 Nov 34.

14   Whitley M.J. 1985 *German Cruisers of World War Two* (hereafter cited as Whitley 1985) p.30 & 170. The light cruiser *Nürnberg*, had been laid down in Nov 33; it would be launched in Dec 34 and completed just under a year later.

15   Whitley M.J. 1991 *German Destroyers of World War Two* p.12, 16, 21 & pp.45-47. However *Z1-4 (Deutsche Werke, Kiel)* would not commission before 1937.

16   Sieche E. *Germany* in Gardiner R. and Chesneau R. (Ed.) 1980 *Conway's All the World's Fighting Ships 1922-1946* p.222. The *Hessen* & *Schlesien* were both de-commissioned in 1934. *Hessen* would be converted into a radio-controlled target vessel during 1935-36, whilst *Schlesien* would, after modification, join her sister Schleswig-Holstein as a cadet training ship. The already de-commissioned *Hannover* would be stricken in 1935.

17   Whitley 1985 p.25 & Whitley 1989 p.214. See also Green W. 1970 *The War Planes of the Third Reich* p.277 & Gaul

In the meantime the position of *Führer der Marineluftstreitkräfte (FdL)* was established on the 1 April 1934 under *FregKpt.*Hermann Bruch.[18] Bruch was responsible for the war readiness and operational deployment of the *Marineluftstreitkräfte* and it is interesting to note the forward deployment of both the *1.(M)/116* (Norderney) and *1.(Mz)/186* (List) to help guard the *Reichsmarine's* Nordsee bases against possible French or British naval action.[19] Bruch's major subordinate command was the *Stab/Fl.G.(See) 116* which, in a break with German military practice, was quickly re-designated the *Stab/Fl.G.(See) 106*. It continued to control the activities of the *1.(M)/116* and *1.(Mz.)/186* but Edert's fighters appear to have come directly under the *FdL.*[20]

The beginnings of a supply organisation *(Nachschubeinheiten-See)* also came into being within the *Gehobene Luftamtes Kiel* during 1934. In June a *Luftwaffen-Munitionsanstalt* was established at Diekhoff, whilst in October *Luftparke (See)* were established at both Holtenau (*FregKpt.a.D.*Hermann Schantz) and Nordenham.[21]

In addition to the new aircraft types, the first marine support craft were introduced from 1934. Initially these took the form of two basic types: a *Flugsicherungsschiff* or aircraft recovery vessel, and a *Flugbetriebsboot* or aircraft service craft. In the first case an existing hull was taken in hand for conversion at the *Flenderwerke* at Lübeck, the result being the 35 metre *Flugzeugbergungsschiffe Phoenix* which entered service in 1934.[22] The first purpose built *Flugsicherungsschiff* was the 38.2 metre *Krischan* which was commissioned on the 10 March 1934.[23] The *Krischan* was capable of handling small single-engine floatplanes such as the He 42, He 60 and W 34/See using a twin-post boom, whilst the *Phoenix* could lift up to 9 tonnes and could accommodate the larger He 59B. However it was appreciated that as aircraft weight increased a greater lifting capacity would be required and therefore both of the additional vessels ordered in 1934 were designed to operate a crane of at least 10 tonne capacity.[24]

For more general harbour duties the first of a range of smaller craft was also acquired in 1934, this being the Flugbetriebsboot A.101 (Klass A I) which was bought from the British Power Boat

in Isby (Ed.) 2005 p.81.

18 Gaul in Isby (Ed.) 2005 p.81. Hermann Bruch was transferred to the *Lw.* on the 1 May 34. His previous posting had been as *I.Offizier* on the *leichte Kreuzer Köln* - see service record for Hermann Bruch in Hildebrand K.F.1990 *Die Generale der deutschen Luftwaffe 1935-1945 Band 1 A-G* (hereafter cited as Hildebrand 1990) pp.119-120.

19 Whitley 1989 p.83. Although both *Deutschland & Admiral Scheer* were based at Wilhelmshaven at this time, German naval strategy was to withdraw all heavy units into the Ostsee and rely upon light screening forces and minefields to keep enemy warships at bay - see Reynolds C.G. 1974 *Command of the Sea: The History and Strategy of Maritime Empires* p.489.

20 Ries 1974 p.163 & Rosch B.C. 1995 *Luftwaffe Codes, Markings and Units 1939-1945* p.94 & 167. At this stage *Luftwaffe* the short range *Aufklärungsgruppen* were numbered *11X* with the second *"1"* denoting the short range nature of the unit, whilst the *X* indicated the parent *Luftkreis*, hence the use of *116* for the initial reconnaissance units within *Luftkreis VI*. The *Fernaufklärungsgruppen* were numbered *12X* with the *"2"* denoting the long range nature of the unit and the *"X"* the parent *Luftkreis*. In adopting a *"0"* as the unit designator it is likely that the *Organisations-Abteilung* were trying to denote a third type of reconnaissance unit with a mixed complement of *Staffeln* as was indeed the case in the *Marineluftstreitkräfte*.

21 Jung et al 1977 p.57. Nordenham was situated 8 kms SW of Bremerhaven; Diekhoff is thought to be close to Stralsund in Mecklenburg .

22 Jung et al 1977 pp.105-106. The *Phoenix* was completed in Nov 32 and re-constructed for use by the *DVS* in 1934. It was fitted with a *Bockkran* of 9 tonne capacity and was capable of carrying a single seaplane. It was assigned to the *E-Stelle Travemünde*. See also *Schiffsatlas* in Caspari H.A. Dr. (Ed.) Undated *E-Stellen Travemünde und Tarnewitz 3.Band – Die Geschichte der Seeflugzeug-Erprobungsstelle Travemünde und daraus hervorgegangenen E-Stelle für Flugzeugbewaffnung Tarnewitz* (hereafter cited as Schiffsatlas in Caspari (Ed.) Undated Bd.3) p.180.

23 Jung et al 1977 p.106. The *Krischan* displaced 133 tonnes and was equipped with a twin boom *Ladebaume* of 4 tonne lifting capacity. It was assigned to the *DVS Zweigstelle List*. See also *Schiffsatlas* in Caspari (Ed.) Undated Bd.3 p.185.

24 Jung et al 1977 p.106. These were *the Klass K.II & Klass K.III*, both of which could lift 10 or more tonnes and had sufficient deck space for two seaplanes.

Co. at Southampton. Equipped with two engines, the A 101 was capable of 26.5 knots for the rescue role and following experience with this small craft two new classes were designed for construction at Lemwerder (Klass A II) and Berlin-Pichelsdorf (Klass A III).[25] A group of slightly larger general purpose craft were also laid down at the *Gebr.Kroger Yacht-und Bootswerft*, Warnemünde, the first of which, the B.101 (Klass B I) was also completed in 1934. The B.101 displaced 18 tonnes and was 15.7 metres in length. It had an enclosed cabin plus an open area in the stern of the boat for more passengers or freight.[26]

---

25   Jung et al 1977 pp.142-144. Only one craft of the *A.I Klass* was purchased from Britain. Four *Klass A.II* were ordered from *Abeking & Rasmussen* of Lemwerder, and four *Klass A.III* from *Naglowerft* of Pichelsdorf.
26   Jung et al 1977 pp.143-144. Only one craft of the *B.I Klass* was delivered.

2E4

The Territorial Organisation of the Secret Air Arm

DECEMBER 1934

Gehobene Luftamtes Königsberg		
Gen.d.Art.(char) Edmund Wachenfeld		
Aufklärungsstaffel (F)	Königsberg-Neuhausen	Hptm.i.G.Fritz Reinshagen
Gehobene Luftamtes Berlin		
GenLt.Leonhard Kaupisch		
Fliegerschule (Land)	Magdeburg	Maj.Alfred Sturm (Jan 35)
Fliegerschule (Land)	Neuruppin	Maj.Hermann Steindorf
Kampffliegerschule	Prenzlau	Obstlt.Richard Putzier ?
Aufklärungsstaffel (F)	Prenzlau	Not known
Jagdgeschwader	Döberitz	Maj.Robert Ritter von Greim
Sturzkampfgeschwader	Schwerin	Not known
Kampfgeschwader	Tutow	Maj.August Ploch ?
Behelfskampfgeschwader	Berlin-Tempelhof	Hptm.Robert Knauss
Flugbereitschaft Ob.d.L.	Berlin-Staaken	Obstlt.Gustav Kastner-Kirdorf
Fliegerstaffel z.b.V.	Berlin-Staaken	Hptm.Theodor Rowehl
Gehobene Luftamtes Dresden		
GenLt.Karl Schweickhard		
Fliegerschule (Land)	Cottbus	Obstlt.Otto Dessloch
Fliegerschule (Land)	Gotha	Obstlt.Albert Vierling
Aufklärungsstaffel (H)	Cottbus	Not known
Aufklärungsstaffel (H)	Gotha	Not known
Aufklärungsstaffel (F)	Größenhain	Hptm.Günther Wieland

Gehobene Luftamtes Münster		
GenLt.Hans Halm		
Aufklärungsfliegerschule	Braunschweig	Obstlt.Walter Somme
Aufklärungsfliegerschule	Hildesheim	Obstlt.Waldemar Reinicke
Kampfgeschwader	Fassberg	Obst.Alfred Keller
Fliegerschule (Land)	Celle	Maj.Kurt-Bertram von Doring
Gehobene Luftamtes München		
GenLt.Karl Eberth		
Fliegerschule (Land)	Würzburg	Hptm.Rudolf Trautvetter
Fliegerschule (Land)	Kitzingen	Maj.Heinrich Lorenz
Kampffliegerschule	Lechfeld	Obstlt.Curt Pflugbeil
Jagdfliegerschule	Schleißheim	Maj.Josef Mai
Aufklärungsstaffel (H)	Goppingen	Hptm.Jens-Peter Petersen
Aufklärungsstaffel (H)	Goppingen	Hptm.Otto Jordan
Gehobene Luftamtes Kiel		
KonAdm.Konrad Zander		
Fliegerschule (See)	Stettin	Georg Pasewaldt
Flugzeugführerlehrgang C	Travemünde	Not known
Fliegerwaffenschule (See)	Warnemünde	Maj.i.G.Ulrich Kessler
Fliegerwaffenlehrgang (See)	Bug auf Rugen	Hptm.Otto Schroeder-Zollinger
Seejagdstaffel (J 1)	Kiel-Holtenau	Maj.Georg Edert
Mehrzweckstaffel (Mz 1)	List auf Sylt	Maj.Max Schöne
Seeaufklärungsstaffel (M 1)	Norderney	Maj.Herbert Olbrich

Although the term *Geschwader* has been used this does not indicate the true size of the unit; most *Gruppen* were at a reduced two-*Staffel* establishment at this time. Substantive military ranks are shown in all cases although publicly these officers were either retired *(a.D.)* or held *DLV* ranks.

Part 2 - Photo Commentaries

Photo 2A-1 Original caption: *"Deutschland"* **1934: Accompanied by the** *Reichskriegsminister,* ***General*** **von Blomberg (2nd from right) and the** *Chefs der Marineleitung, Admiral Raeder* **(2nd from left) Adolf Hitler takes a voyage on board the** *"Deutschland"* **in the North Sea.**

Bundesarchiv Bild 146-1984-030-03 Photo: o.Ang. Scherl Agency

Admiral Erich Raeder's ambition to return Germany to the status of a true "Blue Water" Navy had come a step closer with the commissioning of the *Panzerschiff Deutschland* on the 1 April 1933. At that time two further *Panzerschiffe* were under construction and would commission later in 1934 (*Panzerschiff B – Ersatz Lothringen*) and in early 1936 (*Panzerschiff C – Ersatz Braunschweig*). Meanwhile Raeder had already reached an agreement with *Reichswehrminister* Kurt Schleicher in November 1932 that the *Reichsmarine* be fully modernised by 1938 with six *Panzerschiffe*, six *kleine Kreuziere*, six *Zerstörer/Torpedoboot-Halbflottillen* and three *Schnellboot-Halbflottillen* to which it was hoped to add sixteen *U-Boote* once the political situation allowed.

Although the new Führer lacked naval experience he proved to be more than sympathetic to the *Reichsmarine's* objectives, seeing the modern capital ship as a tangible manifestation of the power of the State. These views were almost certainly confirmed in his presence aboard the *Panzerschiff Deutschland* in April 1934 when *Kpt.z.See* Hermann von Fischel took the ship on a short Norwegian cruise visiting Sognefjord and Hardangerfjord. Also aboard were *Admiral* Raeder, *GenOb.* Werner von Blomberg and *Gen.d.Art.* Werner Frhr.von Fritsch who used this opportunity to tackle Hitler over the rising power of Ernst Röhm and his *SA*. During the voyage the *Deutschland Pact* was agreed which assured Hitler of the support of the *Reichswehr's* high command in the event of his succession to *Reichspräsident* in return for Hitler's suppression of Röhm.

German naval policy remained unchanged. France was the perceived enemy and the design and layout of the planned *Panzerschiffe D* and *E* reflected the challenge presented by the *Marine nationale Francaise's* two new 30-35,000 tonne *batiments de Ligne Dunkerque* and *Strasbourg* which would commission in 1935-36. Meanwhile Hitler had already indicated that he would no longer beholden to the military restrictions of the Treaty of Versailles and this enabled the *Marineleitung* to order substantially larger and more powerful warships. Both *Panzerschiffe D* and *E* were nominally of 17,000 tonnes but in reality would displace twice that amount. To safeguard the *Reichsmarine's* planned developments Hitler would reach an accommodation with the British in 1935 that would allay any fears that the Royal Navy might entertain about a new naval arms race.

All of the *Reichsmarine's* replacement *Panzerschiffe* and *Kreuziere,* bar *Emden,* were designed to carry aircraft; *Deutschland* would be fitted with her catapult during a 1935-36 refit and the *K-Klass Kreuziere* would follow as they returned to the yards. By the end of 1934 27 Heinkel He 60 had been produced including the first examples of the *C-Reihe Bordflugzeug* for use aboard these vessels. Catapult training had also been included for the new crews of these aircraft and the resumption of shipboard naval air operations was awaited with enthusiasm.

Photo 2A-2 Original caption: Portrait of Hellmuth Felmy in the uniform of a *Luftwaffe Oberst.*

Bundesarchiv Bild 183-1998-0720-501 Photo: o.Ang.

When Hermann Göring was appointed *Reichskommissar für die Luftfahrt* in February 1933 he found that the basis for a new German military air arm already existed. The key issues of formulating an air doctrine, deciding on an air organisation, developing combat aircraft, and the training of aircrew and technical personnel had all been accomplished. The credit for this work over a period of fifteen years can be attributed to the three officers who headed the *Reichsheer's* clandestine air staff: *Maj.*Helmuth Wilberg (1919-27), *Maj.*Hugo Sperrle (1927-29) and *Obstlt.*Hellmuth Felmy (1929-33).

Hellmuth Felmy was a graduate of the pre-war *Lehr-und Versuchsanstalt für Militärflugwesen* at Döberitz. He flew operationally from August 1914 to June 1918, with a good deal of his wartime service being spent in the Middle East where he was *Fhr.FA 300 Pascha I*. He was retained by the *Reichsheer* being assigned as a *Kp.Chef.i.Kraftfahr-Abt.5* in 1920 prior to being appointed *Flieger-Referent* in the *Stab 5.Division* in 1921. From 1924 he served in *T 1* prior to a period on the *Stab des Infanterie-Fhrs.V* from 1926. He became *Chef T 2 V (L)*, later *Inspektion 1 (L)*, in February 1929 at a point when the full air staff was created: *Ref.1* – Policy and Directives for the *Fliegerwaffe*, 2 – Personnel and Traditions, Air Politics, 3 – Technical development for the *Fliegerwaffe*, 4 – Administration, 5 – Organisation and Budget, 6 – Air Intelligence, 7 – Air Defence, 8 – Bureau Services & 9 – Training the *Fliegertruppe*.

Considered by many to have one of the finest brains in the *Reichsheer*, Felmy was a competent, capable and knowledgeable officer. He was the guiding force behind the influential *Richtlinien für die Ausbildung in der Reichswehr auf dem Gebiet der Luftstreitkräfte* (Principles for the Employment of Air Forces within the *Reichswehr*) which was published on the 20 December 1930 to effectively set the stage for the on-going debate on the future form of the military air arm. Felmy wanted an independent *Reichsluftwaffe*, a position that was eventually conceded by the *Chef des Heeresleitung* on the 24 February 1932, but he was far less successful in gaining approval for a projected air arm of 80 *Staffeln* with a sizable bomber component to be attained by 1938. An agreement was finally reached on the 14 July 1932 for a peacetime force of 22 *Staffeln* but even this limited programme was to be spread over the years 1934-37.

Felmy had spent twelve years in his wartime rank of *Hauptmann* before being promoted to *Major* in January 1927. Thereafter his seniority had been accelerated to reach *Oberst* in October 1933. His first position in the clandestine *Luftwaffe* was as *Kommandeur der Fliegerwaffenschulen* and *Chef des Stabes des Kommandeurs der Schulen* (Friedrich Christiansen).

Photo 2A-3 Original caption: The battle for the Young-Plan in the *Reichstag* in Berlin! This significant meeting was attended by representatives of all political parties. As a leader of the National Socialists in the *Reichstag*, *Hauptmann* Hermann Göring goes to the reading of the Young-Plan in the *Reichstag*.

Bundesarchiv Bild 102-01908A Photo Georg Pahl

After the abortive *München Putsch* of 1923 the badly wounded Göring had fled to Austria, Italy and ultimately to Sweden. By 1925 he was badly in debt and a confirmed drug addict being admitted to a mental asylum for "an abuse of morphine", a problem that would return to haunt him for the next two years. His renaissance would come in 1928 when he stood for election as a *NSDAP Reichstagsabgerordneter*. He was one of twelve to be elected in May of that year and quickly claimed the Party's public transport portfolio. Through the good auspices of Erhard Milch, Göring was retained as a "consultant" for *DLH*, agreements that were followed soon after by those for *BMW* and *Heinkel* whilst other industrialists would also make contributions. Relieved of his financial worries Göring threw himself behind the *NSDAP's* political campaign proving himself to be a skilled political speaker and orator. In September 1930 the *NSDAP* increased their share of the 577 contested seats in the *Reichstag* from 12 to 107 representatives.

In this image from March 1930 Georg Pahl has captured Hermann Göring on the steps of the *Reichstags* building. By this time Göring was an acknowledged political player of great skill and was acting as Hitler's personal political representative within Berlin. Two years later on the 30 August 1932 he would become *Präsidenten des Deutschen Reichstags* a position of even greater influence in the *NSDAP's* continued rise to power in Germany.

The Young Plan of 1929 marked a further reduction in Germany's war debt. Following on from the Dawes Plan of 1924 which had itself sought to rationalise Germany's economic position following the earlier period of hyper-inflation, the Committee headed by American industrialist Owen D.Young recommended a further 20% reduction in Germany's overall financial obligations and a proposal that two thirds of the debt be postponed, being subject only to the payment of interest on the remaining amount. However the Plan was quickly overtaken by the worldwide effects of the Wall Street Crash of 1929 and by 1932 there was international recognition that Germany could no longer make any reparations payments.

Photo 2A-4 Original caption: In Fascist Germany 1934. Berlin: Leading Nazis at the *Presseball* at the *Festsalen im Zoologischen Garten*: *Reichspropagandaminister* J.Goebbels (left), *Ministerpräsident* H.Göring (centre), *Reichswehrminister* W.von Blomberg (right) with ladies.
Bundesarchiv Bild 183-M0921-500 Photo: o.Ang. AND-ZB/Archiv

The *deutsche Presseball* was one of Berlin's annual society events. First held in 1872, it had used the *Festsalen am Zoologischen Garten* venue from 1912. Hitler never attended these events but as the newly appointed *Reichspropagandaminister, Dr.*Goebbels would use the event of 8 February 1934 to confirm to the world the new political realities within Germany.

Hermann Göring seen here in his uniform as *General der Infanterie*, a rank conferred on him by *Reichspräsident* Hindenburg on the 31 August 1933, was busily accruing personal power at this time: *preußischen Ministerpräsident* (11 Apr 33), *preußischen Innernminister*, later *Reichsminister des Innern* (21 Apr 33), *Reichsminister der Luftfahrt* (5 May 33) and *Präsident des Preußischen Staatsrates* (8 Jul 33). In April 1933 he had founded the *geheime Staats Poliziei (Gestapo)* and the *Forschungsamtes*, two organisations which he would use successfully to further the *NSDAP* cause as well as enhance his personal standing with Hitler. Control over the *Gestapo* would pass to Heinrich Himmler in April 1934 but the *Forschungsamt* remained Göring's "Goose that laid the Golden Egg". It was hidden within the *RLM* where it was employed to tap telephones, intercept and decode diplomatic and commercial messages. As a result Göring was remarkably well informed about all significant matters at all times.

Werner von Blomberg, promoted to the rank of *Generaloberst* by Hindenburg on the 31 August 1933, had quickly become a Hitler convert. He was described in 1933 as *"a reasonable man, except for his blind adoration of Hitler"*. During 1933-34 he would actively support the politicisation of the *Reichswehr* and its ever closer links with the *NSDAP* and its para-military forces although by the time of this photograph he was becoming increasingly concerned about Ernst Röhm who Hitler had elevated to a *Reichsminister ohne Geschaftsbereich* (Minister without Portfolio) with a seat on the key *Reichverteidigungsrat* (Reichs Defence Council). These concerns were shared by Göring, although for different reasons and would result in drastic action on Hitler's part later in the year.

Photo 2A-5 Original caption: Adolf Hitler discusses the government crisis with his staff! From right to left, Hitler's *Stabschef Hautpmann* Röhm, talks excitedly to an intent Adolf Hitler - left in the picture, in the middle - *Reichstag Präsident Hauptmann* Göring. (*Zentralflughafen* Berlin-Tempelhof, 30 November 1932).
Bundesarchiv Bild 102-14081 Photo: Georg Pahl

Hitler consults his closest confidantes in the wake of the *NSDAP's* poor electoral showing in the November 1932 national elections. With the loss of 35 seats it seemed to many that the previously inexorable rise in the popularity of the National Socialists had come to an end. The reality was different: the *NSDAP* remained the largest party in a splintered *Reichstag; Reichskanzler* Franz von Papen's unpopular Government had been unable to secure the cross party support that it required to govern; and Hitler's political acumen was without equal. During the short lived government of Kurt von Schleicher, Hitler moved decisively to neutralise the left wing of the *NSDAP* under Gregor Strasser, whilst refusing to agree to any accommodation short of an appointment as Schleicher's successor. In this he had the support on von Papen who worked behind the scenes to influence the *Reichspräsident*. When it became clear that Schleicher would not be able to achieve a workable coalition, Hindenburg took the decision to appoint Hitler as *Reichskanzler* with von Papen as *Vizekanzler*.

As *Reichstagpräsident*, Göring had played an important part in Hitler's rise to political power. By the skilful use of parliamentary procedures he had been able to effectively undermine von Papen's position in the *Reichstag*, whilst his right of access to the *Reichspräsident* and his inner circle had been important in reassuring Hindenburg of Hitler's integrity, patriotism and respect for tradition during this crucial period. Hitler's confidence in him had also seen him sent to Italy in early November where he met Mussolini on a vital cash raising visit to replenish the Party coffers.

By the time of this photograph, Ernst Röhm already regarded himself as the saviour of the National Socialist revolution. Through his control of the *Sturmabteilung (SA)* he wielded enormous power at grass roots level where working class Germans looked for a fundamental reform of the economic system. In its battles with the Communists and attacks on the Jews, the *SA* had become adept at destabilising established norms of law and order and it increasingly appeared that for any Government to be successful it would be necessary to accommodate Ernst Röhm.

With over 3 million members the *SA* more than rivalled the 140,000 man *Reichswehr*. In recognition of this power base Hitler appointed him to the *Kabinett* as *Reichsminister ohne Geschäftsbereich* in December 1933 and at the same time gave him a place on the *Reichsverteidigungsrat*. This only served to encourage Röhm to go one stage further and in February 1934 he demanded that the *Reichswehr* be absorbed into the *SA* to form a true *Volksheer* and that he should replace von Blomberg as *Reichswehrminister*. It was a step too far. Industrialists, bankers and now the *Reichswehr* all wanted Röhm and the threat posed by his *SA* removed. Within the *NSDAP* it was Göring that led the anti-Röhm faction which crucially included Heinrich Himmler, the *Reichsführer SS*. Vital intelligence on Röhm's activities came from Göring's *Forschungsamt* and this was enough to convince Hitler that he must act. On the 30 June 1934 orders went out that Röhm and his confederates were to be assassinated. In an orgy of killing at least 89 died including other rivals – Gregor Strasser and Kurt von Schleicher. Hermann Göring had performed the role of "Murder Manager" to perfection.

Photo 2A-6 Original caption: The *preußischer Ministerpräsident* Hermann Göring with (to his right) the Italian *Korporativ-Minister* Bottai, and left the vice-secretary of the Italian Fascist Party Professor, his Excellence, Marcipati at the *NSDAP Parteitag* in Nürnberg on the 3 September 1933.

Bundesarchiv Bild 102-02912A Photo: Georg Pahl

The *1933 Parteitage* were held in Nürnberg from the 31 August to the 3 September and as many as a half a million loyal National Socialists, members of the *Reichswehr*, officials and dignatories attended the event which was entitled the *"Reichsparteitage des Sieges"* in celebration of Hitler's assumption of power. The event was recorded and made into the film *"Der Sieg des Glaubens"* by the female Director Leni Riefenstahl which had a wide screening in Germany up to the Night of the Long Knives in June 1934.

Following the assumption of power Göring had extended his activities into foreign relations. Following his visit to Mussolini in November 1932, he made three official visits to Italy in 1933 as

Hitler's special emissary. The most important took place in April when he met Mussolini to re-assure him that Hitler had no designs in respect of Austria. He also visited the Pope at the Vatican, whilst Erhard Milch held talks with *Gen.*Italo Balbo of the *Regia Aeronautica* – talks which would result in the training of German pilots and observers in Italy during July to September 1933. As a result of these visits it is not surprising that he played host to the Italian Fascist delegation at the Nürnberg Rally. His network of foreign contacts would grow immeasurably in the years to come and would prove invaluable as Hitler's ambitions turned outward to the other countries of central Europe.

Göring is wearing his *Sturmabteilung* uniform with the rank of *SA-Obergruppenführer* complete with his Imperial decorations including a Breast Star and his coveted *Pour le Mérite*. In 1923 he had been the *Chef der SA* up until the abortive *München Putsch* of 9 November in which he was wounded and had to flee Germany.

Göring would use in succession three different Ju 52/3m *Verkehrsflugzeuge* all of which were painted red and named *"Manfred von Richthofen"*: WNr.4022 D-2527, WNr.4066 D-ABAQ and WNr.4069 D-ABIK. This is the first of the three, Ju 52/3m fe D-2527 which was renamed *"Kurt Wolff"* in 1935 and registered to *DLH* as D-AGUK. As was the case with the other *DLH* aircraft seconded for Government use, D-2527 was operated by *Flugkäpitan* Hans Baur's *Regierungsstaffel* at Berlin-Tempelhof.

Photo 2A-7 Original caption: The inauguration of the new bison enclosure by the *preußische Ministerpräsident* General Hermann Göring in the State Nature Reserve Schorfheide on Werbelin lake in the Mark! The *preußische Ministerpräsident* and his guests during the visit to the Schorfheide. From left to right: *Reichsfinanzminister* von Schwerin Krossik, *Vizekanzler* [Franz] von Papen, *Staatssekretär* [Hans-Heinrich] Lammers, the *preussiche Justizminister* [Hanns] Kerrl, Hermann Göring and the Italian Ambassador in Berlin [Vittorio] Cerutti.

Bundesarchiv Bild 102-15927 Photo: Georg Pahl

Shortly after his ten day vacation tour in the Balkans during the 15 – 25 May 1934, Göring retired to his newly completed forest refuge at Carinhall, some 80 kms north of the capital. There on the 10 June 1934 he played host to an invited party of forty Government ministers and foreign diplomats whose motorcade he met on the southern fringes of the *staatlichen Naturschutzgebiet* within the largely unpopulated Schorfheide, a huge expanse of heathland interspersed with forests and lakes. Here he launched into a lecture on the elks and bison that he had imported from Ostpressuen and Poland before showing his guests around. He was particularly proud of his new bison reservation as by that time the European Bison was an endangered species with just only 50 animals remaining in captivity. The last examples in the wild had been shot in Poland in 1919 and in the Caucasus in 1927. In recognition of his passion for hunting and conservation Hitler would make him *Reichsforstmeister* on the 3 July 1934.

Dressed flamboyantly in high leather boots, leather trousers and tunic with a silk blouse and wearing a hunting dagger at his waist, Göring seemed oblivious to his guests' private comments about his appearance, Sir Eric Phipps, the British Ambassador, being one of those who found the scene somewhat bizzare. Ten days later Göring was in full *DLV* uniform for the interment of his late wife, when once again hundreds of diplomats and politicians were invited to Carinhall. Ten days after that he was overseeing the assassination of the *SA* hierarchy and other enemies of the new regime. Such were the many faces of Hermann Göring.

Not surprisingly Göring found little time for the new *Reichsluftwaffe*. His main achievement in this respect was the appointment of the industrious Erhard Milch, the *Mitglied des Vorstandes des DLH*, as his *Staatssekretär* on the 2 February 1933. It would be his job to translate Göring's plans for the new air arm into reality. In 1933 Göring envisaged that this would initially be a small force concealed within existing civil organisations such as the *DLV, Deutsche Luftfahrt, DVS* and *DLH*, whilst preparations were made for full scale aerial re-armament from 1935. Göring's initial aircraft construction plan was extraordinarily modest totalling just 295 machines to be delivered from May 1933 to April 1934 whilst additional fighters would be obtained from Italy. However this programme was quickly superseded by Milch's far more ambitious *Rheinland Programm* which called for the delivery of no less than 4,021 aircraft between 1 January 1934 and 30 September 1935. Göring was more than happy with this expansion. With the *NSDAP* in power, money would be no object.

Photo 2A-8 Original caption: In honour of the German participants of the *Europa-Rundflug* 1934 at the *Flugverbandshaus* (in Berlin). From left to right: *Staatssekretär* Milch, *Hauptmann* Seidemann and *Major* von Kehler. Berlin - Speech by *Staatssekretär* Erhard Milch (standing), Hans Seidemann, Richard von Kehler (left to right).

Bundesarchiv Bild 183-2005-0103-517 Photo: o.Ang.Scherl Agency

Following a personal appeal from Adolf Hitler, *Hptm.a.D.*Erhard Milch agreed to a new appointment as *Staatssekretär für die Luftfahrt* on the 2 February 1933. On the 5 May he became Göring's *Staatssekretär* within the newly formed *Reichsluftfahrtministerium (RLM)*. It was an inspired appointment. Milch was a first-class administrator with top class organisational skills. His unbroken record of involvement with commercial aviation during the post war period had given him an excellent knowledge of the aviation industry, its strengths and weaknesses and its personalities. Of equal importance within the new Reich were his excellent connections with the *NSDAP* and the high esteem in which he was held by Hitler himself.

He quickly set about establishing the new Ministry from nuclei provided by the *RWM's Luftschützamt*, the *Waffenamt's Wa.Prw.8* and the *RVM's Luftfahrtabteilung* (briefly re-designated *Abt.I Luftverkehr*). The new *RLM* emerged with five *Amter* (Offices) and two autonomous *Abteilungen* (Branches): the *Luftschützamt*, later *Luftkommandoamt (LA)*, the *Allgemeines Luftamt (LB)*, the *Technisches Amt (LC)*, the *Verwaltungsamt (LD)*, the *Personalamt (LP)*, the *Zentralabteilung (ZA)* and the *Abteilung für zivilen Luftschütz (ZL)*. Given Göring's many other commitments and interests it was Milch that exercised day-to-day control over these departments. He also exerted considerable influence on the nature of the covert *Luftwaffe's* future equipment being a proponent of both the long range strategic bomber and the single-engine dive bomber. He substantially increased the scale and pace of aerial re-armament with the introduction of the *Rheinland Programm* on the 1 January 1934. In accordance with Göring's plan for the development of the new air arm, this new programme placed a considerable emphasis on the production of training aircraft which would equip the new *DLV Flieger-Ausbildungsstellen* and the *Kommando der Schulen's Fliegerschulen*. It would also enable the small *Luftfahrtindustrie* to become accustomed to the volume production of more modern types and for new firms to be introduced to aircraft and aero-engine manufacture.

Staatssekretär Milch is seen here at the *Flugverbundshaus* in the *DLV* uniform of a *Generalmajor*, an honorary rank which had been bestowed on him on the 24 March 1934 to give him seniority over his *Amtschef* – only *MinDir.*Willy Fisch (*Chef LB*) was a civilian. To his left are *Hptm.*Hans Seidemann and *Maj.a.D.*Richard von Kehler, the *Präsident des Deutschen Aero-Clubs*. Seidemann was the highest placed of the twelve-strong national team for the *1934 Europa-Rundflug* which had been won by the Poles. He had been placed third, whilst Theo Osterkamp and Werner Junck had come in fifth and sixth respectively. The *RLM* had commissioned three new aircraft specifically for this event: the Messerschmitt Bf 108, Fieseler Fi 97 and Klemm Kl 36, these being powered by either the Argus As 17 or Hirth HM 8U special racing engines. Seidemann, who had been secretly trained as a military pilot at Lipetsk in 1928-29, was at that time undergoing secret training as a *Generalstabsoffizier* whilst serving as an *Offizier zbV* on the staff of the *Chefs der Heeresleitung*.

Photo 2A-9 Original caption: *Kronprinz* Wilhelm and Enst Udet at the *Volksflugtag* in Berlin on the 1 April 1934. Berlin – Ernst Udet and Wilhelm von Preussen beside an aircraft at the *Volksflugtag* at the Tempelhofer Field.

Bundesarchiv Bild 102-01779 Photo: Georg Pahl

As *Reichskommissar*, later *Reichsminister der Luftfahrt*, Göring had made it his policy to attract as many highly decorated former members of the wartime *Luftstreitkräfte* as possible to the ranks of the emerging *Reichsluftwaffe*. Such men were heroes to German youth and their exploits an inspiration to this new generation of military aviators. Early recruits included *KptLt.a.D.*Friedrich Christiansen (27 *Luftsiege*), *Hptm.a.D.*Robert Ritter von Greim (28 *LS*), *Maj.a.D.*Alfred Keller, *Lt.a.D.*Hans Klein (22 *LS*), *Hptm.a.D.*Bruno Loerzer (44 *LS*), *Hptm.a.D.*Albert Müller-Kahle and *Lt.a.D.*Theodor Osterkamp (31 LS). However the greatest catch, *Oblt.a.D.*Ernst Udet (62 *LS*), proved to be the most allusive.

By 1933 Udet had become far more than a stunt pilot, he was a true celebrity and his love of the good life, of wine and women, made the prospect of a return to uniform and discipline an anathema to him. Göring had made his opening bid at the 25th Anniversary Banquet of the *Deutschen Aero-Clubs* in Berlin on the 1 February 1933 where he promised Udet the dollars needed to buy two of the new Curtiss Hawk II fighter-dive bombers during his forthcoming visit to the USA. Udet arrived in New York in June aboard the *TS Europa* before flying across the USA to Los Angeles where he participated in the National Air Races and then north to Chicago for the World Fair. He first flew the Hawk at Buffalo in October and immediately fell in love with the new aircraft. The two machines were then dismantled and shipped to Germany. Udet carried out his first demonstration to *RLM* officials who were largely unimpressed, but on the 16 December he flew the aircraft at Tempelhof in front of *Staatssekretär* Erhard Milch who immediately asked Udet to attend all future conferences on dive-bombing at the *RLM*.

This image was taken on the 1 April 1934 at the Easter *Volksflugtage* at Tempelhof on the occasion of Udet's first public demonstration of the Hawk. A crowd of 120,000 were delighted and enthralled by his dynamic display: arrival at 300 kph, two consecutive loops followed by vertical slow rolls, a negative flick roll and vertical dive from 800 metres before accelerating to 550 kph in front of the crowd with a final vertical bank. Although wearing the uniform of the *DLV*, Udet was still a civilian. Nonetheless his regular contacts with the *RLM's C-Amt* gave him considerable influence in respect of the development of dive bombers and assault gliders. No aircraft manufacturer would refuse him the opportunity of flying their latest design and in this way he helped to promote the new trainers: the Ar 66, Bu 131, Fw 44, Go 145 and He 72. On the 1 June 1934 he finally succumbed to Göring's relentless pressure and was commissioned into the *Luftwaffe* as an *Oberstleutnant* as an *Offizier zbV* within the *RLM*.

Curtiss 35B Hawk II c/n H-81 D-3165 had been re-registered D-IRIS in April 1934 shortly after the Tempelhof display. It was unfortunately lost on the 15 July 1934 when the seat collapsed and trapped the controls as Udet rolled the aircraft over at 1,000 metres to begin his display at the *National Sozialist Flugschau* at Hamburg-Altona. As the aircraft spun away he had no option but to escape by parachute, the aircraft crashing on the airfield in front of Rudolf Müller who was coming in for an engine-off spot-landing in a Klemm Kl 31. Udet was recovered from a nearby allotment by ambulance but was uninjured. Later displays were flown in the second aircraft, D-3164 which had been re-registered as D-IRIK.

Photo 2A-10 Original caption: The famous *Ozeanflieger Hauptmann* Köhl at the *Nordbayerischen Verkehrs-Flug-Gesellschaft!* Our picture shows the famous *Ozeanflieger Hauptmann* Köhl (center) with his wife (left) and *Direktor* Croneiss of the *Nordbayerischen*

***Verkehrs-Flug-Gesellschaft* having taken over the ocean flyer's hat - From left to right: *Frau* Köhl, Hermann Köhl, not known, Theo Croneiss, Children.**

Bundesarchiv Bild 102-09801 Photo: Georg Pahl

Theodor Croneiss had been born in Schweinfurt on the 18 December 1894. Following the outbreak of the Great War he had joined the *1.bayerischen Chevauleger-Rgt.* but before the end of 1914 had transferred to the *Fliegertruppe*. He saw action over the Dardanelles and was the top scoring German *Experte* on the Ottoman Front with 5 *Luftsiege*. In 1924 *Oblt.a.D.*Croneiss became the *Fhr.Sportflug GmbH für Mittelfranken und Oberpfalz* at Augsburg before becoming the founder and *Direktor* of the *Nordbayerische Verkehrsflug GmbH* on the 25 March 1926. On the basis of cheap ticketing *Nordbayerische Verkehrsflug* was one of the few domestic operators to be commercially successful following the creation of *Deutsche Luft Hansa*. Meanwhile in 1925 he helped finance the struggling Willy Messerschmitt and flew the M 17 successfully in the first *Deutschlandflug* and in the *Oberfrankenflug*. On the 28 April 1926 he was co-founder of the *Messerschmitt Flugzeugbau GmbH* which with support from both the *RVM* and the *Bayerische State* had by the end of the year absorbed the assets of the *Udet Flugzeugbau* to form the *Bayerische Flugzeugwerke (BFW)* at Augsburg. Croneiss placed a contract for the new M 18 *Verkehrsflugzeug* on behalf of his airline with the new firm whose main product line was the U 12 *Flamingo*. In 1927 Croneiss won the *Sachsenenflug* in M 19 D-1221, the *Ostpreussenflug* in M 23b D-1668, and took part in the 1929 *Challenge de Tourism Internationale* and the *1930 Europa Rundflug*.

At the time of this photograph, taken in front of one of *Nordbayerische Verkehrsflug's* M 18 airliners in March 1930, Croneiss had become increasingly active politically. He joined the *NSDAP* on the 1 March 1933 and becoming a *Fliegerreferenten der Obersten SA-Führung* and eventually *Geschwaderführers der Fliegerlandesgruppe X (Bayern)* in the newly re-constituted *Deutsche Luftsport Verbände*. However he was lucky to survive his attempts to undermine Erhard Milch's position as *Staatssekretär für die Luftfahrt* in 1933-34 and he was severely reprimanded by Göring.

Born in Neu Ulm on the 13 April 1888, Hermann Köhl had been a pre-war regular officer in the *Württembergisches Pionier-Battalion Nr.13* but after being wounded in the legs he was unable to carry out his duties and had transferred to the *Fliegertruppe*. He trained as a pilot and made a name for himself through his nocturnal bombing operations over France as a *Staffelführer* within *Kagohl 4*. Wounded in 1917 he returned to action as *Kdr.Kagohl 7* and was awarded the *Pour le Mérite* on the 21 May 1918. Two days later he was forced down behind enemy lines and taken prisoner having completed a staggering 857 *Feindfluge (Operational Missions)*. Post-war he served with *Polizeifliegerstaffel Boblingen* before re-engaging with the *Heer* as *Chef 7./Inf.Rgt.13*, later *Chef 1./Pio.Btl.5* in Neu Ulm. He left the *Reichsheer* in 1925 to work for the *Junkers-Luftverkehr AG* as *Nachtstreckenleiter*, a position he carried over to the *DLH* in 1926 where he pioneered the use of the new blind flying instruments.

In 1927 Ehrenfried Frhr.von Hunefeld purchased two of the new W 33 all-metal monoplanes with the intention of using these to be the first to successfully cross the Atlantic Ocean from east to west. After an abortive first attempt D-1167 *Bremen* departed Ireland on the 12 April 1928 with Köhl, Hunefeld and Irish Captain James Fitzmaurice for New York. After 36.5 hours the exhausted crew force landed on Greenly Island off Labrador in Canada. Köhl was awarded the Distinguished Flying Cross by US President Calvin Coolidge but lost his job with *DLH* over his secrecy surrounding this attempt. Thereafter Köhl became involved in test flying and the development of air-to-air refuelling but fell from favour once he made it clear that he did not favour the *NSDAP*. Rather than curry favour with Göring he retired to a small farm in southern Bayern where he died on the 7 October 1938 at the age of 50.

Photo 2A-11 Original caption: *Generalleutnant* **Walther Wever. Born 11.11.1887. Photographed 1.4.1930 as** *Kdr.d.II./IR 12.* **1921** *Hauptmann im Generalstab d.Gr.Kdos.I, Hptm.i.Generalstab des Chefs des Generalstabes* **des Feldheeres. Died 3.June 1936 in Dresden.**

Bundesarchiv Bild 146-1976-026-04A Photo: o.Ang.

The major reason for the *Luftwaffe's* initial success was the quality of its senior officers. Thanks to *Reichswehrminister* Werner von Blomberg's personal intervention the *RLM's* first *Amtschef* were amongst the finest middle-ranking staff officers available to the *Reichswehr*. During 1933 *Reichsluftfahrtminister* Hermann Göring received *Obst*.Albert Keßelring as *Chef der Verwaltungsamt (LD), Obstlt.i.G.*Hans-Jurgen Stumpff as *Chef der Luftpersonalamt (LP)* and *Obstlt.*Wilhelm Wimmer as *Chef der Technisches Amt (LC)*.

The only weak link was *Obst.i.G.*Erberhard Bohnstedt, the existing *Chef des Luftschützamt (LA)* who had originally been assigned to this post by *Gen.d.Inf.*Kurt von Equord-Hammerstein, the *Chef der Heeresleitung*, in an attempt to stop the *Reichsluftwaffe* from emerging with a truly separate identity The most logical alternative to Bohnstedt would have been *GenMaj.*Helmuth Wilberg who had done so much to promote the military air arm in the period 1919-27. However he had retired on the 30 November 1932. In response to Göring's request for a new *Chef LS*, Blomberg offered him a choice between Erich Frhr.von Manstein and Walther Wever, both of whom were considered to be outstanding officers. Stumpff would later state: *"Wever, I thought, was the better choice for the Luftkommando Amt, since I felt Manstein was too stubborn. Göring gladly accepted my recommendations and requested Wever's transfer from (Gen.d.Inf.Kurt Frhr.von) Hammerstein."*

Despite his non-aviation background Wever quickly became an air power enthusiast. He learned to fly at the age of 46 and having read Giulio Douhet's *Command of the Air* and Hitler's *Mein Kampf* he quickly came to the conclusion that the new *Reichsluftwaffe* would need to be an offensive air arm equipped with long range bombers capable of independent operations. He was an excellent "people manager" who had the knack of getting the very best from his subordinate officers. As a former member of the Imperial *Größer Generalstab* he possessed a wealth of staff experience both at an operational level as well as in command and ministerial appointments. As an *Oberst i.G.* he was appointed as *Chef des LS-Amt* on the 1 September 1933.

Photo 2B-1 Original caption: At the *Ehrenmal* **in the Unter den Linden, 1934.**

Bundesarchiv Bild 146-1973-023-07 Photo: Georg Pahl

On the 1 February 1934 Werner Frhr.von Fritsch was promoted to *Gen.d.Art.* and made *Chef der Heeresleitung* by *Reichspräsident* Hindenburg. Blomberg and Hitler had favoured the pro-NSDAP Walther von Reichenau but this had been resisted by *Gen.d.Inf.*Gerd von Rundstedt, the *Oberbefehlshaber von Gruppenkommando 1* in Berlin and by Hindenburg who preferred an apolitical appointment. Fritsch was an officer of exceptional military ability whose post-war appointments had included *Chef T 1* (1926-28), *Kdr.1.Kavallerie-Division* (1931-32) and *Bfr.Wehrkreis III* in Berlin (1932-34). He was extremely popular within the *Reichsheer* with an authority even greater than his mentor Hans von Seeckt. A strict Protestant with deeply held religious beliefs, he has been described as a humanitarian although later in the year his morality would not extend to his brother officers of Jewish faith whom he had dishonourably discharged. Together with *Gen.d.Art.*Wilhelm Ritter von Leeb, the *OB Gr.Kdo.2* in Kassel, Fritsch and Rundstedt were the most important army officers in the *Reichswehr* at that time.

Blomberg supported Hitler's policy of military expansion and rearmament and initially this took the form of actively supporting Göring in the creation of the *Reichsluftwaffe*. Following his appointment in January 1933 he removed the newly formed *Luftschützamt* from the direct control of the *Chef der Heeresleitung* to the *Reichswehrministerium* prior to its eventual reorganisation and transfer to Göring's *RLM* where in 1934 it was re-titled the *Luftkommando-Amt (LA)*. He also instructed the *Reichsheer and Reichsmarine* to transfer some 220 officers, including all those on the *geheime Fliegerliste* to the new *Luftwaffe* following its covert activation on the 27 April 1933. For the new *Chef LA*, Göring would be offered a choice between Erich von Manstein and Walther Wever, both outstanding staff officers suitable for eventual promotion of *Chef der Heeresleitung*. The final choice was *Obst.*Wever who became *Chef des Luftschützamt* in September 1933. At Blomberg's instigation other staff officers would follow including *Obst.i.G.*Heinrich Danckelmann and *Obstlt.i.G.*Ludwig Wolff.

*Reichspräsident GFM.a.D.*Paul von Hindenburg finally died on the 2 August 1934. With Blomberg, Göring and Fritsch's active support Hitler summarily assumed the position of *Reichspräsident* and in so doing became the *Oberbefehlshaber der Reichswehr*. Quite independently von Reichenau devised a new oath of allegiance: *"I swear by God this holy oath, that I will render to Adolf Hitler, Führer of the deutsches Reich, unconditional obedience, and that I am ready, as brave soldier, to risk my life at any time for this oath."* This oath was then taken by all serving members of the *Reichswehr* during the afternoon and evening of the 2 August 1934 thus confirming Hitler's new personal status as supreme military commander.

In October 1934 Hitler ordered Blomberg to treble the size of the *Reichsheer*. Blomberg and Fritsch decided that this would be accomplished using the existing seven *Wehrkreise*, each of which would in effect become a *Korps* headquarters for three divisions- in total 21 *Divisonen*. However this plan was quickly superseded by a plan for a *Friedensheeres* of 36 *Divisonen*, the additional personnel coming from conscription, a measure that was announced to the World by Hitler on the 16 March 1935. Three more *Wehrkreise* were activated, two of these coming from the disbanded 2. and 3.*Kavallerie-Divisionen* at Breslau and Kassel, and an additional one at Hamburg. Earlier in April 1934 Göring had ordered the formation of five, later six, *Höheren Luftamter* as the territorial basis for the *Reichsluftwaffe*; in March 1935 these would be re-titled *Luftkreise* in a similar manner to the *Reichsheer's* existing *Wehrkreise*.

Photo 2B-2 Original caption: The *Deutschlandflug* 1933. Pilot (Theodor) Osterkamp visits his aircraft with his bride. Aviatrix Gudrun Pagge and Theodor Osterkamp.
Bundesarchiv Bild 183-2008-1016-504 Photo: o.Ang.Scherl Agency

In addition to the serving officers who were transferred in 1933-34 it was essential that the covert *Luftwaffe* recruited suitable men from other walks of life. Due to the Allied restrictions many former *Luftstreitkräfte* personnel had been unable to join the *Reichswehr* and some of these had made a post-war career in the various Police forces which unlike the purely criminal investigation services of Britain and the USA had an armed para-military element – the *Landespolizei* and *Schützpolizei*.

Meanwhile to meet the needs of the first flying units and in particular the increasing numbers of *Fliegerschulen*, *Obstlt.i.G.*Hans-Jurgen Stumpff's *Personalamt* had worked quickly to secure the services of experienced professional aviators from commercial aviation. These men included Joachim-Friedrich Huth, Werner Junck, Fritz Morzik, Georg Pasewaldt, Carl-August von Schoenebeck and Theo Osterkamp. These aviators had nearly all seen active service during the Great War as *Leutnante* and senior *Unteroffiziere* and as such were employed as the *Reichsluftwaffe's* first generation of unit commanders seeing service in the flying schools and the covert operational units from the 1 April 1934.

Theodor Osterkamp had volunteered for training as a *Marineflieger* in August 1914 and had seen service as an observer with *Marine-Fliegerabteilung II* and *I* in Flanders. Having made a name for himself in this role and been commissioned, he had re-trained as a pilot in 1917 before joining Gotthard Sachsenberg's *Marine-Feldjagdstaffel I* where he quickly scored 5 *Luftsiege*. In June 1917 he became *Führer Marine-Feldjagdstaffel II* which he led with such skill that he could report the destruction of 100 enemy aircraft by July 1918 of which he had been responsible for sixteen. Awarded the *Pour le Mérite* on the 2 September 1918 his final score was 31 *LS*. Post-war he had served with Sachsenberg in Kurland before his formal discharge in January 1920. *Lt.d.Res.a.D.*Osterkamp was an early recruit to the *Reichsmarine's* clandestine *See-Versuchsabteilung (Severa) GmbH* (later *Luftdienst eV*) and he was *Leiter Seeflugstation Kiel-Holtenau* (1926-31) and *Leiter Seeflugstation Norderney* (1931-35). He was commissioned into the covert *Luftwaffe* with the rank of *Hauptmann* on the 1 August 1933 and he is seen here soon afterwards in his new *DLV* uniform with the rank of *Fliegerkäpitan*. As a *Sportflieger* he took part in the *Europa-Rundfluge* competitions of 1930, 1932 and 1934. Promoted to *Major (Fliegerkommandant)* in April 1934 he would become *Käpitan 5./JG 132 Richthofen* at Jüterbog-Damm a year later.

Photo 2B-3 Original caption: Social evening by leading members of the *Reichswehr* and the *SS* in the former *militärarztlichen Akademie* at Invalidenstrasse 48, Berlin. Clockwise around the table: *Fliegerchef* Karl Eberth, *Käpitan zur See* Wilhelm Canaris, *SS-Gruppenführer* and *Chef der SD* Reinhard Heydrich, the *Chef des Heeresverwaltungsamtes Generalmajor* Friedrich Karmann, the *Kommandeur der Kriegsakademie Generalleutnant* Curt Liebmann and *Fliegerkommodore* (Ralph) Wenninger.

Bundesarchiv Bild 183-H26899 Photo: o.Ang.

The *Reichsluftfahrtministerium* was established on the 5 May 1933 but it took almost a year for its organisational structure to be finally established. *FregKpt.*Ralph Wenninger, the former *Leiter der Luftschützgruppe/Marineleitung* and *Chef des Stabes des Luftschützamtes/RWM* became the *Leiter der Zentral-Abteilung (ZA)* on the 1 April 1934. The ZA's core function was the handling of the *RLM's* external relationships with political and diplomatic agencies at home and abroad. It consisted of the *Adjutanter d.RLM, Kommandant d.RLM, Bürodirecktor d.RLM*, the *Attachegruppe* (Attache Dept.), *Abwehrgruppe, Gruppe Rechtswesen, Gruppe Politische Angelegenheiten, Pressegruppe* and the *Gruppe Sanitätswesen*. Ralph Wenninger did not transfer to the covert *Reichsluftwaffe* until the 1 October 1934 when he was simultaneously promoted to *Käpitan zur See* and *Oberst*.

Fliegerchef Karl Eberth was one of the five retired *Reichsheer Generale* who were re-called for duty with the *Reichsluftwaffe* in April 1934. Ebert was a former *bayerischen Artillerieoffizier* from well before the Great War. He spent the whole of the war period as a *Generalstabsoffizier* before being retained by the *Reichsheer* for service with *Artillerie-Rgt.7*. His final appointment had been as *Artillerie-Führer VII* at München and before he was retired on the 30 November 1930 with the honorary rank of *Generalleutnant*. On the 1 April 1934 he was appointed *Präsident des Höheren Luftamtes München* with overall responsibility for aviation matters within Bayern, Württemberg, Baden and Hessen. His staff consisted of a *Chef des Stabes* (Chief of Staff), *Führungs-Abt.* (Command Branch), *Personal-Abt.* (Adjutant Branch), *Gerichts-Abt.* (Legal Branch), *Verwaltungs-Abt.* (Administrative Branch) and a *Luftfahrt-Abt.* (Civil Aviation Branch). The day to day aspects of his work insofar as civil aviation was concerned were delegated to the individual *Luftamtes* at Frankfurt/Main, München, Nürnberg, Stuttgart and Wiesbaden. The remaining *Höheren Luftamter* were located at Königsberg/Ostpr., Berlin, Dresden and Hannover. In July 1934 Göring created an additional functional rather than territorial *Höheren Luftamt* at Kiel for all matters pertaining to marine aviation.

The remaining officers around this dinner table in early 1935 include Wilhelm Canaris who was *Leiter des Amtes Ausland/Abwehr* within the *RWM* with overall responsibility for intelligence and counter-intelligence work on behalf of the *Reichswehr*, and Reinhard Heydrich who would gain notoriety as the ruthless *Leiter des Sicherheitsdienst* within Heinrich Himmler's *SS*. He had played a leading role in the execution of the Night of the Long Knives in June 1934 and was responsible for all internal security matters on behalf of the *NSDAP*.

Photo 2C-1 Original caption: Heavy plane crash near Dresden. The aircraft on the Berlin-Wien route, departed the *Zentralflughafen Tempelhof* and crashed shortly before landing in Dresden, all 8 occupants were killed. [06/10/1930]. Our picture shows the *Messerschmitt-Type*, which includes the crashed airliner D-1930 which was flown by pilot Erich Pust.

Bundesarchiv Bild 183-R08592 Photo o.Ang. (Scherl)

The bad feeling that was to persist between *Staatssekretär* Erhard Milch and the aircraft designer *Professor* Willy Messerschmitt has its origins in Milch's decision as *Leitender Mitarbeiter der Deutsche Luft Hansa* to cancel the outstanding *DLH* order for ten BFW M 20 airliners in 1931 following the loss of M 20b WNr.443 D-1930 at Dresden on the 6 October 1930 and WNr.442 D-1928 at Breslau on the 14 April 1931. This decision forced the *Bayerische Flugzeugwerke AG (BFW)* into bankruptcy at the beginning of June 1931 and effectively ruined Messerschmitt and his colleague Theo Croneiss.

Fortunately Messerschmitt's patents had been held by the dormant *Messerschmitt Flugzeugbau GmbH* which was re-activated with private finance, money from the sale of manufacturing rights for the M 23 to Romania and the re-instatement of production of the M 20 and M 28 after a successful legal battle to force *DLH* to honour its orders for those types. After several other battles including an attempt by Ernst Heinkel to acquire the Augsburg factory in 1932, it became possible to re-establish the *BFW AG* on the 1 May 1933 albeit with just 82 employees. Invitations to tender designs for the covert *Reichsluftwaffe's* new combat aircraft should then have followed but Milch's distrust of Messerschmitt initially restricted *BFW's* involvement in Germany's aerial re-armament to teh licence construction of just 30 Dornier Do 11 *Kampfflugzeuge* and 24 Heinkel He 45 *Fernaufklärer*. Despite the success of his M 37 *Reiseflugzeuge* (Bf 108) in the *Europa-Rundflug* of 1934, Messerschmitt found it almost impossible to tender for new work from the *RLM* and it was only with lobbying of Göring by his close friend *Reichsleiter* Rudolf Hess that he was allowed to submit a design proposal to meet the *Luftkommando Amt's Rustungsflugzeuge* requirement for a single seat *Jagdflugzeuge* to replace the Heinkel He 51 which was just entering series production. The result was a development contract for the Bf 109 which would compete for a production contract with the Ar 81, He 112 and Fw 159.

Photo 2D-1 Original caption: Our successful *Seekampfflieger Oberleutnant* Christiansen – A studio portrait of Friedrich Christiansen with medals (including the *Pour le Mérite*, awarded on 11 December 1917).

Bundesarchiv Bild 146-2013-0006 Photo: o.Ang. Postenkartenvertrieb W.Sanke, Berlin

Examination of the *Reichsluftfahrtministerium's* Officer Roster for the 1 June 1933 shows a considerable dependence on former military and naval officers who were either transferred from recruited from civilian positions within the *Reichswehrministerium* or were appointed directly from the civilian sector. For example *Maj.a.D.*Hilmer Frhr.von Bülow was already *Chef der Abteilung Fremde Luftstreitkräfte in der Truppenamt* and he simply transferred to a similar position within the *Luftkommando Amt (LA)* in June 1934, whilst *Oblt.z.See a.D.*Hans-Jochen von Arnim, a former naval aviator who had been employed by *Junkers-Luftverkehrs AG* and the *Oberschlesischen Luftverkehrs AG*, would eventually be assigned to the *Kommando der Schulen*.

*KptLt.a.D.*Friedrich Christiansen was another former naval officer who had been engaged in civil aviation, in his case as *Kommandant* of the *Flugschiff* Dornier Do X during the trans-Atlantic flights of 1931-33. In March 1933 he was recruited for service in Göring's newly formed *RLM* where he became a *Ministerialrat* and eventually *Inspekteur der Schulen* with the rank of *Kpt.z.See*.

This was a particular important appointment given Göring's emphasis on training during the secret establishment phase of the *Reichsluftwaffe*.

Born on the 12 December 1879 in Wyk auf Fohr on the Nordsee coast of Schleswig-Holstein, Friedrich Christiansen was the son of a sea captain. He went to sea at the age of 15 and by the age of 22 was *2.Offizier* on the large sailing vessel *Preussen*. Following a short period of compulsory naval service in 1901-02 he was discharged into the *Reserve* and returned to the *Handelsmarine* where he gained his Master's papers and employment on the High Seas. He learned to fly, receiving his pilot's certificate in March 1914.

Following the outbreak of hostilities he was recalled for service as a flying instructor at Kiel-Holtenau and as such was one of the earliest naval aviators in a service that had placed its pre-war hopes in *Luftschiffe* rather than heavier-than-air aeroplanes. In January 1915 he was posted to the *Seeflugstation Zeebrugge* in occupied Belgium where he served as a pilot flying artillery shoots and reconnaissance patrols off the coasts of France, England the Netherlands, together with attacks on Dover, Deal, Ramsgate and Margate on the 19 March 1916. He was commissioned as a *Leutnant der Reserve der Matrosen-Artillerie* on the 18 February 1916 and appointed *Staffelführer* prior to assuming more extensive responsibilities as *Oberleutnant, Geschwaderführer* and *Stationsleiter Flandern I* from September 1917. Zeebrugge was the largest and most active of the *Marineflieger's Seeflugstationen* in Flanders and the home for between 35-50 *Seeflugzeuge*. During this period he completed 440 *Feindflüge* in the course of 1,164 flying hrs, executed a daring rescue mission for the crew of the *Torpedoboot S 20* in July 1917, and in a series of successful joint missions with the *U-Booten* based in Belgium captured five steamships. He had a number of *Luftsiege* including the British airship C-27 which he destroyed off Lowestoft on the 11 December. For these achievements and more he was decorated with the *Plm* on the 11 December 1917. In the final year of the war *KptLt.*Christiansen used the advanced new Hansa Brandenburg W 29 fighter seaplane to inflict serious losses on British naval vessels and aircraft in the Nordsee and off the English coast. His personal score was 27 *LS*.

Photo 2D-2 Original caption: The *Fest der Flieger*, 1934 in the *Festsalen im Zoologischen Garten*. The following aviation pioniers were honoured: (from left to right): Thelen, Mackenthun, *GehRat.*Schutte, Bruno Loerzer (*Präsident des DLV*), Staatssekretär Milch, Prof.von Parseval and Hans Grade.

Bundesarchiv Bild 183-2008-0414-500 Photo: o.Ang. Scherl Agency

Given the emphasis to be placed on the training of flight personnel, the politicisation of the existing *Deutsche Luftfahrtverband eV (DLV)* was one of *Reichskommissar* Göring's key objectives in 1933. On the 25 March 1933 he established the *Deutschen Luftsportverband eV,* a new organisation which absorbed all the formerly independent flying clubs and air sport related organisations. These included the *Technische Hochschulen's Akamedischen Fliegergruppen*, the *Ring Deutscher Flieger* and the *Sturmvogel*. Also included were the newly created *NSDAP Fliegersturme* of both the SA and SS. In this way Göring pre-empted attempts by Ernst Röhm and Heinrich Himmler to establish their own "private" air arms which in the fullness of time may have even challenged the legitimacy of the still covert *Reichsluftwaffe*.

Göring appointed *Hptm.a.D.*Bruno Loerzer, his wartime friend and colleague, as *Reichsluftsportführer* and *Präsident des DLV*. The new *DLV's* objectives were to promote flying and aviation within Germany, train flight and technical personnel for future integration into the *Reichsluftwaffe*, to provide proficiency training for existing flight and technical personnel and to supervise and promote sport aviation within Germany and in international competitions. As Göring saw the *DLV* to be a *Luftwaffe-Reserve* in the making, it quickly became a uniformed para-military force organised on a territorial basis with a total of sixteen *Fliegerlandesgruppen* which reported to Loerzer's headquarters in Berlin. The *DLV* established an increasing number of *Segelflugabteilungen* (Glider Detachments), *Fliegerausbildungs-* (Pilot Training) and *Fliegerübungsstellen* (Pilot Proficiency Centres) for its 30,000 members. Eventually its *Fliegerjugend* (Youth Wing) would grow to a similar size offering opportunities for model aircraft making and competition and glider training.

In this photograph from 1934 *Staatssekretär* Erhard Milch and *Reichsluftsportführer* Bruno Loerzer, both wearing their new *DLV* uniforms, honour the pioneers of German aviation: Robert Thelen who was awarded Pilot Certificate Nr.9 on the 11 May 1910 and who made a number of pre-war record breaking flights, before becoming a test pilot for *Albatros* and from 1926 *Leiter der Prufabteilung/DVL* at Berlin-Adlershof; *Prof.*August von Parseval who with *Zeppelin* and *Schütz-Lange*, pioneered airship design building 22 non-rigid or semi-rigid military airships between 1905-18, thereafter remaining active in airship design; *Hptm.a.D.* Walter von Mackenthun who as a *Leutnant* became Germany's first *Militärflieger*, *Fhr. Jasta 15* and thereafter the force behind Germany's first airlines - *Deutsche Luft-Reederei (DLR), Deutscher Aero Lloyd (DAL)* and *Deruluft*. Choosing not to join *Deutsche Luft Hansa*, he was the Editor *Luft-Magazins* from 1926 and in 1927 established the *Verein Alte Adler* – an association for pre-war aviators; *Flugpionier* Hans Grade who was who first flew in a triplane of his own design in 1908 before establishing Germany's first flying school in 1910, post-war he had established *Grade Automobilwerke AG* to build small sports cars. In 1934 he was looking to re-enter aviation with designs for a *Volksflugzeuge* (People's Plane).

Photo 2D-3 Original caption: The first *Nazi Flugtag* in Staaken near Berlin on 9 April 1933. *National Sozialisten* in preparation for the take-off of a new self-built glider at Staaken. *Flieger SA.*

Bundesarchiv Bild 102-14501 Photo: Georg Pahl

Within the *NSDAP's* para-military formations it was Ernst Röhm's *Sturmabteilung (SA)* who first ordered the formation of a aviation detachment when he established the *SA-Fliegersturme*. Expertise was sought from within the established aviation community and *Lt.a.D.Dr.rer.pol.* Günther Ziegler, former Director of *Sportflug GmbH* and the *Deutsche Verkehrsfliegerschule (DVS)*, was appointed as *Referent beim Stab der Obersten SA-Führung* in April 1931, being succeeded in this capacity by *Oblt.a.D.*Theodor Croneiss, an active Director of the *Bayerische Flugzeugwerke AG* and the *Nordbayerische Verkehrsflug GmbH*, who was appointed *Fliegerreferent der Obersten SA-Führung* in 1933.

Meanwhile in November 1931 Heinrich Himmler ordered that a small number of *Schütz Staffel (SS)* personnel were to be given flight training within a newly formed München based *SS-Fliegersturm*. A particularly influential figure in this new organisation was *Hptm.a.D.*Eduard Ritter von Schleich, the *Schwarzer-Ritter*, who had achieved 35 *Luftsiege* in a distinguished military career that had included time as *Fhr.d.Militärflugschule 1, Fhr.d.Schusta 28, Fhr.d.Jasta 21, Fhr.d.JGr.3* and ultimately *Kdr.d.bayerischen JG IV*. He was awarded the *Pour le Mérite* on the 4 December 1917. Post-war he had remained active in civil aviation and was employed by the *Trans-Europa Union, Junkers-Luftverkehr* and *Deutsche Luft Hansa* before he became the *Ltr.d.Fliegerschule Eibl* in 1930. He was appointed *Fhr.d.SS-Fliegerstaffel Süd* in October 1931.

Both the *SA/SS-Fliegersturme* were absorbed into the *DLV* in September 1933, presumably following agreements between Göring, Röhm and Himmler. This move should be seen as a wider rationalisation of the *NSDAP's* hierarchy's roles and responsibilities, for example in April 1934 Göring passed control of the *Gestapo* to Himmler. However it was also indicative of the on-going rivalries and power battles within the upper echelons of the *NSDAP* which would ultimately lead to the suppression of the *SA's* senior leadership in June 1934.

This photograph from the 9 April 1933 is indicative of this period when elements of the *NSDAP* briefly maintained their own "air arms". Members of the Berlin based *SA-Fliegersturm* are seen with a bungee-launched primary glider at a *National Sozialist Flugtag*. From September trained pilots the *SS/SA* were entitled to wear the *SS-SA Fliegerabzeichen* on their new *DLV* uniform.

Photo 2E-1 Original caption: Opening of the Winterhilfswerkes 1934-1935 by the leader in the *Reichstag* on the 9 October 1934. Berlin, *Reichstag* (Kroll Opera House) Adolf Hitler speech, from the left on the government benches Wilhelm Frick, Hermann Göring, Joseph Goebbels, behind Eltz of Rübenach, Richard Walther Darré, Franz Seldte, Hjalmar Schacht and Werner von Blomberg.
Bundesarchiv Bild 102-04121 Photo: Georg Pahl

On the 17 May 1933 Hitler addressed the *Reichstag* with the words: *"Germany is entirely ready to renounce all offensive weapons if the armed nations, on their side, will destroy their offensive weapons... Germany would also be perfectly ready to disband her entire military establishment and destroy the small amount of arms remaining to her, if the neighbouring countries will do the same... Germany is prepared to agree to any solemn pact of non-aggression, because she does not think of attacking but only of acquiring security."*

Adolf Hitler was appointed *Reichskanzler* at a time of an international desire for universal disarmament. In 1932 sixty nations had come together in Geneva to attend the Conference for the Reduction and Limitation of Armaments. Ever the astute politician, Hitler seized upon this theme to justify his eventual decision to rearm Germany. He would offer arms reduction in the certainty that such a proposal would be rejected; he would then counter with proposals for limited rearmament to gain parity; then if all of his proposals were rejected he would be able to withdraw Germany from the League of Nations having assumed the moral high ground and continue with his underlying desire to expand the *Reichswehr*.

Hitler formally withdrew Germany from both the Disarmament Conference and the League of Nations on the 14 October 1933. Not surprisingly the French had not been willing to forego their military superiority over the Germans, especially as neither Britain nor the USA were willing to provide the necessary assurances if the French voluntarily disarmed. The national plebiscite on Hitler's decision and his proposal for a single party *Reichstag* – naturally that of the *NSDAP* – was carried with a massive 95% and 92% approval respectively. The turn-out on the 12 November had been astonishingly high – 96%. Thus in one bold policy move, Hitler had not only secured his own political position and that of the *NSDAP*, but also the approval of the Germany people to his isolationist foreign policy and re-armament.

This photograph was taken nearly a year later on the 9 October 1934. By this time, Hitler's position was virtually unassailable. He had neutralised the threat from the communist left politically, whilst the extreme right within his own party had been bloodily removed. Following the death of Hindenburg he had merged the position of *Reichspräsident* with that of *Reichskanzler* with the full backing of the *Reichswehr*'s most senior officers. Economic recovery was firmly underway reducing long term unemployment and boosting national productivity. Much of this economic regeneration would of course be associated with re-armament and this was especially true in the *Luftfahrtindustrie* where in the nineteen months from 31 January 1933 employment had risen from 3,988 to 43,094 workers.

Key members of Hitler's Kabinett can be seen on the far side of the podium: *Reichsinnernminister Dr.*Wilhelm Frick, *Reichsluftfahrtminister* Hermann Göring, *Reichsminister für Volksaufklärung und Propaganda Dr.*Josef Goebbels, *Reichsverkehrsminister* Paul Frhr.Eltz von Rübenach. *Leiter Rasse-und Siedlungshaupt Reichsbauernführer* Richard Darre, *Reichsarbeitsminister* Franz Seldte,

*Reichswirtschaftsminister Dr.*Hjalmar Schacht and *Reichswehrminister GenOb.*Werner von Blomberg.

Photo 2E-2 Original caption: Labour service men visited the *Jagdstaffel "Richthofen"* at Döberitz in Berlin for the first time on 3 August 1935. *Flugplatz Döberitz* - members of the *Reichsarbeitsdienstes* with *Jagdgeschwader "Richthofen"* help push a *Schulflugzeugs* Heinkel He 72 *Kadett* (Registered: D-ELIF, with the legend *Reklame-Staffel Mitteldeutschland des DLV* on the rear fuselage).

Bundesarchiv Bild 102-04676A Photo: Georg Pahl

The *Reichsheer's* first air units had been the three *Reklamestaffeln* that had been established in response to *Reichswehrminister* Wilhelm Groener's concerns over the realism of the *Reichswehr's* air defence training in 1930. Outwardly these units belonged to the *Deutsche Luftfahrt GmbH* but in reality they were staffed by experienced instructor pilots from Lipetsk and were officially subordinate to their parent *Wehrkreis I* (Königsberg), *III* (Berlin) and *VII* (München) respectively. Each *Staffel* consisted of four aircraft, initially the Albatros L 82c *Sportflugzege*, and these aircraft were subsequently employed to provide a degree of realism during military manoeuvres whilst at other times they maintained an overt cover by towing banners which advertised a variety of different consumer products. The *Reklamestaffel Ostpreussen* was located at Königsberg, the *Reklamestaffel Mitteldeutschland* at Berlin-Staaken and the *Reklamestaffel Süddeutschland* at Nürnberg-Fürth, whilst their activities were co-ordinated by the *Stab/Reklameabteilung* in Berlin. The initial command personnel were *Maj.(Char.)* Gustav Kastner-Kirdorf (*Kdr.*), Karl-Friedrich Knust (*Ostpreussen*), Edgar Petersen (*Mitteldeutschland*) and Gerhard Ulbricht (*Süddeutschland*).

Edgar Petersen had joined the *Reichsheer* in August 1926 and had immediately begun flight training with the *Deutsche Verkehrsfliegerschule (DVS) Zweigstellen* at *Stettin* and *Schleißheim*. Good enough to be employed as an instructor he was re-assigned to the *Fliegerschule Lipetsk* where he served in this capacity on the Fokker D.XIII from 1929-31. He then served as *Käpitan Reklamestaffel Mitteldeutschland* at Staaken, later Döberitz, from 1932-34. In 1934 he was posted to the *Infanterieschule Dresden* and in April of that year the assets of the *Reklamestaffeln Mittel-*and *Süddeutschland* were amalgamated at Döberitz to create the *Reichsluftwaffe's* first covert *Jagdgruppe* – the *Fliegergruppe Döberitz* which was equipped with the Arado Ar 65E *Jagdflugzeuge* under the command of *Maj.*Robert Ritter von Greim.

This photograph shows one of the *Reichsheer's* new *Schulflugzeuge* which were ordered in quantity under *Staatssekretär* Erhard Milch's *Rheinland Programm* of July 1934. The Heinkel He 72 *Kadett* was an *A Schulmaschine*, the *A-Reihe* being powered by the 150 hp Argus As 8R *Reihenmotor*, whilst the *B-Reihe* (seen here) had a 160 hp Siemens und Halske Sh 14A *Sternmotor*. Following the appearance of two aircraft in 1933, the *Ernst Heinkel Flugzeugwerke AG* went on to complete eighty aircraft in 1934 and production would continue at the new factory at Rostock-Marienehe for two more years by which time 235 had been built. The He 72 was an A2 Class aircraft with an all up weight between 500 and 1,000 kgs and as such was registered in the D-E Series introduced in March 1934.

Photo 2E-3 Original caption: Junkers Ju 52 named *"Hermann Göring"* (Registered D-AJIM) of the *Regierungsstaffel*, later the *Fliegerstaffel des Führers*.

Bundesarchiv Bild 146-1989-014-30 Photo: o.Ang.

By the early thirties many air power theorists had decided that the use of military aircraft for aerial bombardment could well be decisive in a future conflict. This view had been popular within *Obstlt.*Hellmuth Felmy's *Inspektion 1 (L)* and from 1933-34 it was embraced enthusiastically by Hermann Göring, Erhard Milch and Walther Wever. The *National Sozialist* view of air power centred on the creation of a *Riskio-Flotte* or Deterrent Air Force, a powerful force of bombing aircraft that would be able to lay waste to a hostile nation's cities and infrastructure. Given the widely held international concerns over the threat posed by bombing, such an approach had merit. Theorists such as *Dr.*Robert Knauss also argued that such an approach was highly cost effective, indeed a far better use of resources than the *Reichsmarine's* costly *Panzerschiff-Programm.*

On the basis of the Lipetsk trials, the Dornier Do F had been selected by *Obstlt.*Wilhelm Wimmer's *Wa.Prw.8F* as the *Reichsluftwaffe's* first *Nachtbomber-Land.* This twin-engine monoplane was of modern design with a retractable undercarriage. It could carry a maximum load of five SC 250 bombs under the fuselage or up to thirty SC 50 bombs in six vertical bomb magazines within the fuselage. A 1,000 kg offensive load could be carried over 1,200 kms or a 1,500 kg load over 690 kms. This made it suitable for attacks on Paris from air bases in western Germany. In all orders were placed for 1,000 of these new aircraft, but service units quickly found the type to be dangerously deficient. Under certain flight conditions the wing would flex and vibrate which required turns to be limited to 45 degrees of bank, whilst the aircraft exhibited poor directional stability. Nor were the aircraft's Siemens und Halske Sh 22 radial engines any more satisfactory, the rush to mass produce this metric version of the Bristol Jupiter radial having resulted in poor quality control, and if these problems were not enough the complex electro-mechanical retraction system for the main undercarriage proved unreliable.

Following several fatal crashes, *Obst.*Wimmer *(Chef LC)* and *Maj.*Wolfram Frhr.von Richthofen *(Chef LC II)* held a key meeting with *Obst.*Hugo Sperrle *(Kdr.Fliegerdivision Nr.1)* and *Obst.*Alfred Keller *(Kdr.Fliegergruppe Fassberg)* on the 19 December 1934 at which it was decided to halt production of the Do 11D in favour of the slightly improved Do 13C. In the interim production of the reliable Junkers Ju 52/3m was stepped up, with the aircraft being modified with *Sonderausrüstung II* (defensive armament) and *III* (drop ordnance racks and bomb sight) as the Ju 52/3m g3e. The resultant *Behelfsbomber* could carry six SC 250 or twenty-four SC 50 internally over a range of 750 kms or 900 kgs over 1,200 kms, and it was this type that actually formed the primary equipment of the newly formed *Fliegergruppe Fassberg* and *Tutow* from June 1934.

This image probably dates from 1935-36 and shows Ju 52/3m ge WNr.4050 *Hermann Göring*, an unarmed VIP transport that was employed by *GenOb.*Werner von Blomberg as *Reichswehrminister.* It is thought that this particular aircraft crashed at Frankfurt on the 19 September 1936.

Photo 2E-4 Original caption: *Panzerschiff Deutschland* **– launched 19 May 1931, change of name to *Lützow* on the 15 November 1939, wrecked 4 May 1945, sunk in 1947; in the *Kaiser Wilhelm Kanal* passing the *Levensauer Hochbrucke.***

Bundesarchiv Bild 134-C0095 Photo: o.Ang.

The new *Panzerschiff Deutschland* passes through the *Kaiser Wilhelm Kanal* in the winter months at some point before the formation of the *Kriegsmarine* in 1935. Displacing 11,700 tonnes (Standard load) the vessel had a draught of 5.81 m in this configuration. Her main armament of six 28 cm SK C/28 in two triple turrets together with her secondary armament of eight 15 cm SK C/28 in single mountings can be clearly seen. Although designed to accommodate a catapult and two shipboard aircraft these have yet to be fitted. The *Reichsmarine* was justifiably proud of its new Flagship which was the first of three such vessels to be commissioned. The *Admiral Scheer* was commissioned on the 12 November 1934 and the *Admiral Graf Spee* on the 6 January 1936.

The *Kaiser Wilhelm Kanal* was constructed across the base of the Jutland Peninsula between 1887-95 to permit the transfer of naval vessels from Kiel in the Ostsee to the Brunsbuttelkoog on the Elbemundung. This strategic waterway avoided the potentially vulnerable routing of shipping through the Skagerrak and Kattegat and at 85 kms in length it shortened the distance between Hamburg and

Kiel by 685 kms. As the size of the *Kaiserliche Marine's Linienschiffe* increased the *Kanal* was widened and deepened to a depth of 11 m between 1905-14. It normally took 7-8 hours for a vessel to negotiate the seaward end locks and pass through the *Kanal* at a speed of 8 kts. In addition to its naval traffic the *Kanal* was a particularly important route for mercantile shipping with 13.4 million tons passing through in 1934. The chief cargoes carried were coal, ores, lumber and cereals.

Photo 2E-5 Original caption: *Leichter Kreuzer "Karlsruhe"* - **Launched 20 August 1927, sunk off Kristiansand 9 April 1940.**

Bundesarchiv Bild 134-B0309 Photo: o.Ang.

After the design of the *kleine Kreuzer Emden* was finalised in 1921 there was a major re-think in future cruiser design within the *Reichsmarine*. Under the successive direction of *Admirals* Behncke and Zenker a requirement evolved for a powerfully armed light cruiser capable of use as a fleet scout or ocean raider. Germany's naval architects were accordingly instructed to design the largest, fastest and heaviest gunned ship that was possible within a hull of 6,000 tonnes – this being the limit set under the terms of the Treaty of Versailles.

Armed with nine 15 cm SK C/25 in three triple turrets the *Königsberg-Klasse* had a considerable superiority in hitting power when compared to existing British light cruisers and was slightly superior to the new French *Duguay-Trouin* Class. The planned roles favoured a concentration in firepower to the rear of the vessel and to this end two turrets were located aft, albeit in a rather unusual offset arrangement. Two single 8.8 cm FlaK L/45 constituted the secondary armament, whilst the increasing threat from air attack was countered with four twin 3.7 cm SKC/30 mountings. A heavy torpedo outfit of four triple 50 cm banks was also included. The design incorporated a catapult between the two funnels for a He 60 *Bordflugzeug* but this was not fitted initially due to the Treaty restrictions. As the preferred diesel engines would not be available in time, conventional steam turbines were installed with secondary diesel cruising motors   a complex machinery installation that was to cause problems. Bunker capacity for 1,184 tonnes fuel oil and 261 tonnes of diesel fuel was provided. A reasonable protective scheme was incorporated but with all this weight the architects were forced to compromise in these vessels structural integrity despite the fact that 85% of the structure was electrically welded to keep within the design parameters. This too would become a problem for Blue Water operations. However at the time the appearance of these fine new ships was a valuable boost to morale within the *Reichsmarine*.

Kleine Kreuzer Karlsruhe (*Kreuzer C*) was the second of three ships of the *Königsberg-Klasse* - *Königsberg* (*Kreuzer B*) was commissioned on the 17 April 1929 and *Köln* (*Kreuzer D*) was commissioned on the 15 January 1930. *Karlsruhe* was built by the *Deutsche Werke, Kiel* (*Bau-Nr.207*) at a cost of RM 36 million during 1927-29. She commissioned on the 6 November 1929 under *FregKpt.*Eugen Lindau and after her shake-down cruise and trials she was assigned to the *Inspektuer des Bildungswesens der Marine* as a training ship for officer candidates from May 1930 until June 1936.

Of those *Marineoffiziere* with *Sonderausbildung (Fliegeroffiziere)* it is known that *KptLt.* Otto Schroeder-Zollinger held the position of *Torpedo Offizier* aboard the *Königsberg* during 27 September 1932 and 30 September 1933 and that *KorvKpt.*Hermann Bruch was *I.Offizier* aboard the *Köln* during the period 4 April 1932 until the 31 March 1934. Other *Fliegeroffiziere* that served aboard these *kleine Kreuziere* during 1930 were *KptLt.*Werner Goette (*Köln*) and *Oblt.z.S.*Hans Metzner (*Karlsruhe*).

Part 2 Appendices

Appendix A

Rank Equivalencies

5 DECEMBER 1933

REICHSHEER	REICHSMARINE	DEUTSCHE LUFTSPORTVERBAND
Generalfeldmarschall		
Generaloberst	Generaladmiral	
General der …	Admiral	Reichsminister
		Staatssekretär
Generalleutnant	Vizeadmiral	Fliegerchef
Generalmajor	Konteradmiral	Fliegervizechef
		Kommodore
Oberst	Käpitan zur See	Fliegerkommodore
Oberstleutnant	Fregattenkäpitan	Fliegervizekommodore
Major	Korvettenkäpitan	Fliegerkommandant
Hauptmann	Käpitanleutnant	Fliegerkäpitan
Rittmeister		
Oberleutnant	Oberleutnant zur See	Schwarmführer
Leutnant	Leutnant zur See	Kettenführer
Stabsfeldwebel	Stabsfeldwebel	
Oberfeldwebel	Oberfeldwebel	Obermeister
Feldwebel	Feldwebel	Meister
Unterfeldwebel	Obermaat	Untermeister
Unteroffizier	Maat	Flugzeugführer
Stabsgefreiter	Matrosenoberstabsgefr.	
	Matrosenstabsgefreiter	
	Matrosenhauptgefreiter	
Obergefreiter	Matrosenobergefreiter	Hilfsflugzeugführer
Gfreiter	Matrosengefreiter	Oberflieger
Oberschutze		
Schütze	Matrose	Flieger

Der Reichsverteidigungsminister und Befehlshaber der gesamten Wehrmacht LP Nr.1555/33 g.kdos.II, Berlin, den 5.12.1933

Appendix B

Reichswehr Personnel known to have Trained in Italy

1 JULY - 30 SEPTEMBER 1933

Leiter - Maj.Curt Pflugbeil

Jagdfliegerlehrgang	Beobachterlehrgang
Nicolaus von Below	Hans Grunow
Anselm Brasser	Martin Gutzmann
Siegfried von Eschwege	Hans Heidemeyer
Adolf Galland	Johannes Hubner
Ortwin Giesse	Heinrich von Klitzing
Kurt von Greiff	Arthur Menke
Adolf Haring	Friedrich Moricke
Dietrich Heisterman von Ziehlberg	Frithjof Pasquay
Jobst-Heinrich von Heydebreck	Friedrich Prager
Claus Hinkelbein	Gundolf Frhr.Schenk zu Schweinsberg
Lothar von Janson	Ulrich Schmidt
Hans-Günther von Kornatzki	Heinrich Trettner
Ernst Kusserow	
Siegfried Lehmann	
Kurt Leonhardy	
Otto Pilger	
Georg Rieke	
Hermann Schmidt	
Erich von Selle	
Karl Frhr.von Wechmar	
Otto Winterer	
Hans-Hugo Witt	

Appendix C

Reichsheer Fliegeroffiziere with the Reklameabteilung

1930-34

Nicolaus von Below Oct 33 (Staaken) JG 132	Hans-G.von Kornatzki Apr 34 (Döberitz) JG 132
Axel von Blomberg Oct 33 (Staaken) JG 132	Siegfried Lehmann Oct 33 JG 132
Hans Busolt Oct 33 (Furth) JG 132	Günther Lützow Oct 34 (Döberitz) JG 132
Friedrich Dreyer Nov 30 – Dec 33	Siegfried Mahrenholtz Nov 30 – Jan 34 Inf.Rgt.
Sie'frd von Eschwege Dec 33 (Kap.Furth) JG 132	Edgar Petersen 32 – 34 (Kap.Staaken) Inf.Schule
Lothar von Janson Oct 33 (Kap.Königsberg) JG 132	Gerhard Ulbricht Oct 30 – Nov 33 (Kap.Furth) DVS
Gustav Kastner-Kirdorf Dec 33 (Kdr.Abt.) RLM	Otto Winterer Oct 33 – Jan 34 (Staaken) Rechlin
Friedrich-Karl Knust Oct 30 (Kap.Königsberg)	

Appendix D

Aircraft Registered to the Reklameabteilung der DVL

Junkers A 35	1084	D-1109	Ex-Flugsicherung	
Albatros L 82c	10163	D-1878	Ex-Deutsche Luftfahrt	Destroyed Jun 34
Albatros L 82c	10167	D-1927	Ex-Deutsche Luftfahrt	
Albatros L 82c	10168	D-1932	Ex-Deutsche Luftfahrt	
Albatros L 82c	10169	D-1933	Ex-Deutsche Luftfahrt	
Albatros L 82c	10170	D-1934	Ex-Deutsche Luftfahrt	
Albatros L 82c	10171	D-1935	Ex-Deutsche Luftfahrt	
Albatros L 82c	10172	D-1938	Ex-Deutsche Luftfahrt	
Albatros L 82c	10173	D-1940	Ex-Deutsche Luftfahrt	
Albatros L 82c	10174	D-1945	Ex-Deutsche Luftfahrt	
Albatros L 82c	10175	D-1946	Ex-Deutsche Luftfahrt	
Albatros L 82c	10177	D-1951	Ex-Deutsche Luftfahrt	
Albatros L 82c	10178	D-1953	Ex-Deutsche Luftfahrt	
Junkers F 13 ko	2079	D-2316	Ex-DLV	

Appendix E

Aircraft Registered to Luftbild Gmbh, Berlin

Rumpler C I	8486	D-75		
Junkers F 13 f1e	545	D-OKUF	Ex-lsd OLAG (A-96) (formerly D-332)	
Junkers F 13 d1e	734	D-373	Ex-DLH	
Dornier Do B Merkur	95	D-969		To DVL/Adlershof

Appendix F

Aircraft Registered to the Reichsamt für Flugsicherung

Junkers A 20	868	D-708	Ex-RLM & DVS	
Junkers A 20	1053	D-900	Ex-RLM & DVS	
Junkers A 35	1059	D-987	Ex-DVS	
Junkers A 35	1062	D-989	Ex-RDL & DVS	Destroyed 34
Junkers A 35	1084	D-1109	Ex RDL & DVL	To Reklame-Abt.
Albatros L 75b	10135	D-1543	Ex-DVS (Zentralstelle für Flugsicherung)	
Albatros L 75e	10150	D-1755	Ex-DVS (Zentralstelle für Flugsicherung)	
Junkers F 13 he	2056	D-1959	Ex-RDL & DVS	To DVS
Focke Wulf A 47a	121	D-2295	Zentralstelle für Flugsicherung	

The *Reichsamt für Flugsicherung* was responsible for the promotion of flight safety throughout Germany. Its aircraft were probably used to check the accuracy of wireless navigation aids at the main civil airports.

Known Dornier Do F Registrations

The Dornier Do F had been selected in 1932 as the *Luftwaffe's* first dedicated night bomber. The first production aircraft appeared in 1933 and a number were registered to the *Deutsche Reichsbahn* as freight transports and although commonly referred to as the Do F they were in reality Do 11C/Da aircraft. The Do 11C/D was produced in quantity for the *Luftwaffe* during 1933-34. The first 32 aircraft were c/n 261-292 and these were initially registered numerically on the *LFR-B*. Later aircraft c/n 301-349 (49) 531-545 (15), 561-572 (12) & 615-626 (12) were registered on the new 1934 *LFR*. The last three batches were built at *Dornier's* new Wismar facility and it seems that in all 120 Do 11 *Kampfflugzeuge* were completed plus a further 30 by *BFW* at Augsburg.

Meanwhile problems with the Do 11D had led to a redesigned aircraft which appeared in 1933 as the Do 13 c/n 293-295 & 350. This took time to fully develop and it seems likely that only a dozen Do 13E were actually completed as such. The remaining aircraft on order were completed as Do 23F/G for psychological reasons. *Dornier* built 144 Do 23 *Kampfflugzeuge* at Friedrichshafen c/n 387-530 and 54 at Wismar c/n 573-614 (42) & 626-638 (12) during 1934-35.

DO F (3)							
D-AGIR	Do 23 294	D-AHOS		D-ANEX	Do 11D 261	D-3025	
DO 11 (11+34)							
D-3029		D-3039		D-3052		D-3065	
D-3032		D-3042		D-3056		D-3070	
D-3035		D-3048		D-3061			
D-ABEL	Do 11da	D-AFOT	Do 11da	D-ANAK		D-AVAL	Do 11D
D-ABEX	Do 11dc	D-AGIF	Do 11da 281	D-ANEF	D-AVUV	D-AVYF	Do 11D
D-ABIQ		D-AGOZ	Do 11D	D-APAT		D-AXAK	Do 11D
D-ABOL	Do 11D	D-AGYH		D-AQYN	Do 11D	D-AXOL	(Do 23 ?)
D-ABOS	Do 11da 284	D-AGYM	Do 11da	D-ASAT	Do 11D	D-AXUX	
D-ADAN	Do 11da	D-AHER	Do 11da	D-ASIT		D-AZIT	
D-ADUL	Do 11da	D-AHIF	310	D-ASON	Do 11D	D-AZUN	Do 11da
D-AFAZ		D-AJOL	Do 11da	D-ATEV			
D-AFEZ	Do 11da	D-AKAP					

DO 13B-E (4)							
D-AHYL	293	D-AQET		D-AQIR		D-ARIT	

DO 23F/G (50)							
D-ABAK		D-AKUS		D-APEX		D-ARYQ	
D-ABOP	Do 23G 352	D-AKYF		D-APII		D-ASEO	
D-ACAQ		D-AKYK		D-APIP		D-ASIL	
D-ADAQ		D-ALEV		D-APIQ		D-ASIN ?	
D-ADAT		D-ALIR		D-APIT		D-ATEF	
D-AFOI		D-ALUZ		D-APIX		D-ATIX	
D-AFYL		D-ALYH		D-APYN		D-ATOF	
D-AGYT		D-ALYR		D-APYR		D-ATOZ	
D-AGYV		D-AMIR		D-AQEE	Do 23G	D-ATWA	
D-AHON		D-ANIT	Do 23G	D-AQOH		D-AVIT	
D-AHOQ		D-ANOQ		D-AQOZ		D-AXIM	
D-AJYF		D-ANYH		D-ARXO		D-AZIP	
D-AKIR		D-ANYQ					

Appendix H

Extract from the 1934 Luftfahrzeugrolle

D-UBAF to UHAR

D-UBAF	He 70 V3	457	(D-3314)	D-UDIN	W 34 hi W			
D-UBAJ	W 34 hi	2766		D-UDIR	W 34 hi W			
D-UBAL	He 70			D-UDIZ	Hs 122A-0 V3			
D-UBAM	He 114			D-UDON	Junkers G 24			
D-UBAR	Focke Wulf A 17			D-UDOP	Junkers G 24ba	848	(D-1017)	
D-UBAS	W 34 hi	2766	(D-3342)	D-UDOR	He 70D-0			
D-UBAS	He 70			D-UDOV	He 70			
D-UBAV	Hs 122 V1			D-UDUR	Ju 160	4240		
D-UBAX	Ju 49			D-UDYF	Do B Merkur	87	(D-1102)	
D-UBAZ	Ju 49	3701	(D-2688)	D-UDYM	He 70F-2	1277		
D-UBEK	He 70D			D-UFAL	He 70G-2			
D-UBEQ	He 70e	712		D-UFAS	W 34 hi	2772		
D-UBER	W 34 hi	2792		D-UFAZ	He 70G-1			
D-UBES	Ju 52 cc	4004	(D-2317)	D-UFEX	He 70F-2			
D-UBEZ	He 70			D-UFIF	He 70			
D-UBIF	L3 Delphin III	152		D-UFIK	Focke Wulf A 38			
D-UBIK	He 70			D-UFIL	He 70E			
D-UBIN	He 70d	709		D-UFIR	Ju 160A-0	4208		
D-UBIQ	Ju 160D-0	4244		D-UFIZ	He 70			
D-UBIR	Ju 87A-0 V4	4924		D-UFOH	Ju 160B-0	4239		
D-UBIT	Focke Wulf A 38			D-UFON	BFW M 20a	392	(D-1480)	
D-UBOF	He 70G-1	1692		D-UFOY	He 70			
D-UBON	Ju 160B-0	4217		D-UFUO		He 70		
D-UBOT	Focke Wulf A 17			D-UFUX	Ju 160 V2	4203		
D-UBOX	He 70G-1	911		D-UGAP	Do B Merkur Bal	161	(D-1087)	
D-UBUK	Ju 52/3m			D-UGAT	He 114 V2	1971		
D-UBUS	Ju 46 hi	2733	(D-3411)	D-UGAZ	Ju 160A-0	4214		
D-UBUZ	He 70G-2			D-UGEQ	He 70			
D-UBYL	He 70G-1			D-UGES	W 34			
D-UBYN	Hs 122 V2	5		D-UGEV	He 70			
D-UBYR	Ju 87 V1			D-UGEX	He 70G-2			

D-UBYV	Ju 160	4241		D-UGIK	He 70		
D-UDAL	BFW M 20a	421	(D-1676)	D-UGIR	W 34		
D-UDAO	Ar 81 V			D-UGIZ	Ju 160D-0	4220	
D-UDAS	He 70D	710		D-UGOR	He 70D	711	
D-UDEK	Ju 160D-0	4218		D-UGUS	W 34/Ju 46 hi	2744	(D-2419)
D-UDER	W 34 hi	2808		D-UGUV	Ju 160B-0	4238	
D-UDET	DSF Habicht			D-UHAF	He 70G-2		
D-UDEV	Hs 122			D-UHAG	He 70		
D-UDEX	Ar 81 V3			D-UHAH	He 118 V2	1294	
D-UDEZ	W 34			D-UHAM	BFW M 23b	516	
D-UDIM	He 70G	1132		D-UHAR	W 34 W		

From March1934 single engine C Class Aircraft (those with an all up weight in excess of 5,000 kgs) were registered in the D-U Series – multi engine aircraft above 5,000 kgs were registered in the D-A Series. This incomplete extract shows that registrations were not allocated sequentially. In fact aircraft of a particular type used registrations at random from throughout the available block. These were interspersed with allocations to other types so that it was impossible for a foreign power to accurately calculate the number of aircraft of any given type that had been manufactured. Further confirmation of this practice can be seen in the case of aircraft that had been re-registered from the numerical *LFA-B* sequence as shown above.

Appendix I

Production Summary

A. AIRFRAMES

HEINKEL He 45B/C/D

Two seat light reconnaissance bomber

Production continuing:	8 aircraft delivered 1933 against an initial order for 20 machines, 142 delivered in 1934 against new orders for 320 machines. (Total production by 28 Feb 35 180 machines).
Manufactured by:	Bayersiche Flugzeugbau (24), Gotha (66), Heinkel (60). Focke Wulf was contracted to build 159 aircraft.
Production variants:	He 45B (He), He 45C (Bf/Fw/Go) & He 45D (Bf).

HEINKEL He 46C

Two seat short range reconnaissance and army co-operation aircraft

Production continuing:	1 aircraft delivered 1933 and 83 in 1934 against orders for 270 machines. (Total production by 28 Feb 35 111 machines).
Manufactured by:	Heinkel (84). MIAG, Fieseler, Gotha and the Flugzeugbau Halle were all contracted.
Production variants:	He 46C (He).

HEINKEL He 70E/F

Three seat reconnaissance bomber

Production continuing:	9 aircraft delivered in 1934 against an order for 72 machines. (In all 16 machines delivered by 28 Feb 35).
Manufactured by:	Heinkel (9).
Production variants:	He 70E (He), He 70F (He).

ARADO Ar 64D

Single seat fighter

Production complete:	1 aircraft delivered 1933 and 18 in 1934 against an initial order for 60 machines, later reduced in Jan 34 to 19 machines.
Manufactured by:	Arado (19).
Production variants:	Ar 64D (Ar)

ARADO Ar 65E/F

Single seat fighter

Production continuing:	1 aircraft delivered 1933 and 69 in 1934 against an order for 85 machines.
Manufactured by:	Arado (70)
Production variants:	Ar 65E (Ar) & Ar 65F (Ar).

HEINKEL He 51A

Single seat fighter

Production continuing:	2 aircraft delivered 1933 and 26 in 1934 against orders for 141 machines.
Manufactured by:	Heinkel (28). Arado was contracted to deliver 70 aircraft.
Production variants:	He 51A (He),

DORNIER Do Y

Four seat heavy day and night bomber

Production complete:	5 aircraft delivered in 1933 with three delivered to Yugoslavia.
Manufactured by:	Dornier (5).
Production variants:	Do Y (Do).

DORNIER Do 11C/D & Do 13C

Four seat night bomber

Production complete:	22 aircraft delivered 1933 and 57 in 1934 against an order for 150 machines.
	(76 aircraft delivered by 28 Feb 35).
Manufactured by:	Bayerische Flugzeugbau (5), Dornier (74).
Production variants:	Do 11C (Do), Do 11D (Bf/Do) & Do 13C (Do).

JUNKERS Ju 52/3M g3e

Four seat auxiliary day and night bomber

Production continuing:	17 aircraft delivered 1933, including 2 bombers, against an order for 36 machines.
	179 delivered in 1934 against a Jan 34 order for 450 machines.
	(259 aircraft delivered by 28 Feb 35 with 64 in Feb 35 alone).
Manufactured by:	Junkers (192).
Production variants:	g3e (Ju)

HEINKEL He 50A

Two seat dive bomber

Production complete:	1 aircraft delivered 1933 and 20 in 1934 against an order for 51 machines.
Manufactured by:	Heinkel (21). BFW, Focke Wulf and Weser were all contracted.
Production variants:	He 50A (He),

HEINKEL He 42D/E

Two seat floatplane trainer

Production complete:	14 aircraft delivered 1933 and 28 in 1934.
Manufactured by:	Heinkel (42).
Production variants:	He 42D (He) He 42E (He).

HEINKEL He 60A/B/C

Two seat Reconnaissance Floatplane

Production continuing:	8 aircraft delivered 1933 and 19 in 1934 against an order for 20 machines, extended in Jan 34 to 81 machines.
Manufactured by:	Heinkel (27).
Production variants:	He 60A (He), He 60B (He) & He 60C (He)

DORNIER Do 15 MILITÄR WAL

Four seat Reconnaissance Flying Boat

Production complete:	13 aircraft delivered 1934 against an order for 21 machines.
Manufactured by:	Dornier-Friedrichshafen (13).
Production variants:	Do 15 (Do).

HEINKEL He 59B

Four seat Torpedo-Bomber Reconnaissance Floatplane

Production continuing:	1 aircraft delivered 1933 and 13 in 1934 against initial orders for 21 machines.
Manufactured by:	Heinkel (14).
Production variants:	He 59B (He).

HEINKEL HD 38D

Single seat floatplane fighter

Production complete:	11 aircraft delivered 1933. Total production 12 machines.
Manufactured by:	Arado.
Production variants:	HD 38D (Ar).

HEINKEL HE 51W

Single seat floatplane fighter

Production continuing:	14 aircraft delivered 1934 against a Jan 34 order for 14 machines.
Manufactured by:	Heinkel.
Production variants:	He 51W (He).

ALBATROS L 101D

Two seat primary trainer

Production complete:	46 aircraft delivered 1933. Total production 83 aircraft.
Manufactured by:	Focke Wulf (46)
Production variants:	Al 101D (Fw).

ALBATROS L 102B

Two seat primary trainer

Production complete:	8 aircraft delivered during 1933 including an unknown number of L 100.
Manufactured by:	Focke Wulf (8)
Production variants:	Al 102B (Fw).

BUCKER Bu 131A

Two seat primary trainer

Production continuing:	A very small number delivered in 1934.
Manufactured by:	Bucker.
Production variants:	Bu 131A (Bu).

FOCKE WULF Fw 44B

Two seat primary trainer

Production continuing:	13 aircraft delivered 1933 against an initial order for 19 machines, an unknown number in 1934.
Manufactured by:	Focke Wulf (44).
Production variants:	Fw 44B (Fw).

HEINKEL He 72A/B

Two seat primary trainer

Production continuing:	2 aircraft delivered 1933 followed by 80 in 1934.
Manufactured by:	Heinkel (82).
Production variants:	He 72A (He), He 72B (He).

KLEMM TYPES

Two seat primary trainer

Production complete: 126 Klemm types aircraft delivered 1933 and c.240 in 1934.

Manufactured by: Klemm (366).

Production variants: L 25 (Kl), L 26 (Kl), L 27 (Kl), Kl 31 (Kl) & Kl 32 (Kl).

ARADO Ar 66C

Two seat basic trainer

Production complete: 16 aircraft delivered 1933 and up to 233 in 1934.

                         (301 machines delivered by 28 Feb 35).

Manufactured by: Arado (cirtca 233), Gotha (?)

Production variants: Ar 66C (Ar/Go).

JUNKERS W.33

Four seat crew trainer and light transport

Production complete: 8 aircraft delivered 1933 and more than 20 in 1934 against an order for 199 machines.

                         (Production completed in Feb 35 with 199 machines built).

Manufactured by: Henschel (87 W33/34), Junkers (28).

Production variants: W.33he (Ju).

JUNKERS W.34hi

Four to six seat crew trainer and light transport

Production continuing: 15 aircraft delivered 1933 and more than 42 in 1934 against orders for 1,191 machines.

                         (83 machines delivered by 28 Feb 35).

Manufactured by: Henschel (87 W33/34), Junkers (57)

Production variants: W.34hi (Ju).

BAYERISCHE FLUGZEUGWERKE Bf 108A

Two seat sports aircraft

Production continuing: 6 aircraft delivered in 1934.

Manufactured by: Bayerische Flugzeugbau (6).

Production variants: Bf 108A (Bf).

B. AERO-ENGINES

BMW VI
Twelve cylinder liquid-cooled vee engine

Production continuing:	6,300 by BMW 1934-37.
Manufactured by:	BMW
Production variants:	BMWVIU 6,0 Z (690 hp) and BMW VI 7,3 Z (750 hp).
Applications:	BMW VIU 6,0 Z - Do 13, Do 15, Do 23, He 45, He 59 and He 60.
	BMW VI 7,3 Z - Ar 65E/F, HD 38, He 51A/W & He 70E/F.

BMW 132
Nine cylinder air-cooled radial engine

Production continuing:	5,500 by BMW 1934-37
Manufactured by:	BMW and Daimler-Benz.
Production variants:	BMW 132 (550 hp) and BMW 132A-3 (725 hp).
Applications:	132 - W.34hi
	132A-3 - Ju 52/3m g3e

SIEMENS UND HALSKE SH22B
Nine cylinder air-cooled radial engine

Production continuing:	Figures unavailable
Manufactured by:	Siemens
Production variants:	Sh 22B (650 hp).
Applications:	Sh 22B - Ar 64D, Do 11C/D, He 46C, He 50A and W.34hi.

JUNKERS L5
Six cylinder water-cooled in-line engine

Production complete:	1,000 units manufactured 1925-33.
Manufactured by:	Junkers
Production variants:	L5 (300/310 hp) and L5G (425 hp).
Applications:	L5 - He 42D & W 33.
	L5G - He 42E & W 33he.

ARGUS AS 10C

Eight cylinder air-cooled inverted vee engine

Production continuing:	Figures unavailable
Manufactured by:	Argus
Production variants:	As 10C (240 hp)
Applications:	Ar 66, Ar 76, Bf 108, Fw 56 and Go 145.

SIEMENS Sh 14A

Seven cylinder air-cooled radial engine

Production continuing:	Figures unavailable
Manufactured by:	Siemens
Production variants:	Sh 14A (150 hp).
Applications:	Fw 44B, He 72B, Kl 31 and Kl 32.

ARGUS AS 8

Four cylinder air-cooled inverted in-line engine

Production continuing:	Figures unavailable
Manufactured by:	Argus
Production variants:	As 8 (95 hp)
Applications:	L 100, L 101, Al.102, He 72A, Kl 25, Kl 26, Kl 27 and Kl 31.

HIRTH HM 60R

Four cylinder air-cooled inverted in-line engine

Production continuing:	Figures unavailable
Manufactured by:	Hirth
Production variants:	HM 60R (80 hp)
Applications:	Bu 131A and Kl 25.

Appendix J

Planned Activation of Combat Units for the Reichsluftwaffe

28 JULY 1932

The Chief of the Troop Office   Berlin, the 28.7.1932
Nr.1845/32 Top Secret In.1, Chef/V   12 copies
                                                                           2nd copy

Related: 1. T 2 (Organisation) Nr.549/32 Top Secret IIIB of 15.7.32
               2. Armed Forces Office Nr.5855/32 Top Secret Armed Forces A Ia of 21.7.32
               3. The Chief of the Troop Office Nr.562/32 Top Secret T 2 Chief/III of 14.7.32

Regarding: Formation of the peacetime Army

The following orders are issued for the formation of military air units within the new peacetime Army:

The establishment of the earlier approved sub-organisations under a 3-year –Plan is confirmed as follows:

33/34	Training units (by separate outline)
34/35	1 Air Brigade Commander
	Air Group Command East:
	1 Reconnaissance Squadron
	1 Fighter Squadron
	Air Group Command Centre:
	1 Reconnaissance Squadron
	1 Fighter Squadron
	Air Group Command South:
	2 later 6 Reconnaissance Squadrons
35/36	For Air Group Command East:
	1 Reconnaissance Squadron
	1 Fighter Wing Headquarters
	1 Fighter Squadron
	For Air Group Command Centre:
	1 Reconnaissance Squadron
	1 Fighter Wing Headquarters

36/37	1 Fighter Squadron For Air Group Command South: 2 later 6 Reconnaissance Squadrons For Air Group Command East: 1 Reconnaissance Squadron 1 Fighter Squadron For Air Group Command Centre: 3 Reconnaissance Squadrons 1 Fighter Squadron For Air Group Command South: 1 Reconnaissance Squadron 1 Bomber Group Headquarters 3 later 10 Bomber squadrons

Distribution of the newly formed units on a longer time period than 3 years can be ordered.

It will be particularly helpful to arrange for the subordination of the testing stations to the military and prepare special services (Dissolution Commission, Construction Supervision, Air Supply Office, Air Academy).

For the transition year the continued use of civilian technical staff will be required.

Appendix K

Transfer of the Luftschützamt to the Luftministerium

15 MAY 1933

**The German Minister of Defence
and Commander of the Armed Forces**

Berlin, the 10.5.1933
40 copies
23rd copy

Air Defence Office Nr.617/33 Top Secret Insp.1 (L) II A
Regarding: Formation of the Air Ministry

1. The German President has on the 27.4. ordered the formation of the Air Ministry.

2. The Air Ministry incorporates the:
    a) the Air Defence Office in the German Armed Forces Ministry
    b) the Office of the German Air Commissioner
These Offices will be brought together under the German Minister for Aviation.

3. The Air Defence Office (LA) transfers with all field offices with effect from 15.5. from the from RWM and enters the current establishment of the Air Ministry.

4. The *Chief of the Air Defence Office* retains the management of air protection office in the Air Ministry. He will conduct his duties in the Air Ministry in direct consultation with the Minister of Aviation.

5. The LA will consist of the following organisation in the Air Ministry:
    1. The Air Command Branch (Tactics, Missions, Operations)
    2. The Air Organisation Branch
    3. The Air Training Branch
    4. The Air Defence Branch
    5. The Personnel Branch
    6. The General Branch (General Troop Matters)
    The whole Air Technical Branch (formerly L 2 in LA) – with the Supply Department and Air Equipment Inspectorate which will come to the General Branch in the Air Defence Office – is in the General Air Office of the Air Ministry.

6. The responsibilities of the former LA - except for the Technical Branch in Para 5 - go over to the Air Defence Office of the Air Ministry.

7. Until the formation of a new personnel budget in the Air Ministry, the approved budget of my staff of the LA (Armed Forces Ministry Nr.344/33 Top Secret Insp.1 (L) V of 10.3.1933) for the formation of the Air Defence Office in the Air Ministry will prevail.

8. From the 5.5.33 the personnel of the LA will be separated from the jurisdiction of the Chiefs of the Army High Command and Navy High Command. They will continue to be treated equally to the personnel of the Army or Navy in all personnel matters. They stay on their pay scales in the Army or Navy prior to the establishment of a dedicated staff budget in the Air Ministry. After discontinuation of the period of camouflage, new regulations will take place for the air forces.

Attracting more staff for the Air Defence Office in the Air Ministry as well as for its field offices, schools and units must be made through transfers from the Army and Navy. The scheme in detail, as well as that of the later staff exchange will take place later.

9. The handling of all Air Force and Air Defence matters takes place within the Air Defence Office of the Air Ministry, which has to keep the Army High Command and Naval High Command continuously informed. My earlier "Instructions for the organization of Air Defence Office" and associated regulations for cooperation between the Chiefs of the Army and Navy High Commands and the Chief LA (Armed Force Ministry Troop Office Nr.150/33 Top Secret T 2 Organisation III B/Insp.1 (L) V of 21.3.33) are repealed.

The Chief of the Air Defence Office in the Air Ministry continues to advise the Chiefs of the Army and Navy High Commands..

The position of special advisors for Air and Air Defence issues in the Army and Navy High Commands are discontinued. In case of war, and exercises special staffs will be placed at their disposal.

The Air Defence Office of the Air Ministry has served on all major joint Army and Naval High Commands, the same applies entirely for these posiions.

To enable continuous joint working the personnel of the Air Defence and the General Office of the Air Ministry, and of the Army and Navy High Commands are to participate in Staff Journeys, War Games and Troop Exercises, which is also the case for the personnel of the Army and Naval High Commands, especially command staffs and naval staff officers in the Air Ministry. To this end, I have made joint proposals.

To all possible extent, given the need for camouflage, air and air defence forces are to be used to the exercises of the Army and Navy High Commands.

The Ministry of Aviation has directed me to inform the Chief of the Ministerial Office (Armed Forces Ministry) three times weekly about all significant events in the Air Ministry.

10. Budget. The delegated funds of the Army and Navy budget go over to the Air Ministry.

Signed von Blomberg
Certified accurate
Bohnstedt, Oberst

Appendix L

Activation Programme for the Friedensluftwaffe

12 JULY 1933

Order from the Minister of German Aviation for the 1st Activation Period (1934)
12.7.1933

The Minister for German Aviation
Air Defence Office.Nr.1565/33 Top Secret A 2 I.

Berlin, the 12.7.1933
22 Copies
3rd Copy

Regarding: Activation Programme for the peacetime Luftwaffe

1. To the Chief of the Army High Command
2. To the Chief of the Naval High Command

1. Under the arrangements of all existing programs for the construction of the peacetime Luftwaffe the preparation of the following headquarters and formations is ordered for the 1.Formation Period (1934):

   a.   Land formations and associated headquarters:
       2 Air Group Commands
       3 Long range Reconnaissance Squadrons
       2 Army Co-operation Squadrons
       2 Fighter Wing Headquarters
       6 Fighter Squadrons
       2 Bomber Wing Headquarters
       5 Bomber Squadrons
       <u>5 Auxiliary Bomber Squadrons</u>
       21 Squadrons

   b.   Naval and Coastal formations
       1 Headquarters Commander of Naval Air Forces
       1 Reconnaissance Squadron
       1 Fighter Squadron
       1 Multi-role Squadron
       1 Long range Reconnaissance Squadron (equipment)
       <u>1 Auxiliary Squadron</u>
       5 Squadrons

2. The establishment of these formations – beginning on the 1.7.34 – must take place under the preservation of camouflage, but at the same time take the form of having a civil commitment. Military formations must not appear to be so from the outside.

The formations are based on existing plans. Newly created civil aviation institutions (notably Flying Schools), or those employed for public air transport should be used as cover, stocks being established at appropriate places (Bomber units).

Complete planned peacetime accommodation and full installation is therefore not possible initially.

3. Locations for the 1934 Formations will be advised as soon as they been finally agreed.

4. The second phase of the 1st Formation Period during the 2nd Programme year (1935) will provisionally include the establishment of:

Land formations   2 Long range Reconnaissance Squadrons
                         5 Army Co-operation Squadrons
                         17 active and auxiliary bomber squadrons

Naval formations   1 Reconnaissance Squadron

Certified accurate:

Speidel   I.V.
(Hauptmann)   Signed Milch

Bibliography

PRIMARY SOURCES

Index of official papers and documents sourced in the main text. These have been organised in date order by Ministry and then by Office.

BA/MA   Bundesarchiv/Militärarchiv – RH (Reichs Heer) RL (Reichs Luftwaffe) (Germany)
DZ/MGFA   Dokumentenzentrale des Militärgeschichtlichen Forschungsamtes (Germany)
MA/DBR   Militärchiv/Deutsche Bundesrepublik (Germany)
NARA   National Archives and Records Administration (USA)

Flugmusterei

Flugmusterei, *Letter 4 Dec 19* in BA/MA RH 2/2275
Flugmusterei, *Letter 13 Nov 19* in BA/MA RH 2/2275

Kriegstagbücher

KTB Santa Elena (BA/MA F 3290/PG 63 520 – 25)

Reichspräsident

Telegram 088/Teleg.4012 from Hindenburg in Mosley 1974 p.195

Reichswehr/Verteidigungsminister

RWM to Marineamt – Vorschlage für die Entwicklung der Luftfahrtindustrie, 11 Januar 1927 in BA/ MA RH2/2187
Aktennotiz des Reichswehrministers Groener vom 3.12.1930 in Suchenwirth 1968 p.37
RWM Befehl Nr.401/33, Geheim, dated 21 Marz 1933 in (Author Unknown) *Geschichte des deutschen Generalstabs* in Suchenwirth 1968 p.46
Reichsverteidigungsminister u.Bfr.d.gesamten Wehrmacht Nr.617/33, Geheim, I, (H) II A, 10.5.1933 in Unknown Geschichte des deutschen Generalstabs in Maaß 1955 p.17
Reichsverteidigungsminister und Befehlshaber der gesamten Wehrmacht Nr.1007/33 vom 15.5.1933 in DZ/MGFA Akte II L 49
Der Reichsverteidigungsminister und Befehlshaber der gesamten Wehrmacht LP Nr.1555/33 g.kdos.II, Berlin, den 5.12.1933 in DZ/MGFA, Akte II L 49

Heeresleitung

Seeckt Denkschrift, 1923 in Volker 1962
Seeckt, letter to Truppenamt et al, 1 Dec 1919 in BA/MA 2/2275
Seeckt Letter to Waffenschulen, 8 Nov 24 in BA/MA RH 12-12/22
Seeckt Bemerkungen des Chefs der Heeresleistung (1923) in NARA File T-177, Roll 25

Hans von Seeckt - Letter to the Waffenamt and Branch Inspectorates, 24 Jan 1924 in BA/MA RH 12-2/21

Truppeneinheiten des Feldheers National Archives, von Seeckt Papers File M-132, Roll 340

Heeresausbildungsabteilung Denkschrift, 29 Nov 1926 Heeresmotorisierung und Kriegsgliederung einer motorisierte Division in BA/MA RH 8/b 923

Chef d.Heeresleitung Letter to the Waffenamt, Juli 1931 in BA/MA RH 8/v.993

Direktive Nr.401/33 Geheim, 21 Mar 33 as issued by the *Inspektion 1 (L) i.RWM*

Truppenamt

Truppenamt T-Luft "Richtlinien für die Führung des operativen Luftkrieges"

Truppenamt T 4 Directive to the Waffenschulen, 1920 in BA/MA RH 12-2/54, 9

Truppenamt T 4 "Ausbildung der aus Führergehilfen im Aussicht genommenen Offiziere" 31 Juli 1922 in BA/MA 12-21/94, 4

Truppenamt "Zussammenstellung der Gesamtstärken und Ausrüstung der Kommandobehorden und Studie eines Offizieres über die Fliegerwaffe und ihre Verwendung (1925)

T 2 III (L) "Richtlinien für die Führung des operativen Luftkrieges" Mai 26

TA-L, Referat VI "Militärische Faktoren für die Bewertung der modernen Luftmachte" dated 9 Apr 1926, in BA/MA RH 2279

T 1, letter of November 1926, in BA/MA RH 12-1/15

TA-L, Ausbildung Lehrgang L 1927 (30 November 1926) in BA/MA RH 2/2299

Grundsatze für den Einsatz der Luftstreitkräfte 1930 in BA/MA RL 2/II 364 Entwurf

Chef des Truppenamts Nr.1845/32 geh.Kdos., In.1, Chef/V, Berlin, den 28.7.1932 Ausbau des Friedensheeres in Nowarra 1980 p.45

Heereswaffenamt

HWA Nr.2840/28, geh.Kdo. "Z" Wa B 6 in Suchenwirth 1968 p.18.

Waffenamt, Organisation and Personnel Roster 1928/29 in BA/MA RH 8/v.3667.

Waffenamt Correspondence: Conference Memo, 18 Februar 1932 in BA/MA RH 8/v 9916

Luftschutz And Flakartillerie

Luftschutzübungsreise 1924 in BA/MA RH 2/2244

Unterstellung der Luftschutztruppen (September 16, 1933) in NARA T-405/Reel 1/Frames 4828144-46

Entwicklungsprogramm 13.12.30 RL 4 Chef des Ausbildungswesens/General der Fliegerausbildungs und Luftwaffen-Inspektion/Waffengeräte in BA/MA Folder 257

Richtlinien für die Gefechts-und Schießübungen der Kw.Batterien 1931 in NARA T-405/Reel 1/ Frames 4827245-47

Entwicklungsprogramm der Flugabwehr-Waffen des Heeres June 12, 1932 in BA/MA RL 4/Folder 257

Ausbildung der Schw.Battr. in den Monaten Marz, April u.Mai (February 12, 1933) in NARA T-405/ Reel 1/Frames 4927962-63

3.(Preuß.) Fahabteilung, Berlin-Lankwitz, den 21.8.33 in NARA T-405/Reel 1/Frames 4827931-32

Unterstellung der Luftschutztruppen (September 16, 1933) in NARA T-405/Reel 1/Frames 4828144-46

Ausbildungsplan für das Winterhalbjahr 1.11.33 bis 31.3.34 (September 20, 1933) in NARA T-405/ Reel 1/Frames 4827776-77, 4827784-85

Taktische Ausbildung der Offiziere im Winter 1933/34 (October 10, 1933) in NARA T-405/Reel 1/ Frames 4827952

Werbung von Offizieranwartern (August 15, 1934) in NARA T-405/Reel 1/Frame 4828531

Bemerkungen zur Ausbilding (November 1934) in NARA T-405/Reel 1/Frames 4827276-81

Bemerkungen zur Ausbildung 1933 T-405 German Air Force Records: Luftgaukommandos, Flak, Deutsche Luftwaffenmission in Rumanien in NARA Reel 1/Frames 4827259-65

Entwicklung und Einsatz der deutschen Flakwaffe und des Luftschutzes im Weltkrieg Kriegswissenschaftliche Abt.d.Lw. 1938

Individually Written Reports

Hagen von dem Maj., November 1928 *Reisebericht* in BA/MA RH 2/1822

Speidel Hptm, *Berichte* in MA/DBR, R 06 10/4

Spies R. 1927 *Report on Bombing Accuracy and Patterns* in BA/MA RH 2/2187

Reichsverkehrsministerium

Anhang "Statistik des planmaßigen deutschen Luftverkehrs im Kalenderjahr 1928" in RVM 1929

Anhang XI Zusammenstellung der im Funkverkehr anzuwendenden Abkurzungen in 29/44 RVM 1929

Betriebsordnung für den internationalen Flugfunkdienst nebst Ausführungbestimmungen für den deutschen

Betriebsordnung für den internationalen Flugfunkdienst 29/40 in RVM 1929

Betriebsordnung für den internationalen Flugfunkdienst 29/50 in RVM 1929

Betriebsordnung für den internationalen Flugfunkdienst in 29/52 RVM 1929

Flugfernmeldediesnst Anhang IV in 29/43 RVM 1929

Flugzeuge, Verzeichnis der in die deutsche Luftfahrzeugrolle eingetragenen Flugzeuge in RVM 1929

Funkverkehrsbezirke der deutschen Flughäfenfunkstellen, 6 Apr 29 in RVM 29/15

Luftfahrfeuer der Nachtflugstrecke Berlin-Schkeuditz in 29/38, dated 21 Sep 29 in RVM 1929

Verzeichnis der deutschen Notlandeplätze nach dem Stande vom 1.Mai 1929 in RVM 1929

Reichsminister Des Innern

Reichsminister des Innern - II C 864 Berlin 5 Marz 1920 Heraushebung der nichtmilitärischen Einrichtungen der Polizeifliegerstaffeln in Schilling and Rettinghaus 1994 p.109

Marineleitung

Letter Adm.Zenker to VizAdm.Raeder 1927 in Mallmann Showell 1999 p.5

Marineleitung Denkschrift, Mai 1929 Braucht Deutschland große Kriegsschiffe? in Rahn 1976 p.281-286

Reichsluftfahrtministerium

Abschrift einer Aktionnotiz des Ministerialdirektors Fisch (RLM) vom 22.5.1933 zur Vorlage für Staatssekretär Milch über ein am Vormittag gefuhrtes Telefongespräch mit Major Reinicke (LB-Amt) in Volker 1967 p.26.

Milch Diary 1925-35 in Irving 1973

Luftkommandoamt

LA Nr.1305/33 g.Kdos. A 2 I, vom 29 Jun 33 in Hooton 1994 p.102

Aufstellungsprogramm der Friedensluftwaffe LA Nr.1565/33 geh.Kdos. A 2 I, vom 12 Jul 33 in Nowarra 1980 p.52

Anlagen zum Winterkriegsspiel 1934-35 in BA/MA RL 2 II/77 in Corum p.153

Vortrag des Generalmajors Wever bei Erdffnung der Luftkriegsakademie und Lufttechnischen Akademie in Berlin-Gatow am 1.November 1935 in Corum 1997 p.137

LA.Nr.617/33 g.Kdos.L 1 (H) II A Bildung des Luftministeriums 10 Mai 33 in Maaß 1955 p.15

RdL. LA Nr.1941/159/33 g.Kdos. A II 2 A, 14 August 1933 Ersten Aufstellungsabschnitt der Fliegerwaffenschulen in Zapf 2001 p.260

LA Nr.500/34 g.Kdos. La II ZA v. 10.2.34 in Jung et al 1977 p.57

Technisches Amt

Organisation of the RLM Technisches Amt (B.II) as of 15.06.1933 in BA/MA Freiburg, RL 3/2220

Liste der Tarnbezeichnungen der aufzustellenden Verbände der Luftwaffe LC Nr.1594/34 zbV. geh. Kdos. 12.4.1934 in Nowarra 1980 pp.54-55

Flugzeugbeschaffungsprogramm vom 1.7.1934, Stand vom Dezember 1934 in DZ/MGFA, Akte L II 1296

Besprechungsprotokolle LCII, LC-Besprechungen (Akte E 20): 19.12.1934 Besprechung zwischen Kommodore Sperrle, Keller und Amtschef LC über Sachlage Do 11 in DZ/MGFA, Akte E 1635

Aktennotiz vom 18.7.1934 betr. Telefongespräch Oberst Sperrle/Geerdts in DZ/MGFA Akte E 1635

Personalamt

RdL LP Nr.1860/34 g.Kdos. II 2, Berlin, den 8.3.1934 in DZ/MGFA, Akte II L 49, Teil 2

RdL LA Nr.1090/34 g.Kdos. L.A.II 2 A, Berlin, 20.April 1934 Aufstellung des Jagdgeschwaders 132 in Döberitz in Mombeek E. and Roba J-L. Undated p.12

Verwaltungsamt

RdL LD III, LD Nr.8177/34 gKdos., Berlin, den 28.3.1934 in DZ/MGFA, Akte II L 49, Teil 2

Royal Air Force

Command 467 *Permanent Organisation of the Royal Air Force - Note by the Secretary of State for Air on a Scheme outlined by the Chief of the Air Staff 11 Dec 19*, HMSO

Air Staff Memorandum August 1923 (Supplement in March 1924) *"Air Strategy in Home Defence: The Correct Objective"*

Other Documents

Blomberg's Directive, TMWC, XXXIV pp.487-491 in Shirer 1963 p.210
Junkers Diary, 24 Aug 1933 in Junkers Nachrichten, 1962 in Irving 1973 p.35
The Liebmann Papers in the *Institut für Zeitgeschichte ED 1*
Phipps Papers, I 1/14 in Overy 1984 p.37 & 248
Telegram Phipps to Simon, 24 Oct 1933 in DBFP (3) Vol.V in Irving 1973 p.36
SHAA File 2B133 in Hooton 1994 p.90
SHAT File 4N96-I in Hooton 1994 pp.32-33
SHAT File 4N97, Dossier 2 in Hooton 1994 p.52
Test Programme 1.2.25-30.6.25 Bb.Nr.25/2.25.F BA/MA Freiburg, Document RM8v/3604

Dienstvorschriften

H.Dv.300   Die Truppenführung
H.Dv.487   Führung und Gefecht der Verbündenen Waffen, 1921

Source: *Das Archiv für technische Dokumente 1900-1945: Heeres-Druckvorschriften* in www.superborg.de 2005

L.Dv.3   Militärstrafgesetzbuch.
L.Dv.10   Der Kampfflugzeug, 1934
L.Dv.152   Zündervorschrift (Nur für Abwurfmunition) 1936
L.Dv.212   Ju 52/3m Beschreibung, Einbau-und Prüfvorschrift für So, 1935
L.Dv.221   Do 11 Bedienungsvorschrift So, 1935
L.Dv.224   He 59 Beschreibung, Einbau-und Prüfvorschrift der So 3 1935
L.Dv.232   He 60 Beschreibung, Einbau-und Prüfvorschrift für So
L.Dv.233   He 60 Bedienungsvorschrift für So 1 1936.
L.Dv.304   He 59 Flugzeughandbuch 1935
L.Dv.305   He 59 Baubeschreibung 1935
L.Dv.313   He 50 Flugzeughandbuch
L.Dv.314   He 50 Flugzeugbeschreibung.
L.Dv.321   Beschreibung, Einbau-und Behandlungsvorschrift für die geschützte Betriebsstoffbehalteranlage Do 11D, 1935
L.Dv.316   He 70F Flugzeughandbuch 1937
L.Dv.307   Ar 65 Flugzeughandbuch,
L.Dv.308   Ar 65 Bauschreibung
L.Dv.309   Ar 65 Reparaturanleitung
L.Dv.317   He 70F Flugzeugbeschreibung 1937.
L.Dv.327   Beschreibung, Einbau-und Behandlungsvorschrift für die geschützte Betriebsstoffbehalteranlge He 60
L.Dv.328   Ar 65 Beschreibung, Einbau-und Behandlunsvorschrift für die geschützte Betriebsstoffbehalteranlage
L.Dv.347   Ar 66 Flugzeughandbuch
L.Dv.348   Ar 66 Bauschreibung
L.Dv.359   He 42E Flugzeughandbuch

L.Dv.360   He 42E Flugzeugbeschreibung
L.Dv.365   He 60E Flugzeughandbuch

Source: *Das Archiv für technische Dokumente 1900-1945: Luftwaffen-Dienstvorschriften* in www.superborg.de 2005

LC BB.Nr.2763/33 0 1 g.Kdos., Kennblatt des Technischen Amtes im RLM für das Flugzeugmuster Ju 52 1933 in Dierich 1973 pp.318-320

LC BB.Nr.1850/35 0 1 g.Kdos., Kennblatt des Technischen Amtes im RLM für das Flugzeugmuster Do 11A 1935 in Dierich 1973 pp.320-322

Interviews and Testimony

Interrogation Report of Gen.d.Flak.Walter von Axthelm "Part I AA Program 1930-31" Appendix C in *519.601A-12 AFHRA* in Westermann 2001 p.40

Contributions by Gen.d.Flg.a.D.Rudolf Bogatsch & Gen.d.Flak.a.D.Walther von Axthelm in Maaß 1955 p.20

Affidavit Dr.Ernst Brandenburg, 29 Oct 49 in Irving 1973 p.17

Information provided by GenLt.a.D.Hermann Bruch in Maaß 1955 pp.32-33

Commentary by Gen.d.Flg.a.D.Paul Deichmann to Richard Suchenwirth in Suchenwirth 1968 pp.172-173

Contribution by Gen.d.Flg.a.D.Hellmuth felmy in Maaß 1955 p.25

Interview of Gen.d.Flg.a.D.Hellmuth felmy with Suchenwirth R. Prof., 16 Feb 54 in Suchenwirth 1968 p.26

Interview with Gen.d.Flg.a.D.Hellmuth felmy, 25 Jun 54 in D/II/1, Karlsruhe in Suchenwirth 1969 pp.1-2

Interview of MinDirektor a.D.Wilhelm Fisch by Prof.Richard Suchenwirth, 20 Dec 1957 in Suchenwirth 1968 p.10.

Information provided by Min.Dir.a.D.Willy Fisch in Maaß 1955 p.18

Information from Gen.d.Flg.a.D.Hans Geisler in Maaß 1955 p.36

Information provided by GenLt.a.D.Walther Grosch in Maaß 1955 p.19

Information provided by GenLt.a.D.Johannes Graf von Hachenburg in Maaß 1955 pp.37-38

Information provided by Obst.a.D.Alois Heldmann in Maaß 1955 p.51

Information provided by GenIng.a.D.Walter Hertel in Maaß 1955 p.46

Information provided by Gr.Ltr.Kehrberg in Kreipe and Koester 1955 p.47

Interview with GFM.a.D.Albert Keßelring & Prof.Suchenwirth, 30 Jan 56 in D/II/1 Karlsruhe in Suchenwirth 1969 p.131

Information from GenLt.a.D.Bruno Maaß and Gen.d.Flg.a.D.Josef Kammhüber in Maaß 1955 p.18

Interview between GFM.a.D.Erhard Milch and Prof.Richard Suchenwirth, 29 September 1954 in D/I/2, Karlsruhe in Suchenwirth 1969 p.5

Information provided by GenLt.a.D.Andreas Nielsen & Obst.a.D.Rudolf Koester in Maaß 1955 pp.48-49

Information provided by GenObStÄrzt.a.D.Prof.Dr.med.Oskar Schroeder in Maaß 1955 pp.32-33

Information from Gen.d.Fl.a.D.Hans-Georg Seidel & GenLt.a.D.Josef Schmid in Maaß 1955 p.34

Information from Gen.d.Flg.a.D.Hans Siburg in Maaß 1955 p.21

Interview of GenOb.a.D.Kurt Student with Prof.Richard Suchenwirth, 12 Mar 55 in D/II/1 Karlsruhe

Interview between Frhr.Götz von Richthofen (Wolfram's son) and James Corum, 4 Sep 93 in Corum 1997 p.68

GFM.a.D.Erhard Milch Hauptgrunde für den Zussammenbruch der deutschen Luftwaffe im Weltkrieg II in Maaß 1955 p.24

Interview between GenOb.a.D.Hans-Jürgen Stumpff & Prof.Richard Suchenwirth, 22 Nov 54 in D / II/1 Karlsruhe in Suchenwirth 1969 pp.2-3

Hans-Karl von Winterfeld (DLH Verkehrs-Inspektion), unpublished memoirs in Irving 1973 p.33

SECONDARY SOURCES

Karlsruhe Document Collection

Bülow Frhr.von H. GenLt.a.D. *Die Abteilung Fremde Luftmachte im Reichswehr-und Reichsluftfahrtministerium 1927-1937*

Gundelach K. Hptm.a.D., Koester R. Obst.a.D. & Kreipe W. Gen.d.Flg.a.D. *Ausbildung in der Fliegertruppe* in B/III/1b

Hertel W. GenIng.a.D. *Die Beschaffung in der deutschen Luftwaffe* in C/IV/6b

Maaß B. GenLt.a.D. *Organisation der Fliegerstellen im RWM 1920-1933* in A/I/2

Seeckt von H. GenOb. *Memorandum to Reichskanzler, Dr.Wilhelm Cuno, dated 23 Nov 22* in C/ III/1

Siburg H. Gen.d.Flg.a.D. *Vorbereitende Maßnähmen der Marineleitung auf dem Gebeits des Seeflugwesens in den Jahren 1920-1933* in A/V/1

Thomsen GenIng.a.D. *Junkers Flugzeugwerke Fili in der Naehe von Moskau 1924-127* in C/III/1

Wimmer W. Gen.d.Flg.a.D. *Stellungnähme zu Luftfahrt-Ausbildung in der Reichswehr von Hellmuth Felmy, Teil I* in B/III/1a

USAF Numbered Historical Studies

All these titles are available to download from www.afhra.af.mil/studies/ numberedusafhistoricalstudies151-200. Where the author has obtained published sources the publisher is indicated.

Grabmann W. GenMaj.a.D. 1956 *German Air Force Air Defence Operations Vol.I 1933-41* USAF Historical Studies No.164 MLRS Books2006

Heitman H. 1955 *The Planning and Development of Bombs for the German Air Force 1925-1945* USAF Historical Studies No.192

Hertel W. Dipl.Ing.GenIng.a.D.1955 *Procurement in the German Air Force* USAF Historical Studies No.170

Kreipe W. Gen.d.Flg.a.D. and Koester R. Obst.a.D. 1955 *Technical Training within the German Luftwaffe* USAF Historical Studies No.169

Maaß B. GenLt.a.D. 1955 *The Organisation of the German Air Force High Command and Higher Echelon Headquarters within the German Air Force* USAF Historical Studies No.190 Sunflower University Press, Manhattan

Nielsen A. GenLt.a.D.1959 *The German Air Force General Staff* USAF Historical Studies No.173 Sunflower University Press, Manhatta

Renz von O.Gen.d.Flak.a.D. 1958 *The Development of German Anti-Aircraft Weapons and Equipment of all types up to 1945* USAF Historical Studies No.194

Schwabedissen W. GenLt.a.D. *Problems of Fighting a Three-Front War* USAF Historical Studies No.178

Suchenwirth R. 1959 *Historical Turning Points in the German Air Force War Effort* USAF Historical Studies No.189 Arno Press, New York

Suchenwirth R. Prof. 1968 *The Development of the German Air Force 1919-1939* USAF Historical Studies No.160 Sunflower University Press, Manhattan

Suchenwirth R. Prof. 1969 *Command and Leadership in the German Air Force* USAF Historical Studies No.174 Sunflower University Press, Manhattan

Printed Books

Absolon R. (Ed.) 1984 *Rangliste der Generale der deutschen Luftwaffe nach dem stand vom 20.April 1945* Podzun-Pallas-Verlag GmbH, Friedberg

Adkin F.J. 1983 *From the Ground Up* Airlife Publishing Ltd., Shrewsbury

Air Ministry 1948/49 *AP 248 - The Rise and Fall of the German Air Force 1933-1945* WE Inc., Old Greenwich

Althoff W.F. 1990 *Sky Ships: A History of the Airship in the United States Navy* Orion Books, Crown Publishers, Inc., New York

Anderton D.A. 1981 *The History of the US Air Force* The Hamlyn Publishing Group Limited, London

Andrews C.F. 1969 *Vickers Aircraft since 1908* Putnam & Company Ltd., London

Angolia J.R. and Hackney C.R. 1984 *The Pour le Mérite and Germany's First Aces* Hackney Publishing Co., Friendswood

Baker D. 1990 *Manfred von Richthofen: The man and the aircraft he flew* Outline Press (Book Publishers) Limited, London

Baker D. 1996 *Adolf Galland: The Authorised Biography* Windrow & Greene Ltd., London

Barker R. 1981 *The Schneider Trophy Races* Airlife Publishing Ltd., Shrewsbury

Barnes C.H. 1970 *Bristol Aircraft since 1910* Putnam & Company Ltd., London

Barraclough G. (Ed.) 1978 *The Times Atlas of World History* Times Books Limited, London

Beauvais H., Kossler K., Mayer M. and Regel C. 2002 *German Secret Flight Test Centres to 1945: Johannisthal, Lipetsk, Rechlin, Travemünde, Tarnewitz, Peenemünde-West* Midland Publishing, Hinckley, part of Ian Allan Ltd, Shepperton – Bernard & Graefe Verlag, München

Bekker C. 1974 *The German Navy 1939-1945* The Hamlyn Publishing Group Ltd., London – 1972 Gerhard Stalling Verlag, Oldenburg and Hamburg

Belcarz B. and Peczkowski R. 2001 *White Eagles: The Aircraft, Men and Operations of the Polish Air Force 1918-1939* Hikoki Publications Ltd., Ottringham

Below N. Obst.a.D.2001 *At Hitler's Side – The Memoirs of Hitler's Luftwaffe Adjutant 1937-1945* Greenhill Books, Lionel Leventhal Limited, London – 1980 *Als Hitlers Adjutant 1937-45* von Hase & Koehler Verlag, Mainz

Bender R.J. 1972 *Air Organisations of the Third Reich: The Luftwaffe* R.James Bender Publishing, Mountain View

Bender R.J. and Petersen G.A. 1975 *Hermann Göring from Regiment to Fallschirmpanzerkorps* R.James Bender Publishing, San Jose

Bingham V. 1998 *Major Piston Aero Engines of World War II* Airlife Publishing Ltd., Shrewsbury

Blanchard W.O. and Visher S.S. 1931 *Economic Geography of Europe* McGraw-Hill Book Company, Inc., New York

Bodenschatz K. Oblt. 1935 *Jagd in Flanderns Himmel – Aus den sechsen Kampfmonaten des Jagdgeschwaders Freiherr von Richthofen* Verlag Knorr & Firth GmbH, München

Boog H., Rahn W., Stumpf R. and Wegner B. 1990 *Die Deutsche Reich und die zweite Weltkrieg Vol.6 Der globale Krieg* Deutsche Verlags-Anstalt, Stuttgart

Bowers P.M. 1966 *Boeing Aircraft since 1916* Putnam and Company Ltd., London

Bowers P.M. 1979 *Curtiss Aircraft 1907-1947* Putnam & Company Ltd., London

Bowyer C. 1979 *Guns in the Sky: The Air Gunners of World War Two* J.M.Dent & Sons Ltd., London

Boyd A. 1977 *The Soviet Air Force since 1918* Macdonald and Jane's (Publishers) Ltd., London

Braatz K. 2005 *Gott oder ein Flugzeug: Leben und Sterben des Jagdfliegers Günther Lützow* NeunundzwanzigSechs Verlag, Moosburg

Bridgman L. (Ed.) 1946 *Jane's All the World's Aircraft 1946* Random House UK Ltd., London

Brütting G. 1976 *Das waren die deutschen Stuka-Asse 1939-1945* Motorbuch Verlag, Stuttgart

Brütting G. 1986 *Das Waren die deutschen Kampfflieger-Asse 1939-1945* Motorbuch Verlag, Stuttgart

Budingen E. (Ed.) 1938 *Kriegsgeschichtliche Einzelschriften der Luftwaffe Vol.1 Entwicklung und Einsatz der deutschen Flakwaffe und des Luftschutzes im Weltkriege* Ernst Siegfried Mittler und Sohn, Berlin

Caldwell D. 1996 *The JG 26 War Diary Vol.1 1939-1942* Grub Street, London

Carlsen S. and Meyer M. 1998 *Die Flugzeugführer Ausbiludung der deutschen Luftwaffe 1935-1945 Bd.I Von der Grundausbildung bis zur Blindflugschule* VDM Heinz Nickel Verlag, Zweibrücken VDM Heinz Nickel Verlag, Zweibrücken

Carlsen S. and Meyer M. 2000 *Die Flugzeugführer Ausbiludung der deutschen Luftwaffe 1935-1945 Bd.II Fliegerwaffenschulen und Erganzungsgruppen* VDM Heinz Nickel Verlag, Zweibrücken

Carson A. 1986 *Flight Fantastic: The Illustrated History of Aerobatics* Haynes Publishing Group, Sparkford

Caspari H.A. Dr. (Ed.) Undated *E-Stellen Travemünde und Tarnewitz 2.Band – Die Geschichte der Seeflugzeug-Eprobungsstelle Travemünde und daraus hervorgegangenen E-Stelle für Flugzeugbewaffnung Tarnewitz* Luftfahrt-Verlag Walter Zuerl, Steinebach-Worthsee

Caspari H.A. Dr. (Ed.) Undated *E-Stellen Travemünde und Tarnewitz 3.Band – Die Geschichte der Seeflugzeug-Eprobungsstelle Travemünde und daraus hervorgegangenen E-Stelle für Flugzeugbewaffnung Tarnewitz* Luftfahrtverlag Axel Zuerl, Steinebach-Worthsee

Cescotti R. 2001 *The History of German Aviation: Bombers and Reconnaissance Aircraft 1935 to the Present* Schiffer Publishing Ltd, Atglen – *Kampfflugeuge und Aufklärer – Entwicklung, Produktion, Einsatz und zeitgeschichtliche Rahmenbedingungen von 1935 bis heute*

Chamberlain G. 1984 *Airships - Cardington: A history of Cardington airship station and its role in world airship development* Terence Dalton Limited, Lavenham

Chesneau R. 1984 *Aircraft Carriers of the World 1914 to the Present: An Illustrated Encyclopedia* Arms and Armour Press, Lionel Leventhal Ltd., London

Christienne C. and Lissarague P.1980 *A History of French Military Aviation* Smithsonian Institution Press, Washington

Churchill W.S. 1948 *The Second World War Vol.I The Gathering Storm* Cassell & Co.Ltd., London

Citino R. 1987 *The Evolution of Blitzkrieg Tactics: Germany defends itself against Poland, 1918-1933* Greenwood Press, New York

Clarke I.F. 1966 *Voices Prophesying War 1763-1984* Oxford University Press, London

Cole C. and Cheesman E.F. 1984 *The Air Defence of Great Britain 1914-1918* Putnam, The Bodley Head, London

Collier B. 1957 *The Defence of the United Kingdom* Imperial War Museum, London (was HMSO)

Conradis H. 1960 *Design for Flight: The Kurt Tank Story* Macdonald & Co. (Publishers) Ltd., London

Constable T.J. and Toliver R.F. 1968 *Horrido! Fighter Aces of the Luftwaffe* Arthur Barker Ltd., London

Coombs L.F.E. 1997 *The Lion has Wings: The race to prepare the RAF for World War II 1935-1940* Airlife Publishing Ltd., Shrewsbury

Cooper M. 1978 *The German Army 1933-1945: It's Political and Military Failure* Macdonald and Jane's Publishers Limited, London

Cooper M. 1981 *The German Air Force 1933-1945: An Anatomy of Failure* Jane's Publishing Company Limited, London

Corum J.S. 1992 *The Roots of Blitzkrieg: Hans von Seeckt and German Military Reform between the World Wars* University of Kansas Press, Lawrence

Corum J.S. 1997 *The Luftwaffe: Creating the Operational Air War 1918-1940* University Press of Kansas, Lawrence

Corum J.S. 2008 *Wolfram von Richthofen – Master of the German Air War* University Press of Kansas, Lawrence

Craven W.F. and Cate J.L. (Ed.) 1948 *The Army Air Forces in World War II Vol.1 Plans and early operations January 1939 to August 1942* University of Chicago Press, Chicago

Cross R. 1964 *The Bomber Aircraft Pocketbook* B.T.Batsford Ltd., London

Davis B.L. 1971 *German Army Uniforms and Insignia 1933-1945* Arms and Armour Press, Lionel Leventhal Limited, London

Davis B.L. 1975 *Flags and Standards of the Third Reich: Army, Navy and Air Force* Macdonald and Jane's, London

Davis B.L. 1991 *Uniforms and Insignia of the Luftwaffe Vol.1: 1933-1940* Arms and Armour Press, Cassell, London

Dean M. 1979 *The RAF and the Two World Wars* Cassell, London

Degelow C. (Trans.Kilduff P.) 1979 *Germany's Last Knight of the Air: The Memoirs of Major Carl Degelow* William Kimber & Co. Limited, London

Delaney J. 2000 *The Blitzkreig Campaigns: Germany's Lightning War Strategy in Action* Caxton Editions, Caxton Publishing Group, London

Desouetter D.M. Undated *All About Aircraft* Faber and Faber Ltd., London

Dierich W. 1973 *Kampfgeschwader 51 "Edelweiss": Eine Chronik aus Dokumenten und Berichten 1937-1945* Motorbuch Verlag, Stuttgart

Dobinson C. 2001 *AA Command: Britain's anti-aircraft defences of World War II* Methuen Publishing Ltd., London

Dornier GmbH 1983 *Dornier: Die Chronik des ältesten deutschen Flugwerks* Dornier GmbH, Friedrichshäfen

Douhet G. 1972 *Command of the Air* Arno Press, New York

Dressel J. and Griehl M.1997 *The Luftwaffe Album: Bomber and Fighter Aircraft of the German Air Force 1933-1945* Arms and Armour Press, Cassell Group, London

Eberhardt von W. (Ed.) 1930 *Unsere Luftstreitkräfte 1914-1918: Ein Denkmal deutschen Heldentums* Vaterlandischen Verlag E.A.Weller, Berlin

Edmonds J.E. Brig.Gen.Sir 1987 *History of the Great War: The Occupation of the Rhineland 1918-*

1929 HMSO, London

Emiliani A., Ghergo G.E. and Vigna A. 1975 *Regia Aeronautica: perido prebellico e fronti occidental* Intergest, Milano

Faber H. (Ed.) 1979 *Luftwaffe: An analysis by former Luftwaffe generals* Sidgwick and Jackson Limited, London

Falck W. Obst.i.G.a.D. 2002 *Wolfgang Falck: The Happy Falcon – An Autobiography of the Father of Night Fighters* Eagle Editions Ltd., Hamilton

Fleischer W. 2003 *German Air-Dropped Weapons to 1945* Motorbuch Verlag, Stuttgart

Francillon R.J. 1979 *Japanese Aircraft of the Pacific War* Putnam & Company Limited, London

Francillon R.J. 1979 *McDonnell Douglas Aircraft since 1920* Putnam & Company Ltd., London

Francillon R.J. 1982 *Lockheed Aircraft since 1913* Putnam & Company Ltd., London

Franks N., Bailey F. and Duiven R. 1996 *The Jasta Pilots: Detailed listings and histories August 1916 - November 1918* Grub Street, London

Friedman N. 1988 *British Carrier Aviation – The Evolution of the Ships and their Aircraft* Conway Maritime Press Ltd, London

Fuller J.F.C. 1920 *Tanks in the Great War 1914-1918* Murray, London

Fuller J.F.C. 1923 *The Reformation of War* Dutton & Co., New York

Futrell R.F. 1989 *Ideas, Concepts, Doctrine; Basic Thinking in the United States Air Force, 1907-1960 Vol.I.* Air University Press, Maxwell AFB

Galland A. GenLt.a.D. 2001 *The First and the Last – Germany's Fighter Force in the Second World War* Cerebus Publishing Limited, Bristol - 1954 Die Ersten und die Letzen

Gander T. & Chamberlain P. 1978 *Small Arms, Artillery and Special Weapons of the Third Reich: An Encyclopedic Survey* Macdonald and Jane's Publishers Limited, London

Gardiner R. and Chesneau R. (Ed.) 1980 *Conway's All the World's Fighting Ships 1922-1946* Conway Maritime Press Ltd., London

Gersdorff von K. and Grasmann K. 1985 *Die Deutsche Luftfahrt 2: Flugmotoren und Strahltriebwerke* Bernard & Graefe Verlag, Koblenz

Girbig W. 1980 *...mit Kurs auf Leuna: Die Luftoffensive gegen die Triebstoffindustrie und der deutsche Abwehreinsatze 1944-1945* Motorbuch Verlag Stuttgart

Goerlitz W. 1951 *Der Zweite Weltkrieg 1939-1945 Bd.V* Steingruben Verlag, Stuttgart

Goerlitz W. 1953 *History of the German General Staff 1657-1945* Frederick A.Praeger, New York - *Geschichte des deutschen Generalstabs von 1657-1945* Bechtermunz Verlag, Frankfurt am Main

Goerlitz W. (Ed.) 2000 *The Memoirs of Field Marshal Keitel, Chief of the German High Command 1938-1945* Cooper Square Press, New York

Golding H. (Ed.) Undated *The Wonder Book of the Navy* Ward, Lock & Co.Ltd., London

Gordon H.J. 1957 *The Reichswehr and the German Republic 1919-26* Princeton University Press

Gordon Y. and Khazanov D. 1999 *Soviet Combat Aircraft of the Second World War Vol.2 Twin-Engined Fighters, Attack Aircraft and Bombers* Midland Publishing Ltd., Leicester

Green W. and Fricker J. 1958 *The Air Forces of the World: Their History, Development and Present Strength* Macdonald & Co. (Publishers) Ltd., London

Green W. 1970 *The War Planes of the Third Reich* Macdonald and Jane's Publishers Limited, London

Grey C.G. 1940 *A History of the Air Ministry* George Allen & Unwin Ltd., London

Grey C.G. 1943 *The Luftwaffe* Faber and Faber Ltd., London

Griehl M. 2008 *Deutsche Flugzeugbewaffnung bis 1945* Motorbuch Verlag, Stuttgart

Groener-Geyer D. 1955 *General Groener Soldat und Staatsmann* Societats Verlag

Gunston B. 1995 *World Encyclopaedia of Aero Engines* Patrick Stephens Limited, Haynes Publishing, Sparkford

Hallion R.P. 1989 *Strike from the Sky: The History of Battlefield Air Attack 1911-1945* Airlife Publishing Ltd, Shrewsbury – Smithsonian Institution, Washington

Haute van A. 1974 *Pictorial History of the French Air Force 1909-1940* Ian Allan Ltd., Shepperton

Hecks K. 1990 *Bombing 1939-45: The Air Offensive against Land Targets in World War Two* Robert Hale Limited, London

Heinkel E. 1956 *He 1000* Hutchinson & Co. (Publishers) Ltd., London

Henig R. 1998 *The Weimar Republic 1919-1933* Lancaster Pamphlets, Routledge, Abingdon

Herlin H. 1960 Udet A Man's Life Macdonald & Co. (Publishers) Ltd., London - 1958 *Udet - eines Mannes Leben*

Hermann 1943 *The Rise and Fall of the Luftwaffe* John Long Ltd., London

Hermann F. *Der Erde* im *Flammen*

Hildebrand K.F.1990 *Die Generale der deutschen Luftwaffe 1935-1945 Band 1 A-G* Biblio Verlag, Osnabrück

Hildebrand K.F.1991 *Die Generale der deutschen Luftwaffe 1935-1945 Band 2 H-N* Biblio Verlag, Osnabrück

Hildebrand K.F.1992 *Die Generale der deutschen Luftwaffe 1935-1945 Band 3 O-Z* Biblio Verlag, Osnabrück

Hitler A. 1927 *Mein Kampf: 4 ½ Jahre Kampf gegen Luge, Dummbeit und Seigbeit* Verlag Franz Eher

Hoeppner von, E. W. Gen.d.Kav.a.D. 1921 *Germany's War in the Air: The Development and Operations of German Military Aviation in the World War* The Battery Press, Nashville

Hoffschmidt E.J. 1969 *German Aircraft Guns WWI – WWII* WE Inc., Old Greenwich

Hogg I.V. 1970 *Barrage: The Guns in Action* Macdonald & Co. (Publishers) Ltd., London

Hogg I.V. 1978 *Anti-Aircraft: A History of Air Defence* Macdonald and Jane's Publishers Limited, London

Höhne H. 1972 *The Order of the Death's Head – The Story of Hitler's SS* Pan Books Ltd., London, Martin Secker and Warburg Ltd., London – 1966 *Der Orden unter dem Totenkopf* Verlag der Spiegel, Hamburg

Holley I.B. 1964 *Buying Aircraft: Material Procurement for the Army Air Forces* US Army in World War II Special Studies Office of the Chief of Military History, US Army, Washington

Homze E.L.1976 *Arming the Luftwaffe: The Reich Air Ministry and the German Aircraft Industry 1919-1939* University of Nebraska, Lincoln

Hooks M. 1999 *Images of Aviation: Lufthansa* Tempus Publishing Limited, Stroud

Hooton E.R. 1994 *Phoenix Triumphant: The Rise and Rise of the Luftwaffe* Arms and Armour Press, London

Imrie A. 1971 *Pictorial History of the German Army Air Service* Ian Allan Ltd. Shepperton

Imrie A. 1989 *German Naval Air Service* Arms and Armour Press, London

Irving D. 1973 *The Rise and Fall of the Luftwaffe: The Life of Luftwaffe Marshal Erhard Milch* Futura Publications Limited, London - Weidenfeld & Nicolson Limited

Irving D. 1978 *The War Path: Hitler's Germany 1933-1939* Papermac, Macmillan Publishers Limited, London

Irving D. 1989 *Göring: A Biography* Macmillan London Limited, London

Isby D.C. (Ed.) 2005 *The Luftwaffe and the War at Sea 1939-45: As seen by officers of the Kriegsmarine and Luftwaffe* Chatham Publishing, Lionel Leventhal Ltd., London

Ishoven van A. 1975 *Messerschmitt: Aircraft Designer* Gentry Books Limited, London

Ishoven van A. 1977 *The Fall of an Eagle: The Life of Fighter Ace Ernst Udet.* William Kimber & Co.Limited, London

Ishoven van A. 1977 *Messerschmitt Bf 109 at War* Ian Allan Ltd., Shepperton

Jackson R. 1983 *The Sky their Frontier: The Story of the World's Pioneer Airlines and Routes 1920-40* Airlife Publishing Ltd., Shrewsbury

James J. 1991 *The Paladins: A Social History of the RAF up to the outbreak of World War II* Futura Publications, Macdonald & Co (Publishers) Ltd., London

Jarrett P. (Ed.) 1997 *Biplane to Monoplane: Aircraft development 1919-39* Putnam Aeronautical Books, Brassy's (UK) Ltd., London

Jarrett P. (Ed.) 1997 *Aircraft of the Second World War: The Development of the Warplane 1939-45* Putnam Aeronautical Books, Brassy's (UK) Ltd., London

Johnson B. 1978 *The Secret War* British Broadcasting Corporation, London

Johnson J.E. 1964 *Full Circle: The Story of Air Fighting* Pan Books Ltd., London – Chatto & Windus Ltd.

Jung D., Wenzel B. and Abendroth A. 1977 *Die Schiffe und Boote der deutschen Seeflieger 1912-1976* Motorbuch-Verlag, Stuttgart

Kahn D. 1978 *Hitler's Spies: German Military Intelligence in the World War II* Hodder & Stoughton Limited, Sevenoaks – Macmillan Publishing Co., Inc.

Kaiser J. 2010 *Der Ritterkreuzträger der Kampfflieger Bd.I* Luftfahrtverlag-Start, Bad Zwischenhahn

Kaiser J. 2011 *Der Ritterkreuzträger der Kampfflieger Bd.II* Luftfahrtverlag-Start, Bad Zwischenhahn

Keller von Obstlt.a.D. 1929 *Die heutige Wehrlosigkeit Deutschlands im Lichte seiner Verteidigung gegen die Fliegerangriffe im Kriege 1914/18* Verlag Offene Worte, Berlin

Ketley B. and Rolfe M. 1996 *Luftwaffe Fledglings 1935-1945: Luftwaffe Training Units and their Aircraft* Hikoki Publications, Aldershot

Kens K. and Nowarra H.J. 1961 *Die deutschen Flugzeuge 1933-1945: Deutschlands Luftfahrt-Entwicklungen bis ende des Zweiten Weltkrieges* J.F.Lehmann Verlag, München

Kesselring A. 1974 *The Memoirs of Field-Marshal Kesselring* Purnell Book Services, Limited, London, William Kimber and Co. Limited - Keßelring A. 1953 *Soldat bis zum letzten Tag*

Kiehl H. 1983 *Kampfgeschwader "Legion Condor" 53: Berichte, Erlebnisse u.Dokumente 1936-1945* Motorbuch Verlag, Stuttgart

Kilduff P. 1991 *Germany's First Air Force 1914-1918* Arms and Armour Press, Cassell, London

Kilduff P. 1999 *The Illustrated Red Baron: The Life and Times of Manfred von Richthofen* Cassell & Co., London

Kington J.A. and Selinger F. 2006 *Wekusta: Luftwaffe Meteorological Reconnaissance Units and Operations 1938-1945* Flight Recorder Publications Ltd., Ottringham

Kinsey G. 1978 *Seaplanes - Felixstowe: The Story of the Air Station 1913-1963* Terence Dalton Limited, Lavenham

Knappe S. and Brusaw E. 1993 *Soldat – Reflections of a German Soldier 1936-1949* BCA, Airlife Publishing Ltd., Shrewsbury

Knauss R. (pseudonym Maj.Holders) 1932 *Luftkrieg 1936: Der Zertrummerung von Paris* Verlag Tradition Wilhelm Kolk

Koch H-A.1954 *Die Geschichte der deutschen Flakartillerie 1935-1945* Podzun-Pallas-Verlag GmbH, Friedberg

Koos V. 2006 *Typenbucher Deutsche Luftfahrt: Ernst Heinkel Flugzeugwerke 1922-1932* HEEL Verlag GmbH, Königswinter

Koppenberg H. 1935 *The Development of Dessau during 1934*

Kosin R. 1983 *The German Fighter since 1915* Putnam, Conway Maritime Press Ltd., London - *Die Entwicklung der deutschen Jagdflugzeuge* Bernard & Graefe Verlag, Koblenz

Kotowski G. 1963 *Friedrich Ebert: eine politische Biographie* Franz Steiner Verlag, Wiesbaden

Kranzhoff J A 1997 *Arado – History of an Aircraft Company* Schiffer Publishing Ltd., Atglen - *Arado: Geschichte eines Flugzeugwerks* Aviatic Verlag, München

Kurowski F.1979 *Seekrieg aus der Luft* Verlag E.S.Mittler & Sohn GmbH, Herford

Kurowski F. 1995 *The History of the Fallschirmpanzerkorps Hermann Göring: Soldiers of the Reichsmarschall* J.J.Fedorowicz Publishing Inc., Winnipeg

Lamberton W.M. 1960 *Fighter Aircraft of the 1914-1918 War* Harleyford Publications Limited, Letchworth

Lamberton W.M. 1962 *Reconnaissance and Bomber Aircraft of the 1914-1918 War* Harleyford Publications Limited, Letchworth

Lange B. 1970 *Das Buch der deutschen Luftfahrttechnik* Verlag Dieter Hoffmann, Mainz

Lange von C. (Ed.) 1941 *Flakartillerie greift an: Tatsachenbereite in Wort und Bild* Verlag Scherl, Berlin

Larkins W.T. 1996 *Battleship and Cruiser Aircraft of the United States Navy 1910-1949* Schiffer Publishing Ltd., Atglen

Layman R.D. 1989 *Before the Aircraft Carrier: The Development of Aviation Vessels 1849-1922* Conway Maritime Press Ltd., London

Lee A. 1972 *Goering; Air Leader* Gerald Duckworth & Company Limited, London

Lenton H.T. 1975 *German Warships of the Second World War* Purnell Book Services Ltd., Macdonald and Jane's (Macdonald & Co.) (Publishers) Ltd.), London

Liddell Hart B.H. 1925 *Paris, or the Future of War* E.P.Dutton & Company, New York

Liddell Hart B.H. 1928 *The Remaking of Modern Armies* Little, Brown & Co, Boston

Liddell Hart B.H.& Pitt B. (Ed.) *History of the Second World War Vol.1* Purnell Publishing, London

Lumsden A.S.C. 1994 *British Piston Aero-Engines and their Aircraft* Airlife Publishing Ltd., Shrewsbury

MacBean J.A. and Hogben A.S. 1990 *Bombs Gone: The development and use of British air-dropped weapons from 1912 to the present day* Patrick Stephens Limited, Thorsons Publishing Group, Wellingborough

Macksey K. 1978 *Kesselring: The Making of the Luftwaffe* B.T.Batsford Ltd., London

Mahlke H. Obstlt.i.G.a.D. *Memoirs of a Stuka Pilot* Frontline Books, Pen & Sword Books Ltd., Barnsley

Mallmann Showell J.P. 1979 *The German Navy in World War Two: A Reference Guide to the Kriegsmarine 1935-1945* Arms and Armour Press, Lionel Leventhal Limited, London

Mallmann Showell J.P. 1999 *German Navy Handbook 1939-1945* Sutton Publishing Limited, Stroud

Mankau H. and Petrick P. 2001 *Messerschmitt Bf 110 - Me 210 - Me 410: Die Messerschmitt-Zerstörer und ihre Konkurrenten* Aviatic Verlag GmbH, Oberhaching

Markham G. 1989 *Guns of the Reich: Firearms of the German Forces 1939-1945* Arms and Armour Press, London

Marwick A. 1965 *The Deluge* Macmillan Publishers Ltd., London

Mason H.M. 1973 *The Rise of the Luftwaffe 1918-1940* Cassell & Collier Macmillan Publishers Ltd., London

Mason T. 1993 *British Flight Testing: Martlesham Heath 1920-1939* Putnam Aeronautical Books, Conway Maritime Press Ltd., London

Masson le H.1969 *Navies of the Second World War: The French Navy Vol.1* Macdonald & Co. (Publishers) Ltd., London

Matuschka E. 1983 *Organisation des Reichsheeres in Handbuch zur deutschen Militärgeschichte 1648-1939* Militärgeschichtliches Forschungsamt, Freiburg

Maurer M. 1969 *Combat Squadrons of the Air Force World War II* Office of Air Force History, Washington

Meekcoms K.J. and Morgan E.B. 1994 *The British Aircraft Specifications File: British Military and Commercial Aircraft Specifications 1920-1949* Air Britain (Historians) Ltd., Tonbridge

Meier-Welcker H. 1967 *Seeckt* Bernard and Graefe

Meinck G. 1959 *Hitler und die deutsche Aufrüstung 1933-1937* Franz Steiner Verlag, Wiesbaden

Mellenthin von F.W. GenMaj.a.D.1977 *German Generals of World War Two* University of Oklahoma Press

Merrick K.A. 1977 *German Aircraft Markings 1939-1945* Ian Allan Ltd., Shepperton

Messenger C. 1989 *The Art of Blitzkrieg* Ian Allan Ltd., Shepperton

Milsom J. 1975 *German Military Transport of World War Two: Lorries and Cars of the German Army, 1933-1945* Purnell Book Services Ltd., London, Arms and Armour Press, Lionel Leventhal Limited, London

Mitcham S.W. 1985 *Hitler's Legions: The German Army Order of Battle, World War II* Leo Cooper, Martin Secker and Warburg Limited, London

Mitcham S.W.1988 *Hitler's Field Marshals and their Battles* Guild Publishing for William Heinemann

Mitcham S.W. 1989 *Eagles of the Third Reich – Hitler's Luftwaffe* Airlife Publishing Ltd., Shrewsbury – 1988 Presidio Press, Novato

Mondey D.1971 *Pictorial History of the USAF* Ian Allan Ltd., Shepperton

Mollo A. 1981 *The Armed Forces of World War II: Uniforms, insignia and organisation* Orbis Publishing, London

Mombeek E, Smith J.R. and Creek E.J.1999 *Luftwaffe Colours: Jagdwaffe Vol.1 Sctn.1 Birth of the Luftwaffe Fighter Force* Classic Publications, Crowborough

Mombeek E. and Roba J-L. Undated *In the Skies of France – A Chronicle of JG 2 Richthofen Vol.1: 1934-1940* ASBL, Linkebeek

Moore J. (Ed.) 2001 *Jane's Fighting Ships of World War I* Random House Group Ltd., London

Morareau L. 2002 *Les Aéronefs del'Aviation Maritime (1910-1942)* ARDHAN – Association pour le Recherche de Documentation sur l'Histoire de l'Aéronautique Navale

Morrow J.H. 1982 *German Air Power in World War I* University of Nebraska Press

Morse S. (Ed.) 1982 *The Illustrated Encylopedia of Aircraft* Orbis Publishing Ltd., London

Mosley L. 1974 *The Reich Marshal: A Biography of Hermann Göring* Weidenfeld and Nicolson, London

Moyes P.J.R. 1964 *Bomber Squadrons of the R.A.F. and their aircraft* Macdonald and Jane's (Publishers) Ltd., London

Müller W. 1990 *The Heavy Flak Guns 1933-1945* Schiffer Publishing Ltd, West Chester - Die Schwere Flak 1933-1945 Podzun-Pallas-Verlag, Friedberg

Müller W. 1995 *German 20 mm Flak in World War II* Schiffer Publishing Ltd, Atglen - *Waffen-*

Arsenal und Fahrzeuge der Heere und Luftstreitkräfte: 2cm Flak im Einsatz 1935-1945 Podzun-Pallas-Verlag, Friedburg

Müller-Hildebrand B. 1954 *Das Heer bis zum Kriegsbeginn* Mittler, Darmstadt

Murray W. 1985 *Luftwaffe: Strategy for Defeat 1933-45* George Allen & Unwin (Publishers) Ltd., London

Nauroth H. 1988 *Stukageschwader 2 Immelmann: Eine Dokumentation über das erfolgreichste deutsche Stukageschwader* Verlag K.W.Schultz, Preußisch Oldendorf

Naval Intelligence Division 1945 *BR 529C Geographical Handbook Series: Germany Vol.IV Ports and Communications*

Navair 00-80P-1 1970 *United States Naval Aviation 1910-1970*

Nayler J.L. and Ower E. 1930 *Aviation of To-Day: Its History and Development* Frederick Warne & Co.Ltd., London

Nemecek V. 1986 *The History of Soviet Aircraft from 1918* Willow Books, William Collins & Co.Ltd., London

Neulen H.W. 2000 *In the Skies of Europe: Air Forces allied to the Luftwaffe 1939-1945* The Crowood Press, Marlborough – 1198 Universitas Verlag

Neumann G. (Ed.) 1921 *Die Deutschen Luftstreitkräfte im Weltkriege* E.S.Mittler und Sohn, Berlin

Nowarra H.J. 1963 *The Messerschmitt 109: A Famous German Fighter* Harleyford Publications Limited, Letchworth

Nowarra H.J. and Brown K.S. 1964 *von Richthofen and the Flying Circus* Harleyford Publications Limited, Letchworth

Nowarra H.J. 1966 *Marine Aircraft of the 1914-1918 War* Harleyford Publications Limited, Letchworth

Nowarra H.J. 1980 *Heinkel He 111 – A Documentary History* Jane's Publishing Company Limited, London – 1979 *Die He 111: Vom Verkehrsflugzeug zum Bomber* Motobuch-Verlag, Stuttgart

Nowarra H.J. 1980 *Die Verbotenen Flugzeuge 1921-1935 – Die getarnte Luftwaffe* Motorbuch Verlag, Stuttgart

Nowarra H.J. 1981 *Nahaufklärer 1910-1945: Die Augen des Heeres* Motorbuch Verlag, Stuttgart

Nowarra H.J. 1982 *Fernaufklärer 1915-1945: Enstehung, Entwicklung, Einsatz* Motorbuch Verlag, Stuttgart

Nowarra H.J. 1987 *Aircraft & Legend: Junkers Ju 52* Haynes Publishing Group, Sparkford

Obermaier E. 1966 *Die Ritterkreuzträger der Luftwaffe Bd.I Jagdflieger 1939-1945* Verlag Dieter Hoffmann, Mainz

Obermaier E. 1976 *Die Ritterkreuzträger der Luftwaffe Bd.II Stuka- und Schlachtflieger 1939-1945* Verlag Dieter Hoffmann, Mainz

Odhams Undated *Britain's Wonderful Fighting Forces* Odhams Press Limited, London

Ohlinger E. *Bomben auf Kohlenstadt* Oldenburg, Berlin

Orange V. Prof. 2001 *Park – Then Biography of Air Chief Marshal Sir Keith Park* Grub Street, London

Ostertag R. 1986 *Deutsche Minensucher: 80 Jahre Seeminenabwehr* Koehlers Verlagsgesellschaft mbH, Herford

Otte A. 1988 *Die Weissen Spiegel: Vom Regiment zum Fallschirmpanzerkorps* Podzun-Pallas-Verlag GmbH

Overy R.J. 1984 *Goering: The Iron Man* Routledge & Kegan Paul plc, London

Padfield P. 1984 *Dönitz: The Last Führer* Panther Books, Granada Publishing Ltd., London

Patzwall K.D. 1986 *Luftwaffen-Rangliste 1945* Militair Verlag Klaus D.Patzwall, Norderstedt

Pearcy A. 1993 *Flying the Frontiers: NACA and NASA Experimental Aircraft* Airlife Publishing Ltd., Shrewsbury

Pile F. 1949 *Ack-Ack: Britain's Defence against air attack during the Second World War* George G.Harrap & Co.Ltd., London

Pletschlacher P. 1978 *Die Königlich Bayerischen Fliegertruppen* Motorbuch Verlag, Stuttgart

Postma T. 1979 *Fokker: Aircraft Builders to the World* Jane's Publishing Company Limited, London

Poturzyn von J.M.1924 *Jahrbuch für den Luftverkehr 1924* München

Pozzuoli C. 1988 *La Figura e l'Opera di Guilio Douhet* Caserta-Puzzuoli

Preston A. and Batchelor J 1977 *Battleships 1856-1919* Phoebus History of the World Wars Special, Phoebus Publishing Co./BPC Publishing Ltd., London

Preston A. (Ed.) 1989 *Jane's Fighting Ships of World War II* Bracken Books, Bestseller Publications Ltd., London

Prien J. 1992 *Einsatz des Jagdgeschwaders 77 von 1939 bis 1945: Ein Kriegstagebuch nach Dokumenten, Berichten und Erinnerungen Teil 1 1934 bis Mai 1941* Struve's Buchdruckerei und Verlag, Eutin

Prien J., Stemmer G., Rodeike P. and Bock W. 2000 *Die Jagdfliegerverbande der Deutschen Luftwaffe 1934 bis 1945 Teil 1 Vorkriegszeit und Einsatz über Polen - 1934 bis 1939* Struve's Buchdruckerei und Verlag, Eutin

Priller J. 1980 *JG 26: Geschichte eines Jagdgeschwaders. Das JG 26 (Schlageter) 1937-1945* Motorbuch Verlag, Stuttgart

Quarrie B. 1989 *Encyclopaedia of the German Army in the 20th Century* Patrick Stephens Limited, Thorsons Publishing Group, Wellingborough

Rabenau von F. Gen.d.Art.1940 *Seeckt: Aus seinem Leben* Hase & Koehler, Leipzig

Radinger W. and Schick W. 1999 *Messerschmitt Bf 109 The World's Most Produced Fighter – From Bf 109 A to E* Schiffer Publishing Ltd, Atglen - *Messerschmitt Me 109: Das Meistgebaute Jagdflugzeug der Welt - Entwicklung, Erprobung und Technik: vom Bf (Me) 109A bis 109E* Aviatic Verlag, Oberhaching

Rahn W. 1976 *Reichsmarine und Landesverteidigung, 1919-28 Konzeption und Führung der Marine in der Weimar Republik* Bernard und Graefe Verlag, München

Ramsey W.G. (Ed.) 1987 *The Blitz Then and Now Vol.1* 1987 Battle of Britain Prints International Limited

Reichsverkehrsministerium 1929 *Nachrichten für Luftfahrer* Verlag Gebr.Radetzki, Berlin

Reynolds C.G. 1974 *Command of the Sea: The History and Strategy of Maritime Empires* Robert Hale & Company, London

Rieckhoff H.J. GenLt.a.D.1945 *Trumpf oder Bluff? 12 Jahre deutsche Luftwaffe* Inter Avia, Geneva

Ries K. 1970 *Luftwaffe Bd.1 Die Maulwürfe 1919-1935* Verlag Dieter Hoffmann, Mainz

Ries K. 1974 *Luftwaffen-Story 1935-1939* Verlag Dieter Hoffmann, Mainz

Verlag Dieter Hoffmann, Mainz

Ries K. 1977 *Recherchen zur Deutschen Luftfahrzeugrolle Teil 1: 1919-1934* Verlag Hoffmann, Mainz

Ries K. 1986 *Luftwaffe Photo-Report 1919-1945* Motorbuch Verlag, Stuttgart

Ries K. 1988 *Deutsche Flugzeugführerschulen und ihre Maschinen 1919-1945* Motorbuch Verlag, Stuttgart

Ries K. and Dierich W. 1993 *Fliegerhorste und Einsatzhäfen der Luftwaffe: Planskizzen 1935-1945*

Motorbuch Verlag, Stuttgart

Robertson B. (Ed.) 1959 *Air Aces of the 1914-1918 War* Harleyford Publications Limited, Letchworth

Roberston B. 1978 *The RAF: A Pictorial History* Robert Hale Limited, London

Robertson B. 1981 *The Army and Aviation: A Pictorial History* Robert Hale Limited, London

Rosch B.C. 1995 *Luftwaffe Codes, Markings and Units 1939-1945* Schiffer Publishing Ltd., Atglen

Ross A. (Ed.) 1993 *75 Eventful Years: A Tribute to the Royal Air Force 1918-1993* Wingham Aviation Books, Canterbury

Schack von Wittenau Graf, S.1981 *Pionierfluge eines Lufthansa-Käpitans 1926-1945* Motorbuch Verlag, Stuttgart

Schliephake H. 1971 *The Birth of the Luftwaffe* Ian Allan Ltd., Shepperton

Schliephake H. 1977 *Flugzeugbewaffnung – Die Bordwaffen der Luftwaffe von den Anfangen bis zur Gegenwart* Motorbuch Verlag, Stuttgart

Schilling F. and Rettinghaus H. 1994 *Die Geschichte der Luftpolizei* Flugzeug Publications GmbH

Schmitt G. 1988 *Hugo Junkers and his Aircraft* transpress VEB Verlag für Verkehrswesen, Berlin

Schmitt-Rops H. 1930 *Das Funkwesen in der Luftfahrt*

Schneider H. 1940 *Flugzeug-Typenbuch: Handbuch der Deutschen Luftfahrt und Zubehör-Industrie Hauptausgabe A 1939/40* Herm.Beyer Verlag, Leipzig

Seaton A. 1982 *The German Army 1933-1945* Weidenfeld and Nicolson Ltd., London

Seeckt von H. GenOb.a.D. 1930 *Thoughts of a Soldier* Ernest Benn, London – 1928 *Gedanken eines Soldaten* Verlag für kulturpolitik, Berlin

Seeckt von H. GenOb.a.D. 1938 *Aus Meinem Leben 1866-1917* Hase & Koehler Verlag, Leipzig

Seifert K-D. 1999 *Die deutsche Luftfahrt 28: Der deutsche Luftverkehr 1926-1945 – auf dem Weg zum Weltverkehr* Bernard & Graefe Verlag, Bonn

Sekigawa E.1974 *Pictorial History of Japanese Military Aviation* Ian Allan Ltd., Shepperton

Shackleton M.R. 1939 *Europe: A Regional Geography* Longmans, Green and Co.Ltd., London

Shirer W.L. 1963 *The Rise and Fall of the Third Reich: A History of Nazi Germany* Martin Secker & Warburg Ltd., London

Shirer W.L. 1969 *The Collapse of the Third Republic: An Inquiry into the Fall of France in 1940* Pan Books, London - William Heinemann Ltd. and Secker and Warburg Ltd., London

Simpkin R. 1987 *Deep Battle: The Brainchild of Marshall Tukhachevskii* Brassey's (UK) Ltd.

Sinnott C. 2001 *The RAF and Aircraft Design 1923-1939: Air Staff Operational Requirements* Frank Cass Publishers, London

Smith H. 1981 *Aircraft Piston Engines: From the Manly Balzer to the Continental Tiara* Sunflower University Press, Manhattan

Smith J.R. and Kay A. 1972 *German Aircraft of the Second World War* Putnam & Company Limited, London

Smith J.R. 1971 *Messerschmitt: An Aircraft Album* Ian Allan Ltd., Shepperton

Smith J.R. 1973 *Focke Wulf: An Aircraft Album* Ian Allan Ltd., Shepperton

Smith J.R., Creek E.J. and Petrick P. 2003 *On Special Missions: The Luftwaffe's Research and Experimental Squadrons 1923-1945* Classic Publications, Ian Allan Publishing Ltd., Hersham

Smith P.C. 1974 *The Story of the Torpedo Bomber* Almark Publishing Co.Ltd., London

Smith P.C. 1981 *Impact! The Dive Bomber Pilots Speak* William Kimber & Co.Limited, London

Snyder L.L. 1976 *Encyclopaedia of the Third Reich* Promotional Reprint Company Ltd., for Bookmart Limited, Leicester - McGraw-Hill Inc.

Solltau G. 1989 *Die Flakabteilung I./12: Geschichte und Schicksal 1914-1945* Kameradschaft des ehemaligen Flakregiments 12

Spate W. 1989 *Top Secret Bird: The Luftwaffe's Me 163 Comet* Pictorial Histories Publishing Co., Missoula

Stark R. 1988 *Wings of War – A German Airman's Diary of the Last Year of the Great War* Vintage Aviation Library, Greenhill Books, Lionel Leventhal Limited, London - 1932 *Die Jagdstaffel unsere Heimat: Ein Flieger-Tagebuch Aus D.Letzten Kriesjahre*

Stroud J.1966 *European Transport Aircraft since 1910* Putnam and Company Ltd., London

Sturtivant R. and Cronin D. 1998 *Fleet Air Arm Aircraft, Units and Ships 1920 to 1939* Air Britain (Historians) Ltd., Tunbridge Wells

Sturton I. (Ed.) *Conway's Battleships – The Definitive Visual Reference to the World's All-Big-Gun Ships* Conway Maritime, Anova BooksCompany Ltd., London

Swanborough G. and Bowers P.M. 1976 *United States Navy Aircraft since 1911* Putnam & Company Ltd., London

Swanborough G. and Bowers P.M. 1989 *United States Military Aircraft since 1909* Putnam Aeronautical Books, Conway Maritime Press Ltd., London

Sweeting C.G. 2001 *Hitler's Squadron: The Führer's Personal Aircraft and Transport Unit 1933-45* Brassey's Inc., Dulles

Tarnstrom R.L. 1982 *Handbooks of the Armed Forces: Scandinavia*

Taylor J.W.R. and Moyes P.J.R. 1968 *Pictorial History of the RAF Vol.One 1918-1939* Ian Allan Ltd., Shepperton

Taylor H.A. 1974 *Fairey Aircraft since 1915* Putnam & Company Ltd., London

Terraine J. 1974 *The Mighty Continent: A View of Europe in the Twentieth Century* Futura, London

Terraine J. 1985 *The Right of the Line: The Royal Air Force in the European War 1939-1945* Hodder and Stoughton Limited, London

Terzibaschitsch S. 1980 *Aircraft carriers of the US Navy* Conway Maritime Press Ltd, London

Teske H. (Ed.) 1966 *General Ernst Köstring: Der militärische Mittler zwischen dem deutschen Reich und der Sowjetunion* Frankfurt am Main

Tessin G. 1974 *Deutsche Verbande und Truppen 1918-1939* Biblio Verlag, Osnabrück

Thetford O. 1976 *Aircraft of the Royal Air Force since 1918* Putnam & Company Ltd., London

Thetford O. 1977 *British Naval Aircraft since 1912* Putnam & Company Ltd., London

Thiele H. 2004 *Luftwaffe Aerial Torpedo Aircraft and Operations in World War Two* Hikoki Publications Ltd., Crowborough

Thomas F. and Wegmann G.1991 *Die Ritterkreuzträger der Flugabwehrtruppen Bd.1 u.2.*Die Deutsche Bibliothek, Biblio-Verlag

Thomas G. 1966 *Geschichte der deutsche Wehr und Rüstungswirtschaft, 1918 to 1945* Harald Boldt Verlag, Boppard am Rhein

Thompson A. 2013 *Küstenflieger: The Operational History of the German Coastal Air Service 1935-1944* Fonthill Media

Titz Z. 1971 *Czechoslovakian Air Force 1918-1970* Arco Aircam Aviation No.30 Arco Publishing Company, Inc., New York

Townsend P. 1970 *Duel of Eagles* Corgi Books published by Transworld Publishers Ltd., London – Weidenfeld & Nicolson Ltd.

Treadwell T.C. 1985 *Submarines with wings: The past, present and future of aircraft carrying submarines* Conway Maritime Press Ltd., London

Trenkle F. 1986 *Die deutsche Luftfahrt 7: Bordfunkgeräte - Vom Funksender zum Bordradar* Bernard & Graefe Verlag, Koblenz

Turner P.St.J. 1970 *Heinkel: an aircraft album* Ian Allan Ltd., Shepperton

Turner P.St.J. and Nowarra H.J. 1971 *Junkers: an aircraft album* Ian Allan Ltd., Shepperton

Ullmann M. 2002 *Luftwaffe Colours 1935-1945* Hikoki Publications Ltd., Ottringham

Vajda F.A. & Dancey P.1998 *German Aircraft Industry and Production 1933-1945* Airlife Publishing Ltd, Shrewsbury

Vogt H. 1994 *Schlachtfeld Luftfahrzeug: Der Einsatz der schwarzen Männer im II.Weltkrieg* Flugzeug Publications GmbH

Volker K-H. 1962 *Die Entwicklung der militärischen Luftfahrt in Deutschland 1920-1933* Deutsche Verlags-Anstalt, Stuttgart

Volker K-H. 1967 *Die deutsche Luftwaffe 1933-1939: Aufbau, Führung und Rüstung der Luftwaffe sowie die Entwicklung der deutschen Luftkriegstheorie* Deutsche Verlags-Anstalt, Stuttgart

Volker K.H. 1968 *Dokumente und Documentarfotos zue Geschichte der deutschen Luftwaffe* Deutsche Verlags-Anstalt, Stuttgart

Wagner W. 1980 *Kurt Tank - Konstrukteur und Testpilot bei Focke Wulf Die deutsche Luftfahrt 1* Bernard & Graefe Verlag, Bonn

Wakefield K. 1999 *Pfadfinder: Luftwaffe Pathfinder Operations over Britain, 1940-44* Tempus Publishing Inc., Charleston

Wallace Clarke R. 1994 *British Aircraft Armament Vol.2 RAF Guns and Gunsights from 1914 to the present day* Patrick Stephens Limited, Haynes Publishing, Sparkford

Walter J. 2004 *Guns of the Third Reich* Greenhill Books, Lionel Leventhal Limited, London

Westarp Graf von E.J. Obstlt. (Ed.) 1941 *Westarpscher Taschenkalendar 1941/42 für die Luftwaffe sowie für Luftschutz, Luftverkehr und Luftsport* Verlag Alfred Waberg, Grimmen

Westermann E.B. 2001 *Flak: German Anti-aircraft Defenses 1914-1945* University Press of Kansas, Lawrence

Wheeler-Bennett J.W. 1964 *The Nemesis of Power: The German Army in Politics, 1918-1945* Macmillan & Co., London

Whitley M.J. 1985 *German Cruisers of World War Two* Arms and Armour Press Ltd., London

Whitley M.J. 1989 *German Capital Ships of World War Two* Arms and Armour Press Ltd., London

Whitley M.J. 1991 *German Destroyers of World War Two* Arms and Armour Press Ltd., London

Whitley M.J. 1995 *Cruisers of World War Two: An International Encyclopedia* Arms and Armour Press, Cassell, London

Zapf J. 2001 *Flugplätze der Luftwaffe 1934-1945 und was davon übrig blieb Bd.1 Berlin & Brandenburg* VDM Heinz Nickel, Zweibrücken

Zapf J. 2006 *Flugplätze der Luftwaffe 1934-1945 und was davon übrig blieb Bd.5 Mecklenburg-Vorpommern* VDM Heinz Nickel, Zweibrücken

Zeng IV de, H.L., and Stankey D.G. 2008 *Bomber Units of the Luftwaffe 1933-1945: A Reference Source* Vol.2 Classic, Ian Allan Publishing, Hersham

Articles and Periodicals

Die deutsche Luftfahrt – Jahrbuch 1936 Naturkunde und Technik, Frankfurt am Main

Geyer M. 1975 'Das Zweite Rüstungsprogramm (1930-1934)' in *Militärgeschichtliche Mitteilungen,* 1

Knauss R. 1933 'Eine geheime Denkschrift zur Luftkriegskonzeption Hitler-Deutschlands von Mai 1933' in Heinemann B. Maj. and Schuncke J. Maj. (Ed.) 1964 *Zeitschrift für Militärgeschichte* Nr.1 pp.72-86

Lichte A. 1976 'Der Reichseingriff in die Junkers-Werke' in *Junkers Nachrichten H5/6* 1976

Mecozzi A.Maj. 'Les Grandi Unita Aviatori' in *Rivista Aeronautica* Mar 29

Overy R.J. 1979 'The German Motorosierung and Rearmament: a Reply' in *Economic History Review* Vol.32

Seydel Hptm.a.D. 1921 'Flak' in *Militärwochenblatt Nr.33* in Corum 1997 p.63

Speidel W. Gen.d.Fl.a.D. 'Reichswehr und Rote Armee' in *Vierteljahrshelfte für Zeitgeschichte* Vol.1 Jan 1953

Thienemann E. 'Der deutsche Minenraumdienst' in *Marine Rundschau* Vol.I Feb 1961 in Suchenwirth 1968 p.41

Trautvetter 'Über die Begriffsbestimmungen für den deutschen Luftfahrzeugbau' in *Der Luftweg* H.8/1922

Andersson L. 1989 'Secret Luftwaffe: German Military Aviation Build-up between the Wars' in *Air Enthusiast* No.41

Green W. and Swanborough G. 1971 'Fighter A to Z' in *Air Enthusiast* Vol.1 No.7

Green W. and Swanborough G. 1980 'Fighter A to Z' in *Air International* Vol.18 No.2

Green W. and Swanborough G. 1980 'Fighter A to Z' in *Air International* Vol.18 No.3

Imrie A. 1973 'The Staaken E./420' in *Aircraft Illustrated* Vol.6 No.4

Jarrett P. 1990 'Beardmore's Heavy Metal Monsters Pt.1' in *Aircraft Monthly* Vol.18 No.2

Jarrett P. 1990 'Beardmore's Heavy Metal Monsters Pt.2' in *Aircraft Monthly* Vol.18 No.3

Stroud J. 1984 'Die Junkers Grossflugzeuge' in *Air Enthusiast* No.24

Weal J. 1980 'Dr Dornier's Great White Wal' in *Air Enthusiast* No.13

Websites

www.adl-luftfahrthistori.de	Luftfahrt History
www.airhistory.org.uk	Golden Years of Aviation
www.axishistory.com	Axis History
www.digizeitschriften.de	Statistisches Jahrbuch für das Deutsche Reich
www.feldgrau.com	Feldgrau – Research on the German Armed Forces 1918-1945
www.frontflieger.de	Die Soldaten der deutscher Fliegertruppe
www.greatwar.com	Great War Militaria
www.lexicon-der-wehrmacht.de	Lexicon der Wehrmacht
www.reocities.com	Axis Biographical Research
www.technikmuseum-magdeburg.de	Technikmuseum Magdeburg
www.wikipedia.org	Wikipedia
www.ww2.dk	Luftwaffe 1933-45
smartblotch.files.wordpress.com	The Rohrbach Chronicles

Index

Index of General & Miscellaneous Terms

Index of People

Index of Places

Index of Aircraft & Engines

Index of Military Equipment & Weapons

Index of the *Reichsluftfahrtministerium* (RLM) (German Air Ministry)

Index of the *Reichsverkehrsministerium* (German transport ministry) (RVM)

Index of the *Reichswehr* (German Armed Forces)

Index of the German *Heer* including constituent parts

Index of the German *Reichsmarine* (Navy)

Index of Airlines

Index of Civil & Paramilitary Flying Organisations

Index of Other Organisations